THE NEW PRACTICAL REFERENCE LIBRARY

EDITOR IN CHIEF

CHARLES H. SYLVESTER

FORMER CITY SUPERINTENDENT OF SCHOOLS, STATE INSPECTOR OF HIGH SCHOOLS, PROFESSOR OF LITERATURE
AND METHODS OF TEACHING IN STATE NORMAL SCHOOL, AND STATE INSTITUTE CONDUCTOR,
WISCONSIN; AUTHOR OF "ENGLISH AND AMERICAN LITERATURE."

ASSOCIATE EDITOR

ELLSWORTH D. FOSTER, LL. B.

FORMER SUPERINTENDENT OF SCHOOLS; CONDUCTOR OF TEACHERS' INSTITUTES; MEMBER FACULTY BENTON
HARBOR (MICH.) COLLEGE AND NORMAL; AUTHOR OF "CYCLOPEDIA OF CIVIL GOVERNMENT."

ASSISTANT EDITORS

KENNETH L. M. PRAY, A.B.
PHILADELPHIA "RECORD"

ANNA McCALEB, Ph.B.
UNIVERSITY OF CHICAGO

HELGA LEBURG HANSON, A.B.
NORTHWESTERN UNIVERSITY

ALBERTUS V. SMITH, Ph.B.
UNIVERSITY OF CHICAGO

VOLUME V

TORONTO   CHICAGO

HANSON-BELLOWS COMPANY

1914

SCHOOLS. In its broadest sense, the term *school* is used to designate a place where instruction is given in the arts, sciences and professions, and includes grammar schools, high schools, academies, colleges, universities and technical schools. Most commonly, however, the name is restricted to institutions below college rank. The modern schools of the western nations are very different in their aims and methods from the schools of the ancients or from the schools of the oriental peoples to-day. For a discussion of the origin of schools, their growth, their aims and methods, their similarities and differences in different countries, and their importance in the life of nations, see EDUCATION; EDUCATION, HISTORY OF; EDUCATION, COMPULSORY; EDUCATION, NATIONAL SYSTEMS OF; COLLEGE; UNIVERSITY; COMMON SCHOOLS; SCHOOLS, CORRESPONDENCE.

Schools, CORRESPONDENCE, educational institutions in which instruction is given to pupils by letter. This system of education is the result of a general demand for the extension of higher instruction to many persons who are unable to attend high schools, normal schools or colleges. It is especially intended for students of small means, who are prevented by financial or other considerations from continuing their studies beyond grammar school or high school courses.

The scheme was first successfully developed in Germany, about 1856, though it had been suggested and tentatively applied in England some years before. In the United States the Chautauqua Literary and Scientific Circle was the first to adopt the idea, and its correspondence university, organized in 1884, gained immediate popularity, though it never achieved financial success. Its plan consisted in the formation of circles, or clubs, which were furnished from time to time with text-books prepared by eminent instructors, together with plans of study, which were worked out by the students in classes or groups, the results being reported to the headquarters of the school. Certificates were given upon the completion of the courses. The University of Chicago soon after its organization developed the scheme somewhat more completely. Its correspondence department is an integral part of its organization and offers courses in thirty departments. Any student may take by correspondence one-third of the work required for a degree. Differing from all

150

of these is the plan of Northwestern University, which gives credits for preparatory work done through an affiliated school, the Interstate School of Correspondence. No work of college grade is offered. Preparatory work taken through the correspondence school is accepted as full preparation for admission to college courses in the branches covered. Other institutions in all parts of the world have taken up the idea and carried it out upon one of the plans outlined above, especially as an adjunct of university extension or upon an entirely independent basis.

The work of all these schools is carried on by various means. In some, special text-books are prepared, which include in themselves the suggestions and aids to study required by the particular subjects covered. In others, text-books like those used in residence schools are furnished the student, but they are supplemented by special instruction books, embodying the suggestions necessary for the successful prosecution of correspondence and home study.

The rapid growth in the extent of correspondence instruction may be traced to the natural advantages which the plan has over even the most thorough class instruction. Among these are the following: (1) It reaches a far greater number of students than any regular school could possibly reach. (2) It furnishes instruction to them at comparatively little expense and with no loss of time from other occupations. (3) The work is adapted to all classes of students. (4) It gives to each student personal and individual instruction by teachers specially prepared and trained for the work. (5) The successful prosecution of a correspondence course requires unusual development of a firm purpose and of perseverance on the part of the student. (6) It teaches him thoroughness, accuracy and self-reliance. (7) Not least among its advantages is the fact that it trains him in the writing of clear, concise English.

The system is not without its drawbacks, but the mature student, who has had sufficient experience to ascertain his own inclinations and talents and to attain a serious purpose in life, will find in the very disadvantages of correspondence instruction a means for his own development. Furthermore, many of the defects noticed in the system in its early years are being overcome by remedies suggested by experience and study. Thus, a feeling of fellowship among the students is carefully fostered. Confidential notes, queries and suggestions from teacher to pupil and *vice versa* tend to become a helpful substitute for personal contact and acquaintance. Reference books and laboratory supplies are furnished with courses that require these helps, and a plain statement of the circumstances under which the study is being carried on gives the instructors the data from which to give helpful advice as to the amount and character of the work to be pursued. See CHAUTAUQUA LITERARY AND SCIENTIFIC CIRCLE; UNIVERSITY EXTENSION; EDUCATION.

Schopenhauer, *sho'pen how ur,* ARTHUR (1788–1860), a German philosopher, born at Danzig. After completing a course of literature and philosophy in the University of Göttingen, he published his essay on *The Fourfold Root of the Principle of Sufficient Reason.* He then devoted most of his time for the next four years to the preparation of his greatest work, *The World as Will and Idea.* After this he was for a time tutor in the University of Berlin, but as a teacher he was unsuccessful, and he retired to his home in Frankfort-on-the-Main, where he spent the remainder of his life in perfecting his system of philosophy.

The system of Schopenhauer has for its foundation the proposition that the only necessary reality in the universe is will, which includes not only conscious desire, but unconscious instinct and the forces which appear in inorganic nature, as well. What are called appearances exist only in the mind and are merely forms under which this universal will manifests itself. Throughout nature, from the lower animals downward, this will works unconsciously, and it attains consciousness only in the higher stages of being, as in man. This will makes all experience not according to law, but to its purpose of realizing its own desires. When so directed by its fancy, this will expresses itself rationally. At other times it is wholly unreasonable. Against the caprices of this will man is powerless. Resignation is the only means of attaining peace. Salvation lies in ignoring the demands of the sensuous nature and in striving to free ourselves naturally from the will to live. Schopenhauer was an idealist and a pessimist, and in its last analysis the ethical feature of his philosophy coincides quite closely with the Buddhistic doctrine of Nirvana, or annihilation.

Schubert, *shoo'burt,* FRANZ (1797–1828), one of the greatest composers of modern times. He was born at Vienna and commenced his musical education in his seventh year. He soon acquired proficiency on the piano and on different stringed

instruments, so that in a short time he was able to take the part of first violin in the orchestra at the court chapel. After leaving this post he supported himself by teaching music, devoting himself, in obscurity and neglect, to composition. He finally secured assistance from a college friend, though still suffering from poverty, lack of opportunity and unappreciative criticism. Still his lyric sense did not fail him, and he continued to write the songs which were

FRANZ SCHUBERT

to make him famous. Besides his six hundred songs, he left about four hundred other compositions, including fifteen operas, six masses and several symphonies. His symphonies take a high rank, the *Seventh* (in C major) being ranked by Mendelssohn and Schumann with Beethoven's. Liszt described him as the most poetic of musicians. His music was of the inspirational sort, many of his most famous compositions being written in a reckless hurry, notably *Hark, Hark, the Lark* and the famous *Serenade in D Minor.* His *Erl King* is considered one of the greatest songs ever written.

Schumann, *shoo'mahn,* ROBERT (1810–1856), a celebrated musical composer and critic, born at Zwickau, Saxony. He studied law at Leipzig, but in 1830 he finally devoted himself to music. The celebrated pianist Clara Wieck, the daughter of his teacher, became his wife in 1840. In 1834 he commenced his *Neue Zeitschrift für Musik,* a journal which was to herald an ideal music, and which for ten years exercised an important influence upon the development of the art, aiding the advancement of such musicians as Chopin, Brahms, Berlioz, Schubert and Mendelssohn. In the year following his marriage he published nearly one hundred fifty songs, many upon Heine's words, and all marking an advance upon previous composers in the fidelity with which the music reproduced the delicate shades of meaning in the poems. Notable among his works in this period were the *Symphonic Studies* and the songs, *Woman's Love and Life* and *Poet's Love*. He then commenced his great series of orchestral works, his symphony in B flat being first performed at the close of 1841. Under stress of work, however, his reason failed him, and after an attempt to drown himself in 1854 he was confined in a lunatic asylum, where he died. His music has a dreamy, moody quality, which is both novel and attractive.

Schumann-Heink, ERNESTINE, née ROESSLER (1861–   ), a German contralto. She made her début in 1878 in Dresden, where she continued to sing for four years, but later made appearances in various parts of Germany with remarkable success. She first sang in America in 1898, was received with enthusiasm, and repeated her successes upon several later visits, in grand opera, light opera, concert and recital.

Schurman, *shoor'man,* JACOB GOULD (1854–   ), an American educator, born at Freetown, Prince Edward Island. He was educated in Canada and at London and Edinburgh universities. Later he studied at Heidelberg and Berlin. At the age of twenty-six, he was appointed professor of philosophy and English literature in Acadia College, Nova Scotia, and six years later he became professor of philosophy at Cornell University. From this position he became dean of the Sage School of Philosophy at Cornell, and in 1892 he was elected president of the university. He was a member of the United States Philippine Commission of 1899 and devoted nearly a year to the study of conditions in the islands. He is the author of *Kantian Ethics and the Ethics of Evolution, The Ethical Import of Darwinism, Belief in God, Agnosticism and Religion, A Generation at Cornell* and *Philippine Affairs, a Retrospect and Outlook.* In 1912–1913, he was United States Minister to Greece and Montenegro.

Schurz, *shoorts,* CARL (1829–1906), a German-American soldier, orator and political leader, born at Liblar, Prussia. He was educated at Cologne and at the University of Bonn, where he became associated in the publication of a liberal newspaper. He was compelled to go to Switzerland during the revolutionary period of 1848. Later he served as correspondent for German papers in Paris and London and

emigrated to the United States in 1852. He settled in Watertown, Wis., took part in the campaign of 1856 and was defeated for lieutenant governor of the state on the Republican ticket in the following year. He opened a law office at Milwaukee in 1859 and soon attained

CARL SCHURZ

note for his remarkable eloquence, both in the English and the German languages. He was made brigadier general in the Federal army in 1862 and fought at Bull Run, Chancellorsville, Gettysburg and Chattanooga. At the close of the war he made a tour through the South and reported conditions which influenced Congress to radical measures of reconstruction. Later he became newspaper correspondent and finally editor of the Saint Louis *Westliche Post.* In 1869 Schurz was elected to the United States Senate, where he opposed the policy of President Grant and led in the Liberal Republican movement of 1872. He was appointed by President Hayes secretary of the interior, and at the close of the administration he became editor of the New York *Evening Post.* He repudiated the Republican platform and nominations in 1884 and after that time was independent in politics, though generally favoring the Democratic party. He was an early supporter of civil-service reform and was president of the National Civil Service Reform League from 1892 to 1901.

Schuyler, *ski'lur,* PHILIP (1733–1804), an American soldier and statesman, born at Albany,

N. Y. He served in the French and Indian War and at its close was elected to the colonial assembly; he then represented his state in the controversy over the territory of Vermont, then known as the Hampshire Grants. He was elected a delegate to the Continental Congress in 1775, and soon after the Battle of Bunker Hill he became a major general in the Continental army. He was placed in command of the expedition to Canada, but on account of illness was obliged to relinquish it to Richard Montgomery. Later he fought against indians and Tories in New York and made a treaty of alliance with the Six Nations. Being hampered and accused by superior officers, he resigned his commission in disgust, demanded a court of inquiry and was acquitted with high honor. He remained in the army, but was superseded by General Gates; to Schuyler, however, largely belongs the credit for the defeat and capture of Burgoyne and his army. He finally resigned unconditionally in April, 1779, and represented New York in Congress as a leading Federalist. Afterward he was elected to numerous state offices and finally to the United States Senate. He married in 1755 Catherine Van Rensselaer, and his daughter Elizabeth became the wife of Alexander Hamilton.

Schuylkill, *skool'kil,* a river rising in the northeastern part of Pennsylvania, in the Blue Mountains, and flowing southeastward into the Delaware, 5 mi. below the city of Philadelphia. Its length is 120 miles, and it is navigable as far as Philadelphia for boats of 300 or 400 tons.

Schwanthaler, *shvahn'tah lur,* LUDWIG MICHAEL (1802–1848), a German sculptor, born at Munich. In 1835 he was made professor in the Academy of Arts in Munich. Among his more important works may be specified the fifteen figures of the *Battle of Arminius,* for the northern pediment of the Walhalla at Regensburg; the colossal bronze statue of Bavaria, seventy feet high, in front of the Ruhmeshalle, Munich; a statue of Mozart at Salzburg; one of Jean Paul at Bayreuth, and one of Goethe at Frankfort.

Schwatka, *shwot'ka,* FREDERICK (1849–1892), an American explorer, born at Galena, Ill. He graduated at West Point in 1871 and was occupied with garrison duty on the frontier until 1877. Meantime, he continued his studies and was admitted to the bar in Nebraska and received a degree in medicine in 1876. Two years later, under leave of absence, he started out upon a search for the Franklin polar expedi-

tion. After a most remarkable journey, filled with the greatest privation and heroism, he returned with evidence of the final destruction of the Franklin expedition. Later he explored the Yukon River in Alaska and also made several expeditions through the unknown parts of Mexico. He was honored by many learned societies in both America and Europe.

Scilly, *sil'ly,* **Islands,** a group of islands situated at the entrance of the English Channel, about 30 mi. w. by s. from Land's End. There are six islands of some importance, and the others are mere points of rock, the entire group containing about 140 islands. The inhabitants are engaged in fishing and in the cultivation of flowers and vegetables. Population in 1911, 2500.

Scio, *si'o,* or **Ski'o,** the ancient Chios, an island belonging to Turkey, situated in the Aegean Sea, 53 mi. w. of Smyrna, and separated from the coast of Asia Minor by a channel about 7 miles wide in the widest place. The island is 32 miles long from north to south, and in the widest place it is 18 miles wide. It has an area of 320 square miles, and the surface is mountainous, the highest elevation having an altitude of about 4000 feet. The chief products are wine, oil, cotton, silk, oranges and other fruits. The island is one of the most beautiful in the eastern Mediterranean, but it is subject to severe earthquakes. Previous to 1822 it was the most prosperous island in the Grecian Archipelago, but during a revolt that year nearly all of the population was massacred or sold into slavery, and the island has never recovered from this disaster. It is supposed by some to be the birthplace of Homer. Population, about 60,000.

Scioto, *si ot'o,* **River,** a river rising in the northwestern part of Ohio and flowing eastward and then southward into the Ohio River. Its length is about 225 miles, and it is 450 feet wide at its mouth. The Scioto is navigable for boats for 130 miles, and its valley is noted for its fertility, being one of the best cultivated portions of the state.

Scipio, *sip'e o,* PUBLIUS CORNELIUS (237–about 185 B. C.), surnamed *Scipio Africanus the Elder,* one of the most illustrious of Roman warriors. At the battle at the Ticinus against the Carthaginians, in 218 B. C., he is said to have saved the life of his father, and two years later he was one of the few who escaped from the fatal Battle of Cannae. In 212 B. C. he was unanimously elected aedile, and in the following year he became proconsul in Spain. His first successful enterprise of importance was the conquest of New Carthage, the stronghold of the Carthaginians in Spain. The next year (209) he totally defeated Hasdrubal, Hannibal's brother, and in 207 he won a decisive victory over Mago and Hasdrubal, the son of Gisco. The result was to drive the Carthaginians from Spain, and Scipio was empowered to lead an army against Carthage itself. The Carthaginians recalled Hannibal from Italy, but the great Battle of Zama (202 B. C.) resulted in the total defeat of the Carthaginians, who, on the advice of Hannibal, sought for peace. On his return to Rome Scipio was honored with a triumph and received the surname of *Africanus*. After the successful close of a war with Antiochus, king of Syria, in 189 B. C., Scipio retired into private life.

Scipio, PUBLIUS CORNELIUS AEMILIANUS (about 185–129 B. C.), surnamed *Scipio Africanus the Younger*, son of Lucius Aemilius Paulus and adopted son of Publius Cornelius Scipio, the son of Scipio Africanus Major. In 151 B. C. he accompanied the consul, Lucius Licinius Lucullus, to Spain as military tribune, and two years later, on the outbreak of the Third Punic War, he commanded in Africa under Manius Manilius. His services were so important that in 147, although he was not of the legal age, he was unanimously chosen consul and leader of the forces against the Carthaginians. In 146 he took, and by command of the senate, burned, Carthage, for which he was honored with a triumph at Rome and with the surname of *Africanus*. In the last years of his life he made himself many enemies among the people by opposing the measures of the popular party, especially the agrarian law of Tiberius Gracchus. He was found dead in his bed, probably murdered by a political enemy.

Scissors, *siz'zurz*. See SHEARS.

Scissorsbill or **Skimmer**, a bird of the gull family, named because of its peculiar elongated, compressed bill, of which the lower mandible much exceeds the upper in length and shuts into the latter somewhat after the fashion of a knife blade into its handle. This beak is of an orange color at its base and black at its tip. The bird is found along the Atlantic coasts of America and Africa and is often seen skimming along the water, thrusting the lower bill into the water searching for food. The general color of the bird is dark above and white below, with a band of white across the wings.

Scoresby, *skorz'by*, WILLIAM (1789–1857), an Arctic explorer, born in Yorkshire. His first voyages were made with his father, a whaler, and in 1806, as chief officer of his father's ship *Resolution*, he penetrated to 81° 30′ north latitude, the northernmost point reached up to that time. Another important voyage was undertaken in 1822, and during this he charted accurately the coast of East Greenland.

Scorpio, *skor'pe o*, the eighth sign of the zodiac. In ancient astrology the symbol (♏) was meant to represent the arrow-shaped sting of the scorpion.

Scor'pion, an animal having a long body, abruptly ending in a long, slender tail formed of six joints, the last of which bears a very sharp and poisonous sting. A sting from this animal gives excruciating pain, but it is very seldom, if ever, fatal to man. The eyes of the scorpion, which are of the simple kind, number six, eight or twelve. The female carries her young on her back for several days after they are hatched and tends them carefully for about a month, until they are able to shift for themselves.

SCORPION

Scorpions generally live in dark places and under stones. They are found in the United States and various other parts of the world.

Scorpion Fish, a genus of fishes belonging to the gurnard family. The *red scorpion fish* is a familiar form. The *spotted scorpion fish* is a second species, and, like the preceding form, it occurs in British waters, as well as in the Mediterranean, the Atlantic and the tropical seas. Another species is the common market fish of southern California, measuring a foot in length and colored brown and olive.

Scorpion Fly, an insect related to the dragon flies. The name *scorpion fly* is derived from the appendages attached to the abdomen of some species. The male in the common species, for example, has the sixth and seventh joints of the abdomen attenuated and capable of extensive motion, while the last joint forms a pair of forceps, resembling those of the earwigs. When at rest this tail is curled over the back, but when irritated the forceps are used as weapons of offense or defense.

Scotch Ter'rier, a small dog, with a thick-set, rough-coated body, a long, narrow head,

SCOTCH TERRIER

with pricked ears and dark eyes. It weighs from fourteen to twenty pounds and is black, red and black brindled, or reddish-brown in color.

Scot'land, the political division occupying the northern part of the island of Great Britain, separated from England by the Cheviot Hills and the Solway Firth. Its greatest length from northeast to southwest is 287 miles, and its breadth varies from less than 30 to 140 miles. Its area is 29,785 square miles, or a little less than that of South Carolina. Scotland is remarkable for the irregularity of its coast line and for the groups of islands bordering it upon the west and north. The most important of these are the Hebrides, the Orkneys and the Shetlands, each of which is described under its proper title. On the eastern coast the most prominent indentations are Moray Firth, the Firth of Tay and the Firth of Forth, while on the south and west are Solway Firth, the Firth of Clyde, the Firth of Lorne, the Sound of Sleat and Loch Broom. With the exception of the sound, each of these indentations terminates in an estuary.

SURFACE AND DRAINAGE. The surface of Scotland is divided naturally into three divisions—the highlands, occupying the northern portion of the country; the central lowlands, immediately southeast of the highlands, and the southern uplands, which include the southern counties. The highland region, which embraces fully one-third of Scotland, is noted for its numerous mountains and hills, the highest of which are the Grampian Hills, containing steep precipices and narrow valleys through which flow rapid streams or in which lie deep and clear mountain lakes. The highest elevation in this region and in Great Britain is Ben Nevis, which attains an altitude of 4406 feet. The central lowlands differ from lowlands in most other countries in being widely diversified by low hills, beautiful valleys and numerous lakes and streams. This region and the highlands have for centuries been famous for their beautiful scenery, and it was this portion of Scotland that Scott immortalized in his poems, *Lady of the Lake, Lay of the Last Minstrel* and *Marmion*, and in a number of his novels (See SCOTT, WALTER, Sir). In the southern uplands are found numerous ranges of low mountains, one of which, the Cheviot Hills, forms a portion of the boundary between Scotland and England. Another range extends southward into England. These are low mountains, and the highest peaks do not attain an altitude of 3000 feet, but a number reach a height of 2700 feet or over. The surface in this part of the country is less broken and irregular than in the highland region.

The most important streams flow to the east and enter the North Sea. The largest of these is the Tweed, and others worthy of mention are the Forth, the Tay, the Dee, the Don, the Spey and the Findhorn. Those entering the sea on the west are the Clyde, the Ayr, the Doon, the Dee, the Nith, the Annan and the Esk. The Tay has the greatest volume of water, but the Clyde has been canalized and thus made navigable for ocean ships as far as Glasgow. This renders it by far the most important commercial waterway of Scotland. The country is noted for its large number of beautiful mountain lakes. Among the most noted of these are Lomond, Katrine, Tay, Earn, Rannoch, Awe, Shiel, Ness and Maree, in the western and northern highlands, Leven in the central lowlands, and Saint Mary's, Ken, Dee and Doon, in the southern uplands.

CLIMATE. See GREAT BRITAIN, subhead, *Climate*.

MINERAL RESOURCES. The southern portion of Scotland is rich in minerals. By far the most important of these is coal, which is mined in large quantities in the County of Lanark, in which Glasgow is situated. Iron ore is found in the County of Ayr, to the west of the coal fields. Mineral oil in small quantities is obtained in some portions of the lowlands, and in other sections building stone of good quality is quarried.

FISHERIES. Surrounded, as it is, by cool waters and dotted with a large number of cold, clear streams and lakes, Scotland abounds in fish, and the taking of them constitutes an important industry of the people. The annual catch is valued at about $15,000,000. The varieties taken in largest quantities are herring, haddock and cod. Important whaling fleets also have headquarters at Dundee, and from this port considerable seal fishing is carried on.

AGRICULTURE. Its rugged surface, barren soil and cool climate render a large part of Scotland unsuitable for agriculture. In the lowlands all available land is tilled, and in the highlands and upland regions much of the country is devoted to stock raising. The highlands are well adapted to sheep, and the wool produced is of considerable value. Among the important crops are oats, barley, turnips, potatoes and hay. Forage crops are also raised for fodder. The country is known for its excellent breeds of cattle, among which are found the Ayrshire, the Jersey, the polled Angus and the Galloway (See CATTLE). Scotland is also the home of the Clydesdale horse.

MANUFACTURES. The manufactures are important and furnish occupation for fully one-fourth of the inhabitants. The most important manufacturing industries are those producing woolens, cottons and linens. These are followed by the iron and steel industries, whose center is at Glasgow; along the Clyde are found the largest shipyards in the world. Glasgow is also noted for its manufacture of chemicals, and throughout the country are found breweries and distilleries, some of which have become famous for their products. Edinburgh is noted as one of the great publishing centers of the English-speaking world. In other localities sugar refining and the manufacture of paper, glass, gloves, hosiery and various small wares give employment to a large number of people.

TRANSPORTATION AND COMMERCE. See GREAT BRITAIN, subhead *Transportation and Commerce.*

INHABITANTS AND LANGUAGE. The people of Scotland are known as Scots, or Scotch. Those occupying the northern portion of the country, particularly the highlands, are of Gaelic descent, and among them the Gaelic language is still spoken, though most of the younger people have learned the English (See

CELTS). The southern portion of the country contains a large number of people of English descent. Population in 1911, 4,759,445.

GOVERNMENT AND RELIGION. For the purpose of local government Scotland is divided into 18 counties. The country forms a political division of the United Kingdom, coördinate in its rights and privileges with England, and it has representatives in both branches of the British Parliament. See GREAT BRITAIN, subhead *Government.*

In religion the larger part of the population are followers of the Presbyterian faith, though other Protestant churches have considerable following, and in the larger cities the Church of England is maintained, but neither this Church nor the Roman Catholic Church has as numerous a following, in proportion to the number of inhabitants, as in England or Ireland.

EDUCATION. See EDUCATION, NATIONAL SYSTEMS OF, subhead *Great Britain.*

CITIES. The important cities are Edinburgh, the capital, and Leith, its seaport; Glasgow, the chief industrial center; Dundee, and Aberdeen. Each of these is described under its title.

HISTORY. The part of the island of Britain which lies north of the Firth of Forth and the Clyde was known by the Romans from the first century A. D. as Caledonia. The name Scotia (Scotland), limited in the early periods to Ireland, was used from the tenth century on for a part of Scotland, and after the thirteenth century it was applied to the present realm of Scotland. The oldest inhabitants of the country were the Picts. When the Romans, during the time of the emperor Claudius, conquered the southern part of Britain, the northern part, Caledonia, remained independent. When Agricola was in Great Britain he made several incursions into Caledonia and won some victories, but after his recall these advantages were lost by the Romans. As a protection on the north for their British territory, the Romans during the time of Emperor Hadrian built a wall between the Firth and the Tyne. Under Antoninus Pius a second wall was built farther north. In spite of these fortifications, however, Britain was constantly, after the third century, disturbed by invasions of the Picts. About the middle of the fourth century, the Scots, who had come from Ireland and settled in the northwestern part of Caledonia, began to take part in these invasions.

The history of Scotland during the time of

the Anglo-Saxon conquest of Britain is enveloped in mystery. In the seventh century, when we again have historical accounts of the country, it is found divided into four kingdoms, those of the Scots, the Picts, the Britons and the Saxons. About the second half of the sixth century, Christianity had been introduced among the Picts, and the Scots had brought Christianity with them from Ireland. In 843 the king of the Scots, Kenneth, made himself ruler also of the Picts, and the kingdom thus formed was known for a time as Alban and later as Scotland. Early in the ninth century, Scotland began to be disturbed by the Danes and the Normans, who had made invasions of the country and had formed settlements on the islands about the coast.

The last king who was descended from Kenneth was Malcolm II. He was followed by Duncan, who was killed in 1040 by Macbeth. Malcolm III, known as Malcolm Canmore, the son of Duncan, defeated Macbeth and slew him, in 1057. When England was conquered by the Normans, in 1066, Malcolm took the part of Edgar Atheling, the legitimate ruler, and gave asylum to many of the Anglo-Saxon nobles. He was for this reason involved in long conflicts with William the Conqueror and was at length obliged to submit and do homage for his kingdom. The most noteworthy of the sons of Malcolm was the youngest, David I (1124–1153), who introduced into Scotland feudalism as it was in practice in England. David's grandson and successor, Malcolm IV, was unable to maintain in full the power which David had gained.

William the Lion (1165–1214), by reason of his claims on territory in the northern part of England, came into conflict with Henry II of England, was taken captive at Alnwick in 1174 and received his freedom only on taking the oath of allegiance to the English king. William was followed by his son Alexander, who, taking advantage of the disturbed condition of England under John, invaded that country, was defeated and was compelled to do homage to the English king. Alexander III, by his defeat of the king of Norway, added to the kingdom the Isle of Man and the Hebrides.

After the death of Alexander and that of his granddaughter, Margaret, called the Maiden of Norway, numerous pretenders to the crown arose, among whom the most powerful were John Baliol and Robert Bruce (See BALIOL, JOHN; BRUCE, ROBERT). Edward I, chosen as arbiter between these two claimants, decided in favor of Baliol, who then in turn swore allegiance to the English crown. When Edward made his overlordship too oppressive, Baliol attempted with the help of France to make Scotland independent; but Edward invaded Scotland, and after a victory at Edinburgh he took Baliol to England with him as a prisoner. Scotland was now ruled by an English regent. Resistance under William Wallace was for a time effectual, and a great victory was gained at Stirling in 1297. Eight years later, however, Wallace, deserted by the Scotch nobles, was defeated and taken prisoner. Another popular leader was found in Robert Bruce, who declared himself king of Scotland, as Robert I, and in 1314 completely defeated an English army under Edward II at Bannockburn. For fourteen years from this date, Scotland was practically independent. Robert's son, David II, who succeeded him, was a minor, and new disturbances at once began in Scotland. War broke out with England in 1333, and after the Battle of Halidon Hill (1333) and that of Neville's Cross (1346), the Scottish kings were obliged to do homage to England.

With the accession of Robert II in 1371 began the Stuart dynasty. The kings of this line were for the most part strong and able men, but the fact that many of them came to the throne during their minority allowed the nobles to gain undue prominence. James I (1406–1437), who had been taken prisoner by the English before his father's death, was not allowed to return to Scotland until 1424. He proved, on gaining the authority, to be a man of much strength of character, and he introduced order into his kingdom, put down the nobility and greatly encouraged commerce and industry. James IV (1488–1513) became involved in a war with England on account of his support of the pretender, Perkin Warbeck (See WARBECK, PERKIN), but soon concluded a truce, and married, in 1503, the daughter of Henry VII of England. However, after the accession of Henry VIII to the English throne, James, who had formed an alliance with France, invaded Northumberland, but was defeated and killed at the Battle of Flodden Field.

The king's death plunged the nation into a state of anarchy; his successor, James V, had not yet reached the age of two years. His cousin, the duke of Albany, was appointed regent, but from an early part of the reign James was almost entirely in the hands of the earl of Angus, who had married the queen dowager and had almost complete control of affairs till 1528, when James, then in his seventeenth year, managed to escape to Stirling, take the government into his own hands and drive Angus into England. His alliance was sought by England, France and Spain, and in 1537 James married the daughter of Francis I. The young queen died a few weeks after her arrival in Scotland, and in the following year James married Mary of Lorraine, daughter of the duke of Guise. Henry VIII made several attempts to induce James to join the Reformation, but James remained a supporter of the old faith as against the reform doctrines.

The eventful period which followed the accession of Mary was dominated by the Reformation movement and by the questions affecting the union of Scotland and England. A scheme to marry the young queen to Edward, son of Henry VIII, was defeated, and the old league with France was renewed (See MARY STUART).

James VI, the son of Mary, was but a child, and a succession of regents governed the kingdom. On the death of Elizabeth of England, in 1603, James succeeded to the throne as the nearest heir, through his descent from Margaret, daughter of Henry VII and wife of James IV (See JAMES I of England).

There were seven Scottish Parliaments called by James after his accession, wherein he was represented by a commissioner sitting as president. His chief energies were directed to an attempt to draw England and Scotland into a closer union, by means of harmonizing the laws of the two countries and by establishing episcopacy in Scotland. In furtherance of the latter object he visited Scotland in 1617 for the only time after the union of the crowns. There were many acts passed for promoting trade and commerce, and the nation about this time seems to have been seized with a mania for colonization, as many thousands of the inhabitants left their native land for the Irish province of Ulster or the more distant shores of Nova Scotia. James died in 1625 and was succeeded by his son, Charles I (See CHARLES I).

Foreign wars and domestic troubles prevented Charles from visiting Scotland till 1633, when he was crowned at Edinburgh. The church was now entirely governed by the bishops, and civil affairs were managed by the privy council. At the outbreak of the civil war in England, Scotland took the part of the Parliament against the king, the Solemn League and Covenant being entered into between the Scottish Presbyterians and the English Parliament (See COVENANTS).

After the execution of Charles, in 1649, the Scots proclaimed his son king, under the title of Charles II. The young king was then in Holland, and commissioners were sent over from Scotland to inform him that the governing body was willing to join his cause if he would take the covenant. This Charles agreed to do, and he was invited over to his northern kingdom. He arrived in Scotland, was crowned at Scone in 1651 and immediately marched into England. Cromwell, who had already defeated him once in Scotland, followed, and at Worcester utterly scattered the royalist force and compelled Charles to become a fugitive (September 3, 1651). Cromwell returned to Scotland for a time, and on his departure for England he left Monk to complete the work. Cromwell's death was followed by his son's fall, Monk's march to London at the head of the army and the restoration of Charles II (1660). It soon became apparent that Charles was determined to carry out the favorite scheme of his father and grandfather, of establishing the episcopacy in Scotland. This attempt was violently opposed and led to a cruel persecution, which lasted with more or less severity during the whole of the reign of Charles. Hundreds were executed; others were fined, imprisoned and tortured, and whole tracts of the country were placed under a military despotism of the worst description. Under James II the chief events in Scotland were the rising, defeat and execution of Argyll; the declarations of indulgence by which many of the Presbyterian ministers returned to their charges, and the continued persecution of the strict Covenanters. At the Revolution of 1689, William, James's son-in-law, and Mary were proclaimed king and queen of Scotland, and religious freedom was again restored.

The death of William III in 1702 transferred the crowns of the two nations to Queen Anne, sister of Mary. In 1703 the Parliament of Scotland issued a declaration which showed an intention, in case of the death of the queen, to appoint a different sovereign from the English king, and the ill feeling between the two countries grew so strong that English statesmen became convinced that a union was essential for the peace of the two countries. A joint commission was appointed to draw up articles of union in 1706. In the Scottish Parliament the articles encountered a strong opposition, but a majority finally carried the measure in January, 1707. The chief provisions of the Act of Union were that the two kingdoms should be united under the name of Great Britain; that sixteen Scottish peers and forty-five Scottish members of the House of Commons should be elected to the Parliament sitting in London; that the Established Presbyterian Church of Scotland should be maintained; that Scotland should keep unchanged her own laws and customs relating to property and private rights, and that all the rights of trade, free intercourse and citizenship should be the same for Scotch and English subjects. Henceforth the history of Scotland is identified with that of England. See GREAT BRITAIN, subhead *History*. Consult Geikie's *Scenery of Scotland*, also Scott's *Heart of Midlothian, Lay of the Last Minstrel, Lady of the Lake* and *Marmion*.

LANGUAGE AND LITERATURE. Down to the fifteenth century the term *Scottish language* meant the Gaelic, or Celtic, tongue, while the language of lowland Scotland was looked upon as English. Such it really was—Northern English, with certain peculiarities of its own. The term *Scottish* came to be applied to it as possessing these peculiarities and as having a somewhat distinctive literary use. This language has been divided into three periods. During the *early* period, extending to the end of the fifteenth century, there was little difference between the language of Scotland and that of England north of the Humber. In the *middle* period, which extended to the Union, it was influenced in a slight degree by the Gaelic, and in a more pronounced manner by French and Latin, consequent on the French alliance and the revival of learning. During the *modern* period, it has been to a considerable extent affected by modern literary English, though the genuine vernacular may still be heard in many districts.

The *Sir Tristram*, a metrical romance dating from the end of the thirteenth century, doubtfully attributed to Thomas the Rhymer, is by some regarded as the earliest piece of Scottish literature, but the first undoubted specimen of Scottish literature is the *Bruce* of Barbour (about 1375). Down to the middle of the sixteenth century four names stand out prominently, namely, Henryson, Dunbar, Gavin Duglas and Sir David Lindsay. Then, with the exceptions of Alexander Scott, Arbuthnot, Rolland of Dalkeith, Sir William Alexander and Drummond of Hawthornden, about a century and a half elapsed before any eminent poet arose. In the third period of the language the first notable name is that of Allan Ramsay (1686–1758), author of *The Gentle Shepherd* and of numerous shorter pieces and songs. To this same age belongs also nearly the whole of that remarkable body of song known as the Jacobite minstrelsy. The most prominent Scotch writers, aside from those mentioned, are

Fergusson, Robert Burns, Hector MacNeill, Sir Walter Scott, James Hogg, Robert Tannahill, Joanna Baillie, George MacDonald, Robert Louis Stevenson, John Watson and J. M. Barrie. Besides these there is a long list of philosophers, legal writers and physicians, such as Adam Smith, Barclay and Liddell.

Scott, ROBERT FALCON (1868–1912), English naval officer and Antarctic explorer, who shares with Amundsen the honor of having reached the South Pole. Capt. Scott became a naval cadet in 1881, and for nineteen years he served continuously in the navy, reaching the rank of commander. In 1901 he led an expedition to the south polar regions, where he remained until 1904. On his return to England he was promoted to the rank of captain in recognition of his achievement. In 1909 he was appointed to

ROBERT FALCON SCOTT

command the British Antarctic Expedition, whose object was to make extensive investigations in the polar regions and also to locate the South Pole. Scott and three companions reached the Pole on January 18, 1912, but on their return trip they lost their lives from exposure in a terrific blizzard. The fate of Capt. Scott and his companions, as recorded in their diaries, will always remain one of the most glorious and most tragic in the world's history of exploration and discovery. See SOUTH POLAR EXPLORATION.

Scott, WALTER, Sir (1771–1832), a Scotch poet and novelist, born in Edinburgh. He entered the high school of Edinburgh in 1779, and in October, 1783, he was matriculated at the University of Edinburgh, but neither at school nor at college did he manifest any special ability. At the age of sixteen he began in his father's office an apprenticeship to legal business, and in 1792 he was admitted as a member of the Scottish bar. In 1797 he married a Miss Charpentier, the daughter of a French refugee; in 1799 he was appointed sheriff of Selkirkshire, and in 1806 he became a principal clerk of the Court of Session. His first ventures in literature were a translation of Bürger's *Lenore*, and *The Wild Huntsman*, which he published in 1796. Then followed the ballads of *Glenfinlas*, *The Eve of Saint John* and the *Grey Brother*; a translation of Goethe's *Götz von Berlichingen*; the three volumes of the *Minstrelsy of the Scottish Border*, and an edition of the old metrical romance of *Sir Tristram*. In 1805 he became prominent as an originel poet, with the *Lay of the Last Minstrel*, an extended specimen of the ballad-style, which at once became widely popular. In 1808 he published *Marmion*, another poetic romance which greatly increased his reputation, and in 1810 appeared the *Lady of the Lake* in which his poetical genius seems

SIR WALTER SCOTT

to have reached its height. His subsequent poetical productions, *The Vision of Don Roderick*, *Rokeby*, *The Bridal of Triermain* and *The Lord of the Isles*, did not attain the same success.

On the decline of his popularity as a poet,

and on his realization of the fact that Byron was surpassing him in his own field, Scott turned his attention to the prose romance, for which the greater part of his early life had been a preparation. The appearance of *Waverley*, in 1814, forms an epoch in modern literature, as well as in the life of Scott. This romance, or novel, was rapidly followed by the series known as *The Waverley Novels*, which comprises such masterpieces of historical fiction as *Guy Mannering*, *The Heart of Midlothian*, *The Bride of Lammermoor*, *The Legend of Montrose*, *Ivanhoe*, *The Monastery*, *Kenilworth*, *Quentin Durward* and *The Talisman*.

The desire of becoming an extensive landed proprietor, and of founding a family, was always strong with Scott, and this desire he began to gratify in 1811, when he purchased a small farm of about 100 acres, lying on the south bank of the Tweed. By degrees, as his resources increased, he added farm after farm to his domain till he had completed the estate to which he gave the name of Abbotsford. In 1820, when he was made a baronet by George IV, he reached the zenith of his fame and material prosperity. But this prosperity was founded on no solid basis, and the crash came in 1826, when Constable & Co., Edinburgh publishers, were obliged to suspend payment, hopelessly involving Ballantyne & Co., with whom it then appeared Scott was a partner. The liabilities which were thus incurred by him amounted to about $600,000; this sum, although he might have compromised with his creditors, Scott assumed as a personal debt. He worked like a galley slave in order to clear off the debt, his novels and historical writings following each other with incredible rapidity, and within two years he was able to pay his creditors $200,000. The strain was too great, however, and in 1830 he had an attack of paralysis, from which he never fully recovered. A trip to Italy did him little good, and he returned to Abbotsford to die. He was buried in his family burial aisle, amidst the ruins of Dryburgh Abbey. Some years after his death his debt was entirely liquidated by the sale of copyrights. The biography of Scott written by his son-in-law, John Gibson Lockhart, has become a classic.

Scott, WINFIELD (1786–1866), an American soldier, born near Petersburg, Va. He was educated for the law and admitted to the bar, but never practiced. Entering the army, he served with distinction in the War of 1812, won the Battle of Chippewa and was severely wounded in the Battle of Lundy's Lane. In

1832 and the following years, General Scott was employed in operations against the indian tribes, and in 1841 he was appointed commander in chief of the United States army. His fame rests chiefly upon his brilliant conduct of the Mexican War, in which he gained victories at Cerro Gordo, Contreras, Churubusco, Molino del Rey and Chapultepec, made himself master of the City of Mexico and concluded an advantageous peace. He was twice an unsuccessful candidate for the presidency. On the outbreak of the Civil War he remained true to the Federal government, but was too infirm to take any actual command. He retired from active service in 1861, and in 1864 he published his autobiography.

Scour'ing Rush. See HORSETAIL RUSH.

Scran'ton, PA., the county-seat of Lackawanna co., and the third city of the state in population, is situated on the Lackawanna River, 162 mi. n. of Philadelphia and 145 mi. n. w. of New York, on the Delaware, Lackawanna & Western, the Central of New Jersey, the Delaware & Hudson, the Erie and other railroads. It is the center of a fine and extensive system of electric railways. The city is beautifully situated on both sides of the little river, on rather high, undulating land, with broad streets. Scranton has three parks and a public square, in which the courthouse is situated. The Everhart Museum will soon be an additional attraction. The chief public buildings are the postoffice, the city hall, the courthouse, the Albright Memorial Library, the Y. M. C. A. building, the Masonic Temple, the Board of Trade and the Connell buildings. A number of churches are noted for their architecture, as are also the Home for the Friendless, the high school and the Taylor Hospital, a fine institution of its class. There are several other hospitals.

Scranton is in the center of the northern anthracite coal region and is one of the most important coal-distributing points in the country. There is also an extensive trade in miners' supplies. The industrial plants represent a capitlal of more than $30,000,000 and are numerous and extensive, including blast furnaces, rolling mills, foundries, machine shops, glass works, silk mills, breweries, locomotive works and manufactories of knit goods, lace, carpets, buttons, pianos and numerous small articles. There are thirteen banking institutions, with deposits of $30,000,000. The public schools are excellent. There are several private and denominational schools. The city is also the home of the International Correspondence Schools, the largest institution of its kind in the world.

The first settlement within the present limits of the city was made in 1788 and was named Slocum Hollow. But Scranton was really founded in 1840 by two brothers, Joseph and George Scranton; hence, its name. In 1850 it was incorporated as a borough, and it was chartered as a city in 1866. Since 1880 its growth has been rapid. Population in 1910, 129,867.

Screw, a simple machine, consisting of an inclined plane wound around a cylinder. The projecting spiral plane is called the *thread*, while the cylinder forms the *body* of the screw. To show that the thread is formed by an inclined plane, cut a paper triangle with one square corner and a length of at least three times its height. Draw a heavy pencil line along the edge of the slanting side of the triangle; then, beginning at the wide end, roll the paper around a pencil, taking care to keep the edge of the triangle even with the end of the pencil. The dark line along the slanting side forms the thread of the screw. The distance between the threads is called the *pitch*, or *interval*. In the figure, W represents the weight; P, the point at which the power is applied, and p, the pitch.

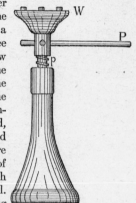

To determine the weight that can be raised by a screw with the application of a given power, multiply the power by the circumference of the circle which it describes, and multiply this product by the number indicated by the denominator of a fraction showing the pitch. The circumference of the circle is found by multiplying its diameter by 3.1416. To illustrate: To find the weight which can be raised by a power of 25 pounds, acting upon a lever 3 feet long and attached to a screw having a pitch of $\frac{1}{4}$ of an inch, multiply the diameter of the circle, which is 6 feet, by 3.1416, and multiply this product (18.8496) by 12, to reduce the number to inches. The product equals 226.1952 inches. This number, multiplied by 4, the denominator of the fraction indicating the interval, or pitch, equals 904.7808. The power, 25 pounds, multiplied by this number, gives 22,619.52 pounds, the weight that can be lifted. Because of the great power gained by the screw, it is used in raising buildings, in presses, and for holding together parts of machinery, pieces of wood and other articles.

Screw Pine or **Pandanus,** a genus of plants growing in the tropical parts of the Eastern Hemisphere. They take their name from the spiral arrangement of the long, pineapple-like leaves. In some species, peculiar roots are sent out from various parts of the stem, and these, entering the ground, serve as props for the trunk. One Indian species produces flowers whose fragrant buds are used for flavoring purposes and as a basis for perfumes. Another furnishes strong fibers, from which the natives make sugar bags; and in another species, the tips of the shoots are edible as well as the seeds.

Screw Propel'ler, an apparatus which, being fitted to ships and driven by steam, propels them through the water, and which, in all its various forms, is a modification of the common screw. Originally the thread had the form of a broad, spiral plate, making one convolution round the spindle, or shaft, but now it consists of several distinct blades, forming portions of two, three or four threads. The usual position for the screw propeller is immediately before the stern post, the shaft passing parallel to the keel into the engine room, where it is set in rapid motion by the steam engines. The successful introduction of the screw propeller is due to F. P. Smith and to John Ericsson, both of whom, independently and about the same time (1838), secured patents. Numerous modifications of the screw propeller have been proposed and adopted since it was first introduced, and since 1870 it is really the only form of propeller used, except in some cases in shallow inland waters.

Scribe, *skreeb,* AUGUSTIN EUGÈNE (1791–1861), a French dramatic writer. His first distinct success was achieved in 1816, and thenceforward his pen was never idle. His dramatic pieces comprise all the departments of the lighter kind of drama, and from their gaiety and interest of plot, as well as because of the felicitous manner in which modern French life is depicted in them, they have acquired popularity over the European continent and have also been introduced on the American and English stage, in the form of translations or adaptations. Two of the best known among them are *The Glass of Water* and *Adrienne Lecouvreur.*

Scribe also wrote the libretti for *Fra Diavola, Robert le Diable, The Huguenots* and many other operas.

Scrof'ula, a word that has been vaguely used, but is now confined to certain forms of tuberculosis, which are due entirely to infection by the bacillus of consumption. During the Middle Ages it was believed that scrofula could be cured by a touch of the king, and the disease was then known as *king's evil.* Touching for king's evil was practiced, among others, by Edward the Confessor of England and Louis IX of France, and it was tried as late as 1775 by Louis XVI of France.

Scru'ple, a measure of weight in the Troy system, equivalent to 20 grains, $\frac{1}{3}$ part of a drachm, $\frac{1}{24}$ part of an ounce and $\frac{1}{288}$ part of a pound.

Scud'der, HORACE ELISHA (1838–1902), an American author, born in Boston, Mass. After his graduation from Williams College he taught school in New York City and then removed to Boston. He edited for a time the *Riverside Magazine for Young People,* and in 1890 he became editor of the *Atlantic Monthly,* succeeding Thomas Bailey Aldrich. His chief writings include a sympathetic *Biography of Lowell, The History of the United States, George Washington* and a number of children's books, among which are *Seven Little People and Their Friends* and *The Bodley Books.*

Scu'do, an Italian coin, of different values in different states and at different times, but, especially, a modern coin equal to five lira, or francs, or about 96 cents.

Scul'pin, a small fish found in the northern seas and on the Pacific coast of America. Their color varies in different species. The shape resembles that of the bull-head catfish, and the body is covered with warty projections. Common species are the *daddy-sculpin* of Greenland waters and the *grubby* of the coast of New England.

Sculp'ture, the art of imitating living forms in solid substances. The word means, strictly, a cutting, or carving, in some hard material, as stone, marble, ivory or wood; but it is also used to express the molding of soft substances, as clay or wax, and the casting of metals or plaster.

PROCESSES. In producing a work of sculpture two processes are involved, "modeling" and "casting," the former alone being truly the work of the artist. In most sculpture it is customary for the artist to make for himself an image of life size, fashioned in wet clay. For a head or bust a flat board, set on a high stand, with a piece of wood standing at right angles to it, is used. Lead piping is sometimes employed to raise the height of this piece of wood, and around this structure the clay is roughly built up, a cylindrical mass for the neck and an egg-shaped form for the head. For a full-length figure an "armature" is prepared, consisting of an iron rod through the center, attached to which are other irons, in the case of statues, or lead piping, for statuettes. These are bent to the required positions, the whole, when complete, representing in line the pose and character of the intended figure. Upon and around this framework the figure is first roughly built up with clay, care being taken to add just as much as is requisite and to follow the general form and direction of the muscles. The essential difference between modeling and carving is that in the former the artist works from within outward, by the addition of material, while in the latter he works from without inward by the taking away of material. The sculptor's work proper generally ends with the completion of the clay model. The next process is that of casting. Plaster of Paris of the consistency of thick cream is poured over the model, to the depth of from two to three inches, the inner layer being colored. When this is set, the clay is carefully removed, and what is termed a "waste mold" is formed. This is carefully washed and when dry is oiled. Into this mold, plaster of Paris is poured, and when this has set hard, the waste mold is chipped off. The plaster of Paris has taken the place of the clay and formed what is called a "cast." A head is usually cast in halves, and a similar treatment is adopted in the case of complete figures. This is termed "piece molding." Parts which project very much are removed and cast separately, being afterward attached by means of plaster of Paris. The reproduction of this plaster cast in marble or stone is a mechanical operation, usually intrusted to a skilled workman. To aid him he employs a "pointing machine," with which he takes exact measurements. Some sculptors work on the marble after a rough copy of the original is made, and some never touch it, but simply supervise the work. For casting in metal, a plaster mold is first made as already described. Within this is fixed a rudely-formed solid, but removable, mass, called a "core," the space between it and the surface of the mold being filled with the molten metal. Another method for smaller work is used, in which the mold is lined with wax and the core inserted close up to the wax lining. The wax is then melted out and the molten metal poured into the mold to take its place, the core being afterward removed.

Three forms of sculpture are usually recognized. When the object stands free, it is said to be *in the round*; when it projects slightly from a solid surface it is said to be *in relief*; when it is cut into or sunk down into the surface it is said to be *in intaglio*.

HISTORY. *Egypt.* It is to Egypt that we must turn for the first signs of a developed form of sculpture. The distinctive characteristics of Egyptian sculpture are colossal size, stability and symmetry, the expression being that of calm repose and solemnity, with a suggestion of the supernatural. A conventional uniformity without life or action reigns everywhere. Most of the sculpture is relief and is defective in perspective and proportion, but the figures have a remarkable dignity and are true to life (See SPHINX). The best period of Egyptian sculpture was from 1450 to 1000 B. C. In the British Museum is to be found a splendid collection of Egyptian sculptures, extending from 2000 B. C. to the Mohammedan invasion, 640 A. D.

Assyria. The best period of Assyrian sculpture, as a style, is inferior to that of Egypt. Its characteristics are an intense and vigorous spirit of representation, without the least reference to ideal beauty of any kind. As compared with Egyptian work it is more realistic, but less true. It is powerful and energetic, but lacks grandeur; overladen with detail and ornamentation, it does not attain to the sublime in its repose, nor to beauty in its movement. Persian sculpture (560–331 B. C.) differs but little from Assyrian, and is usually included with it.

Greece. Greek sculpture, in its infancy, is strongly stamped with Oriental character, as may be seen by a careful examination of the reliefs from the temple of Assos, now in the Louvre, and the metopes from Selinus, casts of which are in the British Museum. But from the end of the sixth century B. C., the development of Greek art was rapid and continuous. In the sculptures for the Temple of Aegina, executed about 475 B. C., and now preserved at Munich, the figures of the warriors are no longer of the stiff, conventional type, with attitudes correct but lifeless; there is energy of movement in their action, and they have a living truth of gesture, only to be gained by artists who had studied the human form long and attentively. Upheld on the one hand by a noble mythology, that magnified, without distorting, human attributes, and supported on the other by an increasing knowledge of nature, the ultimate perfection of Greek art became only a question of time. It came to perfection in Phidias, whose statues of Athene, in the Parthenon at Athens (438 B. C.), and of Zeus, in the temple at Olympia, mark the period of the highest style of Greek art (See ELGIN MARBLES). Other sculptors of this period were Myron, known by his *Discobolus*, and Polycletus, a close rival of Phidias. The special character of the art that flourished at Athens under the rule of Pericles (fourth century B. C.) consists in a perfect balance and combination of elements sublime and human. Sculpture had reached that point when a faultless imitation of nature was within its reach, but it had not yet abandoned its spiritual connection with a splendid mythology. We have, therefore, in the sculpture of this period, the highest type of human beauty, joined to a godlike calm and reticence of motion. Examples of the grand style of this epoch are the sculptures of the Parthenon (See PARTHENON) and the Nike Apteros Temple, on the acropolis; the colossal bronze head of Artemis, in the British Museum; the Venus of Milo, in the Louvre, and the exquisite relief representing the parting of Orpheus and Eurydice, in the museum at Naples. Greek art, however, rapidly moved toward a still closer imitation of actual human life. The people, after the Peloponnesian War, spoiled by the luxury and pleasures which the prosperity of the Age of Pericles had opened to them, were not satisfied with the severe forms of the older masters. The sculptors now cultivated the soft, the graceful and the flowing and aimed at an expression of stronger passion, and they began to be fascinated by the force and variety of human feeling, as well as by the beauty of the human form. Jupiter, Juno and Minerva, favorite subjects of the Phidian era, were exchanged for Venus, Bacchus and Amor. The representatives of this latter style were Scopas, his younger contemporary, Praxiteles, and Lysippus. The most important works of Scopas that survive are the decorations of the mausoleum at Halicarnassus, erected by Artemisia over the remains of her husband Mausolos, prince of Caria, 352 B. C. These sculptured decorations, now in the British Museum, present in the designs for the frieze, depicting a battle between Greeks and Amazons, an invention of graceful and energetic movement and a record of rapid and violent gesture such as clearly distinguish the work from that which it succeeded. The *Venus of Milo* and the celebrated group of Niobe and her chil-

dren are works attributed to Scopas. The works of Praxiteles are especially valuable as expressing a tenderness of feeling which this new and closer sympathy with human emotions had developed. He is known to us chiefly through copies of his works, or of the works of his school, the most celebrated of which are preserved in the Vatican; but the sweetness and delicate grace of his style are admirably displayed in the statue of Ceres discovered at Cnidus, now in the British Museum. Lysippus represented the human form and athletic power in the highest perfection. From the death of Alexander the Great, 323 B. C., onward to the conquest of the Romans, 146 B. C., the progress of Greek sculpture is only a further, and often a weaker, development of the same ideal. The celebrated group of the *Laocoön*, the head of the *Dying Alexander*, the *Dying Gladiator* and *Apollo Belvedere* are some of the works of this epoch that are preserved to us.

Italy. The history of sculpture in Italy is only a continuance of its story in Greece. It was Greek art, produced by Greek workmen, that adorned the palaces of the emperors; and the Roman sculptors, in so far as they had any independent existence, can only claim to have impoverished the ideal they received from Greece. Many of the best-known statues in existence were produced in the Graeco-Roman period; such are the *Borghese Gladiator*, in the Louvre, the *Venus de Medici*, at Florence, and the *Farnese Hercules*, at Naples. From the time of Hadrian (138 A. D.), art rapidly declined, and this debased Roman was the only style employed in Italy until the revival in the twelfth century. With the general awakening which began in Italy and spread over Europe, came a revival of sculpture, as of all other arts. The stiff, conventional figures of the Middle Ages were invigorated by the spirit of activity which marked the new movement. This revival of sculpture began with Nicola Pisano, who was born at Pisa about 1206 and whose work is preserved in the pulpits which he carved at Pisa and Siena. He was followed by his son Giovanni Pisano (died 1320), whose great work is the allegorical group in the Campo Santo of Pisa; but both of these sculptors worked on classic lines. Jacopo della Quercia (1374–1438), whose beautiful reliefs, adorning the façade of the Church of San Petronio at Bologna, show a feeling for grace not before expressed, was, in a certain sense, the founder of the modern school. Lorenzo Ghiberti (1381–1455) developed a more pictorial style with extraordinary success; but sculpture awaited the advent of Donatello (1386–

1468) to find its true direction and to reach its full triumph. Luca della Robbia (1400–1481) and Andrea Verrocchio (1435–1488), the master of Leonardo da Vinci, may also be named. The special tendencies of Italian sculpture may be said to have reached their full expression in the work of Michelangelo (1475–1564). Here all previous efforts to interpret passion and feeling were summed up and concluded. It was toward a complete understanding of the resources of physical expression that all Italian art had been tending, and it is only more fully exhibited in Michelangelo because he was the greatest master that Italy produced. The chief characteristic of his style was the use of colossal, highly developed forms, combined with intense dramatic action. His works are the statues in the chapel of the Medici at Florence, the *Captives*, in the Louvre, the colossal *David*, at Florence, the *Moses*, in Rome, and the *Madonna*, in Bruges. For a long period after Michelangelo Italian sculptors were content to imitate and sometimes to exaggerate his manner. The only immediate successor of Michelangelo worthy of note is Cellini (1500–1571), of Florence. Lorenzo Bernini (1598–1680), the master of the "barocco" style, exemplifies a straining after grace and elegance by means of affectation. In the eighteenth century Italy became the headquarters of the classical revival which spread thence throughout Europe. The leading spirit in this movement was Canova (1757–1822), who, although he failed to restore to his art its earlier masculine strength, at least sought in the study of the antique for greater simplicity and elegance in representation. Canova's most finished productions are notable for an affectionate tenderness of sentiment, rather than imagination, and his figures are never formed after the highest ideal. His most characteristic works are the *Graces, Hebe* and the *Cupid and Psyche*; his finest work is the colossal group of *Theseus Slaying a Centaur*, at Vienna. Canova formed Thorwaldsen (1770–1844), the great Danish sculptor, and his name and influence dominated the art of sculpture throughout Europe for many years. Modern Italian sculpture has leaned toward realism, the leading representatives being Gallori, Magni and Ximenes, and of those who avoided this tendency, the best-known are Consani, Albani and Fedi.

France. The early art of France was influenced by the styles prevailing at that time. Thus the sculptures of French cathedrals show Byzantine, Romanesque and Gothic influences, the finest examples in the last being at Amiens.

Awakening in the fifteenth century, it produced, as forerunners of the Renaissance, Bouteillier and Colombe (1431–1514), and in the sixteenth century, Jean Goujon (1530–1572), whose best work is the *Fountain of the Innocents* in Paris, and whose *Diana* shows all the faults and beauties of the style. Cousin (1501–1589), Pilon (1515–1590), Pierre Puget (1622–1694), Coysevox (1640–1720) and Girardon (1630–1715) continued the style which, while aiming at elegance and grace, lost simplicity and roundness. The Danish school which produced Thorwaldsen, owes its rise to French influence. Later yet came Houdon (1741–1828), Bosio (1769–1845), Rude (1785–1855), Barye (1795–1875), a sculptor of animals, and Carpeaux (1827–1875), whose chief work, *La Danse*, is in front of the new opera house in Paris. Among recent artists are Saint Marceaux, Frémiet, Falguière, Mercié, Dalou, Rodin, Dubois, Bartholdi, Barrias, Bartholomé and Riviere.

Germany. There was no early school of German sculpture, apart from the general Gothic style of all northern European countries, but with the Renaissance of the fifteenth century arose Adam Krafft (1480–1507) and Peter Vischer, two contemporary sculptors of Nuremberg, and Albert Dürer (1471–1528), painter and sculptor. Then came a break until the rise of the modern school, which owes its existence to the influence of Thorwaldsen. The chief names are Dannecker (1758–1841), with his *Ariadne*, and Schadow (1764–1850), with *Girl Tying Her Sandal*. Rauch (1777–1857) was the real founder of the modern German school. His monument to Frederick the Great, in Berlin, with its many accessory figures, is his finest work, and from his school came Rietschel (1804–1861), Schwanthaler (1802–1848), August Kiss (1802–1865), Bandel (1800–1876) and Drake (1805–1882). Among sculptors of recent fame are Begas, Eberlein, Zumbusch, Kundmann, Weyr, Tilgner, Strasser, Wolff, Hildebrand and Schilling.

England. Of examples of sculpture executed before the eighteenth century England possesses very few. Several tombs exist, and some of the cathedrals, notably Wells, Exeter and Lincoln, possess figures executed presumably by Englishmen at an earlier date. It is not, however, until the reign of Charles I that names of artists appear, notable among them being Nicholas Stone (1586–1647) and Grinling Gibbons (1648–1721), who was the first real artist of the English school. Banks (1735–1805) is the father of ideal English sculpture, but he died unappreciated, leaving

John Flaxman (1755–1826) to achieve the task of bringing the classical spirit into English art and of founding the school of the nineteenth century. His love for severe simplicity and true form was imbibed in Rome, and it is best seen in his *Shield of Achilles*, in his *Michael Overcoming Satan* and in his *Cephalus and Aurora*. His most famous pupil was Baily (1788–1867), whose *Eve at the Fountain* is much admired. John Gibson (1791–1866), a pupil of Canova, more properly belongs to the Italian than to the English school, his whole artistic life having been passed in Rome. His finest works are *Psyche Borne by Zephyrs*, *Narcissus*, *Hylas Surprised*, now in the National Gallery, and a large relievo of *Christ Blessing Children*. His introduction of color in statuary raised much discussion. Foley (1818–1874), whose chief work is the equestrian statue of General Outram, now at Calcutta, and Patrick Macdowall (1799–1870), with *Love Triumphant*, are the last names of the classic school. The tendency of sculpture in England at the present day is toward a more original and naturalistic treatment. Alfred Stevens (1817–1875) is the author of the finest decorative work in England, the monument of the duke of Wellington in Saint Paul's. Of late sculptors who have contributed to England's reputation are Boehm, Woolner, Watts, Leighton, Armstead, Simonds, Brock, Thorneycroft, Ford, Gilbert, Bates, Franklin, Stark and Pomeroy.

Other Countries. The Renaissance began earlier in the *Netherlands* than in the other northern countries, and had its center at Dijon, in Burgundy, where a number of important mas-, ters were active, among whom was Claux Sluter. In the seventeenth century the school of Antwerp gained prominence and produced such sculptors as François Duquesnoy (1594–1644) and his pupil Artus Quellinus (1609–1688), who showed Italian influence. The eighteenth century noted a decline of sculpture in the Netherlands. *Scandinavia* followed the other nations in the general plan of development. The influence of the Netherlands and France was felt in the eighteenth century. The most important names are Sergel (1740–1814), Bystrom (1783–1848) and Bissen (1798–1868). In the nineteenth century, Thorwaldsen (1770–1884), the great Danish sculptor, stands as the chief exponent of the antique tendency in sculpture. Sculpture in *Russia* is of very recent growth. Two names are worthy of mention, Lanceray and Lieberich (1828–   ).

151

United States. The first American sculptors of importance are Greenough (1805–1852), a portrait statue artist of marked achievement: Powers, whose *Greek Slave*, *Il Penseroso* and *Proserpine* are well known; Crawford, who produced *American Revolution* and *Indian Chief*. Of later artists in the same group are Palmer, Story, Randolph Rogers, John Rogers, Rinehart and Hosmer. These, with the intensely patriotic Henry Kirke Browne and J. Q. A. Ward, form a school of distinctive American art, noticeable both in theme and execution. Others of less fame are Clevenger, Bartholomew, Meade and Launt Thompson. Since about 1875, American sculpture has been greatly influenced by the French, though some of the more important artists have had German and Italian training. Of the German-American group, Keyser, of Baltimore, is the most important. Howard Roberts and Levi Warner were among the first to display the French influence. Of most recent fame are Augustus Saint Gaudens and Daniel C. French, both masters of the art, whose works have placed them in the front rank of modern sculptors. Notable among the works of French are the bronze statue of Washington, executed as a gift of American citizens to France, and the bronze doors of the Boston Public Library. Saint Gaudens's greatest works are the *Shaw Memorial*, on the Boston Common, and the bronze equestrian statue of Sherman, at the principal entrance of Central Park, New York. The latter is counted among the half-dozen greatest equestrian statues of the world. Frederick MacMonnies, a pupil of Saint Gaudens, has recently achieved honor, both at home and abroad. Herbert Adams, Partridge, Paul Bartlett, Bitter, Niehaus, Rhind, Proctor, Kemys, Barnard and Lorado Taft are among the younger men who have reflected credit upon American sculpture. On the whole, it may be said of American sculpture that it has started along a path which leads to works of permanent value, namely, independent and consistent labor. It does not disregard the classic forms, but it adds to them an individuality and flexibility which well represent the free and vigorous character of American life. Such buildings as the Library of Congress at Washington and such decorative achievements as the sculpture of our recent expositions testify both to the demand for good art and the ability of our own sculptors to meet that demand. According to the opinions of great art critics our school of sculpture can now compare favorably with the new school of any country.

A more comprehensive view of the subject of sculpture may be had by reading the biographies of the important sculptors mentioned in this article.

Scur'vy, a disease formerly very prevalent among sailors, because of their being compelled on long voyages to live exclusively upon salt meat and hard bread, with impure water. In recent years the disease is little known, because of better sanitary provisions and more abundant supplies of food. It is due to poor nourishment and is rarely seen, except among the poor and careless. Severe cases of scurvy are accompanied by swellings in different parts of the body and by swollen gums, which become ulcerated and bleed, making it almost impossible to eat. In fact, unless suitably treated, it progresses to exhaustion and death. Before there have been any serious losses of tissue, however, the disease may be cured by proper treatment, and no serious ill effects will remain.

Scutari, or **Skutari,** *skoo tah're,* a city of Albania. Scutari lies near the southern extremity of Lake Scutari, at the point where the Bojana River issues from the lake. Its industries are of little importance, but it was for many years a great Turkish fortress. In the Balkan War of 1912–1913, Scutari was taken by the Montenegrins, but was assigned to the new kingdom of Albania. Population, about 20,000.

Scylla, *sil'la,* in classical mythology, a beautiful girl, who, through the jealousy of Circe, was turned into a terrible six-headed monster. She lived under a rock in the sea opposite Charybdis, and every time a ship went by she stretched out her six heads and seized six men.

Scythe, *sithe,* an instrument used for mowing. It consists of a long curving blade, with a sharp edge, made fast at the proper angle to the lower end of a more or less upright handle, called the *snath*. This is bent into a convenient form for swinging the blade to advantage. Most snaths have two short projecting handles, fixed to the main handle. The real line of the handle is that which passes through the hands and ends at the head of the blade. This may be a straight line or a crooked one, generally the latter, and by moving the short handles up or down on the main handle, each mower can place them so as to best suit the size and position of his body. The *cradle* used for cutting grain has a very wide scythe and a frame of fingers fastened to the snath for catching the grain as it is cut and for laying it in even rows for binding. A bush scythe is shorter and stronger than a grass scythe. Mow-

ing and reaping machines have now replaced the scythe and cradle in most civilized countries.

Scythians, *sith'e anz,* a name vaguely used by ancient writers. It was sometimes applied to all the nomadic tribes which wandered over the regions to the north of the Black and Caspian seas, and to the east of the latter. In the time of the Roman Empire the name Scythia covered Asia from the Volga to the frontiers of India.

Sea. See OCEAN.

Sea Anem'one, the popular name of a number of animals belonging to the Coelenterata. They are among the most interesting organisms met on the sea beach, and in aquaria they form a great attraction. All of them appear as fleshy cylinders, attached by their bases to rocks or stones, and presenting, at their free extremities, mouths surrounded by circlets of arms or tentacles. With these tentacles, in some cases exceeding two hundred in number, they seize their food, which they paralyze by means of stinging cells, common to this branch of the animal kingdom. The appearance of the anemones with their tentacles extended is very beautiful, as they are of all varieties in color and resemble not a little a fully expanded flower, which, however, closes suddenly when touched in any way. Although the sea anemones are attached to rocks, they appear able to detach themselves and move about at will. Some species are used as food in Mediterranean countries.

Sea Bear. See FUR SEAL.

Sea Cow. See MANATEE.

Sea Cucumbers or **Holothuria,** a family of animals, covered with a tough leathery skin perforated with holes, through which the foot-tentacles are protruded (See ECHINODERMATA). The animals are capable of extending themselves to several times their ordinary length, and they will reproduce to an extraordinary degree parts of the body which are cut away or destroyed. They abound along the eastern coast of Asia, and some species are edible. See TREPANG. (See illustration on next page.)

Sea Eagle, the name given to one or two different members of the eagle family which are generally found living near the sea coasts and subsisting mainly upon fish. They make inland journeys in search of food and sometimes seize hares and other small animals. In the most common species, the *white-tailed eagle,* or *erne,* found in all parts of Europe, the head is covered with long, drooping feathers of ashy brown color, while the body is dark brown, streaked in places with lighter tints. See EAGLE.

Sea Hare, the name of a genus of mollusks. These animals are slug-like in appearance and derive their popular name from the prominent

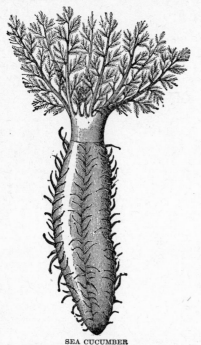

SEA CUCUMBER

character of the front pair of tentacles, which somewhat resemble the ears of a hare. Four tentacles exist, and the eyes are situated at the base of the hinder tentacles. The shell is either absent or is of very rudimentary character and is concealed by the mantle. The sea hares are widely distributed throughout most seas and generally inhabit muddy or sandy tracts. They emit a fluid of a rich purple hue, which, like the ink of the cuttlefishes, has the property of diffusing itself quickly throughout the surrounding water. They are also known to discharge an acrid fluid of milky appearance, which has an irritant effect on the human skin.

Sea Horse. See HIPPOCAMPUS.

Seal, an aquatic mammal, living chiefly in the sea, though a few specimens are found in some of the larger lakes of Europe. The seal has a body which is large at the front and tapers toward the tail, like that of the whales. It has four legs, which are almost covered by the skin of the body, while in place of the feet are fins or flippers. The hind legs are used in swimming, and the fore legs support the animal in an erect position when he is on the

land. The mouth is large and is surrounded by numerous feelers, resembling those of the cat. The eyes are large, with an almost human expression, and the ears are small or entirely lacking. The body is covered by thick, woolly fur and long, shining hair, and all is so oily and smooth that it enables the seal to move easily through the water. Seals are air-breathing animals, but they can remain under water for a considerable time. They are expert divers and swimmers, but are exceedingly awkward on land. They frequent rocks in shallow places and icebergs, where they come at breeding time and remain to rear their young. Most species are easily tamed, and they often form great attachment for their keepers and are easily taught ingenious and amusing tricks.

Seals inhabit the cool waters of the temperate and polar regions and usually return to the same spot year after year to breed. They live in herds, and before they were hunted many of these herds were of enormous size. In many places, however, they have now been nearly exterminated by hunters, who seek them for their skins and their fat, which is known as blubber. There are numerous species, but commercially these are all grouped under the fur seal and hair seal. The latter is the common seal of the Atlantic coast. It has long, silky hair and is valued for its skin and blubber. It

SEAL

is captured in large quantities off Newfoundland, Labrador, Norway and Jan Meyan Island. See ELEPHANT SEAL; FUR SEAL.

Seal, an engraved stamp, bearing a device or inscription pertaining to the owner; also, the impression of such a stamp on a plastic substance, as wax. A seal upon a document was originally a substitute for a signature. The use of seals is of the highest antiquity, and one of the earliest and commonest forms is the signet ring, impressions being made in fine clay, beeswax and lead. Later flat seals, called *bullae*, made of gold, silver and lead, were used and were attached to documents by silk or woolen bands. Sealing wax was invented in the seventeenth century. Each state has a seal, with a distinct device or legend. The attestation of deeds and other documents by a notary's seal stamped is customary.

Sea Lemon, a genus of mollusks, destitute of shell and possessed of gills, which form a circle of plumes in the middle of the back, at the hinder end of the animal. The name *sea lemon* has been given to this mollusk because of its lemon color and somewhat lemon-like shape. It is found at low water mark, under stones and in similar places.

Sea Lilies. See CRINOIDEA.

Sealing Wax, a resinous preparation used for securing folded papers and envelopes, and for receiving impressions of seals set to instruments. Ordinary red sealing wax is made from shellac melted with rosin, to which are added Venice turpentine and vermilion. Inferior qualities consist of a proportion of common resin and red lead, and black and other colors are produced by substituting appropriate pigments. Sealing wax was invented in the seventeenth century.

Sea Lion, a seal, of which there are several species, the largest reaching a length of fourteen

timid creatures that herd together in large numbers.

Sea Mouse, a genus of small marine worms that inhabit deep water, especially in the North Atlantic. The hairs, or bristles, which fringe the sides of the body show beautiful iridescent hues. These animals may be obtained by dredging, although they are frequently cast up on shores after storms.

Search, RIGHT OF, in maritime law, the right claimed by a nation at war, to authorize the commanders of its lawfully commissioned cruisers to enter private merchant vessels of other nations met with on the high seas, to examine their papers and cargo and to search for enemy's property or contraband of war; or the right claimed by a nation to search vessels of other nations and to seize citizens of the former in the service of the latter. England's insistence on the right of search was one of the causes leading to the War of 1812.

Search Warrant. SEE WARRANT.

Sea Robin. See GURNARD.

Sears, *seerz,* BARNAS (1802–1880), an American educator, born at Sandisfield, Massachusetts. He was educated at Brown University and Newton Theological Seminary. After teaching two years at Madison University, he went to

SEA LION

feet. Different species are found in the Southern Pacific and in the Northern Pacific. The common black sea lion of California is a small species that is often confined in zoological gardens. This is the animal that has been one of the attractions on the rocks near the Cliff House at San Francisco. The sea lions are

Germany and studied at Halle, Leipzig and Berlin. On his return, he became professor of theology at Newton Seminary, of which institution he was later made president. In 1848 he succeeded Horace Mann as secretary and agent of the Massachusetts Board of Education. In 1855 he was chosen president of Brown

University, holding the position for twelve years, when he became agent of the Peabody Educational Fund. He edited the *Christian Review*, was the author of *The Life of Luther*, contributed to the *Bibliotheca Sacra* and wrote a number of pedagogical and educational treatises.

Sea Serpent, *sur'pent*, a great marine monster, often reported to have been seen; there is no proof that such an animal exists. Various accounts assert that it is sixty feet or more in length and that it swims with its head and part of its body out of water. The whole story, however, is generally regarded as a myth, and the explanation of it is that people have been deluded by the sight of shoals of fish, logs of wood or seaweed.

Sea'sickness, a nervous attack, produced by the motion of the sea. It shows itself in headache, nausea, vomiting, general weakness and sometimes great depression. Usually an attack passes quickly off, as the person becomes accustomed to the sea, and will not recur, at least during the continuance of that voyage. Some more susceptible people are always more or less ill when on the water and become more violently so whenever the motion of the vessel increases. Children and aged persons are more frequently exempt than others. Many remedies have been suggested for seasickness, but none of them seems to be effective in all cases. A person should take pains to keep the bowels regular, should not overload the stomach and should take active exercise in the open air. If, however, the attack is severe, the patient should go to bed for a day or two. However, long confinement in a stateroom is bad, and it very often happens that the attacks will disappear entirely on return to the open air.

Sea Snake, a name common to a family of poisonous marine snakes of several genera. They frequent the seas of warm latitudes. Although usually dull brownish or greenish, some are beautifully colored, especially the species found in India. They delight in calms and are fond of eddies and tideways, where the ripple collects the fish and medusae, on which they feed.

Seasons, *se'z'nz*, the four grand divisions of the year—spring, summer, autumn, winter. These have distinctive characters, best seen in the temperate zones. Within the tropics they are marked not so much by differences of temperature as by wetness and dryness and are usually distinguished as the wet and dry seasons. Astronomically speaking, in the Northern Hemisphere spring extends from the vernal equinox to the summer solstice; summer extends from the summer solstice to the autumnal equinox; autumn lasts from the autumnal equinox to the winter solstice; winter extends from the winter solstice to the vernal equinox. The characters of the seasons are reversed to the inhabitants of the Southern Hemisphere. See EQUINOX; SOLSTICE, and the articles on each of the four seasons.

Sea Squirts, *skwurts*, or **Ascidians**, a name commonly given to certain low-grade mollusks, which resemble double-necked bottles, of a leathery or gristly nature, and are found at low water on a sea beach or are dredged from deep water attached to stones, shells, seaweed and fixed objects. The name has been applied to them from their habit of squirting jets of water when touched or irritated in any way. There are numerous species, all of which pass through peculiar phases of development, the young sea squirt appearing like a tadpole.

SEA SQUIRTS
Colony on branch of seaweed.

Sea Surgeon, *sur'jun*, or **Surgeon Fish**, one of a family of fishes numbering eighty species, so named because on the side of the fish near the tail is a sharp spine, resembling somewhat a surgeon's lancet. The sea surgeon is found on the Atlantic coasts of South America and Africa and in the Caribbean Sea. Its average length is from twelve to nineteen inches.

Seattle, *se at't'l*, WASH., the county-seat of King co., and the largest city in the state, is situated on Puget Sound, 129 mi. inland from the Pacific Ocean, 347 mi. w. of Spokane, 1822 mi. w. of Saint Paul, 185 mi. n. of Portland and 804 mi. by water n. of San Francisco. It is on the Great Northern, the Northern Pacific, the Chicago, Milwaukee & Puget Sound, the Oregon & Washington and other railroads. The city occupies a beautiful site, between Puget Sound on the west and Lake Washington on the east. It is built upon a series of hills, which in some places rise to the height of 300 feet and are separated by broad valleys or terraces.

The main streets run north and south, and the cross streets, east and west. An excellent street car system connects all parts of the city and the important suburbs. The streets have been graded at great expense and are well paved. The city is substantially built, most of the buildings in the business center being constructed of steel and brick or stone. Among the important buildings are the new Catholic Cathedral, costing $500,000, the courthouse, the Federal building, the Carnegie Library, the Alaska building, the White building, the city hall, Butler Hotel, Hotel Washington and the buildings of the state university. The city has fifteen parks. Chief among these are Denny, Kinnear, Lincoln, Volunteer, Washington and Woodland. All of these will ultimately be connected by a system of boulevards.

The University of Washington is the most important educational institution within the city and the state; among the others are Seattle Seminary, Immaculate Conception College, Academy of Holy Names and several schools maintained either by denominational or private enterprise. An excellent system of public schools, including six high schools, is maintained.

Seattle is one of the most important industrial and commercial centers on the Pacific coast. On the water front are found the extensive docks and railway stations devoted to the handling of freight and to the wholesale trade. This is the most convenient port for all traffic going to Alaska and for much of that between the United States and China Japan, Hawaii and the Philippine Islands, and since the occupation of the Philippines by the United States the oriental trade of Seattle has rapidly increased. There is also an extensive local trade by water between the city and numerous other towns on Puget Sound. The harbor is one of the best and will be greatly increased by a ship canal, under process of construction, to connect the Sound with Lake Washington. The largest ocean steamships can reach Seattle docks in all seasons of the year. The most important industries consist of the manufacture of lumber and timber products, shipbuilding and the manufacture of iron and steel products, flour and grist mill products and various articles made of wood. The United States navy yard located across the Sound, 14 miles distant, contains the largest dry dock on the Pacific coast. The repair works here give employment to about 1000 men and in this yard have been constructed some of the best battleships of the navy.

HISTORY. The city occupies the site of a former Indian town. The first settlement by white men was in 1852, and the next year the town was laid out and named after an Indian chief. It was incorporated in 1865, and previous to the completion of the transcontinental railways its growth was slow. In 1889 a fire destroyed the main portion of the city, causing a loss of over $10,000,000. Within a year a new and better city had been built, with wider streets and more modern buildings. The discovery of gold in Alaska and the acquisition of the Philippines suddenly brought Seattle into prominence as a commercial center, and it has continued to increase in population and wealth ever since. Population in 1910, 237,194.

Sea Urchin or **Echinus**, a genus of marine animals, typical of the great branch which is

UNDER SURFACE OF SEA URCHIN

named from it (See ECHINODERMATA). The body of the sea urchin is more or less globular and covered with a shell which is often studded with movable spines. Sea urchins, of which there are many species, are found in shallow water in almost all parts of the world, those of the tropical regions being larger and covered with heavier spines.

Sea'weed, the common name for any plant which grows in water. See ALGAE; KELP.

Sebas'tian, DOM (1554–1578), king of Portugal, ascended the throne in 1557, at the death of his grandfather, John III. In 1578, after assuming the power himself, he led his nobility into Africa on a wild expedition against the Moors, and perished in battle, with nearly all his followers. He had no immediate heir, and Portugal was soon annexed by Philip II of Spain, but the masses of the people refused to believe in Sebastian's death, and several pretenders to his name received a measure of popular support. The belief in the future return of Dom

Sebastian lingered long in Portugal, finally taking the form of a myth and giving rise to a considerable literature of poems and romances.

Sebastian, SAINT, a Christian churchman who suffered martyrdom under Diocletian. He was a captain of the praetorian guard, but being a Christian he encouraged those who were to suffer death for their religion. Diocletian, on hearing of this, ordered Sebastian to be tied to a stake and shot with arrows. Irene, a Christian, is said to have taken him to her home and cared for him till his wounds were healed. The Italian painters, especially Veronese and Domenichino, have made the young martyr, with his body containing arrows, the subject of several pictures. When Sebastian, after his recovery, accused Diocletian of cruelty, the young soldier was condemned to be beaten to death with rods (288).

Sebas'topol, a Russian city, situated on the southwest side of the Peninsula of Crimea, on the Black Sea. It has an excellent harbor, whose entrance is strongly fortified. The important buildings include the Cathedral of Peter and Paul and the Vladimir Cathedral. The city contains a number of monuments commemorating the Crimean War, and it also has a cemetery, in which over 127,000 soldiers are buried. The city was practically destroyed during the Siege of 1855. Since then it has been rebuilt on modern plans. It has railway communication with Moscow and is one of the most important Russian ports on the Black Sea. Population in 1909, 71,100.

Secession, *se sesh'un*, in United States history, a term applied to the act of a state in withdrawing from the Union. The idea of secession appeared at many times during the early career of the republic, being suggested as early as the constitutional convention of 1787. At every important change in policy from that time forward, the minority party suggested secession as a means of compelling the party in power to change its course. It was suggested at the Louisiana Purchase, at the War of 1812, at the passage of the tariff of 1828 and at various times during the slavery controversy. It was actually carried out, however, only in 1860, after the election of Abraham Lincoln, and at that time it brought on the Civil War. See CIVIL WAR IN AMERICA; CONFEDERATE STATES OF AMERICA; UNITED STATES, subhead *History*.

Secession, WAR OF. See CIVIL WAR IN AMERICA.

Sec'onda'ry Schools, schools ranking in grade between the common schools and the colleges. In the United States they include high schools, academies, and seminaries whose courses of study do not extend beyond preparation for college. The high schools are under city or township control, and in the newer states the most advanced are affiliated with state universities, so that their graduates can enter those institutions without examination. Academies and seminaries are usually under denominational control. Many of these schools maintain, in addition to a college preparatory course, departments in commerce and finance, art and music. The secondary schools of Germany are known as *realschulen*. See COMMON SCHOOLS; EDUCATION, NATIONAL SYSTEMS OF.

Sec'retary Bird, a South African bird of prey that derives its popular name from the peculiar plumes which project from the back and sides of its head and give it the appearance of having bundles of old-fashioned quill pens stuck behind each ear. It has very long legs and stands nearly four feet in height. Though somewhat resembling a heron in its general appearance, it is more closely related to the vulture, and as it kills rats, mice, troublesome insects and even snakes, it is protected by law.

Secre'tion, in animal physiology, the separation of certain elements from the blood and the forming of them into special fluids, differing from the blood itself, as bile, saliva, mucus. Secretion is the work of organs of various form and structure, but all may be classified as membranes or glands. Secretions are of two kinds, those that have a special work to do, known as *true secretions*, as the saliva and bile; and those that are discharged from the body as worthless or harmful, known as *excretions*. The latter require no special cells, as they exist in the blood and must be separated from it. If an excretory organ becomes useless, some other organ will do its work, but if an organ of secretion be removed, its product is no longer found in the system. See GLANDS; MEMBRANES.

Se'cret Service, that branch of the organization of the government whose duty it is to detect criminal and fraudulent practices and to gain information upon subjects of a private nature. In most foreign governments this service is in the hands of a separate department, but in the United States each of the several executive departments has its own secret service. The most important is that connected with the treasury and it is engaged chiefly in the detecting and arresting of coin and note counterfeiters and in preventing the violation of revenue laws.

Sec'ular Games, a great festival, probably of Etruscan origin, anciently celebrated at Rome to mark the commencement of a new *saeculum*, or generation. In 249 B. C. it was decreed that the secular games should be celebrated every hundredth year after that date; but this decree was frequently disregarded.

Seda'lia, Mo., the county-seat of Peltis co., 100 mi. e. of Kansas City, on the Missouri, Kansas & Texas and the Missouri Pacific railroads. The city is situated on a plain almost a thousand feet above sea level, in an agricultural region containing, also, deposits of zinc, iron, lead, fire clay, emery and limestone. The city has a extensive trade in hay, potatoes, grain, fruit and poultry. Repair shops of the Missouri Pacific are located here. There are also foundries, machine shops, implement works, woolen mills, flour mills, grain elevators, broom factories, a brewery and other factories. The streets are regularly laid out and lined with beautiful shade trees. The principal structures are the Federal building, the courthouse, the high school, the municipal buildings and the railroad hospital. There are twenty-five churches, public and parish schools, the George R. Smith College, Saint Anthony's Academy, a public library and two school libraries. The city was laid out by General George R. Smith in 1861 and was a military post during the Civil War. It was incorporated in 1864 and was chartered as a city in 1889. Population in 1910, 17,822.

Sedan, *se dahN'*, BATTLE OF, a famous battle of the Franco-German War, fought at Sedan, a town in France. Marshal MacMahon, on his way to relieve Bazaine at Metz, was forced by the Germans to take refuge in the fortress of Sedan, which was then surrounded by the enemy. On Sept. 1, 1870, the French issued from their position and the battle began. Driven back to the town of Sedan, the French defended themselves gallantly, but were finally forced to surrender. Over 85,000 men, with the emperor, Napoleon III, were made prisoners. It was the capture of Sedan which led to the overthrow of the Second Empire in France. See FRANCE, subhead *History*.

Sed'ative, anything which tends to quiet a part or the whole of the nervous system or any of the organs of the body. Different drugs act upon different organs, and some affect the whole systems. In many cases drugs that act as sedatives upon one organ are irritants upon another, and often when small doses are sedatives, large doses excite or irritate. Besides the drugs, cold, heat and friction are local sedatives, and frequent use is made of them. See NARCOTIC; ANESTHETIC, and articles on the several drugs.

Sedges, *sej'es*, plants which look like grasses, but which grow in tufts in wet places and which are coarse and rough. They differ from the grasses, however, in having triangular stems, and in their flowers, which resemble minute lilies in form and structure. Most of the hay cut in swampy places is made up of sedges, which are never so succulent and nutritious as the grasses. There are numerous species of the sedge family so nearly alike that only botanists can distinguish them. They are distributed throughout all parts of the world. The Egyptian papyrus belongs to this family.

Sedgwick, *sej'wik*, CATHERINE MARIA (1789–1867), an American author, born at Stockbridge, Mass. For fifty years she conducted a private school for the education of young ladies. Her first work of fiction, *A New England Tale*, was popular, and *Redwood* was compared favorably with the novels of Cooper and was translated into several European languages. Other works of hers were *Hope Leslie, The Linwoods* and *Letters from Abroad*. She was a prolific writer and contributed much to the annuals and magazines.

Sedgwick, JOHN (1813–1864), an American soldier, born at Cornwall, Conn., and educated at West Point. He served in the Seminole wars and in the Mexican War, and at the outbreak of the Civil War he was given command of a brigade, serving with great efficiency in the Peninsula Campaign, at Antietam and at Chancellorsville, Fredericksburg and Gettysburg, where he distinguished himself by a difficult forced march, in order to reach the scene of battle. He was with General Grant in the famous Virginia campaign of 1864 and was killed at Spottsylvania Court House.

Seeder. See SOWING MACHINE.

Seeds, the name given in botany to the ripened ovules of plants. Each seed consists of an embryo and a supply of food, protected by a more or less hardened coat. The embryo is a minute plant, one part of which has the power to grow up to the light and air, where it develops leaves and flowers, and the other of which has the power to develop roots, which grow toward the darkness in search of food and moisture. In the seed the food supplies are in some cases placed around the embryo, while in others they are stored in the embryo itself. The coverings of the seeds are so marked that a person knowing them can easily recognize the species from which they came.

Some seeds are hard and dry or stony, while others develop appendages such as wings or silky hair, that are evidently intended to aid in the dis-

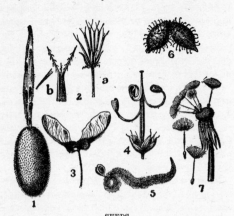

SEEDS

1, squirting cucumber; 2, bidens: *a*, the full head, *b*, fruit enlarged; 3, maple; 4, geranium; 5, clematis; 6, cocklebur; 7, dandelion.

tribution of the seeds. In a few species there is an extra covering, called an *aril*, which is either fleshy or sack-like, as may be seen in the mace of a nutmeg.

See′land or **Zealand,** the largest and most easterly island belonging to Denmark, between the Peninsula of Jutland and Sweden. Its outline is very irregular. The greatest length from north to south is 80 miles, and its greatest breadth is 65 miles. The area is 2680 square miles. Most of the island is low, the greatest elevation not exceeding 400 feet. The land is covered with forests or fertile fields and is the seat of Copenhagen. Population in 1911, 1,096,897.

Seer, the standard measure of weight in India, varying in different parts of the country. The imperial, or standard, seer is exactly equivalent to the kilogram, or about 2.205 pounds; it is the fortieth part of a maund. As a standard liquid measure, the seer is equal to about 6 gills.

Seguin, *sa gaN′,* EDOUARD (1812–1880), a French-American physician, born in France, where he devoted himself to the study of idiocy and the training of idiots. After the Revolution of 1848 he settled in the United States and achieved remarkable results in his treatment of idiots. His writings on the subject still hold the position of text-books.

Seidl, *zi′d′l,* ANTON (1850–1898), a famous musical conductor, born at Pest and educated at Leipzig and Vienna. He became a close friend and assistant of Richard Wagner and was an admirer and follower of that master.

In 1885 he was called to New York to conduct German opera, and there he developed a strong orchestra. His fame spread abroad and in 1897 he was one of the directors at Covent Garden, London, and in the same year at the Baireuth festival. With the possible exception of Theodore Thomas, he did more than any other American conductor to popularize musical culture.

Seidlitz, *sed′lits,* **Powders,** a medicine, named after the Seidlitz spa in Bohemia. These powders are usually put up in blue and white papers, the blue containing tartrate of soda and potash (Rochelle salt), with bicarbonate of soda; and the white, tartaric acid. The contents of the blue paper are dissolved in half a tumbler of water, and the acid powder is then added. The draught is taken during the effervescence, which begins at once. The medicine acts mildly on the bowels.

Seine, *sayn,* a river of France, which rises in the Department of Côte-d'Or and flows north-northwest and enters the English Channel between Havre and Honfleur. It is 475 miles long and is navigable for 350 miles. It enters the channel by an estuary 6 miles wide. Below Paris the Seine is noted for its winding course and for the beautiful scenery along its banks. Its most important tributaries from the south are the Yonne and the Eure, and from the north, the Aube, the Marne and the Oise. The Seine is connected by canals with the Scheldt, the Meuse, the Rhine, the Rhone and the Loire.

Seismograph, *sise′mo graf,* an instrument for measuring the force and direction of earthquakes and other earth movements. It records both the horizontal and the vertical movements by means of an index, the record being traced on smoked glass. There are various forms of seismographs. One which is used in the observatory on Mount Vesuvius consists of a delicate electric apparatus, which is set to work by the agitation or change of level of a mercurial column, which records the time of the first shock, the interval between the shocks, and the duration of each; their nature, whether vertical or horizontal; the maximum intensity, and, in the case of horizontal shocks, the direction.

Select′men, in New England, officers chosen annually to manage the affairs of a town. A town has usually from three to seven selectmen, who constitute both a legislative and an executive authority.

Sele′ne, in Greek mythology, the goddess of the moon, daughter of Hyperion and sister of Helios (the sun) and Eos (the dawn). She was also called Phoebe, and in later times she was identified with Artemis. In art she was often represented as a beautiful woman, with large wings, a long robe and a coronet.

Sele′nium, a rare chemical element, discovered by Berzelius in 1817 in the refuse of a sulphuric acid manufactory near Fahlun, in Sweden. It occurs in several minerals, chiefly in combination with sulphur, copper, lead, mercury and silver, and it is closely related, in its general chemical properties, to sulphur and tellurium. Selenium takes fire when heated to a tolerably high temperature in air or in oxygen, burning with a blue flame and a disagreeable odor. With hydrogen selenium forms the very disagreeably smelling gas, *seleniureted hydrogen*. In metallic form it is a conductor of electricity, and its power of conductivity is increased by sunlight. See PHOTOPHONE.

Self-Denying Ordinance, an enactment passed by the British Parliament in 1645, decreeing that no member of Parliament shoul hold office in the army during the war against Charles I. The object was to give the control of the army to the radical independents, rather than to the Presbyterians. Cromwell, who was a member of Parliament and an officer in the army, was declared an exception to the rule and was allowed to keep his position.

Se′lim I (about 1467–1520), sultan of the Ottoman Empire. The people raised him to the throne in place of Bajazet, his father, who was afterward poisoned, with the brothers and nephews of Selim. In 1514 Selim entered upon a war with Persia and obtained large accessions of territory. He next directed his arms against the Mamelukes of Egypt, and in 1517 he became master of Syria and Egypt. The rights and insignia of the caliphate were at this time granted to Selim by the last descendant of the Abbassid caliphs in Egypt, and in consequence the sultans of Constantinople became the chiefs of Islam, the representatives of Mohammed.

Selim III (1761–1808), sultan of the Ottoman Empire, succeeded his uncle, Abd-ul-Hamid, in 1789. He attempted reforms in his government after European methods, but wars with Russia and Austria prevented their being carried out. These wars were brought to a close by treaties, which cost Turkey some territory. Selim then entered with great ardor upon his system of reforms; but the fanatic zeal of the people, kindled by the preaching of the dervishes, burst into open revolt, and he was deposed by the

Janizaries (1807). An attempt to regain his throne ended in his murder. Selim's efforts for the reformation of Turkey were not altogether fruitless, for manufactures had begun to flourish, and a number of improvements of real benefit to the nation were effected.

Seli′nus, one of the most important of the Greek colonies in Sicily, founded probably about 628 B. C., on the southwest coast of the island. Thucydides mentions its great power and wealth and the rich treasures of its temples. It was conquered by the Carthaginians in 409 B. C., and about 250 B. C. it was destroyed by them. There are still important ruins of ancient Greek temples here, and valuable sculptures belonging to them have been preserved.

Seljuks, *sel′jooks*, a Turkish dynasty which was very powerful in Asia in the eleventh and twelfth centuries, and which was named after Seljuk, a chieftain of the Ghuz Turks. Persia was conquered by the Ghuz Turks in 1030, and this was the basis of the Empire, which later extended over Armenia, Turkestan, Syria and Asia Minor. In the First and Second crusades, the Christians came into conflict with the Seljuks. The Ottoman Empire in Asia was founded on the ruins of the Seljuk Empire.

Selkirk, *sel′kurk*, or **Selkirkshire**, formerly known as Ettrick Forest, an interior county of England, of interest because within it are the scenes of Scott's *Lay of the Last Minstrel*.

Selkirk, or **Selcraig**, ALEXANDER (1676–1723), an English mariner, the prototype of Robinson Crusoe. He took part in buccaneering expeditions in the South Seas, and in consequence of a quarrel with his captain he was put ashore, at his own request, on the island of Juan Fernandez. There he lived alone for four years and four months, until he was taken off by the captain of a privateer. He returned home in 1712, and his adventures became known to the public. Defoe's *Robinson Crusoe* appeared in 1719, but Crusoe's experiences have but little in common with those of Selkirk. Selkirk afterward rose to the rank of lieutenant in the navy.

Selkirk Mountains, a range in the southeastern part of British Columbia, west of the Rocky Mountains and almost parallel to them, extending north of the United States boundary to the great loop of the Columbia River. The range is about 200 miles long and 80 miles wide. The scenery is magnificent, and there are many precipices, glaciers and rugged peaks, the highest of which is Sir Donald, 10,645 feet. The slopes are covered with dense forests.

Sel'ma, ALA., the county-seat of Dallas co., 50 mi. w. of Montgomery, on the Alabama River, at the head of navigation, and on the Louisville & Nashville, the Southern and other railroads. The city is in a cotton-growing region and contains cotton, cottonseed oil, flour and planing mills, railroad shops, iron works and other factories. The Alabama Baptist Colored University is located here, and the city has the Dallas Academy, the public library, private business schools, a good Y. M. C. A. building and the county courthouse. The first settlement was made in 1823. During the Civil War the city was an important Confederate depot of supplies, and several engagements were fought here. Population in 1910, 13,649.

Semaphore, *sem'a for*, a device used for signaling in navies, in the army and on railroads. Before the invention of the telegraph, many kinds of semaphores were in use, but electric communication has rendered them unnecessary in most instances. The simplest form of semaphore is that employed on railways. It consists of an upright standard, from 3 to 18 or 20 feet in height, as conditions may require, to the top of which one or more boards, called *arms*, are attached. These arms are fastened to the standard so that they can be raised or lowered from the office of the telegraph operator. The long arm is painted usually red or white,

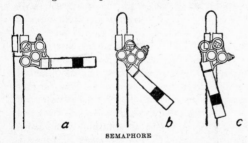

SEMAPHORE

a, stop; *b*, caution, go slowly; *c*, way clear, go ahead

and the short arm contains an iron frame, in which are placed red and green glasses, one above the other. When the arm of the semaphore is dropped it indicates a clear track; if raised to an angle of 45° it indicates caution; if raised to a horizontal position it indicates that the train should stop. At night the colored glasses in the short arm give the necessary signals. When the arm is dropped a white light is shown; at an angle of 45° a green light, and when in horizontal position, a red light. See RAILROAD.

Sembrich, *sem'briK*, MARCELLA (1858–   ), a Polish operatic soprano whose real name was Marcelline Kochanska. She was educated at Vienna and made her début at Athens in 1877. She was immediately successful and soon made tours of both Europe and America, winning the unanimous praise of the critics for the purity and flexibility of her voice.

Semele, *sem'e le*, in Greek mythology, a daughter of Cadmus, beloved by Jupiter. Jealous of her husband, Juno persuaded Semele to entreat her lover to attend her with the majesty in which he appeared on Olympus. As he had sworn to gratify her every wish, Jupiter, though horrified at this request, came to her accompanied by lightnings and thunderbolts, when Semele was instantly consumed by fire. Bacchus was her son by Jupiter.

Sem'inole, a sub-tribe of the Creek indians, early established in Florida. Their heroic efforts to hold their territory and to prevent themselves from being removed west of the Mississippi were so successful that it was only after a terrible war of seven years (1835–1842), which cost the United States $10,000,000 and 2000 lives, that the Seminole were transported to Indian Territory and finally settled there. See OSCEOLA; FIVE CIVILIZED TRIBES.

Semir'amis, a queen of Assyria, whose history is much mingled with fable. The legend tells that she was a daughter of the fish goddess Derceto by a Syrian youth, and that she was exposed to die by her mother, but was fed by doves until discovered by the chief of the royal shepherds, who adopted her. Her beauty was so great that Onnes, the governor of Nineveh, fell in love with her and made her his wife. She accompanied him in the siege of Bactra, and here her beauty, wit and bravery won the love of King Ninus, the founder of Nineveh. He demanded that Onnes should give her up to him, but Onnes refused, and finally in his despair he hanged himself. Semiramis then became the bride of Ninus, who shortly after resigned to her the crown and had her proclaimed queen of Assyria. She built Babylon and made it the mightiest city in the world, and she conquered many of the neighboring countries. After a reign of forty-two years, she was deposed, and some accounts say she was killed by her son. It is probable that Semiramis is to a large extent a mythological person, corresponding to the goddess Astarte or to the Venus of the Romans.

Sem'ites or **Semitic Nation,** an important West-Asiatic group of peoples, including the Hebrews, the Assyrians, the Arameans, the Arabians, the Babylonians and the Phoenicians. They are closely akin in their physical and mental characteristics, in their religion and in their language (See SEMITIC LANGUAGES). The name is derived from that of Shem, the son of Noah, but is not rightly applied to all of the peoples who are given in *Genesis* x as the descendants of Shem.

Semit'ic Languages, the languages belonging to the Semites, or Semitic peoples. The Semitic languages form an important linguistic family, which is usually divided into a northern and a southern section. To the northern belong the ancient dialects of Assyria and Babylonia (recovered by means of the cuneiform inscriptions); the Hebrew, with the Samaritan and Moabitic; the Phoenician and Carthaginian; and lastly the Aramaic, which includes the Chaldee and the Syriac. The northern Semitic languages are now almost entirely extinct as spoken tongues, though Hebrew is to some extent still used in writing. The most important of the south Semitic tongues, and the only one now in extensive use, is the Arabic, which as a spoken language may be divided into the four dialects of Arabia, Syria, Egypt and Barbary. To this southern branch belongs also the Ethiopic, or ancient ecclesiastical language of Abyssinia. The most prominent characteristic of the Semitic tongues is the peculiarity that their roots regularly consist of three consonants, which always remain unchanged, the various words and word forms being produced by the insertion of vowels between the consonants of the root. Another peculiarity is the absence of compound words. See PHILOLOGY.

Semmes, *semz,* RAPHAEL (1809–1877), an American naval officer. He entered the navy in 1832, having previously studied law, took part in the Mexican War and on the outbreak of the Civil War joined the Confederate service. In command of the *Sumter,* and afterward of the *Alabama,* he captured many prizes (See ALABAMA, THE). In an encounter with the Federal ship *Kearsarge,* off the coast of France, the *Alabama* was sunk, and Semmes was later placed in charge of the James River squadron. He was imprisoned after the war, but gained his liberty at the amnesty. The rest of his life was devoted to law practice. He was the author of *Service Afloat and Ashore, Cruise of the Alabama and Sumter* and several other books.

Sen'ate, originally the supreme legislative body of ancient Rome, first instituted, according to tradition, by Romulus. Under the Republic the consuls, the consular tribunes and the censors had the power of choosing the senators; but they were restricted to those who had previously held magistracies, and as the magistrates were chosen by popular election, the senate was ultimately a representative body. In the administration of affairs the senate was supreme, and during national crises it could invest the consuls with absolute and dictatorial authority. Its numbers varied from 100 to 1000, being often increased or diminished to suit the wishes of various emperors and dictators.

In modern times the term is applied to the upper, or less numerous, branch of the legislature in various countries, as in the United States, France, in most of the separate states of the Union and in some of the Swiss cantons. It is also used to designate the governing body of certain universities. See UNITED STATES, subhead *Government.*

Sen'eca, a tribe of indians, originally inhabiting the western part of New York State. Upward of 2600 are now on New York reservations, and a small band are in the former Indian Territory. See FIVE NATIONS, THE.

Seneca, LUCIUS ANNAEUS (3–66), called Seneca the philosopher; a Roman philosopher, born at Corduba (Cordova). When quite young he went to Rome, where he made rapid advances in knowledge under the tuition of his father. At an early age he became interested in philosophy, and later he adopted Stoicism, which he ardently followed. At the age of thirty-nine he was banished to Corsica, where he remained eight years, devoting his time to philosophy and writing. On his recall he was made praetor and appointed one of the tutors of the emperor Nero. At first Seneca exerted a strong influence over his pupil. But on the death of Burrus, Nero's military governor, Seneca's influence began to decline, and soon it ceased to have any effect upon the course of his wayward pupil. Later, Seneca was accused of conspiracy and forced to commit suicide. His works comprise treatises on *Anger*; on *Providence*; on *Tranquillity of Mind*; on the *Steadfastness of the Wise Man*; on *Clemency,* addressed to Nero; seven books on *Benefits*; seven on investigations of nature, and twenty books of moral letters. The tragedies which bear Seneca's name are very inferior to his prose writings, and it is doubtful whether he is really the author of them.

Seneca Falls, N. Y., a village in Seneca co., about 40 mi. w. by s. of Syracuse, on the Seneca River, near Cayuga Lake, and on the New York Central railroad and a number of electric railways. The name is derived from the falls in the river, which are about 50 feet high. These afford good water power, and there are machine shops, woolen mills, fire engine and pump works and furniture and other factories. There is also a large trade in dairy and farm products. Cayuga Lake Park is a summer resort of some prominence. The city has a public library, business schools and three banks. It was settled in 1791 and was incorporated in 1831. Population in 1910, 6588.

Seneca Lake, a lake in the western part of New York, about 25 mi. s. of Lake Ontario, into which its outlet discharges. The lake is 37 miles long, from 2 to 4 miles wide and 630 feet deep. It is noted for the beauty of its scenery and is navigable for steamers throughout the year. At the head of the lake is the celebrated Watkins Glen.

Senegal, *sen e gawl'*, a French colony, situated in West Africa, between the Gambia River on the south and the Senegal on the north, and extending eastward from the Atlantic coast to the Niger territories, the eastern boundary being indefinite. The region is mostly low, and in some sections the soil is unfertile, but in some portions of the Senegal valley there are luxuriant forests. The climate is hot and unhealthful. The products consist of cocoanuts, rubber, raisins, millet and maize. The capital is Saint-Louis, which is connected by railway with Dakar and Rufisque. There are no manufactures, and the commerce is comparatively unimportant. Population in 1911, 1,172,000.

Senegal, a river of western Africa, which rises in the interior, near the sources of the Niger, from which its sources are separated by the highlands of the Mandingo country. Its course is northwest and west through the Senegambia and Niger territories, and it enters a lagoon on the Atlantic Ocean near the town of Saint-Louis. Its total length is about 1000 miles, and it is navigable for about 700 miles, or as far as the Cataracts of Felou.

Sen'egam'bia and Niger Territories, a dependency of France, situated in western Africa and extending from the Senegal River on the south to the Spanish possession of Rio de Oro and westward indefinitely. The region includes that portion of old Senegambia that was not included in the colony of Senegal. The eastern part of the region is hilly or mountainous, but the coast is low. The chief rivers are the Senegal and the Gambia. The region is well watered, and the vegetation along the lower Senegal is luxuriant. The government of the territories is under one administration. See AFRICA, subhead *Political Divisions*.

Senn, NICHOLAS (1844–1908), an American surgeon, born in Switzerland. He came to the United States at an early age and settled in Ashford, Wis., where he began the study of medicine. He graduated from the Chicago Medical College in 1868 and later studied in Germany, graduating in medicine at Munich. He first served as a house physician at the Cook County, Illinois, Hospital, and then practiced medicine in Wisconsin. In 1884 he became professor of the principle and practice of surgery in the Chicago College of Physicians and Surgeons and held the same position later in the Rush Medical College. He held many important positions and wrote many valuable books on surgery, which are considered authorities on the subjects treated. Among these are *Varicocele, Experimental Surgery, Surgical Bacteriology, Principles of Surgery, The Pathology and Treatment of Tumors* and *Practical Surgery for the General Practitioner*. Doctor Senn was elected to membership in most of the leading medical organizations in the United States. He was also a member of a number of European societies.

Sen'na. See CASSIA.

Sennacherib, *sen nak'e rib*, an Assyrian king, son of Sargon, whom he succeeded in 705 B. C. He suppressed the revolt of the Babylonians, reduced part of Media, exacted tribute from Tyre and other Phoenician cities, advanced upon Philistia and Egypt and finally proceeded against Hezekiah, king of Judah, who had revolted. Yielding to panic, Hezekiah paid the tribute exacted, but when Sennacherib again invaded Judah, a miraculous visitation caused the death of thousands of his troops. Sennacherib was a great builder, and his greatest architectural work was the palace of Koyunjik, which covered eight acres.

Sensa'tion, a mental impression received through the excitation of a sensory nerve. The conditions necessary to a sensation are (1) a stimulus acting upon the ends of a sensory nerve; (2) the transmission of this stimulus to the nerve center with which the excited nerve is connected; (3) reaction of the brain upon the stimulus. Sensations are divided into two classes, general and special. General sensations are those which are related to the welfare of the body and serve as warnings or stimuli to action. Hunger, thirst and fatigue are good illustrations. Special sensations are those received through the organs of special sense and are more directly connected with mental states than are general sensations.

INTENSITY. The intensity of a sensation depends upon two classes of conditions—those which are external and those which are internal. The external conditions are (1) the intensity of the stimulus; for instance, the sensation from the light of a candle is not as intense as that from an electric light; (2) the mass or amount of the stimulus; a boy derives more pleasure from a spoonful of sugar than from a few grains; (3) newness of surroundings; because everything is new to him the child has stronger sensations from a certain stimulus than does the adult; (4) prolongation of the stimulus; the intensity is weakened by the prolongation of the stimulus beyond a given time. An odor which is at first keen is scarcely perceived after a few moments. Looking continually at a bright object fatigues the eye, and the color appears more dim, and listening continually to a monotonous sound lessens the intensity of the stimulus.

The internal conditions are (1) attention; sensation becomes more vivid if we give it our attention; (2) condition of mind and body; sensations are weakened by weariness and by some diseases, while they are sometimes intensified by such diseases as irritate the nerves; (3) contrast; sudden changes from one extreme to another increase the intensity, as in passing from a dark room to one brilliantly lighted, or in the hearing of a loud sound when one is in quietude.

THRESHOLD. Sensations are received only from those stimuli which are strong enough to cause reaction of the brain. Some animals, such as the dog and cat, have certain organs of sense highly developed. The dog can detect odors which man does not recognize. The animals of the cat family have a keen sense of hearing and can hear sounds which will not affect man. The lowest stimulus which produces a sensation through an organ of special sense is termed the *threshold* of sensation for that organ; for instance, sixteen vibrations per second is the lowest number which will enable the human ear to perceive sound. An animal which can detect a lower number has a correspondingly lower threshold of hearing. The threshold is lowered by training; therefore it is very important that due attention be given the development and

training of the senses in the education of children.

DEVELOPMENT. At birth the organs of special sense are dormant, and they develop slowly. The best authorities consider touch as the fundamental sense, and it is the one earliest developed. Taste and sight follow closely, and the development of touch aids in their perfection and makes them more acute. While taste and smell are inseparable in the act of tasting, the sense of smell is of later development than the sense of taste. Hearing is developed later than the other senses, but next to sight it is the sense which gives us the widest range of knowledge.

Since each sense produces its own peculiar sensations, it follows that all senses should be trained. The training of the eye and ear to the neglect of touch, taste and smell is a serious error and deprives children of the chance to acquire at first hand much valuable knowledge. Because sight and hearing are so easily trained, parents and teachers are prone to neglect the development of the other senses. See PERCEPTION.

Senses, SPECIAL. The sensory nerves (See NERVOUS SYSTEM, subhead *Sensory Nerves*) convey to the brain two classes of impulses, those arising from conditions within the system, such as fatigue, exhilaration, hunger, thirst and the various feelings caused by disease, and those arising from contact with external objects, which give us a knowledge of the outside world. The former are classed as *general*, and the latter as *special* sensations.

The special senses comprise those organs, sensory nerves and brain centers which respond only to special stimuli. In the order of their complexity they are (1) touch and the temperature sense; (2) the muscular sense; (3) taste; (4) smell; (5) hearing, and (6) sight. The organs of special sense bring to their respective brain centers impulses which these centers alone can translate, and this translation gives us the knowledge of sight, sound, touch, etc. It is supposed by some physiologists that the impulses are all alike and that the different interpretations are due solely to the brain centers; but there is no definite knowledge as to the method by which the impulses conveyed to the brain from the different organs are translated into mental impressions. That these impressions are wholly due to the brain centers is certain. A blow on the back of the head, or the stimulation of the optic nerve by electricity will cause a sensation of light in the darkest room, and the stimulation of the auditory nerve will cause a ringing in the ears amid perfect quiet.

There is no sharp line of separation between the general and special senses. By the increase of the stimulus, what is a special sensation, as touch, may be changed to pain. This is well illustrated by the increase of pressure at one point on the hand. A light pressure gives rise to the sense of touch, but when increased beyond this limit, it becomes painful, and we experience the pain only. The special sensations are also envolved from the general, as their development from the lower orders of animals illustrates. All impressions arising through the nerves of special sense have a physiological and a psychological phase. These phases are explained in the article SENSATION. Also see EAR; EYE; SMELL; TASTE; TOUCH.

Sensitive Plant, a peculiar plant, a native of tropical America, but often grown in greenhouses of colder climates. At the approach of night the leaflets all fold together, and the common footstalk bends toward the stem; at sunrise the leaves gradually unfold and recover their usual state. The same phenomena take place if the plant is touched roughly, except that it recovers itself in a short period. Many species of different families show similar sensitiveness in lesser degree.

Sen'sory Nerves or **Af'ferent Nerves.** See NERVOUS SYSTEM.

Seoul or **Seul,** *sa ool',* the capital of Korea, situated on the north bank of the Han of Seoul River, 25 mi. n. e. of its port, Chemulpo. The city is enclosed by high walls; the streets are narrow and dirty, and the houses are generally low and of poor construction. The only buildings of importance are the royal palaces and other government buildings and a few temples. A railway connects Seoul with Chemulpo. Population in 1911, 278,958.

Sep'ara'tor, CREAM, a machine for removing the cream from milk. There are several machines for this purpose, the most common of which is a recent invention. It operates upon the centrifugal principle. The separator consists of a revolving bowl, or drum, into which the milk is passed. There are separate tubes for removing the cream and the skim milk. The faster the drum revolves the more rapidly and completely the cream is separated. The capacity of the separator is from 175 to 3000 pounds of milk in an hour.

Se'pia, the name of a cuttlefish, also of a pigment used by painters to produce a beautiful brown color. This is prepared from the secretion of an organ in the cuttlefish, called the *ink bag.* Originally the color is black, but it is changed to brown by dissolving it in caustic potash. This solution, after boiling and filtering, forms the sepia of commerce. The black coloring matter obtained from these ink bags is placed upon the market in cakes and sticks as India ink. See CUTTLEFISH; INDIA INK.

Se'poy, the name given to a native British Indian soldier. The Sepoys form an important part of the British regular and irregular forces, and they number in all over 140,000. Though not generally equal in courage and dexterity to European soldiers, the Sepoys are hardy, have great endurance and are very temperate.

Sepoy Rebellion. See INDIA, subhead *History.*

Seppuku, *sep poo'koo.* See HARA-KIRI.

Septem'ber, the ninth month of the year, containing thirty days. In the Roman calendar it was the seventh month, from which fact its name, September, is derived.

Septim'ius Seve'rus, ARCH OF, a triumphal arch in Rome, erected in 203 A. D. by the Senate and dedicated to the emperor Septimius Severus and his two sons, Caracalla and Geta, in commemoration of the victory over the Parthians and Arabians. The arch is 75 feet high and bears inscriptions and reliefs relative to the campaigns of Severus. It is located at the end of the Sacred Way, on the Forum.

Septuagint, *sep'too a jint',* the name commonly given to the ancient Greek version of the Old Testament. It was originally believed to have been made in seventy-two days, by the order of Ptolemy II Philadelphus, but it is now known to have been written at different times and by different workers, part of it possibly as late as 100 B. C. It is still in use in the Greek Church, but its greatest value at the present time to the Western Church is for the criticism and comparison of the text with the various other versions of the Old Testament.

Se'quin, a Venetian gold coin, first struck about the end of the thirteenth century, equivalent in value to about $2.30. Coins of the same name, but differing in value, were issued by other states.

Sequoi'a, a species of trees belonging to the cypress family, found on the Coast Ranges and the Sierra Nevada mountains in California and Oregon. There are but two species, the *redwood,* and what is popularly known as the *big tree.* The latter name is given to a small number of trees found only on the western slope of the Sierra Nevadas in California. These trees grow in groups, popularly called groves, and stand amidst smaller trees of different kinds. Ten groves are known, but only two of these are easily accessible. They are the Calaveras grove in Calaveras County, and the Mariposa grove, sixteen miles south of Yosemite Valley. The Calaveras grove contains 800 trees, and the Mariposa has 365 large trees and a number of smaller ones. The grove of the Kings and the Keweah rivers is by far the largest known, but its trees are not so large as those in the other groves named.

The average height of the big trees is 275 feet, but there are a number which attain a height of 300 to 325 feet. The average diameter is 20 feet, though the largest trees have diameters of 25 and 30 feet. The trunk is straight and slightly tapering, bearing on the upper half or third a crown of branches. Branches are seldom found below 125 or 150 feet. The bark is cinnamon red on the old trees and reddish-purple on the young. It has an average thickness of eleven or twelve inches, but on some of the largest trees it is two feet in thickness and is deeply grooved and very rough. The bark does not burn readily and serves to protect the trees from forest fires. The branches are short and thick and divide into tufts of fine spray, which bear short, flat leaves, closely crowded together. The fruit is a cone about two inches long and one and one-half inches in diameter. Each cone produces a large number of seeds, which are very small. The wood is soft and of a slightly reddish hue.

In 1854 one of these trees was cut down. The task was accomplished by boring off the trunk with augers, and it took five men twenty-two and one-half days to do the work. A pavilion was built on the stump and is now used as a dance hall. It affords ample room for twenty couples on the floor and for the musicians and a fair number of spectators. Another fallen tree in this grove was over 400 feet in height and measured 30 feet in diameter at its base. The heart has been burned out, and a man can ride through the hole in the trunk on horseback for a distance of 90 feet and emerge through an opening caused by the breaking off of a limb. In the Mariposa grove a roadway has been cut through one of the standing trees, the tunnel being large enough to afford ample room for the largest coach; yet this does not seem to affect the strength or life of the tree.

The age of the big trees is not definitely known, but it is very great. They are probably the oldest living objects upon the earth. The largest of them are estimated to be from 2500 to 3000 years old. If this estimate is correct, a number of these trees must have attained a good size before the beginning of the Christian era. See REDWOOD.

Seraglio, *se rah'lyo*, (properly, serai), the palace and surrounding buildings, formerly serving as the royal palace of the Turkish sultan at Constantinople. Since 1839 it has not been used by the sultan, and it is now going to ruin. It stands in a beautiful situation, on a point of land projecting into the sea. Its walls embrace a circuit of about nine miles, including several mosques, the museum of Constantinople, the harem, and buildings capable of accommodating 20,000 men. Amongst the Turks the name is often used to designate any residence of the sultan.

Sera'pis, an Egyptian deity whose worship was introduced into Egypt in the reign of Ptolemy I. Plutarch and Tacitus relate that Ptolemy, having seen in a dream the image of a god, which he was ordered to remove from the place in which it stood, sent to Sinope and brought thence a colossal statue, which he set up in Alexandria. It was declared to represent the god Serapis and appears to have been originally a statue of Pluto or Jupiter. The name Serapis is composed of the names Osiris and Apis. A magnificent temple was built at Alexandria for the reception of the statue of Serapis, and this temple—the Serapeum—was the last hold of the pagans in that city after the introduction of Christianity. The Egyptians themselves never ackowledged him in their pantheon; but he was the principal deity in the Greek and Roman towns of Egypt. Forty-two temples are said to have been erected to him in Egypt under the Ptolemies and Romans; his worship extended also to Asia Minor and was introduced into Rome by Antoninus Pius. The image of Serapis perished with his temple at Alexandria, which was destroyed in 389 by the order of Theodosius.

Serapis, THE. See BON HOMME RICHARD, THE.

Serayevo, *se rah'ye vo.* See BOSNA-SERAI.

Serfs, a term applied to a class of laborers existing under the feudal system, whose condition, though not exactly that of slavery, was little removed from it. Under feudalism, from the vassals of the king downward, the whole community was subject to certain degrees of servitude, and it was only on condition of specific services to be rendered to his superior that any individual held his land. In the case of the lower classes this servitude amounted to an almost complete surrender of personal liberty. There were two classes of laborers, the villeins and the serfs proper. The former occupied a middle position between the serfs and the freemen. A serf could not be sold, but could be transferred along with the property to which he was attached. A serf could obtain his freedom by purchase, by residing for a year and a day in a borough or by military service. By these various means the serf population gradually decreased, and in most parts of the Continent they had disappeared by the fifteenth century. Serfdom in England and Scotland was extinguished very gradually, existing almost in its original form as late as 1574; and even in the eighteenth century a species of serfdom existed among Scottish miners. Serfdom in Russia did not originate in feudalism, but in royal enactment; it was abolished by a manifesto of Alexander II, on March 17, 1861.

Serinagur, *se re'na gur'*, or **Srinagar,** a city of India, capital of Kashmir, situated in the Kashmir valley, on both banks of the Jehlum River, 170 mi. n. e. of Lahore. It is an exceedingly picturesque town when seen from a distance, but the streets are narrow and dirty and contain but little of interest. In the environs are beautiful gardens, and also the lake made famous by Moore in his *Lalla Rookh*. The chief industries are the manufacture of shawls and attar of roses. Population in 1911, 126,344.

Se'rous Membranes, certain double membranes in the human body, as the pleura, the pericardium and the peritoneum, which form a sort of closed sac surrounding certain organs, the interior surfaces of the sac secreting a small quantity of serous fluid. Their chief function is to allow free action to the organs and prevent the injurious effects of friction. The synovial membranes of the joints belong to this class. These membranes are liable to various diseases. See PLEURISY; PERITONITIS.

Serpent, *sur'pent*. See SNAKE.

Serpent Charming, an art of great antiquity, confined in practice exclusively to certain countries. The power exercised by the charmers over poisonous serpents is unquestionably remarkable, and though there is little doubt that the common practice of the charmer is to extract the fangs from the snakes before exhibiting them, yet there is good authority for believing

152

that it is not always done. The instrument usually employed in serpent charming is a kind of pipe, which is varied by whistling and the use of the voice. The effect of this medley of sounds is to entice the serpents from their holes, so that the serpent charmer can pin them to the ground with a forked stick. In India and other places the art of serpent charming is an hereditary profession and is practiced for the purpose of gaining a livelihood by amusing the public. Besides the evident power music has upon the serpents, they appear to be influenced in a marked degree by the eye of the charmer, who controls them by merely fixing his gaze upon them.

Serpentine, *sur'pen tine*, a rock composed of magnesia, silica and water, usually of beautiful shades of green, but sometimes of a brown, red or yellow color. Much of serpentine is veined or spotted with streaks of white, and these varieties are known in the United States as *verde antique* marble. Serpentine takes a high polish and is quite extensively used in finishing the interiors of public buildings. It is not a good stone for exteriors, because it contains more or less iron, which, on weathering, discolors the stone. It is found in Switzerland, Italy and a number of localities in the United States. It takes its name from its mottled green appearance, which was formerly supposed to resemble the skins of some serpents.

Se'rum Ther'apy, the treatment of disease by means of blood serum, containing germs of the disease which by creating antitoxins in the blood of the patient render him immune. Cultures of the specific germ are made, and some animal, usually a healthy horse, is inoculated. The serum from this animal is tested on a rabbit, for instance, and if found to protect the little animal from inoculation with active disease germs, the serum is felt to be safe for human beings. Vaccination is an example of serum therapy. This method of treatment has been used with varying success in pneumonia, cholera, typhoid, diphtheria and several other bacterial diseases and is thought to promise great results in the future. See GERM THEORY OF DISEASE.

Serval, *sur'val*, a South American flesh-eating animal, about three feet in length, nearly related to the leopard. Its general body-color is a bright golden, tinged with gray and marked with black spots. The serval, or *tiger cat*, as it is sometimes called, is readily domesticated. Its fur commands high prices. (See illustration on next page.)

Serve′tus, Michael, or **Miguel Servede** (about 1511–1553), a learned Spaniard, memorable as a victim of religious intolerance. He was born at Ludela, in Navarre. He was the son of a notary, who sent him to Toulouse to study civil law. Here he began to give his attention to theology, and having formed views of the Trinity antagonistic to the orthodox doctrine, he removed to Germany, where he printed a tract entitled *De Trinitatis Erroribus,* followed a year later by his *Dialogorum de Trinitate Libri duo.* Finding that his opinions were

SERVAL

obnoxious in Germany, he escaped to France, under the name of Michael of Villeneuve, and began the study of medicine. At Paris Servetus met Calvin for the first time, and an arrangement was made for a theological discussion between them, but Servetus failed to appear. In Vienne, in 1553, he published his matured theological system, under the title of *Christianismi Restitutio* (Restoration of Christianity). He was arrested for heresy and imprisoned, but contrived to escape and purposed to proceed to Naples. He was arrested at Geneva, however, on a charge of blasphemy and heresy, and his various writings were sifted in order to insure his condemnation. The divines of all the Protestant Swiss cantons unanimously declared for his punishment, and Calvin was especially urgent and emphatic as to the necessity of putting him to death. As Servetus refused to retract his opinions, he was burnt at the stake. He is numbered among the anatomists who made the nearest approach to the doctrine of the circulation of the blood before the time of Harvey.

Servia, *sur′ve a,* an independent kingdom, located in the southeastern part of Europe, bounded on the n. by Austria-Hungary, on the e. by Rumania and Bulgaria, on the s. by Turkey and on the w. by Austria-Hungary. The northern boundary is formed by the Save and the Danube rivers, and the eastern, by the

Drina. The greatest length and breadth of the country are about equal, being about 160 miles. The area is 18,630 square miles, or a little less than the combined areas of Vermont and New Hampshire. The surface is high and mountainous, the country being traversed by spurs of the Carpathian Mountains in the northeast, the Balkan in the southeast and the Dinaric Alps in the west. None of these is high, and the loftiest summit is only 6325 feet. The whole country is drained into the Danube, either directly through the Morava, which flows through the center of the kingdom, or indirectly by the rivers that form a part of its boundary. The climate in the elevated regions is rigorous, but in the valleys and lowlands it is mild and equable. There is plenty of rainfall, and the mountains are covered with forests.

The chief mineral productions are lead, zinc, quicksilver, copper, iron and coal, though none of these is extensively mined. Agriculture is the chief occupation of the people, and good crops of corn, wheat, flax, hemp and tobacco are raised. Fruit growing is also an important industry, some districts being noted for the production of wine, and others for the production of prunes. Silkworms are raised in large numbers, and in the hilly regions extensive pastures make the raising of live stock an important industry. The manufactures consist of carpets, embroidery and other textiles, jewelry, filigree work and woodenware. Nearly all manufacturing is carried on in the homes and by hand tools or primitive machinery, but the inhabitants display great skill in their special lines of work.

A trunk line of railway from Vienna to Constantinople extends across the country, and a branch reaches from Nissa to Sofia in Turkey. Aside from this, transportation is either by river or ordinary highways. The exports amount to about $14,000,000 a year, and the imports are about two-thirds of that sum. The chief exports are live stock, agricultural products, fruits and lumber and timber products, while the imports consist of manufactured goods and some food products and machinery. The chief trade is with Austria-Hungary, Germany and Great Britain.

The government is a constitutional monarchy. The people are represented in a legislative assembly called the *Skupshtina*, the members of which are chosen at a general election. There is also a council of state, one-half of whose members are appointed by the Skupshtina and the others by the king. The capital is Belgrade, in the northern part of the kingdom, and the Greek Church is the State Church. Population in 1910, 2,911,701, nine-tenths of whom are Serbs, a Slavic people closely related to the Croatians of Austria-Hungary. There is quite an extensive Servian literature, but the great mass of the inhabitants are uneducated.

In ancient times Servia formed a part of the Roman province of Moesia. After this it was occupied in succession by Huns, Ostrogoths, Lombards and other tribes. In the seventh century the country was entered by the Servians, but in the century following it acknowledged the supremacy of the Byzantine emperors. Later Servia became independent, and in the middle of the fourteenth century it included all of Macedonia, Albania and Thessaly, the northern part of Greece and Bulgaria. After this its power declined and it became tributary to Turkey, remaining in this condition for about 200 years. In 1718 the greater part of the territory was ceded to Austria, but a few years later was again transferred to Turkey. The oppression of the Turkish government led to several wars, and from 1812 to 1878 the country was ruled by a number of monarchs who were vassals of the sultan. In 1877, during the Russo-Turkish war, Servia rebelled, and by the Treaty of Berlin in the following year her independence was recognized by the European powers. The present constitution was adopted in 1889. See BALKAN WAR.

Servius Tul′lius, the sixth of the legendary kings of Rome. According to the tradition he was the son of a slave, given by the elder Tarquin to his wife. He married Tarquin's daughter, and on the death of his father-in-law (578 B. C.) he was raised to the throne. He defeated the Veientines and the Etruscans and divided the population of Rome into tribes, instituting at the same time the *comitia centuriata* and *tributa*; he also beautified the city and built several temples.

Sesame, *ses′a me,* **Grass.** See GAMA GRASS.

Ses′amum, tropical plants, from the seeds of which a coarse flour is made and an oil is extracted. Both are used as articles of food in the parts of India and Africa where the seeds are produced. Sesamum is now grown in the United States, to which it is supposed to have been brought by negroes from Africa.

Sesos′tris. See RAMESES II.

Seti I, *sa′te,* a king of Egypt, the second ruler of the nineteenth dynasty, the father of

Rameses II (See RAMESES II). On the walls of the Hall of Columns at Karnak, which he built, are described his campaigns in Asia against the inhabitants of Syria and Palestine. He built the Temple of Osiris at Abydos.

Se′ton, ERNEST THOMPSON (1860–   ), an American author, artist and lecturer, born in Shields, England. From 1866 to 1870 he lived in the backwoods of Canada, and from 1882 to 1887 he lived on the western plains. He was educated at the Toronto Collegiate Institute and at the Royal Academy in London, England. In 1891 he became official naturalist to the government of Manitoba. He was one of the chief illustrators of the *Century Dictionary* and has illustrated many books on birds and animals. Best known of his works, however, are his stories about animals, mostly written for magazines. These include *Wild Animals I Have Known; The Biography of a Grizzly; Lobo, Rag and Vixen; Lives of the Hunted; Two Little Savages: Monarch, the Big Bear,* and *Animal Heroes,* and they deal with animal life in a way which was original with him. The truth of Seton's accounts of animals has been questioned by many naturalists, but the stories have certainly aroused a new interest in animals and led to increased study of their habits.

Setter, a hunting dog, so named from the habit of crouching or "setting," on observing the game which it is trained to hunt. The distinct races are the English, Irish and Russian setters, the first two being considered the best

SESAMUM
Showing fruit and seeds enlarged.

breeds. In appearance the setter resembles the spaniel somewhat, having long, silky hair and drooping ears, but in habits it resembles the pointer. (See illustration on next page.)

Set′tlement, in law, 1, A deed by which property is settled; especially the general will or disposition by which a person regulates the disposal of his property, usually through the medium of trustees and for the benefit of a wife, children or other relatives; or the disposition of property at marriage in favor of a wife. 2, Legal residence, or establishment, of a person in a particular parish, town or locality, which entitles him to maintenance if he is a pauper and subjects the parish or town to his support. The settlement of a pauper is the place of his birth, and this remains his settle-

SETTER

ment until he has acquired another settlement. In the United States, a settlement may be acquired in various ways, namely, by birth; by the legal settlement of the father, in the case of minor children; by marriage; by continued residence; by the payment of requisite taxes; by the lawful exercise of a public office; by hiring and service for a specified time, or by serving an apprenticeship.

Seul, *say ool'*. See SEOUL.

Sevanga, *se vahn' ga,* **Lake.** See GOKTSCHA.

Seven Days' Battles. See PENINSULA CAMPAIGN.

Seven Pines, BATTLE OF. See FAIR OAKS, BATTLE OF; PENINSULA CAMPAIGN.

Seven Sleepers, according to a famous ancient story, seven Christian youths of Ephesus, who, by a command of the emperor Decius, were imprisoned in a cave in which they had taken refuge. Here a sleep fell upon them, and they did not awaken for two hundred years. On emerging from the cave, during the reign of Theodosius, they were amazed to find a totally new civilization all about them. They related their story to the multitude, gave them their blessing and died. The Mohammedans have a similar legend.

Seventeen-Year Locust. See CICADA.

Seventh Day Ad'ventists, the largest sect of the Adventists, numbering more than 115,000 members and supporting more than 2000

churches. According to their doctrine, the seventh day of the week, the Christian Saturday, is the Sabbath. They believe that the dead sleep till the day of judgment; that the unsaved are destroyed; that the care of bodily health, total abstinence and the eating of vegetable food only are religious duties. They have established sanitariums in various states, and their missionary work extends into almost every country in the world. In the United States their headquarters are at Takoma Park, a suburb of Washington, D. C.; previous to 1903 the headquarters were at Battle Creek, Mich. Chief among their periodicals are the *Advent Review and the Sabbath Herald* and *The Signs of the Times.* Their publications are numerous and embrace discussions of the Bible and of their own peculiar doctrines, histories of their sect and treatises on health and disease.

Seven Weeks' War, the struggle between Prussia and Austria in 1866, which determined that Prussian influence was to be predominant in Germany. Bismarck, feeling that war must come soon, determined to force the question, and used as a pretext the Schleswig-Holstein question (See SCHLESWIG-HOLSTEIN). Italy and most of the North German states joined Prussia, while Austria was aided by Bavaria, Württemberg, Saxony, Hesse and Hanover. The Prussians were from the first victorious, and after the Battle of Königgrätz, or Sadowa, Austria was obliged to sue for peace.

Seven Wise Men, seven sages who lived in Greece in the sixth and seventh centuries before Christ. As generally set down, they were Periander, Pittacus, Thales, Solon, Bias, Chilo and Cleobulus. Maxims of prudence and elementary morality are regarded as embodying a summary of their wisdom. Among these maxims are, "Know thyself," "Nothing in excess," "Consider the end."

Seven Wonders of the World, an old designation of seven structures, remarkable for their splendor or magnitude, generally said to have been the pyramids of Egypt, the walls and hanging gardens of Babylon, the temple of Diana at Ephesus, the statue of the Olympian Jupiter at Athens, the Mausoleum at Halicarnassus, the Colossus of Rhodes and the Pharos, or lighthouse, at Alexandria.

Seven Years' War, a famous war between Prussia and other European powers, which lasted from 1756 to 1763. As the result of a war with Prussia, Maria Theresa of Austria had been forced to cede Silesia to Frederick the Great. To recover her lost territory she concluded an alliance with Russia, secured the support of Poland and Saxony and attempted to form a closer union with France. In the meantime war broke out between France and England (1755), and George II, in order to protect his German states, concluded an alliance with Prussia, while France agreed to aid Austria against Frederick. Being informed of these negotiations, Frederick resolved to anticipate his enemies. In August, 1756, he invaded Saxony, occupied the chief towns and compelled the Saxon army to surrender. This step created a stir in the European courts, and in 1757 Austria, Russia, France, Sweden and the German Empire were in arms against Frederick, while he had no allies but England and a few German states. In 1757 Frederick marched into Bohemia and gained a bloody battle at Prague. Soon after, however, the Austrians under Daun defeated Frederick at Kolin, relieved Prague and forced the Prussians to retreat to Saxony. The French army, after defeating Frederick's allies under the duke of Cumberland, united with the imperial forces; Frederick met them at Rossbach and routed both armies, then hurried back to Silesia, which was occupied by the Austrians, and vanquished a superior army under Daun at Leuthen, thus recovering Silesia. While Frederick was thus occupied in the south and west, his general, Lehwald, had successfully repelled the Swedes and Russians on the north and east.

The next campaign was opened in February, 1758, by Ferdinand, duke of Brunswick, who, at the head of Frederick's allies, opposed the French in Lower Saxony and Westphalia. He defeated the French at Crefeld in June and ultimately drove the enemy beyond the Rhine. Frederick defeated the Russians at Zorndorf and was defeated in turn by Daun at Hochkirch, but before the end of the year he drove the Austrians from Silesia and Saxony.

In 1759 Frederick suffered at Kunersdorf a defeat such as he had never sustained before, and his position became extremely precarious. The British victories over the French helped matters somewhat, and the campaign of 1760 opened well for him. George II of England died in this year, however; Pitt was removed from power and Prussia thus lost her only ally. It seemed as if nothing could save her, but in 1762, when Frederick's fortunes were at their worst, Elizabeth of Russia died and was succeeded by Peter III, who was an enthusiastic admirer of Frederick. Russia made a treaty with Prussia, but Peter was deposed before Russia could lend Frederick any substantial aid. However, Russia did not again join Austria, and as both sides were practically exhausted, peace was concluded at Hubertsburg in 1763. Matters were adjusted as they had been before the war, and Frederick was allowed to retain Silesia. The struggle between France and England in Europe was accompanied in America by the conflict known as the last French and Indian War (See FRENCH AND INDIAN WARS).

Sev'ern, the second largest river in England, formed by the union of two small streams which rise in Mount Plinlimmon, Montgomeryshire. After a circuitous southerly course of about 210 miles, it falls into the British Channel. It receives the Tern, the Upper Avon and the Lower Avon, from the west, and the Teme and the Wye, from the east. It is navigable to Welshpool, about 178 miles above its mouth and 225 feet above sea level. Below Gloucester the banks become so low that destructive inundations have frequently occurred.

Seve'rus, LUCIUS SEPTIMIUS (146–211), a Roman emperor. Under Commodus he commanded the legions in Pannonia, and on the murder of Pertinax in 193 he was proclaimed emperor by his troops. Severus accordingly marched to Rome to subdue the partisans of Julianus, who had purchased the imperial purple from the praetorians. On his approach, Julianus was assassinated by his own soldiers, and Severus banished the praetorians and ridded himself of the rivalry of Albinus, commander of the Roman forces in Britain. He then marched to the East against Pescennius Niger, who had also been elected emperor by a powerful army. After many obstinate battles, Niger was routed on the plains of Issus. Having sacked Byzantium and conquered several Eastern peoples, Severus returned to Rome. He next, with his two sons, Caracalla and Geta, marched to the East to repel an invasion of the Parthians and subjugated Seleucia, Babylon and Ctesiphon. After subduing an insurrection in Britain and building a stone wall from the Tyne to the Solway Firth, as a defense against the Caledonians, he died at York.

Sevier, se veer', JOHN (1745–1815), an American pioneer, politician and soldier, born in Rockingham County, Va. He left school at sixteen, was married in the following year and at twenty-one emigrated to the Shenandoah Valley, where he founded the village of Newmarket. He became celebrated as an indian fighter and in 1772 moved to the Wautauga settlements, further west. During the Revolution he rendered valuable service to the Americans in conflicts with the indians on the frontier, and also fought at King's Mountain. At the close of the war, he was made brigadier general. When the State of Franklin was set up, in the present territory of Tennessee, he became governor, and when it was reannexed to North Carolina, he represented the district in Congress. Sevier was chosen first governor of the State of Tennessee in 1796 and served until 1801 and again from 1803 to 1809. He was elected to Congress from 1811 to 1815 and was on several occasions commissioner to the indians of the southwest.

Seville, *se vil'*, a city of Spain, situated on the Guadalquivir River, 62 mi. n. n. e. of Cadiz. It is built in Moorish style, has narrow streets, lined with old Moorish houses, which are usually built around interior courtyards with fountains in the center. Many of the dwellings are of two stories, and nearly all of them are white. The city is notable for its abundant and beautiful vegetation. It was formerly enclosed by a wall, but only a few remains of this are now visible. The principal parks or squares are the Plaza de San Fernando and the Plaza de Triomfo, upon which is the cathedral. The city also has a number of boulevards, noted for their beauty. Among the buildings of note are the Cathedral of Seville, which ranks next to Saint Peter's at Rome in size; the Giralda, a peculiar structure in the form of a square tower over 300 feet in height and dating from the sixteenth century; the palace of the Moorish kings, or the Alcazar, and the chapel of the Catholic kings.

The chief educational institutions include the University of Seville, the provincial school of art, the provincial museum and the provincial library, which has over 80,000 volumes, and the Columbian Library, founded by the son of Columbus. The civil hospital is noted as one of the largest institutions of the kind in the world. The leading industries include the manufacture of tobacco, silk, ironware, soap and chocolate. The city has an important trade with the surrounding country. It is one of the oldest cities of Spain and was a place of considerable importance under the Romans. During the eleventh century it was the capital of a Moorish state. Later it was captured by Saint Ferdinand of Castile, and was for a long time the capital of the Castilian dominion. At the time of the discovery of America, it was the leading commercial port of Spain. Population in 1910, 155,366.

Sevres *sa'vr'*, a town of France, in the Department of Seine-et-Oise, 7 mi. n. w. of Paris. It is famous chiefly for its porcelain, which is manufactured in a government factory established in 1756. Population of the town in 1911, 9000.

Sewage and Sewerage. *Sewage* is the proper name for the waste matter which passes through drains or conduits away from single houses or from villages and towns; *sewerage* is the name for the system of pipes or drains designed to carry off the refuse. Sewage is made up of solid and liquid matter from houses, the fluid waste from domestic and manufacturing operations, generally much of the surface drainage and sufficient water to carry away the waste. In small villages and in farming communities, each house disposes of its own sewage, usually in the soil, and this under ordinary circumstances is a safe method; but wherever people are crowded together it is necessary to dispose of all refuse matter promptly and completely (See GARBAGE). The customary way, especially in the smaller cities, is to float the sewage off in airtight tubes, to such a distance that it will be harmless. Except in very level countries, the force of gravity is sufficient to carry away the sewage, but in some places pumping stations are necessary to distribute it properly. It is evident that plenty of water is necessary to carry away the refuse successfully, and in many places drains are so arranged that surface water is conducted to the sewers, where it assists in carrying off the solid matter. Such a plan, however, is open to objections, as at times the sewer pipes are partially empty and poisonous gases collect and escape through the drainage openings. A better plan is to keep the drainage system separate from the sewers.

Small sewers are usually made of terra cotta or vitrified clay, but when they are more than two feet in diameter, iron pipes are used or brick sewers are constructed. In large cities the more expensive stone masonry and concrete are substituted for brick. The sewers should be properly ventilated, so that noxious gases may not rise through the pipes to the houses and cause sickness. Yet the danger from gas is not so great as the danger from polluting the soil or water supply of the town with the sewage. If the waste matter can be carried far out into some large body of water, it may be deposited with safety, because the water in time disinfects the refuse; but where the sewage is thrown into small streams or small bodies of water, the possibilities for conveying disease to other places, if not to the one whence the sewage originated, can scarcely be overestimated. To throw sewage upon the soil is eventually to bring again the contamination which resulted from the use of cesspools. While air and soil will disinfect sewage, if time is allowed, yet their power as disinfectants is limited. See SANITARY SCIENCE.

Sew'ard, WILLIAM HENRY (1801–1872), an American statesman, born in Florida, Orange co., N. Y. He graduated at Union College in 1820, studied for the bar and began practicing in Auburn in 1823. He gradually drifted into politics, and in 1830 he was elected a member of the New York senate. Displaying marked abilities as a politician, he was in 1838 chosen governor of his native state, where he served with marked ability until 1842, when he resumed his private practice. In 1849 Seward was elected to a seat in the United States Senate. There he was the friend and adviser of President Taylor and distinguished himself by his firm resistance to the extension of slavery, opposing in eloquent speeches the Compromise of 1850 and the Kansas-Nebraska Bill.

Reëlected as a Whig in 1856, he took a prominent part in the formation of the Republican party, and in 1860 he was the leading candidate for the presidential nomination, but being defeated in the convention by Abraham Lincoln, he exerted himself to secure Lincoln's election and was appointed secretary of state. In this post he discharged his duties with great ability until 1869. He adjusted the Trent affair (See TRENT AFFAIR) and the Alabama Claims (See ALABAMA, THE), secured the withdrawal of the French from Mexico and purchased Alaska from Russia. He was dangerously wounded in April, 1865, when Lincoln was assassinated. Seward wrote a *Life of John Quincy Adams* and an *Autobiography*.

Sewel'lel, a small rodent, about fifteen inches long, living in wet regions of California, Oregon and Washington. It has characteristics that unite it both with the beaver and with the squirrels or marmots. The sewellel is reddish-brown in color, with small eyes, short tail and very strong jaws. It lives in colonies in underground burrows and feeds on vegetable substances.

Sewerage. See SEWAGE.

Sewing, *so'ing,* **Machine.** The first known attempt to make a sewing machine was that of Thomas Saint, an Englishman, in 1790, but his machine was not practical. In 1830 a machine was made in France which was successfully used in making clothes for the army, but it was destroyed by a mob, because the tailors thought that its use would take away their employment. Two years later Walter Hunt of New York made a number of machines on a plan similar to that found in the successful machines of the present day, but he failed to take out a patent. The first successful sewing machine placed upon the market was that of Elias Howe, of Boston, which was patented in 1846, and the use of the sewing machine dates from that year.

This machine consisted of a needle, with an eye near the point, and below the cloth, a shuttle, which carried another thread on a small spool, called the *bobbin*. The needle was attached to an arm vibrating on a pivot so as to force the needle through the cloth. The shuttle carried the lower thread through the loop made by the upper thread and locked it as the needle tightened the loop with its upward movement. While numerous patterns of machines have been invented since, all double threaded machines are constructed on the principle invented by Howe. The Singer machine, which soon followed the Howe, had an improved plan for operating the needle and for moving the cloth along as it was sewed. This machine also used the treadle as motive power. Previous to the invention of the Singer, all sewing machines were operated by turning a crank by hand.

Single-threaded machines make what is called a chain stitch. Of these the Wilcox and Gibbs is the most successful pattern. While these machines are easily operated, they have the defect that if one stitch becomes broken the entire seam is liable to be raveled. There are now sewing machines constructed for nearly every line of work done by the needle, such as sewing on buttons, making buttonholes and sewing boots and shoes and harnesses.

Sex'tant, an improved form of quadrant, capable of measuring angles of 120°. It consists of a frame of metal and ebony, stiffened by cross-braces and having an arc embracing 60° of a circle. It has two mirrors, one of which is fixed to a movable index, and various other appendages. It is capable of very general application, but it is chiefly employed at sea for measuring the altitudes of the heavenly bodies and their apparent angular distances, and for determining latitude.

The principle of the sextant, and of reflecting instruments in general, depends upon an elementary theorem in optics, namely, if an object be seen by repeated reflection from two mirrors which are perpendicular to the same plane, the angular distance of the object from its image is double the inclination of the mirrors. To find the angle between two stars, hold the instrument so that the one is seen directly through the telescope and the unsilvered portion of the mirror, and move the index arm so that the

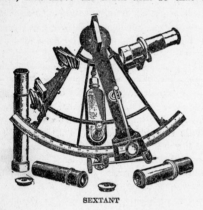

SEXTANT

image of the other star seen through the telescope by reflection is nearly coincident with the first. The reading on the arc gives the angle required, half-degrees being marked as degrees, because what is measured by the index is the angle between the mirrors, and this is half that between the objects. By knowing the position of the star in the celestial sphere, the latitude of the ship can be found, by comparing its altitude, as shown in the sextant, with this position.

Seychelles, *sa shel'*, **Islands,** a group of islands in the Indian Ocean, about 750 mi. n. e. of the northern extremity of Madagascar. The islands are generally mountainous and are of volcanic origin, the highest point having an elevation of about 3000 feet. They are covered with productive soil, and valuable crops of sugar cane, coffee, cacao, rice and vanilla are grown. They have been occupied by the British ever since 1794. Population in 1911, 26,000.

Seymour, IND., a city in Jackson co., 60 mi. s. by w. of Indianapolis, on the Baltimore & Ohio Southwestern, the Pittsburg, Cincinnati, Chicago & Saint Louis and other railroads. It is in a farming and dairying region, and it also contains railroad shops, wool, flour and lumber mills, carriage works and other factories. The city has a public library, a high school, Saint

Ambrose Academy, eleven churches and two national banks. Population in 1910, 6305.

Seymour, HORATIO (1810–1886), an American statesman, born in Pompey Hill, Onondaga co., N. Y., and educated at Geneva Academy and at a military academy. He was admitted to the bar, and after serving three terms with marked ability in the New York legislature, in 1852 was elected governor on the Democratic ticket, serving one term. At the outbreak of the Civil War, he sought a basis for compromise, but in the end was decidedly in favor of the maintenance of the Union and, again elected governor in 1862, showed conspicuous energy and ability in raising troops. He opposed the assumption of unusual war powers by President Lincoln, but took stern measures against draft riots and in general upheld the administration. In 1868 he was overwhelmingly defeated for the presidency by General Grant and retired to private life.

Shackleton, SIR ERNEST HENRY (1874–   ), an English explorer, born at Kilkee, Ireland, and educated at Dulwich College, London. He served as lieutenant in the British navy and was second in command to Captain Scott in the British Antarctic Expedition of 1901. He was knighted for distinguished services as commander of the Antarctic Expedition of 1907–9. This expedition relocated the magnetic south pole, explored Mount Erebus, determined the extensive glaciation of the Antarctic continent, reaching latitude 83° 23' south, a little over 100 miles from the South Pole. This expedition was of great importance, as it resulted in a gain in accurate knowledge of the Antarctic regions. The scientific observations of this party put an end to further speculation as to the character of the land at the South Pole. *The Heart of the Antarctic* is the record of this expedition. Shackleton has lectured in Great Britain, Canada and the United States and has received many medals and other honors.

Shad, a name of several fishes, of the family of herrings, including two species, the common, or allice, shad, and the white shad. The *common shad* inhabits the sea near the mouths of large rivers, and in the spring ascends them for the purpose of depositing its spawn. The form of the shad is the same as that of the other herrings, but it is of larger size, and in some places it receives the name of *herring king*. Its color is a dark blue above, with brown and greenish lusters, the under parts being white. An American species of shad, varying in weight from

4 to 12 pounds, is highly esteemed for food and is consumed in great quantities in the fresh state. Shad are found all along the coast from

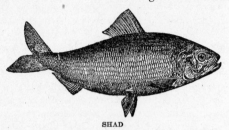

SHAD

New England to the Gulf of Mexico and have been successfully introduced on the Pacific coast.

Shad Bush. See JUNEBERRY.

Shad'dock. See GRAPE FRUIT.

Shad Fly. See MAY FLY.

Shaef'fer, NATHAN C. (1849–   ), an American educator, born at Maxatawny, Berks County, Pennsylvania. He was educated at Franklin and Marshall College and at the universities of Berlin, Tübingen and Leipzig. In 1875 he became principal of the Keystone State Normal School, and in 1893 he was elected superintendent of public instruction for Pennsylvania. He has also occupied a number of important official positions, being a member of the Commission of Industrial Education, president of the Medical Council of Pennsylvania and chancellor of the Pennsylvania Chautauqua at Mount Vernon. He is the author of *Thinking and Learning to Think* and *History of Education in Pennsylvania*, and he was editor of *Bible Readings for Schools* and the *Pennsylvania School Journal.*

Shaf'ter, WILLIAM RUFUS (1835–1906), an American soldier, born at Galesburg, Mich. He was reared on a farm and received only a common school education. At the outbreak of the Civil War he entered the Union army and was brevetted brigadier general for gallant conduct in action. At the close of the war he entered the regular army, serving in various posts until the outbreak of the Spanish-American War, in which he commanded the land operations in Cuba, which resulted in the surrender of the Spanish army at Santiago. Later he commanded various departments, and he retired in 1901, with the full rank of major general.

Shaftesbury, *shafts'bur ry,* ANTHONY ASHLEY COOPER, First Earl of (1621–1683), an English statesman. He was a member of the parliaments of 1640, and when the civil war broke out he joined the Parliamentary cause, after having shown slight royalist leanings. He had a prominent position under Cromwell during the Protectorate, but after Cromwell's death he saw that a restoration of the legitimate monarchy was what the country really wished and used his influence to that end. Charles II created him first Baron Ashley, later made him earl of Shaftesbury and gave him a prominent part in the government. He served as chancellor of the exchequer and later as a member of the hated Cabal. In 1679 he became president of the council, and in the same year he succeeded in passing the Habeas Corpus Act. He was, however, dismissed from the council, and two years later he was indicted for high treason, but acquitted. Obliged, by his connection with treasonable plots, to flee to Holland, he died there shortly after. He is the Achitophel of Dryden's *Absalom and Achitophel.*

Shagreen', a kind of untanned leather, prepared from skins of horses, asses and camels, and made in Russia and in the East. The granular appearance is caused by imbedding in it, while it is soft, the seeds of a species of plants. Afterward the surface is smoothed down and then soaked, and the indented places swell up in relief. The skins of shark, sea otter, seal and other animals have also been used for making shagreen. Shagreen was formerly used for covering sword scabbards, and it is now used as a covering for camera boxes, instrument cases and various like articles.

Shah Jehan, *je hahn',* (?–about 1665), the fifth Mogul emperor of Delhi, who reigned from 1627 to 1658, when he was deposed by his son Aurungzebe. During his reign the Mogul Empire attained a great magnificence; he founded Delhi, where he erected the celebrated peacock throne; and he built the Pearl Mosque and the Taj Mahal at Agra, as a mausoleum to his favorite wife. See TAJ MAHAL.

Sha'kers or **Shaking Quakers,** a sect which arose at Manchester, in England, about 1747, and which has since been transferred to America. The formal designation which they give themselves is the United Society of Believers in Christ's Second Appearing. That of Shakers was given them in ridicule, but it is nevertheless passively accepted by them. The founder of the sect as it at present exists was Ann Lee, an expelled Quaker, born in Manchester in 1756. She came to America in 1774 with seven followers and formed the first settlement at Watervliet, near Albany. They agree with the Quakers in their objections to taking oaths, their neglect of certain common courtesies of society and their rejection of the sacraments. They believe in the immediate revelations of the Holy Ghost (gifts); maintain that the old law is abolished, the new dispensation begun; that intercourse between heaven and earth is restored; that God is king and governor; that the sin of Adam is atoned and that man is made free from all errors except his own; that every human being will be saved; that the earth is heaven, now soiled and stained, but ready to be brightened by love and labor into its original state. At first the motions from which they derive their name were of the most violent, wild and irregular nature—leaping, shouting and clapping of the hands; but at present they move in a regular, uniform dance, to the singing of a hymn, and march around the hall of worship, clapping their hands in regular time. The societies are divided into smaller communities, called families, each of which has its own male and female head. Celibacy is enjoined upon all, and married persons on entering the community must live together as brother and sister. All property is held in common, and all bind themselves to take part in the family business—the men either as farmers, builders, gardeners, smiths, painters or as followers of some other handicraft; and the women in some household occupation or in the work of education. In America there are about twenty communities, with between two and three thousand members, chiefly in the New England states.

Shakespeare, *shayk'speer,* WILLIAM (1564–1616), an English poet and dramatist, the greatest of English poets, one of the greatest of the world's poets. He was born at Stratford-upon-Avon, a town in Warwickshire. His father was John Shakespeare, a burgess of Stratford, who combined his business as a butcher, a woolstapler and a glover, with dealings in timber and corn. His mother was Mary Arden, daughter of Robert Arden of Wilmecote, a prosperous yeoman farmer. They had eight children (four sons and four daughters), of whom William was the third. When the third child was born, and for some time afterward, the family was prosperous, for in 1568 John Shakespeare was high bailiff of Stratford. From this fact it may safely be inferred that his son received the best education which the grammar school of Stratford could give. After leaving school the first absolutely authentic event in Shakespeare's life is his marriage with Anne Hathaway, daughter of a yeoman in the hamlet of Shottery, near Strat-

ford. The marriage bond is dated Nov. 28, 1582, at which date Shakespeare was in his nineteenth year, while, from the date on her tombstone, it is known that his wife was eight years older. On May 26 following, their first child, named Susanna, was baptized, and in February of 1585, a son and daughter were born, who received the names of Hamnet and Judith. From this date until Shakespeare was established in London as a player and dramatist, there is a gap of seven years, during which we are again left to tradition and conjecture. To account for his leaving Stratford it has been suggested that his marriage with Anne Hathaway had proved unsuitable and unhappy, but there is no positive evidence in support of this belief. Then, again, there is the famous legend of the deer stealing, for which it is said he was prosecuted by Sir Thomas Lucy, of Charlecote. In retaliation he wrote, according to Rowe, a satirical ballad, which so enraged the baronet that Shakespeare thought it prudent to leave Stratford. The more probable reason is that his increasing domestic responsibilities, together with the acquaintance he presumably had with the players from London who visited Stratford, induced him to push his fortune in the city. He soon became a well-known player and a dramatist of such distinction as to call forth an envious reference in 1592 from a fellow dramatist. This is found in *A Groatsworth of Wit*, written by Robert Greene, and published a few weeks after his death by Chettle.

The first certain date in Shakespeare's life after his arrival in London is 1593. In that year he published his *Venus and Adonis*, with a dedication of this, "the first heir of my invention," to Henry Wriothesly, earl of Southampton; and in the following year he dedicated to the same patron his other poem of *The Rape of Lucrece*. As suggesting that this patronage was substantial in its nature, there is a story to the effect that the earl at one time gave to Shakespeare £1000 ($5000) to complete some purchase he had on hand. Whatever truth there may be in the story, it is certain that about this time Shakespeare began to grow in fortune and in fame. In connection with this increase of fortune it is noteworthy that the affairs of his father, John Shakespeare, seem also to have improved, for in 1596 he applied at the herald office for a grant of arms, which application was conceded in the following year. In 1596 Shakespeare's only son Hamnet died and was buried at Stratford, where the family continued to reside. The tradition is that Shakespeare visited his native town once

WILLIAM SHAKESPEARE
From the portrait, Stratford upon Avon, England

a year during the time that he lived in London. However this may be, it is clear that his interest in Stratford was not founded entirely in sentiment or family affection, for in 1597 he bought there a substantial house, called New Place, and in a return of grain and malt he is described as the holder of ten quarters. There is also documentary evidence to prove that he was possessed of property in the parish of Saint Helen's, Bishopgate.

While these things indicate the growth of his material prosperity, there is proof that his fame as a lyrical poet and dramatist was also being securely established, for in 1598 there was published the *Palladis Tamia*, by Francis Meres, in which twelve of his plays are enumerated, and in which mention is made of his "sugared sonnets among his private friends." Yet, notwithstanding this literary activity, he was still a player, for when Jonson's comedy of *Every Man in His Humor* was produced in 1598, Shakespeare took part in the performance. In the following year he was a shareholder in the Globe Theater, and his practical turn is still further evidenced by the fact that he bought (1602) 107 acres of arable land in the parish of Old Stratford for £320 and acquired (1605) for £440 the unexpired term of a lease of the tithes of Stratford, Old Stratford, Bishopton and Welcombe. Along with these material possessions he received the style and title of William Shakespeare, Gentleman, of Stratford-upon-Avon; but in London he was still a player in 1603, since when Ben Jonson's play of *Sejanus* was produced in that year, Shakespeare occupied a place in the list of actors. His father had died in 1601; his eldest daughter Susanna had married, in 1607, a practicing physician named John Hall; in the same year his brother Edmund, who was also a player, died in London and was buried in Southwark, and in 1608 his mother, Mary Shakespeare, followed her husband to the grave. In February, 1616, his youngest daughter, Judith, married; on the 25th of the following month he executed his will; and in another month he was dead.

The cause of his death is unknown, but in Stratford there was a tradition "that Shakespeare, Drayton and Ben Jonson had a merry meeting and, it seems, drank too hard, for Shakespeare died of a fever there contracted." By his will he left the bulk of his property to Susanna Hall and her husband, his daughter Judith, his sister Joan and his godson, while a few friends and fellow players were also remembered. To his wife he bequeathed specifically the "second best bed

with the furniture"; for there would probably be ample provision made for her, as a widow had right of dower in her husband's freehold property. He was buried in the chancel of Stratford church, on the north wall of which a monument, with bust and epitaph, was soon afterward set up. Over his grave was placed a slab with the inscription:

> Good frend, for Jesus sake forbeare
> To digg the dust encloased heare;
> Bleste be the man that spares thes stones
> And curst be he that moves my bones.

Tradition says that these words were written by Shakespeare himself shortly before his death, but of this there is no proof. As for Shakespeare's character, as estimated by his contemporaries, it found fit expression in the words of Ben Jonson. "I loved the man," he said, "and do honor to his memory, on this side idolatry, as much as any. He was indeed honest, and of an open and free nature, had an excellent phantasy, brave notions and gentle expressions."

In classifying the plays of Shakespeare by the aid of such chronology as is possible, modern critics have found it instructive to divide his career as a dramatist into four marked stages. The *first period* (1588–1593) marks the inexperience of the dramatist and gives evidence of experiment in characterization, looseness in the construction of plot, with a certain symmetrical artificiality in the dialogue. To this stage belong *Titus Andronicus* and Part I of *Henry VI*, both of which, it is thought, Shakespeare merely retouched; *Love's Labour's Lost*; *The Comedy of Errors*; *The Two Gentlemen of Verona*; *A Midsummer Night's Dream*; parts II and III of *Henry VI* in which it is thought probable that Marlowe had a hand, and *King Richard III*. The *second period* (1594–1601) is that in which, with increased security in his art, the dramatist sets forth his brilliant pageant of English history, his brightest conception of the comedy of life and more than proves his capacity for deeper things by one great romantic tragedy. To this stage belong *King Richard II*, parts I and II of *Henry IV*, *King Henry V*, *King John*, *Romeo and Juliet*, *The Merchant of Venice*, *The Taming of the Shrew*, *Merry Wives of Windsor*, *Much Ado About Nothing*, *As You Like It* and *Twelfth Night*. The *third period* (1602–1608) shows that the dramatist, having mastered all the resources of his art and tasted life to the full, is strangely fascinated by mortal mischance, so that even his comedy becomes bitter, while his tragedy is black with the darkest tempests of passionate human experience. To this stage in his development belong *All's Well That Ends Well, Measure for Measure, Troilus and Cressida, Julius Caesar, Hamlet, Othello, King Lear, Macbeth, Antony and Cleopatra, Coriolanus* and *Timon of Athens.* The *fourth period* (1609–1613) is that in which Shakespeare, after having passed through a season which was probably darkened by his own personal experiences, attained the glad serenity of mind which enabled him to write his last romantic plays. To this period belong *Pericles*, which is only partly from Shakespeare's hand, *Cymbeline, The Winter's Tale, The Tempest* and *King Henry VIII.* Of non-dramatic pieces Shakespeare was the author of *Venus and Adonis, The Rape of Lucrece*, the *Sonnets* and *A Lover's Complaint.* It is agreed that only a few of the poems in the collection published under the name of *The Passionate Pilgrim* were written by him. There has been much discussion as to how many of the plays usually credited to Shakespeare were really written by him, and systematic attempts have been made to prove that Bacon, not Shakespeare, was the author of the greater part of them. Such a theory is generally regarded as without foundation. See halftone, STRATFORD-UPON-AVON.

Shale is the solidified mud of ancient waters, having a slaty structure and usually containing a large proportion of clay. Shale is frequently found deposited between seams of coal and commonly bears fossil impressions. The variety known as bituminous shale burns with flame and yields an oil, which, mixed with paraffin, is of great commercial importance. Alum is also manufactured from alum shales. See ALUM STONE.

Sha′ler, NATHANIEL SOUTHGATE (1841–1906), an American geologist and educator, born in Newport, Ky. He graduated from the Lawrence Scientific School of Harvard University, served for a time in the Federal army and later became assistant in science at Harvard. He became full professor of zoölogy in 1887 and dean of the Lawrence Scientific School four years later. He wrote many articles for the magazines, besides several books, of which the following are perhaps the best known: *First Book in Zoölogy; Kentucky*, in the American Commonwealths Series; *The United States of America, A Study of the American Commonwealth; Nature and Man in America; Outlines of the Earth's History,* and *The Individual: A Study of Life and Death.*

Shamanism, *shah′man iz m,* a general name applied to the idolatrous religions of a number

of barbarous nations in northern Asia, best represented by the Tunguses. The shaman is a priest who performs sacrifices and works magical spells, in order that the people may keep on good terms with the gods. The worshipers believe in a Supreme Being, but to this they add the belief that the government of the world is in the hands of a number of secondary gods, both benevolent and malevolent toward man, and that it is absolutely necessary to avert their malign influence by magic rites and spells.

Shamo, *shah mo′.* See GOBI.

Shamo′kin, PA., a borough in Northumberland co., about 45 mi. n. by e. of Harrisburg, on the Philadelphia & Reading and the Pennsylvania railroads. It is in the anthracite coal fields and also contains foundries, machine shops and knitting, flour and planing mills. There are eighteen churches, four banks, two high schools, a public library, electric lights and electric street railways. The town was laid out in 1835, and the borough was incorporated in 1864. Population in 1910, 19,588.

Sham′rock, the name commonly given to the national emblem of Ireland. It is a plant whose leaf has three leaflets, and it is generally supposed to be the plant called white clover, but some think it to be the wood sorrel. It is said that Saint Patrick picked a shamrock leaf and used its three divisions to illustrate his idea that the Father, the Son and the Holy Spirit could be three and yet be one God. The plant commonly called the shamrock in Ireland is one of the hop clovers, a slender, trailing species, with small, yellow heads.

Shanghai, *shahng hi′,* a seaport of China, and its most important commercial center, situated 160 mi. e. s. e. of Nanking, on the left bank of Hwang-pu, by which it is joined to the Yang-tse-kiang River. The Chinese part of the city is enclosed within a wall about 24 feet high. In this part the streets are narrow and dirty and the buildings are low and crowded together; but north and northeast of the Chinese quarter is a large foreign settlement, occupied by British, French and Americans. Along the water front this part of the city presents the appearance of a modern European or American town. It has theaters, newspaper offices, club houses, street railways and electric light plants. This portion of the city also contains a fine cathedral, municipal offices and hospitals. The governing authorities of the foreign settlement are chosen from Americans, English and French who reside there, and the residents are under the protection of the consuls of their respective governments.

Shanghai is one of the most important commercial centers of Asia and its exports amount to over $200,000,000 annually. The imports are from Great Britain, India and other British colonies and consist of cotton goods, woolen goods, metals, petroleum, electrical apparatus and other machinery and numerous small wares. The exports are chiefly raw silk, manufactured silk, tea, rice, sugar, cotton, wool, paper and hides. The population is estimated at 600,000, about one-half of whom live within the boundaries of the foreign quarters.

Shan'non, the largest river of Ireland, which rises at the base of Cuilcagh Mountain, in County Cavan, flows southwest and south through loughs Allen, Boderg, Bofin, Ree and Derg, divides Connaught from Leinster and Munster and enters the Atlantic by a wide estuary, at the mouth of which are Loop Head, in Clare, and Kerry Head, in Kerry. Its length is about 250 miles. The estuary begins a little below Limerick and is navigable for large vessels, while small craft ply nearly the whole length of the river.

Shark, the general name for a group of fishes, celebrated for the size and voracity of many of the species. They are common in almost all oceans, though most abundant in warm waters. The body is long, and the tail is thick and fleshy. The mouth is large and is armed with several rows of compressed, sharp-edged teeth. The skin is usually very rough and is covered with a multitude of little pimples, instead of scales. They are the most formidable and voracious of all fishes; they pursue other marine animals and seem not to care whether their prey be living or dead. They often follow vessels and shoals of fishes in their periodical migrations. The *basking shark* is by far the largest species, sometimes attaining the length of forty feet, but it has none of the ferocity of the others. The *white shark* is one of the most formidable and voracious. It is common in many of the warmer seas, reaching a length of over thirty feet. The *hammer-headed sharks*, which are chiefly found in tropical seas, are very voracious and often attack man. They are noteworthy for the remarkable shape of the head, which resembles somewhat a double-headed hammer, the eyes being at the extremities. Other forms are the *porbeagle*, the *blue shark*, the *fox shark*, the *sea fox*, the *sea ape*, or *thresher*, and the *Greenland*, or *northern*,

shark. In China and Japan the smaller sharks serve as food, and in China and India the fins form an important article of commerce. Oil is made from the livers of some species.

Sharon, *shair'on*, PA., a borough in Mercer co., 75 mi. n. w. of Pittsburg, near the Ohio boundary line, on the Shenango River and on the Pennsylvania, the Erie and other railroads. Coal is extensively mined in the vicinity, and there are rolling mills, furnaces, foundries, boiler works, machine shops and other factories. Stone quarrying is also an important industry. The borough contains the Hall Institute, the Saint Scholastica Academy and a public library. It was settled in 1795 and was incorporated in 1841. Population in 1910, 15,270.

Sharps'burg, PA., a borough in Allegheny co., 5 mi. n. e. of Pittsburg, on the Allegheny River and on the Pennsylvania and the Baltimore & Ohio railroads. It is in a coal-mining region and contains a rolling mill, foundries, machine shops, varnish works, glass factories, lumber works and other factories. There are public and parish schools, a high school and a public library. The first settlement was made in 1826, and the borough was incorporated in 1841. Population in 1910, 8153.

Shaw, HENRY WHEELER (1818–1885), an American humorist, better known as Josh Billings, born in Lanesborough, Mass. He received a common school education and entered Hamilton College, but soon left there to go west. For some time he was a deck hand on the Ohio River steamboats, and later he became an auctioneer. After settling in Poughkeepsie, N. Y., he began writing for papers and gained considerable popularity. In 1863 he began lecturing and became as successful on the platform as in literature. Collections of his writings were published, and he also edited yearly the *Farmers' Allminax*, which had a large circulation.

Shaw, GEORGE BERNARD, (1856–   ), a prominent Irish critic, essayist and dramatist. He was born in Dublin and in 1876 settled in London, where he began a brilliant journalistic career. He took an active interest in politics, being favorable to Socialism, and was an early member of the Fabian Society. After he had written four novels he began writing plays. Mr. Shaw's dramas have always created interest and aroused discussion, favorable and otherwise. He is daring, witty and satirical. His satire is frequently biting and he deals with the hypocrisy of modern society and the frailties of human nature with an unsparing hand. Typical plays are *Arms and the Man*, *Man and Superman* and *Candida*.

GEORGE BERNARD SHAW

Shawnee', a wandering tribe of Algonquian indians that was early broken up, some of the tribe finding a home in Oklahoma, but most of them remaining east of the Mississippi.

Shawnee, OKLA., the county-seat of Pottawatomie co., is located 39 mi. e. of Oklahoma City, on the North Canadian River and the Santa Fé, the Chicago, Rock Island & Pacific, the Missouri, Kansas & Texas and other railroads. The Chicago Rock Island & Pacific shops are located here and furnish work for hundreds of workmen. The city has substantial schoolhouses and churches, and the Baptist State University is located here. Population in 1910, 12,474.

Shays's Rebellion, an insurrection in Massachusetts in 1786–1787, resulting from the financial distress which followed the close of the Revolutionary War. The special grievances of the insurgents were the high salaries paid to officials, high taxes and extortionate fees of lawyers and officers. In September, 1786, a mob of six hundred gathered at Springfield, forced the supreme court to adjourn and attempted to capture the arsenal, but in January the state militia under General Benjamin Lincoln succeeded in putting down the uprising. Ten of the leaders were condemned to death, but later they were pardoned by Governor John Hancock.

Sheboy'gan, WIS., the county-seat of Sheboygan co., 52 mi. n. of Milwaukee, on Lake Michigan, at the mouth of the Sheboygan River, and on the Chicago & Northwestern railroad. It is an important shipping point for the surrounding farming and dairying section. There are large cheese warehouses, coal and salt docks, fisheries, chair and furniture factories, foundries, machine shops, bottling works, brickyards and various other establishments. The city has a public library, a good Federal building, a county asylum for the insane, a home for the friendless and the Saint Nicholas hospital. There are two parks and about a score of churches. The place was settled in 1836, the village was incorporated in 1846 and the city was chartered in 1853. Population in 1910, 26,398.

Sheep, a cud-chewing animal, nearly allied to the goat. It has hollow horns, like those of

SOUTHDOWN SHEEP

the cow, and its body is covered with wool. The sheep is one of the most useful animals to man; its wool serves for clothing, its flesh is an excellent article of food, its skin is made into leather and its milk is used in some countries to make butter and cheese. There are many varieties of domestic sheep, but it is not known from what wild species they were originally bred, though it is probable that the smaller short-tailed breeds are descended from the wild species known as the *moufflon*. Domestic sheep are found in all parts of the civilized world, but they are most extensively raised in the temperate regions, where they are kept chiefly for the wool and flesh. The first sheep were brought to America by Columbus in 1493. The Spaniards introduced them into Mexico and Florida, and from these early flocks large herds descended. Other breeds were also brought by the English into the northern colonies, so that early in the history of the country the farms were stocked with sheep.

All breeds can be grouped under three classes, the coarse-wooled, the medium-wooled and the fine-wooled. Among the *coarse-wooled* breeds the Leicesters, Cotswolds and Lincolns are the most common. These breeds are characterized

COTSWOLD SHEEP

by their long, coarse wool, white faces and straight backs. The *medium-wooled* breeds are usually large in size and have compact fleeces, the wool being about one-half the length of that of the coarse-wooled breeds. One of the best known of these is the Southdown, which is easily distinguished by its large, compact body and its brown face and legs. The medium-wooled breeds are valuable for both wool and mutton and are very generally raised. The merino is the most important of the *fine-wooled* breeds. This sheep was introduced into America from Spain, where it has been bred for many centuries. It is small in size and has short legs, and the skin is wrinkled about the neck and shoulders. The wool is short, very fine and quite oily. It is the most valuable wool taken from sheep, and a fine cloth is manufactured from it. The merino is delicate and will thrive only in a dry climate. These sheep are raised in large numbers in Australia, in New Zealand and in some of the Rocky Mountain states.

There are numerous other breeds of sheep, but with one or two exceptions they are of no economic importance. One of these is the sheep from which the so-called fur known as *astrakhan* and *Persian lamb* is obtained. The wool of this sheep is very fine and curly, which gives these furs a peculiar appearance.

Australia, British South Africa, Argentina and the United States are the great wool-growing countries of the world. In the United States, Montana, Wyoming, New Mexico and Ohio are the leading states. There are about 9,000,000 sheep slaughtered in the United States each year, and the country produces about one-fourth of the world's output of wool. See MEAT PACKING; MUTTON; WOOL.

Sheep Lau'rel. See KALMIA.

Sheepshead, *sheeps'hed,* the name of a fish caught on the shores of Connecticut and Long Island. It is allied to the gilt-head and the bream, and it is considered a delicious food. It receives its name from the resemblance of its head to that of a sheep. The color is a silvery white, and the fish is rarely more than two feet in length.

Sheep Tick, one of the well-known insects, which, in the pupa state, are shining oval bodies that become attached to the wool of the sheep. From these issues the tick, which is horny, bristly, of a rusty ocher color and wingless. It fixes its head in the skin of the sheep and extracts the blood, leaving a large round tumor.

SHEEP TICK

Shef'field, a municipal and parliamentary borough of England, in the West Riding of Yorkshire, situated on hilly ground, at the junction of the Sheaf and the Don, about 160 mi. n. of London. It possesses many fine buildings, among which are the ancient parish Church of Saint Peter's, in the Perpendicular style, recently restored; Saint Mary's Catholic Church; Albert Hall, and the Cutler's Hall. Of educational and literary institutions there are the Free Grammar School; the Church of England Educational Institute; University College, formerly the Firth College; the Wesley College; the School of Art, and the Saint George's Museum, founded by Mr. Ruskin. The trade of Sheffield is chiefly connected with cutlery, for which it has long been famous, and the manufacture of all forms of steel, iron and brass work. The steel manufacture includes armor-plating, rails, engine castings and rifles. There are also manufactures of engines, machinery, plated goods, Britannia metal goods, stoves and grates. Sheffield is supposed to have been originally a Roman station. Edward I granted it a charter as a market town in 1296. It is only since 1800 that it has developed such importance as a manufacturing center. Population in 1911, 454,632.

Sheik, *sheek* or *shayk*, a title of dignity originally belonging to the chiefs of the Arabic tribes, but now used among Moslems as a title of respect. The head of a Mohammedan monastery and the head man of a village are sometimes called sheiks. The chief mufti at Constantinople is the *sheik-ul-islam*.

Shek'el, an ancient weight and monetary unit. The weight is believed to have been about 126 or 130 grains troy or, according to a so-called *double measure*, 252 or 260 grains troy. The value of the silver coin was about 56 cents. There were also half-shekels of both silver and copper. A shekel (weight) of gold was worth $9.10.

Shel'by, ISAAC (1750–1826), an American frontiersman and soldier, born near Hagerstown, Md. Before he was twenty-one his strength and daring had caused him to be appointed deputy sheriff of his county. In 1771 he went with his father to Tennessee, took part in the contest with the indians in 1774, and at the outbreak of the Revolution became captain of the Virginia militia. Later, as colonel of North Carolina troops, he distinguished himself at King's Mountain and coöperated with Greene in his campaign against Cornwallis. At the close of the war he settled in Kentucky, became first governor of the state in 1792 and was again elected in 1796 and from 1812 to 1816. At the head of Kentucky troops he was conspicuous in the War of 1812.

Shel'byville, IND., the county-seat of Shelby co., 26 mi. s. e. of Indianapolis, on the Big Blue River and on the Cleveland, Cincinnati, Chicago & Saint Louis and the Pittsburg, Cincinnati, Chicago & Saint Louis railroads. The city is in an agricultural, stock-raising and dairying region, and it contains flour mills, creameries, furniture factories, lumber and planing mills, ice factories and various other works. It has a Carnegie library, twelve churches, two national banks and several loan associations. The Forest Hill cemetery is also of interest. Population in 1910, 9500.

Shel'don, EDWARD AUSTIN (1823–1897), an American educator, a graduate of Hamilton College. He began his educational career as a teacher in a school for orphans and children of poor parents in Oswego. He later became superintendent of schools of Syracuse, New York, but at the end of two years returned to Oswego as clerk of the board of education. He became acquainted with the methods of teaching originating in England and known as *object lessons*, and he introduced this work into the Oswego

schools, being the first to use it in the United States. The Oswego City Training School was made a state normal school, and Mr. Sheldon was elected its president, which position he retained until his death. His work was very influential in revolutionizing methods of instruction throughout the country. He is considered one of the pioneers of the *new education* in the United States.

Shell, a hollow projectile, filled with a bursting charge of gunpowder or other explosive composition and fitted with a fuse by which to fire it at the desired time. Shells are usually made of cast iron or steel; for mortars or smooth-bore cannon they are spherical, but for rifled guns they are usually elongated. *Common shells* are simple hollow projectiles, filled with powder. On explosion they act like a mine. They are very effective in breaching earthworks or masonry. *Palliser shells* are made of mottled iron, with pointed heads, nearly solid and chilled white by being cast in iron molds. They are intended for use against armor-clad vessels; the chilled point, in virtue of its intense hardness and great crushing strength, penetrates to an extraordinary depth. *Steel* shells of similar power have also been made. *Shrapnel shells* are shells filled with bullets and with a small bursting charge just sufficient to split the shell open and release the bullets at any given point. *Segment shells* are of the nature of shrapnel. They contain iron segments, built up round the inside of the shell. From their construction they are inclined to spread much more than shrapnel on bursting, and they should consequently be fired to burst close to the object.

Shel'ley, PERCY BYSSHE (1792–1822), an English poet, born at Field Place, Horsham, Sussex, the son of Sir Timothy Shelley, a landed proprietor of ancient family. He was educated at Sion House Academy, Brantford, at Eton and at University College, Oxford. At Sion House and at Eton he was persecuted somewhat by his fellows, and thus he early began to show that fierce hatred of oppression which characterized him throughout his life. While at Oxford he showed himself possessed of uncommon literary ability; but he fell into disfavor with the authorities on the publication of a pamphlet called *The Necessity of Atheism* and was expelled. In 1811, shortly after his expulsion from college, he eloped to Edinburgh with Harriet Westbrook, the daughter of a retired innkeeper, but sixteen years of age. The marriage turned out unhappily, and after nearly three years of a wandering, unsettled life they separated. In November, 1816, Harriet committed suicide by drowning. Shelley was deeply affected by this event, but soon after he married Mary Godwin, with whom he had visited the Continent in 1814. Partly because his lungs were affected and partly because he feared that he should be deprived of the children of his second marriage, on account of his atheism, as he had been deprived of those of his former marriage, Shelley left England finally in March, 1818, and the whole short remainder of his life was passed in Italy. On July 8, 1822, he was sailing with a Mr. Williams

PERCY BYSSHE SHELLEY

in the Bay of Spezzia when a storm arose and both were drowned. According to the quarantine laws of Tuscany the bodies were burned, and the ashes of Shelley were deposited by his friends in the Protestant burying ground of Rome.

From his youth Shelley's life was a constant battle in defense of the radical revolutionary principles he had adopted. He believed in the possibility of establishing an ideal society, in which such institutions as marriage and property should be subordinate to the development of individuals. In some of his poems, *Queen Mab*, his earliest important work, *The Revolt of Islam* and *Prometheus Unbound*, he embodied his beliefs on the reconstruction of society. The poems of Shelley, however, which have remained most popular, are characterized, rather, by a del-

158

icate fanciful beauty, than by any openly expressed spirit of revolt. Shelley was one of the great lyric poets of England, and his gift of wonderful melody, grace and lightness shows best in such poems as *Ode to the West Wind, The Cloud, Ode to Liberty, Ode to a Skylark, To Night* and *Lines to an Indian Air*.

Shells, the hard outer coverings which form the chief protection of many of the lower animals. The mollusks, the Echinodermata, the Crustacea and even certain insects, as the beetles, and certain mammals, as the armadillos, have such coverings. Perhaps the most interesting and typical shells are those of the mollusks, which are divided, as to form, into two classes—the univalves and the bivalves. The most common examples of the univalves are the shells of common snails, which assume a variety of graceful shapes and beautiful colors. Some are long spirals, tapering to a point; some are tightly wound wheels, like a watch spring, and some are short, round spirals, with wide openings. Some of these shells are delicate, with a pearly luster, while others are thick, heavy and shiny, as if made from china. Of the bivalves—shell formed of two parts, joined by a hinge—the best examples are the clam and oyster shells. The most easily noted characteristics of these very common shells are the different layers of which they are composed—the outer horny layer, or epidermis, and the beautiful inner pearly layer. There are endless varieties of both univalve and bivalve shells, some so small as to be indistinguishable as shells, some very large; and all of these have been put to many uses. They have been used as ornaments by civilized and uncivilized peoples, as material for the making of buttons and other objects, and as money. The study of shells and of shelled animals is called *Conchology.* See Cowrie; Wampum.

Shen′ando′ah, Pa., a borough in Schuylkill co., about 100 mi. n. w. of Philadelphia, on the Pennsylvania, the Lehigh Valley and the Philadelphia & Reading railroads. There are also electric railways to the neighboring towns. It is in a rich anthracite coal field, and mining is the principal industry. The Greek Catholic church here was one of the first of that denomination in the United States. The borough contains about a score of churches, a public library, gas and electric lights, two national banks, a savings bank and three building and loan associations. Shenandoah was settled in 1850 and was incorporated in 1866. Population in 1910, 25,774.

Shenandoah River, a river formed in West Virginia by the junction of the North, the Middle and the South Rivers. It flows northeastward and enters the Potomac at Harper's Ferry, just above the passage of the latter river through the Blue Ridge Mountains. The length of the Shenandoah is 300 miles. Its valley is bounded on the southeast by the Blue Ridge Mountains and is noted for its fertility and beauty. This valley was the scene of numerous military operations during the Civil War. See SHERIDAN, PHILIP HENRY.

Shepard, HELEN GOULD (1868-   ), an American philanthropist, daughter of Jay Gould. She was for many years identified with philanthropic work of all kinds. Among her most famous benevolences was the gift to the United States Government, at the opening of the Spanish-American War, of $100,000, for the improvement of the equipment of the hospital and commissary service. She also made large contributions to Rutgers College and to New York University, the Hall of Fame being one of her gifts to the latter institution. Mrs. Shepard has also been a liberal patron of the Young Men's Christian Association. She married Finley J. Shepard, January 22, 1913.

Shepherd, *shep'urd,* **Dog,** a variety of dog employed by shepherds to assist in tending flocks. It is generally of large size, of powerful, lithe build and remarkable for its intelligence and usefulness. The tail is rather long and possesses a bushy fringe, the muzzle is notably sharp and the eyes large and bright. Of all strains of shepherd dog, the Scotch collie is most celebrated.

Shepherd's Purse, a plant belonging to the mustard family. It is an annual weed, with small white flowers and flat, heart-shaped pods. It is found everywhere in temperate climates.

Sherbrooke, *shur'brook,* a city in Quebec Province, situated at the junction of the Saint Francis and Magog rivers, 101 mi. e. of Montreal, and on the Grand Trunk and the Boston & Maine railroads. The rivers furnish good water power, and the city is quite an important industrial center. Among the leading manufactures are woolen cloths, flour, foundry products, tools, lumber, wood pulp, paper and malt liquors. Population in 1911, 16,405.

Shere Ali, *sheer ah'le,* (1825-1879), ameer of Afghanistan. He succeeded his father, Dost Mohammad, in 1863. The ameer's relations with the English government in India were not very friendly, and when, in 1878, a Russian mission was received with honor at Kabul, while afterward permission was refused for a British mission to cross the frontier, the British invaded Afghanistan, thus beginning the second Afghan war. Shere Ali fled from Kabul to Turkestan, where he died.

Sher'idan, WYO., a city and the county-seat of Sheridan co., on the Chicago, Burlington & Quincy, 178 mi. w. n. w. of Newcastle. Coal is mined in the vicinity, and the city has a brewery and manufactures of agricultural implements. It is the seat of a college. Population in 1910, 8408.

Sheridan, PHILIP HENRY (1831-1888), an American soldier, probably the greatest cavalry

PHILIP SHERIDAN

leader of the Civil War, born in Albany, N. Y. He graduated at the Military Academy, West Point, in 1853, and from 1855 to 1861 he served on the frontiers of Texas and Oregon. At the outbreak of the Civil War he was a captain in the Thirteenth Infantry, but in the following year he was made colonel of the Second Michigan Cavalry. Later in the year he was placed in command of the Army of the Ohio, and in the battles of Perryville, Murfreesboro, Chickamauga and Chattanooga, he showed the greatest ability and bravery. In April, 1864, Grant appointed him chief of cavalry of the Army of the Potomac, and he made several daring cavalry raids into the Shenandoah Valley. His ride from Winchester to Cedar Creek, a distance of twenty miles, which turned a Federal defeat into a brilliant victory, is his most famous exploit. During the final advance upon Richmond he was Grant's right-hand man. He fought the Battle of Five Forks, which necessitated Lee's evacuation of Richmond and Petersburg; and as Lee fled he constantly harassed and attacked him, until he compelled his surrender at Appomattox Court House, Apr. 9, 1865. After the war he held various military commands. In March, 1869, he became lieutenant general, and in February, 1883, on the retirement of Sherman, commander of the army.

Sheridan, RICHARD BRINSLEY (1751–1816), an English dramatist, born in Dublin. He was sent for a short time to a school in Dublin, and in 1762 he went to Harrow, where he did not distinguish himself. His first famous comedy, *The Rivals,* was produced in 1775, and this was followed by *The Duenna,* a comic opera, and *The School for Scandal,* the greatest comedy which had been produced since Shakespeare. Although a member of Parliament, Sheridan never became a statesman; but he soon rose high as an orator. His greatest effort was his speech on the impeachment of Warren Hastings.

Sher'iff, in the United States, the principal administrative officer of a county. The principal duties of the sheriff are to maintain peace and order, to attend courts as administrative officer, to guard prisoners and juries, to serve processes and execute the judgments of the courts and to preside at inquisitions. In most states the sheriff is elected by the popular vote.

Sherman, *shur'man,* TEX., the county-seat of Grayson co., 64 mi. n. of Dallas on the Frisco, the Atchison, Topeka & Santa Fé, the Texas & Pacific and other railroads. The city has an elevation of about 1000 feet above the sea. It is in the fertile Red River valley and is not far from the great Ardmore coal fields of Oklahoma. It ships large quantities of cotton and grain and contains a large cotton gin, several cottonseed oil mills, flour and lumber mills, machine shops, brick works and other factories. The higher educational institutions are the North Texas Female College, the Carr-Burdette Christian College for women, Mary Nash Female College, Austin College for boys, Sherman Institute, Saint Joseph's Academy and a commercial college. The municipality has a public library and owns and operates the waterworks. Sherman was settled in 1848 and was chartered as a city in 1895. Population in 1910, 12,412.

Sherman, JAMES SCHOOLCRAFT (1855–1912), a lawyer and congressman, born at Utica, N. Y. He was mayor of Utica in 1884, and member of Congress from 1887 to 1907, with the exception of one term. In 1908 he was elected Vice-President on the Republican ticket. In 1912 he was renominated, but died six days before the election.

Sherman, JOHN (1823–1900), an American statesman, born in Lancaster, Ohio. He was

JOHN SHERMAN

admitted to the bar in 1844 and began practice at Mansfield, where he was elected to Congress in 1855. As a speaker he was an acknowledged power from the first, was a member of important committees and rendered valuable aid to the government, in financial affairs. In 1861 he became United States senator, and as chairman of the ways and means committee he did much to strengthen the public credit during the Civil War and after. He was appointed secretary of the treasury in 1877 and succeeded in accumulating a sufficient gold reserve for the resumption of specie payment. He served continuously as United States senator from 1881 until 1897, when he became secretary of state. He resigned in April, 1898, and retired to private life.

Sherman, ROGER (1721–1793), an American legislator, one of the signers of the Declaration of Independence, born at Newton, Mass. As a boy he was apprenticed to a shoemaker, but in 1743 he entered business with his brother at

New Milford, Conn. Later he was admitted to the bar, having prepared himself by his own study, and was then elected to the Connecticut legislature. In 1774 he entered the Continental Congress and was one of the committee of five chosen to draw up the Declaration of Independence. He also helped in the preparation of the Articles of Confederation and served continuously in the Congress until 1787, when he was made a delegate to the constitutional convention. At this meeting he took a prominent part and in 1791 he was chosen to the House of Representatives. The same year he was elected to the Senate, where he remained until his death.

Sherman, WILLIAM TECUMSEH (1820–1891), an American general, born at Lancaster, Ohio,

WILLIAM TECUMSEH SHERMAN

and educated at the military academy, West Point. He served in Florida, Mexico and elsewhere till 1853, when he resigned his commission. On the breaking out of the Civil War he offered his services to the United States government and was appointed colonel of the Thirteenth Infantry. He was present at the Battle of Bull Run, greatly distinguished himself at Shiloh and subsequently took a prominent part in the operations under Grant around Vicksburg and Memphis. Transferred to Tennessee, he rendered Grant great service in the operations around Chattanooga, and early in 1864 he led his forces in a raid across Mississippi, devasting the country from Jackson to Meridian. In March, 1864, he succeeded Grant as commander of the military division of the Mississippi, and at the beginning of May, simultaneously with Grant's advance in the East, he entered upon his invasion of Georgia. On September 1, after a number of battles, he received the capitulation of Atlanta and on December 21 entered Savannah. Then, turning northward into the Carolinas and fighting more battles, he received the surrender of General Joseph E. Johnston at Durham's Station, Apr. 26, 1865, a surrender which brought the war to a close. Sherman was made a major general in 1864, lieutenant general in 1866 and general in 1869. He was retired in 1884.

Sher'ry, a Spanish wine, made in the neighborhood of Cheres, in the Province of Andalusia, near Cadiz. Dry sherry is the most highly prized. It is a strong wine, esteemed for its delicate flavor. Sherry is more largely imitated and adulterated than any other wine. See WINE.

Sherwood, *shur'wood,* WILLIAM HALL (1854–1911), an American musician, born at Lyons, N. Y. He had a remarkable musical education, both in the United States and in Europe, and upon his return to America became a teacher in the New England Conservatory, afterward in New York, and later director of the pianoforte department in the Chicago Conservatory. In 1897 he founded the Sherwood Piano School in Chicago and became its principal.

Shet'land or **Zet'land Islands,** a group of islands, lying between the Atlantic Ocean and the North Sea, northeast of Scotland. They are about 100 in number, of which 23 are inhabited. The largest of the Shetlands is Mainland. The area of the whole group is about 550 sq. mi., and the population in 1901 was 28,195. The surface is rugged, and the coasts have many indentations, lined with abrupt cliffs of gneiss, sandstone and granite. The climate is variable, but moderate, as to both heat and cold. Fishing forms the chief industry, the cod, the ling and the herring being the principal articles of commerce. The rearing of cattle, sheep and ponies is also an important industry, the Shetland ponies being especially famous. The principal agricultural products are oats and barley, while in the manufactures, hosiery and shawls take the lead.

Shiites, *she'ites,* one of the two great sects of Mohammedans. They do not acknowledge the *Sunna* as a law, and they believe that Ali, the fourth caliph after Mohammed, was his first lawful successor. The Persians are Shiites.

Shil'laber, BENJAMIN PENHALLOW (1814–1890), an American humorist, best known under the pen name of *Mrs. Partington,* born at Portsmouth, N. H. He became a printer and was engaged in this occupation at Dover, N. H., and at Boston until 1847, when he joined the editorial staff of the Boston *Post.* He contributed to this paper humorous sketches which found their way to all parts of the country. From 1856 to 1866 he was joint editor of the Boston *Saturday Evening Gazette,* but thereafter devoted himself to independent literary work. Among his well-known books are *Life and Sayings of Mrs. Partington, Partingtonian Patchwork* and *Ike and His Friends.*

Shil'ling, an English silver coin, equal in value to 12 bronze pence, or one-twentieth of a pound sterling, and approximately equal to 24 cents, to 1.25 French francs and to 1.11 German marks. The convenient size and value of the English shillings made them popular in the American colonies, but, like the pound unit, in the colonies they varied greatly in value. A few coins of this denomination were issued by the colonies, notably the famous Pine Tree Shilling of Massachusetts. The shilling is still used as a money of account in parts of the United States, its most common value being about 12½ cents, or ⅛ of one dollar.

Shi'loh, BATTLE OF, one of the most memorable battles of the Civil War, fought about 2 mi. w. of Pittsburg Landing, on the Tennessee River, in Tennessee, around a log chapel known as "Shiloh Church." Grant and Sherman commanded the Federals, and A. S. Johnston and Beauregard led the Confederates. On April 6, 1862, the Confederates took the Federals by surprise and drove them from their lines, with heavy loss in men and guns; but the second day the Federals, having received reënforcements under generals Lew Wallace and D. C. Buell and largely outnumbering the Confederates, regained their first position and forced the Confederates to retreat to Corinth. The total losses of the Federals were 13,000 men, including Gen. W. H. L. Wallace, killed, and Gen. B. M. Prentiss, captured. The Confederates lost 10,700 men, including Gen. A. S. Johnston, one of their most talented commanders.

Shinney. See HOCKEY.

Shin'toism, one of the two great religions of Japan. In its origin it was a form of nature worship, but the essence of the religion is now ancestor worship and sacrifice to departed heroes. After the introduction of Buddhism, the priests of Shintoism became magicians and fortune tellers. After the overthrow of the shogun, Shintoism again took the place of Buddhism.

Shiogoon' or **Tycoon'.** See SHOGUN.

Ship, in general, any large sea-going vessel. In a more restricted sense, it signifies a vessel intended for distant voyages, in distinction to a *boat,* a term which includes all navigable vessels. In a still more limited sense, a ship is a sailing vessel, with a bowsprit and three masts (fore, main and mizzen), each having three parts (lower mast, topmast and topgallant mast), all rigged with a certain number of square sails. When there is a fourth mast it is called a jigger. But the development of steam navigation has greatly enlarged the scope of the term ship, so that it now includes steam vessels, as well as all kinds of sailing craft, such as men-of-war, transports, merchantmen, barks, brigs, schooners, sloops, galleys, cutters and barges.

The Phoenicians, the greatest commercial people of antiquity, made considerable progress in the art of shipbuilding; the Romans also had a well-developed art, and before them, the Egyptians. But with the tide of barbarism which swept over Europe at the downfall of the last great ancient empire, the science of shipbuilding was almost lost, and the Western peoples, to whom the world's progress was henceforth entrusted, were compelled to begin anew and build up, from their own resources, new models. The chief events which gave impetus to the development of the art were the invention of the compass, the discovery of America and the finding of a passage to India. Spain, the great maritime nation of the early modern era, followed by France and Holland, and later still by England, made the first important advances. The last of these nations has the credit for building the first three-decker (1637), known as the *Sovereign of the Seas.* Superiority in the art shifted again to France, who, by the latter half of the 18th century, had produced models vastly in advance of anything before constructed. After the independence of the United States was achieved she rapidly forged to the front and soon took the lead in the art of shipbuilding. In 1832, Scott Russell demonstrated the theoretical principles upon which the speed of ships is based, and these were immediately applied with success by both American and foreign builders. The Baltimore clipper schooners were the first results of the application of true principles of construction. They had sharp bows and deep stern, were very long and lay low in the water, had long, slender masts and large, skilfully cut sails. The construction of square-rigged vessels on these principles gave faster, safer ships than had been known before, and these played a large part in

exhausted. Great Britain still leads all nations in the tonnage of ships built, but the United States leads in the number constructed, as is shown by the following figures: In 1900 there were built in Great Britain, 1433 ships, with a total tonnage of 944,267 tons. The same year there were built in the United States 1447 ships, with a total tonnage of 393,790 tons. The names of Cramp and Roach are known the world over as builders of the finest types of merchant vessels and battle ships. These yards are both

SHIP

A, mast; B, topmast; C, topgallant mast; D, royal mast; E, yard; J, bowsprit; K, jib boom; L, flying jib boom; P, crosstrees; R, spanker boom.

1, course; 2, topsail; 3, topgallant sail; 4, royal; 5, spanker; 6, fore topmast staysail; 7, jib; 8, flying jib.

the development of the oriental trade of both England and America.

Until this time the only means of propulsion known were oars and sails, but with the application of steam, a new revolution in the art of shipbuilding took place. Wood gave place to iron, and iron finally yielded to steel, as the material of construction. The *Great Western*, launched in 1837, was the first steamship built expressly for regular trips between England and America. She was propelled by paddles, but soon thereafter Ericsson's screw propellers were adopted almost universally. From that time progress was rapid, till, at the beginning of the twentieth century, the possibilities of the science seem to be nearly

situated on the Delaware River, but there are also large shipbuilding yards at San Francisco, New York and other ocean ports.

The modern ocean liners are models of beauty, safety and convenience. Some of these are over 800 feet in length, have a capacity of 12,000 to 45,000 tons and have engines which generate from 30,000 to 70,000 horsepower. These largest vessels are propelled by steam, but mammoth sailing ships are also constructed, rarely, however, with a capacity of over 5000 tons. Steel ships now predominate, as they are much lighter, easier of construction, more manageable upon the water, less easily damaged and far more durable. In wooden ships, the keel is the base

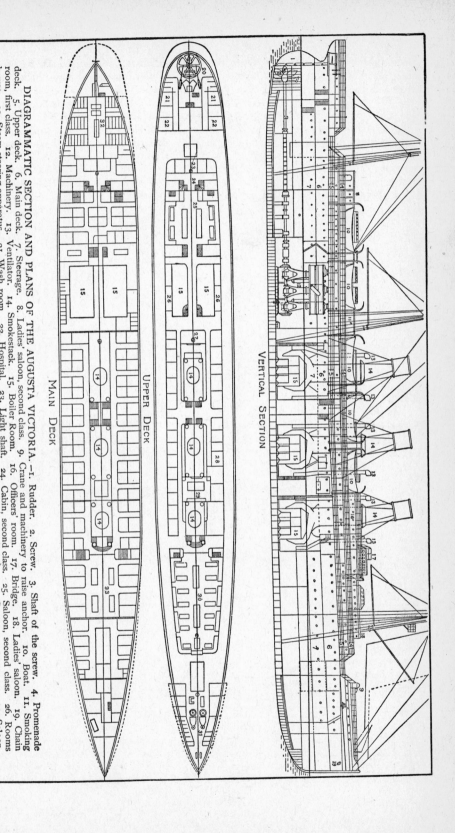

DIAGRAMMATIC SECTION AND PLANS OF THE AUGUSTA VICTORIA.—1. Rudder. 2. Screw. 3. Shaft of the screw. 4. Promenade deck. 5. Upper deck. 6. Main deck. 7. Steerage. 8. Ladies' saloon, second class. 9. Crane and machinery to raise anchor. 10. Boat. 11. Smoking room, first class. 12. Machinery. 13. Ventilator. 14. Smokestack. 15. Boiler Room. 16. Officers' room. 17. Bridge. 18. Ladies' saloon. 19. Chain hawse. 20. Steam steering apparatus. 21. Wash room. 22. Hospital. 23. Light shaft. 24. Cabin, second class. 25. Saloon, second class. 26. Rooms for ship's crew. 27. Bakery. 28. Slaughter house. 29. Kitchen. 30. Saloon, first class. 31. Anchor windlass. 32. Steerage passengers. 33. Saloon, first class. The majority of the unnamed divisions on the Upper Deck and Main Deck are staterooms for passengers. The stairways leading from one deck to another are indicated by horizontal black rulings.

VERTICAL SECTION

UPPER DECK

MAIN DECK

of the structure; from it rise, on both sides, many ribs, consisting of strong timbers curved to the shape desired in the hull. Over these are bolted the outer planks, the spaces between which are calked, to prevent leaking. Beams

CUTTER

extend from side to side on the interior to support the decks. In steel ships the sides or walls and all the adjacent parts are mutually self-supporting and are not dependent upon the keel, as are the parts of a wooden ship. The keel and ribs are of steel, and the sheathing or plating consists of large steel sheets. The girders and supports are all of iron and steel, and in the hull, only the floors of the decks, the partitions and some of the fixtures and furnishings are of wood.

From what has been said it is evident that the science of ship designing is at once important and intricate. The conditions that confront the naval architect are innumerable and present problems that demand for their solution the application of high mathematical principles and computations, combined with the most minute experimental observations. The ship must have graceful lines, must possess a certain capacity for cargo and also must be able to carry a certain number of passengers; her engines must be capable of propelling her at a certain speed, and her shape must be conducive to allowing such speed with economy of fuel; she must be able to stow enough coal to last during the trip at a rate of about 500 tons a day, for fast boats like the *Deutschland*, and about 260 tons for the larger, slower boats. She must be safe, but light, must withstand shocks firmly and must be built so that she will return to erect position when turned slightly to the side.

The average cost of a fully equipped man-of-war is about $3,000,000, and that of a merchant or passenger ship somewhat less.

The completion of the *Lusitania* and *Mauretania* is considered to mark a new era in ocean transportation. Steam turbines take the place of the old-styled reciprocating engine; each ship is driven by four propellers and makes an average speed of about 25 knots, or nearly 30 miles, an hour. The *Mauretania* has a width of 88 feet, is 60 feet deep, has gross tonnage of 33,000 tons and a displacement of 46,640 tons. She will accommodate 550 first-class passengers, 375 second-class and 1300 third-class passengers, and requires a crew of 800. The electric lighting plant required over 200 miles of cable and a dynamo larger than that necessary for a good-sized town. Her consumption of coal averages about 2000 tons a day and 350 men are required to attend to the fires. These ships are fitted with every convenience and luxury that can be found in the most select hotels of Europe or the United States, as well as with the latest devices to insure safety. They make the voyage between New York and Liverpool in less than five days. Since the completion of these ships, the *Olympic* has

BRIG

been built by the White Star line and the *Imperator* and *Vaterland* by the Hamburg-American line. All three of these are longer than the *Mauretania* (790 feet) and the *Lusitania* (760 feet), and the *Vaterland* (950 feet) is the longest boat in the world. The *Titanic* was a sister ship to the *Olympic*. See TITANIC.

A good idea of the interior arrangements of a large steamship may be obtained from the three accompanying diagrams, which are taken from the plans of the fast-sailing propeller *Augusta Victoria*, which has a displacement of 7642 tons and 12,500 horsepower. There are staterooms for 270 passengers in the first cabin; for 150 in the second cabin, and for 700 in the steerage. See WAR SHIP.

Ship Canal. See CANAL.

Ship Railway, a railway for the transportation of ships overland from one body of water to another. Ship railways are of ancient origin, and the first of which there is any record was built across the Isthmus of Corinth about 400 B. C. This could carry boats 150 feet long and with a draft of over 8 feet. It was in operation for more than three centuries.

The modern ship railways that have been most successful consist of inclines connected with canals, where the ship is hauled from one level to another, instead of being lifted by means of a canal lock (See CANAL). The most extended ship railway ever planned was that projected by Captain James B. Eads across the Isthmus of Tehauntepec. This railway was to take the place of an isthmian canal, and the plans for its construction were all perfected, but the sudden death of Captain Eads prevented the carrying out of the project. Another railway on the same plan was projected across the Isthmus of Chignecto, New Brunswick, in 1875. When completed this railway will be seven miles long. The work was begun in 1888, but lack of funds has prevented its completion. The plan is to load ships upon cradles, or cars, by running the cars under water to such a depth that the ships can be easily floated upon them; then, after the ship is supported in position, the car and ship will be raised to the level of the road by means of hydraulic presses. The cars will then be hauled to their destination by locomotives constructed especially for the purpose.

Ship Worm or **Tere'do**, the common name of a mollusk which has a somewhat wormlike appearance. The shell is small and consists of two valves, which are situated near the anterior end. In length the worm averages about a foot, and it is half an inch in diameter. It has gained notoriety from its boring habits, and occasionally it causes great destruction to ships and submerged wood by perforating the wood in all directions. In boring, each individual carefully avoids the tube formed by its neighbors, but often only a very thin film is left between cavities, which are lined with a limy secretion. Various plans have been tried to protect wood from this destructive animal, such as copper-sheathing and treating with creosote, but the plan which appears to be most successful is that of driving a large number of short nails with large heads into the timber. The rust from the heads of the nails appears to prevent the operation of the worms.

Shiraz, she'raz, a city of Persia, situated 115 mi. n. e. of Bushire, on the Persian Gulf. The site is an elevated plain 5000 feet above sea level and is in the midst of a region noted for its rose gardens, vineyards, cypress groves and orchards. The city is surrounded by an old wall, and one hundred years ago it was the residence of the ruler and was the chief center of science and art for Persia. It was then celebrated for its magnificent buildings and its elegant manufactures. It has now lost much of its importance and has been seriously damaged by earthquakes. The manufactures include textiles, rose water, glass, silverware and inlaid work. The population is estimated at from 30,000 to 50,000.

Shire, she'ra, a river of southeastern Africa, draining Lake Nyassa into the Zambezi, which it enters on its left bank, after a course of about 270 miles nearly due south. It is navigable in the lower part of its course, but above the head of navigation it contains many falls and rapids, during the course of which it descends 1200 feet.

Shit'tim Wood, the wood of which the Tabernacle in the wilderness was principally constructed. It is the wood of the shittah tree of the Bible, which is supposed to be the *Acacia seyal* of the Sinaitic peninsula. It is light, but cross-grained and enduring, and is of a fine orange-brown color.

Shod'dy, a fiber made by cutting up and shredding woolen, worsted or mixed rags. The rags are thoroughly cleansed, then shredded and carded, by processes similar to those used in the manufacture of wool (See WOOLEN MANUFACTURE). When it leaves the cards the fiber is in the form of long, fluffy rolls. These are packed into bales under hydraulic pressure, and in this form they are shipped to manufacturers.

Shoddy is used in the manufacture of cheaper grades of cloth, where it is combined with wool. A variety which is a sort of wool powder is also used to add weight and substance to certain woolen cloths. During the Civil War a large amount of shoddy was put into the clothing furnished the Union soldiers by contractors. Because of the wealth obtained by some of these contractors and because of their ambition for social prominence, the epithet *shoddy* is now used to describe anything which pretends to be better than it is.

Shoes. See BOOTS AND SHOES.

Sho'gun, Shiogoon or **Tycoon,** originally the military commander of one of the four districts into which the Japanese Empire was divided. These commanders eventually became practically absolute rulers of their districts and superseded the mikado in power, but by the revolution of 1868 the office of shogun was abolished and the central power was reëstablished.

Shooting Star. See METEOR,

Short Ballot, a phrase signifying the means by which it is sought to simplify the ballot and render the result of an election more truly representative of the popular will. To accomplish these ends it is proposed to place on the ballot only the names of those officials who are to determine public policy, leaving to appointment all those whose duties are merely administrative. It is further urged that very few offices be filled at one election. Questions of public policy are also presented to the voter for his approval. Public interest in this proposed reform is shown by the rapid extension of the commission form of government among cities, for this plan necessarily includes the underlying principles of the short ballot. See MUNICIPAL GOVERNMENT.

Short'hand, the method of writing by which the process is so abbreviated as to keep pace with speech. It is also known, according to the principle underlying the particular system, as stenography (compressed writing) and phonography (sound writing). It was practiced by the ancient Greeks and Romans, not only on account of its brevity, but for purposes of secrecy; but all knowledge of the art was lost from the tenth century until the end of the sixteenth, when modern shorthand had its birth in the publication by Dr. Timothy Bright of his *Characterie* and by Peter Bales of his *Arte of Brachygraphie*. In these early systems arbitrary signs were used in most cases to denote each word. The earliest system of shorthand of any practical importance was that of John Willis, whose *Arte of Stenographie* (1602) became very popular. It was based on the common alphabet, with the addition of arbitrary signs; and this, indeed, was the character of the numerous systems which obtained until the time of Pitman. Willis had many imitators, some of whom made slight improvements in his system, but William Mason, whose system was published in 1672, was the only one who made any real advance. In 1751 Thomas Gurney published his *Brachygraphy*, founded on Mason's system, and the use of Gurney's system has been perpetuated by his descendants, who have been the official shorthand writers of the Houses of Parliament since the beginning of the nineteenth

century. In 1767 appeared the *Universal English Shorthand* of John Byrom, an *a, b, c* system, characterized by "simple strokes and no arbitrary characters"; and in 1786 the *Stenography* of Samuel Taylor was published. This, which is the best of all the *a, b, c* systems, contributed largely to make stenography popular, and it was the system which was almost universally used until Isaac Pitman gave his *Phonography* to the world in 1837. Taylor's system possessed more easy and natural outlines and was therefore capable of being written with a greater degree of speed than any previous system, and it contained no arbitrary characters. Harding, who re-edited the system in 1823, introduced a few.

Pitman had a number of predecessors, whose systems, like his own, were strictly phonetic. These systems, however, never obtained any footing, while Pitman's almost immediately became popular; the Benn Pitman system, a variation of the original Pitmanic, is now used by more reporters and shorthand writers than any other. Like all other phonetic systems, Pitman's rejects the ordinary orthography and writes words according to the sounds; thus, *though* becomes *tho*, *plough* becomes *plow*, and *enough* becomes *enuf*. Discarding the common alphabet, which formed the basis of the stenographic systems, it has adopted an alphabet of its own, consisting of a series of straight lines, curves and dots, each representing a distinct sound. This alphabet is the basis of a highly ingenious and complex system, which aims at securing the greatest degree of brevity consistent with legibility. In rapid writing in Pitman's system the vowels are generally omitted.

In recent years several new systems have been introduced and have met with more or less success. Many of these are modifications of the original Pitmanic system, such as Graham's (1858) and Munson's (1867). There are also many constructed upon a new and so-called "rational" basis. Of these now widely used in the United States, the best-known are the Cross, or Eclectic, the Pernin, the Gregg and the McKee. All differ from each other as greatly as from the Pitmanic systems. The Cross, or Eclectic, is formed largely upon the basis of position of strokes, though several new strokes are also used. The Pernin is evolved from geometrical figures and does not use the Pitmanic shading. The Gregg system, which has been gaining adherents rapidly in the West, has five striking features—(1) no shading;

(2) slope same as in long-hand; (3) no position writing; (4) vowels and consonants conjoined; (5) curves are used and few angles. The McKee, commonly known as the New Standard system, retains the Pitmanic shading, and its vowels are composed of circles and ellipses in different sizes. It does not use positions.

At the present time there are about two hundred complete and more or less distinct systems in America, while in all foreign countries systems have grown up, adapted in phonetic properties or in script style to the sounds or characters of the particular language. It is interesting to note that the Pitmanic system has been adapted to Spanish, French, German, Italian, Dutch, Welsh, Japanese, Chinese and Hindustanee uses.

Shorthand has now been developed to the point where it easily keeps pace with speech, a fair average for an accomplished reporter being from 150 to 175 words a minute. Speed records have been made and authenticated of from 200 to 275 words a minute, for a period of ten or fifteen minutes in succession, and higher rates have been reached for shorter periods.

Shosho'nean Indians, the great group of tribes who lived west of Kansas, north and west as far as Oregon and south and west to California. Those east of the Rocky Mountains were hunting tribes, of fierce and warlike disposition, while those living west of the mountains were degraded and lived on small animals, fish, roots and seeds. The savagery of the Shoshoni, also called *Diggers,* or *Snake* indians, was thoroughly disgusting, but some of the southern members of the group, living in northwestern Arizona, were Pueblo indians and were successful agriculturists and skilled makers of pottery. Bannock, Comanche, Ute and Shoshoni are among the principal tribes. See MOKI.

Shoshone Falls, a waterfall on the Snake River, about 25 miles above the mouth of the Salmon Falls River. The river flows for some distance through a deep canyon, where it has a number of small falls and cataracts. These terminate in the main fall, which is 950 feet wide and about 200 feet high. Next to Niagara these are the greatest falls in the United States.

Shoshone River. See SNAKE RIVER.

Shoshoni, *sho sho'ne,* or **Snake,** a tribe of North American indians, inhabiting a considerable stretch of territory in Idaho, Utah and Nevada. They are a degraded tribe and live partly by hunting and fishing, but many of them live on roots and small animals.

Shot, a term applied to all solid projectiles fired from cannon, and also to hollow projectiles without bursting charges, as the Palliser shot. Solid shot have gradually disappeared since the introduction of rifled guns, which fire elongated shot, with more or less conical heads. Some of the shot fired by the immense guns now used weigh more than a ton. Smooth-bored ordnance still use solid round shot and case shot. Shot is also the name given to the small round pellets of lead, used with sporting guns, for shooting small quadrupeds and birds. This kind of shot is made by dropping the melted lead through the holes of a colander, set at a considerable height above water, the drops naturally assuming the globular form. See GRAPE SHOT.

Shot, PUTTING THE. See ATHLETICS.

Shot'gun, a smoothbore gun, which fires a charge of small shot and which is used chiefly for hunting small game. Originally these were muzzle-loaders, and none were manufactured in the United States. In 1836 the first breech-loader was invented, and since that time by numerous improvements shotguns have been brought to as great perfection as any other small arm. Brass or brass and paper shells, fitted with percussion caps, contain the charge. The shotguns were generally double-barreled in construction, but recently they are made single-barreled, with magazines, on the same principle as a repeating rifle. Hammerless guns, which discharge the shell by a mechanism hidden in the breech, are popular. The common sizes of shotguns are 10 and 12 bore, though guns of smaller bore are not uncommon. The best shotguns have Damascus twist, or laminated steel, barrels. In the former, alternate rods of steel and iron are welded together into a single bar, which is twisted to strengthen the fiber. Three bars, in one of which the twist runs opposite to that of the others, are then rolled into a strip, which is coiled about a steel core, into the form of a hollow cylinder, firmly welded together. Laminated barrels are made of similar strips, hammered solidly together and then bored to the desired size. The two barrels are fastened together, so that their charges would cross at about 120 feet from the muzzles. Finally, the barrels are browned or blued and fitted with stocks and locks.

Shovelboard, *shuv''l bord.* See SHUFFLE-BOARD.

Shoveler, *shuv''l ur,* or **Spoonbill,** a river duck, so named because the end of its bill is widened out, like a shovel or spoon. It feeds in the mud of shallow waters, using its bill to stir up the mud and capture small animals.

SHOVELER

The male bird is rather gay in color, but the female is much more modest in her appearance. One species is found in the United States during summer.

Shovel Fish, a genus of fishes belonging to the sturgeon family and found in North American rivers. It is so named from the flattened form of the head.

Shreveport, *shreev'port*, LA., the parish-seat of Caddo parish, 325 mi. n. w. of New Orleans and 15 mi. from the Texas state line, on the Red River and on the Queen & Crescent, the Texas & Pacific, the Missouri, Kansas & Texas and several other railroads. It is the second city in the state and is the commercial center of the northwestern part. Cotton is the principal product of the surrounding rich agricultural region, and the city contains cotton compresses, a cottonseed oil mill, machine shops, ice factories and lumber and stockyards. It also exports considerable live stock, hides and wool. Some of the prominent structures are the hospital, the Federal building, the courthouse, the First National Bank and the Cooper building. Shreveport was settled in 1833 and was incorporated in 1839. During the Civil War it was the capital of the state, after the capture of Baton Rouge. Population in 1910, 28,015.

Shrew, a genus of small mammals, quite different from the common mice and from the dormice, and found in almost every region of the northern hemisphere. The *common shrew* may readily be distinguished by its prolonged muzzle, by its teeth, colored brown at the tips, and by its reddish-brown fur. It feeds upon insects and their larvae and inhabits dry places, making a nest of leaves and grasses. It feeds

chiefly by night. Shrews are voracious in their habits and frequently kill and devour one another. They secrete a fluid of disagreeable odor, which prevents larger animals from eating their flesh. In former days the bite of the shrew was accounted venomous, while its body, variously treated, was regarded as a cure for many complaints. One American species, the *mole shrew*, resembling a mole in some of its habits, feeds on flesh of all kinds. Another American species is the *shrew mouse*, smaller and lighter in color, which dwells around marshes and wet regions. The *water shrew*, the largest American shrew, attains a total length of about five inches. The snout is not so pointed as that of the common shrew. The color is black on the upper parts and white underneath. A prominent swimming fringe of stiff, white hairs

COMMON SHREW

is found on the tail and on the toes, and this forms a distinctive feature of the species. Its food resembles that of the common shrew. It makes its burrows in the overhanging banks of rivers and lakes and dives and swims with great facility.

Shrew Mole, a genus of mammals belonging to the family of shrew mice, but also by some zoölogists placed in the mole family. It is found in North America, usually near rivers and streams, and burrows after the fashion of the common mole, which it resembles, also, in its fine and closely set fur. The average length of the shrew mole is about seven inches.

Shrike, a name applied rather loosely to different birds with strong, hooked bills. In the United States but two species are found— the *great northern shrike*, or *butcher bird*, and the *loggerhead shrike*. These birds resemble each other strongly in appearance and differ but little in size. Their general color is gray on the upper and white on the under parts, but the quills of the tail are black, and a black band crosses the forehead and surrounds the eyes. The shrikes are about nine or ten inches in length and feed principally upon mice, small birds, frogs and insects. These birds have a peculiar habit of catching their prey and impaling it upon thorns or suspending it upon the branches of trees, in order to tear it in pieces

SHRIKE

with greater ease. This habit has given them the name of butcher birds. Shrikes are fighters and defend their rude, bulky nests with great vigor.

Shrimp, a genus of small crustaceans, closely allied to the crawfish. The common shrimp is found in the North Atlantic Ocean, on both

SHRIMP

English and American coasts, and in the Pacific. It is about two inches long, greenish-gray in color, with brown dots. On the Pacific coast it is pink. It is highly prized for food.

Shrove Tuesday, the day before the first day of Lent, or Ash Wednesday, so called because confession is specially made and "shrift" is received. It was at first a day of considerable festivity, and from the common practice of eating pancakes then, the day came to be called *Pancake Tuesday.* Since 1857 Shrove Tuesday has been celebrated in New Orleans by a street pageant, known as the *Mardi Gras,* representing, in elaborate tableaux, noted scenes in history and literature, by a masquerade ball and by other gay entertainments.

Shuf'fleboard or **Shovelboard,** a game played by two or four persons, on a sand-sprinkled board, thirty feet long, with raised edges. Across the board, five inches from each end, a line is drawn. Eight circular pieces of iron, about two and a half inches in diameter and weighing a pound, are used by the players, who slide them

the length of the board. Each side has four pieces, and the players slide them in rotation. If a piece is left projecting over the edge of the board, it scores three points. If it rests between the finishing line and the edge or on the line it scores two points. If no piece is inside the line, then the one nearest to it scores one. The game is twenty-one points.

Another form of shuffleboard is popular on ocean steamers. A place on the deck is marked out, as in the accompanying diagram. The players stand nine or ten paces away, and each in turn pushes one of his pieces along the deck with a crutch-shaped cue, in an endeavor to leave the pieces on the numbered squares. If a piece rests on one of the semi-circular places, ten is taken

−10		
6	1	8
7	5	3
2	9	4
−10		

SHUFFLEBOARD

off the player's score; on the squares the count is as indicated by the numbers. The game is exactly 50 points. If more than fifty are made, the additional ones are deducted from the score.

Siam, *si am',* a kingdom of southeastern Asia, extending from about 12° to 20° 30′ north latitude, and from 98° to 106° east longitude. A projection extends into the Malay Peninsula, reaching south to the 4th degree of north latitude, and is known as Lower Siam. Siam proper is bounded on the n. and e. by Anam, or French Indo-China, on the s. by the Gulf of Siam and on the w. by Burma. Lower Siam separates the Indian Ocean on the west from the China Sea on the east. The northern boundary is somewhat indefinite, but the area of the country is estimated at 236,000 square miles, about one-fourth of this comprising Lower Siam. In general, Siam proper is a low plain, sloping gently toward the south and consisting of the valleys of the Menam River and its tributaries, together with the Mekong, which forms the western boundary, and the valleys of its tributaries. The watersheds between these are low and in some places scarcely noticeable. In the main, the land along the streams and near the coast is low and swampy. On the southeastern border is Tonle Sap Lake, a large part of which is in Cambodia. On the western boundary is a rocky ridge, constituting a low mountain chain, the extension of which forms the backbone of the Malay Peninsula.

The climate is tropical, but owing to the position of the country in reference to the sea, it is not as hot as one might expect from the latitude. The humidity is great, and in general the climate is trying, if not unhealthful, to Europeans. There are two seasons, the wet and the dry, the former lasting from May to October, and the latter occupying the remainder of the year. The rainfall is heavy, in some sections amounting to 240 inches a year, but during the dry season, in the northern part of the country, no rain falls for several months. Here the atmosphere is drier, and the nights are cool.

The mineral resources of the country consist of gold, copper, tin, rubies and sapphires, of the last of which Siam is estimated to furnish one-half of the world's supply. The northern part of the country is covered with dense forests, containing teak and other tropical woods, but the great wealth of the country lies in its agricultural regions, which are confined to the lowlands of the southern half. By means of the numerous rivers and canals, these can be amply watered and even flooded when necessary. The chief crop is rice, and Siam is one of the largest producers of this grain. Cotton, tobacco, sugar cane, coffee and pepper are also raised. The jungles abound in wild animals, including the tiger, the rhinoceros, the leopard, the gibbon, the crocodile, the python and numerous other serpents. Siam is also the home of the white elephant, which is worshiped by many of the inhabitants of southern Asia.

The rivers constitute the chief avenues of commerce, though some railways have been constructed and several hundred miles are in operation. The telegraph and the telephone have also been introduced. The chief export is rice, and the annual shipments vary in value from $15,000,000 to $20,000,000. Other important articles of export are teak and precious stones. The timber cutting is under the care of English experts, who have supervision of the forests.

The population, according to the census of 1908, is 8,117,000, at least 1,500,000 of whom are Siamese. There are about 600,000 Chinese and the same number of Malays, the latter inhabiting Lower Siam. In the north are numerous tribes known as Laotians and others related to the Shan tribes. The Siamese are darker than the Chinese, but lighter than the Malays. They have straight black hair and are usually indolent. In religion they are Buddhists. Their language consists largely of words of one syllable and is similar to the Hindu and languages of other cultured nations of this part of the world.

The Chinese control most of the commerce and other business enterprises. Many of these have intermarried with the Siamese, and a mixed population is the result.

The government is an absolute monarchy. The king is assisted by a ministry, consisting of members appointed by himself, who have charge of the various departments of government. In addition to these there is a legislative council which includes the ministry, ex-ministers and others who are nominated by the king. Within recent years the government has made marked advance along lines similar to those followed by the best European nations. This is largely due to the advice of foreigners, especially Englishmen, whom the king has called to his assistance. For the purpose of local government the country is divided into provinces, over each of which is a governor. Much of the territory subject to the king is nominally under the control of France or Great Britain, and other portions are ruled by the chiefs of native tribes, though these are subject to the central government at Bangkok. The Malay provinces are ruled by rajahs, who are usually subject to a local agent, who represents the king. Bangkok is the capital and the only city of importance. Consult Knox's *Siam and Java* and Annie H. Leonowen's *Siam and the Siamese*.

Siamese, *si am eez'* or *si am ees'*, **Twins** (1811–1874), the best-known example of two individuals having their bodies connected from birth. A thick, fleshy ligament extended from the lower end of the breast bone of each. They were born in Siam and were named Eng (right) and Chang (left). They were on exhibition in Europe and America a number of times, and ultimately settled in the State of North Carolina. They married two sisters. Chang received a paralytic stroke in 1870, and three years later he was affected with an inflammatory disease of the respiratory organs. He died unexpectedly while his brother was asleep, and Eng died a few hours afterward. The Siamese twins attracted great attention during their lifetime, particularly from physiologists and medical men, some of whom thought that the ligament connecting them might have been cut without causing the death of either. The Hindu twins, joined in about the same manner, were separated by an operation in Paris (1902). One lived; the other died of tuberculosis.

Sibe'ria, a division of the Russian Empire, extending from the Ural Mountains on the w. to the Pacific Ocean on the e., and from the Chinese Empire on the s. to the Arctic Ocean on the n. The southern boundary is distinctly marked by the Thian-Shan Mountains, along the western portion, the Altai, in the center, and the Yablonoi, farther east, while the extreme eastern portion of this boundary is formed by the Amur River. The area is about 4,800,000 square miles, or one and one-half times that of the United States, exclusive of Alaska and island possessions.

The entire region is a vast plain, sloping gradually to the north, but it is naturally divided into western and eastern portions, the western part containing scarcely any elevations, the watershed between the Obi and the Yenesei being so slight that it is scarcely perceptible. The Stanovoi Mountains extend along the eastern coast and rise abruptly from the sea (See STANOVOI MOUNTAINS). A spur of this range, extending into the peninsula of Kamtchatka, has some peaks that are estimated to have an elevation of nearly 15,000 feet. Between the Stanovoi Mountains and the Lena River are a number of broad elevations, more resembling plateaus than mountain ranges, so that this portion of Siberia has a somewhat mountainous character. The highest peaks are found along the southern border, where the White Mountain, in the great Altai, near the southeastern boundary, reaches an elevation of 14,800 feet, and other elevations along the ridges forming this boundary, range from 9000 to 12,000 feet.

Siberia has a number of long rivers. In their order, from the west eastward, these are the Obi, the Yenesei and the Lena, flowing into the Arctic, and the Amur, flowing into the Pacific. It is estimated that no other country, except Brazil, has so many long rivers as Siberia. The Amur is navigable for about 2400 miles; but the rivers flowing into the Arctic are of little value commercially, because they are closed by ice during the greater portion of the year. However, steamers ascend these and their tributaries during the summer months and afford the inhabitants of their valleys opportunity to communicate with the outside world.

The climate of Siberia is characterized by short, warm summers and long and intensely severe winters. Central Siberia is considered to have a colder climate than any other habitable portion of the globe, the thermometer in winter sometimes registering 60° and even 75° below zero. In the northeastern part of the country, the soil remains frozen throughout the year, with the exception of a few inches near the surface, that thaw during the summer. It is sup-

posed to be frozen for several hundred feet below the surface. In excavations that have been made, layers of ice intervening between layers of soil have been found to considerable depths, and geologists are of the opinion that these ice sheets are remains of the past glacial age (See GLACIAL PERIOD). In the eastern part of the country there is very little rain or snow, and over a good part of the region it is impossible to use sledges; but in the western portion there is rainfall sufficient for successful agriculture.

According to its vegetable life, Siberia can be divided into three regions. The great tundra, occupying the northern portion of the country, has its surface covered with mosses and lichens, except during the short summer, when numerous flowering plants spring up and come to rapid maturity. South of this, occupying the central portion, is the wooded belt, which extends the entire length of the country and contains trees of stunted growth. This gradually merges into the woodland and forest belt, which extends across the entire southern part. This region is believed to contain the most extensive forests known, aside from those of the Amazon basin. Here are found large areas of pine, spruce, maple, oak, beech, birch and poplar. The summers in this part of Siberia are sufficiently long to admit of the growing of nearly all crops raised in cool temperate regions. Siberia abounds in fur-bearing animals, and the taking and curing of furs is a valuable industry for the inhabitants of some of the colder regions.

The mineral wealth is undeveloped. Mining operations are carried on in the Ural Mountains, where gold, silver and platinum are found. Gold mines are also worked to some extent in the eastern and northeastern parts of Siberia, and there are extensive deposits of salt, sulphur, coal, lead and copper, none of which has yet been developed.

Agriculture is the chief occupation of the inhabitants, and this is most extensive in western Siberia, where large crops of wheat, hay, oats, barley and potatoes are raised. The raising of live stock is also important. There are few manufactures in the country, and these are generally carried on in the homes of the workmen or in small shops. The most important manufacturing center is Tomsk, which contains a number of mills and factories and supplies a large region with porcelain, flour, carpets, iron ware and refined sugar.

The Trans-Siberian railroad, extending the entire length of Siberia and connecting Vladivostok, on the Pacific, with Moscow and Saint Petersburg, is an important factor in the development of the country. By means of this line of transportation, goods from other lands can now easily be imported, and the products of the inhabitants can reach foreign markets at rates of transportation that enable them to be sold with a margin of profit (See TRANS-SIBERIAN RAILWAY). As stated above, the large rivers are navigable during a portion of the year; there are also caravan routes between the leading Siberian cities and trade centers in Mongolia and Manchuria. Merchandise is carried over these routes on the backs of camels and horses. With the exception of the trade with the Chinese Empire, nearly all of the commerce is with European Russia. However, Vladivostok is becoming an important port, and considerable trade with the United States and some other countries passes through it.

Western Siberia is much more densely populated than the other portions of the country. Over 60 per cent of the population are Russians. The other inhabitants include, chiefly, Germans and Aryan gypsies, while in the eastern portion are a number of tribes closely allied to the Samoyeds and Finns. In eastern Siberia are Tartars, Chinese, Manchus and Koreans.

Western Siberia was taken by the Russians in 1582, and from that time to the present the purpose of the Russian government has been to extend its dominions eastward. It was a long time before the Pacific coast was reached, and the last acquisition of territory, which was obtained from China, was not made until 1861. Following the Chino-Japanese War, in 1896, Russia secured a lease of Port Arthur and other portions of Manchuria, but her failure to keep the treaty agreement to vacate certain ports after 1900 led to the war with Japan in 1904, as a result of which Russian aggressions in the East were checked, and Port Arthur, a part of the island of Sakhalin and some other territory were relinquished. For government and cities, see RUSSIA.

Sib'yl, the name common to certain women mentioned by Greek and Roman writers, said to have been endowed by Apollo with a prophetic spirit. Their number was variously stated, but was generally given as ten, of whom the most celebrated was the Cumaean sibyl (from Cumae in Campania). She was said to have written the collection of prophecies, famous under the name of *Sibylline Books*, which she offered to Tarquin the Proud for sale. When the king, on account of the high price asked, refused to buy them, she threw three of the nine books into the fire, and on a second refusal she destroyed three more, after which the king, alarmed, paid for the three remaining the price originally asked for the whole. These books were preserved in the Temple of Jupiter Capitolinus and were consulted on occasions of national danger. In 83 B. C. they were destroyed by fire along with the temple, and the Senate sent delegates to the Italian and Greek cities, to collect whatever Sibylline verses they could find. After the rejection of those which were considered spurious, about 1000 of them were retained and preserved in the new Temple of Jupiter Capitolinus. This collection of Sibylline oracles seems to have been burned by Stilicho shortly after 400 A. D. The so-called Sibylline oracles which have come down to modern times are of Jewish or Christian origin, dating from about 170 B. C. to 700 A. D.

Sicilian, *sis sil'e an,* **Ves'pers,** the name given to the outbreak of the insurrection in Sicily on Easter Monday, 1282, against the French. Charles of Anjou had established himself, through the favor of the pope, in possession of the Two Sicilies. He ruled with great severity, and the oppressed people applied in vain to the pope for relief. At last, enraged by the insult offered a young bride by a French soldier, the inhabitants of Palermo flew to arms and fell upon the French, who were all massacred. Before the end of April, Messina and other towns followed the example of Palermo, and the Sicilian Vespers ended in the overthrow of the domination of Charles of Anjou.

Sicilies, *sis'il liz,* KINGDOM OF THE TWO, a former kingdom of Italy, consisting of Naples, or Southern Italy, and Sicily (See SICILY). About 1037, while Greeks and Saracens were struggling for the possession of Lower Italy and Sicily, the sons of Tancred de Hauteville, a count in Lower Normandy, entered Lower Italy with their followers. Robert Guiscard, one of these brothers, subdued Apulia and Calabria, taking the title of duke, and his youngest brother, Count Roger, conquered Sicily. Roger's son and successor, Roger II, completed the conquest of all Lower Italy by subduing Capua, Amalfi and Naples, and in 1130 he took the title of king, calling his kingdom the Kingdom of the Two Sicilies. In 1189 the race of Tancred became extinct, and the German emperor, Henry VI, of the House of Hohenstaufen, claimed the kingdom in the right of his wife, the daughter of Roger II. The kingdom remained with the family of Hohenstaufen until 1266, when Pope Urban IV, feudal overlord, bestowed it upon Charles of Anjou, brother of Louis IX of France.

Sicily freed herself in 1282 from the oppressions of the French (See SICILIAN VESPERS) by the aid of King Pedro of Aragon, and Naples was separated from it, Sicily being subject to the kings of Aragon, while Naples remained under the rule of the House of Anjou. Alfonso V of Aragon in 1442 gained possession of Naples, which he bestowed on his natural son Ferdinand. In 1504 Sicily was united to Naples under the Spanish crown, but in 1713 the Peace of Utrecht again divided the Two Sicilies, Naples falling to Austria, Sicily to Savoy. Philip V of Spain reconquered Sicily, but was forced to cede it to Austria in 1720, Savoy receiving Sardinia in exchange, by which means the Two Sicilies became a part of the Austrian dominions. In 1734 Don Carlos, son of Philip V, invaded Naples, conquered both the continental and the insular part of the kingdom and was crowned at Palermo in 1735 as Charles IV. This change was sanctioned by the Treaty of Vienna (1738), and till 1860 this line of the Bourbon family maintained possession of the Two Sicilies, except for a few years during the Napoleonic period, when Joseph Bonaparte and Joachim Murat reigned on the mainland as kings of Naples. Francis I, Ferdinand II and Francis II were despotic tyrants, who forced the people into periodic revolts, which were put down with much severity. In 1860, however, an insurrection broke out in Sicily, and an expedition of volunteers from Piedmont and other Italian provinces, under Garibaldi, sailed from Genoa to the assistance of the insurgents. The result was that the Neapolitan troops were driven from the island. Garibaldi, following up his success, crossed over to the mainland, where he met little or no opposition; Francis II fled from Naples; the strong places in his hands were reduced, and by a popular vote the Kingdom of the Two Sicilies ceased to exist, as such, and became a part of the kingdom of Italy. See ITALY, subhead *History*.

Sicily, *sis'il ly,* the largest island of the Mediterranean, belonging to Italy, from the southwestern extremity of which it is separated by the narrow Strait of Messina. It has an area of about 9700 sq. mi. The north and east coasts are steep and cliffy and are provided with good harbors, the finest being that of

Palermo. The greater part of the surface consists of a plateau of varying elevation, and the highest point is the active volcano of Etna, in the eastern part of the island. The climate, as in the other regions of the Mediterranean, is mild and agreeable, except when the island is visited by the sirocco. The soil is very fertile. Three-fourths of the cultivated surface is covered with cereals, chiefly wheat, though oats and barley are also grown. Cotton, sugar and tobacco are also cultivated to some extent. Fruits of every variety are extensively grown, including large quantities of oranges and lemons. The vine flourishes almost everywhere, and much wine is produced. The chief exports are fruits, wine, sulphur, olive oil and sumach. Tunny and sardine fisheries are carried on round the coast. Manufactures are but little developed. The chief seats of foreign commerce are the three principal towns, Palermo, Messina and Catania. The system of roads and railways is still defective. Education is extremely backward; life and property are by no means secure, and brigandage still exists.

At the dawn of history, the older races inhabiting Sicily, the Sicani and the Siculi, were hemmed in by Phoenician and Greek colonies. The Greeks, who entered the island in the eighth century B. C., founded the great cities of Syracuse, Agrigentum and Messina, drove the Phoenicians to the northwest coast and spread their influence and culture over the whole island. Greek art and literature flourished, and many Greek names of distinction are connected with Sicily. The Carthaginians later took the place of their kinsmen, the Phoenicians, and between them and the Greeks a struggle ensued, which ended in favor of the latter (480 B. C.). War with the Carthaginians brought the Romans to Sicily, and they extended their rule over the whole, Sicily becoming a Roman province in 212 B. C. On the decline of the Roman Empire, the island was overrun by the Goths, who retained possession till the sixth century A. D., when Sicily became part of the Byzantine Empire. In the beginning of the ninth century, the Saracens became masters and continued so till their expulsion in the eleventh century by the Normans, who remained long enough in possession to establish the feudal system in all its rigor. For a continuation of the history of Sicily, see SICILIES, KINGDOM OF THE TWO. Population in 1911, 3,672,258.

Sick'le, a reaping hook, consisting of a curved blade of steel, with a handle, the edge of the blade being in the hollow of the curve. In using the sickle, the workman holds the handle in the right hand and grasps with the left hand as much grain as can be cut at one stroke. The sickle is then placed around this bunch of grass, just below where it is held, and is drawn backward towards the handle. The sickle has been largely superseded by the cradle, and the cradle in turn has given place to reaping machines. See SCYTHE.

Sickles, DANIEL EDGAR (1825–1914), an American soldier and politician, born and reared in New York City. He began the practice of law in 1846, was elected to the state legislature, and later became corporation counsel of the city of New York. In 1851 he was chosen to Congress, and at about this time he gained notoriety for a quarrel with Philip Barton Key, whom he killed. At the outbreak of the Civil War, he raised a regiment and became its colonel, took part in the Peninsula Campaign and fought at Antietam, Fredericksburg, Chancellorsville and Gettysburg, being seriously wounded in the last-named battle. He was retired in 1869 with the full rank of major general, became minister to Spain and from 1892 to 1894 served in Congress as a Democrat.

Sid'dons, MRS. SARAH (1755–1831), an English actress, the daughter of Roger Kemble, manager of an itinerant company of players, was born in Wales. In 1774 she met with the first recognition of her great powers as an actress, at Cheltenham, in her presentation of Belvidera in *Venice Preserved.* Her success at Cheltenham procured for her an engagement at Drury Lane, but her first appearance there was a comparative failure, and she went again on circuit in the provinces. On her second appearance at Drury Lane, in 1782, her success was complete. She was universally acknowledged to be the first tragic actress of the English stage, and this distinction she retained until her retirement in 1818. Her greatest characters were Queen Catherine, in *Henry VIII,* and Lady Macbeth, although in whatever rôle she appeared she never failed to captivate her audience.

Sidereal, *si de're al,* **Time,** time measured by the apparent motion of the stars. A *sidereal day* is the time from the passage of a star across the meridian till its next passage; it is exactly the period of the revolution of the earth on its axis. It is the most constant unit of time. Its length is 23 hours, 56 minutes, 4.098 seconds. A *sidereal year* is the period in which the fixed stars apparently complete a revolution and come to the same point in the heavens; it is the exact period of the revolution of the earth around the sun. There are 366.2563612 sidereal days in a sidereal year.

Sid'erite or **Spath'ic Iron** or **Chalybite,** an important ore of iron, of grayish-brown or brownish-red color, sometimes becoming nearly black. It occurs in rocks of various ages and in connection with other ores. The largest deposits are usually found in gneiss, mica, schist and clay slate. See IRON.

Sidney, OHIO, the county-seat of Shelby co., 40 mi. n. of Dayton, on the Miami River, on the Miami & Erie Canal and on the Cincinnati, Hamilton & Dayton and the Cleveland, Cincinnati, Chicago & Saint Louis railroads. The city is in an agricultural region and contains more than one hundred manufacturing establishments. The principal products are road scrapers, whips, corn shellers, horse collars, fly nets, carriages and carriage parts, brooms, churns, flour and leather. It was settled shortly after 1800 and was incorporated in 1819. Population in 1910, 6607.

Sidney, PHILIP, Sir (1554–1586), an English soldier, courtier and poet, one of the most conspicuous figures at the court of Queen Elizabeth. After graduating at Oxford, he traveled through Europe, and on his return he was most cordially received by Queen Elizabeth. During an absence from court, forced upon him by his outspoken opposition to a projected marriage of the queen, he wrote his famous romance of *Arcadia.*. It is said that at one time, when, with Sir Francis Drake, he planned to set out on an expedition to the West Indies, Elizabeth commanded him to remain in England, saying that she could not lose the "jewel of her kingdom." Sidney had a part in England's attempt to defend the Dutch against the Spaniards, and at the Battle of Zutphen he was mortally wounded. While he was being carried from the battlefield, he called for water, but when it was brought to him, he motioned it away and said to a wounded soldier whom he saw regarding him wistfully, "Thy need is greater than mine." Sidney's death was deeply mourned throughout England. Though his writings have much merit, it is chiefly as a perfect type of the English gentleman that he is remembered.

Siege, *seej,* an attempt to capture a city or fort by preventing reënforcements or supplies from being sent to it. A siege is resorted to whenever a place is considered too strong to be taken by assault or, in other cases, where there is no need of haste and time can be allowed to reduce the fortification. If on a coast, the harbor and port is blockaded by ships outside the range of its guns, while land forces in intrenchments cut off help from the interior (See BLOCKADE). In intrenching itself, the army runs its works parallel to the line of defense, so that the guns of the latter may not sweep lengthwise, and it then covers them so as to be bombproof. Usually a siege of this character terminates in an assault, for the besiegers have been bringing their parallels of offense nearer and nearer to the walls of the fort, while at the same time they, perhaps, have tunneled under them and are ready to destroy a part of the walls by exploding a mine. Sometimes the work is done openly, under the protection of artillery fire (See BOMBARDMENT); and at times, as in the siege of Port Arthur, the besieging army takes hills and erects fortifications which command the defending works, so making surrender a necessity (See FORTIFICATION). There have been many famous sieges in history, marked by heroic resistance of garrisons and inspiring bravery of assailants. Such are the fourteen months' siege of La Rochelle by Cardinal Richelieu in 1628; the four years' siege of the rock of Gibraltar by the French and Spanish during the years 1779–1783, and the siege of Port Arthur by the Japanese in 1904.

Siena, *se a'na,* or **Sien'na,** a city of Italy, situated on the frontier of Tuscany, 59 mi. s. of Florence. It occupies an elevated site between two streams and is surrounded by old walls. The streets are narrow and crooked, but among the buildings are found a number of ancient palaces and churches of considerable architectural importance. The cathedral, dating from the thirteenth century, occupies a height overlooking the city and is one of the most striking and beautiful structures in Italy, outside of Rome. Other churches of note are those of San Giovanni, of San Francesco and San Domenico, with the chapel of Saint Catharine. The educational institutions include a university that was famous during the Middle Ages, the institute of fine arts and a public library, containing 75,000 volumes. During the Middle Ages this was an important art center and was the birthplace of a number of famous painters and sculptors. The industries are comparatively unimportant and include the manufacture of textiles, hats and small wares. Population in 1911, 41,673.

Sienese, *se en nees',* **School of Painting.** See PAINTING.

Sienkiewicz, *syen kya'vech,* HENRYK (1846–), a Polish novelist, educated at the University of Warsaw. His first publication was *Nobody is a Prophet in His Own Country,* a humorous story. He wrote descriptions of his visit to California, a drama and a number of short stories before the publication, in 1880, of a novel, *The Tatar Bondage. With Fire and Sword, The Deluge* and *Pan Michael,* his next works, are truly great historical novels, and the fame which they brought their author was increased on the publication, in 1895, of *Quo Vadis.* This became immensely popular, and several dramatic versions were made of it. In 1900 he published another novel, *Knights of the Cross.* In 1905 he was awarded the Nobel prize in literature. The authorized translation of Sienkiewicz's works into English has been made by Jeremiah Curtin.

Sierra Leone, *se er'ra le o'ne,* a British colony on the west coast of Africa, located between Liberia, on the s., and French Guinea, on the n. It is an irregular-shaped territory, with a coast line of about 180 miles and an area of about 4000 square miles. Near the coast the surface is flat and rocky, and in the interior it is hilly, some elevations attaining a height of from 2000 to 3000 feet. The country is watered by a number of streams, flowing to the Atlantic. The climate is exceedingly hot and unhealthful, especially along the coast. The soil is fertile, the rainfall heavy, and abundant crops of rice, corn, plantains, yams, cassava and pumpkins are raised. Sugar cane, coffee, ginger, indigo and cotton can also be grown with profit. Tropical fruits are native, and bananas, pineapples, oranges and pomegranates are found in abundance. Some parts of the colony are covered with dense forests. The chief exports include pepper, oil seed, palm oil, kolanuts, rubber, cocoa, ginger, hides, ivory, rice and beeswax.

The colony was founded in 1787 by a company of fugitive slaves and was settled for the purpose of founding an asylum where escaped slaves could live under a free government. Population in 1911, 75,572, of whom only 700 were whites. The capital is Freetown. Sierra Leone Protectorate, established in 1896, extends inland for about 180 miles and has an area of about 26,000 square miles and a population estimated at 1,000,000.

Sierra Madre, *mah'dray,* the name given to two mountain ranges of Mexico, which run almost parallel with the coast on either side. Following the curves of the coast, they come closer together as they extend farther southward, and a little south of the City of Mexico they are prac-cically connected by a range of volcanoes. The western range averages over 8000 feet in height and has peaks that are more than 10,000 feet high. The eastern range is considerably lower.

Sierra Nevada, *ne vah'da,* a mountain range of Spain, extending for about 60 mi. in a north-east-southwest direction, near the southeastern border of the country. The range is located about 25 miles from the Mediterranean coast and rises very abruptly. The Sierra Nevadas are the highest mountains in the Spanish penin-sula, and the highest peak is the Mulhacen, 11,-420 feet. The summits of the range are covered with snow during the greater part of the year, and it is from this fact that they obtain their name, which means *snowy range.* The lower elevations and the valleys between the mountains are fertile and are covered with orchards of olives, chestnuts and oranges.

Sierra Nevadas, a mountain range in Cali-fornia, extending north and south along the east-ern boundary of the state, from Tehachapi Pass, on the south, to the southern part of Oregon. By some geographers the Sierra Nevadas are considered to belong to the same range as the Cascade Mountains, which extend northward through Oregon and Washington. The Sierra Nevadas form an almost unbroken range, with an average width of 70 miles; and they contain numerous lofty peaks, reaching altitudes of from 10,000 to nearly 15,000 feet. The most promi-nent of these peaks are Mount Whitney, 14,980 feet, the loftiest summit in the United States, outside of Alaska; Fisherman Peak, 14,448 feet; Mount Corcoran, 14,093 feet, and Kaweah Peak, 14,000 feet. There are also several peaks that exceed 13,000 feet. The Sierra Nevadas con-tain many deep, narrow valleys, with nearly vertical walls, in some instances thousands of feet in height. Of these, Yosemite Valley is a good type. These valleys, combined with the lofty peaks, make the scenery of the Sierra Neva-das unusually grand. There are several passes traversing the range. The best known of these are the Truckee Pass, through which the South-ern Pacific Railway reaches the Sacramento Valley; the San Joaquin Pass, in the center of the range, and the Tehachapi Pass, at the south.

Sieyès, *se a yais',* EMMANUEL JOSEPH (1748–1836), better known as the Abbé Sieyès, was born at Fréjus and pursued his studies for the Church at Paris. He was active in furthering the progress of the Revolution and soon acquired great influence in the National Assembly. He

originated the idea of the new geographical divi-sion of France into departments, arrondissements and communes. In 1799, on his return from a mission to Berlin, by which he secured the neu-trality of Prussia, he became a member of the Directory. He subsequently suppressed the Jacobin Club and was active in bringing about the overthrow of the Directory and the substi-tution of the consular government, by the Revo-lution of the 18th Brumaire, the new constitu-tion being devised by him. But Sieyès soon found his speculations completely overmatched by Bonaparte's practical energy, and though a consul provisionally, he saw it desirable to termi-nate his political career. He retired, with the title of count, and he was given valuable grants of property and a sum of 600,000 francs. At the second restoration of the royal line, Sieyès was banished and did not return till after the Revolution of 1830. He was then elected a mem-ber of the Academy.

Sigel, *se'gel,* FRANZ (1824–1902), an Ameri-can general, born in Baden, Germany. He was a veteran soldier of the German revolution of 1848; went to England in 1851, and came to America the next year. From 1853 until the outbreak of the Civil War, he was a teacher and journalist. In 1861 he entered the Federal army and organized a regiment of infantry and a bat-tery of artillery. He fought with distinguished valor at Pea Ridge, Bull Run, in the Shenandoah Valley and at Maryland Heights. After his victory at Pea Ridge he was made major general. From 1865 until his death he was a prominent citizen of New York City, where he filled various public offices and wrote for the press.

Sigismund, *sij'is mund,* (about 1368–1437), Holy Roman emperor and king of Bohemia. On the death of his father-in-law, king of Poland and Hungary, he was crowned king of Hungary. Subsequently, he was involved in war with Tur-key, and after a defeat by Bajazet, at Nicopolis in 1396, he fled to Greece. On his return to Hungary in 1401 he was made prisoner, and the throne was given to a rival. Sigismund escaped, raised a powerful force and reduced Hungary to subjection. In 1411 he became emperor and in 1419 was crowned king of Bohemia. Among the events of his reign were the Council of Con-stance, by which Huss was burned, and the Huss-ite war.

Sig'nal Corps, *kor,* a branch of the United States army whose duty it is to send messages and convey the information necessary in military campaigns. A signal system was established just before the outbreak of the Civil War, and during that conflict the signal corps rendered excellent service. Since 1891 the Signal Corps has been separate from the Weather Bureau. It numbers about 800 men, whose uniform bears an orange stripe, that distinguishes it from the infantry. The implements used by the corps are captive balloons, telegraphs, telephones, wireless telegraph apparatus of the lightest construction, flags, signal lights and the heliograph (See HELIOGRAPH). At Fort Riley, Kansas, is the school of instruction in the signals used in the army, navy and merchant marine. With a battle line possibly one hundred miles long, the outcome of a modern campaign is often dependent on the information collected and given by the signal corps, which is now recognized as one of the most important branches of the service. See SIGNALING.

Sig'naling, an art of great importance in war and commerce, especially between vessels at sea. From the simple form in which barbarous peoples signaled from one place to another, a high art has been developed, by which messages of great length and on almost every conceivable subject may be sent with perfect accuracy for a distance of many miles. In the United States army one of the simplest methods of signaling is called *wigwagging*. To do this a soldier faces the station to which he is signaling and, holding a flag or handkerchief, or at night a torch, on a staff, vertically in front of him, waves it to the right for 1; to the left for 2; downward before him for 3. The end of the word is indicated by 3, and the same signal in combinations is an abbreviation. Letters are indicated by different combinations of 1 and 2; as, 12 is *E*; 212 is *S*, and 1122 is *J*. These are the usual combinations, but for signaling in the face of an enemy these may be changed so that messages can be sent in cipher. After each letter a pause is made. Such signals in clear weather, through a good glass, may be recognized at a distance of twenty-five miles. Signals may be communicated, also, by light flashed from the surface of a mirror (See HELIOGRAPH). Wigwagging signals may be sent by a mechanical contrivance, in which wooden or metal arms are moved upward and downward (See SEMAPHORE).

Marine signals are of various kinds, to be used, respectively, in the day, in the night and in the fog, and an international code makes all intelligible; private codes are also used by nations and by corporations (See FLAG). Among the international signals used by vessels at sea

is that of distress, which is given by firing a gun, at intervals of about a minute, or by the use of a square flag, with a ball above or below it, in the day; or in the night time, by flames, as from a burning tar barrel or oil barrel. Rockets or shells of any color or description, fired one at a time at short intervals, convey the same information. See FOG SIGNALS; WEATHER BUREAU.

Sign Language, a system of communication by gestures and movements of the hands and fingers and without speaking. The simplest system is that used by the American indians of different tribes. Their gestures and symbols were so natural and sprang so directly from their feelings, that tribes often hundreds of miles apart, who rarely came in contact with each other, were able to communicate with little difficulty. The following are typical indian signs: *Strength* and its allied ideas, in all their applications, were represented by the motion of breaking a strong stick. *Wolf* was represented by two fingers extended at the side of the head, indicating the two erect ears. *White man* was represented by drawing a finger across the forehead, to indicate the presence of a hat or cap. Another common system is that used by the deaf and dumb. This differs from the sign language of the indians in being almost wholly arbitrary, though many of the signs were developed originally by logical steps from imitations of actions and from natural symbols of emotion; for instance, the idea of *food*, or eating, or hunger, may be expressed by raising the hand to the mouth.

Signorelli, *se'nyo rel'le,* LUCA (1441–1523), (called also, from his birthplace, *Luca da Cortona*), a celebrated Italian painter, born at Cortona and educated under Piero della Francesca, at Arezzo. He was the first to apply anatomical knowledge to painting, and he thus became the precursor of Michelangelo. Among his early works are *Pan*, now in the Berlin Museum; a *Madonna*, now in the Uffizi, and frescoes in the Sistine Chapel. His greatest productions are a series of magnificent frescoes in the cathedral of Orvieto, comprising the *History of Antichrist*, the *Resurrection of the Dead* and *Hell and Paradise*.

Sigourney, *sig ur'ny,* MRS. (1791–1865), an American author, whose maiden name was Lydia Huntley. In 1815 she published a volume entitled *Moral Pieces in Prose and Verse*, which was quickly followed by other works, most of which were very popular. Among her principal poems are *Traits of the Aborigines of America*, *Zinzendorf*, *The Western Home* and *Pocahontas*.

Sigs'bee, CHARLES DWIGHT (1845-   ), an American naval officer, born at Albany, N. Y. He was educated at Annapolis and took part, under Farragut, in the Battle of Mobile Bay in 1864. As director of an expedition for exploring the bottom of the Gulf of Mexico, he introduced many original methods and received high honors from his government and from foreign countries. He became a captain in the navy in 1897 and was in command of the battleship *Maine* at the time of its destruction in Havana harbor, Feb. 15, 1898. In the Spanish-American War he commanded the auxiliary cruiser *Saint Paul* and afterward was in command of the battleship *Texas*. In 1900 he was appointed chief officer of naval intelligence, became rear admiral in 1904 and later was made a member of the naval general board.

Sigurd, *se'gurd*, in northern mythology, the hero of the *Volsung Edda*, identical with the Siegfried of the Germans. He was the son of Sigmund, a descendant of Odin, and was brought up at the court of his step-father. When he had grown to young manhood, he was given the sword of his father Sigmund, which Odin himself had bestowed, and he set forth to slay the dragon Fafnir and to gain possession of the fabulous wealth which Fafnir guarded. After killing this monster, he ate its heart and was thus enabled to understand the language of the birds. By the birds he was told of a sleeping maiden, Brunhilde, a Valkyr, who had been condemned by Odin to a deep sleep in a palace surrounded by flames, until she was awakened by some hero. Sigurd mounted the hill on which the palace stood, rode through the flames, which died down all about him, entered the palace and awakened the sleeping maiden, who proved to be so beautiful that he at once fell in love with her.

Promising that he would shortly return to claim her, he again set forth on his adventures, and this time he journeyed to the land of the Niblungs. The wife of the king of the Niblungs, a sorceress, brewed for Sigurd a potion which caused him to forget Brunhilde and to fall in love with her daughter Gudrun, whom he married. Gudrun's brother, Gunther, was desirous of marrying Brunhilde, but she could not be won without a struggle. Sigurd, assuming the form of Gunther, won Brunhilde, but when she came to the court to be married to the prince of the Niblungs, Sigurd, in spite of his love potion, recognized her and was filled with remorse. Brunhilde, unable to forgive him for his apparent faithlessness, had him put to death, and then in remorse she killed herself on his funeral pyre.

Sikhs, *seeks*, (from a Sanskrit word meaning *disciple*), a religious sect in northwestern Hindustan, which worships one invisible God. Its founder was Nanak Shah, born in 1469, in the Province of Lahore. He labored to lead the people to a practical religion, to a pure worship of God and to love of mankind. He sought, also, to combine Mohammedans and Hindus into one brotherhood. The real founder of the Sikh state was Govind Sinh, or Singh, the ninth ruler from Nanak. He abolished the system of castes and gave all men equal rights. His followers, owing to their valor in the protracted contest with the Mohammedans, received the title of Sinhs, or lions. Govind Sinh wrote the *Dasema Padshah ke Granth*, or book of the tenth prince, which, besides treating of religious subjects, contained the history of the author's exploits. The Sikhs hold it in equal veneration with the Adi-Granth. Govind Sinh died in 1708, and the Sikhs gradually yielded to the superior power of the Mohammedans. A small number of the Sikhs escaped to inaccessible mountains and preserved the doctrines of their fathers and an inextinguishable hatred toward the Mohammedans. After Nadir Shah's return to Persia, they left the mountains and subdued all Lahore. The Sikhs then broke up into a number of independent communities, each governed by a *sirdar*; but in 1792 Ranjit Singh established himself as despotic ruler of the Sikhs, with the title of Maharajah. The territory of the Sikhs now comprehended the whole Punjab, part of Multan and most of the country between the Jumna and the Sutlej. After Ranjit Singh's death, in 1839, a period of anarchy followed. In 1845 (First Sikh War) the Sikhs attacked the British under Sir Hugh Gough, at Mudki, where they were repulsed (December 18), and three days later they were defeated at Ferozeshah. A treaty was signed by which Great Britain held the city of Lahore and a British resident took supervision of the government. In 1848 the Second Sikh War broke out. Lord Gough advanced with an army against the enemy, but he received a severe check at Chillianwalla, Jan. 13, 1849. Both armies were then reinforced, and on February 21 at Gujorat, the power of the Sikhs

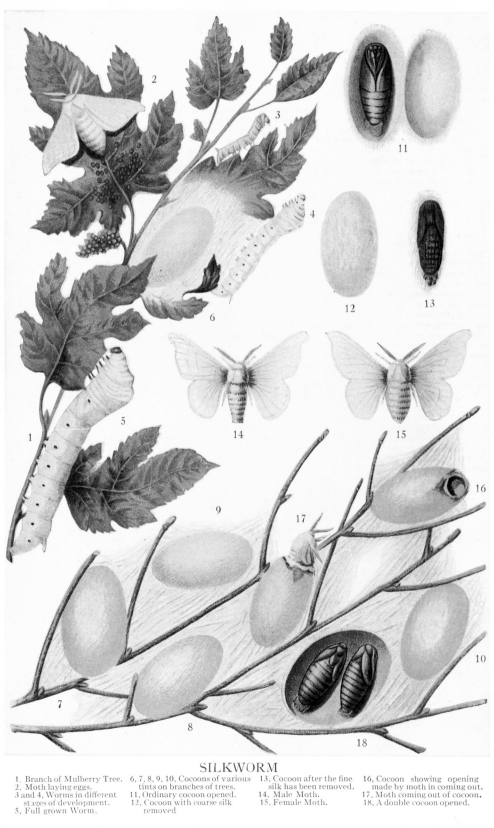

SILKWORM

1, Branch of Mulberry Tree.
2, Moth laying eggs.
3 and 4, Worms in different stages of development.
5, Full grown Worm.

6, 7, 8, 9, 10, Cocoons of various tints on branches of trees.
11, Ordinary cocoon opened.
12, Cocoon with coarse silk removed

13, Cocoon after the fine silk has been removed.
14, Male Moth.
15, Female Moth.

16, Cocoon showing opening made by moth in coming out.
17, Moth coming out of cocoon.
18, A double cocoon opened.

was completely broken, and the Punjab was annexed to the British Empire in India. The Sikhs are mostly of Jât origin, are of fine physique and possess great powers of endurance, as well as courage. In 1911 their number was 3,014,466 in India, more than half of whom are in the Punjab, and they compose the mass of the gentry in the region between the Five Rivers.

Si Kiang, *se kyahng'*, or **Hong Kiang,** a river of China, which rises in the Province of Unnan, flows east and southeast and enters the China Sea near Canton. Its length is estimated at 900 miles, and it is navigable for large vessels for about 75 miles. It enters the sea by a number of mouths.

Sile'nus, a Grecian divinity, the foster-father and constant companion of Bacchus, and the leader of the satyrs. He was represented as a robust old man, generally intoxicated, so that he had to be held by his friends upon his ass.

Silesia, *si le'she a*, a province of Prussia, occupying the extreme southeastern part of that kingdom. Silesia was formerly independent, and at the beginning of the fourteenth century it was divided into seventeen independent states, each ruled by a duke. This resulted in the overthrow of each of the kingdoms, and Silesia became subject to the Bohemian kings. In 1740 Frederick II of Prussia laid claim to a part of Silesia, and in 1763, at the close of the Seven Years' War, the larger part of the country was given to Prussia; the remainder, continuing under the possession of Austria and known as Austrian Silesia, forms a small division in the northwestern part of Austria. For climate, surface and products, see GERMANY.

Sil'ica, a compound of oxygen and silicon, forming one of the most frequently occurring substances in the materials of which the earth's crust is composed. Silica forms a principal ingredient in nearly all the earthy minerals and occurs either in a crystallized form or in amorphous masses. In its naturally crystallized form it is known as *rock crystal*. When of a delicate purple, these crystals are known as *amethyst*. Silica is also met with in the form of chalcedony and carnelian. It enters largely into the lapidary's art, and it constitutes jasper, agate, cat's eye, onyx and opal. In opal the silica is combined with water. The resistance offered by silica to all impressions is exemplified in the case of flint, which consists essentially

of silica, colored with some impurity. Silica is found to constitute the great bulk of the soil which serves as a support and food of land plants, and it enters largely into the composition of many rocks. Many natural waters present silica in a dissolved state. It is, however, not soluble in pure water. The action of an alkali is required to bring it into a soluble form, and hot water dissolves it in larger quantities than cold. Silica forms a number of hydrates which have acid properties and from which a great number of salts, known as silicates, are obtained.

Sil'icon, excepting oxygen, the most abundant element in the solid earth. Never appearing native, it is very common as silicon dioxide or as silica and in various other minerals (See QUARTZ; FLINT; SAND). In one form silicon is a brown powder, but it may also exist in a modified form, consisting of shining metallic scales.

Silk, the peculiar, glossy thread spun by the caterpillars of certain species of moths, of which the silkworm moth is the most conspicuous. The common silk moth possesses a short body, stout legs and white wings, which are marked by black lines running parallel with the wing borders. When extended, the wings measure about two inches across.

FORMATION OF THE FIBER. In the wild state the female deposits her eggs in summer on the leaves of the mulberry tree, but in silk culture the moths are placed on pieces of paper or of muslin, on which they deposit their eggs. For hatching artificially the eggs are placed in a room heated gradually up to a temperature of about 80° F. The room must be kept scrupulously clean and well ventilated. In eight or ten days the young appear. The caterpillars are then covered with sheets of paper or loose muslin, over which finely chopped young mulberry leaves are scattered. The caterpillars soon find their way through the meshes of the cloth or openings in the paper to the leaves, upon which they begin to feed.

When first hatched, the worms are black and about a quarter of an inch long. The caterpillar stage lasts from six to eight weeks, and during this period the worm generally casts its skin four times. After casting its skin the last time the caterpillar is about two inches long, and in ten days it attains its full growth of three inches. The body consists of twelve segments, with six fore legs and ten legs on the hinder segments of the body, provided with hooks. The mouth is large, with powerful jaws, and the color is a greenish-gray.

At this stage the caterpillar becomes languid, refuses food and prepares to spin its cocoon. If left to itself it will sew two leaves together and spin the cocoon between them, but in silk culture the worms are usually placed in racks containing small cells, to the sides of which the cocoon is attached. The silk thread is formed from a sticky fluid contained in two tubular glands, one on each side of the body, connected with a prominent opening in the lower lip, called the *spinneret*. This opening has two apertures, and as the fluid issues from these in minute streams and comes in contact with the air, it hardens into a strong, glossy thread. When examined under the microscope, one of these threads is seen to be composed of two strands, lying side by side. This appearance is caused by the two minute strands that issue from the spinnerets, uniting as they come in contact and forming one thread. The time required for spinning the cocoon is from three to five days. While doing the work the caterpillar attaches itself to the support by its hind legs and places the thread by moving its head from point to point. The average length of thread in a perfect cocoon is about 1000 yards, though it may vary from 800 to 1000 yards.

If left to themselves in a warm place, the cocoons will hatch in about three weeks, but those from which silk is to be obtained are not allowed to hatch. This is prevented by placing them in a warm oven or in hot water, which kills the pupa. It requires twelve pounds of cocoons to yield one pound of raw silk, and one ounce of silkworms' eggs will produce 100 pounds of cocoons. The female moth produces from 300 to 500 eggs. For the successful cultivation of the silkworm, vigorous and healthy mulberry trees are necessary, the white mulberry being the favorite species. China, Japan, India, Italy, France and Spain are important silk-producing countries, though silk culture is found in several others.

The silk industry seems to have originated in China, and the Chinese were the first to make known the value and usefulness of the fiber produced by the silkworm.

MANUFACTURE. In the manufacture of silk, the first operation is the unwinding of the cocoons and the *reeling* of the silk. For this purpose they are placed in shallow vessels containing hot water, which softens the gummy matter of the cocoons. The ends of the filaments are then conducted by guides to large reels moved by machinery. Four or five threads, from as many different cocoons, are thus brought together, and, uniting by means of the gum, form one thread.

The outside fiber is coarser than that which it encloses and is usually taken off separately. The silk thus produced is called *raw silk*. Before it can be woven into cloth the raw silk must be *thrown*. Throwing is often a special trade, but it is usually conducted by machinery in large mills. It consists in spinning, twisting and reeling. Previous to throwing, the silk is carefully washed, wound on bobbins and assorted as to its quality. In the throwing machine it is again unwound from the bobbins, twisted by the revolutions of a flyer and then wound on a reel. The twist of the silk is regulated as required by varying the relative velocities of the flyer and reel. The silk thus prepared is called *singles* and is used for weaving common or plain silks and ribbons. The next operation, called *doubling*, is the twisting of two or more of these threads on one bobbin. This is done in a throwing machine, and the silk thus spun is called *tram* silk, commonly used for the weft of richer silks and velvets. Two or more of these threads of tram silk twisted in the throwing mill together constitute *organzine*, a species of silk thread used for warps of fine fabrics. But in tram silk the threads are all twisted in one direction, forming individual strands like twine, whereas in organzine the collected threads are twisted in an opposite direction to the twist of the strands, like cable or rope. The silk in this condition is called *hard*, in consequence of the gum, which is, however, separated by careful boiling.

Silk is woven on looms similar to those used in weaving cotton and wool (See WEAVING). In the United States power looms are employed wholly, but in Europe many hand looms are still found, while in China they are used entirely. The fineness and softness of silk fiber make it possible to manufacture from it a greater variety of fabrics than from any other fiber, and these products range in fineness from the gossamer web to the heavy plush used for winter garments. Ingenious looms have been invented by American and French operators, as well as special attachments for weaving intricate patterns, which are now produced at moderate cost.

The manufacture of sewing silk is really a continuation of the process of throwing. It is made by continuing to double and twist the threads together, until a thread of the desired size and strength is obtained. This branch of the silk industry is confined to the United States, and it has become of considerable importance.

The manufacture of waste silk is also an important industry. Only about seven-tenths of the silk on a cocoon can be wound onto the reel. The remainder, together with the coarse fiber taken from the outside of the cocoon and the silk obtained from defective cocoons and those from which the moths have been allowed to escape, constitute the waste. This is subjected to a number of processes, such as washing, combing and spinning, until it forms the spun silk of commerce, which is used for silk yarn and for woof in some silk fabrics.

The leading countries in the production of raw silk are China, Japan, Italy and France, while the leading countries in its manufacture, in the order of their importance, are France, the United States, Germany and Switzerland. The annual output of silk manufactories in the United States averages about $185,000,000. The color plate shows the various stages of evolution of the silkworm and silkworm moth.

Silk, ARTIFICIAL. Artificial silk is made of a substance that has practically the same chemical composition as pure silk. In the preparation of it, cotton is carded into wadding and is soaked in a mixture of 15 parts nitric acid to 85 parts sulphuric acid; then all traces of the acid are removed by strong pressure. The cotton is then dissolved in a mixture of alcohol and ether, and forms *collodion*. This is allowed to stand for some weeks or months, in order to improve its quality. The collodion is run between steel rollers, which force the liquid through minute tubes into a weak solution of nitric acid. The streams of collodion, as they come in contact with the acid, are changed to fibers, which are wound directly upon reels. This fiber is then subjected to a number of processes, consisting of washing, twisting and reeling, until it is formed into yarn suitable for weaving.

Artificial silk has many of the characteristics of pure silk, but it is not considered as durable, and it is not extensively used, though the manufacturers claim that it can be produced at a cost varying from one-quarter to one-half of that of pure silk.

Silk'worm. See SILK.

Silkworm Gut, a substance prepared from the silky secretion of the caterpillars of the ordinary silkworm, taken from the insect's body, It constitutes the lustrous and strong line, so well known to anglers as *gut*. See ANGLING.

Silo, a specially prepared structure in which green, coarse fodder can be preserved in a succulent condition, for future use as food for farm stock. In shape, silos may be square or rectangular, but the cylinder form is now universal,

since it is more economical per unit of capacity, and permits of more solid packing, there being no square corners hard to fill compactly. The entire structure must be as nearly air tight as possible, since the presence of air causes decomposition; the inside walls must be perpendicular and smooth to permit uniform settling of the inclosed mass of silage; and this must be of considerable depth so that there will be sufficient pressure to keep the mass compact. Consequently the height should be between twenty-five and thirty feet, while the diameter may vary according to the needs of the farmer constructing it. Wood has been the material generally used in building silos but concrete is rapidly winning favor, as it is cheap, and furnishes an air-tight, water-proof and vermin-proof structure. In recent years silos have become very common. See Volume VI, department AGRICULTURE, subhead *The Dairy*.

Silu'rian System, a division of rocks, originally including the formations between the Archaean and Devonian systems, and named for the Silures, a people of ancient Britain. Later the system was restricted to the formations between the Cambrian and Devonian systems, and it is subdivided into Lower Silurian and Upper Silurian. An English geologist recently adopted the name Ordovician for the Lower Silurian (See ORDOVICIAN SYSTEM), but in the United States the Upper and Lower Silurian divisions are still recognized. The formations are of wide extent and are found in all the continents. The rocks are largely limestones and sandstones and have been divided into a number of series and stages with local names. In the United States the most noted of these are the Niagara, the Onondaga and the Lower Helderberg. The formations of this system make up the greater part of the Appalachian Mountains and the sides of the celebrated Delaware Water Gap, and extend southward as far as Tennessee. The gypsum and salt beds of New York and the iron ore along the Appalachian Mountains belong to these formations. See DEVONIAN SYSTEM; PALEOZOIC ERA.

Sil'ver, one of the precious metals, ranking next to gold in value. It appears to have been known almost as early as gold, and, without doubt, for the same reason, because it occurs very frequently in a state of purity in the earth and requires but an ordinary heat for its fusion. Pure silver is of a fine white color. It is softer than copper but harder than gold, and is about ten and one-half times as heavy as water. Its chemical symbol is *Ag*. It is next in malleability to gold, having been beaten into leaves only $\frac{1}{100000}$ of an inch in thickness. It may be drawn out into a wire much finer than a human hair. It excels all other metals as a conductor of heat and electricity. Silver melts when heated completely red hot, and it may be boiled and volatilized by a very strong and long-continued heat. *Oxide of silver* is produced by dissolving silver in a solution of nitric acid and precipitating with an alkali. The compound called *horn silver* or *chloride of silver* is obtained by dissolving silver in nitric acid and mixing the solution with a solution of common salt. When exposed to the light it turns to a blackish color, hence its great use in photography. *Bromide of silver* is the most sensitive to light of all known solids. It is used for coating the "dry plates" employed in photography. When silver is long exposed to the air, it acquires a covering of a violet color, which deprives it of its luster; this coating is sulphide of silver. Silver readily forms alloys with iron, steel, lead, tin and mercury. Of the combinations of acid and silver, the most important is *nitrate of silver*, obtained by dissolving silver in nitric acid. If the silver and acid are pure, the solution of silver nitrate is colorless, very heavy and caustic; it stains the skin and all animal substances an indelible black; after evaporation it deposits, on cooling, transparent crystals of nitrate of silver.

ORES. There are five important silver ores, namely, native silver, vitreous silver, or silver glance, black silver, red silver and horn silver. Native silver occurs principally in veins, traversing gneiss, clay slate and other paleozoic rocks, but not usually in great quantity. It often forms a natural alloy with gold. Vitreous silver presents itself in various shapes and is of a blackish-lead-gray color, with a metallic luster. It is malleable, about as hard as gypsum, and is subject to tarnish. It is more or less pure silver sulphide and has been found almost exclusively in veins, along with ore of lead, antimony and zinc. It occurs in Saxony, Bohemia, Hungary, Mexico and Peru; and it is an important source of silver. Black silver generally occurs in granular masses, of an iron-black color. It is about as hard as gypsum and presents a smooth surface when cut with a knife. This mineral is a composition of silver with antimony and sulphur and traces of iron, copper and arsenic. It is found in veins, along with other ores of silver, and is a valuable ore for the extraction of silver. It occurs chiefly in Saxony, Bohemia, Hungary and America. Red silver is found in crystals and often in masses, in grains and even as a fine powder. It is a double sulphide of silver and antimony, containing, on an average, sixty per cent of silver. It occurs in veins with other silver ores, galena and blende. It is found in various parts of Saxony, in Bohemia, in Hungary and in Norway, but chiefly in Mexico, Peru and the western United States. Horn silver, or silver chloride, occurs in crystals and also in crusts and granular masses. It contains about seventy-six per cent of silver. It is found in the upper parts of veins in clay slate and also in beds with other silver ores or with iron ocher. It is not abundant in Europe, but occurs in large masses in Mexico and Peru. The above are the ores of silver from which silver is chiefly extracted; but considerable silver is obtained from ores of lead and copper, which are worked primarily for these metals.

REDUCTION OF ORE. Silver is extracted from its various ores by smelting or amalgamation. The former method is founded on the great affinity of silver for lead, which, when melted with silver, acts as a solvent and extracts it from its union with other metals. The silver is afterward separated from the lead by the process of cupellation, which consists in exposing the melted alloy to a stream of atmospheric air, by which the lead is converted into an oxide, while the silver remains untouched. The method by amalgamation depends upon the property of mercury to dissolve silver without the aid of heat. One or the other process is employed, according to the nature of the ores. The ores which are treated by smelting are usually those consisting principally of silver-bearing sulphide of lead. By this method the ore is first pulverized and roasted, to expel the sulphur, and is then freed from the lead. The ores best adapted to the process of amalgamation are native silver and vitreous silver. The ores are first selected to form a proper mixture, with reference to the quantity of silver and sulphur they contain. The sulphur is then removed by adding to the mixture of an ore ten per cent of common salt, by which, during the further operation, the sulphur is oxidized, and the acid thus formed unites with the base of the salt and forms sulphate of soda; while the hydrochloric acid thus set free combines with the silver in the ore that was not in the metallic state, and forms chloride of silver. In this state the ore is reduced to a fine powder by various mechanical processes. It is then submitted to the action of mercury, with which it forms an amalgam. This amalgam is subjected to the action of heat in a distilling furnace, by which the mercury is vaporized and the silver remains. Silver is sometimes separated from copper by the use of a porous cup. This is effected by means of lead, which when brought into fusion with the alloy combines with the silver. The silver-bearing lead thus obtained is subjected to the usual processes of cupellation, and the coarse copper, from which the silver has been separated, is refined. Large quantities of silver are now obtained from silver-bearing lead ores, by a process known as Pattinson's process, which depends on the property, which pure lead possesses, of crystallizing at a temperature at which an alloy of silver and lead is still fluid, so that the solid crystals of lead can thus be removed.

PRODUCTION. The silver mines of North and South America are incomparably more important than those of all the rest of the world. The Mexican mines were worked before the Spanish conquest and then produced large quantities of silver. Their total yield has been estimated at over $3,000,000,000. Great deposits of silver have been discovered in Nevada, Arizona, California, Colorado, Idaho, Montana, New Mexico and Utah. Silver ore, chiefly silver-bearing galena, has also been found in great quantities in the Barrier Ranges of New South Wales. Some of the mining concerns here are the largest in the world. Considerable quantities of silver are also produced in Europe. The average production of Germany is estimated at about $8,000,000. The annual production of silver for the world is about $109,-000,000. Of this, Mexico produces about $35,000,000, and the United States, about $30,000,000.

Silvering. See GILDING.

Simcoe, *sim'ko*, LAKE, a lake of Ontario, Canada, between Lake Ontario and Georgian Bay, an arm of Lake Huron. It is about 30 miles long and 18 miles wide at its widest part, and it discharges itself into Lake Huron by the Severn River. It contains a number of islands, and its banks are well wooded. Many summer villas are located here.

Simile, *sim'i le*, a figure of speech, which consists in the comparing of two things which are supposed to have some resemblance, the comparison being pointed out by some such word as *like* or *as*. For the distinction between metaphor and simile, see METAPHOR.

Simms, WILLIAM GILMORE (1806–1870), an American author, born at Charleston, S. C.

He studied law and was admitted to the bar in 1827, but abandoned that profession for literature and journalism. In 1827 he published his first volume of poems; but his best poem, *Atalantis, a Tale of the Sea*, appeared in 1833. This was followed by a series of romances founded on Revolutionary incidents in South Carolina and by several border tales and historical romances. Among his novels may be mentioned *Martin Faber, Guy Rivers, The Yemassee, The Partisan, The Kinsman*, subsequently called *The Scout, Count Julian* and *Eutaw*. He was editorially connected with several periodicals and filled a number of political offices.

Simonides, *si mon'e deez*, (556–468 B. C.), a Greek lyric poet. He visited Athens, and after the death of Hipparchus, who had treated him very generously, he proceeded to Thessaly, where he obtained the patronage of powerful families. He afterward returned to Athens, and at a competition for the best elegy upon those who fell at Marathon, he gained the prize over Aeschylus. When eighty years of age he was victorious in another celebrated poetical contest, his fifty-sixth victory of this nature. Shortly after this he was invited to the court of Hiero at Syracuse, where he remained till his death. Only fragments of the works of Simonides have come down to us, one of these, the beautiful inscription for those who fell at Thermopylae: "Go, stranger, and tell the Lacedaemonians that we lie here in obedience to their laws."

Simon Peter. See PETER.

Simoom′ or **Simoon′,** a hot, suffocating wind, that blows occasionally in Africa and Arabia, generated by the extreme heat of the parched deserts or sandy plains. The air, heated by contact with the noonday burning sand, ascends, and the inflow of colder air from all sides forms a whirlwind, or miniature cyclone, which is borne across the desert, laden with sand and dust. Its intense, dry, parching heat, combined with the cloud of dust and sand which it carries with it, makes this wind very destructive to both vegetable and animal life. The effects of the simoom are felt in neighboring regions, where winds owing their origin to it are known under different names, and it is subject to important modifications by the nature of the earth's surface over which it passes. See KHAMSIN; SIROCCO.

Sim′plon, a mountain pass of Switzerland, near the frontier of Piedmont, Italy. Through the pass the famous Simplon road was constructed by Napoleon in 1800–1806. The summit of the pass has an elevation of 6590 feet, and for many years this has been one of the most important routes across the Alps.

The Simplon Tunnel, a railway tunnel through the Alps at this point, was commenced in 1898 and was completed in February, 1905. It is a double tunnel 12½ miles long, each tunnel having a single track. This is the longest railway tunnel in the world.

Simp'son, JAMES YOUNG, Sir (1811–1870), the most eminent medical practitioner of his day and the discoverer of the anesthetic properties of chloroform. He was born at Bathgate, in Linlithgowshire. His first paper on chloroform was read before the Medico-Chirurgical Society of Edinburgh on March 10, 1847, and the anesthetic soon came into general use. He received honors from numerous scientific societies in America and Europe, and in 1853 he was elected a foreign associate of the Academy of Medicine of Paris. In 1856 he received the laureateship and gold medal of the French Academy of Sciences, with the Monthyon prize of 2000 francs, awarded for the "most important services done to humanity."

Simpson, JERRY (1842–1905), an American politician, born in New Brunswick, Canada. He removed to Oneida County, N. Y., in 1848, and was a sailor for twenty-three years, being captain of vessels on the Great Lakes. He removed to Kansas in 1878 and then to New Mexico. Though originally a Republican, he was elected by the Populist party to the Fifty-second Congress from Kansas and was again elected in 1897.

Sims, JAMES MARION (1813–1883), an American surgeon, born in South Carolina. He studied medicine at Charleston and Philadelphia, and having begun practice, had his attention drawn to some of the special diseases of women, for the treatment of which he gained a distinguished name, introducing new instruments and operations. He was instrumental in the establishment of a woman's hospital in New York. Subsequently he practiced for some years in Europe and had charge of a large hospital at Sedan, after the defeat of the French there in 1870.

Sinai, *si'nay* or *si'ni*, a peninsula projecting into the Red Sea, between the Gulf of Suez and the Gulf of Akabah. Its length from north to south is 140 miles, and the breadth at its northern end is about the same. The peninsula is tri-

angular. The surface is mountainous, the entire region consisting of barren mountains and valleys. The highest peaks are Jebel-Katherin, 8537 feet; Jebel-un-Shomer, 8449 feet, and Jebel-Musa, or Mountain of Moses, 7363 feet. Horeb, or the Mount Sinai of the Old Testament, has been identified by different authorities with each of these three peaks, and which one is the true Sinai is not known.

Sindh or **Sind,** a province of British India, constituting the Presidency of Bombay. See BOMBAY.

Sin'dia or **Scindiah,** the hereditary title of the head of the Mahratta dynasty, ruling in Gwalior, which was founded in 1738 by Ranojee Sindia, a chief who raised himself from obscurity by his own merits. He died in 1754. In 1781 Madaji Sindia negotiated a peace between the British and the Mahrattas, and having introduced European discipline and tactics into his army, he possessed himself of Delhi, Agra and the person of the Mogul emperor, in whose name he subsequently acted. He was the most powerful member of the Mahratta confederacy.

Sin'ding, CHRISTIAN (1856–   ), a Norwegian composer, educated in Germany and Austria. His compositions are remarkable for their demands in technique, their brilliant runs and chord passages and their striking Norwegian themes.

Sin'gapore', a British colony, forming one of the Straits Settlements and consisting chiefly of the island and city of Singapore, with a few smaller islands. The principal island is about 25 miles long and 14 miles wide and has an area of 206,000 square miles. Its location gives it a hot climate throughout the year, though it is not unhealthful. The chief interest centers in the city of Singapore, a well-built town, with a large and easily accessible harbor, which is bordered by a beautiful park. The chief public buildings consist of the Cathedral of Saint Andrew's, the townhall, the courthouse and the Roman Catholic Cathedral. Singapore is the meeting point of numerous important ocean routes. It is a free port and carries on an extensive trade. Population in 1911, 311,985, of whom over sixty per cent were Chinese.

Singhalese, *sin ga leez'* or *sin ga lees'*. See CEYLON.

Sing'ing, the art of making music with the human voice; also the music thus produced. The mechanism by which this music is made consists of the lungs, which supply the air; the muscles of the diaphragm, or chest, which force the air through the throat, and the vocal chords of the throat, whose vibrations produce the sound. Difference in pitch of voice is due to the length of the vocal chords; difference in quality is due to the differences in the shape of the cavities of the mouth and nose and to the different use of the muscles of the larynx. The compass of the human voice is from about C below the bass clef to F above the treble, though no single voice has this compass, the average being about twelve to fifteen tones, and the greatest, slightly over three octaves. The total range of the voice is divided into four parts, the *soprano*, consisting of the highest tones, beginning at about E on the treble clef; the *alto*, or *contralto*, including those from about G on the bass clef to C on the treble clef; the *tenor*, including about the range of the contralto, but extending somewhat lower, and the bass, including all the lower notes, beginning at about C above the bass clef and extending downward. See MUSIC.

Single Tax, the name given by common consent to the economic reform which proposes the abolition of all taxes on personal property and the raising of public revenues, local, state and national, by a single tax on land values, irrespective of improvements, this tax eventually to become equal to the annual rental value of the land. The theory of the single tax is based upon Ricardo's "law of rent," which, briefly, is this: "The economic rent of a given piece of land depends upon (or is determined by) the excess of its product over that which can be obtained with an equivalent effort from the least productive land in cultivation." By taking this economic rent (that is, the excess of product of a particular piece of land, over that which can be obtained from the least productive land in use— or at the so-called "margin of cultivation") for public purposes (taxes), those who are now holding the lands without using them, in order to secure in the future a higher value, would no longer be able to do so with profit, since the benefit which they have been receiving would now be confiscated to the State. Thus, vast areas of land would be thrown open to practically free employment; the opportunities for labor would be nearly equal, and the reward to labor would be approximately the whole product, except what would be taken for interest on the capital invested. In proof of their assertions, single taxers point to statistics. For instance, the unimproved land within the limits of the city of Chicago constitutes a large part of the total area and would furnish employment for thousands of persons. They justify the confiscation of land values (for the taking of the whole rental value would amount to the confiscation of the land), partly on the basis that this value is created by the community and cannot be rightfully monopolized by individuals. Furthermore, they contend that private ownership of land must eventually reduce the majority of mankind virtually to a condition of slavery; for wealth can be produced only by the application of labor to land (that is, to all natural agencies, including earth, air, water); therefore, either the owner of the labor (man) or the owner of the opportunity to labor (land) can control the laborer and can make such terms with him as he pleases. This condition is brought constantly nearer by the withholding from use of large tracts of land, while the growth of population and other conditions constantly increase the competition of laborers for employment, that is, for the right to use the land. Believing as they do that the original act of reducing land to private ownership was wrong and worked an injustice, not only upon those from whom the land was taken, but upon all who came after, they believe the State has a perfect right to reverse this step and retake for the community, by taxation, the value of land, without compensating the present owners.

The single-tax theory has gained many adherents, especially in England and the United States, during the last quarter of a century, chiefly through the propaganda of Henry George, an American economist who first thoroughly elucidated the principles of the theory, though the idea had been before developed in a crude way by French economists. George's first great work on the subject was *Progress and Poverty*. It immediately became popular and has been translated into all the languages of the civilized world (See GEORGE, HENRY). But the theory has never been given a practical test, though it has been partially applied in New Zealand and in small divisions of other countries. At Fairhope, Ala., is a small colony of single taxers who are attempting to work out their principles in practical life. Their efforts have been attended with some success. Some of the important demands of the single taxers are being accepted and incorporated in the laws of several of the states, especially the abolition of the tax on personal property, the reform being urged in many instances on the ground that this form of property is so easily concealed that persons of small means pay vastly more, in proportion to their ability, than those of wealth, and, further, that the methods of assessment place a premium upon perjury and corruption.

The main objections that are urged to the single tax are the following: (1) That it would relieve a large class of persons from support of the government; (2) that the tax would be inelastic; (3) even though the justice of the principle of the single tax be granted, for the sake of argument, the fact that private ownership of land has been recognized for centuries and has led to the development of many interwoven interests, would make it inexpedient for the community to recover possession of the land by the means proposed. See TAX; RENT.

Sing Sing, N. Y. See OSSINING, N. Y.

Sin'ople, red quartz containing iron. It is of a blood-red or brownish-red color, sometimes with a tinge of yellow. It occurs in small, very perfect crystals and in masses resembling some varieties of jasper.

Siouan, *soo'an,* **Indians,** those related Indian tribes who covered the land of the upper Mississippi and Missouri valleys, far into Canada, and embraced detached tribes east of the Mississippi. Among other numerous tribes are the Dakota, the Omaha, the Winnebago, the Assiniboin, the Osage and the Ponca. They have been bitterly hostile to the whites, and their fierce and warlike dispositions have made some of them troublesome enemies, though no Ponca nor Omaha has fought against the United States.

Siout, *se oot'.* See SIUT.

Sioux, *soo,* or **Dako'ta,** the largest tribe of Indians dwelling west of the Mississippi. They have several times engaged in hostilities with the United States settlers and troops, chiefly because the government broke faith with them. In 1862 more than a thousand settlers were killed. In 1876 a body of them, which had taken up a position in the Black Hills, defeated the United States troops under General Custer. They number about 2400. See SIOUAN INDIANS. See INDIANS, AMERICAN.

Sioux City, IOWA, the county-seat of Woodbury co., is located on the Missouri River, at the mouth of the Big Sioux River, 156 mi. n w. of Des Moines, and on the Illinois Central, the Chicago & Northwestern, the Chicago, Saint Paul, Minneapolis & Omaha, the Great Northern, the Chicago, Milwaukee & Saint Paul and the Chicago, Burlington & Quincy railroads. The city is a very important agricultural and livestock market. It has two large meat packing plants and a number of smaller ones. The

stockyards also do an immense business. It has 34 wholesale and jobbing houses and 150 factories, two breweries, railroad repair shops and other industrial establishments. Two bridges cross the Missouri River, one, a combination bridge affording facilities for railroads, street cars, vehicles and foot passengers. Sioux City is the seat of Morningside College and other educational institutions, has six hospitals, a Federal building, a city hall and a public library. It has 56 churches, a Y. M. C. A. building, an auditorium seating 3000, two theaters and lodges of all the principal societies. Sioux City was first incorporated in 1858, became a city of the first class in 1886 and adopted the commission plan of government in 1910. Population in 1910, 47,828.

Sioux Falls, S. D., the county-seat of Minnehaha co., about 90 mi. n. of Sioux City, Iowa, and 8 mi. from the Iowa state line, on the Big Sioux River and on the Great Northern, the Illinois Central, the Chicago & Northwestern, the Chicago, Rock Island & Pacific and other railroads. The river has a series of falls, descending about 100 feet in half a mile and furnishing extensive water power. The city contains boiler and sheet iron works, flour mills, a biscuit factory, breweries, carriage works, brickyards and other establishments. There are stone quarries in the vicinity, and the city has large wholesale houses and conducts a valuable trade. The educational institutions include the Sioux Falls College, a Lutheran normal school, All Saints' School and the state school for the deaf. The city is the seat of an inter-denominational orphans' home and the state penitentiary. The public buildings include the municipal buildings, the county courthouse and over thirty churches. The city has waterworks, gas and electric lights. Sioux Falls was chartered as a city in 1883. Population in 1910, 14,094.

Siphon, *si'fon,* a bent tube, with arms of unequal length, used for drawing liquids from one vessel to another at a lower level. The principle upon which the siphon works is illustrated by the figure. The water in the short arm, DC, is sustained by the pressure of the atmosphere on the surface of the liquid in the cup. The column of water in the long arm, AB, is heavier than that in the short arm, but it is resisted by an equal upward pressure of the atmosphere at A. Since both AB and CD are acted upon by the same pressure, and since AB is heavier than CD, the water flows out of the tube at A, and it will continue to flow until the water in the cup has reached the end of the short arm. The principle of the siphon is often used in carrying water over slight elevations and in emptying casks and other vessels. A rubber tube makes an excellent siphon, since it can be easily bent to fit any conditions. Like the pump, the siphon will not work if the highest point in the tube exceeds thirty-three feet above the surface of the water, since the pressure of the atmosphere will not force the water to a greater height than this.

Sir-Daria, *seer dahr′ ya.* See SYR-DARYA.

Si′ren, an instrument for producing continuous or musical sounds and for measuring the number of sound waves, or vibrations, per second, which produce a note of given pitch. In its original form it consists of a disk, with a circular row of oblique holes, revolving close to the top plate of a wind chest, perforated with corresponding holes, sloping in the opposite direction, so that the jets of air from the latter, passing through the former, keep the disk in motion. These jets of air also produce a note, corresponding to the rapidity with which the plate is revolved or the frequency with which the holes in the plate coincide with those in the chest. The number of coincidences or vibrations in a given time is shown by indices connected with the axis of the disk.

Sire′nia, an order of marine mammals related to the whales. They have no hind limbs, and their fore limbs are merely paddles. Their food is chiefly seaweeds, and they live in the mouths of rivers. See MANATEE; DUGONG.

Si′rens, in Greek mythology, the name of several sea nymphs, who, by their singing, fascinated sailors who passed by their island and then destroyed them. When Ulysses approached their island, which was near the coast of Sicily, he stuffed the ears of his companions with wax, while he bound himself to the mast and thus escaped. The sirens then threw themselves into the sea, where they became formidable rocks. Another story is that they threw themselves into the sea because vanquished in music by Orpheus.

Sir′ius, the brightest star in the heavens, also called the Dog Star, situated in the mouth of the constellation Canis Major, or the Greater

Dog. It is estimated to have more than 13 times the sun's magnitude.

Siroc′co, the Italian name for a hot wind. The term is properly applied to any warm wind of sufficient duration to produce a general climatic change. Siroccos are common over the southern portion of the United States, the countries of southern Europe and other portions of the world, but the term is particularly applied to the warm wind of the Sahara. The sirocco here should be distinguished from the simoom, which is much more violent, though both winds produce dust storms.

Sisal, *sis sahl′,* or **Grass Hemp,** a species of agave, yielding a valuable fiber. It is a native of Mexico and Central America, and is specially cultivated in Yucatan. Sisal is grown upon stony ground, and the leaves, from which the fiber is prepared, are between two and three feet long. The pulp is cleaned away from each side of the leaf, and the remaining fiber is then washed and sun-dried. It has considerable commercial value, in the manufacture of cordage and coarse cloth.

Sisters of Charity. See CHARITY, SISTERS OF.

Sisters of Mercy. See MERCY, SISTERS OF.

Sistine, *sis′tin* or *sis′teen,* **Madon′na.** See MADONNA; RAPHAEL.

Sisyphus, *sis′e fus,* a mythical king of Corinth, who promoted navigation and commerce, but was deceitful and tyrannical. For his wickedness he was punished in the lower world by being obliged to roll a heavy stone to the top of a hill; it always rolled down again, thus rendering his punishment eternal.

Sit′ka, an important town of Alaska, situated on the west coast of Baranof Island, 1130 mi. n. of Seattle and 160 mi. s. w. of Juneau. The town has a picturesque site, near a number of mountain peaks covered with perpetual snow. The climate is mild, considering the latitude. The chief buildings are the Greek church, begun in 1816; a church connected with the Presbyterian mission, and the school buildings of the Russian-Greek church, the United States government and the Presbyterian industrial training school. Other institutions of importance are the barracks, an agricultural experiment station, the governor's residence, the United States land office and a marine hospital. The chief industries of the town are mining, lumbering and salmon canning. Sitka was the old Russian capital of Alaska and until 1906 was the seat of government for the territory under the United States; in that year the capital was transferred to Juneau.

Sitting Bull, (1837–1890), a famous chief of the Sioux, born at Willow Creek, Dakota. He early became prominent because of his hostility to the white settlers in the Northwest, and was conspicuous in many attacks upon their settlements. At the Battle of Mussel Shell, in the Yellowstone region, in 1868, his forces were defeated, and from this time until 1876 he was fighting friendly indians and raiding Montana settlements. In the latter year a campaign was undertaken against him, during which General Custer and his force were massacred. Later he escaped to Canada, but on promise of pardon he surrendered to General Miles in 1881. He was killed while attempting to prevent an arrest.

Siut or **Siout,** *se oot'*, (also written Assiut), the chief town of Upper Egypt and the capital of the Province of Siut, situated on the west bank of the Nile, 248 mi. s. of Cairo, and on the Cape-to-Cairo railroad. It is a well-built town and is an important trade center. It also has manufacturing industries of considerable value and is widely noted for its red and black pottery and pipe bowls. A large dam has been constructed across the Nile at this point, to regulate the flow of water for irrigation purposes. Near the city are a number of ancient tombs, cut in the rocks. Population in 1907, 39,442.

Siva, *shiv'va*, the name of the third of the three great Hindu deities (Brahma, Vishnu and Siva), represented as the destroyer and also as the creator, or regenerator. He is frequently represented with five faces and two, four, eight or ten hands, with a third eye in the middle of his forehead and with a trident in one hand. He rides on a white bull, and serpents usually hang about him. See BRAHMA; VISHNU.

Six Nations, THE. See FIVE NATIONS, THE.

Six'tus, the name of five popes, of whom Sixtus IV and Sixtus V were the most noted. SIXTUS IV, Francisco della Rovere, pope 1471–1484, was a patron of art and learning. Among the works commemorating his reign are the Ponte Sisto and the famous Sistine Chapel in the Vatican. SIXTUS V, Felice Peretti, pope 1585–1590, was born in the diocese of Ferno. As pope he actively pursued criminals and purged Italy of bandits and mendicants. He was an able financier; though he found the papal treasury exhausted at his accession, he left at his death three millions of dollars available to his successor. He also greatly enriched the Vatican library, collecting from the mon-

asteries countless valuable manuscripts and placing them in the hands of competent translators. He caused new additions to be built to the existing library and had the arrangement of its treasures so perfected that it has been since that time the admiration of all who visit Rome. The Vatican press was founded by him. By it he had printed the works of Gregory the Great, Saint Bonaventure and other learned divines; also, the Septuagint and the Vulgate, which were published in 1590. The Scala Santa, by which, according to tradition, Christ ascended to the hall of Pilate at Jerusalem, was raised by Sixtus's direction. In his brief reign, this pope accomplished more for Rome and the Catholic Church than any of his predecessors in a like period.

Skagerrak, *skah'ger rak*, a broad arm of the North Sea, which washes Norway on the north, Jutland on the south and Sweden on the east, where it communicates with the Cattegat. Its length is about 150 miles; its breadth, 80 miles. Its depth varies from 30 to more than 200 fathoms. There are several good harbors on the Norwegian and Swedish coasts. See CATTEGAT.

Skalds or **Scalds,** *skaldz* or *skawldz*, the poets and historians of the Scandinavian race. They sang the praises of the gods and celebrated the exploits of the national heroes. A list of over two hundred of the most distinguished is still preserved in the Icelandic language.

Skat, *skaht*, a game of cards, played with a euchre deck by three, four or five persons, for sixty-one points. The cards in the tricks taken count as follows: ace, eleven; ten spot, ten; king, four; queen, three; knave, two. The four knaves, which are called *matadors*, are the highest trumps and rank in order of suits, clubs, spades, hearts and diamonds. Only three take part in active play at each deal. Five cards are dealt to each of the three players. The next two cards are laid face down on the table, then five more are dealt to each of the same players. The two which are laid face down on the table are called the *skat*. Suit must be followed if possible; if not, any card may be played. By means of bidding and passing the bid, in which the rank of the suits is considered, the one who is to lead is selected. The counting is complicated, and the method should be studied from a manual. The game was invented in 1817 in Altenburg and is very popular among Germans and is played to a considerable extent in the United States, but its difficulty has prevented it from becoming more generally popular.

Skate, a name popularly applied to several species of the ray fish. The common skate agrees with the other members of the genus in possessing a flat, broad body, the chief portion of which is made up of the expanded pectoral fins, which are concealed under the skin. The tail is long and slender, and the snout is pointed, with a prominent ridge, or keel. The teeth are arranged in a mosaic, or pavement-like, pattern. This fish, although commonly seen of moderate dimensions, may attain a weight of two hundred pounds or more. See RAY.

SKATE

Skates and Skating. A skate consists of a frame, shaped somewhat like the sole of a shoe, underneath which is fastened a metallic runner. Skating seems to be of great antiquity, mention being made of it in the Edda. In Holland, from time immemorial, skates have been used by all classes of people upon the canals and rivers, for the facility of locomotion they afford. Great variety in the manufacture of skates has been introduced within a comparatively short period. In the improved forms the wood of the older skate has been replaced by metal, and the skate is attached to the foot by spring fastenings, which obviate the need for straps. A kind of skates termed "parlor skates," or roller skates, in which the metal runner is replaced by small wheels, is used on a prepared asphalt or other smooth flooring. In the United States there are few outdoor sports that attract as much attention or draw such large crowds as skating, and most of the northern cities make provision at public expense for children and adults who wish to skate on the lagoons in the public parks. Contests are held for local championships, and the winners of these take part in contests between different sections of the country. Not a few times there have been representatives from Europe, but they have usually been defeated by the Americans.

Skeat, *skeet,* WALTER WILLIAM (1835–   ), a British author, born in London, educated at

King's College School, London, and at Christ's College, Cambridge, where he graduated in 1858. Skeat is a most successful editor of early English literature and has a profound knowledge of the etymology and history of the English tongue. His chief works include a Mœso-Gothic glossary, the four Gospels in Anglo-Saxon and Northumbrian versions; editions of *The Vision of William concerning Piers the Plowman; Piers the Plowman's Creed; The Lay of Havelok the Dane,* and Barbour's *Bruce,* for the Early English Text Society. He has also edited, for the Clarendon Press, *Specimens of Early English Literature* and portions of Chaucer's *Canterbury Tales.* To Skeat much of the interest in Chaucer is due. In 1879–1882 he published an etymological dictionary of the English language, which marked an epoch in this branch of knowledge. He has also written original poems, and he has translated Uhland's songs and ballads.

Skel'eton, THE, or framework of the human body, is composed of 200 bones, of which 74 belong to the *axial* skeleton—head, neck and trunk—and 126 to the *appendicular* skeleton—the extremities. This number does not include certain small bones developed in tendons as they pass across bony angles.

AXIAL SKELETON. The *spine,* or the vertebral column, is made up of 26 bones, of which 7, called the cervical vertebrae, are located in the neck; 12, the dorsal or thoracic vertebrae, lie in the thoracic region, or chest, and support 24 ribs and the sternum; 5, the lumbar vertebrae, lie in the loin or lumbar region; the sacrum, made up during early life of 5 sacral vertebrae, which grow into one solid mass in the adult, lies in the sacral or pelvic region, forming a kind of keystone, by which the weight of the body is transmitted to the pelvic girdle and the lower extremities; the coccyx, made up during early life of 4 rudimentary vertebrae, forms the lowest part of the spinal column. Each vertebra contains an opening, through which the spinal cord passes; a projection from the back, which with its neighbors forms the ridge of the spine; projections on each side, which in the dorsal vertebrae support the ribs, and four processes for points of contact with the vertebrae next above and below. The upper vertebra, or atlas, has a pair of hollows, into which knobs on the under part of the skull project, to allow the nodding of the head. The second vertebra, or axis, has a peg that fits into an opening in the atlas and thus allows the head to be turned from side to side. Strength, combined with great elasticity and flexibility, is provided for the spinal column by anterior, posterior and lateral ligaments, by pads of cartilage placed between the vertebrae and by an alternation of anterior and posterior curves in the four principal regions.

The *ribs*, 12 on each side, form the walls of the chest. They are tipped in front with cartilages, which in the 7 upper, or true, ribs, join them to the sternum. Of the remaining 5, or false, ribs, the upper 3 are fixed to the cartilages above, but not to the sternum, and the lower 2 are free, or floating. All articulate with the spinal column. The cartilages allow the ribs to be easily compressed, hence tight clothing should be avoided.

The *sternum*, or breast bone, occupies the front of the chest, articulates at its upper extremity with the two clavicles, or collar bones, and gives direct articulation to the seven upper ribs on each side.

The axial skeleton is completed by the skull and the hyoid bone. The *skull*, situated on the top of the spinal column, is composed of 28 bones, 6 of which are located in the ears; 8— the frontal, 2 temporal, 2 parietal, 1 occipital, 1 ethmoid and 1 sphenoid—form the cranium and enclose the brain; 14—the vomer, 2 palate, 2 nasal, 2 lachrymal, 2 malar, 2 superior maxillaries, 1 inferior maxillary, 2 turbinated—form the face. The bones of the cranium are united by sutures, which somewhat resemble dovetailing in carpentry, thus allowing a symmetrical development or growth at the edges. The bones themselves are made up of two layers, with a porous substance known as the arachnoid membrane lying between. This arrangement gives the cranium power to resist blows and to prevent a jar from being easily communicated to the brain.

The *hyoid* is a bone situated at the base of the tongue, to which it is attached. No fewer than ten muscles arise from or are inserted into it. It articulates with no bones, but is suspended from the skull and supports the larynx by a ligament.

APPENDICULAR SKELETON. This skeleton comprises the shoulder girdle, with the upper extremities (64 bones), and the pelvic girdle, with the lower extremities (62 bones). The *shoulder girdle* includes the clavicle, or collar bone, and the scapula, or shoulder blade. The *clavicle* is a slender bone, shaped like the small italic *f*, extending from the sternum to the scapula, to each of which it is attached by cartilage. It aids in preventing the shoulder from falling toward the chest and also gives freedom to the shoulder movement. The *scapula* is a flat, irregular, triangular bone, lying outside the ribs, in the back of the chest, but separated and suspended from it by muscles.

The upper extremities include the following bones on each side: the humerus, the forearm, the carpus and the metacarpus. (1) At the upper extremity of the *humerus*, or arm bone, are found a head, a neck and two projections, while at its lower extremity it articulates with the ulna and radius. (2) The *forearm* contains the *radius* and the *ulna*, the former on the outside and the latter on the inside, both uniting with the humerus by a hinge joint. At their lower extremities the bones of the forearm join the carpus, the radius directly and the ulna indirectly, through the intervention of a small fibro-cartilage. The ulna is heaviest at the end which joins the humerus, and the radius is heaviest at the end which joins the carpus. (3) The *carpus*, or wrist, consists of 8 small, irregular bones, arranged in two rows, united by ligaments, and lying between the forearm and the palm. (4) The *metacarpus*, or palm, includes the five metacarpal bones, numbered from the thumb to the little finger. The fingers, or *digits*, are provided with three bones each, except the thumb, which has only two. These bones are known as the *phalanges*. The thumb has the advantage of moving freely on the carpus, by means of a saddle joint. The other carpal and metacarpal bones play slightly upon their fellows by means of gliding joints.

The *pelvic girdle* comprises the innominate, immovably united to the sacrum. The *innominate* is composed of three bones (ilium, ischium and os pubis), which unite in adult life along a Y-shaped line, located in the cup of the hip joint. The *ilium* spreads out a broad concave surface, in which the intestines are supported; the *ischium*, or haunch bone, forms the projection of the buttock and supports the body while sitting; the *pelvis*, or basin, furnishes the bony support upon which rest the organs of the abdomen.

The lower extremities join the innominate bones in the hip joints. They include, on each side, the femur, the patella, the leg and the foot. (1) The *femur*, or thigh bone, is the longest bone in the body; at the upper end of the shaft is a head, a neck, an angle and a large and a small projection; at the lower end are two knobs (external and internal), articulating with

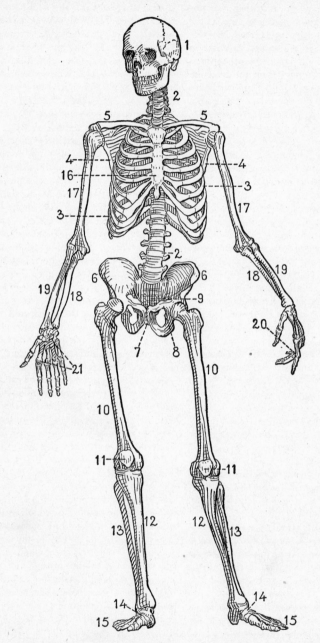

THE SKELETON. 1. Cranium. 2. Vertebræ. 3. Ribs. 4. Scapula or shoulder blade. 5. Clavicle or collar bone. 6. Hip bone. 7 Coccyx. 8. Pubes. 9. Sacrum. 10. Femur or thigh bone. 11. Patella or kneecap. 12. Tibia. 13. Fibula. 14. Metarsal bones. 15. Phalanges. 16. Sternum. 17. Humerus. 18. Ulna. 19. Radius. 20. Phalanges. 21. Metacarpal bones.

THE SKELETON

the tibia and the fibula in the knee joint. (2) The *patella*, or kneepan, is a chestnut-shaped bone, placed in the tendon of the muscle, at the point where the tendon glides over the external surface of the femur. (3) The *leg* contains two bones, the *tibia*, or shin bone, and the *fibula*. The tibia is the larger bone and is in front of the fibula. It is the only leg bone which articulates with the femur. At the lower extremity is a horizontal, smooth surface, for articulation with the ankle. The fibula is a slender bone, located on the outside of the leg, covered entirely by muscles, except at its upper and lower extremities, and articulating above and below with the tibia. The knee joint is a compound articulation. (4) The *foot* is made up of a series of bones, arranged in three groups—the *tarsus*, or ankle, made up of 7 bones; the *metatarsus*, made up of 5 metatarsal bones, and 5 digits, in each of which are found 3 bones, except in the great toe, which contains only 2. See JOINTS.

Skel'ton, JOHN (1460–1529), an English poet. He studied at both Oxford and Cambridge, and from both he received the laureateship, an academical honor. Henry VII made him tutor to Prince Henry, afterward Henry VIII, and he was held in high estimation for his learning. His works comprise, among others, the drama, or morality, of *Magnyfycence*; a satire on Wolsey, entitled *Why come ye not to Courte?*; the *Tunnynge* (the brewing) *of Elynor Rummyng*, a humorous picture of low life, and the *Book of Phylyp Sparrow*.

Skepticism, *skep'te siz'm*, in philosophy, doubt of the existence of a knowable reality. The causes of this doubt are, first, that judgments regarding an assumed reality must be made from sense-perceptions, which may or may not be unerring and which, because of their nature, vary with individuals and in different experiences of the same individual; second, that the knowledge thus obtained must therefore lack permanence and universality and have no real worth. Notable among the skeptics of the ancient world were Protagoras and Pyrrho, the latter of whom taught that it is advisable continually to suspend judgment, since absolute knowledge is impossible. A celebrated modern skeptic was David Hume, who questioned the validity of every act of consciousness.

Ski, *ske*, the Scandinavian snowshoe, consisting of a runner, or slat, of wood, six to ten feet long, about one-fourth of an inch thick and a little broader than a man's foot. It is slightly curved upward at the tip, and sometimes

has a narrow groove along the middle of the lower surface, to keep it from slipping sideways. Skiing is great sport, and in both Norway and the United States clubs compete every winter. Among the contests are long runs, for twenty miles or more, short runs at high speed, and jumping. The jump is made on a hillside and is really a long flight through the air, from which the jumper must alight on his feet and continue his course without falling.

Skimmer. See SCISSORSBILL.

Skin, THE, the outer covering of the body. It has a total area of from twelve to twenty square feet and varies in thickness from one-eighth to one-hundredth of an inch, according to location. It is composed of two layers. The outer layer, the *epidermis*, or *cuticle*, is itself made up of several layers of cells of various shapes and sizes. The surface layer is composed of horny scales and is thickened on the palms of the hands and on the soles of the feet. The inmost layer of the cuticle seldom varies in thickness, and it fits closely to the true skin. It contains the coloring matter which gives the characteristic tint to individuals and races. There is at all times a continual building of new cells and a throwing off of old ones from the surface. The hair and nails are a modification of the cuticle.

The true skin, the *dermis*, or *cutis*, in its outer layer contains very many minute projections, called papillae, on which the inmost layer of the cuticle is molded. They are most abundant where the sense of touch is most acute, as they contain nerve fibers (See NERVOUS SYSTEM). The skin also contains the *sudoriferous*, or *sweat, glands*, and the *sebaceous glands* (See GLANDS). The former, consisting of small, round masses, surrounded by blood vessels in the fat tissue under the skin, send up a duct through the cutis to the surface of the body, where it pours its secretion through a slanting, valve-like opening. These glands are distributed over the whole surface of the body, but are most abundant and largest in the palm of the hand, on the sole of the foot and on the brow. Sebaceous glands, abundant in those parts of the body supplied with hair and about the entrances to the body, as the nose, the lips and the external ear, are wholly wanting in the palms of the hands and the soles of the feet. Their secretion keeps the skin soft and pliable. The skin serves as an organ of touch; a regulator of temperature, by the evaporation of the sweat that is always being poured onto the surface of the body; a protection for the deeper tissues, and an organ of excretion, secretion and absorption

Skin Graft'ing. See AUTOPLASTY.

Skink, the common name of certain small lizards. They have long bodies, entirely covered with rounded scales, and are natives of warm climates. One species, the *adda*, is celebrated throughout the East as being useful in the cure of various diseases to which the inhabitants of Egypt, Arabia and other eastern countries are subject. It is about six inches in length and reddish in color, banded with darker shades.

Ski'o. See SCIO.

Skir'ret, a plant sometimes cultivated in gardens for its roots, which furnish a palatable food and from which a spirituous liquor is made. It is a perennial plant, a native of China and Japan. The flowers are white, and the roots, which resemble parsnip, may be used from the end of September onward. The skirret is very popular in Europe, but is little known in the United States.

Sku'a, a powerful bird of the gull family, living on northern seacoasts. In plumage it is usually brown, with blackish head and white breast. The skuas are found in numbers in Iceland, where they are often seen in pastures or on plowed lands, hunting for their food, which consists of insects, larvae, berries and grain. They often chase smaller birds of prey and compel them to give up the fish they have caught.

Skull. See SKELETON; FACE, THE.

Skunk, a flesh-eating animal of North America, that belongs to the weasel family. The

SKUNK

skunk is about the size of a large cat and feeds on eggs, small birds and mammals. It is a great enemy to poultry, making its raids at night. The skunk's fur is of a dark-brown hue, streaked longitudinally with black and white, and its tail is long and bushy. The animal is notorious for the strong and disgusting odor which it emits from certain glands. The secretion of these glands can be forcibly ejected at

the will of the animal, and this is its chief means of defense. The skunk is sometimes hunted for the sake of its fur, which is purified for commercial purposes by heat. It is often sold under the name "Alaskan sable." The *striped skunk* and *white-backed skunk* are two of the best-known species.

Skye, the largest island of the Hebrides, forming a part of the County of Inverness, Scotland. It is separated from the mainland by the Strait of Loch Alsh and the Sound of Sleat. It has an area of 535 square miles. Its shores are irregular, bold and beautiful, and the surface is mountainous, a number of peaks rising to a height of 2000 to 3000 feet. The island is not well suited to agriculture, but is quite generally given to sheep raising. Population in 1911, 15,500.

Skye Ter'rier, a small dog, with a long, low body, covered with a coat of dark gray hair. It is nine or ten inches high and about twenty-two inches long. The long, fine, silken hair nearly touches the ground, hanging down on the sides quite straight. In its proper place, this dog is a bright and cheerful companion. The *Paisley*, or *Clydesdale*, *terrier*, a variety of terrier brought into notice within the last few years, is a Skye with a light and silky coat; it is kept entirely as a house dog.

Sky'lark. See LARK.

Slag, a compound formed in the processes of extracting metals from their ores. It is mainly a compound of silica with alumina or lime, or both, together with various other substances in small quantity. It always contains more or less of the metal from the extraction of which it results. The presence of silica gives a glassy appearance to the mass. Slag is sometimes cast into blocks and used for road making and building, and when reduced to powder it is used in making mortar. In some parts of Europe slag is employed to impart a glaze to bricks. Some kinds of iron slag are made into an imperfect glass, which is used for making vases, match safes and other small articles.

Slander. See LIBEL.

Slate, a well-known hard variety of rock, which splits into thin plates, the type being roofing slate. The prevailing color is gray of various shades, but it may be green, purple, red or black. Slate yields to the knife, but the different varieties vary in hardness. Slate occurs in all countries where there are metamorphic rocks. It is commonly divided into elevated beds of various degrees of thickness; and from the natural divisions of the rock these beds often form peaked and serrated mountains. The finest variety, which is used for the covering of roofs, is generally embedded in other slate rocks, of a coarser kind. Quarries of slate of this description are worked extensively in Vermont and Pennsylvania. The finest grades are used for writing slates and blackboards. In the making of marbleized slate, the background is painted on the stone, which is allowed to dry and is then dipped into water, upon which coloring matter has been spread. The coloring matter adheres to the slate and thus produces the pattern, which is fixed by baking the slabs in a kiln.

Sla'ter Fund, a fund given by John Fox Slater for assistance in educating negroes of the South. The original gift, made in 1882, was $1,000,000. This was placed in charge of a board of trustees, who were to expend the interest in assisting schools already established. By provisions of the donor the income is to be expended directly on school work and not upon buildings or grounds. The larger part of the fund is used in assisting worthy students in their preparation for teaching, especially in manual training schools and agricultural and mechanical colleges. See PEABODY EDUCATIONAL FUND.

Slaughterhouse, *slaw'tur haus,* **Cases,** a group of cases decided by the Supreme Court of the United States in 1872, by which it limited the power of the Federal Government to usurp the powers of the state. The cases arose through an attempt by the legislature of Louisiana to restrict the butchering business in New Orleans, ostensibly in the interests of public health. The law in fact granted a complete monopoly of the business to one corporation. Suit was brought in the Federal circuit court to overthrow this statute, on the ground that it infringed the Fourteenth Amendment of the Constitution, but the Supreme Court decided that the purpose of the amendment was not to deprive the states of their police power, and that this power necessarily remained unimpaired. It also declared that there is a citizenship of the United States which is distinct from that of the state, and that the conditions of the latter are subject to regulation by the state.

Sla'very, the system by which some persons are held as the property of others. Slavery existed among the Hebrews, but in a very mild form. Among the Greeks and Romans it was a rooted institution, its character of mildness or severity varying in different times and places. The slaves of the ancient Romans were either captives or debtors that were unable to pay, and originally they had no rights at all. They could be put to death for the smallest misdemeanor. Slaves were exceedingly numerous, and in later times they almost monopolized the handicrafts and occupations, those of clerk, doctor and literary man included. Hosts of slaves were employed in the gladiatorial exhibitions. Slave revolts occurred often, but were always put down, not always without some difficulty. But even in Rome slaves were often set at liberty. It was not till the time of the Empire that any great change took place in the institution itself. Emperor Augustus granted the slave a legal status, and Antoninus took from the masters the power of life and death over their slaves. The rise of Christianity modified the rigid chattel conception of the slave, and, accordingly, the law soon gave him personality and protection. Finally, Justinian, in the sixth century A. D., enlarged the *coloni,* men personally free, but tied to the soil like serfs. Thereafter slavery, though practiced by Rome's Teuton conquerors, was gradually replaced in medieval Europe by feudal vassalage, or serfdom. This persisted to modern times, surviving in Russia until 1861 (See FEUDAL SYSTEM).

Slavery and the slave trade were again extended in Asia and Africa by the Mohammedans, who subjected Christians and heathens, whites and blacks, alike. After the institution had become all but extinct in Europe, it had a new birth in the American colonies of European origin. The first shipment of negroes to the New World took place in 1503, when the Portuguese carried some to Saint Domingo. From that time to the present century a traffic in negroes across the Atlantic was carried on by all the colonial powers, the English being particularly active.

Slavery soon affected the social, economic and political character of the colonies, especially in the South, where it was found particularly profitable, to such an extent that in spite of the theory of equality then in vogue, abolition was deemed unwise and unnecessary by a large part of the people. The first persons who liberated their slaves and labored to effect the abolition of the slave trade were the Quakers in the United States and England, early in the eighteenth century. In 1783 a petition was addressed to the British Parliament for the abolition of the trade, which Wilberforce eloquently supported. But the soul of all the efforts for the abolition of the traffic was Thomas Clarkson. On Feb. 4, 1794, the French National Convention declared all the slaves in the

French colonies free. The African Society, founded by Wilberforce and Clarkson, redoubled its efforts to procure the suppression of this traffic, and in March, 1807, the famous Abolition Act was passed. Jan. 1, 1808, was fixed as the time when this trade, on the part of the British, should cease. The abolition of the slave trade by most of the other European powers was gradually provided for by treaty. These treaties were mainly enforced by a British squadron maintained off the west coast of Africa. In 1831 the British government emancipated all the slaves of the Crown, and in 1833 a bill was passed for the emancipation of all the slaves in British colonies. By this bill the slaves were to receive their freedom on Aug. 1, 1834, and a compensation of $100,000,000 was to be distributed as a gift among the slaveholders, to make up for any loss they might sustain by the arrangement.

The United States Constitution provided for the abolition of the slave trade in 1808, but a furious struggle was waged against slavery itself for a half-century thereafter. It culminated in the Civil War, as a result of which abolition was declared by proclamation in 1863 and by Constitutional amendment in 1865. In 1873 the Spanish government abolished slavery in Porto Rico, and in 1886 abolition in Cuba took place. In Brazil slavery existed till 1888.

The efforts made to suppress the slave trade on the east coast of Africa have not hitherto proved quite successful. Those chiefly engaged in the trade are Arabs, who sell the slaves in the African countries bordering on the Mediterranean and at the ports of the Red Sea. They are all ultimately destined for Mohammedan masters. See UNITED STATES, subhead *History*; CIVIL WAR IN AMERICA; COMPROMISE OF 1850; CRITTENDEN COMPROMISE; DRED SCOT DECISION; EMANCIPATION PROCLAMATION; FUGITIVE SLAVE LAWS; KANSAS-NEBRASKA BILL; SQUATTER SOVEREIGNTY; MISSOURI COMPROMISE; UNDERGROUND RAILROAD; WILMOT PROVISO; ABOLITIONISTS; POLITICAL PARTIES IN THE UNITED STATES; SERFS. Consult, also, articles upon great men connected with the slavery struggle, such as GARRISON, WILLIAM LLOYD; PHILLIPS, WENDELL; WEBSTER, DANIEL; CLAY, HENRY; CALHOUN, JOHN CALDWELL; STEPHENS, ALEXANDER HAMILTON, and many others.

Slavo′nia. See CROATIA AND SLAVONIA.

Slavs, *slahvz,* or **Slavo′nians,** a branch of the Aryan, or Indo-Germanic, family. They have broad heads and a pale white, swarthy or light brown skin. In height they are below the average Aryan. In the fourth century Slavs lived in great numbers in the neighborhood of the Carpathians, and thence they appear to have spread northward to the Baltic and southward to the Adriatic.

The Slavs in the districts in which they still exist form two great groups, the southeastern and the western. The former includes the Bulgarians, the Servians, the Croats, the Slavonians and the Russians. In the latter group are the Czechs, the Serbs and the Poles. The total number of Slavs is about 125,000,000, the majority of whom are Russians. With few exceptions the Russian and Bulgarian Slavs belong to the Greek Church; the western Slavs are mostly adherents of the Roman Catholic Church.

Sledge, *slej,* a vehicle moved on runners, for the conveyance of loads over frozen snow or ice or over the bare ground; called also a *sled.* The same name is given to a kind of traveling carriage, mounted on runners, otherwise called a sleigh, much used in Russia, Canada and other northern countries during winter. See SLEIGH.

Sleep, the state in which the activity of the brain proper appears to be naturally and temporarily suspended. Dreaming, sleepwalking and other phenomena show that some activity of the mind is possible, even in sleep. All parts of the body which are the seats of active change require periods of rest. In the case of the brain, it would be impossible that there should be short periods of activity and repose, that is, of consciousness and unconsciousness; hence the necessity of sleep, a condition which is a remarkably perfect example of what occurs at varying intervals in every actively working portion of our bodies. Sleep, therefore, affords the interval during which nervous energy expended during the waking hours is renewed.

The respective influences of habit, age, temperament and occupation have much to do with the duration and character of sleep in different individuals. Physiologists are all agreed that dreamless sleep is the most refreshing, the lighter sleeper being disturbed by the most trifling noises. In some diseased conditions sleep may be prolonged for indefinite periods, while, on the contrary, periods of active wakefulness may occur and extend for days, weeks or months, without a single interval of sleep. Insensibility may be caused by too much blood in the brain or by too little blood; sleep, it is probable, is caused by the blood leaving the brain for other parts of the body.

Sleep'lessness. See INSOMNIA.

Sleepwalking. See SOMNAMBULISM.

Sleeping Sickness. This disease is the last stage of trypanosoma infection, and is prevalent in certain sections of Africa. The parasite which causes it is communicated to man by the bite of a species of tsetse fly. It is always fatal, no cure being known for it. In recent years, whole sections in Africa have been depopulated by its ravages. The sleeping sickness stage begins when the disease reaches the nervous system. The patient becomes apathetic, the apathy deepens into stupor, and he literally sleeps to death.

Slidell', JOHN (1793–1871), an American politician, born in New York City and educated at Columbia College. He removed to New Orleans in 1819 and became United States district attorney. In 1853 he was elected to the United States Senate, but resigned upon the secession of Louisiana and was appointed special commissioner of the Confederacy to France. He was captured with James M. Mason, however, while aboard the British steamer *Trent* and was arrested and taken to Fort Warren, Boston. He was later released and sailed for England; there he took up his interrupted negotiations with foreign governments, but without success. After the war he lived in England until his death. See TRENT AFFAIR.

Slide Rule, an ingenious instrument, composed of two sliding pieces, each engraved with one or more arithmetical linear scales, so related to one another, that by drawing one of the pieces out until a point representing a certain number upon its scale coincides with the point representing another number upon the other scale, the quotient of the latter by the former may be read on inspection from the second scale, opposite the figure 1 on the first. In a variety of similar ways the product of two or more numbers, the square or cube root of a number, the square or cube of a number, natural sines and tangents (See TRIGONOMETRY) and logarithms are found without effort in an incredibly short time.

Slime Molds, a group of plants of exceedingly simple structure, which live upon rotting bark and decaying wood, in moist, shady places. They are not easily distinguished from animals and, in fact, have been described under both titles. In no other plant is protoplasm found in such large quantity, and thus the slime molds give a very excellent opportunity of studying the action of protoplasm. During one period of its life the slime mold develops spores which, when dry, retain life for an indefinite period; but as soon as they are moistened, they swell quickly, burst and discharge their protoplasm. This protoplasm lengthens and develops a delicate hair at one end, and by means of this hair it swims freely about. The form modifies until it closely resembles an amoeba; then many of the plants unite and make the slimy plasmodium, which slides about over decaying vegetable matter until ready again to produce spores and go through the circle of its life. The largest plasmodia may be several inches square, but most of them are very much smaller.

Slings, instruments for throwing stones or bullets. One common kind consists of a strap, with two strings attached to it. The stone or bullet is lodged in the strap, and the sling is whirled rapidly round in a circle, the ends of the strings being held in the hand. The missile is thrown when one of the strings is allowed to fly loose. The velocity with which the projectile is discharged is the same as that with which it is whirled round in a circle whose radius is the length of the string. The sling was a very general instrument of war among the ancients.

In making a catapult, an elastic band is fastened to each end of a forked stick. With the handle of the Y-shaped stick in the left hand, a stone being held by the thumb and finger in the center of the cord, the missile is sent with a great force when the band is stretched to its limit and let go. The catapult, or slingshot, may be a dangerous weapon, and in most c'ties boys are forbidden to use it.

In the making of *bolas,* six small stones or bullets, wrapped tightly, each in a piece of cloth, are tied, one to each of six pieces of string, about two and a half feet long. The strings are tied together at the ends opposite to the stones. The tied end is taken in the hand; the stones are swung swiftly around the head and then let go into the air. The stones separate, and if the implement is thrown into a flock of birds, it frequently succeeds in entangling some of the number. The bolas used by the Paraguay indians, the Patagonians and the Gauchos of the Argentine Republic consists of a rope which has, at either end, a heavy stone, or bullet, of metal or hardened clay. It is thrown so as to entangle the animal at which it is aimed.

Slip, an inclined plane, upon which a vessel is supported while being built or upon which she is hauled up for repair; also, a contrivance for hauling vessels out of the water for repairs. One form of slip consists of a carriage, or cradle, with truck wheels, which run upon rails on an inclined plane. The ship is placed on the carriage while in the water, and the carriage, together with the ship, is drawn up the inclined plane by means of wheels and pinions, operated by hand or steam power.

Slipperwort, *slip'pur wurt.* See CALCEOLARIA.

Slo'cum, HENRY WARNER (1827–1894), an American soldier, born at Delphi, N. Y., and educated at West Point, where he graduated in 1852. He resigned in 1856 to engage in the practice of law, but at the outbreak of the Civil War he was appointed colonel of a New York regiment. He fought at the first Battle of Bull Run, where he was severely wounded, and was afterward made brigadier general of volunteers. He served in the Peninsula Campaign, being promoted to the rank of major general, fought at the second Battle of Bull Run, South Mountain, Antietam, Chancellorsville and Gettysburg, and was with Sherman in his marches to Atlanta and to the sea. He resigned from the army in 1865, resuming his law practice. He was twice elected to Congress.

Sloe, *slo,* a well-known shrub or small tree of the plum genus, possessing a very hard, tough wood. It blossoms with white flowers in the early spring, and it has a black, round fruit about the size of a pea. These berries are used for preserves and liquors and for dyeing black. The sloe abounds in Great Britain and most parts of Europe, and it has been naturalized in the New England states.

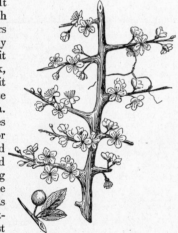

SLOE BRANCH AND FRUIT

Sloth, a mammal inhabiting South and Central America. The claws of the sloth are long and curved, and the feet are turned inward. This adaptation is of great service to the animal in its life in the trees, but it makes walking on the ground almost impossible. The sloths live on the leaves, buds and bark of trees. The

best known species is the *ai,* which has three toes and is of a brownish-gray color, with darker tints on the face and limbs. The fur is very coarse. The *unau,* or *two-toed sloth,* has an average length of about two feet, and its color is a lighter gray than that of the ai. The tail in

SLOTH

both species is usually lacking, or at the most it is of a rudimentary character.

Slot Machine, the name given to two machines, similar only in the fact that they are manipulated by the dropping of a coin through a slot. One kind of slot machine is a gambling device, usually consisting of a wheel, bearing symbols, which is set to revolving by the impact or weight of the money, the player having previously wagered the amount of his deposit upon the chances of the wheel stopping when a certain symbol reaches a certain point.

The other type of slot machine is, in fact, an automatic salesman. The coin is dropped in a slot, setting wheels and levers in motion, so that a package of candy or gum or a trinket is released and falls into an open receptacle.

Sloyd (Swedish, *slojd*), a system of manual training which was first introduced into the schools of Finland and Sweden and which has been quite generally adopted in other countries. The original plan limited the work to the manufacture of small household utensils, such as wooden spoons, knives and forks, by whittling; but in 1876 Otto Solomon, director of the normal school at Naas, extended the system by the introduction of mechanical drawing, the employment of more tools and the use of more difficult exercises. The system used in the United States is patterned after Solomon's idea and constitutes the foundation of most of the manual training work for boys in elementary schools. The material used is wood, cardboard or iron, but a special line of instruction is prepared for each class of material. See MANUAL TRAINING.

Slug, the name applied to several genera of mollusks, resembling the snails, but lacking an external shell, though many of them possess a rudimentary organ of this nature, concealed more or less completely by the mantle. The slugs have four tentacles, and the eyes are borne on the tips of the larger pair. The great gray slug usually frequents hollow trees and undisturbed heaps of vegetation. The black slug is more common and usually smaller in size.

Small Arms, firearms that may be held in the hand, as distinguished from those which must be fired from a carriage or other mount (See ARTILLERY). Under the name *small arms* are included the pistol, the revolver, the musket, the shotgun and the rifle, upon each of which will be found a special article in its proper place. Soon after the invention of gunpowder its use was applied to hand arms, although the earlier ones were very heavy and could be handled only by two men. A lighted fuze was used to touch off the charge, a process that hindered rapidity of fire. This gave way to a matchlock and that to the flintlock, which in turn was superseded by the percussion lock, which is still in use. During the Civil War the United States government used four million small arms in numerous varieties, but since that time all of these have been discarded for more improved forms. American manufacturers have perfected their plants until no less than $10,000,000 of capital are invested, and about one million rifles and an equal number of other small arms are made every year.

Small'pox, a contagious fever, accompanied by ulcerating sores, that often leave the patient scarred permanently. Smallpox has been known and described since the early Middle Ages, and at times it has been one of the most terrible scourges. It is violently contagious, very few who are exposed escaping the disease, unless they have been vaccinated. No infant is too young to take the disease, and no adult is too aged. The contagion lies in the sores, or *pustules,* and it is also probably given off through the breath and the pores of the skin. The disease manifests itself about twelve days after exposure, and it varies in duration according to the severity of the attack. In minor cases the recovery is rapid and complete, but in severe cases death may intervene very quickly. Unless

great care is exercised during the disease and after, the patient may be left with bad scars or with serious affection of some of the organs, particularly of the eyes. Since Jenner's discovery of vaccination, however, the ravages of smallpox have been practically stopped in all countries where it has been possible to secure very general preventive measures. Exposure to the disease should be followed by immediate vaccination, unless that has very recently been done. There is usually little excuse now for a person who takes the disease. See VACCINATION.

Smell. The sense of smell originates in the olfactory lobes of the brain, and the olfactory nerves coming from these centers are distributed to the mucous membrane of the upper part of the nasal cavities. In order that odors may be perceived, air must pass through the nostrils; hence a person sniffs when he desires to perceive an odor more keenly. The sense of smell in man is not nearly so keen as in many of the lower animals, though he can probably detect more odors than any of these animals. Odors are numerous and difficult to classify, and they are named from the substance from which they arise, as the odor of musk and the perfume of violets. The nerves of smell are stimulated by an odor when it first acts upon them, but if long continued, the stimulus is lost, and the person fails to recognize the odor. The nature of odor is not well understood. That it arises from gaseous or volatile matter all agree, and some authorities consider that it can arise from matter in a gaseous state alone. Others think differently, and in support of their theory they point to the fact that substances like musk can fill a large space with odor for weeks and not diminish perceptibly in weight. The sense of smell is closely allied to the sense of taste, which it undoubtedly aids. See NOSE; SENSES, SPECIAL; TASTE.

Smelt, a family of fishes allied to the salmon. They are slender and delicate and usually measure about eight inches in length. They receive their name because of their odor, which is like that of a cucumber. Smelts live around the coasts of Europe and North America. In the United States they abound along the New England and the Californian coasts. In England they are given the name *starlings* and are considered excellent food.

Smet, PETER JOHN DE (1801–1872), one of the most distinguished missionaries of the Jesuit order, born in Termonde, Belgium. In 1821 he sailed for America and in 1828 went to Saint

Louis and assisted in establishing the University of Saint Louis. Ten years later he was sent to establish a mission among the Pottawatomies. He attached himself to the yearly caravan of the American Fur Company, as missionary among the Flathead indians of the Rocky Mountains, in 1840, and after a year he returned to Saint Louis, but soon set out anew for indian conversions. On different occasions he efficiently interceded to prevent and end strife between the United States and the indians.

Smetana, *sme tah'na,* FRIEDRICH (1824–1884), a Bohemian composer and pianist, the founder of the Bohemian school of composition. He founded a musical academy at Prague, after studying under Liszt, but went to Sweden in 1856 and became conductor of the Gothenburg Philharmonic concerts. There he remained until 1866, when he became kapellmeister at the National Bohemian Theatre. In his later years, his mind gave way, and he died in the Prague lunatic asylum. Smetana's works have a true Bohemian atmosphere; they are thoroughly original and contain not a few passages of striking power and beauty. He composed several operas, *The Bartered Bride, Two Widows, Dalibor* and others, besides many compositions for the piano and orchestra.

Smi'lax, a group of plants belonging to the lily family. Most of them are climbing or trailing, and numerous species are found in Asia and America. Sarsaparilla is obtained from the roots of several species, and the roots of others are edible. The green brier and the carrion flower are found in the United States. The cultivated plant known to gardeners as smilax is really an asparagus.

Smiles, SAMUEL (1812–1904), an English writer, born at Haddington, Scotland, and educated for the medical profession. He practiced for some years as a surgeon at Leeds and then became editor of the *Leeds Times.* He is the author of many works on industrial enterprise, the chief of which are *Life of George Stephenson, Workmen's Earnings, Strikes and Wages, Live of the Engineers, Self Help, Character, Duty* and *Thrift.* These works are characterized by their good moral teaching, and they are written in a clear and simple style.

Smith, ADAM (1723–1790), a distinguished writer on political economy. His first publication, *The Theory of Moral Sentiments,* appeared in 1759 and won him at once a high reputation. In 1763 he attended the duke of Buccleuch on his travels, and during a long stay in France he became acquainted with Turgot, Necker, D'Alembert and others. On his return to Scotland in 1766, he retired with his mother to Kirkcaldy, where, after ten years of close study, he wrote his celebrated *Inquiry into the Nature and Causes of the Wealth of Nations.* Numerous editions, both of the *Moral Sentiments* and the *Wealth of Nations,* have been published, and the *Wealth of Nations* has been translated into most European languages.

Smith, ALEXANDER (1830–1867), a Scotch poet. His first published work was his *Life Drama,* a volume of poems which attracted wide attention. In 1854 he was appointed secretary of the University of Edinburgh, and the following year he produced, in conjunction with Sydney Dobell, a volume of *Sonnets on the Crimean War.* This was followed by his *City Poems,* and by his longest and best poetical work, *Edwin of Deira.* In 1863 he published a collection of papers entitled *Dreamthorp,* which was succeeded by *A Summer in Skye* and *Alfred Hagart's Household.*

Smith, EDMUND KIRBY (1824–1893), an American soldier, born at Saint Augustine, Fla., and educated at West Point. He served in the Mexican War with distinction and later became an instructor at West Point. At the opening of the Civil War he resigned from the United States army and became brigadier general in the Confederate service, serving with Johnston in the Shenandoah Valley in 1861 and under Bragg in the west in the following year. In October, 1862, he was made lieutenant general and was given charge of all the Confederate forces west of the Mississippi. In February, 1864, he was made full general and opposed General Banks in the disastrous expedition up the Red River. He finally surrendered to General Canby, in May, 1865. After the war he became interested in commercial enterprises, was chancellor of the University of Nashville from 1870 to 1875 and was later professor in the University of the South at Sewanee, Tenn.

Smith, FRANCIS HOPKINSON (1838–   ), an American engineer, artist and author, born in Baltimore. As an engineer he became a successful contractor and constructed several important government works on the Atlantic seaboard. As an artist he has attained some distinction. A few of his pictures are *In the Darkling Wood, Peggothy on the Harlem* and *A January Thaw.* Besides the work in water colors, his charcoal drawings and his illustrations have become well known. Of late years his fame as an author has eclipsed that in his other professions. *Colonel Carter of Cartersville* had a great success and was later dramatized. Among his other books are *Caleb West, A White Umbrella in Mexico, The Fortunes of Oliver Horn, The Under Dog, Tides of Barnegat, Peter, Forty Minutes Late* and *Kennedy Square.*

Smith, GERRIT (1797–1874), an American capitalist and philanthropist, born at Utica, N. Y., the son of Peter Smith, partner of John Jacob Astor in the fur trade. He graduated from Hamilton College, was admitted to the bar and gained distinction in his profession, settling at Peterboro, N. Y. He was elected to Congress in 1853, but soon retired and devoted himself to philanthropy, dividing his large land holdings among poor families, in parcels of fifty acres each. He also advocated liberality in religion and finally became a prominent anti-slavery worker, being an intimate friend of John Brown. Though a stanch Unionist, he favored a liberal policy of reconstruction and was one of the signers of Jefferson Davis's bail bond.

Smith, GOLDWIN (1823–1910), an English-Canadian writer, educated at Oxford. He was

GOLDWIN SMITH

called to the bar, but never practiced law. From 1858 to 1866 he was regius professor of modern

history at Oxford. As a lecturer he attracted great attention, on account of his strongly democratic views and his striking originality. Having, during the American Civil War, strongly defended the cause of the North, he was at the close of the war invited to visit the United States, to deliver a course of lectures, and his visit resulted in his accepting the professorship of history at Cornell University, Ithaca, N. Y. He resigned the appointment in 1871 and moved to Toronto, where he was appointed a member of the senate of the University of Toronto. He wrote and lectured extensively on political and economic questions. His views were often unpopular, but his earnestness and high ideals earned for him universal respect. Among his chief works are *Lectures on Modern History; The Empire,* and *History of the United States.*

Smith, JOHN (1580–1631), commonly known as Captain John Smith, one of the founders of the English colony in Virginia, born at Willoughby, in Lincolnshire. After many adventures as a soldier of fortune in Europe, Asia and Africa, he went out with the first expedition of the London Company to America in 1606. Dissensions broke out before it had reached its destination, and Smith was condemned to be hanged; but he escaped this fate and became an active member of the colony. He made important geographical discoveries, obtained supplies from the natives and was finally intrusted with the guidance of the colony, where he displayed notable executive ability. In 1609 he was obliged to return to England. He subsequently visited the American coast for the purpose of trade, and he gave the name *New England* to the region now so called. He published several histories of Virginia and descriptions of his discoveries, his chief works being, *A True Relation . . . . of Virginia* and *A General Historie of Virginia.*

Smith, JOSEPH (1805–1844), the founder of the Church of the Latter Day Saints, or the Mormon sect, was born in Sharon, Vt. When he was ten years of age his parents removed to Palmyra, N. Y. When he was 22 years of age Smith announced that in a vision an angel revealed to him the spot where the Bible of the western continent was buried. Following the directions thus obtained, Smith claimed that there was delivered to him the volume containing the doctrine on which Mormonism is founded The new sect met with persecution and the Mormons were gradually driven westward In 1844 Smith was arrested for alleged violations of the law, and lodged in jail in Carthage, Ill., where he was shot by a mob. See MORMONS.

Smith, SAMUEL FRANCIS (1809–1895), an American preacher and writer, best known as the author of the national hymn, *My Country, 'Tis of Thee*. He was born in Boston, Mass., and graduated from Harvard College in 1829 and from Andover Theological Seminary in 1832. He was pastor of the Baptist Church, Waterville, Mo., and professor of modern languages in Waterville College, 1834–1842. Later he was pastor at Newton, Mass.; editor of the *Christian Review*, Boston, and editor of the publications of the Baptist Missionary Union (1854–1869). He is the author of *The Morning Light is Breaking* and other hymns. He published the *Life of Rev. Joseph Grafton, Missionary Sketches*, a *History of Newton* (Mass.) and *Rambles on Mission Fields*.

Smith, SYDNEY (1771–1845), an English humorist, born at Woodford, Essex. He graduated at New College, Oxford, and was ordained in the established church. Moving to Edinburgh in 1798, he helped to found the Edinburgh *Review*, to which he made frequent contributions in later years. In 1803 he moved to London, where he gained note as a preacher, writer and lecturer. He was gradually promoted in the church, until in 1831 he was appointed to a subordinate position in Saint Paul's. His principal writings are his *Letters on the Subject of the Catholics, to My Brother Abraham, who Lives in the Country, by Peter Plymley*, a satirical essay in the interests of Catholic emancipation. These and other less famous writings abound in clear logic, irony and good humor.

Smith, WILLIAM (1769–1839), an English geologist, born at Churchill, in Oxfordshire. While a civil engineer he became interested in the study of rocks and soils, and he finally formulated the principle that stratified rocks exhibit a definite order of succession and that the different horizons in a series may be identified by their included fossils. He published several works in support of his theories and prepared a geological map of England and Wales, showing the arrangement and rock formations of the whole country. From this work he has been called the "father of English geology." His services were recognized officially by a government pension.

Smith, WILLIAM FARRAR (1824–1903), an American soldier, born at Saint Albans, Vt. He graduated at West Point in 1845 and later became an instructor there. Soon after the outbreak of the Civil War, he was given command of a volunteer regiment and participated in the first Battle of Bull Run and in the Peninsula Campaign, as brigadier general of volunteers. He was promoted to be major general of volunteers and colonel in the regular army, for gallantry at Antietam, fought at the Battle of Gettysburg and was made chief engineer with the Army of the Cumberland, performing notable service at the Battles of Chattanooga. He also served in the Army of the Potomac in Grant's famous Virginia campaign and was brevetted major general in the regular army, retiring in 1867. He became president of the International Telegraph Company and later president of the board of police commissioners in New York City.

Smith, WILLIAM SIDNEY, Sir, (1764–1840), an English admiral, born in Westminster. After serving with distinction as a volunteer in the Swedish navy against Russia and then against France, he returned to England and was given command of a small flotilla, with which he cruised against the French privateers in the Channel. Appointed then to the *Tiger*, he did good service in Syria and subsequently in Egypt against Bonaparte, receiving a severe wound at the Battle of Alexandria. He was created rear admiral in 1805, and in 1806, as commander of a small squadron, he inflicted signal injuries on the French, off the coast of Naples. Next year he accompanied Admiral Duckworth to the Dardanelles, where he distinguished himself by the destruction of a Turkish squadron. As a reward for his services he received a pension of $5000 a year.

Smith College, an institution for the higher education of women, at Northampton, Mass., chartered in 1871. All undergraduate courses of study lead to the degree of Bachelor of Arts. The degree of Master of Arts is conferred for postgraduate work. In connection with many of the departments, clubs are organized for advanced or special work. The faculty numbers about 140, and there are about 1500 students. The college is a contributor to the American Schools of Classical Study at Rome and Athens, to the marine biological laboratory at Woods Hole, Mass., and to the zoölogical station at Naples.

Smith'son, JAMES (1765–1829), founder of the Smithsonian Institution. He was educated at Pembroke and Oxford and was a fellow in the Royal Society. By his will he left to his nephew,

H. J. Hungerford, about $515,000, stipulating that if the legatee died without issue, the whole amount should pass to the United States, to found at Washington an institution for the "increase and diffusion of knowledge among men." His nephew died childless, and the money reverted to the United States. See SMITHSONIAN INSTITUTION.

Smithso'nian Institution, an institution for the promotion of knowledge, located at Washington, D. C., and authorized by an act of Congress of 1846 to carry into effect the provisions of the will of James Smithson, an Englishman who bequeathed the United States over $515,000, for the purpose of establishing such an institution (See SMITHSON, JAMES). The funds are administered by a board of regents, consisting of the president of the United States, the chief justice of the Supreme Court, three senators, three members of the House of Representatives and six citizens who are not members of Congress. Two of these must be residents of the District of Columbia, but of the other four no two can reside in the same state. The president of the board of regents has the title of chancellor, and this office is usually bestowed on the chief justice. The executive head of the Institution is the secretary, who is chosen by the board of regents.

The plan and organization of the Institution are due to the wisdom and foresight of Prof. Joseph Henry, who was its first secretary and who administered the affairs of the Institution for thirty years (See HENRY, JOSEPH). The funds of the Institution are applied to assisting original research in all lines of knowledge, particularly along scientific lines, and to the publication of the annual reports of the Institution and other papers and books. The three series of publications systematically issued are *Contributions to Knowledge, Miscellaneous Collections* and *Annual Reports*. These are distributed free of charge to public libraries, educational institutions and individuals engaged in literary or scientific research. In connection with this distribution the Institution has established a system of international exchanges, so that it obtains similar publications from nearly all countries of the world.

In addition to the work of the Institution proper, the secretary has charge of the National Museum, which is maintained by the government; also of the Bureau of Ethnology, which is a department in the Institution, of the Astrophysical Observatory and of the National Zoölogical

Park. The Institution occupies beautiful buildings on the Mall, extending from the Capitol to the Washington Monument. Here are found the original building of the Institution and the National Museum, while the Bureau of Ethnology occupies rented quarters in another part of the city, and the Zoölogical Park is about two miles north. See NATIONAL MUSEUM OF THE UNITED STATES.

Smoke, the visible vapor that arises from a substance burning. In its more extended sense the word *smoke* is applied to all the volatile products of combustion, which consist of gases charged with minute portions of carbonaceous matter, or soot; but the term is frequently employed to express merely the carbonaceous matter which is held in suspension by the gases. There are many practical difficulties in the way of consuming smoke, but experience has shown that none of them are insuperable. If sufficient air is supplied to furnish oxygen, the combustible parts of smoke can be made to burn and leave only invisible vapors and gases. Smoke from the many furnaces of a large city often becomes a public nuisance, and in many places laws have been passed requiring the adoption of some device for burning the soot, but no one method has been found successful in all cases.

Smokeless Powder, an explosive used in the place of gunpowder in cannon and other firearms. It is so named because it burns with little smoke. The smokeless powders are prepared by the dissolution of gun cotton and nitrocellulose in ether, the compound being then dried. In the drying process it hardens and has a horn-like appearance. The cake is then made into flakes, cords or grains, according to the use for which it is intended. The nitrocellulose consists of sawdust, or wood pulp, soaked in a mixture of sulphuric and nitric acids. While there are several varieties of smokeless powder, they all contain nitrocellulose and gun cotton, or nitroglycerine, with one or both of these substances. They vary in strength according to their composition.

Smol'lett, TOBIAS GEORGE (1721–1771), a novelist and miscellaneous writer, born near Dumbarton, Scotland. He was educated at the University of Glasgow and was apprenticed to a surgeon. His interest, however, was rather in literature than in surgery, and in 1739 went to England with a tragedy, *The Regicide,* which he was unable to have performed. After some years' service as surgeon's mate, on board the *Cumberland,* he returned to England and again took up literature. The first of his novels, *Roderick Random*, appeared in 1848, and its success was immediate and great. Among his later works the most noteworthy are *Peregrine Pickle* and *Humphrey Clinker*. His novels, carelessly constructed, often coarse and usually marked by a humor which descends frequently into burlesque, depend for their interest largely on their thrilling scenes and on their occasional admirable character drawing.

Smug'gling, the practice of defrauding the government by the introduction of articles into consumption without paying the duties chargeable upon them. It may be committed upon either the excise or customs revenue. See CUSTOMS DUTIES.

Smuts, small fungi which live in certain plants as parasites. They attack wheat, oats, barley and, particularly, indian corn. Smuts are propagated by means of spores and often do immense damage to crops. The spore settles upon the young plant when its tissues are tender. It penetrates to the interior and grows toward the end of the stalk, dividing wherever the stalk divides and sending a filament into each branch, thus finding its way eventually to the tips of the shoots which bear the fruit. In corn the smut does not appear to damage the plant until the kernels are well formed. Then in the course of a few days those at the end of the ear swell, burst and throw out a large quantity of black powder. This powder is merely the perfected spores, which can be carried long distances by the wind. They fall upon manure heaps, lodge in the soil or find homes in other suitable places, where they develop a different spore, which, carried to the corn plant the next season, begins its career again, as has been described. When smut appears in a field, the only safe thing to do is to destroy all the ears affected by it. Seed from a field thus affected should not be planted.

Smyrna, *smur'na*, a seaport of Asiatic Turkey, situated on the Gulf of Smyrna, 200 mi. s. s. w. of Constantinople. It occupies a site consisting partly of level ground and partly of the slopes of Mount Pagus, and when seen from the sea it presents an attractive appearance. The city is divided into five quarters—the Frank, or European, quarter, which extends along shore and contains the modern buildings; the Greek, the Armenian, the Turkish and the Jewish quarters. The Turkish quarter occupies most of the high ground. The city has a fine wharf and carries on an important foreign trade, exporting raisins, sponges, carpets and rugs, opium, tobacco,

licorice and numerous other articles. Most of its trade is with Great Britain. The city is connected with Constantinople by rail and with a number of other important towns in Asia Minor. Population, estimated at 200,000, about one-third of which are Greeks and one-third Turks.

Snail, a small mollusk, with a shell of one part, or valve. Two general divisions are rec-

SNAIL

ognized—land snails and water snails. The shells of land snails are arranged in whorls, which may rise to a point or may be comparatively flat. The shell is covered with a thin membrane, which gives it its color and serves as a protection from the weather. The portion of the snail that protrudes from the shell is called the "foot." The head is on the forward end of the foot and contains two sets of tentacles, or feelers, the larger of which are tipped by the eyes. The snail moves slowly, by contracting one portion of the foot after another, and it is aided in its movements by a slimy fluid which it secretes. Land snails live in damp, shady places and prefer moss and decaying wood, but may be found on rocks. In cold or extremely dry weather, land snails retire into their shells and close the opening with a membrane. In France a species of small snail is cultivated as a food.

Snake, an indian tribe. See SHOSHONI.

Snake, a reptile, easily distinguished by its long, slender body, which tapers gradually to a tail and which is covered with horny scales, but never with bony plates. Snakes have no limbs, though in some species rudimentary hind limbs may be detected. The ribs are very numerous, some snakes having more than 300 pairs. These give form to the body, aid in breathing and are also, in connection with the scales, organs of locomotion. Snakes crawl upon the ground, by swinging their bodies in loops from side to side, and most of them are able to raise their heads and a large portion of their bodies into the air. They have hooked, conical teeth, which serve to hold their prey, but are useless for chewing. While some species are fatally venomous, the majority of them are perfectly harmless. In the venomous serpents two long poison fangs are firmly fixed in a movable bone, above which is a gland for the secretion of poison. The teeth are perforated by tubes, through which the poisond is forced. The tongue of a snake is forked, can be pushed far out of the mouth and is probably an organ of touch, rather than of taste. Snakes have no eyelids and no external ears, and their nostrils are on the snout. The lower jaw is loosely articulated to the upper, and the tissues about the mouth are so elastic that a snake can swallow an animal really much greater in diameter than itself. Some snakes lay eggs, but others produce the young alive. In most species the mother takes great care of her young, and it is said that in one species, at least, the mother, when alarmed, will open her mouth and allow the young to run to cover within her body.

Each locality of the temperate and torrid zones has its own peculiar species of snakes, some of which live only in warm, arid regions; some live in moist, shady places, and others live in water. All the species are vastly more numerous and much larger in the tropics than in the temperate regions. There are over 1500 species known, and about 20 poisonous species are found in the United States. Of these the large majority, however, live only in the southwestern portions of the country. Two rattlesnakes and the copperhead are the only poisonous natives of the Northern states. See ADDER; ANACONDA; BLACKSNAKE; BOA; COBRA; COPPERHEAD; MOCCASIN SNAKE; PYTHON; RATTLESNAKE; VIPER.

Snake Bird. See DARTER.

Snake Dance. See MOKI.

Snake River, a large river of the northwestern United States. It rises in Yellowstone Park, flows southeast, then west, northwest, north and finally westward, emptying into the Columbia, in southeastern Washington. Its total length is about 1300 miles. A number of beautiful rapids and cataracts are found at different places in the river. This river was formerly called the Lewis River. It was called Shoshone River by the indians.

Snake'Root, the popular name of numerous American plants of different species and genera, most of which are, or formerly were, used as remedies for snake bites. Among the varieties are the *wild ginger* of Canada, the *Indian snakeroot* and the *Seneca snakeroot* of eastern North America.

Snapping Turtle, a species of fresh-water tortoise, common to all parts of the United

States. It sometimes reaches a length of three feet and is notable for its fierceness. One species, found around the lower Mississippi Valley, is called the *alligator-snapper* and is

SNAPPING TURTLE

noted for the strength of its large jaws. It feeds on small animals and receives its name from its habit of snapping at everything within its reach.

Snipe, a common name for certain wading birds that are usually seen along the shores of rivers and lakes. They are slender and active, both on land and on the wing. All have narrow bills, longer than the heads, and their eyes are set far back. Usually the plumage is brownish or grayish and spotted or streaked with white

SNIPE

or black, the whole blending closely with the colors of the ground, so that they are not easily seen. Snipes are considered good game birds everywhere. The *jacksnipe* is a large common species that is found, throughout the summer time, in the Northern states. When the bird is aroused near its nest, it flies in a zigzag way up and down, making with its wings at the same time a curious drumming sound.

Snorri Sturluson, *snor're Stoor'loo son,* (1179–1241), an Icelandic poet and historian. He early turned his attention to the history of the kings of Norway and made a collection of sagas, entitled the *Heimskringla,* or the *Ring of the World,* in which are interspersed songs of his own composing. It contains a record of the Norwegian kings from the earliest time to the death of Magnus Erlingsson (1177) and was first printed in the seventeenth century. It has been translated into several languages. Snorri is also supposed to be the author of the *Prose Edda*. See EDDA.

Snow, frozen vapor falling to the earth in flakes. Whenever precipitation occurs at a temperature below 32° F., snow is formed. Snow is not frozen rain, but consists of minute crystals formed by the freezing vapor. These take various shapes, but are patterns of a six-pointed star, which in large flakes are very beautiful. By collecting such flakes on a coal-black surface, these crystals can be studied with an ordinary magnifying glass. Each flake contains a number of crystals, so arranged as to form beautiful designs. The size of the flakes depends upon the temperature and the amount of moisture in the atmosphere. They are largest when the atmosphere is heavily charged with moisture and the temperature is just below the freezing point. The amount of water in snow is about one-tenth that in rain; that is, a snowfall of ten inches would be equivalent in water to a rainfall of one inch.

Snow occurs in cool temperate regions in the winter, and it falls on the summits of high mountains and in the polar regions throughout the year. The heaviest snowfall is in mountains of the cool temperate regions, where the amount is several feet each winter, as in the Alps and in some portions of the Rocky Mountains, particularly in the State of Washington and in British Columbia. The melting of this snow supplies water for springs and streams (See RIVER; SPRING). When frozen together in great masses, this snow forms glaciers (See GLACIERS). The line of perpetual snow is often known as the *snow line* and depends upon altitude and latitude. It will be lower in cool climates than in warm. See RAIN.

Snow'berry, the popular name of a tropical American shrub. The fruit consists of snow-white berries. The name is also applied to a bushy shrub of the woodbine family, a native of North America, bearing white berries.

Snowbird, a name given to several finches that early in the spring go far north to nest, returning late in the fall. They gather in large flocks and feed in the snow on the seeds of grass and large plants. The *snowbunting*, often called the snowbird, is common in the northern United States. It has a gray back, white breast and black and white tail and wings, and is a very pretty bird.

Snow'bunt'ing. See SNOWBIRD.

156

Snowdrop, a well-known garden plant, belonging to the amaryllis family. It bears solitary, drooping and white, bell-shaped flowers, which appear early in spring. It is a native of the Alps, but is quite common in gardens in the northern United States.

Snow Line, the line, or level, on a mountain side, above which there is snow during all the year. The position of this line varies in different localities, and in the same locality in different years. It is about 2000 feet above sea level in Greenland and about 19,000 feet in the Himalayas of Asia.

Snowplow, a plow for clearing away the snow from roads, sidewalks and railways. Snow-plows for clearing the snow from roads and sidewalks are usually triangular and are hauled by horses. They push the snow to each side of the path and are useful when the snow does not reach a great depth, after which the accumulation of snow on each side of the path renders their use somewhat difficult. Snow plows used on railways are of two kinds—the triangular plow, which is attached to the front end of the locomotive or a special car and removes the snow by being forced through it, and the rotary plow. The triangular plow differs from that used on ordinary roads in that the sides form an oblique edge, which points downward to the middle of the track. As the plow is forced through the snow it lifts it up and then throws it out on each side of the track. The rotary plow consists of a large wheel, with buckets attached to an axis that rotates at right angles to the rails. As the wheel revolves, the buckets scoop up the snow and empty it into a hopper, from which it is thrown to a great distance by a powerful fan. The rotary plow is operated

SNOWBUNTING

by a special engine and is pushed along by a locomotive. Its effectiveness does not depend upon the speed with which it is moved forward, and it is successful in clearing the heaviest drifts, even when they are packed by strong winds.

Snowshoe, *sno'shoo,* a kind of flat shoe, either made of wood alone, or consisting of a light frame, crossed and recrossed by thongs, the broad surface of which prevents the wearer from sinking in the snow. Snowshoes are usually from 3 to 4 feet in length and from 1 to 1½ feet broad, across the middle. Rapid progress is made with them by experienced runners, but the beginner finds them difficult to handle. See SKI.

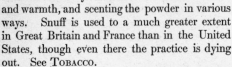

SNOWSHOE

Snuff, a powdered preparation of tobacco, inhaled through the nose. It is made by grinding, in mortars or mills, the chopped leaves and stalks of tobacco, in which fermentation has been induced by moisture and warmth, and scenting the powder in various ways. Snuff is used to a much greater extent in Great Britain and France than in the United States, though even there the practice is dying out. See TOBACCO.

Sny'ders, FRANS (1579–1657), a Flemish painter, born at Antwerp. He studied the rudiments of his art under Breughl and Van Balen. Later he visited Italy, but in 1609 finally took up his abode at Antwerp. Snyders, who is considered never to have been surpassed in his delineation of game, fish and fruit, excelled, also, in hunting scenes and combats of wild beasts. Some of his works are *Diana's Hunt,* *Two Lions Pursuing a Roebuck* and *Prometheus and the Eagle.*

Soap, a chemical compound of fat or oil with potash or soda, used for washing and cleansing and for medicinal purposes. There are many different kinds of soaps, but those commonly employed may be divided into three classes—(1) toilet soaps; (2) coarse household soaps; (3) soft soaps.

SOAP MAKING. The soap stock comes to the factory in cars. It consists of tierces of tallow and stearin from stockyards and wholesale meat markets. For the finer varieties of soap there are barrels of cocoanut oil, palm kernel oil and palm oil. The tallow is weighed, and then the barrels are run into an iron trench, with open ends downward. A hot blast of steam is forced up into the trenches, and the tallow melts and drops down through holes in the bottom of the trench to the soap vats below. Barrels of rosin are then dumped into the vats. It is this product that gives laundry soap its rich, yellow color and most of its odor. Rosin is not used in toilet soaps.

The next department is the *leach house.* Here are a number of steaming vats, fifteen feet in diameter and twenty feet deep. Each vat is partly filled with dissolving caustic soda or lye, which is kept moving. From the bottom of the lye vats a pipe runs to the great soap kettles on the floor below. Some of these kettles are large enough to hold over 275,000 pounds of soap. In the bottom there is a great spiral coil of steam pipes, which serve to raise the soap to the boiling point. The lye, the tallow and the rosin are supplied in exact proportions and thoroughly cooked together. Then the workmen let in some strong brine, and it sends the soap out of solution and floats it to the surface of the kettle. Just enough water is added to allow the impurities to settle.

After standing several days, the soap is let out through a pipe, which carries it downstairs to the *crutcher.* At the top of the crutching machine the soap passes through a sieve, where the impurities are strained out. Then it passes downward into a cylinder, set flush with the floor, and an augur-like screw churns it until it looks like thick pudding. Carbonate of soda is added, and the soap becomes much lighter in color. This chemical also imparts to the soap its cleansing properties. When the soap has been thoroughly churned, the mass streams down into iron boxes, which form it into cakes 4½ feet long, 3½ feet wide and 15 inches thick. In this form it is placed on a traveling platform, which carries it between two upright posts, across which are strung sharp, steel wires, as far apart as the width of an ordinary bar of soap. The wires cut the big cake into slabs, and these in turn are trimmed and cut into bars by other wires. They are then sent to the drying room. When dry, the soap is ready for packing.

The making of toilet soaps is a longer operation and one that requires greater care. The substance, either tallow, cocoanut oil or palm oil, is boiled with lye in 10,000 pound kettles. After the soap has been hardened, it is chopped up in a machine. It is then put on racks and left until it has been dried, after which it goes to the grinding room. Here the scraps of soap are treated with various colors and perfumes. Then the mass is ground between rollers of stone until it is smooth and stringy. It comes out in fine ribbons and is ground and reground until the color is perfectly distributed. The tar soaps are made by adding tar to the soap shavings. On leaving the grinding machine the soap goes into the hopper, a device which forces it, by means of an augur screw, through a narrow hole, in the form of a cylindrical stick. When these sticks are about four feet long they are taken into another room, molded into cakes and wrapped in paper. Transparent soap is made by using alcohol in the process. Formerly the glycerine, lye and salt left in the bottom of the kettles were all wasted, but a process has been devised for saving the glycerine, which is sold principally to dynamite makers. The salt is also saved and used over and over again.

Soapstone or **Ste'atite,** a soft rock with a soapy feel. It has a variety of colors, from light to dark gray and almost black. A soft white variety forms the French chalk used by tailors. Powdered soapstone is sometimes used to prevent friction in machinery. Soapstone is easily cut into statues, which are hardened by baking and colored to imitate more expensive stones. The stone is used in making stoves and foot stoves. In New England, where small blocks of the stone are often heated and put in sleighs to protect the feet from cold, it is known as *freestone.*

Social Dem'ocrats, an advanced body of socialists. They originated and are chiefly represented in Germany, where they form a strong political party. The Social Democratic Labor Party was established in 1869. In 1875 it formulated a program, which set forth that labor is the source of all wealth and all culture and that the uplifting of labor must come through the laboring classes. The party aims at the development of a socialistic society, the removal of all social and political inequality, the administration of justice by the people and the establishment of gratuitous and universal education. Religion, only, is to be regarded as a private concern. The Social Democrats in the United States have made great gains in the last few years, the vote for their presidential candidate in 1904 being 402,286, against a vote of 87,814 in 1900. The Socialist party polled 448,453 votes at the presidential election in 1908, and 901,725 in 1912.

Socialism, *so'shal iz'm,* the name given to a theory which has for its object the reform of society on the principal of coöperation, instead of the principle of competition, by which society is now largely controlled. While socialism and anarchism have in view the same end—the improvement of society—they seek this end through directly opposite means. Anarchism seeks general equality among men and the largest freedom of the individual, by abolishing all systems of law and government; socialism, on the other hand, seeks the same end by increasing the powers of the State and making government paternal. Socialism would extend government ownership to all utilities connected with production and distribution. The advocates of socialism base their theory on the history of society, in which they see the following economic stages, each of which they claim is a successive step in an evolution of society which will ultimately lead to their ideal.

THE GENS. It is generally conceded by historians that the primitive forms of society rested upon communism, or common ownership of both products and means of production. This was but natural, since the tribal life of this period was based on kinship. The leader of each tribe or gens was a patriarch, and most of his followers were his descendants. There was no such thing as social inequality; woman held her true position in the family, and the amassing of wealth by any individual at the expense of the others was unknown. If one prospered, all shared his prosperity, and in case of suffering from scarcity of the necessaries of life, all suffered alike.

SLAVERY. During the period of communism all discoveries and inventions which aided in the production of wealth were the property of the community. The power to acquire wealth was gained slowly, but by degrees the communal system was changed, because it was seen that such a system retarded the progress of wealth production, and because tribes learned that it was better to keep captives taken in war and compel them to labor, than it was to kill them when captured. By degrees two classes arose, those who labored and those who received the benefits of labor, and rights in private property were recognized. Slavery became thoroughly established, and in Rome and Corinth the slaves at one time far outnumbered their masters. Finally, the economic conditions reached a stage where slavery became unprofitable, and this was one of the principal causes leading to the end of Roman domination. With the fall of the Roman Empire, new economic conditions arose. The invasion of the barbarians from the north resulted in establishing a different order of society. The rise of the feudal system caused serfdom to succeed slavery and formed one of the most important conditions of society during the Middle Ages. The serf was but little above the slave. He was bound to the soil without any rights which his master was bound to respect, except that he could not be sold like the chattel slave of the former period.

THE WAGE SYSTEM. In the course of centuries many of the serfs obtained their freedom, and there arose a class of private owners and craftsmen in all the nations of western Europe. At the abolition of the feudal system in England, the individual peasants in the country and the free craftsmen in the towns were in sufficient number to give tone and character to the entire industrial system of the country. Gradually these individual proprietors were deprived of their property, and the only resource left them was to sell their labor to the best possible advantage. Purchasers of labor, or employers, found it to their advantage to concentrate their energy and capital on the production of a single commodity or, at the most, on very few commodities. This gave rise to the system of exchange, which became national, then international.

Many producers of the same commodity entered the market, and this resulted in the modern competitive system, in which each strives to undersell his competitors. In order to do this he must manufacture his product at the least possible cost. This necessity has a tendency to depress wages, as the wage-earner must earn for his employer more than he receives. The constant discovery of new processes and the invention of labor-saving machinery have also been powerful factors in building up the present industrial system, in which capital is combined under the control of large corporations, and in which labor has become highly specialized. For a time the only interest between the capitalist and the wage-earner was a pecuniary one, and ever since the recognition of rights in private property there has been more or less strife between the property-holding and the propertyless classes. In recent years this has led to thorough organization in both classes, the corporation representing the first, and the labor union, the second.

This theory of socialism sees in the present economic conditions the limit of this state of society and claims that just as conditions have made each of these successive stages inevitable, so the present conditions make inevitable the return to the economic system of the early ages. In proof of this tendency they point to the public ownership of utilities; to the gradual, but constant, increase of coöperation, or profit-sharing, in many industries, and to the sale of stock to employes by large corporations.

Socialism has reached its greatest development in Germany, where the socialists have attained sufficient strength to enable them to influence, to some extent, public measures. In other countries of continental Europe, and in England, Australia, Canada and the United States, its followers are also increasing in numbers. Many of the large universities now maintain chairs of sociology, and the wide discussion given the various theories of society is tending towards such changes in social and economic conditions as will lead to the abolition of existing evils and the establishing of more just and equitable relations between capital and labor.

Social Set'tlements, the name given to those houses, or centers, in the poorest districts of great cities, where cultured men and women live, in order to come in contact with, and improve the condition of, the poorer classes. The activities of these societies include efforts at the development of the physical, mental, moral, spiritual and social interests of the poor. The oldest and most famous of the social settlements is Toynbee Hall in London, founded in 1884 and named in honor of Arnold Toynbee, who had taken the first steps toward its organization. In the United States, Hull House and the Chicago Commons in Chicago, and the College Settlement and University Settlement in New York have undertaken, and in large measure have carried out, remarkably broad plans for the guidance and uplifting of the unfortunate poor. See ADDAMS, JANE.

Society Islands or **Tahiti,** *tah' he te,* **Archipelago,** a group of islands located in the Southern Pacific Ocean, between the Low Islands, on the east, and the Friendly Islands, on the west. The group consists of a number of islands arranged in two groups, the Leeward group, or Society Islands proper, and the Windward group. Of the Leeward group the chief islands are Huahaine, Raiston, Tahao and Bora Bora. Of the Windward group Tahiti and Morea are the important islands. The islands are of volcanic origin, and some of them rise several thousand feet above the sea. Most of them are surrounded by coral formations. The islands are densely wooded, and cocoanuts, bananas, sugar cane, vanilla, oranges and other tropical fruits are cultivated. The climate is mild and healthful. The population is about 18,000, most of whom are Malays. The islands are a possession of France.

Society of Jesus. See JESUITS.

Sociology, *so'she ol'o jy,* the name given to the science whose field is the study of society, including the fundamental facts upon which society is based; the history of modern societies, and the description and classification of present social phenomena. It thus includes in its broadest sense the study of the general progress of civilization, including history, economics, jurisprudence and politics. It is based, of necessity, largely upon statistics, and its conclusions are arrived at through an historical and psychological study of the individuals that compose society and of the movements which in the past have affected its form and nature. See ANARCHISTS; BROOK FARM; COMMUNISM; COOPERATION; ENVIRONMENT; FACTORY AND FACTORY LEGISLATION; GEORGE JUNIOR REPUBLIC; ILLITERACY; IMMIGRATION; LABOR ORGANIZATIONS; MONOPOLY; POLITICAL ECONOMY; POPULATION; SOCIAL SETTLEMENTS; STATISTICS; SUICIDE; TRUSTS; WOMEN'S RIGHTS; CONVICT LABOR; PRISON; SOCIALISM; CAPITAL PUNISHMENT.

Socrates, *sok'ra teez,* (469–399 B. C.), an ancient Greek philosopher, born at Athens. For a time he followed the profession of his father, who was a sculptor; then he was a common soldier for several years, after which he became interested in philosophy and devoted himself to the education of the youth of his native city, hoping thereby to make more useful citizens and a more firmly established and morally sound State. By means of conversation, which was simple, yet brilliant, he so illuminated commonplace facts that the great truths underlying them became apparent. Because of his pure morality, honesty and interest in all mankind, he was highly esteemed; yet he was hated by those who opposed his ideas of government and religion and was finally accused of corrupting the youth of the State with heretical religious views. He was tried before a court of citizen jurors and was sentenced to death. A month later he drank the cup of fatal hemlock and expired.

Socrates made no attempt to formulate a system of philosophy, nor to commit his ideas to writing. What we know of his doctrines is learned from Xenophon's *Memorabilia* and Plato's *Dialogues.* The great influence which he wielded is largely due to the fact that his ideas were made practical in his life. He was governed always by his high sense of virtue and obeyed conscientiously the promptings of an inner voice, which he declared to be a never-failing counselor. He attained to an intellectual strength and a spiritual peace that make him remarkable among the world's greatest thinkers.

So'da, a term applied in common language to several compounds of sodium, but most properly to the carbonate of sodium. This substance appears commercially either crystallized in lumps or in a crude powder called *soda ash.* It is obtained from the ash of plants growing near the sea, from native sources or by chemical process, the latter source being by far the most common. In the chemical process the first step is the decomposition of common salt by means of sulphuric acid; the second, the conversion of the sulphate of sodium so produced into crude carbonate of soda, by strongly heating with chalk and carbonaceous matter; the third, the purification of the pure carbonate, and fourth, the treatment of the by-products, hydrochloric acid and calcium sulphide. See GLAUBER'S SALT.

Soda Water, an effervescent drink, generally consisting of ordinary water charged with carbonic acid gas, which has been forced into it under pressure. It rarely contains any soda, but receives its name from the manner in which the carbonic acid was originally manufactured, which was by a combination of soda and weak sulphuric acid. The gas is now made by treating marble or chalk with sulphuric acid, after which it is forced into the water, one volume of water taking about five volumes of the gas. Plain soda water is sparkling and pungent and slightly sour in taste, but as the beverage is usually served it is flavored with fruit syrups and other substances.

Pop, ginger ale and other similar drinks consist of water flavored with various extracts and charged with carbonic acid gas, which is kept under pressure in the bottle. When the cork is removed the gas escapes rapidly and causes the effervescence.

So'dium, a metallic element discovered by Sir Humphry Davy in the year 1807. It is silver-white, and has a very high luster. It melts at 204° F. and oxidizes rapidly in the air, though not so rapidly as potassium. It decomposes water instantly, but does not spontaneously take fire when thrown on water, unless the water be somewhat warm or unless the progress of the globule of sodium upon the surface of the water be impeded. When heated in air or oxygen it takes fire and burns with a very pure and intense yellow flame. It is perhaps more abundant in our globe than any other metal, for it constitutes two-fifths of all the sea salt existing in sea water and is present in the water of springs, rivers and lakes, in almost all soils and in the deposits of rock salt. Sodium is also contained in sea plants and in land plants growing near the sea. It occurs, also, in most animal fluids. It is used as an agent in the manufacture of aluminium and magnesium, and as a reagent in chemical operations. Common salt is a compound of chlorine with sodium (See SALT). Sodium also occurs as oxide of sodium in a good many minerals; but it is most common in the form of carbonate, nitrate and borate of soda. Of the numerous salts of sodium, many are important medicinal agents, and others are valuable in other ways. *Sodium arsenate* is used as a substitute for arsenic and is an important element in fly poisons; *sodium bromide* and *sodium iodide* are prescribed for quieting the nerves; *sodium bicarbonate* is one of the important ingredients of baking powder and is used in the manufacture of mineral waters; *sodium hypophosphite* is another remedy which is prescribed for restoring health to the nervous system. See SALTPETRE; WATER GLASS.

Sod′om, one of the five cities situated in the plain of the Jordan River, and referred to in the thirteenth and fourteenth chapters of *Genesis*. It was in Sodom that Lot settled when he separated from Abraham. The city was plundered by Chedorlaomer and was afterwards rescued by Abraham. According to biblical accounts, this and three other cities in the vicinity were destroyed in a miraculous way because of their wickedness. It was at this destruction that Lot and his two daughters were spared, while his wife, not obeying the divine command, was turned into a pillar of salt (*Gen*. XIX, 23–30). The exact location of Sodom is unknown, and authorities differ in regard to it, some believing it to have been at the north end of the Dead Sea and others at the south end. In Scripture Sodom is usually associated with Gomorrah.

Sodom, APPLE OF, a fruit mentioned by early writers as growing on the shores of the Dead Sea. It was beautiful to the eye, but when eaten it filled the mouth with ashes. Although no satis-factory explanation has ever been given, it is supposed by some to have been a gall produced on dwarf oaks by an insect.

Soerabaya, *soor′a bi′a.* See SURABAYA.

Soerakarta, *soo′ra kahr′ta.* See SURAKARTA.

Sofia or **Sophia,** *so′fe ah,* the capital of Bulgaria, situated on the River Bogana, near the Balkan Mountains, 325 mi. n. n. w. of Constantinople, on the line of railway extending from Constantinople to Budapest. The city is built on modern plans and has broad, straight streets. The important buildings are the old mosque of Sofia, ruins of which still remain; the Mosque of Buyuk-Jami, used for a museum; the palace of the prince, and the government buildings. The city is the seat of a university founded in 1888. The chief industries include the manufacture of silk and other textiles and of pottery. Sofia occupies the site of ancient Sardica, and in 1878 it was made the capital of Bulgaria. Population in 1910, 102,812.

Soft-Shelled Tur′tle, the name of a large class of turtles inhabiting fresh water in many parts of the world. They are entirely aquatic in their habits and have strong, webbed feet. In the winter they spend their time in the mud underneath the water, and there they lay their eggs. The flesh of these turtles is considered especially good. The name is derived from the peculiar leathery character of the shell.

Soil, in geology, the loose surface layer of the earth's crust; in agriculture, that portion of this loose surface layer which is suitable for tillage and in which plants can grow. The process of forming soil has been in operation since the first solid masses of the earth's surface appeared, and the same agencies which began its formation at that time are still at work and are producing the same results. These agencies are the atmosphere, water, plants and animals.

The atmosphere aids in the formation of soil by mechanical and chemical action—by mechanical action, when strong currents of wind wear away rock in certain localities and deposit the particles in others; by chemical action, when under conditions of moisture the oxygen of the air takes certain substances of which the rock is composed and destroys them, thus causing the rock to crumble.

Water is the most powerful agent in the formation of soil, since it does more than all other agencies in decomposing rocks. It decomposes rocks by wearing them away, as in the case of water in streams, and by breaking up rocks into particles as a result of freezing. At the foot of all cliffs masses of rock fragments are found (See TALUS). These are formed by the water's entering crevices in the rock and freezing and breaking the particles off. These particles are in turn broken up by weathering and by similar action of the water. Water also acts chemically, since oxygen readily attacks substances which the water dissolves from the rock. The combined action of water and atmosphere is known as weathering, and this is by far the most important process in the formation of soil.

Plants contribute to the formation of soil by the decay of roots, leaves and stubble, and frequently by the decay of the entire plant. The roots also assist in breaking up rocks by growing in crevices; and the absorption of nutriment by the plant also decomposes rocks to a limited extent. Animals contribute to the formation and enrichment of soil by their excrement, by the decay of their carcasses and by burrowing. A good illustration of this is found in the earthworm, which bores its hole by passing the soil through its body. During this process the soil is pulverized and enriched. The holes thus made allow the air to enter the soil, and in this way a fresh supply for soil breathing is furnished (See EARTHWORM). Thousands of insects make the soil their home, and in numerous ways they contribute to its fineness and fertility.

The composition of soil depends upon that of the rock from which it was formed. When the soil overlies the decomposing rock, it is usually of the same nature, but along river beds and in localities which are the beds of ancient lakes, the soil may be of entirely different composition from that of the surrounding rock, since it was transported a long distance by water (See ALLUVIUM). A sandy soil is one whose composition is nearly three-fourths sand. A clayey soil is about half clay, while a lime soil is about one-fifth lime. A peaty or vegetable soil is made up of peat or vegetable matter. Loams are soils containing a mixture of clay, sand, lime and decayed vegetable matter, known as *humus.*

All soil contains water, the amount depending upon the condition of the country in regard to rainfall, and the nature of the soil itself. In soils most suitable for tillage the water exists in the form of a thin film around each minute particle of soil, similar to the film formed around a marble when it is dipped in water. Soils containing clay retain the water much longer than those composed principally of sand or gravel. When too much water is present it gathers in excavations made in the soil and is known as free water. The presence of free water is injurious to growing crops, since it drowns the roots and prevents their obtaining the necessary amount of nourishment. See AGRICULTURE.

Soko'to, a native kingdom, situated in Central Africa and occupying the northern part of Nigeria east of the Niger and north of Benuwe. It includes a number of petty kingdoms, or provinces, governed by partially independent rulers. The population is estimated at about 10,000,000. The chief commercial center is Kamo. Sokoto was the former capital and now has a population of about 10,000. Nearly all of the state is under British influence.

So'lar Engine or Solar Motor, an apparatus for utilizing the heat of the sun as a motive power, by causing it to convert the water in a small boiler into steam. Many attempts have been made to utilize the sun's heat as a motive force, but until 1901 none of these was successful. In that year a motor was constructed and placed upon a farm near Pasadena, Cal., where it was used for pumping water and for performing other light work. This motor consisted of a large mirror, constructed in the form of an umbrella, with a part of the top cut off; the mirrors were set at an angle, to catch all the sun's rays striking upon it and to reflect them upon a long steam boiler, set in the center like the handle of the umbrella. The mirror faced the south, and in the morning it was adjusted so as to catch rays of the rising sun. When sufficient steam was generated to operate the engine, it was connected with a system of clockwork, and the mirror was made to turn with the sun, so that when the machine was once started, it needed scarcely any attention during the day. This motor developed fifteen horse power. With the reduction in the expense of their manufacture, solar motors of this pattern will make very desirable machines for pumping water for irrigation.

Solar Mi'croscope, an instrument by means of which a magnified image of a small transparent object is projected on a screen, the light employed being sunlight. It is really a magic lantern, in which the microscope objective takes the place of the object-glass, and a mirror for collecting the sun's rays takes the place of the light. The solar microscope must be used on the south side of a building, and for the best results the mirror should be attached to a clock, so that it will turn with the sun and will reflect the rays upon the condenser continuously. See MAGIC LANTERN.

Solar System, in astronomy, the name given to that system of which the sun is the center, that is, to the sun and the bodies that revolve about it. To this system belong the eight great planets and their satellites, the asteroids lying oustide of Mars, comets and meteorites, the whole being bound together by the mutual attractions of the several parts. The size of this great solar system is utterly beyond comprehension. Herschel's illustration was that if the earth were represented by a pea, the sun would be a ball two feet in diameter, 327 feet away on one side, and Neptune a plum a mile and a quarter away on the other. See elsewhere in this work articles on each of the planets and on each group of bodies that belong to the solar system.

Solders, *sod'urz,* alloys used in joining the surfaces or edges of metals. It is a general rule that the solder should always be easier of fusion than the metal intended to be soldered by it. The usual solders are compound and are of two kinds, hard and soft. The *hard solders* are ductile, will bear hammering and are commonly prepared of the same metal as that which is to be soldered, with the addition of some other, by which a greater degree of fusibility is obtained. Under this head comes the hard solder for gold, which is prepared from gold and silver or from gold and copper or from gold, silver and copper. The hard solder for silver is prepared from equal parts of silver and brass, but it is made to fuse more easily by the mixture of one-sixteenth of zinc. The hard solder for brass is obtained from brass mixed with a sixth or an eighth or even a half of zinc, and this may also be used for the hard solder of copper.

The *soft solders* melt easily, but are partly brittle, and therefore they cannot be hammered. Of this kind are the following mixtures: Tin and lead in equal parts; bismuth, tin and lead in equal parts; bismuth, two parts, tin and lead, each one part.

In soldering, the surfaces to be united must be made perfectly clean and free from oxide. This is commonly done by scraping the surfaces; and in order that the formation of any oxide may be prevented during the process, borax, sal ammoniac or resin is used, either mixed with the solder or applied to the surfaces.

Soldiers' Homes, homes provided for disabled soldiers and sailors. The United States supports such institutions at the following places: Dayton, Ohio, Milwaukee, Wis., Togus, Me., Hampton, Va., Leavenworth, Kan., Santa Monica, Cal., Marion, Ind., Danville, Ill., Hot Springs, Dak., and Jackson City, Tenn., the total membership being about 30,000. The following states provide homes for disabled volunteer soldiers: California, Colorado, Connecticut, Idaho, Illinois, Indiana, Iowa, Kansas, Massachusetts, Michigan, Minnesota, Missouri, Montana, Nebraska (2), New Hampshire, New Jersey (2), New York (2), North Dakota, Ohio, Oregon, Pennsylvania, Rhode Island, South Dakota, Vermont, Washington, Wisconsin and Wyoming, the total membership being about 15,000. The requirements for admission are (1) honorable discharge from the United States service; (2) disability which prevents the applicant from earning a living; (3) agreement to abide by the rules and regulations of the institution and to perform whatever duties are required. Soldiers and sailors whose pensions exceed $16 per month are not usually eligible.

Solemn League and Covenant. See COVENANTS.

Sol'id. In geometry this term signifies a magnitude which has three dimensions, length, breadth and thickness. The best usage now substitutes the term *volume* for solid, since the latter conveys the idea of substance, or matter, while geometry has to do only with imaginary figures, or space. (See CONE; CUBE; CYLINDER; GLOBE; PRISM; PYRAMID; SPHERE; TETRAHEDRON.)

In physics the term solid signifies a body which has a shape of its own and resists forces tending to change that shape. It is thus distinguished from liquid, which offers little resistance to forces that tend to change its shape.

Solitaire, *sol e tair',* or **Patience,** *pa'shens,* a game of cards played by one person. There are many games of this sort described in books, most of which consist in arranging the cards after fixed rules, in an endeavor to classify them according to suits, and the player's interest lies in the extent to which he may succeed.

So'lo. See SURAKARTA.

Sol'omon (the Prince of Peace), son of David, king of Israel, by Bathsheba, formerly the wife of Uriah. He was appointed by David to be his successor, in preference to his elder brothers. By his remarkable judicial decisions and his completion of the political institutions of David, Solomon gained the respect and admiration of his people; while by the building of the Temple, which gave to the Hebrew worship a magnificence it had not hitherto possessed, he bound the nation still more strongly to his throne. The wealth of Solomon, accumulated by a prudent use of the treasures inherited from his father, by successful commerce, by a careful administration of the royal revenues and by an increase of taxes, enabled him to meet the expense of erecting the Temple, of building palaces, cities and fortifications, and of supporting the extravagance of a luxurious court. Fortune long seemed to favor this great king; and Israel, in the fullness of its prosperity, scarcely perceived that he was continually becoming more despotic. Contrary to the laws of Moses, he admitted foreign women into his harem; and from love of them he was weak enough in his old age to permit the free practice of their idolatrous worship and even to take part in it himself. Toward the close of his reign troubles arose in consequence of these delinquencies, and the growing discontent, coming to a head after his death, resulted in a division of the kingdom, which his feeble son, Rehoboam, could not prevent. The forty years' reign of Solomon is still celebrated among the Jews for its splendor and its happy tranquillity, as one of the brightest periods of their history.

Solomon Islands, a group of islands in the Western Pacific, lying s. e. of Bismarck Archipelago, e. of New Guinea and between New Britain and New Hebrides. The larger islands are of volcanic origin, and most of the smaller ones are of coral formation. Their total area is about 16,950 square miles. The population is estimated at 180,000, nearly all of whom are Malays and Papuan negroes. Two of the islands are controlled by Germany, and the others by Great Britain.

Solomon's Song (called also the *Song of Songs*, or *Canticles*), one of the canonical books of the Old Testament. From the earliest period this book has been the subject of much controversy. It seems to have been a recognized part of the Jewish canon in the time of Jesus. Till the beginning of the present century the author of the book was almost universally believed to be Solomon, but modern critics attribute it to an author of northern Israel, who wrote it about the middle of the tenth century B. C., shortly after the death of Solomon, in a spirit of protest against the corrupt splendor of the court of Zion. By the Jews it has been regarded as a spiritual allegory, in which God is the lover, and the people of Israel, the beloved. By the early Christian Church the lover represented Christ, and the beloved was the soul of man.

So′lon (638?–558? B. C.), one of the seven wise men of Greece, and the great legislator of Athens. One of his earliest public actions was

his instigation of the Athenians to the recovery of Salamis, after which he was chosen chief archon (594 B. C.) and was invested with unlimited powers. He established a new constitution, divided the citizens according to their wealth and added to the powers of the popular assembly. He made many laws relating to trade and commerce, and he either entirely abrogated all debts or so reduced them that they were not burdensome to the debtors, abolishing the law which gave a creditor power to reduce his debtor to slavery. When he had completed his laws he bound the Athenians by oath not to make any changes in his code for ten years. He then left the country, to avoid being obliged to make any alteration in them, and visited Egypt, Cyprus and other places. Returning after an absence of ten years, he found the state torn by the old party hate; but all parties agreed to submit their demands to his decision. It soon became evident, however, that Pisistratus would succeed in gaining the chief power, and Solon left Athens. Though Athens now fell under the despotic rule of Pisistratus, much of Solon's legislation remained effective. See GREECE, subhead *History*; ATHENS, subhead *History*.

Solstice, *sol′stis*, in astronomy, the point in the ecliptic at the greatest distance from the equator, at which the sun appears to stop or cease to recede from the equator, either north in summer or south in winter. There are two solstices—the summer solstice, the first degree of Cancer, which the sun reaches about the 21st of June, and the winter solstice, the first degree of Capricorn, where the sun is about the 22d of December. The time at which the sun is at either of these points also receives the same name.

Solu′tion, the transformation of matter from either the solid or the gaseous state to the liquid state, by means of a liquid called the *solvent*, or *menstruum*. When a liquid adheres to a solid with sufficient force to overcome its cohesion, the solid is said to undergo solution, or to become dissolved. Thus, sugar or salt may be brought into solution by water; camphor or resin, by spirit of wine; silver or lead, by mercury. Solution is facilitated by increasing the extent of the surface exposed to the solvent, which may be most easily done by reducing it to powder. Heat, by diminishing cohesion, usually favors solution; but there are exceptions to this rule, as water just above the freezing point will dissolve nearly twice as much lime as it dissolves at the boiling point. If a solid body be introduced in successive small portions into a definite quantity of a liquid capable of dissolving it, the first portions disappear most rapidly, and each succeeding portion dissolves less rapidly than its predecessor, until solution altogether ceases. In such cases the forces of adhesion and cohesion balance each other, and the liquid is said to be *saturated*.

Sol'way Firth, *furth,* an arm of the Irish Sea, forming a part of the boundary between England and Scotland, and extending inland in a northeastern direction for about 35 miles. Its width at the entrance is about 23 miles. The rivers flowing into it are the Esk, the Derwent, the Dee, the Nith and the Annan. A large portion of the Solway is left dry at ebb-tide. It abounds in fish and has several valuable salmon fisheries.

Sol'yman II or **Suleiman II,** *soo'lay mahn,* surnamed *the Magnificent* (about 1495–1566), sultan of the Turkish Empire, the son of Selim I, whom he succeeded in 1520. Having put down a revolt which occurred in Syria and Egypt and having concluded an armistice with Persia, he besieged and took Belgrade in 1521. The next year he captured the island of Rhodes, which had been in the possession of the Knights of Saint John for over two hundred years. Turning his arms against Hungary, he won the Battle of Mohacs and captured Buda and Pesth. In 1529 he advanced on Vienna, but was forced to raise the siege, with great loss. His armies next gained considerable territories from Persia. In 1541 he overran a great part of Hungary, but an armistice was concluded in 1547. Late in his reign he attempted the capture of Malta and began another war against Hungary, during which he died.

Somaliland, *so mah'le land,* or **Somali,** a territory in eastern Africa, bordering on the Gulf of Aden and the Indian Ocean and extending from the foot of the Red Sea to Cape Guardafui, and southward as far as the Juba River. The breadth varies from 50 to 180 miles. Most of the land is high, consisting of plateaus bordered with high mountain ranges and separated by broad desert tracts or fertile plains. The climate is healthful, except along the coast. The soil is fertile, and wherever tilled it produces good crops. Politically this region is divided among France, Great Britain and Italy, the northern portion, at the head of the Gulf of Aden, being known as *Somali Coast Protectorate* and belonging to France; the central portion, bordering on the south shore of the gulf, being known as *British Somaliland,* and the larger portion, bordering on the Indian Ocean, as *Italian So-*

maliland. See AFRICA, subhead *Political Divisions.*

Somers, *sum'urz,* **Islands.** See BERMUDA ISLANDS.

Somersworth, *sum'urz wurth,* N. H., a city in Strafford co., 5 mi. n. of Dover, on the Salmon River and on the Boston & Maine railroad. It has large cotton and woolen mills and boot, shoe and other factories. There is a public library, and the waterworks system is owned and operated by the city. The place was settled in 1729, and the city was chartered in 1893. Population in 1910, 6704.

Somerville, *sum'ur vil,* MASS., a city in Middlesex co., adjoining Boston, Chelsea and Cambridge, on the Mystic River and on the Boston & Albany and the Boston & Maine railroads. The city is built on seven hills and covers an area of about four and one-fourth square miles. It is primarily a residence place and contains many fine homes. There are fine public parks and a number of places of considerable historical interest. In Powder House Park is an old building, constructed about 1703 and used for a long time as a powder house. Central Hill was occupied by a redoubt during the siege of Boston, and on Prospect Hill Washington is supposed to have first unfurled the American flag. The city has more than thirty churches, a large public library, two high schools, an industrial school for boys and business schools. The Somerville Hospital is partly supported by the city, and there are homes for the aged, a day nursery and an almshouse. Other prominent buildings are the city hall and the state armory.

There are various manufacturing establishments, of which the packing houses and the boiler tube works are some of the most important. Other products are liquors, desks, picture frames and jewelry. The place was settled about 1630, was incorporated as a town in 1842 and was chartered as a city in 1872. Population in 1910, 77,236. Consult Samuels's *Somerville, Past and Present.*

Somerville, MARY (1780–1872), a Scotch writer on mathematics and the physical sciences. At the request of Lord Brougham, and with the object of popularizing Laplace's *Mécanique Céleste* for the Society for the Diffusion of Useful Knowledge, she prepared her first work, *Mechanism of the Heavens.* It proved above the class for whom it was intended, and it was published independently in 1831. This work brought her many honors, including honorary membership of the Royal Astronomical and other learned societies, and a pension from the government. She wrote a preface to this work on the relation of the sciences, which was afterward expanded into a separate work, *The Connection of the Physical Sciences*. In 1848 she published a *Physical Geography*.

Somme, *sohm*, a river of France. It rises in the Department of Aisne and flows southwest into the English Channel, about 15 mi. beyond Abbeville. Its length is 140 miles. It is canalized through a part of its course and is connected by canal with the Oise and the Scheldt.

Somnam'bulis'm or **Sleepwalking**, a peculiar activity of the mental functions during sleep, in which the subject moves and acts as one awake, though without consciousness. In such a state the organs of sense are inactive, and the intellectual powers are blunted. Walking in sleep is the most noticeable, but not the most marvelous, characteristic of somnambulism. The somnambulist may perform many voluntary actions, which show that to all appearance he is conscious of the things that surround him. He may get out of bed, dress himself, go out of doors and walk, frequently over very dangerous places, in perfect safety; in fact, he may expose himself without fear to perils which in his waking moments would seem insurmountable. On waking in the morning he is either utterly unconscious of having stirred in the night or remembers it as a mere dream. In some cases somnambulists have held intelligent conversations. Sensitive and excitable people are subject to the complaint, which often appears in conjunction with other nervous affections and appears to be hereditary. The condition incited by hypnotism is an artificial somnambulism. See HYPNOTISM.

Som'nus (Latin, "sleep"), in ancient mythology, the god of sleep, son of Nox (night) and twin brother of Mors (death). He was supposed to bring sleep both to gods and men

Son'net, a species of poetical composition, consisting of fourteen rhymed verses, arranged according to rule. It is of Italian origin and consists of two stanzas of four verses each, called the *octave,* and two of three each, called the *sestet.* The octave of the proper sonnet consists of two quatrains, the rhymes of which are restricted to two—one for the first, fourth, fifth and eighth lines; the other for the second, third, sixth and seventh. In the sestet, which is commonly made up of two tercets, there may be either two or three rhymes, variously distributed. The form described above is the Petrachan, or Italian, form, but the verses may also be arranged in the

Shakespearean form, of three quatrains of alternate lines, finished with a couplet, or in the irregular form practiced by Coleridge and others.

The sonnet generally consists of one principal idea, elaborated. The lightness and richness of the Italian, Spanish and Portuguese languages enable their poets to express every feeling or fancy in the sonnet; but in English it has been found most suitable to grave, dignified and contemplative subjects. Among the most successful writers of English sonnets are Shakespeare, Milton, Wordsworth, Mrs. Browning and Rossetti. Mrs. Browning's *Sonnets from the Portuguese* are the most celebrated group of poems of this kind in our literature, and as examples of the most famous single sonnets from other authors may be mentioned Milton's *On His Own Blindness*; Wordsworth's *On Milton*; Shakespeare's "Let me not to the marriage of true minds"; Keats's *On Looking into Chapman's Homer*; Shelley's *Ozymandias*. Milton's *On His Own Blindness* is here given complete:

When I consider how my light is spent
  Ere half my days, in this dark world and wide,
  And that one talent which is death to hide
Lodged with me useless, though my soul more bent
To serve therewith my Maker, and present
  My true account, lest he returning, chide;
  "Doth God exact day-labor, light denied?"
I fondly ask. But Patience, to prevent
That murmur, soon replies, "God doth not need
Either man's work, or his own gifts. Who best
  Bear his mild yoke, they serve him best. His state
Is kingly; thousands at his bidding speed,
  And post o'er land and ocean without rest;
  They also serve who only stand and wait."

Sons of Liberty, in American history, the name given to a society during the pre-Revolutionary period, organized for the purpose of opposing the policy of the British ministry. It was at first secret in its methods, but it afterward adopted the name by which it is known, suggested to it by a speech in behalf of the Americans by Colonel Isaac Barré in Parliament. The association had no central headquarters, but performed its most notable service in New York. Until the Revolution it took the lead in opposing by violence and active agitation all measures instituted by the British government for the more strict control of the colonies.

Sons of Vet'erans, a patriotic society organized at Philadelphia in 1879, for a purpose similar to that of the Grand Army of the Republic. Membership is limited to lineal male descendants, over eighteen years of age, of honorably discharged soldiers, sailors or marines, who served in the Union army during the Civil War. The society is divided into 29 state *divisions*, including about 2000 local *camps*, with a membership of more than 100,000.

Sonsonate, *sohn'so nah'tay,* a city of Salvador, Central America, situated 50 mi. w. by s. of the city of San Salvador, in a rich agricultural district. It has railway connection with Acajutla. The industries include shell work and a trade in sugar. Population in 1911, 18,000.

Soot, a black substance formed by combustion, which rises in fine particles and adheres to the sides of the chimney or pipe conveying the smoke. The soot of coal and that of wood differ very materially in their composition, the former containing more carbonaceous matter than the latter. Coal soot contains substances usually derived from animal matter, and it has been used for the preparation of the carbonate of ammonia. Its chief basis is charcoal, in a state in which it is rendered soluble by the action of oxygen and moisture; and hence, combined with the action of the ammoniacal salts, it is used as a fertilizer and acts very powerfully.

Sophia, *so'je ah,* CHURCH OF SAINT, in Constantinople, the most celebrated ecclesiastical edifice of the Greek Church, now used as a mosque. It was built by Emperor Justinian and was dedicated in 558. It is in the Byzantine style of architecture, has a fine dome, 184 feet high and 105 feet in diameter, and is richly decorated in the interior, the vaults and arches being covered with superb mosaics on a gold ground. The exterior of the church is plain and unimposing.

Sophists, *sof'ists,* the name of a class of wandering teachers who, in the latter part of the fifth century B. C., represented the disorganized schools of Greek philosophy. Their teaching included all branches of learning, but with few exceptions they themselves did not originate positive doctrines. Their attitude was critical and sometimes skeptical, and they sought to overthrow existing institutions and systems of thought. Starting with the assumption that all men have equal rights, they argued that government and laws are man-made institutions, which have been established in the interests of those making them; therefore, obedience to law is determined by the interests of the individual and is not a moral obligation. This theory made the individual a law unto himself in all his acts. In regard to man's relation to society, this theory exerted at the time considerable influence and found expression in the political and social disorganization that characterized the period. Among the most

celebrated of the Sophists were Protagoras, Gorgias, Thrasymachus and Hippias.

Sophocles, *sof'o kleez,* (about 496–406 B. C.), the second, in order of time, of the three great Greek tragic dramatists, born at Colonus, a village in the immediate vicinity of Athens. The rank of his family is not known, but he received an education equal to that enjoyed by the sons of the best Athenian families. Sophocles first appeared as a dramatist in 468 B. C., when he took the first prize, in competition with Aeschylus. Aeschylus retired to Sicily, and Sophocles accordingly held all but undisputed supremacy until the appearance of Euripides, who took the first prize in 441. Sophocles, however, excelled both his rivals in the number of his triumphs. He took the first prize about twenty-four times, the second frequently, the third never. In 440 B. C. he was chosen one of ten generals in the war against the aristocrats of Samos.

One hundred thirty plays in all are ascribed to Sophocles, of which seventeen are not considered authentic. Eighty-one of his dramas, including the seven now extant, were brought out after he had attained the age of fifty-five. The chronological order of the existing plays is given as follows: *Antigone, Electra, Trachiniae, Oedipus Tyrannus, Ajax, Philoctetes* and *Oedipus at Colonus.* Sophocles brought the Greek drama to the highest point of perfection of which that form of art is susceptible. His subjects are human, while those of Aeschylus are heroic, and in his management he shows himself a perfect master of human passions. The tendency of his plays is ethical, and he subordinates the display of passions to an end. He also introduced scenic illustration and a third actor. No tragic poet in ancient or modern days has written with more elevation and purity of style, and his versification stands alone in dignity and elegance.

Soprano, *so prah'no.* See MUSIC.

Sorata, *so rah'ta,* or **Illampu,** *il yahm'poo,* one of the highest peaks of the Andes, situated in Bolivia, on the east side of Lake Titicaca. It rises in two summits, whose respective heights are 21,490 and 21,275 feet. The mountain is an extinct volcano.

Sorbonne, *sor bohn',* an institution of learning, located in the Latin Quarter in Paris. It was established in the thirteenth century by Robert de Sorbon. The original school was intended for the instruction of priests who would pledge themselves to teach without pay. In its early history it became one of the most important theological schools of Europe, and it exercised a decided influence on French history, its faculty being called on constantly to pronounce opinions on the most important questions. The Sorbonne was given to the city of Paris during the nineteenth century, and a magnificent new building was erected. The present organization maintains a department of theology and faculties of literature and science.

Sorghum, *sor' gum,* a genus of grasses, some species of which are known by the general name of millet. In the United States one species, with large succulent stems, is cultivated for its sap, from which a molasses popularly known as sorghum is made.

Sor'rel, the name of a genus of plants of the buckwheat family, common in Europe and America. The green foliage of all the species has a bitter taste and is used for medicinal purposes and in soup and salads. The plant grows about a foot high and has small red flowers. It is usually found in dry soil and in meadows and pastures, and some species, such as the *field sorrel* and the *sheep sorrel,* are very troublesome in fields. It is eradicated by means of cultivation and by the use of lime and other fertilizers in the soil. Other varieties of this plant are called *red sorrel, sour weed* and *horse sorrel.*

Sorrel Tree, a tree which inhabits the range of the Alleghanies from Virginia to Georgia. The leaves are long, finely toothed and strongly acid in taste and are often used in making a cooling drink for invalids. The flowers are small, white and egg-shaped. The wood is hard and fine grained and is used in making various articles, as tool handles.

Sothern, *suth'urn,* EDWARD H. (1859-   ), an American actor, born in London. His father was a famous actor, and young Sothern made his first appearance on the stage in small parts in his father's company, but met with no notable success until 1885, when he appeared in *One of Our Girls. The Highest Bidder,* two years later, was also very successful, and from that time Sothern rose steadily in popularity, as star in his own company. Particularly popular were his presentations of *A Prisoner of Zenda* and *Under the Red Robe.* In 1900 he assumed his first tragic rôle, as Hamlet, and in later years, with Julia Marlowe, he made tours of the United States, presenting various Shakespearean plays, among them *Romeo and Juliet* and *Much Ado About Nothing.* He married Miss Marlowe, 1911.

Soul, *sole,* the spiritual part in man, which distinguishes him from the brutes; the immaterial part of man, as opposed to his body. Soul is sometimes used as synonymous with *mind,* but generally it is used in a wider sense, as being a whole to which belong the faculties that make the mind. *Soul* and *spirit* are more nearly synonymous, but each is used in connections in which it would be improper to use the other. Nearly all philosophies agree in regarding the soul as that part of man which enables him to think and reason and which renders him a subject of moral government; but they differ when it comes to a question of origin and detail.

Soult, *soolt,* NICOLAS JEAN DE DIEU (1769-1851), duke of Dalmatia and marshal of France, born of humble parentage in the Department of Tarn. He joined the army as a common soldier. Raised from the ranks, he became successively lieutenant and captain in his regiment. In 1803 he had the command of one of the camps of the army intended for use against England, and he was one of the marshals created immediately after the formation of the Empire in 1804. In the war against Austria in 1805, he distinguished himself at Ulm and Austerlitz, and he acquired new fame in the Prussian campaign. He was given a command in Spain, but in 1813 he was recalled, in consequence of Napoleon's disasters, to take the command of the fourth corps of the grand army, and he commanded the infantry of the guard at Lützen. On the news of Wellington's victory at Vittoria, he was sent back to reorganize the French force in Spain, and he did his utmost to oppose Wellington's triumphant career, till Napoleon's abdication. After the restoration he gave in his adhesion to Louis XVIII, who made him minister of war. On Napoleon's return he joined him, and although he was banished for this, he was later recalled, and under Louis Philippe he held several offices. In 1847 he was made marshal general of France.

Sound, that which a person hears; a perception brought to the brain through the organs of hearing. It is produced by vibrations of the sounding body. The reeds of an organ, the strings of a violin, the wires of a piano, the head of a drum and all other sound-producing bodies vibrate in producing sound.

HOW SOUND TRAVELS. The vibrations of the sounding body start similar vibrations in the body through which the sound travels. When a bell is rung, the vibrations of the bell start vibrations in the atmosphere, which move in every direction from the bell and carry the sound. Sound will travel through any elastic substance, but it will not travel through a vacuum.

Sound travels through air, at a temperature of 32° F., at the rate of 1090 feet per second, and this velocity increases 1.1 feet for every additional degree in temperature; at 60° the velocity is 1120 feet. Sound travels through hydrogen about four times as fast as through the air, and it moves through water at about 4700 feet per second; through copper, its velocity is a little over eleven times as great as through the air, and through steel it is about fifteen times as great. By noticing a flash of lightning and counting the number of seconds between it and the report of the thunder, the distance of the cloud can be determined. The sound requires five seconds to traverse a mile, so the distance in miles is one-fifth the number of seconds.

LOUDNESS OF SOUND. The loudness of sound depends upon the size of the vibrations; the greater the vibration, the louder the sound. Large bodies in vibration produce louder sounds than small ones. The intensity decreases in proportion as the square of the distance from the sounding body increases. When the distance from a sounding body is doubled, the sound is reduced to one-fourth. Speaking tubes confine the sound within narrow limits, so that the sound waves are conveyed much farther than they would be in the open air.

REFLECTION OF SOUND. When sound waves strike a hard surface, they are thrown back, or reflected, in the same way as are rays of light from a mirror. Curved walls, like the domes of buildings and the rounded ceilings and ends of audience rooms, reflect sound waves to a common point, and a person standing at this point can often hear a whisper that is uttered in some other part of the room. For this reason the name *whispering galleries* has sometimes been applied to such places. Ear trumpets are simply instruments for gathering waves of sound and reflecting them to a common point, and they are equivalent to an increase in the size of the ear. By their means sounds can be heard that could not otherwise be perceived.

An echo is produced when the reflecting surface is so far away that the sound which it throws back is distinct from the original sound. Remarkable echoes occur among mountains, where the ranges upon both sides of the valley are in such position that the sound is reflected back and forth several times. Audience rooms that are too large or are not well proportioned are often difficult to speak in, because of the echoes.

NOISE AND MUSIC. The difference between noise and music is the difference between regular and irregular vibrations. Musical tones are produced by regular vibrations, and these must not fall below sixteen per second. The pitch of a tone depends upon the number of vibrations per second. These numbers arranged in certain order constitute the musical scale, as follows, the C which has 256 vibrations being the one which is known as middle C:

C	D	E	F	G	A	B	C
256	288	320	341	384	427	480	512
Do	Re	Mi	Fa	Sol	La	Ti	Do

The difference in pitch produced by doubling the number of vibrations is called an *octave*. The quality of a musical tone depends upon the character of the sounding medium, which affects the nature of the vibrations. Hence, while several musical tones may have the same pitch, each may be distinguished from the others by its peculiar quality. See MUSIC.

Sounding, the operation of finding the depth of water and the quality of the bottom, especially by means of a plummet sunk from a ship. In navigation two plummets are used, one called the *hand lead*, weighing about 8 or 9 pounds, and the other, the *deep-sea lead*, weighing from 25 to 30 pounds. The former is used in shallow waters, and the latter is used at a distance from shore. The nature of the bottom is commonly ascertained by using a piece of tallow, stuck upon the base of the deep-sea lead. The scientific investigation of the ocean and its bottom has rendered more perfect sounding apparatus necessary, and it has led to the invention of various successful contrivances for this purpose.

Sousa, *soo'za,* JOHN PHILIP (1854–   ), an American composer and band leader, born at Washington, D. C. He conducted the Marine Band at Washington at two different times, but in 1892 he formed the organization identified with his name, which has met with great success throughout the world. As a composer of military marches he has won great fame. Among the best are *The Liberty Bell, The High School Cadets, Stars and Stripes Forever* and *The Diplomat.* He is the author of several light operas, notably *El Capitan, The Bride Elect, The Charlatan* and *The Free Lance.*

South Africa, UNION OF, a British colony established May 31, 1910, by the legislative union of the Cape of Good Hope, Natal, Orange Free State and the Transvaal. The executive is the governor-general, who is assisted by a council of ministers. Laws are passed by Parliament, composed of a senate and a house of assembly. Parliament must meet every year.

The Senate has 40 members, 8 elected by each of the provinces and 8 appointed by the governor-general. The assembly has 121 members, the number from each province being determined by its proportion of population. Each province has an administrator appointed by the governor-general for five years, and a council elected for three years. The governor-general resides at Pretoria, and the legislature meets at Cape Town.

South African Republic. See TRANSVAAL.

South African War (1899–1902), between Great Britain, on the one hand, and the South African Republic and the Orange Free State, on the other. In 1885 gold was discovered in the Witwatersrand, and the discovery drew an increasing number of foreigners to the Transvaal each year. By 1899 the Uitlanders, as the Boers called the foreigners, outnumbered the original settlers by seven to three. Most of these foreigners were British subjects, and the Boers suspected them of hating the Dutch. Under the leadership of their president, Paul Kruger, the Boers planned from the beginning of this migration to keep the Uitlanders from gaining control of the government. The naturalization laws, which before 1885 had been liberal, were restricted, until in 1887 the term of residence before a foreigner could be naturalized was fixed at fifteen years. The foreigners of course claimed that they were entitled to a voice in the government and that the restrictions imposed upon them were unjust. Jameson's Raid (See JAMESON, LEANDER STARR) in 1896 brought matters to a crisis, and although the British government had Jameson punished, the Boers used the incident as an excuse for further restrictions on the Uitlanders. These foreign inhabitants petitioned Great Britain, but the negotiations which the British government attempted to make with the Boers failed in the end, and it became apparent that the question could not be decided peacefully. War was declared in October, 1899, the Orange Free State joining cause with the South African Republic.

When hostilities began, the British had about twelve thousand men in Natal, besides small forces at other points. At the outset the Boers seemed to have a decided advantage. British forces were shut up in Ladysmith, Mafeking and Kimberley, and the other troops were unable by their successes in the field to offset these reverses. A large addition was at once voted to the English army in South Africa, and Sir Redvers Buller, on his arrival in Africa with reënforcements, at once moved to the relief of Ladysmith. In December Roberts and Kitchener were sent out, and on their arrival a new campaign was mapped out. The British cavalry force was increased, and thus one of the early drawbacks of the British was remedied. By the last of February, 1900, the sieges of Kimberley and Ladysmith had been raised, the relief of the latter place giving rise to much of the hardest fighting of the war. From this time on, fortune was with the British. In March, Bloemfontein was taken, and while there Roberts proclaimed the Orange Free State British territory, under the name of the Orange River Colony. The British force then moved toward Pretoria, taking, on the way, Kroonstadt and Johannesburg, and in June Pretoria was occupied. President Kruger fled at the occupation of Pretoria (See KRUGER, STEPHANUS JOHANNES PAUL). The three months which followed the capture of Pretoria were devoted by the British to an attempt to capture all the Boer forces in the neighborhood, and by the first of August it seemed as if all organized warfare had ceased. Roberts therefore issued a proclamation in September, 1900, declaring the South African Republic British territory under the name of the Transvaal Colony. In spite of their reverses in fortune, however, the Boers refused to make peace, and a constant guerrilla warfare was carried on under De Wet and Botha. Kitchener, who had been left in command on Roberts's return to England, gained for himself much unpopularity by gathering into large camps, called concentration camps, the Boer women and children and compelling them to live under conditions which caused much sickness and death.

By May, 1902, the Boers had been forced to the point where they accepted the terms of peace on which England insisted. All Boers were obliged to lay down their arms and acknowledge themselves subjects of Edward VII, and in return a promise was made that no one should be considered subject to any proceeding for acts in connection with the war. Provision was also made for the teaching of the Dutch language in the public schools in all cases where it was desired by the parents, and it was provided that the military administration of the two colonies should give place as soon as possible to a civil government. See TRANSVAAL.

South Amboy', N. J., a borough in Middlesex co., on Raritan Bay, at the mouth of the

Raritan River, opposite Perth Amboy, and on the Pennsylvania, the Central of New Jersey and other railroads. The river here is crossed by a long drawbridge. The surrounding region contains large quantities of sand and clay, and the city has manufactures of pottery, terra cotta, asphaltum and brick. Large quantities of coal are shipped by the Pennsylvania railroad through this port. The borough was incorporated in 1898. Population in 1910, 7007.

South Amer'ica, the fourth largest grand division, situated between 12° 45′ north latitude and 55° 30′ south latitude, and between 35° and 81° 30′ west longitude. Its greatest length from north to south is about 4800 mi., and from east to west it is about 3300 mi. The area is 7,700,000 sq. mi. South America is a large peninsula, joined to North America by the narrow isthmus of Panama, and it is bounded on the n. by the Caribbean Sea and the Atlantic Ocean, on the e. by the Atlantic Ocean and on the w. by the Pacific Ocean. With the exception of the southern portion of the western coast, which is bordered by islands and indented by numerous fjords, the coast line is remarkably regular. The large indentations are, on the north, the Gulf of Darien; on the northeast, the mouth of the Amazon, and on the southeast, All Saints Bay, the Bay of Rio de Janeiro, the mouth of the Rio de la Plata, Bahia Blanca, Gulf of San Mantias and Gulf of Saint George. There are few islands belonging to the continent. Those worthy of mention are Trinidad, off the northern coast, the Falkland Islands, east of the southern extremity of the continent, and the Galapagos, on the equator, west of Ecuador.

SURFACE AND DRAINAGE. There are three systems of mountains in South America, the greatest of which are the Andes, on the Pacific coast, stretching in a continuous chain for over 4000 miles. Next to the Himalayas this is the highest mountain range in the world, the highest point being 25,000 feet (See ANDES). The second system is that of the highlands of Guiana, which lie north of the Amazon valley. Here are several irregular groups of mountains, about 2000 feet high, which separate the plains of the Orinoco from those of the Rio Negro and the Amazon. The Brazilian highland, the third system, is very broad and is crossed by low ranges of mountains. Its average height is less than half that of the Andes. From the configuration of its surface, the continent may be divided into five physical regions: (1) The low country skirting the shores of the Pacific Ocean,

from 50 to 150 miles in breadth, and 4000 miles in length; the two extremities of this territory are fertile, the middle is a sandy desert. (2) The basin of the Orinoco, a country consisting of extensive plains, or steppes, called *llanos*, either destitute of wood or merely dotted with trees, but covered with a very tall herbage during a part of the year; during the dry season the heat is intense here, and the parched soil opens into long fissures, in which lizards and serpents lie in a state of torpor. (3) The basin of the Amazon, a vast plain, embracing a surface of more than 2,000,000 square miles, possessing a rich soil and humid climate; it is covered almost everywhere with dense forests, which harbor innumerable tribes of wild animals and are thinly inhabited by savages, who live by hunting and fishing. (4) The great southern plain, watered by the Plata and the numerous streams descending from the eastern summits of the Andes; open steppes, which are here called *pampas*, occupy the greater portion of this region, which is dry, and in some parts barren, but in general is covered with a strong growth of weeds and tall grass, which feed large herds of horses and cattle and afford shelter to a few wild animals. (5) The country of Brazil, eastward of the Paraná and the Uruguay, presenting alternate ridges and valleys, thickly covered with wood on the side next the Atlantic, and opening into steppes, or pastures, in the interior.

The three important river systems of South America are the Amazon, the Orinoco and the Plata, the Amazon being the largest river on the globe. All of these rivers flow into the Atlantic. The Amazon rises in the Andes and is 4000 miles long. It is navigable for about 2300 miles (See AMAZON). The Orinoco rises in the Parine Mountains and is 1400 miles long. The Orinoco and the Amazon systems are connected by a small river called the Cassiquiare. The Plata is formed by the confluence of the Paraná and the Uruguay rivers and is 185 miles long; at its mouth it is about 125 miles wide. The principal smaller rivers are the San Francisco, the Rio Negro, the Colorado and the Essequibo. The largest lake is Titicaca, in the Andes, covering an area of about 4000 square miles and over 12,000 feet above the level of the sea. There are several small lakes in the mountain regions, but none is of special importance. For a detailed description, see subhead *Surface and Drainage*, in the articles treating of the different South American countries.

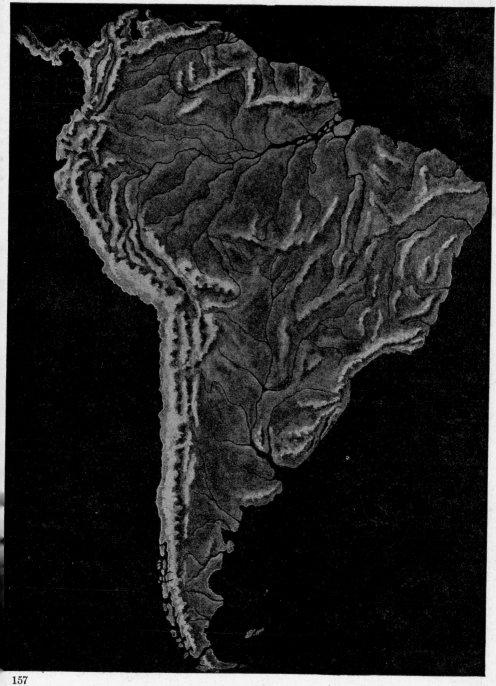

RELIEF MAP OF SOUTH AMERICA

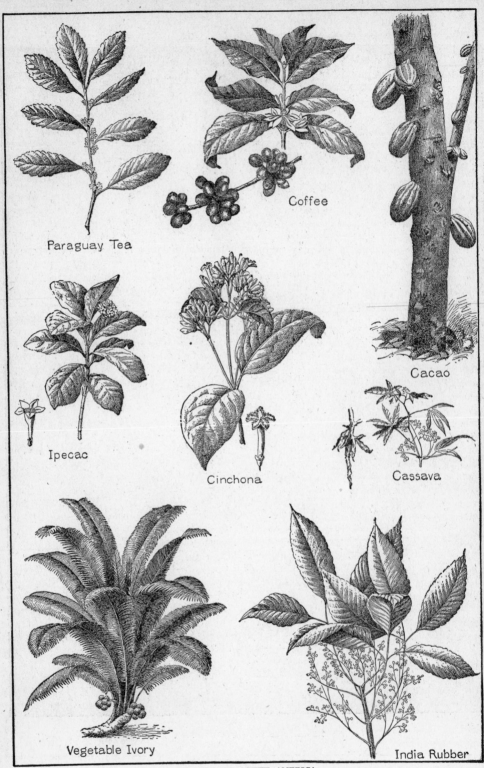

Paraguay Tea

Coffee

Cacao

Ipecac

Cinchona

Cassava

Vegetable Ivory

India Rubber

PLANTS OF SOUTH AMERICA

MINERAL RESOURCES. The mineral wealth of South America consists in gold, silver, copper, mercury, diamonds and other valuable minerals. The desert coast of Chile is rich in guano, nitre, valuable iodine compounds and borax. Chile is also rich in copper and silver, and the coal mines are being developed rapidly and give promise of great wealth. There are celebrated silver mines in Bolivia and considerable supplies of gold in Venezuela and Guiana. Some rich gold mines have been discovered in the southern part of Argentina. Brazil has extensive deposits of coal and iron, and previous to the discovery of the diamond field in South Africa it was the chief source from which diamonds were obtained. Emeralds are also found in Venezuela.

CLIMATE. Considering its extent in latitude, South America has a remarkably equable climate. The extremes of heat and cold which characterize North America are not found here. The northern portion of the continent, although lying within the tropical regions, has the intense heat greatly modified by its elevations, and some of the highest peaks in the Andes, even under the equator, contain snow throughout the year. The temperature during midwinter averages about 80° in the north and 35° in the south. The lowlands along the Orinoco, the Amazon and the coast of Brazil have a hot climate. The southern portion of the continent is free from sudden changes or extremes, because of the nearness of the oceans and the influence of the mountains along the western coast. The rainfall is heaviest in the Amazon basin and diminishes toward the south, until the arid region, constituting a large part of Argentina and Patagonia, is reached. The southern portion has a damp climate, characteristic of the cool temperate regions. The seasons are just the opposite of what they are in the northern hemisphere, the summer occurring in December, January and February, and the winter in June, July and August.

VEGETATION. The vegetable kingdom in South America has a magnificent development, particularly in the vast tropical territory east of the Andes, the basins of the Amazon, the Orinoco and their tributaries, where the genera and species are very abundant, the forests large and the forms gigantic. Besides palms, there are dye-woods of all sorts, cedar, mahogany and ebony; farther south are the araucarias of Chile and the beech forests of Argentina. There are numerous kinds of fruit trees, the fruits of which are usually very large and covered with extremely thick shells. Among these may be mentioned the cannon-ball tree and the Brazil nut tree. Ferns and water lilies are also numerously represented, and splendid specimens of both are found. The jungle, or undergrowth, in the forests is impenetrable in many places. Cinchona is found on the higher ground within the tropics. A holly is grown, the leaves of which are soaked in water and produce a beverage called *Paraguay tea*. During the rainy seasons the pampas and llanos are covered with a thick growth of grass and other vegetation.

ANIMAL LIFE. The zoölogy of South America is extensive and peculiar, embracing a fourth of all the known mammals, among which, however, are almost none of the wild animals so abundant in Africa and Asia. The most powerful of the carnivora is the jaguar, which is indeed the only formidable beast of prey in the whole continent. Of the other animals may be mentioned tapirs, peccaries, sloths, ant-eaters, armadilloes, llamas, chinchillas and monkeys. The armadillo is said to be the only wild animal that increases with the increase of population. Many of the species are peculiar to South America and are not found elsewhere. Among birds the most notable are various parrots, humming birds, flamingoes, toucans and aracaris. Chief among the reptiles are alligators, boas, turtles and rattlesnakes. In the tropical regions the insects are very numerous, including many species of butterflies, of large size and gorgeous hues. The beetle family is also well represented, some species being much larger than those found in other regions.

INHABITANTS. The aborigines of South America are undoubtedly of the same race as those of North America, as there exists a very striking general physical resemblance between the native races throughout the whole of the American continent, from Cape Horn to Bering's Strait (See INDIANS, AMERICAN). They are almost all of a copper color, with long black hair, deep-set black eyes, aquiline nose and often handsome, slender form. In South America these red men are far more numerous than in North America, and though many are half-civilized, a greater number are in a state of barbarism. A considerable portion of the population also consists of persons of Spanish and Portuguese blood, and along with these are a far greater number of mixed Indian and European blood, civilized and forming an important element in the various states of the continent. To these are now being added

Llama

Boa

Condor

Ocelot

Peccary

Great Ant-Eater

Tapir

Rhea

ANIMALS OF SOUTH AMERICA

Pottery

A Native Home

Dagger
and Spear

An Indian
Woman

POPULATION CHART
Native Races; Few White People.
European and American;
Thickly Settled.

An Indian Man

Typical Open-Air Market Place

TYPES OF SOUTH AMERICAN NATIVE CIVILIZATION

considerable numbers of Spanish and Italian immigrants.

POLITICAL DIVISIONS. The political divisions, in their order from north to south, are Panama, Colombia, Venezuela, British Guiana, Dutch Guiana, French Guiana, Brazil, Ecuador, Peru, Paraguay, Uruguay, Argentina, or Argentine Republic, Bolivia and Chile. Each of these is described under its title.

HISTORY. Columbus first touched the continent at the mouth of the Orinoco in 1498. The next navigator to explore this continent was Hojeda, a Spaniard, who followed the coast from near the equator to Venezuela. He was accompanied by Americus Vespucius, who published the first account of the New World (See AMERICUS VESPUCIUS). Spain and Portugal had almost entire control of the continent until the beginning of the nineteenth century. The Spanish colonies declared their independence in 1810, and after a ten years' war a number of republics were established. In 1823 Brazil became independent of Portugal and retained a monarchical form of government which lasted until 1889, when the form of government was changed to a republic. The only foreign possessions on the continent are those of British, French and Dutch Guiana.

Southampton, *suth hamp'ton,* a seaport town of England, situated on a peninsula at the mouth of the Itchen, 18 mi. n. w. of Portland and 79 mi. s. w. of London. The city has a beautiful site and is noted for its picturesqueness. It was formerly a walled town, and some of the wall and several gates still remain. The most important buildings are God's House, a hospital, and the churches of Saint Michael and Holywood. The town is the most important English seaport on the channel. It has an excellent harbor and was formerly an important station for steamers crossing the Atlantic. The manufactures include carpets, machinery and yachts. The city is also a favorite seaside resort. Population in 1911, 119,012.

South Austra'lia, a state of the Commonwealth of Australia, occupying the central portion of the continent and extending from the Great Australian Bight, on the south, to the Timor and Arafura seas, on the north. It is bounded on the e. by Victoria, New South Wales and Queensland and on the w. by Western Australia. Its extreme length from north to south is 1850 mi., and its breadth from east to west varies from 550 to 700 mi. Its area is

903,690 sq. mi., making it second in size of the Australian states.

South Australia occupies the central portion of the great Australian plain, and with the exception of some low mountains in the south whose highest summits, Mount Lofty and Mount Razorback, attain an elevation, respectively, of 2300 and 2800 feet, the country is low and nearly level, rising by a gentle slope to a plateau of 600 to 1000 feet in the interior. The southern part contains a number of shallow lakes, including Eyre, Torrens, Gardiner and Everard. These are partially salt. The Murray River flows through the southeastern part and is the only stream of importance in the state.

The climate is hot, but usually healthful. Along the coasts, both north and south, there is considerable rainfall, on the north coast amounting to 63 inches in the year; but in the interior the rainfall is often not more than 10, and sometimes only 5, inches. For these reasons agriculture is confined chiefly to the southeastern portion of the colony. Agriculture forms the chief industry of the inhabitants. Wheat is the most important crop, followed by barley and oats. Large quantities of oranges, grapes and other fruits are grown, and the manufacture of wine has become an industry of considerable importance. The mineral resources are comparatively unimportant. Gold, silver and copper are found, but copper is the only metal mined to any extent. There are but few manufactures, and these are confined to supplying the local needs.

The executive department consists of a governor and a council of 6 members. The legislature comprises two bodies—the legislative council, of 18 members, and the house of assembly, of 42 members, all elected by popular suffrage, the right to vote being extended to women. The northern part of the state is organized into what is called the *Northern Territory* and is governed by a commissioner appointed by the state. Adelaide is the capital. See AUSTRALIA; AUSTRALIA, COMMONWEALTH OF.

South Bend, IND., the county-seat of Saint Joseph co., 86 mi. e. by s. of Chicago, on the Saint Joseph River and on the Grand Trunk, the Lake Shore & Michigan Southern, the Vandalia and other railroads. The University of Notre Dame and Saint Mary's Academy are located two miles north of the city. Some of the important institutions of South Bend are the Saint Joseph's Academy, the Northern

Indiana Medical and Surgical Institute, two hospitals, more than thirty churches, four national banks and six building and loan associations. Other important structures are the Federal and the county buildings, the city hall, the Y. M. C. A. building and two theaters. The city is in a rich farming region and is the chief industrial center of northern Indiana. The principal manufactures are wagons, plows and other agricultural implements, clover hullers, sewing machines, flour, woolen goods, watches, and concrete blocks. The first white settlement was made by Alexis Coquillard in 1824. The town was incorporated in 1835, and the city was chartered in 1865. Population in 1910, 53,684.

South Beth'lehem, PA., a borough in Northampton co., 40 mi. n. of Philadelphia, on the Lehigh River, opposite Bethlehem, and on the Lehigh Valley, the Philadelphia & Reading, the Central of New Jersey and several electric railways. It has good transportation facilities, is near deposits of coal and iron ore, and contains iron and steel works, machine shops, foundries, zinc and brass works, wood-working establishments and other factories. Lehigh University is located here, and the borough also contains the Bishop Thorp Seminary for girls, the Saint Luke's Hospital, and public and school libraries. Population in 1910, 19,973.

South'bridge, MASS., a town in Worcester co., 20 mi. s. by w. of Worcester, on the Quinebaug River and on the New York, New Haven & Hartford railroad. Some of the prominent buildings are the townhall, the public library and the Y. M. C. A. building. There are manufactures of spectacles, eye glasses, shuttles, knives, cottons and woolens. It was separated from Charlton in 1801 and was incorporated as a town in 1816. Many of the inhabitants are French Canadians. Population in 1910, including two villages, 12,592.

South Car'oli'na, the PALMETTO STATE, one of the South Atlantic states, bounded on the n. and n. e. by North Carolina, on the s. e. by the Atlantic Ocean and on the s. w. and w. by Georgia. In shape the state is almost an isosceles triangle, with the apex pointing southward. The longest meridian and the longest parallel are about 225 miles each, and they intersect near Columbia. The gross area is 30,989 sq. mi. Population in 1910, 1,515,400.

SURFACE AND DRAINAGE. South Carolina has three natural divisions of surface, known respectively as the "low country," the "middle country" and the "upcountry." The first division consists of low lands along the coast, extending in some places a hundred miles inland. Most of this region is but a few feet above sea level, and low islands and salt marshes border the coast. The "middle country" consists of rolling land broken here and there by sandhills. Along the western border of this region is a belt of sandhills partially covered with pine forests and known as the "Pine Barrens." Beyond this the country rises abruptly to the Piedmont plain. The "upcountry" includes the northern and western parts of the state and is rich in minerals. In the northwest the Blue Ridge Mountains rise abruptly to a height of over 2000 feet above the plateau, Mount Pinnacle, the highest peak in the state, having an altitude of 3436 feet.

The drainage is to the southeast. The principal rivers are the Savannah, the Pedee, the Congaree and the Santee. Below the Fall Line these streams are deep and sluggish. At the Fall Line and above they furnish abundant water power and cities with thriving manufacturing industries are found on them.

MINERAL RESOURCES. The mineral resources of South Carolina are extensive and varied. The mineral yielding the greatest income is phosphate rock, which occurs at intervals in a belt that follows the coast and extends from a point near the source of the Wanda River to the mouth of the Broad River. The rock occurs as land rock and river rock. The latter is mined from the beds of streams. Clay products rank next to phosphates in value. Considerable building stone is quarried, and gold is mined in a few localities, the annual output amounting to about $50,000. Kaolin is found in large quantities and there are valuable deposits of iron ore, marble, granite, asbestos, soapstone and mica, with smaller quantities of silver, lead, copper and graphite. The mineral fuels include gas, petroleum and coal. There is an abundance of granite in the Piedmont sandhills, but only a few granite quarries.

CLIMATE. South Carolina has a delightful climate. The winters are short, hardly ever lasting longer than six weeks. The summers, while long, are not hot or enervating, and the nights are always cool. Snow falls only in the mountains. The average annual temperature is 63°; the average rainfall, 52.31 inches.

AGRICULTURE. South Carolina is still an agricultural state. The chief productions are cotton, rice, tobacco, corn and oats. The state is one of the foremost in the production of rice

and is third in the production of cotton. The sea-island cotton is the best in the world and is produced in large quantities in the strip of islands near the coast. Enough corn is raised to supply the local demand. Truck gardening and fruit growing are rapidly developing industries. Watermelons are grown in abundance, peaches are cultivated in the Piedmont section and olives and oranges grow along the coast. Among native fruits are apples, pears, quinces, plums, apricots, almonds and cherries. The hillsides of the Piedmont section are covered with fine vineyards. There are extensive pine and cypress forests in the mountain section and in the low country.

MANUFACTURES. Nearly one-half the annual products of South Carolina now consist of manufactured goods. Cotton manufacturing is by far the most important industry, the state being second, among the southern states, to Georgia in the value of her cotton products. The manufacture of lumber and timber products ranks second. Other industries are the manufacture of fertilizers, of cottonseed oil and of naval stores. There are extensive fisheries at Charleston, Georgetown, Beaufort and Port Royal.

TRANSPORTATION. The Savannah, the Pedee, the Congaree and the Santee are navigable to the Fall Line. The mouths of these rivers form good harbors and there is a good harbor at Charleston. The state is well supplied with railroads, which traverse it from the northeast to the southwest and from the northwest to the southeast. The entire mileage exceeds 3500 miles, and with the exception of the counties along the coast the state is well provided with railroad facilities. Columbia, Sumter and Greenville are the chief railway centers. The lines are practically under the control of three systems, the Atlantic Coast Line, the Seaboard Air Line and the Southern. Charleston has an important foreign trade.

GOVERNMENT. The legislature consists of a senate, containing one senator for each county, and a house of representatives of 124 members, elected on the basis of population. The senators are elected for four years, and the representatives for two years. The sessions are annual and are unlimited. The executive department consists of a governor, a lieutenant governor, a secretary of state, a comptroller-general, an attorney-general, a treasurer, an adjutant and inspector-general and a superintendent of public instruction, each elected for two years; an insurance

commissioner elected by the General Assembly for two years; a commissioner of agriculture, commerce and industries, appointed by the governor for four years, and three railroad commissioners elected by the people for alternate terms of two, three and four years each. The courts comprise a supreme court of one chief justice and three associates, elected by the general assembly for eight years, and a circuit court for each judicial circuit into which the state is divided. The judges for the circuit courts are elected by the legislature for four years.

EDUCATION. Since 1870 marked improvement has been made in the school system. Before the Civil War there were free common schools, but they were supported mainly by private funds. In 1868 a public school system was provided for by the state. Separate schools are maintained for the white and colored races. The South Carolina Historical Society, founded at Charleston in 1855, has a valuable library and some important manuscripts. There are several denominational colleges and academies and a state college at Columbia.

CITIES. The principal cities are Columbia, the capital; Charleston, Greenville, Spartanburg, Anderson, Rock Hill and Sumter, each of which is described under its title.

HISTORY. In 1562 French Huguenots settled at Port Royal, S. C., but the colony was dispersed by the Spaniards, and settlement was not again attempted in the territory for nearly one hundred years. In 1663 it was granted by the king of England to eight proprietors, and the first permanent settlement was made on the Ashley River, but it was later removed to Charleston. In 1729 the proprietors of the Carolinas, which had been governed together (See NORTH CAROLINA), sold their interest to the Crown, and the region was divided into two separate royal provinces. During the eighteenth century, South Carolina maintained a semi-independence of the Crown and was aggressively patriotic during the pre-Revolutionary struggle, being the first state to form an independent constitution (May, 1776). Many of the most important battles of the war occurred within its borders, and it also furnished many famous commanders, among whom were Thomas Sumter and Francis Marion. The Federal Constitution was ratified after somewhat bitter discussion, in May, 1788.

South Carolina was always strongly Anti-Federalist in sentiment and came into serious collision with the national government at the passage of the

Clay tariff act in 1832, secession being averted only by compromise. It was the first to secede (December 20, 1860), and the first battle of the war was fought at Fort Sumter in the following April. Though the voting population of the state was but 47,000, it furnished 60,000 men to the Confederate army, of whom one-fifth were killed. It refused to ratify the Fourteenth Amendment, but adopted a constitution allowing negro suffrage, in 1868, and was readmitted to the Union. It suffered especially under the carpetbag régime, the state debt being increased from five to twenty million dollars in five years. Among recent incidents in its history have been the Charleston earthquake, August 31, 1886; the famous storm and tidal wave, 1893, and the South Carolina and West Indian Exposition of 1901 and 1902. It has been consistently Democratic in both state and national politics since 1876. Consult Ransom's *Resources and Industries of South Carolina.*

South Carolina, UNIVERSITY OF, founded as the South Carolina College in 1801 and opened in 1805, was before the War of Secession one of the most advanced colleges in the Union. During the war the college was closed and the buildings were used as a hospital, first by the Confederate and afterwards by the Federal government. Reopened as a university in 1866, it was closed again after a few years in consequence of unsettled political conditions, until 1880, when it was again opened as a college. It was in 1906 reorganized as the University of South Carolina, and has since experienced rapid development. It now includes the schools of art, science, engineering and law, a school for teachers and a graduate school, with also extended elective courses of study. The faculty numbers about thirty-five, and there are over 400 students. The library includes about 50,000 volumes.

South Carolina Exposition, officially known as the *South Carolina Interstate and West Indian Exposition,* an exhibition of products and industries, opened in Charleston, S. C., Dec. 1, 1901, and closed May 1, 1902. The purposes of the exposition were to show the industrial progress of the South during the century and to demonstrate the great opportunities for future trade with the countries of South America, Central America and the West Indies.

Eleven buildings were erected, and the United States government, many of the states of the Union and several of the republics of South America and the West Indies made exhibits. The attendance was about 675,000.

South Dako'ta, the SUNSHINE STATE, one of the North Central states of the Union, bounded on the n. by North Dakota, on the e. by Minnesota and Iowa on the s. by Nebraska and on the w. by Montana and Wyoming. Its extreme breadth from north to south is 225 miles; its extreme length from east to west is 360 miles, and its area is 77,615 sq. mi., of which 747 sq. mi. are water area. Population in 1910, 583,888.

SURFACE AND DRAINAGE. The surface, for the most part, is a gently undulating prairie, rising from a plain east of the Missouri River to a plateau in the western portion of the state and to the Black Hills in the southwest. Two long and narrow table lands from 1500 to 2000 feet above sea-level, covered in places with boulder-strewn hills, extend nearly north and south; one, the Coteau des Prairies, is near the eastern border, and the other, the Coteau du Missouri, lies just east of the Missouri River. Between these plateaus is the famous basin of the James, or Dakota River. West of the Missouri River the surface is more uneven, and hills and buttes are numerous. All of this region is drained by branches of the Missouri. The Black Hills region comprises an area of about 5000 square miles, extending into Wyoming. The highest point is Harney Peak, 7216 feet in altitude. The central zone is of granite and around it are rows of hills made in the up-turned edges of sedimentary rock layers.

To the southeast of the Black Hills are the famous Bad Lands, though the name is a misleading one, for it is simply the abbreviation for "bad-for-travelling lands," as the early French explorers called them. This region is made up of soft clays, marls, shales and sands, in which the forces of erosion have produced deep, steep-walled gulches and ravines, and numerous hills and buttes. In the broader valleys, where the slope is not so steep, nutritious grasses grow. The North Dakota bad lands extend into the northwestern part of the state. These clays are more highly colored and the scenery is more beautiful than in the southwest.

The state is drained by the Missouri River system. The Missouri itself flows through the state in a southeasterly direction. Parallel to the Missouri and 100 miles east is its tributary the James or Dakota River. The remaining principal tributaries of the Missouri all enter from the west; in order from north to south they are the Little Missouri, the Cannon Ball, the Grand, the Owl or Moreau, the Big Cheyenne and the White. All the rivers flow toward the southeastern corner of the state, and a part of the eastern boundary is formed by the Big Sioux.

CLIMATE. The climate, being continental, is characterized by extremes of heat and cold, but as the air is clear and dry, the heat of summer and the cold of winter are not so uncomfortable as in states to the east where the air is damp. The average annual temperature of the east half of the state is 44.5°; of the west half, 45.6°. The mean annual rainfall for the eastern half of the state is 22.3 inches, and for the western half, 17.3 inches. The unusual amount of sunshine and the invigorating qualities of the air make the climate very healthful.

MINERAL RESOURCES. The Black Hills are said to comprise the richest 100 square miles on earth, yielding about one-twelfth of the gold produced by the United States each year, and ranking South Dakota fourth in the list of gold-producing states. Silver, mica, lead, spodumene, tungsten, tin, copper, iron, manganese, graphite, and other rare and valuable minerals are also found in this region. Here, too, are found valuable limestone, granite, sandstone, marble and gypsum. Excellent building and paving stone, called red quartzite, known also as Sioux Falls jasper, is quarried at Sioux Falls and Dell Rapids along the Big Sioux River. Cement is manufactured from the beds of chalkstone near Yankton and great quantities of excellent brick and fire clays are found.

AGRICULTURE. The rich plains of the eastern half of the state have been famous for years for wheat, corn and other farm products, and the grazing plains of the western portion for live stock. With the advent of railroads into the western plains and the application of improved "dry farming" methods, the entire state is fast becoming agricultural. Irrigation is practiced to some extent in the vicinity of the Black Hills, especially in the valley of the Belle Fourche River.

MANUFACTURES. Agriculture supplies the raw material for the most important manufacturing industries, the making of flour, cheese, butter and condensed milk.

TRANSPORTATION. Railroads reach all parts of the state, and new lines are being built in the newer sections. The important roads are the Chicago Milwaukee & St. Paul; the Chicago & Northwestern; the Chicago, Burlington & Quincy; the Illinois Central; the Great Northern and the Chicago, Rock Island & Pacific.

GOVERNMENT. The legislature consists of a senate of not less than 25 nor more than 45 members, and a house of representatives of not less than 75 nor more than 135 members. The sessions are biennial and are limited to sessions of 60 days, except in cases of impeachment. The executive department consists of a governor, a lieutenant-governor, a secretary of state, an auditor, a treasurer, a superintendent of public instruction, a commissioner of schools and public lands and an attorney-general, all elected for two years. The courts consist of the supreme court, consisting of five judges elected for six years, and state district courts, one in each district, presided over by judges elected for four years. County judges are elected, one in each county, for two years.

EDUCATION. The state educational institutions are controlled by a board of regents consisting of five members appointed by the governor for a term of six years. These comprise the state university, located at Vermilion; the state college of agriculture and mechanic arts, located at Brookings; the state school of mines, located at Rapid City; the northern normal and industrial school, located at Aberdeen; and three state normal schools, located at Madison, Spearfish and Springfield. There are also denominational schools of higher education. The common schools of the state are supported from the interest on the investment of funds derived from the sale of school lands, from a local tax, a general tax and from other sources.

INSTITUTIONS. The leading institutions are the insane asylum at Yankton, school for the feeble-minded at Redfield, school for the deaf at Sioux Falls, institution for the blind at Gary, soldiers' home at Hot Springs, reform school at Plankinton and penitentiary at Sioux Falls.

CITIES. The principal cities are Pierre, the capital; Sioux Falls, Aberdeen, Lead, Mitchell, Watertown, Huron, Deadwood, Yankton, Rapid City and Brookings.

HISTORY. For the early history of South Dakota, see NORTH DAKOTA, subhead *History*. The state of South Dakota was formed by the division of Dakota Territory in November, 1889, after a great immigration to the region had caused it to become important as a wheat-producing territory. Since its admission into the Union, the state has progressed rapidly along all lines of development. Laws providing for primary elections, municipal ownership of telephones, the regulation of railways, for the compulsory education of Indian children and regulating the education of the deaf and blind have been enacted.

South Dakota, UNIVERSITY OF, a state university established at Vermilion, by the territorial legislature of Dakota, under the name of the University of Dakota. When the territory was divided into North and South Dakota and these states were admitted to the Union, the name was changed to that which the institution now bears. The present organization includes a collegiate department, also colleges of law, medicine, music and commerce, and a preparatory department. The collegiate department has courses in classics, literature, civil and mechanical engineering and sciences. and it has control of the state geological survey. The university is open to women on equal terms with men. The faculty numbers over 50, and there are about 500 students. The income is derived from state appropriations and from the Congressional land grant, and it amounts to about $90,000 a year

Southern Cross, one of the most brilliant constellations in the Southern Hemisphere. It consists of four stars of the first magnitude, so arranged as to present the appearance of a cross. The right and left stars point directly east and west, while the upper and lower ones form the pointers to the south pole. When these pointers are on the meridian the cross is most nearly perpendicular.

Southern Ocean. See ANTARCTIC OCEAN.

South'ey, ROBERT (1774–1843), an English poet and miscellaneous writer, the son of a linen draper of Bristol. He was sent to Westminster School in 1788 and soon gave proof of distinguished talents; but he was dismissed in 1792 for a satirical paper on flogging, published in a school journal. Shortly afterward he entered Balliol College, Oxford, where he remained but two years. He formed an acquaintance with Coleridge, and they were married on the same day to two sisters; but the scheme for the founding of an ideal community on the banks of the Susquehanna, in the carrying out of which their marriage was the first step, failed for lack of funds. In 1804 Southey fixed his permanent residence at Greta, near Keswick, in the heart of the English lake district, where he had Wordsworth and Coleridge for neighbors. From this period his intellectual activity was untiring, and he continued for a period of almost forty years to issue annually at least one, and often several, works, besides contributing largely to different periodicals. A government pension of £160 was allowed him in 1807, which was increased in 1835 to £460. In 1813 he was appointed poet laureate. Having lost his first wife, he married, in 1839, Caroline Anne Bowles, herself a writer of some eminence. Soon afterward he sank into a state of imbecility, from which he did not recover. Among his poetical productions may be mentioned *Joan of Arc, Thalaba, Madoc, The Curse of Kehama, Roderick, the Last of the Goths* and a *Vision of Judgment.* Several of his minor pieces have in them more of true poetry than his longer poems. His prose works are remarkable for their excellent style. Among these may be mentioned his *Life of Nelson, Life of Wesley, History of Brazil* and *The Doctor.* His letters are admirable.

South Had'ley, MASS., a town in Hampshire co., on the Connecticut River, 3 mi. n. e. of Holyoke. Mount Holyoke College is located here. The industries include manufactures of paper, fertilizers and brick. Population in 1910, 4894.

South McAl'ester, Okla., a town of the Choctaw nation, about 85 mi. s. w. of Fort Smith, Ark., on the Chicago, Rock Island & Pacific and the Missouri, Kansas & Texas railroads. There is also an electric line to neighboring mining towns. Cotton is extensively cultivated, and there are valuable coal mines in the vicinity. The city has a large wholesale trade and contains cotton gins and large cotton compresses, several foundries and other factories. Most of the business blocks are substantially built of limestone and sandstone. Population in 1900, 3479; estimated in 1904, at 8000.

South Milwau'kee, WIS., a city of Milwaukee co., on the Chicago & Northwestern railroad, 10 mi. s. s. e. of Milwaukee. Wire and cable, horseshoes and steam dredges are manufactured in the city. Population in 1910, 6092.

South Mountain, BATTLE OF, a battle of the Civil War, fought September 14, 1862, near Sharpsburg, Md., between a Confederate force of 18,000 from Lee's Army of Northern Virginia and a Federal force of 28,000 from McClellan's Army of the Potomac. The Confederates were compelled to retreat, after offering a stubborn resistance, and took up a position along Antietam Creek, where another severe battle was fought September 16. The losses at South Mountain were, of the Federals, 1800, of the Confederates, 2600.

South Nor'walk, CONN., a city in Fairfield co., 14 mi. s. w. of Bridgeport, on Long Island Sound, at the mouth of the Norwalk River, and on the New York, New Haven & Hartford railroad. It has a beautiful location overlooking the sound and is an attractive residence place.

There is a large coastwise trade, and the city contains manufactures of paper boxes, hats, boots and shoes, stone and earthen ware and various iron products. Shipbuilding is also carried on, and oysters are extensively grown. The munici-

with Omaha, but has a separate municipal government. The five large meat-packing houses are the principal industrial establishments, and in the packing business the city is surpassed only by Chicago and Kansas City. It has a free

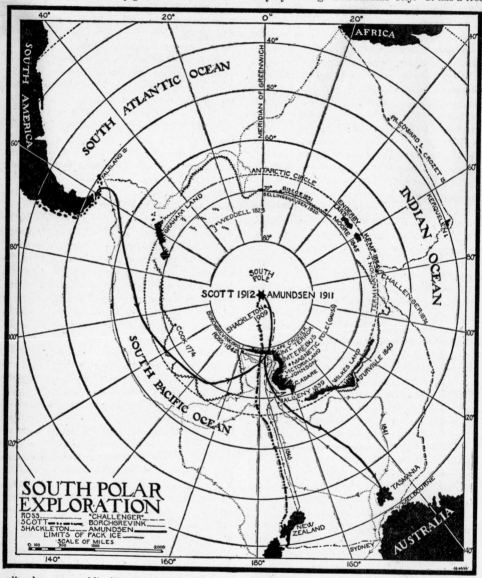

SOUTH POLAR EXPLORATION

ROSS .... "CHALLENGER" ....
SCOTT .... BORCHGREVINK ....
SHACKLETON .... AMUNDSEN ....
LIMITS OF PACK ICE ....
SCALE OF MILES
0 100   300   1000   2000

pality has two public libraries. Population in 1910, 8968.

South Omaha, *o'ma haw,* NEB., a city in Douglas co., adjoining Omaha, on the Missouri River and on the Union Pacific, the Missouri Pacific, the Chicago, Burlington & Quincy, the Chicago, Rock Island & Pacific and several other railroads. It practically forms one city

library and good public schools. The place was settled in 1882 and has grown rapidly since the establishment of the union stockyards two years later. Population in 1910, 26,259.

South Po'lar Ex'plora'tion. The first discovery of land in the proximity of the Antarctic Circle was made accidentally by Dirk Cherrits, a Dutch navigator, who, in endeavoring to enter the Strait of Magellan, was driven southward to latitude 64°, whence he discovered the South Shetland Islands. Captain Cook is the first who is known to have sailed within the Antarctic Circle. He reached the southernmost point attained by him, on Jan. 30, 1774, 71° 10' south and 107° west. In 1821 Bellinghausen, the Russian, discovered Peter the Great and Alexander islands. Enderby Land and Kemp Land were discovered by Biscoe in 1831–1833. The first of these is the easternmost point of a supposed continuous coast and lies in about latitude 67° 30'. Sabrina Land and Balleny Islands were discovered in nearly the same latitude by Balleny in 1839. In 1840 two important exploring expeditions, one American, the other French, reached the Southern seas. The American expedition, under Wilkes, passed very near the southern magnetic pole, the position of which, at the time, he calculated to be 70° south latitude and 140° east longitude; it also traced land from longitude 154° 27' to 97° 30' east, which Wilkes concluded to be continuous. The French expedition, under Dumont d'Urville, found traces of what they believed to be a continuous coast from 136° to 142° east, to which they gave the name of Adelie Land. An English expedition under James Clark Ross in 1839 passed the Antarctic Circle in about longitude 178° east, and in 172° 36' east longitude and 70° 41' south latitude he found a continuous coast, trending south, with mountain peaks 9000 to 12,000 feet in height. He gave the country the name of South Victoria Land. In 77° 32' south latitude, 167° east longitude, he discovered an active volcano, Mount Erebus, 12,400 feet high.

The prominence given to Arctic expeditions often diverts our attention from those made to the south polar regions, yet such expeditions have occurred with comparative frequency since Ross's time. While many of these exploring parties have succeeded in reaching high latitudes, only a few of them have attempted explorations or discoveries within the Antarctic Circle. From 1872 to 1876 the British scientific expedition for deep-sea exploration made its celebrated voyage in the *Challenger*, under the direction of Sir Wyville Thompson, and reached the point indicated on the accompanying map in 1874 (See CHALLENGER EXPEDITION). In 1894–1895 the Norwegian whaler *Antarctic* landed a company at Cape Adare, Victoria Land. In 1897–1899 the Belgian Antarctic Expedition, under Captain Adrian de Gerlache, in the *Belgica*, was caught in the ice pack and drifted as

far south as latitude 71° 36'. This was the first company to spend the winter far enough south to lose sight of the sun. In the same year the German expedition for deep sea exploration in those waters found the Antarctic Ocean to be of great depth. But the most important of the later attempts was that of the British Antarctic Expedition (1898–1900) under the direction of the Norwegian scientist, Borchgrevinck. This explorer reached the farthest point south yet attained, 78° 50', only 800 miles from the pole. The south magnetic pole was located, and the party also made several expeditions inland. Borchgrevinck reached New York in February, 1902, and gave an interesting account of his discoveries.

In 1901 three expeditions were sent to the south polar regions by the German, the British and the Scandinavian governments, respectively. Each expedition was charged with a special line of work. That from Great Britain had for its object geographical exploration and discovery and was in charge of Captain R. F. Scott, of the royal navy; the German expedition, in charge of Professor Von Drygalski, was designed to make a scientific study of the magnetic phenomena and the life of the region, while the Norwegian expedition was to combine both of these features to a greater or less extent. An accident to their ship compelled the Norwegian party to abandon it before any results had been attained. The British expedition spent two winters in the south polar regions, establishing their camp near Mount Erebus. By sledge journey they succeeded in approaching nearer the south pole than any previous party. The German expedition did not attempt to approach so near the pole, and after spending one winter in scientific research it was recalled by the government. As the result of these efforts, the south magnetic pole was relocated, and much valuable geographical, magnetic and zoölogical information obtained. The British ship *Discovery* returned in 1904.

One of the most noted of all Antarctic expeditions was that under Lieutenant Ernest H. Shackleton during 1908 and 1909. Shackleton divided his forces into three parts. One located the south magnetic pole, another ascended Mount Erebus, and the third, led by himself, penetrated the interior of the Antarctic continent to within 111 miles of the south pole, when the expedition was obliged to turn back because of lack of provisions. Shackleton demonstrated that the interior of this continent is a high plateau having an altitude in places of more than 10,000 feet, and that in all probabilities the south pole lies in this plateau. Although the expedition practically solved the problem of the south pole, another British expedition was fitted out in 1910 under Captain Scott. Scott and four companions reached the pole on January 18, 1912, but on the return trip they lost their lives after terrible suffering from cold and hunger. Though the leader was lost, the expedition achieved valuable results. Its scientific records should prove of great benefit to science.

In 1910 the Norwegian navigator Amundsen embarked with the determination to reach the south pole and after a remarkable experience reached the southernmost part of the earth on December 14, 1911, returning early in 1912 with the story of his adventures.

South Port'land, MAINE, a city in Cumberland co., on Casco Bay, opposite Portland. There are four bridges and an electric railway to Portland. It is in a farming region and contains iron works, machine shops, acid works and small shipyards. The state school for boys is located here. South Portland was originally a part of Cape Elizabeth and was incorporated as a city in 1889. Population in 1910, 7471.

South Sea Company, a company organized in England in 1711 by the lord treasurer Harley, with the exclusive right to trade in the South Sea. In less than ten years after its establishment, the South Sea Company had taken over the entire national debt, which had by that time become £30,000,000. A number of the directors of the company began to dispose of their shares in 1720, and the weakened confidence which resulted from this, together with the failure of Law's Mississippi Scheme in France, brought about the collapse of the entire scheme. Thousands of shareholders were ruined, and the great financial ability of Walpole was able only partially to restore order and confidence in the country.

Sovereign, *suv'ur in,* a gold coin, of the value of one pound sterling, the monetary unit of Great Britain, equivalent to 20 shillings, or about $4.8665 in United States money. Its weight is about 123.275 troy grains, of which .916 is pure metal. Half-sovereigns, 2-pound pieces and 5-pound pieces are also coined in the same proportion of weight and purity. The crown is equal to a quarter-sovereign. The sovereign of to-day bears the likeness of the ruler. See CROWN; GUINEA; SHILLING; PENNY; FARTHING; POUND.

Sovereignty, *suv'ur in ty.* The word *sovereignty* is used in two different senses—to denote what is technically called *internal* sovereignty, that is, supremacy over the citizens of a state, and to denote *external* sovereignty, that is, complete independence of any other state. When used with reference to the internal affairs of a state, sovereignty may be either *legal* or *political.* The latter refers to the power which has ultimate control over all the state activities; thus, in the United States the people would be the political sovereign. Legal sovereignty refers to the organ of government which expresses the will of the political sovereign.

Internal sovereignty is considered to have certain attributes. (1) It is *absolute,* that is, there can be no limitation upon its powers or activities. Practically, it will be seen, no government has absolute internal sovereignty, since every modern government is limited, either by a constitution or by some act or decree which granted rights which by prescription or for some other cause are now inviolable. (2) Sovereignty is said to be *indivisible,* that is, there cannot be two sovereigns with authority over the same territory. In a federal government either the whole people are the sovereign and the state and central governments are the instruments of its sovereignty, or each state is a sovereign and the central government acts only in certain matters for the general good. An externally sovereign state theoretically is one which is absolutely independent of all other states; but in practice this is impossible, and states which have practically surrendered every power in their relation to other states are still considered sovereign. See STATE; GOVERNMENT.

Sowing, *so'ing,* **Machine** or **Seeder,** a machine for planting grain. Among the simplest and earliest forms of this machine is a cylindrical vessel, with small holes at regular intervals around its circumference. This was used for sowing round seeds, such as turnip seed. The machine was placed on wheels and was drawn over the land at a regulated speed; by its mere rotation the seed was delivered with considerable uniformity. A later pattern of machine had a fixed seed box, from which the delivery of the seeds was regulated by a revolving brush.

The style of seeder in most common use for wheat, oats and other small grains is the *drill.* This consists of a narrow box, eight or ten feet long, with circular openings in the bottom, from three to four inches apart. Connected with each of these openings is a hollow iron tube, extending down to the ground. In front of each tube is a device for making a small furrow, called the *lister*, consisting of two thin, flat pieces of steel, which meet in front and turn upward with a curve. Back of each lister is a wheel or other device for covering the grain. The box contains a revolving brush, for the purpose of distributing the grain evenly through the holes in the bottom. This can be gauged so as to allow any quantity to pass through and is thus adaptable for the sowing of different grains. As the machine is moved forward the brush revolves, and the grain falls through the drills into the furrows. A team of two horses can operate one of these drills, and on good ground it will seed from eight to ten acres in a day.

Sow Thistle, *sou this''l,* the name applied to several thistles, growing in the eastern and northern parts of the United States. They are very abundant as weeds and are used as food by many animals and as a pot herb in Europe. The most common species grows to a height of two or three feet and has a branching stem and small yellow flowers, about three quarters of an inch in diameter. Like the Canada thistle, it spreads very rapidly, by means of its creeping roots and light seeds, blown about by the wind. It is usually found in pastures or grain fields and can be eradicated only by careful cultivation and by the planting of other crops to smother its growth. One species is common in Massachusetts and southern New York.

Spahis, *spah'hees,* the name given to the irregular Turkish cavalry, which is said to have been organized by Amurath I and which gave place in 1826 to regular cavalry. Their usual arms were the saber, the lance and the javelin. The French call a body of light cavalry raised in Algeria, *spahis.* The name *sepoys,* given to the native troops in British India, is the same word.

Spain, a country situated in the southwestern part of Europe, between 36° and 43° 48′ north latitude and between 9° 20′ west and 30° 19′ east longitude. It is bounded on the n. by the Bay of Biscay and France, from which it is separated by the Pyrenees Mountains; on the e. by the Mediterranean Sea; on the s. by the Mediterranean, the Strait of Gibraltar and the Atlantic Ocean, and on the w. by Portugal and the Atlantic Ocean. Its greatest breadth from north to south is 540 miles, and its greatest length from east to west, 620 miles. The area, exclusive of islands and colonies, is 190,000 square miles; but including the islands and colonies,

it is 194,783 square miles, or a little more than the combined areas of California and Indiana. The coast line, which contains few deep indentations, measures 1400 miles.

SURFACE AND DRAINAGE. The principal feature of the surface is the great interior plateau, separated by valleys from lofty mountain chains, which border the coast on the south and southeast and form the boundary between France and Spain on the north. This plateau, which occupies nearly three-fourths of the Iberian Peninsula, has an elevation varying from 1000 to 3000 feet above the sea and is crossed by a number of mountain ranges, called *sierras,* the most important being the Castilian Mountains in the center, generally known as the Sierra de Guadarrana and the Sierra de Gredos. A watershed, extending from northeast to southwest, divides this tableland into two unequal portions, the southern portion being nearly twice the size of the northern. The surface is cut by the valleys of streams, which have worn deep channels, so that the interior presents many marked contrasts of scenery. Upon the north of the plateau and separated from it by the valley of the Ebro are the Pyrenees Mountains, forming an unbroken barrier between France and Spain, and their westward prolongation, the Cantabrian Mountains, which form the northern border of the plateau (See CANTABRIAN MOUNTAINS; PYRENEES). The valley of Andalusia, on the south, separates the plateau from the Sierra Nevadas, which have a northeast-southwest trend along the Mediterranean coast; in their highest peak, Mulahacén, which attains an elevation of 11,420 feet, they have the highest land in Europe excepting in the Alps. See SIERRA NEVADA.

The rivers generally rise in the interior or the plateau, and the longer streams flow into the Atlantic, since the watershed is nearer the Mediterranean. Chief of these are the Minho, the Douro, the Tagus and the Guadiana. Of the streams flowing into the Mediterranean, the Ebro and the Guadalquivir are the most important, the last being the largest river on the peninsula. This river is navigable as far as Seville. There are no lakes of importance in the country.

CLIMATE. Although nearly surrounded with water, Spain has a continental climate, which is characterized by dryness, by a wide range of temperature between summer and winter and by rapid variations of temperature during the seasons. In the north, along the ocean, the climate is quite equable; the winters are mild and the summers are cool, and rainfall is quite evenly distributed throughout the year; but in the interior the climate is dry and is characterized by cold winters and hot summers, the thermometer here sometimes showing a temperature of 107°, while during the winter the rivers are frequently frozen over. That portion of the country bordering on the Mediterranean is strongly affected by the hot winds from Africa and has a higher mean temperature than any other part of Europe. Here there is little rainfall, and, as in the interior, irrigation is necessary for successful cultivation of the soil.

MINERAL RESOURCES. Spain is one of the richest of European countries in minerals, and her mines have been noted for centuries. The chief metals are silver, lead, iron, copper and quicksilver. Iron has been mined extensively in the northwestern part of the country, and it is also found in the south central part and in other localities. Much of this ore is shipped to Great Britain. The quicksilver mines of Almaden, near the south central part of the country, have been famous for centuries and are the largest of the kind in the world. Large quantities of lead and copper are obtained from the southern provinces, and coal is generally distributed over the country, the coal mines being worked almost wholly by foreign capital. The yearly output has an average value of $40,000,000. On the whole, the mines are not fully developed, and the mining industry is not prosecuted with vigor or great profit.

AGRICULTURE. Agriculture is the chief industry and engages the attention of from one-half to three-fourths of the inhabitants. The peculiarities of surface and climate divide the country into a number of agricultural districts, whose interests are widely diversified. The portion of the country bordering on the Mediterranean and forming the southeastern provinces is generally known as the gardens. Here every foot of available land is brought under tillage, in some places the rock being blasted and hammered into powder for the purpose of making soil. Every available fertilizer, even to the street-sweepings, is used. Artificial irrigation is practiced in the most elaborate and scientific manner, and large crops of oranges, lemons, grapes and other fruits, as well as grains, are raised. In the interior the dryness of the climate and the deep channels through which the rivers flow, make agriculture unprofitable, because water cannot be secured for irrigation, and this vast area is given over to grazing or is left as waste land; but in the northwestern part of the country bordering on the Atlantic, diversified farming and stock raising are successful. Here all of the fruits common to central Europe grow in abundance, and there is sufficient moisture for the raising of cereals and hay and for keeping the pasture lands in good grass; consequently, this region is noted for its live stock. For centuries Spain has been one of the leading countries of Europe in the production of wool. It was here that the merino sheep, famous for the excellent quality of its wool, originated. However, the numbers of these sheep have been greatly depleted within the last decade.

In general, the land is held in large estates, owned by the nobility and rented to tenants on such terms as to keep them in extreme poverty. With the exception of a small district in the southeastern part of the country, methods and means for tilling the soil are decidedly primitive. The inhabitants are generally indolent, and but poor returns are received for the expenditure of labor and capital.

MANUFACTURES. The manufactures are limited and are not sufficient to supply the home demand. Catalonia, in the northeastern part of Spain, is the leading manufacturing province. Following this, in the order of importance, are the districts of Galicia, Asturias and Vizcaya, which have an abundance of water power. A few of the large towns in the interior, including Madrid, Seville and Toledo, also have some manufactures. Barcelona is the chief manufacturing city of the country, and the leading industries include the manufacture of textiles, metal, paper and leather, and lace making. The provinces Valencia, Murcia and Andalusia manufacture some silk and woolen goods. Cordova was formerly famous for its leather, but it no longer holds a leading position in the leather industry. The manufacture of tobacco is of importance in Madrid, Seville, Valencia and some other towns. There are also manufactures of gold and silverware and jewelry. Other industries of some importance are the manufacture of beet sugar, of glass and of olive oil.

TRANSPORTATION AND COMMERCE. On account of the mountainous condition of the interior, the construction of railways is very expensive, and comparatively few lines have been completed. Two railways connect Spain with France, and Madrid, the capital, is the center of the railway system. The entire mileage for the country is about 8400 miles. The roads are generally poor, and means of transportation in the interior are entirely inadequate to the needs of the people. In all, Spain has about 100 good harbors, and most of the trade is carried on by sea, though but little of it is in Spanish vessels. The Mediterranean ports have regular steamship connection with all the leading ports of Europe, with the Philippine Islands and Cuba and with the Atlantic ports of the United States.

The commerce is comparatively small. The exports consist of raw material and some manufactures and agricultural products, particularly raisins, fruits and wool. The imports include food supplies, raw material for manufactures and manufactured goods. The chief countries engaged in the foreign trade are, in the order of their importance, Great Britain, France, Argentina, Portugal and Germany. Since the Spanish-American War there has been but little trade with the United States.

GOVERNMENT. The government is a constitutional monarchy, the present constitution having been adopted in 1876. The executive power is vested in a king, who is assisted by a council of ministers. The throne is hereditary in the royal family; the king is irresponsible, and his ministers are required to countersign all of his official acts, thereby assuming responsibility for them. The national legislature, known as the *Cortes*, consists of a Senate and a Chamber of Deputies. The Senate is composed of three classes of senators—those who are entitled to seats by their own right, including the adult sons of the king and the adult sons of the immediate heir to the throne, Spanish nobles whose annual income is at least $12,000, and the captain-generals of the army, the admirals of the navy, the archbishops and the presidents of the councils of state, war, navy and supreme court and of the tribunal of accounts; 100 senators nominated for life by the Crown; 180 elected by a limited suffrage for a term of five years. The number of members by right, together with Crown appointees, cannot exceed 180. The terms of one-half of the elective class expire every five years; but on dissolution of the Senate by the king, the terms of all expire. The Chamber of Deputies is composed of 431 members, chosen for five years at popular election. Annual sessions are held; the king can dissolve the Cortes at any time, but he must call another within three months. The houses have equal legislative powers.

158

The judiciary includes a supreme court of cassation; a number of district courts, which are under the jurisdiction of the supreme court, and tribunals below the district court. Local courts consist of courts of justices of the peace and municipal courts. For the purpose of local government the country is divided into provinces and communes, each having its own assembly, the members of which are elected by popular vote.

ARMY AND NAVY. The army was reorganized in 1903 and was placed on an effective basis of 80,000 men. The navy, which was nearly destroyed in the Spanish-American War, is being slowly rebuilt. In comparison with the navies of other European nations, it is very weak. In all ranks there are 16,700 men, and the number of ships does not exceed 40.

COLONIES. The colonial possessions consist of the island of Fernando Po and a few small adjoining islands, off the coast of Africa; the Muni River settlements, along the banks of the Muni and Gambia rivers, on the west coast of Africa, bordering the Gulf of Guinea, and Rio de Oro, on the west coast of Africa, bounded on the south by the Senegambia and Niger territories and on the north by Morocco. The entire area of these possessions is about 80,000 square miles. All are sparsely populated.

INHABITANTS AND LANGUAGE. The Spanish people are descendants of the Iberians, who are the oldest inhabitants of the peninsula, and a few of their representatives are still found among the Basques, in a little province bordering on France. The country was invaded by the Romans, but they did not succeed in making any permanent impression upon the native inhabitants. However, the invasion by the Mohammedans and their occupation of the peninsula for seven hundred years made decided changes in the native races and in the language, which contains many Arabian words. Spain formerly consisted of a number of kingdoms, each with its local interests, habits and customs, and these differences have continued from one generation to another and have prevented that union in language and purpose which usually characterizes the people of a nation. The prevailing language is Spanish, and the religion is that of the Roman Catholic Church, which is the State Church and includes nearly all of the inhabitants. There are a few Protestants, but they are allowed but little liberty in practicing their religion. The people are of medium stature and dark complexion, with black eyes and usually straight black hair.

ART. See PAINTING, subhead *Seventeenth Century*.

LITERATURE. Spanish literature began, like the literature of most other countries, in songs descriptive of the great deeds of heroes. The earliest of these songs which is extant is one on the Cid (See CID, THE), the manuscript of which dates from the fourteenth century. Fiction writing began in the fourteenth century, and from that century or the next dates the *Amadis of Gaul*, the most famous of medieval romances. The Golden Age of literature in Spain began in the sixteenth century, and lasted until the second half of the seventeenth. Of the scores of famous men who wrote during this period, the greatest were the poets Calderon de la Barca (See CALDERON DE LA BARCA, PEDRO) and Lope de Vega (See VEGA CARPIO, FELIX LOPE DE) and the novelist Cervantes (See CERVANTES SAAVEDRA, MIGUEL DE). Literature declined in Spain during the late seventeenth century, and the eighteenth century produced few writers of note. The imitation of French literature, which grew up in the latter half of the eighteenth century, had in some ways beneficial effects, as in the drama particularly there were productions of worth. The romantic movement which swept over Europe in the early nineteenth century affected Spain with the other countries, and poets, as well as prose writers, showed its influence. Of the last half of the nineteenth century the most notable literary form in Spain was the novel (See CABALLERO, FERNAN).

CITIES. The chief cities are Madrid, the capital; Barcelona, Valencia, Malaga, Cadiz, Seville and Granada, each of which is described under its title.

HISTORY. When the Phoenicians landed in Spain and began colonization, probably at the end of the twelfth century B. C., they found the country inhabited by a race of mingled Celtic and Iberian stock, to whom the name Celtiberians has been given. After the Phoenicians came the Greeks, but the history of Spain did not really begin until the third century B. C., when the Carthaginians conquered almost the entire peninsula. Hamilcar Barca, Hasdrubal and Hannibal were the three great generals who established the empire of Carthage in Spain (See HAMILCAR BARCA; HASDRUBAL; HANNIBAL). As a result of the Punic wars, the Carthaginians were driven from Spain and the Romans came into possession of the territory. Not until 19 B. C., however, was the entire peninsula brought into subjection to Rome. Three provinces were formed from the conquered territory, and these were prosperous and powerful under the Roman rule.

In the early part of the fifth century A. D., the Visigoths entered Spain and there established a kingdom. For three centuries the Gothic rule continued, but in 711 the Arabs overthrew the Visigothic king and made the greater part of Spain a dependency of the caliph. Gradually, in the mountainous districts of the Pyrenees, independent Christian kingdoms were established, and these small states were constantly at war among themselves for supremacy. In the eleventh century, Aragon and Castile emerged as the most powerful, and little by little they absorbed the other states. Fortunately for these two new powers, the Ommiad dynasty of the Moors, which had been in power for almost three centuries, became extinct in the eleventh century, and the subsequent division of the Mohammedan territory into small independent states favored the expansion of the Christian states. By the early part of the thirteenth century the Moorish dominion in Spain had been almost entirely overthrown by the united efforts of Castile, Navarre and Aragon, and even the Kingdom of Granada, the only Moorish kingdom which remained, was forced to admit the supremacy of Castile.

By the marriage of Isabella of Castile to Ferdinand of Aragon, these two countries were united (1479), and they were thus enabled to undertake the conquest of what remained of Moorish power in Spain. After a ten years' war, Ferdinand and Isabella in 1492 entered Granada, the Moorish capital, and thus became the sovereigns of all Spain, with the exception of Navarre. Twenty years later Navarre, except the part north of the Pyrenees, was also taken by Ferdinand, and Spain became one power. The discovery, during the reign of Ferdinand and Isabella, of the New World, by navigators sent out by those sovereigns, added much to the greatness of the rising kingdom.

The grandson of Ferdinand and Isabella, Charles, was also the grandson of Maximilian of Austria, and his accession in 1516 was the inauguration of the Hapsburg dynasty on the Spanish throne (See CHARLES V, Holy Roman Emperor). Charles was ruler, also, of the Netherlands and Milan, and these were made part of the Spanish territory which he left to his son, Philip II. The tyranny and bigotry of Philip (See PHILIP II) and of his successors, Philip III (1598–1621) and Philip IV (1621–1665), were among the immediate causes of the decline of Spain, which under Charles had been one of the great countries of Europe. The loss of the Netherlands was a great blow to the country (See NETHERLANDS, THE, subhead *History*), and the wars with England worked great damage to the Spanish navy (See ARMADA). With Charles II (1665–1700), the Hapsburg dynasty became extinct in its male line, and only by the disastrous War of the Spanish Succession were the claims to the throne settled (See SUCCESSION WARS, subhead *War of the Spanish Succession*). At the close of the struggle Philip of Anjou was recognized as king, as Philip V, and the Bourbon dynasty was thus begun. The war had hastened the decline of Spain, by depriving her of many of her colonial possessions, and although during the reign of Philip an attempt was made, directed by Alberoni, to restore the country to its earlier conditions, an alliance of the great European powers frustrated the plan.

Ferdinand VI (1746–1759) and Charles III (1759–1788) both introduced reforms into the government and strengthened the state somewhat, but Charles IV (1788–1808) was not as strong a ruler as his two predecessors, and all that had been gained under them was lost. In 1808 affairs had come to such a state that Charles felt that safety for himself and for Spain lay only in his abdication, and he therefore gave up the throne to his son Ferdinand. Napoleon, who had been pouring troops into the Spanish capital, was by this time strong enough to compel both Charles and Ferdinand to renounce all claims to the Spanish crown, which he conferred on his brother, Joseph Bonaparte. The Spanish people refused to recognize the Bonapartes as their rulers and declared for Ferdinand, and the active resistance which followed on their declaration was the first step toward Napoleon's overthrow (See PENINSULAR WAR). In 1814 Ferdinand again entered Madrid as king, and a reactionary policy was immediately adopted by him. From this time until 1868 the Bourbon dynasty reigned uninterruptedly, and liberals and absolutists in turn held the chief power in the State. In 1868 a revolt arose, headed by Prim, and the queen, Isabella, was driven from the country (See ISABELLA II). The attempt of the Spanish to find for themselves a ruler, led indirectly to the Franco-German War (See FRANCO-GERMAN WAR). From December, 1870, to early in 1873, Amadeus, son of Victor Emmanuel of Italy, reigned as king at Madrid, and after his abdication a republic was organized

(See CASTELAR, EMILIO). The republic proved unpopular, and in 1875 the monarchy was reëstablished, with Alfonso XII, son of Isabella, as king. Alfonso reigned for ten years, and his posthumous son, Alfonso XIII, succeeded him, with Christina, his mother, as regent. A rebellion in Cuba was met with the greatest severity, and complications ensued which led, in 1898, to war with the United States (See CUBA, THE REPUBLIC OF; SPANISH-AMERICAN WAR), the result of which was the loss to Spain of Cuba, Porto Rico and the Philippine Islands. Alfonso XIII, when he took the rule himself, found the building up of his exhausted country no easy task. But he proved himself a capable ruler, with wide ambitions for Spain (See ALFONSO XIII). Population in 1910, 19,588,688. Consult Hale's *Spain*, in Story of the Nations Series; also, Katharine Lee Bates's *Spanish Highways and Byways*.

Spalding, *spawl'ding,* JOHN LANCASTER (1840–), a Roman Catholic archbishop, born at Lebanon, Ky. He was educated at Mount Saint Mary's College and at the University of Louvain, Belgium. He became a priest and was appointed chancellor of the diocese of Louisville in 1871, bishop of Peoria in 1877 and titular archbishop of Scyphopolis (Palestine) in 1909. He is the author of *Things of the Mind; Means and Ends of Education; Religion, Agnosticism and Education;* and other volumes.

Span'iel, the name given to several varieties or breeds of dogs. Their distinguishing characteristics are a rather broad muzzle, remarkably long and full ears, plentiful and beautifully-waved hair. The prevailing colors of most breeds are liver and white, though some are red and white, black and white, or deep brown or black on the face and breast, with a tan spot over each eye. The *King Charles* is a small variety of the spaniel, common as a lapdog. It is usually black and tan or brown and has a large head and a small, well-coated body. The *Maltese* is also a small species of spaniel. The *water spaniels*, large and small, differ from the common spaniel only in the roughness of their coats. They are fond of the water and make excellent retrievers. Other species are the *cocker spaniel*, the *Irish water spaniel* and the *field*, or *black*, *spaniel*. Spaniels possess considerable intelligence, affection and obedience, which, combined with beauty, make them highly prized as house dogs.

Span'ish-Amer'ican War, the war between Spain and the United States in 1898. Its fundamental cause was the inability or unwillingness of Spain to govern Cuba according to principles of freedom and justice. It was a result of nearly a half-century of disagreement and negotiation, during which the United States had often proposed to purchase the island, in order to remove the menace to American industries and peace, while the island itself had been in almost constant turmoil from rebellion and accompanying oppression. The last insurrection began in 1895, and in spite of the most determined efforts upon the part of Spain, through severe measures undertaken by her governors-general, Campos, Weyler and Blanco, the Cubans had succeeded is establishing a semblance of an independent government and had maintained more or less successful warfare against the Spanish army.

The interest of the United States government became more and more centered upon Cuban affairs, and finally the United States battleship *Maine* was sent to Havana to protect American interests. On the night of February 15, 1898, the vessel was destroyed by an explosion. Though responsibility could not be placed upon Spanish officials, the American people were convinced that it was the result of a deliberate plot, and public sentiment forced Congress soon to declare war (April 25). Meanwhile, it had declared that "the people of Cuba are and of right ought to be free and independent," demanded that Spain relinquish her authority in the island, and authorized the president to use the army and navy of the United States to accomplish that end. The first gun of the war was fired April 23 by the *Nashville*, in the capture of a Spanish merchantman. The navy at once began a blockade of Cuban ports, while volunteer troops to the number of 200,000 were soon recruited, drilled and equipped at several camps.

The first important engagement was at Manila Bay, where Commodore George Dewey, in command of the Asiatic squadron, completely annihilated the Spanish fleet. Troops were immediately sent to the Philippines under General Merritt, and an attack by the land and naval forces led to the fall of Manila on August 13. Meantime, a Spanish fleet under Admiral Cervera had reached Cuban waters and had taken a position in the harbor of Santiago, on the southern coast of Cuba, where it was blockaded by an American fleet under Sampson and Schley. It was during this blockade that Lieutenant Hobson and a crew of volunteers attempted to blockade the entrance to the harbor by sinking the collier *Merrimac* (See HOBSON, RICHMOND PEARSON). In June, General Shafter,

with a force of 17,000 men, had landed a little east of Santiago and invested the town. The enemy gradually retired within their fortifications in Santiago, offering the only important resistance at the hills of San Juan and El Caney, which were finally gained by the Americans on July 2 (See ROUGH RIDERS; EL CANEY, BATTLE OF). On the following day Cervera, under orders from his government, attempted to break the blockade; but after a long running fight his whole squadron was beached or destroyed, and he himself with 1700 men was captured (See SANTIAGO, BATTLE OF). The siege of the city was continued until July 15, when General Toral surrendered the whole District of Santiago.

On July 25 General Miles raised the United States flag over Porto Rico, and on the following day Spain made overtures for peace. August 12 a protocol was signed, and in December a final treaty of peace was accepted, by which Spain relinquished all claims to Cuba and surrendered Porto Rico, the Philippines and Guam to the United States, for a consideration of $20,000,000 and special commercial privileges until 1909.

The total expense of the war to the United States was $165,000,000; 2910 American soldiers lost their lives, of whom all but 306 died from disease. This fearful death rate from causes other than battle caused an investigation of the war department, which, however, resulted in a general acquittal of the responsible officials. See UNITED STATES OF AMERICA, subhead *History*; CUBA, subhead *History*; PORTO RICO; PHILIPPINE ISLANDS.

Spanish Succession, *suk sesh' un*, WAR OF THE. See SUCCESSION WARS.

Spar'row, the name of a large group of finches, which have, in general, a brown plumage streaked with black. The common *English house sparrow*, which is about six inches long, is extremely hardy and very obnoxious. It was brought into the United States about the year 1869 and has increased astonishingly in numbers, until now it is probably more numerous than any other wild bird. One pair will raise several families of four or five each year. These sparrows live in and about cities and towns, where their big, clumsy nests of straw and hay are always objectionable. Though once thought to be aids to the farmer, it is now known that they eat few insects, but live chiefly upon grains and the refuse they gather in the streets. The *lark sparrow*, or *lark finch*, is a sweet songster of the western part of the United States, which nests on the ground and feeds on seeds and insects. The *chipping sparrow*, the *ground sparrow*, the *vesper sparrow* and the *white-throated sparrow* are all favorite summer residents of

ENGLISH SPARROW

northern United States and southern Canada. The last named is a beautiful little bird, whose cheery note is heard during the spring migrations and about his nesting places during the summer.

Sparrow Hawk, the common name of several small, active and strong hawks. They watch for their prey from tree tops or other elevated positions. They are useful and beneficial because of the large quantity of insects and small noxious animals which they destroy.

Sparta, *spahr'ta,* or **Lacedaemon** *las e de'-mon,* a celebrated city of ancient Greece, the capital of Laconia and the chief city of the Peloponnesus. It was a scattered city, consisting of five separate sections. Unlike Athens, it was plainly built and had few notable buildings. Consequently there are no imposing ruins to be seen here, as at Athens.

The Spartans were a stern and rugged warrior race, despising toil and danger and esteeming military glory the highest of honors. They were temperate in eating and drinking, and their food was of the plainest sort. By law they were debarred from trade and agriculture, and the chief occupation of their day was military drill and physical exercise. The form of government was aristocratic, and the executive power was vested in two kings and five ephors. The Spartan child was trained to endure any hardships, to be self-controlled and obedient to authority. From the age of seven to twenty he lived in a public institution and took his meals at the public table. From twenty to thirty he lived under arms in barracks, and although at thirty he was required by law to marry, he still ate at the public table.

According to tradition, the Spartan state was founded by Lacedaemon, son of Zeus. The most celebrated of its legendary kings was Menelaus (See MENELAUS). It is accepted as an historical fact that the Spartans were the descendants of the Dorians, who invaded the Peloponnesus not later than 1000 B. C. (See GREECE, subhead *History*). Such of the former inhabitants of the state as did not emigrate were allowed to keep the poorest lands about the city and to work as tradesmen or mechanics, but they were given no part in the government. About 900 B. C. Lycurgus appeared and gave the country a code of laws under which it prospered; and it was about this time that the Spartans entered on their career of conquest. They extended their sway over all the territory of Laconia, a portion of the inhabitants of which they reduced to the condition of slaves (See HELOTS). They also waged war with the Mycenaeans, the Arcadians and the Argives, against whom they were so successful that before the close of the sixth century B. C. they were recognized as the leading people in Greece. Early in the following century the Persian wars began (See GREECE, subhead *History*), during which a rivalry grew up between Athens and Sparta. This rivalry led to the Peloponnesian War, in which Athens was humiliated, and the old ascendency of Sparta was reëstablished (See ATHENS, subhead *History*). Soon after this the Spartans became involved in a war with Persia by joining Cyrus the Younger in his rebellion against his brother Artaxerxes and Athens, Thebes, Corinth and some of the Peloponnesian states seized the opportunity to declare war against Sparta. The final outcome of this struggle was the defeat of Sparta at Leuctra in 371 B. C.

During the following century Sparta steadily declined, although one or two determined attempts were made to restore its former greatness. The principal of these was made by Cleomenes, but his endeavors failed, because there were in Sparta less than a thousand inhabitants of true Spartan descent, and the majority of these were in a state of beggary. When Philip of Macedon entered Greece, Sparta struggled vigorously against him, but Macedonia was victorious in the end. With the rest of Greece, Sparta passed under the dominion of the Romans in 146 B. C.

The old constitution of Lycurgus was reëstablished under Roman rule, and the city prospered until the fifth century, when it was sacked by the Goths.

Spar'tacus, a Thracian gladiator, the instigator and leader of a revolt of the slaves in Italy, between 73 and 71 B. C. He had been compelled, like other barbarians, to serve in the Roman army, but he had deserted and become the head of a band of robbers. At length he was taken prisoner and placed in a gladiatorial school at Capua, with two hundred other slaves. They formed a conspiracy, effected their escape and were joined by the disaffected slaves and peasantry of the neighborhood, so that in a few months Spartacus found himself at the head of over sixty thousand men. Two consuls were sent with armies against him, but Spartacus defeated them in succession and led his forces toward Rome. In this crisis Crassus was placed at the head of the army and managed to hem in the revolted slaves near Rhegium. Spartacus broke through the enemy by night and retreated, but later he had to encounter the army of Crassus. His soldiers were overcome, and Spartacus himself fell fighting.

Spar'tanburg, S. C., the county-seat on Spartanburg co., 93 mi. n. w. of Columbia, on the Charleston & Western Carolina and on several branches of the Southern railroad. The city is on an elevation of over 800 feet. It has an excellent water supply, a good sewage system, gas and electric lights and electric street railways. There are also suburban railways to the neighboring towns. It is in a rich cotton-growing region, containing, also, deposits of limestone, granite, gold and iron. There are many large cotton mills and also broom factories and soap works. Converse College and Wofford College are located here, and the city has the Kennedy Library and a state institution for the deaf, dumb and blind. Population in 1900, 11,395; in 1910 it had increased to 17,517.

Spath'ic Iron. See SIDERITE.

Spav'in, a disease of horses, which affects the hock joint, the joint in the hind leg between the knee and the fetlock. Spavin may occur in two forms. The first, which is called *bog,* or *blood, spavin,* arises from an injury and is accompanied by swelling and inflammation. In the other form, known as *bone spavin,* there is an injury which causes a bony substance to be deposited about the joint, in some cases causing permanent stiffness.

Spawn, the eggs of fishes, frogs and reptiles. The number of eggs produced by fishes varies greatly in different species; for instance, in the spawn of a single codfish, as many as 3,500,000 eggs have been found. Usually before spawning the fish forsake the deep waters for the rivers and return after the eggs have been deposited.

Speaker, a person who presides over a deliberative assembly, preserving order and regulating the debates. The speaker of the House of Representatives formerly exercised great power through the appointment of committees and his right of recognition of any member rising to speak. Since 1910, however, the speaker is merely the presiding officer and appoints none the standing committees which practically control legislation. The speaker of the House of Commons is always a member of that House, but he has no vote, except in case of a tie, and no right to speak in debate.

Speaking Trump'et, an instrument used for conveying the sound of the voice to a distance. It consists of a hollow piece of metal or other material, of nearly conical form, open at both ends and slightly turned out at the narrow end to form a mouthpiece. A cheap pattern, made of pressed board and in common use at races and games, is called a *megaphone.*

Specie, *spe'she,* **Pay'ments,** RESUMPTION OF, in American history, specifically, the steps taken by the United States between 1875 and 1879 for gradual redemption of United States notes, of which there were at that time $382,000,000 outstanding, as a result of the issues of paper money during the Civil War. It had been found necessary in 1861 to suspend the redemption of these notes in metallic money, by reason of the extraordinary demand for gold caused by the war. This practically removed all restriction upon the issuance of paper money, since it it was necessary from time to time to increase the monetary circulation, in order to meet the ordinary demands of trade. As the volume of this paper money increased, its value naturally decreased, causing not only a rise of prices, but a general uncertainty in financial and commercial circles. This reflected upon the credit of the national government. In order to improve the situation, an act was passed in 1866 providing for the gradual retirement of greenbacks and the payment of them in specie, but this was not satisfactory. Another act was passed in 1875, providing for complete resumption of all notes presented on January 1, 1879, and for the gradual accumulation of gold in the treasury by means of the sale of bonds, for the purpose of redeeming these notes. As the supply of gold increased, the value of greenbacks or government notes proportionately rose, and when the government offered to redeem its notes in gold, few were presented. Return to specie payments caused some hardship to the debtor classes, since as the value of currency increased, prices decreased, and those having private debts which were incurred during times when the value of notes was low, were compelled to pay them in money of constantly increasing value.

Species, *spe'shiz,* any one group of animals or plants, the members of which generally bear a close resemblance to one another in the essential features of their organization and which reproduce fertile plants or animals practically like themselves, though subject to some variation. The early scientists differed in their ideas of what constituted a species, and the use of the term has changed. Haeckel defines it: "The species is the whole succession of organisms which exhibit the same form in the same environment." The determination of species is sometimes a difficult matter. In some instances the differences between one form and another are very marked, and the gap between the related forms is not filled by a series; as, for instance, the New Zealand lizards, which are the sole living representatives of an order or a class. Other organisms present great difficulties in classification, because of the many more or less different forms. Accordingly, as new discoveries are made, the limitations of species are changed; new ones are established, and old ones are broken down. In scientific classification, species unite to form groups, or *genera,* which, in turn, are included in *orders,* the orders forming *classes,* and so on. When individuals of a species differ sufficiently, *varieties* may be established (See GENUS; VARIETY).

Specific, *spe sif'ik,* **Grav'ity.** See GRAVITY, SPECIFIC.

Specific Heat, a term applied to the ratio between the quantity of heat required to raise a given mass of any substance one degree in temperature, and the quantity of heat required to raise an equal mass of water one degree in temperature. The specific heat of a substance may be found approximately by heating it to a given temperature and immersing it in an equal weight of water, whose temperature is known. When the two substances have reached a uniform temperature, divide the number of degrees of heat which

the water gained, by the number which the substance lost, and the result is the specific heat of the substance.

Spec'tacled Bear, the sole representative of the bears in South America, inhabiting the high mountain forests of Chile and Peru, so called from the light-colored rings round its eyes. The rest of the face and body is black.

Spectacles, a well-known and invaluable optical instrument, supposed to have been invented by Roger Bacon in the thirteenth century, and used to correct or offset some defect in the organs of vision. Spectacles consist of two oval lenses, mounted in a light metal frame, which is made up of the *bows,* the *bridge* and the *temples,* though the bows are often omitted. The lenses are usually concave, convex or concavo-convex, though lenses forming segments of a cylinder are used in some cases of astigmatism (See LENS). In long-sighted persons, the defect of the eye is counteracted by convex lenses; in short-sighted persons, by concave lenses. In so-called *divided spectacles,* each lens is composed of two semicircles of different foci, neatly united one above the other; one half is used for looking at distant objects, and the other is used for examining those near the eye. Spectacles can be made with such skill and in such variety that almost any defect in vision arising from irregularity in the shape of the eye can be corrected by them. One should never select spectacles without consulting a skilled oculist, since the eyes are seldom alike, and a lens that is suited to one eye is not suited to the other. Unless spectacles are adjusted to the eyes, they are liable to be injurious rather than beneficial. See EYE.

Spec'ter Bats, a family of insectivorous bats of South America, which have a simple, fleshy, leaf-like appendage to the nose, and a forefinger of two joints. They attain a considerable size, and the family comprises the vampire bats.

Spec'troscope, an instrument for separating rays of light into their prismatic colors (See LIGHT, subhead *Spectrum*). The essential parts of an ordinary spectroscope are the *collimator tube,* at the left, with a narrow slit at the outer end and a double-convex lens at the inner; the *prism,* which occupies the stage in the center, and the *telescope,* at the right. The frame is constructed for the purpose of adjusting and holding these parts in position. The slit in the collimator tube can be enlarged or diminished by the use of a screw with a very fine thread, which is connected with a movable plate. The lens in this tube collects the rays of light admitted through the slit and causes them to strike the prism parallel to one another. The spectrum is viewed through the telescope. However, instruments may be so constructed as to project the spectrum on a screen.

The spectroscope is used for the purpose of determining the composition of the heavenly bodies, such as the sun and stars, and the composition of substances when adulteration is suspected. The spectroscope used by astronomers is attached to a telescope and contains a number of prisms, arranged in the form of a circle, so that the light passes through each one successively. By this means the spectrum is enlarged. It is viewed through the eyepiece of the telescope. See SPECTRUM ANALYSIS.

Spec'trum. See LIGHT, subhead *Spectrum*.

Spectrum Anal'ysis, the process of finding the composition of substances by means of the spectroscope (See SPECTROSCOPE). Burning bodies produce three kinds of spectra, known as the continuous spectrum, the bright-lined spectrum and the dark-lined, or absorption, spectrum. For instance, a *continuous* spectrum is formed by a glowing or burning body near the instrument or by the sun when its rays are analyzed by a single prism. If a candle or gas light is burned near a prism, it forms a continuous spectrum. A *bright-lined* spectrum is formed when gases which are not under great pressure are burned. The lines thus formed have a definite position in the spectrum and never change in the same substance. The *dark-lined* spectrum is formed by the absorption of light as it passes through the vapor of some substance between the burning body and the spectroscope. Experiment has shown that the vapor of any substance absorbs the rays of light which that substance produces in the spectrum when it is burned. These dark lines are known as *Fraunhofer* lines, from the name of their discoverer, and a number of them appear in the spectrum of the sun. Since these occupy a definite position on the screen, they are designated by the letters of the alphabet, as *a, b, c.*

The process of spectrum analysis is as follows: The dark lines in the solar spectrum are produced by its light passing through the vapor of certain substances. Since, in the spectrum of iron, bright lines cover certain dark lines in the solar spectrum, therefore we infer that the atmosphere of the sun contains the vapor of iron. The presence of other substances in the sun has been discovered in a similar manner. In testing the composition of any substance by means of the spectroscope, a small quantity of the substance is burned and its spectrum is noted. In case the substance contains impurities, the lines which these impurities form will also appear on the screen, and their presence is thus noted. The great value of the spectroscope for ascertaining the purity of substances is in its ability to detect minute quantities. It is estimated that as small a quantity as $\frac{1}{2500000}$ of a grain of lithium can thus be detected.

Spec'ulum Met'al, metal used for making the specula mirrors of reflecting telescopes (See TELESCOPE). It is an alloy of two parts of copper and one of tin, its whiteness being improved by the addition of a little arsenic.

Speech, spoken language; uttered sounds intended to convey meaning and produced by the organs of voice, namely, the larynx and the mouth and its parts, including the tongue and the teeth. In speech there are two great classes of sounds, known as vowels and consonants. *Vowels* are produced by sounds coming primarily from the larynx and passing with comparative freedom through the mouth cavity, though modified in certain ways. *Consonants* are formed by the greater or less interruption of the current of air from the larynx in the mouth. Vowels can be uttered alone and independently of consonants, and their sounds can be prolonged at will; consonants have no importance in speech apart from vowels. Both vowel and consonant sounds are very numerous in the different languages of the world, but any one language has only a fraction of those that may be used. A single sound may convey an idea of itself and thus form a word, or several may be combined to form a word; and if the word is uttered by several distinct successive changes in position of the vocal organs, it is a word of several syllables. Words, again, are combined to form sentences or complete statements, and the aggregate of words used by any people or community in mutual intercourse forms its language.

Speed'well, the common name of a group of plants, natives of temperate climates all over the world. The species, consisting of herbs, undershrubs or shrubs, number one hundred eighty. One species, which is a favorite flower of Great Britain, is a creeping herb, with bright blue flowers. *Common speedwell* was once extensively used as a substitute for tea and as a tonic. *Germander-leaved speedwell* has much the same properties as common speedwell, and it is a general favorite, on account of its being among the first flowers in the early spring. The finest species come from New Zealand and have variously colored flowers and beautiful foliage.

Spoke, *speek,* JOHN HANNING (1827–1864), an English traveler. In 1857 he set out with Burton on an expedition to ascertain the position of the great lakes of the interior of Africa. Lake Tanganyika was discovered, and when Burton fell ill, Speke proceeded north and discovered the south end of the Victoria Nyanza. For this discovery he was awarded the gold medal of the Royal Geographical Society. In 1862, accompanied by Captain Grant, he explored the western and northern margin of the lake and found a river flowing north out of the lake, which proved to be the White Nile. His discoveries and adventures were described by him in his *Journal of the Discovery of the Source of the Nile* and *What Led to the Discovery of the Source of the Nile.*

Spelling Reform. See PHONETICS.

Spelt′er. See ZINC.

Spencer, *spen′sur,* MASS., a town in Worcester co., 12 mi. w. of Worcester, on the Boston & Albany railroad. It is in a beautiful farming region, about 1000 feet above sea level. One of the largest boot and shoe factories in the world is located here, and there are woolen mills and manufactories of vinegar and other articles. The public institutions include a number of churches and parish schools, the David Prouty High School and the Richard Sugden Public Library. The place was settled in 1720 and formed a part of Leicester until 1753. Population in 1910, 6740.

Spencer, HERBERT (1820–1903), a distinguished English philosopher. Because of delicate health during childhood and youth, he was educated at home and lived most of the time out of doors. In this way he acquired a dislike for schools and so completed his education under tutors. During this time he was much interested in making collections of insects and in rearing moths and butterflies and in studying the botany of the locality.

At the age of seventeen, Spencer became an engineer on the London & Birmingham railway and continued in this occupation for about ten years, when he gave it up and became sub-editor of the *Economist* in London, which position he held for four years. During this time he made the acquaintance of George Eliot, John Stuart Mill and other celebrated scholars and thinkers. It was while editor of the *Economist* that his first work of importance, *Social Statics,* appeared. Spencer conceived the idea of publishing a philos-

ophy whose scope should include all existing knowledge, and upon this he faithfully labored throughout his life and was finally able to see it completed and published.

Spencer was remarkably well fitted by nature for the task which he had set himself. He was a patient observer and had acquired a vast quantity of facts in all sciences and possessed the power of seeing relations between facts to a remarkable degree—to a much greater degree

HERBERT SPENCER

than Darwin or other specialists. Whatever opposition may in the future be given the principles which he attempted to establish, intelligent men will always look upon his effort to systematize knowledge with the greatest respect and give to him the credit accorded to no other man in this field of labor.

Like Darwin, Spencer was a thorough believer in evolution and did much through his lectures and writings to establish and extend the theory (See EVOLUTION). He believed in the unity of all things, and he set forth this belief in so convincing a manner that his popularity grew in spite of the violent opposition which some of his statements caused. His works have been particularly well received in the United States. Among those best known are *First Principles, Principles of Biology, Principles of Psychology, Principles of Sociology, Principles of Ethics* and *Education.* Besides these, he wrote numerous books on various subjects and three volumes of *Essays, Scientific, Political and Speculative.*

Spencer, SAMUEL (1847–1906), an American capitalist and railroad promoter, born at Columbus, Ga. He was educated at the University of Georgia and the University of Virginia. In 1887 he was made president of the Baltimore & Ohio railroad and soon became interested as stockholder, director or manager of many important railroad systems, especially in the south and southwest, among which are the Alabama Great Southern, the Cincinnati, New Orleans & Texas Pacific, the Georgia Southern & Florida, the Mobile & Ohio, the Southern Railway and the Central of Georgia. He was killed in a railway accident, while riding in his own car over his own road.

Spencer Gulf, a large indentation on the southern coast of Australia. Its length is 200 miles, and its greatest breadth is about 90 miles, while at its inner extremity it narrows to about 3 miles. The minor indentations on its coast are Hardwicke, Fort Lincoln and Franklin harbors. At the head of the gulf is Fort Augusta.

Spen'ser, EDMUND (1552–1599), an English poet, born in London. He was admitted as a

EDMUND SPENSER

sizar of Pembroke Hall, Cambridge, in 1569 and graduated as M. A. in 1576. On leaving the university he is thought to have resided in the north of England, where he unsuccessfully wooed a lady, whom he celebrates under the name of Rosalind in his *Shepheardes Calendar,* published in 1579. The year before, he had gone to London, where he was introduced to Sir Philip Sidney, to whom he dedicated this poem. In 1580 he went to Ireland, as secretary to Lord Grey, deputy of the island, and he had a part in restoring peace after Desmond's rebellion. Soon afterward, Lord Grey, in conjunction with the earl of Leicester and Sir Philip Sidney, procured for Spenser a grant of upward of three thousand acres in the County of Cork, out of the forfeited lands of the earl of Desmond, and he fixed his residence at Kilcolman.

He was then engaged in the composition of the *Faerie Queene,* of which he had written the first three books. With these he accompanied Raleigh the next year to England, where they were published in 1590, with a dedication to Queen Elizabeth. He then passed two or three years in Ireland, where, in 1594, he married. His courtship is celebrated in eighty-eight sonnets, and his marriage in *Epithalamium,* the finest wedding song in the English language. After another visit to London, during which he published three more books of the *Faerie Queene* and his *Foure Hymnes,* Spenser returned to Ireland, and in September, 1598, he was appointed sheriff of the County of Cork. The rebellion of Tyrone, however, took place in October; Spenser's house was fired by the populace, and, according to some accounts, his child perished in the flames. The poet arrived in England with body and spirit broken by these misfortunes, and he died in the following January. He was interred in Westminster Abbey, near Chaucer. As a poet, although his minor works contain many beauties, Spenser will be judged chiefly from the *Faerie Queene.* In the full title the poem is described as "disposed in twelve books, fashioning twelve moral virtues," and six of these were completed, besides two cantos on *Mutabilitie.* It is supposed that part of the unfinished poem may have perished when the poet's house was sacked and burned. Because of his great influence on his successors Spenser has been called "the poet's poet."

Spense'rian Stanza, the stanza adopted by Edmund Spenser in his *Faerie Queene.* It consists of a strophe of eight ten-syllable lines and one twelve-syllable line, and has a three-fold rhyme, the first and third lines forming one; the second, fourth, fifth and seventh, another; and the sixth, eighth and ninth, the third. It is the stateliest of English measures and was adopted by Byron in his *Childe Harold.*

Spermaceti, *spurm'a se'te,* a fatty material, obtained chiefly from cavities in the skull of the sperm whale. During the life of the animal the spermaceti is in a fluid state, forming part of the oily liquid which is found when the head of the whale is opened. On exposure to the air the spermaceti solidifies and separates from the oil. Some of the larger whales have been known to yield twenty-four barrels of spermaceti, and from seventy to a hundred barrels of oil. After being purified the spermaceti forms a white, crystallized, brittle, semitransparent substance, somewhat resembling tallow. It is chiefly employed as an ingredient in ointments and is also largely used in the manufacture of candles. See SPERM WHALE.

Spermatophytes, *spurm'a to fite's.* See PHANEROGAMOUS PLANTS.

Sperm Oil, the oil of the sperm whale, which is separated from the spermaceti and the blubber. This kind of oil is much purer than train oil and burns away without leaving any charcoal on the wicks of lamps. In composition it differs but slightly from common whale oil.

Sperm Whale or **Cachalot,** *kash'a lot,* a species of whale belonging to the section of the

SPERM WHALE

whale order denominated *toothed* whales. The sperm whale is generally met with in the Pacific, but occasionally it is also found on the coast of Greenland. The large blunt head in an old male is sometimes 30 feet long and forms about a third of the total length of the body. The *blow holes,* or S-shaped nostrils, are situated in the front part of the head. The weight of an adult animal is estimated at about 200 tons. This whale is valuable for its oil and for a substance taken from the head, known as *spermaceti.* See SPERMACETI; WHALE.

Sphene, *sfeen,* a mineral composed of silicic acid, titanic acid and lime. Its colors are dull yellow, green, gray, brown and black. It is found in crystals and without them. The primary form of its crystal is an oblique rhombic prism. The crystals, commonly from one-fourth to one-half an inch long, are found in granite, gneiss, mica slate and granular limestone.

Sphere, *sfeer,* a geometric solid contained under a single surface, which in every part is equally distant from a point called the center.

It may be conceived to be generated by the revolution of a semicircle about its diameter, which remains fixed and which is called the *axis* of the sphere. A section of a sphere made by a plane passing through its center is called a *great circle* of the sphere; and when the cutting plane does not pass through the center the section is called a *small circle* of the sphere. The volume of a sphere is two-thirds that of its circumscribing cylinder, that is, $\frac{4}{3}\pi$ r^3. Spheres are to one another as the cubes of their diameters. The surface of a sphere is equal to four times the area of one of its great circles, or 4π r^2.

Sphe'roid, a body or figure resembling a sphere, but not perfectly spherical. In geometry it is a solid generated by the revolution of an ellipse about one of its axes. When the generating ellipse revolves about its longer or major axis, the spheroid is *oblong,* or *prolate*; when about its less or minor axis, the spheroid is *oblate.* The earth is an oblate spheroid, that is, flattened at the poles, so that its polar diameter is shorter than its equatorial diameter.

Spheroid'al State, the condition of a small quantity of liquid, when, on being placed on a highly heated surface, as red-hot metal, it assumes the form of a more or less flattened spheroid and evaporates without boiling. The spheroid in this condition does not touch the surface of the metal, but floats on a layer of its own vapor and evaporates rapidly from its exposed surface. It is heated mainly by radiation from the hot surface, because conduction is impossible, since the layer of intervening vapor conducts heat very feebly. The formation of a layer of non-conducting vapor explains why it is possible to dip the wetted hand into molten iron with impunity.

Sphinx, *sfinx,* a fabulous monster which figures both in the Grecian and Egyptian mythologies. The Sphinx of the Greeks is represented with a body like that of a lion, with wings and with the breasts and head of a woman. Legend tells that Juno, provoked with the Thebans, sent the sphinx to punish them. The sphinx proposed a riddle and devoured any one who failed in an undertaking to interpret its meaning. The question proposed was, What animal walks on four legs in the morning, two at noon and three in the evening? This was at last explained by Oedipus, who said that man walked on his hands and feet when young, or in the morning of life; at the noon of life, he walked erect, and in the evening of his days he supported himself upon a stick. Whereupon, her riddle being read, the sphinx destroyed herself. The sphinx was used by the Greeks for artistic and decorative purposes and seems to have been in some sense symbolic.

The Egyptian sphinx had a human head (male or female) on the body of a lion and was always in a recumbent posture, with the fore paws stretched forward. The largest sphinx, that near the group of pyramids at Gizeh, is about 150 feet long and 63 feet high; the body is hewn out of stone, but the paws, which are thrown out 50 feet in front, are constructed of masonry. There are also sphinx figures in Egypt with rams' heads and hawks' heads. The Egyptian sphinx was probably a purely symbolic figure, with no historical connection with the Greek fable, and the Greeks may have applied the term to the Egyptian statues merely on account of an accidental external resemblance to their own figures of the sphinx. See PYRAMID.

Sphinx Moth, a species of hawk moth, deriving its popular name from a supposed resemblance which its caterpillars present to the Egyptian sphinx, when they raise the fore part of their bodies. See HAWK MOTH.

Sphygmograph, *sfig'mo graf*, an instrument which, when applied over an artery, indicates the force and frequency of the pulse, by registering them on a strip of paper moved by clockwork. It reveals in a very delicate and beautiful manner, by the tracing of a pencil on the paper, in the form of irregular waves, the force of the heart beats, and in making experiments with different kinds of medicines it shows their effect on the nervous system.

Spice, *spise*, certain aromatic, pungent seeds, barks, roots and fruits, used commonly in cooking, as seasoning for food. Among the spices are pepper, mace, nutmeg, cloves, ginger, allspice, cinnamon, capsicum, mustard and mint. Spices contain little nourishment, but they have certain volatile oils, which affect the nervous system and stimulate the digestive organs, thus aiding digestion. Most of the spices are natives of the old world, especially of the East, where the trade has long been an important one. Spices were used in ancient times, the Greeks and Romans employing them extensively and carrying on an important trade in them.

Spice Islands. See MOLUCCAS.

Spi'ders, the common name of animals often classed with the insects, but really constituting a class by themselves, the Arachnida. The spider's head and chest are united to form one segment; no wings are developed, and the abdomen

is furnished with from four to six cylindrical or conical glands or spinnerets, from the minute openings in which, extremely fine, silky filaments are drawn. With these filmy, threads the spider makes its web, which is intended to entangle prey or to serve as a house for the industrious little animal. Spiders have four pairs of legs and no antennae. Their mandibles are terminated by a little hook; near which is a gland secreting a poisonous fluid, by which the spider kills its prey. The female spider is much the larger, and the males rarely approach, for fear of being devoured. The eggs are numerous and are usually hidden in cocoons, which are

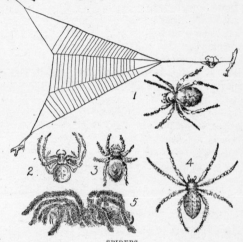

SPIDERS

1. Triangle spider and web.
2. Crab spider.
3. Jumping spider.
4. Large orb weaving spider.
5. Tarantula.

carried by some mothers until the eggs hatch; often the countless young live upon the mother's back in such masses that they make her appear very much larger than she is. Spiders are exceedingly interesting animals, and many species have developed remarkably intelligent ways of living. The tropical species are very large and powerful, some of them being able to capture small birds. The common garden spiders spin perfect geometric webs. When a fly is entangled in one of these, the owner darts out, throws another web about the intruder, kills it, sucks its blood, throws away the body and repairs the web in a very short space of time. Some species run with great speed, and others leap many times their own length, to seize their prey. They are quarrelsome and often fight to the death. If their limbs are torn off, others may grow again. The water spiders are interesting inhabitants of fresh-water pools, where they live in skilfully constructed nests, looking like small diving bells, suspended mouth downward in the water. See TARANTULA; TRAPDOOR SPIDER.

Spider Monkey. See MONKEY.

Spikenard, *spike'nahrd,* or **Nard,** a highly aromatic plant, growing in the East Indies. The root has a strong smell and a sharp, bitterish taste. This is the true spikenard of the ancients, and it has enjoyed celebrity from the earliest period, on account of the valuable extract, or perfume, obtained from its roots, which was used in the ancient baths and at feasts. It is highly esteemed in the East as a perfume, and it is used to scent oil and ointments. In the United States the name is applied to a plant with large, spicy, fragrant roots, used to some extent as a medicine, especially as a tonic. It grows extensively in southern Canada and in the northern sections of the United States.

SPIKENARD

Spinach, *spin'aje,* a genus of plants, of which there is only one species, common spinach, widely cultivated for its leaves, which are used as greens. It is wholesome and agreeable, but contains little nutriment. There are two principal varieties cultivated in gardens, the prickly-fruited and the smooth-fruited. What is called *New Zealand spinach* is sometimes used instead of common spinach, as is also *Australian spinach.*

Spinal Cord, the nervous cord which extends from the brain along the back side of the spinal column, and from which all the important nerves and systems of nerves branch. At the center of the cord is a tiny canal, which is connected directly with the cavities of the brain. Next to it is the gray matter, and around this is the so-called white matter, which is composed only of nerve fibers. See BRAIN; NERVOUS SYSTEM; NERVES.

Spin'dle, in spinning, a piece of wood for twisting and winding the fibers drawn from the distaff; or the pin used in spinning wheels, for twisting the thread, which, when twisted, is wound on the spindle. See DISTAFF; SPINNING.

Spindle Tree, a genus of small trees or shrubs containing about three hundred species. The leading species are from ten to thirty feet in height, and in autumn they become attractive by reason of their great profusion of seed vessels, which are generally of a delicate pink or white color. The common spindle tree is found wild in Great Britain, in France and throughout the north of Europe. The wood is of a white color, finely grained and hard. It was once esteemed as a material for musical instruments and spindles, hence its name. A species in the United States is the *burning bush,* which grows in moist woods and produces a small, bright-red fruit.

Spin'et. See PIANO.

Spin'ning, the art of making thread or yarn by twisting the fiber of wool, flax, cotton, silk or other material. In the earliest times spinning was accomplished by the use of the distaff and the hand spindle. The fiber, when spun, was wound upon the distaff, and the spindle, consisting of a round stick tapering at each end, with a notch for fixing yarn or thread at the upper end, was held in the hand and rotated by a movement against the right leg, while the left hand of the spinner gathered and supplied the fiber. The first improvement upon this device was the fixing of the spindle horizontally in a frame, causing it to rotate rapidly by means of a band that passed around a large wheel. This was the beginning of the spinning wheel, which is supposed to have been invented sometime in the sixteenth century (See SPINNING WHEEL). The treadle was added later, thus giving the spinner both hands with which to manipulate the thread.

The first spinning wheels contained only one spindle, but those with two spindles were afterwards invented. The next great invention in spinning consisted of the spinning jenny, invented by Hargreaves (See SPINNING JENNY). This made possible the spinning of a large number of threads at once. Later Hargreaves's invention was improved upon by the invention of the water frame, which made an evener and finer yarn. The mule-jenny, which is the basis of all spinning machines now in use, consists of a combination of the spinning jenny and the water frame. By means of these inventions the art of spinning was very materially advanced, and one operator could produce as much yarn in a day as fifty or more working by the old method.

The size of the yarn and the forms of the twist are determined by the speed with which the machine operates and the rapidity with which the thread is drawn out, rapid motions producing a fine, hard-twisted yarn, while slow motions produce a coarse and more loosely twisted yarn. While it is possible to regulate spinning machines so as to have them produce yarn of different grades, yet in large manufactories it is found more economical to construct each machine for the manufacture of a particular grade of yarn and to devote it entirely to that purpose. By this means more simple machines can be constructed, and the work can be done more rapidly. See CLOTH; WEAVING.

Spinning Jenny, the name given to the first spinning machine by means of which a number of threads could be spun at once. It was invented about 1767 by James Hargreaves, a Lancashire weaver, and consisted of a number of spindles turned by a common wheel or cylinder worked by hand. Later it was replaced by the mule-jenny. See SPINNING.

Spinning Wheel, a machine for spinning wool, cotton or flax into threads by the hand. It consists of a wheel, a band and a spindle. The wheel for spinning flax has a distaff attached and is driven by the foot; but the wheel for spinning wool is driven by hand. The spinner turns the wheel with the right hand, and holds the wool, which is in the form of rolls about three feet long and a half-inch in diameter, in the left hand. The degree of fineness of the yarn is determined

SPINNING WHEEL IN THE HOME OF GOVERNOR CARVER

by the rapidity with which the thread is drawn out by a backward movement of the spinner.

Spinoza, *spe no' za,* BARUCH or BENEDICT (1632–1677), a Dutch-Jewish philosopher, born in Amsterdam. In spite of an orthodox training he fell under the influence of Descartes, and through his heretical doctrines came into such unpleasant relations with the rabbis that he ceased to attend the synagogue. Expelled from the Israelitish community, he fled from Amsterdam to the suburbs to escape the enmity of the fanatical Jews, and after five years' seclusion he removed to Rhynsburg. Finally he set-

tled in The Hague, where he died. By his skill as a grinder of optical lenses, he managed to earn a living. He refused a pension from the French king and a professorship in Heidelberg, because their acceptance might interfere with his freedom of thought and conduct, but he accepted a legacy from his friend De Vries. This annuity enabled him to devote a large part of his time to the study of philosophy. In 1670 he published anonymously his *Tractatus theologico-politicus,* a practical political treatise, designed to demonstrate the necessity, in a free commonwealth, of freedom of thought and speech. This work called forth such a storm of adverse criticism that Spinoza published nothing further. After his death all his unpublished writings were published. *Ethics Demonstrated in the Geometrical Order,* which he had completed in 1674, is his most famous work and the one containing his metaphysical system. The essence of this system is that God is identical with the universe.

Spire, a term specifically applied to the tapering portion of a steeple, which rises above the tower, but sometimes loosely applied to the steeple itself. The earliest spires, in the architectural sense, were merely pyramidal or conical roofs, on the buildings in the Romanesque style of architecture of the eleventh century, specimens of which still exist. These roofs, becoming gradually elongated and more and more acute, resulted at length in the elegant, tapering spire. The spires of medieval architecture, to which alone the term is appropriate, are generally square, octagonal or circular in plan; they are sometimes solid, more frequently hollow, and are variously ornamented with bands, with panels, more or less enriched, and with spire lights.

Spir'itualis'm, the belief that communication can be held with departed spirits. Spiritualism is of ancient origin, but in its limited and modern form, it dates from the year 1848. In this year a Mr. and Mrs. Fox, who lived with their two daughters at Hydeville, N. Y., were disturbed by repeated and inexplicable rappings throughout the house. At length it was accidentally discovered by one of the daughters that the unseen "rapper" was so intelligent as to be able to reply to various pertinent questions and was so communicative as to declare that he was the spirit of a murdered peddler. When this discovery was made known, a belief that intercourse could be obtained with the spirit world became epidemic, and numerous "spirit circles" were formed in various parts of America. The manifestations thus said to be obtained from the spirits were rappings, table turnings, musical sounds, writings and the unseen raising of heavy bodies.

The peculiarity of these phenomena was that they were always more or less associated with a *medium*, that is, one who was supposed to have an organization sensitively fitted to communicate with the spirit world. Daniel D. Home possessed unusual powers and was said to be able to float up to the ceiling or out of the window into the next room. Such claims not only attracted the curious and converted the unthinking, but also received the attention of legal and scientific men. Judge Edmonds and Professor Hare undertook to expose their fallacy, but both had to admit the genuineness of some of the evidence; while in England the truth of the phenomena gained the assent of such eminent converts as A. R. Wallace, Sir William Crookes and Professor DeMorgan. The believers in spiritualism are quite numerous in England and the United States, where they number about 250,000 and have many newspapers, magazines and books to explain and enforce their belief. Notwithstanding this testimony, spiritualism has been greatly discredited by the fact that many, indeed, probably a majority, of public mediums have been convicted of fraud. The belief is not widely accepted by educated people. See CLAIRVOYANCE.

Spi′rom′eter, a contrivance for determining the capacity of the human lungs. The instrument most commonly employed consists of two cylinders, one inverted and of a size that will allow it to move freely up and down within the other. The lower cylinder is filled with water, and to the top of the upper a tube and an air cock are attached. By blowing into the tube the air from the lungs is expelled into this cylinder, which rises. A graduated scale marks the number of inches which the cylinder rises, and the diameter being known, the number of cubic inches of air expelled from the lungs is easily determined.

Spit′head, a celebrated roadstead on the south coast of England, a favorite anchorage of the British navy. It is the western division of the strait that separates the Isle of Wight from the mainland. It is protected from all winds except those from the southeast, and its noted security warranted the name which has been applied to it, the *King's bedchamber*. It receives its name from the Spit, a sandbank stretching south from the Hampshire shore for 3 miles. It is 14 miles long and about 4 miles in average breadth. Spithead has been strongly defended since 1864 by fortifications, completing those of Portsmouth.

Spitz or **Pomeranian Dog,** a small dog, about the size of the spaniel, with a sharp-pointed face and an abundant, usually white coat, sometimes of great beauty. The spitz is useful for no kind of work, but it has long been popular as a pet and fancy dog. It is closely allied to the Eskimo dog, and the larger varieties were formerly used as wolf dogs.

Spitzbergen, *spits burg′en,* a group of islands in the Arctic Ocean, situated about 400 mi. n. of Norway, between Franz Josef Land and Greenland. The largest islands are West Spitzbergen, Northeast Land, Edge Island, King Charles Land, King Charles Foreland and Hope Island. The highest elevations reach an altitude of 5000 feet. The islands are icebound during the greater part of the year and are remarkable for the extensive glaciers found upon them. Recently they have become somewhat important as affording a starting point for numerous polar expeditions. See NORTH POLAR EXPLORATION.

Spleen, THE, the largest of the ductless glands, situated in the upper part of the abdomen, to the left of the stomach and between it and the diaphragm. It is covered by an outer coat from the peritoneum and an inner fibrous coat, composed of connective tissue. The spleen is a soft, bluish-red organ, varying in shape and size, but usually oval, with a weight of six or seven ounces. The functions of the spleen are not well known, but from its enlargement at the close of the digestive process it seems to act as a storehouse for some of the elements of the food, gradually furnishing them to the system. It is said to produce blood corpuscles, as the splenic vein contains a large amount of white corpuscles. The theory that it destroys red blood corpuscles is not held now. The spleen may be removed from the body of an animal without destroying life.

Splicing, *splise′ing,* the process of joining two ropes without the use of a knot. The three chief varieties of splice are the short splice, the long splice and the eye splice. In making the *short splice* (Fig. 2) the ends of two ropes are unlaid for a short distance and are then fitted closely together; by the help of a marlinspike, the ends of each are laced over and under the strands of the other. The *long splice* is made in the same manner, but the rope is unlaid for a greater distance; hence the splice is stronger. The *eye splice* (Fig. 3) is made by bending over the end of the rope and lacing the strands into the rope where it is unlaid. The eye may be oval or circular. The *becket hitch* (Fig. 1) is the easiest method of attaching a small line to a rope. The *single wall* (Fig. 4) is the simplest method of preventing the end of a rope from fraying.

Splu'gen Pass, a mountain pass through the Alps, extending from the Cantòn Grisons in Switzerland to Lombardy, Italy. Its summit has an altitude of 6945 feet, and the pass forms a part of the boundary between Switzerland and Italy. The road to this pass is carried a portion of the way through three covered galleries. This road was constructed by the Austrian government in 1819–1821.

Spof'ford, AINSWORTH RAND (1825–1908), an American librarian, born in Gilmanton, N. H. He received a classical education and became associate editor of the Cincinnati *Daily Commercial*. In 1861 he was appointed first assistant librarian in the Library of Congress; in 1864 he became librarian in chief, which position he held until 1899. As a librarian Mr. Spofford became widely known for his comprehensive knowledge of books and their contents. He wrote largely for the periodical press and edited, with others, a *Library of Choice Literature* (10 vols.), a *Library of Wit and Humor* (5 vols.) and *A Practical Manual of Parliamentary Rules*. During his administration the national library increased from 70,000 to over 600,000 volumes.

Spoils System. See CIVIL SERVICE AND CIVIL SERVICE REFORM.

Spokane, *spo kan'*, WASH., the county-seat of Spokane co., situated on the Spokane River, 347 mi. e. of Seattle and 1475 mi. w. of Saint Paul, and on the Great Northern, the Northern Pacific, the Union Pacific and other railroads. The city covers a tract of a little over 20 square miles and is beautifully situated on both sides of the river, which here flows through a gorge and forms a series of cascades, which are capable of developing large water power, as well as affording beautiful scenery. The streets are broad and regular and cross each other at right angles. In the business section of the city they are paved. The city has an excellent system of street rail-

ways, which connect all parts with the business center.

Among the important buildings are the city hall, the courthouse, the office of the *Review*, the auditorium, the Masonic Temple, Spokane Club building and Athletic Club building. Among the churches the Roman Catholic and Protestant Episcopal cathedrals are especially worthy of mention. The city contains a number of small parks, which add greatly to its beauty. Fort Wright, an important military post, is also within the city limits and occupies a site of over 1000 acres. Among the educational institutions are Gonzaga College and the Academy of the Holy Name, both Roman Catholic, Burnot Hall, Saint Stephen's and the Lyons School for boys. Of all these institutions Gonzaga College is the most important. The city maintains an excellent system of public schools, and its high school is one of the prominent buildings. There is a Carnegie library, besides the libraries connected with the various schools.

Spokane is an important distributing center for a wide range of country, including eastern Washington, northern Idaho and northeastern Oregon. Within this territory are many important mines, as well as large areas of rich agricultural lands. These conditions give the city a large trade. The falls are capable of developing about 60,000 horse power, and about one-half of this is now utilized in generating electric power, some of which is used in the city and some carried to the Coeur d'Alêne mines, 100 miles distant. There are numerous manufactures of considerable importance. Chief among these is the manufacture of lumber, which is one of the leading industries of this locality. There are also sewer pipe works, flour mills, brickyards, terra cotta works, foundries, machine shops, furniture factories and factories for the manufacture of pottery and numerous other minor articles.

The first settlement was made at Spokane in 1873 and was named Spokane Falls. The town grew slowly until the opening of the Northern Pacific Railroad in 1881. In 1889 a fire nearly destroyed the business center. Like many other western towns, the city also suffered from overdevelopment; but when these crises were past, Spokane entered upon an era of steady and continuous prosperity. It is the most important town in eastern Washington. Population in 1910, 104,402.

Sponge, *spunj*, a jelly-like animal, belonging to the order Coelenterata. There are numerous species (See COELENTERATA), but what is known to commerce as a sponge is the skeleton of the animal. When examined, a common sponge is found to contain a large number of tubes, which extend into it in all directions. The smaller tubes unite to form larger ones; and if the sponge is cut open, it is found that these all join together, making one or more large tubes, that extend through the body from side to side. In the living sponge these tubes are lined with the flesh of the animal, and in the cavities in the small tubes are found many digestive tracts, or stomachs, in which the food is assimilated. In the network

SPONGE

of fibers forming the sponge proper, are found many spicules of silica and lime. In some of these the spicules of silica are so numerous as to give them a glass-like appearance, and when arranged in rows, like stars, these are beautiful objects; such are the *glass-rope* sponge and *Venus's flower basket*. Sponges reproduce themselves by means of eggs, which are formed by the layer of tissue which secretes the skeleton.

The best sponges are obtained from the Mediterranean and Red seas, where they live in deep, clear water, from 150 to 200 feet below the surface. The methods of securing sponges vary in different localities. In some parts of the Mediterranean they are still obtained by diving. The old method of diving is to have two men go out in a boat, one of whom attaches a weight to his feet and descends to the bottom of the sea, where by rapid movements he gathers a few sponges and places them in a basket. He then gives a signal to the man in the boat, who hauls him up. By more recent methods a diving dress is used, which enables the collector to remain under water a long time. Where the water is not too deep, the sponges are secured by the use of spears or prongs, attached to long handles. The fisher uses a bucket with a glass bottom, which, when placed on the surface of the water, enables him to see to a depth of sixty or more feet. When a sponge is discovered he breaks it off with his prong and brings it to the boat. After being collected, the sponges are

159

either buried in warm sand or allowed to lie in the sun, until the flesh has thoroughly decomposed. They are then cleaned and beaten, in order that all the decomposed matter may be expelled, and they are then dried and placed on the market.

Sponge, FRESH-WATER, a small fresh-water animal, about half an inch in length, which may be found in the bottom of almost any clean ditch or in ponds and lakes, attached to rocks, plants or submerged boards. Its form is that of two rather blunt cones, placed base to base. It is closed at one end, which is attached to a support; at the other it opens into a comparatively large mouth; at the sides there are numerous small pores, which perforate the walls. Water flows into the sponge through these small pores and is thrown out through the larger mouth-like opening. The food is brought into the sponge with the in-coming water currents, and after it has been digested the refuse is thrown out through the mouth. The fresh-water sponge has a skeleton composed of small needles or spicules, one of which is enclosed within a single cell and probably remains there until it has completed its full growth, when it is thrown out from the exterior of the sponge.

Sponta'neous Combus'tion, the burning of substances without the application of fire or other apparent cause. Jute, heaps of rags and similar substances, when saturated with oil, turpentine or varnish, and bituminous coal, when moistened with water, often begin burning in this manner. Cases of spontaneous combustion of the human body have been related, but leading scientists declare such a thing impossible.

Spontaneous Generation, *jen'ur a'shun*, or **Abiogenesis,** *ab'e o jen'e sis*, the doctrine that life may originate from dead matter, without the intervention of already existing protoplasm. In the seventeenth century this was the dominant view, and noted scientists have at intervals advocated the theory, but now the more general opinion is that living matter is invariably derived from some preëxisting living matter. Of course it has never been claimed that anything excepting the simplest forms of life could be generated spontaneously, and as before the invention of the microscope the presence of bacteria and other minute organisms could not be detected, there was good reason for the belief that life did spring spontaneously from dead matter.

Spoon'bill, a wading bird of the heron family. It takes its name from the shape of its bill, which is somewhat like a spoon, being curiously widened and bent slightly downward at the tip. Spoonbills are shy birds, living in flocks in wooded marshes, generally not far from the mouths of rivers, and on the seashore. The *roseate spoonbill* is a beautiful American bird, with a plumage of fine rose color, except for the

SPOONBILL

whitish neck and bright red wings. These birds have been much hunted for their plumes. In the United States the name *spoonbill* is sometimes given to the shoveler duck.

Spoon'er, John Coit (1843–   ), an American lawyer and statesman, born at Lawrenceville, Ind. At the age of sixteen he removed to Madison, Wis., where he attended the state university, graduating in 1864. Thereafter he served until the close of the Civil War in the Union army. He was admitted to the bar in 1867 and practiced law at Hudson, Wis., from 1870 to 1884. He was elected to the state legislature and in 1885 was chosen United States senator, served one term, was defeated for reëlection, was again elected in 1897 and was reëlected in 1903. In the United States Senate he distinguished himself as a debater and constitutional lawyer, being recognized as a leader of that body.

Spoon Worm, a name given to several different species of worms which have a spoon-like appendage near the mouth. All the species are remarkable for their wonderful power of contraction and expansion and for the extraordinary manner in which they can alter their shape. They are inhabitants of the sea and are much used as bait by fishermen.

Spots'wood or **Spottiswood,** Alexander (1676–1740), an English colonial governor in America, born at Tangier, Africa. He entered the British army, served with distinction and was appointed lieutenant governor of Virginia in 1710. For the following twelve years he was active in developing the commercial and educational interests of the colony, being responsible for the introduction of iron works and for vast improvements in the production of tobacco. He was superseded in 1722 on account of minor difficulties, but remained in America and became deputy postmaster-general in 1730.

Spott'sylva'nia Court House, Battle of, a battle of the Civil War, fought near Spottsylvania Court House, Va., about 50 miles from Richmond, between the Federal army under Meade and the Confederate Army of Northern Virginia under Lee, in May, 1864. After the battle in the Wilderness, Grant had ordered a movement around Lee's right wing to Richmond. Lee, however, was prepared for this maneuver and was in formation at Spottsylvania Court House before Grant reached that point. The contest was opened by General Hancock, for the Federals, on May 7, but his attack and those of his associates were fruitless. The fighting was continued intermittently until May 12, when desperate assaults were made by the Federals upon all parts of the Confederate line, but were repulsed with terrible slaughter. Grant remained in his position a week and at last withdrew, starting upon another movement around Lee's right flank toward Richmond. The Federal losses at Spottsylvania were nearly 7000, while those of the Confederates were somewhat larger. It was during this battle, on May 11, that General Grant sent his famous dispatch to General Halleck at Washington: "I propose to fight it out on this line if it takes all summer." See Civil War in America.

Sprain, a strain of the ligaments in any part of the body. Sprains are very frequent in the joints of the fingers, arms and lower limbs, in the latter of which the ankle is most frequently affected. Sometimes the ligaments are only strained, but in other cases they may be torn or broken, and the sprain may vary in degree, not only with the severity of the injury, but also according to its location. Sprains in some joints are much more difficult to heal than in others. Inflammation, swelling and pain follow a sprain and sometimes are exceedingly severe. The application of hot or cold water will often take out the soreness, and complete rest will bring a cure, unless the ligaments have been so badly torn that splints are necessary, as in a case of fracture.

Sprat, a small fish of the herring family, rarely more than six inches long. At one time the sprat was thought to be the young of the herring, the pilchard or the shad, but it can be easily distinguished from the young of any of these fishes by means of the sharply-notched edge of the abdomen. It is found in the North Atlantic and Mediterranean and on coasts of the southern United States. It is considered a delicious, well-flavored and wholesome fish.

Spree, *spray,* a river of Germany, which rises in the eastern part of Saxony, flows north and northeast through the Province of Brandenburg, traverses the city of Berlin and joins the Havel a little below Charlottenburg. Its length is about 250 miles, and it is navigable for vessels of 500 tons for a short distance above Berlin, while vessels of lighter draft can ascend the river for 110 miles. It is connected with the Oder by the Friedrich Wilhelm Canal.

Spring, an elastic body used for relieving concussion, for furnishing motive power or for controlling the motion of machines. Springs are made of various materials, such as steel wire, coiled spirally; steel rods or plates or strips of steel, suitably joined, as in the springs for carriages and railway cars; masses of India rubber, which, because of its elasticity, will resume its former position as pressure is removed. There are many patterns of springs, ranging from the delicate hairspring in the watch to the heavy springs found in locomotives. In the ordinary gunlock, the spring imparts motion to the hammer by being suddenly released from a strong tension. In the spring balance, the spring indicates the weight of the object placed on the scale pan. In the safety valve, it indicates the pressure of steam in a boiler and causes the valve to open at the proper time. Numerous other uses of the spring are also common.

Spring, a stream of water flowing from the earth, or a stream of water at the place of its source. Springs have their origin in the water that falls upon the earth in the form of rain or snow, which sinks through porous soils till it arrives at a layer of rock through which it cannot pass, where it forms subterranean reservoirs at various depths. When the pressure of the water which fills the channels through which it has descended is sufficient to overcome the resistance of the overlying mass of the earth, the water breaks through the upper strata and gushes forth in a spring. It may find some natural

channel or crevice through which to issue. In descending and rising through various mineral masses, the water of springs often becomes charged with gaseous, saline, earthy or metallic substances, as carbonic acid gas, sulphureted hydrogen gas, nitrogen, carbonate of lime, silica and carbonate of iron. When these substances are present in considerable quantity, the springs become what are known as *mineral springs.* Warm and hot springs are common, especially in volcanic countries (See THERMAL SPRINGS). Some springs run for a time and then stop altogether, after a time run again and again stop; these are called *intermittent springs.* Others do not cease to flow, but discharge a small quantity of water for a certain time and then give out a greater quantity; these are called *variable springs.* Springs are most numerous in mountainous and hilly regions, where the underground water finds ready outlets. See ARTESIAN WELL.

Spring, the season of the year between winter and summer, beginning with the vernal equinox, about March 21, and ending with the summer solstice, about June 21. In the public mind

SPRINGBOK

in the United States, spring comprises the months of March, April and May.

Spring'bok, a species of antelope, closely allied to the gazelle, formerly found in vast herds in

South Africa. Both the flesh and the hide are valuable, and it is therefore much hunted. It is a beautiful animal, of graceful form and fine colors—dull brown on the upper parts and pure white beneath, with a broad band of deep red where the colors meet on the flanks. It is larger than the roebuck, and its neck and limbs are much longer and more delicate. The horns curve in a lyre-shape, and are small in the female.

Spring'er, WILLIAM McKENDREE (1836–1903), an American politician and jurist, born in Sullivan County, Ind. He was educated in the public schools and at Illinois College in Jacksonville, Ill., also at Indiana University. He engaged in journalism and was admitted to the bar in 1859. In 1872 he was chosen to the state legislature and in 1875 began a service of twenty years in Congress, where he rose to a position of leadership in the Democratic party. In 1895 he became United States judge and later chief justice of the United States court of appeals in Indian Territory, but five years later he resumed private practice in Washington.

Spring'field, ILL., the capital of the state and the county-seat of Sangamon co., 185 mi. s. w. of Chicago, on the Baltimore & Ohio Southwestern, the Chicago & Alton, the Illinois Central, the Wabash and other railroads. The city is compactly built and regularly laid out, with wide, beautiful, shaded streets. The most prominent structure is the state capitol, with its massive dome, 364 feet high. The magnificent Lincoln monument and mausoleum, which contains the remains of the president, his wife, two children and one grandson, is located about a mile and a half from the capitol, in Oak Ridge Cemetery. The old capitol, now serving as the county courthouse, and the Lincoln residence, which is owned by the state, are interesting features.

The educational institutions include the Bettie Stuart Institute, Concordia Seminary, Saint Agatha's School, the Sacred Heart Academy and the Springfield business college. Other important buildings are the Executive Mansion, the city hall, the postoffice, the high school, Odd Fellows' Temple, an orphanage, two hospitals and a sanitarium. There are city, state and supreme court libraries and those of the State Historical Society and the Illinois State Museum of Natural History. A state fair is held here annually. The surrounding country is a rich farming and coal-mining region, and the city contains a large watch factory, engine and boiler works, car shops, lumber mills, foundries, machine shops and other factories. Springfield

was settled in 1819, was chosen as the county-seat in 1823, was incorporated as a town in 1832, was made the state capital in 1837 and was chartered as a city in 1840. Population in 1910, 51,678.

Springfield, MASS., the county-seat of Hampden co., 99 mi. w. by s. of Boston and 136 mi. n. e. of New York City, on the Connecticut River and on the Boston & Albany, the Boston & Maine, the Central New England and the New York, New Haven & Hartford railroads. It is a beautiful city and an attractive residence place, with wide and well-shaded streets. Forest Park covers an area of about 463 acres, and there are many small parks and public squares, containing a soldiers' and sailors' monument, statues of Miles Morgan and President McKinley and Saint-Gaudens's statue of *The Puritan.* Springfield has often been called "the City of Homes," for a smaller percentage of the population live in rented houses than in almost any other New England city.

Among the noted structures are a new Carnegie library, an art museum, a science museum, a county law library, and a hall of records. The city has two high schools, one of which is a well equipped technical high school, good public day schools and about ten evening schools. The unique features of the educational system of Springfield consist in the evening trades school, supported at public expense, a vocational school for boys, and three schools specially adapted to the needs of feeble-minded or backward pupils. The higher institutions of learning include the International Y. M. C. A. Training School, the American International College, two boarding schools for girls and three business colleges. The city contains the Mercy, Springfield and Wesson Memorial Homeopathic and Maternity hospitals. The two last were founded and endowed by D. B. Wesson and are splendidly appointed. There are about fifty churches, and among other prominent buildings are the union railway station, the Federal building and the courthouse.

A United States arsenal was established here in 1795, and it now employs from 1400 to 3000 men. It has a number of banks, savings banks, trust companies and insurance companies. The Smith & Wesson revolver works are located here. The manufactures include railroad cars and supplies, paper, envelopes, buttons, art goods, electrical supplies. automobiles. cotton goods and many small wares. Within a radius of 25 miles are the cities of Holyoke, Northampton, Chicopee and Hartford, as well as many large towns and villages. Its location in reference to these towns makes Springfield an important commercial center. The place was settled in 1636 by people from Roxbury, under the leadership of William Pynchon. During King Philip's War it was attacked and burned, Oct. 4, 1675. It was the scene of a riot in January, 1787, between the state troops and Shays's insurgents. The city was chartered in 1852. Population in 1910, 88,926. Consult Green's *Springfield* (1636-1886); also Tower's *Springfield Present and Prospective.*

Springfield, Mo., the county-seat of Greene co., is situated 130 mi. s. w. of Jefferson City, on the Saint Louis & San Francisco and the Kansas City, Clinton & Springfield and other railroads. The leading industrial establishments are lumber and flour mills, wagon factories and railroad and car shops. Drury College, Loretto Academy and a state normal are located here. A ten-story office building, the Colonial Hotel, the Frisco building, the courthouse, the Federal building, the high school, three hospitals, the zoölogical gardens and a large national cemetery are interesting features. The place was settled about 1819 as an Indian trading post and was incorporated in 1833. Population in 1910, 35,201.

Springfield, OHIO, the county-seat of Clark co., 45 mi. w. of Columbus, on Lagonda Creek and Mad River and on the Erie, the Detroit Southern, the Cleveland, Cincinnati, Chicago & Saint Louis, the Pittsburg, Cincinnati, Chicago & Saint Louis and a number of electric railroads. The city is in a fertile farming district, has good water power and has been for many years a very important center for the manufacture of agricultural implements. The industries also include foundries, machine shops, flour and paper mills, publishing houses and various other establishments. Wittenberg College is located here, and the city has a ladies' seminary, several Catholic parish schools and two business colleges. Noteworthy structures are the city hall, the Federal building, the courthouse, the Bushnell Library and the Y. M. C. A. buildings. Near the city are the state homes of the Masons, Odd Fellows and Knights of Pythias. Other features of interest are the fine soldiers' monument, Snyder Park and Fern Cliff Cemetery. The town was laid out in 1801 and was chartered as a city in 1850. Population in 1910, 46,921.

Spring Val'ley, ILL., a city in Bureau co., 100 mi. s. w. of Chicago, on the Illinois River and on the Chicago, Burlington & Quincy, the Chicago, Rock Island & Pacific and the Chicago & Northwestern railroads. Coal mining is the chief industry, while there are also foundries, machine shops and manufactories of pumps and other articles. The municipality has a public library and owns and operates the waterworks. The place is near the Cherry Mine, where in 1909 occurred a terrible mining disaster. Population in 1910, 7035.

Spring'ville, UTAH, a city in Utah co., 50 mi. s. by e. of Salt Lake City, on the Rio Grande Western and the San Predo, Los Angeles & Salt Lake railroads. It is on an elevation of 4920 feet, near the eastern end of Utah Lake, in a beautiful valley, which is well watered and contains fruit and stock farms. The city has a beet sugar factory and other establishments. It contains an academy, a Latter Day Saints' Church and a Presbyterian Church. The place was founded in 1850. Population in 1910, 3356.

Spruce, *spruce,* the name given to several species of cone-bearing trees. The *Norway spruce* yields the valuable timber known under the name of *white,* or *Christiania, deal.* It is a native of a large part of northern Europe, and is a noble tree, of conical habit of growth, reaching sometimes the height of 150 feet. The *white spruce* and the *black spruce* are both natives of North America. The latter attains the height of seventy or eighty feet, with a diameter of from fifteen to twenty inches. Its timber is of great value, on account of its strength, lightness and elasticity, and it is often employed for the yards of ships and the sides of ladders. The *hemlock spruce* is a noble species, rising to a height of seventy or eighty feet and measuring from two to three feet in diameter. It grows abundantly in the northern part of the United States and in Canada. The wood is employed for laths, fences and coarse indoor work. The bark is exceedingly valuable for tanning. The *Douglas spruce,* or *fir,* of northwestern America, reaches a height of 100 to 180 feet in its native forests. See LUMBER.

Spruce Beer, a fermented liquor, made from the leaves and small branches of the spruce fir, or from the essence of spruce, boiled with sugar or molasses and fermented with yeast. There are two kinds, the brown and the white, of which the latter is considered the better, as being made from white sugar, instead of molasses. Spruce beer forms an agreeable and wholesome beverage, and it is also used as a medicine.

Spurge Family or **Euphorbiaceae,** *u for'be-ay'se ee,* a natural order of herbs, shrubs or very large trees, which grow in all regions of the globe, those of the temperate regions being nearly all herbs. Most of them have a biting, milky juice, from which many valuable products are obtained. The flowers are always small and inconspicuous, but in many species there are large, bright-colored bracts, that resemble the petals of flowers. In the accompanying diagram, at the right is shown a single sterile flower, taken from the group at the left. The latter shows the single fertile flower in the midst of a number of sterile ones, all surrounded by the cup-shaped involucre, which bears the bright-colored bracts. The stems of the Euphorbiaceae vary greatly in appearance, and in some species they strongly resemble cacti. The fruit is dry or slightly fleshy

EUPHORBIA

and is three-lobed. Most of the tropical species are known as euphorbias. The poinsettia is a common American species.

Spurgeon, *spur'jun,* CHARLES HADDON (1834-1892), the greatest Non-conformist preacher of his time, born at Kelvedon, Essex, and educated at Colchester. He removed in 1853 to a chapel in New Park Street, Southwark, which, as it became too small for his audience, he abandoned; he engaged the Surrey Music Hall and ultimately built the well-known Metropolitan Tabernacle, which will accommodate about 6000 persons. Besides his ordinary ministrations and the publication, after 1855, of a weekly sermon, he founded many benevolent societies, including the Stockwell Orphanage and the Pastors' College. In 1887 he severed his connection with the Baptist Union, on account of what he called the

"down grade" tendency of the Church. He was the author of numerous volumes, of which the best known are *The Saint and his Saviour, John*

CHARLES HADDON SPURGEON

Ploughman's Talk, Feathers for Arrows, The Treasury of David Types and Emblems, The Metropolitan Tabernacle Farm Sermons, The present Truth, Storm Signals and *Salt Cellars.* His *Speeches at Home and Abroad* was published in 1878.

Spy, a term applied to a person employed by one army or party to enter the enemy's camp or quarters and to gain valuable information concerning his plans and equipment. The spy is allowed by usage to use any means, fair or foul, such as deceit, disguise or treachery, to accomplish his purpose. Military law decrees that, if a spy is captured, he shall die an ignominious death. See HALE, NATHAN.

Squadron, *skwahd'ron,* a division of a regiment of cavalry. A squadron, which consists of from 120 to 200 men, may be of two, three, or four troops, each commanded by a major. The term is applied, also, to a division of a fleet, consisting of a detachment of ships of war, numbering from two to eight, employed on a particular service or station, and under the command of a flag officer. See TACTICS.

Squall, *skwawl,* a sudden and violent outburst of wind, usually accompanied by rain or hail.

Squalls usually occur in connection with thunderstorms, which they precede by a few minutes. The squall is accounted for by the downward reaction of the expansion of the air in a storm cloud. This reaction, combined with the onward movement of the storm, forces the air next to the earth forward with such velocity as to cause a brisk wind, which may become violent. Squalls extend over larger areas than tornadoes, but are seldom destructive, unless accompanied by hail.

Square, in geometry, a figure with four equal sides and equal angles. This figure is considered the unit for the measurement of areas, though actually the unit of area measurement is no longer considered to be perfectly square, but merely to contain the same amount of surface space as would a square figure whose sides were of the length of the corresponding linear unit. To *square* a figure, a polygon, for example, is to reduce the surface to a square of equivalent area by mathematical means. This can be done by finding the area of the polygon and extracting the square root, the result being one side of the required square. The squaring of a circle is impossible, but it was one of the first problems to engage the attention of the mathematicians of antiquity. In arithmetic and algebra the square of a number is the product obtained by multiplying a number by itself. Thus, 64 is the square of 8, for $8 \times 8 = 64$.

Squash, *skwosh,* the fruit of a vine belonging to the same family as the melon and cucumber. It is closely related to the pumpkin and has many varieties, which differ greatly in size, in shape and in quality. Some varieties mature early in the season and are known as summer squashes, while others are not usable until late in the fall. The summer squashes grow into fancy forms and are variously colored in white, yellow and green. The later varieties are darker in flesh and have harder and darker shells.

Squash Bug, a name given to two species of insects, best known as destroyers of squash, pumpkin and other similar plants. The species which is particularly destructive in the United States is a cylindrical beetle, with wing cases striped with black and yellow.

Squatter, *skwot'tur,* **Sovereignty** or **Popular Sovereignty,** terms used in American history to denote the right of the inhabitants of any territory to govern themselves without Federal interference. The first term specifically relates to that right as applied to an unorganized territory, inhabited by so-called "squatters," that is, persons who had taken up land without purchasing titles. The doctrine of "squatter sovereignty" became of importance during the slavery controversy, when it was championed especially by Stephen A. Douglas, who incorporated it into the Kansas-Nebraska Bill. This declared that the people of the territories should have the right to decide whether slavery should be admitted or excluded. Though the theory was first proposed in order to protect the rights of slaveholders and to allow the extension of slavery, it was ultimately repudiated by the South, which was upheld by the dictum of Chief Justice Taney in the Dred Scott case. It finally led to a division between the Northern and Southern Democrats.

Squid, a popular name for many species of ten-armed animals, especially for the cuttlefish. They have a tapering body and a fin on each side of the tail and are often of a bluish color, speckled with purple. The American squids range from Newfoundland to the Virginia coast and are much used as bait by codfishers.

Squill, a plant belonging to the lily family, closely allied to hyacinths and onions. The term squill is more particularly applied to the sea onion, which has a large, bitter, bulbous root, like that of the common onion. It is a native of the sandy shores of the Mediterranean. The bulb has been known as a medicine from the earliest ages and is still used as a remedy for croup in children.

SQUILL

Squinting or **Strabismus,** *stra biz'mus,* a condition of the sight in which the axis of vision in one eye is turned from its proper position in relation to the other. The normal position of the eye and its direction towards objects are controlled by four straight muscles; one is attached above the eyeball; one beneath, and one on each side. If one of these muscles becomes paralyzed, that on the opposite side turns the eye out of its proper position and causes squinting. If one eye is defective or deformed, squinting is apt to arise from overstraining the other.

Squirrel, the name given to a large family of small rodents, or gnawing animals. The family is divided into two groups, the ground squirrels and the tree squirrels. Squirrels are found in all parts of the world except Australia, but are much more numerous in America than in Europe. Tree squirrels are light and agile little creatures, with strong jaws, sharp teeth and long, bushy tails. *Ground squirrels* seldom ascend trees, but burrow in the ground. In color squirrels are usually of a rich, ruddy brown or a dark gray on the upper parts, merging into reddish or grayish-

RED SQUIRREL

white on the under parts of the body; but the color varies with the season and climate. The head is large, and the eyes are projecting and bright. The *common squirrel* inhabits Europe and the north of Asia; while the *cat squirrel*, the *gray squirrel*, the *black squirrel*, the *red squirrel* and the *great-tailed squirrel* are American species. One oriental species is remarkable because it is the only animal which assumes a purely ornamental coat in the breeding season. It is gray in the summer and takes on a brilliant orange coat in early winter, changing to gray again in early spring.

Squirrels subsist on nuts, acorns and seeds, of which they lay up a store for winter in hollow trees or in the earth. Their nests, which consist of woody fiber, leaves and moss, are usually situated in the forks of trees, and the young, of which there are three or four to a pair in a season, are born in June. When engaged in eating, they sit on their haunches, with their tails thrown upward on the back, grasp the eatables with their fore paws and gnaw with their powerful teeth. The fur of some of the American species, especially of those of the north, is an important article of commerce.

Squirrel Monkey, a monkey inhabiting Brazil, resembling in general appearance and in size the common squirrel. A well-known species is grayish-olive in color, the under surface being gray, the ears white and the tail tipped with black.

Squirrel-Tail Grass. See WILD BARLEY.

Srinagar, *sre'na gar'*. See SERINAGUR.

Sta'dium, originally the race course of Olympia, Greece, where various athletic contests were held, but later a name given to all places throughout Greece where games were celebrated. Around the stadium were mounds of earth and sometimes seats, from which the spectators could see the contests, and the floor was sand or loose earth. The course was straight and was about 600 Greek feet long. The length of the stadium as a measure of distance is 125 paces, or 625 Roman feet, equivalent to 606 feet, 9 inches, in English measure.

Stadtholder, *stat'hold ur,* (Dutch, *Stadt-houder*, "cityholder"), a title formerly given in the Netherlands to the governor of a province. In 1580, when Holland and Zealand revolted against Spain and united to accept William, prince of Orange, as their ruler, they called him *stadtholder*. Upon the assassination of Prince William, the title was conferred on his son, Prince Maurice, and it remained as the title of the ruler until Holland was annexed by France, in 1802. It was finally dropped in 1814, when the prince of Orange was declared king of the Netherlands.

Stael-Holstein, *stay'el hole'stine,* ANNE LOUISE GERMAINE, Baroness de, commonly called *Madame de Stael* (1766–1817), a French author, the daughter of Necker, minister of finance to Louis XVI. Her education was directed with puritanical severity by her mother, but this was counteracted by the indulgence of her father, who encouraged his daughter to converse with the eminent philosophers who frequented his house. In 1786 she married Baron de Staël-Holstein, Swedish ambassador at the French court. The marriage was not very happy, and she lived for a time apart from her husband. In 1788 she printed her *Lettres sur Jean Jacques Rousseau*. At the outbreak of the Revolution (1789) she exercised considerable political power, by reason of her father's high position at court and through her own wit and womanly charm; but during the Reign of Terror she fled to her father's estate in Switzerland, after vainly endeavoring to save her friends and the royal family. During the period of the Directory, Madame de Staël returned to Paris, where she again became an influence in politics. Subsequently she was banished by Napoleon, on account of her bold advocacy of liberal views. Her husband died in 1802, and in 1811 she secretly married a young officer, De Rocca. This second marriage became known only after her death. Among her writings are the novels *Delphine* and *Corinne, On Germany, Thoughts on the French Revolution* and *Ten Years of Exile.*

Staff, a body of officers whose duties are in connection with an army or regiment as a whole and who are not attached to particular subdivisions. The staff of the general of the army of the United States consists of six aids, with the rank of colonel of cavalry; that of a lieutenant general consists of two aids and one military secretary, ranking as lieutenant colonels of cavalry; that of a major general consists of three aids, with rank of captains or lieutenants; the staff of a brigadier general consists of two aids, ranking as lieutenants.

The so-called *general staff* of the United States army was organized by an act of 1903. The chief of staff is commander and supervisor of all departments of the army, under the president. Under the chief of staff are the military secretary, the inspector-general, the quartermaster-general, the commissary-general, the surgeon-general, the paymaster-general, the chief of engineers, the chief of ordnance, the judge-advocate-general, the chief signal officer and the chief of the bureau of insular affairs.

Staff, a covering for buildings, made of hydraulic cement and sand, bound together by fibers of jute. Staff was used for covering the buildings of the Paris Exposition in 1889, the buildings of the World's Columbian Exposition at Chicago in 1893 and the buildings of the Louisiana Purchase Exposition at Saint Louis in 1904. It is comparatively cheap and light and can be molded into any desired form, but it is not suitable for the exterior of permanent buildings, as it lasts only a short time. See CEMENTS.

Stag or **Red Deer,** a large and handsome deer which is a native of Europe and northern Asia. In Great Britain it is now found wild only in the Highlands of Scotland. In summer the back and flanks of the stag are of a yellowish-brown color, while these parts in winter are reddish-brown. A full-sized male stag, with antlers well developed, stands about four feet high at the shoulder and has lofty, branching horns three

feet in length, while the female is smaller and has no horns. These deer feed on grass, buds and young shoots of trees, and in winter they roam in herds. The male is known distinctively as the hart, or stag, the female as the hind, and the young as the calf. The stag is represented in North America by the wapiti. See DEER.

Stag Beetle, a large beetle, especially distinguished by the enormous size of its horny and toothed mandibles, which somewhat resem-

STAG BEETLE

ble the horns of a stag. It is seen flying about in the evening, in the middle of summer, especially around oak trees. There are several species.

Stag'hound, a large and powerful hound, formerly used in Europe for hunting the stag, or red deer, and now nearly extinct. It was bred, as is supposed, from the bloodhound and greyhound. The modern staghound is a variety of the foxhound.

Stained Glass, an ornamental glass, produced by the oxides of metal, mixed with the ingredients used for common glass, applied with a brush and fastened in a kiln for firing. Another method is to dip a transparent glass into colored glass, when both are in a molten state. Opaline glass for art windows is made by pouring colored glass of different kinds upon white opaque glass and then pressing the whole between a heavy iron roller, thus causing the different glasses to fuse.

The first step in the making of ornamental windows is the design. A small sketch is first made, from which several copies are taken. It is then enlarged to the full size of the window and properly colored. The copies are cut into small sections, and pieces of glass are cut out, like these sections of the pattern. After this the glass is selected, and the various colors are painted upon the glass, to suit the general design. Sometimes a figure, a face, a flower, a monogram or some other design is to be painted in the window, in which case the colors are laid on the pieces of glass with mineral paint, which fuses into the glass when heated, after which the glass bits are taken to the kiln and fired. When all the sections are assembled on the uncut pattern, the original drawing is brought in for comparison. In joining the pieces together, a frame of lead is made for each piece, and lead strips are run through a pair of rollers, to secure uniformity in thickness and width and to make grooves in each side of these strips. As each piece is leaded, it is placed over the pattern, until the window is assembled as a whole. Then the leads are soldered together with a common soldering, after which a cement of lead and oil is spread along the leads, to make the whole water-tight. The window is cleaned with whiting and is then ready to be placed in position. In some of the medieval cathedrals of Europe are windows of great value, which were the designs of great artists and were finished with a perfection which has not been equaled until the present time.

To-day the United States leads the world in the manufacture of stained glass. The revival of the art is due especially to John La Farge and Louis Tiffary. The process of manufacture has materilay changed, and many wonderful effects in iridescence have been obtained. The picture is really a glass mosaic work, in which various effects are produced by what is known as modeled glass, by using several thicknesses, sometimes as many as eight. Streakings of different colored glass (pot metal) is also used to obtain pictorial effects. An excellent example of modern stained glass is the beautiful window in the Bartlett Gymnasium of the University of Chicago, where the artist has chosen *Wilfred, Knight of Ivanhoe, crowned by the fair Rowena*, as his subject. See GLASS.

Stainer, *stine'ur,* JOHN, Sir (1840–1901), an English organist and composer. He early received important appointments as organist and in 1872 accepted such a position at Saint Paul's, London. During his later years he published many compositions, including numerous cantatas and oratorios, the best of which are *The Daughter of Jairus, Saint Mary Magdalene* and *The Crucifixion.*

Stalac'tite, a mass of rock suspended from the roof of a cavern, and produced by the evaporation of water which holds in solution compounds of lime, silica and iron. The water percolates through the rock, and as it evaporates, these substances solidify. Stalactites usually take the form of icicles, but occasionally they form columns extending from the roof to the floor of the cavern. Similar masses of small size are frequently to be seen, also, hanging from stone

bridges. Simultaneously with the formation of the stalactite, a similar but upward growth, called a *stalagmite,* takes place at the spot where the successive drops of water fall and evaporate. See CAVE.

Stalag'mite. See STALACTITE.

Sta'men. See FLOWERS.

Stam'ford, CONN., a city in Fairfield co., 33 mi. n. e. of New York City, on Long Island Sound and on the New York, New Haven & Hartford railroad. The location is attractive, and many New York business men have their homes here. There is regular steamship connection with New York City, as well as electric lines to neighboring towns. The place is especially well known for its manufactures of locks and keys, and it also produces various other articles, including drugs, pianos and typewriters. It contains the Ferguson Library, a city hospital, Saint John's Hospital and Home and several private sanitariums. The educational institutions include the Catherine Aiken School for girls, Betts Academy for boys and several other private institutions. Stamford was settled in 1641 by a company from Wethersfield, on the site of an old indian village called Rippowam. It was made a borough in 1830 and was chartered as a city in 1894. Population in 1910, 25,138.

Stamp, a term specifically applied to the public mark or seal, made by a government or its officers upon paper or parchment, whereon private deeds or other legal agreements are written and for which certain charges are made for purposes of revenue. The name is also applied to a small piece of stamped paper issued by the government, to be attached to a document liable to duty, or to letters, papers or packages to be transmitted by mail.

Stamp Act, an act regulating the imposition of stamp duties; specifically, an act passed by the British Parliament in 1765, requiring all documents, commercial instruments and newspapers to be written or printed on paper stamped by the British government. After the close of the French wars, there grew up in England a feeling that taxes ought to be raised in America as a contribution to the war debt, and for the military defense of the colonies, and that the matter should be placed under the control of Parliament. The colonies expressed their willingness to raise money in answer to requisitions upon their assemblies, but they denied the right of Parliament to tax them, as it was a body in which they were not represented. The act was proposed in March, 1764, and was passed in March, 1765.

When the news was received in America, riots in opposition broke out. In October the colonies held a convention and sent a memorial to the king, acknowledging his sovereignty, but denying the right of Parliament to tax them. In March, 1766, the act was repealed, but the taxing power of Parliament was reiterated. This episode was one of the immediate causes of the Revolution.

Stamp Weed. See INDIAN MALLOW.

Stan'bery, HENRY (1803–1881), an American lawyer, born in New York City. He was educated at Washington College, Pa., was admitted to the bar in 1824 and for a time practiced in Lancaster, Ohio. He became the state's first attorney-general in 1846, and twenty years later he was appointed by President Johnson attorney-general of the United States. He resigned in 1868 to act as counsel for President Johnson in his impeachment trial, and he then resumed practice in Cincinnati.

Standard Time. See TIME, STANDARD.

Stan'dish, MILES (1584–1656), an American colonist and soldier, born in Lancashire, England. He served in the English army in the Netherlands, and, though not a member of the Leyden congregation, sailed with the *Mayflower* colony to Massachusetts in 1620. He became the strongest leader of the Pilgrims in their struggle against the indians. During the first winter his wife died, and the traditional account of his effort to secure a second wife has been made familiar by Longfellow in *The Courtship of Miles Standish*. In 1625 he was sent on a mission to England, but returned in the following year and settled at Duxbury, Mass., where he died. Standish was the military head of the colony, and for a long time was its treasurer. A monument surmounted by a statue has been erected to his memory at Duxbury.

Stan'ford, LELAND (1824–1893), an American capitalist and politician, born in Watervliet, N. Y. He was admitted to the bar and removed to Wisconsin in 1849, but he went to California in 1852 and engaged in gold mining and mercantile business. He was one of the promoters of the Central Pacific Railroad, was made president of the company and superintended the construction of the line. He was elected governor of California in 1861 and was United States senator from 1884 until his death. He founded the Leland Stanford Junior University at Palo Alto, Cal., in memory of his son. See LELAND STANFORD JUNIOR UNIVERSITY.

Stanislas I Leszczynski, *stan'is laws lyesh-chin'y'ske,* (1677–1766), king of Poland. His father was grand treasurer to the Polish crown, and he himself was palatine of Posen, when he was recommended to the Warsaw assembly by Charles XII of Sweden as a candidate for the vacant throne of Poland. He was accordingly elected and crowned (1705), but after the disastrous Battle of Poltava (1709), when his patron Charles XII was defeated, he had to flee from Poland. Ultimately he found refuge in France, where his daughter Maria became the wife of Louis XV. Assisted by the French king, he sought to establish his claim to the throne of Poland in 1733, but again he had to retire into France, where he was given possession of the duchies of Lorraine and Bar, which he held until his death.

Stanislas II Augus'tus (1732–1798), the last king of Poland. Sent by Augustus III of Poland on a mission to Saint Petersburg, he became a favorite with Catharine, afterward empress of Russia, by whose influence he was crowned king of Poland in 1764. The nobility, however, were discontented with this interference on the part of Russia, and compelled the king to abdicate in 1771. He protested against the various partitions of Poland, formally resigned his sovereignty in 1795 and died in Saint Petersburg, as a pensioner of the Russian emperor.

Stan'ley, ARTHUR PENRHYN (1815–1881), second son of Edward Stanley, rector of Alderley, afterward bishop of Norwich, born at Alderley, Cheshire. He was educated at Rugby and Balliol College, Oxford, and became leader of the "broad Church" party. Stanley had a keen sense of humor, was charitable and sympathetic, and had a large circle of friends and acquaintances. He tried to build up the Church on a broad basis, and from his pulpit he exercised a wide influence. He was the author of numerous works, among which are *Life of Arnold, Memoir of Bishop Stanley, Commentary on the Epistles to the Corinthians, Memorials of Canterbury Cathedral, Lectures on the Eastern Church, Lectures on the Jewish Church, Memorials of Westminster Abbey, Essays on Church and State* and *The Athanasian Creed.*

Stanley, HENRY MORTON, Sir (1841–1904), an African explorer, born at Denbigh, Wales. His father, John Rowlands, died when the boy was but two years old. In 1857 he shipped as cabin boy to New Orleans and was there adopted by a merchant, whose name he assumed. Stanley enlisted in the Confederate army, and was taken prisoner in the Battle of Shiloh (1862). He escaped, and after a visit to his home in Wales he volunteered into the United States navy and became an ensign on the ironclad *Ticonderoga*. At the close of the war he went West as a newspaper correspondent, and as correspondent for the New York *Herald* he joined the Abyssinian expedition of 1868. He afterward traveled in Spain, and it was while there in 1869 that he was asked by the proprietor of the New York *Herald* "to go and find Livingstone." After visiting the Crimea, Palestine, Persia and India, he reached Zanzibar in the early part of 1871, and thence

HENRY MORTON STANLEY

he proceeded across Africa, in search of Livingstone (See LIVINGSTONE, DAVID). He met and relieved Livingstone at Lake Tanganyika in November of the same year and returned to England. He then acted as the *Herald's* correspondent during the Ashanti War in 1873.

As correspondent of the London *Daily Telegraph* and the New York *Herald*, in 1874 he undertook an expedition into Africa, where he explored the equatorial lake region, and for the first time he traced the Kongo River from the interior to its mouth. For the purpose of developing this vast region he returned in 1879 under the auspices of the International African Association, founded by the king of the Belgians. In this territory stations were planted, steam navigation was established and in 1885 the territory received the name of the Kongo Free State (See KONGO FREE STATE). In 1887 Stanley organized an expedition for the relief of Emin Pasha,

who, after the Mahdist rising in the Sudan, was cooped up with his Egyptian followers in the equatorial province of Egypt. This time he entered Africa on the west by way of the Kongo; and after a series of extraordinary marches through a forest region, he met Emin Pasha in the neighborhood of the Albert Nyanza. After a return journey, to bring up the rear column, which he had left on the Aruwimi, Stanley finally, in May, 1889, set out from the Albert Nyanza and brought the pasha and his followers to the coast. Upon his return to England he was immensely popular and was sent to Parliament in 1895, where he worked earnestly for the development of British interests in Africa. He wrote *How I Found Livingstone, Through the Dark Continent, In Darkest Africa* and *The Congo and the Founding of its Free State*.

Stanovoi, *stahn o voi'*, **Mountains,** a mountain chain situated in the northeastern part of Asia and extending in an easterly and northeasterly direction from about the 54th parallel of north latitude into the northeastern extremity of Asia, near Bering Strait. The chain extends along the coast of Siberia bordered by the Okhotsk Sea, and a spur runs southeasterly into the Peninsula of Kamtchatka. On the west the Stanovoi merge into the Yablonoi system (See YABLONOI MOUNTAINS). In some places the slopes are covered with dense forests, but the summits are generally bare. The highest mountains do not exceed 8000 feet in altitude, and the entire length of the chain is about 3000 miles.

Stan'ton, EDWIN McMASTERS (1814–1869), an American statesman, born at Steubenville, Ohio. He acted for three years as clerk in a book shop, attended Kenyon College from 1831 to 1833, subsequently studied law and was admitted to the bar in 1836, beginning practice at Cadiz, Ohio, later removing to Steubenville, Ohio, and Pittsburg, Pa. In 1856 he opened an office at Washington, D. C., where he acquired a large practice in the Supreme Court. After Lincoln was elected president, Stanton entered Buchanan's cabinet as attorney-general. Shortly after the outbreak of hostilities between the North and South, President Lincoln appointed him head of the war department (January, 1862), and his acceptance of the office marked the beginning of a vigorous military policy. He remained in the cabinet at President Johnson's request after Lincoln's death, but soon came into disagreement with his chief over the reconstruction policy and was asked to resign. Stanton refused, with the support of the Senate, and was suspended, but declined to give up his office until the failure of impeachment proceedings against Johnson. He was appointed justice of

EDWIN M. STANTON

the Supreme Court by President Grant, but died a few days later.

Stanton, ELIZABETH CADY (1815–1902), a woman suffragist and reform advocate, born in Johnstown, N. Y. She was educated in the local academy and by private teachers. Her father was an eminent lawyer and a member of Congress. The daughter inherited a legal mind and strong reasoning powers. She married Henry B. Stanton, a prominent Abolitionist and a man in full sympathy with her ideas. She met Lucretia Mott while attending the World's Anti-Slavery Convention in London, and thereafter she labored with her in behalf of woman's rights. In 1848 Mrs. Stanton called the first woman's rights convention ever held in America, to assemble at her home in Seneca Falls, N. Y. Three years later she became associated with Susan B. Anthony, and they labored together in the cause of woman's rights for the remainder of Mrs. Stanton's life. Mrs. Stanton had a charming personal appearance and was a good writer and a fluent speaker. She attained a national reputation as an author and lecturer and exerted a strong influence in behalf of the cause which she advocated. She held many prominent positions in women's organizations and was active in securing higher education for women. Some of her best-known writings are *The Solitude of Self* and *Self-Government the Best Means of Self-Development.*

Sta'ples, THE. See FARNE ISLANDS.

Starch, a substance of very great importance, stored as food in many plants. It occurs in seeds, as in those of wheat and other cereal grains and of leguminous plants; in many roots and underground stems; in the stem and pith of many plants, as in the sago plant; in some barks, as in that of cinnamon, and in pulpy fruits, such as the apple. Finally, it is contained in the juice of most vegetables, in a state of suspension, and is deposited when the expressed juices are allowed to stand. The starch of commerce is chiefly extracted from wheat flour and potatoes. When pure, starch is a snow-white powder, of a glistening appearance, which makes a crackling noise when pressed with the finger. It is composed of transparent, rounded grains, the size of which varies in different plants, those of the potato being among the largest, and those of wheat and rice the smallest. It is insoluble in cold water, alcohol and ether; but when heated with water it is converted into a kind of solution, which, on cooling, forms a stiff, semi-opaque jelly. If this is dried up, it yields a transparent mass, which softens and swells into a jelly, if water is again applied. Starch is employed for stiffening linen and other cloth. When potato starch is roasted at a moderate heat in an oven, it is converted into a species of gum, employed by calico printers. Starch is convertible into sugar by boiling with dilute sulphuric acid. Starch forms the greatest portion of wheat flour, and is, consequently, the chief ingredient of bread.

Star Chamber, formerly an English court of civil and criminal jurisdiction at Westminster, said to have taken its name from the star-decorated room in which it was held. It consisted originally of a committee of the privy council and was remodeled during the reign of Henry VII, when it consisted of four high officers of state, with power to add to their number a bishop, a temporary lord of the council and two justices of the courts of Westminster. It had jurisdiction over forgery, perjury, riots, maintenance, fraud, libel and conspiracy cases, and it could inflict any punishment short of death. Its trials were without jury, and the abuses which this made possible led to the abolition of the court during the reign of Charles I.

Star'fish, a name given to an interesting sea animal, belonging to one of the lower orders (See ECHINODERMATA). The starfish has five arms attached to a central disk, and each arm is anatomically complete in itself. Its nervous system consists of a ganglion around the mouth and five cords running along the lower side of the arms, to terminate in an eye at the end of each arm. The starfish is found sometimes in shore pools, about low-water level, but its favorite haunts are on the floor of the sea, at a depth of a few fathoms. It is covered with a tough leathery skin, beset with prickles, and the skin is supported by a series

STARFISH

of plates, beautifully joined together. On the under surface of each arm, there is a series of small holes, through which the tubular feet can be protruded when the starfish wishes to move. A number of different animals resemble the starfish proper, but differ in the number of arms and in other respects.

Stark, JOHN (1728–1822), an American soldier, born at Londonderry, N. H. While still a young boy, he was captured by the Saint Francis indians and adopted into the tribe. He fought in the last French and Indian war, and at the opening of the Revolution he raised a regiment, which he led to Cambridge, and took a prominent part in the Battle of Bunker Hill. He was present at the battles of Trenton and Princeton, but resigned his commission in April, 1777. At the approach of Burgoyne, however, in the fall of the same year, he raised a regiment of New Hampshire troops and completely routed a force of Tories and Hessians at Bennington, August 16. He was also present at the Battles of Saratoga and was made a brigadier general. Stark was a member of the André court-martial and served at the head of important departments until the close of the war. He was one of those who,

in 1776, pledged their private fortunes to pay the soldiers, in order to induce them to enlist for a second term.

Star'lings, a family of birds, widely distributed throughout the world and allied to the crows. The common starling is found in almost all parts of Europe. It is between eight and nine inches in length, of a blackish blue or purplish color, with each feather marked at the extremity with a wide triangular speck. The common starling has been introduced into the United States and now is a well-known bird about New York and other eastern cities, where it is distinguished from the blackbirds and grackles by its short tail and yellowish-white beak. Starlings have a variety of notes, and some species have clear whistles or rich songs. They thrive in captivity and improve in their songs.

Star-Nosed Mole, a North American genus of moles, distinguished by bearing at the extremity of the muzzle a remarkable structure of fleshy and somewhat cartilaginous rays, disposed in the form of a star.

Star of Bethlehem, a common spring garden plant of the lily family, with white, waxy and starlike flowers. It is a native of Europe, but it is naturalized in the United States.

Star of Bethlehem, the star which, according to Biblical tradition, heralded Christ's birth. *Matthew* II, 1–2.

Star Route Frauds, frauds disclosed in connection with the postal service during the administration of President Hayes. The name *star route* was given to routes over which the mail was carried on horseback or in wagons, owing to the fact that they were marked with a star in the records of the postal department. Through the activity of a certain clique of government officers, including several congressmen and senators, the compensation for carrying the mails over these routes was increased more than fourfold, the profits being divided between the contractors who carried the mail and the members of the ring. The leaders were prosecuted during the early part of Garfield's administration, but only one was ever punished. However, the operations of the conspirators were ended.

Stars, those self-shining bodies seen in the heavens at night, like bright, twinkling spots, always occupying the same relative position in the sky. Because these bodies are unlike the planets and comets and appear to remain immovable, they are called "fixed stars," though the name is no longer considered appropriate, for it is known that many of them actually do move, and it is probable that all are in motion. In order to distinguish the stars from one another, the ancients divided the heavens into different spaces, containing groups of stars (See CONSTELLATIONS). The stars are classified according to their brightness as of different magnitudes, those of the first magnitude being the brightest. All the stars beyond the sixth or seventh magnitude are called *telescopic stars*, as they cannot be seen by the naked eye. Astronomers recognize stars as small as those of the sixteenth magnitude. As to the absolute size of the stars, little is known; but the light given out by Sirius, the brightest fixed star in the heavens, is estimated at $63\frac{1}{2}$ times that of the sun.

The colors of the stars vary considerably, red, yellow, blue and green being noticeable, and it is supposed that they differ considerably in composition, though they are probably made up of the same matter that composes the earth. Stars are very irregularly distributed over the heavens; in some regions scarcely one is to be seen, while in others they seem densely crowded together, especially in the portion known as the galaxy, or Milky Way (See MILKY WAY). Of the stars visible to the naked eye at one time, the number probably does not exceed a few thousands, but seen through the telescope, their number is so great as to defy calculation. The distances of the stars from the earth are very great. The shortest distance yet found, that of α Centauri, a double star in the Southern Hemisphere, has been calculated at 20,000,000,000 miles, so that light takes $3\frac{1}{2}$ years to travel from it to our earth. Many stars have been observed whose light appears to undergo a regular periodic increase and diminution of brightness, amounting, in some instances, to a complete extinction and revival. These are called *variable* and *periodic* stars. It is found that some stars, formerly distinguished by their splendor, have entirely disappeared. Such stars are called *temporary*. Many of the stars that usually appear single are found, when observed with telescopes of high magnifying power, to be really composed of two, and some of them have three or more stars close together (See DOUBLE STARS). When we look at the stars, they appear to be placed on the inside of a hollow sphere that revolves around us, and the pivot on which the sphere turns is near the North, or Polar, Star. This apparent rising and setting of the stars is due to the rotation of the earth. See BEAR, GREAT; SOLAR SYSTEM; PLANET, and articles therein referred to; also ASTRONOMY, Vol. VI.

Star Spangled Banner, An American patriotic hymn, written by Francis Scott Key in 1814. At the time Key was a prisoner on board the British frigate *Surprise*, which was one of the vessels then attacking Baltimore. The tune to which the words are set is known as "Anacreon in Heaven," and was composed by John Stafford Smith about 1770.

Starvation, *stahr va'shun.* When food is not supplied in sufficient quantities to supply the waste that is continually taking place in the various organs of the body, the tissues themselves are used to supply energy, and starvation follows. The accompanying conditions are emaciation, lowered vitality and temperature and a general weakness. Death in animals, according to Chossat, occurs when the body has lost two-fifths of its weight. Man seldom lives longer than a week or ten days when deprived of food, but the time may be lengthened by taking a little water only. It may also be lengthened by the person's remaining in bed, well covered with clothing, thus lengthening the loss of temperature and the exhaustion of muscular tissue.

State, an organized political society whose population dwells in a fixed and permanent territory and under a single government. The origin and rise of the conception of *State* is obscure, but is now believed to have been a gradual process, powers being surrendered, often unconsciously, by the members of a community as they came to realize more fully the utility of coöperation and unity. Accordingly, scholars now are agreed that the object of the State is to secure the benefits which flow from peace, security and coöperation. With regard to the question whether a State should be *paternalistic* or *individualistic* in character (that is, whether it should extend its functions and minister to the every need and desire of its citizens, or should confine itself to the simple and fundamental functions, such as the preserving of peace and the punishment of crime), no general principle can be stated, but every new question in that connection should be decided with reference to the "greatest good to the greatest number."

In a broad sense, the study of the State involves a study of all political theory, and in that sense it has engaged the minds of the greatest philosophers in history, beginning with Plato and Aristotle, who wrote in the days and spirit of the city-state; Aquinas and Dante, who in the Middle Ages discussed the problem of the relation of Church and State; Machiavelli, the champion of a strong monarchical government; Locke and

Rousseau, the exponents of the theory of natural right; Hobbes, the defender of absolutism, and Montesquieu, who sought to find the basis of good government by studying the history of government.

The name *state* is given to each one of the political divisions composing the United States of America. The name is, however, somewhat loosely applied, since, though they do have full control of all local affairs, many powers essential to the full sovereignty of a state, such as declaring war, levying import duties and negotiating treaties, have been surrendered by them to the central government.

State, Department of, one of the nine executive departments of the United States government, in charge of the secretary of state, appointed by the president and confirmed by the Senate. This department was the first one organized under the Federal government. The secretary is first in importance and prestige in the president's cabinet and is first in line of succession to the presidency. The department has charge of all foreign affairs, both of state and of the consular service. Its business is transacted through eight bureaus, each of which is under the direction of a commissioner. The secretary also publishes all ordinances of Congress and proclamations and decrees of the president and affixes the presidential seal to all documents. See United States, subhead *Government.*

Stat'en Island, an island forming the southeastern part of New York State and the southern part of Greater New York, of which it constitutes the borough of Richmond. It is situated at the entrance of New York harbor, 5 miles southwest of Manhattan Island, and is separated from Long Island by the Narrows and from New Jersey by Staten Island Sound, or Arthur Kill, and Kill van Kull, which connects New York Bay with Newark Bay. The island is 13 miles long and has a hilly surface, the highest elevation being about 300 feet. It contains many fine residences and villas. The largest village on the island is New Brighton, which is on the northern shore. Forts Wadsworth and Tompkins are located on the island, near the Narrows.

States-General, the name applied to the representative assembly of France, made up of members from the nobility, clergy, and Third Estate. Under Charlemagne there was an assembly which included the nobility and the clergy, but this body was not, as far as can be

determined, summoned after the beginning of the tenth century, until 1302, when Philip the Fair called together the three orders, to gain help in his contest with the pope. As absolutism grew in France, the States-General became less and less important. From 1614 the body was not assembled until the famous meeting of 1789 (See French Revolution).

The name States-General is also applied to the legislative assembly of Holland.

States of the Church. See Papal States.

States' Rights, a term used in United States political history to denote the view of those who hold that the Union is a compact of sovereign and independent states, the central government being only their agent. Carried to its logical conclusion, it upheld the right of any state to nullify an oppressive or unconstitutional act of Congress. The doctrine was formerly widely held, especially in the South before the Civil War, where it was used to combat the authority of Congress to interfere with slavery. It was also held, though in more moderate terms, by northern statesmen, including Jefferson, Madison and many New England Federalists. Various constitutional authorities have upheld the doctrine, though it is admitted that the Civil War finally removed it from the field of political discussion.

State University of Iowa. See Iowa, State University of.

Stat'ics, that branch of dynamics which treats of the properties and relations of forces in equilibrium, equilibrium meaning that the forces are in perfect balance, so that the body upon which they act is in a state of rest. The word *dynamics* is employed as expressing the science which treats of the laws of force or power, thus corresponding closely to the old use of the term *mechanics*; and this science is divided into *statics* and *kinetics,* the first being the science which treats of forces considered as producing rest and the second as treating of forces considered as producing motion. See Dynamics.

Statis'tics, a collection of facts; especially those facts which illustrate physical, social, moral, intellectual, political, industrial and economic conditions or changes of condition, and which admit of numerical statement and of arrangement in tables. The collection of statistics may have the object merely of ascertaining numbers or of learning what happens in an average of a great number of cases, as is the case of insurance statistics; or of detecting the causes of phenomena that appear in the consideration of a great number of individual cases—such phenomena, for example, as the decline of a certain trade or the prevalence of a certain disease. In all civilized countries the collection of statistics forms an important part of the administrative duties of government.

Stat'ute, a law proceeding from the government of a state; the written will of the legislature, solemnly expressed according to the forms necessary to constitute it the law of the state. In the United States a statute which contravenes a provision of the constitution of a state by whose legislature it was enacted, or of the United States Constitution, is void. See LAW.

Staun'ton, VA., the county-seat of Augusta co., 55 mi. n. of Lynchburg, on the Baltimore & Ohio and the Chesapeake & Ohio railroads. The city is surrounded by an agricultural region and contains manufactures of organs, flour, chemicals, wagons, agricultural implements and general machine shop products. The leading public buildings are the city hall, the courthouse, the Masonic Temple and the Columbian Hall. The state institutions for the insane, the deaf and dumb and the blind are located here, and the city has several seminaries for girls, a military academy and parish and other private schools. The place was settled in 1745 by people from northern Ireland and was chartered as a city in 1871. During the Civil War it was an important strategic point. Population in 1910, 10,604.

Stavanger, *stah'vang ur,* a seaport of Norway, situated on an inlet of the North Sea, known as Bukken Fjord, 100 mi. s. of Bergen. It is one of the oldest cities of Norway and contains a cathedral which is one of the finest specimens of Gothic architecture in the country. The city is noted for its large merchant fleet. Population in 1910, 37,261.

Stead, *sted,* WILLIAM THOMAS (1849–1912), English editor born at Embleton. After nine years' experience as editor of the Darlington *Northern Echo,* he became assistant editor of the *Pall Mall Gazette* under John Morley, and when the latter retired Stead became editor. He introduced the interview and many American methods into English journalism, and made a reputation for his originality. In 1890 he founded the monthly *Review of Reviews,* of which he was editor until his death. He vigorously opposed the Boer War, though his attitude cost him the friendship of Cecil Rhodes. He wrote numerous books and magazine articles, including some on spiritualism, to which he be-

came a convert. Whatever he undertook, his unbounded enthusiasm and enterprise gave him the strength of a crusader; he always fought for what he believed. He made several visits to America, on the last of which he lost his life by the sinking of the *Titanic.*

Steam, *steem,* the vapor of water. Steam forms at all temperatures, even below freezing point (See EVAPORATION). In the ordinary use of the word, however, steam means the vapor of water when it is at or above boiling point; that is, 100° C. or 212° F. Steam is lighter than water, and at boiling point it occupies about seventeen hundred times as much space. Pure steam is invisible and should be distinguished from the clouds formed by the issuing of steam from the spout of a teakettle or the escape pipe of an engine, for these clouds are caused by the condensation of the steam into minute particles of water. The expansive force of steam increases with the increase of temperature. This is taken into consideration in the operating of engines. *Pure steam,* or *dry steam,* acts like pure gas. Dry steam is secured by heating it to a temperature above that of boiling water. The dome of the boiler is a chamber for collecting the dry steam. *Wet steam,* or *saturated steam,* is of the temperature of boiling water and contains particles of water suspended in the vapor. *Waste,* or *exhaust steam* has been used; *live steam* is that ready for use.

The great expansive force of steam, and the ease with which it can be condensed, make it the most valuable gas for the motive power of engines (See STEAM ENGINE). Steam is also used for warming buildings, for cooking, in meat packing and in establishments for extracting substances such as glue from animal tissues.

Steam Engine, a machine for using the expansive force of steam as a motive power. The first recorded attempt to use steam as a motive power is attributed to Hero of Alexandria, in the second century B. C. Hero constructed an apparatus consisting of a hollow metallic ball, mounted on hollow trunnions, upon which it revolved. Tubes with their outer ends drawn to a small size and opened at right angles to the axis of the ball were inserted so that they resembled the spokes of a wheel. The trunnions were connected with a closed kettle, in which water was boiled. As the steam filled the ball and escaped through the tubes, its reaction against the air caused the ball to revolve. This apparatus worked on the same principle as Barker's Mill (See BARK-

ER'S MILL). From the time of Hero's experiment until about the beginning of the eighteenth century, nothing more was known concerning the use of steam as a motive power. In 1705 Thomas Newcomen of England was granted a patent for an engine which consisted of a boiler, from which the steam was conveyed by a pipe to the interior of a cylinder, the upper end of which was open to the air, and in which the piston worked. The piston was attached to a walking beam, to the opposite end of which the pump rod was attached. Clumsy as this machine was, it worked fairly well for pumping water. The piston was raised by the pressure of steam and was forced down by the pressure of the air, after the steam in the cylinder had been condensed by the use of cold water. The valves were worked by hand until a boy who was tending the valves became tired of his task and by a system of sticks and cords so connected them with the walking beam that the engine became self-acting. Later his device was attached to all engines. This engine was greatly improved by Watt (See WATT, JAMES).

The steam engine as we know it to-day is constructed upon Watt's plan, with the exception that the attachments and gear for working the valves have been considerably improved.

PARTS. The essential parts of a steam engine are the boiler (See BOILER); the working parts, consisting of cylinder, piston, valves and gear; the necessary appliances for connecting the piston with the machinery to be operated. These usually consist of a connecting rod, a crank and a shaft, or fly wheel.

The cylinder is an iron box, whose inner surface has been carefully turned. Upon one side, a box called the *steam chest*, A, is fastened, and from this openings, called the *steam ports* (1 and 2), lead to each end of the cylinder. Steam is admitted through the pipe, H. Between the steam ports is the *exhaust port*, 3. The valve, B, is connected by the eccentric rod, G, with the eccentric, which gives it its sliding motion (See ECCENTRIC). The cylinder contains the piston, D, to which is fastened the piston rod, E. As this leaves the cylinder it passes through the *stuffing box*, F, which is packed with cotton waste or other material, to make it steam-tight. The valve alternately opens and closes the steam ports and the exhaust port. The diagram shows steam entering the cylinder through 2 and escaping to the exhaust port through 1. The piston is moving towards the left. When it reaches its farthest point in

that direction, the valves are reversed, 1 being opened into the steam chest, and 2 into the exhaust port, thus forcing the piston back to the opposite end of the cylinder. The outer end of the piston rod is connected with a *cross head*, to which the connecting rod is also attached. The cross head slides between guides and holds the piston rod firmly in position. The

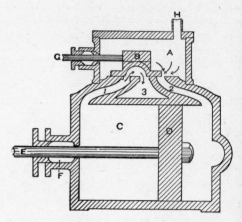

connecting rod joins the cross head to the crank and thus changes the reciprocating motion of the piston into the rotary motion of the shaft. The shaft contains the necessary attachments for operating the valves and governor, so that the engine is automatic. All that is necessary to start the engine is to open the *throttle valve*, which admits the steam to the steam chest through the pipe H. The movement is regulated by the governor (See GOVERNOR).

CLASSIFICATION. Engines are classified according to the position of the cylinder axis, according to their method of using steam and according to the work for which the engine is designed. A vertical engine has the axis of the cylinder in a vertical position, and the piston has an up and down motion. A horizontal engine has the piston axis in a horizontal position. This is the most common pattern of stationary and locomotive engines. The inclined engine has the cylinder in an inclined position. This pattern was formerly quite common, but it has now nearly disappeared. The use of electricity has led to the construction of a pattern of large engine which combines the vertical and horizontal types, one cylinder being vertical and the other horizontal. Some of these engines have a capacity of 5000 or 6000 horse power.

According to their method of using steam, engines are *condensing*, or *low pressure*, and *non-*

condensing, or *high pressure*. A condensing engine is one in which the exhaust steam is conducted to a condensing chamber, where it is condensed, the water being returned to the boiler. This is called the low-pressure engine, because the air pump connected with the condensing chamber enables the exhaust steam to escape into a vacuum. In the high pressure engine the exhaust steam escapes into the air, consequently it must overcome the pressure of air, which, at sea level, is equal to about fifteen pounds to the square inch.

The *compound* engine uses the steam successively in two or more cylinders before it is allowed to escape, while a *simple* engine uses the steam but once. Compound engines, known as *triple expansion* engines, are the most common form of marine engines. They are usually vertical

admit the steam alternately at the two ends of the cylinder, the same as in the steam engine, and operate much more rapidly and effectively. The hammer is so perfectly adjusted that it can be made to strike a blow of any required force. Steam hammers are used in large forgings, such as gun forgings, shafts for vessels and other like purposes. One erected in the Krupp iron works at Essen, Germany, weighs over 150 tons. The steam hammer was invented by Thomas Nasmyth of England, in 1839, and was patented three years later.

Steam'ship. See Ship.

Steam Shovel, *shuv'el*, an excavating machine for use on dry land. It consists of a hoisting engine and movable crane, with a scoop, or shovel, so attached to the crane that it can be moved in any direction. The bottom of the

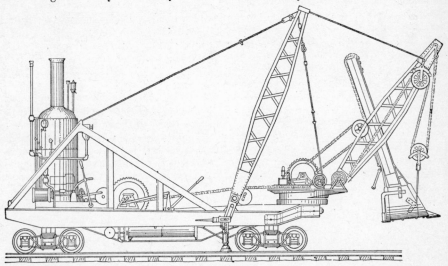

STEAM SHOVEL

and use the steam three times. A *single* engine has but one cylinder, or if compound, but one set of cylinders, while a *double* engine has two cylinders, each independent of the other. Locomotives and some stationary engines are double. See Locomotive; Traction Engine.

Steam Hammer, a hammer operated by the action of steam, without the aid of any other machinery. The important parts of a steam hammer are the frame, the cylinder, the piston, the piston rod, the hammer proper and the anvil. In the early pattern of steam hammer, the hammer was operated by admitting the steam to the lower end of the cylinder and raising the piston. The steam was then cut off and the hammer fell by its own weight. Later patterns, however,

shovel is attached by a hinge and held in place by a spring. In use the shovel is lowered to the earth, then pulled forward and slightly downward by a chain that winds over a cylinder. This movement fills it. When filled it is raised by the crane and swung over the point where it is to be emptied. By pulling a cord the spring holding the bottom in place is released, and the shovel empties itself. The capacity of steam shovels varies from one to five cubic yards, but from one and a half to two and a half cubic yards are the sizes generally used. These machines are extensively employed in digging cuts on railways, excavating canals, and in the iron mines of the Lake Superior region for digging the ore and loading it upon cars. The entire structure, including the engine, is mounted on a car, so that it can be moved as required.

Steam Turbine, *tur'bin,* a form of motor which uses the expansive force of steam to produce motion, by bringing the steam in contact with floats on an axis, similar to the floats of an ordinary water turbine (See TURBINE WHEEL). The steam turbine is enclosed in a steel case, which has veins between the floats and extending inward almost to the axis. The veins and floats are curved in opposite directions, so that the current of steam is reversed by coming in contact with them, and the reaction caused by this reversal of the current forces the floats along and causes the axis to rotate. The steam turbine is really several turbines attached to the same axis, each succeeding one having a slightly larger diameter, in order to adapt it to the pressure of the expanding steam. Steam turbines are used for light power and also upon steamships, where they have taken the place of the common steam engine very satisfactorily. The first steamer equipped with this form of motor crossed the Atlantic early in the spring of 1905. The use of the turbine relieves the ship from the strain arising from the action of an ordinary engine and also enables the vessel to maintain a more uniform rate of speed.

Steam Whistle, *whis''l,* an arrangement connected with the boiler of a steam engine, for the purpose of making a loud whistling sound. In the locomotive steam whistle a tube, fixed to the head of the boiler and opening into its interior, is commanded by a stop cock; the tube ends in a portion perforated with holes and surrounded by a thin brass cup. The tube and cup are so adjusted as to leave a narrow opening all round. Above this opening a thin brass cup is fixed in an inverted position, so as to present a sharp edge to the opening. When the stop cock is opened, the steam rushes through this orifice with great violence, and in coming in contact with the sharp edge of the cup it produces a loud, shrill sound. The tone of the whistle depends upon the size of the cylinder and the thickness of the metal from which it is made. Small cylinders of thin metal give a sharp, shrill tone, and large cylinders give a low tone, such as is given by steamboat whistles. Steam whistles can be made to give off musical tones, by graduating the length of the pipe or cup. Such an instrument is called a *calliope*.

Stearic, *ste ar'ik,* **Acid,** one of the most important and abundant of the fatty acids. As stearin it exists, in combination with glycerine, in beef and mutton fat and in several vegetable fats. Stearic acid, which is inodorous, tasteless, insoluble in water, but soluble in alcohol, forms white scaly crystals and combines with alkalies, earths and metallic oxides, to form stearates. It burns like wax and is used in making candles.

Ste'arin, the chief ingredient of suet and tallow, or the harder ingredient of animal fats, olein being the softer one. It is obtained from mutton suet by repeated solution in ether and crystallization. It may also be obtained from tallow pressed between hot plates and from dissolution of the substance in hot ether, which on cooling deposits the stearin. It has a pearly luster and is soft to the touch, but not greasy. It is insoluble in water, but soluble in hot alcohol and ether. When treated with superheated steam, it is separated into stearic acid and glycerine, and when boiled with alkalies the stearic acid combines with the alkali and forms soap and glycerine. When melted, stearin resembles wax.

Ste'atite. See SOAPSTONE.

Sted'man, EDMUND CLARENCE (1833–1908), a prominent American poet and critic, born at Hartford, Conn. He studied at Yale, took up journalism and was war correspondent of the New York *World* during the Civil War. Later he became a stockbroker in New York and was a member of the Stock Exchange. He contributed to the more important magazines and published his first volume of verse in 1860. His critical work, *Victorian Poets,* appeared in 1875 and has gone through many editions; the *Poets of America* appeared in 1886, but it proved less interesting. Among his volumes of verse are *Poems, Lyrical and Idyllic*; *Hawthorne and Other Poems,* and *Alice of Monmouth.*

Steel, a variety of manufactured iron, possessing peculiar properties of hardness, elasticity and strength. Steel is of a grayish-white color, has a granular texture of even structure, can be tempered to any degree of hardness and can be made highly elastic. It is also ductile and malleable and possesses greater tensile strength than any other variety of iron. It welds readily and can be bent into almost any desired form without breaking. Steel is invaluable in the arts and is more extensively used than any other variety of iron.

VARIETIES. Steel is made by combining a certain proportion of carbon with iron, and there are numerous varieties, due to the different methods of manufacture. The most important of these are blister steel, Bessemer steel and open-hearth steel.

Blister Steel, or Tool Steel. This variety

is made by the oldest process by which steel is manufactured from iron. Wrought iron bars are laid between layers of charcoal in iron retorts that are lined with fire brick. The air is excluded, and the retorts are placed in a furnace and heated to a yellow heat, the temperature being maintained six or eight days, according to the grade of steel desired. The process is known as *cementation*, and the term *blister steel* is derived from the appearance of the bars, which, when taken from the retorts, are covered with blisters. A small quantity of carbon is added to the wrought iron during the process, thus converting it into steel. With the best quality of wrought iron, this process produces the highest grade of steel. When melted and cast into ingots, this constitutes the *cast steel* from which edged tools are made.

Bessemer Steel. This variety of steel takes its name from Sir Henry Bessemer of England,

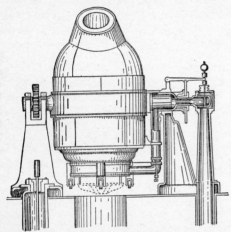

BESSEMER CONVERTER

the inventor of the process of its manufacture. In principle it is directly the reverse of the cementation process, which produces steel by burning the carbon into wrought iron. Bessemer conceived the idea of making steel by burning carbon out of cast iron, which contains too large a proportion. The furnace in which this is done is known as the *converter*. It is an egg-shaped iron vessel, about fifteen feet high and eight feet in diameter, narrowing at the top to an opening about eighteen inches in diameter. The furnace is lined with fire brick and mounted on trunnions, so it can be tilted to a horizontal position by a hydraulic piston. In most patterns the top is curved, so as to bring the opening to one side. The bottom contains a

number of tuyeres, each perforated with holes half an inch in diameter. The tuyeres are connected with an air chamber, which is supplied with air through one of the trunnions, connected by pipes with a powerful blowing machine. The converter is charged directly from the blast furnace or from iron that is melted in a separate furnace, called the *cupola*. In being charged, the converter is tipped upon its side. As it resumes an upright position, the blast is automatically turned on, and air is forced through the molten metal with a pressure varying from fifteen to twenty-five pounds to the square inch. This burns out the silicon and carbon and produces such violent boiling of the metal as to cause the converter and its foundations to vibrate perceptibly. When the silicon and carbon have been consumed, the blast is shut off, the converter is again tilted upon its side and a small quantity of *spiegeleisen*, an alloy of highly carbonized iron and manganese, is added. After this has been thoroughly mixed with the metal, the charge is poured into ladles, from which it is run into casting molds. The ingots thus formed are reheated and rolled into forms desired for use. The process of converting the charge into steel requires from eight to twenty minutes, and the time is determined by the furnace man, who is able to tell by the color of the flame at the mouth of the converter when the process is completed.

Open-hearth steel is that made in a furnace resembling very closely the puddling furnace (See IRON, subhead *Wrought Iron*). This steel is made from pig and scrap iron, and the changes in the metal are about the same as those in the production of Bessemer steel. It is produced in large quantities and is second in importance only to Bessemer steel. Open-hearth steel is employed for the frames of buildings, boiler plates, ship plates and castings, while Bessemer steel is almost universally in use in the manufacture of rails.

USES. The discovery of the Bessemer process made it possible to produce steel at such low cost as to extend its use widely, and now it has almost entirely replaced wrought iron in all forms of structural work. The extension of railway lines has also greatly increased the demand for rails. In all, the world's output of steel is over 34,500,-000 tons annually. Of this amount the United States produces about 15,000,000 tons, which is more than the amount produced by any other country. See IRON.

Steel, JOHN, Sir (1804–1891), a Scottish sculptor, born at Aberdeen. He received his art education in the Royal Academy, Edinburgh, and in Rome. He gained a prize for the seated statue of Sir Walter Scott, now part of the Scott Monument in Edinburgh, and from the time of its completion, in 1846, his success was assured. Among his well-known works, also in Edinburgh, are the statues of Wellington, Professor Wilson, Allan Ramsay, Thomas Chalmers and Queen Victoria, and the Scottish memorial to the Prince Consort, on the unveiling of which, in 1876, Steel was knighted.

Steele, RICHARD, Sir (1672–1729), an English essayist, born at Dublin, Ireland. By the influence of his uncle, who was secretary to the duke of Ormonde, Steele was educated at the Charter House, where he formed a friendship with Addison, and at Oxford. In 1694 he entered the Life Guards, and some years later, by dedicating a poem to Lord Cutts of the Coldstream Guards, he gained the rank of captain. Shortly before this time (1701) he published a prose treatise called *The Christian Hero*, a treatise for his own moral instruction. Its severe morality, however, brought ridicule upon its author, who was by no means over-strict in his own conduct, and it seems to have had no effect on his character. His next attempt at literature resulted in the comedies of *The Funeral*, *The Lying Lover* and *The Tender Husband*, and a number of years afterward he added to these *The Conscious Lovers*. In 1707 he was appointed, by the influence of Addison, to the editorship of the *Gazette*, and two years later he started a light miscellany called *The Tatler*, which, with its successors, *The Spectator* and *The Guardian*, established the fame of Steele and his fellow-worker, Addison, as the first of English essayists. He started various other journals, such as *The Reader*, *The Englishman*, *Town Talk* and *The Plebeian*, but they never attained the success of the first two.

Steel'ton, PA., a borough in Dauphin co., 3 mi. s. e. of Harrisburg, on the Susquehanna River and on the Pennsylvania and the Philadelphia & Reading railroads. The chief industrial establishments are the iron and steel works of the Pennsylvania Steel Company; but there are also lumber and flour mills, brickyards and machine shops. The place was laid out in 1866 and was incorporated in 1880. Population in 1910, 14,246.

Steel'yard, in mechanics, a balance, or weighing machine, consisting of a lever of unequal arms. The most common kind, often called the Roman balance, is a lever of the first class (See LEVER). One may find the weight of an object by suspending it from the end of the shorter arm, or placing it in a scale-dish suspended from that arm, and sliding a balance weight, whose weight is known, along the longer arm, until the instrument remains in equilibrium in a horizontal position; the weight of the substance attached to the short arm of the lever is indicated by observing the position of the movable balance-weight, with respect to a graduated scale marked upon the long arm of the steelyard. A ring or hook is attached to the fulcrum, so that the instrument may be conveniently hung upon a fixed support; if it is small it may be held in the hand, and a vertical index or pointer, similar to that attached to the beam of a balance, is sometimes added.

Steen, JAN (1626–1679), a Dutch painter, born at Leyden. He studied under Nicolas Knupfer and Van Goyen and married the daughter of the latter. From the conflicting accounts of his career it appears that he was at one time a tavernkeeper, and the tradition is that he led a drunken and dissolute life; but in disproof of this his numerous paintings attest that he must have been a laborious and careful worker. He stands in the foremost rank among Dutch painters, as regards execution, composition, color, and the action, gestures and expression of his figures. His chief paintings are to be seen in the galleries of The Hague and Amsterdam, and one, *The Music-master*, is in the National Gallery, London.

Steer'ing, the control of the direction of a ship when in motion. It is accomplished by a contrivance usually composed of three parts, namely, the rudder, the tiller and the wheel, except in small vessels, where the wheel is unnecessary. The rudder, or helm, is a long and flat piece or frame, suspended edgewise down the hind part of a ship's stern-post, where it turns upon a kind of hinge to the right or left, serving to direct the course of a vessel, as the tail of a fish guides its body. The tiller is a bar of timber or iron, fixed horizontally to the upper end of the rudder and projecting within the vessel. The movements of the tiller are effected in small vessels by hand, assisted by a sort of tackle, called the *tiller rope*. In larger vessels there are, properly speaking, two ropes or chains, which, being wound about the axis or barrel of a wheel, act upon the tiller with the powers of a windlass. In the enormous modern vessels, the rudder is moved by hydraulic or steam power, so that the steersman is compelled to make little exertion.

Stein, *stine,* HEINRICH FRIEDRICH KARL, Baron von (1757–1831), a Prussian statesman. He studied at Göttingen, entered the mining department of the Prussian government, became head of the mines and manufactures department in Westphalia and in 1804 became a minister of state. For the severity of his criticisms on the administration, he was dismissed (1807), but in a few months he was recalled, with power to introduce his reforms. Accordingly he abolished serfdom by edict, made military service obligatory on all classes and rearranged the financial and administrative affairs. By means of these reforms he laid the basis of Prussia's future greatness. He afterward visited Saint Petersburg, and was instrumental in bringing about the coalition which crushed Napoleon. After the military struggle was over, he lived in retirement.

Steinbock, *stine'bok,* or **Steen'bok,** a small antelope, found in South Africa. It is ashen-gray on the sides, white underneath and stands about two feet in height; the male has short horns. The name is also applied in Europe to the ibex.

Stems, the parts of plants which bear leaves. Though stems in some plants are all underground, in most cases they serve to keep the leaves and flowers of plants in the sunlight; they always form channels by which the liquids in circulation can reach the leaves from the roots. The stems of some plants live but one year; others live two years, and still others may live on indefinitely from year to year. The methods of growth vary with the species, sometimes being directly upward from a terminal bud, making a cylindrical, upright tube; sometimes branching regularly, but still standing upright. Other stems are weak and rise by climbing only, either by their rootlets, or tendrils, or by twining round and round some slender support. The tuber of the potato or the root-stock of Solomon's seal are examples of underground stems. Other condensed forms are found above ground, as may be seen in the peculiar tips that the cactus family exhibits. The living parts of the dicotyledonous plant are confined to the narrow zone just under the outer bark and outside the main core of the tree. In monocotyledonous plants, however, the stem grows in restricted areas throughout the whole diameter. Cross sections of stems show very clearly the structure of the two forms; the dicot-

yledons show concentric rings of woody matter, while monocotyledonous plants are of rather uniform pithy structure, with fibrous bundles.

Stencil, *sten'sil,* a thin plate of brass, cardboard or other material, used for printing letters and ornamental designs. The designs are cut in the stencil, which is laid on the article or surface to be marked. A brush, filled with paint, is rubbed over the stencil. By this means the design is quickly and cheaply stamped. Stencils are now used almost wholly for ornamental work, rubber stamps having taken their place in lettering.

Stenography, *sten og'ra fy.* See SHORT-HAND.

Stephen, *ste'ven,* (about 1097–1154), king of England, son of Stephen, count of Blois, and Adela, a daughter of William the Conqueror. His uncle, Henry I, gave him the earldom of Montaigne, in Normandy, and large estates in England, in return for which he took the oath to secure the succession to Henry's daughter, Matilda. But when his uncle died, in 1135, he hastened from France to England, laid claim to the crown for himself and was crowned in London. In 1139 Matilda landed in England with her half-brother, the earl of Gloucester, and a civil war ensued, in which Stephen was taken prisoner and Matilda was acknowledged queen. The conduct of the new sovereign, however, excited an insurrection against her government, and she was shut up in Winchester Castle, while the earl of Gloucester was taken prisoner. Stephen was exchanged for the earl, and the war was renewed. When Matilda retired to Normandy, the contest was taken up by her son Henry. Finally the struggle was brought to an end in 1153 by the Treaty of Wallingford, in which it was agreed that Stephen should reign until his death, and that he should be succeeded by Henry.

Stephen, LESLIE, Sir (1832–1904), an English critic and biographer. He was educated at Eton, King's College, London, and Trinity Hall, Cambridge, and after his graduation he became a fellow and tutor. Subsequently devoting himself to literature, he became the editor of the *Cornhill Magazine,* a position which he gave up in 1882 that he might edit the *Dictionary of National Biography.* Among his works are *Essays on Free Thinking and Plain Speaking;* three series of *Hours in a Library; The History of English Thought in the Eighteenth Century; The Science of Ethics;* lives of Pope, Swift, Hobbes and George Eliot, in the English Men of Letters Series, and a *Life of Henry Fawcett.*

Stephens, ALEXANDER HAMILTON (1812–1883), an American statesman, born near Crawfordsville, Ga. He spent his childhood amid the greatest poverty, received his education at Franklin College, through the assistance of a charitable organization, and in 1834 was admitted to the bar. He later repaid his helpers with interest. Stephens was elected to the Georgia legislature in 1836 and to Congress in 1843, where he at once assumed prominence as a fearless advocate of the rights of the South, though at the same time a lover of the Union. In 1860 he opposed secession, not because he believed it wrong in principle, but because he deemed it inexpedient at the time. At the Georgia secession convention he delivered a great speech for the Union, but followed his state into the Confederacy and became vice-president of the new government. He headed the Confederate peace commission at Hampton Roads, in February, 1865. At the close of the war he was imprisoned five months at Fort Warren. In 1866 he was elected to the United States Senate, but was not allowed to take his seat. He entered Congress, however, in 1873, and remained there until 1882, when he was chosen governor of his state. In every position in which he was placed Stephens acted with the highest of motives and with deep conviction. His career constantly exemplified rare moral courage and devotion to principle.

Stephens, JOHN LLOYD (1805–1852), an American author, born at Shrewsbury, N. J. He graduated in 1822 at Columbia College, studied law and practiced for eight years at the bar in New York. To recruit his health he made an extended journey through Europe and the East, an account of which he supplied in letters to the *American Monthly Magazine.* These were afterward published in fuller narrative form, under the title of *Incidents of Travel in Egypt, Arabia Petraea, and the Holy Land* and *Incidents of Travel in Greece, Turkey, Russia and Poland.* In 1839 he was sent by the United States government to negotiate with the governments of Central America; as the result of his experiences and investigations in that country he published *Incidents of Travel in Central America, Chiapas and Yucatan.* After another visit to Central America he issued *Incidents of Travel in Yucatan,* and both of these books were valuable contributions to our knowledge of the ruined cities and monuments of this part of

America. He was afterward chiefly associated with the company which constructed a railway across the Isthmus of Panama.

Stephenson, *ste'ven son,* GEORGE (1781–1848), an English engineer and inventor. While an engine-wright at Killingworth, he constructed a locomotive for the tramways and

GEORGE STEPHENSON

succeeded in inducing the projectors of the Stockton & Darlington railway to adopt it. The result was that in 1825 the first railway was built, over which passengers and freight were borne by locomotives. He was then employed to construct the Liverpool & Manchester railway, the directors of which accepted his locomotive, called the *Rocket,* which at the trial trip in 1830 ran 29 miles in an hour. Stephenson was afterward identified with numerous railway undertakings, and he was also the inventor of a miner's safety lamp. See LOCOMOTIVE.

Stephenson, ROBERT (1803–1859), an English engineer, son of George Stephenson, born at Wallington Quay, England. He received both a practical training in the colliery at Killingworth and a liberal education in technical schools, after which he became his father's assistant and was engaged in surveying several railway lines. Later he took charge of his father's factory at Newcastle and greatly aided him in improving the locomotive. Subsequently his services were in great demand as a railway engineer, and he became celebrated as the builder of great bridges. He was the designer of the tubular bridge. The most celebrated of these bridges are the Britannia Bridge over the Menai Straits, the Conway Bridge and the first Victoria Bridge across the Saint Lawrence at Montreal. This was replaced by a steel truss bridge in 1898. See BRIDGE, subhead *Tubular Bridges*.

Steppes, *steps*, a Russian name applied to those extensive plains which, with the occasional occurrence of low ranges of hills, stretch from the Dnieper across the southeast of European Russia, round the shores of the Caspian and Aral seas, between the Altai and Ural mountains, and occupy a considerable part of Siberia. In spring they are covered with verdure, but for most of the year they are dry and barren. See PLAINS.

Ster'eop'ticon. See MAGIC LANTERN.

Ster'eoscope, an optical apparatus which enables one to look at the same time upon two photographic pictures, nearly the same, but taken under a slight difference of angular view, so that each eye looks upon one picture only. The effect is similar to that produced by natural vision. A reflecting form of stereoscope was invented by Wheatstone in 1838. Subsequently Brewster invented the refracting stereoscope, based on the refractive properties of the halves of double-convex lenses. This is the one now in general use.

Ster'eotyp'ing, the process of copying pages of type or of engraving in type metal and of making stereotype plate. The type are set and locked in the form, then sent to the foundry, where the face is brushed clean with a soft brush dipped in oil. A thick, soft paper, especially prepared for the purpose, is then pressed down upon the type with a heavy iron roller. The face of the type is forced into the paper, so as to make a perfect mold of the page. This mold is called a *matrix*. After drying, the matrix is taken from the type and placed in a casting box, and melted type metal is poured over it, making a plate which is a perfect copy of the type. The stereotype plates made for ordinary printing presses are flat, but those made for the presses used in large newspaper establishments are in the form of half-cylinders (See PRINTING PRESS). Several casts can be made from the same matrix, and in all large cities there are firms which make a business of supplying country papers with plates for printing a portion of the paper. The ordinary time for making a stereotype plate is about ten

minutes. Since such plates are inexpensive and are so quickly made, they are specially valuable for printing daily papers. See PRINTING.

Sterling, *stur'ling*, ILL., a city in Whiteside co., 109 mi. w. of Chicago, on the Rock River and on the Chicago & Northwestern and the Chicago, Burlington & Quincy railroads. There are also electric railways to the neighboring towns. The city is in a fertile agricultural region, has good water power and contains manufactories of wire goods, gas engines, undertakers' supplies, hardware, pumps and other articles. It has a number of churches, a township high school, a parish school, a business college and a public library. Population in 1910, 7467.

Stern'berg, GEORGE MILLER (1838–   ), an American surgeon and student of bacteriology, who studied the yellow fever in Cuba, wrote authoritatively on the disinfection and cure of contagious diseases, and during the Spanish-American War, as surgeon-general of the United States Army, directed medical affairs and practically relieved Cuba from the scourge of yellow fever.

Stern'burg, HERMANN SPECK VON, Baron (1852–1908), German diplomat, born in Leeds, England. He was educated in Germany, joined the army and fought through the Franco-German War. He rendered able service during the Boxer troubles in China and was for two years consul-general for India and Ceylon. In January, 1903, he was sent as minister plenipotentiary and envoy extraordinary to the United States on a special mission, and in July, 1903, he became the regularly appointed ambassador to the United States.

Sterne, *sturn*, LAURENCE (1713–1768), an English author. After his graduation from Cambridge he was ordained, and for twenty years he performed the clerical work in the livings of Sutton and Stillington, in Yorkshire. In 1759 appeared the first two volumes of his longest work, *Tristram Shandy*, which, by their humor, whimsicality and happy audacity of tone and treatment, gained instant popularity. The publication of this work was continued, the ninth and last volume appearing in 1767, and Sterne found himself exceedingly popular in London, whither he had moved. His other writings are *A Sentimental Journey Through France and Italy* (1768) and a number of sermons, besides letters published after his death. Though disfigured by indecency, Sterne's *Tristram Shandy* and *Sentimental Journey*, especially the former, contain some of the finest humor in English literature.

Steth'oscope, an instrument used by medical men for distinguishing sounds within the thorax and other cavities of the body. In its simplest form it consists of a hollow cylinder of hard rubber, with one extremity funnel-shaped. To the other extremity flexible rubber tubes with earpieces are attached. The funnel is pressed against the chest of the patient, and the earpieces are placed in the ears of the listener. The stethoscope is used by physicians for determining the condition of the heart and lungs.

Stettin, *stet teen'*, a city of Prussia, situated on both sides of the Oder, 79 mi. n. n. e. of Berlin and near an inlet of the Baltic Sea. The chief objects of interest are the Church of Saint Thomas, dating from the thirteenth century; the government building, which was the castle of the old dukes of Pomerania; the old townhall, and a fine fountain. The city is one of the most important manufacturing centers of the Province of Pomerania and is the site of some of the largest shipbuilding yards in the world. Its other industrial plants include machine shops, foundries, sugar refineries, textile factories and works for the manufacture of paper, cement and chemicals. It is the third seaport in rank among the cities of the German Empire. Population in 1910, 236,113.

Steuben, *stu'ben* or *stoi'ben*, FRIEDRICH WILHELM AUGUST HEINRICH FERDINAND, Baron von (1730–1794), a Prussian general, who fought in the American Revolution. He was born in the fortress at Magdeburg and at the age of fourteen entered the Prussian army. In 1758 he was made adjutant-general, and he fought with distinction during the Seven Years' War, becoming at its close grand marshal of the prince of Hohenzollern-Hechingen. In 1777, at the solicitation of Benjamin Franklin, he went to America and offered his services to Congress. He immediately was dispatched to Valley Forge, where, during the winter, he drilled the army in military tactics, in which he had received special instruction from Frederick the Great. He was made inspector-general and instituted many important reforms. He fought at the Battle of Monmouth, was a member of the André court martial, put an end to the marauding invasions of Benedict Arnold in Virginia and took a prominent part in the siege of Yorktown. At the close of the war he was granted large tracts of land by several states and a pension of $2400 by Congress. For a time he lived in New York City, but later removed to an estate near Oriskany, N. Y., where he died. His *Manual of Tactics*, published in 1780, was long the official manual in the United States army.

Steubenville, *stu'ben vil*, OHIO, the county-seat of Jefferson co., 43 mi. s. w. of Pittsburg, Pa., on the Ohio River and on the Pennsylvania, the Pittsburg, Cincinnati, Chicago & Saint Louis and the Wheeling & Lake Erie railroads. The city is in a section having deposits of coal, gas and petroleum, and it has extensive manufactures of iron, glass and pottery. Some important features are the city hall, the courthouse, a Carnegie library, Gill Hospital and Stanton and Altamont parks. The town was laid out in 1798, on the site of a fort named in honor of Baron Steuben, and it was chartered as a city in 1851. Population in 1910, 22,391.

Ste'vens, THADDEUS (1792–1868), an American statesman, born at Danville, Vt. He graduated at Dartmouth College, taught school and was admitted to the bar, practicing at Gettysburg and Lancaster, Pa. He was elected to the legislature as a Whig in 1833, where he served with rare energy and ability, and was elected to Congress in 1849. There he was a leader of the anti-slavery forces for two terms and again from 1859 until his death. As one of the Republican leaders in Congress he was the chief advocate of emancipation and negro suffrage and of the radical reconstruction measures, and he led the impeachment of President Johnson. Though bitter and sarcastic in debate, he was famous for his undiscriminating charities.

Ste'venson, ADLAI EWING (1835–1914) an American politician, born in Christian County, Ky. He was educated in the common schools and at Center College, Danville, Ky., and removed in 1852 to Illinois, where he was admitted to the bar five years later. In 1874 he was elected a member of Congress from Illinois by the Democratic party, and in 1885 he was appointed first assistant postmaster-general. In 1892 he was elected vice-president, and at the conclusion of his term he was appointed a member of the commission to try to secure international bimetallism. He was nominated for vice-president in 1900, but was defeated.

Stevenson, ROBERT (1772–1850), a Scotch engineer, born at Glasgow. His first work was the erection of a lighthouse on Little Cumbrae. He was for forty-seven years inspector of lighthouses, and during that time he built twenty-three lighthouses on the Scottish coast, introduced many improvements in the construction of bridges, canals, harbors and railways and invented the system of *intermittent* and *flashing* lights. His greatest work was the Bell Rock lighthouse. See LIGHTHOUSE.

Stevenson, ROBERT LOUIS BALFOUR (1850–1894), a Scottish poet, essayist and writer of fiction, born in Edinburgh. He studied law and was called to the Scottish bar, but found his true calling in literature. A leisurely journey through France and Belgium by canoe supplied material

ROBERT LOUIS STEVENSON

for *An Inland Voyage* (1878), and a walking tour in southern France was described in the following year in *Travels with a Donkey.* During these years were published, too, in various periodicals, the stories and essays, some of them among his best, which were afterward collected as the *New Arabian Nights, Virginibus Puerisque* and *Familiar Studies of Men and Books.*

Learning in 1879 of the severe illness of Mrs. Osbourne, whom he had met some years previously, he decided to go to California, her home. He made the voyage in the steerage of an emigrant ship, and finished the journey across the continent in an immigrant train. These experiences he described in *The Amateur Emigrant* and *Across the Plains.* In 1880 he married Mrs. Osbourne. During the next ten years his quest for health took him to various points, and in 1890 he settled permanently in Samoa, where he soon became a commanding figure among the

natives. Meanwhile he had published *Treasure Island,* a story of stirring adventure which met with immediate success; *Prince Otto,* a romance; *Doctor Jekyll and Mr. Hyde,* an account in story form of the dual personality which exists in every man; *Kidnapped; The Master of Ballantrae; A Child's Garden of Verses* and *Underwoods,* a second volume of verse, and the *Merry Men and Other Tales.* During his years in Samoa he wrote *David Balfour,* which is a sequel to *Kidnapped,* and *Saint Ives,* and he began *Weir of Hermiston,* which, although unfinished at his death, is by most critics regarded as his greatest work.

Stevenson's uncomplaining spirit, his cheerfulness and diligence in the face of disadvantages so great that to a less courageous man they might have seemed overwhelming, make him one of the most attractive of literary personalities. As a story-teller he rivals Scott, while his exquisite style places him in the front rank of the writers of his time.

Stevens Point, WIS., the county-seat of Portage co., 100 mi. n. of Madison, on the Wisconsin River and on the Wisconsin Central and the Green Bay & Western railroads. The city is an important trade center for an extensive region and lies just north of the great potato-producing district. There is good water power, and more than one hundred industrial establishments, which include saw mills, foundries, knitting works and manufactories of furniture, paper and other articles, are located here. The city has a Carnegie public library and is the seat of one of the state normal schools. The place was settled in 1836. Population in 1910, 8692.

Stew'art, ALEXANDER TURNEY (1803–1876), an American merchant, born near Belfast, Ireland, of Scotch parents. He was educated at Trinity College, Dublin, but emigrated to America in 1823. He taught school for two years in New York City and then established a drygoods business, which rapidly grew until it became the largest business of its kind in the world, including both wholesale and retail branches and agencies and affiliated stores in all important centers of Europe and America. After the death of Mr. Stewart, however, the business rapidly declined.

Stewart, WILLIAM MORRIS (1827–1909), an American lawyer and politician, born at Lyons, N. Y. His early childhood was spent in Ohio, where he received an elementary education. He entered Yale College, but later withdrew to go to California during the gold-seeking craze of 1849. He took up mining claims and later studied law; he was admitted to the bar in 1852 and became attorney-general of California two years later. In 1860 he removed to Virginia City, Nev., where he engaged in the practice of law and in mining, being interested in the famous Comstock lode. In 1863 he was elected United States senator, served two terms and served again from 1887 to 1905, being a conspicuous advocate of free coinage of silver.

Stib'nite or **Antimony Glance,** an ore consisting of antimony and sulphur. The color is lead-gray or blackish, and the mineral is very brittle. This ore is the source of most of the antimony of commerce.

Stick'leback, the popular name for certain small fishes. The name is derived from the presence of spines on the back, taking the place of fins. These fishes are found in ponds and streams, in salt and fresh waters of Europe; they are very active and voracious and live upon aquatic insects and worms. The sticklebacks are among the very few fishes which build nests for their young. The nest is composed of straw, sticks and similar materials. In the top a small hole is formed, and in this the eggs, yellow in color and about the size of poppy seeds, are deposited. The most common species is the *three-spined stickleback, banstickle,* or *tittlebat,* which is distinguished by the body being protected at the sides with shield-like plates and by the possession of three spines on the back. It varies from two to three inches in length. There are few fish of more interesting habits than the stickleback.

Stick'seed, a weed, native to Europe, but now common throughout America, especially in waste grounds and poor soils. It grows to a height of two feet, has a hairy stem, bears small flowers late in summer and produces nutlets covered with small projections, which cling to passing animals and thus distribute the seed. Persistent digging and cultivation may eradicate the weed. A plant closely allied to this and resembling it is called *beggars' lice* and sometimes *beggars' ticks.* See WEEDS.

Still'water, MINN., the county-seat of Washington co., 18 mi. n. e. of Saint Paul, on the Saint Croix River and on the Northern Pacific, the Chicago & Northwestern and other railroads. It has a beautiful location, near the Dalles, which extend about 30 mi. to the north along the river. The Minnesota state prison is located here, and the municipality contains a Carnegie library, a fine city hall, two convents and a

city hospital. It is the industrial center of the Saint Croix lumber region and has a large trade in logs, which are floated down the river. The industrial establishments include lumber mills, grain elevators, flour and feed mills, foundries and machine shops and manufactories of wagons, boats, farm implements, shoes and other articles. Stillwater was settled in 1843. It was incorporated as a village in 1848 and chartered as a city in 1854. Population in 1910, 10,198.

Stilt, a plover, with exceedingly long, slender legs, which give it its common name. The American species is white, with black head and pink legs. Few birds have greater power of flight, either in distance or rapidity. The stilt is always a peculiar-looking bird, whether walking or flying, with its long legs awkwardly stretched out.

Stilts, long sticks, upon which a person may stand when walking. The stilts used by children for playthings usually have long handles, which pass under the arms and are held by the hand. In countries where stilts are used for practical purposes, they are bound to the side of the leg, and the wearer carries a long pole to assist him in keeping his balance. The inhabitants of the lowlands in southern France find stilts a necessity a good part of the year, as much of the land is under water.

Sting'fish. See WEEVER.

Sting Ray, a ray, remarkable for its long, flexible, whip-like tail, which is armed with a projecting bony spine, very sharp at the point, and furnished along both edges with sharp cutting teeth. One species is common on the eastern coasts of North America. Some species are found in the waters around northern South America, where they grow ten or twelve feet in length. This fish sometimes inflicts serious wounds with its tail.

Stirling, *stur'ling,* a city of Scotland, on the right bank of the Forth, 31 mi. n. w. of Edinburgh and 26 mi. s. w. of Perth. The object of greatest interest is Stirling Castle, built upon a commanding height. Within the walls enclosing the castle are the palace of James V, the Parliament House and the royal chapel. The industries include the manufacture of carpets, woolen goods and rope. On the border of the city is Bannockburn. Stirling was the former residence of the Scottish kings and has been celebrated in song and story by Sir Walter Scott and other writers. Population in 1911, 20,000.

Stoat, *stote.* See ERMINE.

Stock, CAPITAL, that which represents the capital of a corporation. The total stock is divided into equal shares, usually of a par or face value of $100. The ownership of a share of stock includes the rights to vote at the meetings of stockholders and to receive a part of the profits of the company. These profits, when paid to stockholders, are called dividends. Stock may be either common, on which the dividend is determined by the net profits, or preferred, on which the dividend is at a fixed rate. Full dividends on preferred stock must be paid before the owners of common stock receive any profits. Ownership of a majority of the common stock is necessary to control; owners of preferred stock usually have no voting power. See BROKER; CORPORATION; STOCKJOBBING.

Stock'bridge, a member of the Mahican confederacy of Algonquian tribes. They were originally gathered in a mission at Stockbridge, Mass., but are now living in Shawano County, Wisconsin, with a part of the Munsee. They are intelligent and industrious, and they live in all respects like white farmers.

Stock'holm, the capital of Sweden, situated at the east end of Lake Malar, on a number of rocky islands and peninsulas, which are separated by fiords and surrounded by forests. The older portions of the city have narrow streets, but the newer parts are laid out on modern plans and contain numerous squares, which are ornamented with monuments and statuary. There are also a number of beautiful parks about the city. The most important structure is the royal palace. Other buildings of importance are the customhouse, the exchange bank, the townhall, the parliament house and the national library, national museum and academy of arts and sciences. Among the churches worthy of mention are the Stor Kyrka; the Riddarholms Kyrka, which is the burial place of the Swedish kings, and the Katarina Kyrka. The city also contains a monument to Gustavus III and statues of Gustavus Adolphus and Charles XII. There are a number of important educational institutions, including a polytechnic school, a school of forestry and a medical institute. The royal library has over 300,000 volumes and a large collection of pamphlets. Among the learned societies are the Royal Swedish Academy of Sciences and the Swedish Academy. Stockholm is an important industrial center and has manufactures of furniture, tobacco, soap, sugar, malt liquors, and foundry and machine shop products. Shipbuilding is also carried on to some extent. The city has a large trade, and its imports outrank those of any other city of Sweden. Population in 1911, 346,599.

Stock'jobbing, the practice of dealing in stocks or shares, especially by persons who buy and sell at a certain rendezvous, known as the Stock Exchange, on their own account and not for clients, as do the stockbrokers, properly so called. This business, as well as dealing in margins through brokers (See BOARD OF TRADE), has come somewhat into disrepute, owing to the fact that many, if not most, of the transactions are of a purely gambling nature. For instance, A agrees to sell B $50,000 worth of bank stock, to be transferred in twenty days, for $60,000. Now if the price of bank stock on the day appointed for transfer should be only 118 per cent, he may then purchase the necessary amount of stock for $59,000 and thereby gain $1000 by the transaction. Should the price of bank stock, however, advance to 125 per cent, he will have to pay $62,500 for the necessary amount of stock and will thus lose $2500. These fluctuations being almost entirely unforeseen, the whole transaction is largely one of chance. If, however, A owned the stock and sold it for a definite price to B, the transaction would be perfectly legitimate, and part of the business of the Stock Exchange is done in this way.

Stock'ton, CAL., the county-seat of San Joaquin co., 78 mi. n. e. of San Francisco, on an arm of the San Joaquin River, at the head of navigation, and on the Santa Fé, the Western Pacific and the Southern Pacific railroads. The city is in a great agricultural and dairying region, noted for its natural beauty and equable climate. It is the trade center of the San Joaquin valley and handles large amounts of lumber, grain, live stock, fruits and vegetables. There are oil and natural gas wells in the valley, and the manufactures include agricultural implements, flour, foundry products, window glass, leather, beer, woolens, canned goods and fuel briquettes, which are made from coal. The state hospital for the insane, Saint Mary's College and Saint Agnes Academy are located here. The city has a public library and a county law library, and the other notable structures are the courthouse, the high school, the postoffice, the Masonic Temple and the County and Pacific hotels. The place was founded by Charles M. Weber in 1849 and was named in honor of Robert Field Stockton of the United States navy. Population in 1910, 23,253.

Stockton, FRANCIS RICHARD (1837–1902), an American humorous writer, born at Philadelphia. He was educated in the Philadelphia high school and after graduation applied himself to wood-engraving and contributed numerous illustrations to books and magazines. But he soon abandoned this pursuit for journalism. He was employed successively on the Philadelphia *Post*, the New York *Hearth and Home*, *Scribner's Monthly* (afterward the *Century Magazine*) and *Saint Nicholas*. His reputation rests, however, upon his short stories and humorous sketches. He tells the most impossible tales with a realistic effect which is irresistibly humorous. He has also written several novels and a number of children's stories. His first work which attracted general notice was *Rudder Grange*. His best-known stories are *The Lady or The Tiger?*, his most popular story; *The Late Mrs. Null*, *The Casting Away of Mrs. Lecks and Mrs. Aleshine*, *The Merry Chanter*, *Captain Horn* and *The Girl at Cobhurst*.

Stockton, ROBERT FIELD (1795–1866), an American naval officer, born at Princeton, N. J. In 1811 he entered the United States navy, served in the War of 1812 and was employed on numerous special commissions until the outbreak of the Mexican War. At that time he commanded the Pacific squadron and in coöperation with General Fremont captured Los Angeles and San Diego, organized a government in California and practically assured United States supremacy in that territory. He resigned in 1850 and was for a time thereafter member of the United States Senate from New Jersey.

Stod'dard, RICHARD HENRY (1825–1903), an American poet, critic and essayist, born at Hingham, Mass. He learned the trade of an iron molder, but began to write in prose and verse for periodicals and ultimately devoted himself to literature. Among his numerous writings are *Footprints*, *Songs of Summer*, *The King's Bell*, *The Book of the East* and *Memoir of Edgar Allan Poe.*

Stoddard, WILLIAM OSBORN (1835–   ), an American novelist and writer of stories of adventure for boys, born at Homer, N. Y. He graduated at the University of Rochester, became a farmer and later was an editor in Chicago. Enlisting as a private in the Civil War, he was appointed a secretary to President Lincoln. After the War he went into business,

and as an inventor he obtained several patents. He wrote more than fifty volumes of verse, biography and fiction. Among the titles of his books are *Lives of the Presidents*, *The Fight for the Valley*, *Long Bridge Boys*, *The Spy of Yorktown* and *Zeb, a New England Boy.*

Stoicism, *sto'e siz'm*, a system of philosophy developed by Zeno and his followers in the latter part of the fourth century B. C. The system takes its name from the porch, or *stoa*, at Athens, where Zeno taught. Zeno lived to a great age and was highly esteemed, and his system was continued and perfected by his followers. Stoicism became firmly established in Rome, and numbered Cicero, Seneca, Marcus Aurelius and other eminent Romans among its followers. The ethical doctrines of the Stoics completely overshadowed all the rest of their philosophy, and these were characterized by their severity. Their ethical system claimed as its first principle the absolute freedom of the will. Virtue was the highest good, and action, not contemplation, was the supreme problem for man to solve. While virtue was sufficient for happiness, the Stoics did not believe that happiness of pleasure should be made the end of human endeavor. Emotion was considered to be productive of evil only, and because of this it should be entirely subdued. That man alone was wise who completed the performance of his duty, was without passion, although not without feeling, was not indulgent, but was just toward himself and toward others.

The doctrines of Stoicism have exerted a wide influence in all ages, and in a modified form they are still found in the ethical codes of many social and political organizations. In the modern sense a *Stoic* is one who is not easily excited and is apparently or professedly indifferent to pleasure or pain. See ZENO.

Sto'la, a garment worn by the Roman women over the tunic. It fell as low as the ankles or feet, was fastened round the body by a girdle, leaving broad folds above the breast, and had a flounce sewed to the bottom. It was the characteristic dress of the Roman matrons.

Stomach, *stum'ak*, an organ of digestion, formed by the expansion of a portion of the alimentary canal. The human stomach is situated on the left side, just below the diaphragm. It has four coats—the serous, or outer; the muscular, which serves to force the food, after it is made into chyme, toward and through the pylorus, to keep the orifice closed till the food is digested and to mix the food thoroughly with the gastric juice; the cellular coat, and the inner, or mucous, coat, which is soft, smooth and velvety and contains the glands which secrete the gastric juice. It has been estimated that there are 5,000,-000 openings of these glands in this membrane. The stomach has two openings, the cardiac, through which the food enters from the oesophagus, and the pyloric, through which the food enters the intestines. See DIGESTION.

Stone, a hard concretion of some species of earth, as lime, silex, clay and the like; also the material obtained by quarrying rocks. The principal component parts of stones are silex, alumina, lime and magnesia; sometimes the oxides of iron, manganese, nickel, chromium and copper also enter into their composition. Stones are of various degrees of hardness and weight; they are brittle, and some are fusible; but they are not malleable, ductile or soluble in water. Stones are of extensive use for a great variety of purposes, such as building, paving, grinding and ornamental purposes. See BUILDING STONE.

Stone, ARTIFICIAL, a concreted material, applied to numerous purposes, as making building blocks, flagstones, tiles, statuary, vases, grindstones and sewer pipes. There are many varieties, most of which have a base of hydraulic cement, with which sand and pulverized stone of different kinds are mixed. See CONCRETE.

Stone Age, a term used to denote the period during which people used stone for their tools and weapons. The expression *age*, as here used, implies merely a time, longer or shorter, earlier or later, during which stone implements were used by the particular people to whom reference is made. People in isolated regions, like the islanders of the South Pacific and the Eskimos of the extreme north, have remained in their Stone Age to the present time. From the relics that are found in various parts of Asia, Africa and America, it seems evident that stone was the first material used by any people, and that man everywhere began his warfare with nature by the use of stone. The implements which have been found naturally divide the Stone Age into two epochs. During the first of these, the implements were rude and are found in caves and elsewhere, in connection with the bones of extinct animals. The relics of the later period are of many varieties of stone, and many are highly polished. A greater variety, too, is seen; axes, hammers, knives, daggers, spear and arrow heads, saws, chisels, borers and scrapers all have been found. We know that

the people of the Stone Age had some domestic animals and that they built rude houses and, in some cases, put together large mounds of stone as burial places for their dead. See BRONZE AGE; IRON AGE; LAKE DWELLINGS.

Stone Chat, a common European bird, which lives upon moors and in other open places. Its color is generally black, though the belly is a

STONE CHAT

yellowish-white and the breast a light chestnut-brown. It is a small bird of the warbler family, that is able to run with great rapidity. The bird is occasionally seen in North America.

Stoneham, *stone' am*, MASS., a town in Middlesex co., 8 mi. n. of Boston, on the Boston & Maine railroad. The place has a public library, a good high school building and a public park, included in the metropolitan park district. The chief industries are large boot and shoe factories, machine shops, tanneries and furniture works. It was settled about 1670 and was incorporated as a separate town in 1725. Population in 1910, 7090.

Stonehenge, *stone' henj*, an extensive group of standing stones, in Salisbury Plain, Wiltshire, England, two miles from Amesbury. They form two circles and two ovals. The outer circle, which is about three hundred feet in circumference, consisted, when entire, of thirty upright stones, each about sixteen feet high, placed at intervals of three and one-half feet, with thirty squared stones mortised upon them. The inner circle, which is eight feet from the outer, consisted of about thirty stones, six feet in height, without imposts. The first oval consists of five groups of three stones, two uprights with an impost. Before each group stood three smaller upright stones. Inside the inner oval is a large slab, supposed to have been an altar. The whole is surrounded by a double mound and ditch, and there is also an avenue leading from the northeast, bounded by a mound and ditch. These circles were probably formed in connection with the Druidical or some other old religion.

Stone River, BATTLE OF. See MURFREES-BORO, BATTLE OF.

Stones, PRECIOUS. See PRECIOUS STONES.

Sto'ny Point, N. Y., a town in Rockland co., at the head of Haverstraw Bay, on the Hudson River, 42 mi. n. of New York City, on the West Shore and other railroads. It is on a rocky promontory, which was fortified by the Americans early in the Revolution. The fort was captured, strengthened and garrisoned by the British under Clinton in May, 1779. Washington then ordered General "Mad Anthony" Wayne to regain this position. On July 16, with 1200 men, he surprised the fort at midnight, entered it with a rush and forced the garrison to surrender at the point of the bayonet. The Americans did not fire a gun; they lost 15 men killed and 83 wounded; the British lost 63 killed and 553 captured. Soon after the capture the fortifications were destroyed and the place was abandoned. The ruins of the fort are included in a small national park created in 1902. Population in 1910, 3651.

Storage Battery or **Accumulator**, a name applied to a kind of electric battery by means of which electric energy can be stored and rendered portable. The cells of such batteries contain grooved lead plates and lead electrodes. The grooves in the plates are filled with different substances, a paste of red lead for the positive plate and litharge for the negative plate. The plates are moistened with water containing sulphuric acid. The batteries are charged by connecting them with a dynamo, and will retain the electricity until it is required for use. Most storage batteries have many plates.

Stork, a tall and stately wading bird, of the heron family. The common stork is found during the summer time throughout the greater part of Europe, but it passes the winter in Africa and Asia. With the exception of the black on the wings and the red beak, legs and toes, the bird is pure white, and as, when standing erect, its head is about four feet from the ground, it is really handsome. It is a familiar bird, sometimes building its nest upon the roofs of inhabited houses, and it is consequently regarded almost as a sacred bird, the symbol of piety and family love. In sleeping, the storks stand upon one foot, and they thus are often seen in the day time, even in crowded cities. They have no voice, and the only sounds they make are peculiar clatterings of the bill. The practical reason for favoring them is that they are very good scavengers.

STORK

Storms, violent disturbances of the atmosphere, usually accompanied by rain, snow and hail, sometimes by thunder and lightning. Storms are general or local, and they are occasioned by the unequal heating of the atmosphere, which causes unequal pressure over adjoining areas.

Fair and foul weather follow each other in continuous succession over most of the world. The frequency and violence of the changes may vary at different seasons of the year, but in general these are due to local causes. A study of the weather maps issued by the United States Weather Bureau shows that there are always in the country one or more areas of low pressure, surrounded by areas of high pressure. The areas of low pressure are those of low barometer and high temperature. They may have a diameter of from 500 to 1000 miles, and the winds blow toward them from all directions. In the center of the low pressure areas, condensation takes place, followed by rain or snow.

In the temperate latitudes of the northern hemisphere the storm center moves eastward, its course usually being from southwest to northeast, while in the tropics its direction is westward. In the southern hemisphere, these directions are reversed. The storm centers which move across the United States are usually lost in the Atlantic, only a few of them reaching Europe. When they do extend thus far they usually strike the continent north of the British Isles, but in a few instances they have been known to strike the British Isles and even extend as far south as France and Spain. The rain-bearing wind usually comes from the southwest or south, and the area of low pressure is succeeded by one of high pressure, from which the wind blows outward. A north or northwest wind produces a clear sky, a high barometer and a low temperature. In the northern Mississippi valley, such a wind will often cause a drop of 15° or 20° in the thermometer in less than an hour.

Storms of this character are cyclonic in their nature; that is, they are caused by currents of air moving from all directions into the area of low pressure, and they have a rotary motion on a large scale. They are more frequent in winter than in summer and are most frequent in the spring and autumn months. On land they are seldom violent, but over the sea, in the tropical latitudes, they often attain such violence as to be destructive to shipping. These storms should not be confounded with the so-called cyclones of the United States, which are tornadoes and cover only a very small area.

General storms can usually be predicted from one to two days in advance of their occurrence. They are preceded by a falling barometer, a rise in temperature and cloudiness in the west, which usually begins with the formation of long streaks of cirrus clouds. Storms may last from one to ten days, according to the area which they cover and the rapidity with which the area of low pressure moves forward, but their duration seldom exceeds three days. See Cyclone; Hurricane; Monsoon; Rain; Tornado; Wind. Consult Archibald's *Story of the Atmosphere*, Davis's *Elements of Meteorology* and Tarr's *Physical Geography*.

Sto'ry, Joseph (1779–1845), an American lawyer and jurist, born at Marblehead, Mass. He graduated from Harvard in 1798 and was admitted to the bar in 1801. For a time he turned to literary pursuits, but without success. Devoting himself to law and politics, he was chosen to the legislature and then to Congress, where he served from 1808 to 1811. In that year he was appointed a justice of the United States Supreme Court, and in 1829 he became professor of law at Harvard, a position which he held for

the rest of his life, though continuing to perform his duties on the bench. His law works include a number of special treatises, commentaries and judgments, which, with his decisions as a jurist, have done much to mold American legal and legislative practice.

Stoss, Veit (?1440–1533), a German sculptor, born at Nuremburg, considered the greatest wood carver of Germany. Owing to his eccentric character he had many quarrels with the city authorities of Nuremberg, and he was several times imprisoned. He died at an old age, totally blind. Most of his works are religious and show a deep spiritual feeling, which was lacking in the artists of his time. His works are found in the public buildings and in cathedrals of the principal cities of Germany. Some of the best-known examples of his art are the *High Altar*, the *Taking of Christ, Christ on Mount of Olives, Crowning of the Virgin by God and Christ, Pieta* and a *Madonna*.

Stoth'ard, Thomas (1755–1834), an English painter, born in London. His first work was book illustration, in which he showed great skill. He afterward drew designs for the *Town and Country Magazine*, Bell's *British Poets* and the *Novelist's Magazine*. Among his works, which number over five thousand designs, the more important series and single designs are for Boydell's *Shakespeare*, illustrations of *Robinson Crusoe, The Pilgrim's Progress, The Rape of the Lock* and Cowper's *Poems*; while his best-known works are *The Canterbury Pilgrims, The Flitch of Bacon* and *Greek Vintage*.

Stoughton, *sto'ton,* Mass., a town in Norfolk co., 18 mi. s. of Boston, on the New York, New Haven and Hartford railroad. It has a public library, a high school and a number of private schools, and it contains several beautiful residence sections. The industrial establishments include woolen mills, rubber works, boot and shoe factories and machine shops. Population in 1910, including the villages of West Stoughton and North Stoughton, 6316.

Stout, James Huff (?–1910), a lumberman, manufacturer and politician, resident of Menomonie, Wis. He had large business and manufacturing interests and was for several terms a member of the state senate. Mr. Stout rendered unusually valuable service to his state through his work in the development of the industrial, physical and art sides of elementary and secondary education. It was through his financial support that Menomonie, Wis., was the first public school system in the United

States to furnish a complete, well-organized system of instruction in art, manual training, domestic art and science and physical training, for every child of school age, from the kindergarten to the high school. The Stout Training School, a high-grade normal school for the preparation of kindergartners, manual training and domestic science teachers, has been established in Menomonie and is maintained through his support. Mr. Stout also inaugurated the system of traveling libraries in Wisconsin, by providing thirty such libraries for the use of the people in his own county. He was also instrumental in securing the enactment of the law establishing a state library commission, through which the library system of the state has been established and developed.

Stove, a device for storing and sending out heat. The stove consists of an enclosure, usually in the form of a box, with an opening for the flue and another for putting in the fuel. The first stoves were made of brick and tile or stone and were very large. The first iron stoves were made in France, early in the eighteenth century, and were introduced into England about 1716, where they were so modified as to enable them to burn coal. In 1745 Benjamin Franklin invented a stove which had a downward draft that distributed the heat evenly over the sides. This was a great improvement over any stoves that had preceded it, and some years later he invented another for burning coal; but stoves were not in general use in the United States until after 1825. Previous to that time nearly all dwelling houses were warmed by fireplaces. Country churches were not warmed, but women carried foot stoves to church. These were small tin or sheet iron boxes, with their sides perforated and enclosed in wooden cases. Just before starting for church the women had these stoves filled with burning coals.

There are now many patterns of stoves upon the market, designed for burning wood, hard coal, soft coal, kerosene and gas. Gas stoves are in very general use for cooking, in cities where illuminating gas is used. Gasoline stoves manufacture the gas from gasoline before using it and are convenient for use in places where illuminating gas cannot be obtained, and for use in summer weather, as they do not heat the rooms in which they stand.

Stowe, HARRIET ELIZABETH BEECHER (1811–1896), an American novelist, best known as the author of *Uncle Tom's Cabin*. This book, published in 1852, had perhaps a greater influence than any other piece of fiction ever written, was translated into more than twenty languages and had an unprecedented sale. Though loose in construction and marred by signs of hasty composition, *Uncle Tom's Cabin* is nevertheless a strong book, because it tells vividly a story of vital interest. It was dramatized shortly after its publication and has had wonderful popularity as a play.

Mrs. Stowe, sister of Henry Ward Beecher, was born at Litchfield, **Conn.**, where her early life was spent. Her family moved in 1832 to Cincinnati, and four years later she was married to Rev. Calvin E. Stowe of that city. Her knowledge of the condition of the slaves was gained by visits to slave states and possibly by encounters with escaping slaves. *Uncle Tom's Cabin* was by no means her only work, but the others are practically unnoticed, because of the success of the one. Among the others may be mentioned *The Minister's Wooing, Oldtown Folks, Dred* and *My Wife and I.*

Strabismus, *stra biz'mus.* See SQUINTING.

Stra'bo (about 64 B. C.–about 19 A. D.), a Greek geographer, a native of Pontus. His earliest writing was his *History*, of which but a few fragments remain. His great work, however, on geography, in seventeen books, has been preserved entire, with the exception of the seventh book, of which there is only an epitome. The first two books are introductory, the next eight treat of Europe, the six following treat of Asia and the last discusses Africa.

Stradivarius, *strah'de vah're us,* ANTONIO (1649–1737), a celebrated violin maker, born in Cremona, Italy. He was a pupil of Nicolo Amati, in whose employment he remained until 1700, when he began making on his own account. It was he who settled the typical pattern of the Cremona violin, and his instruments, for tone and finish, have never been excelled.

Straf'ford, THOMAS WENTWORTH, Earl of (1593–1641), an English statesman. He sat in Parliament for Yorkshire for a number of years and in the first Parliament of Charles I strongly opposed the royal aggressions. In 1628, before the Petition of Right was presented, he drew up a bill similar to that document; and as this was not accepted by the king, Wentworth later supported the Petition of Right. As he felt, however, that Parliament was going too far in its opposition to the king, he joined the king's side, was made baron, then viscount and president of the Council of the North and privy councilor. In all of Charles's later attempts to make the royal authority absolute, Wentworth, with Laud, was his strongest supporter. In 1633 he went to Ireland as lord deputy and attempted to impress his system of "thorough," by which he meant thorough devotion to the interests of the king. Although Ireland was commercially and industrially the better for his rule, the despotism employed in putting into practice his system made him exceedingly unpopular.

After his return to England in 1639 Wentworth was made earl of Strafford and became even more powerful in the king's council. When the Scots rebelled against the king, Strafford went to Ireland to raise an army, to help put down the insurrection, and this act was later used against him in his impeachment. One of the first acts of the Long Parliament was the impeachment of Strafford. It became plain that the House of Lords was not likely to render judgment against him, and the Commons were therefore obliged to change their proceedings to a bill of attainder. This was passed by both houses, and Charles I, despite the fact that he had promised that Strafford should come to no harm, was forced to sign it. Strafford was beheaded in May, 1641.

Stramo′nium, also called THORN APPLE, JIMSON WEED and STINK WEED, an herb which grows to the height of about three feet. It has an erect stem, numerous branches, and large, triangular leaves, and it bears large white flowers. The seeds are flat and of a dark brown color. This is the plant from which the drug stramonium is obtained. The active principle is contained in the leaves and seeds. The drug is a powerful poison, but it is quite generally used in medicine, for relief in asthma and for purposes similar to those for which belladonna is used, as it resembles belladonna very closely in its properties.

Strassburg, *strahs′boorK*, a city of Germany and the capital of Alsace-Lorraine, situated on the Ill River, 250 mi. e. by s. of Paris and about 370 mi. s. w. of Berlin. It is one of the most strongly fortified towns of the German Empire and is practically encircled by forts and ramparts. For centuries the city has been noted for its cathedral, the oldest part of which dates from the beginning of the eleventh century, and which was completed in the fifteenth century. In the tower is the famous Strassburg clock (See STRASSBURG CLOCK). Other buildings of note are the Church of Saint Thomas; the municipal museum of art, which was formerly

an episcopal palace, and the imperial palace. The leading educational institution is the University of Strassburg, now known as the Emperor William University. Its library contains over 800,000 volumes, and in addition there is a municipal library of over 115,000 volumes. The city is connected with the Rhine by canals, and it also has communication with a number of the waterways of France. The industrial establishments include tobacco and cigar factories, organ works, machine shops, printing houses, tanneries and foundries.

Strassburg is supposed to have been founded by the Romans, who named it Argentoratum. In the sixth century its name was changed to Strassburg, and in the beginning of the tenth century it came under the control of the German emperors. It was united with France in 1861, but at the close of the Franco-German War, along with Alsace-Lorraine it became a part of the German Empire. Population in 1910, 178,891.

Strassburg Clock, the famous clock in the tower of the Strassburg Cathedral. The present one is the third to acquire fame. The first was built in 1352; the second in 1570, and the last, early in the nineteenth century. This is 30 feet high and 15 feet wide at the base. At the bottom is a large globe of the heavens, which shows the course of the stars and the passing of each important one across the meridian of Strassburg. Behind this globe is a calendar, which shows the day of the month and the occurrence of all the religious festivals. Above the calendar are automatic figures, one of which is drawn across the platform on each day. Thus, Apollo crosses on Sunday, Diana on Monday, etc. Above these figures is the dial, which tells the time of day. Next above is a planetarium, and above this is a globe which shows the phases of the moon. On the next floor are several figures, which strike the quarter hours. These represent the different periods of life—infancy, youth, old age and death. Above all is a figure of Christ. At noon on each day, the twelve apostles pass before him in procession, and at the same time a cock appears and crows three times. See STRASSBURG.

Strat′ford, Ontario, the county-seat of Perth co., situated on the Avon River and on the Grand Trunk railway, 88 mi. w. of Toronto. It is quite an important industrial center and has foundries and machine shops, railroad shops, chemical works, woolen factories, hosiery factories and a boot and shoe factory. Population in 1911, 12,946.

Stratford de Red'cliffe, STRATFORD CANNING, Viscount (1786–1880), an English diplomat, cousin of George Canning. His first diplomatic post was that of secretary to an embassy at Constantinople, and he later became minister at Constantinople. He was minister to the United States in 1820 and to Russia four years later, and in 1841 he went as ambassador to Turkey. At the court of Constantinople he attained great influence, and his struggle with the Russian ambassador, Prince Menshikoff, over the question of Russian influence in Turkey was of great political importance. The Crimean War was the result of this contest, and Canning remained at Constantinople during the war. He was raised to the peerage as Viscount Stratford de Redcliffe in 1852.

Stratford-upon-A'von, a municipal borough of England, famous as the birthplace of Shakespeare, situated 8 mi. s. w. of Warwick. The town is characterized by broad streets and old wooden houses. It contains the parish church, in which Shakespeare lies buried, and the house in which he was born, and in which are preserved portraits, early editions and other objects of interest related to the poet. The Shakespeare Memorial Building, including a theater, the old Guild Hall and the Shakespeare Monument, are other objects of interest. Anne Hathaway's cottage is about one mile west of the town. Population in 1911, 8500.

Strathco'na and Mount Royal, DONALD ALEXANDER SMITH, Lord (1820–1914), a Canadian statesman, born in Scotland. In 1838 he became associated with the Hudson Bay Company, doing work for many years on the Labrador coast and in the northwest, where he was first made chief factor and then resident governor and chief commissioner of the company in Canada. Following this, in 1870, he was elected to the Manitoba legislature and to the Canadian House of Commons, and later he was appointed member of the Northwest Territorial Council. He resigned from the Manitoba legislature, but remained in parliament, except between 1880 and 1887, until 1896, when he was appointed high commissioner to London. His interest in railroads is responsible to a large extent for the rapid railway development in Canada and the completion of the Canadian Pacific railroad.

Strat'ified Rocks, certain rocks which are composed of several layers, more or less parallel, which were originally loose substances, as sand or clay, deposited by water. Common stones of this nature are sandstone, shale and limestone. When the strata do not lie horizontally, but are inclined, they are said to *dip* toward some point of the compass, and the angle they make with the horizon is called the *angle,* or *dip,* or *inclination.* When strata protrude above the surface, or appear uncovered, they are said to *crop out.* They are said to be *conformable* when their planes are parallel, whatever their dip may be, and they are *unconformable* when their planes are not parallel. See DIP.

Straus, *strous,* OSCAR SOLOMON (1850–   ), an American merchant, reformer and diplomat, born in Georgia, of Jewish parents. He graduated from Columbia University and began the practice of law. He entered upon a business career in 1881 and accumulated a large fortune. As a Democrat he was appointed minister to Turkey in 1887, but affiliated with the Republican party in 1896 and was reappointed to the same post by President McKinley. In 1902 he

LORD STRATHCONA

succeeded ex-President Harrison as a member of the permanent court of arbitration at The Hague. From 1907 to 1909 he was secretary of the department of commerce and labor, and in the next year was ambassador to Turkey. Mr. Straus has always been interested in reform

STRATFORD-UPON-AVON AND SHAKESPEARE'S BIRTHPLACE

movements and is the author of numerous books on political problems in the United States.

Strauss, *strous,* DAVID FRIEDRICH (1808–1874), a German philosopher, born at Ludwigsburg, Württemberg. He studied in Tübingen University, became assistant to a country clergyman in 1830 and was appointed temporary professor in the seminary at Maulbronn. This last position he resigned, and he went to Berlin, to study under Schleiermacher and Hegel. In 1835 he published a *Life of Jesus,* in which he attempted to prove that the gospel narratives had a mythical origin and growth and contained no miracle or prophecy, the Christ of faith being a mere idea. To his numerous critics he replied in *Streitschriften* (Polemical Writings) and *Zwei friedliche Blätter* (A Pacific Pamphlet). His appointment to the chair of Church history and dogmatics in the university at Zurich caused so much opposition that he had to refuse it, but was given a pension of 1000 francs as a recompense. His second great work was *Die christliche Glaubenslehre* (The Christian Doctrines). He also wrote a life of Ulrich von Hutten, and other works.

Strauss, JOHANN (1825–1899), a German composer, son of Johann Strauss, a Viennese dance music writer and conductor (1805–1849). In 1863 he became conductor of the court balls at Saint Petersburg, and in 1872 he conducted an orchestra of one hundred performers at the World Peace Jubilee in Boston. He wrote over four hundred waltzes, many of them world-famous, especially *The Beautiful Blue Danube, Artist's Life* and *Wine, Woman and Song.*

Strauss, RICHARD (1864–   ), a German composer and conductor, the most distinguished exponent of the school of music founded by Richard Wagner. He was born in Munich and had a thorough musical education under the best European masters. He was conductor of the royal opera at Weimar from 1889 to 1894; at Munich until 1899, and since then at Berlin. As a composer he is the leader of the "moderns," whose theories are an extension of Wagner's. His best known operas are *Salome* and *Elektra,* two tragedies, and *The Rose Cavalier,* an attempt, not wholly successful, to write a comedy. His tone poems, *Don Juan, Don Quixote, Till Eulenspiegel's Merry Pranks* and *Death and Transfiguration,* are often considered his best works. His songs are similar to those of Schumann, in that the accompaniment is meant to express, as fully as the words, the sentiment of the writer. Strauss has made several tours of Europe and America, and has been warmly received everywhere.

Straw, the dried stems of certain plants, chiefly rye, wheat, barley, oats and buckwheat. Its chief use is in the manufacture of mats, coarse cloths, paper and various other articles, and it is also employed for fodder and for bedding. The so-called Panama hats are made from the straw of a Central American plant resembling the palm. In the United States straw is especially valuable for the manufacture of paper, for which purpose rye straw is the best.

Straw'berry, the most common and extensively cultivated of small fruits. The strawberry grows wild in nearly all temperate climates, and the numerous cultivated varieties have been developed from the seeds of wild strawberries, especially from the species found in Chile. The fruit is really the end of a large, juicy stem, in which are imbedded the little fruits, which we call the seeds of the berry.

Growing strawberries is an important industry in most of the states of the Mississippi Valley and in several of the North Atlantic states. The best results are obtained from young plants. In the Gulf States the berries begin to ripen in February, and by the time the crop farthest south is harvested, that in the states directly north is ready, so that these states furnish the Northern markets with berries until June, when those from Wisconsin and Minnesota appear. Thus the wide range over which this fruit can be successfully cultivated enables it to continue on the market during most of the summer months. The berries are usually packed in pint or quart boxes, which are shipped in crates. The quantity of strawberries raised in the United States exceeds the combined crop of all other small fruits.

Straw Plait, straw, plaited or braided into strips or tissues of some size, for making hats, bags, ornaments and matting. In the manufacture of straw hats the straw must be of a certain length between the knots and must not be brittle; and these qualities are found most frequently in the wheat grown in Tuscany, where the well-known Leghorn hats are made. When the grain is still green the straw is pulled up by the roots, dried in the sun, bleached by means of sulphur fumes, split by a machine, and plaited into hats by women and young children, as a domestic industry. In the United States, the making of hats and other articles from imported plait is now an extensive industry.

Streator, *street'or,* Ill., a city in La Salle co., 94 mi. s. w. of Chicago, on the Vermilion River and on the Atchison, Topeka & Santa Fé, the Chicago & Alton, the Chicago, Burlington & Quincy and several other railroads. It is an important railroad center, in an agricultural section, which is also near deposits of coal, fire clay and building stone. The leading factories are glass works, foundries, machine shops, car shops and brick and tile works. Streator is built largely on a bluff along the river, has an attractive park near the center of the city, a Carnegie library, a high school, an opera house and good churches and school buildings. The place was settled in 1860 and was chartered as a city in 1882. Population in 1910, 14,253.

Street, George Edmund (1824–1881), an English architect. Having studied architecture under Gilbert Scott, in 1850 he began work on his own account. He favored the English Gothic style, and in this his principal works were built. The chief of these were the new law courts in the Strand, London, for which he was appointed architect in 1868. His architectural structures are numerous and important; among them were the Crimean Memorial Church in Constantinople and the Synod House in Dublin. He was a member of the British and American Institutes of Architecture, and a Royal Academician. He published *The Brick and Marble Architecture of North Italy in the Middle Ages* and *Some Account of Gothic Architecture in Spain.*

Street Rail'way, a railway laid in the streets of a city or town, especially for the transportation of passengers. The street railway is a distinctively American idea, though it was developed from the tramway (See Tramway). The first street railway was laid in New York City, from the Bowery to Harlem, in 1831 and 1832. The car used was an old-fashioned stagecoach, and it was hauled by horses. Afterwards steam power was tried, but it was not successful, and the horses were reinstated. The success of this line led to the construction of others in New York and other cities, and before 1860 street railways were common in all large cities of the United States. Since that time they have been extended through most of the cities of Europe.

Various forms of motive power have been used, such as horses, compressed air, steam, cables and electricity, but omitting elevated and underground lines, the cable and electricity are the only forms worthy of notice. The first street railway operated by cable was constructed in San Francisco in 1873. In a cable railway the motive power is furnished by a stationary steam engine, which winds an endless wire cable around a drum. This cable passes under the middle of the track, in a conduit containing pulleys, upon which it runs. A slot leads from the surface to the conduit, and through this a bar extends. This bar has a grappling device and is attached to the motor car of the train, which is usually called the *grip car.* By means of a lever the grappling device can be made to grab the cable or release it at will. Cable lines are especially advantageous in cities like San Francisco and Seattle, where many of the streets have steep grades. Except in such locations the cable has now been displaced by electric cars. See Electric Railway; Elevated Railway; Underground Railway.

Strength of Materials. The strength of any material is the resistance which it opposes to alteration of form or to fracture by any application of force. Materials are subject to many forms of strains, and some are better qualified to resist strains of a certain kind than others. Stone, for example, is admirably constituted for supporting immense weights, but it would not offer much resistance to a direct pull. Cast iron is superior to wrought iron in resisting a pull, or tensile stress, but the latter excels the former in its resistance to a thrust, or compressive stress.

A material is exposed to five distinct strains— a tensile, or stretching, strain, in the direction of its fibers, as in the case of ropes and tie beams; a transverse strain, acting perpendicularly or obliquely to its length, as in levers and joists; a crushing strain, by pressure, as in the case of pillars and posts; a torsional, or twisting, strain, acting in a perpendicular direction, at the extremity of a lever or otherwise, as in axles and crank shafts, and a shearing force, applied laterally, as in the case of a shearing machine for cutting through iron plates and bars.

Wrought iron and steel offer the greatest resistance to tensile strains; the strength of wood in this direction varies according to its seasoning and specific gravity. The heavier the wood is, in general, the stronger it is. The transverse strength of beams is determined largely by their elasticity. The property varies greatly in different materials. Wood has a greater elastic range of action than iron or steel bars and it consequently sinks or deflects to a greater degree under a given weight. Any strain beyond the *elastic limit* entails fracture. Increased stiffness or transverse resistance of beams is rapidly obtained with an increase of depth of the beam. With the exception of wood, materials offer a greater resistance to a crushing force than to a tensile strain. Cast iron is superior to wrought iron in this respect and is consequently much employed in the construction of foundations. Torsional stress tries the solidity and tenacity of metals more than any other kind of stress. But the torsional strength of shafts increases very rapidly as the diameter is enlarged. The distribution of material in hollow forms conduces to the greatest strength and stiffness, in combination with the minimum consumption of material. A familiar instance of the hollow construction is the stem of grasses, and especially the bamboo, while another example is that of the hollow bones of animals.

Strike, the action taken by workmen in any branch of industry when they cease from work, with the object of compelling their employer to accede to certain demands made by them; distinguished from a *lockout*, which is the retaliatory measure adopted by the employers to resist such demands, by stopping the operation of their plants and throwing their workmen out of employment. See LABOR ORGANIZATIONS.

Strob'oscope, an apparatus for viewing a moving object. The simplest form of stroboscope consists of a pasteboard cylinder, with vertical slits at equal intervals, mounted upon an upright axis. By placing a series of pictures within the cylinder, so that they can be viewed through the slits, and by causing the apparatus to revolve, one can produce an effect similar to that of moving pictures, provided the interval between successive images formed upon the retina of the eye is shorter than the time each picture is exposed. Many forms of this simple instrument have been invented and are used as toys and for amusement. With the advancement of photography and the perfection of the magic lantern, a more elaborate form of stroboscope has come into use (See KINETOSCOPE)

Strom'bus, a name now given only to the shells of a few large mollusks, though originally extended to cover several genera. The giant strombus, or fountain shell, of the West Indies, often forms an ornament in houses and is largely used in cameo and porcelain work.

Strontium, *stron'she um,* a yellowish metal, first separated from its compounds by Davy in 1808. It is a malleable, ductile metal, that burns with a crimson flame when heated in air.

Though less abundant than barium, it occurs in nature in similar forms of combination. Strontium carbonate was first discovered in the lead mines of Strontian in Argyleshire. In the process of sugar refining it is used to extract the sugar. By dissolving this in nitric acid, strontium nitrate is made, and this is used extensively in the manufacture of fireworks, as it burns with a bright red flame.

Strophanthin, *stro fan'thin,* a crystalline substance with a strongly bitter taste, obtained from the seeds of a plant, native to Africa, where it is used as an arrow poison. It affects the muscles and increases their contractile power. Physicians use it as a tonic in heart disease.

Struve, *stroo've,* FRIEDRICH GEORG WILHELM VON (1793–1864), a Russian astronomer, born at Altona and educated at Dorpat University. On the completion of the Russian observatory at Pulkova, near Saint Petersburg, in 1839, he was nominated its director, and here he continued his researches on the nebulae and double stars. His works, which are considered excellent authority by astronomers, are of a highly technical nature.

Strychnine, *strik'nin,* a substance found in nux vomica and various plants of the genus *strychnos.* It is extracted in the form of colorless, four-sided prisms, which have no odor, but are intensely poisonous. One-eighth of a grain of strychnine is sufficient to kill a large dog; three-eighths of a grain produce spasms in man; one-half a grain has been known to be fatal, while a grain is almost certainly so. The symptoms of strychnine poisoning are difficulty in breathing, followed by twitching of the limbs and convulsions, in which the body becomes rigid and is often bent strongly backward (See ANTIDOTE). Strychnine is intensely bitter and will communicate its taste to 20,000 times its own weight of water. In very small doses it is a valuable tonic.

Strychnos, *strik'nos,* the botanical name of a genus of shrubs or trees, which are found principally in the tropical parts of Asia and America. They produce some of the most violent poisons known. See NUX VOMICA; STRYCHNINE; CLEARING NUT.

Stu'art or **Stew'art,** a royal family of England and Scotland. The founder of the house seems to have been a Norman baron named Fitzflaald, a follower of William the Conqueror, whose second son, Walter, entered the service of David I of Scotland and became steward of the royal household. The name of the office was adopted by the family as a surname. Walter obtained large grants of land from David. James, the fifth steward, was chosen as one of the regents, on the death of Alexander III, and died in the service of Bruce in 1309. His son, Walter, the sixth steward, married Marjory, daughter of King Robert I, a union which secured to his family the crown of Scotland in the event of the extinction of the royal line. Walter died in 1326 and was succeeded by his son Robert, who, on the death of David II without issue, succeeded to the crown as Robert II. With James VI the Stuart family succeeded to the throne of England. (For its history subsequent to this time see JAMES I; CHARLES I; CHARLES II; JAMES II; MARY II; ANNE.) James II was driven from the throne of England, and for years there was a struggle to replace the Stuarts on the throne. Mary of Modena, second wife of James II of England, gave birth to James Edward, commonly called the Old Pretender (See STUART, JAMES EDWARD). In 1715 an unsuccessful attempt was made by the Jacobites, or Stuart party, to set this prince on the throne of his ancestors by force of arms. He married a granddaughter of John Sobieski, king of Poland, by whom he had two sons, Charles Edward, the Young Pretender, and Henry Benedict Maria Clement, who became a cardinal in 1747.

Stuart, CHARLES EDWARD, called *The Young Pretender* (1720–1788), eldest son of James Edward Stuart, the Old Pretender. He was promised aid by France in an invasion of Great Britain, and accordingly in 1745 he landed in Scotland. With the help of the Scotch Highlanders, who joined him promptly, he won a victory over the royal forces, but when he entered England he found little support and was finally obliged to retreat without attempting to enter London. At Culloden, in 1746, he was completely defeated by the duke of Cumberland, and for five months he remained hidden in various places in the Scotch Highlands and in the Hebrides, protected by the loyalty of the Scotch. His life after his return to the Continent was most dissolute.

Stuart, GILBERT (1755–1828), an American painter, noted for his portraits of famous Americans. He was born in Narragansett, R. I. He had little chance for study under good masters until 1775, when he went to London. There he remained until 1792, and during the last part of his stay his genius was fully recognized. In 1795 he painted the first of those portraits of Washington on which, more than on any of his other work, his fame rests. It is by the various Stuart portraits that Washington is chiefly

known. Among Stuart's other sitters were John Adams, Jefferson, Madison, Monroe, John Jay, John Jacob Astor, William Ellery Channing and Josiah Quincy. See WASHINGTON, GEORGE, *portrait.*

Stuart, JAMES EDWARD, called *Chevalier Saint George* or *The Old Pretender* (1688–1766), son of James II of England. He was born a short time before his father was deposed, and in fact, his birth and the fear that on his accession England would become permanently a Catholic country, had much to do with the overthrow of James. In 1715 an attempt was made to secure the throne for him, but it was easily put down. The remainder of his life was spent mostly in Rome. His wife was a granddaughter of John Sobieski of Poland.

Stuart, JAMES EWELL BROWN (1833–1864), an American general, born in Patrick County, Va. He graduated at the United States Military Academy in 1854; was promoted rapidly from one rank to another until 1861, when he was appointed captain. He resigned from the United States Army, however, when Virginia seceded, and was made lieutenant colonel of Virginia troops. He was in chief command of the Confederate cavalry in the first Battle of Bull Run in 1861, and in September of the same year he was promoted to be brigadier general in the Confederate army. In June, 1862, he conducted a daring reconnoissance of McClellan's army on the Chickahominy. He fought at the second Battle of Bull Run, led the advance of Jackson's Maryland invasion and fought at South Mountain, Antietam and Fredericksburg. After the fall of Stonewall Jackson, Stuart succeeded to the temporary command of Jackson's corps at Chancellorsville. In the campaign of 1864 he was mortally wounded at Yellow Tavern, near Richmond, where he attempted to check Sheridan's advance.

Stuart, RUTH McENERY (1856–), an American story-writer, born in Avoyelles parish, La., and educated in New Orleans. She married Alfred O. Stuart, a cotton planter, in 1879, and in 1885 she moved to New York. Her writings include *George Washington Jones, The Story of Babette, The Women's Exchange, Sonny* and *The River's Children.*

Stubbs, WILLIAM (1825–1901), an English historian and divine, educated at Ripon Grammar School and at Oxford University. After his graduation he became a fellow of Trinity College. In 1862 he was appointed librarian of Lambeth Palace and in 1866 became professor of modern history at Oxford. He edited many valuable historical works in the Rolls Series and wrote *Seventeen Lectures on the Study of Mediaeval and Modern History*, besides producing the *Constitutional History of England*, his greatest work.

Stuc′co, a fine plaster, used as a coating for walls, to give them a finished surface. The stucco used for interior docorations is made of pulverized white marble, mixed with water, or of calcined gypsum or plaster of Paris, mixed with glue. That used for external purposes is of a coarser kind and is prepared in various ways, the different kinds being generally distinguished by the name *cements*, some of which take a polish almost equal to the finest marble. The Greeks and Romans used stucco to a great extent, both for internal and external decoration in their buildings.

Sturgeon, *stur′jun*, a family of fishes characterized by having a gristly skeleton and a body covered with hard scales. The general form of the sturgeon is elongated and rather slender; the snout, long and pointed. The body is covered with numerous bony plates, in longitudinal rows, and the exterior portion of the head is also

STURGEON

well mailed. The mouth, placed under the snout, is small and funnel-shaped, without teeth. The food is sucked in. The eyes and nostrils are on the side of the head. On the back is a single dorsal fin, and the tail is forked. The sturgeons are sea fish, but ascend the larger rivers in great abundance and are the objects of important fisheries. The flesh of most of the species is wholesome and agreeable food; their roe is converted into caviare, and their air bladder affords the finest isinglass.

The common sturgeon inhabits the North American and European seas, migrating during early summer into the larger rivers and lakes. Its flesh is firm and well flavored, somewhat resembling veal. The general body color is yellow, and its length is five or six to eight feet, but it may reach twelve feet. Its food consists of mollusks, small crustaceans and small fishes. The sterlet is found in the Volga and the Danube. Its flesh is the most delicate, and its roe yields the best caviare. The great, or white, sturgeon, is found in the Danube, the Volga and other rivers running into the Black and Caspian seas. It

frequently exceeds fifteen feet in length and weighs about 1200 pounds. The flesh is not much esteemed, but the finest isinglass is made from its air bladder. There are several species peculiar to North America. One of these, the fresh water sturgeon, inhabits the great lakes and connected streams.

Sturm, *stoorm*, JOHN (1507–1589), a celebrated educator, born at Schleiden, Prussia. He began teaching at Louvain, afterwards went to Paris, and was then appointed director of the gymnasium at Strassburg, which position he occupied for forty years. It was in connection with this school that Sturm gained his wide reputation as an educator and reformer. He organized the gymnasium into twelve classes, or grades, extending from the lowest primary to the college, and each of these classes had the work so planned that it prepared for the one next higher. His methods of teaching were clear, practical and forceful, and his course of study was so well planned that the pupils in his school made remarkable progress. The work attracted the attention of educators in every country of Europe, and from Germany it was transferred to England and was the basis of organization of such schools as Eton and Rugby. From England his influence extended to America. Sturm is justly considered the originator of what has developed into the graded school system of the present day. He was the ablest educator of the Reformed Church during his age.

Stuttgart, *stoot′gahrt*, a city of Germany, capital of the Kingdom of Württemberg, is situated near the left bank of the Neckar, 90 mi. w. by n. of Munich and 38 mi. s. e. of Karlsruhe. The surrounding country is exceptionally beautiful, and the city is noted for its broad streets, spacious squares and fine buildings. The most noted structures are the new palace; the old palace, dating from the sixteenth century; the royal library, which has over 400,000 volumes; the Stiftskirche, which dates from the twelfth century, and a Jewish synagogue. The city buildings consist of the industrial museum, the townhall, the hall for the choral society, the art museum, the palace of justice and the polytechnic institute. The educational institutions include a conservatory of music, an academy of fine arts, a veterinary college and a cabinet of natural history. Among the leading industries are the manufactures of textiles, chemicals, furniture, paper, pianos and chocolate. The city is, next to Leipzig, the greatest center of the German book trade. Population in 1910, 286,218.

Stuyvesant, *sti've sant,* PETER (1592–1672), a Dutch governor of New York (New Netherlands), born in Holland. In 1647 he was made director-general of the colony of the New Netherlands, a position he held until 1664, displaying noteworthy ability and energy in organization

PETER STUYVESANT

and administration. In 1664 the colony fell into the hands of the English and became known as New York. Stuyvesant went to Holland the next year, but soon returned and passed the rest of his life on his farm, called Bouwerij, from which the present Bowery in the city of New York has its name.

Sty'lites or **Pillar Saints,** a class of Christian saints, who, by way of penance, passed the greater part of their lives on the top of high columns. This method of self-torture was introduced by Simeon the Stylite (Saint Simeon Stylites), a Syrian monk, who lived in the open air near Antioch, on the top of a column 60 feet high and only 4 feet in diameter at the top. Here he remained for many years and preached to the crowds that gathered at the foot of the pillar. It appears, however, that he must have descended at times, since he cured the sick by his touch and performed sundry other miracles, wrote epistles and took part in political quarrels. He died in 459. His example was imitated by many persons in Syria and Palestine, and the mania continued until the twelfth century.

Styp'tic, a remedy that has the virtue of clotting blood or of closing the opening in a wounded blood vessel. Oak bark decoction, gallnuts in powder or infusion, matico and turpentine are vegetable styptics; salts of iron, the sulphates of copper and zinc, the acetate of lead and the nitrate of silver are mineral styptics.

Styx, in Greek and Roman mythology, the name of a river of the lower world, over which the dead were ferried by Charon. Styx was also a rivulet in Arcadia, whose water was considered poisonous.

Suabia, *sway'be a.* See SWABIA.

Suaheli or **Swahili,** *swah he'ly,* a name given to the inhabitants of the Zanzibar coast of eastern Africa and the adjacent islands, a people of mixed Arabic and native African origin. They form the most important part of the subjects of the sultan of Zanzibar, and their language is the common medium of communication in eastern Africa.

Suakin, *swah'kin,* or **Suakim,** *swah'kim,* a seaport of the Egyptian Sudan, situated on the Red Sea, about 630 mi. from the Strait of Bab-el-Mandeb. It is built partially on an island and partially on the mainland. It was formerly a commercial port of considerable importance and exported large quantities of ivory, tobacco and gums; but the rising of the Mahdists in the Sudan nearly destroyed the trade, and it has not yet been fully recovered. It is an important station for pilgrims bound for Mecca.

Sublimation, *sub'lim ma'shun,* a process by which solid substances are, by the aid of heat, converted into vapor, which is again condensed into the solid state by the application of cold. The substance formed by the process of sublimation is called a *sublimate.* Sublimation bears the same relation to a solid that distillation does to a liquid. Both processes purify the substances to which they are severally applied, by separating them from the fixed and grosser matters with which they are connected. The vapor of some substances which undergo the process of sublimation condenses in the form of a fine powder, called *flowers;* such are the flowers of sulphur and the flowers of benzoin. Other sublimates appear in a solid and compact form, as camphor, hydrochlorate of ammonia and all the sublimates of mercury.

Submarine Ca'ble. See CABLE, SUBMARINE.

Submarine Navigation, *sub'ma reen' nav'e ga'shun.* When the diving bell had shown that air for respiration can be supplied to persons in adequately arranged vessels under water, ingenious men began to speculate on the possibility of navigating closed ships or boats in similarly exceptional circumstances. The first submarine boat on record was constructed in the beginning of the seventeenth century by a Dutchman named Cornelius Drebell, or Drebelle. It was propelled by oars and was tried in the Thames by order of James I. It carried twelve rowers, besides passengers. One of the most successful machines contrived for submarine navigation was that of Bushnell of Connecticut, which was projected in 1771 and completed in 1775. His vessel was propelled by screws, somewhat resembling those now in use for steam vessels, and there was sufficient air to last for half an hour. In 1800 Robert Fulton, who was at that time a resident of France, constructed a submarine boat, of which he made many trials, some of them at the expense of the French government, on the Seine, at Brest and at Rouen. Compressed air was used for respiration, and he remained at a depth of 25 feet for four hours, propelling the boat in any direction: he also successfully attached a torpedo containing gunpowder to the bottom of an old vessel lying in Brest harbor, and destroyed her.

The vessel patented in 1859 by Mr. Delaney, of Chicago, was egg-shaped, and diminished nearly to a point at each end. It had two iron tanks in the interior; one had air pressed into it by an air pump; the second contained water. The engineer of the boat, by pumping water into or out of the second tank, through the action of the air in the first, could raise or lower the boat to different depths in the water. In 1863 the Confederates in Charleston made use of a submarine boat against the blockading Federal squadron. This boat, called a "David," after the inventor, was built of boiler plates and was propelled by hand by eight men, at a maximum speed of four knots; two side rudders were used for sinking and raising the boat when in motion; it was cigar-shaped, and when advancing to attack, the top was just on a level with the surface of the water. Three trial trips were made, and each time it sank and failed to rise, the crews perishing; the fourth trial, however, was successful, and passing out of the harbor the boat succeeded in blowing up the *Housatonic*, but could not get clear and was carried down. Several of these "Davids" were afterward constructed by the Confederates, but none of them again succeeded in inflicting any serious damage upon the Federal ships.

For some years afterward, although several experiments were carried out in France and America, no successful results were arrived at, but in 1866 a submarine boat was built at Stockholm by Nordenfelt. This boat was driven by steam and ran 16 miles at a speed of 5 knots, but was immersed for only five minutes at a time; it descended, however, 30 feet, and this was repeated several times. A similar boat was constructed for, and bought by, the Greek government. Two others somewhat larger were built by Nordenfelt for the Turkish government and were tried at Constantinople in 1887; they were 100 feet long and 12 feet in diameter, with a displacement of 160 tons; when not immersed they had a speed of 12 knots, traveling a distance of 100 miles without recoaling; they had a crew of six men and descended successfully to a depth of about 50 feet. A still later Nordenfelt boat was tried at Southampton in 1887; this was 125 feet long, with a diameter of 12 feet, a displacement of 230 tons and a speed of 15 knots, when not immersed; with the cupola under water, however, this speed was reduced to 5 knots. Although these boats at the time seemed to answer all expectations, further experiments seem to have shown that they could not be depended upon for real practical work, and the original boat, after lying some time in Copenhagen without finding a purchaser, was finally bought and broken up as old iron in 1891. By the choice of steam as his motive power the inventor created difficulties not easily overcome and prevented the satisfactory development of that type of boat. One result of this choice was that the boat, when proceeding without communication with the atmosphere, was entirely dependent upon the energy developed by the boiler. That this method of accumulation is disadvantageous is clear from thermo-dynamic principles. Not only is the great weight of the engines and boiler a disadvantage, but the continual radiating heat from the boiler renders a prolonged stay in one of these boats impossible when under the surface. An attempt has since been made in England, with the Honigman natron boiler, but with no better results; and later inventors have adopted electric accumulators, with electric motor and engines, as the motive power.

The nearest approach to a workable submarine boat has been made in two boats, built in France, named the *Goubet* and *Gymnote*, and in one, the *Peral*, built at Cadiz. All three have been subjected to exhaustive trials, and with all three a fair measure of success has been obtained. The *Peral*, so called after the designer, a lieutenant in the Spanish navy, was first tried at Cadiz in May, 1889. According to official reports, it attained a speed of 7 knots, and it is believed that a speed of 11 knots could be reached. It covered, during two trials, 120 miles without exhausting all the electricity in the accumulators; it answered its helm well, and no difficulty appears to have been experienced in sinking or again rising to the surface, although it was found necessary to rise to the surface before venturing to alter course. A torpedo was also successfully discharged at a target 400 meters off, while during the six hours she remained closed up, the air on board remained perfectly sweet. In the case of the *Gymnote* and the *Goubet*, with which, since 1889, a series of trials have been carried out at Toulon and Cherbourg, the results have been much the same. No difficulty was experienced in sinking and rising to the surface, when run on a perfectly straight course; when it was necessary to turn, the boats were brought to the surface and placed on their new course before again sinking. When they were moving at a depth of 15 feet below the surface, no trace of their course could be perceived on the top of the water, although in the case of the *Gymnote* at Toulon, she was clearly visible and all her movements were followed, from a captive balloon 150 feet in the air. The *Goubet* has a displacement of about 2 tons, is 16 feet 5 inches long and 5 feet 10 inches deep, and has a beam of $3\frac{1}{2}$ feet; outside the boat at the stern it carries a torpedo, charged with 110 pounds of dynamite; it carries a detachable keel weighing 900 kilograms, the dropping of which, in the event of the pumping out arrangements at any time breaking down, would enable the vessel to rise immediately. Its crew consists of only two men. The vessel is fitted with reservoirs with compressed air, electric accumulators and motor.

In the summer of 1901 the *Gustave Zede* made a voyage from Toulon to Ajaccio, in Corsica, a distance of 190 miles, in three days. She struck the bottom of a large ship with a dummy torpedo, without revealing her presence to any one on board. The *Zede* is 148 feet long and 10.75 feet in diameter, and is cigar-shaped. The success of these submarine boats has led the French government to construct twenty on the pattern of the *Zede*. Great Britain is also experimenting with submarine boats, for the purpose of adding them to her navy.

In 1877 John P. Holland, of Paterson, N. J., constructed a submarine boat that was fairly successful. This boat is provided with diving rudders and a horizontal shaft at the stern, which are used to produce and maintain submergence. The boat is also provided with a camera lucida, by means of which the one steering can see objects above the surface. The United States Naval Department in 1900 authorized the construction of five boats of the Holland type for use in the navy. In 1897 Simon Lake, of Baltimore, designed a submarine boat of an entirely different pattern. His boat is shaped very much like the hull of a yacht and has wheels attached, on which it moves over the bottom of the ocean. This boat, called the *Argonaut*, has proved successful and may be considered the forerunner of a type of submarine boats well adapted for wrecking, laying the foundations of piers and other forms of work under water. Submarine navigation has made considerable advancement during the last decade, and there is every prospect of its becoming successful. See TORPEDO.

Subpoena, *sub pe'na*, (Latin, "under penalty"). See WITNESS; WRIT.

Sub'ways. See UNDERGROUND RAILWAY.

Succession, *suk sesh'un*, **Wars**, wars which have arisen from conflicting claims for the possession of a crown. In modern European history the most important of these struggles were the War of the Spanish Succession (1701–1714), the War of the Polish Succession (1733–1735), the War of the Austrian Succession (1740–1748) and the War of the Bavarian Succession (1778–1779). The first and third only will be treated of in this article.

THE WAR OF THE SPANISH SUCCESSION. Shortly before the death of Charles II of Spain, who had no direct heirs, several competitors laid claim to the throne, the two principal being Louis XIV of France, son of the eldest sister of Philip IV, and Emperor Leopold of Austria, son of a younger sister of Philip IV. The other powers were greatly interested in this question, since the union of either France or Austria with Spain would have endangered the balance of power in Europe. After much negotiation Philip of Anjou was put forward by Louis XIV to represent the French claim, and Leopold nominated his second son Charles as his substitute, both declaring that Spain should never be incorporated with their respective dominions. The king of Spain eventually recognized Philip as his heir, and on the king's death, in November,

1700, Philip was proclaimed at Madrid. He was recognized by most of the European powers except Austria, which in 1701 began a war against France. However, the arrogant and aggressive behavior of Louis, his recognition of the son of James II as king of England and his declaration that the accession of Philip to the Spanish throne did not prevent his succession in France, caused England, Holland and Austria to combine against him and Philip in 1702. Prince Eugene of Austria had already opened the contest and had won some victories over the French. In 1702–1703, Marlborough, at the head of an allied army, reduced the French strongholds along the Meuse and in the Low Countries; in 1704 he joined his forces with Eugene, and together they defeated the Franco-Bavarian army at Blenheim. Barcelona was captured by an English force in 1705, and the earl of Peterborough gained some brilliant successes in this quarter. In 1706 the French were defeated by Marlborough at Ramillies, and by the Austrians at Turin. By 1707 the French and Spanish had driven the allies out of Spain, but in the following year Marlborough and Eugene reunited their forces and severely defeated the French at Oudenarde.

The resources of France were now crippled, and Louis made overtures of peace, which were rejected. The struggle was renewed with great vigor; Villars proceeded against Marlborough and Eugene, but he was defeated by the allies at Malplaquet in September, and matters continued to look very unfavorable for Louis. The war dragged on until the accession of the Archduke Charles to the Austrian throne changed the whole aspect of affairs, and the struggle, so far as Great Britain, France and Holland were concerned, was brought to an end by the Peace of Utrecht in 1713. Peace between Great Britain and Spain soon followed, the former gaining Gibraltar and Minorca; and in 1714 the emperor, Charles, forsaken by his allies, was reluctantly compelled to sign a treaty at Baden, recognizing Philip V as the king of Spain.

THE WAR OF THE AUSTRIAN SUCCESSION. This arose on the extinction of the male line of the House of Hapsburg, by the death of Emperor Charles VI in 1740. By diplomatic negotiations before his death and by means of the settlement called the Pragmatic Sanction, Charles had endeavored to secure the Austrian succession for his daughter, Maria Theresa. But there were several other claimants for the Austrian possessions, which included Bohemia,

Hungary, northern Italy, part of the Netherlands and Austria proper. Besides Maria Theresa, the other claimants of importance were Charles Albert, elector of Bavaria, and Philip V of Spain; while the chief European powers which took an interest in the succession were France, Prussia and England. The first movement was made by Frederick II of Prussia, who, in December, 1840, marched his army into Silesia and secured that province as his share of the spoil. In the following year an agreement was entered into between France, Spain, Bavaria, Prussia, Saxony, Sardinia and Naples, by the terms of which a French-Bavarian army entered Upper Austria, another French army invaded the Austrian possessions in the Netherlands, and the forces of Spain and Naples occupied the Austrian territory in northern Italy. This having been done, the coalition arranged that Charles Albert should be crowned as emperor of Germany, under the title of Charles VI, and this was accomplished at Frankfort.

Meanwhile, Maria Theresa appealed for help to the Hungarian Diet, with such effect that a Hungarian force promptly invaded Bavaria and captured the city of Munich. She also formed an alliance with England, in accordance with which the English government furnished her with money, sent a fleet to Naples to demand the withdrawal of Neapolitan troops from Austrian territory, and supplied a portion of the army which defeated the French forces at Dettingen (1743). After this event negotiations for peace were begun, but with so little success that another league was formed, including England, Holland, Austria, Saxony and Sardinia, and a general European war broke out. Among the more important events of this general conflict were the Second Silesian War, begun by Frederick II; an attempted invasion of England by France, in favor of the Pretender, and the brilliant campaign in the Netherlands conducted by Marshal Saxe, terminating (May, 1745), in the victory of Fontenoy, where the English and allies were defeated. In 1745, however, Emperor Charles VII died, and his son, Maximilian Joseph, gave up all claim to the Austrian throne and concluded peace with that country; in the same year the husband of Maria Theresa was elected emperor, under the name of Francis I. War was still continued against Austria by the French forces under Marshal Saxe, but ultimately a definite treaty of peace between all the powers was signed in

1748, at Aix-la-Chapelle. See AIX-LA-CHAPELLE, TREATIES OF.

Suc'cory. See CHICORY.

Suck'er, a name applied popularly to several fish, because of the manner in which they use their mouths in eating. The best known is the *common sucker* of the streams and lakes of North America. There are several species, none of which is very large. All have roundish mouths on the lower side of the head, and thick, puckered lips, with which they suck up food from the mud from the bottom. In some places they are very abundant. The flesh is not firm and is filled with many small bones.

Sucre, *soo'kray,* or **Chuquisaca,** *choo'ke-sah'ka,* **Char'cas** or **La Plat'a,** a city of Bolivia. It is called the capital and is the seat of the supreme court, but the president and foreign representatives reside at La Paz. It has a fine cathedral and a university reputed to be the oldest in South America. There are mining and agricultural industries. The city was founded by one of Pizarro's officers in 1539. Population in 1910, 23,416.

Sudan or **Soudan,** *soo dahn',* a name applied to an extensive region in the central part of Africa, south of the Sahara. Its boundaries are indefinite, but it extends eastward from the Atlantic to the valley of the Upper Nile and southward to about the 5th parallel of north latitude. It is watered by the Niger in the western part and the Bahr-el-Ghazal in the eastern part, and Lake Chad is located near the center. The region contains lofty mountains and broad plains, which are in some places nearly void of vegetation, while in others they are interspersed with patches of forest and open country. In other localities there are high plateaus. The loftiest mountain range is the Adamawa, whose highest summit is 10,000 feet above the sea. Much of the Sudan is covered with a luxuriant growth of vegetation. The climate is hot, and in the lowlands along the coast and streams it is extremely unhealthful for Europeans. Bananas, yams, indigo, African rice, indian corn and tropical fruits are extensively cultivated. The region is occupied by a large number of native tribes, who until recently were organized in independent kingdoms. Since 1902 nearly all of the territory has been placed under the protection of some European power, the western part, or Egyptian Sudan, sometimes called English Sudan, being under the protection of Great Britain, and most of the eastern part becoming a possession of France;

but a few small areas in this part of the Sudan are subject to Germany. See AFRICA, subhead *Political Divisions;* SAHARA.

Sue, *sü,* MARIE JOSEPH EUGÈNE (1804–1857), a French novelist. He adopted his father's profession of medicine, became a surgeon in the army, was transferred to the navy and left the service in 1829. His first work was a sea novel, *Kernock the Pirate,* which was quickly followed by *Plick and Plock, Atar-Gull, The Salamander* and the *Lookout of Koatven.* He now entered the department of historical fiction and published several novels. But his most famous works are *The Mysteries of Paris* and *The Wandering Jew.* His later novels are *The Foundling, The Seven Capital Sins* and *The Mysteries of the People.* In 1850 Sue was elected to the Constituent Assembly as an advanced radical. After the seizure of power by Napoleon III, in 1851, he left France and retired to Annecy, where he died.

Suetonius, *swe to'ne us,* **Tranquil'lus,** GAIUS, a Roman writer who flourished about 100 A. D. Little is known of the circumstances of his life. He distinguished himself as an advocate and enjoyed the patronage of the younger Pliny. He became secretary to the emperor Hadrian, but was dismissed on account of his intimacy with the empress Sabina. His chief work, the *Lives of the Twelve Caesars,* gives an interesting account of the private life and personal character of the twelve Roman emperors from Julius Caesar to Domitian, and it is of great value to us from the light which it throws on domestic manners and customs.

Suez, *soo ez',* a seaport of Egypt, situated at the head of the Gulf of Suez, 76 mi. e. of Cairo, with which it is connected by rail. It is also at the southern entrance of the Suez Canal. The houses are built of sun-dried brick. The city contains a number of mosques and, in the European quarter, several substantial hotels, warehouses and other buildings. The town derives its importance from its position on the Suez Canal, since the opening of which it has materially increased in population and commercial importance. Population, about 18,000.

Suez Canal, a ship canal across the Isthmus of Suez, connecting the Mediterranean with the Red Sea. It extends from Port Said, on the Mediterranean, to Suez, on the Gulf of Suez, a distance of one hundred miles. It is 420 feet wide at the surface and 31 feet deep. About sixty miles of the channel is through shallow lakes. It is a sea level canal and has no locks.

Work on this canal was begun in 1859, and the structure was completed in 1869. The original expense was about $95,000,000.

The Suez Canal was undertaken and carried to completion under the direction of Count Ferdinand de Lesseps, a French engineer. It is the largest ship canal in the world. Its construction shortened the sailing distance between England and India more than 5000 miles, and it has materially increased the traffic between

European and Asiatic countries. The canal is lighted by electric lights, so that ships can navigate it by night as well as by day. About 4000 vessels pass through it each year. It is under the management of an international commission and is open to ships of all nations on equal terms. See CANAL.

Suffrage, *suf'fraje,* the act or right of participating in the election of officers or the making or approval of laws. The old belief that suffrage is the natural right of every adult citizen of a state is no longer accepted by political philosophers, and most modern states claim the right to restrict suffrage at their pleasure. The principal qualifications now required are intellectual ability, religious affiliation, property possession, moral character and residence. All states do not lay such restrictions, and no state requires them all. In America, at different times and places, all have been in force. The first to disappear was the religious test, which made its last stand in South Carolina, but was abolished by 1790. The freehold, or real property, qualification was general, but it was generally abolished before the Civil War. See ELECTION; WOMAN SUFFRAGE.

Sugar, a sweet substance found in the juices of plants, particularly sugar cane, sorghum, beets and sugar maple, also from cocoanut and other palms. The sugar of commerce is practically all obtained from sugar cane and beets.

CANE SUGAR. This is prepared from the sugar cane. The leading countries in the production of this plant are Cuba, Java, Porto Rico, Brazil, Argentina and certain sections of the United States, particularly Louisiana and Hawaii. The cane found in the tropical regions is the richest in sugar. That of the West Indies furnishes about 225 pounds of sugar to a ton of cane, while that from Louisiana yields only about 160 pounds. In the manufacture of sugar the cane is first crushed between heavy rollers, which press out the juice. The rollers are in two or three sets, called *mills,* each mill so adjusted that it presses the cane harder than the one before it. As the crushed stalks pass from one mill to another, they are moistened with water of varying temperature, in order that the remaining juices may be liberated; the crushed stalks, or *bagasse,* are used for fuel under the boilers. By this process about nine-tenths of all the cane sugar is manufactured. The juice is immediately treated with sulphurous acid gas, and it is then mixed with lime; the gas bleaches it and permits excessive liming, which materially aids in the clarification of the juice. The lime prevents inversion, or the separation into fruit sugar and grape sugar. The juice is then filtered, after which it is ready for reduction by evaporation.

For the first sugars, the juice, after being reduced to a syrup in evaporators, is boiled in vacuum pans (See VACUUM PAN) until the water is all driven off and crystallization takes place, forming a *masscuite,* which is pure sugar mixed with a small per cent of syrup. This masscuite is dropped into a mixer, where it is stirred and kept from caking by revolving paddles, from which it is fed to revolving cylinders called *centrifugals,* on the sides of which is a basket of wire netting. As the cylinder revolves at a high rate of speed the masscuite is washed, the amount of washing varying with the quality of the sugar manufactured. The liquid portion is forced out through the meshes of the basket, and this, after several reboilings, constitutes the molasses of commerce. The solid crystals of sugar are left within the centrifugal. The sugar is then dropped onto conveyers and taken to the granulator to be thoroughly dried, the granulator being a revolving cylinder heated by steam, through which the sugar is fed by gravity. Sugar thus made is placed on the market as *granulated sugar*. *Loaf sugar* is made by packing the fresh sugar in molds, where it is allowed to form blocks, which are sawed to the desired shape. Cheaper grades of sugar, known as seconds and thirds, are made from the syrups taken from the first sugars. The first is placed on the market as *coffee sugar*, and the latter is known as *brown sugar*; both are sold principally to the large refineries.

BEET SUGAR. In the manufacture of beet sugar the diffusion process is used. The beets are first sliced by machinery, then placed in iron cells, where a constant circulation of water is kept up, the juice being drawn from the cell holding the fresh chips, and the fresh water being introduced into the last of a series of cells, just before dropping the chips. The liquid thus obtained is first treated with carbonic acid gas; it is then mixed with lime, after which carbonic acid gas is forced through it a second time. The gas combines with the lime and other impurities and causes them to settle at the bottom of the tank. The liquid is then passed through bag filters, when it is ready for evaporation. The remaining processes are the same as those used in making cane sugar. A ton of beets will make from 320 to 400 pounds of sugar. The waste chips are fed to cattle.

MAPLE SUGAR. Maple sugar is obtained from the sap of the sugar, or rock, maple (See MAPLE), and it is highly prized on account of its delicate flavor. The sugar season begins in the spring, as soon as the sap commences to circulate in the trees. The sap is obtained by boring a small hole in the trunk of the tree, from an inch to an inch and a half deep, placing in this an iron spile, containing a hook, to which a bucket is attached. The sap drips through the spile into the bucket. The sap is collected and evaporated in the sugar houses, constructed specially for the purpose. The evaporating apparatus is constructed on such a plan that the sap flows in at one end and the syrup flows out at the other. Four gallons of sap make a pound of sugar. Maple sugar is placed on the market in the form of syrup and sugar. It is now used only as a delicacy and commands a very high price. The leading states in its production are Vermont, New York and Ohio.

SORGHUM. This is a variety of cane used in the manufacture of syrup. It will grow in much cooler climates than sugar cane, but the amount of sugar obtained from it is not sufficient to be worthy of consideration, when compared with the sugar made from cane and beets. The sap is suitable for the manufacture of syrup only, and the process used is similar to that employed in the manufacture of cane sugar.

REFINING. Much of the sugar imported into the United States is received in the crude form, known as *raw* sugar. This is dissolved in water to which a small quantity of lime has been added. This solution is then heated by steam and passed through filters which consist of deep vats with perforated bottoms containing a thick layer of animal charcoal. The filter removes the coloring matter. Syrup is collected underneath the tanks and boiled in vacuum pans, until the water has been driven off and crystallization takes place. The masscuite is then treated the same as that from cane and beet sugar in the preparation of granulated sugar.

The largest sugar refineries in the United States are located in New York, New Orleans, Philadelphia and San Francisco. In the entire world there are produced about 16,000,000 tons of sugar every year. This total is almost equally divided between cane sugar and beet sugar. The leading countries producing sugar cane have already been given. Those leading in the manufacture of beet sugar are, in the order of their importance, Germany, Russia, Austria, France and Belgium. This industry is comparatively new in the United States, but it is gradually growing. The country produces about 500,000 tons of beet sugar a year. The United States consumes about 4,000,000 tons of sugar in a year, and less than one-fourth of this is produced in this country, the remainder being imported. The quantity used averages over 77 pounds per year for each individual. See SUGAR CANE; BEET; MOLASSES.

Sugar Cane, a plant of the grass family from which about two-fifths of the sugar of commerce is obtained. Sugar cane is supposed to be a native of the tropical regions in Asia, but it is not at present found in the wild state. In general appearance sugar cane resembles maize or Indian corn. It grows to heights varying from five to eighteen feet, according to soil, climate and cultivation. The stalks vary from one to two inches in diameter, and are jointed like corn stalks. At each joint there is a bud or eye, which, when the cane is planted, sprouts and produces a new plant. The leaves grow to about three feet in length and are about two inches wide at the base, tapering gracefully to a point. When young the plant presents a fresh,

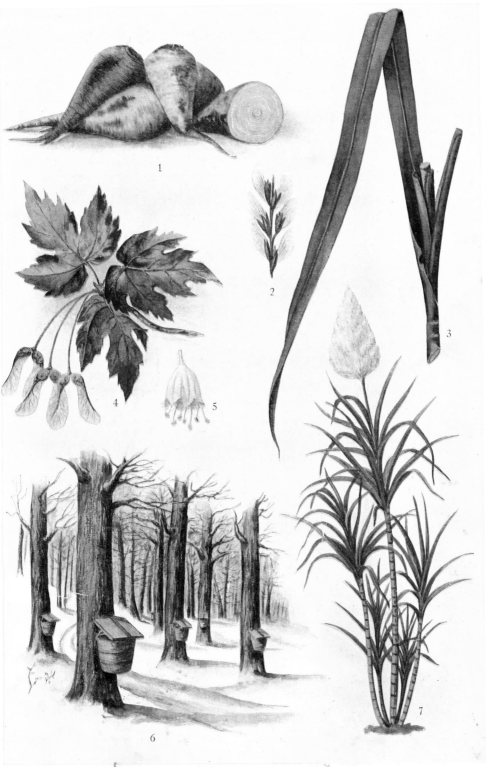

SUGAR

1, Sugar Beets.
2, Blossom, Sugar Cane, enlarged.
3, Leaf of Sugar Cane.
4, Leaf and Fruit, Sugar Maple.
5, Blossom, Sugar Maple.
6, Maple-Sugar Orchard.
7, Sugar Cane.

green appearance, but as it matures some of the leaves turn a purplish hue, and those at the bottom turn yellow, wither and fall off.

Sugar cane is grown extensively in the tropical regions of Asia, Cuba and other West India Islands, Hawaii and Louisiana and to a less extent in several countries of Europe and the other Gulf states. The soil should be very fertile and carefully prepared. In this country the soil is plowed and thrown up into ridges from five to seven feet apart. A deep furrow is plowed in the top of the ridge, and the cane is laid in this for covering. The best results are obtained by planting only the upper joints of the cane. Two or three cuttings may be laid side by side in the furrow. The cane is covered with a plow and sometimes the ground is rolled. In Louisiana it requires about eight months for the crop to mature. During growth the land is frequently cultivated to keep it free from weeds and to prevent evaporation.

At harvest time the cane is cut about two inches from the ground and stripped of leaves. The top is then cut off and the stalks are piled in rows for hauling to the factory. In Cuba and other tropical countries where there is no danger from frost, the crop is allowed from ten to eighteen months in which to mature. Small crops are obtained from one planting, but the first crop is the most valuable and for good results the field should be replanted every third year. See SUGAR.

Suicide, *su'e side,* the intentional killing of one's self. The question as to the moral justification of suicide has exercised the minds of ethical philosophers from the days of Plato, Marcus Aurelius and Seneca down to the present time. Some schools of thought, notably the Stoics, defended suicide under certain conditions.

From the medical point of view, suicide is in the majority of cases a symptom of disease of the brain. However, sane men may and do commit suicide, and many states make such an attempt a crime. Aiding in a suicide is in many states the equivalent of manslaughter, and suicide usually is ground for forfeiture of life insurance. The two predominating causes of suicides are found to be alcoholism and melancholy. Four-fifths of all patients suffering from melancholia have suicidal feelings, and two-fifths of them make actual attempts on their lives. It is a risk that should be provided against in every case of melancholia or alcoholic insanity. The tendency to suicide is often inherited, but is far more frequently the result of environment and suggestion.

162

The competition and worry incident to the modern business life and the lack of leisure to consider things higher than mere existence, doubtless influence the suicide rate. Attempts at suicide are sometimes made while the patient is quite unconscious or in a state of altered consciousness, so that there is no recollection of it afterward. Sometimes it is suggested by the sight of a weapon or water or any means of destroying life.

The modes of committing suicide vary in different countries, in the two sexes and in different professions. Hanging is the most common method in most European countries, except Italy, where drowning and shooting predominate. Suicide is much more common among men than among women, being in the proportion of 3 or 4 to 1; and this applies to all countries and races. The rate of suicide seems to increase with age, at least up to the seventieth year; there are instances of suicide at five years of age, and some at more than ninety. Suicide in all civilized countries is becoming more common year by year. It is most common among the widowed and least frequent among the married. The military profession furnishes much the largest proportion of suicides in all countries, being usually twice or thrice that of any other calling, and in Italy it is fourteen times larger than the average; next comes domestic service, then the liberal professions.

Among notable suicides (omitting cases referred to in Scripture) may be mentioned:

Sappho	B. C. 7th c.	Clive	1774
Empedocles	435	Rousseau (?)	1778
Demosthenes	322	M. Roland	1793
Hannibal	183	Pichegru	1804
Mithridates	63	Romilly	1818
Cato the Younger	46	Castlereagh	1822
Brutus and Cassius	42	Admiral Fitzroy	1865
Mark Antony	30	E. M. Ward, painter	1879
Cleopatra	30	Louis II of Bavaria	1886
Nero	A. D. 68	Crown Prince of Austria	1889
Otho	69	Balmaceda	1891
Earl of Essex	1683	Boulanger	1892
Chatterton	1770		

Suleiman II, *soo la mahn'.* See SOLYMAN II.

Suliotes, *soo'le ote's,* a mixed people of Albanian and Greek origin, who, to escape the tyranny of the Turks in the seventeenth century, settled in the mountains of Parga, south of Albania, where they formed an independent republic. They lived partly by rearing cattle and partly by plunder. Their chief village, Suli, was occupied by the Turks in 1822, and many of the Suliotes then dispersed throughout Greece. See BOZZARIS, MARCO.

Sulk'y, a two-wheeled carriage, of skeleton construction, with a seat for one, placed directly over the shafts. The sulky is used for driving horses, while in training or in races. The most modern patterns contain skeleton wheels, ball bearings and pneumatic tires. The recent remarkable records in horse racing are due partly to the improvement in the sulky.

Sul'la, LUCIUS CORNELIUS (138–78 B. C.), a Roman dictator. He served with distinction under Marius in the Jugurthine and Cimbrian wars and was chosen praetor. For his services in the Social War, he was appointed consul in 88 B. C., and the Province of Asia, with the conduct of the war against Mithridates, fell to his lot. Marius also wanted this command, and to carry his point he resorted to acts of violence, by which Sulla was compelled to escape from Rome. But Sulla reëntered the city at the head of his army, drove Marius to Africa and then sailed for the East at the beginning of 87 B. C. He expelled the armies of Mithridates from Europe, crossed into Asia and was everywhere victorious, gaining wealth for himself and his soldiers and forcing Mithridates to conclude a peace. Sulla now hastened to Italy, where, although Marius was dead, the Marian party was still strong, and after a number of combats, he entered Rome in triumph in 82. A frightful proscription followed, and Rome and all the provinces of Italy were filled with the most revolting scenes of cruelty. After satisfying his vengeance by the murder or proscription of thousands, he caused himself to be named dictator for an indefinite period (81 B. C.). He now ruled without restraint, repealed and made laws, abolished the tribuneship and settled his veterans in various parts of Italy. In 79 he laid down his dictatorship and retired to Puteoli, where he abandoned himself to all sorts of debauchery.

Sul'livan, ARTHUR SEYMOUR, Sir (1842–1900), an English musician, born in London. He completed his musical education at the Royal Academy of Music. In 1858 he went to Leipzig, and on his return, in 1862, he at once attracted attention by his music to Shakespeare's *Tempest*. He wrote several oratorios and many songs and anthems, one of the most famous being *The Lost Chord*. Perhaps his most popular compositions were the burlesque operettas which he produced in collaboration with W. S. Gilbert. Among the most popular are *H. M. S. Pinafore, Pirates of Penzance* and the *Mikado*. In 1886 he set to music an arrangement of Longfellow's *Golden Legend*, which was one of his finest compositions. He was knighted in 1883.

Sullivan, JOHN (1740–1795), an American soldier, born at Berwick, Maine. He early removed to Durham, N. H., where he practiced law until the opening of the Revolution. He was made a brigadier general, participated in the siege of Boston and in Arnold's expedition to Canada and was captured at the Battle of Long Island. Being exchanged, he fought at Trenton, Princeton, Brandywine and Germantown, coöperated with the French fleet at Newport and in 1779 conducted an expedition against the Tories and indians of western New York, inflicting a crushing defeat at Newtown (now Elmira). He was elected to Congress in 1780, became president of the State of New Hampshire in 1786 and was later United States district judge.

Sul'ly, JAMES (1842–   ), an English psychologist and educator, born at Somerset. He was educated in Independent College and Regent Park College, London. Later he studied at several German universities. In 1892 he was elected professor of philosophy of mind and logic in University College, London. He also was awarded the position of lecturer on education at the College of Preceptors. He is widely known in England and America through his works on psychology and teaching. The most widely read of these are *Sensation and Intuition, Outlines of Psychology, The Teachers' Handbook of Psychology, The Human Mind, Studies of Childhood* and *Children's Ways*.

Sully, MAXIMILIEN DE BÉTHUNE, Duke de (1560–1641), first minister of Henry IV of France. He distinguished himself in Henry's campaigns before he came to the throne, and after Henry's accession he was appointed comptroller of finance. By his excellent administration he largely reduced taxation and eventually paid off a great state debt. His industry was unwearied, and he did much to encourage agriculture, which he regarded as the mainstay of the state. After the murder of Henry IV (1610) he retired from court and resigned most of his charges. He was created a marshal by Louis XIII in 1634. His *Memoires* have been published in English.

Sulphates, *sul'fate's*, salts of sulphuric acid. Of the sulphates, some are very soluble, some sparingly soluble and some insoluble. The most important sulphates are sulphate of aluminium and potassium, or alum; sulphate of ammonium, employed for making carbonate of ammonia; sulphate of copper, or blue vitriol, much used in surgery and in dyeing, and for preparing certain green coloring matters; sulphate of iron, or green vitriol, used in making ink and very extensively used in dyeing, in calico printing and in medicine; sulphate of manganese, used in calico printing; sulphate of quinine, much used in medicine; sulphate of zinc, or white vitriol, used in surgery, in the preparation of drying oils for varnishes and in calico printing. See CALOMEL; CORROSIVE SUBLIMATE; EPSOM SALTS; GLAUBER'S SALT; GYPSUM.

Sulphonal, *sul'fo nal,* a white powder, used by physicians to produce sleep. It is poisonous, but does not have the injurious effects that follow the use of chloral.

Sulphur, *sul'fur,* an elementary, non-metallic substance which has been known from the earliest ages. Because of the low temperature at which it burns, it was called *brimstone,* a corruption of *brennestone.* It frequently occurs in a pure state in beds of gypsum or clay, but it is generally associated with sulphate of strontium. It also occurs in chemical combination with oxygen and various metals. It is found in greatest abundance and purity in the neighborhood of volcanoes, modern or extinct, as in Sicily; and as an article of commerce it is chiefly imported from the Mediterranean. It is also found in California, Mexico and Iceland. Native sulphur is usually separated from the earthy matter by a process of distillation, the sulphur vapors being liquefied by a condenser. The product obtained from native sulphur or from iron pyrites is afterward refined by a further process of distillation.

Pure sulphur is commonly met with in two forms—as a compact, brittle solid, and as a fine powder. It is nearly tasteless and of a greenish-yellow color, and when rubbed or melted it emits a peculiar odor. It is insoluble in water and is not very readily soluble in alcohol, but it is taken up by spirits of turpentine, by many oils and by carbon disulphide. It is a non-conductor of electricity and is readily melted and volatilized; it fuses at 232° F., and between 232° and 280° it possesses the greatest degree of fluidity. It possesses the peculiar property of solidifying at a higher degree, or when raised to 320°. From 480° to its boiling point (792°) it again becomes fluid, and at 792° it rises in vapor, which condenses in close vessels in the form of a fine, yellow powder, called *flowers of sulphur.* The roll sulphur of commerce is made by pouring sulphur in fluid state into cylindrical molds, where it is cast.

Sulphur exists in several different forms, and these modifications are characterized by differences in specific gravity, in solubility in various liquids and in many other points. It is employed in the manufacture of gunpowder, matches, vulcanite, and sulphurous and sulphuric acids. It is also employed in medicine and for various other purposes. Sulphur combines with oxygen, hydrogen, chlorine and other elements, forming various important compounds. *Cinnabar,* or sulphide of mercury; *galena,* or sulphide of lead; *pyrite,* or sulphide of iron; *barite,* or sulphate of barium, and *gypsum,* or calcium sulphate, are common and useful compounds. *Sulphur chloride* is produced by passing chlorine gas into a retort containing melted sulphur. It is used for vulcanizing caoutchouc. Sulphur forms two combinations with oxygen, the *dioxide* and the *trioxide.* The former, a colorless gas which may be liquefied and solidified by cold and pressure, is the product of combustion. It is used in the arts for bleaching silk, wool, straw, parchment and such other substances as are destroyed by the action of chlorine. Sulphur trioxide is a white, crystalline solid, produced by the oxidation of the dioxide. *Sodium thiosulphate* is produced by the boiling of sulphur with soda lye, sulphur dioxide being passed into the solution until it is completely decolorized. It is largely used in the arts as an antichlor and for fixing photographs. *Carbon disulphide* is a volatile liquid, with a poisonous vapor, produced by the action of sulphur upon carbon at high temperatures. It is used for dissolving caoutchouc and gutta-percha, for extracting essential oils from plants and seeds and for extracting bitumen from minerals.

Sulphureted Hydrogen, *sul'fu ret'ed,* or **Hydrosulphuric Acid** or **Hydrogen Sulphide,** a colorless, inflammable gas, produced by the putrefaction of sulphurous organic matters. Many mineral waters contain it naturally. It may be artificially produced by burning sulphur vapor in hydrogen or by passing hydrogen through sulphur. It has a sweet taste, but a very nauseous odor, as of rotten eggs. It has poisonous effects, when breathed, and experiments have shown that a small portion of it in the air is injurious. If a white filter-paper soaked in a solution of acetate of lead be exposed to sulphureted hydrogen the paper will turn black. This forms a good test for the presence of the gas in the air.

Sulphuric, *sul fu'rik,* **Acid** or **Oil of Vitriol,** an acid discovered by Basil Valentine toward the close of the fifteenth century. It was formerly procured by the distillation of dried sulphate of iron, called *green vitriol*, and because the corrosive liquid which came over in the distillation had an oily consistence, it was called *oil of vitriol*. The principle laid down by Roebuck in 1746 is still used in its manufacture, though in the United States, notably at Mineral Point, Wis., a new method, called the "contact method," employing platinum to separate the acid from its salts, seems likely to replace the old. The Roebuck method consists in burning sulphur, or more frequently iron pyrites, in closed furnaces, and leading the fumes, mixed with oxides or nitrogen, into large leaden chambers, into which jets of steam are continuously sent. The oxides of nitrogen are produced by the action of sulphuric acid upon niter contained in pots, which are placed between the sulphur ovens and the chambers. The sulphur dioxide takes away part of the oxygen from the oxides of nitrogen, which are again oxidized by the air in the chambers. The sulphur trioxide produced unites with the steam to form sulphuric acid. The acid produced in the chamber is condensed in leaden vessels until it reaches a certain gravity, when it is run into glass and known as the *brown acid* of commerce. Sometimes it is then run into platinum vessels, where the condensation is continued until the specific gravity has increased to 1.84.

Pure sulphuric acid is a dense, oily, colorless fluid, exceedingly acid and corrosive, decomposing all animal and vegetable substances by the aid of heat. It unites with alkaline substances and separates most of the other acids from their combinations with the alkalies. It has a very great affinity for water and unites with it in every proportion, producing great heat; it attracts moisture strongly from the atmosphere, becoming rapidly weaker if exposed. The sulphuric acid of commerce is never pure, but it may be purified by distillation. With bases, sulphuric acid forms salts called sulphates, some of which are neutral and others acid. Through concentration of sulphuric acid as far as is possible without decomposition, and through the cooling of the liquid so obtained, crystals of the true acid are formed. The ordinary acid is a hydrate of varying composition. A very strong form of sulphuric acid, known as *Nordhausen acid*, is prepared by heating green vitriol in closed vessels; it is a solution of trioxide in sulphuric acid, or it may be regarded as *pyro-sulphuric acid*. It is chiefly used in the arts for dissolving indigo.

Sulphuric acid is used extensively in the arts and is, in fact, the chief agent for obtaining most of the other acids, by extraction from salt. In the chemical laboratory, the uses to which it is put are innumerable, and in the separation of copper, cobalt, nickel, silver and platinum from their ores, it is an important agent. Phosphorus, bromine, iodine, ether, starch, glucose, sugar, phosphorescent drinks, parchment paper, celluloid, nitroglycerine, guncotton, coal tar colors and many dyes are all prepared by its aid. It is used in calico printing and in tanning, in dyeing, in refining tallow and many of the oils and in the preparation of all the sulphates. When to all these important uses we add its function as a medicinal agent, it is evident that sulphuric acid is really the most important of all the acids.

Sulphuric E'ther. See ETHER.

Sul'tan (Arabic, "mighty one," "lord"), the ordinary title of Mohammedan rulers. The ruler of Turkey assumes the title of *sultan-es-selatin*, or sultan khan, "sultan of sultans." The title sultan is also applied to the sultan's daughters, and his mother, if living, is styled *Sultan Valide*.

Sulu, *soo loo,* **Islands,** a group of islands extending from the northeastern point of Borneo to the Philippines, and consisting of more than 190 islands, whose combined area is about 1600 square miles. The archipelago is divided into six groups. Named in their order from the northeast, these are Basilan, Samales, Sulu, or Jolo, Siarsi, Kinatussan and Tawi-Tawi. Sulu is the most important island. Nearly all of the group are covered with forests, which contain considerable teak and sandalwood. The chief cultivated crops are rice, cacao, maize and various sorts of roots. Cocoa, bananas, breadfruits, mangoes and oranges are native to the islands, Quite a large industry is carried on in the sale of the pearl shell known as *Manila shell*. The natives are chiefly Moros and are ruled by chiefs who are subject to the authorities of the United States. In 1899 a portion of these islands became the possession of the United States, in connection with the Philippines, ceded by Spain. The population of the Province of Sulu in 1910 was about 60,000.

Sumac, *su'mak,* or **Sumach,** a genus of shrubs and small trees, containing about one hundred species, widely distributed throughout the world, in temperate and tropical climates. The most general North American species is the *Virginian,* or *stag-horn, sumac,* distinguished by crooked, downy branches and small, red berries. The *smooth-leaved sumach*, which is also common in the United States, has acid leaves and ornamental red berries. Both of the preceding are used for dyeing purposes. Two closely allied species, both called *poison ivy* and *poison oak*, from the fact that their leaves are poisonous to some persons, are found in almost all parts of the United States. They are creeping or climbing vines, bearing groups of three leaflets. *Poison sumach*, or *dogwood*, grows in American swamps. It is a shrub, from fifteen to twenty feet high, producing clusters of greenish-white flowers. Its leaves are extremely poisonous to some persons, producing serious inflammation or eruption of the skin. A Japanese poisonous variety produces a sap, from which the well-known lacquer is made.

SMOOTH-LEAVED SUMACH

Sumatra, *soo mah'tra*, a great island in the Indian Ocean, immediately under the equator, separated from the peninsula of Malacca by the Straits of Malacca, and from Java by the Straits of Sunda. Its greatest length is about 1050 miles; its breadth, about 240 miles; its area, about 180,000 square miles. Banca and other islands adjoin the coast. The west side of the island is mountainous, with peaks ranging in height from 2000 feet, in the south, to 5000 feet farther north, and culminating in Indrapura, a volcano 12,400 feet high. Gold, copper, tin and iron are found in abundance, and deposits of coal exist. The chief rivers are the Rokan, the Musi, the Jambi and the Indragiri, all of which form extensive deltas at their mouths. Sumatra enjoys great equability of climate, but in many low-lying parts it is unhealthy; rain falls almost incessantly in the south. Mangroves grow near the coast; and at higher elevations, myrtles, palms, figs and oaks of various species are met with. The camphor tree prevails in the north, and among vegetable curiosities are the upas tree and the gigantic rafflesia. Pepper, rice, sugar, tobacco, indigo, cotton and coffee are cultivated for export, and camphor, benzoin, catechu, gutta-percha and caoutchouc, teak, ebony and sandalwood are also exported. The animals include the elephant, the tapir, the two-horned rhinoceros, the tiger, the orang-outang and other apes, some species of deer and antelope, and numerous birds and reptiles. Of the domestic animals, the chief is the pig, next to which rank the cow and the horse.

The island is for the most part under the authority of the Dutch, and their possessions are divided into six governments. The most important native state is Achin, in the extreme north of the island. Sumatra has a very mixed population, consisting of Malays, Chinese, Arabs and many native tribes, most of whom are Malays. The Battas are a peculiar and interesting race, approaching the Caucasian type. Writing has been known among them from a very early period, and their ancient books are written in a brilliant ink on paper made of bark. Most of the inhabitants are Mohammedans. Population, estimated at about 3,500,000, including 5000 Europeans, 100,000 Chinese and about 10,000 other foreigners. The chief towns are Palembang, Benkulen, Padang and Achin. There are about 200 miles of railroads in the island.

The Dutch acquired their territories in Sumatra in the sixteenth and seventeenth centuries. The British formed a settlement at Benkulen in 1685, and in 1811 they seized the Dutch possessions on the island. These were restored in 1815, and by treaties in 1834 and 1871 the Dutch were allowed the right to enlarge their territories by treaty or by conquest and annexation. The tidal wave accompanying the volcanic eruption of Krakatoa in 1883 caused great destruction on the south coast of Sumatra.

Sumbawa, *soom bah'wa*, an island in the Indian Archipelago, lying s. by w. from Celebes. It is about 160 miles long from east to west and has an area of about 5200 sq. mi. The surface is mountainous and contains a number of volcanoes, the most important being Temboro, with an altitude of 9050 feet. The island is fertile, and the population numbers about 150,000. It is tributary to the Dutch.

Sum'mer, the season of the year between spring and autumn, beginning with the summer solstice, about June 21, and ending with the autumnal equinox, about September 22. In the United States the summer season is covered by the months of June, July and August.

Sum'mit, N. J., a city in Union co., 12 mi. w. of Newark, on the Delaware, Lackawanna &

Western railroad. It has a pleasant situation and is the home of many New York and Newark business men. The place contains a silk factory and cultivates roses and fruit. It has a home for invalids, an orphanage, a public library, good schools and several academies. Population in 1910, 7500.

Sum'mons. See WRIT.

Sum'ner, CHARLES (1811–1874), an American statesman, born at Boston, Mass., and educated

CHARLES SUMNER

at Harvard University. In 1834 he was admitted to the bar, and, devoting himself to legal and literary studies, in 1836 he published three volumes of Judge Story's decisions, subsequently known as *Sumner's Reports*, and edited a periodical called the *American Jurist*. He visited Europe in 1837, but returned in 1840 to Boston, where he resumed his legal practice. In 1845 he first gained note as an orator by his famous address on *The True Grandeur of Nations*. He then took up the anti-slavery cause, and in 1851 he was elected to the Senate of the United States by a coalition of Free-Soilers and Democrats; he remained there until his death, an active and distinguished champion of freedom.

In May, 1856, after delivering a speech on *The Crime Against Kansas*, vigorously attacking the slaveholders, he was violently assaulted by Preston S. Brooks, a member representing a slaveholding state (South Carolina). His injuries compelled him to absent himself from public

duties for nearly four years, and they eventually caused his death. He was a supporter of Lincoln and Hamlin, and in 1861 he became chairman of the Senate committee on foreign relations, where he served with marked ability for ten years. Sumner advocated the view of reconstruction known as the theory of "state suicide" (See RECONSTRUCTION), opposed President Johnson, was the author of the so-called Civil Rights Bill and voted for the impeachment of the President. He opposed the home and foreign policy of President Grant and supported Greeley in 1872. After the former's reëlection in 1872, Sumner seldom appeared in debate.

Sumner, EDWIN VOSE (1797–1863), an American soldier, born at Boston, Mass. He was educated at Milton Academy and, entering the United States army, distinguished himself in frontier warfare, especially in the Black Hawk War. He participated in the Mexican War, winning the rank of brevet colonel for his gallantry at Cerro Gordo and Molino del Rey. After the war he fought the indians in the West, and in 1861 he was placed in command of a corps of the Army of the Potomac. He won distinction in the Peninsula Campaign, was wounded at Antietam and commanded the right wing of the Federal army at Fredericksburg. Thereafter, at his own request, he was assigned to the Department of Missouri, but died while on his way to assume his duties.

Sump'tuary Laws, laws to repress extravagance, in order to prevent poverty, to enrich the State, to protect certain interests or to prevent immorality and crime. They were common in ancient times, being directed especially, in both Greece and Rome, against extravagance in dress or in entertainments. Sumptuary laws were revived by Charlemagne, and in France various laws and decrees of a similar nature were passed, down to the reign of Louis XV. In England these laws were passed from the reign of Edward III to the time of the Reformation. In the United States, the Federal and state constitutions forbid, generally, the passage of such laws, except in the promotion of public health and safety. The policy of protection is sumptuary in principle. Sumptuary legislation is foreign to the spirit of modern politics and contrary to the elementary principles of economics.

Sum'ter, S. C., the county-seat of Sumter co., 43 mi. s. e. of Columbia, on the Atlantic Coast Line and the Southern railroads. The city is in an agricultural region, producing cotton, tobacco and vegetables. It contains more than fifty industrial establishments, including cotton factories, planing mills and manufactures of telephones, golf sticks, coffins and caskets. The city has a public high school and several academies. Population in 1910, 8109.

Sumter, FORT. See FORT SUMTER.

Sumter, THOMAS (1734–1832), an American soldier, born in Virginia. He went in early childhood to South Carolina, where he took a prominent part in the wars with the Cherokees. He was with Braddock's expedition in 1755 and at the outbreak of the Revolution became lieutenant colonel of a South Carolina regiment of riflemen. He served in his own state against Tories and indians, later was at the head of a regiment of North Carolina troops and finally became brigadier general of the State of South Carolina. In the campaign against Cornwallis, he distinguished himself for quickness and bravery in attack. He fought two battles with a troop of cavalry under Colonel Tarleton, his force being almost annihilated in the first and decisively victorious in the second. He was sent to the Federal Congress in 1789, served two terms and was again elected in 1797. From 1801 to 1809 and from 1811 to 1817 he was in the United States Senate, and for a time he was minister to Brazil. General Sumter was the last surviving general officer of the Revolution.

Sun, the source of heat and light for the earth, and the center of the solar system, of which the earth is a part. In spite of its importance to us, it should be remembered, however, that it is only one of thousands of stars and by no means one of the large ones. Arcturus, for instance, is possibly 100 times the diameter of the sun and gives out 6000 times more light. The North star is probably 200 times as strong as the sun. Yet the sun is more than 865,000 miles in diameter, or 110 times the diameter of the earth, and in volume it is 1,300,000 times the size of the earth. Its density, however, is about $\frac{1}{4}$ that of the earth, and, accordingly, its weight is only 334,000 times as much. Its gravity is 27 times that of the earth, so that if it were possible for a man to get to the surface of the sun, he would weigh more than two tons and would probably be crushed by his own weight. The sun's distance from the earth is about 93,000,000 miles. It turns on its axis once in about 26 days, the equatorial regions rotating more rapidly than the regions farther away from the equator. This curious fact is thought to prove that the sun is a gaseous mass, but it is not thoroughly understood by astronomers.

The vast unknown interior of the sun is, of course, wholly invisible to us, but astronomers can note the shining surface, which they call the *photosphere*; a cloak, or envelope, of burning hydrogen, called the *chromosphere*, which shows red through the spectroscope; irregular *prominences*, connected by the chromosphere and extending up through it, vast planes of hydrogen, thousands of miles high, beside which our earth is but a speck, and a still more vast luminous envelope, called the *corona*, seen in total eclipses, where it shows in hairy, radiating lines, long near the equator and shorter about the poles. The surface of the sun does not appear clear and equally brilliant in all parts, but is mottled with small patches of greater light distributed in streaks and groups. The spots, which seem to consist of a dark center, surrounded by radiating lines, are irregular in shape and vary greatly in size, from 1000 to 100,000 miles in diameter. They are not constant in shape, but often split into two parts. Though there are always some spots visible, yet there are periods, recurring at regular intervals, in which the spots are much more numerous. Sometimes a spot is visible for but a few hours, while again it may last for months. The spots probably are depressions in the surface, in which the cooler gases have collected. Two kinds of prominences are seen— the eruptive, like shooting flames, and the cloud-like, which seem to float above the surface. The composition of these prominences and of the corona was discovered by the use of the spectroscope during an eclipse; they are thought to be principally burning hydrogen, yet other gases are probably mingled with it.

From the diagram on next page, the comparative size of the earth and the moon's orbit and the relative shapes and sizes of the visible parts of the sun may be seen. It should be understood that this diagram is a section only, and the corona, chromosphere and protuberances extend in every direction from the center of the sphere. The discoveries made by the use of the spectroscope have been marvelous and have enabled astronomers to learn what materials enter into the composition of the sun. It has been shown that iron, tetanium, calcium, manganese, nickel, cobalt, chromium, barium, sodium, magnesium, copper, hydrogen, zinc, sulphur, cerium, strontium and potassium are to be found in a gaseous state. The sun is, then, probably composed of heated gases held together by gravity. It is not thought that the sun burns as we see a piece of wood burn, for there has been time since the earth was first inhabited for the sun to burn and cool off, if that were the case; but there has been no appreciable falling off in temperature. What keeps up the heat we do not know, though many

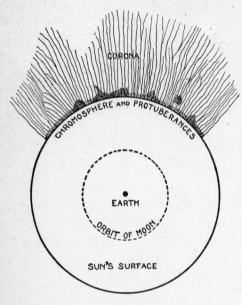

theories have been advanced to account for it. The sun certainly gives off heat in enormous quantities, and it may be possible that millions of years hence it will begin to cool and in time lose all its heat. See SOLAR SYSTEM.

Sun Bear, a bear found in India and the East Indian Archipelago, in dense mountain jungles. The *Tibetan sun bear* is a black species, with a white patch on the breast. The *Bornean sun bear* has an orange-colored patch. The *Malayan sun bear*, or *bruang*, is a very small species. All the sun bears are slender, and their fur is not so heavy and thick as that of the other bears. See BEAR.

Sun'bird, a bird which is confined to the tropical regions of Asia and Africa, and which, in brilliant plumage and habits, somewhat resembles the humming bird. The sunbirds are usually seen in pairs, in groves and gardens, sucking honey from the flowers. Some species build in holes in trees or in thick bushes, while others make dome-like nests, which they suspend from the limbs of trees.

Sunbury, *sun'ber y*, PA., the county-seat of Northumberland co., 54 mi. n. of Harrisburg, on the Susquehanna River and on the Pennsylvania and the Philadelphia & Reading railroads. The borough is in a lumbering and coal-mining region and has railroad shops, silk, woolen, lumber and flour mills, coffin works, foundries and machine shops. The important structures are the Packer Hospital, the courthouse, the jail and the parish house. The place was settled in 1772, on the site of Fort Augusta and of an old indian village. Population in 1910, 13,770.

Sun'da Islands, a name used somewhat indefinitely, but in general applied to two groups of islands, known as the Greater Sunda and the Lesser Sunda Islands. The greater islands include Sumatra, Borneo, Celebes, Java, Medura, Banca and Billiton, and the lesser group includes Bali, Lombok, Sumbawa, Flores, Sandalwood Islands, Ombai, the Timor group and a number of others. With the exception of a part of Borneo, the islands of both groups belong to the Netherlands.

Sun Dance, a curious ceremony, formerly practiced by the Sioux indians in order to propitiate the sun god. It was accompanied by terrible tortures, which the young men inflicted upon themselves to please their gods. They cut the flesh and skin of their bodies in parallel strips, passed thongs under the raised skin between, and fastening these thongs to a pole, danced till the thongs tore out and the men fell exhausted. The United States government no longer permits this dance.

Sunday (the sun's day), the first day of the week; the Lord's day.

Sunday Letter. See DOMINICAL LETTER.

Sunday Schools or **Bible Schools,** schools for the purpose of giving religious instruction, have existed in various forms since the first century B. C., but to Robert Raikes, an Englishman, is due the credit of originating the modern Sunday School, about 1780. Before he died, in 1811, there were 400,000 children in the Sunday Schools of Great Britain alone. The system met with opposition, as it seemed, to some persons, to interfere with the duties of the home and the keeping of the Sabbath, yet in spite of a council of bishops, called to stop the movement, it spread over the world. In 1824 the American Sunday School Union was formed, and through its influence, within ninety years, 125,000 Sunday schools had been organized and over $15,000,000 had been expended in distributing Bibles and other religious works. In 1913, there were in the world 297,866 Sunday schools, 2,624,896 teachers and over 26,000,000 scholars. In the Roman Catholic Sunday schools in the United States there are about 1,000,000 scholars.

The first national convention of the Sunday

School Union met in New York City in 1832. In its meeting in 1872 the uniform lesson system was inaugurated. Dr. John H. Vincent, with Mr. Jacobs of Chicago, took the initiatory steps which led to the publication of the *International Series of Lessons,* which are now in use by most Protestant denominations in the world. Various experiments have been tried to check the withdrawal from the Sunday schools of those pupils who do not wish to repeat the course previously studied. The use of graded courses, now almost universal, has been the most successful. In 1878 an international convention was organized, which meets once in three years. The World's Sunday School Convention of 1913, the seventh of its kind, met at Zurich, Switzerland. Ministers, teachers and missionaries from twenty-five countries were present. The Chautauqua movement has brought about increased interest in Bible study and in the training of teachers for Sunday School work.

Sun'derland, a seaport of England, situated at the mouth of the Wear, 14 mi. n. e. of the city of Durham. It is a modern town and is well built. Its harbor and docks are large, and it is one of the important seaports of the United Kingdom. Large quantities of coal are mined in the vicinity, and much of it is shipped from this port. There are also extensive shipbuilding works, fisheries, iron works and glass factories. Other industries include the manufacture of earthenware, machinery, chemicals, ropes and chains. Population in 1911, 151,159.

Sundew, plants growing in bogs and marshes, having leaves clothed with reddish hairs, bearing glands, which discharge drops of clear, glutinous fluid, glittering like dewdrops, whence the name. A characteristic of these plants is their habit of capturing insects by their sticky secretion. The leaves are clustered in a rosette at the bottom, are roundish in shape and are covered all over with sticky hairs. When the insect alights on one of these leaves, the hairs close quickly about it and imprison it. See BUTTERWORT; VENUS'S FLYTRAP; PITCHER PLANTS.

Sun Dial, a device for measuring time by a shadow cast by the sun. The dial consists of two parts, the *face,* or *plane,* and the *back,* or *gnomon.* The gnomon is usually a flat piece of metal, fixed to the center of the plane and pointing towards the north pole, its position being such that it is parallel to the earth's axis. The circumference of the dial is divided into hour spaces, with divisions of halves and quarters. At noon the shadow of the gnomon would fall upon the

north point of the circumference; at six o'clock in the morning it would fall upon the west point, and at six o'clock in the evening, upon the east point. The hour in the day is determined by the position of the shadow in reference to the points named. The sun dial is the oldest known device for measuring time, but since the invention of clocks, sun dials have been regarded simply as curiosities. See CLOCK.

Sun'fish, a remarkable and beautiful genus of fishes, short and almost circular in form. The sunfish appears like the head of a large fish separated from its body, and when swimming it turns upon itself like a wheel. It grows to a large size, often attaining a diameter of four feet, and sometimes of twelve feet. The back is bluish, with round silvery spots, the under parts, silvery, and the fins, bright red. The skin is hard and leathery, but the flesh is soft, white and palatable. The liver is large and yields an oil highly valued among the sailors as a cure for rheumatism. The sunfish is found in all seas, from the Antarctic Circle to the Arctic Circle. The common little flattened fish of the streams of North America are often called sunfish. They are bright colored in the breeding season and have black spots on the gill covers. These sunfish are related to the bass, and all species are good eating.

Sun'flower, a genus of plants of the helianthus family, so called from the ideal resemblance of the yellow flowers to the sun, with his golden rays. The root is mostly perennial, the stem upright and often tall, and the leaves, heart-shaped. The flowers are large, and the disk of the head is brown, surrounded by numerous yellow petals. The species are numerous, but almost all are inhabitants of North America. The gigantic sunflower common in gardens is a native of Peru. The stem is from six to fifteen feet in height; the flowers, sometimes one foot in diameter, are usually turned toward the south. The seeds form an excellent nourishment for poultry and for cage birds; and an edible oil has also been expressed from them. The rockrose and the common marigold are also sometimes called sunflowers.

Sun'nites, the so-called orthodox Mohammedans, in contradistinction to the Shiites, or heterodox Mohammedans. They form by far the larger of the two divisions, embracing the Mohammedan inhabitants of Egypt and the rest of Africa, Syria, Turkey in Europe, Asia and Arabia. They chiefly differ from the Shiites in receiving the Sunna (a collection of traditions relating to Mohammedanism) as of equal importance with the Koran, while the Shiites reject it absolutely. The Sunnites are subdivided, on account of some minute differences of custom and law, into four minor sects. The Persians are the principal Shiites.

Sun'stroke, a sudden and severe injury to the health, resulting from exposure to hot sun or to other intense heat. It may have two different effects. One, known as *heat exhaustion*, or *heat prostration*, may be recognized by great exhaustion, weakness, faintness and even nausea, followed or accompanied by a remarkable fall in temperature. In these cases the temperature of the body should be raised by external applications of heat and by internal stimulants. The other, known as *heat stroke*, or *sunstroke*, comes on more suddenly than does heat exhaustion; the patient usually loses consciousness soon, and the temperature rises rapidly, often reaching 115° F. The body is flushed and perspires freely. In this case the temperature of the body should be lowered as rapidly as possible, by sprinkling ice water over the chest and body and by rubbing the limbs with ice or ice water. The patient should then be placed upon a bed and wrapped in warm blankets. If the temperature again rises, the same process should be continued, until the body reaches its normal condition. Both of these effects are largely preventable. Those who are required to labor in excessively hot places should dress in thin, loose clothing, should sleep in well-ventilated rooms, should avoid stimulants and should drink plenty of water, but not ice water.

Su'pe'rior, WIS., the county-seat of Douglas co., at the west end of Lake Superior, on the Saint Louis River, opposite Duluth, Minn., and on the Northern Pacific, the Great Northern, the Chicago & Northwestern and other railroads. The city has three deep, connecting, well-sheltered harbors and conducts a large trade. There are almost two hundred industrial establishments, including flour and lumber mills, shipyards, packing houses and manufactories of wagons, furniture and various iron and steel products. The city is connected with Duluth by two railroad bridges and a ferry. It has two public libraries, a state normal school, a business college, two high schools and three hospitals. In the latter part of the seventeenth century the great explorer Du L'Hut established a trading post here. The town was first laid out in 1855 and became a city thirty years later. Population in 1910, 40,384.

Superior, LAKE, the largest expanse of fresh water in the world, and the most westerly and most elevated of the Great Lakes of North America. It washes the shores of the State of Minnesota on the west, those of Wisconsin and the northern peninsula of Michigan on the south, and those of Canada on the north and east. Its greatest length is 420 miles, its greatest breadth, 167 miles, and its area, 32,000 square miles. It is 600 feet above sea level, and has a depth of 1200 feet. In shape it forms an irregular crescent, dotted with numerous islands toward its northern and southern sides. The northern shore consists of cliffs, varying in height from 300 to 1000 feet, but the southern shore is low and sandy, although occasionally interrupted by cliffs, among which are the fantastic Pictured Rocks, 300 feet high, one of the greatest natural curiosities of the United States. The waters of the lake are remarkable for their transparency and are well stocked with fish, principally trout, whitefish and sturgeon. The outlet is at the southeast, by Saint Mary's River, through which Lake Superior discharges into Lake Huron. The region surrounding the lake is rich in minerals, copper and iron being found in abundance.

Supernaturalism, *su'pur nat'u ra liz''m,* a term used, chiefly in theology, in contradistinction to *rationalism*. In its widest extent supernaturalism is the doctrine that religion and the knowledge of God require a revelation from God. It considers the Christian religion an extraordinary phenomenon, out of the circle of natural events, as communicating truths above the comprehension of human reason. Rationalism maintains that the Christian religion must be judged, like other phenomena, by reason.

Supremacy, *su prem'a sy,* ROYAL, a term which is applied to the authority of the English sovereign over the Established Church of England. Up to the reign of Henry VIII the headship of the pope had been acknowledged in England as in other Roman Catholic countries, but Henry abolished this and proclaimed himself supreme head of the Church, specifically stating, however, that he assumed no spiritual powers. Although during the reign of Mary the papal authority was again acknowledged, Elizabeth for the second time abolished it and repassed the Act of Supremacy. There were from time to time various statutes passed, providing that an oath of supremacy be taken in connection with the oath of allegiance.

Supreme' Court, the name given to the highest judicial body in the system of government of

the United States. It now consists of nine justices (including the chief justice), appointed for
life, by the president and Senate. The salary of
the chief justice is $13,000, and that of each
associate justice is $12,500. The justices may
retire at the age of seventy, on a pension. The
court constitutes one of the most unique and
remarkable features of the American system,
having power to nullify, by declaring unconstitutional, any act of the national Congress or of
the state legislatures. It has final jurisdiction in
admiralty, patent, copyright and revenue cases,
and it has original jurisdiction in cases where a
state is a party. The annual session at Washington begins the second Monday in October.
See UNITED STATES, subhead *Government.*

Surabaya or **Soerabaya,** *soo'ra bah'ya,* a seaport of Java, situated on the north coast, opposite the island of Madura and at the mouth of
the Surabaya River. The chief buildings are
the government house, the mint and storehouses.
It has a large and safe harbor, which is defended
by strong fortifications. Shipbuilding docks
and a naval station are located here. The trade
is large, and, next to Batavia, it is the most important commercial center of the Dutch East
Indies. Population in 1905, 150,198, of whom
8063 were Europeans.

Surakarta or **Soerakarta,** *soo'ra kahr'ta,* or
So'lo, a city of Java, situated on the Solo River,
and connected with Surabaya by railway. It is
the residence of the emperor of Surakarta province. Shipbuilding is the chief industry. The
trade is important, and the city exports considerable quantities of rice, cotton, coffee, sugar,
tobacco and cocoanuts. Population in 1905,
118,378, of whom 1572 were Europeans.

Surat, *soo raht',* a city of British India, situated on the Tapti River, near its mouth, 150 mi.
n. of Bombay. The city contains a number of
mosques and Hindu temples, the palace of the
former nabob and an old castle. It was formerly of considerable commercial importance,
but Bombay gradually absorbed most of its
trade. It has some manufactures of textiles.
Population in 1911, 114,863.

Surgeon, *sur'jun,* **Fish.** See SEA SURGEON.

Surgery, *sur'jur y,* that branch of medicine
which is concerned with the removal of injured
parts or organs or with the healing of lesions by
means of operations on the parts affected, either
by hand or with instruments. Surgery early
became separated from medicine, for practical
ends, and a mischievous distinction between
medical and surgical cases arose. Thus were

developed such separate sciences as surgical and
medical anatomy, surgical and medical pathology and surgical and medical clinics. But
the progress of science has extended the domain
of surgery, and it has made the relation between
it and medicine more intimate.

The origin of surgery may almost be said to be
coeval with the human race. Herodotus says
that the medical art in Egypt was divided into
numerous branches, representing each member
of the body. The Greeks knew and practiced
several important operations, in a mode little
behind modern practice. The Romans followed
the Greeks and improved upon their methods,
besides inventing new operations of considerable
difficulty. On the decline of the Roman Empire, the medical art in Europe fell entirely into
the hands of the monks, and when, in 1163, the
Council of Tours prohibited the clergy from performing any operations, surgery became incorporated with the trade of barber and was reduced
to the simplest operations, chiefly that of letting
blood. The earliest revival of the science arose
from the contact of Europeans with the Eastern
nations, particularly the Arabs, and before the
close of the eleventh century, Salerno, in Italy,
acquired celebrity for a school of medicine.
From that time on there was a continual growth
in surgical skill and knowledge, but in the nineteenth century the development was greater
than in all the previous time.

The most astonishing advances in surgery
were made possible by the discovery of anes-
thetics and of the influence of bacteria upon
wounds. In 1846 ether was first used by American physicians, and a year later chloroform was
introduced by an Edinburgh physician. At
once it became possible to perform operations
that required considerable time, and which had
previously been impossible because of the pain
attendant upon them. Yet for a long time, blood
poisoning made fatal most operations in which
the wound was exposed to the air. After Pas-
teur discovered that bacteria were the cause of
putrefaction and many diseases, it was understood that most wounds would heal rapidly if
bacteria were kept from them. Following this
idea, the most surprising operations were successfully performed, and the patients speedily
recovered. Now no organ seems so delicate or
so vital that the surgeon fears to treat it with a
knife. The skull is opened and the brain exposed; the heart and lungs are laid bare; wounds
in the stomach and intestines are closed, and
vicious sores are taken away from these organs

without fear. So numerous and delicate are these operations that no one man attempts to perform them all, but each surgeon confines himself to those for which he has been specially trained. Many operations of the present time are of the bloodless kind and are performed by manipulation, rather than by cutting.

In a modern operation every care is taken, and success is more probable in a well-appointed hospital than at even the best of homes. In the hospital everything is prepared for its special use; instruments are all ready at hand, and every one is thoroughly sterilized before using; in fact, everything to be used about the person is made rigidly clean. During the progress of the operation excessive bleeding is guarded against, and after the work has been performed provision is made for proper drainage of the wound, which is then closed in such a way that there can be no possibility of infection. See ANTISEPTIC; BACTERIA AND BACTERIOLOGY; GERM THEORY OF DISEASE; MEDICINE.

Surinam, *soo re nahm'*. See GUIANA, DUTCH.

Surmul'let, a name of fishes allied to the perches, often called *red mullets*, abundant on the coasts of Europe. The common red mullet of the Mediterranean is about twelve inches long, is esteemed as very delicious food and was much prized by the Romans.

Sur'rey, the name given to a light, four-wheeled carriage, with a box-shaped body. It has two seats and side braces. See CARRIAGE.

Surrey, HENRY HOWARD, Earl of (about 1517–1547), an English soldier and poet. He succeeded to the courtesy title of earl of Surrey when his father became duke of Norfolk in 1524. Shortly before Henry VIII's death, Surrey and his father were suspected of aspiring to the succession and were arrested and lodged in the Tower. Surrey was tried, condemned and executed on Tower Hill. He wrote many elegies and love songs; but his chief importance to literature lies in the fact that in his translation of two books of the *Aeneid* he introduced blank verse into English.

Surveying, *sur vay'ing*, the art of running lines for the purpose of locating boundaries, measuring land and making maps or charts. *Plain surveying*, which is confined to small areas, such as that used in measuring land and fixing the sites of buildings and other structures, does not take into consideration the curvature of the earth; but *topographical* surveying, which is on a much more extended scale and is for the purpose of producing maps that will show ele-

vations and depressions of land, the location of bodies of water and other objects, must necessarily take note of this fact, as must *railroad* surveying, which is for locating and determining the course and grades of lines of railway. The purpose of *marine* surveying is the locating of shoals and other objects dangerous to navigation, the mapping of the mouths of rivers and entrances to harbors and the determining of depths of water in the courses over which vessels usually pass. Surveying on a large scale is usually under the direction of the national government. See COAST AND GEODETIC SURVEY.

Survey of Public Lands. See LANDS, PUBLIC.

Su'sa, an ancient city of Persia, the capital of the Province of Susiana, or Elam, situated in the plain between Kerkha and Dizful. It was a royal residence of splendor and importance and occupied a large site, which was strongly fortified. It contained a palace and the treasury of the Persian kings and was their chief residence from the time of Darius I for many years. It is the city referred to as Shushan in the book of *Daniel*. Excavations have revealed much of its former beauty and grandeur, and it is visited by many pilgrims.

Sus'quehan'na River, a river of Pennsylvania, formed by the union of north and east branches, which issue respectively from lakes Schuyler and Otsego, in Otsego County, New York. The general course of the Susquehanna is southwest, until it reaches the boundary line of Pennsylvania, when it crosses the state in an irregular course from north to south; after flowing a short distance through Maryland it enters the head of Chesapeake Bay. The stream cuts its way through numerous ranges of mountains, forming gaps or passes, and along its course are many places of scenic interest. The most important tributaries are the Chemung, the Lackawanna, the West Branch and the Juniata. There are many important towns along its banks, including Binghamton and Owego, in New York, and Wilkesbarre and Harrisburg, in Pennsylvania. The entire length of the stream and its branches is about 400 miles. Because of the many rapids and shallows it is not navigable.

Sut'lej, a river of India, the most easterly and the largest of the five rivers of the Punjab, rises in Tibet, in a small stream that is tributary to Lake Manasarowar. Its source is near the sources of the Indus, the Ganges and the Brahmaputra. In the upper part of its course it flows westward through the Himalaya region;

then it flows along the western foot of the Siwalik Hills, whence it has a generally southwest course until it unites with the Chenab, to form the Panjnad, or Five Rivers. After a course of about 50 miles it joins the Indus. The entire length of the stream is about 1000 miles. In the upper part of its course it is a mountain torrent, but at Felor it attains a width of over 2000 feet and a depth of from 12 to 18 feet. Up to this point it is navigable for river craft. In the lower part of its course the waters are generally used for irrigation.

Suttee', a practice, common in India from early times, of a wife burning herself with the body of her husband. It was especially common among the upper classes. The Hindu writings did not call for this sacrifice, but it was almost universal until the time of the English occupation of India. In 1829 it was abolished.

Suvaroff, *su vah'rohf*, or **Suvoroff**, *su vo'-rohf*, ALEXEI VASSILIEVITCH, Count (1729–1800), a Russian general. He entered the army in his seventeenth year and rapidly rose to distinction, taking part in the Seven Years' War and the Turkish war of 1773–1774. In the Turkish War of 1787–1792, as chief in command, he gained the title of Count Suvaroff-Rymnikski, by his great victory on the banks of the Rymnik. The most important, and perhaps the most sanguinary, of his actions during this war, was the storming of Ismail in 1790, which was followed by the indiscriminate massacre of the inhabitants. He was next employed against the kingdom of Poland, and he conducted a campaign of which the partition of the country was the result, and for which he received a field marshal's baton and an estate in the dominions which he had helped to annex to the Russian Crown. The last and most celebrated of his services was his campaign in Italy in 1799, when his courage and genius for a while repaired the disasters of the allied forces. He gained several brilliant victories, drove the French from all the towns and fortresses of Upper Italy and was rewarded with the title of Prince Italiski.

Swa'bia or **Suabia**, a duchy of medieval Germany, named from the Suevi. During the time that it formed a part of the Frankish Empire, the territory was governed by a duke, but after the dissolution of the Frankish Empire it was placed under a count and became well-nigh independent. In the tenth century it was made a duchy of the German Kingdom, and in the twelfth and thirteenth centuries, while under the rule of the House of Hohenstaufen, it was the wealthiest and most powerful of the duchies. When the Hohenstaufen line became extinct, in the thirteenth century, the duchy declined in importance. From the fourteenth to the sixteenth century, the leagues of the various cities were of more importance than the duchy itself. At present a part of Bavaria is known as Swabia.

Swallow, *swol'lo*, the general name of a family of birds somewhat resembling the swifts.

BARN SWALLOW

They have long, powerful wings, short, broad beaks and comparatively small and weak legs and feet. They take their insect food on the wing, being aided by the wide gape of their bills. Swallows, of which there are a number of species, are found all over the world, except in the coldest regions. They are exceedingly rapid and graceful on the wing, turning, doubling, flying aloft, skimming the water's surface and even drinking while on the wing. They are migratory birds and return with great regularity to the north for their nesting. The *barn swallow* builds mud nests on the rafters of barns and the *eave swallow* builds similar nests under the eaves of houses. It is a very common species in the United States. The familiar *purple martin*, the *tree swallow* and the *cliff swallow* are all common residents of the United States. The so-called *chimney swallow* is really a swift, as is the swallow which produces the edible birds' nest. See MARTIN; SWIFT. The *window swallow* is a common European species.

Swallowing. See DEGLUTITION.

Swamp, *swomp*. See MARSH.

Swamp'scott, Mass., a town of Essex co., on Massachusetts Bay and on the Boston & Maine railroad, 13 mi. from Boston. It has two parks, a public library and the Phillips School, besides numerous attractive summer residences. Many of its inhabitants are engaged in business in Lynn. Population in 1910, 6204.

Swan, *swon,* the largest bird of the duck family, always famous for its grace and beauty on the

SWAN

water. Among the Greeks and Romans the swan was venerated as the sacred bird of Apollo and the Muses. It was once thought that the swan sang beautifully just before its death; but as a matter of fact, all swans have harsh and rather unpleasant notes. They are strong, fierce fighters, defending their nests against preying animals and even against man. In North America there are two wild species, both of which are white, with black bills and legs. The *whistling swan* has an orange spot in front of the eye, and the *trumpeter swan* lacks this mark. The latter, which was at one time quite common in western United States, furnishes most of the swan's down for the market. In Australia is a *black swan.* Though formerly the flesh of swans was thought to be fine, it is now considered too coarse for the table, and domestic swans are kept only for their beauty.

Sweat, *swet,* a fluid excreted through the pores of the skin; also known as perspiration. The nature of this fluid and the processes by which it is excreted are discussed in the article SKIN. Changes or abnormalities in the composition of sweat or in the process of excretion are symptoms of many common diseases. In those accompanied by high fever, the perspiration is likely to be diminished; this is the condition known as anidrosis. In others, such as rheumatism, cholera, malaria, tuberculosis and certain stages of other diseases, the sweating is profuse; this condition is known as hyperidrosis.

Sweatshop System, the system by which subcontractors undertake to do work in their own houses or small workshops, employing others to do it, making a profit for themselves by the difference between the contract prices and the wages they pay their assistants. The object of the subcontractor, or sweater, being to secure as large a margin of profit as possible, the tendency of the system is to reduce the wages of the workers to the lowest possible limit. Considerable of this sort of sweating has been done in industrial history, but it disappears under the advance of incorporations, trades unions, factory inspection and legislation. The system appears in the United States among cigar makers, cloak makers and shop tailors, and it has given rise occasionally to strikes, out of which have come temporary relief. The evils attendant upon this system are overcrowded tenements, bad sanitary conditions, inadequate pay and long hours of labor. In some states, however, legislation has forbidden the use of dwelling tenements for workshops, the overcrowding of workrooms and the employment of children. See LABOR ORGANIZATIONS.

Swe'den, a kingdom in northern Europe, situated between 55° 20′ and 69° 3′ north latitude and between 11° 6′ and 24° 10′ east longitude. It is bounded on the e. by Russia, the Gulf of Bothnia and the Baltic Sea; on the s. by the Baltic; on the s. w. by Cattegat and Skagerrak, and on the w. and n. by Norway. Its greatest length is 970 miles; its greatest width, 225 miles, and its area, 172,876 sq. mi., or about the same as that of California, Maryland and Delaware combined. The coast line is a little over 1400 miles.

SURFACE AND DRAINAGE. The Scandinavian Alps, or Kiolen Mountains, form the northern portion of the boundary between Sweden and Norway. These are low mountains consisting in some places of scarcely more than a high plateau. The highest summits are Sarjektjakko, 6855 feet, and Kaskasatjakko, 6809 feet. From the mountain barrier the land slopes by successive terraces toward the east and southeast. The coast is low, level and in some places marshy. It is estimated that nearly one-third of the surface of the country is below a level of thirty feet, while only a small portion of it has a level of 2000 feet and over. The southern part of the country is generally low.

Sweden has a large number of rivers, and with scarcely an exception these flow in a southeasterly direction. The Tornoa and its northern tributary, the Muonio, form the boundary with

Russia. Other important streams in their order, passing southward, are the Lulea, the Skelleftea, the Unea, the Indals and the Dal, flowing into the Gulf of Bothnia; the Klar, rising in Norway and flowing southerly into Lake Venner, and the Gota, discharging the waters of this lake into the Cattegat. The country has a large number of lakes. The most important of these are lakes Venner and Vetter. The former, having an area of over 2100 square miles, is the third largest lake in Europe. The northern part of the country is studded with lakes, which in form are generally long and narrow. These, as well as most of the streams, are too small to be available for navigation.

CLIMATE. Considering its latitude, Sweden has a mild climate, though there is a marked difference in the mean annual temperature in its northern and southern extremities, the mean temperature at Stockholm for January being 24½°, and for July, 63°. In general the summers are hot, and the winters extremely cold; in the northern part of the country the thermometer sometimes falls as far as 40° below zero. There is scarcely any transition between winter and summer or between summer and winter. Spring and autumn, which characterize most temperate countries, here are very short or are lacking altogether. The rainfall averages about 20 inches for the entire country, but it is much heavier in the south, where it is about 35 inches, than in the north, where it seldom exceeds 13 inches. The greatest amount of rain falls during August.

MINERAL RESOURCES. Sweden has an abundance of minerals, and for many years mining has been one of its most important industries. Iron ore is distributed over the country, but the mines in the north are the most valuable. These produce magnetite, or magnetic iron ore, and the quality of the metal mined from it is such as to make Swedish iron in demand the world over (See IRON, subhead ORES). Other metals found in paying quantities are copper, zinc and silver. Alum, manganese, sulphate of iron and cobalt are also found, and there is an inferior quality of coal in the southern part of the country, small quantities of which are mined. The mining industries of the country give employment to about 31,000 people.

AGRICULTURE. Only a small portion of the land is suitable for cultivation. A large part of the remainder is covered with forests, and some of the rest is suited to grazing. Agriculture gives employment to about three-fourths

of the inhabitants. The farms are generally small, ranging from 5 to 45 acres in extent. The best lands are in the southern and central parts of the country, and here the farms, when well tilled, produce as much per acre as the best farms in England. The chief crops are oats, rye, potatoes, barley and wheat. Large quantities of hay are cut, and other forage plants are raised to some extent. In the parts of the country where pasturage is good, the raising of live stock is an important branch of industry; here dairying receives the attention of a large number of farmers, and considerable quantities of butter are exported to Great Britain. Sugar beets are cultivated in the south, and flax, tobacco and hops are raised successfully in various localities. Agriculture is aided by the government, which establishes agricultural schools and sends teachers of agriculture throughout the country. Notwithstanding this, in many places the industry lags, and primitive methods and implements are still employed.

OTHER INDUSTRIES. The fisheries are of considerable importance, though they do not yield a sufficient supply of fish to meet the demands of the country. Of the manufacturing industries, those connected with the cutting and preparation of lumber and its products are by far the most important. Saw mills are found throughout the country, and the lumber industry employs a larger number of people than any other branch of manufacture. Other important industries include the manufacture of flour, of textiles and foundry and machine shop products. Sweden is noted for its manufacture of iron, which is exported to nearly all countries of the world. The leading industrial centers are Stockholm, Göteborg and Norrköping, all of which have large textile establishments. The most important iron works are at Eskilstuna and Motala.

TRANSPORTATION AND COMMERCE. Transportation facilities are good. The roads are in excellent condition, and the country has over 7600 miles of railway lines, which connect all of its leading commercial centers and join them with the important seaports of Norway. Canals connect many of the lakes and rivers, so that there are over 2500 miles of inland waterways. All of these means of transportation give the country adequate facilities for moving its products.

The commerce is large, considering the size and population of the country. Most of it is maritime, and Swedish ships carry not only the trade of the country, but a considerable part of that of other nations. The leading exports are minerals, metal goods and machinery, live stock, hair, hides and other animal products, lumber and its products, which far exceeds the others. The imports consist of minerals, principally coal, metal goods, machinery, textiles, grain, flour and other food products. The foreign trade is carried on chiefly with Great Britain, Germany and Norway.

INHABITANTS AND LANGUAGE. The Swedes are descendants of the Scandinavian branch of the Teutonic peoples who formerly inhabited the northern part of Europe. They are usually tall and well proportioned and have a light complexion, blonde hair and blue eyes. They are characterized by their industry, sobriety, cheerful disposition and general intelligence. Wherever they have gone they have won a reputation for honesty and thrift. The language is somewhat different from that of Norway and Denmark. Because of the union of that branch of the Scandinavians forming the Swedes with the Svears of the north and the Gotars of the South, the blending of the native languages of these people with the old Scandinavian tongue produced a language somewhat more sonorous than the dialects found in Denmark and Norway, which very closely resemble each other.

EDUCATION. An excellent system of public schools is maintained, under the direct supervision of the government. Attendance is compulsory, and there is scarcely a person of school age who cannot read and write. In addition to the common schools, two universities are maintained, one at Upsala and the other at Lund. There are also fourteen normal schools and a number of technical schools, of navigation, textiles, mining, medicine, veterinary science, agriculture and forestry. The deaf and blind are cared for in special institutions maintained by the state.

LITERATURE. The earliest writings in Swedish literature which have been preserved are ancient provincial laws, some of which date from the thirteenth century. There are, too, ballads which were written at a very early date. Like the other countries of Europe, Sweden was affected in the later Middle Ages by the romantic movement in literature, and tales of chivalry were the result. In the sixteenth century little was produced except religious works, but in the century that followed Swedish writers began to be influenced by the writers of other countries, and a more varied literature resulted. The middle eighteenth century produced Swedenborg and Linnaeus, who were,

however, of more importance to religion and science than to pure literature. Gustavus III was a patron of letters, and many writers of note were members of the court he assembled. The romantic movement which swept over Europe in the early nineteenth century affected Sweden with the other countries, and the first half of that century was the most noteworthy period in the history of Swedish literature. Tegnér (1782–1846), the author of *Frithiof's Saga*, is the greatest poet Sweden has produced. Among nineteenth century writers the best known outside of her native country was the novelist, Fredrika Bremer.

SCULPTURE. See SCULPTURE.

GOVERNMENT AND RELIGION. The government is a constitutional monarchy. The throne is hereditary in the male line of descent, but in case there is no direct heir, a king is chosen by the national legislature. The king is required to be a member of the Lutheran Church and is bound to observe the laws and enforce the same. The legislative department consists of a Dadiet, comprising two houses, the upper chamber of 150 members chosen by the legislators of the various provinces, for nine years, and the lower chamber of 230 members, chosen for three years. The suffrage is restricted by property qualifications. In choosing the members of the lower chamber about one-third are chosen from the towns and two-thirds from the country. Previous to 1905 Sweden was united with Norway under the same king, but at Norway's request this union was severed.

The Lutheran Church is the established church, and nearly all the inhabitants are followers of this creed. Other religions, however, are tolerated, and there are a few communicants of the various evangelical denominations, as well as some Roman Catholics.

CITIES. The chief cities are Stockholm, the capital; Gothenburg and Malmö, each of which is described under its title.

HISTORY. Authentic history of Sweden begins about 1000 A. D., but for three centuries after that time the country was in a turmoil, owing to the constant struggles between the two Teutonic peoples, the Swedes and the Goths, who occupied, respectively, the northern and the southern parts of the peninsula. In the twelfth century Christianity spread through the country, and in their attempts to advance the new religion the Swedes made themselves masters of Finland. In 1397, by the union of Kalmar, Queen Margaret (See MARGARET) united Sweden, Denmark and Norway as one kingdom. The Swedes were restive under the union, but not until 1523, under Gustavus Vasa, were they able to make themselves independent (See Gustavus I).

From this time the nation made a steady advance in the face of difficulties, despite the succession of weak rulers, the first of whom was Eric XIV, who ruled from 1560 to 1568. Under John III (1568–1592) occurred a reaction to Catholicism, from the Lutheranism which Gustavus had established as the State religion. The people showed their adherence to the new religion, however, by demanding the abdication of John's son, Sigismund, who attempted to restore Catholicism as the State faith. Charles IX (1604–1611) did much to counteract the bad effects which the previous reigns had had on the country, and his son and successor, Gustavus Adolphus (1611–1632), brought Sweden to a point which it had never reached before. With all of its growth in patriotism, commerce and culture, Sweden had made no attempt at territorial expansion, and it was not accorded by the other states of Europe a very high position. Gustavus Adolphus was ambitious, and his ambition, with his faith in Protestantism, was sufficient to draw him into the war which was raging in Germany (See Gustavus II Adolphus; Thirty Years' War). Even after the death of Gustavus Adolphus, his policy was carried out, and for some time Sweden was recognized as one of the great powers of Europe. Slight accessions of territory were made under several of the rulers by successes in war, but in 1675 the Swedish armies were completely defeated by the elector of Brandenburg at Fehrbellin.

The first great sovereign after Gustavus Adolphus was Charles XII (king from 1697 to 1718), whose extraordinary military genius drew the eyes of all Europe to Sweden (See Charles XII). After his death the country became greatly enfeebled by the struggles of various political factions, and even Gustavus III (1771–1792), who put down the factions and increased the royal power, was unable to restore it fully. Finally, Gustavus IV (1792–1809) proved himself so weak, and yet so stubborn, that he was deposed and was compelled to renounce the crown for his heirs (See Gustavus IV Adolphus). Charles XIII, the uncle of Gustavus, was elected king, and as he had no heirs, Bernadotte, one of Napoleon's marshals, was chosen crown prince, in the hope of conciliating Napoleon (See Charles XIV John). The effectual aid which Berna-

163

dotte rendered the allies in the final overthrow of Napoleon gave Sweden a claim on the Congress of Vienna, and Norway was accordingly taken from Denmark and given to Sweden. Bernadotte came to the throne in 1818, and although, because of his selfish desire for his own advancement, he was never personally popular, he greatly increased the prestige and prosperity of his realm. He was succeeded in 1844 by his son, Oscar I, under whom, as under the two succeeding kings, Charles XV (1859–1872) and Oscar II, prosperity continued. In 1905 Norway broke away from Sweden and became an independent country (See Norway, subhead History). Population in 1910, 5,522,474. Consult Thomas's Sweden and the Swedes; also, Sweden, its People and its Industry, edited by Sunborg.

Swe′denborg, Emanuel (1688–1772), the founder of the New Jerusalem Church, or sect of Swedenborgians, the son of Jasper Swedberg, bishop of West Gothland. He was born at Stockholm, but little is known of his youth. His studies embraced mechanics, mathematics, mining, chemistry, physiology and most of the natural sciences. He spent four years in scientific travels through England, Holland, France and Germany, and on his return he was appointed assessor in the Royal College of Mines by Charles XII, a position he held only till 1749, though he retained the salary through life. Swedberg invented a rolling machine to transport cannon over the mountains to the siege of Frederickshall, and this service, with his treatises on algebra, on the value of money, on the orbit and position of the earth and planets and on tides, gained for him the favor of the government; in 1719 Queen Ulrica raised the Swedberg family to the rank of nobility, and the name was changed to Swedenborg.

Swedenborg visited the mines of Sweden, of Saxony and of Austria and Hungary. A work on the origin of things, followed by a treatise on mining and smelting (Opera Philosophica et Mineralia), was published in 1734 and attracted much attention among the scholars of Europe. He increased his knowledge by new travels (1736–1740), in Germany, Holland, France, Italy and England, and after his return he published the Oeconomia Regni Animalis (Economy of the Soul-kingdom), which contains the application of the system of nature, unfolded in his philosophical works, to man. He was first introduced to an intercourse with the spiritual world in detail, according to his own statement, in 1743 at

London. The eyes of his inward man, he says, were opened to see heaven, hell and the world of spirits, in which he conversed, not only with his deceased acquaintances, but with the most distinguished men of antiquity. His works are very numerous, among the more important of them being the *Arcana Coelestia*, the *New Jerusalem*, *Angelic Wisdom*, the *Apocalypse Explained* and *Heaven and Hell*.

Swedenborgians, *swe′den bor′je anz*, the followers of Swedenborg, particularly the members of what is called the New Jerusalem Church, or New Church. The belief of the Swedenborgians is as follows: Jesus Christ is God, in whom is a trinity, not of persons but essentials, answering to the soul, the body and the operation of these in a man; that the Scriptures contain an internal or spiritual meaning, which is the Word existing in heaven; that the key to this is the correspondence between natural and spiritual things, as between effects and their causes; that man is saved by shunning evils as sins and by leading a life according to the ten commandments; that man is a spirit clothed with a natural body for life on earth, and that when he puts it off at death he continues to live as before, but in the spiritual world, first in an intermediate state between heaven and hell, but afterwards, when his character, whether good or evil, becomes harmonious throughout, among his like, either in heaven or hell; that the Lord's second coming and the last judgment are spiritual events, which have already taken place. Swedenborgians are found in the United States and in many of the countries of Europe. See SWEDENBORG, EMANUEL.

Sweet Alyssum, *a lis′ um*, a well-known flowering annual. It grows from four to ten inches high, and blossoms from June to September, in long clusters or bunches of small, white, sweet-scented flowers, of which bees are very fond. It is easy to raise, growing in any ordinary soil, either from seeds or cuttings. One variety has double flowers, another is noted for its varigated

SWEET ALYSSUM

leaves, still another, being dwarfed and bushy, is used to set off rockeries.

Sweet′bread. See GLANDS.

Sweet′bri′er, a name applied to several species of rose, natives of Europe, but naturalized in the United States. Sweetbrier grows wild, but it is often planted in hedges and gardens, on account of the sweet smell of its small leaves and pink flowers. It is also called the *eglantine*.

Sweet Flag, a rush-like plant, found in marshy places throughout the northern hemisphere. The leaves are all long and sword-shaped, and the slender, green stem bears a greenish spike of flowers. The root, which is long, cylindrical and knotted, has a strong aromatic odor and a warm, pungent, bitterish taste, and it has been employed in medicine since the time of Hippocrates. It is also used by confectioners as a candy and by perfumers in the preparation of aromatic vinegar, hair powder and other articles. By some persons it is called *calamus root*, but it is a very different plant from the real calamus.

Sweet Gum. See LIQUIDAMBAR.

Sweet Lo′cust. See HONEY LOCUST.

Sweet Pea, a garden plant. It is cultivated on account of the beauty of its flowers, which are purple, rose, white or variegated, and remarkable for sweet fragrance. Sicily is said to be its native place. There are about one hundred fifty known varieties.

Sweet Pota′to, a plant of the Convolvulus family, a native of the tropics, but now cultivated in all the warmer parts of the world. Columbus brought sweet potatoes to Spain as a gift to Queen Isabella, and by the middle of the sixteenth century they were in general cultivation in Spain. The sweet potato has smooth, creeping stems, heart-shaped leaves and a flower that resembles the morning-glory in all but its beauty. The root is large, yellowish and considered an excellent food. In the United States, Georgia, North Carolina, South Carolina and Alabama lead in the production of sweet potatoes, but they are raised much farther north; and because of their excellence they are seen everywhere in the markets during the fall and winter months.

Sweet Wil′liam, a species of pink, an old inhabitant of flower gardens which has produced numerous varieties. It grows wild in dry and sterile places in middle and southern Europe.

Sweyn, *swain*, a king of Denmark, father of Canute the Great. He died in 1014, after having established himself in England, though without being crowned there.

Swift, the common name of a bird, very much resembling the swallow in outward appearance and habits, but in structure much different and classified by some naturalists with the humming birds, or goatsuckers. Like the swallows, the

SWIFT

swifts live principally upon the wing, catching insect food and even gathering material for their nests while in full flight. The common North American swifts are the so-called chimney swallows, which build their nests in fireless chimneys of houses, sometimes almost filling the cavity with the dried twigs, which are fastened together with a sticky glue, the saliva of the birds. The swifts hunt over a large territory during the day, and at night they return to their home in the chimney, where they move restlessly about, chattering throughout the night. Their tails are spiny-pointed and are used in climbing and propping themselves against the wall. The famous edible birds' nest is built by a swift, almost entirely from its own saliva. The *cliff swift* of Guatemala builds a strange nest, about two feet long and two inches in diameter, with a chamber about six inches in diameter at the top, where the eggs are laid. The entrance is from the lower end.

Swift, JONATHAN (1667–1745), the greatest of English satirists, born in Dublin of English parents. His education at Kilkenny and later at Trinity College, Dublin, was most irregular, and it was only by a special dispensation that he was granted a degree. In 1689 he became secretary to Sir William Temple of Moor Park, Surrey, but his pride made this relation a most trying one, and after five years he gave it up and returned to Ireland to secure a Church living. With that of Kilroot, which was given him, he shortly became dissatisfied, and he

returned to Moor Park, where he remained until Temple's death. During this time arose his love for the *Stella* of his writings, Miss Hester Johnson, a relation of Sir William Temple's and an inmate of his home. In 1699 Swift accepted an invitation from the earl of Berkeley to accompany him to Ireland as chaplain and secretary, and he was presented by that nobleman with the living of Laracor. During his residence there he invited to Ireland Miss Johnson, who, with her friend Mrs. Dingley, lived at the parsonage during Swift's absences and in the neighborhood when he was at home.

The famous *Tale of the Tub*, published in 1704, brought Swift wide notice, and by its satire against literary and religious pedantry he injured his chances for advancement in the Church. During a stay in England from 1710 to 1713 Swift wrote the *Journal to Stella*, a work which throws much light on his life. In these years also he became acquainted with Miss Hester Vanhomrigh, called by him *Vanessa*, a

JONATHAN SWIFT

young lady of fortune who fell in love with him and proposed marriage. When he returned to Ireland, she followed him and took up her residence in his neighborhood. At length, through secret means, she became aware of his attachment for Stella, and in desperation she visited Stella and demanded the truth. Swift's anger and the rupture of their friendship brought about her death in a short time.

In 1724 the publication of the *Drapier Letters* made Swift the hero of the Irish people, and two years later the appearance of *Gulliver's Travels* greatly increased his fame. His exertions to better the condition of the poor in Ireland remained constant until 1742, when the affliction which he had long been dreading came upon him, and his mind failed. His insanity continued until his death, three years later.

Swift's fierce satire, absent from none of his work and growing more savage in his later years, is to be accounted for partly by his intense hatred of all sham and injustice, partly by the tragic gloom of his own nature.

Swim'ming. A large proportion of the animal tribes are furnished with a greater or less capacity for swimming, either in water or on its surface, but man is unqualified for swimming without learning to do so as an art. The art of swimming consists chiefly in keeping the head, or at least the mouth, above water, and using the hands and feet as oars and helm. It forms a most healthful, invigorating and agreeable exercise, and the means which it affords a man of preserving his own life or the lives of others, in situations of peculiar peril, is also a great recommendation.

Lack of confidence is the greatest obstacle in the way of most of those who begin to learn to swim. The beginner cannot persuade himself that the water will support him, and feeling that he must sink, he stiffens his back and throws his head out of the water; or he doubles up in such a way that he begins to sink, after which his flounderings only hasten his descent. As a matter of fact, very little motion of the limbs is necessary to keep the human body afloat, and this is especially true if the person rests upon his back and puts his head well into the water. The head, shoulders and back are the heaviest parts of the body, and all efforts to keep them high in the water or outside, are at the expense of strength. If the learner will not consider the possibility of sinking; will give up the idea of supporting himself by muscular strength, and depend upon the water to buoy him up like a cushion, he will learn to swim as easily as he learned to walk when a child. He should remember to keep the body straight; to move the arms and limbs together, from the shoulders and hips, without doubling or bending the body any more than he is compelled to do. He should throw himself out at full length, face

downward, allowing the water to rise above his shoulders and neck, and then strike boldly out in water that is not over his head. If he sinks a few times, he has merely to stand on his feet and try again. After he has learned to swim in the simplest way, the other and better methods, such as swimming on the back or on the side, or using the overhand stroke, will be easily acquired.

If a person is in danger of drowning, and a swimmer goes to his rescue, the latter should remember that the drowning person is not apt to be conscious of what he is doing and may seize his rescuer and drag him down. If, however, there is no great excitement, the swimmer can support and carry the other very easily, if the latter will rest his hands upon the hips of the swimmer and, stretching at full length, keep perfectly quiet. This is a convenient method of bringing out any one who is attacked with weakness or cramp. If the drowning person is unconscious, his body may be drawn along by the hair or pushed ahead of the swimmer, if far from shore; if near, he can be seized by the arm and drawn out. For treatment of the drowned, see DROWNING.

Swin'burne, ALGERNON CHARLES (1837–1909), an English poet. He was born in London and was educated at Balliol College. Oxford. His first productions, the dramas of *The Queen Mother* and *Rosamond*, published in 1861, attracted but little attention. They were followed by two tragedies, *Atalanta in Calydon* and *Chastelard*, and by *Poems and Ballads*, which excited considerable criticism. After that time Swinburne was prominently before the public. Among his numerous later works may be mentioned *A Song of Italy*; *William Blake*, a critical essay; *Ode on the Proclamation of the French Republic*; *Songs of Sunrise*; *Bothwell*, a tragedy; *A Century of Roundels*; *A Study of Victor Hugo*; *Essays and Studies*; a poem on the *Armada*; *Studies in Prose and Poetry*, and a *Study of Shakespeare*.

Swine. See HOG.

Swing, DAVID (1830–1894), an American clergyman, born at Cincinnati, Ohio. He was educated at Miami University, Oxford, Ohio, and was made professor of languages there, which position he held until 1866, when he became pastor of the Fourth Presbyterian Church of Chicago. In 1874 he was charged with heresy, but after a celebrated trial he was acquitted. He resigned his pastorate and withdrew from the Presbyterian ministry. He organized a new church, and from 1878 until his death he held independent services at Central Music Hall, Chicago. He published *Old Pictures of Life.*

Swin'ton, WILLIAM (1833–1892), an American educator and author, born in Scotland and educated at Knox College, Toronto, and at Amherst, Mass. He began his career as a professor in a woman's seminary at Greensboro, N. C., but during the Civil War he went to the front with the Army of the Potomac, as war correspondent for the New York *Times*. In 1869 he became professor of English language and literature in the University of California. He was the author of *Campaigns of the Army of the Potomac, The Twelve Decisive Battles of the War, A Condensed History of the United States* and a number of other text-books.

Swiss Guards, *gahrdz*, bodies of Swiss troops, which, since Switzerland gained her independence in the fifteenth century, have been employed in many European countries as bodyguards and for duty about courts. The most famous are the French Swiss Guards, organized in 1616 and annihilated in the defense of the Tuileries, Aug. 10, 1792. Their heroism is commemorated in Thorwaldsen's *Lion of Lucerne*, carved in the face of a rock at Lucerne, Switzerland. The French Swiss Guards were reorganized by Louis XVIII in 1815 and were defeated and dispersed in the Revolution of 1830.

Swit'zerland, a republic of central Europe, lying between 45° 50' and 47° 50' north latitude and between 5° 48' and 10° 28' east longitude. It is bounded on the n. by Germany, on the e. by Austria-Hungary, on the s. by Italy and France and on the w. by France. Its greatest length from east to west is 200 miles, and its breadth is 125 miles. The area is 15,976 square miles, or a little less than one-half that of the State of Maine.

SURFACE AND DRAINAGE. The characteristic physical features of Switzerland are its lofty mountain ranges, enormous glaciers, magnificent lakes and wild, romantic valleys. The loftiest mountain chains belong to the Alps and are situated chiefly in the south. The central nucleus is Mount Saint Gotthard, which unites the principal watersheds of Europe and sends its waters into four large basins—north by the Rhine to the North Sea, southwest by the Rhone to the Mediterranean, southeast by the Po to the Adriatic and east by the Danube to the Black Sea. In like manner it forms a kind of starting point for the loftiest ranges of the Alps—the Helvetian, or Lepontine, Alps, to which it belongs itself; the Pennine Alps, which include Mont Blanc, the culminating point of Europe, beyond the Swiss frontiers in Savoy; and the Rhaetian Alps, which stretch east and northeast across the Canton of Grisons into the Tyrol. Besides the Alps, properly so called, the only range deserving of notice is that of the Jura, which is linked to the Alps by the small range of the Jorat. See ALPS.

Owing to the mountainous nature and inland position of the country, none of the rivers acquire such a size within its limits as to become of much navigable importance. The Rhine, formed by two head streams in the Canton of Grisons, flows north into the Lake of Constance and thence west to Schaffhausen, where it forms the celebrated falls of that name. Below these falls its navigation properly begins (See RHINE). Its principal affluent in Switzerland is the Aar. The Rhone, rising in the Rhone glacier, flows northwest into the Lake of Geneva. Immediately after issuing from the lake at the town of Geneva, it receives the Arve, and about 10 miles below it quits the Swiss frontier. The waters which the Po receives from Switzerland are carried to it by the Ticino; those which the Danube receives are carried to it by the Inn. The largest lakes, that of Geneva in the southwest and that of Constance in the northeast, as well as that of Maggiore on the south side of the Alps, belong partly to other countries. Within the limits of Switzerland, and not far from its center, are Lake Neuchâtel, with Morat and Bienne in its vicinity; Thun, with its feeder, Brienz; Lucerne, Sempach, Baldegg, Zug, Zürich and Wallenstättersee. All these internal lakes belong to the basin of the Rhine and are famous for their beautiful scenery.

CLIMATE. The climate varies with the elevation. The mountains serve as a barrier to winds, and in the lower valleys and on the central plains, a temperate climate, with a mean annual temperature of about 50°, prevails. This average diminishes about 3° for every 1000 feet of altitude, and in the higher altitudes the climate is cold and during winter is especially severe. On the south side of the Alps the snow line is a little over 10,000 feet above the sea level, but on the north side it descends to about 8500 feet. The summits of the higher mountains are covered with perpetual snow and are usually enveloped in clouds. The rainfall is heavy, varying from 33 inches, in the central plain, to nearly 100 inches, in other localities. While the climate is healthful and to a degree stimulating, it is not particularly favorable to agriculture.

MINERAL RESOURCES. The mountains are masses of granite and gneiss and contain untold resources of building material. Sand and limestone are also found in many places, and rock salt is obtained in three cantons. The metal-bearing ores are few and of little importance. Anthracite coal is found near Bern, in Fribourg, and is mined to a limited extent, but on the whole the mining industries of the country are of slight importance, and nearly all the coal, as well as iron and other metals, is imported.

AGRICULTURE. About two-thirds of the population are owners of land. However, the higher altitudes are unsuited for cultivation. The chief crops are hay and forage plants, wheat, rye, oats and potatoes; but the land is unable to produce enough of any of these to supply the demand, and large quantities are imported. Fruit is generally cultivated, and from it wine and spirit-uous liquors are made; in the south, almonds, walnuts, olives, chestnuts and, in some places, lemons are grown. The raising of live stock is, however, a more important branch of agriculture than tilling the soil. Large numbers of excellent breeds of cattle are raised, and the manufactures of cheese and condensed milk are important industries. Cattle are also quite extensively exported for breeding purposes, but most of the beef is imported. On the mountains large numbers of goats are raised, and these are valuable for their milk, flesh and skins. The lakes and streams are well stocked with fish, and fish culture is given careful attention by the government. Nearly one-fifth of the country is covered with forests.

MANUFACTURES. The manufacturing industries are of more importance than the agricultural and furnish employment to nearly as many people. The mountain streams furnish an abundance of water power, the people are industrious and generally skilful, and the numerous railways give them ample opportunity for marketing their wares. Manufactures of textiles and metal wares are among the most important industries. The chief centers of the cotton industry are Zurich, Appenzell, Glarus and Saint Gall. The Swiss fabrics are noted for their fineness and for the high quality of their dyes, and they consequently find a wide market. The silk industry is centered at Basel and Zurich. Next in importance to the textile and metal industries is the manufacture of watches, in which the Swiss

have been noted for many years. The chief centers of watch making are Geneva, Chaux-de-Fonds and Locle. Before the invention of machinery for the manufacture of watches, Swiss watches were in demand in all civilized countries and were considered superior to all others, but competition with the machine-made watches of the United States has greatly crippled the hand industry, and in recent years watch-making machinery has been quite generally introduced into the country. Other industries of importance include wood carving, the tanning and manufacture of leather and the manufacture of musical instruments and jewelry.

TRANSPORTATION. The rivers are too swift and shallow for navigation, hence all transportation is by railroads or carriage roads. Considering the number of mountains, the country is remarkably well supplied with railways, there being about 3500 miles in operation, two-thirds of which is owned by the State. Through the Saint Gotthard and Simplon tunnels, connection is made with Italy. Steamers ply on all of the larger lakes, and the carriage roads are in excellent condition, so that transportation facilities are adequate for both freight and passenger traffic.

INHABITANTS AND LANGUAGE. Switzerland was the home of a prehistoric race, the remains of which have been found in their lake dwellings; but the first people of whom we have record were the Helvetians, who were found in this locality when the Romans, under Julius Caesar, crossed the Alps in 58 B. C. This people was of Celtic origin (See CELTS). The present inhabitants are descendants from the ancient Helvetians and following generations, in whom was mingled the blood of the Teutonic people from the north and of the Roman element from the south. German is the prevailing language, except in the west, where French is quite generally used; in the extreme south both French and Italian are spoken, and in some cantons the Romansch tongue prevails. The Swiss are a hardy race, noted for their industry, honesty and skill.

EDUCATION. The schools are of a high order, and a compulsory education law is strictly enforced in most of the cantons. In addition to its public schools, the country contains a number of noted universities, particularly those at Zurich, Bern, Geneva and Fribourg. There are also academies at Geneva and Lausanne, and a federal polytechnic school is located at Zurich. The excellence of this school draws pupils from all European countries.

GOVERNMENT. Switzerland is a federal republic, consisting of 22 cantons, with the capital at Bern. The executive power is vested in the Federal Council of 7 members, elected for three years by the two houses of the national legislature. The government is divided into 7 departments, each of which is in charge of a member of this council. The president of the council is also president of the state and is elected by the councilors annually. The legislative powers are vested in the Federal Assembly, which consists of two houses, the National Council and the Council of Estates. These bodies hold separate sessions in the discussion of all legislative matters, and they have joint sessions for electoral and judicial purposes. Each canton has a local government of its own and is given jurisdiction over its own affairs. One peculiar feature of the Swiss government is the referendum, by which it refers to popular vote questions of national importance. The initiative is coupled with the referendum, and by this the people have a right to draw up and present to the national legislature such measures as they think should be enacted into law.

In religion the inhabitants are divided between the Protestant and Roman Catholic churches, about three-fifths of them being Protestants. All forms of worship are tolerated.

CITIES. The chief cities are Bern, the capital; Zurich, Geneva, Basel and Lucerne, each of which is described under its title.

HISTORY. The oldest inhabitants of Switzerland mentioned in written history were the Helvetians (See HELVETII). They were subjugated between 58 B. C. and 10 A. D. by the Romans, and later they were almost exterminated. Before the fall of the Roman Empire of the West, Switzerland was occupied by the German Confederation of the Alemanni, by the Burgundians and by the Lombards. By the year 534, under the successors of Clovis, it had become a part of the empire of the Franks. Under Charlemagne's successors it was divided between the Kingdom of France and the German Empire, but ultimately the whole country fell to Germany. Under most of the German sovereigns, however, the dependence of Switzerland on Germany was merely nominal, and the local governors conducted themselves as sovereign princes and compelled the inhabitants of their districts to acknowledge them as lords. It was very unwillingly that the Swiss submitted to the rule of these imperial vassals, and in the thirteenth century this unwillingness resulted in the formation,

by the three forest cantons of Uri, Unterwalden and Schwyz, of a league to resist the usurpations of the Austrians. Open hostilities began in 1315, and the struggle which followed is remarkable for the bravery and heroism of the Swiss. It is to the period just preceding the first victory of the Swiss at Morgarten in November, 1315, that the legend of William Tell belongs (See TELL, WILLIAM). The victory at Morgarten relieved the Swiss cantons for seventy years of any invasions by the Austrians, and when, in 1386, war broke out, the outcome was similar to that of the earlier campaign, for in the Battle of Sempach (1386) and of Näfels (1388) the Austrians were completely defeated. It was in the Battle of Sempach that legend tells that Arnold Winkelried sacrificed his life for the sake of his country. Meanwhile new districts had been added to the league, and in the period that followed the Battle of Sempach the Swiss Confederation gradually wrested from Austria much of its power.

The third war with Austria terminated in 1460 in favor of the Confederation, which obtained Thurgau, Austria being thus deprived of all its possessions in the territory which modern Switzerland includes. In 1474, at the instigation of Louis XI of France, the Swiss turned their arms against Charles the Bold of Burgundy, invading his country and defeating his army. Charles, in turn, invaded Switzerland, but the Swiss were again completely victorious and inflicted defeats on the Burgundians at Granson and at Morat and assisted in the final defeat of Charles at Nancy, in 1477. In 1481 Fribourg and Solothurn became members of the confederacy, which about this time began to make defensive alliances with the neighboring states.

The last war with Austria broke out in 1499. The struggle was severe, but the Swiss were finally the victors in six hard-fought battles, and by the Peace of Basel they were practically separated from the Empire, a separation to which, however, formal and international sanction was not given until 1648. Early in the sixteenth century Basel, Schaffhausen and Appenzell were admitted into the federation, and the number of cantons was thus brought up to thirteen, at which it remained until 1798.

In 1519 the doctrines of the Protestants were first promulgated in Switzerland by Zwingli (See ZWINGLI, ULRIC). Protestantism spread rapidly through the country, especially in the northern counties, and in 1531 the religious differences of the country had become so pronounced that war broke out between the Catholics and the Protestants. The Protestants were defeated at Kappel, and Zwingli was killed. By the Peace of Westphalia, which in 1648 closed the Thirty Years' War, Switzerland was declared to be wholly independent of the German Empire.

Through the remainder of the seventeenth and the greater part of the eighteenth centuries considerable disorder existed in Switzerland. The religious and political differences of the cantons virtually prevented peaceful growth. In the last years of the eighteenth century the ferment of the French Revolution spread to Switzerland, and in 1798 the ancient confederation was replaced by the Helvetic Republic, which lasted four years. In 1803 Napoleon organized a new confederation, with nineteen cantons, and in 1814, by the Congress of Vienna, four other cantons were added. The Congress of Vienna acknowledged the independence of the confederacy and proclaimed its perpetual neutrality and the inviolability of its soil. Again in 1830 and in 1848, Switzerland was affected by the revolutionary movement in France, and a new federal constitution was introduced in the latter year. This constitution remained in force until 1874, when it gave place to the present constitution. Under this instrument Switzerland has attained prosperity and has won the respect of the world. In 1891 a celebration was held of the six hundredth anniversary of the old Swiss League. Population in 1910, 3,741,971. Consult Mrs. Arnold Hug's *Switzerland*, in the Story of the Nations Series; also A. T. Storey's *Swiss Life in Town and Country*.

Sword, *sord*, a weapon used in hand-to-hand encounters, consisting of a steel blade and a hilt, or handle, for wielding it. The blade may be either straight or curved, one-edged or two-edged, sharp at the end, for thrusting, or blunt. The ancient Greek swords were of bronze and later of iron. The Romans in the time of Polybius (150 B. C.) had short, straight swords, of finely tempered steel. The straight, long sword was used by the Christians of the West in the Middle Ages, while the Poles and all the tribes of Slavonic origin employed, and still prefer, the crooked sword, or scimitar, which was also used by the Saracens and is still the common sword in the East. The double-handed sword of the Middle Ages was an unwieldy weapon, and probably originated from the wearing of plate armor. The sword is of much less importance in warfare than formerly, but European cavalry are still armed with it. The use of the sword

has been abolished in the United States army, and the saber takes its place as an accouterment for officers. The saber is 30, 32 or 34 inches in length. From the former importance of the sword, it came to be connected with various matters of ceremonial, and it is the emblem of power, or authority, or of triumph and protection. Damascus, Toledo and Milan were anciently famous for their sword blades.

Swordfish, *sord' fish*, a fish allied to the mackerel. There is but one species, and that occurs in the Mediterranean Sea and the Atlantic Ocean. It attains a length of from twelve to fifteen, or even twenty, feet, the elongated upper jaw, or sword, forming about one-half of its length. Its body is covered with minute scales. Its color is a bluish-black, above, and silvery white on the under parts. To kill it with the harpoon is considered fine sport by the Neapolitan and Sicilian fishermen, who prize its flesh. The swordfish attacks other fishes with its powerful weapon and often inflicts fatal wounds. Even the timbers of ships have been found to be perforated by the sword-like jaw, which has been broken off and left sticking in the wood.

Syb'aris, an ancient Greek city, located at the southern extremity of Italy, on the Gulf of Tarentum, supposed to have been built about 720 B. C. It rose to an extraordinary degree of prosperity, and in ancient times the inhabitants were famed for their luxury. At the time of its greatest strength, it was an important commercial center and had strong democratic tendencies. But little is known of the history of Sybaris, except that during the sixth century B. C. it became one of the most powerful and wealthy of the Grecian cities. It was destroyed by the Crotonians, who turned the waters of the river Crathis against it in 510 B. C. Excavations since 1879 have brought to light the site of the ancient city. But little of interest has been found, however.

Syc'amore, a wide-spreading tree, cultivated in Palestine and the countries of the eastern Mediterranean. The wood is regarded as indestructible, from the fact that it was used by the ancient Egyptians in making mummy cases. In England the tree called the sycamore is a maple. In the United States the sycamore is the buttonwood or plane tree. See PLANE TREE.

Syd'ney, the capital of New South Wales and the chief naval station of Australia, situated on the southern shore of Port Jackson, 5 mi. from the entrance of the harbor. The city has a beautiful site on a land-locked harbor with rocky shores, and it is defended by modern fortifications. The new town is well laid out and contains a number of public gardens and promenades. In the center of the city is Hyde Park, from which the principal streets lead. The chief buildings are the government building, the parliament house, the mint and the city library, together with the buildings of some of the public institutions, including a museum, a school of art and several hospitals and asylums. The leading educational institution is the University of Sydney, in Victoria Park, and among the churches, the Cathedral of Saint Andrew and the Roman Catholic Cathedral of Saint Mary are worthy of mention. The manufactures include machinery, foundry products, cars, locomotives, stoves, boots and shoes, clothing, textiles, tobacco and malt liquors.

Sydney is the seat of government for New South Wales and is the oldest city in Australia, having been founded in 1788 as a penal colony. In 1842 it was incorporated as a city, and after the discovery of gold in the colony, in 1851, it grew rapidly. Next to Melbourne, it is the most important city of Australia. It is connected by steamship with all the important ports and has an extensive trade. Population in 1911, of Sydney proper, 112,921; including the suburbs Balmain, North Sydney, Paddington, Redfern, Glebe and a number of others, 629,503.

Sydney, the county-seat of Cape Breton co., Nova Scotia, situated on Cape Breton Island, at the head of an excellent harbor, 275 mi. n. e. of Halifax. It is near extensive coal mines, to which it owes much of its prosperity. It is the terminus of the Intercolonial and the Sydney and Glace Bay railways. The chief industries are shipbuilding, meat packing and the manufacture of iron and steel. It is the chief town of Cape Breton Island and is a naval station of some importance. Population in 1911, 17,800.

Syllogism, *sil'lo jiz'm,* in logic, a form of reasoning or argument, consisting of three parts, the first two of which are known as *premises* and the third as the *conclusion*, which is derived by joining in thought the two premises. Each premise contains two terms, of which one is common to both and is the means of bringing together the other terms. This common element is called the *middle term.* The subject of the conclusion is known as the *minor term*, and the predicate, as the *major term.* Correspondingly, the proposition containing the minor term is the *minor premise*, and the proposition

containing the major term is the *major premise.* In arranging the syllogism, it is customary to place the major premise first. The following is a good illustration of the arrangement and the method of combining the terms in a syllogism:

Autumn comprises September, October and November. (*Major Premise.*)

In the north central states the pleasantest season is autumn. (*Minor Premise.*)

Therefore, in the north central states the pleasantest season comprises September, October and November. (*Conclusion.*)

Here the middle term, *autumn*, brings into necessary connection the minor term, *in the north central states the pleasantest season,* and the major term, *September, October and November.*

There are six rules for the construction of a syllogism:

(1) Every syllogism must have three terms; no more, no less. If there were, for example, four terms, there would be no middle term, and consequently no conclusion would be possible.

(2) Every syllogism must have but three propositions. If there were more than three propositions, there would be more than three terms, and Rule 1 would be violated.

(3) The middle term must be distributed; that is, it must be referred to as a whole at least once in the premise.

(4) No term that is not distributed in one of the premises must be distributed in the conclusion. The error to which disregard of this rule leads is illustrated in the syllogism:

All rabbits are rodent mammals.

No hares are rabbits.

Therefore, no hares are rodent mammals.

Here the major term, *rodent mammals*, which is not referred to universally in the major premise, is distributed in the conclusion; that is, an assertion has been made concerning the entire class of rodent mammals, namely, that hares do not belong to this class, which is false.

(5) No conclusion can be drawn from negative premises. For example, if A is not B, and E is not F, no inference of the relation between A and F can be made.

(6) If one premise is negative, the conclusion must be negative.

Sylves'ter II (999–1003), pope, was born in Auvergne and at an early age entered the monastery of Saint Gerard in Aurillac. He was made archbishop of Ravenna in 998 and in the following year was raised to the papacy. He had the reputation of being the most learned man of his time, maintained the power of the Church, was a great promoter of learning and composed a number of works, particularly on arithmetic and geometry.

Sym'bol, a sign by which one knows or infers a thing; an *emblem*. It is generally a definite, visible figure intended to represent or stand for something else. The common *astronomical symbols* are signs conveniently representing such things as astronomical objects, phases of the moon and astronomical terms. Some of these symbols are so ancient that we can find no satisfactory account of their origin. The symbols for the chief heavenly bodies are as follows: Sun, ☉, Mercury ☿, Venus ♀, Earth ♁ and ⊕, Moon ☽, Mars ♂, Ceres ⚳, Pallas ⚴, Juno ⚵, Vesta ⚶, Jupiter ♃, Saturn ♄, Uranus ♅, Neptune ♆, Star ✶. Each asteroid, except those given above, is represented by a circle, with a special number within it. The phases of the moon are indicated in this manner: ● new moon; ☽ moon in first quarter; ◉ full moon; ☾ moon in last quarter.

The *mathematical symbols* are the numerous ones used to make operations in mathematics easier. Some are mere symbols of value, like the numerals and the letters of the alphabet; others are of operation, such as +, the sign of addition; —, of subtraction; ×, of multiplication, and ÷, of division. There are also signs of deduction, such as ∴ (therefore), and of aggregation ([ ]). Besides these, there are the signs of denominate numbers and the special signs used in geometry, trigonometry and the other branches of mathematics, all of which may be easily found in any good text-books on the subjects.

Sym'pathet'ic Nerves. See NERVOUS SYSTEM, subhead *Sympathetic System*.

Synagogue, *sin'a gog*, the recognized place of public worship among the Jews. It is supposed to have originated during the Babylonish captivity. The synagogues were so constructed that the worshipers, as they entered and as they prayed, looked toward Jerusalem. At the extreme east end was the holy ark, containing copies of the Pentateuch; in front of this was the raised platform, for the reader or preacher. The men sat on one side of the synagogue, and the women sat on the other, a partition 5 or 6 feet high dividing them. The chief seats, after which the scribes and Pharisees strove, were situated near the east end. The constitution of the synagogue was congregational, not priestly, and the officebearers were not hereditary, but were chosen by the congregation. A college of elders managed the affairs of the synagogue and possessed the power of excommunication. The officiating minister was the chief reader of the prayers, the law and the prophets. The servant of the synagogue, who had general charge of the building, generally acted on week days as schoolmaster to the young of the congregation. The right of instruction was not strictly confined to the regularly appointed teachers, but the ruler of the synagogue might call upon any one present to address the people, or even a stranger might volunteer to speak. The modern synagogue differs little from the ancient. Instead of elders, there is a committee of management; and the women are now provided with seats in a low, latticed gallery. The *Great Synagogue* was an assembly, or council, of 120 members, said to have been founded and presided over by Ezra after the return from the captivity. Their duties are supposed to have been the remodeling of the religious life of the people and the collecting and editing of the sacred books of former times.

Synchronograph, *sin'kro no graf*, an apparatus used in machine telegraphy, for the rapid transmission of signals by means of an alternating current. The effect is produced by a metallic disk, mounted on the same axis with the generator that supplies the current or on another axis, whose relative speed to that of the generator is known. The current is supplied to this disk through a brush, which comes in contact with the circumference. The opening and closing of the circuit is produced by a perforated tape, passing between the brush and the circumference of the disk. The synchronograph can be used with most forms of receiver employed in machine telegraphy, and as many as four thousand words a minute have been transmitted by it, though this record was made during a special experiment, and it is somewhat higher than can be obtained in regular work. See TELEGRAPH.

Syncope, *sin'ko pe*. See FAINTING.

Syndicalism, a term denoting the revolutionary activities of one wing of the labor movement. It seeks the overthrow of present economic conditions, substituting therefor the industrial commonwealth, in which labor shall have control of all the means of production and appropriate to itself all the profits arising therefrom. Syndicalism teaches that there are only two classes in modern society—the capitalists and the laboring classes. There being no bond of sympathy between them, labor can only secure the enjoyment of its rights by the overthrow of the capitalist class. Hence it advocates industrial war. It would organize labor in industrial unions—based on industries as a unit, not labor unions—drilling and preparing them by incessant strikes, seeking to win their strikes by "direct action" (which means all sorts of aggressive actions), until they are ready for the "general strike" to accomplish their great purpose.

Synge, John Millington (1871–1909), Irish dramatist and poet, born in Dublin and educated there at Trinity College. After spending a number of years in Paris, he returned to Ireland, where he soon became associated with W. B. Yeats and Lady Gregory in the movement for the revival of the Irish drama and language. His first plays, *Riders to the Sea* and *In the Shadow of the Glen*, produced in 1905, are remarkable for their sense of the overpowering simplicity of tragedy. *The Playboy of the Western World*, though not his best work, is best-known. *Deirdre*, a play based on a classic Irish legend, is undoubtedly his greatest achievement. *The Well of the Saints, The Tinker's Wedding*, a few short poems and essays and a volume on *The Aran Islands* are his other writings. A man of great imagination and remarkable delicacy of style, Synge is by many considered the greatest of Irish poets of his time.

Syn'thesis, the union of various elements to form a compound. In philosophy, the term is applied to the process by which a conclusion is reached through the building of a system of reasoning upon certain premises. It is, therefore, opposite to analysis, which consists in finding the elements or facts or characteristics of which a conclusion or notion is composed. In chemistry synthesis consists in building up a complicated compound from certain elements, and in this case, also, it is opposite to analysis, which consists in the separating of a compound into its constituents.

Syr'acuse, a city of Italy, situated on the e. coast of the island of Sicily, 30 mi. s. s. e. of Catania. The town is built upon the little island of Ortugia, and is connected with the mainland by a mole. The present town is of little importance. The buildings of interest are the cathedral, built about an ancient Doric temple, a building known as the Temple of Diana, and a few old palaces. The city contains a museum of antiquities that is of great interest. Ancient Syracuse at one time had over 500,000 inhabitants and was the most important city of the western Grecian world. Most of the ancient town was on a high, triangular plateau, with precipitous sides. The colony was founded by the Corinthians under Archias, 734 b. c. It was captured by the Romans, after a three years' siege, in 212 b. c., and it continued as a Roman possession until the downfall of the Empire. In 878 the city was destroyed by the Saracens, and the main portion of it has never been rebuilt. Population, about 21,000.

Syr'acuse, N. Y., the county-seat of Onondaga, co., situated at the foot of Onondaga Lake, 148 mi. w. by n. from Albany and about the same distance east of Buffalo, on the New York Central, the West Shore and the Lackawanna railroads, and on the Erie and the Oswego canals. The city is built upon a series of low hills and has a beautiful location. It has a large number of public parks, some of which are only small plots at the intersection of streets; but Burnet Park, on the west, contains over 100 acres, and Lincoln Park, on the east, has about 20 acres. The state fair grounds are also located here and are maintained by the state of New York. The most important public buildings are the city hall, the court house, the Federal building, the new high school, a Carnegie library, the state asylum for feeble-minded children, the county orphan asylum and the buildings of Syracuse University. See Syracuse University.

Syracuse is the fourth city in the state in industrial importance. Its industries include the manufacture of clothing, machinery, iron and steel, malt liquors, steel pipe, automobiles and automobile accessories, chemicals, pottery, boots and shoes, agricultural implements and typewriters, in which it excels any other city. The salt industry is extensive. The salt is procured from springs on the borders of Onondaga Lake, and the industry has been maintained from the earliest times. Though it has somewhat fallen off in recent years, the annual production is about 2,000,000 bushels. Near the city are extensive works for the manufacture of soda, coke, tar, ammonia, carbolic acid, nitric acid and other chemicals.

Syracuse is on land formerly occupied by the Onondaga indians. The locality was visited by a Jesuit missionary in 1642. The first settlement at Syracuse proper was made in 1805, but the town did not reach any importance until after the completion of the Erie Canal. It was incorporated as a village in 1825, and in 1847 it was chartered as a city. Population in 1910, 137,249.

Syracuse University, an institution of higher learning, founded at Syracuse, N. Y., in 1870, under the auspices of the Methodist Episcopal Church. It comprises the college of liberal arts, the college of fine arts, the college of medicine, the college of law and the college of applied science. It has a graduate department, conferring the master's and doctor's degrees, and it maintains a summer session of six weeks and a table at the marine biological laboratory at Wood's Hole, Mass. An observing station of the United States Weather Bureau was established here in 1902. On the campus there has been erected the largest stadium in the United States. It has a faculty of 250; an attendance of over 3500 and a library of over 90,000 volumes.

Syr-Darya, *seer dahr′ya,* or **Sir-Daria** or **Sihon,** a river of western Asia, which rises on the west slope of the Thian-Shan Mountains and flows westward, then northwestward, into the Sea of Aral. It is about 1200 miles long and is the largest river of Asiatic Russia, though it is of little value to navigation.

Syr′ia, that portion of Asiatic Turkey bounded on the n. by the Taurus Mountains, on the e. by the Syrian Desert, on the s. by Arabia, on the s. w. by Egypt and on the w. by the Mediterranean Sea. Its area is variously estimated at from 75,000 to 109,000 sq. mi. For surface, climate, products and cities, see TURKEY.

At an early period in its history Syria became a part of the Assyrian Empire, and it afterwards passed, successively, to the Persians, the Greeks and the Romans; then it formed a part of the Byzantine Empire; in 1036 it was captured by the Arabs; in 1078, by the Seljuk Turks, and a little over 200 years later, by the Crusaders, who remained in possession of Jerusalem until 1293. After this, through the capture by the Mamelukes, Syria became united with Egypt, and through Egypt, to the Turkish Empire, to which it was added in 1517. It was conquered by Mehemet Ali in 1833, but was restored to Turkey seven years later, and it has remained under Turkish dominion ever since. The country has been disturbed by rebellions and wars a number of times, but whenever these were serious they have been quelled by the assistance of European powers.

Great interest attaches to Syria, because it was the original home of the Hebrews, the Hittites, the Phoenicians and other nations connected with Old Testament history. It was within this region that Abraham dwelt, that the Hebrew kingdom was established and that David and Solomon reigned. Later that portion known as Palestine drew the attention of the world, because it was the land in which Jesus Christ lived and in which Christianity was founded.

Syr′iac, a dialect or branch of the Aramaic, and thus one of the Semitic family of languages. It was a vernacular dialect in Syria during the early centuries of the Christian era, but it ceased to be spoken as a living language about the tenth century, being crowded out by that of the Arabian conquerors. A very corrupted form of it, however, is still spoken by a few scattered tribes, principally by the Nestorians, of Kurdistan and Persia. Syriac literature had its rise in the first century A. D. At first it was chiefly connected with theological and ecclesiastical subjects, Biblical translations and commentaries, hymns and liturgies, but in course of time it embraced history, philosophy, grammar, medicine and the natural sciences. The oldest extant work in the language is an incomplete translation of the Bible. The greater part of the Syriac literature has been lost, but much valuable material still remains unedited.

Syrian Christians or **Church of the Syrian Rite,** that section of the Christian Church which had its stronghold in Syria, and which was originally included in the patriarchate of Antioch, and subsequently in that of Jerusalem. Up to the end of the fourth century, the Syrian Church was in a very flourishing condition, having at that time a membership of several millions; but controversies arising over the incarnation, it split up into several sects, such as the Maronites, in Lebanon; the Jacobites, in Mesopotamia; the Christians of Saint Thomas, in India, and the Nestorians, in Kurdistan. The term Syrian Christians is frequently specially applied to the latter community.

Sy′ros. See SYRA.

Szegedin, *seg′ed en,* a city of Hungary, situated on the west bank of the Theiss, at its junction with the Maros, 96 mi. s. e. of Budapest. It is the second city in population in the kingdom and is in the midst of an extensive fertile region. The city was nearly destroyed by fire in 1879 and has been rebuilt on modern plans. It has broad streets, numerous public squares and a number of fine public buildings, including the townhall, the government buildings and a theater. The river is lined with excellent wharves, and the city has an extensive trade. The chief industries include the manufacture of soap and prepared foods. Population in 1910, 118,-328.

T, the twentieth letter in the English alphabet, resembles in form the Phoenician character from which, through the Greek and Latin, it is derived, and with which it is identical in sound. In its phonetic value *t* corresponds most nearly to *d*, and the two are often interchanged in related languages. In combinations with *h*, *t* is pronounced in two ways, as in *thought* and as in *this*. When followed by *i*, *t* often has the sound of *sh*, as in *motion*, and in some words it is silent, as in *listen*.

Tab′ernacle, in Jewish antiquities, the tent or sanctuary in which the sacred utensils were kept during the wanderings of the Israelites in the desert. It was in the shape of a parallelogram, 45 feet long and 15 feet wide, and it was 15 feet high. Its smaller ends were placed east and west, and its entrance was in the east. Its framework consisted of forty-eight gilded boards of shittim-wood, bound together by golden rings and set into silver sockets. The ceiling and walls

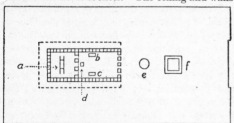

PLAN OF TABERNACLE

a. Ark in the Holy of Holies.
b. Table of show-bread.
c. Golden candlestick.
d. Altar of incense.
e. Laver, or basin for washing.
f. Altar of burnt offering.

were covered with a curtain of linen, made in ten pieces. Outside this was a curtain of goats' hair, made in eleven pieces. Over this covering was thrown one made of skins. The interior was divided by a curtain into two compartments, the outer, the "sanctuary" proper, and the inner, the holy of holies. In the sanctuary was placed, on the north, the table of showbread; on the south, the golden candlestick, and in the middle, near the inner curtain, the altar of in-

cense. In the center of the holy of holies stood the ark of the covenant. The tabernacle was situated in a court 150 feet long and 75 feet wide, surrounded by costly screens 7½ feet high, supported by pillars of brass 7½ feet apart, to which the curtains were attached by hooks and fillets of silver. In the outer, or eastern, half of the court stood the altar of burnt offering, and between it and the tabernacle itself was the laver, at which the priests washed their hands and feet before entering the sanctuary. On the first day of the second year after the Israelites left Egypt, the tabernacle was dedicated. During all their wanderings a cloud rested on it by day, a pillar of fire by night. The Levites had charge of it, taking it down and putting it up at the various stopping places. The tabernacle lost its value and glory after the Philistines captured the ark. It was superseded by the Temple, at Jerusalem.

Tabernacles, Feast of, the last of the three great festivals of the Jews (the Passover, the Feast of Weeks, or Pentecost, and the Feast of Tabernacles), which required the presence of all the males in Jerusalem. Its object was to commemorate the dwelling of the Israelites in tents during their sojourn in the wilderness, and it was also a feast of thanksgiving for the harvest and vintage. The time of the festival fell in the autumn, when all the chief fruits were gathered in, and hence it is often called the "feast of the ingathering." Its duration was strictly only seven days, but it was followed by a day of holy convocation of peculiar solemnity. During the seven days the people lived in booths erected in the courts of houses, on the roofs and in the court of the Temple. It was the most joyous festival of the year.

Table Mountain, a mountain situated in South Africa, overlooking Cape Town and Table Bay. Its height is 3582 feet. It takes its name from its peculiar shape, having a broad, flat top. Table Mountain adjoins Devil's Mount, on the east, and the Sugarloaf, on the west. It is frequently covered with a white cloud, which is called the "tablecloth."

Taboo', a word used to indicate any object which by religious command may not be touched. The art and the practice were most common in the South Sea Islands. The taboo is applied not only to things which, because of their evil nature, it is unsafe to come in contact with, but also to things which are sacred. Thus, the person of the chief or king is usually tabooed, as is any piece of consecrated ground. In former times in Polynesia, where the taboo was most in force, the penalty for breaking it was often death; in minor cases, the penalty was a confiscation of the goods of the guilty man. Of course the practice was much abused, and it gave a priest or chief almost unlimited power over his people and enabled him by pronouncing a certain object tabooed, to gain possession of it for himself.

Tabor, *tah'bor,* MOUNT, a mountain situated in the northern part of Palestine, on the shores of the Lake of Galilee. It rises almost abruptly from the plain of Esdraelon to a height of about 1000 feet, and it forms nearly a perfect cone. The altitude of the summit above sea level is about 1850 feet. From the summit an extensive view of the surrounding country can be obtained. Recent excavations show that the sides of the mountain contain many remains of ancient structures, and this mountain is supposed by some to be the scene of the Transfiguration.

Tabriz, *tah breez',* or **Tebriz,** a city of Persia, located on an elevation about 4500 feet above the sea, 30 mi. e. of Lake Urumia. It is surrounded upon three sides by hills. Many ruins attest the destruction caused by earthquakes, showing that it was formerly of much greater importance than at present. There is but little of interest within the city, the chief object being the large, blue mosque. The suburbs are beautified by gardens and orchards. Much of its former commerce has been diverted to ports on the Caspian Sea. Its leading articles of export are grapes, shawls and rugs. Population, estimated at 170,000.

Tacitus, *tas'e tus,* PUBLIUS CORNELIUS (about 55–about 117), a Roman historian. Of his education and early life, little is known. He seems to have been first appointed to public office in the reign of Vespasian. Under Titus, by whom he was treated with distinguished favor, he became quaestor or aedile; he was praetor under Domitian, and he was consul under Nerva. In 78 he married the daughter of Gnaeus Julius

Agricola, the celebrated statesman and general whose life he afterward wrote. He was several years absent from Rome on provincial business, and he probably then made the acquaintance of the German peoples. After his return to Rome he lived in the closest intimacy with the younger Pliny, and he had a very extensive law practice, acquiring a high reputation as an orator. Four works from his pen are still extant: his *Annals,* in sixteen books (of which books, seven to ten, inclusive, are lost), which contain an account of the principal events in Roman history, from the time of the death of Augustus to that of Nero; his *Histories,* of which there are extant only four books and a part of the fifth, which treat of the year 69 and a part of 70; his *Germania,* an account of the geography, manners and institutions of the various German tribes, and his *Agricola,* a masterpiece of biography. His style is exceedingly concise, so much so as to make it often difficult to gather his full meaning without great care. He had a wonderful knowledge of men, and he excelled as a character painter.

Tacking, in navigation, an operation by which a ship is enabled to beat up against a wind, by a series of zigzag courses, the sails being turned obliquely to the wind, first on one side and then on the other. *Going about* is another term for tacking, and while the change is in progress the vessel is said to be *in stays.*

Tacoma, WASH., the county-seat of Pierce co., 28 mi. s. of Seattle, is at the head of Commencement Bay, on Puget Sound and on the Tacoma Eastern, the Oregon & Washington and several divisions of the Northern Pacific railroads. The city has one of the finest harbors in the world and a beautiful location along the bay. The snow-capped Olympic Mountains stretch along the west, and Mount Ranier, locally known as Mount Tacoma, rises to a height of over 14,000 feet on the southeast. The Puyallup River empties into the bay here and helps to form the spacious harbor. Many steamship lines connect the city with all parts of the world, more than twenty boats making regular trips to the Orient alone. The city is near one of the richest farming regions of the Northwest, containing, also, valuable timber lands and extensive coal mines. Along the harbor are many large electrically operated coal bunkers and immense grain elevators. In the exportation of wheat, Tacoma is the second largest port on the Pacific coast; the other leading articles of trade are flour, lumber, fish and fruit. The chief manufactories are of lumber and lumber products; other large industrial plants include flour mills, foundries, car and machine shops, smelters, refineries, shipyards, and manufactories of furniture, wagons and various other articles.

The city is an important educational center. Here are the University of Puget Sound, Pacific University, Washington College, Whitworth College, Vashon College, Annie Wright Seminary, Academy of Visitation and Tacoma Academy. The public high school has a manual training department; a Carnegie library and the Ferry Museum of Art are also important educational features. There are two large parks, Wright and Point Defiance, the latter containing about 660 acres. The state hospital for the insane is located a few miles southwest, and the city also contains three hospitals and an orphanage. The other important structures are the city hall, the courthouse, the chamber of commerce, the Union Club House, the Northern Pacific Railway building, the Tacoma Theater, the Tacoma Hotel and the high school. The place was settled about 1869. It was made the terminus of the Northern Pacific Railroad in 1873 and was organized as a city ten years later, by the consolidation of New Tacoma and Old Tacoma. The city more than doubled its population between 1900 and 1910. Population in 1910, 83,743.

Tacon'ic Mountains, a range of mountains forming a part of the boundary between New York and Massachusetts and extending northward into Vermont, where they connect with the Green Mountains. The Taconic range is an eastern extension of the highlands of the Hudson. The mountains are low, with rounded tops, and their sides are generally covered with forests or cultivated fields.

Tac'tics, the science and art of conducting a battle.

MILITARY TACTICS. Three different arms of the service, each complete in itself, are to be used separately and in combination (See INFANTRY; CAVALRY; ARTILLERY). *Infantry* is slow in its movements, but gives a resistless rifle fire and can be used where neither cavalry nor artillery can advance. At a distance of 900 yards, modern rifle fire is decisive, but it can be used to some effect at a distance of over one and a half miles. It is customary for infantry to advance in columns until they reach the zone of firing, and then to spread into a single, open-order line, so that a volley may not be so destructive. Each subdivision has been assigned, before entering action, a definite

part of the enemy's lines as its target; but the range not being known, it must be assumed. The advance of the infantry is usually by short rushes, under the protection of rough ground, trees, buildings or whatsoever may be used to advantage. Between advances the men lie down behind ridges or hastily built defenses of earth and deliver their fire, either in volleys or in a certain number of rounds at will. Each man must think for himself, as it is impossible to keep any definite formation. At a distance of 900 yards, as has been said, the advance is usually broken, or the defenders are forced to retreat from their position. All the time while leading up to this climax of the battle, a steady fire has been kept up, and the line of the enemy has been continually searched for weakened spots, on which the fire might be concentrated. It often happens that in the ardor of an infantry charge, the men are carried to close quarters with the enemy and even scale the wall of the defense, especially when it has been weakened or broken by artillery fire.

Cavalry has its chief advantage in its swiftness, and its chief use, therefore, is before the main battle or after the climax has passed, in pursuing a retreating enemy or in covering the retreat of its friends. If the main battle is on an open plain, cavalry can advance at will, but it forms an easy target for the enemy's artillery and could not, while armed only with swords and lances, be relied upon to defeat a strong infantry force. When cavalry meets cavalry, the first shock usually is decisive, though sometimes a hand-to-hand conflict follows, in which individual prowess wins. Sometimes cavalry makes a successful dash against artillery, particularly if it can reach the rear and unprotected side of the batteries. The cavalry usually acts in coöperation with the artillery and follows up by its charges the effective work of the great guns.

Field artillery cannot protect itself on the flanks nor change position without pausing in its fire, and accordingly it is oftentimes at a disadvantage; but when placed properly and well served, it is an indispensable thing in the opening of a battle, where its great powers of destruction pave the way for the infantry and cavalry. Moreover, it forms the most effective cover for the retreat of its own army. Field guns are usually placed on a height, with a wide outlook, or they may be concealed behind a hill or obstruction, where, by an indirect fire over this protection, they reach the enemy.

The first shots are experimental, but the officers observe the direction and range through their field glasses, and they direct the aim for more accurate marksmanship. No other branch of the service requires such careful drill, for the artilleryman must not only handle his gun with skill, but the officers must understand thoroughly the theory of projectiles, must be able to put this theory in practice and must show good judgment in the location of batteries and in the direction of the fire.

After all, there are many elements, besides the general effectiveness of the three arms of the service, that enter into the decision of a modern battle. The personnel of the officers, the careful preparation, the element of surprise in the enemy's movements and the unknown conditions of ground, all call for well-balanced judgment and quick decision on the part of the commanders. The spirit and training of the troops, the relation between them and the subordinate commanders and the health of the men, are also important factors.

NAVAL TACTICS. As in land operations, the commander in a battle at sea tries to hold off the enemy at every point, and so to overmatch him in one particular place that the line of battle can be broken. If once, in a sea fight, the line of battle is broken, it gives a much better opportunity than in land combat to destroy the disordered forces. The invention of steam changed the whole form of naval tactics, because it then became unnecessary to maneuver for the wind; and the continued improvements in naval artillery practically did away with the necessity of meeting at close quarters. The invention of the *Monitor* and other ironclads made the wooden vessel of little importance; and more recently the torpedo boats and submarines have made the life of even the giant battleship insecure. In a modern sea fight all the various ships, each armed in its own peculiar way, must be maneuvered so as to use its points to the greatest advantage, guarding its weaknesses and taking advantage of its points of superiority wherever possible. The sea affords no shelter for troops and gives little opportunity for concealing the size of the forces or the plan of battle. Some vessels are so arranged that they can fire straight ahead or astern, rather than broadside, and such ones are used in a way to profit by that quality. But in the majority of cases the greatest power of a vessel is in its broadside fire, as every vessel avoids, if possible, being struck by shot which travel its entire length. Ships in battle usually pass each other in column; if two alone be fighting, both sail in circles; if the attack is made against coast defense or against a stationary fleet, all sail in the form of an ellipse, these maneuvers bringing the most guns into action to the best advantage. Close quarters are always avoided, for fear of torpedoes, which consequently are used chiefly at night. The great warships are rather unwieldy, as they cannot be stopped or turned in several times their own length, so that it is dangerous to change speed or formation in the heat of battle. In the United States navy, a fleet is divided into *squadrons* of from two to eight ships; a *division* is half a squadron of six ships or more, and a *section* is made up of two ships of a squadron. When all the ships of a fleet are advancing abreast, they are said to be arranged *in line*; they are *in column* when they advance in single file, and they are in *echelon* when all advance along a course diagonal to the line which would pass through all the ships.

Taf'feta, a term which has been applied to various kinds of plain silks, but which is applied to-day to a specific variety, which is thin, glossy and of a fine, plain weave, distinguished from grosgrain, corded silk, and from surah, twilled silk.

Taft, LORADO (1860–   ), an American sculptor, born at Elmwood, Ill. In 1879 he graduated at the University of Illinois, and in the following year he went to Paris, where he studied for three years at the Ecole des Beaux-Arts. In 1886 he settled in Chicago, where he became instructor in sculpture in the Art Institute and lecturer in the university extension department of the University of Chicago. His works comprise a statue of Schuyler Colfax, in Indianapolis; a statue of General Grant, and decorations for the Horticultural Building at the World's Columbian Exposition, which included two groups, *The Sleep and the Awakening of the Flowers* and *The Painting of the Lily.* Taft is the author of the *History of American Sculpture,* the best work yet written on that subject.

Taft, WILLIAM HOWARD (1857–   ), American jurist and statesman, the twenty-seventh president of the United States, was born in Cincinnati, O., and educated at Yale University and at Cincinnati College, from whose Law School he graduated when twenty-three years of age. For the seven years following his graduation, Mr. Taft practiced law, and during this time was appointed to a number of minor offices. In 1887 he was appointed judge of the Supreme

Court of Cincinnati. Three years later he resigned to become solicitor-general of the United States, and in 1892 he was appointed United States circuit judge for the sixth circuit. Two years later he was urged by President McKinley to become president of the Philippine Commission, and resigned his position in the circuit court to accept the appointment. In July, 1901, Mr. Taft became first civil governor of the Philippines, and under his administration the plans for the government of the Islands, including the Philippine Congress and the appointment or election of many local officers, were projected and put into force. Mr. Taft's work in the Philippines is conceded by all to be the greatest piece of constructive

WILLIAM HOWARD TAFT

statesmanship of modern times. During this time he also visited Pope Leo XIII in Rome and made satisfactory arrangements with him about the purchase of extensive tracts of land held in the Philippines by various Roman Catholic religious orders. In 1904 he was appointed secretary of war. In 1906 he was the agent of the United States for reintroducing American government into Cuba. He has also had much to do with establishing and carrying forward the work of the Panama Canal. In 1907 he again visited the Philippines to be present at the opening of the first Philippine Congress. On his return trip he visited the emperor of Japan and the czar of Russia. In the summer of 1908 he visited Panama and averted an insurrection, if not a war, between

164

that country and Colombia and Venezuela. In November, 1908, Taft was elected President of the United States. During his term of office the Payne-Aldrich Tariff Bill became a law, a corporation tax was provided, and an attempt made to negotiate a reciprocity treaty with Canada. The Payne-Aldrich law, though the result of popular demand for lower tariffs, materially increased many important duties. Besides the unpopularity of this law, the administration was injured by the withdrawal of Roosevelt's supporters from the Republican party. Though he was renominated for president by the Republicans, he was defeated at the polls. In the spring of 1913, after the expiration of his term of office, he accepted a professorship at Yale University.

Tahiti, *tah'he te,* **Archipelago.** See SOCIETY ISLANDS.

Tail'or Bird, a bird so named from its curious habit of sewing leaves together to form a nest. It belongs to the family of true warblers

TAILOR BIRD

and inhabits India and the Eastern Archipelago.

Taine, *tayn.* HIPPOLYTE ADOLPHE (1828-1893), a French historian and critic, born at Vouziers. In 1854 his first work, an *Essay on Livy,* was praised by the Academy; in 1864 he was appointed professor in the School of Fine Arts in Paris, and in 1878 he was elected to a seat in the Academy. His *History of English Literature,* one of the best and most philosophical works on the subject, appeared in 1864, and it was followed by *English Idealism, English Positivism, The Philosophy of Art, Notes on England* and *The Origin of Contemporary France,* this last a work of great research and value in three sections, dealing respectively with *The Ancient*

Régime, The Revolution and *The Modern Régime.*

Taj Mahal, *tahzh ma hahl',* a famous mausoleum in India, outside the city of Agra, built by Emperor Shah Jehan about 1650. This is a masterpiece of Indian architecture. It is of white marble, 185 feet square, situated in the center of a court 315 feet square. The four corners of this court are adorned with four elegant minarets, and over the whole is an exquisite white marble dome, 58 feet in diameter and 80 feet high, rising over four corner chapels, each crowned with a dome The interior decorations consist of beautiful stones in arabesque patterns, mosaics and inlaid work of unsurpassed beauty. It is said to have cost from $10,000,000 to $50,000,000. See ASIA, full-page plate, *Some Types of Civilization in Asia.*

Talc, a magnesian mineral, consisting of broad, flat, smooth layers or plates, soapy to the touch, of a shining luster; it is translucent and often transparent, when in very thin plates. There are three principal varieties of talc, *common, earthy* and *indurated.* Talc is a silicate of magnesium, with small quantities of potash, alumina, oxide of iron and water. It is used in many parts of India and China as a substitute for window glass. A variety of talc, called *French chalk,* or steatite, is used for tracing lines on wood and cloth.

Tal'ent, a unit of weight and money used by the Greeks, Hebrews and other ancient peoples. As a unit of both weight and value it varied widely among the Greek states, but two standards predominated. In one of these the talent weighed 37.8 kilograms, and in the other about 26 kilograms. Upon the latter unit the largest coin used by the Greeks was based, its value being a little more than $1000. As a weight among the Greeks it was divided into 60 *minas* and 6000 *drachmas.* The Romans also had monetary units called *great talents* and *little talents,* the former being worth about $480 and the latter about $365. In other countries at different times the talent varied in weight from 30 to 43 kilograms.

Tal'ipot Palm, the great fan palm, a native of Ceylon and India. The cylindrical trunk reaches a height of sixty to one hundred feet and is crowned with a tuft of fan-like leaves, usually about eight feet in length and fourteen feet in breadth. These leaves are used for covering houses, in making umbrellas and fans and as a substitute for paper. From the pith, a food resembling sago is made. When the tree has attained its full growth, the flower spike bursts from its envelope with a loud report. When the fruit has matured, the tree generally dies.

Talisman, *tal'iz man,* a figure cast or cut in metal or stone, and made, with certain superstitious ceremonies, at some particular moment of time, as when a certain star is at its culminating point, or when certain planets are in conjunction. The talisman thus prepared is supposed to exercise extraordinary influences over the bearer, particularly in averting disease. In a more extensive sense, the word is used, like amulet, to denote any object of nature or art, the presence of which checks the power of spirits or demons and defends the wearer from their malice. Relics, rosaries and images of saints were employed as talismans in the Middle Ages.

Tal'lade'ga, ALA., the county-seat of Talladega co., 60 mi. e. of Birmingham, on the Southern, the Louisville & Nashville and other railroads. The city is in a fertile agricultural region, producing vegetables, live stock and large quantities of cotton. In mineral resources the county is one of the richest in the state, and it contains coal, iron, marble and a fine limestone, which is used for lithographic work. The manufactories include cotton mills, machine shops, tanneries, grist mills and fertilizer factories. The state schools for the deaf, dumb and blind, Talladega College and Isbell Female College are located here. The municipality has electric and gas lights and owns and operates the waterworks. It is one of the oldest settlements in the state and is situated on the ground where General Jackson, with an army of state troops, defeated a force of Creek indians in 1813. Population in 1910, 5854.

Tal'lahas'see, FLA., the capital of the state and the county-seat of Leon co., 165 mi. e. of Jacksonville and 25 mi. n. of the Gulf of Mexico, on the Sea Board Air Line, the Georgia, Florida & Alabama and other railroads. The city has a fine location near picturesque lakes, and it contains broad and well-paved streets. The Florida State College for Women, the state normal and industrial college for colored students and the Leon County Academy are here. The city contains the Walker, the state and the supreme court libraries. Other prominent features are the state capitol, the courthouse, the postoffice and Bloxham Park. Cotton, tobacco, sugar cane and fruit are grown in the vicinity, and dairying and stock raising are also carried on. The principal manufactures are cigars and cottonseed oil. The site was chosen as the seat of the territorial government in 1822, the town was laid out in 1824 and the city was chartered in 1827. Population in 1910, 5018.

Talleyrand-Perigord, *tah la rahN' pa re gor',* CHARLES MAURICE, Duke de, Prince of Benevento (1754–1838), a French statesman. He was educated for the Church, and in 1788 he was consecrated bishop of Autun, despite the immorality of his life. On the meeting of the States-General in 1789, he was elected deputy for Autun, and in the following year he was elected president of the National Assembly. In 1791 he was sent to London, charged with diplomatic functions, and during his stay there he was proscribed for alleged royalist intrigues. Forced to leave England by the provisions of the Alien Act, in 1794 he sailed for the United States; but he returned to France in 1796, and in the following year he was appointed minister of foreign affairs.

He devoted himself entirely to Bonaparte, whom he had early recognized as the master spirit of the time, and after Bonaparte's return from Egypt, Talleyrand contributed greatly to the events which led to the fall of the Directory and the establishment of the Consulate. He was then reappointed minister of foreign affairs, and for the next few years he was the executor of all Napoleon's diplomatic schemes. After the establishment of the Empire, in 1804, he was appointed to the office of grand chamberlain, and in 1806 he was created prince of Benevento. After the Peace of Tilsit, in 1807, a coolness arose between him and Napoleon, and it became more and more marked. In 1809 he resigned his office, and in 1814 he helped to secure Napoleon's abdication. He took part in the Congress of Vienna, and in 1815, when the allies again entered Paris, he became minister of foreign affairs. After a short time he resigned this position and retired into private life. When the revolution of July, 1830, broke out, he advised Louis Philippe to accept the throne, and he held several diplomatic offices under the new government.

Tal'low, a solid fat, obtained from animals, especially cattle and sheep. It is obtained by subjecting the carcasses to steam heat in closed kettles. Beef tallow of the best quality comes from the fat around the kidneys; that of a cheaper grade is obtained from the caul and other tissues. Tallow is purified by being heated to a high temperature and then strained. When cold, it is white and hard, resembling lard, except that it is somewhat whiter. The most extensive use of tallow is in the manufacture of

soap. It is also employed to some extent in the manufacture of candles and in dressing leather. A specially prepared tallow is used in making oleomargarine. See OLEOMARGARINE.

Tallow Tree, the name of several trees which produce a tallow-like substance, used for making candles. One of the largest and most beautiful, and the most widely diffused, of the plants is found in China, where it is called the

TALLOW TREE

candle tree and the *wax tree*. From a remote period it has furnished the Chinese with the material out of which they make candles. The capsules and seeds are crushed together and boiled; the fatty matter is skimmed as it rises, and it condenses on cooling. The tallow tree has been introduced into the United States, and is almost naturalized along the low sea coasts of the Carolinas.

Talma, *tal mah',* FRANÇOIS JOSEPH (1763–1826), a French tragedian. In 1787 he made his début at the Comedie Française, but attracted no particular attention. His greatest successes were achieved at the Theatre de la Republique, which he, with his followers, founded in 1791. He enjoyed the intimacy of Napoleon and was the friend of Chénier, Danton, Camille Desmoulins and other revolutionists. Talma was the greatest modern tragic actor of France, and he was one of the earliest advocates of realism in scenery and costume.

Talmage, *tal'maje,* THOMAS DE WITT (1832–1902), an American pulpit orator, born at Bound Brook, N. J. After holding several charges he became pastor of an important Presbyterian church in Brooklyn (1869–1894), which came to be known as "The Tabernacle." Talmage soon earned the reputation of being a powerful preacher. The Tabernacle was burned and rebuilt in 1872 and 1889, but after the third loss by fire (1894), Talmage preached in the Academy of Music, New York City, and he then went to Washington, D. C., where he was assistant pastor of the First Presbyterian Church (1895–1899). He lectured in America and England. His sermons were published every week and were translated into many tongues. Many of them have been issued in volumes bearing fantastic titles. Talmage was editor of *The Christian at Work* (1873–1876), *The Advance* (1877–1878), *The Christian Herald* (1890–1902), and he was the author of several published works.

Tal'mud, THE, the body of the Jewish civil and canonical law not comprised in the Pentateuch. It consists of two parts, the Mishna, or the laws written in Hebrew, and the Gemara, or commentary on the law, written in Aramaic, into which crept many anecdotes, proverbs, legends and some history, till it might be called a cyclopedia of rabbinical knowledge. The former, comprising sixty-three treatises, is composed of six main divisions: (1) on tithes, agriculture, etc.; (2) on festivals, feasts and the Sabbath; (3) on marriage, vows and oaths; (4) on penal laws and ethics; (5) on sacrifices, including a description of the Temple of Jerusalem; (6) on purifications. The Gemara included the discussions on the Mishna by the rabbis of Babylon and Palestine, from the third to the sixth century, when the two were brought together in a final compilation. The Talmud is especially valuable to students of religion, history and language. Translations are found in English, French and German, and the study of it is spreading in England and the United States. In the Gemara doubts are resolved, duties explained and the most minute circumstances relative to the conduct of life are fully discussed.

Ta'lus, the heap of broken rock that forms at the base of cliffs and steep mountain slopes. It varies from a few inches to many feet in thickness, depending upon the size of the cliffs and the length of time which it has been under formation. The rocks are broken off by weathering, usually by the repeated freezing and thawing of water in their crevices. Where the fragments are coarse, the inclination of the talus is very steep; where they are fine, it is more gradual. An old talus contains more fine rock than a new one, since the fragments are continually undergoing decomposition and forming soil. See SOIL.

Tamaqua, *ta maw'kwa,* PA., a borough in Schuylkill co., 38 mi. n. of Reading, on the Little Schuylkill River and on the Central of New Jersey and the Philadelphia & Reading railroads. It is near extensive mines of fine coal and has flour mills and foundries, machine shops, powder and planing mills and other factories. The waterworks are owned and operated by the municipality. The place was settled in 1799 and was chartered as a borough in 1852. Population in 1910, 9462.

Tam'arind, a large and beautiful tree, of the East and West Indies, belonging to the Legu-

TAMARIND

minosae. Its pods are filled with a sweet, delicately flavored pulp, which is considered a delicacy. This pulp, with the seeds it contains, is preserved in sugar, packed in layers in casks and shipped in large quantities into Europe and America. The wood is beautiful, especially in the roots, and it is so hard that it is difficult to work.

Tam'arisk, the common name of shrubs and small trees which are very abundant all round the Mediterranean and are naturalized on some parts of the south coast of England. The common tamarisk attains a height of from sixteen to twenty feet, bears small flowers of a bright rose color, and has a very attractive appearance, which makes it much sought after as an ornament for shrubberies and parks. In the deserts of Arabia and Africa, the tamarisk is used for fuel and other purposes.

Tambourine, *tam boor een'*, a musical instrument, consisting of a piece of parchment, stretched over the top of a broad hoop, which is furnished with little bells. It is sounded by sliding the fingers along the parchment, or by striking it with the back of the hand or with the fist or the elbow. It is a favorite instrument among the peasants of Spain and Italy and was long used in Egypt.

Tam'erlane. See TIMUR.

Tam'il, the name of a race which inhabits South India and Ceylon. They are regarded as among the original inhabitants who occupied the country before the Aryan invasion from the north, and who adopted the higher culture of the invaders. The Tamil language is spoken, not only in South India and Ceylon, but also by a majority of the Indian settlers in places farther east, as Pegu and Penang. There is an extensive literature, the greater part of which is in verse.

Tam'many Society, a Democratic political organization of New York City. It derives its name from an indian chief, who is said to have signed the treaty with Penn, and round whom many fanciful legends of virtue and nobility afterward gathered. Washington's Pennsylvania troops chose him as their patron saint, in place of Saint George; and on his "day," May 12, 1789, the society—organized at first as the Columbian Order, to rival the Cincinnati—was founded. The organization soon became a party "machine," and by its aid, Aaron Burr was raised to the vice-presidency. In 1805 the Tammany Society was formally chartered, its professed objects being charity and the extension of the franchise. By 1822 the society had grown so large that the management was transferred to a general committee of three delegates from each ward. Tammany took a leading part in city politics from the first, and it flourished steadily. The number of the general committee rose to over 1400, delegates ultimately being sent from each district and precinct; finally, a central "committee on organization" was chosen, whose chairman was "boss" of the hall. The most notorious of these "bosses" was William M. Tweed, whose gigantic frauds, and those of the "ring" of which he was the chief, were finally exposed in 1871. This catastrophe sadly crippled the power of Tammany, but its influence was by no means killed, and it has since proved alternately a source of power and of insecurity to the Democratic party. Tammany controlled New York City elections, with rare exceptions, until 1913, when it was defeated by a non-partisan movement which resulted in the election of Mayor Mitchell.

Tam'pa, FLA., the county-seat of Hillsboro co., 240 mi. s. by w. of Jacksonville, on Tampa Bay, at the mouth of the Hillsboro River, and on the Atlantic Coast Line and the Sea Board Air Line railroads. The city has an attractive location and a healthful climate, and it has become a popular winter resort. Special features of interest are the De Soto Park, where the United States volunteers camped during the Spanish-American War; the Tampa Bay Hotel, a very large resort hotel; the old government reservation, and the Convent of Holy Names. Large quantities of phosphate, fruits, vegetables, turpentine, rosin, lumber, fish and cattle are exported, while the city is second only to New York in the importation of tobacco. Cigar making is the principal industry. The raw material comes chiefly from Havana, and the work is done largely by Cuban immigrants. The city has four banks, eighteen churches, county and Catholic high schools and several parish schools. Tampa was settled as a military post during the wars with the Seminole. It was incorporated and made a port of entry in 1886. About the same time the tobacco business began to be developed, and the city has since grown very rapidly. Population in 1900, 15,839. Since 1900 the city has grown rapidly. Population in 1910, 37,782.

Tampa Bay, a body of water on the western coast of Florida, entering Hillsboro and Manatee counties. Its length is about 35 miles; the width varies from 6 to 15 miles. It constitutes a safe, spacious and easily accessible harbor. A line of keys protects it from storms. On Egmont Key, at its entrance, is a lighthouse 86 feet high. The bay contains many small islands and abounds in fish and turtles. The chief town is Tampa. Other ports are Port Tampa and Gulf City.

Tampico, *tam pe'ko*, a seaport of Mexico, situated on the Gulf of Mexico, 225 mi. n. n. w. of Vera Cruz, at the mouth of the Tampico River. The city has a good harbor, which is protected by a breakwater and a jetty. The town is well laid out; it has broad streets and a number of public monuments, and it contains naval and military hospitals. Most of the buildings are after the Spanish style of architecture. It is an important commercial port and carries on a good trade with Great Britain and the United States. Population in 1910, 18,000.

Tanager, *tan'a jur,* a family of birds, closely related to the finches. Its representatives in the United States are of five species, only two of which, however, reach the northern boundary. The *scarlet tanager,* except for its black wings and tail, is covered with brilliant scarlet plumage, which makes him the brightest of all the birds of the northern United States. Its nest is a rather loose structure, placed in trees, and its eggs are pale blue, spotted with brown. The *summer tanager* is rose-red all over, brighter in tint below, though the female is rather dull in color, being a yellowish-green.

Tananarivo, *ta nah'na re'vo.* See ANTANANARIVO.

Tan'cred (about 1050–1112), one of the most famous heroes of the First Crusade. He distinguished himself at the siege of Nicaea, at the Battle of Dorylaeum, at the capture of Jerusalem and at Ascalon, and he was made prince of Galilee by Godfrey de Bouillon. He is represented by Tasso, in the *Jerusalem Delivered,* as the flower and pattern of chivalry.

Taney, *taw'ny,* ROGER BROOKE (1777–1864), an American jurist, born in Calvert County,

ROGER BROOKE TANEY

Md., the son of a wealthy planter. He was educated at Dickinson College and was ad-

mitted to the bar in 1799. Elected to the state senate in 1816, as a Federalist, he later passed into the Democratic party and supported Andrew Jackson, who in 1831 appointed him attorney-general of the United States and in 1833 secretary of the treasury. He encouraged and carried out the removal of the government deposits from the United States Bank, but in June, 1834, the Senate, establishing an entirely new precedent, refused to confirm his nomination as head of the treasury department. The balance of parties changed, however, and in 1836 the Senate confirmed his appointment as chief justice of the United States, to succeed John Marshall. He displayed marked ability as a jurist and great learning as a lawyer, though he reversed the previous tendency of the court toward centralized government and stood firmly for state sovereignty. Many of his decisions were severely criticised, especially that in the Dred Scott case (See DRED SCOTT DECISION) and the one denying the right of the president to suspend the writ of *habeas corpus.*

Tanganyika, *tahn'gan ye'ka,* a large lake, situated east of the central part of Africa, lying on the borders of the Kongo Free State and German East Africa. Its greatest extent is from northwest to southeast. Its length is about 400 miles, and its width varies from 20 to 40 miles. The lake occupies a narrow basin, enclosed by an almost continuous series of hills and mountains. It is fed by a number of rivers and discharges its waters by the Lukuga, on the west, into the Lualaba, or Upper Kongo. The surface is noted for its changes of level caused largely by periods of rainfall and dry weather. The lake was discovered by Burton and Speke in 1858, and it later was explored by Livingstone, Stanley and other travelers. The chief towns on the shore are Ujiji, Bismarckburg and Albertville. The lake is navigated by steamers and is connected with Lake Nyassa by a carriage road 210 miles long. The Cape-to-Cairo railway as projected will touch the southern end of the lake.

Tangier, *tan jeer',* or **Tangiers** or **Tanja,** a seaport and the diplomatic capital of Morocco, situated near the western entrance of the Strait of Gibraltar, 36 mi. s. w. of the town of Gibraltar. Its site is at the head of a spacious bay, and when seen from the sea, the town presents a striking appearance, rising in the form of an amphitheater. The houses are nearly all of one story and are built along lanes or narrow streets, many of which are too steep to admit of the use of carriages. There are a few modern residences, occupied by Europeans and by the most wealthy merchants. The city also contains a number of mosques, a Roman Catholic church and several Jewish synagogues. It is lighted by electricity. The harbor is fairly good, and the trade is considerable, though in the last half-century it has materially fallen off. The city is the center of a caravan trade of some importance, and most of its exports go to the cities of southern Europe. In 1662 it became a possession of Great Britain, but was abandoned after twenty-two years. Population, estimated at about 30,000, of whom 6000 are Christians and about 5000 Jews.

Tan'ja. See TANGIER.

Tannhäuser, *tahn' hoi zur,* in old German legend, a knight who gained admission into a hill called the Venusberg, in the interior of which Venus held her court. For a long time he remained buried in sensual pleasures, but at last he listened to the voice of the Virgin Mary, whom he heard calling upon him to return. The goddess allowed him to depart and he hastened to Rome, to seek the pope's absolution. The pope, however, when he learned the extent of the knight's guilt, declared that it was as impossible for him to obtain pardon as it was for the wand in the pope's hand to bud and bring forth green leaves. Despairing, the knight retired from the presence of the pontiff and entered the Venusberg once more. Meanwhile the pope's wand actually began to sprout, and the pope, taking this as a sign from God that there was still an opportunity of salvation for the knight, hastily sent messengers into all lands to seek for him. But Tannhäuser was never again seen. Richard Wagner has adopted this legend, with modifications, as the subject of one of his operas.

Tan'nin or **Tan'nic Acid,** a substance prepared by extraction from powdered gallnuts, by means of a mixture of alcohol, ether and water, from which it is obtained by evaporation. It is almost colorless and odorless, has a bitter taste and is used as an astringent in medicine, as a mordant in dyeing and, in combination with other substances, as coloring matter in ink. Similar substances are prepared from other vegetable growths and are sometimes called *tannic acid.* Such are *alder tannin, caffetannic acid* (prepared from coffee berries) and *fraxitannic acid,* made from the leaves of the ash tree.

Tan'ning, the process of converting raw skins into leather. This is accomplished by producing a change in the gelatin of the skin, so as to prevent decay and make the texture tough and waterproof. The substances generally used in tanning are oak bark, hemlock bark and, in some countries, bark from the fir and the pine. These barks contain tannin, and it is the combination of this substance with the gelatin of the skin that produces leather. See LEATHER.

Tan'rec or **Ten'rec,** a genus of insect-eating mammals, resembling in outward appearance the European hedgehog, as they are covered with bristles about an inch in length. They live in burrows, which they excavate by means of their strong claws, and they hibernate like the hedgehog. They live in Madagascar.

Tan'sy, a well-known plant of the Compositae order, abundant in Great Britain and throughout Europe, and naturalized in the United States. It is a tall plant, with divided leaves and button-like heads of yellow flowers. Every part of the plant is bitter. Tansy tea is an old popular medicine, believed to be a fine tonic. Tansy is now cultivated in gardens, mainly for the young leaves, which are shredded down and employed to flavor puddings and cakes.

Tan'talus, in Greek mythology, a son of Jupiter, and king of Phrygia, Lydia, Argos or Corinth, who was admitted to the table of the gods, but forfeited their favor, either by betraying their secrets, stealing ambrosia from heaven or presenting to them his murdered son Pelops as food. As punishment he was placed in a lake whose waters receded from his lips when he attempted to drink; and he was tempted by delicious fruit, which withdrew when he attempted to eat. According to other account , a huge rock forever threatened to fall and crush him.

Tantras, *tahn'tras,* a name of certain Sanskrit sacred books, each of which has the form of a dialogue between Siva and his wife. The Tantras are much more recent productions than the Vedas, the oldest dating after the Christian era, although their believers regard them as a fifth Veda, of equal antiquity and higher authority. The Tantrikas, or followers of the Tantras, indulge in mystical and impure rites, in honor of Siva.

Taoism, *tah'o iz'm,* a religion of China. Lao-Tse, who lived at the same time as Confucius, is commonly regarded as the founder of the faith, although it is probable that the religion had existed before his time, and that he simply gave it a more definite form. The religion teaches humility, gentleness and economy; that evil must be met by goodness, and that injury must be recompensed by kindness. After the entrance into China of Buddhism, Taoism adopted many of the peculiarities of the new faith. See CHINA, subhead *Government and Religion.*

Tapajos, *ta pah zhohs',* a river of Brazil, which rises in the middle west of the south central part of the country and flows northward into the Amazon. Its length is about 1100 miles, and it is navigable for small boats to within a few miles of its source.

Tap'estry, a fabric consisting of a warp, upon which colored silk, worsted and gold threads are fixed, to produce a pattern, being worked with a needle instead of a shuttle. It is made entirely by hand, and it has a greater solidity and excellence of design than ordinary woven cloth. Tapestry also differs from woven cloth in that the patterns, or designs, are not repeated; in the finer pieces they consist of beautiful figures, illustrating historical events (See BAYEUX TAPESTRY). During the fifteenth and the following centuries, beautiful tapestries were made in Flanders, France and Italy, and they were used in the decoration of the walls of palaces and churches. They were hung from the wall near the ceiling and were left loose, in order to have the best effect. The most famous tapestry factory, that of the Gobelins in Paris, was established in 1630, under Louis XIV. The finest pieces come from Arras, in France; hence tapestry is often called arras. Many valuable pieces of ancient times are now preserved in the museums.

Tapeworm, *tayp'wurm,* the name given to certain internal parasites, found in a mature state in the alimentary canal of warm-blooded vertebrates. Tapeworms are composed of a number of flattened joints, or segments, attached to a head, which is furnished with a circlet of hooks, or suckers, that enable it to maintain its hold on the mucous membrane of the intestines, in which it dwells. The other segments are simply buds, given off by the head, the oldest being farthest removed from it; each is capable of reproducing a perfect worm. The tapeworm has neither mouth nor digestive organs, and it absorbs its nutrition through the skin. The length of the animal varies from a few inches to several yards. The buds will not undergo development in the animal in which the adult lives, but they must be swallowed by some other warm-blooded vertebrate, where they develop, perforate the tissues and enter some organ, or are carried by blood vessels to some solid part of the body, where they surround themselves with a sac and remain

in this condition until their host is eaten; then they find their way into the intestinal tract of another vertebrate.

Tap'io'ca, a mealy substance, prepared from cassava meal, which, while moist or damp, has been heated, for the purpose of drying it, on hot plates. By this treatment the starch grains swell; many of them burst, and they unite to form small, irregular masses, or lumps. In boiling water tapioca swells up and forms a jelly-like mass. It is used for puddings and other desserts.

Tapir, *ta'pur,* the name of a genus of hoofed animals related to the hog. The common *South*

TAPIR

American tapir is about the size of a small ass and has a brown skin, covered with short hair. It inhabits forests, lives much in the water, conceals itself during the day time and feeds on vegetables, which it gathers with its flexible proboscis. There are several other American species. Fossil tapirs are scattered throughout Europe, and among them is one which in size must have nearly equaled the elephant.

Tar, a thick, dark-colored, viscid product, obtained by the destructive distillation of such substances as wood, coal, peat and shale. Wood tar, such as the Archangel, Stockholm and American tars of commerce, is obtained by burning billets of wood slowly in a conical cavity, at the bottom of which is a cast-iron pan, into which the tar exudes.

Tar is made from pine trees. The green pine trees are cut up, roots and all, into pieces three or four feet long and a few inches in diameter. These sticks are piled up on end, in the shape of a wigwam, one pile above another, until the top dwindles to a point. Damp earth and sand are heaped over the pile to a depth of several inches, and it is sometimes further covered with boughs. A flue is made at the top, to furnish the necessary draft, and a number of small holes, or dampers, are left at the bottom. When everything is ready, the pile is ignited; as the fire spreads through the wood, the apertures at the bottom are gradually closed up, and a slow combustion goes on for about ten days. It is necessary to watch the fire very closely, to see that it does not go out or burn too fiercely. At the end of the firing period, the spout at the bottom of the tar hole begins to trickle with a slow-moving, brown liquid, which has a pungent odor. This is the beginning of the flow of tar. During the first few hours the flow is usually filled with sand or charcoal, and it is properly discarded. When the stream is fairly clear, it is run into retorts, where it is distilled; wood spirit and pitch oils are given off. The black residuum is poured, while hot, into barrels, where it soon hardens and becomes the ordinary tar of commerce. About 17.5 per cent of the wood burned is converted into tar, and the flow lasts sometimes for two or three weeks. As high as 150 barrels of tar are taken from a single "hole." Tar is much used in making tar pavements, tar roofs, tar paper and in calking ships and sidewalks. See COAL TAR.

Taranto, *ta rahn'to,* a fortified seaport, situated in the southern part of Italy, 44 mi. s. w. of Brindisi, on an island which was formerly a peninsula and separated the Gulf of Taranto from what is known as the Little Sea. It is a poorly built town, but it contains a few structures of interest, among them the Cathedral of Saint Cataldo, a museum of antiquities and a nautical school. The chief industries are those connected with oyster and other shell fisheries. The town has a fine harbor and considerable trade. Taranto was founded by the Greeks in 708 B. C. and is on the site of ancient Tarentum, which became a powerful city before it was captured by the Romans, in 272 B. C., after which it was a Roman province until the downfall of the Empire. Population in 1911, 70,000.

Taran'tula, a common name given to the trapdoor spider in the United States or to any large spider of the tropics. The real tarantula is a native of southern Europe, whose bite was at one time supposed to be dangerous, curable only by dancing to a wild, peculiar music. A tarantula bite, however, is really not much worse than the sting of a wasp.

Tarbell, *tahr'bel,* IDA MINERVA (1857–   ), an American author, born in Erie co., Pennsylvania. Shortly after her graduation from Allegheny College, she became associate editor of *The Chautauquan.* From 1891 to 1894 she studied in Paris, and in the latter year she became an associate editor of *McClure's Magazine.* In 1906 she took a similar position on the *American*

Magazine. Her works include a *Life of Abraham Lincoln* and several other biographies, but she is best known as the author of a *History of the Standard Oil Company.* She also contributed to magazines numerous articles on history and current topics, besides some short stories.

Tare, the common name of different species of the pea family, known also by the name of *vetch.* There are numerous species and varieties of tares, or vetches, but that which is found best adapted for agricultural purposes is the common tare, of which there are two principal varieties, the *summer tare* and the *winter tare.* They afford excellent food for horses and cattle, and hence they are extensively cultivated throughout Europe. One species is found in the United States. The tare mentioned in the Scriptures (*Matt.* XIII, 36) is supposed to be the darnel.

Taren'tum, PA., a borough in Allegheny co. 21 mi. n. e. of Pittsburgh, on the Allegheny River and on the Pennsylvania railroad. It is in an agricultural and coal-mining region, and it has paper mills, glass factories, foundries, machine shops, flour mills and planing mills. The municipality has a national bank, public and parish schools, a high school and a public library, and it owns and operates the electric lighting plant. Population in 1910, 7414.

Target, *tahr'get.* 1, A shield, or buckler, of a small kind, such as those formerly in use among the Highlanders, which were circular in form, cut out of ox hide, mounted on strong wood,

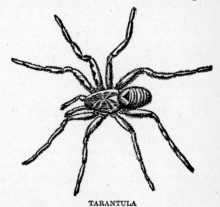

TARANTULA

strengthened by bosses and spikes and often covered externally with a considerable amount of ornamental work. 2, The mark set up to be aimed at, in archery, musketry or artillery practice. These targets are generally square or oblong metal plates, on which is marked a central circle, with two or more wide rings around it. The center is called the *bull's eye*. It is the marksman's aim to put his shots as near the central point as possible; if he hits the bull's eye he is credited with 5 points; if he hits within the first circle, 3 points; within the second, 1 point.

Targum, *tahr'gum,* a term applied to a translation of parts of the Old Testament into the Chaldee, or Aramaic, language, originating probably when the Jews began to use Aramaic instead of Hebrew. Only three are extant on the Pentateuch, one of the Prophets, others on the *Psalms, Job,* the *Proverbs, Song of Songs, Ruth, Lamentations, Esther* and *Ecclesiastes.* The real value of these lies in the ideas to be gained of the life of the people. Etheridge translated the Targums on the Pentateuch into English.

Tar'iff, a list of dues. The word had a curious origin, being derived from *El Tarifa,* the Rock of Gibraltar. The Spaniards levied duties on all vessels passing the straits, and a list of these duties was called *tariff dues;* hence the modern use of the word.

In the United States the term is applied almost exclusively to the regulation of import duties, and for a century it has been one of the chief causes of political contention. Prior to the adoption of the Constitution, some of the individual colonies had assessed a tax on imports; but the first tariff bill under the national government was passed in 1789. It was introduced into the House of Representatives of the First Congress by James Madison. The object was to tax imports "for the support of the government, for the discharge of the debts of the United States and for the encouragement and protection of manufactures." This bill was signed by President Washington on July 4, 1789. It provided for the levying of specific duties on some goods and of *ad valorem* duties on others (See CUSTOMS DUTIES). The act was frequently amended, the duties always being raised, until 1824, when a bill was passed providing an average rate of 37 per cent. Meanwhile the loose-constructionists, under Clay, had declared for a protective tariff, in opposition to the strict constructionist Republicans (Democrats), who claimed that the Constitution gave no power to levy anything but a revenue tariff. The result of their agitation was the "tariff of abominations" of 1828, which represented a decided advance toward prohibitive duties.

It was protested against by the Southern states, on the ground that it would lead foreign nations to discriminate against American raw materials, upon the export of which the South depended; also, because they believed it to be unconstitutional. In 1832 the South Carolina legislature declared the acts of 1824 and 1828 null and void, and prohibited the collection of duties.

In the following year Henry Clay introduced a compromise tariff bill. The object of this bill, as expressed in its preamble, was "to prevent the destruction of the political system, to arrest civil war and to restore peace and tranquility to the nation." It provided for a gradual reduction in duties. In response to firm action by Congress and by President Jackson, the nullification acts were repealed by South Carolina. From 1840 to 1845 several tariff bills were drafted and discussed, but only one, which provided for a rate of about 33 per cent, was passed. In 1846 the Walker tariff bill was passed, reducing the rate of duty to 25½ per cent.

The Democratic party in their platform of 1856 declared openly for free trade, and in the following year they passed an act which reduced the average duty to about 20 per cent. In 1860 the Republican convention declared for a protective tariff, and in 1861, under the stimulus of war, Congress passed a bill which raised the tariff to about 27 per cent. During the next two years the tariff was raised several times on special articles; in 1864 all duties were raised by 50 per cent, and another increase was enacted in 1866. A gradually growing discontent with the maintenance of the Morrill tariff, or so-called "war tariff," led, in 1882, to the appointment of a tariff commission to ascertain the effect of, and to recommend changes in, the existing tariff laws, but the resulting bill (1883) was satisfactory to nobody. The Democrats came to power in 1884 and introduced, in 1888, the Mills bill, a measure intended to reduce taxation and simplify the collection of revenue, but it failed to become a law. The Republicans returned to power in 1888, and two years later they passed the McKinley bill, which generally raised the duties.

In 1894 the Democrats were in control and passed the Wilson-Gorman tariff act, which materially reduced the tariff, and became a law without the president's signature. This act was superseded by the Dingley act in 1897, which again inaugurated a high tariff. In 1909 the Payne-Aldrich act was passed at a special session of Congress. This act purported to lower the tariff, but it was not satisfactory to a great majority of the people, and resulted in

IMPORTS

TOTAL—$1,653,264,000

- COTTON GOODS $65,153,000
- SEEDS $25,641,000
- FRUITS, NUTS $45,377,000
- CHEMICALS, DYES $92,029,600
- WOOL $33,078,000
- COFFEE $117,826,500
- SILKS $96,746,000
- IRON, STEEL $26,551,000
- PRECIOUS STONES $41,298,000
- TOBACCO $31,919,000
- COPPER $35,843,500
- SUGAR $115,515,000
- TIN $46,215,000
- INDIA RUBBER AND GUTTA PERCHA $105,037,500
- OILS $31,349,000
- LEATHER $16,166,700
- ART WORKS $36,092,000
- WOOD $52,502,000
- TEA $18,207,000
- COCOA $15,931,500
- HIDES AND SKINS $102,476,000
- VEGETABLE FIBRE $59,659,900

EXPORTS

TOTAL—$2,204,322,000

- IRON AND STEEL $268,154,000
- HOPS $4,648,000
- ANIMALS $15,448,000
- SOAP $4,536,000
- FURS $15,000,000
- MEAT AND DAIRY PRODUCTS $156,260,000
- OIL CAKE $28,229,000
- CARS, VEHICLES $42,633,000
- NAVAL STORES $26,755,000
- CORN $28,957,500
- FARM MACHINERY $35,640,000
- TOBACCO $48,305,000
- COAL $52,649,000
- CHEMICALS, DYES, ETC. $25,117,000
- MINERAL OILS $112,472,000
- LEATHER $60,756,800
- WHEAT FLOUR $51,000,000
- WOOD $96,782,000
- RAW COTTON $365,849,000
- GOLD AND SILVER SPECIE $122,219,000
- WHEAT $28,477,000

the returning of a Democratic majority to the House of Representatives in the Sixty-second Congress. The bill provided for the appointment of an advisory tariff commission. In 1913 President Wilson called a special session of Congress to revise the tariff. The bill passed by this Congress, known as the Underwood-Simmons Tariff Act, provided for many changes in the rates. The duties on cotton goods and on woolen goods were greatly lowered and wool was placed on the free list. Sugar pays a slight duty until May 1, 1916; after that date it is free. Also on the free list are many chemicals and metals, cement, asphalt, wood pulp and rag pulp not exceeding 2½ cents a pound in value, lumber, coal, boots and shoes, original works of art. Over 930 rates were reduced, 86 were increased, and 307 remained unchanged. Of the 86 increases, 51 were in the chemical schedule, and the remainder were taxes on perfumes, precious stones, gold and silver ware, articles made of fur and other luxuries. To compensate for the loss of revenue caused by the numerous reductions in the tariffs, the Underwood law provided an income tax. See INCOME TAX; FREE TRADE; PROTECTION.

Tar'kington, NEWTON BOOTH (1869–   ), an American novelist, born in Indiana and educated at Princeton University. *The Gentleman from Indiana,* his first book, won him a very favorable reputation, which was heightened on the publication of *Monsieur Beaucaire,* a fascinating romance. Among his later books are *The Two Vanrevels, Cherry, The Conquest of Canaan* and *The Guest of Quesnay.* In 1902 he was elected to the Indiana legislature.

Tarpeian, *tahr pe'yan,* **Rock,** a precipitous rock, forming part of the Capitoline Hill at Rome, over which persons convicted of treason were hurled. It was so named, according to tradition, from *Tarpeia,* a vestal virgin of Rome, the daughter of the governor of the citadel on the Capitoline, who, covetous of the golden bracelets worn by the Sabine soldiery, opened the gate to them, on the promise of receiving what they wore on their left arms. Once inside the gate they threw their shields upon her, instead of the bracelets. She was buried at the base of the Tarpeian Rock.

Tarpon, *tahr'pon,* a herring-shaped fish, found on the southern coasts of the United States and in the West Indies. It reaches a length of five or six feet and a weight of from 100 to 400 pounds, and it is of giant strength. Though too coarse, ordinarily, for food, it is a great attraction to anglers. Its scales, which are of great size, are now largely used in ornamental work.

Tarquin'ius, LUCIUS, surnamed *Priscus* (the elder), in Roman tradition, the fifth king of Rome. His father, Demaratus, was a Corinthian who settled in Tarquinii, one of the chief cities of Etruria, and married an Etruscan wife. Having removed with a large following to Rome, Tarquinius became the favorite and confidant of the Roman king, Ancus Martius, and at the latter's death Tarquinius was unanimously elected king. According to Livy, he made war with success on the Latins and Sabines, from whom he took numerous towns. His reign was also distinguished by the construction of the Cloaca Maxima, the Forum and the wall about the city and by the commencement of the Circus Maximus and the Capitoline temple. After a reign of about thirty-six years, he was killed by assassins employed by the sons of Ancus Martius (578 B. C.).

Tarquin'ius, LUCIUS, surnamed *Superbus* (the proud), the last of the legendary kings of Rome, the son of Tarquinius Priscus. He succeeded Servius Tullius. He abolished the privileges conferred on the plebeians; banished or put to death the senators whom he suspected; never filled up the vacancies in the senate, and rarely consulted that body. However, he continued the great works of his father and advanced the power of Rome abroad by wars and alliances. After a reign of nearly twenty-five years, a conspiracy broke out, by which he and his family were exiled from Rome (510 B. C.). He tried repeatedly, without success, to regain his power, and at length he died at Cumae. See ROME.

Tarrakai, *tah rah ki'.* See SAGHALIEN.

Tar'rytown, N. Y., a village of Westchester co., on Tappan Bay, which is an extension of the Hudson River, and on the New York Central & Hudson River railroad. It has a beautiful situation, and many of the residences of the town are handsome mansions. The Tarrytown Lyceum, which has a library of more than 4000 volumes; the Institution of Mercy, and Irving Institute are among the chief features of the town. Automobiles are manufactured. The first settlement was made on the site of Tarrytown in 1645, and the town was incorporated in 1870. "Sunnyside," the home of Washington Irving, is about two miles south of the village, and near it is Sleepy Hollow, made famous by that author. Population in 1910, 5600.

Tarshish, *tahr'shish,* a place frequently mentioned in the Old Testament. It is now generally identified by Biblical critics with the Tartessus of the Greek and Roman writers, a district in southern Spain, near the mouth of the Guadalquivir, settled by the Phoenicians.

Tarsus, *tahr'sus,* an ancient city of Asia Minor and the former capital of Cilicia, situated on both banks of the river Cydnus, about 12 mi. from the sea. At the beginning of the Christian era it was an important city and was especially celebrated for its learning and its educational institutions. It was the birthplace of the apostle Paul and was visited by him at least once after his conversion. The present town contains a few remains of the ancient city and has a population of about 15,000.

Tartan, *tahr'tan,* a well-known species of cloth, checkered, or cross-barred, with threads of various colors. It was originally made of wool or silk and constituted the distinguishing badge of the Scottish highland clans, each clan having its own peculiar pattern. An endless variety of fancy tartans is now manufactured, some of wool, others of silk, others of wool and cotton and some of silk and cotton. The pattern had its origin in Asia and is probably the oldest pattern known.

Tartar or **Argol,** the hard crust found adhering to the sides of casks in which wine has been incompletely fermented (See CREAM OF TARTAR). *Tartar of the teeth* is an earthy-like substance, which occasionally is deposited from the saliva, in the form of a hard coating upon the teeth, near the gums. It consists of animal matter, phosphate of lime and mucus from the saliva.

Tartar, *tahr'tur,* **Emet'ic,** a name given to the double tartrate of potassium and antimony, an important compound which is used largely in medicine. At first it is sweet to the taste, but the aftertaste in the mouth is very disagreeable. It is an active emetic and cathartic, and it is of great value in reducing fever; but from its depressing influence on the heart, physicians are growing more careful in prescribing it.

Tartar'ic Acid, a compound of carbon, hydrogen and oxygen, that exists in grape juice, in tamarinds and in several other fruits. It is obtained in its commercial form principally from the bitartrate of potassium (See CREAM OF TARTAR). Tartaric acid crystallizes in large rhombic prisms, transparent and colorless and very soluble in water. It is inodorous and is very sour to the taste. A high temperature decomposes it,

giving rise to several new products. The solution of tartaric acid acts with facility upon those metals which decompose water, as iron and zinc. Tartaric acid is largely employed as a discharge in calico printing and for making soda water powders and baking powders. It is valuable in medicine, for its cooling properties.

Tartars or **Tatars,** a term usually applied to certain roving tribes which inhabited the steppes of central Asia. More specifically, however, Tatar, or Ta-ta, appears to have been the name of a tribe of Mongols who occupied, about the ninth century, a district of Chinese Tartary, on the Upper Amur. The true Tartars formed part of the horde of Genghis Khan and of the successive hordes of similar origin who followed them.

Tartarus, *tahr'tur us,* a deep and sunless abyss, according to Homer and the earlier Greek mythology, as far below Hades as earth was below heaven. It was closed by iron gates, and in it Jupiter imprisoned the rebel Titans. Later poets described Tartarus as the place in which the spirits of the wicked received their due punishment, and sometimes the name was used as synonymous with Hades, or the lower world in general.

Tartary, *tahr'tur ry,* a name applied in the Middle Ages to the wide band of country extending through Central Asia, from the seas of Japan and Okhotsk, in the east, to the Caspian Sea, on the west, including Manchuria, Mongolia, Turkestan and all the south part of Russian Asia. In a restricted sense it is identical with Turkestan. It received its name from the Tartars, or Tatars.

Tashkent' or **Tashkend,** a city of Asiatic Russia, situated on a tributary of the Syr-Darya, 90 mi. n. w. of Khokan. It is one of the oldest towns of central Asia and consists of the native, or Asiatic, quarters and the Russian quarters, the latter being constructed on modern plans. The city contains a castle, a number of mosques and old temples, a bazaar and several colleges. The manufactures include silk and cotton goods and gunpowder. The city is a place of considerable trade, and it transships merchandise received from Bokhara, Persia, Kashmir and India. Population in 1909, 201,191.

Tasma'nia, a state of the Australian Commonwealth, consisting of the island of Tasmania and a few adjoining islands, situated 150 mi. s. of the eastern extremity of Australia, from which it is separated by Bass Strait. The island of Tasmania measures 200 miles from north to south and 245 miles from east to west. The area of the main island is 24,331 sq. mi., and of the state, 26,385 sq. mi., or about that of West Virginia and Delaware combined. The coasts are bold and irregular, being often indented by fiords and estuaries, some of which form excellent harbors. The interior consists of a central highland, or plateau, with an average elevation of from 3000 to 4000 feet, bearing along its western and northwestern borders a number of mountain ridges and peaks, the highest of which is Mount Cradle, 5070 feet high. Another range of lower altitude is also found along the east coast, and a number of isolated summits exceeding 4000 feet are found in various parts of the island. The plateau contains a number of lakes, the largest, Great Lake, being 12 miles long. All of these lakes are noted for the beauty of their surroundings. The island, considering its size, is well supplied with rivers. The largest of these discharge into the ocean by broad estuaries, which form good harbors.

The climate of Tasmania is remarkably pleasant and even delightful through most of the year. The mean winter temperature is about 47°, and the summer temperature is about 62°, though in the extremely hot weather the thermometer rises in rare instances to 110°. The rainfall varies in different parts of the island, being heaviest on the west and lightest on the east and southeast. The average fall for the island is about 21 inches.

The island is rich in minerals and contains large deposits of copper ore, silver ore, tin and gold. All of these ores are worked, but the income from the copper is more than that from any other mineral source. There is also considerable coal in the island, and this is mined to a limited extent. Large areas are covered with forests of valuable timber trees, and lumbering in some localities is an important industry. The soil and climate are suitable for agriculture, and this engages the attention of the larger portion of the inhabitants. The chief crops are oats, wheat and hay. Hops are raised with success, and the raising of fruit is becoming an important industry. Large numbers of cattle, hogs and sheep are raised, and the annual wool clip usually exceeds 9,000,000 pounds. The island has over 620 miles of railway in operation, two-thirds of which belongs to the state. The main line connects Hobart, the capital, with the next most important port, Launceston. There are numerous branch lines to other towns in the interior. Most of the trade is with Victoria, New South Wales and Great Britain.

The government is similar to that of the other Australian states. The governor is appointed by the British crown and is assisted by a council. The legislative authority rests in a parliament, which consists of a legislative council of 18 members, chosen for six years, and a house of assembly, chosen for three years. The members of the legislative council are chosen by a restricted franchise, the qualification of the electors being based upon the holding of property of a certain value, those having a certain yearly income or those belonging to such classes as lawyers and physicians.

Tasmania was discovered in 1642 by the navigator Abel Janszoon Tasman, and it was named Van Diemen's Land, in honor of Anthony van Diemen, who was governor of the Dutch East Indies. It was visited by Captain Cook in 1777 and in 1803 was colonized by a company of convicts from England. The following year Hobart was founded. For about twenty years the island was under the authority of New South Wales. In 1825 it was given a separate governor and continued as a colony of the British crown until the formation of the Commonwealth of Australia, when it became a member of that federation. Population in 1911, 191,211.

Tasmanian Wolf, a carnivorous marsupial animal, inhabiting Tasmania. In size it is generally about four feet in length, though some specimens attain a much greater size. It has an elongated, and somewhat dog-like, muzzle, and a long, tapering tail; the fur is grayish-brown, with a series of bold transverse stripes, nearly black in color, beginning behind the shoulders and ending at the tail. It is nocturnal in its habits, is fierce and most determined in disposition and is very destructive to sheep and other animals.

Tas'so, TORQUATO (1544–1595), an Italian poet, son of Bernardo Tasso, born at Sorrento. He was early sent to the school of the Jesuits, at Naples, and he subsequently pursued his studies under his father's superintendence at Rome, Urbino and Venice. At the age of sixteen he was sent to the University of Padua to study law, but at this time, to the surprise of his friends, he produced the *Rinaldo*, an epic poem in twelve cantos. The reception given this poem induced Tasso to determine to devote his life to literature, and he went to Bologna, where he studied philosophy and worked on his great poem, *Jerusalem Delivered*. After some years spent in the service of Cardinal Luigi d'Este, he received an appointment at the court of Alfonso, duke of Ferrara.

Here he lived happily for years, produced his pastoral drama, *Aminta,* and completed the *Jerusalem Delivered* (1575).

About this time he became a prey to morbid fancies and believed that he was persistently calumniated at court and systematically misrepresented to the Inquisition. To such a pass, indeed, did this mania come, that the duke was obliged to have him placed in confinement. He escaped and fled from Ferrara, but again returned. So outrageous had his conduct now

TORQUATO TASSO

become, that he was seized by the duke's orders and confined as a madman. He remained in the asylum from 1579 to 1586, until he was released at the solicitation of Vincenzo Gonzaga. Broken in health and spirit, he retired to Mantua and then to Naples. Finally, in 1595, he proceeded to Rome, at the request of the pope, who desired him to be crowned with laurel in the capitol, but the poet died while the preparations for the ceremony were being made. Tasso wrote numerous poems, but his fame rests chiefly on his *Rime,* or lyrical poems, his *Aminta* and his *Jerusalem Delivered.*

Taste. The sense of taste is located in the tongue and upper and back part of the mouth, and the special organs are the filaments of the gustatory nerve, which is a branch of the glosso-

pharyngeal (See CRANIAL NERVES) and has its origin in the centers of taste in the brain. The distal ends of these nerves are known as *taste bulbs,* or *taste buds.* They are found in the papillae of the mucous membrane of the tongue, palate and back surface of the epiglottis. These papillae take three forms, the filiform, the fungiform and the circumvallate. The *filiform* are most numerous on the front two-thirds of the tongue. The *fungiform* are found principally at the tip and sides of the tongue. They are less numerous than the filiform, but are much larger. The *circumvallate* are only eight or ten in number and are situated at the base of the tongue. They are V-shaped and consist of a central projection, surrounded by a wall, from which circumstance they take their name.

The sensation of taste arises from the stimulation of these nerves, and the stimulus is supplied only by substances in solution. Solids or gases must be dissolved before they can be tasted. The larger the area covered by the substance, the keener the taste; therefore, when one wishes to experience the pleasure of an agreeable taste, he spreads the substance over as large an area as possible. On the contrary, when one wishes to escape the unpleasantness of a disagreeable taste, he swallows the substance as quickly as possible. Four tastes are generally recognized—bitter, sweet, sour and salty. It is supposed by some authorities that the filaments in some papillae are sensitive to one taste, and that those in others are sensitive to another, but nothing is definitely known about this. The sense of taste can be highly educated, as is shown in the development made by buyers of butter, tea, wine and other articles of food. It is also closely related to the sense of smell. See SMELL; SENSES, SPECIAL; TONGUE.

Ta'tars. See TARTARS.

Tat'tersall's, the great London market for horses, the headquarters of the turf, established by Richard Tattersall about 1780. A subscription room is open for betters on the turf, where they make and settle their bets.

Tattoo'ing, a practice common to several uncivilized nations, ancient and modern, and to some extent employed among civilized peoples. It consists in pricking a design into the skin and introducing into the wound colored liquids or gunpowder, so as to make it indelible. The designs are sometimes simple dots and lines, sometimes most elaborate. The practice of tattooing is very prevalent among the South Sea Islanders, who use an instrument edged with small teeth, somewhat resembling a fine comb. The natives of Africa also engage in the practice. Degrees of rank are sometimes indicated by the greater or less surface of tattooed skin. Sailors of all nationalities have adopted the tattooing practice, but with them the designs used have no emblematic meaning.

Tauchnitz, *towK'nits,* CHRISTIAN BERNHARD, Baron (1816–1895), a German publisher. His establishment at Leipzig, founded in 1837, is widely known for the *Collection of British Authors* issued from it, which numbers about 3500 volumes and is continually increasing. Tauchnitz was appointed in 1872 British consul-general for Saxony.

Taunton, *tahn'ton,* MASS., one of the county-seats of Bristol co., 36 mi. s. of Boston, on the Taunton River and on the New York, New Haven & Hartford and several electric railways. The city is regularly laid out, with finely-shaded streets, and it has many handsome residences. It contains a large city library, the county law library and that of the Old Colony Historical Society. The public institutions also include Bristol Academy, Morton Hospital, an old ladies' home and one of the state insane asylums. Other features of interest are the city hall, the courthouse, the postoffice, the jail, a theater, the Odd Fellows' Hall, more than a score of churches and Taunton Green and Woodward Springs Park. The city is an important business center for a number of towns, and the principal manufactures are of cotton goods and silverware. There are numerous establishments making stoves, locomotives, carriages and various smaller articles. Miss Elizabeth Pole found an indian village here in 1737, called *Tecticutt,* meaning Great River, and she purchased the land from the indians for the first white man's settlement. It was called Cohannat, but was incorporated two years later under its present name. It was made a shire town in 1746 and was chartered as a city in 1865. Population in 1910, 34,259.

Tau'rus (the bull), the second sign of the zodiac, which the sun enters about April 20. The constellation, containing about 141 stars, is a brilliant one, that may be seen overhead in the evenings of December and January. Several of its stars are remarkable, as Aldebaran, a red star of the first magnitude, the Hyades, and the Pleiades. The symbol is ♉.

Taurus, a range of mountains extending along the south shore of Asia Minor for about 500 miles, thence running north by east. For the greater part of its course the range follows the Mediterranean shore, and it is supposed that the islands of Rhodes, Crete and some others are the highest elevations of the prolongations of these mountains. In different sections the range has received various names, and that portion extending northwesterly beyond the Sihun is called the Anti-Taurus. Mount Argaeus, 13,300 feet high, is the highest peak in Asia Minor.

Tax, a contribution levied, by authority, from the income of private persons, to defray the expenses of government or for other public services. A tax is said to be *direct* when it is demanded from the very persons who it is intended or desired should pay it, as, for example, a poll tax, a land or property tax, an income tax. It is said to be *indirect* when it is demanded from one person, in the expectation and intention that he shall indemnify himself at the expense of another; as, for example, the taxes called customs, which are imposed on certain classes of imported goods, and those called excise duties, which are imposed on home manufactures or inland production. In the United States and elsewhere, a tax on general property, both real and personal, forms the largest part of local revenues, municipal revenues being almost entirely raised from this source; while customs duties and excise duties furnish a large share of national revenue. Owing to the ease with which personal property may be concealed and the tax upon it avoided, the consequent inducement to perjury and the attendant injustice, many states of the Union have abolished it in part, substituting higher rates upon real estate, income, inheritances and certain kinds of traceable intangible property, such as franchises or mortgages (See SINGLE TAX; INHERITANCE TAX; INCOME TAX; CUSTOMS DUTIES; EXCISE TAX; POLL TAX).

Adam Smith laid down four principles of taxation, which have been generally accepted by political economists. These are: (1) The subjects of every state ought to contribute to the support of the government as nearly as possible in proportion to their respective abilities; (2) the tax ought to be certain, not arbitrary; (3) every tax ought to be levied at the time, or in the manner, most convenient for the contributor; (4) every tax ought to be so contrived as to take out and to keep out of the pockets of the people as little as possible over and above what it brings into the public treasury of the state.

Tax'idermy, the art of preparing the skins of animals so that they present a lifelike appearance. The process involves the skinning of the animal, the treatment of the skin with preservative substances, the stuffing of the skin with a false body and limbs and the modeling and mounting of the animal, to give it a natural shape and a pleasing attitude. It is customary to measuse the animal carefully and to make tracings, or casts, before any work is done on the body. The skin is removed from the entire body, even to the tips of the toes; it is turned back over the skull, so that the brain may be removed, and the flesh is scraped away. The bones of the limbs are drawn out, carefully scraped and then pushed back into their proper places. The skin is poisoned, or preserved, with powdered arsenic or alum or with arsenical soap, and dirt and bloodstains are carefully cleaned from the feathers, hair or skin. The eye-sockets, mouth, nostrils and ears are filled with cotton, to preserve their shape, and an artificial body is made. Wires are fitted into the limbs, neck and skull. The skin is drawn over properly, the incisions are sewed up and the animal is carefully molded and mounted. To mount skins properly is a very difficult process and requires skilful handling and a fine artistic sense, but in the museums of great cities are many expensive groups of stuffed animals that are startlingly lifelike in appearance.

Specific directions may be found in taxidermists' guides, and government publications have been issued for free distribution, in order that specimens might be sent to its various collections. Rowley's *The Art of Taxidermy* and Hornaday's *Taxidermy and Zoölogical Collecting* are reliable treatises.

Tay, the longest river in Scotland, and the largest, in volume, in the British Isles. It rises on the north side of Ben Lui, flows in a north-easterly direction through Loch Tay, then flows eastward, then southeastward, and finally enters the North Sea through the broad estuary known as the Firth of Tay. The entire length of the stream is about 120 miles. It is navigable for ocean vessels as far as Dundee and for smaller craft to Perth. At Dundee the Firth of Tay is crossed by one of the largest bridges in the British Isles. The river is noted for its salmon fisheries and for the beauty of its scenery.

Tay'lor, BAYARD (1825–1878), an American writer and traveler, born at Kennett Square, Pa. He learned the trade of a printer, contributed to various magazines and after a journey through Europe on foot in 1844 and 1845 published *Views Afoot*, which gained him a position on the staff of the New York *Tribune*. He afterward traveled extensively, giving his experiences in

El Dorado; *A Journey to Central Africa*; *The Lands of the Saracen*; *A Visit to India, China and Japan*; *Northern Travel*; *Travels in Greece and Russia*; *Byways of Europe*, and *Egypt and Iceland*. He also published several novels; various

BAYARD TAYLOR

volumes of verse, such as *Rhymes of Travel*; *A Book of Romances, Lyrics, and Songs*; *Poems and Ballads*; *Poems of the Orient*; *The Masque of the Gods*, and a translation of Goethe's *Faust* in the original meters, probably the best English translation of that work. One of his best-known poems is the *Bedouin Love Song*. Taylor resided in Germany for long periods, was for some time United States secretary of legation at Saint Petersburg and later was United States minister at Berlin, where he died.

Taylor, JEREMY (1613–1667), a noted English divine, the son of a Cambridge barber. He entered Caius College at the age of thirteen, graduated in 1631 and in 1633 took a master's degree and entered holy orders. Among his most noted works are *The Liberty of Prophesying*; *The Life of Christ, or the Great Exemplar*; *The Rule and Exercises of Holy Living*; *The Rule and Exercises of Holy Dying*, the last two forming the choicest classic of English devotion. *Ductor Dubitantium, or the Rule of Conscience on* *all her General Measures*, said by **Taylor** to be the foundation of his fame, is the most learned of his works. Coleridge says Taylor was "the most eloquent of divines; had I said, of men, Cicero would forgive me and Demosthenes nod assent."

Taylor, Zachary (1784–1850), an American statesman, twelfth president of the United States. He was born in Orange County, Va.,

ZACHARY TAYLOR

but was taken in infancy by his father, Col. Richard Taylor, a Revolutionary veteran, to Kentucky, where he remained on his father's plantation until 1808, when he was appointed first lieutenant in the Seventh Infantry of the United States army. In 1810 he was made a captain, and in 1812 his successful defense of Fort Harrison against the indians was one of the first marked military achievements of the war with England. In 1814 he was promoted to the position of major, and for many years he discharged the duties of indian agent in the West. He served in the Black Hawk War in 1832, and becoming colonel, he was appointed to a command against the Seminole indians in Florida. There, in 1837, he won the Battle of Okeechobee. For this he was brevetted brigadier general and was made commander in chief in Florida.

When war with Mexico threatened, Taylor was ordered to the Texan frontier. Under President Polk's orders he advanced across the disputed territory to the Rio Grande, gained the victories of Palo Alto (May 8, 1846) and Resaca

de la Palma (May 9), and occupied Matamoras, May 18. He was made major general, and February 22–25, 1847, he gained a brilliant victory at Buena Vista, over Santa Anna. For this he received the thanks of Congress and a gold medal. He was nicknamed "Old Rough and Ready" and became a national hero.

General Taylor was nominated for president in 1848, on the strength of his war record, and he was elected. The California question, complicated with the slavery topic, was the chief matter requiring attention during his administration, and before they had been satisfactorily disposed of, he died, July 9, 1850, Millard Fillmore becoming president. His son, Richard Taylor, was an officer in the Confederate army, and one of his daughters was the wife of Jefferson Davis. Consult Howard's *General Taylor*.

Tchad, *chad*, or **Chad** or **Tsad,** a large freshwater lake, situated in central Africa, and surrounded by the territories of Bornu, Kanem, Wadai and Baghirmi. It lies in the French military territory of Tchad and has an area of from 6000 to nearly 40,000 sq. mi., according to the rainfall. The lake has no regular outlet. It is generally shallow, and its margins are overgrown with reeds and other water plants. In the southeastern part are a number of islands. The chief rivers flowing into it are the Shari, on the south, and the Yeu, on the west. The waters abound with fish, crocodiles and turtles of large size.

Tcherkessia, *chur kes'se ah*. See Circassia.

Tea, *tee*, a plant whose leaves are used in making a beverage of the same name. The name is also applied to the leaves. The tea plant is a shrub, which in its native state grows from twenty to thirty feet in height, but under cultivation is cut down so that it seldom exceeds six feet and is made to branch freely. The leaves are dark green and from three to five inches long. The flowers resemble a small rose. These and other parts of the plant are shown in the color plate. The native country of the tea plant is not known, but it is found growing wild in Assam, a province of India, and in some portions of Japan. It is now cultivated in nearly all parts of China and Japan and in India and Ceylon.

The crop is harvested three times a year, the second harvest yielding tea of the best quality. The leaves are picked by hand, and are placed in baskets which the pickers carry suspended from their necks. The leaves are then spread in the sun and partially dried, after which they are heated over a charcoal fire. They are then placed upon a table and rolled in the hands, during which they attain the form in which they are placed upon the market.

Different grades of tea may be prepared from leaves of the same plant. All of these are divided into two classes, *green teas* and *black teas*. In the former the color of the leaf is preserved by a quick drying; in the latter the leaf is allowed to wilt thoroughly before drying, and during the process it turns black. Cheaper grades of green tea are often given their color by being treated with a weak solution of prussic acid or other objectionable substances.

Tea is one of the oldest of the non-intoxicating beverages, and, possibly with the exception of coffee, it is the most widely used. It has a mildly stimulating effect and acts especially on the nervous system. A small quantity tends to calm and rest a person, but when taken in strong solutions it produces wakefulness and tends to produce nervous irritability. Strong tea is a valuable antidote for poisoning, by morphine or antimony. See Vol. VI, INDUSTRIES.

Teachers' Institute, a meeting of teachers, intended to offer a short course of training in methods and devices of teaching school. Almost all states now offer these institutes in from three-day to three-week sessions, chiefly in the summer months, though often in fall and spring as well.

Teak, *teek*, a tree, a native of different parts of India, as well as of Burmah and of the islands from Ceylon to the Moluccas. It grows to an immense size and is remarkable for its large leaves, which are from twelve to twenty-four inches long and from six to eighteen inches broad. The wood, though porous, is strong and durable; it is easily seasoned and shrinks but little. It contains a resinous oil, which enables it to resist the action of water and to repel the attacks of insects of all kinds. It is extensively used in shipbuilding and for many other purposes. Mahogany is perhaps the only more valuable wood.

Tebriz, *ta breez'*. See TABRIZ.

Technical and Industrial Education, a phrase which, strictly speaking, embraces all instruction that has for its object the direct preparation for a career or vocation, but, popularly speaking, applies only to such instruction as bears directly on the industrial arts. Technical education is advanced or collegiate, whereas industrial education is the function of the primary and secondary schools. The problems of industrial education are a direct outgrowth of the decline of the apprenticeship system and the development of the factory system. A medieval apprentice, who was bound to his master for a period of years, thoroughly learned all the details of an industry. The modern factory hand, on the contrary, usually learns only certain stages of the process. The movement for industrial education shows the modern tendency to make the worker more than a machine and to give him the training which he needs to be most successful in his chosen field. It aims to do for the industrial worker what the professional school does for the lawyer and surgeon. There are three distinct steps in the development of industrial education: (1) manual training; (2) technical high schools; (3) trade schools. To these three steps must be added vocational guidance, the continuation schools and the coöperative plan, all of which are now recognized as important in education.

MANUAL TRAINING. Manual training is properly only the ground work for future vocations in that it teaches the use of the hands and their coördination with the brain. It is elementary, but it is a necessary foundation for entrance to technical schools. See MANUAL TRAINING.

TECHNICAL HIGH SCHOOLS. Technical high schools have long been a part of the German educational system and strong arguments have been advanced in favor of their development in the United States. Such schools aim to prepare trained workers for leadership in the industrial world, for positions of higher rank than those of skilled mechanics. Cleveland and Chicago have taken the lead in introducing industrial courses in high school work, and both cities have such special schools.

The textile industry in the United States supports a number of schools which are closely allied to the high schools. Prominent among these are the Textile School of the Pennsylvania Museum at Philadelphia, and three schools in Massachusetts, at Fall River, New Bedford and Lowell, all three cities being great cloth manufacturing centers. These schools, which are partly supported by the state, turn out mature students able to fill important positions in the textile mills. Secondary schools, such as the Lewis Institute at Chicago, the Drexel Institute at Philadelphia, and the Pratt Institute at Brooklyn, now offer similar courses of training.

TRADE SCHOOLS. Trade schools have been developed to take the place of the apprenticeship system. The first important one in the United States, the New York Trade School, was founded in 1881, and was intended primarily for the mechanics in the building trades. A number of

ALEXANDER AUGUSTUS FREDERICK, PRINCE OF TECK
Successor to Duke of Connaught as Governor-General of Canada, 1914

other important schools were established in the next thirty years, but not until 1910 was there a notable increase in the number of trade schools. Many of the schools, like the Baron de Hirsch School in New York, are privately endowed. In Milwaukee, Philadelphia, Indianapolis, Worcester and Portland, Oregon, are trade schools supported wholly or in part by the municipality.

VOCATIONAL TRAINING. This is a system which combines special elementary instruction in the industrial arts with the usual courses of study. It is considered especially desirable in the primary and grammar grades in order that the natural aptitudes of children may be discovered at an early age and so guided that they may find employment to the best advantage.

COÖPERATION. The coöperative plan, by which students spend part of their time working in factories and shops, has been carefully tried out at the University of Cincinnati and has also been applied with success to high school students. The pupils are regularly enrolled in the high school, and at the same time receive their practical experience in a trade.

CONTINUATION SCHOOLS. The term continuation school is generally applied to any kind of school for people who have a regular occupation. The term is applied especially to schools, whether day or evening, which give a technical education to people working in industrial plants. In the United States much of the continuation work has been done by religious and charitable organizations, but it is rapidly becoming a part of the public school systems.

TECHNICAL EDUCATION. Engineering schools, schools of applied science and institutions of technology have reached a high point of organization on the continent of Europe. In the United States their development has been exceedingly rapid, and has resulted in a type of institution that in some respects is superior to those found abroad. Among the most noted are Rensselaer Polytechnic Institute, at Troy, New York; Sheffield Scientific School, at Yale; the Massachusetts Institute of Technology, at Boston; School of Mines, at Columbia University; Sibley College of Mechanical Engineering and Mechanic Arts, in Cornell University; Michigan School of Mines, at Houghton, Mich.; Case School of Applied Science, at Cleveland, Ohio; and Armour Institute of Technology, at Chicago, Ill.

Teck, ALEXANDER AUGUSTUS FREDERICK, PRINCE OF (1874–   ), British soldier, brother of Queen Mary, and through his mother, who

was a grand-daughter of George III, distantly related to King George V. He married in 1894 Princess Alice of Albany, granddaughter of Queen Victoria. His Highness was educated at Eton and Sandhurst. He served in the Matabeleland campaign of 1896, and in the South African War was several times mentioned in despatches for bravery, won the Queen's medal, and was created a member of the Distinguished Service Order. He was gazetted governor-general of Canada on May 7, 1914.

Tecum′seh or **Tecumtha** (1768–1813), a celebrated Shawnee indian chief. In 1805 he began to formulate his plans for organizing the indians of the West into a confederation, and about 1811 he had collected a large force on the Wabash River. The defeat of his brother by General Harrison, at Tippecanoe, disturbed his plans, and he went to Canada at the outbreak of the war of 1812 to aid the British. He was killed in the Battle of the Thames River.

Te Deum, from the opening phrase, *Te Deum Laudamus,* "We praise Thee, Lord," a name of the well-known Latin hymn, usually ascribed to Saint Ambrose and Saint Augustine. It is used in the Roman Catholic and Anglican rituals.

Teeth, the hard, bony appendages which are fastened to the jaw in most vertebrates, and assist in mastication. In man and the higher mammals, two sets of teeth are developed, the temporary, milk or deciduous teeth, and the permanent set. In fishes the teeth fall off and are renewed repeatedly. In man the teeth are embedded in sockets in the upper and lower jawbones. There are thirty-two in all, sixteen in each jaw. The four central teeth, or *incisors,* have chisel-shaped crowns, with sharp edges; on each side of these four is a pointed *canine* tooth, which in the upper jaw is called an eye-tooth; on each side of these two are *bicuspids;* then come the *molars,* three on each side. The last of these molars, owing to their arrival between the seventeenth and twenty-fifth years, are called *wisdom teeth.*

Each tooth has a crown, the visible part, and a root, or fang, the hidden part. The central cavity is filled with a soft pulp, containing blood-vessels and nerves. Dentine, a hard substance, composed of phosphate and carbonate of lime, makes up the greater part of the tooth. The outer covering of the fang, called *cementum,* is a substance resembling bone, while the covering of the crown is a hard enamel. In young teeth the enamel is covered by a delicate membrane, called the "skin of the teeth," which is worn off in adult life. If the enamel which covers the tooth becomes cracked or broken, the underlying dentine is exposed and soon breaks down; and when the decay reaches the pulp which contains the blood-vessels and nerves, toothache results. By constant and regular care of the teeth, much pain and suffering may be avoided. After every meal the teeth should be cleaned with a soft brush and plenty of pure water, and frequently some simple tooth wash or powder, which contains no injurious substances, should be used.

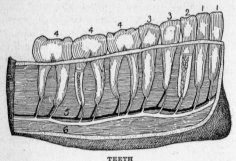

TEETH

1, incisors; 2, canine; 3, bicuspids; 4, molars (the molar at left is the "wisdom" tooth); 5, a blood vessel; 6, a nerve.

Children should be taught to clean their teeth every day, at least, so as to avoid decay and to preserve the general health, which is often injured by unhealthy conditions of the teeth and gums. A dentist should examine a person's teeth at least once a year, that he may repair any decay before it becomes serious.

Tegner, *teg nair'*, Esaias (1782–1846), a Swedish poet. He studied at the University of Lund, became professor of Greek literature there and later was appointed bishop of Wexio, where he died. Among his works the most important is his *Frithjof's Saga*, an epic poem, repeatedly translated into English. Longfellow translated it, as he did also *The Children of the Lord's Supper*.

Tegucigalpa, *tay'goo se gahl'pa*, the capital of Honduras, in Central America, on the Choluteca River, about 78 mi. from its mouth. It is in an important agricultural region, and the mineral resources of the surrounding country, while not as great as formerly, are still considerable. The city has a cathedral, a national university and a seminary. Population, about 18,000.

Teheran or **Tehran,** *te h'rahn'*, the capital of Persia, situated 70 mi. s. of the Caspian Sea and 210 mi. n. of Ispahan, on an elevated plateau, about 4000 feet above the sea. The city is near the snow-covered Elburz mountains, and is enclosed by a wall, which has twelve gates. The

town is poorly built, and most of the dwellings are low mud structures, only the wealthier classes living in modern houses. There are numerous mosques and bazaars, and the newer part of the city has modern boulevards lighted by gas and traversed by street railways. These present a marked contrast to the filthy, narrow streets of the older portion. The important buildings are the royal palace and the government buildings connected with it; also, the royal museum, which contains jewels of great value. Among the educational institutions are the King's College and a polytechnic school. The population in winter is about 200,000, but in summer a large number of the inhabitants remove to a more healthful location.

Telautograph, *tel aw'to graf*, an instrument for transmitting handwriting, drawings and figures by the electric current. It was invented by Prof. Elisha Gray. It consists of a transmitter and receiver at each station, connected with the transmitters and receivers of other stations by two lines of wire, carrying the electric current. The writing or drawing is produced by an ordinary lead pencil, which has two silk threads, at right angles to each other, attached near its point. These cords make the necessary connection with the transmitter, which, by means of a permanently magnetized steel gear wheel, exactly reproduces in the receiver the movements of the pencil. The receiver is operated by a motor, which obtains its power from a local battery and is so adjusted that its movements correspond exactly with those of the transmitter. See Telegraph.

Telegraph, *tel'e graf*, a device for conveying communication at a distance, either by writing or with signals. In its broadest sense, the telegraph includes any system of signals, such as semaphores, the heliograph and flags (See Heliograph; Semaphore; Signaling), but in the sense in which the term is ordinarily used, it means the electric telegraph in common use.

Electro-Magnetic Telegraph. The electro-magnetic telegraph consists of the following essential parts: (1) a battery or other source for generating an electric current; (2) a line wire or other conductor for conveying the current from one station to another; (3) an apparatus for transmitting the message, and (4) an apparatus for receiving the message. The line wire usually consists of iron wire, which has been galvanized to protect it from the weather (See Galvanized Iron), and it is supported upon poles from twelve to twenty feet in height, being attached to them by glass or porcelain insulators. Theoretically there should be two wires, in order to complete the circuit, but in practice the earth is made to take the place of one of these, by attaching the wire leading from one pole of the battery to an iron plate buried in the ground or to the rails of a railway track. The transmitting apparatus consists of a lever, placed on a pivot; it has a knob on the upper side of one end, and immediately under this is a wire containing a platinum point, which, when the lever is pressed down, meets another similar point on the table, connected with the opposite pole of the battery. The receiving apparatus consists of a core of soft iron, wound with a coil of insulated wire, thus making an electro-magnet; and above this is an armature, which is attached to a lever that has an upward and downward motion.

The principle upon which the telegraph operates is that of the making and unmaking of an electro-magnet, by the passage and interruption of the current (See ELECTRO-MAGNETISM). The

by the operator at Saint Louis are exactly reproduced in the sounder at Chicago, and the operator at that station reads the message by the sounds produced in his instrument.

In nearly all telegraph stations there is an additional apparatus, known as the *relay*. This is represented by D in each station. The relay is simply an electro-magnet of greater power than that used in an ordinary sounder. This magnet is connected with the local battery and is used along the line when the distance is so great that the current from the ordinary working battery is not strong enough to carry the message successfully from one station to the other. The relay is connected with the local battery, and in case of transmitting the message from Saint Louis to Chicago, by means of the relay, a weaker line battery can be successfully used. The current passing through the relay at D attracts the lever E in the same manner that the lever of the sounder is attracted. This makes a connection between the line battery C and the local battery F,

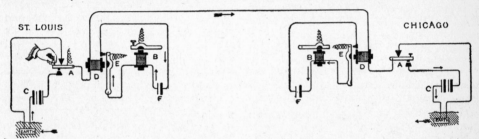

diagram shows the various parts of a telegraph, in such relative position as to indicate the equipment of two stations. In each station A represents the transmitting lever, known as the *key*; B, the receiving apparatus, or *sounder*, and C, the battery. When the operator in Saint Louis wishes to transmit a message to Chicago, he presses down the key, which is ordinarily held up by the spring. As the platinum point on this key connects with the metallic point beneath it, it closes the circuit and sends a current over the line wire to the station in Chicago. This magnetizes the electro-magnet in B at that station and causes it to bring down the armature above, so that the lever strikes upon a metallic point with a sharp click. As long as the key at Saint Louis remains closed, the lever on the sounder in Chicago will remain attached to the magnet, but the instant the transmitting key is opened, the circuit is broken, and the spring in the sounder B brings this lever back into its former position. Thus the vibrations produced

which is also connected with the sounder, and when the relay is used the sounder has the benefit of the current from the local battery and is thus easily operated, while without this aid it would fail to respond to the movements of the transmitting key at a distant station.

The above description is of the simplest form of telegraph, and the apparatus named answers all purposes for small stations, but in large cities and on lines having a great amount of business messages cannot be transmitted with sufficient rapidity by this apparatus, hence devices for rapid telegraphy have been invented. The device in most common use consists of a transmitting and receiving apparatus constructed on a similar plan and moving with the same rate of speed. The message is prepared on a paper tape, by a machine containing keys similar to those on the typewriter. The dots punched out on this paper correspond to those in the telegraph alphabet. The transmitting machine contains an electric brush, which comes in contact with the rim of a steel wheel. The paper forms an insulator between the brush and wheel, except where the dots appear. As this tape is run over the wheel, the dots complete the circuit, which is indicated in the receiving apparatus by a steel point, which passes over a similar tape, chemically prepared, so that whenever the electric current passes through it a bluish-black dot or dash will be made. Thus the message is reproduced in the telegraph alphabet. By means of this apparatus many times the number of words can be transmitted in a given time that would be possible by the ordinary operating key.

DUPLEX TELEGRAPH. In 1872 Thomas A. Edison invented a device for sending two messages in opposite directions over the same wire at the same time. Since that time this invention has been perfected and extended, so that four or more messages are readily sent at once over the same line. This is accomplished by having different sets of instruments, which respond to currents of different strength, each set of instruments being connected with special batteries. Since no set of instruments will respond to the batteries connected with the others, the messages are transmitted without interruption or confusion.

OTHER SYSTEMS. The electric telegraph, known as the Morse system, is the one in general use, but a number of other systems have been invented at different times. One of these, known as Bonelli's telegraph, is worked by means of five wires. The message is set up in brass types in one line. The letters are common block letters, and points like the teeth of a comb are pressed against the raised portions of the type. As the line of type is drawn through the transmitting frame under these points, each point sends a current along its wire to a corresponding point pressing against prepared paper at the receiving station, making a mark on the paper which corresponds to the raised portion of the type which sends the message. This telegraph has not proved successful, because of the expense of installing and operating it. Other systems in use vary from the Morse system principally in the receiving apparatus employed. This is particularly true of the apparatus used in connection with ocean cables. Instead of a sounding instrument, the apparatus consists of a needle which moves over a dial. This is a much more sensitive receiver than the ordinary sounder, and for this reason it is more desirable in connection with such long lines as ocean telegraphs.

HISTORY. Several attempts were made to in-

vent a telegraph previous to 1831, but none was successful. In that year Prof. Joseph Henry (See HENRY, JOSEPH) discovered that a piece of soft iron could be instantly magnetized by passing an electric current through a coil of wire surrounding it; also that it could be as quickly demagnetized by breaking the circuit. The following year Prof. Samuel F. B. Morse conceived the idea of making use of this principle as a means of communication (See MORSE, SAMUEL F. B.), and while on a return voyage from Europe he made the drawings and perfected the plan for the necessary apparatus. Professor Morse gave his first exhibition of this apparatus in 1837. Three years later a patent was obtained, and the inventor applied to Congress for an appropriation to construct a telegraph line from Washington to Baltimore. The majority of Congressmen did not believe that Morse's idea was practicable, and it was not until some years later that the desired appropriation was secured. The first telegraph line was completed in May, 1844, and its success far exceeded the expectations even of the inventor. In the perfection of his apparatus Professor Morse was assisted by Professor Henry and Mr. Alfred Vail, a skilled mechanic. The system of signals known as the Morse Alphabet then adopted has remained in use. It consists of a series of dots and dashes which represent the letters and figures in ordinary use. The first instrument used a receiver which recorded the message on a paper tape that passed over a cylinder, down upon which a pencil point was brought when the circuit was closed; but operators soon discovered that they could read more rapidly and accurately by the ear than by the eye, and this form of receiving apparatus was replaced by the *sounder*, now in almost universal use. The tape receiver is still retained for recording stock quotations and those from other market reports and for a few other special purposes. The additions to Morse's invention have been for the purpose of extending its usefulness and have not in any way modified the principle upon which his plan was based. The electric telegraph is now in use throughout the civilized world, and ocean cables have been laid to such an extent that it is possible to communicate with almost any part of the world within the space of a few minutes. See CABLE, SUBMARINE; TELEGRAPH, WIRELESS; TELAUTOGRAPH.

Telegraph, WIRELESS, a system of telegraphy by means of which messages are sent from one station to another without the use of wire as a conductor of the electric current. That electrical currents can be transmitted through space by the atmosphere has been known for more than a century, but that this phenomenon could be turned to practical purposes is a comparatively recent discovery. Wireless telegraphy, in the sense in which the term is now used, has been wholly developed since 1890. Three systems have been tried. The first used the earth as a conductor of the electric current and was successful only to a very limited extent. The second

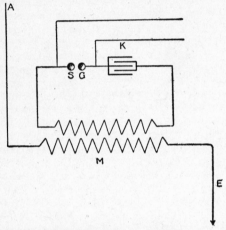

MARCONI'S TUNED TRANSMITTER

A, Aërial, or perpendicular, wire; *E*, earth, or ground, wire; *K*, syntonizing apparatus; *M*, special Marconi transformer; *S G*, spark gap.

method depended upon the principles of the alternating current transformer, and it has been used in connection with the first. By this method messages have been sent 40 miles, but it has never been made practicable for commercial purposes.

The third method, and that now in successful operation, sends messages through space by means of electric waves. This is known as the Marconi system, from its inventor, who has brought it to its present state of perfection (See Marconi, Guglielmo). In 1888 the German physicist Hertz determined by experiment the specific features of certain electric vibrations which have since been known as the *Hertzian waves*. These vibrations have been the basis of all subsequent development in wireless telegraphy. While Marconi has developed wireless telegraphy and made it a successful means of communication, he is not the inventor of most of the apparatus employed in its working.

Briefly described, the Marconi system of telegraphy consists in setting in motion certain electric waves by means of a transmitter. The waves pass through the ether and are received

and recorded at another station. The plan of operating is very similar to that of the ordinary Morse telegraph, but the instruments used are constructed for the purpose of transmitting electric waves through the ether and recording them from the same medium.

The Apparatus. The apparatus consists of a transmitter and a receiver. The transmitter has a strong battery, such as that used in connection with a telegraph or telephone; an ordinary telegraph key; a powerful induction coil and one or more tall masts, to which vertical wires are so attached that they extend beyond the upper end of the mast. The receiver consists of a mast, a balloon or kite for supporting the receiving wire, a special instrument called the *coherer*, a local battery of one cell, a delicate relay and an ordinary telegraph sounder, or recorder.

The breaking of the electric current produces certain vibrations. When these pass off into space they are transmitted through ether in concentric circles and travel with the same velocity as light. To understand this principle one must remember that ether is a substance entirely distinct from the air (See Ether). While the atmosphere pervades space to a certain height above the earth's surface, ether fills all space and makes it possible for light to be transmitted from the heavenly bodies to the earth. Light is the result of one sort of vibrations in ether, and electricity is now believed to be the result of another class of vibrations in this same mysterious substance. The ether waves set in motion by the discharge of an electric current may be illustrated by the waves arising from throwing a stone into a pool or lake. The waves recede from the point of disturbance in concentric circles. As the diameter of the circle increases, the height of the wave diminishes, until, finally, the undulation entirely disappears. The transmitter in the Marconi system is so constructed as to give the electric current the greatest possible strength before the circuit is broken. This break occurs between two brass balls connected with the induction coil. A wire from one of these balls extends upward from the mast, and from the other another wire extends to the earth. The discharges are produced by the operator opening and closing the key, as in the ordinary telegraph. The stronger the current, the farther the ether vibrations produced by its discharge will be transmitted. A more powerful current is therefore required for long than for short distances.

The receiver takes up, or absorbs, the electric vibrations that come to it through the wire supported either on a mast or by means of a kite or balloon. This wire is connected with a recording instrument, and the vibrations which it receives produce the same effect on this instrument as they would in the ordinary system of telegraphy. It is in connection with the receiving instrument that the most delicate and ingenious piece of apparatus is found. This is known as the *coherer*. It consists of a glass tube about two inches long and about the size of a small lead pencil. Near the middle of the tube are two metallic plugs, usually of silver, with a wire connected with each. The space between the plugs is partially filled with finely powdered filings of nickel and silver, containing just a trace of mercury. This little apparatus, invented by Calzecchi, and improved by the French physicist Brantley, is the crux of the whole system. Without it, wireless telegraphy would be impossible. The current absorbed by the receiving wire is by far too weak to operate the receiving instrument and must be strengthened by a local battery, and the coherer is the instrument through which this is done. The nickel and silver filings, when not affected by the current from the receiving wire, act as a non-conductor between the two metallic plugs, one of which is connected with the receiving wire and the other with the receiving instrument and the local battery. When the current from the receiving wire reaches the tube, these filings become rigid and form a conductor connecting the current from the receiving wire with that of the local battery, and this operates the relay, which in turn, by means of the stronger battery, operates the sounder or recorder as may be desired. When the current is completed in the recorder, it causes a vibrator, called the *tapper*, to strike the coherer and to jar the filings back to their original position, thus breaking the current of the local battery. The receiving instrument records the Morse alphabet.

From the above description it will be seen that the only difference between the Marconi and the Morse systems is in the medium used to transmit the electric vibrations. The Marconi system requires a much stronger current, and cannot transmit as many words in the same time as the Morse system. Since these electric waves travel in circles, any instruments within the radius of the circle can receive the message sent; hence the transmitter can send the same message to many stations at the same time, if this is desired.

Mr. Marconi has found that masts from 150 to 200 feet in height work most advantageously in transmitting. He at first used wires extending from 300 to 400 feet above the ground for receiving, but later he found that a wire from 150 to 200 feet high was fully as successful.

SYNTONIZING, OR TUNING. The fact that the same message could be received by any number of stations within reach of its transmitter seemed at first to deprive wireless telegraphy of that secrecy necessary to the transaction of business, and thus to render it valueless for commercial or government purposes. Marconi has overcome this difficulty by a system of "tuning." That is, he has invented a device by which he can so adjust the transmitter and receiver that they work together, and messages from the transmitter, to which a receiver is not tuned, will have no effect upon it. This is accomplished through the use of the coherer, and the adjustment is so perfect that messages sent from the same transmitter in different languages at the same time have each been recorded by their respective receivers without error.

USES. Wireless telegraphy is in general use for commercial and press purposes. Its use on ocean steamers has proved so valuable that any steamship carrying passengers on the ocean or on the Great Lakes is not considered to be fully equipped without a wireless apparatus. Numerous stations are maintained on the seacoast and on the Great Lakes, so that steamers on the latter are seldom more than 100 miles from a station. In a number of instances it has been the means of saving passengers and crews of wrecked vessels. It is also of great value in the lighthouse service. See LIGHTHOUSE.

In 1901 Marconi sent the first wireless message across the Atlantic, between Cornwall, England, and Saint John's Newfoundland. Since then, companies have been formed to compete with the cable companies in the trans-Atlantic service. Messages are transmitted by wireless at 17 cents a word, while messages by cable cost 25 cents a word. In 1910, Marconi succeeded in receiving signals at a high-power station in Argentina, from Glace Bay, N. S., and from Clifden, Ireland, each about 5600 miles distant.

The French government has stations in Algeria and Tunis, and is planning to establish others in French Guinea, Liberia, Timbuctoo and the French Congo. See TELEGRAPH.

See TELEGRAPH. Consult Maver's *Wireless Telegraphy* and Trevert's *The A B C of Wireless Telegraphy*.

Telemachus, *te lem'a kus.* See ULYSSES.

Telephone, *tel'e fone,* an instrument for transmitting sound, especially the sound of the human voice, by means of an electric current or the vibration of a cord or wire. The simplest telephone consists of two vibrating membranes, connected by a cord passing through small openings in the respective centers. Such a telephone is easily made with two tin fruit cans. Punch a small hole in the center of one end of each can, the other end being removed; join them by a twine, held in place in each can by a large knot, and draw the cord taut. Conversation can be carried on through this instrument at a distance of several hundred feet, and disks of membrane specially mounted for this purpose and joined by copper wire will work successfully for a mile or more.

THE ELECTRIC TELEPHONE. The electric telephone was invented by Alexander Graham Bell and was first exhibited to the public in 1876. The essential parts are the transmitter and the receiver. The transmitter consists of a funnel-shaped mouthpiece, directly back of which is a metal disk. A button of hard carbon is attached to the center of this disk on its inner surface; opposite to it and fastened to the frame of the instrument is a second button. The space between these buttons is filled with granulated carbon. These buttons are the electrodes of the transmitter, the current passing from one to the other by means of the granulated carbon. By this device the vibrations produced in the metal disk by the voice of the speaker are exactly reproduced. The receiver consists of a straight or bar electro magnet with a coil at the end next to the metal disk and having only one pole. By completing the circuit through the carbons in the transmitter, the disk in the receiver is caused to vibrate in unison so that the voice of the speaker, including accent and inflection, are heard by the one holding the receiver.

While in the extended telephone systems now in use many accessory parts are necessary, the ones described above are the essentials and constitute the working part of the telephone. Telephone systems consist of main lines and branches, all of which are connected at the central office with an elaborate switchboard, by means of which the operator makes the connections for the users of the system. Each local telephone has, also, a battery, which is essential to the operation of the signaling apparatus. While numerous other patterns of telephones have been invented, they are all based upon the principle of the Bell telephone, which is now in almost universal use in the United States and Europe. The instruments have been brought to such a degree of perfection that one can converse over a line a thousand miles in length.

Telephone, WIRELESS. The principles of wireless telegraphy have been applied successfully to the telephone by Dr. Lee De Forest, of New York. It is found that the ether waves generated by the telephone are more easily controlled than those of the wireless telegraph. The apparatus used is similar to that of the ordinary telephone, with the addition of an apparatus for transforming the transmitting current, and the *audion*, an especially delicate instrument, which makes use of a highly heated gas to transmit the waves to the receiver. See TELEGRAPH, WIRELESS.

Telescope, an optical instrument for viewing distant objects. The simplest telescope con-

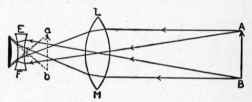

sists of a straight tube, with a double convex lens, LM, at one end, and a concave lens, EF, at the other. The convex lens constitutes the object glass, and the concave lens, the eyepiece. The eyepiece is placed between the objective and the image formed by it. Rays of light from the object AB are refracted by the objective LM and would form an inverted image beyond EF; but this lens tends to disperse the rays, and the eye sees the image at ab. The telescope tube is usually jointed, so that the eyepiece can be placed at different distances from the objective, in order to obtain a sharp focus of the image. Opera glasses and field glasses are made by joining together two telescopes of this pattern. This telescope was invented by Galileo in 1609.

Astronomical telescopes are of two classes, the reflecting and the refracting. The *reflecting telescope* consists of a concave mirror, placed at one end of a tube of the same diameter. The tube is pointed toward the object to be viewed, and the image formed by the mirror is placed in the tube at the proper point, by a prism. This reflects the image so that it is viewed through an eyepiece placed in the side of the tube. The eyepiece is usually so constructed as to magnify the image formed by the mirror. This was the first pattern of astronomical telescope, and to its use many of the early discoveries in astronomy are due; but owing to the difficulty in its manipulation, it has now been almost entirely replaced by the refracting telescope.

The *refracting astronomical telescope* is similar in construction to the smaller instrument, but contains many accessories, for the purpose of adjusting it to different lines of work and for pointing it to any position desired. The tube is supported on a standard and is so adjusted that it is nicely balanced and can be easily directed to any point in the heavens. It is also connected with a system of clockwork, by which its movements can be so adjusted as to enable it to follow the motions of any heavenly body. The eyepiece is a convex lens and magnifies the image. The objective is very large and therefore collects a large number of rays of light; hence, the telescope assists in viewing heavenly bodies in two ways, by collecting a larger number of rays of light than the eye, and by magnifying the image formed.

The most noted telescopes in the world are those of the Yerkes Observatory, at Lake Geneva, Wis., the Lick Observatory, Mount Hamilton, Cal., the observatory at Pultowa, Russia, and the National Observatory, at Washington, D. C.

The Yerkes telescope belongs to the University of Chicago and was presented to the university by Charles T. Yerkes. It is the largest telescope in the world in practical use. The great lens has 40 inches of clear aperture, is over 3 inches in thickness, and weighs about 760 pounds. The tube is of sheet steel, 42 inches in diameter at the objective end, 52 inches in diameter in the middle, and weighs 12 tons. The pier on which the tube rests and revolves is of cast iron and stands about 44 feet in height; the length of the tube is 64 feet. The dome in which the telescope is situated has a diameter of 80 feet and a height of 100 feet. The telescope is manipulated entirely by electricity, and the observer at the eye end, by simply pressing a button, can move the telescope in any direction. The floor of the observatory is raised and lowered by electric motor power, so that the observer can reach the eye end of the telescope without difficulty. The building in which the telescope is set is 300 feet long and 80 feet wide. The large telescope is set in one end, and in the other end two smaller glasses are placed, one 15 inches in diameter, the other 12 inches.

Tell, WILLIAM, a famous peasant hero of Switzerland, now proved to have been a mythical personage. He is said to have belonged to the Canton of Uri, and to have united with others belonging to this canton and to the cantons of Unterwalden and Schwyz in resisting the Austrians. On his refusal to do homage to Gessler's hat, set upon a pole, he was seized and condemned to death, but he was granted his life on condition of shooting, with an arrow, an apple placed on the head of his own son. This he did successfully, admitting at the same time that his second arrow had been intended for Gessler in case of failure. He was therefore kept a prisoner, but while being conveyed across a lake in Gessler's boat, he managed to leap ashore, and soon after killed Gessler, who had landed in pursuit of him.

Tem'pe, VALE OF, a narrow valley in the northern part of Greece, extending between Olympus, on the north, and Ossa, on the south. The river Salambria flows through the valley, and its scenery is remarkably beautiful. This valley was much celebrated by the ancient poets.

Temperance, originally moderation in the use of all things; in popular language, moderation in the use of alcoholic liquors, or total abstinence. Among primitive people excessive use of intoxicants has always been associated with religious rites, and indulgence in an appetite for liquors has been prohibited. Among the ancient Chinese, Carthaginians, Persians and Hebrews there were laws against excess, and the Buddhists taught total abstinence. In modern times the temperance movement has often had a deep religious significance, but its appeals have been based chiefly on grounds of health, economy and morality. The United States, Great Britain, Norway and Sweden, Germany, France, Austria and many other nations now have organizations whose object is to lessen or destroy the consumption of liquors and to secure the passage and enforcement of laws which aid this result.

In the United States, the first organizations were the American Temperance Society, founded 1826, the New York State Temperance Society, founded 1829, and the Sons of Temperance, founded 1842. The Independent Order of Good Templars, founded in 1851, has spread over the world. In 1868 was established the Woman's Christian Temperance Union, and in the next year was formed the National Prohibition Party. Another great factor in the fight for prohibition has been the Anti-Saloon League, founded in 1893 by Howard H. Russell. The efforts of these and many other associations have resulted in a widespread temperance movement, and have secured legislation on the subject in practically every state of the Union. Ten states, with a population of over 16,000,000, now have laws prohibiting the sale or manufacture of intoxicants, and every one of the remaining states has some "dry" territory under some form of local option. See GOOD TEMPLARS, INDEPENDENT ORDER OF; LICENSE; LOCAL OPTION; PROHIBITION PARTY, NATIONAL; WOMAN'S CHRISTIAN TEMPERANCE UNION.

Tem′perature, the state of a body with regard to heat, or the state of a body considered with reference to its power of communicating heat to other bodies (see CLIMATE). In physiography it often refers to the atmospheric heat of a locality at a particular time. When we speak of a body having a "high" or a "low" temperature, it is implied that the condition of heat in the body may be compared with some standard. The means of such comparison is the thermometer. (See THERMOMETER.)

Tem′pering, in metallurgy, the process of giving to metals, principally iron and steel, the requisite degree of hardness. The term is especially applied to the process of giving to steel the necessary hardness for cutting, stamping and other purposes. If heated beyond a certain degree and suddenly cooled, steel becomes very hard and brittle. The process of tempering consists essentially in plunging the steel, when it is red hot, into cold water or other liquid, to give an excess of hardness, and then gradually reheating it until the hardness is reduced or brought down to the required degree. The excellence of all cutting steel instruments depends on the degree of temper given to them. Different degrees of temper are indicated by different colors which the steel assumes. Thus, steel heated to 450°, and suddenly cooled, assumes a pale straw color. This steel is employed for making razors and surgical instruments. See ANNEALING; STEEL.

Tem′plars, KNIGHTS, an order of knights which was established in 1118, for the protection of pilgrims in Palestine. Subsequently its object became the defense of the Christian faith and of the Holy Sepulcher against the Saracens. The name Templars was adopted because the quarters assigned to the order were in a palace in Jerusalem, known as Solomon's Temple. The grand master, the chief of the order, had the rank of a prince, and the order acknowledged the pope alone as its protector. Compelled, in 1291, to leave the Holy Land, the Templars transferred their chief seat to the island of Cyprus. The order was abolished on the charge that the members had ambitious designs on European thrones, and that they held heretical views.

Tem′ple, in architecture, an edifice designed for the performance of public worship. Magnificent and wonderful temples were erected in ancient Greece and Rome, the Romans taking the Greek structures for models. The Egyptian temples also were marvelous structures. The most remarkable temple in the world, however, was that built by Solomon, on Mount Moriah, in Jerusalem. It was an oblong stone building, 60 cubits in length, 20 in width and 30 in height. On three sides were corridors, rising above each other to the height of three stories. The fourth, or front side, was open and was ornamented with a portico, 10 cubits in width, supported by two brazen pillars. The interior was divided into the most holy place, or Holy of Holies, and the sanctuary, or Holy Place. The former contained the ark of the covenant and was separated by a curtain from the sanctuary, in which were the golden candlesticks, the table of the showbread and the altar of incense. The Temple was surrounded by an inner court, which contained the altar of burnt offering. Colonnades, with brazen gates, separated this court of the priests from the outer court, which was likewise surrounded by a wall. This Temple was destroyed by Nebuchadnezzar in 586 B. C.; and after the return of the Jews from the Babylonish captivity, a second Temple, much inferior in splendor, was erected. Herod the Great rebuilt it on a larger scale, surrounding it with four courts, rising above each other like terraces, the lowest of which was 550 cubits square and was surrounded on three sides by a double row of columns and on the fourth by a triple row. In the middle of this enclosure stood the Temple, of white marble richly gilt, 100 cubits long and wide and 60 cubits high, with a porch 100 cubits wide. This magnificent edifice was destroyed by the Romans in A. D., 70 and now nothing of the original structure remains. The Turks have built a mosque there, with a dome, which is known as the Dome of the Rock, or the Mosque of Omar.

Temple, TEX., a city in Bell co., 35 mi. s. w. of Waco, on the Gulf, Colorado & Santa Fé and the Missouri, Kansas & Texas railroads. It is surrounded by some of the richest farming land in the state and has a very large trade in cotton. There are cottonseed oil mills, cotton compresses, flour mills, bottling works and manufactories of agricultural implements and other articles. The city has a public library, a business college, an academy, two hospitals and a number of churches. The place was settled in 1881. Population in 1910, 10,993.

Temple, FREDERICK (1821–1902), archbishop of Canterbury and primate of England, born in Leukas, one of the Ionian Islands. He was educated at Tiverton and Oxford, was ordained for the ministry in 1846, and was principal of the training college at Kneller Hall from 1848 to 1855, when he was appointed head master of Rugby, which position he held for eleven years. He was appointed archbishop of Canterbury in 1896. His last important public service was at the coronation of King Edward VII. He published *Reviews and Essays* and three volumes of *Sermons Preached at Rugby Chapel.* Doctor Temple was a priest of the new school, a rationalist, and was always progressive and always distinguished by vigor and originality of thought and action.

Tenacity, *te nas'e ty,* the measure of the resistance of bodies to tearing or crushing. Tenacity results from the attraction of cohesion, which exists between the particles of bodies; and the stronger this attraction is in any body, the greater is the tenacity of the body. Tenacity is consequently different in different materials, and in the same material it varies with the state of the body in regard to temperature and other circumstances. The tenacity of wood is much greater in the direction of the length of its fibers than in the transverse direction. With regard to metals, the processes of forging and wire-drawing increase their tenacity in the longitudinal direction (See WIRE); and mixed metals have, in general, greater tenacity than those which are simple.

Ten'ant, in law, one who occupies or has temporary possession of lands or tenements, the titles of which are in another, the landlord. A *tenant at will* is one who occupies lands or tenements for no fixed term other than the will of the landlord. A *tenant in common* is one who holds lands or tenements along with another or other persons. Each has a distinct share in the title, and on the death of a tenant his share goes to his heirs or executors. A *tenant for life* is one the duration of whose possession of lands or tenements, or whose interest in them, is determined by the life of the tenant or of another. See LEASE.

Tender, in law, an offer of compensation or damages made in a money action. To make a tender valid, the money must be actually produced. A tender made to one of several joint claimants is held as made to all. A tender of money for any payment is called a *legal tender,* if made in current coin of the country. In the

United States, if the tender is made in silver coins less than one dollar, the amount tendered cannot exceed ten dollars; if made in gold and silver coins, above one dollar, it may be for any amount; if made in United States bank notes, it is legal tender for any amount and for any debt, except for duties on imports and interest on the public debt.

Ten'dons, the name given to the sinews, or cords, by means of which the muscles are attached to the bones. They consist of bundles of white, fibrous, inelastic and very strong tissue, arranged in bands, separated by areolar or connective tissue. Tendons are often quite long, especially where the parts are slender, those in the fingers extending from the muscle in the upper part of the forearm.

Tenement, according to statute, any building in which three or more families live. In popular thought, however, the word tenement is restricted to houses occupied by several different families of the poorer classes of city population. As a large per cent of city dwellers is necessarily housed in tenements, all large cities are confronted with the tenement house problem. They are rightly concerned in the health and safety of their citizens. More and more it is seen that the environment in which people live has a far-reaching influence over their moral and physical well-being. Accordingly, cities must supervise their tenements. Light and ventilation—such important factors in combating disease—are now insisted on everywhere, and a part of the lot must be left vacant, so as to provide inner courts open to the air and weather. All rooms must have windows opening on such courts or on public streets. Sanitary closets must be provided and arrangements made for a suitable degree of family privacy. Fire protection is looked after, and the height of the buildings is limited.

Teneriffe, *ten ur if',* the largest of the Canary Islands. It has an irregular, triangular form. It is 60 mi. long from northeast to southwest and has an area of 785 sq. mi. The island is of volcanic formation and is celebrated for the high peak of Teneriffe, which rises to an altitude of 12,200 feet. The coast is generally abrupt and presents a succession of elevated cliffs, pierced by narrow elevations, resembling fiords. The only good harbor on the island is that of Santa Cruz, on the northeast. See CANARIES.

Tenghiz, *ten geez'.* See BALKASH.

Teniers, *te neerz',* DAVID, the Younger (1610–1690), a famous Flemish painter, the son of

David Teniers, also a painter of note. His works, most of which were scenes of peasant life, were very popular in his own day, and he had many honors conferred on him and became very wealthy. In 1650 Archduke Leopold William, the governor of the Spanish Netherlands, made him court painter, and he took up his residence at Brussels. The pictures of the archduke and his wife and of various scenes of court life were characteristic of this period of Tenierss' life. In his later years he returned to rural scenes and landscapes. He left about eight hundred pictures, some of which appear in every European collection of note. The closeness to nature and the beautiful coloring of his paintings assure him rank as one of the foremost of the genre painters.

Tennessee, the BIG BEND STATE, a South Central state, bounded on the north by Virginia and Kentucky, on the east by North Carolina, on the south by Georgia, Alabama and Mississippi and on the west by Arkansas and Missouri. The average length of the state is 385 miles; average width 109 miles; gross area 42,050 square miles. Population in 1910, Population in 1910, 2,184,789.

SURFACE AND DRAINAGE. What is known as East Tennessee extends from the Unaka or Smoky Mountains to the crest of the Cumberland Plateau, and contains some of the largest ridges of the Appalachians. Between the eastern ridges and the plateau stretches a valley region about one hundred miles in width, broken by minor elevations and depressions. West Tennessee lies between the Tennessee and Mississippi rivers. The narrow valley of the Tennessee River is skirted on the west by a gravelly ridge running north and south across the state. From this divide a rolling plain slopes toward the west, terminating in steep bluffs, beyond which are the alluvial bottom lands of the Mississippi. Middle Tennessee is the portion of the state between the crest of the Cumberland Plateau and the Tennessee River. Its chief structural features are the fertile central basin and the sandy, gravelly highland rim surrounding it.

The state is well drained by three great river systems. The Tennessee, formed by the confluence of the French Broad and the Holston, receives the Clinch, the Little Tennessee, the Elk and the Duck. The Cumberland flows into Tennessee from Kentucky, bends southward around Nashville, passes back into Kentucky and flows into the Ohio. The Mississippi River, which forms the western boundary of the state, has several important tributaries in Tennessee.

CLIMATE. The climate is mild and delightful, warmer in the lowlands of the west and cooler in the highlands of the east. The mean temperature at Memphis is 61.3°; at Nashville, 59.3°; at Knoxville, 57.4°. The average annual rainfall is 54 inches.

MINERAL RESOURCES. The mineral resources are varied and rich. The coal field coincides in extent with the Cumberland Plateau. The annual output of coal is about 6,500,000 short tons. Iron ore is next in importance, Tennessee being the seventh state in the Union in the production of iron. Phosphate rock of great value abounds in the western portion of the central basin and in the northern and western parts of the highland rim. The marbles of East Tennessee are noted for their purity and variety. The copper mines at Ducktown produce about 10,000,000 pounds a year, and large quantities of sulphuric acid as a by-product. Other minerals are slate, limestone, sandstone, lithographic stone, zinc and brick and pottery clays.

AGRICULTURE. Agriculture is the most important industry. The Mississippi bottoms are unsurpassed in fertility. They produce cotton, Indian corn, alfalfa and other crops in abundance. The most important crops of the state are corn, wheat and cotton. Other products are hay, tobacco, oats, potatoes, sorghum, peanuts and garden vegetables. Pears, peaches, apples and strawberries are extensively cultivated. Trucking for the Northern markets is an important industry in some portions of West Tennessee. Livestock raising is an important industry and dairying is increasing in importance.

MANUFACTURES. The manufactures are extensive and are rapidly increasing. Wheat and corn are ground in all parts of the state. Nashville is the principal center of the milling industry. Lumbering is an important industry in all parts of the state and much furniture, agricultural implements and other articles of wood are manufactured. The largest hard wood cabinet factories in the United States are located at Knoxville. There are many large factories for iron and steel products. Other manufactures are tobacco, cotton and woolen goods, cottonseed oil and cake, leather and leather goods, clothing, wagons, carriages, plows and other agricultural implements.

TRANSPORTATION. Tennessee has a railway mileage exceeding 3900 miles. The principal roads are the Nashville, Chattanooga & St.

Louis, the Louisville & Nashville, the Southern and the Illinois Central. The Cumberland, Tennessee and Mississippi are navigable rivers, the last furnishing communication with the entire Mississippi valley.

GOVERNMENT. The legislature consists of a senate and a house of representatives. The number of representatives cannot exceed ninety-nine and the number of senators is limited to one-third the number of representatives. The members of both houses are elected for two years. The legislature meets biennially; regular sessions are limited to seventy-five days and special sessions to twenty days. The executive department consists of a governor, elected by the people for two years; a secretary of state, elected by the legislature for four years, a treasurer and a comptroller of the treasury, elected by the legislature for two years, and an attorney-general appointed by the judges of the supreme court for eight years. The superintendent of public instruction and the commissioner of agriculture are appointed by the governor and confirmed by the senate for a term of two years. The courts consist of a supreme court, with five judges, a court of civil appeals, with five judges, all elected by the people for eight years, and circuit, chancery and other inferior courts, the judges of which are elected by the people of their respective districts for eight years.

EDUCATION. The public schools of the state are maintained by the interest on the permanent school fund, appropriations from the state treasury, and taxes levied in the several counties. Many cities and towns supplement these funds by local taxation. The state appropriates to public education one-fourth of its annual revenues. This is apportioned to the elementary schools, county high schools, the four state normal schools, the state university, and to school libraries. White and colored children attend separate schools. The institutions of higher education are the University of Tennessee, Knoxville; the George Peabody College for Teachers and Vanderbilt University, Nashville; University of the South, Sewanee; University of Chattanooga, Chattanooga; Fisk University, Nashville (for colored students), and a large number of private and church colleges.

INSTITUTIONS. The school for the deaf and dumb is at Knoxville; the school for the blind and the state industrial school are at Nashville. The hospitals for the insane are at Bolivar, Nashville and Knoxville. The penitentiary, at Nashville, has a branch at Petros, where the convicts work in the state coal mines. The state Confederate soldiers' home is at Nashville.

CITIES. The chief cities are Nashville, the capital; Memphis, Knoxville, Chattanooga, Jackson, Clarksville, Columbia, Johnson City and Bristol.

HISTORY. Probably the first white man to visit Tennessee was DeSoto. Later LaSalle built a fort at the site of Memphis. During the eighteenth century English explorers from the eastern colonies ventured into the region, among them Daniel Boone, James Robertson and others, and established posts for trade with the Indians. In 1772 the Wautauga Association was formed, under which the territory was governed almost independently for several years. It was, however, annexed to the State of North Carolina in 1776. Indian troubles were frequent, and the fact that the government of North Carolina did not take active measures to end these outbreaks, together with the indignation aroused at the presumption of North Carolina in ceding the territory of Tennessee to the Federal government, without consulting the inhabitants, led to the formation of a state known at "Frankland" or "Franklin," with John Sevier as governor. However, North Carolina soon regained possession. After 1790 the territory was known as the "Territory South of the Ohio," until June 1, 1796, when it was admitted as a state.

The progress of the new state was rapid, thousands of immigrants entering from all the Eastern states. The sentiment of the people of Tennessee was divided at the outbreak of the Civil War, but after a period of hesitation the state seceded in June, 1861. It furnished more than 100,000 soldiers to the Confederate army and about 30,000 to the Federal army, and it was the scene of some of the severest fighting of the war. Andrew Johnson, a War Democrat, was appointed military governor and attempted to reorganize the state as a part of the Union, but met with rebuffs from Congress. For a time after the war there was much disorder, but soon Tennessee entered upon another period of progress, which has since continued. Since 1868 the state has been almost uniformly Democratic. Consult McGee's *History of Tennessee*.

Tennessee, UNIVERSITY OF. The State University, located at Knoxville, was established in 1794 as Blount College. In 1807 the name was changed to East Tennessee College. Two years later it was changed to East Tennessee University, and in 1879 to the University of Tennessee. In 1909 it was recognized as an integra-part of the public school system of the state. It contains the state college of agriculture and mechanic arts, and receives for the support of this college all the Federal funds allotted to the state for this purpose. It also has the Tennessee Experiment Station, supported by Federal and state funds. It maintains a branch station at Jackson, carries on co-operative agricultural experiments in Middle Tennessee, and conducts short courses in agriculture at a number of places in all sections of the state. There are schools of science, liberal arts, education, law, medicine and dentistry, the last two being located at Nashville. The total number of instructors is about one hundred and fifty; the total number of students about one thousand.

Tennessee River, a river of the United States, formed by the Clinch and the Holston, which rise in Virginia and unite in the eastern part of Tennessee. It flows southwestward to Chattanooga, crossing several ridges of the Alleghany Mountains, thence flows westward through the northern part of Alabama, then northward and northeastward and again northwestward, crossing Kentucky and emptying into the Ohio River near Paducah. It is the largest tributary of the Ohio and is about 800 miles long. It is navigable for large steamboats to Florence, Ala., where it is obstructed by rapids. A canal around these has extended the navigation for steamers as far as Kingston.

Tenniel, *ten neel',* JOHN, SIR (1820–1914), one of the most famous illustrators, born in London. He painted one of the frescoes in the Houses of Parliament in 1845, but he painted only a few pictures. From 1851 to 1901 he was connected, as an illustrator, with *Punch,* and produced over two thousand cartoons for that paper, in particular the weekly political cartoon. He also illustrated many Christmas and other books, including *Aesop's Fables, Ingoldsby Legends* and *Alice's Adventures in Wonderland.*

Ten'nis, a game in which a ball is driven continually against a wall, in a specially constructed court, and caused to rebound beyond a line at a certain distance. Several persons strike it alternately with a racket, the object being to keep the ball in motion as long as possible, without allowing it to fall to the ground. The game was introduced into England in the thirteenth century, and it continued to be very popular with the nobility to the reign of Charles II. See LAWN TENNIS.

Ten'nyson, ALFRED, first Baron Tennyson (1809–1892), the greatest representative poet of

the Victorian Age, born at Somersby, Lincolnshire, Aug. 6, 1809. With the exception of four years spent at the Louth Grammar School, his early education and preparation for college were directed by his father, rector of the parish. In 1828 he entered Trinity College, Cambridge, where he distinguished himself as a student, and where, in 1830, he won a medal, with his prize poem, *Timbuctoo.* He had published, in 1827, in conjunction with his brother Charles, *Poems*

ALFRED TENNYSON

by Two Brothers, but this work gave little indication of his peculiar genius; and his first really important work was a volume of *Poems, Chiefly Lyrical,* which appeared in 1830, and which revealed undoubted genius. In this very productive period, two years later, a second volume appeared, which won for its author recognition as a true poet. It contained many of his most beautiful shorter poems, *The Lady of Shalott, Oenone, The Lotus-Eaters* and *A Dream of Fair Women.*

Partly because of adverse criticism, but chiefly because of his deep affliction in the death of his friend, Arthur Hallam, the next nine years of his life were spent in retirement and in complete devotion to his art. As a result of these years of study, brooding and reflection, came the two volumes of 1842, which showed, in such notable poems as *Morte d'Arthur, Dora, Locksley Hall, Ulysses, The Two Voices* and *Break, Break,*

Break, that the poet's power was reaching its maturity. From this year dates Tennyson's supremacy. *The Princess,* with its exquisite lyrics, was published in 1847, and following this in 1850 came *In Memoriam,* in some respects the finest elegiac poem in the language. The suffering and doubt and final triumph of faith, which had been Tennyson's personal experience after the death of Arthur Hallam, and the general tendency of the age to skepticism and materialism, which must finally emerge in a deeper and nobler faith and understanding, find expression in this series of lyrics. In this same year Tennyson succeeded Wordsworth as poet-laureate; and he married Miss Emily Sellwood, to whom he had been for years betrothed.

Maud, and Other Poems was published in 1855, but was not received with marked enthusiasm. This coldness, however, was more than compensated by the revival of popularity in 1859, when the *Idylls of the King* appeared. In 1864 came *Enoch Arden,* perhaps the most popular of Tennyson's poems. During his later years he made several attempts at dramatic composition, but, though his productions are excellent, they cannot rank with the best. In 1889 appeared the volume called *Demeter and Other Poems,* which contained *Crossing the Bar.*

In 1884 he was made a baron. During his remaining years he lived in the retirement he had always chosen, and his life was ended fittingly by a quiet death in his summer home at Alderworth, Sussex, Oct. 6, 1892. He was placed in Westminster Abbey, next to Chaucer and Robert Browning.

Tennyson's marvelous mastery of the form of verse, his keen sensibility to both material and spiritual beauty and his sympathy with the dominant longing of his age for truth, make him at once its truest and greatest exponent and one of the rarest of the world's poets. Consult Stopford's Brook's *Tennyson, His Art and Relation to Modern Life.*

Ten'or. See SINGING.

Ten'rec. See TANREC.

Tent, a portable dwelling, usually made of canvas, but occasionally of skins of animals and of felt. The simplest form of tent is that of a cone, supported by a pole in the center. The usefulness of this tent is increased by raising the roof several feet and having a separate canvas for the walls, which will be circular. This pattern of tent is in very general use in the armies of the United States and other countries. Another common pattern is that having straight walls and square corners, with a roof shaped like the roof of an ordinary building. The frame for this tent has two or more long poles, extending to the highest point in the roof, with standards for the corners. If the tent is large, a number of standards are necessary. See EDUCATOR, *The Boy's Workshop.*

Ten'ure of Office Act, the name given to several different acts of Congress, by which the term of public officials or the manner of their appointment and removal was determined. The first of these was passed in 1820, fixing a four-year tenure for many Federal positions formerly held indefinitely or during good behavior. By making the tenure of office terminate at the change of national administrations, the way was cleared for the introduction of the "spoils system" in national politics.

Probably the most famous act was that passed in 1867, which was the outgrowth of the conflict between Congress and President Johnson. In accordance with the custom established by a century of history, President Johnson had the power to remove cabinet officers, and he dismissed Secretary Stanton from the office of secretary of war. Congress, which opposed President Johnson's plans and upheld the secretary, accordingly passed an act providing that the consent of the Senate was necessary for the removal of all officials whose appointment was subject to the consent of the Senate. Johnson's disregard of this law resulted in his impeachment. The act was decidedly modified in 1869 and was repealed in 1887, after a contest between President Cleveland and the Senate.

Tepic, *ta peek',* a city of Mexico, situated on a plateau about 2000 feet above the sea, and 25 mi. e. by s. of San Blas. Its leading industries include the manufacture of cotton goods and cigars. Population in 1911, 17,000.

Terceira, *ter sa'e ra,* one of the most important of the Azores, situated in the Atlantic Ocean, about 50 mi. n. e of Pico. It has an area of 162 square miles, is of volcanic origin and contains a number of cones, which are more or less active. The highest summit is about 3600 feet above the sea. The interior of the island contains fine pasture land. The inhabitants are engaged in stock raising and agriculture, good crops of wheat, corn, grapes and other fruit being raised. The seat of government is Angra, on the south coast. Population in 1910, 51,000. See AZORES.

Terence, *ter'ens,* (about 185–159 B. C.), in full, Publius Terentius Afer, a celebrated Roman writer of comedies. He was born in Africa, and while a child was bought by Publius Terentius Lucanus, a Roman senator, who took him to Rome, gave him a good education and finally freed him. The first play which he produced, *Andria*, won him recognition and popularity. About the year 161 he went to Greece, where he translated many of Menander's comedies. According to some accounts he died in Greece; according to others he was drowned in his passage back to Italy. Six comedies of Terence's are extant, and these are all he is known to have produced: *Andria, The Eunuch, The Self Tormentor, Phormio, The Stepmother,* and the *Adelphi*, his last piece, brought out in Rome the year before his death.

Terhune, *ter hune′*, MARY VIRGINIA HAWES (1831–　　), an American writer, best known by her pseudonym, Marion Harland. From the time she was fourteen years old she wrote for the press. In 1888 she became editor of *The Homemaker*. She has conducted departments in *Wide Awake, Saint Nicholas* and many other periodicals and in daily newspapers. Among the novels which she has published are *The Hidden Path, Miriam, Judith, True as Steel* and *Moss-Side*.

Termites, *tur′mite's*, a family of insects, commonly known as white ants. They live much

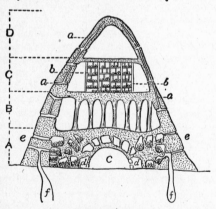

TERMITES' NEST

In the above diagrammatic section of a termite's nest, *D* represents a well-aired, empty attic; *C*, the next story, the nursery, where the young termites are hatched; *B*, a hall, supported by pillars; *A* the ground story; *a*, winding passages in the walls; *b*, the shelves on which the young termites are hatched; *c*, the royal chamber, in which the king and queen are imprisoned; *d*, the chambers of the worker termites *e*, store chambers; *f*, holes in the ground out of which the material used in making the nest is dug

like the ants, though really they have little relationship to them. Termites are confined to the tropics and are especially plentiful in western Africa. They live in colonies, raising large

166

dwellings, in the form of irregular pyramids or cones, to the height of ten or twelve feet. These structures are firmly cemented and are strong enough to bear the weight of several men. Each is divided into various apartments, chambers and galleries, which have their specific uses, like

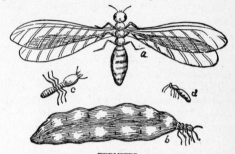

TERMITES

a, perfect male; *b*, female distended with eggs; *c*, soldier; *d*, worker.

the rooms of a house. In every colony there are a king and a queen, both of which are much larger than the rest of the insects; they are constantly kept together in a large chamber in the heart of the hive, where they are attended by a detachment of workers. The queen, whose body is more than a thousand times larger than that of the king, lays the eggs at intervals, and workers carry them off to the small cells in which the larvae are reared. Only the king and queen have wings, except at certain seasons of the year, when a number of winged insects of both sexes are produced and leave the hive; they fly abroad and settle down to form new colonies. There seem to be two classes of neuters, the workers and the soldiers. It is the duty of the former to build the habitations, make covered roads, nurse the young, attend on the king and queen and manage the domestic affairs of the colony. The soldiers have powerfully developed mandibles, and they defend the community with desperate courage from any attacks. In the tropics, some species are terribly destructive, as they sometimes riddle all the timbers of a house before their presence is even known. One species of termites is native of the United States.

Tern, *turn*, a bird of the gull family, seen along lakes and rivers and on the seacoast. These long-winged, graceful birds are sometimes known as *sea swallows*. They may be distinguished by their long, slender, straight bills, pointed wings and forked tails. The legs are relatively shorter than those of the true gulls. They are bold, but wary, birds, whose habit it is to plunge into the water for their prey, sometimes completely immersing their bodies. The largest species, the *Caspian tern*, has a wing expanse of about four feet and is found not only in Europe, Asia and Africa, but also in America. The *common tern* may be seen in all parts of the eastern United States. There are over twenty species common to North America.

Terpsichore, *turp sik'o re*, one of the Muses, the inventor and patroness of the art of dancing.

Terrace, *ter'rase*, in physiography, the name given a stretch of level land along the shore of the sea, a lake or a stream. The surface of the terrace is the former bed of the body of water which it borders. In many river valleys a succession of terraces is found, each of which was the bed of the stream in some former age. The highest terrace is the oldest, and the lowest is the youngest. Terraces are found around the Great Lakes and Lake Champlain. They are usually fertile, but lack moisture. They afford excellent sites for towns and villages and give a pleasing appearance to the landscape.

Ter'ra Cot'ta (Italian, "baked earth"), baked clay or burned earth, a similar material to that from which pottery is made, much used, both in ancient and modern times, for architectural decorations, statues, figures and vases. As now made, it usually consists of potters' clay and fine powdered silica. It is produced in many different colors, the most pleasing being a rich red and a warm cream color. Large numbers of ancient statues, especially statuettes, of terra cotta have been found in recent times. Terra cotta is extensively used by architects for ornamenting buildings.

A large part of terra work is made in plaster of Paris molds. Cornices and other architectural decorations, in which many pieces are just alike, can best be divided into numerous sections and cast. In the process of firing, terra cotta shrinks about one inch to the foot, and allowance must be made for this in the molding. Terra cotta may be glazed or enameled beautifully in white and colors, the work being done exactly as in the case of tile glazing. See POTTERY.

Ter'ra Del Fuego, *fway'go*. See TIERRA DEL FUEGO.

Ter'rapin, the popular name of several species of fresh-water or tide-water tortoises. They are distinguished by a horny beak and scales, covering the upper part of the shell, and partially webbed feet. Terrapins inhabit the tropical and warm temperate countries. They are found in abundance off the Atlantic coast, in the salt-water marshes around Charleston. The *chicken* tortoise, so named from its flavor, is a highly esteemed American species of terrapin. See TORTOISE.

Terre Haute, *ter e hote'*, IND., county-seat of Vigo co., 72 mi. s. w. of Indianapolis, on the Cleveland, Cincinnati, Chicago & Saint Louis, the Vandalia and several other railroads. The city is located on the high terraces of the Wabash River, is regularly laid out, with broad streets, and has several parks. It is the seat of the Rose Polytechnic Institute, the Indiana State Normal School and Saint Mary's Institute, and it contains several orphanages, hospitals and the Rose Dispensary. The public library, the Federal building, the courthouse, the city hall, the opera house and the union station are some of the most prominent structures. The surrounding country is agricultural and contains valuable coal mines. The city is an important railroad center and also has some river trade. The various industrial establishments include distilleries, foundries, machine shops, flour and hominy mills, clothing factories, rolling mills, packing houses, car works, planing mills and manufactories of carriages, glass, electric motors, enameled ware, paving brick, stoves and tools. The place was founded in 1816 and was chartered as a city in 1833. Population in 1900, 36,673. In 1910 it was 58,157.

Ter'rell, TEX., a city in Kaufman co., 32 mi. e. of Dallas, on the Texas & Pacific and the Texas Midland railroads. It is in an agricultural region and has a large trade in cotton, grain, vegetables and live stock. The chief industrial establishments are railroad shops, cotton and flour mills, creameries and agricultural implement works. The North Texas Hospital for the insane and Terrell University are located here, and the city has a Carnegie library, two high schools and a number of churches. The place was settled by Robert Terrell in 1872. Population in 1910, 7050.

Ter'rier, a small dog, remarkable for the eagerness and courage with which it goes into earth and attacks all such animals as foxes, badgers, cats, rats and the like. There are several varieties. In Great Britain two kinds are common, the one rough and wire-haired, known as the *Scotch terrier*, the other smooth-haired and generally more delicate in appearance, known as the *English terrier*. The *skye terrier* is a subvariety of the Scotch terrier, and it is peculiarly prized. The *pepper and mustard* breeds, rendered famous by Sir Walter Scott, are highly valued. The *black and tan* terrier has a sleek and soft coat. All terriers are vigorous, intelligent and have very keen senses. See DANDIE DINMONT; SKYE TERRIER; SCOTCH TERRIER; FOX TERRIER.

Ter'rito'ry, a term applied in the United States to an area similar to a state of the Union, but without the independent position of a state; it is governed directly by Congress, through a governor and other chief officials, appointed by the president, and a legislature of certain limited powers. Territories are usually admitted as states on attaining a sufficient population and adopting a constitution approved by Congress.

Ter'ror, REIGN OF, the term usually applied to the period of the French Revolution from the appointment of the Revolutionary Tribunal and the Committee of Public Safety, in April, 1793, to the fall of Robespierre in July, 1794. See FRENCH REVOLUTION.

Ter'ry, ALFRED HOWE (1827–1890), an American soldier, born at Hartford, Conn. He was admitted to the bar in 1849 and practiced law for a number of years. On the outbreak of the Civil War he entered the service as colonel of the Second Connecticut Militia Regiment. From this position he was rapidly promoted, and in 1865 he was brevetted major general in the regular army. He commanded the Department of Dakota, and in 1876 he led the expedition against the Sioux indians, driving them and their chief, Sitting Bull, into Canada. In 1886 he was made a full major general, succeeding General Hancock, and two years later he retired from the army.

Terry, ELLEN ALICIA (1848–   ), a famous English actress, born at Coventry. She made her first appearance on the stage when only eight years old, playing Manilius in *The Winter's Tale* at the Princess's Theater, under the management of Charles Kean. In 1858 she acted the part of Arthur in *King John*, and in 1863 she made her début as a regular performer, playing Gertrude in *The Little Treasure* at the Haymarket. She married in 1864 and left the stage, but reappeared again in 1867 at the New Queen's Theater, London. In 1879 she made her first appearance at the Lyceum, and for almost a quarter of a century she assisted Henry Irving in his presentations of many of the greatest of classic and modern plays. In Tennyson's *The Cup*, in *Romeo and Juliet, Faust, Eugene Aram* and *Becket*, she proved her right to rank with the greatest of English actresses, but it was as Portia, in the *Merchant of Venice*, that her strongest work

was done. In company with Irving she made many visits to America and always met with great success.

Tertiary, *tur'she a ry,* **Period** or **Tertiary System,** a system of rock formations, joining the Cretaceous below and the Quaternary above, and forming the first division of the Cenozoic Era. The system was named from a former theory, which considered that all strata were divisible into three groups, primary, secondary and tertiary. The system was divided by the English geologist Lyell into four series, or epochs— Eocene, Oligocene, Miocene and Pliocene—each of which is described under its proper title. The United States Geological Survey has grouped these epochs into two, Eocene and Neocene, and this classification is generally adopted in the United States. The rocks of the formation in the United States are found on the Pacific coast, in the western interior, and on the Atlantic and

ELLEN TERRY

Gulf coasts. It was during the Tertiary period that the earth was subjected to those violent changes that resulted in the formation of the highest mountains, the Himalayas, the Caucasus, the Andes and parts of the Rocky Mountains. The climate at the beginning of the period was warm, but the elevation of the continents brought on the age of ice, known as the Glacial period. See CENOZOIC ERA; CRETACEOUS SYSTEM; QUATERNARY PERIOD; GLACIAL PERIOD.

Tertul'lian, Quintus Septimius Florens Tertullianus, the earliest Latin father of the Church, whose works are extant, was born before 160 and died after 220. But little is known of his life, but he had a liberal education. His opposition to worldliness in the Church led him to join the Montanists and to write several books in their defense. His most celebrated work is *The Apology*, a formal defense of Christianity, addressed to the Roman magistrates. The works of Tertullian are chiefly valuable for the light they throw on the doctrine and discipline of the Church in the age in which he lived. Some of his sentences have become proverbial, as, "The blood of the martyrs is the seed of the church"; "How wise an arguer does ignorance seem to herself to be!"

Tes'la, NIKOLA (1857–), an American electrician and inventor. He studied engineering in Paris and was engineer of the Edison station located there. For a time he was employed at Edison's laboratory, near Orange, N. J., but left to open a laboratory of his own. He has shown that electric lamps and motors can be operated on one wire, without a circuit, and he has invented the rotary field motor, the multiphase system of which is used in the 50,000 horse power plant, built to transmit the water power of Niagara Falls to Buffalo and other places. He is considered one of the greatest geniuses in the field of electrical research.

Test Acts, the general term applied to various acts of the English Parliament, which made the holding of public offices conditional on certain religious tests. The name especially belongs to the Corporation Act of 1661, which decreed that all magistrates must take the oaths of allegiance and supremacy and must receive the communion according to the Church of England; and to the Test Act of 1673, which imposed the same tests on the holders of all public offices. These statutes, after various modifications, were finally repealed in 1829.

Testu'do, among the ancient Romans, a cover, or screen, which a body of troops formed with their oblong shields or targets, by holding them over their heads, when standing close to one another. This cover somewhat resembled the back of a tortoise and served to shelter the men from missiles thrown from above. The name was also given to a structure on wheels or rollers, used for protecting those engaged in building or repairing fortifications.

Tet'anus, the disease commonly known as *lockjaw*. In warm climates this is a frequent result of wounds, and it consists in spasmodic contraction of the muscles. This is often strong enough to draw the body entirely out of shape and to hold the lower jaw so closely against the upper that it is impossible to separate them. The disease is a terrible one and is usually fatal, as not more than ten per cent of well-developed cases recover. The disease is infectious and is caused by the presence in the wound of a bacterium common in dirt or the soil of gardens. Treatment by serum has proved effective in curing a number of cases. See SERUM THERAPY.

Tetrazzini, LUISA, a famous Italian soprano, born at Florence. She received her musical education in her native city, and made her debut there in 1895. Since that time she has sung in grand opera in the principal cities of the world, and has gained a wonderful popularity, ranking with the greatest singers of her time. Her favorite operas are *Lucia di Lammermoor* and *La Somnambula.*

Teutonic Knights, *tu ton'ik nite's,* a religious and military order which grew up at the time of the Crusades. The object of its founders, a number of German merchants, was the alleviation of the suffering of the Christian soldiers at the siege of Acre. The society, which received by charter the same privileges as the Templars and the Hospitalers, had its seat first at Acre, but it later removed to Germany, where it set about the conversion of the heathen Prussians. During the fourteenth century the order had much influence and much territory, but during the following century it declined rapidly. However, it existed until 1809, when it was dissolved by Napoleon. A revival of the order, in name at least, took place in Austria in 1834.

Teutonic Races, a term now applied to the High Germans, including the German inhabitants of Upper and Middle Germany and those of Switzerland and Austria; the low Germans, including the Frisians, the Plattdeutsch, the Dutch, the Flemings, and the English descended from the Saxons, Angles and other tribes who settled in Britain; the Scandinavians, including the Norwegians, the Swedes, the Danes and the Icelanders.

Tex'arkan'a, ARK. and TEX., twin cities on the boundary line, one the county-seat of Miller co., Ark., and the other in Bowie co., Tex. They are 145 mi. s. w. of Little Rock, Ark., on the Texas & Pacific, the Kansas City Southern, the Saint Louis Southwestern and other railroads. The towns form one industrial community, but have independent city governments. A pos office, situated on the state line, is used by both cities. They have many fine residences and good business blocks, a Y. M. C. A. building, a railroad hospital and more than thirty churches. The higher educational institutions are the Saint Agnes Academy, the Saint Rose of Lima Academy and the Texarkana Industrial College. The place has a large trade in lumber and cotton, and the leading industrial establishments are various cotton works, railroad shops, lumber mills, machine shops and furniture and pottery factories. Both towns were settled in 1873 and became incorporated cities in 1887. Population in 1900, in Arkansas, 4914; in Texas, 5256. Only a small percentage are of foreign birth, and about 4200 are negroes. Since 1900 the cities have grown considerably. Population in 1910, 15,445.

Texas, the LONE STAR STATE. one of the South Central states is bounded on the n. by New Mexico, Oklahoma and Arkansas; on the e. by Arkansas and Louisiana; on the s. e. by the Gulf of Mexico; on the s. and s. w. by Mexico, from which it is separated by the Rio Grande River. and on the w. by New Mexico. Texas is the largest state in the Union. It is more than one-twelfth the size of the entire United States, exclusive of Alaska and the Philippines, and is larger than either France or Germany. Its average length from n. to s is 760 miles; its average breadth from east to west, 740 miles, and gross area, 265,896 square miles, of which 3498 square miles is water. Population in 1910, 3,896,542.

SURFACE AND DRAINAGE. In general the surface of Texas consists of a series of extended plains and plateaus more or less diversified by mountains and hills and sloping gradually from the northwest to the southeast. The state is divided into four physiographic regions. The first region, belonging to the coastal plain, extends inland from 100 to 200 miles and is prolonged northward to the northeastern corner. This region rises gradually from sea level to an altitude of 600 to 700 feet. The northern part of it is heavily timbered with long-leaved pine, short-leaved pine and hard woods. Second is the Great Black and Grand Prairie reigon, which lies to the west and northwest of the coastal plain. This region has an area of about 31.000 square miles and consists of a gently undulating plain sloping toward the east and southeast, with an altitude of from 400 to 700 feet. The eastern part of this plain is nearly level, but in the west it is more broken, and that

portion south of the Brazos River becomes rugged It contains little timber, but is covered with a soil of remarkable fertility. The third region is the great Staked Plain or Llano Estacado, occupying the northwestern part of the state and bounded by high bluffs and buttes. This is a vast, treeless plateau with an elevation of from 3000 to 4000 feet above sea level. It is in an arid region, but a large part of it supports a good growth of grass, and the region is well adapted to grazing. The fourth, the mountainous region, occupies the western part of the state between the Pecos and the Rio Grande. This contains a continuation of the Rocky Mountains, which extends southward into Mexico. The elevations vary from 3000 to 6000 feet and some of the highest peaks have an elevation of 9000 feet.

The rivers of Texas flow into the Mississippi, the Gulf of Mexico or the Rio Grande. The principal tributary of the Mississippi from Texas is the Red, which forms a part of the northern boundary and drains the northeastern corner of the state The Sabine, forming a part of the boundary between Texas and Louisiana, drains a small portion of the eastern section and flows directly into the Gulf The other streams of importance flowing into the Gulf, in their order southward from the Sabine, are the Neches, the Trinity, the Brazos, the Colorado and the Nueces. The principal tributary of the Rio Grande is the Pecos, which flows across the western part of the state. Along the coast there are numerous lagoons enclosed by low sand bars, and in a number of places there are deep indentations, the most important of these being Sabine Lake, Galveston Bay, Matagorda Bay and Corpus Christi Bay.

CLIMATE. On account of its size and its relief, Texas has a great variety of climate. The southern extremity is only 2° from the torrid zone, but the state stretches northward through 11° of latitude. It is mostly exempt from the extremes of cold and heat. The Gulf breeze blows from the southeast during the summer. The east part of the state is humid, with an annual rainfall of 50 to 60 inches. Toward the west, it gradually diminishes. At El Paso it is about 10 inches. The Gulf coast and prairie region have abundant rainfall. The mean annual temperature is about 70°. One of the climatic features of the state is what is known as the "northers."

MINERAL RESOURCES. Both lignite and bituminous coal are found in a number of places.

The largest deposits are in the northern and east central parts of the state. Another occurs on the Rio Grande and extends into Mexico. These mines are being worked more and more each year. It is estimated that the area of all the coal fields in the state is about 40,000 square miles, and the annual output exceeds 1,000,000 tons. Thurber, Bridgeport and Cisco are among the leading coal mining towns. Petroleum has been found in a number of places, particularly in the southeastern part. The Beaumont, Sour Lake, Humble and Corsicana oil fields are among the most important. The annual output exceeds 13,000,000 barrels. There are also deposits of gypsum, salt and sulphur. Asphalt is found in Montague County and elsewhere. Natural gas is found in a number of regions. There is an abundant supply of granite and other building stone. Lying along the Rio Grande in the extreme southwestern part of the state is an extensive deposit of cinnabar. Iron ore and quicksilver are found in several places. As yet the mineral resources of Texas are comparatively undeveloped.

AGRICULTURE. Texas is well adapted to agriculture and produces large crops of nearly all grains, fruits and vegetables grown in a warm temperate climate. It is the first state in the Union in the production of cotton, producing one-fifth of the cotton supply of the world. This has grown largely in the coastal plain region and the prairie region to the north and west. In the southern part of the coastal plains there are 40,000 acres given to the growth of sugar cane, and 182,000 acres producing rice. In the interior, corn, wheat, oats, potatoes, berries, nuts and orchard fruits are raised. The raising of vegetables for the Northern markets is an important branch of agricultural industry. The western part of the state is devoted to stock raising. Texas has more cattle than any other state in the Union. Alfalfa is also raised in West Texas to a large extent, and irrigation is being profitably used in many places. A magnificent supply of artesian well water renders irrigation possible. West Texas raises and ships large numbers of horses and hogs. In the production of wool, Texas is a leading state. In the value of its agricultural products, Texas is the third state in the Union.

MANUFACTURES. Manufacturing in Texas is yet in its infancy, but the state possesses great natural advantages for this industry. The large area of the state and the heavy freight charge tend also to encourage the manufacture of articles for local use. The manufacture of lumber and of lumber and timber products is the leading industry. Next in importance is the making of cottonseed oil and cake. In the value of cottonseed oil and cake, Texas ranks first in the Union. Other industries are the manufacture of cotton goods, saddles and harness, flour and grist mill products, the making and repairing of railway cars and the canning of fruits and vegetables.

TRANSPORTATION AND COMMERCE. Galveston is the chief seaport and is located on a good harbor. The northeastern and central parts of the state are well supplied with railways. Two trunk lines extend across the state from northeast to southwest into Mexico, and two lines cross it from east to west, reaching the Pacific coast. These are connected by numerous cross-lines and also have spurs reaching the lumber regions and the most important agricultural regions, but the coast counties and those in the northwestern and western parts of the state are yet without adequate railway communication. The entire mileage of the state is about 15,000 miles, and new lines are being constructed from year to year. Texas is the first state in the Union in railway mileage.

The commerce of Texas is extensive. The exports consist of cotton, lumber, oil, rice, hardware, livestock, wool, vegetables and fruits, and far exceed in value the imports, which consist of manufactured goods and food products.

GOVERNMENT. The legislature consists of a senate limited to 31 members, and a house of representatives limited to not more than one member to each 15,000 inhabitants and not more than 150 members in the aggregate. The senators are elected for four years and the representatives for two years. The legislature meets biennially and the session is practically limited to sixty days by the reduced pay of the members after that time. The executive department consists of a governor, lieutenant-governor, comptroller, treasurer, commissioner of general land office, state superintendent of public instruction, and attorney-general, each elected for two years, and a railroad commission of three members, elected for six years. The secretary of state, the adjutant general, and the commissioner of insurance, agriculture, statistics and history, are appointed by the governor.

The courts consist of a supreme court of three judges, elected for six years each, five courts of civil appeal, of three judges each, one court of criminal appeals of three judges, and sixty-three district courts of one judge each; also county courts of each county, and justice courts for precincts, towns and villages. The judges of the district courts are elected for four years, and the county court for two years.

EDUCATION. The state maintains an excellent system of public schools and has the largest permanent school fund in the Union. The perpetual state funds of the state amount to about $65,000,000, the exact value and the exact distribution varying from time to time. The state paid in 1910 for the education of each child of scholastic age, $6.25. This was largely supplemented by local taxation. Separate schools are maintained for white and colored children. The school system is under the direct supervision of a Board of Education and a State Superintendent. In counties of 3000 scholastic population and over there is a county superintendent of schools. In smaller counties the people may, by vote, establish this office. When there is no such officer, the county judge is exofficio the county superintendent of schools. Besides the rural schools, cities and large towns are independent school districts and have, in many instances, excellent systems of graded schools. State normal schools are located at Huntsville, Denton, San Marcos and Canyon City. There is also a state normal school for colored teachers at Prairie View, near Hempstead. The state university is at Austin, but its medical department is at Galveston. The agricultural and mechanical college is at College Station, near Bryan, and the college of industrial arts (for girls) is at Denton. There are besides these institutions a number of important colleges and secondary schools maintained by various religious denominations. The most important of these are Southwestern University at Georgetown, the Polytechnic College at Fort Worth, Baylor University and Texas Christian University at Waco, Trinity University at Waxahachie, Austin College at Sherman, the North Texas Female College at Sherman.

INSTITUTIONS. The schools for the deaf and dumb and blind are at Austin. Institutions are maintained here for both white and colored children. There is a Confederate soldiers home at Austin, and also a home for the widows of the Confederate soldiers. There is a state orphans home at Corsicana. The hospitals for the insane are at Austin, San Antonio and Terrell. The state penitentiaries are at Huntsville and Rusk, and the reformatory for juvenile offenders is at Gatesville.

CITIES. The chief cities are Austin, the capital; San Antonio, Dallas, Houston, Fort Worth, Galveston, Waco, El Paso, Laredo and Denison.

HISTORY. Cabeza de Vaca, a Spanish companion of Narvaez, visited Texas in 1528, but it was more than one hundred fifty years later that the first European settlement was made by La Salle. Many years later missions were founded by Spaniards at San Antonio. In 1730 the indians began war on both French and Spaniards, but did not weaken the hold of either. After 1820 there was a vast immigration of citizens of the United States to Texas, the most important settlement being made at Austin. At about the same time, the revolt of Mexico from Spain occurred, in which the Texans eagerly joined, but oppressive laws by the Mexican congress led to a revolt of Texas from Mexico, under the leadership chiefly of Americans, among them Sam Houston. Texas was successful, though never recognized by Mexico, and a republic was formed, which was disorganized in 1845, when Texas was annexed to the United States and admitted as a state. This led to the Mexican War, which was terminated by the Treaty of Guadalupe Hidalgo, by which Mexico acknowledged the right of the United States in Texas.

In 1861 Texas seceded from the United States and joined the Confederacy, to whose armies she furnished 90,000 soldiers during the Civil War. Under orders from President Johnson in June, 1865, a reorganized government was established, with a constitution abolishing slavery, renouncing the right of secession, conferring civil rights on freedmen and repudiating the Confederate state debt. However, Congress did not recognize the new government, and, by the reconstruction acts of 1867 placed the state under military authority, with General Philip H. Sheridan in command. Until 1870 the carpetbag régime ensued, with disastrous results, but in March of that year Texas was readmitted to the Union. Since that time the state has increased rapidly in population and wealth. Consult Garrison's *Texas*, in the American Commonwealths Series.

Texas, UNIVERSITY OF, a state institution of higher learning, established at Austin, Tex., in 1876, but not opened until 1883. As organized it comprises a college of liberal arts and departments of engineering, law and medicine, the last being located at Galveston. The income of the university is derived from a million and a half acres of land, set apart by the state. The faculty numbers about 140, and there are about 2500 students. The library contains 80,000 volumes.

Thack′eray, WILLIAM MAKEPEACE (1811–1863), an English novelist and humorist, born at Calcutta. At the age of seven he was sent to England for his education, was placed at the Charterhouse School, London, and afterward continued his studies at Cambridge. He left the university without taking a degree and chose the career of an artist; but after spending some

WILLIAM M. THACKERAY

time on the Continent, in study, he became convinced that art was not his vocation, and having lost his fortune, he resolved to turn his attention to literature. His first appearance in this sphere was as a journalist. Under the names of George Fitz-Boodle, Esq., or of Michael Angelo Titmarsh, he contributed to *Frazer's Magazine* tales, criticisms, verses and character sketches which were marked by great knowledge of the world, keen irony and playful humor. It was in this magazine that *The Yellowplush Papers*, *Barry Lyndon*, *The Paris Sketchbook* and *The Irish Sketchbook* first appeared. In 1841 *Punch* was started, and Thackeray's contributions to that periodical, among others *Jeames's Diary* and the *Snob Papers*, were very successful.

In 1846–1848 his novel of *Vanity Fair* was published in monthly parts, with illustrations by himself; and long before its completion its author was unanimously placed in the first rank of British novelists. His next novel was *Pendennis*, completed in 1850. In 1851 he delivered a series of lectures in London on the *English Humorists of the Eighteenth Century*, which were repeated in Scotland and America and were published in 1853. Another novel, *Henry Esmond*, appeared in 1852, and this was followed by *The Newcomes* (1855); *The Virginians* (1858), a sort of sequel to *Henry Esmond*; *Lovel the Widower*; *The Adventures of Philip*, and *Denis Duval*, which was left unfinished at his death. In 1855–1856 he delivered a series of lectures in the United States on *The Four Georges*. In 1860 he became editor of the *Cornhill Magazine*, in which his later novels and the remarkable *Roundabout Papers* appeared, but he retired from that post in 1862.

Thackeray's writings are remarkable always for their unfailing purity and simplicity of style. They are characterized throughout by keen satire, which, however, is not the bitter cynicism of Swift, directed against human nature in general, but a more kindly satire, ridiculing sham and pretense in whatever guise, but sparing everything that is good and genuine. Thackeray undoubtedly ranks as the classical English satirist of the Victorian reign and as one of the greatest novelists, essayists and critics in the literature. His verse, half humorous, half pathetic, and often wholly extravagant, is always characterized by grace and spontaneity.

There is no important biography of Thackeray, but Trollope's *Thackeray*, in the English Men of Letters Series, gives interesting light on his life and ideas.

Thalberg, *tahl′berK*, SIGISMUND (1812–1871), a celebrated German pianist, born at Geneva, Switzerland. He obtained his musical education at Vienna, and from his first public appearance his career was brilliant. He was court musician to Emperor William of Austria and toured England, France, Russia, Italy and America. He was noted for his mastery of the singing tone.

Thaler, *tah′lur*, a silver coin, formerly in use in Germany, of the value of about 75 cents.

Thales, *thay′leez*, (640–548 B. C.), the earliest philosopher of Greece, a native of Miletus, in Ionia, or, according to some, of Phoenicia. He is said to have made several visits to Egypt, where he received instructions from the priests, from whom he probably acquired a knowledge of geometry. After his return, his reputation for learning and wisdom became so great that he was reckoned among the seven wise men, and his sayings were held in the highest esteem by the ancients. He considered water to be the world-substance, from which all objects in the universe were made. See PHILOSOPHY.

Thali'a, one of the nine Muses. She was the patron of comedy and was usually represented with the comic mask and the shepherd's crook in her hand. One of the Graces was also called Thalia.

Thal'lium, a metal discovered by Crookes in 1861. In its physical properties thallium resembles lead, but it is slightly heavier, somewhat softer and may be scratched by the finger nail. It melts under a red heat and is soluble in the ordinary mineral acids. In color it resembles silver, but is less brilliantly white. The tenacity of the metal is less than that of lead, but it is possessed of very considerable malleability. The compounds of thallium are exceedingly poisonous. Small quantities of thallium appear to be widely distributed in nature, the metal frequently occurring in iron and copper pyrites and in native sulphur.

Thames, *temz,* the most important, though not the largest, river of Great Britain. It rises in the south central part of England, flows southeasterly and enters the North Sea through a broad estuary. London is situated on both banks of the Thames, about 60 miles from its mouth. The chief tributaries from the north are the Cherwell, the Thame and the Colne, and from the south, the Medway and the Kennet. The river is navigable for ocean steamers as far as London, though those of the greatest draft do not ascend above Tilbury, about midway between London and the mouth of the river. The Thames is noted for its extensive shipping interests and for the many miles of wharfage along its banks. The entire length of the stream is about 215 miles.

Thames River, BATTLE OF THE, a battle fought on the Thames River, in the township of Oxford, Ontario, Canada, October 5, 1813, between a force of about three thousand Kentucky volunteers, under General Harrison, and a British force of about two thousand, under General Procter and the indian Tecumseh. After having retreated before Harrison for some days, Procter made a stand, but was overwhelmingly defeated, the battle being opened by a famous cavalry charge led by Colonel Richard M. Johnson, who, it is said, personally killed Tecumseh. General Procter was censured for his conduct. The battle practically put an end to indian coöperation with the British in the northwest.

Thane, a title of honor among the Anglo-Saxons. In England a freeman, not noble, was raised to the rank of a thane by acquiring a certain portion of land and receiving a special appointment in the king's hall. Every thane had the right of voting in the witenagemot, not only of the shire, but also of the kingdom, when important questions were to be discussed. After the Norman conquest, thanes and barons were classed together.

Than'et, ISLE OF, an island belonging to England, situated at the mouth of the Thames River. It is 9 miles long and has an area of 41 square miles. The island is celebrated for its watering places, chief among which are Ramsgate, Margate and Broadstairs.

Thanet, OCTAVE. See FRENCH, ALICE.

Thanks'giving Day, in the United States, an annual festival of thanksgiving for the mercies of the closing year. Practically it is a national harvest festival, fixed by proclamation of the president and the governors of states, and ranks as a legal holiday. In 1789 the Episcopal Church formally recognized the civil government's authority to appoint such a feast, and in 1888 the Roman Catholic Church also decided to honor a festival which had long been nearly universally observed, though nowhere with such zest as in the New England states, where it ranks as the annual *family* festival, taking the place which in England is accorded to Christmas.

The earliest harvest thanksgiving in America was kept by the Pilgrim Fathers at Plymouth in 1621, and it was repeated often during that and the ensuing century; Congress recommended days of thanksgiving annually during the Revolution, and in 1784 for the return of peace. President Madison issued a proclamation of the same import in 1815. Washington appointed such a day in 1789, after the adoption of the Constitution, and in 1795 he appointed another day as Thanksgiving Day, for the general benefits and welfare of the nation. Since 1817 the festival has been observed annually in New York, and since 1863 every president has issued each year a proclamation appointing the last Thursday of November as Thanksgiving Day.

Tha'sos, an island belonging to Turkey and situated in the Aegean Sea, south of the coast of Thrace. Its area is about 150 square miles. The entire surface is mountainous, and some of the peaks attain an altitude of 3400 feet. The mountains are covered with forests, but the lowlands and valleys are under tillage. Timber, oil, wax and honey are exported. In ancient times this island contained valuable gold mines. It is supposed to have been colonized by the Parians previous to 700 B. C., and it was for a long time one of the most prosperous of the Roman colonies. Population, about 12,000.

The′ater, an edifice appropriated to the representation of dramatic spectacles. The first theaters of the Greeks, who were the founders of the drama in its modern sense (See DRAMA), were very rude structures. They were usually temporary wooden scaffolds, but in 500 B. C. an accident occurred, and in that same year the Athenians set to work to build the great theater of Dionysus, the first stone structure of the kind. Ruins of theaters exist in almost every city of Greece, and they all show similarity to this first theater in Athens. Among the Greeks and Romans, theaters were the chief public edifices next to the temples, and in point of magnitude they surpassed the most spacious of the temples, having in some instances accommodation for as many as 10,000 to 40,000 spectators (See COLOSSEUM). The Greek and Roman theaters very closely resembled each other in their general form and principal parts. The building was of a semicircular form, resembling the half of an amphitheater, and it was not covered by a roof. In Greece the semicircular area was often scooped out in the side of a hill, but Roman theaters were built on the level. The seats of the spectators were arranged in tiers up the semicircular slope. The part of the theater in which the spectators sat was usually called the *cavea*, or pit, because it was excavated, and this name is still applied to the lowest part of the audience room in a modern theater. The stage, or place for the players, a narrow platform along the straight side of the theater, was in front of the seats. Behind this rose a high wall, resembling the façade of a building, this being intended to represent any building in front of which the action was supposed to take place. This was called in Greek *skēnē*, the stage being called *proskēnion*. The semicircular space between the stage and the lowest seats of the spectators was called *orchestra* and was appropriated by the Greeks to the chorus and musicians, and by the Romans to the senators. Scenery, in the modern sense of the word, was not employed, except in a very rude form, but the stage machinery seems in many cases to have been elaborate; and in particular there was a well-known machine or contrivance of some sort, from which deities made their entrance, as if from the sky. The immense size of the ancient theaters made it impossible for the unaided voice to be heard by the whole audience. To remedy this, the actors wore metallic mouthpieces very

similar to megaphones. In comedy the actors wore a light shoe, called the sock, a term often used to designate comedy, in contradistinction to tragedy, in which a *buskin* or high-heeled shoe was worn by the actor, to make him appear taller. The actors were males, the characters of women being represented by young men. The performances, which always included a series of plays, often lasted from sunrise until sunset. A price was charged for admission until the time of Pericles, when the poorer classes, and later all the citizens, were admitted at the cost of the State. In earlier times women were allowed to witness the tragedies only, but later they attended all representations.

Between the decline of the ancient, and the rise of the modern, drama there is a long interval, in which the nearest approach to theatrical entertainments is found in miracle plays, mysteries and interludes. These performances took place in churches, convents or halls or in the open air. Sometimes the stage was roofed, in which case the ends of it were used by the fashionable patrons, an arrangement which later gave rise to the use of boxes.

In 1548 the Confraternity of the Trinity opened a theater in Paris, in which they performed secular pieces. The first theater erected in Italy seems to have been that of Florence, built in 1581, but the first building that approaches the modern style was one constructed at Parma in 1618. In England there were organized companies of actors as far back as the time of Edward IV; but as there were no regular playhouses, the performances took place in tennis courts, inn yards and private houses. The London Theater was built by James Burbage before 1576, and the Curtain in Shoreditch and the playhouses in Blackfriars and Whitefriars date from about the same time. Shakespeare's plays were brought out at the house in Blackfriars and at the Globe on the Bankside, both of which belonged to the same company, to whom James I granted a patent in 1603. The Globe was a six-sided wooden structure, partly open at the top and partly thatched. Movable scenery was first used on the public stage by Davenant in 1662, and about the same time this manager introduced women to play female characters, hitherto taken by boys and men.

Modern theaters are all very much alike in their internal construction. The house is divided into two distinct portions, the auditorium and the stage, the former for the spectators, the latter for the actors and scenery, which is often of the most elaborate and realistic kind. The floor of the auditorium is always sloped down from the back of the house to the stage. Several tiers of galleries, or balconies, run in a semicircular or horseshoe form round the house. On the ground floor the front rows of seats are generally reserved as dress, or orchestral, stalls, and the back part is called the pit. The seats in the galleries rise terrace-wise from the front, so as to allow the persons in the back rows to see the stage over the heads of those before them. Immediately in front of the stage is the space occupied by the orchestra. Part of the stage flooring is movable, either as traps, through which actors or furniture ascend or descend, or in long narrow pieces, which are drawn off at each side of the stage, to allow the passage of the rising scenes. Adjoining the stage are the dressing rooms for the performers.

The theaters of the United States are as a rule licensed and regulated by the municipal corporations. Theaters are compelled by law to follow a certain plan, to furnish a sufficient number of exits and to have a fireproof curtain in front of the stage and sufficient fire-fighting appliances on the stage. The violation of these laws was responsible for the terrible catastrophe in 1903 in the Iroquois Theater, Chicago, in which six hundred persons were burned to death. Among the largest theaters in the United States are the Metropolitan Opera House, New York, and the Auditorium and Majestic theaters in Chicago.

Theatines, *the'a tinz,* an order of monks, founded at Rome in 1524, principally by Gianpietro Caraffa (afterward Pope Paul IV), bishop of Theate. They bound themselves to preach against heretics, to attend the sick and criminals and not to possess property or to ask for alms. The order formerly flourished in France, Spain and Portugal, but its influence is now chiefly confined to the Italian provinces.

Thebes, *theebz,* an ancient capital of Egypt, in Upper Egypt, on both sides of the Nile, about 300 mi. s. s. e. of Cairo, now represented by the four villages of Luxor, Karnak, Medinet Habu and Kurneh, as well as by magnificent ruins, which extend about seven miles along the river. When Thebes was founded is not known; the period of its greatest prosperity reaches from 1500 to 1000 B. C. The ruins comprise magnificent temples, rock-cut tombs, obelisks decorated with beautiful sculptures, long avenues of sphinxes and colossal statues. The largest of the temples is that at Karnak. Above Karnak are the village and temple of Luxor. The Mem-

nonium, or temple of Rameses II, and the temple and palace of Rameses III, on the other, or left, bank of the river, are objects of great interest. Here are also the colossal statues of Amenoph III, one of them known as the vocal statue of Memnon. In the interior of the mountains which rise behind are found the tombs of the kings of Thebes, excavated in the rock, the most remarkable being that of Seti I, discovered by Belzoni, and containing fine sculptures and paintings.

Thebes, a city of Greece, situated about 40 mi. n. of Athens and about midway between Mount Helicon and the channel separating Euboea from the mainland. The present village is of but little importance, though it commands a fine view. The population is about 3000. Ancient Thebes was one of the most celebrated of Grecian cities. It was the chief city of Boeotia, the birthplace of Pindar, Epaminondas and Pelopidas. It was also prominent in Grecian history. It is said to have been founded by Cadmus 1500 B. C. Under the leadership of Epaminondas it became the leading city and state of Greece.

Theine, *the'in.* See CAFFEINE.

Theiss, *tīse,* a river of Hungary, the longest tributary of the Danube. It rises in the Carpathian Mountains, on the borders of Galicia. The main stream is formed by the union of the Black Theiss and the White Theiss. Its general course is westerly as far as Tokay, thence southwesterly and southerly. During the latter part of its course it flows parallel with the Danube, until it joins that river between Benat and Slavonia. The stream is unusually winding in its course and has a length of more than 800 miles. It is navigable for light boats for about 450 miles.

The'mis, goddess of law and justice among the Greeks, the daughter of Uranus and Gaea (Heaven and Earth) and one of the wives of Jupiter.

Themistocles, *the mis'to kleez,* (about 514–449 B. C.), an Athenian general and statesman. After the Battle of Marathon he convinced the Athenians, most of whom believed that the struggle with Persia was over, that there was still need for preparation, and he induced them to build a fleet. On the invasion of Greece by Xerxes, Themistocles succeeded in obtaining the command of the fleet, and in the Battle of Salamis (480 B. C.) he conquered the Persians and saved Greece. Subsequently he was accused of having enriched himself by unjust means and of being privy to designs for the betrayal of Greece to the Persians; and fearing the vengeance of his countrymen, he, after many vicissitudes, took refuge at the Persian court.

Theocracy, *the ok'ra sy*, literally, "government by God," the name given to a state in which the Almighty is regarded as the sole sovereign, and the laws of the realm are considered to be divine commands, rather than human ordinances. The priesthood therefore become the interpreters of the "divine commands" and act as the officers of the invisible ruler. The typical example of a theocracy is that established by Moses among the Hebrews. The governments of colonial Massachusetts and Connecticut were at times theocratic in nature.

Theoc'ritus, a Greek poet who flourished about 280 B. C. We have under his name thirty idyls, or pastoral poems, of which, however, several are probably by other authors. Most of his idyls have a dramatic form and consist of the alternate responses of shepherds.

Theod'olite, a surveying instrument for measuring horizontal and vertical angles by means of a telescope, the movements of which can be accurately marked. This instrument is variously constructed, but its main characteristics are the same in all forms. Its chief features are the telescope; a graduated vertical circle, to which the telescope is attached; two concentric horizontal circular plates, which turn freely on each other, and two spirit levels on the upper plate, to enable the operator to know when the instrument is level, the whole being on a tripod stand. The lower plate contains the divisions of the circle round its edge, and the upper or vernier plate has two vernier divisions, diametrically opposite. The plates turn on a double vertical axis. To measure the angular distance horizontally between any two objects, the telescope is turned round, along with the vernier circle, until it is brought to bear exactly upon one of the objects; it is then turned round until it is brought to bear on the other object, and the arc which the vernier has described on the graduated circle measures the angle required. By means of the double vertical axis the observation may be repeated any number of times, in order to insure accuracy. The graduated vertical circle is for taking altitudes or vertical angles in a similar way. The theodolite is a most essential instrument in surveying.

Theod'oric (about 454–526), king of the Ostrogoths, the son of Theudemir, king of the Ostrogoths of Pannonia. From his eighth to his eighteenth year he lived as a hostage with the emperor Leo at Constantinople, and two years after his return he succeeded to his father's power. In 488 he invaded Italy, defeated Odoacer and compelled the latter to grant him equal authority with himself. The murder of Odoacer at a banquet soon after opened the way for Theodoric to have himself proclaimed sole ruler. He ruled with great vigor and ability. He attached his soldiers to himself by assigning them a third part of the lands of Italy, while among his Italian subjects, whom he conciliated by introducing an improved administration of justice, he encouraged industry and the arts of peace. Although, like his ancestors, he was an Arian, he never violated the peace or privileges of the Catholic Church.

Theodosius, *the'o do'she us,* (346?–395), a Roman emperor, born in Spain, and selected by the emperor Gratian, in 379, for his partner in the Empire. To his care were given Thrace and the Eastern provinces, which he delivered from an invasion of the Goths, concluding a peace with them in 382. On the defeat and death of Maximus, he became the sole head of the Empire, Gratian having been previously killed in the war against Maximus. In 390 a sedition took place in Thessalonica, and to satisfy his vengeance Theodosius caused the people of the city to be invited to an exhibition at the circus and then had them barbarously murdered, to the number, it is computed, of seven thousand. Saint Ambrose refused him communion for eight months on account of this crime, and Theodosius submitted humbly to the punishment. At his death he left the eastern portion of the Empire to his son Arcadius, the western to his son Honorius.

Theology, *the ol'o jy,* the science which treats of the existence of God, his attributes and the divine will regarding human actions, present condition and ultimate destiny. In reference to the sources whence it is derived, theology is distinguished into *natural,* or *philosophical,* theology, which relates to the knowledge of God from His works, by the light of nature and reason; and *supernatural, positive,* or *revealed,* theology, which sets forth and systematizes the doctrines of the Scriptures. With regard to the contents of theology, it is classified into *theoretical theology,* or *dogmatics,* and *practical theology,* or *ethics.* As comprehending the whole extent of religious science, theology is divided into four principal classes—*historical,* treating of the history of Christian doctrines; *exegetical,* embracing the interpretation of the Scriptures and of Biblical criticism; *systematic*, arranging methodically the great truths of religion; *practical*, consisting, first, of precepts and directions, and second, of the motives by which we should comply with these. *Apologetic* and *polemic* theology belong to several of the above-mentioned four classes at once. The *scholastic* theology attempted to clear and discuss all questions by the aid of human reason alone, laying aside the study of the Scriptures and adopting, instead, the arts of the dialectician.

Theophrastus, *the'o fras'tus,* (372–287 B. C.), a celebrated Peripatetic philosopher, born at Lesbos. He was at Athens, in the school of Plato, and afterwards studied under Aristotle, of whom he was the favorite pupil and successor. On the departure of Aristotle from Athens, after the death of Alexander the Great, Theophrastus became the head of the Peripatetic school of philosophy and composed a multitude of books on morals, metaphysics and science. Two entire works on botany are still extant, but only fragments of his other works, such as those on *Stones* and on the *Winds* and his *Characters*, or sketches of types of character, which is by far the most celebrated of all his productions. To his care we are indebted for the preservation of the writings of Aristotle, who, when dying, intrusted them to his keeping.

Theosophy, *the os'o fy,* according to its etymology, the science of divine things. But the name has generally been applied to the philosophy of those persons who, in their inquiries respecting God, have run into mysticism, as Jacob Böhme, Swedenborg, Saint Martin and others. At the present day the term is applied to the tenets of the Theosophical Society, founded in New York in 1875 by a Colonel Olcott, the objects of which are (1) to form the nucleus of a universal brotherhood of humanity; (2) to promote the study of Eastern literature and science; (3) to investigate unexplained laws of nature and the psychical powers of man, and (4) to search after divine knowledge—the word divine meaning the true nature of the abstract principle, not the quality of a personal God. The theosophists assert that humanity is possessed of certain powers over nature which the narrower study of nature, from the merely materialistic standpoint, has failed to develop. The leaders are Olcott, A. P. Sinnett and Madame Blavatsky, an American Russian. Their so-called occult manifestations are akin to those attributed to spiritualism or telepathy, that is, communication between minds at a distance from each other.

Madame Blavatsky's book, *The Secret Doctrine*, is the authority on modern theosophy.

Therapeutae, *ther'a pu'tee,* a Jewish sect of devotees, probably of the first century after Christ, though thought by some to belong to the third century and to be monks of Egypt. They withdrew into solitary places, where they devoted themselves to a life of religious contemplation.

Therapeu'tics, that branch of medicine which treats of the applications and effects of drugs, and which has for its purpose the relief of pain or the cure of disease. *Rational therapeutics* demands a knowledge of the diseased condition and of the action of the drug or curative agent employed, which is usually determined by actual experiments upon animals or upon man. The manner in which drugs affect the nerve centers, respiration, circulation, blood pressure and body temperature are all matters which must be known. The specific effect of the medicine and the quantity required should be part of a physician's knowledge. A *specific* is a remedy which will positively cure a certain disease, as quinine will cure malaria. The word *therapeutic* in its broadest sense includes every form of treatment, and the word, combined with a qualifying term, may be applied to any system of treatment. Many means besides treatment by drugs are in use. In *natural therapeutics* it is proposed to cure disease through the operation of the laws of nature, the chief duty of the physician being to keep up the patient's strength by food. In *symptomatic therapeutics* the physician attempts to remove bad symptoms without regard to their cause. Other methods or means are known as electro-therapeutics (See ELECTRICITY, USES OF, IN MEDICINE) and suggestive therapeutics (See HYPNOTISM). Surgical treatment is a separate department. See SURGERY; ROENTGEN RAYS; HYDROTHERAPY; MASSAGE. Consult, also, MATERIA MEDICA; PHARMACOPOEIA; MEDICINE.

There'sa, SAINT (1515–1582), a religious enthusiast, born at Avila, in Spain. She entered a convent of the Carmelites in 1534, where she remained for nearly thirty years. Her health was not strong enough at first to follow strictly the rules of the order, but eventually she led a most ascetic life, and accounts of her sanctity spread throughout Spain. She undertook to restore the original severity of the institute, and the first convent of reformed Carmelite nuns was founded at Avila in 1562. During the life of the founder, who took the name Teresa de Jesus in 1562, seventeen convents for women and sixteen for men accepted her reforms. She was canonized by Pope Gregory XV in 1622. Teresa was the author of several works, all of a devotional nature, among them a very curious life of herself.

Thermal, *thur'mal*, **Springs** or **Hot Springs,** springs whose temperature is higher than that of the land where they occur. In high altitudes this temperature may be only a few degrees above freezing point, but in other localities it reaches the boiling point of water, and in some localities thermal springs are subject to eruption (See GEYSER). Most of them are quiet, boiling pools. The crater of the spring extends to a great depth, and the water is heated by coming in contact with the hot rocks below. Most thermal springs hold siliceous and calcareous matter in solution and deposit these around their sides and along their edges, often making beautiful formations. The waters of some thermal springs are valuable for their medicinal properties. Such springs occur in the United States at Hot Springs, Ark., and Hot Springs, S. D. See SPRING.

Thermoelectricity, *thur'mo e lek tris'e ty,* electricity produced at the junction of two metals, or at a point where a molecular change occurs in a bar of the same metal, when the junction or point is heated above or cooled below the general temperature of the conductor. Thus, when wires or bars of metal of different kinds, as bismuth and antimony, are placed in close contact, end to end, and disposed so as to form a continuous circuit, and heat is applied to the ends or junctions of the bars, electric currents are produced. The thermoelectric battery, or pile, an apparatus much used in delicate experiments with radiant heat, consists of a series of little bars of antimony and bismuth, or any other two metals of different heat-conducting power, with their ends soldered together and arranged in a compact form, the opposite ends of the pile being connected with a very sensitive galvanometer. To the combined arrangement of pile and galvanometer the name of *thermomultiplier* is given. The slightest change in temperature generates a current which is manifest in the galvanometer. The so-called thermoelectric pair, which is much used in thermoelectric experiments, is made by soldering together the ends of two metal bars of different heat-conducting power, and bringing the free ends within a conveniently short distance of each other by bending the combined bar into a horseshoe, or magnet, form. As the electric current developed in a single pair is very weak, a considerable number are usually combined to form a thermoelectric pile, or battery. Bismuth and antimony are the metals usually employed, the difference in electro-motive force being greater between them than between any other two metals conveniently obtainable.

Thermograph, *thur'mo graf,* a self-recording thermometer. The American instrument which is the one in most common use, consists of a circular paper disk, graduated on its circumference into hour and minute spaces and divided by concentric circles into spaces indicating degrees of temperature. The disk is moved by clockwork, which causes it to make a revolution once in twenty-four hours. A needle carrying a pen or pencil is so attached to the thermometer that it marks the temperature on the disk, making a complete circuit in a day. See THERMOMETER.

Thermom'eter, an instrument for measuring temperature. The ordinary thermometer consists of a small glass tube, with a fine bore, containing either mercury or alcohol which has been colored. The principle upon which the thermometer works is that when liquids are heated, they expand, and when cooled they contract. The thermometer is made by pouring the mercury or alcohol into a tube through the cup, which is then closed and hermetically sealed, the air having been expelled.

The standard points from which temperature is reckoned are the freezing point and the boiling point of water in the open air at sea level. The thermometer, when being graduated, is placed in melted ice, and the point to which the mercury or alcohol sinks is marked as the *freezing point*. The thermometer is then placed in boiling water, and the height to which the liquid in the tube rises is marked the *boiling point*. Between these points a certain number of divisions, called degrees, are marked. There are, in general use, two scales, determining these degrees. That in common use in England and the United States is known as the Fahrenheit scale. According to this, the freezing point is 32° and the boiling point 212°. In the Fahrenheit scale the zero point is 32° below the freezing point. In the Centigrade scale the freezing point is marked zero and the boiling point 100. The Centigrade scale is much simpler and is in general use on the continent of Europe and for scientific purposes. Another scale, known as the Reaumur, marks the freezing point at zero and the boiling point at 80°. This scale is but little used. To change the Fahrenheit scale to the Centigrade scale, multiply the number of degrees Fahrenheit by $\frac{5}{9}$ and subtract 32. To change the Centigrade to the Fahrenheit scale, multiply the number of degrees Centigrade by $\frac{9}{5}$ and add 32.

Thermopylae, *thur mop'il lee,* a famous pass, leading from Thessaly into Locris, the only road by which an invading army can move from northern into southern Greece. It lies between Mount Oeta and what was anciently an impassable morass, bordering on the Maliac Gulf. It is famous as the scene of the heroic death of Leonidas and his three hundred Spartans, in their attempt to withstand the advance of Xerxes (480 B. C.). Again, in 278 B. C., Brennus, at the head of a Gallic host, succeeded, through the same treachery that secured a victory to Xerxes, in forcing the Greeks to withdraw from the pass.

These'um, any temple dedicated to Theseus. The most famous of these temples was the one built at Athens, northwest of the Acropolis, in 473 B. C. The whole was decorated with beautiful paintings, representing different events in the life of Theseus. The name now commonly refers to a temple at Athens, probably that of Hephaestus, which is the best preserved of Greek temples. It is of Doric style and is made of Pentelic marble.

THESEUM AT ATHENS

There are thirteen columns on the side, nineteen feet high. The frieze is sculptured from the myths of Hercules and Theseus. The building is in excellent condition, owing to the fact that in the early Christian era it was used as a church.

Theseus, *the'se us* or *the'suse,* a mythological king of Athens, son of Aegeus. He was brought up by his mother, in a land removed from Athens, but when he was grown he journeyed to his father's court and was recognized as heir to the throne. At that time Athens was obliged to pay to Crete, as a result of a defeat in war, a yearly tribute of seven youths and seven maidens, who were to be devoured by the Minotaur. Theseus, at his own request, accompanied one of these expeditions, having first promised his father that if he was successful in his attempt to kill the Min-

otaur he would hoist white sails on his return voyage, instead of black. With the aid of Ariadne, the daughter of the king of Crete, Theseus conquered the Minotaur, and then, taking Ariadne with him, he set out on his return. He seems to have been, however, a very inconstant lover and soon abandoned the princess on an island. Forgetful, too, of his father's request, he did not change his sails from black to white, and Aegeus, watching from afar and seeing the same gloomy sails, threw himself into the sea, which has since borne his name. Theseus became king of Athens, and many were the wonderful deeds which he did. For a time he was greatly beloved by his people, but in his later years he grew tyrannical and was at length banished from his kingdom.

Thessalo'nians, EPISTLES TO THE, two New Testament epistles, written by Saint Paul to the church at Thessalonica, in all probability during his long stay at Corinth, therefore not very long after the foundation of the Thessalonian church on Saint Paul's second missionary journey.

Thes'saly, the northeastern division of Greece, consisting, mainly, of a rich plain, enclosed between mountains. In the earliest times Thessaly proper is said to have been inhabited by Aeolic and other tribes. Subsequently it was broken up into separate confederacies, and it seldom exerted any important influence on the affairs of Greece. Thessaly was conquered by Philip of Macedon in the fourth century B. C., became dependent on Macedonia and was finally incorporated with the Roman Empire. After the fall of the Byzantine Empire it came into the hands of Turks, who held it until 1881, when it was formally ceded to Greece by the terms of the Congress of Berlin. The majority of the inhabitants are Greeks.

The'tis, a Greek divinity, a daughter of Nereus and Doris. By Peleus she became the mother of Achilles.

Thiers, *te air',* LOUIS ADOLPHE (1797-1877), a French statesman and historian. He studied law and was admitted to the bar, but soon relinquished law for literature and politics. At Paris he began, after a long struggle with poverty, to write for the *Constitutionnel* and other journals, and before 1830 he had made a great reputation as a political writer. He took part in the foundation of the *National,* and subsequently assisted in editing it, doing much with his articles toward bringing about the Revolution of 1830. During the reign of Louis Philippe he held various offices, and after the Revolution of 1848 he was elected deputy to the Assembly.

He voted for the presidency of Louis Napoleon, but became, later, one of his fiercest opponents, and in 1851 he was arrested and banished. Returning to France in the following year, he remained in comparative retirement till 1863, when he was elected one of the deputies for Paris. During the crisis of the war with Germany and the overthrow of the Empire, he came to the front as the strongest man in France. After the fall of Paris he was declared chief of the executive power, and in August, 1871, the Assembly prolonged his tenure of office and changed his title to that of president. In November, 1872, Thiers declared himself in favor of the Republic, as a definite form of government for France, and thus to some extent he brought about a crisis which resulted in his being deprived of the presidency. He accepted his deposition with dignity and went quietly into retirement. Thiers's chief works are *A History of the French Revolution* and a *History of the Consulate and the Empire*.

Thirlwall, *thurl'wawl*, CONNOP (1797–1875), an English bishop and historian, born at Stepney, Middlesex. He learned Latin at three and could read Greek at four. He was ordained in 1828 and soon after received the living of Kirby Underdale, in Yorkshire. His first important work was a translation of Schleiermacher's *Gospel of Saint Luke*. He owes his reputation to his *History of Greece*, the first edition of which appeared in Lardner's *Cabinet Cyclopedia*, between 1835 and 1844. It was well received, and before the appearance of Grote's *History* it was without a rival in the English language. In 1840 Thirlwall was appointed bishop of Saint David, in Wales, and in six months he could preach in perfect Welsh. His labors in this diocese for thirty-four years resulted in the building of churches, parsonages and schools and the giving of £30,000 from his own pocket. His *Letters to a Friend*, edited by Dean Stanley, show his noble character.

Thirst, *thurst*, the sensation experienced from a lack of water in the tissues of the body. The sensation is chiefly referred to the throat and mouth, but the condition is really one affecting the entire body. Thirst is a common symptom of fever and of those diseases in which there is a loss of water from the body, as in cholera and diabetes, or when there is a loss of blood. It is also produced by highly seasoned food and by exercise that causes free perspiration. The feeling of thirst may be quenched not only by drinking, but by absorption through the skin and by injecting fluids into the veins.

Thirty Ty′rants, the committee of rulers appointed from the aristocratic class at Athens, at the close of the Peloponnesian War. This war was a conflict between democracy, as represented by Athens, and an oligarchical government. as represented by Sparta; and the success of Sparta gave her the power to force upon Athens an oligarchical government. The rule of the Thirty Tyrants was most oppressive, but it lasted for only a year, as in 403 B. C. the old democracy was restored.

Thirty Years' War, a war in Germany, which lasted from 1618 to 1648. It started as a struggle between the Protestant and Catholic princes of Germany, but gradually involved almost all the states of the continent, degenerating at last into a heartless struggle for political power and territory. The religious question had been by no means settled by the Peace of Augsburg of 1555, which, while it allowed religious freedom to the Lutherans, made no provision for the Calvinists, who had become numerous in Germany. In 1608 the Protestants, incited by some infringement on their rights by a Catholic prince, formed a league for their mutual protection, called the Evangelical Union, and in 1609 the Catholics formed the confederation known as the Holy League. In the latter year the emperor published a decree guaranteeing the Protestants of Bohemia the free exercise of their religion. In 1617 there came to the throne of Bohemia a new king, Ferdinand of Styria, and as Ferdinand was an ardent Catholic, the Bohemians feared for their privileges. A dispute arose between the Protestants and Catholics as to the right of the Protestants to build a certain church, and as the king decided against the Protestants, a body of Protestants, led by Count Thurn, entered the royal palace at Prague on the night of May 23, 1618, and hurled two representatives of the Crown from the windows. This incident served to open the war, which had long been ready to break out in Bohemia, and the insurrection soon spread into the adjoining Hapsburg dominions.

The war had scarcely opened when, the Imperial office falling vacant, the Bohemian king, Ferdinand, was elected emperor. With the power and influence he now wielded, it was not very difficult for him to quell the insurrection in his dominions. Frederick V, elector of the Palatinate, who had been chosen king by the Bohemians, was forced to flee; Bohemia was ravaged, and Protestantism was crushed throughout the country. But the struggle continued and spread to Holland and other northern countries and even to England.

In 1625 Christian IV, King of Denmark, supported by England and Holland, threw himself into the conflict, as the champion of German Protestantism. On the side of the Catholics there were at this time two noted commanders, Tilly, the leader of the forces of the Holy League, and Wallenstein, the commander of the Imperial Army (See WALLENSTEIN, ALBRECHT EUSEBIUS WENZEL VON). This period of the war proved disastrous to the Protestant allies, and Christian IV in 1629 concluded, with the emperor, the Peace of Lübeck and retired from the struggle. By what is known as the Edict of Restitution (1629) the emperor Ferdinand now restored to the Catholics all the ecclesiastical lands and offices in North Germany of which possession had been taken by the Protestants in violation of the terms of the Peace of Augsburg. This decree was of course obnoxious to the Protestants, and it was clear that it could be enforced only by war.

The third period of the war, known as the Swedish period, began in 1630, when Gustavus Adolphus, king of Sweden, desirous of promoting Protestantism and of securing the control of the Baltic, took the field against Ferdinand. The influence of Richelieu, whose policy was one of steady opposition to the Hapsburgs, had much to do with bringing about the Swedish interference. While Gustavus Adolphus was trying, in his march through Saxony and Brandenburg, to gain the allegiance of those neutral states, Tilly had advanced to Magdeburg and besieged it. It fell before Gustavus Adolphus could reach it, and all of its inhabitants were massacred.

The only man who could have turned the tide of victory, which from the first ran strongly in favor of the Swedish monarch, was Wallenstein, whom, owing to his unpopularity in many quarters, Frederick had dismissed at the close of the Danish wars. Joined by numerous volunteers and aided by French money, Gustavus Adolphus advanced and routed Tilly at Breitenfeld (September, 1631), victoriously traversed the Main and Rhine valleys, defeated Tilly again near the confluence of the Lech and the Danube (April, 1632) and entered Munich. Meanwhile, the emperor again sought the aid of Wallenstein, by whose ability and energy Gustavus was obliged to retire to Saxony, where he gained the great victory of Lützen (November, 1632), but was himself mortally wounded in the battle.

The war was now carried on by the Swedes

under the chancellor Oxenstierna, till the rout of the Swedish forces at Nördlingen (September, 1634) again gave to the emperor the preponderating power in Germany. The elector of Saxony, who had been an ally of Gustavus, now made peace at Prague, and within a few months the treaty was accepted by many of the German princes. The Swedes, however, thought it to their interest to continue the war, while France resolved to take a more active part in the conflict. Thus the last stage of the war was a contest of France and Sweden against Austria, in which the Swedish generals gained various successes over the imperial forces, while the French armies fought with varied fortune in West Germany and on the Rhine. Meanwhile, the emperor had died (1637) and had been succeeded by his son, Ferdinand III. The struggle continued until, in 1646, the united armies of the French, under the great generals Turenne and Condé, and the Swedes, advanced through Swabia and Bavaria. The combined forces of Sweden, Bavaria and France were then about to advance upon Austria, when the news reached them that the Peace of Westphalia had been concluded and that the long struggle was over (See WESTPHALIA, PEACE OF). The Thirty Years' War left Germany in a state of complete exhaustion. Whole provinces were devastated, and the population was decreased by half

Thistle, *this'l'*, the common name of prickly plants of the family Compositae. There are numerous species, most of which are natives of Europe. The leaves are usually coarse and are armed with spines, or prickles. Thistles spread by means of seeds and creeping roots. The common *cotton thistle* attains a height of from four to six feet. It is often regarded as the Scotch thistle, but it is doubtful whether the thistle which constitutes the Scottish national badge has any existing type, though the stemless thistle is in many districts of Scotland looked on as the true Scotch thistle. Some dozen species of thistle are common in the United States, spreading from New England to Florida. The *Canada thistle* is one of the severest pests of the farmer.

Thistle, ORDER OF THE, a Scottish order of knighthood, sometimes called the Order of Saint Andrew. It was instituted by James V in 1540 and was reorganized by James II of England in 1687. It fell into abeyance during the reign of William and Mary, but it was revived by Queen Anne in 1703. The star of the order is of silver, with eight rays, and with a thistle in the center, surrounded by the Latin motto, *Nemo me im-*

pune lacessit (No one injures me with impunity). The order consists of the sovereign and sixteen knights.

Thistle Bird. See AMERICAN GOLDFINCH.

Thomas, GEORGE HENRY (1816–1870), an American soldier, born in Southampton County, Va. He was educated at West Point, took part in the Mexican War, was appointed professor at West Point in 1850, was recalled to active service in 1855 and was employed in Texas against the indians. When the war of secession broke out, Thomas remained in the Federal army, and was appointed brigadier general of volunteers. Some months later he was sent into Kentucky, where in the following year he won the Battle of Mill Springs. As major general of volunteers he took part in the Battle of Murfreesboro, where he greatly distinguished himself, while at the bloody Battle of Chickamauga, in September, 1863, he saved the Federal army from destruction by his stubborn resistance after the defeat of the Federal right, thus winning the name of "the Rock of Chickamauga." In 1863 he commanded the Army of the Cumberland at Missionary Ridge, and in the following year he coöperated with Sherman in his march on Atlanta. Returning from Atlanta to Tennessee, he defeated Hood and compelled the Confederates to raise the siege of Nashville, for which he was raised to the rank of major general in the regular army.

Thomas, JOSEPH (1811–1891), an American scholar and linguist. With Thomas Baldwin, he was the author of *Baldwin's Pronouncing Gazetteer*. In 1854 he prepared *A New and Complete Gazetteer of the United States*; and in 1855 he brought out *The Complete Pronouncing Gazetteer of the World* (popularly known as *Lippincott's Gazetteer of the World*), containing the pronunciation of the names of nearly 100,000 places. For accuracy and completeness this work has scarcely an equal. In 1864 his comprehensive *Medical Dictionary* appeared, and in 1870 he published his *Universal Pronouncing Dictionary of Biography and Mythology*, which occupies a very high place among books of reference.

Thomas, LORENZO (1804–1875), an American soldier, born at Newcastle, Del., educated at West Point. He served against the indians in Florida, becoming chief of staff, and in the Mexican War he acted as chief of staff for General W. O. Butler, being brevetted lieutenant colonel for gallantry at Monterey. During the Civil War he first acted as adjutant general and then organized several regiments of colored troops in the South. During the controversy between President Johnson and Secretary Stanton, General Thomas was appointed secretary of war, but he did not assume office, on account of Stanton's refusal to vacate. He retired from the army in 1869, with the brevet rank of major general.

Thomas, SAINT, one of the Twelve Apostles of Christ. He is also called Didymus, which means *a twin*. Little is told of him in the Gospels, except the story of his doubting the resurrection of Christ; but early Christian tradition credited him with having spread the gospel in Parthia and having founded the Christians of Saint Thomas, in India.

Thomas, THEODORE (1835–1905), a distinguished German-American orchestra conductor, born at Hanover, Germany. He removed to the United States in 1845 and played in New York for two years, later accompanying Jenny Lind upon her first American tour. He founded an orchestra in 1861, which became famous throughout the world. In 1878 he went to Cincinnati, as director of the College of Music at that city, was for ten years conductor of the Brooklyn Philharmonic Society and then went to Chicago in 1891. There he established one of the world's greatest orchestras, supported by popular subscription. In 1904 a magnificent recital hall was built for the orchestra at a cost of $750,000, but Thomas died soon after, from overwork in connection with its dedication. His great work was the popularization of classic music.

Thomas à Kem'pis (1380–1471), that is, Thomas of Kempe, was born at Kempen, in the archbishopric of Cologne, about 1380. His family name was Hämerken. At the age of twenty he retired to an Augustine convent, near Zwolle, in Holland, where he took the vows. He was a voluminous writer. His works (the printed ones all in Latin) consist of sermons, exhortations, ascetic treatises, hymns and prayers. His name, however, would hardly be remembered, were it not for its connection with the celebrated devotional work called *The Imitation of Christ* (*De Imitatione Christi*), a work which has passed through thousands of editions in the original Latin and in translations. The authorship of this book is generally ascribed to à Kempis.

Thomasville, *tom'as vil*, GA., the county-seat of Thomas co., 200 mi. s. w. of Savannah, on the Atlantic Coast Line and other railroads. The town is picturesquely located, on high ground in the pine belt of the extreme southwestern part of the state. The place contains several large hotels and has attained some prominence as a winter resort. It has a public library and is the seat of the Young Female College and a branch of the state university, called the South Georgia Agricultural and Mechanical College. There is a considerable trade in cotton, sugar cane, tobacco, fruits and vegetables from the surrounding region, while the manufactures are chiefly connected with lumber products. Population in 1910, 6727.

Thompson, *tomp'son,* DAVID (1770–1857), a Canadian explorer, born at Westminster, England, and educated at Oxford. In 1789 he emigrated to America, where he engaged in exploration of the Great Lakes and Hudson Bay region, in the service of the Hudson Bay Company. He crossed the Rocky Mountains in 1807 and followed the course of the Columbia River to its mouth in the Pacific. From 1816 to 1826 he assisted in the survey of the Canadian and United States boundary, and he subsequently explored the Northwest Territory of Canada.

Thompson, DENMAN (1833–1911), an American actor, known chiefly for his presentation of Joshua Whitcomb, the central figure in *The Old Homestead.* From 1888 Thompson constantly presented *The Old Homestead,* and it has always been exceedingly popular.

Thompson, GEORGE (1804–1878), an English abolitionist, born in Liverpool. After 1833 he began a vigorous propaganda, from the platform, of antislavery views, and largely through his untiring agitation the slaves in British territory were finally freed. In 1834 he came to America, gave numerous lectures in all parts of the country in behalf of the antislavery movement and helped in the formation of hundreds of antislavery societies. Later he engaged in many other reform movements, being a prominent member of the Anti-Corn-Law League in England, the British-India Association and the Parliamentary Reform Association. He was for five years a member of Parliament.

Thompson, JAMES MAURICE (1844–1901), an American novelist and journalist, born at Fairfield, Ind. He served in the Confederate army, and after the war he became chief engineer of an Indiana railroad. He was for a long time on the staff of the *Independent* and was a prolific writer. *The Witchery of Archery, A Tallahassee Girl* and *Alice of Old Vincennes* are his best-known works.

Thomson, *tom'son,* JAMES (1700–1748), a Scottish poet, born at Ednam, in Scotland, and educated at Jedburgh and at the University of

Edinburgh. He went in 1725 to London, where *Winter,* the first of his poems on the seasons, was published in the following year. This was followed by *Summer* and *Spring,* and in 1830 these were republished with the addition of *Autumn,* as *The Seasons.* *The Seasons* was of importance in the history of literature because, in its return from the artificiality of eighteenth century poetry to a feeling for the beauty of nature, it marked the beginning of the romantic movement. In 1740 Thomson composed, in conjunction with Mallet, *The Masque of Alfred,* which contains the famous song, *Rule Britannia.* In 1848 his *Castle of Indolence* appeared, a work which reproduces not only the meter, but to a certain extent the spirit, of Spenser's *Fairie Queene,* and this is, in many respects, Thomson's best work. Thomson was greatly beloved for his amiability and kindness of heart.

Thomson, WILLIAM, Sir, Lord Kelvin (1824–1909), one of the greatest mathematicians and

SIR WILLIAM THOMSON

physicists of modern times, born at Belfast. He was educated first at Glasgow University and then at Peterhouse, Cambridge, and at the age of twenty-two he was appointed professor of natural philosophy in the University of Glasgow, a post which he held for fifty years. The same year he became editor of the Cambridge and Dublin *Mathematical Journal,* to which he contributed valuable papers on the mathematical theory of electricity. He was also a distinguished contributor to the *Philosophic Magazine.* Among the most important of his contributions to electrical science are the construction of several delicate instruments for the measurement and study of electricity. It is, however, in connection with submarine telegraphy that Sir William Thomson's name is most generally known, his services being rewarded, on the completion of the Atlantic cable in 1866, with knighthood and other honors. (See CABLE, ATLANTIC.) He also made important additions to our knowledge of magnetism and heat, and invented an improved form of mariner's compass, now in extensive use. He was president of the British Association for the Advancement of Science, and at one time was president of the Royal Society of London. He is the author, jointly with Professor Tait, of a well-known treatise on natural philosophy, and he issued an extensive collection of his mathematical and physical papers.

Thor, in Scandinavian mythology, son of Odin, and the god of thunder. He was the most powerful among the gods, and, owing to his great weight, he was not allowed to cross to earth on the rainbow bridge, by which the other gods crossed. As the special patron god of peasants, Thor entertained them after their death, as Odin, his father, entertained the higher classes. Thor was usually represented as bearing his wonderful hammer, which possessed the property of returning to his hand after he had hurled it. Thursday was named in honor of Thor.

Thoracic, *thor as'ik,* **Duct,** the principal tube of the system of lacteals and lymphatics, extending upward along the spinal column to the seventh cervical vertebra, where it pours the contents which it has gathered from the intestines, the trunk, the left arm, the lower extremities and the left side of the head, into the left subclavian vein. This tube is about twenty inches long and one-eighth of an inch in diameter, is made up of three coats and is well supplied with valves.

Thor'ax. See SKELETON; ABDOMEN.

Thoreau, *tho'ro* or *tho ro',* HENRY DAVID (1817–1862), an American naturalist and writer, born at Boston and educated at Harvard University. For about five years after his graduation he taught school, and then for several years he occupied himself in various ways, in land surveying, carpentering and other handicrafts. He spent no more time on work than was absolutely necessary to provide food and clothing for himself, and he devoted the greater part of his time to study and the contemplation of nature. In 1845 he built for himself a hut in a wood near Walden Pond, Concord, Mass., and there, for

two years, he lived the life of a hermit. After quitting his solitude, Thoreau pursued his father's calling of pencil maker, at Concord. Besides contributing to the *Dial* and other periodicals, he published *A Week on the Concord and Merri-*

HENRY DAVID THOREAU

mac Rivers and *Walden, or Life in the Woods* (1854). After his death appeared *Excursions in Field and Forest, The Maine Woods, Cape Cod* and *Early Spring in Massachusetts.*

Tho'rium, a metal existing in the form of a heavy, metallic, gray powder. It burns in air or oxygen with great splendor and is converted into thoria, or oxide of thorium. It unites energetically with chlorine, sulphur and phosphorus. Hydrochloric acid readily dissolves it, with the evolution of hydrogen gas.

Thorn Apple. See STRAMONIUM.

Thoroughwort, *thur'o wurt.* See BONESET

Thorwaldsen, *tore'vald zen,* BERTEL (1770–1844), a celebrated Danish sculptor, born at Copenhagen. At first he helped his father to cut figure heads in the royal dockyard, then, after some years' study at the Academy of Arts, he won the privilege of studying three years abroad. Going to Rome, he was much impressed by the works of Canova, the sculptor, and Carstens, the painter, who were then residing there. It was not until 1803, however, that he became at all widely known. Then, by a lucky chance, he received a commission from Sir Thomas Hope, to execute in marble a statue of Jason, which the sculptor had modeled. His fortune was now made, and his fame grew rapidly. Commissions flowed in upon him, new creations from his hand followed in quick succession and his unsurpassed abilities as a sculptor became everywhere recognized. In 1819 he returned to Denmark, and his journey through Germany and his reception at Copenhagen resembled a triumph. After remaining a year in Copenhagen and executing various works there, he returned to Rome, visiting, on his way, Berlin, Dresden, Warsaw and Vienna. He remained at Rome till 1838, when he undertook another journey to Copenhagen, being principally moved to this step by the contemplated establishment in that city of a museum of his works and art treasures. His return was a sort of national festival. The remainder of his life was spent chiefly in the Danish capital. The Thorwaldsen Museum, opened in 1846, contains about three hundred of the works of the sculptor. Among his principal works are *Lion of Lucerne*; a group of *Hector, Paris and Helena*; *Psyche*; *Memorial to Baroness Schubart*; *Three Graces*, and *Christ*, in the Free Church at Copenhagen.

Thothmes, *thoth'meez,* **III,** a king of Egypt, one of the most famous rulers of the eighteenth dynasty. He came to the throne about 1538 B. C. During the early part of his reign, his aunt, Hatasu, was his colleague, and his share in the royal power was small. When he became sole ruler, he gratified his spite at her by erasing her name from every monument and temple she had built. Palestine, Syria, a part of Mesopotamia and the region between the Euphrates and the Mediterranean were subdued by him, and an account of his deeds was inscribed on the walls of the Temple of Karnak, which he enlarged. One of the great obelisks which he erected is now in Central Park, New York; another stands on the Thames Embankment, in London.

Thought, *thawt,* the mental power by which we compare ideas and classify them according to their resemblances and differences. The power of thought is the distinguishing feature between the human mind and the minds of lower animals. The first step in thinking is the formation of concepts (See CONCEPT); the second is the formation of judgments (See JUDGMENT), and the third is reasoning (See REASON). There is but one thought process, and the difference in these steps is one of degree only. In the formation of concepts we abstract and compare qualities in sense perceptions and classify these perceptions according to their agreement or disagreement. In the formation of judgments we compare and classify concepts, in reasoning we compare judgments, and from this comparison we form a third judgment. See LOGIC; SYLLOGISM.

The fundamental laws of thought are the law of identity, the law of contradiction and the law of the excluded middle. The *law of identity* means that the same thing or quality is always the same thing or quality, whatever the conditions or circumstances under which it exists. However simple this law may seem, inability to apply it leads to many failures. It is because the boy cannot see that the principles of multiplication and division are the same, wherever they occur, that he has so much difficulty with his operations in common fractions and decimals, and it is because the lawyer cannot discover the underlying principles of law that he loses his case. This law of identity deals with fundamental principles and rules, and in order that it may be applied in all the varying conditions of life, the principles and laws pertaining to the various branches in a course of study should be thoroughly understood.

The *law of contradiction* means that a thing cannot exist in opposite conditions at the same time. A man cannot be dead and alive at the same time. The *law of excluded middle* means that a thing must be or must not be. A coat is either black or not black; an apple is sour or not sour. Gradations in quality form many apparent exceptions to this law, but they should not be so regarded. In forming judgments one should keep the quality under consideration constantly in mind and then determine whether the object compared does or does not agree with this quality. Failure to observe this simple law often leads to indistinct ideas and loose qualifications.

While the child begins to think as soon as he begins to form concepts, the thought power develops slowly during the first few years, and he relies almost entirely upon his powers of observation and memory. To tax a child's reasoning power before he is twelve years of age is unwise, because this can be done only at the expense of the training of the powers of observation and memory, which up to this time are particularly active, and also because the overtaxing of a mental power in its immature state cripples its development in after years. Children whose reasoning powers are overtaxed at an early age seldom make good thinkers or correct reasoners. However, the thought power should not be neglected, but within his capacity the child should be encouraged to compare, judge and classify his ideas.

Thousand and One Nights. See ARABIAN NIGHTS.

Thousand Islands, a group of islands in the Saint Lawrence River, just below its emergence from Lake Ontario. The group contains between 1700 and 1800 islands. Many of them are mere points of rock, while others have an area of several acres and are covered with vegetation. The section of the river containing the islands is known as Thousand Island Park. The scenery is beautiful, and the climate during summer is salubrious. Because of this, many of these islands have been purchased by individuals, and summer villas have been built upon them. Alexandria Bay, the most important town in the park, is a noted summer resort.

Thrace, a name applied at an early period among the Greeks to a region lying north of Macedonia. Besides possessing rich meadows and corn lands, the country abounded in mines, while the Thracian horses and riders rivaled those of Thessaly. Of the rivers of Thrace, the largest and most celebrated was the Hebrus (now Maritza). Abdera, the birthplace of Democritus and Protagoras; Sestos, on the Hellespont, celebrated in the story of Hero and Leander, and Byzantium, on the peninsula on which Constantinople now stands, were the places most worthy of note.

Thrash'er. See BROWN THRASHER.

Thrashing Machine, a machine for separating grain from the straw and chaff; it is used in thrashing small grains, such as wheat, oats, barley and rye. The earliest method of thrashing was by beating out the grain with a stick. Later the grain was trodden out by animals or men. Still later a so-called *sledge* was rolled over the sheaves. This was followed by the flail, consisting of two sticks fastened together at one end by thongs. Using one as a handle, the thrasher brought down the other horizontally upon the grain. The first successful thrashing machine was invented by Michael Sterling, a Scotch farmer, in 1758, but since that time Sterling's pattern has undergone many changes and improvements.

The essential parts of a thrashing machine are the beater, or drum, containing iron teeth projecting from its surface; the *concave*, which is a cast-iron plate, having the shape of a section of the inside of the beater, and fitted with similar teeth, so arranged that the teeth of the revolving beater mesh into them; the *straw carrier* and the *shaker*;

the *blowing drums*, sometimes called rakes, which assist in separating the loosened grain from the straw, and the *winnowing apparatus*, which consists of a blower and a set of screens, that have a vibratory motion and are so graduated that they separate small seeds from the grain. The machine is operated by horse power or steam power. Machines for thrashing on small farms of the Eastern and Central states are usually operated by horse power, while those used on the large wheat farms of the West and Northwest are operated by steam power, usually with an engine of 12 or 15 horse-power capacity. One of these machines will thrash from 1200 to 1500 bushels of wheat in a day.

Thread, *thred*, a slender cord, made of two or more strands, twisted together. Thread is made of cotton, linen and silk, but the manufacture of cotton thread so far exceeds that of the others in quantity and value that this is the sort of thread meant when the term is used without qualification. Cotton thread is made from the long fiber, or sea island, cotton (See COTTON). The process is long and somewhat complicated. The fiber is carefully picked and carded. As the cotton passes from the carding machine, it is packed into a thick, soft card, which is coiled into a can. These coils of ropes pass to the *drawing frame*, which is an arrangement for passing the ropes between a series of rollers, each succeeding set moving faster than the one before, so that the cotton is drawn out fine and thin, like a ribbon. From the drawing frame the cotton passes to the *doubling frame*, which compresses it into a very fine, delicate strip. These strips are then lapped and again drawn out; then recarded, for the purpose of removing any imperfections that may remain. From the second set of cards the thread-like roll or cord is wound upon a bobbin. Six of these are then twisted together, into a large-sized yarn, which is reduced by successive spinnings until it reaches the size of a coarse cotton yarn. From this the thread is spun. Several spinnings are necessary to complete the operation, since thread of the best quality must contain a number of strands, each of which is hard twisted, and all of which are thoroughly twisted together. After spinning, the thread is inspected, then bleached, if white thread is desired, or colored, and wound upon spools for the market.

Thread Worm, a kind of hard worm, which is often an annoying parasite in human beings, especially in children.

Three Rivers, a city of the Province of Quebec, situated on the north bank of the Saint Lawrence River, at its confluence with the Saint Maurice, and on the Canadian Pacific and the Grand Trunk railways, 95 mi. n. e. of Montreal. It is one of the oldest towns in Canada. The chief industry is manufacturing, the principal products being lumber, machinery, iron pipe, tools, boots and shoes, paper and foundry supplies. Population in 1911, 13,691.

Thrush, the highest group of singing birds. There are many species of them, none very large and most of them with a dark plumage, frequently spotted or striped, and with light or spotted under parts. They live in the wooded countries, chiefly on the ground, and in their habits they are gen-

WILSON'S THRUSH

erally solitary, though in the winter and in the season of migration they go in loose flocks. The thrushes are celebrated because of their powers of song and are favorites throughout all parts of the world. In the United States the *brown thrush*, or *brown thrasher*, is one of the best known species. It is rather slender and is brown above, with lighter under parts, streaked with brown. It has a loud, prolonged, clear song. There are eight other species in the United States east of the Mississippi, and among them the *wood thrush*, the *hermit thrush* and *Wilson's thrush* are charming, but shy, inhabitants of the forests and shrubbery. In some localities the wood thrush is called the wood robin. See ROBIN.

Thrush or **Milk Thrush,** a disease technically known as *aphthae*, occurring especially in infants, but occasionally seen in old persons, and consisting of small, white ulcers, resembling particles of curdled milk, and appearing upon the tongue, gums, inside of the lips and on the palate.

Thucydides, *thu sid'e deez,* (about 470– about 400 B. C.), the greatest of the Greek histo-.ians, born in Attica. He was well born and

rich, was the possessor of gold mines in Thrace and was for a time a prominent commander during the Peloponnesian War. For many years he was in exile, as a result of an accusation of remissness in duty; but he appears to have returned to Athens in 403 B. C., the year following the termination of the war. His history of the Peloponnesian War consists of eight books, the last of which differs from the others in containing none of the political speeches which form so striking a feature of the rest, and in being inferior in style. Hence, it has been thought by various critics to be the work of a different author; but it is more probable that it is the author's own, without his final revision. The history is incomplete, the eighth book stopping abruptly in the middle of the twenty-first year of the war. As a historian Thucydides was painstaking and indefatigable in collecting and sifting facts, brief and terse in narrating them. His style is full of dignity, but it is sometimes obscure through its condensations. Thucydides is unsurpassed in the power of analyzing character and action, of tracing events to their causes, of appreciating the motives of individual agents and of combining in their just relations all the threads of the tangled web of history.

Thugs, the name applied to a secret and once widely spread society among the Hindus, whose occupation was to waylay, assassinate and rob all who did not belong to their own caste. This they did, not so much from their cupidity, as from religious motives, such actions being deemed acceptable to their goddess Kâlî. The name is sometimes applied in America to highwaymen in cities or elsewhere.

Thule, *thoo'le,* the name given by the ancients to the most northern country with which they were acquainted. According to some accounts, it was an island six days' voyage to the north of Britannia, and, therefore, it has often been identified with Iceland. Some have imagined it to be one of the Scotch islands, others the coast of Norway.

Thur'low, EDWARD, Baron (1731–1806), an English lawyer, educated at Cambridge and at the Middle Temple. He was called to the bar in 1754 and soon had one of the best practices at the bar. In 1768 he entered Parliament, two years later was made solicitor-general, and in 1771 became attorney-general. He became chancellor of the exchequer in 1778, being raised to the peerage as Baron Thurlow. He was compelled to resign office on the dissolution of the ministry in 1783, but he was still considered the confidential adviser of the king, and on the dissolution of the coalition ministry, at the close of the year, the great seal was restored to him by Pitt. Pitt suspected Thurlow of intriguing with the prince of Wales, and an open disagreement took place between them. Pitt demanded his dismissal, to which the king agreed, and he was deprived of the great seal in 1792. After this he possessed little political influence.

Thur′man, ALLEN GRANBERY (1813–1895), an American statesman and jurist, born at Lynchburg, Va. He was educated at the academy at Chillicothe, Ohio, and was admitted to the bar in 1835. In 1844 he was elected to Congress and served one term, declining a renomination. In 1851 he was appointed associate justice of the Ohio supreme court, became chief justice in 1854 and retained the position two years. He was defeated for governor of Ohio in 1866. In 1869 Thurman became United States senator and again in 1874, rising to a position of leadership among his Democratic colleagues. He was one of the authors of the bill creating the electoral commission in 1876 and was a member of that body. In 1888 he was nominated by the Democratic party for vice-president, but was defeated at the polls.

Thursday, *thurz′day,* Thor's day, the fifth day of the week, so called from the old Teutonic god of thunder, Thor.

Thwaites, *thwayts,* REUBEN GOLD (1853–1913), an American historian, born in Dorchester, Mass. He moved in 1866 to Wisconsin, where he was later editor of the *Wisconsin State Journal.* His writings include *Down Historic Waterways, The Colonies, 1492–1750* and several biographies. He has also edited a number of historical works, among which *The Jesuit Relations,* in seventy-three volumes, is considered an especially careful and scholarly piece of work.

Thyme, *time,* a small plant of the mint family, a native of the south of Europe, frequently cultivated in gardens. It has a strong aromatic odor and yields an essential oil, which is used for flavoring purposes.

Thy′mus Gland. See GLANDS.

Thy′roid Gland. See GLANDS.

Thyrsus, *thur′sus,* among the Greeks, a wand, or spear, wreathed with ivy leaves, and bearing a pine cone at the top, which was carried by the followers of Bacchus as a symbol of devotion. In ancient representations it appears in various forms.

Tian-Shan or **Thian-Shan,** *te ahn′shahn′,* a range of mountains situated in central Asia,

forming a part of the boundary between the Russian possessions and eastern Turkestan. The range extends in a northeastward direction from the Plateau of Pamir to the Desert of Gobi, and it constitutes the watershed between the basins of the Dzungria and the Balkash. It is also closely linked with the Altai Mountains. It forms a part of the great transcontinental barrier, bordering on the northern edge of the central plateau of Asia. The central portion of the range has an elevation of from 15,000 to 20,000 feet. The slopes are usually covered with snow and contain many glaciers. The lower parts of the slopes, to an altitude of from 9000 to 9500 feet, are covered with forests.

Tia′ra, the name given originally to the cap of the Persian kings, but now to the triple crown of the pope. The tiara of the pope is a high cap of gold cloth, encircled by three coronets, with an orb and cross of gold at the top. From either side hangs a fringed and embroidered pendant. The cap was first adopted by Nicholas I, in the ninth century, and later popes added the coronet.

Ti′ber, a river of Italy, which rises in the Tuscan Apennines, flows southward and enters the Mediterranean by two mouths. Its length is 245 miles. The Tiber is noted for the large delta at its mouth and for its historic associations. It traverses the city of Rome, forming the island anciently called *Insula Tiberina.* The stream is subject to floods and carries down large quantities of yellow mud, for which reason it is often known as the Yellow Tiber. Through Rome it has been canalized, and it is also crossed by a number of bridges. During high water it is navigable for about thirty miles north of Rome.

Tibe′rius (42 B. C.–37 A. D.), a Roman emperor, the son of Tiberius Claudius Nero and Livia Drusilla, afterward the wife of the emperor Augustus. Tiberius became consul in his twenty-eighth year and was subsequently adopted by Augustus as his heir. In 14 A. D. he succeeded to the throne, without opposition. Dangerous mutinies broke out shortly afterward in the armies posted in Pannonia and on the Rhine, but they were suppressed by the exertions of the two princes, Germanicus and Drusus. The conduct of Tiberius as a ruler was distinguished by an extraordinary mixture of tyranny with occasional wisdom and good sense. Tacitus records the events of the reign, including the suspicious death of Germanicus, the detestable administration of Sejanus, the praetorian prefect, and the retirement of Tiberius to the Isle of Capri, where he lived an infamous and dissolute life. Sejanus, aspiring to the throne, fell a victim to his ambition in the year 31; and many innocent persons were destroyed, owing to the suspicion and cruelty of Tiberius, to whom spies reported all that went on in Rome.

Tib'et or **Thibet,** an extensive region in south central Asia, lying between the Himalaya Mountains, on the south, and the Kuen-lun, on the north, and extending from India, on the west, to China proper on the east. Its area is variously estimated, but by the best authorities it is considered to be about 750,000 square miles. The entire region consists of a series of elevated plains or plateaus, varying in altitude from 14,000 to 17,000 feet, in the west, and from 8000 or 9000 feet to 14,000 feet, in the east and northeast. The plateaus are rolling or mountainous, and some of the peaks in the surrounding ranges attain altitudes of 25,000 feet and over. The western part of Tibet is largely a desert and contains neither springs nor streams; consequently it is almost wholly devoid of vegetation. These desert characteristics also prevail to some extent in the central and northern parts, because of the cold climate, due to the altitude. However, the southern and eastern parts have plenty of rainfall, are watered by numerous large streams and have an abundance of vegetation. The Indus, the Sutlej, the Ganges and the Brahmaputra have their sources in the southwest, and farther north, the Yang-tse-Kiang and Hoang-ho originate. The country contains numerous lakes, scattered over its area, some of which have no outlet and are salt. Because of the altitude, the climate of the greater part of the region is cold.

The chief mineral products consist of borax, salt, nitre, iron, silver, copper and gold. Turquoise and lapis lazuli are also found. Agriculture and the raising of live stock engage the attention of most of the inhabitants. Because of the altitude, only the hardiest plants can be grown. Barley is the chief cereal. Other crops are wheat, buckwheat, potatoes, turnips, cabbages and pulse. Apples and apricots are raised in the western part, and peaches and some other fruits are grown in the southern. The manufactures are of comparatively little importance. There are no factories or manufacturing centers, and whatever industries are prosecuted are located in the homes of the workmen. Woolen fabrics are manufactured more extensively than anything else. Some of the inhabitants are skilful workers in metals and produce metallic wares and ornamental work. The chief trade is with China and with British India. Nearly all the traffic is in the hands of the government. Means of transport are primitive, and the goods are carried on the backs of pack animals. The chief cities are Lhasa, the capital, Gyangze and Shigatse.

Tibet is the seat of a branch of Buddhism known as Lamaism. Lhasa is the religious and political capital. The religious and civil affairs are in the hands of two lamas, the Dalai lama and the Tishu lama, one residing at Lhasa and the other at Shigatse. The country contains a large number of monasteries, which are the seats of learning and are occupied almost entirely by lama priests, who live a life of celibacy. The population of the country is estimated at from 2,000,000 to 3,000,000, nearly all of whom are Mongolians. While the government is in the hands of the natives, it is controlled in its foreign relations by Chinese agents, and the Dalai lama is virtually the local chief executive. In 1904 and 1905 Tibet was invaded by British forces, and the government was compelled to grant important trade concessions. It has long been a field of commercial and political rivalry between Russia and England.

Tic Douloureux, *tik doo loo roo'*, a species of neuralgia, which affects the facial nerve and is characterized by acute pain, attended with convulsive twitchings of the muscles, and continued from a few moments to several hours. It occurs on one side of the face and may be caused by a diseased tooth, by inflammation in the air passage, by exposure to cold, by dissipation and by other diseases. The natural remedy is removal of the cause, though sometimes warm applications will bring temporary relief.

Tick'nor, GEORGE (1791–1871), an American critic and historian, born at Boston. He graduated at Dartmouth College in 1807 and was admitted to the bar six years later. In 1815 he sailed for Europe and visited the chief capitals, for the purpose of pursuing his literary studies. On his return he was appointed professor of modern languages and literature in Harvard University. After fifteen years he resigned his professorship, and for the next three years he traveled in Europe with his family. In 1849 he published a *History of Spanish Literature*, which was at once recognized by scholars as a work of value and which has been translated into Spanish and German. After some works of minor interest, he produced in 1863 a *Life of Prescott*, the historian, with whom he had maintained a close friendship.

Ticks, a family of parasitic insects, with oval or rounded bodies, and with mouths in the form of suckers, by which they attach themselves to dogs, sheep, oxen and other mammals. Birds and reptiles are also annoyed by the attacks of certain species. The common wood tick is found

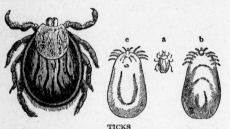

TICKS

Wood tick; *a*, mature dog tick; *b*, gorged with blood, viewed from above; *c*, viewed from below.

widely distributed through damp woods in the United States and is often very annoying to persons. It burrows into the flesh and is often not noticed until gorged with blood, when it is difficult to remove.

Ticon'dero'ga, BATTLES OF. A powerful fortress was built near the site of the village of Ticonderoga, N. Y., by the French in 1755. It was held by Montcalm in 1757 and successfully resisted a vigorous attack by the British under General Abercrombie. It was captured by General Amherst for the English, after a long siege, in July, 1759. One of the first movements in the Revolutionary War was an American expedition against Ticonderoga, undertaken by a body of Green Mountain Boys, under Ethan Allen, and a force of continental troops, under Benedict Arnold. It was captured May 10, 1775, without the loss of a single man. It was on this occasion that Ethan Allen made his famous reply to the British general who inquired by what authority he demanded the surrender of the fort—"In the name of the Great Jehovah and the Continental Congress." It was retaken by Burgoyne in 1777, was later abandoned and was reoccupied in 1780. Ruins of the barracks and fortifications are still to be seen.

The village of Ticonderoga is in Essex co., N. Y., about 100 mi. n. of Albany, on the Central Vermont and the Delaware & Hudson railways. It is situated on an elevated promontory, between Lake Champlain and Lake George. It is the center of a rich graphite region, and for years it furnished almost all of that material produced in the United States. Population in 1910, 2475.

Tides, the periodical rise and fall of the water of the ocean, caused by the attraction of the sun and moon. The tide rises for about six hours, remains stationary for a short time, then begins to recede and continues to fall for the next six hours. The rise is called *flood tide*, and the fall, *ebb tide*. When the water has reached its height, it is called *high water*, and when it has reached its lowest point, it is at *low water*. Every place on the coast has two high and two low tides during the twenty-four hours; but the mean interval between successive high tides is about twelve hours and twenty-six minutes, and the hour of the day at which high or low water is greatest is later each day by about fifty-two minutes.

Tides are caused by the attraction of the sun and moon, but the moon, being so much nearer the earth, exerts by far the greater influence, notwithstanding it is much smaller than the sun (See GRAVITATION). This attraction causes a rise of water, or *tidal wave*, nearest the moon; and as the earth rotates on its axis, the tendency of this wave is to keep directly under the moon. Hence, it travels from east to west, but it lags somewhat behind the moon, on account of the time required to draw the water into its position. Since the attraction of bodies decreases as the square of the distance between them increases, it follows that the points of the moon's greatest and least attraction are at those points on the earth's surface which are respectively the nearest and the far-

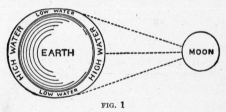

FIG. 1

thest from the moon. At the former point the attraction is greater than the average, and the water is pulled up toward the moon; the solid portions of the earth are attracted the same as the water, so the earth as a whole is drawn toward the moon, away from the point on the opposite side where the attraction is less than the average. The pressure of the water upon either side of this pushes the water up on the side near the moon and forms a tidal wave, which balances that on the opposite side. Therefore we have high tide at the opposite ends of the long diameter of the ellipse, and low tide at the points midway between.

Twice a month, at new and at full moon, the attraction of the moon and sun is combined to act upon the tides at the same points, and the highest tides of the month occur. This is known as *spring tide* and is illustrated in Fig. 2. Near the first and fourth quarters of the moon, the earth, sun and moon are in such relative posi-

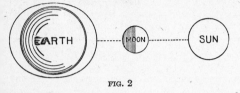

FIG. 2

tions that the attractions of the sun and moon act nearly at right angles upon the earth and we have the lowest tide, called the *neap tide*. This is illustrated in Fig. 3.

In the open ocean the tidal wave is merely a broad swell that is scarcely perceptible, but on

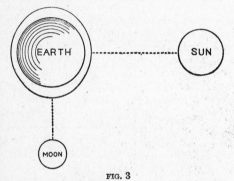

FIG. 3

the coast its height varies according to the shape and the character of the locality. If the coast contains inlets, which narrow towards their head, like the Bay of Fundy, the tidal wave grows higher as it is shortened by the converging shores, and the tide rises very high. If the coast contains a promontory or other projection, which divides the tidal wave, as the Florida peninsula, the tendency is to lower the tide. Because of the irregularity of the coast and of the bed of the ocean, tides do not occur at all places on the same meridian at exactly the same time. Mariners' charts contain the variations in tide for all harbors and are frequently accompanied by tables, which give the time of the tides for each harbor and each month in the year.

Tieck, *teek,* LUDWIG (1773–1853), a German author. He was educated at the University of Halle and at Göttingen and Erlangen, and after his return to Berlin he came forward as a writer of tales and romances. At Jena, in 1799–1800, he entered on friendly relations with the Schlegels, Novalis, Brentano and others, and thus he became associated with what has been called "the Romantic School of Germany." In 1799 he published *Romantic Poems,* and in 1804 his comedy, *Kaiser Octavianus,* appeared. His *Phantasus,* however, gave the first sign of his having freed himself from the mysticism and extravagance of his earlier works. In 1817 he visited England, where he collected material for his *Shakespeare;* and on his return he resided at Ziebingen till 1819, when he removed to Dresden. From this period his writings, as exemplified in his *Tales,* bear the true stamp of genius.

Tien-tsin, *tyen'tsin,* a city of China, situated on the Pei-ho River, where it forms a junction with the Hun-ho, the Hu-to-ho and the Grand Canal, 70 mi. s. e. of Peking, with which it is connected by railway. The city is surrounded by high walls, which are surmounted by towers. The houses in the Chinese quarter are low, and the streets are unattractive. The foreign quarter, which is outside of the Chinese city, is well built and resembles a modern European or American town in nearly all respects. Tien-tsin is an important trade center and one of the chief seaports of the Chinese Empire. It is open to vessels of the leading European nations and the United States on equal terms. During the Boxer outbreak in 1900, Tien-tsin was the point from which the relief expedition of the allied powers started for Peking. Population, estimated at about 750,000.

Tier'ra del Fuego, *fway'go,* or **Terra del Fuego** (land of fire), a group of islands situated off the southern extremity of South America, separated from the mainland by the Strait of Magellan. The islands are really arranged in two groups, the eastern group belonging to Argentina and the western to Chile. Horn Island, the farthest south, contains Cape Horn. The largest island is East Tierra del Fuego, or King Charles South Land. Its greatest length from east to west is 270 miles. All of the islands are mountainous, though there are no evidences of volcanic action among them. The highest peaks are Mount Sarmiento, 6910 feet, and Mount Darwin, 6800 feet. The native inhabitants, or Fuegians, do not exceed 2000 in number. They closely resemble the Patagonians, and by some authorities they are considered to be the lowest in the scale of human existence. Most of the civilized population is found on the eastern group, belonging to Argentina.

Tif'fin, OHIO, the county-seat of Seneca co., 40 mi. s. e. of Toledo, on the Sandusky River and on the Pennsylvania, the Baltimore & Ohio and the Cleveland, Cincinnati, Chicago & Saint Louis railroads. It is the seat of Heidelberg University and of the College of the Ursuline Sisters. The city has a public library, Riverview Park and a fine soldiers' monument. There are deposits of clay and glass sand in the vicinity, and the industrial establishments include machine shops, glass works, potteries, woolen mills, breweries and shoe factories. The place was settled in 1817 by Erastus Bowe, and it was chartered as a city in 1836. Population in 1910, 11,894.

Tiflis' (Russian pronunciation *tyee flyees'*), the capital of Russian Transcaucasia, situated on both banks of the Kur, 275 mi. w. by n. of Baku, with which it is connected by railway. The city occupies a beautiful valley, at the foot of the Caucasus Mountains, and is interspersed with numerous vineyards and orchards. A part

less oval footprint. The average length of a male is about 9½ to 10 feet from the nose to the tip of the tail; the average weight is 500 pounds. It is of a bright fawn color above and a pure white below, crossed irregularly with black stripes. Its colors prevent its form being easily seen in the shades of the jungles. The tiger attains its full development in India, the name of *Bengal Tiger* being generally used as synonymous with those specimens which appear as the typical and most powerful representatives of the species. It generally selects the neighborhood of water courses as its home and springs upon the animals that approach to drink. *Man-eaters* are tigers that have acquired a special liking for human prey. The tiger combines with the strength of a lion, a fierceness, stealth and activity peculiar to itself, so that natives fear it

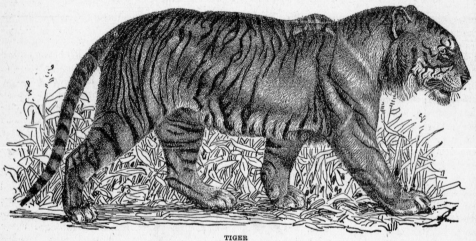

TIGER

of the city has been recently rebuilt on modern plans and contains good hotels, stores, theaters and other buildings, resembling those of the cities of western Europe. The public gardens and botanical garden are objects of rare interest. The educational institutions include the conservatory of music, a railroad institute, a physical observatory and the Caucasian Museum. The manufactures are quite extensive and include the manufacture of tobacco, leather, cotton yarn and malt liquors. The trade is also of considerable importance. Population in 1911, 191,800.

Ti'ger, the largest and most powerful animal of the cat family. The tiger is about the height of the lion, but the body is longer and slenderer, while the head is rounder and has no trace of a mane. The males are considerably larger than the females, and make a more nearly square and

more than any other animal. The natives destroy tigers by means of poisoned arrows or capture them in pits and other traps.

Tig'lath-Pile'ser, the name of several Assyrian kings, the most important of whom is Tiglath-Pileser III. He ruled from 745 to 727 B. c., and was the real founder of Assyrian greatness. His administrative ability was shown in his treatment of his conquered states, which he divided into a number of small districts under Assyrian governors. The king of Judah paid tribute to Tiglath-Pileser, whose name is given in the Old Testament as Pul (II *Kings*, xv, 19).

Ti'gris, a river of western Asia, which rises in the Anti-Taurus Mountains, a few miles east of the Euphrates. It originates in two or more branches, flows generally southeastward and unites with the Euphrates about 90 miles northwest of the Persian Gulf. It is a rapid stream and is navigable for steamers as far as Bagdad and for smaller vessels to Mozul. The river is subject to variations in volume at different seasons of the year, and it attains its greatest height between the middle and the end of May. This river, with the Euphrates, traverses a valley of great historic importance, since it is the scene of many of the events narrated in the Old Testament and also contains the remains of Nineveh and other ancient cities.

Til'den, SAMUEL JONES (1814–1886), an American statesman, born in New Lebanon, N. Y. He was educated at Yale College and at the University of the City of New York and was admitted to the bar in 1841. He was elected to the state assembly in 1845, where he advocated the construction of canals by the state, and in 1846 he was a member of the state constitutional convention. In 1855 more than half the railway corporations in the north were his clients. By 1868 he had become the leader of the Democratic party in New York State. His determined opposition and practical measures broke up the "Tweed Ring" (See TWEED, WILLIAM MARCY), and he himself conducted the successful prosecution. He was elected governor in 1874, served the state with sagacity and honesty and in 1876 was democratic candidate for president. He received a majority of the popular vote and was defeated in the electoral college by one vote, after a long dispute over returns, which was decided by an electoral commission (See ELECTORAL COMMISSION). In 1880 and in 1884 renomination was pressed upon him, but declined. The greater portion of his fortune (which was estimated at $5,000,000), he bequeathed for the endowment of a public library in New York City, but after a long contest over the will, only about $2,000,000 was so applied. Consult Bigelow's *Samuel Jones Tilden.*

Tiles, *tile'z*, a term applied to a variety of articles, made either for ornament, such as inlaid paving tiles, or for use, as draining and roofing tiles. The latter are made similarly to bricks and of similar clay (See BRICK). Floor tiles in which the body of the tile is in one color and a special pattern is produced by the use of other colors, are known as *encaustic tiles*. When designs in floors or walls are made by the arrangement of tiles of different colors, the result is said to be a *mosaic.*

Till'man, BENJAMIN RYAN (1847–   ), an American politician, born in Edgefield County, S. C. He received an elementary education,

but left school in July, 1864, to join the Confederate army. He did not serve long, however, being stricken with illness. After the war he became a planter in his native state, but in 1886 he entered politics, as the champion of industrial and technical education, and succeeded in securing the establishment of several schools. He gained a large following as the advocate of other reforms and was elected governor in 1890. He was reëlected in 1892, his administration being important by reason of the passage of the state liquor dispensary law. In 1895 he became a candidate for the Senate, and after an exciting campaign he was elected. He was reëlected in 1901, in 1907, and again in 1913.

Til'ly, JOHANN TSERKLAES, Count of (1559–1632), one of the most celebrated generals of the seventeenth century. He was born at the castle of Tilly in Belgium and received his military training in the Spanish armies. In 1610 he was selected by Duke Maximilian of Bavaria to reorganize his army, and at the outbreak of the Thirty Years' War he was made commander of the forces of the Holy League. In 1620 he gained the victory of White Mountain, near Prague, and in 1621 he subdued Bohemia. In the years that followed, he overpowered Christian IV of Denmark, who had entered the war on the side of the Protestants, and forced him to withdraw. Tilly became commander of the imperial army in 1630, and in 1631 he stormed Magdeburg. This, his thirty-sixth victory, closed his list of triumphs. On Sept. 17, 1631, he was defeated by Gustavus Adolphus at Breitenfeld, near Leipzig, and in the next year, in a contest with the Swedish king, near the Lech, he was mortally wounded.

Tim'ber, wood used for constructive purposes, as for buildings, telegraph poles, shipbuilding, pulp, paving blocks and the manufacture of furniture. The term is also used to distinguish the standing trees from the wood sawed or manufactured ready for use. See LUMBER.

Timbuk'tu or **Timbuc'too**, a city of Africa, situated on the southern edge of the Sahara and in the military district of French Sudan. It stands on a plain a few feet above the level of the Upper Niger, on whose banks it is situated. Formerly it was a town of considerable importance and was a distributing center for the surrounding country, as well as a starting point for caravans, but it has lost much of its former prestige. The houses are chiefly one-story mud hovels, though the city contains a number of mosques, one of which is a fine structure and dates from 1325.

The town is a prominent telegraph station, and its trade consists in the export of ostrich feathers, gums and other tropical products. Population, about 5000, most of whom are Moroccans.

Time, STANDARD, the system of time-reckoning adopted by law or by general usage over a certain region. The turning of the earth on its axis from west to east causes a constant difference in sun time between places at different meridians; for example, when it is noon, or twelve o'clock, at one place, it is afternoon at places to the east of that point, and forenoon at places farther west. This fact gives rise to many complications, especially in the case of railroads, and in the United States the standard time was settled upon by a convention in 1883. As a difference of 15° of longitude causes a difference of exactly one hour in time, this settlement was effected by choosing a series of meridians, which differed from that of Greenwich, England, by multiples of 15, and making these the centers of time zones. The time in the zone is that of this central meridian. In the United States the time of the territory for $7\frac{1}{2}°$ on each side of the 60th meridian is known as *Atlantic* time; the time of the 75th meridian is called *Eastern*; that of the 90th, *Central*; that of the 105th, *Mountain*, and that of the 120th, *Pacific*. If the dividing line runs through a town, a jog is always made in it so that the town may fall entirely on one side of the line. This irregularity of boundaries is still further emphasized, to accommodate the divisions of the great railway systems. For illustration, the eastern boundary of the Central time belt extends from Detroit to Buffalo, thence southward to Atlanta, thence eastward to Savannah.

At the naval observatory in Washington, D. C., there is a great sidereal clock by which the timepieces of North America are regulated. This clock never runs "fast" or "slow," nor is it influenced by atmospheric conditions, because it runs in a vacuum. Each day at noon and each night at ten o'clock this clock, through the wireless station at Arlington, Virginia, flashes a wireless signal over the country. The speed of the wireless wave is so great that only one-twentieth of a second is lost between Arlington and San Francisco. See ARITHMETIC, Vol. VI.

Timor, *te more'*, the largest of the Lesser Sunda Islands. It lies s. e. of Celebes. Its length is 275 mi., and its area, about 12,350 sq. mi. The island is traversed by ranges of low mountains containing a number of volcanic cones. The loftiest summit has an altitude of 11,800 feet.

The entire surface of the island is hilly or mountainous. Parts of it are well wooded, and others are almost barren. The chief products are bamboo, corn, cotton, tobacco, sweet potatoes, breadfruit, indigo, pineapples, cocoa, sago, lemons, papaws and sandalwood. All tropical fruits grow wild, and agriculture receives but little attention. Though very little of the soil is cultivated, it yields good crops. Politically the island is divided between the Netherlands, which occupies the southwest half, and Portugal, occupying the northeast half. See SUNDA ISLANDS.

Tim'othy, a disciple of Saint Paul, born in Lycaonia, Asia Minor, probably at Lystra, of a Gentile father and Jewish mother. He went with Paul to Philippi and Beroea and remained alone in the latter city, afterward rejoining the apostle at Athens, from which he was sent to Thessalonica. After remaining there some time, he joined Paul at Corinth. Five years later, he was at Ephesus, whence he was sent with Erastus into Macedonia and Achaia, to prepare the churches for Paul's meditated visit. Timothy met the apostle in Macedonia and preceded him on his journey to Jerusalem. He was at Rome with Paul at the time when the epistles to the Colossians, Philippians and Philemon were written. He is said to have been martyred in the reign of Domitian or Nerva.

Timothy or **Cat's Tail,** a well-known grass, which is called *herd's grass* in New England, and which is everywhere highly valued as a fodder grass. It is distinguished by long, cylindrical, closely-packed spikes of flowers, which appear upon strong stems, four to five feet tall. It is perennial, but the stems spring up and mature rapidly, in the same season in which it is sown, if the conditions are favorable. Timothy seed is frequently mixed with clover seed in planting.

Timur, *te moor'*, also called Timur Beg and Timur Lenk and, by corruption, Tamerlane (1336–1405), a celebrated conqueror of Mongol or Tartar race. His ancestors were chiefs of his native district, and Timur, by his energy and abilities, raised himself to be ruler of all Turkestan (1370). By degrees he conquered Persia and the whole of Central Asia, and he extended his power from the great wall of China to Moscow. He invaded India (1398) and overran it from the Indus to the mouths of the Ganges, massacring, it is said, on one occasion, 100,000 prisoners. On his way from India, to meet the forces of Bajazet, the Turkish sultan, he subjugated Bagdad, plundered Aleppo, burned down the greater part of Damascus and wrested Syria from the Mamelukes, after which he invaded Asia Minor with an immense army. Bajazet's army was completely defeated, and the sultan was taken prisoner. The conquests of the Tartar now extended from the Irtish and the Volga to the Persian Gulf and from the Ganges to the Grecian Archipelago. He was making mighty preparations for an invasion of China when death arrested his progress. He was fanatical in his religion, and although no conquests were ever attended with greater cruelty, devastation and bloodshed, he was in a measure a patron of science and art and is reputed author of the *Institutions of Timur* and the *Autobiography of Timur*, both of which have been translated into English. See Mongols.

Tin, a hard, white, ductile metal. Tin appears to have been known in the time of Moses; and the Phoenicians traded largely in the tin ores of Cornwall. The mountains between Galicia and Portugal, and those separating Saxony and Bohemia, were also productive of tin centuries ago and still continue unexhausted. Tin occurs in the Malay Peninsula, the island of Banca, India, Mexico, Chile, Peru, the United States, Australia and other countries, but the most important mines are at Cornwall, England, and on the Malay Peninsula. From the latter, nearly half of the world's supply is obtained.

There are only two ores of tin, the native dioxide, called *tin stone* and *cassiterite*, and the double sulphide of tin and copper, called *tin pyrites*. The former is the only ore used for obtaining metallic tin. It occurs in various crystallized forms—in deep lodes blended with several other metals, as arsenic, copper, zinc and tungsten, when it is known as *mine tin*, or in disseminated masses in alluvial soil, in which state it is called *stream tin*. Mine tin, when reduced to the metallic state, yields *block tin*, while stream tin yields a purer sort, called *grain tin*.

The ore is first ground and washed and is then roasted in a reverberatory furnace, that the sulphur and arsenic may be expelled. Mixed with limestone and fuel, it is again melted in a furnace for about eight hours, the earthy matters flowing off with the lime, while the oxide of tin, reduced to a metallic state, falls by its own weight to the bottom and is drawn off. The tin, still impure, is again moderately heated, when it melts and flows off into the refining basins, leaving the greater part of the foreign metals in a solid state. The molten tin is stirred, in order to disperse the gases, and when partially cool, it separates into layers, the upper consisting of nearly pure tin,

while the under is so impure that it must be melted again. The upper layer is removed, cast into blocks and sold as *block tin*, the purest specimens being called *refined tin*. Pure tin has a fine white color like silver and is a little more than seven and one-fourth times heavier than water. It has a slightly disagreeable taste. Its hardness is between that of gold and lead, and it is very malleable. Tin is very flexible, and when bent it emits a crackling sound, sometimes called the *cry of tin*. It loses its luster when exposed to the air, but it undergoes no further alteration.

Tin will unite with arsenic and with antimony, but does not readily combine with iron. Combined with copper it forms bronze, bell metal and several other useful alloys. With lead it forms pewter and solder of various kinds. *Tin plate* is formed by dipping thin plates of iron into melted tin; they are afterward cleaned with sand and steeped for twenty-four hours in water, acidulated by bran or sulphuric acid. Tin is principally employed in the formation of alloys. Its oxides are used in enameling and for polishing the metals, and its solution in nitro-muriatic acid is an important mordant in the art of dyeing, rendering several colors, particularly scarlet, more brilliant and permanent.

Tin'der, any substance artificially rendered readily ignitible, but not inflammable. Before the invention of matches, tinder afforded the chief means of procuring fire. The tinder, ignited by a spark from a flint, was brought into contact with sticks dipped in sulphur. Tinder may be made of half-burnt linen and of various other substances, such as punk, touchwood or German tinder.

Tintoret'to (1512 or 1518–1594), the commonly used name of Jacopo Robusti, a famous Venetian painter. His father was a dyer, and the name Tintoretto means *little dyer*. He had a surprising passion for large paintings, and his *Last Judgment*, in the ducal palace, is seventy-five feet long, the largest painting in Europe. It is impossible to see it all at once, and so much has it been injured by smoke and "improved" by repainting, that it is hard to realize the artist's own conception. His masterpiece is thought to be *The Crucifixion*, a great painting about forty-five feet long. It shows a marvelous power in drawing the human figure in action, for every person in the picture is busy at something, and none is unnatural in pose. The coloring of this painting is not considered the best of Tintoretto's, nor is it so refined in character as some of his work. There are a great many of his paintings in Venice, where he lived his uneventful life.

Tippecanoe, *tip'pe ka noo'*, Battle of, a battle fought November 7, 1811, near the site of the present village of Battleground, on the Tippecanoe River, in Tippecanoe County, Ind., between a force of 800 Americans, chiefly Indiana and Kentucky militiamen, under William Henry Harrison, and a force of indians, estimated at about 6000, under the command of chiefs White Loon, Stone Eater, Winnemac and the Prophet, brother of Tecumseh. Tecumseh and the Prophet had created much discontent among the indians of the Northwest, and General Harrison had finally found it necessary either to secure a treaty with the indians or to subdue them by force. He finally proceeded to their headquarters at a village on the Tippecanoe and arranged for a meeting with the Prophet, but before the conference could be held the indians had attacked the American camp. After a fierce contest, lasting more than two hours, the indians were driven from the field, and their village was completely destroyed by the Americans. The battle led to a general uprising of the indians in the Northwest, in connection with the War of 1812 between the British and the Americans, and it also gave General Harrison such prestige as a commander that he was named during the following war commander of the American troops in the West and finally was made president, the cry during the campaign of 1840 being "Tippecanoe and Tyler, too."

Tippu Sahib, *te poo'sah'hib*, (1749–1799), sultan of Mysore, son of Hyder Ali. He succeeded his father in 1782. He continued the war in which his father was engaged with the British, and in April, 1783, he forced the British commander to surrender at Bedmore. Tippu was finally defeated near his capital, Seringapatam, and was compelled by a peace, concluded in February, 1792, to relinquish half his territory and to pay a large indemnity. But he was unwilling to submit to this loss and entered into negotiations with the French. Suspecting that Tippu's preparations were connected with Bonaparte's invasion of Egypt, the British determined to anticipate hostilities and declared war against the sultan. Tippu was defeated and retreated to Seringapatam. On May 4, 1799, General Baird took the place by storm and the sultan perished in the conflict.

Tissot, *tis so'*, James Joseph Jacques (1836–1902), a French painter, born at Nantes. The paintings which he produced before he was fifty were taken mostly from Parisian life, but from that time on he devoted himself almost exclusively to religious subjects. His distinction will rest largely upon his water-colors, more than three hundred in number, representing the life of Christ. The series is based upon repeated visits to the Holy Land and departs widely from the conventional treatment of religious subjects, in an attempt to give Christ's real surroundings. The collection was sold to the Brooklyn Institute for $60,000. Tissot also left, at the time of his death, a partially completed set of illustrations of the Old Testament.

Tissues, *tish'uze*, the organized collection of cells of the same sort, or fibers, of which the systems of organs are composed. Thus, we speak of *muscular tissue*, or flesh; *osseous tissue*, or bone; *adipose tissue*, or fat; *cartilaginous tissue*, or gristle; *pigmentary tissue*, or coloring matter seen in the skin; *areolar, cellular*, or *connective tissue*, which is widely distributed in every part of the body and serves to bind together and consolidate other parts and tissues. See Bone; Cartilage; Connective Tissue.

Titanic, with one exception the largest ship ever built. The Titanic was making her first voyage and on April 14, 1912, had reached a point about 1000 miles southeast of Halifax, when it collided with an iceberg and sank four hours later, early in the morning of April 15. The *Carpathia*, hearing the *Titanic's* wireless calls for help, rushed to the scene in time to pick up the lifeboats with 745 passengers, but 1595 persons went to their death on the great liner.

Tita'nium, a metal discovered in 1791. It is found combined with oxygen in several minerals and occurs especially in iron ores, which, therefore, receive the name of titaniferous iron ores. Titanium is a dark green, heavy, amorphous powder, and when heated to redness it burns with a brilliant white flame. The ores of this metal include menachanite, from Menachan in Cornwall, where it was originally found; iserine, from the river Iser in Silesia; sphene; rutile, and brookite. A small quantity of titanium added to steel increases the strength and hardness of that metal. It also increases the luster of silver and improves the carbon points used in arc lamps. See Electric Light.

Ti'tans, in Greek mythology, the sons and daughters of Uranus (Heaven) and Gaea (Earth). They were twelve in number, six sons and six daughters. They rose against Uranus and deposed him, raising Saturn, one of their number, to the throne. They were afterward overcome by Jupiter and were thrown into Tartarus.

Ti'tho'nus, in Greek mythology, a son or brother of Laomedon, king of Troy. He was beloved by Aurora, who besought Jupiter to make him immortal. Her prayer was granted, but she had neglected to ask for continual youth for her lover, and in time he took on all the signs of extreme age. Tithonus's prayer to the gods, to be relieved of the burden of old age, was answered by his being changed into a grasshopper.

Titian, *tish'an,* or **Vecellio,** TIZIANO (1477–1576), one of the most distinguished of the great Italian painters, head of the Venetian school. He was born at Pieve de Cadore, in the Carnic Alps. He studied under Giovanni Bellini of Venice, and in 1507 he was associated with the painter Giorgione in executing certain frescoes.

TITIAN

So closely did he imitate the latter's manner that his works were sometimes taken for those of that master. In 1511 he was invited to Padua, where he executed three remarkable frescoes, still to be seen, and painted the pictures of the *Tribute Money* and *Sacred and Profane Love.* In 1530 the emperor Charles V invited him to Bologna, to paint his portrait; the ruler was so pleased with the work that he would never permit himself to be portrayed by any other artist. Titian excelled as much in landscape as in figure painting, was equally great in ideal heads and in portraits, in frescoes and in oils. As a colorist

168

he is almost unrivaled, and his pictures often reach the perfection of sensuous beauty. Among his principal productions are *The Entombment, The Assumption of the Virgin, The Crucifixion, Descent from the Cross, Mater Dolorosa* and *Christ Crowned with Thorns.*

Titicaca, *te'te kah'ka,* LAKE, the largest lake of South America, situated partly in Peru and partly in Bolivia. It occupies the center of a lofty valley and is surrounded by the mountains forming the main chain of the Andes. It is 130 miles long and 30 miles wide at its widest point. The area is about 3200 square miles, and the height above sea level is 12,500 feet. The outline is irregular. The lake contains several islands and is fed by a number of mountain streams. Its outlet is the Desaguadero, which flows from its southern extremity. The towns of Puno, Juli and Chucuito are on its shores, which also contain many interesting ruins of the old empire of the Incas. Small steamers make regular trips upon the lake.

Tit'lark. See PIPIT.

Ti'tle, that which constitutes the legal ownership of property. Under the common law a complete title has two essential elements, possession and right of possession. A title to real estate may be acquired either by *descent* or by *purchase.* In the former case the holder acquires his right as an heir of a deceased person, who has died intestate. The acquirement of title by purchase includes all other means of acquiring a title. In most states title may be acquired through twenty years' possession.

In England and most of the United States, a system of examination and registration of titles by an authorized officer prevails, and the purchaser of real estate is thus assured of securing a perfect title without personal investigation.

Under the English law a person who purchases real property is entitled to receive a statement in writing, of all the events or changes affecting his title to the land. It is usually a complete history of the title which is to be transferred, showing not only the nature of the seller's interest, but also all mortgages and judgments against it, which affect his title. Such a statement is called an *abstract of title.* Custom has prescribed the same course in the United States.

Titles of Honor, words or phrases attached to the names of certain persons, in virtue of particular offices or dignities possessed by them, or as marks of distinction and special rank. They have existed probably among all peoples. Such were, in Rome, the titles *Magnus* (Great) and

Africanus (African), and the epithets *Caesar*, the name of a family, and *Augustus*, which were gradually applied to all who filled the imperial throne. In modern times such designations as prince, duke, king, lord, Royal Highness, His Excellency, are common.

Tit′mouse, Tit or **Tomtit,** a name given to a large group of small northern birds, of which there are a number of different species inhabiting most parts of the world. They are active little fellows, continually flitting from branch to branch, devouring seeds and insects. The tits live in trees or bushes, and hop, climb or cling, often head downward, prying into crevices in the most curious manner. Their shrill and wild notes are sometimes varied by pleasing musical sounds. In the United States the birds are known as *chickadees*, a name given in imitation of their calls. The *black-capped chickadee* is one of the most familiar and characteristic of northern birds, everywhere a great favorite, particularly as it often stays in rather cold latitudes throughout the winter, when its cheery exclamations are especially welcome. This chickadee is a very sociable, friendly bird, and with a little care it may be kept about quiet homes and will come and feed from the hand of a person.

Ti′tus (40–81), a Roman emperor, the eldest son of Vespasian. He served with credit as a military tribune in Germany and Britain and accompanied his father in the war against the Jews, as commander of a legion. When Vespasian became emperor (69) Titus was left to conduct the war in Judea. He took Jerusalem (70 A. D.), and after visiting Egypt he returned to Rome in triumph and was associated with his father in the government of the Empire. He became sole emperor in 79 and showed himself an enlightened and generous ruler.

Titus, a disciple and assistant of the apostle Paul; the person to whom one of the canonical epistles of the New Testament is addressed. He was a Gentile by origin and was probably a native of Antioch.

Titus, ARCH OF, an arch built by Domitian in 81 A. D., to commemorate the taking of Jerusalem by Titus. It is adorned with reliefs representing various scenes in the campaign and is located on the Sacred Way, facing the Forum.

Titus, EPISTLE TO, one of the three pastoral epistles of the New Testament, believed to have been written by Saint Paul after his first imprisonment at Rome.

Ti′tusville, PA., a city in Crawford co., on the Pennsylvania and the Dunkirk, Allegheny

Valley & Pittsburg railroads. The first oil well in the United States was sunk here in August, 1859. The place now has oil refineries, iron works, silk and lumber mills and engine factories. The city is an important trading center for the surrounding agricultural region. It was settled in 1796 and was made a city in 1866. In 1892 the Oil Creek, swollen by heavy rains, flooded the lower part of the city and caused several oil tanks to give way and allow the oil to spread over the water. This became ignited, and, by flood and fire together, about 60 lives were lost, and about one-third of the city was destroyed. Population in 1910, 8533.

Toad, *tode*, the name applied to various genera of tailless amphibians. Toads have thick, bulky

TOAD

bodies and short legs and are covered with warts. They leap clumsily and generally avoid the water, except in the breeding season. The food of the toad consists of insects and worms. Insects are caught by a sudden shooting out of the tongue, which is provided with a sticky fluid. The young, like frogs, pass through the tadpole stage. The *North American toad* is usually brown or green and is found both on dry land and in swampy regions. The bite and saliva of the *common toad* of Europe was formerly considered poisonous, but no venom or poison apparatus of any kind exists in these creatures. The toad is easily tamed and exhibits a considerable amount of intelligence as a pet.

Toad Flax, a European weed, now common in the United States between New England and Wisconsin. It grows from one to three feet tall and has narrow, whitish-green leaves and bright yellow flowers, which give the plant a brilliant appearance. This is a very troublesome weed, for it spreads rapidly by seeds and rootstocks. It may be eradicated by cultivation, prevention of its seeding and heavy cropping. Other names used to designate the common toad flax are *ramstead, butter-and-eggs, devil's flax* and *snap dragon*. See WEEDS.

Toadstool. See MUSHROOMS.

Tobac′co, a very important plant, belonging to the nightshade family. It has an erect stem, that grows from four to six feet high and produces at the top a cluster of small, rose-colored flowers. The leaves are the important part of the plant. They are oblong and pointed and grow directly

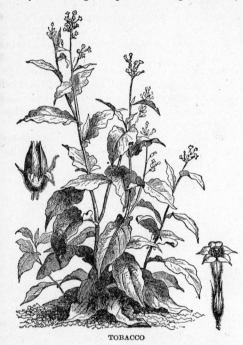

TOBACCO

from the stalk, often attaining a length of eighteen to twenty-five inches and a breadth of eight to ten inches. The plant is slightly poisonous, owing to the presence of nicotine, one of the most virulent poisons known.

The introduction of the use of tobacco forms a singular chapter in the history of mankind. According to some authorities, smoking was practiced by the Chinese at a very early date. At the time of the discovery of America, tobacco was in frequent use among the indians, and the practice of smoking, which had with them a religious character, was common to almost all the tribes. The name *tobacco* was either derived from the term used in Hayti to designate the pipe, or from Tabaca in Santo Domingo, whence it was introduced into Spain and Portugal in 1559, by a Spaniard. It soon found its way to Paris and Rome and was first used in the shape of snuff. Smoking is generally supposed to have been introduced into England by Sir Walter Raleigh, but Camden says the practice was introduced by Drake and his companions, on their return from Virginia in 1585. It was strongly opposed by both priests and rulers. All prohibitions, however, regal or

priestly, were of no avail, and tobacco is now the most extensively used luxury in the world. The United States is the largest tobacco-growing country, and the chief states in the industry are Virginia, Kentucky, North Carolina, Ohio, Connecticut, Pennsylvania, Wisconsin and Tennessee. Tobacco was first cultivated in Europe in Holland, early in the seventeenth century, and it soon extended to other countries, including Austria, Germany, Russia, the Balkan Peninsula, Asiatic Turkey, France, British India, Cuba, Brazil, the Philippine Islands, Japan and Australia.

CULTIVATION. Early in January the beds are covered with fertilizers, and then the seed, which is like a quantity of ground black pepper, is carefully and evenly sown over the ground and whipped in with a brush. A little while after the seed is sown, the bed is covered over with a flimsy cotton fabric, of lighter weight than cheese cloth, to guard against and equalize the frequent changes of weather at this season of the year, and as a protection against the flea bug, which would entirely destroy the young plants as soon as they show above ground. Forty days' time is required for the tobacco to sprout. The plants are large enough for transplanting early in May. The ground is thoroughly pulverized and is laid off into furrows four feet apart, into which the fertilizer is drilled. Then every three feet in the row a hill, or *pot*, is made. The plants are distributed into the pots, and the dirt is settled tightly around the young plant. One good workman will set two acres a day. When the plant is about six weeks old, it is topped to ten or twelve leaves, and almost immediately false leaves, or *suckers*, start at every joint, beginning at the bottom. As many as three successive sets of suckers will start at the base of every leaf, and as these detract from the proper growth of the leaf, it is necessary to go over the crop each week until cutting time and pull off every new sucker. In about three months after planting, the tobacco is ready to cut. When ripe, the green is dappled over with slightly yellow spots. A strong knife, similar to a butcher knife, is used for cutting. As the plants are cut, half a dozen of them are hung over a stick and laid on the ground. These sticks are taken up into a wagon and hauled to the barn. Inside the barn are two furnaces, which are arranged to be fired from the outside of the building. The flues to these furnaces are nearly horizontal and extend back and forth across the inside, to economize the heat better. Sets of horizontal poles, one above another, run across the interior, from which the sticks of green tobacco are suspended. When the barn is full, the doors are closed and the fires are started and are kept burning for four days. Beginning with a very low temperature, the heat is increased to about 100° by the end of the first twenty-four hours. Too sudden heat blackens the stems and otherwise affects the color. Beginning with the second day the temperature is increased about a degree an hour until 125° is reached, and it is held at this temperature from eight to twelve hours, after which the thermometer is started upward again, until 180° is reached, and the heat is held at that until it is noted by frequent examination that the stem of the tobacco is thoroughly killed. Then the fires are drawn, and a quantity of water is thrown in upon the ground, the vapor from which puts the brittle leaves in condition to be handled without injury. The tobacco is then taken out and stored. The lighter and evener the color, the higher price it brings in the market. Some of the best varieties raised in Connecticut and Florida are grown under raised covers of cheesecloth, supported on frames about nine feet high.

In the manufacture of tobacco, the leaves are first thoroughly cleansed with salt and water. The midrib of the leaf is then removed; the leaves are again sorted, and the large ones set apart for making cigars. The leaves are either cut finely, for use in pipes, as is the case with *shag* tobacco, or they are moistened and pressed into cakes, which are designated *cavendish*; or they are pressed into sticks, as *negrohead*; or the leaves are spun in the form of a rope of greater or less thickness; the smallest twist is called *pigtail*. The midribs, separated in the first process of manufacture, are preserved to be converted into snuff. Cigars and cheroots are favorite forms of manufactured tobacco. As the best leaf is grown in Cuba, so also are the best cigars made there. The leaf used for the manufacture of Manila cheroots is grown chiefly on the island of Luzon.

Tobacco Worm, a caterpillar which destroys the leaves of tobacco plants in the United States. It is the larva of a hawk moth, which lays its eggs singly on the tobacco leaves. Several broods are raised in a season, and the later ones often go to tomato plants, where they are known as *tomato worms*. The pupa spends the winter in the ground.

Toba′go, an island of the British West Indies, one of the Windward group, situated 22 mi. n. e. of Trinidad. It has an area of 114 square miles. Part of the surface is mountainous, the highest

altitudes reaching from 1800 to 2000 feet. The soil is productive, and sugar cane, coffee, cacao, tobacco and cotton are raised and exported to a considerable extent, as are cocoanuts and other tropical fruits. Tobago has been a British possession since 1763 and is under the government of Trinidad. Population in 1911, 19,500.

Tobog′ganing, coasting on a toboggan, that is, a sled without runners. Originally the indians of Lower Canada used these toboggans to carry loads over soft snow. Slabs of birch about a quarter of an inch thick are fastened together side by side to make a single board, four to eight feet in length. This is curved upward at the forward end, and hand rails are placed along the side, for the coasters to cling to. The toboggan is steered with the foot or with short sticks held in the hand. In hilly countries, natural slides may be used, but artificial ones are constructed in level countries. The latter are great frameworks of timber, 40 or 50 feet high, from which a slideway, of one or more chutes, packed with ice or snow, runs down to a long level snow- or ice-packed track. The speed attained on these is very high, and the sport an exciting one. In many cities of the northern states, public toboggan slides are erected in the parks; but these are now used more by children and youths with sleds and bobs, than by tobogganists. See Coasting.

Tobol, *to bole′*, a river of Siberia, which rises in the southern part of the Ural Mountains, flows northeasterly for about 750 miles and joins the Irtish near Tobolsk. It is navigable for about three-quarters of its course.

Tobolsk′, a city of Asiatic Russia, capital of the province of the same name, situated in the western part of Siberia, at the junction of the Irtish and Tobol rivers. The important structures in the city are a gymnasium, a seminary, a museum, a prison and a monument to Yurmak, the leader in the Russian occupation of Siberia. The industries include fishing, fur dressing and boat building. Previous to the construction of the Trans-Siberian railway, Tobolsk was an important trade center, but the passage of this line 200 miles south has caused most of its trade to be withdrawn. The city dates from 1587. Its population in 1910 was 20,292.

Tocantins, *to kan teens′*, a river of Brazil, which rises in the south central part of the country, flows northward and enters the southern mouth of the Amazon, generally known at this point as the Rio Para, a few miles above Para. Its chief tributary is the Araguaya, which is nearly as large as the main stream. The length of the Tocantins is about 1500 miles, and it is navigable in different parts of its course, but continuous navigation is prevented by falls and rapids. The tide ascends the stream for about 300 miles from the sea, and for some distance above where it unites with the lower branch of the Amazon it is eight miles wide.

Tocqueville, *tohk veel'*, ALEXIS CHARLES HENRI CLÉREL DE (1805–1859), a French writer and statesman. He, with one colleague, was sent by the government to the United States, to report upon the penitentiary system; the results of the inquiry were published in 1832. His most celebrated work, however, was *Democracy in America*, which was translated into the principal European languages. In 1849 he accepted the portfolio of foreign affairs, but soon resigned it. After the *coup d'état* of 1851, he withdrew from public affairs. *The Ancient Régime and the Revolution*, his second great work, appeared three years before his death.

To'dy, a tropical bird, allied to the kingfishers. There are several species, of which the most elegant is the *royal*, or *king*, *tody*, a native of Brazil. Other species are found in Jamaica and Cuba. The *green tody* is a pretty bird, about the size of the wren.

To'ga (from Latin *tego*, "I cover"), the principal outer garment of the Romans, usually made of white woolen cloth. It was probably of Etruscan origin, and yet it came to be considered the distinctive badge of the Roman citizen. Scholars are divided as to its shape, some making it elliptical, with pointed ends, while others declare that the most usual form was a crescent, the back of which was an elliptical curve, with a circular segment of cloth sewed to its concave side. The toga of ordinary life was white in color. The *toga praetexta* had a broad purple border and was worn by children and by the curule magistrates and censors. When the young Roman was declared to be legally of age, he assumed the ordinary toga, on this account called the *toga virilis*. Persons in mourning and persons under impeachment wore the *toga pulla*, a garment of a dark color; while those who were seeking office were wont to dress themselves out in garments which had been made artificially bright by the help of chalk—hence their name of *candidati*. Under the emperors the toga as an article of common wear fell into disuse; but it continued to be worn by magistrates and people on all official occasions for a hundred years after its general use declined.

To'go, HEIHAICHIRO (1847–   ), a Japanese naval commander, born in Satsuma. Most of his education was received on board the *Worcester*, a British training vessel, and at the Royal Navy College, Greenwich, England. On his return to Japan, he at once came to the front and was sent at first to Hawaii, to guard Japanese interests there. Togo was prominent in the

ADMIRAL TOGO

China-Japanese War and fought with distinction, being promoted first to rear admiral and then to vice admiral. He was also placed in command of the naval dockyards at Maizurn and did much toward the development of the Japanese navy. At the outbreak of the Russo-Japanese War, Togo was given command of the main fleet and covered himself with laurels, gaining brilliant victories over the Russians in the harbor of Port Arthur and in the Battle of the Sea of Japan. See RUSSO-JAPANESE WAR.

Togoland, *to'go lahnt*, a German colony in western Africa, bordering on the north shore of the Gulf of Guinea and bounded on the e. by the kingdom of Dahomey and on the w. by Gold Coast Colony. Its area is estimated at 33,000 sq. mi. The surface is hilly, and a number of streams flow through the colony. A portion of the territory is covered with forests, which contain rubber trees, dye-woods, oil palms and other trees affording valuable forest products. Yams, corn, bananas, ginger, tobacco, cacao and kola are cultivated by the natives. The capital and chief town is Lome. Population, estimated at 900,000, less than 200 of whom are whites.

Tokyo or **Tokio**, *to'ke o*, formerly Yedo, the capital of the Japanese Empire, situated in the east central part of the island of Hondo, on the Bay of Tokyo and on both banks of the Sumida

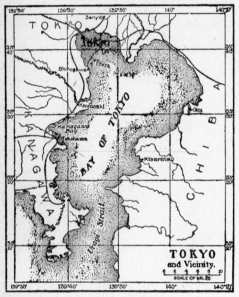

TOKYO AND VICINITY

River. It is divided into sections: the first, or Siro, occupies the center of the city and is the site of the imperial castle; the second, or Soto-Siro, is the district immediately surrounding the castle and occupies quite a proportion of the city; the third, or Midzi, includes the outer portions of the city and is taken up by residences, factories and educational and other institutions. The city, however, extends far beyond the limits of these three divisions, and its outskirts contain long streets, lined with buildings. In the central part of the city, or older town, the streets are narrow and more or less irregular, though in some sections this defect has been partially remedied; but in the newer part of the town the streets resemble more closely those of European and American cities. The commercial portion of the city is east of the castle. Here are found stores, warehouses, banks, office buildings, hotels and other buildings similar to those found in western cities. The arsenal is situated in the northern part of the city and adjoins a garden noted for its rare beauty, and north of this is the

imperial university, which is at the head of the Japanese system of education. Another structure of interest is the imperial museum, which contains many objects illustrating oriental art and history. The shrines which in the past were erected to former rulers are also among the most impressive and beautiful structures found within the city. These are usually adjoining one of the parks.

Tokyo has become in many respects a modern city. It has a well-organized fire department, electric cars, a good police system, daily papers and such commercial arrangements as are found in the cities of Europe and America. Unfortunately the harbor is not deep enough to admit the largest ocean vessels, and this curtails its commerce to a considerable extent, but the manufactures are of importance and are increasing from year to year. The city is connected with Yokohama and other important towns of Hondo by railway.

The old name Yedo was given to a small village which was built at the head of the bay early in the fifteenth century. This became the site of a castle, and at the close of the sixteenth century the town was occupied by Ieyasu, who decided to make it the capital of the Empire. From that time its growth in size and influence was rapid, and it soon became the most important city in Japan. The city has suffered from frequent fires, occasionally from earthquakes and from storms; nevertheless it has continued to increase in population and wealth. Population in 1908, 2,186,079.

Tokyo, University of, an institution of higher learning in Japan, founded in 1868. It has schools of law, medicine, engineering, mathematics, philosophy, history and science, and its faculty is made up largely of Japanese who have been educated in Europe and America. It is a government institution.

Tole'do, Ohio, the county-seat of Lucas co., and the third city of the state, situated at the mouth of the Maumee River, 130 mi. n. of Columbus and 244 mi. e. of Chicago, on the Lake Shore & Michigan Southern, the Cincinnati, Chicago & Saint Louis, the Wabash, the Michigan Central, the Ohio Central, the Pere Marquette, the Grand Trunk and a number of other railways, in all, nineteen lines either entering or passing through the city. The city is built on low land which slopes gradually from the river. It is well laid out, with broad, straight streets, and in the residential sections the streets are lined with shade trees. The park system includes

seven large, and twenty-three small, parks, all
having an area of 848 acres. The largest parks
are Walbridge, on the west side, which has an
excellent zoölogical garden; Ottawa Park, on
the western side; Central Grove Park; Bay View
Park, at the point where the river joins the bay,
and Riverside Park, which is farther up stream.
On the east side are Collins Park and Navarre
Park. Nearly all of these are joined by a system
of boulevards. Among the important buildings
are the courthouse, located in an ample square,
which contains a statue of President McKinley;
the Soldiers' Memorial Building; the Masonic
Temple; the public library, with a collection of
over 50,000 volumes; the Valentine Theater; a
number of fine business blocks, and Saint Paul's
and Saint Patrick's churches. Among the educational institutions are the Toledo Medical
College, Saint John's College and a number of
denominational and private schools; also two
large business colleges. The public school system includes high schools, a manual training
school and a state normal school. An organization known as the Museum of Art maintains a
gallery of paintings.

Toledo is an important industrial center. It
is one of the chief meeting points of the coal
from Ohio and Pennsylvania and the iron ore
mined in Michigan and Minnesota. Its leading
industrial plants include blast furnaces, large plate
glass works, the largest wagon factory in the world,
automobile works, malleable iron works, flour
mills, scale factories and establishments for the
manufacture of cut glass, brushes, staves and the
preparation of spices. The city has an extensive trade, especially in coal, in the shipment
of which it takes high rank among Great Lake
ports. Its harbor contains twenty-five miles of
docks and can be entered by the largest lake
steamers.

The city is built upon ground formerly occupied by the Miami indians. It was first settled
in 1832 and was chartered as a city five years
later. With the settlement of the states in the
Mississippi valley, the town began a steady and
prosperous growth. Population in 1910, 168,-
497.

Toll, *tole,* a tax paid, or duty imposed, for
some liberty or privilege; such as the payment
claimed by the owners of a port, for goods
landed or shipped there; the sum charged by
the owners of a market, or fair, for goods brought
to be sold there; a charge made by those intrusted with the maintenance of roads or bridges,
for the passage of persons, goods and cattle.

Tol'stoy, LYOFF (LEO) NIKOLAYEVITCH,
Count (1828–1910), a celebrated Russian author,
born of a noble and wealthy family at Yasnoya
Polyana. He graduated in 1848 from the University of Kazan, after a course in Oriental languages and law; he lived on his estate for several
years, and in 1851 he accompanied his brother to
the Caucasus. He entered the Russian army,
and during the Crimean War he was with the
Army of the Danube and took part in the siege
of Sebastopol. His account, after the close of the
war, of his experiences while at Sebastopol,
marked him at once as a writer of great power.

LYOFF TOLSTOY

After some years of residence at Saint Petersburg
and at Moscow and after several trips abroad,
he withdrew to his estates, and here, after his
marriage in 1862, he lived in great seclusion.
By his great novels, *War and Peace* (1865–1869)
and *Anna Karenina* (1875–1876), he won for
himself a very high place among writers of fiction. Meanwhile, he had devoted much time
and thought to the education and social improvement of the peasantry. During the years following the publication of *Anna Karenina*, Tolstoy's writings consisted chiefly of treatises on
social and religious questions, and it was not
until 1899 that another important work of fiction,
Resurrection, appeared. This novel aroused wide
and lasting discussion.

Tolstoy's work among the peasants brought
him in time to the conclusion that a man loses
nothing of importance and gains much by engaging in the ordinary labors of the peasants; and

for years he lived the simplest sort of life, working hard and dispensing with all comforts not absolutely necessary. To his religion, too, was applied this process of simplifying, and the result is a religion which accepts nothing except the teachings of Christ himself and which demands, as the highest good, the unhampered working out of each man's individuality.

Tol'tec, a people who lived in Mexico at an early date, and of whom very little exact information has been obtained. It is known, however, that they occupied the entire central plateau of Mexico and acquired considerable advancement in civilization, but were driven out by the conquering Aztecs from the north. See AZTEC.

Toluca, *to loo'ka,* a city of Mexico, situated 36 mi. s. w. of the City of Mexico, on a plateau 8500 feet above the sea. The industrial establishments include cotton factories, flour mills and breweries. It is the site of a weather station and is near the extinct volcano Nevado da Toluca. Population in 1910, 31,247.

Tom'ahawk, a light war hatchet of the North American indians. The early ones were made of stone or deer-horn, put through a handle of wood, or fastened to the handle by sinews, or cords of skin; European traders supplied hatchets of steel. The blunt side of the head was sometimes made hollow, to serve as a tobacco-pipe, a handle of ash, with the pith removed, being the stem. Tomahawks either were used in close combat or were thrown so that the edge would strike the object aimed at. The usage of the indians supplies the phrases *to bury the hatchet* and *to dig up the hatchet,* as equivalents for *to make peace* and *to declare war.*

Toma'to, a plant closely related to tne potato. It is a native of South America, has been introduced into most warm or temperate countries and is cultivated for the sake of its fruit, which is fleshy, usually scarlet or orange in color and irregular in shape. Tomatoes are eaten raw, are used as ingredients in salads or are stewed and cooked in various other ways. For a long time after it was brought from Peru, the tomato was known as the iove apple, and was considered poisonous; in fact, it was not until the early part of the nineteenth century that the tomato was known as an article of food. The yearly crop in the United States is very large, and great quantities are put up in tin cans and sold everywhere in the markets. Maryland, New Jersey, Indiana and California are the leading states in the production of this crop.

Tomb, *toom,* a permanent burial place, usually in the form of an ornamental monument. Tombs are often arranged to cover the burial places of an entire family. The old Roman *columbaria* were underground burial chambers for a large number of persons. The great Egyptian pyramids and the mastabas were tombs, hollowed out in rocks and adorned with beautiful decorations (See PYRAMIDS; MASTABA). Grecian tombs were plain and tasteful. A simple flat stone was set at the grave, often carved with inscriptions and decorated with sculptures. Large monuments to the dead were not found in Greece, but were common in Asia, where Greek influence was felt (See MAUSOLEUM). The tombs of the Romans were more ornamental and were massive (See HADRIAN'S TOMB). In the Middle Ages altar-like tombs, or sarcophagi, often elegantly designed and carved, were common. They were set on the church floor and generally had a life-size figure of the dead, reclining at full length on the top of the monument. The churches in Italy contained the finest examples of this style of tombs, some of which were the most splendid structures in the world. In the modern sense, tomb is generally used to denote a large structure with a spacious interior, in which are receptacles for coffins. Tombs are generally excavated in a hillside, with a door of masonry in front, or built above ground like a small chapel. Family vaults of some pretension are also called tombs. Memorial structures erected in cemeteries over or near a grave, in the form of obelisks, columns and the like, are called monuments.

Tombig'bee, a river of the United States, which rises in the northeastern part of Mississippi, flows south, then southeasterly into Alabama and continues in this direction until it unites with the Alabama to form the Mobile River. The length is 450 miles, and it is navigable for steamboats to Columbus, Miss. The chief tributary is the Black Warrior.

Tomp'kins, DANIEL D. (1774–1825), an American statesman, vice-president of the United States, born at Scarsdale, N. Y. He was educated at Columbia College, studied law and was admitted to the bar in 1797, but turned his attention to politics. He became successively a member of the legislature, a member of Congress, judge of the state supreme court and governor of the state, in which office he served for ten years. He was bitterly opposed to the chartering of the Bank of America in New York, in a long contest in which corruption played an important part against him, and he took the unparalleled step of proroguing the legislature to prevent it, but without success. He persistently advocated the abolition of slavery, which was accomplished in New York, largely through his efforts, in 1827. From 1817 to 1825 he was vice-president of the United States.

Tom′tit. See TITMOUSE.

Tom′-tom, a primitive cylindrical drum, used in the East Indies. It is beaten upon with the fingers or with the open hand, and it is used to beat time to dances or to attract notice.

Ton, *tun,* a measure of weight in the English system, equivalent to 20 hundredweights. A standard hundredweight in both England and America is equal to 112 pounds. Hence the standard ton in commercial transactions is equal to 2240 pounds. In many parts of America the so-called *short* ton, of 2000 pounds, is commonly used, the hundredweight being reckoned at 100 pounds. However, Congress has decided that unless otherwise specified a ton weight is to be 2240 pounds avoirdupois.

Tonawanda, *ton a won′da,* N. Y., a village in Erie co., 10 mi. n. of Buffalo, on the Niagara River, on the Tonawanda Creek, opposite North Tonawanda, on the Erie Canal and on the New York Central and several other steam railroad lines. There are also electric railways to Buffalo and Niagara Falls. It is an important lumber market and has manufactures of steel, lumber and paper. The municipality owns and operates the waterworks and has a free library, a high school and a public park. Population in 1910 8290.

Tone, in music, the sound produced by the vibration of a string or other sonorous body (See SOUND; MUSIC). Nearly every musical sound is composite, that is, consists of several simultaneous tones, with different rates of vibration, according to fixed laws, which depend on the nature of the vibrating body and the mode of producing its vibrations. These several tones are called *partial tones;* that one having the lowest rate of vibration and the loudest sound is termed the *prime, principal,* or *fundamental, tone;* the other partial tones are called *harmonics,* or *overtones.* See HARMONICS.

Ton′ga Islands or **Friendly Islands,** a cluster of islands in the South Pacific Ocean. They consist of three groups, which are divided from one another by two narrow channels and which number, altogether, about 150 islands. The largest island is Tongatabu, in the south group, with an area of 120 square miles, and containing the capital, Nukualofa. Vavao, in the north group, which is named after it, is next to Tongatabu in size; the center group is called Hapai. The trade is considerable, the chief exports being copra, coffee and wool. These islands have been under British protection since 1899, though they are ruled by a native king. Population in 1911, 23,737, of whom 380 were Europeans.

Tongking′ or **Tonquin,** *ton keen′,* a French colony, situated in the northeastern part of Indo-China. It is bounded on the n. by China, on the e. by China and the Gulf of Tongking and on the s. w. by Anam. Its area is between 40,000 and 50,000 sq. mi. The surface along the coast is low, and during the rainy season it is often flooded; but the interior is rather mountainous and contains a number of peaks from 5000 to 6000 feet in altitude. The climate is tropical, and the rainfall is heavy. The soil is very fertile, and where not cultivated it is covered with dense forests. Rice is the most important crop and is followed by sugar cane, tobacco, coffee, papaws, hemp, ramie and cotton. The mulberry tree and the betel palm are also cultivated. There are some minerals, including iron, copper, quicksilver and coal, the last of which is mined to some extent. Europeans have established factories at Ha-noi and Hai-phung, where cotton goods and silks are manufactured. There are also match factories, distilleries, foundries and breweries in the country. Tongking has been a French possession since 1885. The capital is Ha-noi. Population in 1911, 6,119,720.

Tongue, *tung,* the muscular organ of the mouth; also, the principal organ of taste. The tongue is attached at its back extremity to the *hyoid* bone (See SKELETON, subhead *Hyoid Bone*), and its opposite end is free to move in all directions. The interior is composed entirely of muscles, whose fibers extend in nearly all directions and are so arranged as to be mutually helpful. By them the tongue can be flattened, made to assume nearly a cylindrical form, protruded from the mouth or directed to any part of the mouth in which food may lodge. Another set of muscles, the *extrinsic,* join the tongue to opposite supports and cause it to move. The exterior is covered with a mucous membrane, or epithelium, in which are the papillae containing the end organs of the nerve of taste. The back part of the tongue contains a number of glands which secrete mucus, to keep it moist. Besides being the principal organ of taste and articulate speech, the tongue performs an important office in mastication and in swallowing. See TASTE.

Ton'ic, in medicine, any remedy which improves the tone or vigor of the fibers of the stomach and bowels or of the muscular fibers generally. Tonics may be said to be of two kinds, medical and non-medical. *Medical tonics* act chiefly in two ways: (1) indirectly, by first influencing the stomach and increasing its digestive powers, this being the effect of such vegetable bitters as chamomile, cinchona bark, gentian and taraxacum; (2) directly, by passing into and exerting their influence through the blood, as is the case with various preparations of iron, certain mineral acids and salts. The *non-medical tonics* are open air, exercise, friction, cold, in such forms as the shower bath and cold sponge bath, and sea bathing.

Tonnage, *tun'naje,* the number of tons weight which a ship can carry with safety. This is known as *dead weight tonnage.* *Ordinary*, or *gross, tonnage* is not strictly the measure of the weight a ship can carry, but is a gauge of the vessel's dimensions, more or less accurate. The whole interior capacity of the hull of a ship and her deck houses is divided by 100, on the supposition that 100 cubic feet space will hold a ton. In freighting ships, 40 cubic feet of merchandise is considered a ton, though when the weight exceeds 2000 pounds, or 2240 pounds, as the custom may be, the fees are assessed by weight.

Ton'sils, THE, two oblong, soft bodies, situated on the sides of the throat, and made up of minute glands, which give out a secretion that helps the food to pass them. During a cold or a sore throat, they are often enlarged, and when permanently enlarged they may be removed without danger.

Tonsillitis, inflammation of the tonsils. Tonsillitis is rare in infancy or in old age, persons between the ages of ten and forty being most susceptible to it. The inflammation, though seldom fatal, is very painful. The tonsils sometimes become ulcerated, and large accumulations of pus are common. When this last condition occurs the disease is known as quinsy. The causes of the various forms of tonsillitis are not definitely known. The commonest causes are severe colds, which cause a slight inflammation of the tonsils and render them susceptible to other germs. Enlarged or inflamed tonsils should never be exposed to the contagious diseases. An attack of tonsillitis ordinarily lasts five or six days. The first symptom may be a slight chill; then comes a swelling and pain in the throat, with difficulty in swallowing and in breathing. Rest in bed,

hot compresses on the neck, purgatives and an abundance of soft or liquid food are important points in the treatment. The most trustworthy medicines are iron and quinine. See QUINSY.

Tontine, *ton teen'.* See INSURANCE.

Tonty or **Tonti,** *tohN tee',* HENRY DE (about 1650–about 1704), a French explorer and companion of La Salle. He was born in Italy, but early entered the army of France and in July, 1678, accompanied La Salle to Quebec. He assisted him in preparation for several of his great exploring expeditions and was left by La Salle in March, 1680, in charge of Fort Crevecoeur on the Illinois River, but was forced to abandon the position because of mutiny and the hostility of indians, and returned to Green Bay. Later he joined La Salle at Michilimackinac, accompanied him in his great voyage down the Mississippi and was placed in command of Fort Saint Louis, at Starved Rock, near the present village of Utica, Ill. He continued to live among the Illinois indians until 1702.

Toombs, *toomz,* ROBERT (1810–1885), an American statesman, born at Washington, Ga.

ROBERT TOOMBS

He graduated at Union College in 1828, studied law at the University of Virginia and commenced practice in 1830. At the head of a company of volunteers, he served throughout the Creek War. In 1827 he was elected to the state legislature and, except during 1841, served there until 1845. He was then a member of the House of Representatives for four terms, and in 1853 he was elected to the Senate. He opposed the Mexican War and the consequent acquisition of territory by conquest; but in 1861, it was largely through his influence that Georgia passed her ordinance of secession, and he then withdrew from the Senate. He was a delegate to the Confederate congress at Montgomery and subsequently was secretary of state in the Confederacy. He resigned this office soon after, to take a commission as brigadier general in the army, where he distinguished himself at Antietam and in the second Battle of Bull Run. After the close of the war he traveled in Cuba, France and England until 1867, when he returned to the United States and resumed the practice of law in his native town, also taking a conspicuous part in opposition to the Congressional reconstruction. He was an eloquent speaker, a successful lawyer, a brave soldier and an able statesman.

Toothache, tooth'ake, **Tree.** See PRICKLY ASH.

Top, a child's toy, made of a pear-shaped piece of wood, with a metal point, or peg, at the small end, upon which the top is set to spinning by means of a string, wound gradually round the point and well up the side, or by the frequent application of a whip with several strands. Tops were once more popular among young people in the United States than they are at the present time, though still, during every springtime and every fall, in the seasons when the more strenuous outdoor games are not in vogue, they are very common, especially in cities. The *peg top* and the *whip top* are the most common kinds, but many fancy shapes are shown in toy shops; some of these travel on a string and can be made to go through intricate figures; others spin an hour with one winding; some whistle as they spin, and others exhibit changing colors. The inventive boy can make tops that will spin almost, if not quite, as well as those from the store. A peg top can be made of any heavy wood that is not easily split, the point being furnished by a sharp, iron spike, driven through the center of the pear-shaped piece. Often one boy sets his top spinning on a board or walk, and another throws his top at the spinning one, with the intention of striking and splitting it. Sometimes races and endurance tests are held by the possessors of especially fine tops.

To'paz, a mineral, ranked among the gems. It varies from transparent to translucent, has a clear luster and may be yellow, white, green or blue in color. It is harder than quartz and is nearly four times as heavy as water. Chemically, it is a silicate of aluminium, in which the oxygen is partly replaced by fluorine. It occurs in masses and is crystallized in prisms. Crystalline topazes are found generally in igneous and metamorphic rocks and in many parts of the world. Various localities in Maine, Colorado and Utah supply them, and they are common in Ceylon, in parts of India and in Brazil. The Brazilian topazes have deep yellow tints; the Siberian are bluish, and the Saxon topazes are of a pale wine yellow, while those found in the Scotch Highlands are of a sky-blue color. Most of these varieties are not the true oriental topaz, but are varieties of yellow quartz. In ancient times the topaz was a symbol of friendship and was thought to drive away sadness and bestow courage.

Topeka, KAN., the capital of the state and the county-seat of Shawnee co., is 66 mi. w. of Kansas City, on the Kansas River and on the Atchison, Topeka & Santa Fé, the Chicago, Rock Island & Pacific, the Missouri Pacific and the Union Pacific railroads. The city is situated on rolling prairie land, at an elevation of about 900 feet. It is on both sides of the river and covers an area of seven square miles. It is laid out with broad, well-shaded streets and contains several attractive parks and a fair grounds. There are many handsome residences, and it is a clean, well-drained and healthful place. It has electric lights, over thirty-five miles of street railroads and other modern improvements. The most notable buildings near the center of the city are the state capitol and the Federal building, which was constructed in 1882, at a cost of $300,000. Other important structures are the courthouse the city hall, the Y. M. C. A., the Y. W. C. A., the Mills building. The Grand Army Memorial Building, completed in 1914 is constructed entirely of marble and cost over $500,000. The state hospital for the insane occupies five large buildings on extensive grounds west of the city. and the state industrial school for boys has accommodations for two hundred boys on a farm of 210 acres north of the city. Topeka is the seat of Washburn College (Congregational), of the College of the Sisters of Bethany (Episcopal) and of the Kansas Medical College. The libraries of the city are the free public library. in a beautiful building on the state grounds, a large state library and that of the state historical society, the latter two in the state capitol.

The industrial establishments number about 400 and include the railroad shops of the Atchison, Topeka & Santa Fé Railroad, extensive exporting flour mills, foundries, brickyards, machine shops, packing houses, creameries, starch works and manufactories of furniture, clothing and other articles. Three fine hospitals, besides that of the Santa Fé railway, are located here. The place was settled by eastern anti-slavery men in 1854. It was chartered as a city in 1857 and was selected as the state capital in 1861. Population in 1910, 43,684.

Torna'do, a revolving storm that has great force The term was originally applied to the hurricanes prevalent in the West Indies and on the west coast of Africa and in the Indian Ocean, but it has more recently been extended to apply to other storms. In the United States the tornado is frequently, though incorrectly, termed a cyclone. Tornadoes usually form within thunder storms and are caused by conditions similar to those which produce whirlwinds (See WHIRLWIND). They occur on warm days, when the humidity of the air is great. The tornado cloud has a funnel-shaped vortex, in which the velocity of the whirling motion increases as it approaches the center, where it becomes so great as to destroy all objects within the path of the tornado. The direction of the whirl is contrary to that of the hands of a watch, and the tornado moves from southwest to northeast, with a velocity varying from 25 to 40 miles an hour. The danger lies in the path of the funnel-shaped cloud. which is usually but a few rods in diameter. Near the vortex the velocity of the wind is such as to overthrow and often destroy small structures and to draw light objects within the vortex.

Many theories have been advanced to account for these destructive storms, but none seems perfectly satisfactory. The conditions favorable to the development of a tornado are a warm layer of excessively humid air next to the earth, and a layer of cool air above. When an upward current is once started in the warm air, a rotary motion is immediately produced by the inrush of cold air from above. This rapid rotation causes a small area of very low pressure, and the force of the upward current soon increases to a degree that enables it to bear aloft all objects with which it comes in contact. In the center of the vortex the pressure is so light that buildings within the path of the tornado are often wrecked by the expansion of the air within. The condensation begins in the upper air, where the temperature is lowest, and as the whirling column continues to cool by expansion of the rising air, the point at which the condensation takes place gradually approaches the earth, and the cloud continues to form lower and lower, until it comes in contact with the ground The extension of the column downward is not due to the lowering of the cloud, as frequently supposed, but to the descent towards the ground of the point of condensation. While no portion of the United States east of the Great Plains seems free from these storms, they are most frequent in the Mississippi Basin, occurring in the south in the early spring and gradually traveling northward, until in midsummer they occur as far north as Minnesota and North Dakota. See CYCLONE; HURRICANE; TYPHOON. Consult Davis's *Elements of Meteorology.*

Toron'to, the capital of Ontario, the second city of Canada in importance, situated on the n. w. shore of Lake Ontario, 333 mi. s. w. of Montreal and 512 mi. e. of Chicago, on the Grand Trunk and the Canadian Pacific railways. The city has a beautiful location, on ground rising gradually from the lake, until it reaches an altitude of about 200 feet in the highest part. Its extent along the lake front is about 8 miles. The harbor is commodious and is protected by a low island, that extends for about 3 miles from north to south. The city extends back from the lake for about 3 miles and is unusually well planned, nearly all the streets crossing one another at right angles. The streets are broad, most of them well paved and in the residential sections beautified by large shade trees and lawns. The parks include Queen's, or University, Park, in the western part of the city, and several others of less importance. An excellent street car system connects all parts of the city and adjoining suburbs. The most important public buildings are the Parliament buildings, situated in Queen's Park. In Queen s Park there are several fine monuments, the most notable being those erected to Queen Victoria, Sir John A. MacDonald, Sir Oliver Mowat, George Brown, and the monuments to the memory of the Canadians who fell during the Fenian invasion and in the Reil Rebellion. The South African Monument is on University Avenue. Other public buildings include the government house; Osgoode Hall, which is the courthouse of Ontario; the public library, and the provincial insane asylum, also a number of excellent business blocks of modern style. The city is celebrated for its large number of excellent churches. Among these are Saint James Cathedral, with a spire 316 feet high, the Metropolitan Methodist Church, the Cathedral of Saint Michael, Saint Andrew's, the Jarvis Street Baptist and the Bond Street Congregational churches. Among the educational institutions are the University of Toronto, in Queen's Park, Victoria University, Trinity College, Baptist College, Knox College, Saint Machael's College and the provincial normal school.

The industries include the manufacture of agricultural implements, furniture, stoves, bicycles, machinery, boots and shoes, carpets and malt and spirituous liquors. The city also contains extensive car shops and shipyards. The trade is large, and the exports include grains, flour, lumber and manufactured articles. Toronto is a receiving and distributing point for a large agricultural region of unusual fertility. It was founded in 1794, under the name of York, but was captured by the Americans in 1813 and destroyed. In 1834 it was incorporated under the present name. It suffered from the Canadian rebellion in 1837 and from a fire in 1849. Since that time it has been remarkably prosperous. It is without doubt the best-built city in the Dominion. Population in 1911, 376,538.

Toronto, UNIVERSITY OF, an institution at the head of the school system of Ontario, chartered in 1807, under the name of The University of King's College. The further organization, however, was delayed, and the university was not opened until 1843. Six years later, the name was changed to the University of Toronto. The institution has undergone several reorganizations. It now includes faculties of arts, law, medicine and applied science and engineering, and it has instituted courses and examinations for degrees in agriculture, dentistry, music, pedagogy, pharmacy and household science. There are also a number of colleges and schools throughout the province, affiliated with the university, and extension work is maintained by a special committee. Women are admitted. The management of the university is similar to that of the English universities.

Torpe'do, a name for two distinct classes of submarine destructive agents, namely, torpedoes proper, which are movable and which are propelled against an enemy's ship, and submarine mines, which lie stationary in the water. Torpedoes were used at various times during the eighteenth century and with some slight success in the Revolutionary War, but during the Civil War they came into extensive use, and

twenty-three Federal vessels were destroyed by this means. Most of the torpedoes of this epoch either were submarine mines or consisted of a quantity of powder, with an explosive cap fastened to the end of a long spar, which projected under water ahead of the torpedo launch, and exploded when it came in contact with any object. After the war, torpedoes capable of propelling themselves were invented. In some varieties, a gas, generated by chemicals, drove them forward, while others were operated by an electric current along wires which uncoiled as the torpedo advanced. These were followed by contrivances which were fired from torpedo boats and then ceased to be under the operator's control. Such are known as the automobile torpedoes, and of these the Whitehead is the best known. This may be described as being a cigar-shaped vessel, varying from 14 to 19 feet in length and from 14 to 16 inches in diameter. It is made of specially prepared steel and is divided into three compartments; the head contains the gun cotton, which forms its charge, and the fuse for exploding it when it comes in contact with a vessel. The central part contains the engines by which it is propelled and which are worked by compressed air, a sufficient supply of which is stored in the third, or tail, compartment. The propeller is a three-bladed screw, which can move the largest-sized torpedoes at a speed of 24 knots for 220 yards, the distance of 1000 yards being reached at a slower rate of progress. By means of a horizontal balance rudder, the torpedo can be made to sink and to remain during its run at any required distance below the surface of the water, so that it may be discharged from the deck of a ship or from a tube opening into the sea below the water line. At close quarters this is a very destructive weapon against ironclad vessels, striking them beneath their armor, as was demonstrated in the Russo-Japanese War. Although a watchful fleet, protected by search lights and with fast torpedo boat destroyers, can usually protect itself against the torpedo boats, yet the latter serve to keep the fleet constantly in suspense.

The Harvey torpedo is constructed to be pulled through the water, something in the fashion of a ship's log. It has been, however, superseded by the Brennan and other forms of maneuvered torpedo. The Howell torpedo is propelled by a heavy fly wheel, which is spun with great rapidity before the torpedo is fired, and which holds its speed for a long time. Stationary torpedoes, or submarine mines, such as are placed in channels or coasts to prevent the approach of the enemy's vessels, usually consist of a strong metal case, containing an effective explosive, such as gun cotton, and having a fuse or cap which will explode the charge on the slightest contact. The explosion may be effected by means of electricity, the operator firing it at will from the shore. Torpedo nets are sometimes thrown out from the sides of a ship, to protect it from torpedoes, but they are not a perfect defense and cannot be used while the ship is moving. These nets are made of heavy steel rings and are suspended from spars. See Torpedo Boat.

Torpedo, the name of a flat fish, allied to the skates and rays and famous for its power of giving electrical shocks. The fish is able to do this by means of especially developed electrical organs, located on both sides of the head. Scientists are unable to explain just how the electricity is made. The power of the discharge varies with the health and size of the fish. Six

TORPEDO

species of torpedoes are known, and they occur generally in the Mediterranean Sea and in the Indian and Pacific oceans. A large specimen may measure four feet long and may weigh from sixty to seventy pounds.

Torpedo Boat, a vessel which carries one or two torpedoes for use in naval warfare. Since the Civil War the steam launches which carried torpedoes have given way to a highly developed boat, which has a high speed and on whose deck are two torpedo tubes, which may be turned in almost any direction. The *Dahlgren*, one of the best torpedo boats in the United States navy, is 147 feet long and 6 broad, draws about 5 feet of water and has a speed of 30 knots and carries 28 men. The decks of the ship are low and can be made water-tight, so that the waves may wash entirely over without damage. The armor

is light, and the coal bunkers are so distributed as to protect the vital parts of the ship, and the quarters of the crew are crowded, in order to give plenty of space for the powerful engines. The object of the torpedo boat is to approach other ships stealthily under cover of storm, fog and night, and to throw the torpedoes against the enemy. While, owing to the brilliant search lights, the torpedo boat is apt to become a conspicuous mark for opposing gunners, and notwithstanding the dangerous character of the torpedoes themselves, accidents have not been numerous, while the work of the torpedo boats in war has been of the most appalling character. *Torpedo boat destroyers* are merely torpedo boats of large size and high speed, fitted to withstand any weather and meet torpedo boats at an advantage. The armor is heavy and the offensive armament is strong. The destroyers are often fitted with torpedo boats, and so at times they may take the place of the latter; in fact, a combination of the two is not an uncommon thing in navies. See Submarine Navigation; Navy.

Torquemada, *tor ka mah'da*, Thomas de (1420–1498), a Spanish inquisitor-general, born at Valladolid. He was appointed head of the Inquisition after having persuaded Ferdinand and Isabella to ask the pope to establish it. Torquemada was noted for his cruelty. Longfellow makes him the subject of the theologian's tale in *Tales of a Wayside Inn*. Victor Hugo also uses him as a subject.

Torres, *tor'res*, **Strait,** the strait which separates Australia from New Guinea, and is about 90 miles across. It is crowded with islands, shoals and reefs, which render its navigation difficult.

Torricelli, *tor re chel'le*, Evangelista (1608–1647), an Italian scientist and mathematician. Torricelli's name is important in the history of science as the discoverer of the law on which the barometer depends. The principle of this law is that the pressure of the atmosphere sustains a column of mercury of equal area and of the same weight as the column of atmosphere. See Barometer.

Tor'rington, Conn., a borough in Litchfield co., 26 mi. w. of Hartford, on the Naugatuck River and on the New York, New Haven & Hartford railroad. The place has over one hundred manufacturing establishments, producing bicycles, woolens, various brass articles, novelties, needles, hardware and tobacco goods. The municipality has a public library, a fine city hall, a Y. M. C. A. and many good church and school buildings. The place was settled early in the eighteenth century and was chartered as a borough in 1887. Population in 1910, 15,483.

Torsion, *tor'shun,* **Bal'ance,** an instrument employed to measure the intensities of very small forces. It consists of a fine wire or a silk thread, suspended from a fixed point, and having a horizontal needle attached, the force being measured by the resistance to twisting which the filament exhibits when the force acts on the needle. See GALVANOMETER.

Tort, a civil wrong for which the law requires compensation in damages. The right to damages for a tort arises not from breach of contract, as a tort may be committed where no contract has existed. Thus nuisance, libel and slander, trespass and injuries to property are torts. The same act may be both a tort and a crime. Thus a man may be prosecuted by the state for assault and battery and at the same time may have brought against him by the injured man an action for damages.

Tortoise, *tor'tis* or *tor'tus,* a name applied to any species of turtle, but one that should be confined to those that live entirely on land and have arched shells. There are about fifty species living in tropical regions in different parts of the world, the most notable one being a large black species of the Indian Ocean. The shell of some tortoises measures over four feet in length, the animal weighing as much as eight hundred pounds. They are sought for their flesh, which is excellent, and for an oil which they yield. See TURTLE.

Tortoise Shell, a name popularly applied to the horny plates of the shell of the tortoise, especially to those of the hawk's bill turtle, a species which inhabits tropical seas. The horny scales, or plates, which form the covering of this animal are extensively used in the manufacture of combs, snuff boxes and other small articles, and in inlaying and other ornamental work. The shell becomes very plastic when heated, and when cold it retains with sharpness any form which it may be molded to in its heated state. It is now largely imitated by horn and celluloid.

Tory, a political party name, of Irish origin, first used in England about 1679, applied originally to Irish Roman Catholic outlaws, and then generally to those who refused to concur in the scheme to exclude James II from the throne. The nickname, like its contemporaneous opposite, *Whig,* in coming into popular use became much less strict in its application,

until at last it came simply to signify an adherent of that political party in the State who disapproved of change in the ancient constitution, and who supported the claims and authority of the king, Church and aristocracy. In modern times the term has to a great extent been supplanted by *Conservative.* In Revolutionary times in America it was applied to adherents of England.

To'tem, among the American indians, an animal or some other thing, considered as the symbol or designation of an individual, family or tribe. Those who have the same totem are regarded as bound by closer ties than any other

TOTEM POLES

persons. The totem pole is a pole carved rudely with the figure of the totem of any particular tribe. The worship of the totem has been found among other tribes besides the American indians.

Toucan, *too'kan,* a bird found only in tropical or semi-tropical America. It is famous because of its enormous bill, which is both broad and long and which seems entirely too large for the bird that carries it. The upper mandible is curved downward sharply at the tip and is toothed like a saw at the edges. The birds, however, handle this great beak very skilfully upon the soft fruits which constitute their food. The toucans spend their lives in trees, usually in flocks, over which one acts as watchman. Most of them have showy plumage, and some are brilliantly colored. One species, for instance, is a shining black, excepting a big bright yellow patch which covers its throat and breast. (See illustration on next page.)

Touch, *tuch.* The sense of touch has its seat in the sensory nerves of the skin and the mucous membrane of the mouth and in their respective centers in the brain. The sense is most fully developed in the forehead, the face, the tip of the tongue, the fingers and palms of the hands and the toes and soles of the feet. In these regions the sensory nerve filaments are more numerous and also have their extremities more fully developed than in other parts of the body. The ends of these nerves are known as *tactile*

TOUCAN

corpuscles and are best illustrated by those of the fingers. The ridges on the tips of the fingers and palms of the hands are made up of rows of conical papillae (See PAPILLAE), most of which contain a highly developed end organ from the sensory nerve. These nerve filaments are stimulated by contact of the papillae with external objects, and the impulses are interpreted by the sensory centers in the brain (See NERVOUS SYSTEM, subhead *Sensory Nerves*).

Measured by the pressure required to be recognized, the sense of touch is keenest in the forehead, but measured by the power of conveying different impressions, the organs of the fingers are the most perfect. These are capable of being educated, and in the blind and deaf the sense of touch becomes highly developed. By many authorities touch is considered the fundamental sense. We know it is the first of the special senses to be developed, and there is good evidence to prove that it is a valuable aid in developing the sense of sight and the sense of taste. See REFLEX ACTION; SENSES, SPECIAL; TEMPERATURE SENSE.

Touchstone, a variety of black jasper, used for ascertaining the purity of gold and silver.

A series of needles, called *touchneedles*, of which the composition is known, are used for comparison with the article to be tested. When the color of the streak produced by both the needle and the metal tested is the same, the quantity of alloy they contain is supposed to be the same.

Toulon, *too loN'*, a seaport of France, situated on a bay on the Mediterranean, 30 mi. s. e. of Marseilles. After Brest it is the most important naval station of France, and it is defended by strong fortifications. The old town is characterized by narrow, crooked streets, but the new town is built after modern plans and has wide streets, numerous public squares and modern buildings. Some of the important buildings are the Church of Saint Marie Majurere, the townhall, a marine hospital and the arsenal, which covers 660 acres. Population in 1911, 104,582.

Toulouse, *too looz'*, a city of France, is situated on the Garonne River, 130 mi. s. e. of Bordeaux. It is an old town, with narrow streets and poorly constructed buildings, though in some sections it has been modernized and contains fine avenues. The objects of interest are the Church of Saint Sernin, the Cathedral of Saint Etienne and the townhall. The educational institutions include a university, which dates from the thirteenth century, a veterinary college and academies of sciences and arts. Toulouse is an important commercial and industrial center. Its leading industries include the manufacture of gunpowder, tobacco, paper, agricultural implements, carriages, furniture and leather. It also has a cannon foundry. Population in 1911, 149,576.

Tourgee, *toor zhay'*, ALBION WINEGAR (1838-1905), an American author and journalist. He was educated at Rochester University and served in the Union army. He was a member of the state constitutional conventions of North Carolina in 1868 and 1875, was elected judge of the North Carolina superior court in 1868 and became pension agent in 1876. From 1897 to 1903 he was United States consul at Bordeaux, and in the latter year he was sent to Halifax. Among his numerous works of fiction are *A Fool's Errand*, *Bricks Without Straw*, *Hot Plowshares* and *Black Ice*.

Tourmaline, *toor'ma lin*, a mineral occurring crystallized in three-sided or six-sided prisms, terminated by three-sided pyramids, the primary form being a rhomboid. It scratches glass easily and is three times as heavy as water. Tourmaline occurs most commonly in igneous and metamorphic rocks, especially in granite, gneiss and mica-slate. Some varieties are transparent, some translucent, some opaque. Some are colorless, and others are green, brown, red, blue or black. Red tourmaline is known as *rubellite*, blue tourmaline as *indicolite*, and black tourmaline as *schorl*. The transparent varieties include various well-known jewelry stones, as the Brazilian sapphire and the Brazilian emerald. Prisms of tourmaline are much used in polarizing apparatus (See POLARIZATION OF LIGHT), and the mineral possesses powerful electric properties.

Tournament, *toor'na ment* or *tur'na ment*, or **Tourney,** a common sport of the Middle Ages, in which parties of mounted knights encountered each other with lances and swords, in order to display their skill in arms. Tournaments reached their full perfection in France in the ninth and tenth centuries. They were introduced into England soon after the Conquest by the Normans. *Jousts* were single combats between two knights, and at a tournament there would often be a number of jousts, as well as combats between parties of knights. The place of combat was the *lists*, a large open place, surrounded by ropes or by a railing. Galleries were erected for the spectators, among whom were seated the ladies, the supreme judges of tournaments. A knight taking part in a tournament generally carried some device emblematic of a lady's favor. Tournaments gradually went out with the decline of chivalry. So-called military tournaments are now held in the United States and in England. These are assemblages of soldiers, who engage in contests of skill in the use of their arms and accouterments and in athletic sports and games. Exhibition drills are given, and enthusiasm runs high, but there are no longer those tremendous fights to the death which characterized the tournaments of the Middle Ages.

Tourniquet, *toor'ne ket*, an appliance employed in the practice of surgery, to stop bleeding temporarily. A string or cord twisted tight with a stick forms a simple tourniquet.

Tours, *toor*, a city of France, situated on the left bank of the Loire, 145 mi. s. w. of Paris. It has a noted cathedral of the Gothic style of architecture, an archbishop's palace, a museum, a theater and a statue of Balzac, who was a native of the city. The educational institutions include an art school, the College of San Luis de Gonzaga and a library of 125,000 volumes. The industries include the manufacture of iron and steel

products, silk goods, woolen goods, pottery, chemicals and stained glass. Tours is the site of the battle fought between Charles Martel and the Saracens in 732. It was occupied by the Germans in 1871. Population in 1911, 73,398.

Toussaint, *too saN'*, FRANÇOIS DOMINIQUE, called *L'Ouverture* (1743–1803), a soldier and statesman of Haiti. He was born a slave, but managed to acquire a little education, and when the slaves rose in insurrection in 1791, Toussaint served in their army and latterly rose to the position of leader. After the proclamation, in 1793, of freedom to the slaves, the French government, recognizing his military and political ability, made him general in chief of the troops in San Domingo. He defeated the English who had invaded Haiti and in 1799 was forced into a struggle with the mulattoes, whom at last he defeated. He now held supreme civil authority and was completely master of the island, which he ruled justly and firmly. A constitution was drawn up which appointed Toussaint president of Haiti for life, and under his government the commerce and agriculture of the island began to revive. Napoleon, however, feared that although Toussaint was professedly loyal to France, he was aiming at independence, and he therefore sent an expedition to subdue him. Toussaint was at length forced to surrender, was taken prisoner and sent to France. He died in prison there.

Tower, as commonly understood, a building of any shape, the height of which is greater than its horizontal dimensions. In ancient times, although towers were in use, they were chiefly for defense, and few of the towers now in existence date back of the Middle Ages. During that period many towers were erected, both as ornaments for churches and castles and as solitary buildings, and a number of graceful shapes and ornate styles were developed. In Italy the bell towers were usually separate buildings near the churches (See CAMPANILE), but in the northern countries of Europe the tower was usually made a part of the church. Towers on castles and on castle walls were of use as watch towers and places of defense. The Mohammedans make a conspicuous use of towers for religious purposes. See MINARET.

Tower, CHARLEMAGNE (1848–   ), an American writer and diplomat, born at Philadelphia. He graduated from Harvard University in 1872, traveled and studied in Europe for four years and studied law at the University of Pennsylvania, being admitted to the bar in 1878. In 1882 he was elected president of the Duluth and Iron

Range railroad, a position which he held until 1887, when he removed again to Philadelphia and devoted himself to study and writing, in which he achieved some distinction. In 1897 he was appointed minister to Austria, was transferred to Russia in 1899 and in 1902 to Germany, where he served for six years,

Tower of London, a celebrated ancient fortress in London, consisting of a collection of buildings of various ages, on a somewhat elevated position on the north bank of the Thames, outside the old city walls. It covers about thirteen acres and is surrounded by a battlemented wall, flanked with massive towers and encircled by a moat. There is also an inner wall, broken by towers and interspersed with buildings. In the center is the White Tower, the keep of the old fortress, around which are grouped the chapel, the jewel house, the barracks and other buildings. The Tower was a medieval fortress and served at once as a palace, a prison and a place of defense. The White Tower was built by William the Conqueror in 1078 and was successively strengthened by various English sovereigns. The regalia, consisting of the royal crowns and scepters, are now kept and exhibited in the jewel house. The armory contains a fine collection of armor and weapons. In the part called the Bloody Tower, the two young princes, sons of Edward IV, were murdered by order of their uncle, Richard III. The Tower is now chiefly used as an arsenal, and has a small military garrison of the yeomen of the guard.

Townshend, *town'zend,* CHARLES, Second Viscount (1674–1738), an English statesman, who succeeded to the peerage in 1687 and some years later took his seat as a Whig in the House of Lords. After acting as a commissioner for arranging the Scottish Union, he was joint plenipotentiary with Marlborough in the conference at Gertruydenburg, and as ambassador at The Hague he signed the Barrier Treaty. In 1717 he became lord lieutenant of Ireland; and he was secretary of state from 1721 to 1730, when he retired on account of differences with his brother-in-law and colleague, Sir Robert Walpole.

Townshend, CHARLES (1725–1767), an English statesman, grandson of the second viscount Townshend. He entered the House of Commons in 1747 and held in succession the positions of lord of the admiralty, secretary of war and chancellor of the exchequer. He supported Grenville's Stamp Act and introduced the Townshend Acts, regulating the importation of goods into America, which had

much to do with the outbreak of the Revolutionary War.

Toxicology, *toks'e kol'o jy,* the science that treats of the nature of poisons, their effects and antidotes, and also of the legal questions arising from poisoning. See POISON; ANTIDOTE.

Tracery, *tra'sur y,* in architecture, a term which denotes the ornamental decoration used most frequently in a window or gallery. Tracery as an art was first practiced in Gothic architecture during the first part of the thirteenth century in France. It was developed in the windows, but gradually extended to almost every part of the church buildings. Styles varied in different ages and countries and are known as geometrical, flowing and flamboyant.

Trachea, *tray'ke a,* the windpipe or principal air passage of the body. It begins with the larynx, through which it communicates with the mouth and nose, and it ends with the bronchial tubes, through which it communicates with the lungs. All vertebrates that breathe air with lungs have a trachea, which is almost the same in all. In man this tube is about three-fourths of an inch in diameter and four and one-half inches long, and it consists of an external fibrous membrane and an internal mucous membrane. Enclosed between these membranes are from sixteen to twenty cartilaginous rings, extending only around the front and sides of the trachea. Between the ends of these rings and attached to them, extending transversely, is a layer of unstriped muscle, whose function is to decrease the size of the tube, by drawing the ends of the rings nearer together. The surface of the mucous membrane is covered by a layer of ciliated epithelium (See CILIA; EPITHELIUM). The cilia move in such a direction that anything resting on them is drawn toward the mouth. In this way phlegm is removed. Many mucous glands pour their secretion upon the surface of the interior.

Tracheotomy, *tra'ke ot'o my.* See CROUP.

Trachyte, *tra'kite* or *trak'it,* a variety of igneous rock containing potash, feldspar, lime, soda and hornblende, together with an oxide of iron and manganese, besides a few other minerals in small proportion. In composition it is similar to syenite, but in appearance it resembles porphyry, on account of the large crystals of feldspar that are scattered through it. Trachyte is usually light-colored, but it may be of any shade of gray, or black. The rocks of this class are found in South Dakota, Colorado, Montana and Wyoming, but they are more generally distributed in Europe, where they occur in Italy, France and Germany.

Tracta'rianism, the designation of a movement in the Church of England toward "high church," or greater ritualism, against the tendency toward liberalism and rationalism. It originated at the University of Oxford and was promulgated in a series of papers entitled *Tracts for the Times,* published between 1833 and 1841. Newman, Pusey, Keble and the other authors of these tracts were nicknamed Tractarians. It is also known as the Oxford Movement.

Traction Engine, a self-propelling steam engine, designed to haul and operate farm machinery, and sometimes used for hauling wagons and vans over common roads. The ordinary traction engine is a high pressure engine with a horizontal boiler, the whole device mounted upon four wheels. The rear wheels are large and broad and have the tires constructed to prevent slipping. The forward wheels are connected with a steering apparatus. The engine is horizontal and is attached to the top of the boiler. It has an adjustable gear, by which it can be attached to the rear wheels when it is desired to propel the engine over the road. When the engine is used for operating machinery, this gear is detached. Traction engines are usually of twelve or fifteen horse-power, though those of twenty horse-power and larger are sometimes constructed. See LOCOMOTIVE; STEAM ENGINE.

Trade'-mark, a peculiar mark used by a manufacturer to distinguish his own productions from those of other persons. Such marks can now be registered and protected in all the more important countries and even by citizens of one country in another. A mere descriptive title or a geographical name does not constitute a proper trade-mark; it should be some invented word or words, distinctive device, figure, emblem or design, or a written signature. Any mark or name calculated to mislead as to the real name or origin of the goods is invalid. In the United States trade-marks are registered at the patent office, at a fee of $25, the right running for thirty years.

Trade Unions. See LABOR ORGANIZATIONS.

Trade Winds, those perpetual or constant winds which occur in all open seas on both sides of the equator, for a distance of about 30° north and south of it. North of the equator their direction is from the northeast, with occasional slight variations; south of the equator, they proceed from the southeast. The origin of the trade winds is as follows: The great heat of the torrid

zone rarifies and makes lighter the air of that region; in consequence of this rarefaction, the air rises into the higher regions of the atmosphere. The undercurrents coming from the north and south to supply the place of the ascending air, are, on account of the earth's rotation on its axis, deflected from their course as they approach the equatorial region, and they thus become northeast and southwest winds. The belt between the two trade winds is characterized by calms (See CALMS, REGION OF), frequently interrupted, however, by violent storms. Trade winds are constant only over the open ocean, and the larger the expanse of ocean over which they blow, as in the Pacific, the more steady they are. In some places the trade winds become periodical, blowing one half of the year in one direction and the other half in the opposite direction. See WIND.

Trading Companies, a name often given to the great associations, or companies, formed in Europe in the sixteenth and seventeenth centuries, for the exploitation of colonies. They differed from joint stock companies in one respect, namely, that in the latter all the members were united in the conduct of some great undertaking, which was managed by a board of officers and directors representing the whole membership, while in the former, merchants entered them upon certain conditions and then traded individually, each managing his own business. Many of the companies organized as trading companies became joint stock companies in later years. Such were the East India Company, the Hudson Bay Company, the Merchant Adventurers of England, the Muscovy Company and many others. The Virginia Company and the Massachusetts Bay Company, under whose auspices the English colonies were established in America, were organized as trading companies for commercial purposes, but were incorporated as stock companies for the purpose of founding colonies. See JOINT STOCK COMPANIES.

Trafalgar, *trah fal gahr',* a low and sandy cape on the southwest coast of Spain, at the northwest entrance of the Strait of Gibraltar. The famous naval battle in which Nelson lost his life, after defeating a larger French and Spanish fleet, under the command of Villeneuve and Gravina, was fought off this cape, Oct. 21, 1805. The allies lost nineteen ships out of thirty-three.

Trag'acanth, a gum produced by several species of the pulse family, which are natives of the mountainous regions of western Asia. In commerce, tragacanth appears in small, twisted, thread-like pieces or in flattened cakes, which are whitish or yellowish in color and devoid of taste or smell. It is used medicinally for coughs and catarrhs, and commercially it is used in calico printing.

Tragedy, *traj'e dy,* in its broad sense, that form of the drama in which the subject-matter is serious, the language is dignified and the plot is unhappy in its outcome. By the Greeks the term was used somewhat differently; that is, the first two of the above-mentioned characteristics were felt to be necessary to tragedy, but it was not essential that the outcome should be unhappy. The motive of the presentation of tragedy was by the Greeks defined as the purification of the passions, through the arousing of fear and pity. Among the Greeks tragedy was brought to its highest form in the works of Sophocles, Aeschylus and Euripides. In English, Shakespeare and his contemporaries brought tragedy to a point beyond which it seems there is little possibility of its developing. At the present day tragedy as presented on the stage has been to a large extent replaced by lighter, less serious plays.

Among the greatest tragedies which have been produced in modern literature may be mentioned *Athalie* (1691) by Racine, *Faust* (1788–1808) by Goethe, *Wilhelm Tell* (tragi-comedy) (1804) by Schiller, *Hamlet* (1603) by Shakespeare, *Macbeth* (1606–1607) by Shakespeare, *Othello* (1604) by Shakespeare, *King Lear* (1606 or 1607) by Shakespeare, *Romeo and Juliet* (1598) by Shakespeare. See DRAMA.

Trag'opan, the name of certain beautiful wild birds, closely related to common fowls. They are remarkable for a fleshy blue horn above each eye, and for a large throat wattle on the male. The birds can raise and inflate these protuberances at will, especially during the mating season. The forehead and throat are naked or merely hairy. In the five species, the color varies remarkably, some being orange-red and brown, others black with white, black or red marks. They are Asiatic birds, found in the high forests of the Himalayas.

Trailing Ar'butus. See ARBUTUS.

Tra'jan, (51–117), a Roman emperor, the son of a distinguished Roman commander under Vespasian. Trajan served against the Parthians and on the Rhine, where he showed so high a character that Nerva adopted him and created him Caesar in 97. Nerva died in 98, and Trajan, who was then in Germany, succeeded to the throne. He made peace with the German tribes and proceeded to introduce enlightened measures of reform. One of his greatest military achievements was his defeat of the Dacians and the reduction of Dacia to a Roman province. It is supposed that it was in commemoration of this war that he erected at Rome the column which still remains under his name. In 103 he wrote the famous epistle to Pliny, governor of Pontus and Bithynia, directing him not to search for Christians, but to punish them if brought before him, and on no account to listen to anonymous charges. In 114 he set out on an expedition against the Parthians, which resulted in the reduction of Armenia to a Roman province.

Trajan, ARCH OF, an arch at Benevento, Italy, erected in 114 A. D., in memory of the construction of the new road to Brundusium, in the reign of Trajan. The whole arch is 50 feet in height and is one of the best preserved examples of the Roman arch.

Trajan's Column, a column erected in 114 A. D. by the Roman Senate, to the honor of the emperor Trajan. The column stands 100 feet high and is adorned with reliefs commemorating the emperor's victories in the Dacian wars. The summit was crowned with the statue of Trajan, but this was replaced by one of Saint Peter by Pope Sixtus V.

Tram'way, a railway made of wooden stringers, upon which straps of iron are fastened, for the cars to run upon. The cars are hauled by horses or locomotives or are moved by gravity. The first roads of this sort were made of trams of wood or stone. The tramway is the earliest form of railway and was first used in the English collieries (See RAILROAD). The street railway is a modification of the tramway. See STREET RAILWAY.

Transcendentalism, *tran sen den'tal iz'm,* a system of philosophy taught by a school established in New England about the middle of the nineteenth century by some of the foremost American thinkers and writers. The beliefs of the Transcendentalists are hard to define, since they had no fixed creed. Their leading idea was the supremacy of mind over matter, and they maintained that the truth of religion did not depend on tradition or historical facts, but that it has always an unerring witness in the soul. They believed that every person born into the world was possessed of a faculty which enabled him to perceive spiritual truth when this truth was clearly presented. A Transcendental club was founded by George Ripley in 1836, and the school was the outgrowth of this movement.

Among the most eminent Transcendentalists were Ralph Waldo Emerson, James Freeman Clarke, A. Bronson Alcott, Theodore Parker and Margaret Fuller.

Tran'sept, in architecture, the transverse portion of a church, between the nave and the choir, projecting on each side and forming the smaller arms of the cross in the general ground plan. It was a common feature of the church of the Middle Ages and of the Gothic age, when most churches were built on the cruciform plan. The transept of Notre Dame in Paris and that of Amiens are especially beautiful.

Transform'er, a device used for changing the potential of electric currents. The transformer in most common use changes the current from a high to a low potential and is a form of induction coil (See INDUCTION COIL), in which the inner, or primary, coil consists of many turns of fine wire, with an outer, or secondary, coil of a few turns of coarse wire. This transformer is used in electric lighting, for reducing the potential of the current as it is taken from the main wires for supplying incandescent lights in buildings. See ELECTRIC LIGHT.

Tran'sit, in astronomy, 1, the passage of a heavenly body across the meridian of any place, a phenomenon which is usually noted by a transit instrument. The determination of the exact times of the transits of the heavenly bodies across the meridian of the place of observation enables the astronomer to ascertain the differences of right ascensions, the relative situations of the fixed stars and the motions of the sun, the planets and the comets, in respect to the celestial meridians. 2, The passage of one heavenly body over the disk of a larger one; but the term is usually restricted to the passage of the inferior planets, Mercury and Venus, over the sun's disk. The transits of Venus are of great importance in astronomy, as they afford the best means of determining the sun's parallax and consequently the dimensions of the planetary system. These transits are of rare occurrence, four taking place in 243 years, at intervals reckoning from the transit of 1874, in the order of 8, 122, 8 and 105 years, which gives the transit years 1882 (December 6), 2004, 2012, 2117. The transits of Mercury occur more frequently, but they are of far less astronomical interest, as they cannot be used for the same purpose, the planet being too distant from us. Those occurring in the first half of the twentieth century are November 12, 1907; November 6, 1914; May

7, 1924; November 8, 1927; May 10, 1937, and November 12, 1940.

Transit Instrument, an important astronomical instrument, adapted for observing the exact time of the passage of heavenly bodies across the meridian. It consists essentially of a telescope, fixed at right angles to a horizontal axis, which latter has its ends directed exactly to the east and west points of the horizon, so that the optical axis of the telescope may move in the plane of the meridian. A thread passing across the center of the object glass and parallel with the plane of the meridian, enables the observer to note, to the fraction of a second, the time of the passage of a star.

Transmigration, *trans'mi gra'shun*, **of the Soul** or **Metempsychosis,** the passage which, according to some philosophers, the soul, after the death of the body, makes through the bodies of the lower animals or other human bodies or through plants or inanimate objects. In the teaching of the Brahmanic Hindus, it has its foundation in the belief of the connection of all living beings and of the gradual purification of the spiritual part of man and its return to the common source and origin of all things— God. The Buddhists accept a similar doctrine, but with them, the ultimate goal of the soul is not absorption by the Deity, but annihilation, Nirvana. Transmigration also formed part of the teaching of the Egyptian priests. The doctrine probably passed from Egypt into Greece, where it was never generally current, but was confined to the mysteries and some philosophic systems. It occupied an important place in the system of Pythagoras and is supported by Plato and Plotinus. Among the Romans, Cicero alludes to this doctrine, and Caesar informs us that it was believed in by the Gauls, who, he says, in this faith were able to despise death. The doctrine is also found in the Talmud, but only a minority of the Jewish rabbis appear to have adopted it. Various heretical Christian sects have held this doctrine, and it was also professed by the Arabs before Mohammed.

Many men of profound metaphysical genius, both in Europe and America, have affirmed this doctrine and attempted to give it a logical or scientific basis, and for a large class of persons it has a strong attraction. But the theory to the average mind in the Western world is a mere fancy, however deep a metaphysical basis or strong poetic charms it may possess. Transmigration as a general belief will undoubtedly remain with the East.

Trans-Mis'sissip'pi Exposition, an industrial exposition, held at Omaha, Neb., in the summer of 1898, designed to exhibit the progress made by the western states of the Union and to arouse interest in the development of their resources. The site occupied was north of the city limits and contained about 200 acres, which were transformed from monotonous prairie land into a beautiful park. There were about a dozen main buildings, which were veneered with white staff and adorned with reproductions of ancient and modern statuary. The total attendance was over 2,500,000.

Trans'porta'tion. See CARRIAGE; AUTOMOBILE; FLYING MACHINE; ROAD; RAILROAD; CANAL; ELECTRIC RAILWAY; STREET RAILWAY; SHIP; FREIGHT; INTERSTATE COMMERCE ACT. For the legal phases of the subject consult HIGHWAYS; CARRIER, COMMON. See, also, MUNICIPAL OWNERSHIP.

Trans-Sibe'rian Railway, THE, a line of railway originally designed to connect the rail-

Stretensk, 685 miles; Amur, from Stretensk to Khabarovsk, 1373 miles; Usuri, from Khabarovsk to Vladivostok, 474 miles. The Amur section was replaced by a line running farther south through Manchuria, and known as the Manchurian Section. This section extends 952 miles from Nagaden, where it leaves the main line; it also has a southern branch extending to Port Arthur, thus giving the railway access to a port which is free from ice the entire year. The entire distance from Chelyabinsk to Vladivostok is 3961 miles, and to Port Arthur, 4238 miles. The entire system has 6800 miles of road.

The Western Siberian division passes through a level country and was easy to construct, but the Trans-Baikal division presented great engineering difficulties, in the shape of apparently bottomless marshes, and mountainous regions requiring steep gradients. In spite of these obstacles, however, the road was constructed at the rate of 375 miles a year on the average, and the work is well done. Owing to the time re-

TRANS-SIBERIAN RAILWAY
FINISHED —— PROJECTED ---
SCALE OF MILES
0 100 300 500 1000

way systems of European Russia with the port of Vladivostok, on the Sea of Japan. The Trans-Siberian Railway is the outgrowth of a number of plans for establishing means of communication between the Russian possessions in Europe and Asia. The construction of this railway was approved by an imperial rescript given by the Czarovitch, now Nicholas II, March 17, 1891. Work was commenced immediately, and the main line was completed in 1905. The line as originally planned was divided into six sections, as follows: Western Siberian, from Chelyabinsk to Omsk, 878 miles; Central Siberian, from Omsk to Irkutsk, 1134 miles; Trans-Baikal, from Myosava to

quired for constructing the road around Lake Baikal, the line was opened to traffic before this section was completed, and for nearly three years cars were transferred across the lake by ferry. The roadbed is planned for rails of normal width and is everywhere substantial. Drainage is secured by means of iron and clay pipes; bridges over culverts and small streams are solidly built of stone or wood, but those over the large rivers are of the best patterns of steel truss. The bridge over the Irtysh River is nearly four miles long and is considered one of the best railway bridges in the world. The track has a 5-foot gauge, common to all Russian railways, is on a solid roadbed, well ballasted and is in excellent condition. The stations along the line are commodious in plan and artistic in design; they are placed 33 miles apart.

The Trans-Siberian railway is the greatest project of the kind that has yet been carried to successful completion, and it must exert an important influence upon the commerce of the world. By the old routes of travel it required 45 days to go from Saint Petersburg to Peking, by the Suez Canal and the Indian Ocean, or 35 days via New York, San Francisco and the Pacific. By the Siberian railway, one can go from Moscow to Vladivostok, even at the present rate of speed in nine days; and with a rate of speed equal to that of an express train between Chicago and New York, it would require only five days from Saint Petersburg to Peking or eight days from London to Peking.

Transvaal, *trans'vahl,* **The** (formerly the South African Republic), a province of the Union of South Africa, extending from the Limpopo River, on the north, to the Vaal River, on the south. It is bounded on the e. by Portuguese East Africa, on the w. by the British Territory of Bechuanaland, on the s. by Orange Free State, and on the n. by Rhodesia. The area is 111,196 sq. mi., or about that of Nevada.

Most of the country is a high, undulating plateau, with hills and mountain ranges extending through the interior. The tableland varies in height from 4000 to 6000 feet, in the south and east, to between 1500 and 4000 feet, in the north. The Drakenberg Mountains extend north and south across the eastern portion and reach an altitude of 8700 feet in Mauchberg Mountain, the highest peak. The boundary between Transvaal and Portuguese East Africa is formed by the Limpopo Mountains. The Witwatersrand is a height of land, gradually rising to an altitude of 6000 feet, extending across the country approximately in an east and west direction, and forming the watershed between the Limpopo and the Vaal rivers. The southwestern part of the colony is a broad, flat plain. The chief rivers are the Vaal and the Limpopo, with their tributaries. The climate is temperate and, in the main, healthful. It is characterized by intense heat during the summer and by heavy rainfall. These conditions produce malaria in the lower levels, but the winter months are cool and invigorating. The annual rainfall is about 26 inches.

The settlers are largely engaged in stock raising and agriculture. All of the cereals and most vegetables are produced in paying quantities. Extensive grazing regions adapt this country to stock growing, and previous to the war with England, large numbers of cattle, horses, sheep and goats were found in the colony. The mineral wealth, however, is the chief source of income. This consists of gold, which is extensively mined on the Witwatersrand, in the vicinity of Johannesburg and Barborton, and of diamonds, which are obtained in the vicinity of Pretoria. The gold taken from the mines in 1911 was valued at over $170,000,000, and the annual output of diamonds usually exceeds $6,000,000. The province has about 2000 miles of railway, which connects Pretoria, Johannesburg, Pietersburg and Leydenburg with the chief towns in Orange Free State, and these are connected with the trunk line of the Cape-to-Cairo Railway.

The executive head of the government is the administrator, appointed by the governor-general for a term of five years. The administrator presides over the meetings of the provincial council, composed of 36 members elected for three-year terms. An executive committee of four, not necessarily members of the council, acts as cabinet or ministry. The provincial council may legislate on all local matters, including finance, elementary education, agriculture, roads and bridges, and municipal institutions. All legislation is subject to the veto of the governor-general-in-council. The province is divided into 36 electoral districts, each of which sends one member to the Union parliament.

The Transvaal was settled by Dutch emigrants from Cape Colony in 1835 and 1836. These people emigrated northward because they were dissatisfied with the British rule in Cape Colony. Because of wars with the native tribes, the colonists were compelled to apply to British authorities for protection. This was granted, and it became necessary for the British government to assume control of the colonies, in order to preserve peace with the native tribes. To this arrangement the colonists agreed in 1877. Afterwards they protested against annexation to the British dominions, and in 1880, under the Gladstone ministry, it was recommended that the political independence of the country be restored. The South African Republic was proclaimed by the people, in December, 1880. In 1881 a convention was signed by Great Britain, granting independence, except in external affairs. This was superseded by another convention in 1884. Meantime, the Boers were preparing for war, and in a short campaign they administered a serious defeat to the British troops. With the discovery of gold in the Witwatersrand, in 1884, there came a large influx of foreigners, who settled about the mines. The discovery of diamonds also caused an increase of foreign population, and the Boers became alarmed lest these foreigners, *uitlanders*, outnumber the original citizens and assume control of the government. In order to prevent this, the South African Republic refused to grant foreigners franchise and certain other rights, except under great restrictions and difficulties. In 1896 a raid, under the leadership of one Doctor Jameson, which seemingly had for its purpose the gaining of control of the government, so alarmed the Boers that they began to take strenuous measures to defend themselves against the foreigners. While the raid was disavowed by the British government and the leaders of it were nominally punished, the action of Great Britain toward the affair did not satisfy the Boers, and one excess led to another, until war was declared in October, 1899 (See SOUTH AFRICAN WAR). The Boers were defeated, and the South African Republic, under the name of the Transvaal Colony, was annexed to the British dominions on September 1, 1900. Until 1905 the government was under the control of an administrator; but local government was being reëstablished, and complete self-government was restored in 1907, when the first responsible ministry took office. On May 31, 1910, when the Union of South Africa was established, the Transvaal became a province. (See SOUTH AFRICA, UNION OF.) The chief cities are Pretoria, the capital, and Johannesburg. Population in 1911, 1,686,212, of whom 420,831 were whites.

Trapdoor Spider, a name given to certain spiders that have the habit of constructing tubu-

TRAPDOOR SPIDER AND HIS HOME

lar dwellings in the ground, sometimes a foot or more in depth and an inch or so in diameter, closed by a kind of hinged door. They belong to several genera and are found in southern Europe, western North America and elsewhere. The dwelling is lined with the silky substance spun by the insect, and the hinge of the door is formed of the same, the door itself being con-structed sometimes of earthy particles connected by threads, sometimes of leaves and twigs.

Trap′ping, the taking of birds and other animals by traps, or snares, instead of killing them by weapons. Traps are of various kinds, such as the nets that are used for fish; the snares and box traps, to imprison birds and quadrupeds; the dead-fall, which kills by weight, and the steel spring traps, which in various sizes are used for all animals, from the mouse to the bear. The steel trap is the most cruel of all, because it does not usually kill, as does the dead-fall, nor imprison an animal, as the box traps do, but, catching only by the leg, holds its captives in suffering till they are killed and released by the trapper. Some animals when caught by a foot in a steel trap will release themselves by gnawing off the imprisoned member; this is most common among muskrats, and accordingly, hunters set their traps so that the animal will drown soon after being caught.

Trav′eler's Tree, a tree, native of Madagascar, having the appearance of a palm and forming the only species of the genus to which it belongs. It receives its name from the fact that at the base of the leaves there is always a supply of watery, wholesome sap, which furnishes a refreshing drink to travelers. The leaves, which have blades about six feet long and three feet broad, grow on the two opposite sides of the trunk, and as the lower ones fall off the tree takes on the appearance of a huge fan. They are the largest undivided leaves known, except, possibly, those of the Victoria lily. The tree has large, showy flowers, and its seeds, which yield a flour, are used by the natives for food.

Trav′erse City, MICH., the county-seat of Grand Traverse co., 145 mi. n. of Grand Rapids, on the west arm of Grand Traverse Bay and on the Pere Marquette and other railroads. It has an attractive situation and good fishing and enjoys a considerable reputation as a summer resort. The city is in an agricultural and fruit-growing region, and the excellent harbor affords good shipping facilities. The chief industrial establishments are lumber mills and manufactories of wood articles, such as wooden dishes and baskets, while farm implements, leather and foundry and machine shop products are also made. The Northern Michigan Insane Asylum is located here, and the city has a public library. The place was settled about 1850 and was chartered as a city in 1895. Population in 1910, 12,115.

Travertine, *trav'ur tin,* a white limestone, usually hard and partially crystallized, deposited from the water of springs holding carbonate of lime in solution. Travertine is abundant in different parts of Italy, and a large proportion of the edifices of ancient and modern Rome are built of this stone.

Trav'is, WILLIAM BARRETT (1811–1836), an American soldier, born in Edgefield County, S. C. He studied law and was admitted to the bar at Claiborne, Ala. Later he removed to Texas, took a prominent part in its rebellion against Mexico and was captured by the Mexicans, but was finally released. He commanded at the famous defense of the Alamo in February and March, 1836, and was killed just before the fall of the fortress.

Trawl'ing, a mode of fishing, in which a net, in the form of a large bag, with a strong framework keeping the mouth open, is dragged along the bottom of the sea. It is the mode chiefly adopted in deep-sea fishing, and in British waters it has largely developed in recent years, being much prosecuted by small steam vessels, specially built for the purpose. It is not allowed within three miles of the shore. Cod, whiting and other whitefish are taken by it in large numbers, and some kinds of flatfish, as soles, can scarcely be taken in any other way. Trawling can be practiced only on a smooth bottom, as a rough bottom would destroy the net. In Scotland the term trawling is often improperly applied to fishing for herring with the seine. See FISHERIES.

Treadmill, *tred'mill,* an instrument of punishment, consisting of a large wheel, about twenty or twenty-five feet wide, with steps on its circumference. When criminals are placed upon these steps the weight of the men sets the wheel in motion, and they maintain themselves in an upright posture by walking and keeping hold of a horizontal bar placed above them. They are obliged to continue the exercise until the wheel is stopped by the officer in charge. The power thus obtained may be applied to the same purpose as water or steam power. The treadmill has recently been abandoned in most penitentiaries.

Treason, *tre'z'n,* that crime which is directly committed against the supreme authority of the State. It is considered the greatest crime that can be committed. In a monarchy it is the betraying or the forfeiting of allegiance to the monarch. In a republic, such as the United States, where the people as a community, and not any one individual, are sovereign, treason is necessarily confined to levying war against the State, or adhering to and giving aid and comfort to its enemies. It implies the assembling of a body of men for the purpose of overturning or resisting the government by force; but an assembly for deliberative purposes alone cannot commit treason, since the law distinguishes between deliberation and an act of war.

Treasury, *trezh' ur y,* the department of a government which has control of the public revenue. The treasury department of the United States is in charge of the secretary of the treasury, a member of the cabinet, appointed by the president with the approval of the Senate. It has sole charge of the national finances, under the laws of Congress, collects the revenue, makes all expenditures, audits all accounts, has charge of public buildings, national banks, coinage and paper money, and collects financial statistics. The treasury department employs about five thousand officers and clerks. The secretary is second of the cabinet officers in line of succession to the presidency. See UNITED STATES, subhead *Government.* See also CIVIL GOVERNMENT, in Volume VI.

Independent Treasury is the name given to the system adopted by the United States in 1846. It was the result of a long contest over the expediency of establishing a United States bank, and it was passed in the hope that the treasury would be completely divorced from banks, in order that the privilege which the banks received and the influence which they wielded under the former system might be abolished. The new scheme provided for the deposit of United States funds in the treasury at Washington and in certain sub-treasuries in the principal cities. The principle of complete independence from banking, however, has not been fully carried out, since the government, at times when money is scarce, has always deposited funds with the banks, in order to put money in circulation and to reduce the treasury's surplus.

Treaty, *tree'ty,* an agreement, league or contract between two or more nations or sovereigns, formally signed by commissioners properly authorized, and ratified by the several sovereigns, or the supreme power of each State. Treaties are of various kinds, as *commercial treaties, treaties of alliance,* offensive and defensive, and *treaties of peace.* In most monarchies the power of making and ratifying treaties is vested in the sovereign; in the United States it is vested in the president and the Senate, the former conducting the negotiation, the latter ratifying the completed treaty.

Treb'izond, a seaport of Turkey, situated on the Black Sea, 575 mi. e. of Constantinople. The city occupies a plateau and is enclosed by walls erected during the Middle Ages. It contains a number of ruins of ancient structures, among them those of an old castle and several old Greek churches, which have been transformed into mosques. In general, the dwellings are low, one-story buildings. The city contains numerous bazaars and is the seat of an extensive commerce, though the harbor is poor. Population, about 35,000.

Treb'le, in music, the highest vocal or instrumental part in a concerted piece, such as is sung by women or boys or played by instruments of acute tone, as the violin, the flute, the oboe or the clarinet, or on the higher keys of the piano or organ, so-called because it was originally a *third* part, added to the ancient *canto fermo* and the counterpoint. See COUNTERPOINT; MUSIC.

Tree, HERBERT BEERBOHM, SIR (1853–　　), English actor and manager, born in London and educated in England and Germany. He made his first appearance on the stage as Grimaldi, at the Globe Theatre, in 1878, and six years later he scored a great success as the Curate in *The Private Secretary*, given at the Prince's. In 1887 he undertook the management of the Comedy Theatre and of the Haymarket. He visited the United States in 1894. His repertoire includes *The Merry Wives of Windsor*, *The Pompadour*, *The Dancing Girl*, *Hamlet*, *Trilby* and *John-a-Dreams*. He has published *Fallacies of the Modern Stage* and *The Imaginative Faculty*.

Tree Frog, the name of a class of animals differing from sucking frogs in the extremities of their toes, each of which is expanded into a disk, so that the animals can climb trees, wherein they spend their summers feeding upon insects. One species of the Northern and Middle states is brown or gray in color and rarely exceeds two inches in length.

Tre'foil, a name applied to a genus of plants belonging to the same family as the bean. One species, the *bird's foot trefoil*, is common in European pastures and is by some regarded as the shamrock of Ireland. It has been introduced into the United States and is especially common in the South. The name is derived from the form of the leaf, which consists of three lobes, or leaflets.

Trem'olite, a light-colored hornblende, which usually occurs in blades or long columnar crystals.

Trent, a river of England, which rises northwest of the center and flows southeastward, then northeastward, and joins the Ouse to form the Humber, about 15 miles west of Hull. Its length is about 140 miles, and it is navigable for ordinary vessels as far as Gainsborough, and for barges to Burton-on-Trent. It is connected with other rivers by canals, the chief being the Trent and Mersey Canal. Next to the Thames and Severn, the Trent is the most important river of England.

Trent, COUNCIL OF, a celebrated ecumenical council of the Roman Catholic Church, convened to settle various controversies that were agitating the Church during the Reformation period and to correct abuses. It met during the pontificate of Paul III, at Trent, in 1545, but the wars in Germany caused its transference to Bologna in 1546, when it dispersed. Pope Julius III again convoked it at Trent in 1551, but dispersed a year later on the approach of the Lutherans. Eight years afterward it was again called together by Pius IV, and it finished its labors in 1563. This council definitely settled the doctrines of the Roman Catholic Church.

Trent Affair, THE, the name commonly given to an episode during the Civil War, growing out of the seizure by an American war vessel, of James M. Mason and John Slidell, Confederate commissioners, while aboard the British mail steamer *Trent*. Mason and Slidell had run the blockade at Charleston and had gone to Havana, where they embarked for England on the *Trent*. The vessel was overtaken on November 8 by the *San Jacinto*, a Union ship, under Captain Charles Wilkes. He boarded the *Trent*, arrested the commissioners and took them to Boston, where they were confined in Fort Warren. The act, though applauded by the North, was in violation of international usage. The *San Jacinto* should have taken the *Trent* as a prize to a port, to be adjudged. President Lincoln and Secretary Seward recognized the impropriety of the act and released the prisoners, with apology to the British government, and thus probably avoided war. See MASON, JAMES MURRAY; SLIDELL, JOHN.

Trente-et-Quarante, *trahNt ay kahrahNt'* or **Trente-Un.** See ROUGE-ET-NOIR.

Trente-Un, *trahNt uN*, or **Trente-et-Quarante.** See ROUGE-ET-NOIR.

Tren'ton, the capital city of New Jersey and the shire-town of Mercer co., situated on the Delaware river, at the head of navigation, on the Delaware and Raritan Canal and on the Pennsylvania, the Baltimore & Ohio, the Delaware, Lackawanna & Western and other railroads. It is also connected by trolley lines with New York, Philadelphia and the principal cities of New Jersey. It is the seat of the state asylum for the insane, the state reformatory, a reformatory home for girls, a state normal school and the state penitentiary. Its industries include immense pottery works, manufacturing more than one-half of all the pottery and china produced in the United States; also rubber works, manufactories of steel and iron products, furniture factories, watch factories, carriage and wagon works, brickyards and breweries. It possesses exceptional educational advantages, having numerous private and religious academies and business colleges, besides many fine public schools. It has a beautiful public library building, containing about 40,000 volumes, and it is the seat of the state library. Other conspicuous buildings are the state capitol, the county courthouse, the state armory, the Federal building, the Y. M. C. A. building, the Masonic Temple and the high school building. Cadwallader Park and Spring Lake Park contain many beautiful monuments and drives, and another fine boulevard, Riverside Drive, is being projected. Trenton was the scene of a notable engagement in the Revolutionary War (See TRENTON, BATTLE OF). Population in 1910, 96,815.

Trenton, Mo., the county-seat of Grundy co., 83 mi. n. e. of Saint Joseph, on the east fork of the Grand River and on the Chicago, Rock Island & Pacific and the Quincy, Omaha & Kansas City railroads. A good quality of coal is extensively mined, and the Rock Island has railroad shops here. There are also flour mills, machine shops, and butter, cheese, cigar and other factories. The city has a public library and is the seat of Avalon College. The place was settled in 1840 and was chartered as a city in 1893. Population in 1910, 5656.

Trenton, BATTLE OF, an important battle of the Revolutionary War, fought at Trenton, N. J., on the night of Christmas Day, 1776. It was just after Washington's famous retreat across New Jersey. He had crossed the Delaware, and the British had stationed a body of Hessians in the city of Trenton, to watch his movements. Washington, with a part of his command, crossed the Delaware, which was filled with floating ice, and surprised the Hessians in the midst of their Christmas night carousals. With a loss of two men killed and three wounded, the Americans captured about 1000 men, after a brief skirmish.

Washington immediately recrossed the river and soon after fought the famous Battle of Princeton. These successes revived the spirits of Washington's army and practically turned the tide of victory toward the Americans.

Trenton Series, a division of rock formations, including the upper strata of the Ordovician System, known in the United States as the Trenton, Utica, Cincinnati and Hudson formations. The Trenton is a gray or black limestone, and the Hudson and Utica are shales. In Ohio the Hudson is known as the Cincinnati. Rocks of this series also occur in the Rocky Mountains and the Mississippi Valley, where the formations known as the Salina limestone contain zinc and lead ores, found in Wisconsin and Illinois. The petroleum of the Lima, Ohio, oil fields and some of the natural gas are also obtained from the Trenton formations. See GEOLOGY; ORDOVICIAN SYSTEM.

Trepang', the sea slug, a marine animal, popularly known as *sea cucumber,* or bèches-de-mer. It is found chiefly about coral reefs in the Eastern seas, and is a rather repulsive looking animal, somewhat resembling the land slug in shape and varying in length from 6 to 24 inches. Sun-dried trepangs are in special demand in China for making soups. The fishery is carried on in numerous localities in the Indian Ocean, in the Eastern Archipelago and on the shores of Australia.

Trephining, *tre fine'ing,* or **Trepan'ning,** the operation of cutting a circular opening into the skull, by means of a *trephine,* or *trepan.* This instrument consists of a handle, to which is fixed a small, hollow, steel cylinder, from half an inch to an inch in diameter, with teeth on its lower edge, so as to form a circular saw. Trephining relieves the brain from pressure, as in fracture of the skull or in cerebral abscess.

Tres'pass, in law, a term which is applied generally to any offense against the person or property of another, but more especially to a peaceable, but unlawful, entry upon the property of another, the remedy for which is by an action for damages. Any injuries committed against land or buildings are in the most common sense of the word trespasses, as entering another's house without permission, walking over his ground, suffering any cattle to stray upon it, or any act or practice which damages the property or interferes with the owner's or occupier's rights of possession. A creditor or customer can be ordered away by a householder or shopkeeper, and even the civil courts have no power to give a right of entry to officers intrusted with the execution of legal processes, though such officers may maintain possession if once they gain entrance.

Trevel'yan, George Otto, Sir (1838–   ), an English author and politician, the nephew of Lord Macaulay. He was educated at Harrow, graduated at Trinity College, Cambridge, and entered the Indian civil service by competition. He was elected to Parliament in 1865, and with the exception of a short interval, he always followed Gladstone's lead. He is the author of the *Life and Letters of Lord Macaulay*, *The Early History of Charles James Fox* and *The American Revolution*.

Tri'angle, in geometry, a figure bounded by three lines. It is the most important figure in geometry and may be considered the element of all other figures. The *base* of the triangle is the side upon which it rests; the *vertex*, the point of the angle opposite the base; the *altitude*, the perpendicular distance from base to vertex. The three angles of a plane triangle are equal to two right angles, or 180°, and its area is equal to half that of a rectangle or parallelogram of the same base and altitude. If all the three sides are equal, it is an *equilateral triangle*. If two of the sides only are equal, it is an *isosceles triangle*. If all the three sides are unequal, it is a *scalene triangle*. If one of the angles is a right angle, the triangle is *right-angled*. If one of the angles is obtuse, the triangle is called *obtuse-angled*. If all the angles are acute, the triangle is *acute-angled*. If the sides of a triangle are all straight lines, it is a *plane*, or *rectilinear*, *triangle*. If the three lines of a triangle are all curves, the triangle is said to be *curvilinear*. If the sides are all arcs of great circles of the sphere (See Sphere) or are arcs of the same circle, the triangle is said to be spherical. See Angle; Trigonometry.

Trianon, *tre a nohN'*, the name of two villas in Versailles, France. The Grand Trianon is a beautiful one-story palace, built by Louis XIV for Madame Maintenon. The Petit Trianon was built by Louis XV for Madame du Barry and was the favorite residence of Marie Antoinette. In its gardens are still some very beautiful Swiss buildings.

Trias'sic System, a group of rocks, extending from the Carboniferous system, below, to the Jurassic, above, and named from the local formation in Germany, which was characterized by three series. The rocks are sedimentary, but in many places they are disarranged by the breaking through of volcanic matter, which has formed dikes and cliffs of trap. The Palisades of the Hudson afford a good illustration of such formations. Triassic rocks are generally distributed throughout all continents. In North America they are found on both the Atlantic and Pacific coasts. The sandstone of the Connecticut valley and of New Jersey, so highly prized for building, is of this period, but most of the other sandstones of the formation are red and form the group sometimes classified as new red sandstone (See New Red Sandstone). The plant life was similar to that of the Carboniferous period, but the chief characteristic of animal life was in the development of reptiles, which attained their highest perfection during the period, and for this reason some geologists have named it the Age of Reptiles. The difficulty in distinguishing between formations of the Triassic and Jurassic systems has caused the United States Geological Survey to combine the two under the name of the Jura-Trias. See Carboniferous System; Jurassic System; Mesozoic Era.

Trib'une (Latin, *tribunus*), in Roman antiquity, originally, an officer who was connected with a tribe, or who represented a tribe for certain purposes; especially, an officer or magistrate chosen by the people to protect them from the oppression of the patricians, or nobles, or of the Senate and consuls. These magistrates were at first two, but their number was increased to five, and ultimately to ten. There were also military tribunes, each of whom commanded a division or legion of the army.

Trichina, *tre ki'na*, a minute worm, which, when it obtains lodgment in the muscles of man, gives rise to the disease trichiniasis. The worm is found in several of the mammals, especially the pig, and it is generally from the latter that man receives the disease. When a portion of flesh containing the larvae, or worms in their resting stage, is taken into the stomach, these soon become developed into adult worms, which pass into the intestines. In the mature state the male is about one-twentieth of an inch long, and the female is from one-eighth to one-twelfth of an inch in length. The female produces an extraordinary number of embryos, which, by penetrating the mucous coat of the intestine, enter the capillaries and are carried thence into the general circulation; thence they make their way into the muscles, where they rest encased in a limy cyst and give no further trouble. While in their active state, they set up diseased conditions in their host, which often prove fatal. In the illustration, the figure to the left shows larval worms in the encysted state, embedded in the human muscle, and the figure to the right shows

TRICHINAE
Encased and free.

trichinae free in the human muscle. See TRICHINIASIS.

Trichiniasis, *trik'e ni'a sis,* or **Trichinosis,** *trik'e no'sis,* a disease which is caused by eating food containing a small worm known as *trichina spiralis.* This worm inhabits the muscles of pigs, and when their flesh is eaten, the worms are liberated and multiply with extraordinary rapidity, causing fever, stiffening muscles and, very frequently, death from exhaustion or pneumonia. When patients recover, the convalescence is very slow. No means is known of destroying the parasites after they have reached the muscles, but if, as soon as infection is suspected, castor oil or calomel is given in quantities, the embryos will be expelled from the intestines, and health will return. As a general preventive measure, no pork should be eaten by any one, unless it has been thoroughly cooked. Smoking, as in the treatment of hams, is not sufficient to kill trichina. The real cause of the disease was first made known about 1860, though cases of it had been known in Europe since the beginning of the century. It has appeared in the United States and in most parts of Europe, occasionally as an epidemic. See TRICHINA.

Tri'color, the French national flag, or one formed after the model of it. The French tricolor is blue, white and red, in equal vertical sections, the blue being next the flagstaff.

Tricycle, *tri'sik'l,* a three-wheeled variety of velocipede, introduced about 1878. Tricycles were first worked by pedaled levers, but this form

soon gave way to the rotary action, which consists of a cranked axle, to which the pedals are fixed. This axle is connected by chains, running on toothed wheels, with the driving axle. The tricycle is used by invalids and others who are unable to walk.

Triest, *tre est',* or **Trieste,** the chief seaport of Austria-Hungary, situated on the Gulf of Triest, 73 mi. n. e. of Venice and 214 mi. s. w. of Vienna. The city consists of an old town, with narrow streets, which rise rapidly from the harbor to the heights beyond, and a new quarter, which is built on modern plans. The two parts of the city are separated by a street known as the Corso. Some of the important buildings are the townhall, the Cathedral of San Guiesto, which occupies the site of a former Roman temple, and the Greek church. There are also a number of ruins of ancient Roman structures, including those of a theater and an aqueduct. The city has a number of public squares and a public garden. It is the most important trade center of Austria-Hungary on the Mediterranean and has an extensive commerce. Its manufactures include naval stores, machinery, soap, candles, leather and refined petroleum. Population in 1910, 229,510, most of whom are Italians.

Trig'onom'etry, that branch of mathematics which treats of the measurement of triangles and of the relations between their parts. In every triangle there are six things to be considered, namely, the three sides and the three angles. The main object of the theoretical part of trigonometry is to deduce rules by which, when some of these parts are known, the others may be found by computation. To facilitate the study of the relation of these parts, mathematicians have devised a series of *trigonometric functions.* Each of these, though originally discovered in connection with arcs of circles, now has a distinct meaning with relation to the parts of a triangle. Conceive a triangle whose angles are A, B, C, and whose sides opposite these angles are respectively a, b, c. The primary relations expressed by the six important trigonometric functions are, then, as follows: sine of A $(\sin A) = \dfrac{a}{b}$; cosine of A $(\cosin A) = \dfrac{b}{c}$; tangent of A $(\tan A) = \dfrac{a}{c}$; cotangent of $A (\cot A) = \dfrac{c}{b}$; secant $A (\sec A) = \dfrac{b}{a}$; cosecant of $A (\cosec A) = \dfrac{c}{a}$. Two other functions are also sometimes considered, the versine of $A (\text{vers } A) =$

$1-\cos A$; the coversine of A (covers A)$=1-\sin A$. From these tables and others derived from them the relations of any parts of a triangle can be found, having given three parts. For the simplification of operations in trigonometry, tables containing the logarithms of certain numbers, corresponding in value to certain angles, have been formed, so that by referring to these tables the value of any angle can be found immediately, if the value of any one of its functions is known, and *vice versa*.

Trigonometry is divided into three great branches, *plane trigonometry, spherical trigonometry* and *analytical trigonometry*, the first named treating of plane triangles, the second of spherical triangles and the last of trigonometric functions.

The value of trigonometry in many practical pursuits, such as engineering, surveying and geodesy, is almost inestimable, since it makes possible the measurement of distances and magnitudes which could be measured in no other way, on account of physical obstructions or other conditions. Examples of this use may be found in measuring the distance between two objects on the opposite banks of a stream, without crossing, and measuring the height of a mountain above its base.

Trillium, or **Wake Robin,** an early spring wild flower, belonging to the lily family, to the other members of which it bears little resemblance. There are various species, but they all are governed, as their name indicates, by the rule of three; the three-sepaled, three-petaled flower rises out of a whorl of three leaves. The painted trillium, with its white petals veined with pink, and the white trillium, or wood lily, are the most beautiful species. The purplish red trillium, popularly known as "devil in the bandbox," has a very unpleasant odor.

Trin'idad, next to Jamaica, the largest and most valuable of the British West India Islands, situated off the coast of Venezuela, opposite the northern mouths of the Orinoco. It is about 55 mi. long and 40 mi. wide, and its area is 1754 sq. mi. Mountain ranges extend east and west along the borders of the island, but the interior is a comparatively low, undulating plain, near the center of which there is an elevation of 1100 feet. The island is well watered and has plenty of rainfall. Palms, silk cotton trees, breadfruit, bamboo, coffee, cacao, bananas and sugar cane are grown. Coffee, cacao, bananas and sugar cane are exported to a considerable extent. Trinidad has long been noted for its lake of pitch, near Labrea, on the western coast. This lake covers about 90 acres and yields annually over 190,000 tons of asphalt (See ASPHALT). The island is a crown colony, and its government is administered by a governor and a legislative council. Port of Spain, on the northwest side, is the capital. Population in 1911, 330,074, most of whom are of mixed negro and European blood.

Trinidad, COL., the county-seat of Las Animas co., 90 mi. s. of Pueblo, on the Denver & Rio Grande, the Atchison, Topeka & Santa Fe and other railroads. The city is in a valley, on the eastern foothills of the Rocky Mountains, southeast of the Spanish Peaks and north of Fisher's Peak. It is surrounded by a farming and cattle-raising section and is near extensive coal mines. Railroad shops, coke ovens, breweries and wool-scouring plants are located here. The city has a public library, the Rice High School, Saint Joseph's Academy and Saint Raphael's Hospital. Population in 1910, 10,204.

Trin'ity, a theological name given to the doctrine which declares the union of the Father, the Son and the Holy Spirit as Three Persons and One God. The doctrine of the Trinity is nowhere expressly taught in the Scriptures; but in parts of the New Testament it is implied, and it is often indicated in the Old Testament. The definition of the Trinity adopted by the Catholic Church, and generally accepted by orthodox Christians, is that there are in the Godhead three persons, who are one in substance, coeternal and equal in power. The Eastern Church holds that the Holy Ghost proceeds from the Father; the Western, throughout all its divisions, adopting the amended form of the Nicene Creed, holds that it proceeds from the Father and the Son. The three creeds commonly called the Apostles', the Athanasian and the Nicene all contain the points of agreement between the two divisions of the church, while on the point of difference, the Athanasian and the commonly known form of the Nicene, express the faith of the Western Church. The term *persons* is not applied in Scripture to the Trinity, but something analogous to the conception of personality seems to be implied in the apostolical arguments of the epistles.

Trinity Sunday, the Sunday after Whitsunday. It was definitely established as a Church festival by Pope John XXII in 1334. All the principal feasts occur in the half year between Advent Sunday and Trinity, and all the Sundays from Trinity to Advent are called Sundays after Trinity.

Trip' Hammer or **Tilt Hammer**, a hammer operated by tilting the beam to which it is fastened. The beam is hung upon pivots, so that it has an upward and downward motion. The hammer is fastened to one end of this beam, and the opposite end is pressed downward by cams, attached to a revolving cylinder. When the cam has pressed the beam to the lowest point, it releases it, and the hammer falls by its own weight. Tilt hammers are used for light forging.

Trip'le Alli'ance. Three treaties in European politics are known by this name. The first was formed in 1668 by Great Britain, Sweden and the Netherlands, against Louis XIV; the second in 1717 by Great Britain, France and Holland, against Spain, then governed by Cardinal Alberoni; the third was a league formed in 1883 between Austria-Hungary, Italy and Germany. The object of this alliance, which still exists, is the protection of the three states against all outside powers.

Trip'oli, a dependency of Italy, situated in the northern part of Africa. It is bounded on the n. by the Mediterranean Sea, on the e. by Egypt, on the s. by the Sahara and on the w. by the Sahara and Tunis. The southern boundary is not fully determined, but Tripoli at present includes Fezzan and Barca. The area is about 400,000 sq. mi., and the population is about 600,000, chiefly Arabs, Moors, Berbers and Jews, with a few Europeans. Tripoli was acquired by Italy as a result of the war with Turkey in 1912.

Tripoli is one of the Barbary States. Along the coast the surface is low, but it rises toward the interior, a large portion of which is a plateau, covered with sand and limestone. In the southwestern part of the country is an elevation which forms parts of the mountain range known as Jebel-Nefusa, and which rises to nearly 3000 feet above sea level. Beyond this is a large, low plain, which in its broadest part is about 90 miles wide. This region is irrigated by wells and is cultivated. The fertile portion of the country lies along the Mediterranean, in a strip extending on each side of the city of Tripoli, to a width of about 5 miles. Wheat, barley, indian corn and millet are the principal grains grown. The fruits include dates, olives, grapes, pomegranates, lemons, figs, apricots and plums, while melons and other garden vegetables are raised in large quantities. In some sections along the coast, cotton, tobacco, silk, saffron and madder are produced in paying quantities. The summers are hot, though along the coast they are somewhat tempered by sea breezes. The winters are cool, and on the highest mountains snow is sometimes seen.

Tripoli, the capital, contains the bey's castle, which dates from the Middle Ages, a number of Christian churches and European hotels. Among the ancient ruins is a triumphal arch, erected by the Romans in honor of the emperors Marcus Aurelius and Lucius Varus. There are but few manufactures in the city. These consist chiefly of woolen goods and Morocco leather. The city has considerable trade with Europe. The population is estimated at from 25,000 to 30,000.

Tripoli or **Rotten Stone,** a mineral, originally brought from Tripoli and used in polishing metals, marbles and glass. It is a kind of siliceous powder, formed from the decomposition of certain varieties of limestone. It is of a yellowish-gray or white color, rough to the touch, hard in grain, but not compact; it readily absorbs water. It is also found in France, Italy, Germany and in Newton County, Mo.

Tri'reme, a galley, or vessel, with three benches, or ranks, of oars on a side, a common class of warship among the ancient Greeks, Romans and Carthaginians. The trireme was also provided with a large, square sail, which could be raised during a fair wind, in order to relieve the rowers; but this was never employed in action.

Tri'tons, in Greek mythology, the name of certain sea gods. They are variously described, but their bodies are always represented as a compound of the human figure, above, with that of a fish, below. They carry trumpets, composed of shells, which they blow at the command of Neptune, to soothe the waves.

Tri'umph, in Roman antiquity, a magnificent procession, in honor of a victorious general, the highest military honor which he could obtain. It was granted by the Senate only to one who had held the office of dictator, consul or praetor, and then only after a decisive victory or the complete subjugation of a province. In a Roman triumph, the general to whom this honor was awarded entered Rome in a chariot drawn by four horses. He was crowned with laurel and had a scepter in one hand and a branch of laurel in the other. The Senate and the magistrates, the musicians, the spoils and the captives in fetters formed part of the procession which went before him, and he was followed by his army on foot, in marching order. The procession advanced in this order along the *Via Sacra* to the Capitol, where a bull was sacrificed to Jupiter. Banquets and other entertainments concluded the solemnity. A naval triumph differed in no respect from an ordinary triumph, except that it was upon a smaller scale and was characterized by the use of beaks of ships and other nautical trophies.

Trium'virate, three men united in office. The term is particularly applied to two famous coalitions in Roman history, the first in 59 B. C., formed by Caesar, Pompey and Crassus; the second in 43 B. C., formed by Antony, Octavian and Lepidus.

Trog'lodyte (cave dweller), the name given by the ancient Greeks to various races of savages inhabiting caves; especially, to the cave dwellers on the coast of the Red Sea and along the banks of the Upper Nile, in Nubia and Abyssinia. See CAVE DWELLERS.

Tro'gon, the name of a genus of beautiful birds, of which there are about fifty species living in the tropical regions, principally of South America, though a few are found in Asia and Africa. They have loud, unpleasant voices, and they are content to lay their eggs in the top of a rotting stump, without pretense of making a nest. See QUEZAL.

Tro'jan War. See TROY.

Trolling, *trole'ing,* a method of fishing, in which a spoon hook is dragged at the end of a long line behind a boat. This is a favorite method for bass, pickerel and some sea fish. See ANGLING.

Trollope, *trol'lup,* ANTHONY (1815–1882), an English novelist, born in London. He was educated at Harrow, where he proved but a dull student, and in 1834 he entered the postal service. After 1847 various novels appeared, but it was not until his publication of *The Warden* in 1855 that he attracted much notice. *The Warden,* a realistic picture of life in a cathedral town, was followed by others, which had the same setting, *Barchester Towers, Doctor Thorne, Framley Parsonage* and *The Last Chronicle of Barset,* and this series, known as *Chronicles of Barsetshire,* comprises the best of his work. Among his other novels the most notable are *The Way We Live Now, The Claverings* and *The American Senator.* Trollope's works are all characterized by keenness of insight, realism of detail and genial humor.

Trolls, *trole'z,* in Northern mythology, a name of certain supernatural beings, in old Icelandic literature represented as a kind of giants, but in modern Scandinavia regarded as a kind of mischievous imps or goblins, of diminutive size.

Trom'bone, a deep-toned brass instrument, of the trumpet kind, consisting of three tubes. The first, to which the mouthpiece is attached, and the third, which terminates in a bell-shaped orifice, are placed side by side; the middle tube is doubled and slides into the other two like the tube of a telescope. By the manipulation of the slide, the tube of air is altered in length, and the pitch is accordingly varied. Trombones are of three kinds, the alto, the tenor and the bass, and their full, rich tones make them favorite instruments in bands and orchestras.

Tromp, MARTIN HARPERTZOON (1597–1653), a Dutch admiral. He had won a reputation by victories over the Spaniards before the outbreak of the war with England, in 1652, in which he gained his greatest fame. His defeat of Blake off Goodwin Sands in November, 1652, made the Dutch for a time supreme in the Channel, and in the following spring he fought bravely against the English fleet under Blake, Penn and Monk. In August, 1653, he engaged in another battle with the English, during which he was killed.

Trondhjem, *tron'yem,* a seaport of Norway, situated at the mouth of the Nid, on the Trondhjem Fjord. The city is quite strongly fortified, has a number of large warehouses and a cathedral, which is one of the finest in Norway. It has an academy of sciences, a public library of over 110,000 volumes and a museum of natural history collections. Its manufactures include machinery, rope, spirituous and malt liquors and tobacco. There are also large sugar refineries and shipyards. The town is an important commercial center and exports large quantities of fish, especially herring, and wood and woodenware. Population in 1910, 45,335.

Trophy, *tro'fy,* in antiquity, a monument or memorial in commemoration of some victory. It consisted of some of the arms and other spoils of a vanquished enemy, hung upon the trunk of a tree or a stone pillar by the victorious army. The custom of erecting trophies was most general among the Greeks, but it passed at length to the Romans. It was the practice, also, to have representations of trophies carved in stone or in bronze. In modern times trophies have been erected in churches and other public buildings, to commemorate victories or heroic action in war.

Trop'ic Bird or **Boat'swain,** a sea bird with long wings and two long tail-feathers. Its general plumage is white and satiny, and it is often tinged with pink, variegated by blackish patches above and by black marks near the eye. The tropic bird makes no real nest, but deposits

its egg in a hole or crevice in a cliff. It is wonderfully powerful on the wing and passes whole days in the air, without feeling the need of rest.

Tropics, in astronomy, two circles on the celestial sphere, whose distances from the equator are each about 23½°. The northern one touches the ecliptic at the sign Cancer, and it is therefore called the tropic of *Cancer*; the southern one is for a similar reason called the tropic of *Capricorn*. The sun's annual path in the heavens is bounded by these two circles, and they are called *tropics*, because when the sun, in its journey northward or southward, reaches either of them, it appears to turn back and travel in an opposite direction.

Geographically, the tropics are two parallels of latitude, each at the same distance from the terrestrial equator as the celestial tropics are from the celestial equator. The one north of the equator is called the tropic of *Cancer*, and that south of the equator is the tropic of *Capricorn*. Over these circles the sun is vertical when farthest north, or farthest south, that is, at the solstices, and the tropics include between them that portion of the globe called the torrid zone, a zone 47° wide, having the equator for its central line.

Troubadour, *troo'ba dorc*, a name given to a class of early poets who first appeared in Provence, in France. The troubadours were considered the inventors of a species of lyrical poetry, characterized by an almost entire devotion to the subject of romantic gallantry, and generally very complicated in regard to its meter and rhymes. The troubadours flourished from the eleventh to the latter part of the thirteenth century, their principal residence being the south of France, but they also lived in Catalonia, Aragon and North Italy. The most renowned among the troubadours were knights who cultivated music and poetry as an honorable accomplishment.

Trout, *trowt,* the common name of a group of fishes belonging to the salmon family, living in streams and fresh-water lakes. The common trout may be found in northern Europe and North America, in rivers and lakes and even in small streams. A trout weighing one pound is considered a good fish, and though a weight far in excess of that is frequent, many streams produce none nearly so large. The *speckled brook trout*, most highly prized of food fishes, was formerly found in large numbers in the streams of the New England states, northern New York, Michigan and Wisconsin, but it has been nearly exterminated, except in wild regions or in carefully guarded streams. Fish commissions are endeavoring to restock the waters of those states (See

170

Fish Culture). There are several species of lake trout in America, among the finest and largest of which is the *Mackinaw trout*. The

LAKE TROUT

North American lake trout attains a weight of more than 60 pounds.

Trouvere, *troo vair',* a name given to the ancient poets of northern France, corresponding to the *troubadour* of Provence. Their productions partake of a narrative, or epic, character, and thus they contrast broadly with the lyrical, amatory and more polished effusions of their southern rivals.

Troy or **Iliam,** an ancient city in the Troad, a territory in the northwest of Asia Minor, south of the western extremity of the Hellespont, rendered famous by Homer's epic of the *Iliad*. There have been various opinions regarding the site of the Homeric city, the most probable of which places ancient Troy at the head of the plain bounded by the modern river Mendereh, supposed to be the Scamander of Homer, and the Dombrek, probably the Homeric Simois. The Ilium of history was founded about 700 B. C. by Aeolic Greeks, and it was regarded as occupying the site of the ancient city, but this is doubtful. The ancient and legendary city, according to the Homeric story, reached its highest splendor when Priam was king; but the abduction of Helen, wife of Menelaus, king of Sparta, by Paris, one of Priam's sons, brought about its destruction. To revenge this outrage, all the Greek chiefs, afterward famous in history, banded themselves against the Trojans and their allies, and went against Troy with a great fleet. The first nine years of the war were spent by the Greeks in driving the Trojans and their allies within the walls of the capital. The tenth year brought about a quarrel between Achilles, the bravest of the Greeks, and Agamemnon, the Greek commander in chief, which proved for a time disastrous to their party, and which forms the subject of the *Iliad*. In the end the city was taken by means of a large, hollow, wooden horse, in which a number of the bravest of the Greek heroes concealed themselves, while the rest retired to their ships. Thinking that the Greeks had given up the siege, the Trojans incautiously drew the horse within the city and gave themselves up to revelry. The Greeks within the horse issued from their concealment, were joined by their companions without the walls, and Troy was taken and utterly destroyed. This is said to have occurred about 1184 B. C. Not only has the site of the ancient city been disputed, but the legends connected with it are held by some scholars to have no historical foundation; nor has this view been altered by the excavations of Schliemann and his discovery of the remains of a prehistoric city or cities at Hissarlik, the site of the historic Ilium. See HELEN; PARIS; AGAMEMNON; ACHILLES; ULYSSES; HECTOR; WOODEN HORSE.

Troy, N. Y., the county-seat of Rensselaer co., 150 mi. n. of New York City and 6 mi. above Albany, on the east bank of the Hudson River, at the head of navigation and opposite the outlets of the Erie and Champlain canals, and on the Boston & Maine, the Delaware & Hudson and the New York Central railroads. The city stretches along the river on a level alluvial plain, for more than six miles, and it rises to the east on a range of hills about 500 feet high, affording a fine residence section. There are about 100 miles of streets, nearly one-half of which are paved, and the park system includes about 140 acres. Oakwood Cemetery is a large, beautiful burying-ground, containing the graves of Gen. George H. Thomas and other noted men. A prominent feature is the Earl Memorial Chapel and crematory.

The principal educational institutions are the Emma Willard Seminary for the higher education of women and the Rensselaer Polytechnic Institute. The Hart Memorial Library is a fine structure of white marble. There are various charitable institutions, including the Troy and the Samaritan hospitals, Marshall Sanitarium, Troy Orphan Asylum, House of the Good Shepherd, a reformatory, the Day Home and several other homes and orphanages. The Second Presbyterian, Saint Paul's, Saint John's, Saint Mary's, First Presbyterian and Saint Peter's are among the most prominent churches. Some of the other important structures are the Federal building; the city hall; the savings bank building, with its music hall; Rensselaer Hotel; Union Passenger Station; Rowe Memorial Building; the Y. M. C. A.; the high school, and the state armory.

The leading industry is the manufacture of collars, cuffs and shirts. The city produces between eighty and ninety per cent of all the collars made in America. There is an extensive system of laundries, and the various iron and steel works produce laundry machinery, collar-making machinery, stoves, bells, valves, engineering instruments and other goods. The city also contains knitting, paper and flour mills, breweries, brickyards and other establishments. The state dam across the Hudson and the falls of two creeks furnish considerable water power. The financial institutions include one state and six national banks, two trust companies and one savings bank.

The town was laid out in 1787, and the present name was adopted two years later. It was incorporated as a village in 1794 and was chartered as a city in 1816. During the Revolution the American army encamped on the island at the mouth of the Mohawk River opposite Troy and built earthworks on the north side. During the War of 1812 a certain Samuel Willson was engaged in packing meat in barrels for the army. This gentleman was familiarly known as "Uncle Sam," and in connection with him has been given one version of the origin of our national nickname. The story is told that in reply to what was meant by the letters U. S., on one of these barrels of meat, the answer was jokingly given as "Uncle Sam." Population in 1900, 60,651. The village of Lansingburg, with a population of 12,595 in 1900, became a part of Troy the next year. Population in 1910, 76,813.

Troy, OHIO, the county-seat of Miami co., 20 mi. n. of Dayton, on the Cincinnati, Hamilton & Dayton, the Cleveland, Cincinnati, Chicago & Saint Louis and several electric railroads. The city is surrounded by an agricultural region and has a considerable trade in farm and dairy products. There are wagon and bent wood factories and lumber and flouring mills. The waterworks and electric light plant are owned and operated by the city. Population in 1910, 6122.

Troyes, trwah, a city of France, situated on the south bank of the Seine, 98 mi. e. s. e. of Paris. The city has a museum, containing valuable collections of art and natural history objects, and a public library of over 125,000 volumes. The leading industries consist of the manufacture of knit goods and other textiles. Population in 1901, 53,146.

Troy Weight, a weight chiefly used in weighing gold, silver and articles of jewelry. The troy pound contains 12 ounces; each ounce is divided into 20 pennyweights, and each pennyweight is equal to 24 grains. Hence, the pound contains 5760 grains, and the ounce, 480 grains. As the avoirdupois pound (the weight in general commercial use) contains 7000 grains, and the ounce 437½ grains, the troy pound is to the avoirdupois as 144 to 175, and the troy ounce to the avoirdupois, as 192 to 175.

Trudeau, *troo do'*, EDWARD LIVINGSTON (1848–   ), a prominent American physician, himself a sufferer from tuberculosis, who has lived in the Adirondacks for many years and has advocated the open air treatment of that disease in its incipient stages. His contributions to the periodical medical literature have been exceedingly numerous and valuable.

Truffle, *tru'f'l*, a fungus, growing underground. The common truffle is of a fleshy, fungous structure and roundish figure, without any visible root; it is of a dark color, approaching to black, and studded over with tubercles. It varies in size from that of a large plum to that of a large potato. It grows abundantly in some parts of England, Italy and the south of France. It is much sought after as an ingredient in certain highly-seasoned dishes. There being no appearance above ground to indicate the existence of the truffle, dogs are trained to find this fungus by the scent, and to scratch it up.

Trum'bull, JONATHAN (1710–1785), an American patriot and statesman, born at Lebanon, Conn., and educated at Harvard. He was successively judge, deputy governor and governor (1769–1783) of Connecticut and took a prominent part in forwarding the War of Independence. Washington placed great reliance on him and frequently consulted him; to this habit, and his phrase, "Let us hear what Brother Jonathan says," has been traced the name "Brother Jonathan," which is one of the nicknames of the United States.

Trumbull, LYMAN (1813–1896), an American jurist and political leader, born at Colchester, Conn. He taught school for a time, was admitted to the bar in 1837, removed to Belleville, Ill., was elected to the legislature, and in 1841 became secretary of state. He was elevated to the supreme bench of the state in 1848. In 1854 he was elected to Congress, and the following year he was chosen to the United States Senate, where he served continuously until 1873. He soon joined the Republican party, upheld the administration throughout the war and drafted the Thirteenth Amendment. He returned to the Democratic party after the war and voted against the impeachment of President Johnson. He acted with the Populists in 1894.

Trump'et, one of the oldest wind instruments of music. In its modern form it consists of a metal tube (usually brass, sometimes silver), about eight feet long, doubled up in the form of a parabola, and expanding into a bell-shaped end. The instrument is sounded through a cup-shaped mouthpiece. The trumpet tuned on C produces with great power and brilliancy the following series of tones in an ascending scale: C in the second space of the bass clef, G, C, E, G, B, C, D, E and G.

Trustee', in law, a person to whom property is legally committed for the benefit of some other party or parties or for some special purpose. The person for whom, or in whose favor, the trustee holds the estate, or any interest therein, is called the *beneficiary*. No one is compelled to undertake a trust, but if he once accept, he cannot renounce it unless the trust deed contains a provision enabling him to do so, or unless a competent court grants him a discharge, or unless he receives the consent of all those beneficially interested in the estate. Trustees are liable for the consequences of any breach of trust, however innocent, and the estate of a trustee deceased, who has misapplied the trust fund, is liable for the deficiency; but generally speaking, the law only requires of a trustee the same amount of care and prudence he would be expected to display in managing his own affairs. Breach of trust is in most states a crime. Where there are several trustees, each is liable for his own acts and receipts only, unless there is common agreement.

Trusts. This term was originally applied to associations, formed by the transference, by several corporations, of stock to a board of trustees, who thereafter control the policies of all the members of the association. It now has a broader meaning, including not only associations of corporations, but large single corporations or groups of individuals, who possess power to regulate to some extent the market for certain products, and to maintain, within certain limits, prices upon those products. Trusts are of comparatively modern growth, being the result of industrial conditions which have appeared within a half-century. The chief cause of their rise is the great loss occasioned by unlimited competition in industry, due to such wastes as the maintenance of separate bodies of traveling salesmen, separate advertising accounts and separate systems of supervision. Among other influences toward the centralization of capital have been (1) the desire to lessen the cost of production by the consolidation of separate factories, thereby enabling the managers to buy their raw materials in great quantities and, therefore, at a large reduction in price; (2) the personal influence of promoters and financiers, whose profits from such consolidations are often immense; (3) the increased profits resulting from the utilization of the ordinary waste in the manufacture of by-products; (4) the receipt of certain privileges from the government, such as those afforded by the patent laws, the system of protection and bounties.

The first step toward the development of the trust system was so-called "pooling." Under this arrangement a number of independent producers made agreements as to methods of producing and selling, but retained the management of their own factories. In the United States this was soon held to be an unreasonable restraint of trade and therefore contrary to the common law, and in its place arose the real "trust." Under this system the stock of each concern was assigned to a central board of trustees, who voted the stock and therefore determined the policies of the individual producers, trust certificates being issued to the members of the association, in proportion to the value of the stock assigned, and the profits of the whole association being divided *pro rata* on these certificates. The first company to be promoted upon this basis was the Standard Oil Trust, about 1882. But this method left opportunities for waste and inefficient management, and so the next and last step was taken, in which a new company was organized, which bought up the larger part of the stock of each of the constituent corporations. The officers of the new company are therefore able to vote the stock of each of the members and can control, in a much more definite and satisfactory way, their policies.

Within a comparatively few years the movement toward combinations of capital has been greatly accelerated, until in 1900 it is estimated that fully one-fifth of the whole industrial capital of the United States was controlled by so-called trusts. In some respects this tendency to combination has beneficial results, if the power thus gained is handled with care for public, as well as private, interests. In fact, from the standpoint of capital alone, it is almost an unmixed benefit, since it utilizes a far greater proportion of the raw material, at a much less cost than formerly, and at the same time makes the market more stable and certain. One of the greatest

perils connected with this development is the growth of monopoly. For instance, the United States Steel Corporation, which was organized but a few years ago, controls not only a vast majority of the important steel manufacturing plants of the country, but has gained possession of the greatest iron mines and is allied with the strongest railroad systems. Through these it has a power of suppressing competition and of regulating the market, which is a real and growing danger, unless properly curbed. The establishment of monopoly means the maintenance of the power to control prices. This is limited by the natural law that the price cannot be raised above the point where the people will buy. On the other hand, if the monopoly covers a necessary of life, or even a product deemed necessary by a large class of the people, the price may be raised almost indefinitely, without materially reducing sales. The power of the trusts to control wages and conditions of employment also presents important dangers, since as the power of the trusts is extended to a larger and larger proportion of the industry of the country, labor has less and less opportunity to transfer from one employment to another and is therefore increasingly dependent upon capital for existence. The natural result is the development of labor unions (See LABOR ORGANIZATIONS).

The remedies most commonly proposed for these evils are three in number: (1) the application of the common law rule against conspiracy in restraint of trade; (2) the regulation, by state law, of corporations chartered and working within the state; (3) the passage of Federal laws more closely regulating interstate commerce.

The United States government has taken active measures in recent years to curb the trusts. In May, 1911, the Supreme Court handed down an important decision, commanding the dissolution of the Standard Oil Company, on the ground that this company had engaged in conspiracy in restraint of trade. The officials of the trust were given six months in which to complete the dissolution. See CORPORATION.

Tryp'sin, a ferment which occurs in the secretion of the pancreas. It can be taken from the pancreatic juice in the same way that pepsin can be taken from the gastric juice. It has the power of changing proteids into peptones (See PEPTONES; PROTEIDS). Extracts containing trypsin are sometimes administered to those whose digestion is weak; but their most valuable application is for the predigestion of foods.

Tsar. See CZAR.

Tschaikowsky, *chi kov'ske*, PETER ILYTCH (1840–1893), a Russian composer, born at Wolkinsk. He was educated for the law, but in 1862 began the study of music in the Conservatory at Saint Petersburg. In 1866 he was professor in the Conservatory of Moscow, and after 1878 he devoted himself entirely to composition. He visited America in 1890 and conducted the production of his own compositions. His works disclose deep patriotism in both theme and treatment, and they have a light, fanciful character which is exceedingly attractive. Among his important compositions are *Manfred* and *The Tempest*, and the songs *Longing* and *Disappointment*.

Tset'se Fly, a South African insect, akin to the gadfly, whose bite is often fatal to horses, dogs and cows, but is not poisonous to man and wild beasts. The insect is little larger than the common house fly.

TSETSE FLY

Tuamotu, *too a mo'too*, **Islands.** See LOW ARCHIPELAGO.

Tuaregs, *too ah'regz*, wandering people, supposed to be connected with the Berbers in their origin, inhabiting the middle part of the Sahara Desert. They are of a handsome and muscular physique, of warlike habit, and they are followers of Mohammed. Their numbers are estimated at 300,000.

Tuberculosis, *too bur'cu lo'sis*, or **Consump'tion**, a widespread disease that has been known and recognized from ancient times, and that causes about one-seventh of the entire number of deaths in the whole world. The disease is highly infectious. As the bacillus which causes it is almost always present in the air, it is probable that few people, especially in cities, escape infection. Fortunately, however, unless there is some weakness or predisposition toward the disease, the human organism is able to throw off the infection or so to restrict its action that little harm results. Nevertheless, there is no disease whose ravages are so severe or on which so much study is now being placed by scientists, physicians and all interested in public welfare. In 1882 Koch discovered the cause of tuberculosis to be a bacillus, and since that time much has been done to better the condition of consumptives and to restrict the spread of the disease (See GERM THEORY OF DISEASE).

The infectious germ is thrown out of the lungs of a consumptive in the sputum, or spit, and it is not killed by drying. Accordingly, it is taken up by the air in the form of dust and carried anywhere and everywhere. It follows that every precaution should be taken to destroy the sputa of consumptives and the discharges from tuberculous sores; for while consumption is in the popular mind a disease of the lungs, yet it may and does affect any part of the body where the bacilli find lodgment. Tuberculosis of the bones, of the stomach and of the intestines is not uncommon. The disease is not confined to human beings, but may affect cattle, chickens, other domestic animals and, especially, wild animals kept in captivity. Any one of these may serve as a means for distributing the infectious germ. No specific has been found for consumption, though many have been offered to the public. Doctor Koch's studies led him to advocate the use of a serum, or antitoxin, but it has not proved altogether successful. An open air life, with plenty of exercise, in a dry region not subjected to sudden changes of temperature, will do much to mitigate the severity of the disease, and sometimes it will effect a cure. See SERUM THERAPY.

Tuberose, *tube'roze*, a plant, originally brought from the East, now largely cultivated in American gardens, both for its odor and for its beautiful white flowers. The flowers are waxy and are borne in a loose spike, with practically no stems. The tuberose has a bulbous root and an upright, branchless stem, growing to the height of three or four feet. It is cultivated for the perfumers in France and Italy.

Tuc'son *too son'*, ARIZONA, the county seat of Pima co., 130 miles southeast of Phoenix. The city is located on a wide mesa at an altitude of 2390 feet and has a very dry climate. The modern part of the city is well built, with attractive residences, good hotels and public buildings, while the old section is typically Mexican in construction. Tucson is the seat of the University of Arizona and has good public schools, a high school, several sectarian schools, a Presbyterian boarding school for Indians, a Carnegie public library, a Roman Catholic hospital and sanitarium and the Desert Botanical Laboratory, erected by the Carnegie Institution of Washington. It is the largest city in Arizona, is located in an agricultural and grazing region and makes large shipments of cattle. The chief industrial establishments are the railroad shops of the Southern Pacific, flouring mills, ice factory, lumber yards and stockyards. Tucson was probably first settled about 1776, by the Spaniards, when it was known as the Presidio de San Agustin del Tuguison. It was a part of the Gadsden Purchase of 1853, and from 1867 to 1877 it was the capital of the territory. The city has grown rapidly since 1900. Population in 1910, 13,193.

Tucuman, *too koo mahn'*, or **San Miguel de Tucuman,** a city of Argentina, situated 94 mi. n. w. of Santiago, near the foot of a mountain range, on the Upper Dulce River. It is connected by railway with Buenos Ayres, and has a cathedral, a normal school, a national college and other educational institutions. The industries include trade in live stock and the manufacture of spirituous liquors. Population in 1912, 78,695.

Tu'dor, the family name of an English royal line, which reigned from 1485 to 1603. It was founded by Owen Tudor of Wales, who married the widowed queen of Henry V. The first of the Tudor sovereigns was Henry VII; the last was Elizabeth. The reigns of this family were noteworthy for the almost absolute authority exercised. See HENRY VII; HENRY VIII; MARY I; ELIZABETH.

Tudor Style, in architecture, a name frequently applied to the latest Gothic style in England, being the last phase of the Perpendicular, and sometimes known as Florid Gothic. The period of this style is from 1400 to 1537; but the term is sometimes extended so as to include the Elizabethan period, also, which brings it down to 1603. It is the result of the influence of Renaissance styles of the Continent on the Perpendicular style. It is characterized by a flat arch, shallow moldings and a profusion of paneling on the walls.

Tuesday, *tuze'day*, the third day of the week. *Shrove Tuesday* is the Tuesday before Lent, so called because of the custom of making confession on that date.

Tu'fa, the name originally given to a kind of volcanic rock, consisting of accumulations of scoria and ashes about the crater of a volcano. The name is now applied to any coarse, porous rock, cemented into a solid mass by lime or silica. Calcareous tufa is formed by the evaporation of water containing a large quantity of carbonate of lime in solution. It often contains leaves, twigs and other objects around which it has formed.

Tufts College, an institution of higher learning at Medford, Mass., founded in 1852 under the auspices of the Universalists. It comprises a college of liberal arts, and medical, dental and theological departments. It maintains a biological laboratory at South Harpsweed, Me., and the Barnum Museum of Natural History, the gift of the late P. T. Barnum, is especially rich in skeletons and mounted skins of animals. There are 170 instructors and over 1100 students. The library contains over 63,000 volumes.

Tuileries, *tweel re'*, a famous palace, on the right bank of the Seine, in Paris. Catharine de Medici, the wife of Henry II, began the building; Henry IV extended it, and Louis XIV enlarged and completed it. During the Revolution of 1830, the palace was sacked. It was restored to its former splendor by Louis Philippe, but in 1848 it was again pillaged. In 1871 it was finally destroyed by the communists.

Tulane, *tu lane'*, **University of Louisiana,** THE, an institution of higher learning, located at New Orleans. It has an interesting and unique history. It was established in 1847 by the legislature of the state. It continued to receive state support and to be known as the University of Louisiana until 1884. At this time Mr. Paul Tulane gave to administrators appointed by him $1,000,000, which was to be used for the higher education of the people of Louisiana. Mr. Tulane's administrators decided not to found an independent college or university, but to use the entire income from his bequest for the development and maintenance of the already established University of Louisiana. They did so on the condition that the state would forever exempt the property of the Tulane Educational Fund from taxation. The state agreed to do this, and in recognition of the munificent gift of Mr. Tulane the institution was called *The Tulane University of Louisiana*.

Tulane now has a productive endowment of nearly $5,500,000. The institution has invested, in grounds, buildings and equipment, nearly $2,500,000. Its medical department is one of the most famous schools of medicine in America. It is affiliated with the state Charity Hospital, one of the great hospitals of the world, which is supported at a cost of $150,000 annually. The institution in all departments has 216 professors and instructors, and nearly 2500 students. The H. Sophie Newcomb Memorial College, the woman's department of the university, has an endowment of $3,000,000, being the best endowed college for women in the world. The total annual income of the institution is approximately $375,000, and it has occasionally received special grants from the state.

Tu'lip, a genus of plants, belonging to the lily family, growing wild in the warmer parts of Europe and Asia Minor, but now extensively cultivated in gardens everywhere. There are about forty species, of which the most noted is the *common garden tulip,* a native of the eastern shores of the Mediterranean. Upward of one thousand varieties of this plant have been enumerated. The *wild tulip* has yellow flowers and blooms in April and May. The sweet-scented tulip is prized for its fragrance and is grown in the United States.

COMMON TULIPS

Other species are the *scarlet tulip,* with large, purplish spots, surrounded with yellow at the base; the *dwarf tulip*; the *clusiana,* with low, delicate pink and white flowers, and the *Turkestan tulip,* one of the largest and showiest, generally of a vivid scarlet color.

Tulip Tree, a tree, native of the United States, which bears a flower resembling a yellow tulip, each division of which is marked by an orange spot. It is one of the most magnificent of the forest trees of the United States, and next to the plane tree it is the largest of our deciduous trees. It is found from New England to Florida and is known variously as the poplar, whitewood or canoe-wood. Its wood is light, compact and fine-grained, and it is employed for various useful purposes.

Tulsa, Okla., the county-seat of Tulsa co., 118 mi. n. e. of Oklahoma City, on the Arkansas River and the Frisco, Missouri, Kansas & Texas and other railroads. Tulsa lies in a rich agricultural country, but its rapid growth has been due largely to its proximity to the oil and gas fields and coal mines. Glen Pool oil district is probably the richest in the world. Tulsa has many modern homes, fine business blocks, commodious churches, artistic school buildings and thriving factories. The general offices of some of the large oil companies are located in Tulsa The Harry Kendall College, a Presbyterian institution, is located here. Population in 1910, 18,182.

Tumor, *tu'mur,* a surgical term, which in its widest sense means a swelling of any part of the body; more strictly, however, it implies a permanent enlargement, occasioned by a new growth, and not a mere increase in size of a natural part. Tumors may be considered in two well-defined classes, *simple,* benign, or innocent, tumors, and *malignant* tumors. The substance of tumors of the first class resembles some of the tissues of the body; they increase gradually in size, produce little inconvenience, except that which is occasioned by their size, and may be completely cured by a simple surgical operation. Malignant tumors usually terminate fatally.

Tundra, *toon'dra,* a moss-covered plain, bordering on the Arctic Ocean in North America and Siberia. Most of the surface is level or slightly undulating and is swampy. The tundra is covered with a dense growth of mosses and lichens, and during the short summer it bears many small and bright-flowering plants, together with a few ferns and rushes. In some localities the surface is broken by mountains and hills, and in other parts lakes are found. In reality the tundra is a vast peatbog (See Peat), and the annual growth of vegetation is due to the fact that the soil remains frozen, except for about a foot beneath the surface. It is estimated that the entire area of the tundra is from 300,000 to 400,000 square miles. See Plain.

Tung'sten, a heavy metal, discovered in 1781. It has a grayish-white color and considerable luster. It is brittle, nearly as hard as steel, and less fusible than manganese. The ores of this metal are the native tungstate of lime and the tungstate of iron and manganese, which latter is also known as *wolfram.*

Tu'nic, an ancient form of garment, in constant use among the Greeks and Romans. It was worn by both sexes, under the *toga* and the *palla,* and was fastened by a girdle or belt about the waist. The word is popularly applied to any long, loose garment hung from the shoulder and caught at the waist by a belt.

Tuning Fork, a steel instrument, with two prongs, which, when set in vibration, give forth a musical sound of a certain fixed pitch. The ordinary tuning fork sounds only one note, usually the middle, or tenor, C, or the A below it. Some are made with a slider on each prong, which, according as it is moved up or down, regulates the pitch of the note produced.

Tu'nis, a French protectorate in northern Africa, bounded on the n. and e. by the Mediterranean Sea, on the s. e. by Tripoli and on the w.

by Algeria. Its area is about 51,000 sq. mi. Its principal river is the Mejerdah. Between this stream and the northern coast, the country is fertile and generally cultivated. The chief crops are wheat, barley and oats, among the cereals, and olives, lemons, oranges and grapes, among the fruits. Other products of some importance are tobacco and cotton. The country has an agreeable and healthful climate; and since its occupation by the French its commerce has increased, and means of transit have been greatly improved. Primary schools have also been established. There are but few manufacturing industries. The population is estimated at 2,000,000 and consists chiefly of Moors, Arabs, Berbers, Jews, negroes, French and Italians. Nearly all of the people are Mohammedans. The country has about 450 miles of railways, which connect the principal towns with one another and with the coast cities of Algeria. The chief city is Tunis, the capital.

Tun'kers. See DUNKERS.

Tun'nel, an underground passage cut through a hill, a rock or any eminence, or cut under a river or a town, to carry a canal, a road or a railway. In the construction of canals and railways, tunnels are frequently excavated, in order to preserve the desired level and for various other local causes. Tunnels, when not pierced through solid rock, have usually an arched roof and are lined with brickwork or masonry. The sectional form of the passage is various. Among the greatest works of this kind are the tunnels of Saint Gothard, Mount Cenis, the Arlberg and the Simplon. In America the Hoosac Tunnel, the Cascade Tunnel in Washington and those constructed under the Hudson and East rivers by the Pennsylvania railroad, to provide a means of entrance for its trains into New York City, are the most important. The two Pennsylvania tunnels under the Hudson River from Weehawken to New York have an inside diameter of 21 feet 2 inches, and a length under water of 6118 feet. These tunnels were completed in 1910. The Hudson and Manhattan Railroad's tunnels from Jersey City to New York have an inside diameter of 15 feet 3 inches. All of these tunnels are really tubes made of cast iron rings with an average thickness of 16 to 20 inches.

Tun'ny, the largest species of mackerel. These fish live in shoals in almost all the seas of the warmer and temperate parts of the earth. They are taken in immense quantities on the Mediterranean coasts, where the fishing is chiefly carried on. The flesh, which is delicate and

somewhat resembles veal, has been highly valued since ancient times. The common tunny attains a length of ten feet and sometimes exceeds half a ton in weight. Its color is a dark blue on the upper parts and silvery white below. The American tunny is found on the coast from New York to Nova Scotia, and also in the Pacific Ocean off Santa Catalina, where it is known as the tuna. See MACKEREL.

Tu'pelo. See BLACK GUM.

Tup'per, CHARLES, Sir (1821–   ), a Canadian statesman, born at Amherst, Nova Scotia. He studied medicine in Edinburgh at the Royal College of Surgeons and began practice in his native village. He was a member of the executive council and provincial secretary of Nova Scotia from 1857 to 1860. In 1864 he was made prime minister of that province. In 1870 he became a member and president of the Privy Council of the Dominion of Canada, and after 1872 he held, successively, the posts of minister of inland revenue, minister of customs, minister of public works, minister of railways and canals. He later represented Canada as high commissioner at London, and for a time in 1896 he was premier. In 1900 he retired to private life. He was knighted in 1879 and was created baronet in 1888.

Tupper, MARTIN FARQUHAR (1810–1889), an English poet. He was educated at the Charterhouse and under private tutors, and at nineteen he went to Christ Church, Oxford. A stammer hindered him from taking orders; so, after graduating in 1831, he entered Lincoln's Inn, and in 1835 he was called to the bar. He never practiced law, however, but turned to literature. One of his works, *Proverbial Philosophy*, in verse, was very popular and brought him and his publisher a profit of about £10,000 apiece. The poem had, however, no merits of style or of contents.

Tura'nian, a name given to a branch of the human family whose languages seem to have been derived from the same stock. The term was applied, originally, by the Iranians to the people living north of them. The Turanians may be divided into five great classes, one chiefly European and including the Lapps, Finns and Hungarians; a second including the Turks of southeastern Europe and southwestern Asia; a third including the Manchus. The two other groups are of less importance.

Tur'ban, a form of head-dress worn by the Orientals. It varies in form in different nations and among different classes of the same nation. It consists of two parts, a cap without brim, fitted to the head, and a sash, scarf or shawl, usually of cotton or linen, wound

TURBANS

about the cap and sometimes hanging down the neck.

Turbine Wheel or **Turbine**, *tur'bin*, a water-wheel which the water enters and leaves at all points on its circumference. The turbine wheel is enclosed in a close-fitting iron box and is usually attached to a vertical shaft. It operates on the principle of the Barker's mill (See BARKER'S MILL). The circumference of the wheel is provided with floats, all of which point in the same direction. The sides of the box in which the

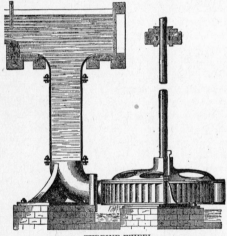

TURBINE WHEEL

wheel is enclosed are called partitions and in number are equal to the floats of the wheel; they point in the opposite direction. The water is admitted to the box through a vertical or oblique iron pipe, called the penstock. The wheel is placed at the lowest possible point, since the power exerted depends upon the pressure of the water. When the water flows through the box, the floats on the edges give it a direction opposite to that in which the floats on the wheel point. As the current of water strikes these floats they tend to turn it in the opposite direction, and the reaction upon the floats causes the wheel to re-

volve. The turbine is the most powerful water-wheel in use, as it utilizes nearly all of the power employed. The largest turbines are found at Niagara Falls.

Tur'bot, a well-known flat fish. It is short and broad and brown on the upper side, which is usually the left side. It sometimes reaches a

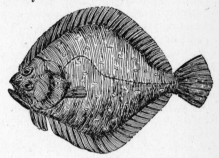

TURBOT

weight of from 70 to 90 pounds. The *American,* or *spotted, turbot,* common on the coasts of New England and New York, may weigh 20 pounds. It is one of the most highly valued of food fishes. See FLATFISH; FLOUNDER.

Turenne, *tu ren'*, HENRI DE LATOUR D'AU-VERGNE, Viscount de (1611–1675), marshal of France, son of the duke of Bouillon and of Elizabeth, princess of Nassau-Orange. He learned the art of war under his uncles, Maurice and Henry of Nassau, in the Dutch service, entered the service of France in 1630, served with distinction in Germany and north Italy and in 1643 received the command of the army of the Rhine in the Thirty Years' War. His successes in this post, as in the Battle of Nördlingen (1645), hastened the close of the war. During the disturbance of the Fronde the victories of Turenne over his former colleague, Condé, greatly aided the French court. In the war against Spain he also distinguished himself, and when war was renewed with Spain in 1667 he conquered Flanders in three months. In the Dutch War of 1672 he had the chief command and showed himself no more noteworthy in his victories than in his ability to repair misfortunes. He was killed while making preparations to engage Montecuccoli.

Turgenieff, *toor gen'yef,* IVAN SERGEYE-VITCH (1818–1883), a celebrated Russian novelist. He was the son of a wealthy nobleman and was educated at Moscow, Saint Petersburg and Berlin. In 1842 he obtained an appointment in the ministry of the interior; but, having written an article displeasing to the authorities, he was shortly afterward banished to his paternal estate.

For some years he led the life of a country gentleman, but he managed to gain a sympathetic and intimate acquaintance with Russian peasant life. His first important publication was translated into English under the title of *Annals of a Sportsman*. It was followed by a great number of short tales and dramas, contributed principally to Russian periodicals. His earliest novels were *Nobles' Nest, or Liza* and *On the Eve*. A powerful politico-social novel, *Fathers and Sons*, was published in 1862 and met with much adverse criticism in Russia. As a result of this criticism his later works showed an even deeper pessimism than had been evident in his earlier writings. These later works include *Smoke, Spring Floods* and *Virgin Soil*, all of which have been translated into English. Turgenieff is ranked with the greatest masters of fiction.

Turgot, *toor go'*, ANNE ROBERT JACQUES, Baron de l'Aulne (1727–1781), a French statesman. He was educated for the Church, but renouncing this purpose he studied law, and in 1771 he was appointed intendant at Limoges, which post he occupied for twelve years. Shortly after the accession of Louis XVI, in 1774, Turgot was appointed comptroller-general of France, and he showed great ability in dealing with the disordered finances of the country. His attempt to make the nobility and clergy contribute to the expenses of government in the same proportion as the common people made him very unpopular and led to his withdrawal.

Tu'rin, a city of Italy, situated on the Po, at its confluence with the Dora Riparia, 79 mi. w. s. w. of Milan. The city occupies a beautiful site, in the midst of a plain, and is surrounded by mountains. It is well laid out, the streets cross each other at right angles, and in the center of the city is the Piazza Castello, on which is the Madama Palace, an old castle built in the Middle Ages, and a royal palace, which dates from the middle of the seventeenth century. Other buildings of interest are the cathedral, dating from the fifteenth century; the Church of San Dominico, dating from the fourteenth century, and the Royal Burial Church, located on a hill east of the city. Turin contains a number of monuments, the most important being a building known as the Mole Antonelliana, erected to the memory of Victor Emmanuel II and used as a museum. It is a square structure, resembling a tower, and is surmounted by a gilded statue, the whole rising to a height of 538 feet. Another monument to Victor Emmanuel is found in the Victor Emmanuel Square, and a third commemorates the completion of the Mount Cenis Tunnel. There are also a number of other monuments of less importance. The educational institutions include the university, with a library of about 300,000 volumes; the Museo Civico, with an important collection of sculptures and paintings; the academy of sciences, with its museum of antiquities, and an art gallery, noted for its valuable collection of paintings. There is also an agricultural college, a military academy, a conservatory of music and an industrial museum. The city maintains several hospitals and an institution for the blind. The manufactures include silk goods, machinery, iron and steel products, porcelain ware, musical instruments, jewelry and chocolate. Turin was the capital of Italy from 1861 to 1865. Population in 1911, 427,106.

Turk'estan', the name given to a large area in the interior of Asia, extending to Siberia and Mongolia on the n., to the Gobi desert on the e., to Tibet, India and Bokhara on the s., and to the Caspian Sea on the w. Some of the boundaries are indefinite, but the region is divided politically into Eastern, or Chinese, Turkestan, and Western, or Russian, Turkestan.

CHINESE TURKESTAN. This country covers an area of 550,350 square miles and has a population estimated at 1,200,000. It includes the Chinese Province of Sin-tsiang and is divided into two large divisions by the extension of the Tian-Shan Mountains; that portion south of the mountains is sometimes known as Kashgaria, and the portion on the north, as Dzungaria. The northern portion has an average altitude of from 3000 to 4000 feet, and the inhabitants are found on the near-by plains and foothills of the mountains, where the fertile land lies. The summers are hot, but in the west the winters are sufficiently cold to bring frost and snow, though in the east snow seldom falls and there is considerable rain. The chief products are wheat, millet, oil-seeds and cotton. Hemp, flax and dye plants are raised, and grapes, melons, pomegranates and some other fruits ripen. The mulberry tree thrives, and considerable silk is produced, but stock raising is the chief industry, and large herds of horses, camels, sheep and cattle are kept. Many of these are exported.

Chinese Turkestan has a large trade, principally with Tibet, China, Kashmir and Russia. The great caravan route from Peking to Siberia passes through this country and follows the line of oases, or wells. The inhabitants are Kirghizes, Kalmucks, Dungans and Kara-Kirghizes, nearly all of these nationalities having originated from the mingling of Turks with Aryans. Kashmir is one of the most important towns and is the chief center of trade with Russia.

RUSSIAN TURKESTAN. This country includes the territories of Samarkand, Ferghana, Syr-Darya and Semiryetchensk, and extends westward from Eastern Turkestan to the Aral Sea and thence to the Caspian. The eastern portion is high, and the surrounding mountains are crowned with perpetual snow; but toward the west the surface descends rapidly, until at the Caspian Sea it is 80 feet below the Mediterranean. The chief rivers are the Amu-Darya and the Syr-Darya, flowing into the Aral Sea. A great part of the country belongs to the Asiatic plain, which extends westward into European Russia. The climate is subject to great extremes of heat and cold. In the summer the thermometer sometimes rises as high as 115°, while in the winter it falls to 25° below zero. During the rainy season the surface is covered with a growth of vegetation which reaches maturity in a short time. The sections along the rivers are irrigated by water courses, and wherever water can be obtained, good crops are grown. Wheat, barley, rice, sugar cane, melons and garden vegetables, as well as fruits of various sorts, are raised in paying quantities. The country is traversed by a number of caravan routes, and the Trans-Caspian railway connects the important towns with one another and with the centers of trade in Russia. The inhabitants are Turkomans, Kirghizes and Russians. The population is estimated at between 5,000,000 and 6,000,000. Tashkent is the chief town and the seat of government.

Turkey, a large game bird of the pheasant family. The origin of its name is uncertain, as it has no connection with Turkey or the Turks. It is a native of North America and was introduced into Europe in the sixteenth century by travelers returning from the New World. Wild turkeys are still found in some American forests, where they feed on berries, fruits, and insects. Their plumage is of golden bronze, with showy violet and green variations. A full-grown male usually weighs from twelve to twenty-five pounds, but the females are smaller. The domesticated turkey resembles the wild turkey, but its plumage is less brilliant in coloring. The turkey builds a nest, lined with leaves, in a hollow on the ground. The eggs, usually eight to twelve at a setting, vary from white to pale buff, spotted evenly with brown, and are more than twice the size of a hen's egg. See color plate, *Game Birds,* accompanying article GAME.

Turkey or **The Ottoman Empire,** a country occupying the southeastern part of Europe, western Asia, portions of northern Africa, and several islands in the Mediterranean Sea. Its boundaries are very irregular, and some of them are not definitely determined; hence, any figures concerning its area and population must be considered as estimates. The following table gives such estimates, according to the latest authorities, showing the possessions, area and population in each of the continents:

POSSESSIONS*	AREA IN SQUARE MILES	POPULATION
Immediate possessions:		
Europe..................	10,000	3,000,000
Asia.....................	693,610	21,000,000
Dependencies:		
Cyprus	3,710	274,108
Samos..................	180	54,840
Egypt	400,000	11,189,978
Total	1,107,500	32,518,926

*The possessions as here listed were held by Turkey at the end of the Balkan War.

The dependencies shown in the above table are practically independent of the Turkish government, excepting that they pay an annual tribute to the sultan. The Empire is usually divided into European Turkey, Asiatic Turkey and African possessions.

EUROPEAN TURKEY. At the beginning of the nineteenth century Turkey in Europe comprised the whole of the Balkan Peninsula. In the course of the next hundred years Turkey lost practically the whole of these possessions. At the close of the Balkan War there remained only Constantinople and Adrianople, with a small strip of 10,000 square miles. This strip is bounded on the north and west by Bulgaria, and on the south by the Aegean Sea, the Strait of Dardanelles and the Sea of Marmora, and on the east by the Black Sea and the Bosporus. The country is generally mountainous, except for the broad valley of the Maritza River, which flows into the Aegean Sea.

ASIATIC TURKEY. Asiatic Turkey contains by far the largest part of the sultan's dominions. It includes Anatolia, or the Peninsula of Asia Minor, and extends eastward as far as Persia. It is bounded on the n. by the Black Sea and Transcaucasia, on the e. by Persia, on the s. by Arabia and the Mediterranean Sea and on the w. by the Mediterranean. These boundaries apply only to the compact portion of the country.

Two long, narrow arms extend southward, one on the east of Arabia, bordering the western shores of the Persian Gulf; the other, a continuation of the country bordering the eastern coast of the Mediterranean, extends southward the entire length of the Arabian Sea and includes the provinces of Hadjaz and Yemen. This region is about 1600 miles long and 160 miles wide.

Asia Minor is a mountainous plateau, with the Taurus Mountains on the south and numerous smaller ranges extending across it in various directions. The extreme eastern part of Asiatic Turkey contains the great valley of the Euphrates, beyond which the country is more or less mountainous, though no very high altitudes are reached. This region contains a few large lakes, among them Lake Urumiah and Lake Van Salt. The Euphrates and the Tigris, draining into the Persian Gulf, are the most important streams of Asiatic Turkey.

AFRICAN POSSESSIONS. The African possessions directly subject to Turkey are Tripoli and Bengazi. While Egypt is considered a Turkish province, its relations to the sultan are very slight, and it is practically under the control of the British government. This is also true of the island of Cyprus.

CLIMATE. The wide extent of the Ottoman Empire gives it a great variety of climate, in regions far separated from one another. The climate of European Turkey is similar to that of other countries bordering upon the Mediterranean, except that the northeastern portions are subject to winds from the north and have colder winters and more snow than other countries of southern Europe. The northern part of Asia Minor also has cold and damp winters, but along the western and southern shores the climate is salubrious and admits of the cultivation of semitropical products. In the interior, especially on the highlands, the winters are somewhat severe. Much of this interior also lacks moisture and partakes largely of the nature of a desert. The southern extensions along the Persian Gulf and Red Sea have a hot, dry climate.

MINERAL RESOURCES. European Turkey has but few mineral deposits of any importance, but Asiatic Turkey is rich in minerals. These include chrome, silver, lead ore, zinc, which is found on the shores of the Black Sea, manganese ore, antimony ore, copper, borax, meerschaum, emery, asphalt and coal, which is mined to a limited extent on the coast of the Black Sea, near Heraclea. Petroleum is found in the middle Tigris valley and in a number of places in Asia Minor, as well as on the north coast of the Sea of Marmora. The island of Rhodes contains valuable deposits of kaolin. Notwithstanding the abundance of mineral resources, the condition of the people and country is such that scarcely any of these deposits are exploited. In 1902 there were only 60 mines in operation in the entire Empire, and these were operated on a small scale.

Agriculture is the chief occupation of the inhabitants, but it is in a backward state, and the most primitive methods are employed. The land is held under four different forms of tenure—crown lands, the income of which belongs to the sultan; Church lands, or pious foundations, the income from which goes to the support of the Church; crown grants, or crown lands, which are rented to the occupants, and freehold property, or land owned by citizens. The last is by far the smallest portion of land under tillage. Because of oppressive taxes, one-tenth of all products not necessary for the support of a family being required for the Church, and other assessments being made for the support of the government, there is but little encouragement to agriculture. The occupants of the land are generally in the extremes of poverty and the depths of ignorance. The climate and soil are well suited to agriculture, and under favorable conditions large crops might be raised. The chief products are tobacco, cereals of all kinds, cotton, figs, almonds, nuts, grapes, olives and all varieties of fruit. Coffee, madder, opium and gums are also raised and exported. Large areas are covered with forests of pine, fir, cedar, oak, larch and other timber trees, and some timber is produced.

Manufactures are limited and are carried on on a small scale. The chief industries consist of the weaving of textiles, particularly silks, carpets and rugs, and the manufacture of attar of roses, wine, leather, paper and some glassware; but in many of these industries the native inhabitants have been obliged to yield to the competition of the machine-made goods of other countries. Several attempts have been made to establish factories on the modern plan, but owing to the ignorance and superstition of the people and the opposition of the government, the enterprises have not met with success.

TRANSPORTATION. The leading seaports, Constantinople and Saloniki, have railway communication with European cities. There are also railways connecting Smyrna, in Asia Minor, with Scutari, on the Bosporus, and several interior towns of the neighboring provinces. Roads are very poor or entirely lacking; hence the facilities for transportation from the interior are entirely inadequate to the demands of the country. Most of the trade is maritime. The chief seaports are Constantinople, Saloniki, Smyrna, Scutari and Beirut. The exports consist largely of silks, carpets, rugs, wool, mohair, raisins, opium, figs, coffee, olive oil, drugs, licorice, sponges and salt fish. The internal trade is almost wholly in the hands of Greeks and Armenians.

INHABITANTS AND LANGUAGE. The Turkish Empire contains a large number of nationalities. In European Turkey about one-half of the inhabitants are descendants of the Osmanli Turks, though they are of a mixed blood, crossed by intermarrying with Slavs, Greeks and Albanians. The remainder of the people in this part of the country are Kurds, Greeks and Jews; but in Asiatic Turkey the Turks predominate, However, these vary quite widely among themselves, being offsprings of Tartars and other races. In the southern part of Asiatic Turkey the Arabs are the predominant race. Throughout the Empire, mingled with these, are Slavs, Serbs, Armenians and Jews. The language varies with the locality and dominant nationality: hence it is hard to determine what the prevailing language of the Empire is. Armenian is spoken and written by a large number of people.

GOVERNMENT AND RELIGION. Turkey is a Mohammedan state, and the fundamental laws of the country are based upon the teachings of the Koran. The government is an absolute monarchy, and the ruler has the title of sultan. He is assisted by two high officials, the grand vizier, who is at the head of the temporal government, and the sheik-ul-Islam, who is the head of the Church. Both of these officials are appointed by the sultan, but the latter has the nominal sanction of the Ulema, a body including clergy and chief officials of the law, over which the sheik-ul-Islam presides. Connected with this body are the Mufti, or interpreters of the Koran. The various departments of government are in the hands of ministers, of whom there are twelve. For local government the Empire is divided into vilayets, or governments, over each of which is a governor. Each vilayet is divided into provinces, and the provinces are again divided into districts, with an occasional subdivision into subdistricts. Several attempts have been made to formulate and adopt a constitution, but none has succeeded. The government is particularly lax in its administration of foreign affairs;

the country is also torn by internal dissensions and revolutions, and massacres are of frequent occurrence. The Ottoman Empire is held together more by the jealousy of the great powers of Europe than by any inherent ties among its people. Foreigners are subject to the laws of their own countries in all cases in which citizens of the Empire are not involved, and the postal facilities are so defective that a number of leading European nations maintain their own postoffices in the larger cities. The country is in the greatest of financial straits, and the government is under the necessity of making frequent arrangements with its foreign creditors. Because of this and of the unstable condition of the government, the sultan is frequently referred to as "the sick man of Europe."

Mohammedanism is the prevailing religion. In European Turkey it is embraced by about one-half of the inhabitants, but in Asiatic Turkey it includes by far the larger proportion of the people. Between the Mohammedans and followers of other creeds there are frequent hostile demonstrations, and converts to evangelical creeds have frequently been massacred in the most cold-blooded manner. Interference of European nations and the United States, however, has secured some protection for missionaries, and mission schools are allowed in some localities.

EDUCATION. Elementary education is obligatory for boys from six to eleven years of age and for girls from six to ten years of age. This, however, is in the hands of the Mohammedan clergy and amounts to but little. There are schools for boys from eleven to sixteen, where higher branches and French are taught, and an attempt has been made to found a university, but so far it has not been successful. There are an imperial art school and a great national school, which has over 400 students. A number of mission schools are of considerable importance. Chief among these is Robert College, an American institution, at Constantinople.

HISTORY. The Ottoman Turks came originally from the region of the Altai Mountains, in central Asia, and in the sixth century A. D. they pushed onward to the west, in connection with other Turkish tribes. Early in the eighth century they came in contact with the Saracens, from whom they took their religion, and of whom they were at first the slaves and mercenaries. In the thirteenth century they appeared as allies of the Seljukian Turks against the Mongols, and for their aid they received a grant of lands in Asia Minor. Othman or Osman, the son of their leader, Ertogrul, became the most powerful emir of western Asia, and after the death of the Seljuk sultan of Iconium, in the year 1300, he proclaimed himself sultan. Thus was founded, upon the ruins of the Saracen, Seljuk and Mongol power, the Empire of the Osman, or Ottoman Turks, in Asia. After Osman, the courage, policy and enterprise of eight great princes, whom the dignity of caliph placed in possession of the standard of the prophet, and who were animated by religious fanaticism and a passion for military glory, raised the Empire to the rank of the first military power, in both Europe and Asia (1300–1566).

The first of these princes was Orkhan, son of Osman He subdued all Asia Minor to the Hellespont and was the first to organize the Turkish power. Orkhan's son, Soliman, first invaded Europe in 1355. In 1361 Orkhan's second son and successor, Amurath I, took Adrianople, which became the seat of the Empire in Europe, and he later conquered Macedonia, Albania and Servia and defeated a great Slav confederation, under the Bosnian king Stephen, at Kossovo. Bajazet (ruler from 1389 to 1402) invaded Thessaly and advanced toward Constantinople. In 1396 he defeated the Western Christians under Sigismund, king of Hungary, at Nicopolis, in Bulgaria; but at Angora, in 1402, he was himself conquered and taken prisoner by Timur, who divided the provinces between the sons of Bajazet. Finally, in 1413, the fourth son of Bajazet, Mohammed I, seated himself upon the throne of Osman. Mohammed was succeeded by his son, Amurath II (1421–1451), who defeated Ladislas, king of Hungary and Poland, at Varna in 1444 (See HUNYADY, JANOS). Mohammed II, the son of Amurath, completed the work of conquest (1451–1481). He attacked Constantinople, which was taken on May 29, 1453, and the Byzantine Empire came to an end. Since that time Constantinople has been the seat of the Sublime Porte, or Turkish government. Mohammed added Servia, Bosnia, Albania and Greece to the Ottoman Empire, and threatened Italy, which was freed from danger by his death. His grandson, Selim I (Sultan from 1512 to 1520), conquered Egypt and Syria. Under Solyman II (1520–1566), the Ottoman Empire reached the highest pitch of power and splendor (See SOLYMAN II), but after his time, the race of Osman degenerated, and the power of the Porte declined.

During the latter part of the sixteenth century and most of the seventeenth century, the chief wars which Turkey waged were with Venice and with Austria. The Battle of Lepanto in 1571, in which the Ottoman fleet was overthrown by the combined fleets of Venice and Spain, was the first great Ottoman reverse at sea; and the Battle of Saint Gotthard, in 1664, in which Montecuccoli defeated the Vizier Kiuprili, the first great Ottoman reverse on land. In 1683 Vienna was besieged by the Turks, but it was relieved by John Sobieski (See JOHN III SOBIESKI), and in 1697 the Turks were defeated at Zenta by the Austrians under Prince Eugene. Two years after this defeat, the Peace of Karlowitz was signed, by which Turkey agreed to renounce its claims upon Transylvania and a large part of Hungary, to give up the Morea to the Venetians, to restore the Ukraine to Poland and to leave Azov to the Russians. Eugene's subsequent victories at Peterwardein and Belgrade obliged the Porte, by the Treaty of Passarowitz, in 1718, to give up Belgrade, with a part of Servia and Wallachia; but the Turks, on the other hand, took the Morea from Venice, and by the Treaty of Belgrade, in 1739, they regained Belgrade, Servia and Little Wallachia, while for a time they also regained Azov.

Russia, which had been making steady advances under Peter the Great and subsequently, now became the great opponent of Turkey. In the middle of the eighteenth century, the Ottoman Empire still embraced a large part of southern Russia. The victories of the Russians in the war between 1736 and 1744 determined the political superiority of Russia, and compelled Turkey to renounce all sovereignty over the Crimea, to yield to Russia the country between the Bog and the Dnieper and to open its seas to the Russian merchant ships. By the Peace of Jassy, 1792, which closed the war of 1787–1791, Russia retained Tauride and the country between the Bug and the Dniester and gained some accessions in the Caucasus.

In the long series of wars which followed the French Revolution, the Ottoman Empire was first opposed to France, in consequence of Bonaparte's campaign in Egypt, and later to Russia, who demanded a more distinct recognition of her protectorate over the Christians. By the Peace of Bucharest in 1812, Turkey ceded to Russia the country between the Dniester and the Pruth. Further disputes ended in the Porte making additional concessions, which tended toward loosening the connection of Servia, Moldavia and Wallachia with Turkey. In 1821 the war of Greek independence broke out (See GREECE, subhead *History*). In 1826 the massacre of the

Janizaries took place at Constantinople, after a revolt (See JANIZARIES). In 1828 the Russians crossed the Balkans and took Adrianople, the war being terminated by the Peace of Adrianople in 1829. In 1831 Mehemet Ali, nominally pasha of Egypt, but real ruler both of Egypt and Syria, levied war against his sovereign and threatened Constantinople; but the Russians, who had been called on for aid by the sultan, forced the invaders to desist. In 1839 Mehemet Ali again rose against his sovereign; but through the active intervention of Austria, Great Britain and Russia, he was compelled to evacuate Syria, though he was recognized as hereditary viceroy of Egypt.

The next important event in the history of the Ottoman Empire was the Crimean War (See CRIMEAN WAR). In 1875 the people of Herzegovina, unable to endure longer the misgovernment of the Turks, broke into rebellion. A year later the Servians and Montenegrins likewise took up arms, and though the former were unsuccessful and obliged to abandon the war, the Montenegrins still held out. Meantime, the great powers of Europe were pressing reforms on Turkey, and at the end of 1876 a conference met at Constantinople, with the view of making a fresh settlement of the relations between her and her Christian provinces. All the recommendations of the conference were, however, rejected by Turkey; and in April following, Russia, who had been coming more and more prominently forward as the champion of the oppressed provinces and had for months been massing troops on both the Asiatic and the European frontier of Turkey, issued a warlike manifesto and commenced hostile operations in both parts of the Turkish Empire (See RUSSO-TURKISH WAR; BERLIN, CONGRESS OF).

The main events in the history of the Ottoman Empire from the Treaty of Berlin to the year 1890 were the treaty with Greece, executed under pressure of the great powers in 1881, by which Turkey ceded to Greece almost the whole of Thessaly and a strip of Epirus (See GREECE, subhead *History*); the occupation of Egypt by Great Britain in 1882, and the revolution at Philippopolis in 1885, when the government of Eastern Rumelia was overthrown, and the union of that province with Bulgaria was proclaimed. In July, 1894, Constantinople was visited by a series of earthquakes, which lasted eight days, two or more occurring each day. Great damage was done to the city and surrounding country, and hundreds of people were killed.

For a number of decades the Turkish government has had frequent revolts to deal with. The massacres occasioned by these uprisings aroused the sympathy of America and Europe, but the European powers would not interfere because it was believed that such interference might cause a general upheaval in Europe. In July, 1908, the Young Turks succeeded in a revolution which compelled the sultan to grant a constitution. The first Parliament under this constitution met in 1909. In April the troops in Constantinople revolted against the Young Turks, but troops from the country near by rushed to the capital, and gained control of the city. Abdul Hamid was compelled to abdicate, and his younger brother, Mohammed Rechad Effendi, ascended the throne with the title of Mehmed V. In 1912 Turkey lost Tripoli to Italy, resulting from a war of aggression on the part of the latter. Hardly had peace been arranged between Italy and Turkey, when war against Turkey was declared by the allied Balkan states. After several months of warfare the European powers interfered to end the struggle, and on May 30, 1913, Turkey accepted the terms of the Treaty of London, which practically ended the rule of Turkey in Europe. (See BALKAN WAR.)

Turkey Buz'zard or **Turkey Vulture**, the commonest of American vultures, so named because at a distance it resembles a turkey in appearance. The turkey buzzard is about two and a half feet long, and its wings extend to about six feet in breadth. It lives in most of the warmer regions of the United States and extends its habitat through Mexico and South America. See VULTURE.

Tur'komans, a nomadic Tartar people, occupying a territory stretching between the Caspian Sea and the Sea of Aral. They do not form a single nation, but are divided into clans.

Turks, a name commonly given to a widely spread race, supposed to have had its original home in Turkestan, but now living in European Turkey and western and northwestern Asia. Besides the Ottoman Turks, or Osmanli, of Turkey, the Turkomans, the Kirghizes, the Usbecks, the Yakuts and others belong to this race.

Turks Islands, a group of small islands forming the southeastern portion of the Bahama chain. Grand Turk, or Turks Island, is the largest and is situated about 110 miles north of Santo Domingo. These islands are noted for their export of salt. Politically they are a British possession and form a dependency of Jamaica.

Tur'meric, a yellow dye, prepared from the root of the turmeric plant, a kind of ginger which is largely used in India and China as an important ingredient in curry powder. The dye is a yellow resinous substance used to dye silk and wool and to color salves and other mixtures.

Turn'er, JOSEPH MALLARD WILLIAM (1775–1851), a great English landscape painter, born in London. From 1789 to 1794 he studied at the Royal Academy, and in 1802 he was elected one of its members. Till this date he had chiefly been known as a landscape painter in water colors, but thenceforth he turned his attention to oil painting, and in the ensuing half-century he produced at the academy exhibitions of more than two hundred pictures. In 1807 he was elected professor of perspective in the Royal Academy. Turner's works claim special merit because of their fine coloring effects. Details are often wanting and drawing is imperfect, but the general effect is wonderful. During the last period of his work, he fell into that vague trifling with mere effects of light and shade and color which has materially lessened the great reputation he had justly acquired by his previous works. He bequeathed most of his pictures and sketches to the nation, on condition of a suitable building being erected within ten years for their reception. They have been placed in the Turner Gallery, occupying two rooms in the National Gallery. Good examples of his art are *Slave Ship*; *The Fighting Temeraire*; *Rain, Steam and Speed on the Great Western Railway*; *Hannibal and His Army Crossing the Alps,* and *The Garden of the Hesperides*.

Turner, NAT (about 1800–1831), an American negro slave, born in Southampton County, Va. From earliest childhood, he claimed to be chosen and inspired for the accomplishment of a great purpose. Accordingly, in 1828 he declared that at a certain sign he would lead an insurrection against his enemies. In 1831, at an eclipse of the sun, he began the carrying out of his plan by killing five members of his master's family. Joined by other slave recruits, he continued the massacre until every person in the neighborhood had been murdered. On the following day the insurrection was broken up by a band of white men and by the arrival of Federal troops. Turner was captured October 30 and was executed within a few days. The insurrection, known as the Nat Turner Insurrection, resulted in the passage of more stringent laws for the management and punishment of slaves in most of the southern states.

Tur'nip, a plant of the mustard family, nearly related to the cabbage and much cultivated on account of its root. It was well known to the Greeks and Romans and has been used as a vegetable in all temperate climates; in some countries it is cultivated on a very large scale, as food for stock. Many varieties, which seem to have come from cultivation, are grown in all parts of the United States.

Turn'stone, a bird of the plover family, which takes its name from the habit of turning up small stones, in its search for marine worms,

TURNSTONE

minute crustaceans and other food. It is found throughout North America, on both the Atlantic and the Pacific coasts, and in other parts of the world.

Tur'pentine, the distilled gum of the pine tree. Turpentine is manufactured by collecting the gum, or crude turpentine, from the trees and distilling it in copper vessels. The season begins when the first spring sap rises, and it ends when winter checks the flow of the sap. In January or February the trees are hacked. The hacks are about six inches deep; they are cut near the roots of the tree, and as close together, to the height of a man's head, as can be done without killing the pine. The hacker leaves a width of bark between each cut, so as to preserve the vitality of the tree. The sap, or gum, fills the cuts with a clear, sticky, thick fluid, and this is removed with a dipper. The sap is deposited in barrels, which are scattered through the woods. The first sap which flows in the spring makes the best resin, and the poorest is the product of the hardened gum which is left on the sides of the cuts. This is removed by the *scraper,* who moves through the woods gathering the leavings.

The still is a copper vat, hooded with a close-fitting, air-tight cover, in which is a funnel, which, in turn, is connected with the *worm* of the still (See DISTILLATION). This worm runs down into another vat, near at hand, and in this vat the fumes, or vapor, of the heated gum are distilled into turpentine. Fire under the copper vat heats the gum, and the volatile parts rise to the funnel, pass into the still and are condensed by the water in the second vat into spirits of turpentine. The residuum left in the vat is the rosin of commerce, which is passed through a series of strainers and sieves to the barrels, which are made on the spot. The turpentine cannot be barreled so easily, for it will work through an ordinary barrel. It is placed in white pine barrels, which have been coated inside with several coats of strong, hot glue, which keeps the turpentine from soaking into the wood. The trees are worked for five or six seasons. All the turpentines dissolve in pure alcohol, and by distillation they yield oils, which are termed *spirits of turpentine*. Oil, or spirits, of turpentine is used to a limited extent in medicine. It is also much used in the arts, for dissolving resins and oils in making varnishes. See RESINS; ROSIN.

Turquoise, *tur′koiz*, a precious stone, of beautiful blue or green color, capable of taking a high polish. It contains a large proportion of clay in its composition, and the color is due to the presence of copper. The turquoise has long been a favorite gem in the East, especially in Persia, where the finest specimens are found. Fine specimens also occur in the Sinai Peninsula and in New Mexico and other sections in the extreme southwestern part of the United States, where mines formerly worked by the ancient Mexicans have been discovered. When exposed to fatty acids, the turquoise loses its color and turns greenish. An imitation, known as *bone turquoise*, is easily distinguished, by examining it under a microscope, which reveals its structure. It is fossil bone colored blue by iron phosphate.

Tur′tle, a name given to reptiles which differ but little from tortoises; in fact, *turtle* is the name commonly given to both genera. Turtles are found in all the seas of warm climates, and they feed mostly on marine plants. The most important species is the *green turtle*, which is from six to seven feet long and weighs from 700 to 800 pounds. Its flesh is highly esteemed as a table luxury. See LEATHERBACK; TORTOISE.

Turtle Dove, *duv*, a small pigeon, about eleven inches long, pale grayish-brown in color, marked with a darker hue above and with a purple tinge on the feathers of its breast. Its cooing note is plaintive and tender. In the United States the turtle dove, or *mourning dove*, is common and quite tame, becoming easily ac-

171

customed to human beings and, if undisturbed, feeding often with domestic fowls.

Tus′caloo′sa, ALA., the county-seat of Tuscaloosa co., 56 mi. s. w. of Birmingham, on the Black Warrior River and on the Queen & Crescent and the Mobile & Ohio railroads. The city is in a cotton-growing region and is near extensive coal mines. The chief industrial establishments are cotton gins and compresses, flour mills, machine shops and creameries. The University of Alabama is just a mile north of the city, and Tuscaloosa Female College, Alabama Central Female College and Verner Military Institute, Stillman Institute, Oak City Academy, University High School and the state insane asylum are all located here. The city was the capital of the state from 1826 to 1846, and the old capitol building is still a feature of interest. The place was settled in 1812 and was incorporated four years later. Population in 1910, 8407.

Tus′cany, a compartimento of the kingdom of Italy, situated in the northern part of the peninsula. It is bounded on the n. by Emelio, on the s. e. by Marches, Umbria and Rome and on the s. w. by the Mediterranean. Tuscany was formerly a grand duchy. In ancient times it was included in Etruria and was the home of the Etruscans. After the subjugation of the Etruscans, it became a part of the Roman Empire. It was the site of a number of cities which, during the Middle Ages, rose to considerable importance and attained their independence. Among these was Florence, which in the thirteenth century became a most prosperous and influential republic. The little state is of importance in history, because from it emanated many influences that affected later civilization, especially along the lines of art and literature. Among the noted names of Tuscany are the Medici, Giotto, Boccaccio, Dante and Petrarch. The dialect of Tuscany became the literary language of Italy, and in the latter half of the sixteenth century the Florentine possessions were formed into the Grand Duchy of Tuscany. In 1745 the state came into the possession of the emperor of Germany, and it was under the rule of the Hapsburgs for most of the time until 1859. In 1861 it became a part of the kingdom of Italy. For climate and products, see ITALY.

Tus′caro′ra, a migrating Iroquoian tribe, which finally settled in New York and was received as a sixth member in the confederacy. See FIVE NATIONS, THE.

Tus′culum, an ancient Latin city, now in ruins, 15 mi. s. of Rome. It was the birthplace of the elder Cato and was a favorite residence of Cicero. Among the remains are the so-called Villa of Cicero, the Forum, a theater, an amphitheater and an ancient castle, or citadel.

Tuskegee, *tŭs kee′gee,* **Normal and Industrial Institute,** an institution for the training of colored persons, established in 1881 at Tuskegee, Ala. The object of the institute is to furnish its students with an education fitting them to become proper leaders of the people of their own race, and thus to bring about better moral and material conditions. The studies of the academic department are closely associated with the practical work in the shops and fields. Instruction and practice are given in mechanical drawing, engineering, blacksmithing, brickmaking, carpentry, canning, founding, harness making, carriage trimming, mechanics, painting, printing, milling, shoemaking, tinsmithing, tailoring, carriage making, farming, sewing, dressmaking, millinery, cooking, laundering, domestic service, mattress making, basketry and nursing. The property immediately belonging to the school consists of more than 60 buildings, over 2600 acres of land, over 1,100 head of live stock and vehicles of every description. The institute has 200 instructors, an attendance of over 1600 students annually and possesses a library containing 20,000 volumes. It has attained a remarkable degree of success under the able direction of Booker T. Washington, its principal. See WASHINGTON, BOOKER TALLIAFERRO.

Tus′sock Moth, a moth whose caterpillars are extremely destructive to the leaves of trees. The female of the white tussock moth is a wingless animal, which lays its eggs as soon as it comes from the cocoon and immediately dies. The caterpillars are very voracious, grow rapidly and are great travelers, moving from tree to tree. If disturbed they drop, suspending themselves by a silken thread. Their cocoons are made of silken hairs from their own bodies. The hairs which appear on the caterpillar in tufts give the name tussock to the moths. Affected trees should be sprayed, and the unattacked ones banded, to prevent the caterpillars from crawling up the trunk.

Twain, MARK. See CLEMENS, SAMUEL LANGHORNE.

Tweed, a river of Great Britain, which rises in the southeastern part of Scotland and flows easterly and then northeasterly into the North Sea. In the lower part of its course, it forms the boundary between Scotland and England. Its

length is 95 miles, and it is navigable for only a short distance.

Tweed, WILLIAM MARCY (1823–1878), an American politician, notorious as the leader of the famous "Tweed Ring" in New York City. He was born in New York City and received but slight education. He early entered politics, became an alderman and in 1853 was elected to Congress. Afterward he held numerous local offices and from 1867 to 1871 was a state senator. As a member of the famous Tammany Hall, he gained immense political influence, and with the help of several unscrupulous supporters he formed a combination for the control of New York City government, in the private interests of the members of the ring. By the bribery of legislators and judges, bills were passed and decisions rendered, which allowed the ring to carry out vast schemes of improvement, through which, by the padding of pay rolls and the auditing of fraudulent bills, they gained immense wealth. The régime lasted for more than six years, and the debt of the city was increased from $20,000,-000 to $101,000,000. Finally, in 1871, through an exposure by the *New York Times* and a vigorous prosecution under a committee led by Samuel J. Tilden, the ring was broken up. Tweed was twice tried, finally convicted and sentenced to twelve years' confinement in the penitentiary and a fine of more than $12,000. He was released two years later on a legal technicality, but was immediately rearrested on a suit for damages to the amount of more than $6,000,000. While confined in jail awaiting trial, he escaped and fled to Spain. He was finally captured, however, and returned to America, where he died in jail.

Tweeds, a twilled fabric, principally for men's wear, with an unfinished surface. It is of two colors, generally combined in the same yarn. The best quality is made all of wool, but in inferior kinds cotton and shoddy are introduced. The manufacture is largely carried on in the southern part of Scotland. It takes its name from the place where it was first made, along the Tweed, in Scotland.

Twelfth-Day, the twelfth day after Christmas, upon which is held the festival of Epiphany. On the evening of this day, called Twelfth-night, various social rites and ceremonies are observed in different countries. One of these is the baking of a twelfth-cake, which contains a bean. When the cake is divided at the feast, the person who receives the piece containing the bean is made king for the occasion.

Twelve Tables, LAW OF THE, the earliest written code of law among the Romans. The traditionary account states that the plebeians complained that they could never hope for strict justice as long as the laws were administered by patrician judges, who were bound only by unwritten laws, which they could interpret to suit themselves. Ten men were appointed, therefore, in 452 B.C, to draw up a code. This code, as drawn up, consisted merely in a compilation of old laws and not of any new legislation.

Twilight, *twi'lite*, the glow in the sky before sunrise and after sunset. Twilight is caused by the refraction of the sun's rays as they pass through the atmosphere. The evening twilight is brightest immediately after sunset and continues to fade until the sun reaches 18° below the horizon, when twilight ceases. The time required for the sun to reach this point varies in different latitudes. In the torrid zone, where the sun's path throughout the year takes nearly the same direction as the parallels, twilight is of short duration, but in summer its duration increases toward the poles, and near the Arctic circle it lasts all night.

Tycho Brahe, *te'ko brah'eh* or *brah*. See BRAHE, TYCHO.

Tycoon' or **Shiogoon'.** See SHOGUN.

Ty'ler, TEX., the county-seat of Smith co., about 100 mi. s. e. of Dallas, on the International & Great Northern and the Saint Louis Southwestern railroads. The city is the center of the fruit-growing region of eastern Texas, and it ships large quantities of cotton, fruit and garden truck. There are also important industrial establishments, including railway shops, canneries, box and crate factories, ice works and potteries. Tyler and East Texas colleges are located here. The especially noteworthy structures are the city hall, the Federal building and the railroad hospital. Bellevue and Lakewood parks are also of interest. The place was settled in 1846 and was chartered as a city in 1875. Population in 1910, 10,400, of which about one-fifth were colored.

Tyler, JOHN (1790–1862), an American statesman, tenth president of the United States, born in Charles City County, Va. He graduated at William and Mary College in 1807, and two years later he was admitted to the bar. He sat in the state legislature from 1811 till 1816, when he was chosen to fill a vacancy in Congress, and he was reëlected in 1817 and 1819. He became a leader of the strict constructionist Democrats, opposed protection and, on the Mis-

souri question, he denied the right of Congress to limit the extension of slavery or to control it at all in the territories. In 1825 he was elected governor of Virginia, and in December, 1826, he became a United States senator. In the Sen-

JOHN TYLER

ate Tyler pursued an independent course, and while, in 1832, he supported Jackson rather than Clay, for the presidency, in February, 1833, he was the only senator who recorded his vote against the "Force Bill," granting extraordinary powers to the president in dealing with South Carolina, though he disapproved of nullification. He denounced the United States Bank, yet he resented the despotic methods by which Jackson overthrew it, supported Clay's motion to censure the president and in 1836 resigned his seat, rather than vote for expunging the resolution from the minutes of the Senate.

He then joined the Whig party, and in 1840 he was elected vice-president on the ticket with General Harrison. President Harrison died a month after his inauguration, and Tyler became president. In the first year of his administration he quarreled with the Whig majority in Congress over the project to reëstablish the national bank. Two bills were passed to this end, and both were vetoed by President Tyler. After the second veto, in September, 1841, all the cabinet except Daniel Webster resigned, he remaining until 1843 to complete the negotiation of the famous Webster-Ashburton Treaty. In 1844 he was succeeded by John C. Calhoun. Besides the Ashburton Treaty, the most important act of

Tyler's administration was the annexation of Texas, in March, 1845, which led to the Mexican War.

At the close of his term, he retired to Virginia and to private life until 1861, when he was president of a peace convention at Washington. Failing in his efforts at a compromise, he joined the Confederate cause and was a member of the Confederate Congress until his death.

Tyler, MOSES COIT (1835–1900), an American educator and historian, born at Griswold, Conn. He was educated at Yale and at Andover Theological School. After completing his education, he served as pastor of Congregational churches at Owego and Poughkeepsie, N. Y. Later he became professor of English at the University of Michigan, from whence he was appointed to the chair of American history at Cornell, which position he held during his life. Professor Tyler was noted as a scholar and a writer. Among his best-known works are a *Literary History of the American Revolution*, the *History of American Literature*, a *Manual of English Literature* and *Glimpses of England*.

Tyler, WAT, an English soldier, one of the leaders in the rebellion of 1381 against the poll tax. He led the men of Kent upon London, where, after fire and pillage, they were partly dispersed by a promise of the king to grant them charters of freedom and amnesty. Tyler, however, remained with a body of the insurgents and was met by the king next day at Smithfield, where, for his apparent insolence in the royal presence, he was stabbed by William Walworth, mayor of London.

Tyndale, *tin'dal,* WILLIAM (?–1536), an English reformer and translator of the Bible. He studied at Oxford and Cambridge and was ordained priest about 1521. Having made himself unpopular by the expression of certain heretical sentiments, he left England for the continent in 1524. After a visit to Luther at Wittenberg, he settled at Cologne, where he completed a translation of the New Testament, which he had probably begun before leaving England. On his expulsion from Cologne, he took refuge in Worms, where he published his octavo edition of the New Testament. In 1530 his translation of the Pentateuch appeared at Marburg. Five years later he was arrested at the instance of Henry VIII and imprisoned in the castle of Vilvorde, near Brussels. After a protracted trial for heresy, he was strangled and burned. Besides his translations, he wrote *The Obedience of a Christian Man.*

Tyn'dall, JOHN (1820–1893), an English scientist. He joined the Irish Ordnance Survey, engaged in railway engineering for several years and was later appointed teacher of mathematics and surveying in Queenswood College. After this he went abroad, studied for a time under Bunsen in Marburg University and under Magnus in Berlin, and on his return to England the publication of the results of his experiments procured him the chair of natural philosophy in the

JOHN TYNDALL

Royal Institution. On the death of Faraday, he became president of the Institution. He made almost yearly trips to the Alps to study glacial phenomena, and in 1872 he lectured throughout the United States, his lectures attracting wide attention. Both his writings and his lectures, while of a high literary order and truly scientific, are of a popular nature. Among his chief works are *Fragments of Science for Unscientific People, The Glaciers of the Alps, Exercise in the Alps, Mountaineering in 1869* and *Heat Considered as a Mode of Motion.*

Tyne, a river of England, formed by the junction of the North Tyne and the South Tyne. It flows in an easterly direction and enters the North Sea. Its length from the union of the head streams is only about 35 miles. It is navigable as far as Blaydon and is of considerable commercial importance, because of the amount of coal shipped on it.

Type, a piece of metal, wood or other material, on one end of which is cast or engraved a letter, figure or other character. The earliest types were made of wood, and in style they resembled the script letters used in copying books before the invention of the art of printing. The parts of a type are (1) the body, (2) the face, (3) the shoulder, (4) the nick and (5) the groove. The *face* is that part that does the printing; the *nick* is to show the right side of the type when set, and the *groove* is to make it stand firmly on its base. In the early days of printing, each printer made his own type, but with the extension of the industry, type casting, or founding, became a business by itself. A few of the large types used in printing are still made of wood, but

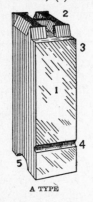

A TYPE

all others are of type metal, which is an alloy, consisting of three parts of lead to one part of antimony, with a small quantity of tin and copper added.

Type are cast by machinery. A steel die, which is an exact pattern of the letter, is first made. This is driven into a piece of soft copper, so as to form a perfect impression of the letter. This is called the *matrix*. The matrix is then placed in a metallic box, called the *mold*. This is placed in the type-casting machine, which opens and closes the mold and fills it with type metal. The metal hardens instantly, and when the mold opens the type drops out. The face is then smoothed on a stone, and the body is nicked and grooved. The type are then tied up in packages, each of which contains only one kind of letter, and are ready for use. All types are about an inch high.

A complete assortment of type is called a *font* and contains large and small capitals, small letters and italics, marks of punctuation and figures; in all, there are about 225 characters for English printing. The size of a font varies according to the work to be done with it. Small fonts contain from 500 to 800 pounds, and large ones have from 20,000 to 50,000 pounds. Type founders have a rule for determining the number of different letters necessary to make each font complete. *Z* requires the smallest number. For every *z* there will be 46 *a*'s, 60 *e*'s, 32 *h*'s, 15 *m*'s, and so on.

There are thirteen sizes of type in ordinary use in printing books and newspapers. These are designated by special names and by the number of points they measure, a point being $\frac{1}{72}$ of an inch. Both methods of naming are given in the illustration.

Nonpareil	6-point
Minion	7-point
Brevier	8-point
Bourgeois	9-point
Long Primer	10-point
Small Pica	11-point
Pica	12-point
English	14-point

The smaller sizes are not used in general printing, although sometimes small Bibles are printed from $5\frac{1}{2}$ point, or agate, and still smaller sizes are used for marginal references in Bibles and other works. The type used in job printing is of various sizes, to suit the taste and conditions of the advertiser. See PRINTING,

Type'setting Machines. See GRAPHO-TYPE; LINOTYPE; MONOTYPE.

Type'writer, a machine used for writing upon paper by means of type, which are manipulated by keys or levers. The essential parts of a typewriter are a set of types; an arrangement of keys, for bringing the types in contact with the paper; a paper carrier, or carriage; a platen, or roller, against which the types strike, and an inking device. The first practical typewriter was due to the ingenuity of three Americans, S. W. Soulé, Carlos Glidden and C. Latham Sholes. Soulé and Glidden abandoned the enterprise before it was completed, and to Sholes the credit is largely due. He patented his invention in 1874 and placed it with the firm of E. Remington & Sons, gunmakers, for manufacture. This machine was placed upon the market as the Remington typewriter and was the first successful typewriter ever produced.

While there are now many patterns of typewriters, all belong to one of two classes, those known as the *basket* machines and those known as *cylinder* machines. In the basket machines, each type is on the end of a bar, hung on a pivot and joined to its respective key by a lever attachment. These type bars are attached to a frame which was formerly circular, forming the basket from which the machine takes its name. In modern machines the frame is an arc of a circle. The bars are of such length that the type on each strikes the platen at the same point. When a key is depressed, the bar strikes the inking ribbon against the paper, making the impression of the character. As the bar drops back to its position, the carriage moves forward one space, thus putting the paper in position for the next letter.

Of the cylinder machines, the Hammond is a good representative. This has the type arranged on a cylinder, and the depression of the key causes the cylinder to revolve until the character desired is brought to a point where it is impressed upon the paper by a little hammer. Each type of machine has its special advantages, but the basket machines far outnumber the others.

Typhoid, *ti'joid,* **Fe'ver** or **Enter'ic Fever,** a disease somewhat resembling typhus fever, but really very different. It is characterized by a serious disorder of the bowels, which causes languor, chills, violent headache, thirst and pains in the limbs, with long continued fever. A rose-colored rash appears on the body; delirium and other serious symptoms arise, and in many cases ulceration or perforation of the bowels causes death. In the treatment of this disease the most important thing is the diet. In mild forms of typhoid, the disease is sufficiently serious to require the greatest care. Typhoid is caused by the presence in the bowels of a bacillus well known to physicians. The bacillus finds its way into the human body usually through water which has been contaminated by sewage or through food that has been infected. The disease is not contagious in the ordinary sense, that it can come from the touch, the breath or skin of the person having it, but the bacilli are present in the excrement from the patient, and as a consequence the utmost care should be observed in every case to destroy all such matter and all cloths used about the patient. It is thought that about three weeks elapse after the bacterium enters the body before the disease begins to manifest itself, and it is probable that infection does not always result from the presence of the bacillus, unless the person is in an enfeebled or weakened condition.

Typhoon, *ti foon',* the violent hurricanes which rage on the coasts of China and Japan and in the neighboring archipelago, occurring from May to November, and most frequent and disastrous in July, August and September. The typhoons are cyclonic storms, which originate somewhat farther south than Manila and move towards the northeast. In severity and character they closely resemble the hurricanes of the West Indies. See HURRICANE.

Typhus, *ti'fus,* **Fever,** known, also, from the place where it occurs, as *hospital fever, jail fever* and by other names, essentially a fever of the poor, ill-fed and badly-housed inhabitants of large cities. It is infectious, and the infection seems to be carried in the breath of the patient. A period of from five to twelve days passes after infection, before the first symptoms show themselves in the patient. Then the disease comes on suddenly, with a chill, followed by a high fever, sharp rheumatic pains and headache. Generally about the seventh day, a rash, of irregular spots of dusky hue, appears over the chest and back, and this has given to the disease the common name of *spotted fever.* Delirium is almost always present during the second week, and after a marked crisis, followed by a sound sleep, the person awakes with the fever gone. Thereafter recovery is rapid. The disease is often fatal, especially where the best of care is not given the patient. The treatment consists in keeping the sufferer in a well-ventilated room, and in preventing exhaustion by light, wholesome diet. The disease is now practically confined to the slums of great cities and to half-civilized nations. Typhus fever should not be confused with typhoid fever, a very different disease.

Tyr, in Northern mythology, the son of Odin, brother of Balder, and the god of war and victory, corresponding to the Mars of the Romans. From Tiu, a variation of his name, Tuesday is named.

Ty'rants, a genus of fly-catching birds, remarkable for their bold and pugnacious disposition. The best-known species is the *tyrant flycatcher,* a native of the United States, more commonly known as the *kingbird.* See KING-BIRD.

Tyre, one of the most celebrated cities of ancient Phoenicia, on the Mediterranean Sea, twenty miles southwest of Sidon. From 1200 to 850 B.C. it was a wealthy and magnificent city and the chief commercial center of the world. It was famous for the dye, Tyrian purple. It was built partly on an island and partly on the mainland; and the insular fortifications formed its chief strength, when besieged and taken by Alexander the Great in 322 B.C. A mole, or causeway, then constructed to the island, was the origin of the isthmus which now connects it with the mainland. The modern Tyre, or Sur, is an insignificant place, of about 6000 inhabitants.

Tyr'ol, a province of Austria-Hungary. It is situated in the heart of the Alps and is noted for its magnificent mountain scenery, in which it rivals Switzerland. Tyrol formed a part of ancient Rhoetia and was conquered by the Romans in 15 B. C. After the fall of the Roman Empire it came under German influence; but in the middle of the fourteenth century it was joined to the house of Austria, with which it has since remained, except during a brief period when it was transferred to Bavaria by Napoleon. For climate and products, see AUSTRIA-HUNGARY.

Tyrone, *ti rone'*, PA., a borough in Blair co., 15 mi. n. e. of Altoona, on the Little Juniata River and on several lines of the Pennsylvania railroad. It is in an agricultural region, which contains, also, timber lands and iron mines. There are manufactures of various paper products, besides large railroad shops, iron works, lumber mills, a tannery and other establishments. The city has nine churches, three banks, public and parish schools and a school library. The Birmingham Seminary is about three miles distant. Tyrone was settled about 1811 and was incorporated in 1857. Population in 1910, 7176.

U, the twenty-first letter and the fifth vowel in the English alphabet. It comes from the Greek alphabet, as the Phoenician had no such character, and it was, until comparatively recent times, used interchangeably with *v*. In time, *v* came to be used for the consonant sound and *u* for the vowel sound, as in the case of *j* and *i*. The true primary sound of *u* was that which it still retains in most of the languages in Europe, that of *oo* in *cool*, the sound being sometimes short, sometimes long. The so-called "long *u*" in English, however, has a distinct *y* sound prefixed to the *oo* sound, as in *use, abuse*.

U'dall, NICHOLAS (1506–1556), the author of *Ralph Roister Doister*, the first regular English comedy. He was master of Eton School from 1534 to 1541, and the play was written for performance by the scholars. He was in favor at court, as a writer of pageants and interludes.

Uffizi, *oof feet'se*, a famous palace in Florence, Italy, containing an art gallery which is one of the most extensive and valuable in the world. This art gallery was founded by the Medici family in the fifteenth century. Valuable additions have been made from time to time, and it now contains some of the most famous of all works of art. Among these are the statues *Venus d'Medici*, *The Dancing Faun* and *The Wrestlers*. Works of the great masters, such as Raphael, Michelangelo, Titian, Correggio, Holbein, Rembrandt and others, are to be seen in this palace.

Uganda, *oo gahn'da*, one of the administrative divisions of British East Africa, forming the western part of the colony. Lakes Albert Nyanza, Victoria Nyanza and Albert Edward Nyanza are wholly or partly within the territory. Uganda was formerly a native kingdom and came under British influence in 1890; it was made a protectorate four years later. The first white man to visit it was Captain Speke, in 1862. It was again visited by Stanley in 1875. The country is mountainous, and in it or upon its borders are most of the important peaks in Africa, including Ruwenzori. Copper and iron abound.

Coffee and rubber are important native vegetable products, and ivory and hides are the chief exports of trade. The natives are quite successful in working iron, but the mines have been exploited to only a limited extent. The population are mostly Bantus and Bagandas, but some of the Kongo pygmies are found in this region. The Bantus are an agricultural people. The Bagandas, who are estimated at 1,000,000, are intelligent and they are largely Christianized. Uganda contains a number of mission stations and schools, some of which are taught by native teachers. A railway from Bombassa to Port Florence, on Victoria Nyanza, furnishes the most direct means of communication with the coast. Several steamers ply on the lake in connection with the railway. Population in 1911, 2,843,300. See BRITISH EAST AFRICA.

Uhland, *oo'lahnt*, JOHANN LUDWIG (1787–1862), a German poet, born at Tübingen. He studied at Tübingen University, practiced law in Stuttgart, was elected a member of the Württemberg Assembly and as a politician was ever an advocate of liberal opinions. He was professor of German literature at Tübingen from 1829 to 1833. In 1848 he was elected to the German National Assembly, but two years later he retired from political life and devoted himself thenceforth to literature. His ballads and romances rank among the literary treasures of the German nation. Of his songs and ballads perhaps *The Good Comrade* and *The Castle by the Sea* are the most universally popular. Besides being a statesman and poet, Uhland was one of the founders of the science of philology.

U'in'ta or **Uintah Mountains**, a range of mountains belonging to the Rocky Mountain system, extending in an east and west direction across the northern portion of the eastern half of Utah and joining the Wahsatch Mountains on the west. The highest summits are Gilbert Peak, 13,687 feet high, Emmons, 13,624 feet high, and Wilson Peak, 13,300 feet high.

Ukerewe. See VICTORIA NYANZA.

Ulm, *oolm,* a city of Germany, in the Kingdom of Württemberg, at the junction of the Blau and the Iller with the Danube. On the opposite shore of the Danube is the village of New Ulm, with which Ulm is connected by two bridges. The most noteworthy building of the city is the cathedral, which was begun in the fourteenth century. It is, after the Cathedral of Cologne, the largest church in Germany, and its spire, 530 feet in height, is the highest in the world. Among the other buildings are a fine townhall of the sixteenth century, the government buildings, the modern palace of justice and the bank. Brass founding, brewing, shipbuilding and the manufacture of paper, hats and tobacco are among the industries of the city, and the ornamental pipe bowls of Ulm are famous. Ulm was one of the free cities of the old German Empire, and during the latter part of the Middle Ages it was of considerable importance. It was one of the earliest of the cities to accept the Reformation. Population in 1910, 56,109.

Ultramarine, *ul'tra ma reen',* a beautiful and durable sky-blue pigment, a color formed of the mineral called lapis lazuli. This substance is much valued by painters, on account of the beauty and permanence of its color, both for oil and water painting.

Ul'tramon'tanism, the views of that party in the Church of Rome who place an absolute authority in matters of faith and discipline in the hands of the pope, in opposition to the views of the party who would place the national churches, such as the Gallican, in partial independence of the Roman papal courts, and would make the pope subordinate to the statutes of an ecumenical council. According to ultramontanism, the pope is superior to general councils, is independent of their decrees and is to be considered the source of all jurisdiction in the Church. The Vatican Council of 1870 virtually established the views of ultramontanism as doctrines of the Church.

Ulysses, *u lis'eez,* called by the Greeks *Odysseus,* one of the most famous of the Greek heroes. Rejected by Helen, Ulysses had married Penelope and had settled down with her to a happy life. Shortly after the birth of his son Telemachus, the Trojan War broke out, and Ulysses, in spite of his vow to help Menelaus, was unwilling to leave his home and engage in the struggle. He therefore feigned madness, but Palamedes visited him and, becoming convinced of his sanity, made use of a strategem. While Ulysses was ploving up the seashore and sowing it with salt, Palamedes placed the boy Telemachus in front of his father's plow. Ulysses by carefully turning aside his team proved that his madness had been merely feigned, and was compelled to join the expedition. At Troy he was one of the bravest of the Greek heroes, and he is an important character in the *Iliad.* The chief interest, however, attaches to his adventures while returning from Troy. Driven to the country of the Lotus-eaters, he with difficulty broke the spell which was cast upon his companions and induced them to continue the voyage. His next disaster was the meeting with Polyphemus the Cyclops, and for his murder of Polyphemus Neptune became very angry with Ulysses and constantly pursued him with his wrath. He was driven upon the island of Circe; he was placed in danger between Scylla and Charybdis, and he was borne, after the death of all of his companions, to the island of the nymph Calypso, where he remained for seven years. On his return to Ithaca he found Penelope in great trouble, but with the aid of Telemachus he overcame her annoying suitors and made himself powerful in his own kingdom again. See CALYPSO; CIRCE: PENELOPE; POLYPHEMUS.

Umballa, *um bahl'la.* See AMBALA.

Umbelliferae, *um'bel if'ur ee,* an important family of flowering plants, containing about 1500 species, most of which are herbs, though a few are shrubs. The flowers are usually inconspicuous and individual, but are arranged in large groups, called umbels, a fact which accounts for the name of the family. It is also known as the parsley family. The leaves contain oil and a resinous matter, which is sometimes of a highly poisonous character. Not infrequently the odor is pleasing, but sometimes it is very disagreeable. Starch and sugar are stored in the roots of some of the species, which are cultivated as important articles of food. Among these the carrot and the parsnip are the best-known examples. Celery belongs to this family, and the leaves of the parsley, fennel and the seeds of the caraway illustrate some of the peculiarities which make the family valuable. Many species are described under their proper names in the text.

Um'ber, a well-known mineral pigment, of an olive-brown color in its raw state, but much redder when burnt. It occurs either naturally in veins and beds or is prepared artificially from various admixtures. The commercial varieties are known as Turkey umber, raw umber, burnt umber and English umber.

Umbrel'la Bird, a black, South American bird, related to the crows and remarkable for its handsome drooping crest of blue-black feathers, which rise from the head and curve toward the end of the beak. Another long tuft of feathers hangs down from the throat.

Unalaska, *oo'nah lahs'ka,* or **Unalashka,** one of the largest of the Aleutian Islands, about 75 mi. long and 20 mi. wide at its widest point. The chief settlement is Unalaska, or Iluliuk, on the north side of the island. Population in 1900, 420. See ALEUTIAN ISLANDS.

Un'cas (?–about 1683), an American indian chief, born in the Pequot settlement of Connecticut. Owing to dissensions among the tribe, he settled east of Lyme, Conn., and founded the Mohegan tribe. In 1637 he combined with the colonists for the destruction of the Pequots and was given a portion of the conquered territory. His friendly intercourse with the colonists aroused the jealousy of the Narragansetts, who made war upon the Mohegans, and for the next few years Uncas was almost continually defending his territory from invasion. He died near Norwich, Conn., and a monument has been erected there in his honor.

Uncial, *un'shal,* **Letters,** letters of large size, used in ancient Latin and Greek manuscripts. These letters were a sort of compound of capitals and small characters, some of them resembling the former, others the latter. Uncial writing is supposed to have been employed in Latin manuscripts as early as the third or fourth century, but was seldom used after the tenth.

Unc'tion or **Extreme Unction,** a sacrament of the Roman Catholic Church, administered to the dying to give them strength and grace physically and spiritually in the hour of death. In this sacrament, the priest, dipping his thumb in the oil, anoints the sick person in the form of the cross upon the eyes, ears, mouth, nose, hands and feet, saying, "Through this Holy Unction and His most tender mercy, may the Lord pardon thee whatever sins thou hast committed by seeing. Amen." He repeats the same, adapting it to the part anointed. The oil used in this sacrament must be blessed by the bishop, a ceremony performed each year on Maundy Thursday.

Un'derground Rail'road, the name given before the Civil War to the method in use in parts of the North for assisting slaves from the South to escape from their masters. Regular routes were laid out, certain houses at convenient intervals being known as stations. Fleeing negroes were taken by friendly Northerners from one of these points to the next, where they were given rest and food and prepared for the next stage in their journey. The most common routes were through Ohio and Pennsylvania, the goal of each being Canada. Among the prominent promoters of these enterprises were Gerrit Smith, Theodore Parker and Levi Coffin. It is believed that fully 25,000 negroes were thus given liberty during the quarter century preceding the Civil War.

Underground Railway or **Sub'way,** a railway in a tunnel excavated for the purpose of placing the roadbed below the level of the street (See TUNNEL). London was the first city to adopt underground railways. In that city the roads now form two systems, the inner circle, thirteen miles in length and connecting the principal railway terminals north of the Thames, and the outer circle, known as the Metropolitan District Railway. In the United States underground systems have been constructed in Baltimore, Boston and New York. The Baltimore system was for the purpose of letting the Baltimore & Ohio railroad into the center of the city. The Boston system carries the street car traffic through the most crowded business districts. The New York subway, over twenty-one miles in extent, reaches the entire length of Manhattan Island and is the largest underground passenger railway in the world. A great freight subway, nearly seventy miles long, has recently been constructed under the central business district of the city of Chicago.

Un'dershot Wheel, a form of water wheel, with a number of float boards disposed on its circumference. It is turned round by the moving force of a stream of water acting on the float boards at its lowest part. In this wheel the water acts entirely by its momentum. The undershot wheel is used where there is a large volume of water and but little fall. See WATER WHEELS.

Underwood, OSCAR (1862–   ), an American statesman, born in Louisville, Kentucky. He was educated at Rugby School, Louisville, and at the University of Virginia. He chose law as a profession, was admitted to the bar in 1884 and began practice in Birmingham, Alabama, where he later became interested in iron manufacture. Entering politics, he was elected to Congress in 1895, and served continuously as representative of the ninth Alabama district until 1914, when he was elected United States Senator. He was a candidate for the presidential nomination in the National Democratic Convention of 1912. From 1911 to 1914 he was chairman of the committee on Ways and Means and majority leader in the House of Representatives. As such, he was a leading factor in the tariff and financial legislation of 1913–1914. In 1914 he was elected United States senator from Alabama.

Un'derwri'ter. See INSURANCE.

Unga'va, a district of Canada, which comprises all of the peninsula of Labrador except the easternmost part, which bears, politically, the name of Labrador. It is partly desolate and rocky, but there are extensive forests, in which are found bears, wolves, foxes, martens and other fur-bearing animals. The interior of the district consists mostly of a tableland 2000 or more feet high. There are a number of lakes drained partly by rivers flowing toward Hudson Strait, partly by others reaching the Atlantic in lower latitudes. The climate is rigorous, but the long winter is bearable, on account of the dryness of the air. No cereal can ripen, but potatoes and other vegetables can be grown. The population (about 4500 in all) consists chiefly of indians, Eskimo and half-breeds. In 1912 Ungava was added to the province of Quebec.

Un'gula'ta, or hoofed animals, an order of mammals which includes the pig, the deer and the horse, as well as elephants, which formerly were classified as Edentata. Most of the ungulates walk on their toes, which are enclosed in a horny hoof. They are able to run with speed and are the only mammals which possess horns. The greater part of the ungulates are called ruminants and have good strong teeth for chewing their vegetable food. See ANTELOPE; BOAR; CAMEL; CATTLE; DEER; ELEPHANT; GIRAFFE; GOAT; HIPPOPOTAMUS; HORSE; IBEX; PECCARY; RHINOCEROS; SHEEP; TAPIR.

U'nicorn, a fabulous animal, frequently mentioned by Greek and Roman writers. It was said to resemble a white horse, but it had one straight horn growing out of its forehead. It was described as a native of India. The figure of the unicorn is much used in heraldry.

Uniform, a dress of a particular style or fashion, worn by members of the same body in order that they may be recognized as belonging to that body.

MILITARY UNIFORMS. In Europe the colors of the military uniform are in general those which were once worn as livery by the royal servants in each country respectively, and are taken from the chief colors in the royal coats of arms. Of recent years, however, experience having proved that in modern warfare the traditional reds, blues and greens are too conspicuous in the field, the

nations are practically adopting the same type of uniform and the same color of material. These uniforms, known as *khaki*, are plainly and substantially made, of drab, clay or dust-colored cotton or woolen cloth.

English. Red has always predominated in the British uniform. At present the infantry wears scarlet, the rifle regiments wear dark green, the cavalry scarlet or blue, the artillery blue with scarlet facings, and the engineers scarlet with blue facings. The British campaign dress is of khaki.

French. In France a radical change took place in the uniform in 1903. For the traditional red full trousers and double-breasted coat, a tunic of dark Prussian blue cloth and trousers of dark bluish-gray were substituted. The only decorative portion of the uniform is the red epaulets.

German. In the German army the infantry wear a single-breasted blue tunic with scarlet facings, the rifle regiments wear dark green tunics with scarlet facings and the cavalry wear a white or light blue tunic with metal or leather helmet. The artillery have dark blue tunics with black facings, while the engineers' uniform is similar. In 1904 the emperor decreed that the service dress for all troops should be of khaki material.

Austrian. In Austria the uniform for the infantry is of dark blue cloth, the rifle regiments wear light gray and the cavalry light blue, while the uniform of the hussars is of light and dark blue.

Italian. In Italy the uniform of the infantry consists of a dark blue tunic and dark gray trousers. The cavalry also wear a dark blue tunic, but the trousers are light gray. The artillery are distinguished by dark blue trousers and by yellow facings on the tunic.

Russian. In Russia the infantry wear a green tunic and green trousers, which are tucked into knee boots. The cavalry wear green tunics and trousers of gray cloth, and the Cossacks usually wear a distinguishing uniform of dark green. The headdress of the Cossacks is a round, high cap of sheepskin.

Japanese. The Japanese winter uniform is dark blue and the summer uniform white. The uniforms for the artillery, infantry and cavalry are the same style, except that the facings for the cavalry are green, for the artillery yellow and for the infantry red. The campaign uniforms are of khaki.

American. Since 1782 the prescribed uniform of the United States army has, in general, been blue, with red facings. In 1902 a cap was substituted for the helmet in the uniforms of the United States soldiers, and full dress, dress and service uniforms were adopted. The proper dress for each occasion is determined by the commanding officer. All officers, during hours when they are on duty (from 9 A. M. to 4 P. M.), wear the prescribed uniform. At other times they may wear civilian dress, but enlisted men may not wear civilian dress without permission of their commanding officers.

The officers wear full dress uniform at all ceremonies when it is desired to do special honor to the occasion. This full dress uniform consists of a double-breasted blue coat with devices and braid on the collar, sleeves and shoulder strap showing the branch of the service and the rank of the officers, and trousers of dark blue cloth. Officers of the cavalry, artillery and infantry wear trousers of sky-blue cloth. Dress uniform is worn by officers at review, inspection and parades and at other ceremonies when the troops are in dress uniform. It is also the habitual uniform at garrison, unless otherwise prescribed by the commanding officer. The dress coat for all except general officers is a single-breasted sack coat of dark blue, trimmed with black braid, but without brass buttons. Shoulder straps and appropriate corps devices on the collar are worn with this coat. The general officer's dress coat is a double-breasted sack coat with brass buttons. The dress trousers are of dark blue cloth without stripe, except for the chief of artillery, who wears light blue trousers with a stripe of scarlet cloth. The service coat is a sack coat of heavy drab and has the insignia of rank on the shoulder strap and the corps device on the collar.

The enlisted men of the army have the same general classes of uniforms as those worn by the officers. The full dress uniform, which is worn at reviews, inspection and parades, consists of a single-breasted sack coat of dark blue cloth, adorned with the breast cord and tassel of the corps, and trousers of sky-blue with a strap of the color appropriate to the corps. The cap has a band of cloth of a corresponding color and the appropriate insignia of metal in front. The dress uniform of a private soldier does not differ from his full dress uniform except that the dress cap has the band removed. The service uniform for enlisted men is worn habitually in the garrison, also for duty under arms, in garrison, at drills, on marches and in the field. It consists of a sack coat of olive drab woolen material for winter and of khaki-colored cotton material for summer wear or in the tropics. The same colored ornaments and chevrons are placed on this coat as on the dress coat.

NAVAL UNIFORMS. In all the modern navies the prescribed uniforms are very much alike. In general, naval uniforms are blue or white, and the differences in the uniforms of the navies of different nations are usually in such details as insignia, epaulets and gold lace. Thus, the uniform of the United States navy as described below may be considered fairly typical.

The uniforms of officers of the United States navy are designated as dress, undress and service dress. The dress uniforms are special full dress, full dress, dress, evening dress A, evening dress B and mess dress. The special full dress uniform consists of a double-breasted blue broadcloth coat with standing collar and eighteen gilt buttons; blue trousers with a stripe of gold lace; epaulets, cocked hat, sword and full dress belt. This uniform is worn on state occasions at home and abroad.

Full dress differs from special full dress chiefly in that a frock coat is worn. This uniform is worn on occasions of ceremony, such as exchanging formal visits with foreign officers.

In the dress uniform the trousers are of plain navy blue cloth or white linen duck and the belt is of plain leather. This uniform is worn at a reception given on board ship by the assistant secretary of the navy, by a member of the president's cabinet other than the secretary of the navy or by any United States officer or diplomatic representative above the rank of charge d'affaires.

Evening dress A is similar in cut to the civilian evening dress, but is of a dark blue color with gilt buttons and epaulets. The waistcoat may be blue or white. This uniform is suitable for occasions of ceremony in the evening to which officers are invited in their official capacity. Evening dress B is like evening dress A except that blue undress trousers are worn and blue cap and white tie. This uniform is prescribed for less ceremonious occasions to which officers are invited in their official capacity.

The mess dress consists of the white mess jacket, cut like the evening dress coat without the tails, white waistcoat and blue or white trousers. It is worn on ordinary social occasions in in the evening to which officers are invited in their official capacity, and where hot weather or other circumstances make it appropriate.

The undress A uniform consists of a double-breasted blue frock coat, similar in cut to the civilian's coat, but with eighteen gilt buttons and with shoulder fixtures for epaulets; undress trousers; blue cap with white cover, if ordered; shoulder straps, sword and plain leather belt. This uniform is worn when reporting for duty and when serving on courts or boards, except boards of survey. Undress B is the same as undress A, except that the sword and belt are not worn; it is prescribed when calling on foreign officers other than commanding officers, at informal daytime receptions and on the decks of vessels going into, or out of, port.

The service dress for officers consists of a service coat of dark navy-blue cloth or serge, or for warm weather a coat of white linen duck or similar material; undress trousers; blue cap with white cover, if ordered, and sword belt and sword. This dress is to be worn at all times when not otherwise provided for.

The uniform worn by enlisted men is designated as blue dress, blue undress, white dress, white undress, blue working dress and white working dress. Dress uniform is worn on all occasions of ceremony and may be of dark blue cloth or white duck or similar material. The coats of the chief petty officers are double-breasted, with gilt buttons. Other enlisted men wear a blue shirt or white dress jumper, with blue cloth trousers. Undress is worn on ordinary occasions and is merely less neat or new uniform, if blue; but white undress has a white collar instead of a blue one. Working dress is old blue or white uniform. It is worn without a neckerchief, while with both dress and undress uniforms enlisted men always wear a black silk neckerchief. Chief petty officers wear caps with visors; other enlisted men wear an ordinary round sailor cap. See INSIGNIA.

U′nion, N. J., a town of Hudson co., on the Hudson River and on the West Shore and the New York, Susquehanna & Western railroads, one mi. n. of Hoboken. The manufacture of silk goods constitutes its chief industry, but there are breweries and a large shirt factory. Population in 1910, 21,023.

Union, S. C., the county-seat of Union co., 65 mi. n. w. of Columbia, on the Southern railway. The city is in an agricultural region, producing cotton, fruit and considerable lumber. It contains several large cotton mills, cotton gins, an oil mill, a knitting mill, a foundry, ice works and other factories. There are fourteen churches, three banks and a public library. The waterworks and electric light plant are owned by the municipality. Population in 1910, 5623.

U′niontown, PA., the county-seat of Fayette co., about 45 mi. s. by e. of Pittsburg, on the Baltimore & Ohio and several lines of the Pennsylvania railroad. The surrounding region contains coal, iron ore, glass sand and natural gas, and the borough has lumber mills, large coke ovens, steel works, foundries, machine shops and glass and other factories. The principal buildings are the hospital, the courthouse, the jail and the county home for the poor. There are four banks, two trust companies, municipal waterworks, electric lights and an electric street railway. The place was settled in 1767, and the borough was incorporated in 1796. Population in 1910, 13,344.

U′nit, a single thing regarded as an undivided whole. In arithmetic the term is also used to denote the least whole number, *one* or *unity*, represented by the figure 1. In mathematics and physics, a unit is any known determinate quantity, by which any other quantity of the same kind is measured, as a foot, a second, a degree, a square yard (See WEIGHTS AND MEASURES). Below are given the more important special units used in physics. The *unit of specific gravity*, for solids or liquids, is the specific gravity of one cubic foot of distilled water at 62° F.; for air and gases, of one cubic foot of atmospheric air at 62° F. The *unit of heat*, or the *thermal unit*, is the quantity of heat required to raise one pound of pure water from a temperature of 39° F. to a temperature of 40° F., or, in the metric system, the amount of heat required to raise a gram of pure water from a temperature of 3.94° C. to 4.94° C. In electricity the *unit of quantity* is that quantity of electricity, which, with an electromotive force of one volt, will flow through a resistance of 1,000,000 ohms in one second; it is called a *farad*. The *unit of electric current* is a current of one farad a second. The *unit of physical work* is that amount of work which will produce a velocity of one meter per second in a mass weighing one gram, after acting upon it a second of time. The *dynamic unit* is the unit expressing the quantity of force or the amount of work done, as the *footpound*. In physical calculations the system of units now in general use is that known as the *C. G. S. System*, based upon the metric system of weights and measures, in which the centimeter is the *unit of length*, the gram is the *unit of mass* and the second the *unit of time*. Consequently, the *unit of area* is the square centimeter; the *unit of volume*, the cubic centimeter; the *unit of velocity*, a velocity of one centimeter per second. The *unit of momen-*

tum is the momentum of a gram moving with a unit velocity.

For definitions of units of measurement in other fields of work, see articles on those units, as FOOT; POUND; DOLLAR.

U'nita'rians, a religious denomination which believes in one God, the Father, and not in a Trinity of Father, Son and Holy Spirit. They accept Christ as a divinely appointed teacher, to be followed, but not worshiped. The Unitarians have no creed; their faith may be summed up in the words, "the fatherhood of God, the brotherhood of man, the leadership of Jesus, salvation by character and the progress of mankind upward and onward forever." The man most influential in the establishment of Unitarianism in the United States was Channing. See CHANNING, WILLIAM ELLERY.

Uni'ted King'dom, THE, officially, the *United Kingdom of Great Britain and Ireland,* the term frequently used to indicate the union of England, Scotland and Ireland under one government. See GREAT BRITAIN.

United States, officially, the *United States of America,* a republic occupying the central portion of North America and extending from 25° 10′ to 49° north latitude and from 66° 58′ to 124° 36′ west longitude.

BOUNDARIES AND COASTAL FEATURES. It is bounded on the n. by the Dominion of Canada, on the e. by the Atlantic Ocean, on the s. by the Gulf of Mexico and Mexico, and on the w. by the Pacific Ocean. Its greatest extent from east to west is 3100 mi., and from north to south, 1780 mi. The total area of the United States proper is 3,026,789 sq. mi. The area of the land surface is 2,973,890 sq. mi. The entire domain of the United States, including Alaska, the Philippines, Porto Rico and Hawaii, is, in round numbers, 3,743,000 sq. mi. It is exceeded in area only by the British Empire, Russia and China. West of the 95th meridian the northern boundary is formed by the 49th parallel of north latitude until the Pacific coast is reached; then it extends southward to the Strait of Juan de Fuca, thus placing Vancouver Island within the Dominion of Canada. East of the 95th meridian the northern boundary is very irregular. That portion of it between the meridian and Lake Superior is formed by the Rainy and Pigeon rivers. Through the Great Lakes the boundary line follows the deepest channel, which divides Lakes Huron, Erie and Ontario nearly equally between the two nations, but gives the larger part of Lake Superior to the United States. Following Lake

Ontario the boundary is formed for a short distance by the Saint Lawrence River, then across New York and Vermont by the 45th parallel; thence it follows the Height of Land in an irregular course to the northeast, until the northerly point of Maine is reached. From there the boundary is completed by the Saint Johns River, a short, arbitrary line and the Saint Croix River. A portion of the southern boundary is formed by the Rio Grande. The entire coast line, exclusive of the Great Lakes, is 12,101 miles. The Atlantic coast is 6017 miles; the Gulf, 3551, and the Pacific, 2533.

The prominent projections are, on the Atlantic Coast, Cape Cod, Cape Hatteras and the peninsula of Florida; on the Gulf coast, Cape San Blas and the delta of the Mississippi, and on the Pacific coast, Cape Mendocino. The important coast waters are, on the Atlantic, Massachusetts Bay, Long Island Sound, Delaware Bay, Chesapeake Bay, Albemarle Sound and Pamlico Sound; on the Gulf, Apalachee Bay and Mobile Bay, and on the Pacific, San Francisco Bay and Puget Sound.

The chief islands on the Atlantic coast are Nantucket, Martha's Vineyard, Long, Manhattan, Staten, Roanoke and Florida Keys; in the Gulf of Mexico, Tortugas, Saint George's, Santa Rosa, the Chandeleur group, Galveston and Padre; on the Pacific, Santa Catalina, the Santa Barbara group and San Juan.

SURFACE AND DRAINAGE. The vast extent of territory embraced within the United States contains a great variety of surface, but this is naturally divided into five regions—the Atlantic Slope, the Appalachian Highlands, the Central Plain, the Rocky Mountain Highlands and the Pacific Slope.

The Atlantic Slope. This region embraces a narrow strip of land extending from the northeastern corner of Maine to Florida. In the northern part it is extremely narrow, and the slope is steep. The irregularity of the coast line produces numerous good harbors, upon which some of the largest cities of the country are located. Chief among these indentations are Boston Bay, New York Bay, Delaware Bay and Chesapeake Bay. South of Long Island this coast region becomes broader and consists of a tract of level land, varying from 75 to 300 miles in width. It is here known as the Atlantic coastal plain. Along the shore and for a short distance inland the surface is low, level and, in many places, marshy. The land then rises gradually until it meets the Piedmont region, or foothills of the

Appalachians. This region consists of the remains of an old, worn-down mountain system, formed previous to the present Appalachian system (See PIEDMONT REGION). Where the plain joins the Piedmont region, there is a marked elevation, known as the Fall Line, because the rivers reaching the Atlantic fall over this uplift, producing numerous rapids and affording excellent water power.

The Appalachian Highlands. This region constitutes the eastern continental barrier and extends from the Gulf of Saint Lawrence to within about 300 miles of the Gulf of Mexico. The trend of the mountains is from the northeast to the southwest. The region consists of a low plateau, from 1500 to 3000 feet in altitude, upon which are a number of parallel ranges of mountains. The northern part of the plateau is quite broken, and the mountains are disconnected, forming separate ranges or groups, as the Green Mountains, the White Mountains and the Adirondacks. South of this division, however, the plateau is continuous and is surmounted by a number of parallel ranges of low mountains, such as the Blue Ridge, the Alleghanies and others. The highest peaks in these highlands are Mount Washington, in the White Mountains, and Mount Mitchell, near the southern extremity of the plateau. On their western slope these highlands descend by a series of foothills to the prairie region in the central plain. See APPALACHIAN MOUNTAINS.

The Central Plain. This occupies the vast interior of the country and embraces that portion of the great central plain of North America included within the boundaries of the United States. It is naturally divided into three regions, the great plain, the lake region and the gulf region.

The Great Plain. East of the Mississippi, this plain occupies that portion of the interior between the Ohio River and the lake region. Here it descends from the western foothills of the Appalachians to the broad, level prairies which compose most of the states bordering on the Mississippi. This stretch of level or slightly rolling land continues westward, until it rises in gradual swells to meet the foothills of the Rocky Mountain highlands, where it attains an elevation of from 3000 to 6000 feet. With the exception of the Ozark Plateau, which extends eastward from the southern boundary of Kansas, crossing Arkansas, the southern part of Missouri and the southern part of Illinois, this level tract of land extends southward into Texas and westward until it joins the Staked Plains in the northwestern

part of that state. With the exception of the forests in northern Minnesota and in the Ozark Region, this entire portion of the country is nearly treeless. Timber is found only along streams and in regions where trees have been planted by settlers. These vast tracts of level, treeless land are generally known as prairies. Their deep, rich soil, abundant rainfall and salubrious climate make the prairies the most valuable agricultural region in the world. See PRAIRIES.

The Lake Region. The lake region constitutes that portion of the United States which drains into the Great Lakes, and thence through the Saint Lawrence River into the Atlantic. The Height of Land, forming the southern boundary of this region, is nearly parallel with the southern shores of lakes Ontario and Erie, extends across the northern part of Ohio, Indiana and Illinois, thence turns northward, to include the eastern portion of Wisconsin, all of Michigan and the northwestern part of Minnesota. The region within the United States is not large. It is either level or rolling, nowhere having high altitudes, and much of it was formerly heavily timbered, but the lumbering interests have greatly reduced the forest area.

The Gulf Region. The Gulf region includes the lowlands bordering on the Gulf of Mexico and extending inland until they meet the foothills of the Appalachian Highlands. In the valley of the Mississippi, this plain extends northward to the Ohio River, and west of the Mississippi it extends northward to the Ozark Mountains. Along the coast the land is low, level and swampy, but with the exception of that immediately in the vicinity of the Mississippi River, it rises gradually toward the interior, until it reaches a height of 300 to 500 feet. The plain includes all of the southern and southeastern parts of Texas, in that state being from 150 to 200 miles in width.

The Rocky Mountain Highlands. This region occupies nearly one-third of the area of the country, and consists of a great plateau, upon which rise several ranges of mountains. This plateau reaches its greatest height and width in Colorado and Wyoming. Here it is nearly 1000 miles wide and from 7000 to 8000 feet in altitude. On its eastern slope it rises from the plain in a series of elevations, until the Rocky Mountains, which form its eastern boundary, are reached. These extend entirely across the country and contain numerous peaks, with altitudes of 14,000 feet or more (See ROCKY MOUNTAINS). The western border of the plateau is formed by the Cascade

Mountains, in the north, and their southern continuation, the Sierra Nevadas. These mountains contain peaks as high as, or higher than, those found in the Rocky Mountains. Their western slope, since they rise from the plateau, is less abrupt than the eastern, which descends to the valley between them and the low ranges (See CASCADE MOUNTAINS; SIERRA NEVADA MOUNTAINS). Between these mountain barriers, the surface of the great plateau is widely diversified by lesser ranges, extending in various directions. These ranges divide this vast inland region into three well-marked divisions, the Columbia Plateau, in the north; the Great Basin, and the Colorado Plateau. The first occupies the mountain regions of Washington, Oregon and Idaho. The Great Basin includes nearly all Nevada and Utah and a small portion of Oregon and California; it is entirely surrounded by mountains, and its rivers find no outlet, hence it contains a number of salt lakes and marshes, the most noted among which is Great Salt Lake. South of this, and occupying a small part of Nevada, nearly all of Colorado, a part of Utah, most of Arizona and New Mexico and the southern part of California, is the Colorado Plateau, marked by many high peaks and the deep gorges of its streams.

The Pacific Slope. Between the Sierra Nevada and Cascade mountains and the coast are low parallel ranges, known as the Coast Ranges. West of these is the narrow strip of land bordering upon the ocean. This low land is much narrower than that bordering upon the Atlantic, but between the mountains are several depressions forming valleys noted for their fertility. Chief among these are the valleys of the San Joaquin and Sacramento rivers, the region around San Francisco Bay and that around Puget Sound. Farther inland, in the southeastern part of California, is Death Valley, a remarkable depression, 300 feet below sea level.

Rivers. The United States is drained by five river systems—the Lake system, the Atlantic system, the Gulf system, the Pacific system and the Great Basin system. The portion of the country drained by the Lake system is comparatively small, and the streams flowing into it are generally short and of little importance, though the Saint Lawrence River, forming the outlet of this drainage area, is one of the most important streams in North America. See GREAT LAKES.

Owing to the position of the Appalachian Highlands, the rivers of the Atlantic system are short and many of them are rapid. However,

the largest of these streams enter the ocean by broad estuaries, which afford excellent harbors, and some of them, particularly the Hudson, the Delaware and the Potomac, cut their way through the mountains, forming deep gorges remarkable for their beautiful scenery. The most important of these rivers, in order, beginning at the north, are the Penobscot, the Kennebec, the Merrimac, the Connecticut, the Hudson, the Delaware, the Potomac, the James, the Pedee, the Santee, the Savannah and the Altamaha. Many of these streams afford excellent water power, and the banks of the Merrimac and many others are lined with manufactories.

The rivers of the Gulf system include the Appalachicola, the Alabama, the Pearl, the Sabine, the Trinity, the Brazos, the Colorado Texas, the Nueces, the Rio Grande and the Mississippi, which drains by far the largest part of the country. See MISSISSIPPI RIVER.

The rivers of the Pacific system are few, and with the exception of the Columbia, draining the northwestern part of the country, and the Colorado, flowing into the Gulf of California, they are all short and small. Proceeding southward from the Columbia, those worthy of mention are the Klamath, the Sacramento, the San Joaquin and the Salinas. The Colorado, formed by the junction of the Green and the Grand in Utah, drains a portion of the plateau between the Rocky and the Sierra Nevada mountains. This stream is remarkable for the gorges which it has formed in the middle and lower parts of its course. See COLORADO RIVER.

The Great Basin system consists of a number of small streams which flow into Great Salt Lake and a few smaller lakes, or which lose themselves in salt marshes in the desert. The Humboldt is the only one of these of any importance.

Lakes. Fully one-half of the area of lakes Superior, Huron, Erie and Ontario belongs to the United States, and all of Lake Michigan is within her boundaries. In addition to these great bodies of water, the northern part of the Appalachian Highlands contains many lakes noted for their clear waters and beautiful scenery. Chief among these is Moosehead, in Maine; Winnepesaukee, in New Hampshire, and Champlain, between Vermont and New York. The northern parts of Michigan, Wisconsin and Minnesota are also studded with lakes, and in the Rocky Mountain region are found numerous lakes, some of which, like Lake Tahoe, are noted for their high altitude, others for their great depth, abundance of fish and beautiful surroundings. The Great Basin has Great Salt Lake and numerous other smaller bodies of salt water. See GREAT SALT LAKE.

Scenery. For variety, beauty and grandeur, the scenery of the United States is unequaled by that of any other country. The Appalachian Highlands are noted for their mountain lakes, sparkling streams and deep gorges, through which rivers find their way to the sea. Notable among the last are the Crawford Notch, in the White Mountains; the Palisades of the Hudson, and the Delaware Water Gap. The central plain presents to view vast areas of fertile fields. The expanse of fresh water afforded by the Great Lakes is nowhere equaled and is approached only by the great lakes in the equatorial regions of Africa. The only cataract comparable with Niagara is Victoria Falls, on the Zambezi, while the Shoshone Falls, Yosemite Falls, the Falls of the Yellowstone and many others in the Rocky Mountain region are unsurpassed in beauty. The extent and grandeur of mountain scenery found in the Rocky Mountains exceeds that of any other single country; the Royal Gorge, Yosemite Valley and the canyons of the Colorado and Yellowstone are features of unusual interest, and the geysers and hot springs of Yellowstone National Park have caused that region to be termed the "World's Wonderland."

CLIMATE. As a whole, the United States has a temperate climate, though in the extreme south some sections are within the subtropical region. The country extends over more than 24° of latitude. This range of latitude, the position and extent of the mountain systems and the differences in altitude, give rise to a great variety of climatic conditions, so that places having the same latitude often vary widely in climate. This is particularly true of places on the Atlantic and Pacific coasts. Here prevailing winds and ocean currents cause a remarkable contrast.

Temperature. On the northern boundary, the average temperature for January is 20°, and for July, 60°. The contrast between the winter temperature on the Pacific and Atlantic coasts in the northern part of the country is very marked, the mean temperature on the Pacific coast being 41°, and on the Atlantic coast, 14°. Toward the south the average temperature rises, and it also becomes more nearly equal at the eastern and western extremities; at the 30th parallel of latitude the difference between the average temperature of the two regions for January is only 2°, and for July, only 9°, while at the extreme southern boundary the January difference is 3°,

and the July difference, but 1°. The central plain is open to the passage of air currents with little or no obstruction; consequently alternating north and south winds sweep over this region, causing sudden and marked changes in temperature. The northern part of the Appalachian Highlands has a cool temperate climate. The winters are usually long and severe, and in New England, New York, some parts of Pennsylvania and northern Ohio, there is a heavy fall of snow. Toward the south the mean temperature rises, and south of Pennsylvania little snow falls, except in the highest mountains. Near the Gulf the temperature seldom falls below freezing point, and the Gulf states, with South Carolina and Georgia, verge upon a subtropical climate. The Rocky Mountain region is cooler than other regions in the same latitude, because of its high altitude. The northern part of this region, as well as the northern portion of the central plain, is subject to intense cold waves during winter, the thermometer occasionally falling as low as 40° below zero; yet, owing to the dryness of the atmosphere, these extremes produce little discomfort. The Pacific coast has a mild climate throughout the year, with a remarkably equable temperature. At sea level the thermometer seldom falls below freezing point, even in the northwestern part of the country, and during summer it seldom rises above 80° or 85°. In the southern part of California, the temperature in summer may be higher than this, though hot waves, even there, last but a short time.

Rainfall. The position of the mountains causes a very unequal distribution of rain. In general, all that portion of the country east of the meridian of 100°, crossing the middle of North and South Dakota and Nebraska, has sufficient rainfall for agriculture. In most of this region the annual precipitation varies from 40 to 60 inches. This is evenly distributed throughout the year, making this region well favored for agricultural purposes. A small region in the eastern part of North Carolina, and another area north of the Gulf of Mexico, have over 60 inches. The northern half of Illinois, Wisconsin, Minnesota, Iowa, most of Kansas, Missouri, Oklahoma and the eastern half of Texas have from 20 to 40 inches of rain, which assures crops; but west of this region the annual precipitation varies from 10 to 20 inches, and agriculture can be successfully prosecuted only by irrigation. However, large areas are well adapted to grazing, since there is sufficient moisture to produce a good growth of grass. The great plateau between the mountains is arid, and the southern half of it, including nearly all of Nevada, the western part of Utah, the western part of Arizona and the southeastern part of California, are practically rainless. This is because the winds are robbed of their moisture as they pass inland from the Sierras. For the same reason the western slopes of these mountains and the valleys between them

and New Mexico. In all, the area of coal measures is almost 300,000 square miles. By far the greater portion of this area contains bituminous coal, but the anthracite variety is confined within the boundaries of Pennsylvania. Coal is now mined in thirty states, and the output exceeds that of any other country, being about one-third the entire output of the world. See COAL.

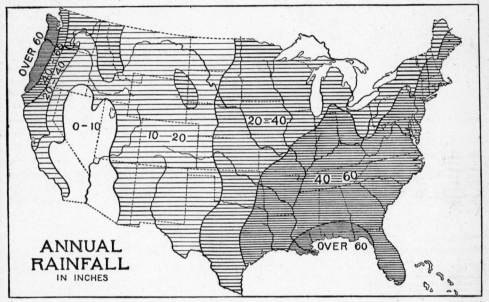

ANNUAL RAINFALL IN INCHES

and the coast ranges are well watered, while along the coast through Washington, Oregon and the northern part of California, there is a region which receives over 60 inches of rain during the year.

MINERAL RESOURCES. The minerals of the United States constitute one of her chief sources of wealth, and in extent and variety they exceed those of any other country. With the exception of some coal and petroleum, most of the valuable minerals are found in the mountainous regions, and there the mining industry is most fully developed. The most important of the mineral fuels are coal, petroleum and natural gas; the chief metals are iron, gold, silver, copper, lead, zinc and quicksilver.

Coal. The most extensive coal measures are found in the central part of the Appalachian highlands, including Pennsylvania and West Virginia and extending westward through the southern part of Ohio, Indiana and Illinois. There are also extensive coal measures in Missouri and Iowa, and areas of lesser extent occur in North Dakota, Montana, Wyoming, Colorado, Utah

Petroleum. Petroleum ranks next to coal in importance as a mineral fuel. The chief oil fields are found in western Pennsylvania, West Virginia, Ohio, Indiana, Kansas, Colorado, Texas, Oklahoma and the southern part of California. The annual output for the entire country is over 160,000,000 barrels, which is exceeded only by that of Russia; but the United States exceeds Russia in the quantity of the products obtained by refining petroleum. See PETROLEUM.

Natural Gas. Natural gas occurs in usable quantities in Pennsylvania, Ohio, Indiana and Kentucky, and in smaller quantities it is found in a number of other states. It is of great advantage, since it furnishes the cheapest and most convenient fuel, especially for many manufacturing purposes, such as smelting iron and steel and manufacturing glass. See NATURAL GAS.

Iron. Iron ranks first in value and importance among the metals produced within the country. The great deposits of ore are in Michigan and Minnesota, around Lake Superior; in eastern New York; in Pennsylvania; in Alabama and Georgia, and in southern Missouri, in the Ozark

Plateau. Deposits of less importance are quite widely distributed, especially in the Rocky Mountain region. Minnesota and Michigan are the leading states in the production of iron ore, and the great centers of iron manufacture are naturally where iron ore and coal can be most cheaply brought together. These are Pennsylvania, Ohio, Illinois, Indiana and Alabama. The United States now leads all other nations in the production of iron and steel, her annual output of pig iron being over 25,000,000 tons. See IRON.

Gold and Silver. All the important gold and silver mines are located in the Rocky Mountain region, throughout which the ores are quite generally distributed. Present methods of extracting the metals from the ore enable miners to work with profit at quantities of low grade ores that were formerly considered worthless, and this has increased the output of both metals. The annual production of gold, including Alaska, is about $95,000,000, and this amount is exceeded only by the mines in South Africa and those in Australia. The leading states in the production of gold are Colorado, California, Nevada, Utah, South Dakota, Idaho, Arizona and New Mexico, and these also contain the chief silver mines. In production of silver, the country is surpassed only by Mexico. See GOLD; SILVER.

Other Metals. The United States produces two-thirds of the world's supply of copper. The most important mines are located in Michigan, on the shore of Lake Superior; in Montana, and in Arizona. Lead is mined in Colorado, Idaho, Illinois, Iowa, Kansas, Missouri, Utah and Wisconsin, and the United States produces more than any other country. Lead and copper ores are frequently found combined with silver ore. Zinc is also found in Illinois, Kansas, Missouri, New Jersey and Wisconsin, the Kansas, Missouri, and Wisconsin mines being the largest producers. Quicksilver is found in California, which produces about all of that substance mined within the country. The United States produces about one-half of the world's supply of aluminum, the reduction works being at Pittsburg and Niagara Falls.

Building Stones. Limestone is very generally distributed throughout the country and is used for a great many purposes, such as the manufacture of lime and the construction of foundations for buildings and of piers for bridges; the finer varieties, such as those obtained in Indiana, are often used for the exteriors of buildings, or when dressed, for trimmings in buildings constructed of other stone or brick. Granite is found in large quantities in the New England states, particularly Maine, New Hampshire and Vermont; there are also large quarries in Minnesota. This is used extensively for building purposes and for tombstones. Granite is very widely distributed through the mountainous regions, and the Rocky Mountain plateau contains sufficient to supply large demands, whenever transportation facilities will warrant working the quarries. Marble is extensively quarried in Vermont and Georgia, and to some extent it is found in Tennessee and other states. The United States produces more marble than any other country. There are large quarries of slate in Vermont, Pennsylvania and several other states. This stone is used for finishing interiors and for roofing. Clays of suitable quality for the manufacture of brick and tile and for pottery are widely distributed.

Miscellaneous Minerals. Gypsum is found in many localities, and salt is obtained from the waters of salt springs and wells, New York and Michigan being the leading states in its production. The manufacture of salt is an important industry in these states.

VEGETATION. The plant life of the United States is characteristic of that of the temperate regions. Originally fully one-third of the country was covered with forests; but in the Appalachian Highlands and the Great Lake region, many sections have been almost wholly denuded, to supply the demand for lumber. In general, the forest areas include the Appalachian Highlands; the region bordering on the south of the Great Lakes and extending westward to the eastern boundary of the valley of the Red River of the North; the region along the Gulf of Mexico, including the eastern third of Texas and most of Arkansas, and the region occupied by the Cascade and Coast ranges of mountains, extending southward from the Dominion boundary as far as the central part of California. The Appalachian forests are characterized by a great variety of hard woods, such as oak, maple, ash, beech and birch. There are also many cone-bearing trees, including spruce, hemlock and the white pine, in the north, and the yellow pine and the cypress, in the south. The forests in the lake region have a great abundance of white pine, which is interspersed with some hard woods, and those of the Pacific coast are notable for peculiar species of cone-bearing trees, which attain great size, particularly the Douglas fir, the redwood, the yellow cedar and the sequoia. For fuller description of forests and their location, see FORESTS, subhead *United States.*

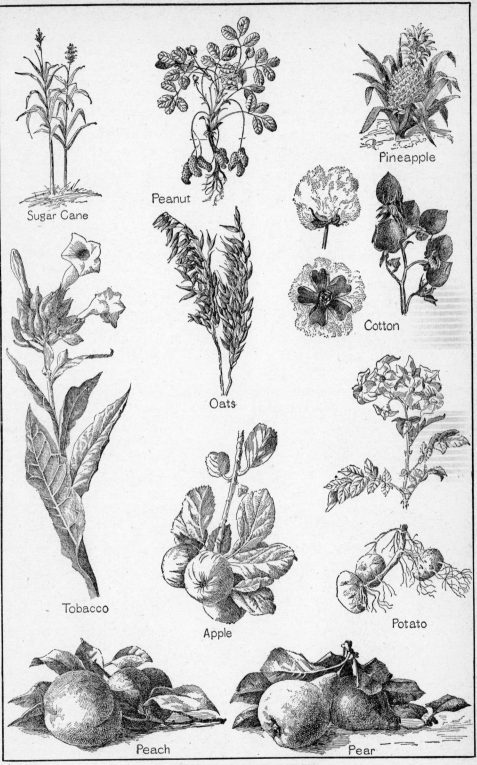

Sugar Cane

Peanut

Pineapple

Cotton

Tobacco

Oats

Apple

Potato

Peach

Pear

PLANT LIFE OF THE UNITED STATES

See, also, full-page illustration, *Plant Life of North America*, in article NORTH AMERICA

In addition to its forests the Appalachian Highland region and Atlantic coast plain have a great variety of smaller plants, many of which are useful, while many are desirable only because of their beautiful flowers. Among the latter are the flowering plants of the mint family, a great number of grasses and a number of shrubs. The great central plain is characterized by the growth of herbaceous plants, most of which belong to the grass family. Many of these grasses are highly nutritious, and previous to the occupation of this region by white men they sustained vast herds of buffalo, which roamed over the prairies. Among these grasses are a great number of flowering plants, noted for their beauty. Within the arid region of the Rocky Mountain plateau are found plants peculiar to desert areas. These consist almost wholly of species of sagebrush, bunch grass and buffalo grass, except in the southern portion of the plateau. Here many species of cactus are found, some of them growing to great size. The Pacific slope is characterized by vegetation peculiarly its own, containing a number of species which are tropical or semi-tropical in nature. Among these are several palms. The southern parts of Texas and Florida have a number of species belonging to the semi-tropical regions, and the vegetation of Florida very closely resembles that of the West Indies. Two plants discovered in America have become of great economic importance. These are maize, or indian corn, and tobacco. The cultivated plants are described under their respective titles, and the areas that they occupy are more fully outlined under the subhead *Agriculture*, in the articles treating of the various states.

ANIMAL LIFE. The native animals of the United States include a large number of species. Among these are 310 species of mammals, 756 species of birds, 816 species of fish, 257 species of reptiles and over 1000 species of mollusks. Among the larger quadrupeds of the carnivorous order are bears, several varieties of wolf, the puma, or mountain lion, the wildcat, the lynx and the coyote. Among the ruminating animals, various species of deer, the buffalo, the mountain sheep and the antelope are the most important. Of these, the buffalo and the mountain sheep are peculiar to North America. However, each of these species is now nearly extinct. There are many species of rodents, of which the beaver is the largest. This animal is also nearly extinct and is found only in the most unfrequented regions of the country. The prairies abound in gophers and prairie dogs, and various species of

squirrels frequent nearly all parts of the country. Among the large birds of prey are the eagle, the hawk and various species of owls. The most important water fowl include the Canada goose, the pelican and ducks. Other game birds of importance are the wild turkey, various species of grouse and pigeons. Song birds exist in large numbers and are found in all parts of the country.

AGRICULTURE. A large part of the country is well suited to agriculture, and for a century the United States has been the leading agricultural nation of the world. According to the census of 1910, there were in the United States 6,361,502 farms, including 878,798,325 acres, of which 478,451,750 acres, or over one-half, were improved land. The capital invested in agriculture, including buildings, implements, machinery and live stock, was $40,991,449,090, or more than double the capital invested in manufactures. The average size of farms throughout the country was 138.1 acres. The smallest average was 78.2, in the eastern half of the central southern group, and the largest 324.5, in the Mountain states. About 4,000,000 farms were worked by their owners, and there were 5,000,000 families living on farms. The number of people engaged in agricultural occupations was over 11,000,000, of which 9 per cent were women.

The great agricultural regions are the prairies of the Mississippi basin, east of the 100th meridian; the land bordering on the Gulf of Mexico, and the valleys of the Pacific slope. The Appalachian region is not so fertile as the others. However, in the valleys and on other low lands there are many valuable farms. In this part of the country the raising of cereals is not profitable, and the region cannot compete with the Mississippi Basin; hence the region is characterized by small farms, whose occupants are engaged in a variety of interests. The arid region, including the states within the Rocky Mountain plateau and the southern part of California, embraces nearly one-third of the country. Over most of this the soil is fertile, and wherever water can be supplied for irrigation, abundant crops are raised. The national government has undertaken works of gigantic proportions, for the purpose of reclaiming as much as possible of this region (See IRRIGATION). The valleys of the Pacific slope, where well watered, produce abundant crops of all plants which can be raised in that climate.

The product map of the United States shows that agriculturally the country is divided into six regions. The words in large type indicate the chief crop or industry in each region. Those in

Porcupine

Hare

Coyote

Deer

Beaver

Raccoon

Crane

ANIMALS OF THE UNITED STATES

See, also, full-page illustration, *Animals of North America*, in article NORTH AMERICA

smaller type indicate other products and industries. A careful study of this map will show that the northern New England states and New York are chiefly engaged in mixed farming and dairying, and that each of the other regions is devoted to one or more principal crops or industries, each of which is worthy of special consideration. For the development of agriculture in the country, see AGRICULTURE, and for more particular accounts, see subhead *Agriculture*, under the articles treating of the different states.

Cereals. As a whole, cereals constitute the most important agricultural product of the country. The great region devoted to these crops comprises the states of the Mississippi Basin, portions of Pennsylvania and West Virginia, and portions of Oregon, Washington and California. The leading wheat-producing states are Minnesota, North Dakota, Kansas, Nebraska and South Dakota. More than half the crop is winter wheat. The annual crop varies from 650,000,000 to about 760,000,000 bushels. In 1913 it was 753,233,000 bushels. The leading corn-producing states are Illinois, Iowa, Missouri, Indiana, Nebraska and Kansas. The annual crop varies from about 2,500,000,000 bushels to 2,900,000,000 bushels. In 1913 it was 2,463,017,000 bushels. The leading states in the production of oats are Illinois and Iowa. In 1913 the crop amounted to 1,122,139,000 bushels. The oats crop is next to the corn and wheat crops in value. Barley is grown quite extensively in California, Minnesota, Wisconsin and a few other states of the North Central region. In 1913 the crop amounted to 173,301-000 bushels. Rice is produced in Louisiana, South Carolina, Texas, Georgia and North Carolina. The annual crop is about 25,000,000 bushels. Considerable buckwheat is grown in some states, and some of the Northern states also produce more or less rye; but in the production of this grain the United States is far behind some of the European countries.

Cotton and Tobacco. Cotton is the chief product of the Southern states and the one from which they derive the greatest amount of money. The crop in 1913 amounted to 14,129,000 bales, of 500 pounds each. The leading states in its production are Texas, Mississippi, Georgia, Alabama, South Carolina and Arkansas (see COTTON). Tobacco is also an important crop, and it is generally distributed over the country. The amount grown in 1912 was 962,855,000 pounds, and it had a value of $104,063,000. This was an increase of 38% in five years. The leading

states in tobacco production, in the order of their importance, are Kentucky, North Carolina, Virginia, Wisconsin, Ohio, Tennessee, Connecticut, Maryland and Pennsylvania. A number of other states also raise considerable quantities. See TOBACCO.

Fruit. Horticulture is an important branch of agriculture, and the raising of fruit is the leading occupation in Florida, Delaware, parts of New Jersey, the western part of New York and the southern part of California, while its production engages the attention of a large number of farmers in Washington, Oregon, the mountainous part of Montana and a number of other states. In Florida pineapples and oranges are the chief fruits. In California oranges, lemons, apricots, grapes, prunes and almonds, among the larger fruits, are of greatest importance, while small fruits are raised in large quantities. Grapes and peaches are grown extensively in New York, and apples and peaches are produced in New York, Michigan, Colorado and numerous other states. Small fruits, including raspberries, blackberries and strawberries, are found in nearly all parts of the country where there is sufficient rainfall for their growth.

Other Crops. In Minnesota, Wisconsin and some other Northern states, considerable flax is grown, mostly for the seed. Sugar cane is raised in Louisiana and a few other of the Gulf states, and the sugar beet is grown in many of the states that have cool temperate climates. Potatoes are raised in large quantities in Wisconsin, Minnesota and New York. Sweet potatoes are grown in Virginia, in the southern part of Illinois and in a number of the Southern states. Vegetables are grown for market in Delaware and New Jersey and in nearly all states in which large cities are located. New York and the states on the Pacific slope are noted for their production of hops.

Live Stock. Much of the arid region is well suited to grazing, and in this section of the country large herds of cattle and sheep are raised. Texas leads in the production of cattle, and Montana is first in the production of sheep. Some of the corn states, particularly Iowa and Illinois, are noted for their beef cattle and hogs. New York, the northern New England states, Iowa, Illinois and Wisconsin are extensively engaged in dairying, and the value of the dairy products is great. The total value of domestic animals in the United States in 1910 was $5,150,000,000. Of this, $1,750,000,000 represented neat cattle; $2,750,000,000 represented horses; $250,000,000, sheep and lambs, and $400,000,000, hogs.

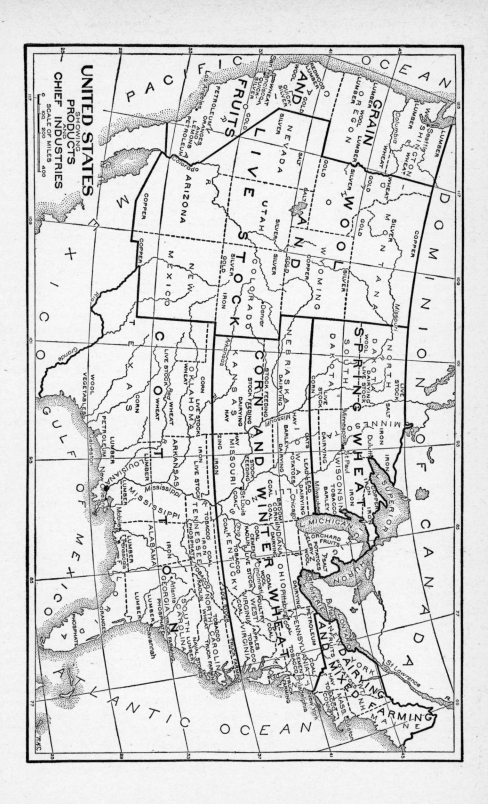

The raising of poultry is also an important branch of agricultural industry, and it engages many people in all parts of the country, though it has received less attention on the Pacific coast than in other regions. In 1909 the value of poultry raised was $202,506,272, and the value of eggs for the same year was $180,768,249. The leading poultry states were Illinois, Missouri, Iowa, Ohio and Indiana.

The methods of agriculture employed, the fertility of the soil and the facilities for transportation make the United States one of the great sources of the world for agricultural products.

FISHERIES. In the extent and value of its fisheries, the United States is the leading country of the world. The industry gives employment to about 212,000 men, has an invested capital of $90,920,000 and an average yearly income of $50,000,000, though some years the output amounts to over $60,000,000. The deep-sea fisheries conducted along the Atlantic coast include those of cod, herring, halibut, bluefish, menhaden and some other varieties, while in the vicinity of Long Island Sound, Delaware Bay and Chesapeake Bay, the oyster industry is extensively developed. Off the coast of Maine, lobsters, clams and scallops are taken in large quantities. On the Pacific coast the salmon fisheries take the lead, and in the Columbia River and in some places around Alaska, the catch is very large (See SALMON). The fisheries of the Great Lakes yield over 100,000,000 pounds a year and give employment to a large number of men. The fish taken in largest quantities are whitefish, lake trout and herring. Many of the rivers and smaller lakes are also well stocked with fish, and the aggregate catch from these bodies of water is considerable, though no accurate figures are obtainable. See FISHERIES; FISH CULTURE.

MANUFACTURES. Since 1860 manufactures have developed more rapidly than any other line of industry in the country. The United States has become the foremost manufacturing country and produces fully one-third of the manufactured products of the world.

Resources and Causes of Development. The chief causes for this rapid and extensive development are the country's abundant agricultural resources, her mineral resources, her extensive forests, the remarkable transportation facilities afforded, the inventive genius of the people and the opportunities for an extensive trade between the states. The extent and variety of agricultural products assure an abundance of food supplies for the people, and the methods of agriculture are such that a comparatively small proportion of the inhabitants can supply food for the entire nation and also for export to foreign lands. This leaves large numbers free to engage in other occupations, and this enables a larger proportion of the people to engage in manufacturing industries than would be possible were the agricultural conditions such that nearly all were dependent for support upon their own efforts in tilling the soil. The abundant supply of coal, iron and other useful metals makes the manufacture of many products convenient and comparatively cheap. This is particularly true of iron and steel and their products, while the presence of clay and various forms of building stone is of equal advantage in the construction of factories and other establishments connected directly or indirectly with manufacturing industries. The great forest areas provide an abundance of lumber and timber for all articles made of wood; hence this line of manufactures has been developed on a very large scale. No other country has such extensive and numerous transportation lines, both by water and by rail; hence the carrying of commodities from one section to another is comparatively easy and cheap (See paragraph *Transportation and Communication,* below).

The American people have always been noted for their mechanical ingenuity, and they have produced a great number of machines and devices which have greatly influenced, and in some cases have revolutionized, the industries of the world. Chief among these are the cotton gin, the sewing machine, the steamboat, the reaping machine, the telegraph and the telephone. To these, many others of lesser importance might be added. Their combined effect has been to simplify and cheapen many processes of manufacturing, transportation and communication, all of which have aided in the development of manufacturing industry.

The freedom of commerce between the states is one of the greatest advantages enjoyed by the country. In no other region of the world is there such an extent of country entirely free from tariff barriers. In addition to this, the country embraces localities whose needs differ widely; consequently there is a demand for interchange of products between these sections, and these conditions have combined to build up a domestic commerce much greater than that known in any other country in the world. This has led to the development of various lines of manufactures.

Location of Manufacturing Districts. The manufacturing districts are very unevenly distributed over the country. In general, those states east of the Mississippi River and north of the Ohio are the leading manufacturing states, and more than four-fifths of all the manufactures in the country are produced within this territory. Without this limit are a few important manufactures, and these are being rapidly developed. Among them are the iron industries of Alabama and Georgia and the cotton industries of Alabama, Georgia, North Carolina and South Carolina. Some of the large cities on the Mississippi are also important manufacturing centers. Chief among these are Saint Louis, Saint Paul and Minneapolis. On the Pacific coast, lumbering, the manufacture of furniture and some other industries are fully developed, while others are increasing in number and importance from year to year.

Leading Industries. Among the many manufactured products of the country the following are the most important: Food products, including flour and meat (See FLOUR; MEAT PACKING); iron and steel; textiles; lumber and its allied products; leather and its finished products; metals other than iron and steel, with various allied products, and paper.

Iron and Steel. In the production of iron and steel the United States leads the world. In 1912 the output of pig iron was 29,726,937 long tons, and of steel, 31,251,303 long tons. The other countries which approach the United States in this industry are Germany, whose output of pig iron for the same year was 17,868,909 long tons, and of steel, 17,301,998 long tons, and Great Britain, which produced 8,751,464 long tons of pig iron and 5,700,000 long tons of steel. Pennsylvania is the leading state in the production of iron and steel, and her output is equal to that of all the other states of the Union. In this industry Ohio ranks second; Illinois, third, and Indiana, fourth.

Textiles. New England is the great center for the manufacture of cotton goods, and Massachusetts is the leading state in this industry. Outside of New England, North Carolina, South Carolina, Georgia and Alabama have within the last two decades established extensive cotton mills. In the output of her cotton goods, the United States is second only to Great Britain. Next in importance to the manufacture of cotton goods is the manufacture of woolens, including carpets and hats. Massachusetts, Pennsylvania and Rhode Island are the states in which this industry is principally located, Philadelphia being one of the greatest centers of carpet manufacture in the world. In the manufacture of silk goods the United States is second only to France, and the great centers of the industry are in New Jersey and Pennsylvania. Extensive factories for the production of knit goods are also found throughout the New England and North Atlantic states.

Lumber. The lumbering industries naturally center in those states containing extensive forest areas. For a full discussion of this industry, see FORESTS; LUMBER.

Leather. Pennsylvania ranks first in the tanning and finishing of leather, while Massachusetts is the leading state in the production of boots and shoes. Perhaps in no other industry is the effect of American invention and perfection of organization better seen than in the manufacture of boots and shoes. Owing to the invention of a number of ingenious machines, this industry has been highly organized, and the United States produces more boots and shoes than any other country. See LEATHER; BOOTS AND SHOES.

Paper. In the manufacture of paper the United States also leads the world. Much of this product is now made from wood pulp, which is generally manufactured in the states that have large supplies of suitable timber for this purpose. See PAPER.

Other Industries. Connecticut leads in the manufacture of small metallic articles, such as needles, pins, clocks and various kinds of hardware. The manufacture of electrical apparatus and appliances has now become very important, and with the extension of electricity as a power the industry is bound to increase in extent from year to year. In the manufacture of chemicals and allied products the United States is inferior to Germany, but the total yearly output of these industries is about $1,500,000,000. In shipbuilding this country is far behind Great Britain and Germany, the annual value of ships constructed being about $75,000,000. In the manufacture of agricultural implements and machinery the United States surpasses every other nation. This industry is most extensive in Illinois, Chicago being the leading center. Other states in which it is large are Ohio, New York and Wisconsin. The yearly output is about $150,000,000. The value of manufactured tobacco products is about $425,000,000, while the annual production of clay, glass and stone products is about $500,000,000. Besides these larger industries there are many smaller ones, considered as miscellaneous, whose annual output exceeds $1,000,000,000 in value, while the hand trades, or those occupations in which the articles are produced by the use of hand tools, have an annual output of about $1,184,000,000.

The recent tendency of manufacturing industries in the United States is to combine into large corporations, so that many industries that were formerly carried on by individuals or in small shops have now been entirely transferred to large factories. For this reason certain industries formerly classed as agricultural were by the census of 1900 classed under manufactures. The most important of these are the dairying industries, concerned with the manufacture of butter and cheese, nearly one-half of which is now made in creameries and cheese factories. See DAIRYING.

TRANSPORTATION AND COMMUNICATION. *Waterways*. The United States has over 12,000 miles of seacoast and more than 18,000 miles of inland waterways. Formerly the inland waterways were of the greatest importance, since by their means the interior of the country found an outlet to the sea. The most important systems of inland waterways are those of the Mississippi River and tributaries and the Great Lakes. Since the construction of railways, the river systems have become less valuable; but the completion of canals, by means of which steamers of deep draft can pass from the lakes to the ocean through the Saint Lawrence, has rendered this waterway of great importance. In connection with it, the construction of the Erie Canal, early in the nineteenth century, opened the way for the transportation of commodities between the Atlantic seaboard and the interior (See SAULT SAINTE MARIE CANAL; WELLAND CANAL; ERIE CANAL). With the exception of the canals named above, many of those first constructed have been abandoned.

Railroads. The first railroads of importance in the United States were constructed in 1830 and 1832, and at the close of the latter year there were 23 miles of railway in the country. In 1911 the mileage was over 244,000 or more than that of the entire continent of Europe. It is nearly one-third of all the mileage of the world. Naturally the older states contain the larger number of lines; the portion of the country east of the Mississippi River is fully supplied with railways, so that nearly all towns have convenient means of communication. In the Appalachian region, the longest lines extend approximately north and south; west of these mountains the general trend of the railways is east and west; in the Mississippi Valley there are a number of north and south lines, connecting Chicago and Saint Louis with important commercial ports on the Gulf of Mex-

ico. Some of these lines extend into Mexico. Six transcontinental lines now extend to the Pacific coast, and the Canadian Pacific, which is only a short distance north of the international boundary line, also renders good service to the inhabitants of the northern part of the country. Electric railways connect many towns situated within a few miles of one another, and these systems are being extended to the rural districts, especially in the eastern part of the country and the southern part of California. On the whole, the country is well supplied with water and rail transportation.

Roads. The development of railways and their importance in the industrial systems of the country has caused neglect of wagon roads, and in the construction of these important means of transportation the United States is far behind European countries. In most states the roads are poor, and in some states, during certain seasons of the year, they are well-nigh impassable.

Communication. Telegraph and telephone lines are found in all parts of the country, and no town of importance is now without one or both of these conveniences. The postal system is also one of the best in the world, taking rank with the systems of Great Britain, Germany and France, and meeting nearly all of the reasonable demands of the country. For a full description, see POST OFFICE.

COMMERCE. *Domestic Commerce*. The domestic commerce of the United States is larger than that of any other country and far exceeds its trade with foreign nations. The widely separated sections of the country, differing from one another in climate, soil and products, create a great demand in each section for the products of others, and in the supplying of this demand an extensive commerce has sprung up. The amount of this trade cannot be obtained, since no record is kept of the shipments of merchandise that are not entered at customhouses; but that it is very great and constitutes one of the leading industries of the country is evident to all who are conversant with commercial and industrial systems.

Foreign Commerce. In her foreign commerce the United States is exceeded by Great Britain and Germany and ranks third among the great commercial nations. For the year ending June 30, 1910, the exports amounted to $1,918,843,196, and the imports to $1,646,377,087. The annual average of exports is about $1,700,000,000, and of imports, about $1,200,000,000. The exports are divided among the various products as follows: Agricultural products, 62-

per cent; manufactures, 30 per cent; forest products, 4 per cent; mining products, 3 per cent. The imports have the following apportionment: Raw material, 38 per cent; food and domestic animals, 21 per cent; manufactures, 16.79 per cent; luxuries, 14.47 per cent.

Most of the foreign trade is carried on with the European nations, in the following order of importance: The United Kingdom, Germany, France, Netherlands, Belgium. Italy and Russia also have a considerable share. Of Asiatic nations Japan has the first place, and China the second. Europe takes about three-fourths

of steamships crossing the Atlantic and the Pacific, practically control their own transportation routes from Liverpool, China, Japan and the Philippines. This gives them great advantage, since they are able to transport merchandise at lower rates than would be possible were it carried by a number of different companies.

POPULATION. *Colonial Period.* During the colonial period settlements were made by English, Scotch, Irish, Swedes, Dutch, French and Germans, but the people from the British Isles far outnumbered all others. With the exception of the Germans, about 100,000 of whom settled in

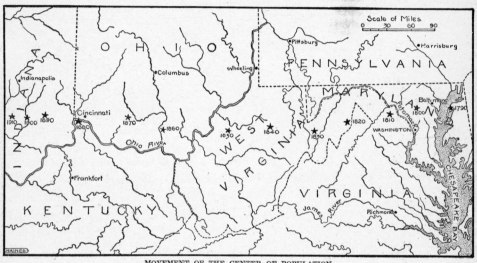

MOVEMENT OF THE CENTER OF POPULATION

of the exports and supplies one-half of the imports. Of the other foreign nations, Canada is the most important in North America, and Brazil, Argentina and Chile lead in South America. The great seaports engaged in European trade are New York, Boston, Philadelphia and Baltimore, while those engaged in trade with China, Japan and the Philippines are San Francisco, Seattle and Tacoma.

While American products are found in all countries of the world, the foreign commerce of the United States is crippled, from the fact that nearly all of it is carried in the ships of other nations, American vessels being engaged almost entirely in the coastwise trade. Were American products carried in American ships, new markets would often be sought, while now it is impossible to extend commerce in this way. Some of the great railway systems, especially those controlling transcontinental lines, by having interests in lines

Pennsylvania, the other nationalities in time blended with the English, so that in language, customs, government and commercial methods the colonies were thoroughly Anglo-Saxon. At the beginning of the Revolutionary War the population is estimated at 2,500,000. During the century and a half of their existence, the political ideas of the colonies were developed and established so firmly that there was little danger of their being changed by immigration in the years that followed, and the country entered upon its national existence with a population firmly united as to nationality and social and political ideas.

Increase in Population. The first national census was taken in 1790. At that time the United States contained in round numbers 4,000,000 inhabitants. About one-fifth of these, or 750,000, were negroes. The growth in population by decades is shown in the following table:

Census	Population, excluding Alaska, Indian reservations and distant island possessions	Increase	
		Number	Per Cent
1910......	91,972,266	15,977,691	21.0
1900......	75,568,686	12,946,436	20.7
1890......	62,622,250	12,466,467	24.9
1880......	50,155,783	11,597,412	30.1
1870......	38,558,371	7,115,050	22.6
1860......	31,443,321	8,251,445	35.6
1850......	23,191,876	6,122,423	35.9
1840......	17,069,453	4,203,433	32.7
1830......	12,866,020	3,227,567	33.5
1820......	9,638,453	2,398,572	33.1
1810......	7,239,881	1,931,298	36.4
1800......	5,308,483	1,379,269	35.1
1790......	3,929,214	....	....

The greatest growth has been in the central and western states, where the increase has been unusually large. This is due to the fertility of the soil in the Mississippi Valley and the oppor-

moved forward more rapidly than it did during the decade between 1900 and 1910. During this decade the center of population advanced westward about 39 miles, being in 1910 in the city of Bloomington, Indiana.

Density. Were the population evenly distributed over the country, excluding Alaska and Hawaii, there would be about 31 people to the square mile. In 1910 the average density was 30.9. Rhode Island, with 508.5 people to the square mile, was the most densely populated; Massachusetts, with 419, was second; New Jersey had 338; Connecticut, 231; New York, 191; Pennsylvania, 171; Maryland, 130; Ohio, 117; Delaware, 103; Illinois, 100.7. All other states had fewer than 100 people to the square mile. Wyoming, with 1.5, and Nevada, with 0.7, were the least densely populated. The per-

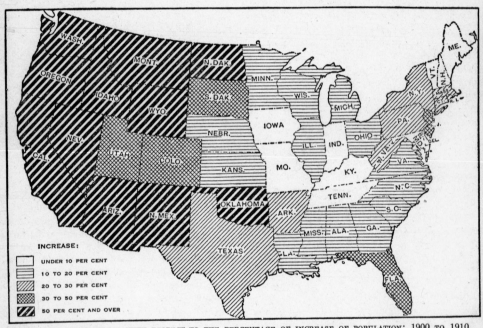

INCREASE:

UNDER 10 PER CENT

10 TO 20 PER CENT

20 TO 30 PER CENT

30 TO 50 PER CENT

50 PER CENT AND OVER

MAP CLASSIFYING STATES WITH RESPECT TO THE PERCENTAGE OF INCREASE OF POPULATION: 1900 TO 1910

tunities and advantages offered by a new country. These attracted large numbers of immigrants.

Movement Westward. In 1790 the center of population was 23 miles east of Baltimore. The center moved westward with varying degrees of rapidity, as indicated by the stars on the map on the preceding page. The center of population has varied slightly from time to time from an east and west line, and during the period in which the states in the Mississippi Valley and farther west were being settled it

centage of increase from 1900 to 1910 is shown in the accompanying map, taken from *Bulletin* 109 of the Bureau of the Census. By this it will be seen that the movement of population has been to the states west of the Mississippi. Washington leads, with an increase of 120.4 per cent; Oklahoma, with an increase of 109.7 per cent, is second and Idaho, with an increase of 101.3 per cent, is third.

Growth of Cities. Since the organization of the government, the population of cities and towns has increased far more, proportionately, than the population of the country at large, and this proportion has been constantly increasing. In 1790, 3.4 people out of every 100 lived in cities of 8000 or more inhabitants. In 1840 this proportion had increased to 8.5 per 100. In 1850, one-eighth of the people dwelt in cities of 8000 or over; in 1890, over one-fourth, and in 1910, over one-third. This rapid growth of cities is due, principally, to the establishment of the factory system, necessitating the bringing together of a large number of operatives; to increased facilities of transportation, and to immigration.

Immigration. Previous to 1800 no statistics of immigration were kept. Good authorities, however, estimate that at the beginning of the Revolutionary War about one-fifth of the people were immigrants and that from 1790 to 1800 about 5000 people entered the country each year. During the first half-century following the adoption of the Constitution, immigration was small; and previous to the Civil War, only about 1,000,-000 foreigners had settled in the United States. After 1870 immigrants began to come by the thousands, and by 1910 they had added nearly 30,000,000 to the population. Previous to 1895 most of the immigrants were from the northern countries of Europe, the majority coming from the British Isles, Germany, Norway and Sweden. Most of them settled in the new states, in the northern part of the Mississippi Valley, where their descendants now constitute a thrifty, law-abiding and industrious people. Since that time, however, the character of immigration has almost entirely changed, and by far the larger proportion of immigrants come from Italy and Austria-Hungary, while smaller numbers are received from other countries of southern Europe. Since the beginning of the century, the tide of immigration has very materially increased. In 1903 the United States received 857,000 immigrants; in 1904, 813,000, and for the year ending June 30, 1910, 1,041,570. In 1850 only 9.7 people in 100 among the population were foreign born, while in 1910 the proportion exceeded 14.

Color. In 1790 the negroes constituted one-fifth of the population and in 1910, less than one-ninth; that is, of the entire population, 9,827,763 were negroes. The great bulk of negroes is found in the states south of the Ohio River, including Texas and Arkansas, though bordering states contain large numbers. In South Carolina and Mississippi, the negroes outnumber the white population. In 1910 there were also 71,531 Chinese and 72,157 Japanese in the United States. The greater proportion of oriental immigrants are confined to the Pacific states. There were also in the country 265,683 indians, most of whom were on reservations.

Present Character. The population of the United States comprises representatives of nearly every race and nation, and the large cities are probably more cosmopolitan than any others in the world. Because of this characteristic, the percentage of illiteracy in the country is higher than it is in some of the European countries, namely, Germany, Switzerland, Scotland, Holland, France and England. In large cities and in some rural communities immigrants settle in communities and for years maintain their language and many of the customs of the Old World; yet in time these conditions yield to American influences. With very few exceptions, English is the language spoken throughout the country, and everywhere it is the official language of the land. Few of those seeking homes in the United States ever return to their native land for permanent residence. In 1900 the population was 76,-303,387, not reckoning the possessions acquired from Spain and Samoa. In 1906 the population was estimated at about 86,000,000. The population of Porto Rico in 1910 was 1,118,012. Hawaii had 191,909 inhabitants and Alaska, 64,356. The Philippines in 1903 had a population of 7,635,426. Thus the population of the United States and its dependencies in 1910 was about 101,000,000.

GOVERNMENT. *General Features.* The national government began with the Continental Congress, which, after the Declaration of Independence, framed the first national constitution, known as the Articles of Confederation. This instrument, however, was soon found to be inadequate to the needs of the country (See CONFEDERATION, ARTICLES OF), and in 1787 the Constitution, establishing the present government, was framed (See CONSTITUTION OF THE UNITED STATES). As organized under the Constitution, the government of the United States is a federal republic, in which the states are self-governing, each having a republican form of government. The powers of the national government are defined by the Constitution, and all powers not specifically delegated to the United States are reserved to the states and to the people. However, the states are prohibited from the exercise of certain powers, among which are making treaties with foreign nations, declaring war and coining money. There are other powers, also, which they are forbidden to exercise except by permission of the national government. The national government is organized in three coördinate departments, legislative, executive and judicial. While these departments, within certain limits, are independent of one another, each is so related to the others as to form, with them, an organic whole. For instance, laws must originate in the legislative department, but the president has the power of veto, and the judicial department can render any law null and void by declaring it unconstitutional. The legislative department also has power to impeach and try United States officers, including the head of the executive department, and the president cannot appoint to certain offices except by the advice and consent of the Senate.

The Legislative Department. The legislative department consists of a Congress, comprising a House of Representatives and a Senate (See CONGRESS OF THE UNITED STATES). The House of Representatives consists of members apportioned among the states according to population, the apportionment being made every ten years. Each state has at least one representative, whatever its population. The members are chosen at a general election, on the first Tuesday after the first Monday of November, in even-numbered years, and they hold their offices for two years. The apportionment in 1911 was one representative to every 211,877 inhabitants, and the number of representatives according to this apportionment was 433. This number includes Arizona and New Mexico. The House of Representatives elects one of its members as the presiding officer, entitled *speaker*, for a term of two years. All bills for raising revenue must originate in this branch of Congress, but in passing bills, the two houses must agree, and they have equal power to reject measures.

The Senate is composed of two members from each state, formerly chosen by the state legislature, but since the adoption of the Seventeenth Amendment, elected by popular vote for a term of six years. Members are so elected that the terms of one-third of the senators expire every two years. The presiding officer is the vice-president of the United States. The Senate has sole power to try cases of impeachment and to ratify treaties with foreign nations. See SENATE.

The Executive Department. The executive department consists of the president, the vice-president and such other officers as the president may select or as may be provided for by law. The president and the vice-president are chosen by

electors for a term of four years (See ELECTORAL COLLEGE). In order that this branch of the government might be efficiently administered, Washington established, in 1789, the following departments: state, war and navy, treasury and postoffice. Since then the following departments have been added: interior, 1849; justice, 1870; agriculture, 1889; and commerce and labor, 1903. In 1913 this last was divided into the department of commerce and the department of labor. With the exception of the department of justice and the postoffice department, the officers at the heads of the departments are styled secretaries. The attorney-general is the head of the department of justice, and the postmaster-general is at the head of the postoffice department. These heads of the departments, taken collectively, constitute the president's cabinet (see CABINET). Each of the departments is explained under its proper title in this encyclopedia. The heads of departments and other important officers are appointed by the president, with the advice and consent of the Senate, while many minor officers are appointed by the president without consulting the Senate, or by the heads of departments.

The president is commander in chief of the army and navy, has the power to call Congress in special session, when necessary, and can veto any bill passed by Congress, though such a bill may be passed over his veto by a two-thirds vote of the members of each house. It is the president's duty to send a message to Congress at the beginning of each session, setting forth the condition of the country and recommending such legislation as he believes is necessary. He also has power to grant reprieves and pardons to persons who are sentenced by United States courts, and it is his duty to see that the laws are executed throughout the country and all of its dependencies. See PRESIDENT.

The Judicial Department. The judicial department consists of the Supreme Court and such other courts as may from time to time be established by law. At present the United States courts consist of the Supreme Court, 9 circuit courts of appeals, 9 circuit courts, 92 district courts, a court of claims, a court of private land claims, a court of appeals for the District of Columbia, the Supreme Court of the District of Columbia, the territorial courts and admiralty courts (See COURTS; SUPREME COURT).

Colonial Possessions. The acquisition of the Philippine Islands and Porto Rico entailed upon the United States a new problem in government. While under the control of the national government, the Philippine Islands are not considered as an organized territory, nor are their inhabitants recognized as full citizens of the United States. They are governed by officers appointed by the president, with the advice and consent of the Senate, the chief officer being styled governor. The other principal officers are members of a commission; each member usually has charge of some department of the government, and the commission as a whole constitutes an executive council, or governor's cabinet. The legislative functions are shared by this commission and local legislatures, members of which are elected by the people. See PHILIPPINE ISLANDS, subhead *Government*; PORTO RICO, subhead *Government*.

State Government. General. The government of each state is based upon a constitution, and in the main follows the plan of the national government. Nearly all states have a legislature of two branches, a senate and a house of representatives. In many the members of the senate are elected for a longer term than the members of the house, and in some states the terms of only a part of the senators expire at one time, so that one-half of them are chosen at each general election. The executive officers of the state are usually a governor, a lieutenant governor, a secretary of state, a treasurer, an attorney-general and a superintendent of public instruction. To these some states add an auditor of public accounts and a comptroller.

The state government deals with all affairs pertaining to the interests of the state, such as laws governing marriage and divorce, the obligation of contracts, the settling of estates, the transference of real property and the regulation of loans, interests and mortgages.

In the matter of courts there is a greater divergence of plan. Almost every state has a supreme court, which has a limited original jurisdiction, and to which cases of certain importance may be appealed from the lower courts. Below this are circuit courts, which usually have jurisdiction over several counties, and in some states there are county courts. Almost all the states have county probate courts for the settlement of estates.

Local. The early colonists established two forms of local government, the *township* form in New England, and the *county* form in Virginia and other southern colonies. These shaped the local government in most of the original states. Under the former plan the township is the unit, and the township officers are chosen at an annual town meeting, in which all voters have a right to

173

participate. All the public business of the local community is in the hands of these town officers. In the county system the township is not recognized, the county being the principal unit of government. The only subdivision is the parish. Under this plan nearly all matters of public interest are looked after by county officers, who are chosen at regular elections. In most states these are known as county commissioners, or county supervisors. Between New England and Virginia a third form of local government grew up. It was the outgrowth of the two systems described above and may be called the *mixed*, or *township-county*, system. Under this scheme certain minor duties devolve upon township officers, while more important local duties rest with county officers. The officers of the county include commissioners, representing the different towns of the county, an auditor, a register of deeds, a treasurer and a superintendent of schools, or school commissioner. Other officers are sometimes added. This system, on the whole, is more satisfactory than either of the others, and it has influenced the systems of local government in practically all of the western states. It combines sufficient local interest with an economy in management that is not possible under the old township system.

Territories. Before the admission of the inhabitants of the national domain to participation in all the activities of the government, a special scheme of government is placed in operation, under which the national domain is divided into so-called *territories*. At first each territory is governed by an executive and judges appointed by the president of the United States. As population increases and the importance of the region develops, the people are given more powers of local government, and finally a legislature, chosen by the people, is established, which may make laws subject to the approval of Congress. Lastly, the territory is admitted as a state, when it has attained a certain population and achieved some industrial or commercial importance. Alaska is the only remaining territory in continental United States.

Finance. The Constitution gives Congress power to levy and collect direct taxes, duties on imported goods and excise taxes. Direct taxation soon proved to be unpopular, and except in extreme cases, such as war, rebellion and famine, was rarely adopted until 1913, when an income tax law was passed. Most of the government's revenue, however, is still derived from import duties and excise taxes on spirituous liquors, tobacco and other articles of manufacture, particularly luxuries. The income is usually ample for the needs of the government. Loans are occasionally obtained through the sale of bonds, which are exempt from taxation and bear a low rate of interest. These bonds are usually payable after a long period, and while the interest is low, the permanency of the investment and the perfect security offered by the government make government bonds very desirable to capitalists.

The most important items of expenditure are pensions, the postoffice, the army, the navy and the interest on the public debt.

POLITICAL DIVISIONS. Within the United States proper there are 48 states and 1 federal district. The external possessions consist of the territories of Alaska and Hawaii; Guam, the Philippines, Tutuila, Porto Rico and a few small islands. At the adoption of the Constitution there were 13 organized states, and these are known as the Original States. The first new state admitted was Vermont, in 1791, and the last, New Mexico and Arizona, which came into the Union in 1911. For description of the outlying territories see articles ALASKA; GUAM; HAWAII; PHILIPPINE ISLANDS; PORTO RICO; SAMOA. The table given below includes only the states within the United States proper. The figures given are taken from the United States census of 1910. Arizona and New Mexico, the latest additions to the list of states, each elect one representative at large.

It is of interest to note that since the Federal census of 1900 three new states have been made out of four territories.

STATE	POPULAR NAME	TOTAL AREA IN SQUARE MILES	ADMITTED TO THE UNION	POPULATION	REPRESENTATIVES IN CONGRESS
Alabama	The Cotton State	51,998	1819	2,138,093	10
Arizona		113,956	1912	204,354	1
Arkansas	The Bear State	53,335	1836	1,574,449	7
California	The Golden State	158,297	1850	2,377,549	11
Colorado	The Centennial State	103,948	1876	799,024	4
Connecticut	The Nutmeg State	4,965	*	1,114,756	5
Delaware	The Diamond State	2,370	*	202,322	1
District of Columbia		70		331,069	..
Florida	The Everglade State	58,666	1845	752,615	4
Georgia	The Empire State of the South	59,265	*	2,609,121	12
Idaho	The Gem of the Mountains	83,888	1890	325,594	2
Illinois	The Prairie State	56,665	1818	5,638,591	27
Indiana	The Hoosier State	36,354	1816	2,700,876	13
Iowa	The Hawkeye State	56,147	1846	2,224,771	11
Kansas	The Sunflower State	82,158	1861	1,690,949	8
Kentucky	The Bluegrass State	40,598	1792	2,289,905	11
Louisiana	The Creole State	48,506	1812	1,656,388	8
Maine	The Pine Tree State	33,040	1820	742,371	4
Maryland	The Old Line State	12,327	*	1,294,400	6
Massachusetts	The Bay State	8,266	*	3,366,416	16
Michigan	The Wolverine State	57,980	1837	2,810,173	13
Minnesota	The Gopher State	84,682	1858	2,075,708	10
Mississippi	The Bayou State	46,865	1817	1,797,114	8
Missouri	The Bullion State	69,420	1821	3,293,335	16
Montana	The Treasure State	146,997	1889	376,053	2
Nebraska	The Tree Planter State	77,520	1867	1,192,214	6
Nevada	The Sage Brush State	110,690	1864	81,875	1
New Hampshire	The Granite State	9,341	*	430,572	2
New Jersey	The Garden State	8,224	*	2,537,167	12
New Mexico		122,634	1912	327,301	1
New York	The Empire State	49,204	*	9,113,614	43
North Carolina	The Old North State	52,426	*	2,206,287	10
North Dakota	The Flickertail State	70,837	1889	577,056	3
Ohio	The Buckeye State	41,040	1803	4,767,121	22
Oklahoma	The Boomer State	70,057	1908	1,657,155	8
Oregon	The Beaver State	96,699	1859	672,765	3
Pennsylvania	The Keystone State	45,126	*	7,665,111	36
Rhode Island	Little Rhody	1,248	*	542,610	3
South Carolina	The Palmetto State	30,989	*	1,515,400	7
South Dakota	The Sunshine State	77,615	1889	583,888	3
Tennessee	The Volunteer State	42,022	1796	2,184,789	10
Texas	The Lone Star State	265,896	1845	3,896,542	18
Utah	The Salt Lake State	84,990	1896	373,351	2
Vermont	The Green Mountain State	9,564	1791	355,956	2
Virginia	The Old Dominion	42,627	*	2,061,612	10
Washington	The Evergreen State	69,127	1889	1,141,990	5
West Virginia	The Panhandle State	24,170	1863	1,221,119	6
Wisconsin	The Badger State	56,066	1848	2,333,860	11
Wyoming	The Equality State	97,914	1890	145,965	1

* Original State.

EDUCATION. The United States has no national system of education, in the sense that there is an educational system administered by the Federal government. However, from the time of the Ordinance of 1787 (See ORDINANCE OF 1787), in which certain sections of land in the Northwest Territory were reserved for educational purposes, the national government has assisted very materially in public education, by granting generous portions of the public domain for the support of universities, agricultural colleges and public schools. In addition to this it maintains the bureau of education, which is a division under the department of the interior. The chief officer, called the commissioner of education, collects statistics and publishes a biennial report, containing educational data of national importance. Further than this his duties are advisory only. However, under the able commissioners who have filled the office since the bureau was established, very much has been done to advance the educational interests of the country.

The administration of the public schools is left to the states, and each maintains its own system of public education. However, these systems so closely resemble one another that, taken together, they practically constitute a national system of education. See COMMON SCHOOLS, also articles on the important universities of the country.

LITERATURE.   See LITERATURE, subhead *American Literature.*

ART. See PAINTING, subhead *Nineteenth Century*; SCULPTURE, subhead *United States.*

CITIES. The census of 1910 gives the following cities as having over 100,000 inhabitants:

1.	New York	4,766,883
2.	Chicago	2,185,283
3.	Philadelphia	1,549,008
4.	St. Louis	687,029
5.	Boston	670,585
6.	Cleveland	560,663
7.	Baltimore	558,485
8.	Pittsburg	533,905
9.	Detroit	465,766
10.	Buffalo	423,715
11.	San Francisco	416,912
12.	Milwaukee	373,857
13.	Cincinnati	364,463
14.	Newark	347,469
15.	New Orleans	339,075
16.	Washington	331,069
17.	Los Angeles	319,198
18.	Minneapolis	301,408
19.	Jersey City	267,779
20.	Kansas City, Mo	248,381
21.	Seattle	237,194
22.	Indianapolis	233,650
23.	Providence	224,326
24.	Louisville	223,928
25.	Rochester	218 149
26.	St. Paul	214,744
27.	Denver	213,381
28.	Portland	207.214
29.	Columbus	181,548
30.	Toledo	168,497
31.	Atlanta	154,839
32.	Oakland	150,174
33.	Worcester	145,986
34.	Syracuse	137.249
35.	New Haven	133,605
36.	Birmingham	132,685
37.	Memphis	131,105
38.	Scranton	129,867
39.	Richmond	127,628
40.	Paterson	125,600
41.	Omaha	124,096
42.	Fall River	119,295
43.	Dayton	116,577
44.	Grand Rapids	112,571
45.	Nashville	110,364
46.	Lowell	106,294
47.	Cambridge	104,839
48.	Spokane	104,402
49.	Bridgeport	102,054
50.	Albany	100,253

HISTORY. *Discovery and Exploration.* At the time of its discovery by Europeans, America was inhabited by savages belonging to the American, or Red, race. The origin and antiquity of these people and the degree of their civilization are still subjects of investigation and dispute (See INDIANS, AMERICAN; MOUND BUILDERS). It is also uncertain at what time and place the American continents were first discovered. Norse seamen are said to have visited the North American coast about 1000 A. D. (See ERIC THE RED), and it is probable that fishermen from northern Europe had made voyages across the Atlantic before that date. But even if both these facts were true, the credit for the real discovery of America must still be given to those navigators who, at the close of the fifteenth century, crossed the Atlantic and explored the shores of the "New World."

The first of these navigators was Christopher Columbus, who in 1492 discovered the Bahama Islands and on later voyages explored the South and Central American coasts. John and Sebastian Cabot in 1497 and 1498, under the auspices of England, skirted the coast of Labrador and perhaps New England, giving Britain the basis for her later claim to the continent of North America. About the same time Americus Vespucius was exploring the coasts of South America, and in his honor America was named. In 1513 Balboa, a Spanish adventurer, discovered the Pacific, and in the same year Ponce de Leon discovered and explored Florida. Verrazano was the first to represent France in this new field, his voyages being made in 1524. Frenchmen and Spaniards then vied for the control of the new-found riches. Narvaez, Coronado and De Soto, in the south, set out to conquer for Spain the vast interior of the North American continent, while in the north, Cartier, and in Florida, Ribaut and the Huguenots, attempted to establish the power of France, but without success.

Meantime, English enterprise had been dormant, but with the advent of Queen Elizabeth to the throne, in 1558, a group of distinguished mariners became anxious to extend English influence in the New World. Of these, Sir John Hawkins, Sir Francis Drake, Sir Humphrey Gilbert and Sir Walter Raleigh were the most important, but they accomplished little of permanent value. It was not till the opening of the seventeenth century that real progress was made toward subduing and colonizing America. At that time, France, under the leadership of such brilliant men as Champlain, Marquette, Joliet and La Salle, extended her influence throughout the region of Canada and into the Mississippi and Ohio valleys, establishing fur-trading posts throughout this territory. In 1565 Spain established a settlement at Saint Augustine, Florida, and made feeble efforts to extend her authority northward, but with little success.

Colonization. (For a detailed account of the development of each of the colonies, see articles upon the several states and also upon the leading discoverers and explorers of the period.)

English Colonies. The chief fact in American history during the seventeenth century is the settlement of English colonies along the Atlantic coast. This was begun in 1607 at Jamestown, Virginia, under the auspices of the London Company, a trading and colonizing corporation similar to the East India Company. This colony was in large measure a commercial and political enterprise, and its settlers were drawn from all classes, but especially from the wealthy and the adventurous. During its early life Jamestown witnessed some of the most important episodes of American history, among them the establishment of the first representative assembly in America (1619), and the institution of negro slavery (1619).

The second English settlement was at Plymouth, Massachusetts, in 1620, and was made by men who had fled from England to avoid religious persecution. In 1628 a settlement was made at Salem by English Puritans. This, too, was a religious movement (See PURITANS). The early history of Plymouth and Salem, the latter called Massachusetts Bay Colony, was somewhat troubled. The colonists early manifested a desire for self-government, which led to bitter contests with the king, but at the same time brought about important progress toward political and religious liberty. However, in 1636 Roger Williams was exiled for his religious belief, and in 1651 a bitter persecution of the Quakers began in Boston. Meantime, Harvard College had been founded in 1638, and the first printing press had been set up in 1639. The success of the early colonies led to other enterprises, and settlements in New Hampshire and Maine resulted. But even the freedom which was nominally established in Massachusetts did not satisfy that community, and in 1633 bodies of settlers from the coast began to travel inland and found settlements along the Connecticut River. These developed into the colony of Connecticut, which in 1637 adopted the first written constitution in America, known as the "Fundamental Orders of Connecticut." New Haven was settled in this year and was united with Connecticut in 1682. Maryland was organized as a proprietary colony, under the Lords Baltimore, and its first settlement was at Saint Mary's, the original purpose being to found a haven of refuge for English Catholics. The territory of the Carolinas was first settled by Virginians, but in 1663 it was granted to eight English noblemen, who divided it into two colonies, which were again united in 1699, but governed separately after 1729.

Pennsylvania was a Quaker proprietary colony, founded by William Penn, Jr., in 1676 and colonized six years later. Its government was organized on an extremely liberal basis and exerted a powerful influence upon other American colonies. The settlement of Rhode Island was the outgrowth of the religious persecution in Massachusetts, being founded by two exiles, Roger Williams and Anne Hutchinson, the former settling at Providence, the latter at Portsmouth. They eventually united their forces. Georgia was the last of the thirteen colonies to be settled; it was founded by James Oglethorpe in 1732, as a refuge for honest debtors. A village was settled at Savannah in the following year.

Other Colonies. New Jersey was first colonized by the Dutch at Fort Nassau, now Gloucester. This was subsequently conquered by the Swedes, restored to the Dutch in 1655 and finally transferred to the English in 1664, becoming a proprietary province under Lord Berkeley and

Sir George Carteret. The Dutch were also the first to establish colonies within the territory of New York, by reason of the voyage of Henry Hudson in 1609. Albany was settled in 1624, and New Amsterdam (New York), two years later. The colony was conquered by the English in 1664. Delaware was long a fighting ground between the Dutch and the Swedes, the latter finally being compelled to relinquish their claim; but the English conquered in 1664.

Colonial Development. During the seventeenth century the scattering colonies of all the nations steadily advanced in strength and constantly extended their borders, until the Atlantic coast from Labrador to Mexico was dotted with prosperous villages and trading centers. During the first half of the eighteenth century, the interests of France and England began to come into conflict, as each attempted to extend its dominion over the fertile interior of the continent. This resulted in a series of wars, known, collectively, as the French and Indian Wars, extending with but slight interruptions from 1689 to 1763 (See FRENCH AND INDIAN WARS). This long conflict had three great results from the standpoint of the colonies: (1) It practically drove France from America and decided that American institutions should be organized chiefly upon British models; (2) it gave the colonists military experience and a feeling of independent power, which made them more willing to stand firmly for their rights against the mother country; (3) it disclosed the necessity for intercolonial union.

During this same time the colonies were developing politically and were manifesting more and more clearly their determination to govern themselves, at least in all local affairs.

The Development of Union. From the earliest times events in America had shaped themselves to the end that the colonies should become not independent units, but parts of a general system. By the middle of the eighteenth century the necessity of such a result had become more evident, only because in the meantime minor issues of a local nature had been decided, and because recent events, in which all the colonies were united, had disclosed to the colonists their common interests and ideals. This development of the spirit of union culminated in 1754 in a congress, held at Albany for the purpose of framing a treaty of friendship with the indiáns, and also of devising a plan for the union of all the colonies. The latter plan, prepared by Franklin, was adopted by the convention, but it was rejected by every colony and by the mother country. The reasons

for its rejection disclosed a state of affairs which found its natural conclusion in the Revolutionary War. Says Franklin, "The Assembly did not adopt it, as they all thought there was too much *prerogative* in it, and in England, it was judged to have too much of the *democratic.*" Thus, the issue was clearly drawn between England and the colonies; the former was set resolutely against the growing spirit of independence and democracy in America; the latter were determined to prevent interference in their affairs.

The Revolutionary War. Causes and Beginnings. The fundamental cause of the Revolutionary War had both economic and political phases. It was laid in the theory of colonization held by every important country in the world at that time, namely, that colonies existed for the mother country and that they had no political or commercial rights except those specifically granted to them. This principle probably would not have been contested, if the tendency of all governments, and especially of England, had not been to repress the growing strength of their colonies and thus to cause distressing economic conditions, which the colonists themselves had no power to remedy. This led to the demand for political self-government, which, when refused, roused a spirit of resistance and, finally, of revolution. This end was hastened by the passage of more and more repressive legislation, such as the enlargement of the Navigation Acts (See NAVIGATION ACTS), the establishment of British garrisons in America and the taxation of the colonies to support these garrisons. To enforce the second policy, a stamp tax was inaugurated, which gave to every colonist a grievance and awakened the famous cry, "Taxation without representation is tyranny." The act repealing the Stamp Act was accompanied by a declaration that the Crown had the right to tax the Colonies, and thus it was of little benefit in appeasing the wrath of the Americans. When followed by the Townshend Acts (See TOWNSHEND, CHARLES), the situation became serious and culminated in open violence (See BOSTON MASSACRE).

It soon became evident to the leading men in the colonies that little was to be expected in the direction of conciliation, and an effort was made to unite the colonies more firmly in opposition to the mother country. One of the important means to this end was the formation of committees of correspondence, which kept the different colonies informed of the march of events throughout the country. The spirit of defiance became more widespread, as was indicated by the destruction of the *Gaspee,* a British man-of-war, stationed near Rhode Island to prevent violation of the customs laws, and by the Boston Tea Party (See BOSTON TEA PARTY). To punish this lawlessness, the British government passed, and attempted to enforce, laws clearly violating the English constitution, and striking at rights especially dear to the colonists. Among these were the Boston Port Bill, closing the port of Boston to all commerce, and acts allowing the trial in England of certain official offenders, permitting the quartering of soldiers upon the colonies and abolishing certain provisions of their charters. To enforce these laws, General Gage and a force of soldiers were sent to Massachusetts.

The colonies were thoroughly aroused, and in reply to a request of the Massachusetts assembly, they sent delegates to a congress at Philadelphia, September 1, 1774. This body, known as the First Continental Congress, passed resolutions of protest against the British policy and agreed not to import goods from England, then adjourned, to reassemble May 1, 1775. Their petition to Parliament was answered by still more oppressive acts; and before the second Congress met, the American cause had gone beyond the stage of discussion or compromise. The colonies, led by Massachusetts, collected military forces and supplies, and when General Gage attempted to seize the stores at Lexington and Concord, and to arrest Samuel Adams and John Hancock, his force was met by a body of minutemen, drawn up on Lexington Common. In the battle which followed the first blood in the Revolutionary War was shed (See LEXINGTON, BATTLE OF). The government of the colonies was soon taken over by the patriots and, guided and inspired by the Second Continental Congress, measures of increasing defiance and independence were taken from time to time. (See articles upon the REVOLUTIONARY WAR IN AMERICA and the decisive battles, for brief outlines of the chief military campaigns; see also articles upon the great statesmen and soldiers of the period.)

Results of the War. At the opening of the struggle the people of the country were not united in the conviction that political independence of Great Britain was the end to be desired. They were still loyal to the mother country and were determined to fight to regain their rights as Englishmen. But the passage of events and the necessary assumption of the ordinary functions of government by Congress and the provisional governments of the Colonies, brought the question of independence prominently forward and finally caused independence to be proclaimed (See DECLARATION OF INDEPENDENCE). Meanwhile, foreign relations had been formed by the appointment of a committee to correspond with foreign governments, and this resulted, in February, 1778, in the signing of a treaty of alliance with France. This treaty is generally considered the turning-point of the war, since it led to such active support by France that England was eventually compelled to make peace, the treaty being signed at Paris, September 3, 1783.

The Articles of Confederation. The financial and internal affairs of the colonies were in a far from satisfactory state. The Continental Congress had assumed only the absolutely necessary functions and had no legal power to compel obedience to its decrees. Appreciating the importance of forming a stronger government to replace that which was being destroyed by the Revolution, Congress appointed a committee in the summer of 1776, to draw up articles for the confederation of the thirteen colonies. These articles, though a vast improvement over the organization which had previously existed, left much to be desired, since the same spirit which had led the colonists to resist the encroachments of British power led them to fear the establishment of a strong power among themselves. The articles therefore provided for no executive head of the government, leaving all power with Congress, which could pass laws only with the consent of the representatives of nine states, a majority of the representatives of each state being necessary to cast its vote. In spite of the apparent weakness of the government which was thus created, state jealousies prevented the adoption of the articles until almost the close of the war, in 1781. Meantime, the financial affairs of the government as a whole and of the several colonies had come to a serious state, since all the governments had been compelled to borrow vast sums of money and, besides, had issued paper notes in payment of debts. This paper money, coming from many sources without adequate security, rapidly depreciated in value, until at the close of the war it was practically worthless. The department of war was in a similarly disorganized state.

The Adoption of the Constitution. Soon after the adoption of the Articles a large faction in the states demanded that a stronger government be immediately organized, but it was several years before they were able to win public sentiment to their view. Finally, in 1786, a convention was proposed by several states, for the purpose of amending the Articles, in order to increase the power of the central government. This convention met in May, 1787, at Philadelphia, and contained in its membership the most able and distinguished statesmen in America, including George Washington, Alexander Hamilton, James Madison, Gouverneur Morris, Robert Morris, Roger Sherman and others. Its sessions were turbulent, owing to the presence of a strong minority party, who feared the centralization of authorit, and it was only through compromise that the Constitution was finally produced and accepted. In its completed form it did not satisfy either party, and the discussion which had taken place in the convention was carried before the people in the contest for ratification. Through the efforts of Jay, Hamilton, Madison, Henry Lee, George Washington and others, it was finally adopted, however, being recognized as the most satisfactory constitution which could at that time be made (See CONSTITUTION OF THE UNITED STATES).

Before its final adjournment, the old Congress of the Confederation performed its most notable work, in passing the famous Ordinance of 1787, for the government of the Northwest Territory (See ORDINANCE OF 1787; NORTHWEST TERRITORY).

Organization of the National Government.
After the ratification of the Constitution by nine states, Congress proceeded to plan the organization of the new government. The election, held in February, 1789, resulted in the unanimous choice of George Washington for president; John Adams, having the next highest number of votes, was made vice-president. The inauguration of the government was delayed until April 30, 1789. Washington took the oath of office at New York, where the first national Congress was assembled.

This body already showed a tendency toward division. The Federalists, that is, those who had advocated the ratification of the Constitution, were opposed by the old Anti-Federalists, now styling themselves Democratic-Republicans, or Republicans, who desired the strict interpretation of the Constitution and a tendency toward decentralization of power. Washington chose for his advisers representatives of both of these factions, Hamilton being the acknowledged leader of the former, and Jefferson, of the latter. Hamilton became secretary of the treasury, and the first important action of the new government was the carrying into effect of principles suggested by him for the

management of the finances of the country. These included the inauguration of tariff duties; the establishment of a national bank; the assumption of debts contracted by the states during the Revolution; the institution of the excise tax; the establishment of a national mint and a system of coinage. All of these measures aroused the greatest opposition, but all were passed, and all soon proved their value and efficacy. Washington set himself to organize the executive departments of the government, and he established precedents which have ever since been followed. During his first term, also, the judicial system was organized, and the first ten amendments to the Federal Constitution were adopted.

In spite of his opposition, Washington was nominated and reëlected unanimously in 1793. Adams was also reëlected vice-president, but was opposed by George Clinton of New York, a Republican. The most important matter connected with Washington's second administration was the relation of the government to foreign nations, especially England and France. The Federalists sympathized with England, and the Republicans sympathized with France, in the war which had begun between them. The visit of Citizen Genet (See GENET, EDMUND CHARLES), Washington's refusal to recognize him and the later proclamation of neutrality, together with the signing of the very unsatisfactory treaty with England, known as the Jay Treaty (See JAY TREATY) and the refusal of England to evacuate her posts in the Northwest Territory or to grant privileges to American commerce, all led to serious domestic disturbances and almost to war; but such an event was averted by Washington's tact and frankness. His second administration was also important for the suppression of the first rebellion against the government, the Whisky Insurrection in Pennsylvania (See WHISKY INSURRECTION); for the unsuccessful expedition of Saint Clair against the indians and the successful expedition of General Wayne, resulting in the cession of a large tract of land by the indians to the United States. A treaty was negotiated with Spain, by which the United States secured the free navigation of the Mississippi. In 1793 Eli Whitney invented the cotton gin, which was to be of greater political importance during the next century than any other single invention of history.

Washington positively refused to accept a third term as president, delivered a famous farewell address and retired to Mount Vernon. He was succeeded by John Adams, a Federalist, who received 71 votes, in opposition to Thomas Jefferson, a Republican, who received but 68. Adams's administration was at first highly popular, on account of the firm stand which it took against the insolent actions of France (See X Y Z Correspondence), but the passage in 1798 of the Alien and Sedition acts (See Alien and Sedition Laws) not only forfeited the popularity of the party, but led to its overthrow. The famous Kentucky and Virginia Resolutions (See Kentucky and Virginia Resolutions) were passed at this time in relation to these laws. The seat of government was changed in 1800 from Philadelphia to Washington. Doubtless the most important appointment of Adams's administration was that of John Marshall to be chief justice of the United States Supreme Court.

At the election in 1800, Adams was defeated, but the two Republican candidates, Jefferson and Burr, had an equal number of electoral votes. The House of Representatives elected Jefferson after a long contest, and Burr became vice-president.

Supremacy of the Anti-Federalists. The ascendency of the Anti-Federalists marks an important change in American politics. At the close of the Revolutionary War there was a notable reaction from the extreme ideas of liberty which that struggle had expressed, and the Constitution placed far more power in the central government than pleased many of the more radical Democrats in the country. But after Adams's administration, another reaction set in, away from centralization, toward democracy. In spite of his theories of strict construction, Jefferson soon was compelled to take steps involving broader powers than either of his Federalist predecessors had assumed. First was the purchase of Louisiana in 1803, the constitutionality of which even he himself doubted. On the other hand, he attempted to reduce the importance of the national government by making but small appropriations for the army and navy; but he was compelled to abandon even this policy when a war with the Barbary powers broke out in 1801. During his first term the Twelfth Amendment to the Constitution was passed, changing the method of voting for president and vice-president.

Jefferson was reëlected in 1804, with George Clinton of New York as vice-president. The most important problem which confronted him during his second administration was the relation of the United States to the commercial war between France and England. He attempted to establish in law his theory that the United States could compel Europe to consider its rights by shutting American ports to the commerce of European nations. This was the cause of the Embargo Act of December, 1807, forbidding American vessels to leave for foreign ports (See Embargo). However, this measure did not accomplish its intended purpose, but instead it seriously injured American commerce. The relations between the United States and Great Britain became more and more strained, because of the persistent attempts of British vessels to impress seamen from American ships. This resulted in several small battles (See Chesapeake, The). During Jefferson's administration, also, Aaron Burr attempted to separate the western states from the Union (See Burr, Aaron); Lewis and Clarke made their famous expedition to the Pacific coast (see Lewis and Clark Expedition); the Cumberland Road was authorized and begun; West Point Military Academy was established; Fulton succeeded in constructing the first successful steamboat, and the slave trade was abolished after 1808.

Jefferson declined a third election and was succeeded by his secretary of state, James Madison, who defeated Charles C. Pickney. The Embargo Act was replaced by the Non-Intercourse Act (See Non-Intercourse Act), before Madison's inauguration, but this did not relieve matters greatly. Madison attempted to carry out Jefferson's policy, but was finally compelled to take more stern measures, and the War of 1812 resulted (See War of 1812). Meantime, Madison was reëlected, with Elbridge Gerry as vice-president, defeating De Witt Clinton. The war was vigorously opposed by the Federalists, especially of New England, and they held a convention at Hartford, in December, 1814, which, it was rumored, threatened secession; but this movement did not gain sufficient strength to be a serious menace to the country. The treaty of peace was signed at Ghent, December 24, 1814.

The end of the war marked, also, the practical end of the Federalist party as an organization, for its unpatriotic stand during the war had won for it the derision of people in all parts of the country. However, the Anti-Federalist party had meantime so changed its position upon constitutional questions that many of the Federalist principles were already firmly incorporated in the government (See Federalist Party). During Madison's term, laws were passed granting a second charter to the United States bank, establishing a protective tariff and appropriating large sums for internal improvements, all measures which the Anti-Federalists had formerly opposed.

The Supreme Court, under Marshall's leadership, had also taken firm ground in favor of a strong national government.

The Era of Good Feeling. In 1816 James Monroe of Virginia, Madison's secretary of state, was elected president, receiving the votes of all the states except Massachusetts, Connecticut and Delaware, which were cast for Rufus King of New York. Since the downfall of the Federalist party had removed many questions from controversy, Monroe's administrations are sometimes known as the "Era of Good Feeling"; but, in fact, just as sincere debate was carried on during this time as at any time before or after, the main questions being the tariff and the admission of Missouri (See MISSOURI COMPROMISE), the latter of which involved the discussion of the rising issue of slavery. Monroe was reëlected in 1820, receiving all the electoral votes but one, which was cast for John Quincy Adams. The most important incident of his second administration was the promulgation of the Monroe Doctrine (See MONROE DOCTRINE). In 1824 a higher protective tariff was passed. The election of 1825 turned upon personal questions and resulted in a contest between Andrew Jackson, John Quincy Adams, William H. Crawford and Henry Clay, the House of Representatives finally electing John Quincy Adams.

John Quincy Adams. This election marks another change in the political history of the United States. The Republican, or Democratic-Republican, party at this time took the name of Democratic, which it has since retained, and the Clay and Adams factions, consisting of the loose constructionists of the old party, took the name of National Republican, which eventually was changed to Whig. Adams's administration was marked by a long controversy between his followers and those of Jackson, who claimed that they had been deprived of the election by a corrupt compact between Adams and Clay. This helped to defeat the Adams faction in 1828 and to elect Jackson. The most important event of this period was the passage of the Tariff of Abominations of 1828 (See TARIFF), which led to the nullification controversy in the following administration (See NULLIFICATION). Adams's term also saw the extension of the policy of internal improvements by the national government, and the beginning of a vast immigration into the western regions.

Democracy Again in Power. Jackson was elected in 1828 by a vote of 178 to 83, with John C. Calhoun as vice-president. This election marks the return of the radical Democratic party to power. The chief contests of his term were over the United States Bank and the tariff, the former being refused a continuance of its charter and the latter resulting in the nullification episode, which was firmly handled by President Jackson, secession being prevented by a compromise bill introduced by Henry Clay. During this controversy the famous debate between Daniel Webster and Robert Y. Hayne occurred. Jackson was reëlected in 1832 over Henry Clay, John Floyd and William Wirt, and Martin Van Buren was chosen vice-president. His second administration was marked by indian disturbances, in the south with the Cherokee and Seminole, and in the west with the Sacs and Foxes under Black Hawk (See BLACK HAWK WAR). The Senate took firm ground against the president, especially for his attitude toward the national bank, and this contest was bitter throughout his term. The question of the independence or annexation of Texas also arose during Jackson's second term and signalized the increasing importance of the slavery controversy, the Texas question resolving itself into a contest upon the part of the South for the extension of slavery territory, and resistance to this policy by the North. The first anti-slavery societies date from this time. President Jackson's terms were also notable for the first important contest over the spoils system, which he had introduced into the national government.

Jackson was succeeded by his follower, Martin Van Buren, who defeated the Whig candidate, William Henry Harrison of Indiana. Richard M. Johnson was elected vice-president. The first year of Van Buren's term was marked by a terrible financial panic, which caused the failure of many banks and corporations and produced great suffering among the people. Van Buren continued the hostility of the Democratic party to the establishment of a national bank and replaced that institution by a system known as the independent treasury (See INDEPENDENT TREASURY).

A Whig Triumph. The financial depression and other issues led to the election of the popular Whig candidate, William Henry Harrison, in 1840, after a memorable campaign, known to history as the "log cabin and hard cider campaign." The anti-slavery party at this election for the first time nominated independent candidates, James G. Birney being the candidate of the Liberty party. Harrison died shortly after his inauguration, and was succeeded by John Tyler, formerly a Democrat. He immediately came into conflict with Congress over the proposed re-establishment of the national bank, and he vetoed two bills drawn to that end. The controversy became so heated that all of Tyler's cabinet except Webster resigned, he remaining merely to complete the negotiation of the famous Webster-Ashburton Treaty (See WEBSTER-ASHBURTON TREATY). In 1843 President Tyler arranged a treaty with the Republic of Texas, providing for the future annexation of that country to the United States, but it was rejected by the Senate. The Texas question became the leading issue in the following campaign, however, which resulted in the election of James K. Polk, the Democratic candidate, over Henry Clay, the Whig, and James G. Birney, the candidate of the Liberty party. Before Tyler left office Congress had approved a resolution for the annexation of Texas.

Texas and the Mexican War. The administration of President Polk was chiefly notable for the precipitation of the Mexican War, as a result of his order to the United States troops under General Taylor to take possession of territory claimed by both Texas and Mexico. Texas was admitted as a state in June, 1845. The war (For a detailed account, see article MEXICAN WAR) resulted in an easy victory for the United States, and by the Treaty of Guadalupe Hidalgo the United States territory was greatly extended. The dispute over the territory of Oregon was also an issue in the campaign in 1844 and was settled by a treaty with England in 1846. During Polk's administration, the Walker tariff of 1846 was passed; it was a return to the principle of tariff for revenue only. The independent treasury was also firmly established. The slavery question again cropped out over the extension of the institution to the territory acquired from Mexico (See WILMOT PROVISO) and in the formation of the Free-Soil party. Gold was discovered in California in 1848 and resulted in a vast immigration to that region.

The Liberty party had been fused with the Free-Soil party, and in 1848 it nominated Martin Van Buren as its candidate for president, against Lewis Cass, the Democratic nominee, and General Zachary Taylor, the Whig nominee. Taylor was elected, with Millard Fillmore as vice-president.

The Downfall of the Whigs. In spite of its triumph at this election, the Whig party soon showed signs of disintegration, being absorbed in part by the Free-Soil movement, which later took form in the Republican party. Meantime,

the Democratic party came under the control of its pro-slavery faction, and the slavery issue was therefore brought to a crisis. For a time in 1850 the controversy seemed to be allayed through the compromise measures, which admitted California as a free state, but gave the South numerous concessions, in the form of the Fugitive Slave Law and the organization of New Mexico and Utah with the right to admit or prohibit slavery as they chose (See FUGITIVE SLAVE LAWS; COMPROMISE OF 1850). President Taylor died before the passage of these acts, and Millard Fillmore succeeded to the presidency. The most important event of his administration was the signing of the Clayton-Bulwer Treaty, regarding the inter-oceanic canal (See CLAYTON-BULWER TREATY). In the election of 1852 the Democrats were successful, Franklin Pierce of New Hampshire becoming president, and William R. King of Alabama, vice-president. The Whig nominees were General Winfield Scott and William A. Graham. The Free-Soil party nominated John P. Hale of New Hampshire and George W. Julian.

Slavery. In spite of the apparent cessation of the slavery controversy, the struggle soon revived, over the organization of the territories of Kansas and Nebraska, and the doctrine proposed by Stephen A. Douglas for the regulation of these territories, known as "squatter sovereignty" (See SQUATTER SOVEREIGNTY). This contest marked the final dissolution of the Whig party, most of the Southern members joining with the Democrats in favor of the extension of slavery, the Northerners, together with other anti-slavery factions, uniting to form the Republican party. During this time a fierce struggle for the possession of Kansas ensued between the anti-slavery and pro-slavery factions (See KANSAS, subhead *History*). It was during Pierce's administration that Commodore Perry negotiated his treaty with Japan.

The election of 1856 again resulted in a Democratic success, James Buchanan being elected president and John C. Breckenridge vice-president, over John C. Fremont and William L. Dayton, the Republican candidates, and Millard Fillmore and A. J. Donelson, the nominees of a new party, known as the Know-Nothings or American party. It was during Buchanan's administration that the slavery struggle came to a head. It witnessed the Supreme Court decision in the Dred Scott case, declaring that Congress had no right to prohibit slavery in the territories; the attempts upon the part of Southern statesmen to gain possession of Cuba, for the extension of slavery (See OSTEND MANIFESTO), and the continuation of the bitter struggle in Kansas, which resulted, in the succeeding administration, in the admission of Kansas as a free state (See LECOMPTON CONSTITUTION). In 1859 occurred John Brown's raid at Harper's Ferry, which roused the most bitter antagonism in the South (See BROWN, JOHN). The Democratic party was now practically divided, and two sets of candidates were nominated, one by the Northern wing and the other by the Southern wing. The former was Stephen A. Douglas, of Illinois, and Herschel V. Johnson, of Georgia; the latter, John C. Breckenridge, of Kentucky, and Joseph Lane, of Oregon. The Republicans nominated Abraham Lincoln, of Illinois, and Hannibal Hamlin, of Maine, while a third party, the successor of the American party, now known as the Constitutional Union party, nominated John Bell, of Tennessee, and Edward Everett, of Massachusetts. Lincoln was elected by a comparatively small plurality and by far less than a majority of the popular vote.

Secession. The election of Lincoln was the signal for the South to take measures to overcome the overwhelming opposition to them in the United States government, and it resulted in the secession of South Carolina on December 20, 1860. Mississippi, Florida, Alabama, Georgia, Louisiana, Texas, Virginia, Arkansas, North Carolina and Tennessee followed within the next six months, and a new nation, known as the Confederate States of America, was organized at Montgomery, Ala., in February, 1861. President Buchanan opposed secession, but denied his right to coerce the seceding states to return to the Union, and therefore he made little effort to protect government property in the South, which was being taken over as rapidly as possible by the seceding states. Efforts at compromise were made during Buchanan's administration, but without effect (See CRITTENDEN COMPROMISE).

Civil War. In his inaugural address President Lincoln urged all sections and classes to come to the support of the government, but expressed his determination to prevent secession. Accordingly, he soon called for volunteers. The Confederate government also called for volunteers and retaliated for Lincoln's proclamation of a blockade by licensing privateers to prey upon Northern commerce. The war began with the bombardment of Fort Sumter on April 14, and its surrender. (For a history of the war, see article CIVIL WAR IN AMERICA; also, articles upon

the important battles and upon the leading soldiers and statesmen of the period.) In April, 1862, Congress purchased and emancipated all slaves in the District of Columbia; two months later it abolished slavery throughout the territories and the public domain, and on January 1, 1863, President Lincoln issued his famous Emancipation Proclamation, which he had announced in the previous September, after the battle of Antietam (See EMANCIPATION PROCLAMATION). During the war the President did not have the undivided support of the North. His suspension of the writ of habeas corpus, the suppression of newspapers and of public gatherings, the Conscription Act of 1863 (See DRAFTING) and the apparent failure of the Union armies in the field during the early years of the war, all led to serious opposition and criticism. The financial problems of the war also necessitated taxes and other extraordinary measures, which became exceedingly unpopular. However in the election of 1864 the Democratic party, in spite of the nomination of a popular general, George B. McClellan, was defeated, on a platform which declared that the war was a failure, and Lincoln was triumphantly reëlected. West Virginia, which had been separated from the old State of Virginia, soon after the beginning of the struggle, was admitted to the Union in December, 1862. The war practically came to a close on the surrender of General Lee in April, 1865, but the rejoicing which that caused was soon overshadowed by universal sorrow at the assassination of President Lincoln, April 14 (See BOOTH, JOHN WILKES).

Reconstruction. The problems which the close of the war would bring were anticipated by Lincoln and by Congress, and steps were taken as early as 1863 to provide for the return of the seceded states to the Union and the reëstablishment of loyal state governments. President Johnson, who acceded to the presidency at the death of Lincoln, carried out as far as possible his predecessor's lenient policy of reconstruction, but in so doing he won the enmity of Congress and was impeached, being saved from conviction by a single vote. Meantime, Congress had passed the Thirteenth Amendment, abolishing slavery, and it had been ratified in December, 1865. It had also passed other laws, placing the Southern states in the position of conquered provinces (See RECONSTRUCTION; JOHNSON, ANDREW; TENURE OF OFFICE ACT, and subhead *History* under each of the Southern states). In 1868, Arkansas, Alabama, Florida, North and South Carolina,

Georgia and Louisiana were readmitted to the Union.

The election of 1868 placed General U. S. Grant in the president's chair, with Schuyler Colfax, of Indiana, as vice-president. The Democratic candidates were Horatio Seymour, of New York, and Francis P. Blair, Jr., of Missouri. Before Grant's inauguration, the Fourteenth and Fifteenth amendments to the Constitution had been passed, granting suffrage to the negroes. The latter was ratified in March, 1870. The first important event of Grant's term was the signing of the Treaty of Washington and the Geneva Arbitration of the Alabama Claims (See ALABAMA, THE), both of which resulted in favor of the United States. The reconstruction policy of Congress led to serious difficulties in the South, which the president sought to remove, but with only partial success (See KU KLUX KLAN). His administration was also marked by the completion of the Pacific railroads and by the accompanying Credit Mobilier scandal (See CREDIT MOBILIER IN AMERICA). This scandal led to a demand for a reform in the civil service, which was made an important issue in the succeeding campaign. This issue, with that of reconstruction and the tendency of the Republicans to centralize power, led to the formation of a new party, the Liberal Republican party, whose candidates, Horace Greeley and B. Gratz Brown, were endorsed by the Democratic convention. However, General Grant was reëlected, with Henry Wilson of Massachusetts as vice-president, Greeley having died before the count of the electoral votes. In the same election the Prohibition party and a labor reform party first appeared.

Soon after his reëlection, Grant was confronted by a difficulty with Spain over the Virginius Massacre (See VIRGINIUS MASSACRE). His second administration was marked by the rise of the Grangers (See GRANGE); by the controversy over the resumption of specie payments (See SPECIE PAYMENTS, RESUMPTION OF); by the exposure of the Whisky Ring (See WHISKY RING); by the coinage acts of 1873; by continued disorders in the Southern states as a result of the carpetbag régime (See CARPETBAGGERS); by a disastrous financial panic in 1873; by a war with the Modocs and Sioux, during which occurred the Custer massacre, and by the Centennial Exhibition at Philadelphia. Discontent with Grant's administration increased. The Democrats gained a majority in Congress and made a hard fight for the election of 1876. Their candidate, Samuel J. Tilden, received a majority of the popular vote,

but was defeated by one electoral vote, as a result of an investigation by a specially constituted electoral commission, which considered the disputed returns from several states (See ELECTORAL COMMISSION).

Industrial Progress and Problems. The successful candidate, President Hayes, immediately withdrew United States troops from the South and thus paved the way for a return of good feeling between the two sections. His term was also notable for the rise of a party representing the laboring classes, which demanded a bimetallic standard of money, the suppression of national bank notes, the institution of an income tax and the prohibition of Chinese immigration. This party became known as the Greenback party. In 1878 the Bland-Allison Bill was passed (See BLAND-ALLISON BILL), and in the following year specie payments were resumed. In 1880 within the Republican party arose a fierce contest for control between the followers of Ulysses S. Grant, who demanded for him a third term, and those of James G. Blaine and John Sherman. James A. Garfield, of Ohio, a compromise candidate, was finally chosen, however, and was victorious over General Winfield S. Hancock, the Democratic nominee, and James B. Weaver, the Greenback-Labor candidate.

The early part of Garfield's administration was marked by the continuation of the party contest and by the disclosure of frauds in the postal service (See STAR ROUTE FRAUDS). President Garfield was assassinated in July, 1881, and died in the following September, Chester A. Arthur becoming president. During his administration the Edmunds law against polygamy was passed; also a bill suspending Chinese immigration for ten years. Civil service reform was forced to the front by the Democratic party, and in 1884 their nominee, Grover Cleveland, of New York, was elected over James G. Blaine by a small popular plurality. The election disclosed an independent movement in the Republican party, which was led by some of the most prominent Republicans in the country. Benjamin F. Butler, of Massachusetts, was the candidate of the Greenback-Labor party, and John P. Saint John was the candidate of the Prohibition party.

President Cleveland proceeded to extend the civil-service reform to a vast number of offices, thus securing the antagonism of many of the political leaders in his own party. The death of Vice-president Hendricks made necessary the passage of a law governing the presidential succession. During the same administration a new

THE PURITAN
St. Gaudens

FOUNTAIN OF THE GREAT LAKES
Taft

COLUMBUS
Bartlett

TWO NATURES
Barnard

MEMORY
French

ETHAN ALLEN
Mead

DEATH AND THE SCULPTOR.   French

GEORGE WASHINGTON
Ward

EXAMPLES OF AMERICAN SCULPTURE

anti-polygamy law, the Interstate Commerce Act of 1887 and a law prohibiting Chinese immigration, were passed. The administration was characterized by an unprecedented use of the veto power, especially upon private pension bills. The campaign of 1888 turned upon the tariff, which President Cleveland had brought forward as an issue by a late message in December, 1887. Cleveland was nominated by the Democrats in that year, but was defeated by the Republican candidate, Benjamin Harrison, though Cleveland received a majority of the popular vote.

Harrison's administration was notable for the remarkable diplomacy of James G. Blaine, for the extension of the policy of reciprocity, for the passage of the McKinley Tariff Bill, the extension of the pension system by a dependent pension law, passed in 1890, by the repeal of the Bland-Allison law and the substitution of the Sherman Silver Purchase Act and by serious labor disturbances at Homestead, Pa (See TARIFF; BERING SEA CONTROVERSY; SHERMAN, JOHN; McKINLEY, WILLIAM; BLAINE, JAMES G.). The monarchy in the Hawaiian Islands was overthrown, and a bill favoring annexation to the United States was passed by Congress. In 1892 the Democratic party returned to power, with Grover Cleveland and Adlai E. Stevenson as its candidates, the Republicans having nominated President Harrison and Whitelaw Reid. The People's party, or Populists, the successor of the Greenback-Labor party, nominated James B. Weaver of Iowa and received 22 electoral votes.

Financial Panic of 1893. The second administration of Cleveland opened with a terrible financial panic, with which most of the early important events of his term were connected, especially his efforts to repeal the Sherman law, his issuance of bonds to replenish the treasury gold reserve and the passage of the Wilson Tariff Law. The treaty of annexation of Hawaii was also withdrawn from the Senate, and the United States government made an effort to reëstablish the monarchy over the islands. His term was also marked by the successful intervention of the United States in a boundary dispute between Venezuela and Great Britain; by a great world's fair at Chicago (See WORLD'S COLUMBIAN EXPOSITION); by the settlement of the Bering Sea controversy; by the extension of the civil service reform and by a great strike of railroad employes, which necessitated the calling out of Federal troops. The Democratic party failed to support the president in his financial policy, and at its convention in 1896 it nominated William J. Bryan, of Nebraska for president, upon a platform demanding the free and unlimited coinage of silver. The Republicans nominated William McKinley, of Ohio. A faction of the Democratic party formed a new organization, known as the National Democratic party, favoring the gold standard, and nominated John M. Palmer of Illinois. The Prohibitionist candidate was Joshua Levering; the Socialist Labor standard bearer was Charles H. Matchett. The Populist party endorsed William J. Bryan, and the Free Silver Prohibition party nominated Charles E. Bentley. McKinley was elected by a large electoral and popular majority.

Expansion. At the organization of the government, the Mississippi River formed the western boundary of the United States, and the area of the country was 828,000 square miles. Only about 300,000 square miles, or a little over one-third of this area, was actually settled. In 1803 the first great addition of territory was made by the purchase of Louisiana (See LOUISIANA PURCHASE). Sixteen years later, this was followed by the acquisition of Florida. With these accessions of territory, the country was openly committed to the policy of expanding her domains, so that in the admission of Texas and the taking over of the territory ceded by Mexico no new policy was established, except in the method pursued. Thus far all territory acquired had been adjoining the United States, but in 1867 Secretary Seward, in the purchase of Alaska, took a radical step, in acquiring territory somewhat remote from the country. A still more radical step was taken in the annexation of Hawaii and the acquisition of the Philippine Islands and Porto Rico. The following table contains data concerning the territory added to the United States:

TERRITORIAL DIVISION	YEAR	AREA ADDED (SQ. MI.)	PURCHASE PRICE
Louisiana	1803	875,025	$15,000,000
Florida	1819	70,107	5,499,768
Texas	1845	389,795	....
Oregon Territory	1846	288,689	....
Mexican Cession	1848	523,802	18,250,000
Gadsden Purchase	1853	36,211	10,000,000
Alaska	1867	590,884	7,200,000
Hawaiian Islands	1897	6,449	....
Porto Rico	1898	3,435	....
Guam	1898	210	....
Philippine Islands	1898	114,958	20,000,000
Tutuila (Samoa Is.)	1899	77	....
Additional Philippines	1901	68	100,000
Panama Canal Strip	1904	474	$10,000,000*
Total		2,900,184	$77,039,768†
Original Territory		827,844	
Total		3,728,028	

*Besides an annual rental of $250,000.
†This does not include $10,000,000 paid to Texas for territory outside of its present boundaries, but included in the state at the time of annexation.

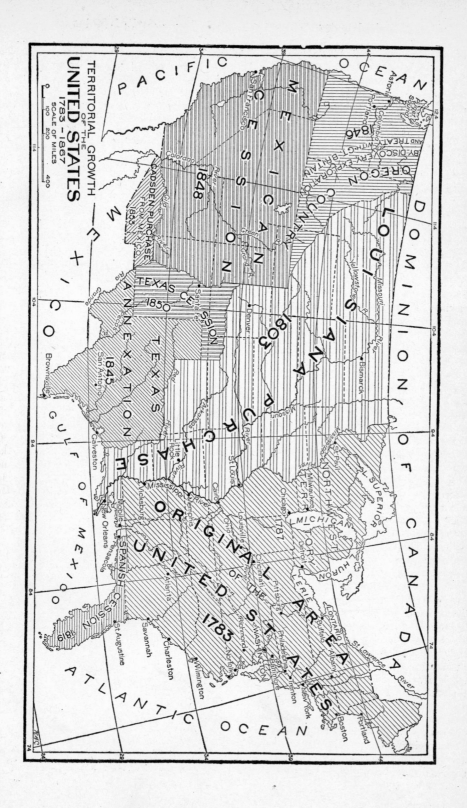

TERRITORIAL GROWTH
OF THE
UNITED STATES
1783-1867
SCALE OF MILES
0   100   200   400

Recent Progress. The most important episode of McKinley's term was the Spanish-American War (See SPANISH-AMERICAN WAR), which arose from the Spanish oppression of Cuba. It resulted in the abolition of Spanish rule in Cuba and the establishment of military government under the United States, which continued until 1902, when the Republic of Cuba was organized. The war also brought into the possession of the United States the Philippine Islands, for which a temporary military government was provided, on account of the continuance of rebellion in the islands. In 1898 Hawaii was annexed to the United States, and in 1900 it was made a territory. A law establishing the gold dollar as the standard of currency was adopted in 1900, and bills reorganizing the army and abolishing the army canteen were passed in 1901. The United States participated in a joint international military expedition to China, to assist in the suppression of the Boxer rebellion, in 1900. The diplomatic events following this expedition emphasized the change in the position of the United States in international affairs.

The chief issues in the campaign of 1900 were imperialism, that is, the question of the retention of the Philippine Islands, and the trust problem. McKinley was again the Republican nominee, and Bryan was the Democratic candidate. McKinley was elected by an increased majority. Soon after his inauguration, President McKinley was assassinated, while attending the Pan-American Exposition at Buffalo and he was succeeded by Theodore Roosevelt, who retained McKinley's cabinet and furthered his policy.

During Roosevelt's administration, the important events were the passage of the Chinese Exclusion Bill; a law providing for the irrigation of the arid lands of the West; the conclusion of a reciprocity treaty with Cuba; the creation of a department of labor and commerce, including a bureau of manufactures and corporations, for the purpose of investigating and regulating trusts; the passage of the bills for the reorganization of the militia, the increase of the navy and the creation of a general staff for the army; the passage of an anti-trust law in 1903; the ratification of a treaty between the United States and Great Britain (See HAY-PAUNCEFOTE TREATY), giving the United States the right to construct and maintain a canal across the Isthmus. (See PANAMA, PANAMA CANAL). Roosevelt's administration was also marked by the successful conclusion of a treaty fixing the boundary between Alaska and the Northwest Territories of the Dominion of Canada, the result being generally favorable to the United States. The campaign of 1904 turned on the personalities of the candidates and on the questions raised by the policy of the Roosevelt administrations. Roosevelt was elected by a large majority over Alton B. Parker, the Democratic candidate. The successful intervention of President Roosevelt to end the Russo-Japanese War, the prosecution of several large corporations for violation of the anti-trust law, the agitation for regulation of railroad rates, the rigid investigations of insurance corporations, and the movement for the conservation of natural resources are important in Roosevelt's second administration.

In the election of 1908, William Howard Taft, the Republican candidate, was successful over Bryan. In the spring of 1909 the President called Congress in special session to revise the Tariff (see TARIFF). The new tariff was unpopular, and was one of the strongest factors in causing the election of a majority of Democrats to the House of Representatives in 1910. This Congress passed acts for the admission of Arizona and New Mexico as states, and considered a reciprocity treaty with Canada which was finally rejected by the Canadians.

The election of 1912 was marked by a split in the Republican ticket. The regular Republicans nominated Taft and Sherman, while the progressives formed a new party, the National Progressive, and nominated Theodore Roosevelt and Hiram W. Johnson of California. The Democratic candidates, Woodrow Wilson and Thomas R. Marshall, were elected by a plurality of more than 2,000,000 votes. For details of the work of the leading statesmen see the articles under their names. The passage of the Underwood-Simmons tariff bill, with the provisions for an income tax, the act creating federal reserve banks, and the trouble with Mexico were the important events of the first year of the new administration. See BANKS AND BANKING; MEXICO, subhead *History;* POLITICAL PARTIES IN THE UNITED STATES; TARIFF.

Bibliography. Among the many books treating of the history and development of the United States, the following are good authority, easily obtained and interesting to the general reader: N. S. Shaler's *The United States of America;* The American Commonwealth Series; The American Statesmen Series; *The Century Book for Young Americans;* John Fiske's *Civil Government in the United States;* Ray Stannard Baker's *Our New Prosperity;* Carroll D. Wright's

Industrial Evolution of the United States; Catherine Coman's *The Industrial History of the United States;* Hugo Münsterberg's *The Americans;* William A. Mowry's *The Territorial Growth of the United States;* and E. Benjamin Andrews's *The United States in Our Own Time.*

United States Indian Industrial School, an institution established by the United States government in 1879 at Carlisle, Pa. Its central purpose was to provide a school where such mental, moral and manual training could be secured by indian boys and girls that they would be led to appreciate the value of modern civilization and desire to attain to it. Besides the training in the common manual trades and elementary instruction in the common branches of study, an "outing" system was provided. Under this plan, as many as possible of the students are sent out into the homes of white pepole as servants. There they live the daily life of the Caucasian, and become acquainted with his common principles and institutions, at the same time saving enough of their wages to ensure them a small working capital at graduation. The physical training and health of the students is also a subject of careful study, and for this work a large gymnasium, athletic field and hospital are provided. Since the organization of the school more than 5000 different indian boys and girls have been in attendance, the recent yearly enrollment being between 1200 and 1500. These students are drawn from 77 different indian tribes, from all parts of the United States and Alaska. The school has more than 400 graduates, many of whom are now employed in helping or teaching in the indian service of the government. The great majority seem to be permanently prosperous and contented in their new life.

United States Military Academy. See MILITARY ACADEMY, UNITED STATES.

United States Naval Academy. See NAVAL ACADEMY, UNITED STATES.

United Workmen, ANCIENT ORDER OF. See ANCIENT ORDER OF UNITED WORKMEN.

Universalists, *u'ni vur' sal ists,* those who hold the doctrine that all men will be saved, in opposition to the doctrine of eternal punishment. A sect of this name was founded about 1750. They believe in the ultimate salvation of all men and created spirits, and they direct their criticism against an eternal hell and, in some cases, against any suffering after death. The name *Universalists* is sometimes applied to the Arminians, in consequence of the *universality* which they ascribe to the operation of divine grace, and of

174

their opposition to the doctrine of *particular* election. There are about 890 Universalist churches in the United States, with 55,000 members.

Universe, *u'ni vurs.* The earth at one time was thought to be the center of creation, and the sun and other bodies were believed to revolve about it. Now it is understood that not only the earth, but the planets and the asteroids, all revolve about the sun, and that the sun itself is but one star out of the many millions in the sky. All these countless stars and the members of the solar system, taken together, make up what we call the universe, a whole so grand that to conceive its limits is utterly impossible. In these volumes such articles as STARS; SOLAR SYSTEM; NEBULAR HYPOTHESIS; EARTH; SUN; MOON; PLANET, and the articles referred to in each of these, will serve to give some idea of what constitutes the universe.

University, a corporation or association of men, organized for the purpose of providing means for study and original research in the higher branches of learning, and empowered to grant degrees that are recognized throughout the civilized world. Universities are among the oldest educational institutions and were established early in the thirteenth century. The first universities were formed by the association of colleges. The oldest are those of Bologna and Paris (See BOLOGNA, UNIVERSITY OF; PARIS, UNIVERSITY OF). The University of Bologna was an association of students; that of Paris, an association of masters and doctors. All the universities established in Europe for several hundred years patterned after one of these plans. Existing European universities are organized upon either the German, the French or the English plan.

GERMAN UNIVERSITIES. This class includes all universities where the German language is spoken, and in addition to those in Germany proper, it embraces the universities of Switzerland and Austria. In these universities the faculties of all departments are independent of one another; and the work of all is characterized by a scientific spirit which leads to the greatest freedom in original research. They are all State institutions and are subject to the control of the minister of ecclesiastical, educational or medical affairs. They derive their support from the government, but each is allowed the greatest liberty in the management of its own affairs and in the determination of its courses of study. The only degrees conferred by German universities are those of doctor and licentiate.

FRENCH UNIVERSITIES. The French universities are modeled after the University of Paris. A number of these were early organized; but during the French Revolution the universities, with all other educational institutions, were abolished. Upon the reorganization of affairs, Napoleon organized the University of France, which was at the head of the educational system. According to his plan, the university had charge of all higher education and was divided into fifteen faculties, located in as many educational districts, with the central authority at the University at Paris. This arrangement continued until 1896, when the districts were made independent, each being given control of its own affairs, under the direction of the minister of education.

ENGLISH UNIVERSITIES. English universities are of two types, those founded during the Middle Ages, such as Oxford and Cambridge, which are unique among the universities of the world in their plan and organization (See CAMBRIDGE, UNIVERSITY OF; OXFORD, UNIVERSITY OF), and those that have been founded since the eighteenth century, such as Durham University and the University of London, which is only a degree-conferring institution. The others resemble the German universities in their plan and organization. This plan has also been adopted wherever English colonization has gone; it is represented in Canada by McGill College, in Montreal, and by the University of Toronto, and in Australia it is exemplified by the universities at Melbourne, Adelaide and Sydney.

AMERICAN UNIVERSITIES. In the United States the term university has been used indiscriminately and is applied to degree-conferring institutions, regardless of their provision for graduate work. Moreover, many schools established in the newer states, either by private or denominational enterprises, have been styled universities, when many of them were scarcely prepared to do the work of a college. According to the plan upon which they have been established, American universities can be grouped into the following classes: (1) Those which have developed from older colleges, such as Harvard, Yale, Pennsylvania, Princeton and The George Washington; (2) those that have been established by act of legislature and are known as state universities, such as the universities of Michigan, Wisconsin and Illinois; (3) those that have been established by benefactions, such as Johns Hopkins and Cornell; (4) those established under the auspices of some religious denomination, such as the Catholic University, at Washington; the University of Chicago, and

Northwestern University, at Evanston and Chicago. All of these institutions maintain undergraduate, or college, departments, and in some of the newer states the state university is under the necessity of maintaining a preparatory school.

Strictly speaking, a university is a school for the higher branches of learning, and it presupposes a college education as requisite to admission. It should contain a college of liberal arts, and faculties of law, medicine and theology; and to these most universities add faculties of sciences and engineering. See COLLEGE; EDUCATION, NATIONAL SYSTEMS OF.

University Exten'sion, a movement for extending the means of a higher education to persons of all classes, by a system of lectures and instruction, carried on by instructors of an established university. University extension originated with Cambridge University, England, in 1872, and it was taken up by the University of Oxford in 1885. In the United States the movement was systematically started by Doctor Melville Dewey in 1888. At that time Doctor Dewey was chief librarian of Columbia University, and he laid before the regents of the University of the State of New York a plan for university extension, in connection with public libraries. Two years later a committee of the New York colleges and universities urged the regents to establish such a system of teaching under state supervision, and in 1821 a bill passed the legislature, appropriating $10,000 for the expenses of organizing the movement. Previous to this, some extension work had been done by the professors of Johns Hopkins University, who, however, conducted it as an individual enterprise, and in 1891 the University of Pennsylvania organized a corps of lecturers, who were to lecture on literature, history, sociology and science in the surrounding towns, wherever local organizations for the study of any of these subjects could be formed. From these beginnings the larger universities took up the work, and it gradually extended over the country. The most successful work has been done by the universities of Pennsylvania, Cornell, Harvard, Yale and Chicago.

The plan includes (1) the arrangement of lecture study courses with syllabi, by the faculties of the university; (2) the organization of local centers, these centers to include people who are interested in pursuing some one of the lecture courses; they decide upon the subject to be studied and engage the lecturer, whose salary and traveling expenses are paid by the center; (3) the lecture, with studies conducted either before or after it, the lecturer carrying on a quiz, in which he gives opportunity for free discussion, asking and answering questions; (4) traveling libraries, which are sent to the different centers; (5) the preparation of papers by members of the center, these papers being read and graded by the lecturer; (6) the giving of credits by the university, for satisfactory completion of the work. These credits are of limited value to those who are seeking degrees. See CHAUTAUQUA LITERARY AND SCIENTIFIC CIRCLE.

U'pas, a tree belonging to the same family as the mulberry and breadfruit, common in the forests of Java and of some of the neighboring islands, and found also in tropical Africa. Many exaggerated stories were formerly current concerning the deadly properties of this plant, its exhalations being said to be fatal to both animal and vegetable life at a distance of several miles. The sap is poisonous and forms the principal element in a mixture used by the natives for poisoning their arrowheads. The fiber of the bark is used in making a kind of cloth.

Upsala, *up sah'la,* a city of Sweden, situated on the Tyris River, 45 mi. n. w. of Stockholm. The river divides the city into the old town, which is on the west bank, and the new town, on the east. These are connected by several bridges. The University of Upsala is located here and is of historical importance, because it is the place where Linné did much of his work (See LINNÉ, KARL VON). It has a library of over 315,000 volumes. The city contains a cathedral which dates from the thirteenth century, and a church which is even older than this. The town is more important educationally and historically than from an industrial point of view. Population in 1911, 26,586.

Up'shur, ABEL PARKER (1790–1844), an American statesman, born in Northampton County, Va. He studied law under William Wirt, was admitted to the bar in 1810, was elected to the state legislature in 1824 and two years later was appointed judge of the general court in Virginia. He was appointed secretary of the navy under President Tyler, and in 1843 he succeeded Daniel Webster as secretary of state, where he served but a year, being killed by an explosion while aboard a United States war vessel.

Up'ton, EMORY (1839–1881), an American soldier, born at Batavia, N. Y., and educated at West Point. He fought at Bull Run and in the Peninsula and Maryland campaigns, and as colonel of a New York regiment of volunteers he won distinction at Fredericksburg, Gettysburg

and in Grant's Virginia campaign. He was wounded at Spottsylvania Court House and again at the Pamunkey River in Sheridan's Shenandoah Valley campaign, and for gallantry at Winchester he was brevetted major general of volunteers. He later served in Wilson's cavalry division in Georgia and was brevetted brigadier general in the regular army. From 1870 to 1875 General Upton was commandant of cadets at West Point Military Academy, and soon afterward he was made colonel in the artillery service of the regular army. He shortly became insane and committed suicide.

U'ral Mountains, a mountain system situated in the Russian Empire, extending southward from the Arctic Ocean along the 60th meridian of east longitude. The Ural Mountains form a portion of the boundary between Europe and Asia. They are low mountains and consist, on their western side, of a number of undulating swells or eminences; but on the eastern side their outline is much more sharply defined, and they descend to the Siberian plain with an abrupt slope. The highest elevations are in the northern and southern sections and exceed 5000 feet. The central section is low, and it is through a pass in this part of the range that the Trans-Siberian railway reaches Siberia. The lower slopes are covered with forests of evergreens, birch and beech, and the mountains are noted for their mineral wealth, which includes gold, silver, copper, iron, lead and platinum. For many years these mountains furnished the larger part of the world's supply of platinum, but the mines are nearly exhausted. There are also large deposits of coal, which have been extensively mined.

Ural River, a river of Russia, which rises on the eastern slope of the Ural Mountains and flows southward through the mountains, after which its course is westward, then southward, until it enters the Caspian Sea by several deltas. The total length is about 1400 miles. The chief tributaries from the west are the Kizil and the Sak-Mara, and from the east, the Sunduk, the Or and the Ilek. The river is shallow and is of but little service to navigation, except during the period of high water.

Ura'nia, in Greek mythology, the muse of astronomy. She is generally represented as holding in her left hand a celestial globe, to which she points with a little staff.

Ura'nium, a rare metal, usually obtained in the form of a black powder, but sometimes in small plates, which have a silvery luster and a certain degree of malleability. It forms several oxides, which are used in painting on porcelain, yielding a fine orange color in the enameling fire. Uranium is the source of radium. See RADIUM.

U′ranus, the seventh planet from the sun, rarely seen, except through a telescope. It was discovered by Sir William Herschel in 1781 and was first called *Georgium Sidus*, in honor of George III, and afterwards *Herschel*, in honor of the discoverer. To the naked eye it appears like a star of the sixth magnitude. In its mean distance it is more than 1,750,000,000 miles from the sun, and the length of its year is equal to about 84 of our years. In its mean diameter it is estimated at about 33,000 miles, and its volume is about 74 times that of the earth; but as its mean density is so much less, the mass of Uranus is only about 12½ times as great as the earth's. The length of the day is supposed to be between nine and ten hours. It is now generally believed that this planet has four satellites, which differ from those of all but one of the other planets, in that their orbits are nearly perpendicular to that of the planet, while the satellites of the other planets revolve in nearly the same plane as the planet to which they belong. Through the telescope, Uranus is merely a pale, greenish disk, with no certain markings; but the spectroscope seems to indicate that Uranus is quite different from other planets in its composition. See PLANET.

Uranus, in Greek mythology, the husband of Gaea, the earth, and by her, the father of the Titans and the Cyclops. He hated his children and confined them in Tartarus, but on the instigation of Gaea, Saturn, the youngest of the Titans, overthrew and dethroned him.

Ur′ban, the name of eight popes, of whom the most notable were the following: URBAN I, SAINT, bishop of Rome from 222 to 230. He was a strong pontiff, and setting himself firmly against the schismatic movement of Hippolytus, he kept it in check. URBAN II, pope from 1088 to 1099, successfully prosecuted the struggle of the papacy against Henry IV, and in 1094 he excommunicated Philip I of France for his matrimonial infidelity. In 1095 he presided at the famous Council of Clermont, which gave the impulse to the Crusades. He died before the success of the First Crusade, which he had organized. URBAN VIII, pope from 1624 to 1644, supported Richelieu's policy against Austria and Spain. He was the founder of the College of the Propaganda and was a patron of Galileo.

Urban′a, ILL., the county-seat of Champaign co., 128 mi. s. by w. of Chicago, on the Wabash and the Cleveland, Cincinnati, Chicago & Saint Louis railroads. It is near Champaign, and the state university is situated between the two cities (See ILLINOIS, UNIVERSITY OF). The surrounding region is agricultural and contains valuable deposits of fire clay. The city has railroad shops, brick works, a lawnmower factory and other factories. Some of the prominent structures are the courthouse, the municipal building, the Masonic Temple, a Y. M. C. A. building, Thornburn High School and two libraries. Crystal Lake Park is also of interest. Urbana was settled in 1824 and was chartered as a city in 1860. Population in 1910, 8245.

Urbana, OHIO, the county-seat of Champaign co., 45 mi. w. by n. of Columbus, on the Erie, the Pennsylvania and the Cleveland, Cincinnati, Chicago & Saint Louis railroads. The city is in an agricultural region and contains manufactories of furniture, bicycle rims, strawboard and other goods. It has Urbana University, a public library and three banks. The town was laid out in 1805. Population in 1910, 7739.

Urine, *u′rin,* the fluid separated from the blood by the kidneys. It carries out of the system many of the wornout tissues, especially the nitrogenous waste. Its composition varies in different animals. Human urine, of a healthy individual, is a clear, amber-colored fluid, slightly acid, and it weighs one and fifteen-thousandths to one and twenty-five thousandths times as much as water. The average quantity discharged in twenty-four hours is about two and a half pints, but the amount varies greatly, being diminished during excessive perspiration, thirst and fever, and being increased by cold, by drinking large quantities of water, by exercise, by certain foods, as salt or sugar, and by certain drugs. The principal solid and the most important ingredient found in urine is urea, the amount of which varies, being greater when animal food is used freely than when the diet is vegetable.

Ur′so, CAMILLA (1842–1902), a famous American violinist, born in Nantes, France. She studied in Paris and came to America at the age of ten, appearing in concert with immense success. She became the most noted female violinist in the world.

Ur′sula, SAINT, a virgin martyr. According to the legend she was a daughter of a prince in Britain and was put to death at Cologne by a horde of Huns, together with 11,000 virgins who accompanied her. According to another reading, the number of her companions was only eleven.

Ursulines, *ur′su linz,* or **Nuns of Saint Ursula,** a sisterhood founded by Saint Angela

Merici, at Brescia, in 1537. These sisters devote themselves to the succor of poverty and sickness and to the education of female children. They had many houses in France during the seventeenth century. The Canadian Ursulines date from 1639; the Irish, from 1771. There are now four houses in Ireland, four in England and twenty-four in the United States, with thousands of pupils. The whole number is 300 convents and 7000 nuns. Their work in Germany has met with great success.

Ur′tica′ria. See HIVES.

Uruguay, *u′roo gway* or *oo roo gwi′*, a country of South America, situated between 30° and 35° south latitude and between 53° and 58° 20′ west longitude. It is bounded on the n. by Brazil, on the e. by Brazil and the Atlantic Ocean, on the s. by the La Plata River and on the w. by Argentina. The country is nearly triangular in outline. Its area is 72,210 sq. mi., making it a little smaller than North Dakota and Delaware combined.

In the north and west there are ranges of low mountains, or hills, which attain an altitude of about 2000 feet, and along the Uruguay River are tablelands, somewhat higher than those in Argentina; but the southeastern part of the country is low and marshy, and the interior is composed of rolling plains. The chief rivers are the Uruguay, which forms the western boundary, and its largest tributary, the Negro, which flows across the country in a southwesterly direction, dividing it into two nearly equal parts. Lake Merim, situated on the northeastern border, is partly in Uruguay and partly in Brazil. The plains in the interior and the hills in the north and northwest are covered with dense forests, and the southeastern portion of the country is overgrown with grass. The chief minerals are iron, zinc, lead, antimony, sulphur and coal, and some gold has been found. There are also quarries of marble and other building stone, but the mineral resources of the country have not been extensively exploited. The rich soil and salubrious climate, accompanied by an abundance of moisture, make the country favorable for agriculture, yet only small areas are under tillage. The chief crops are wheat, corn, barley, millet, oats, rye and flaxseed. Stock raising is the most important industry of the country, and large numbers of horses, mules, cattle and sheep are reared. In 1901 there were over 17,624,000 sheep in the country, and the wool crop for the previous year was 32,750 metric tons. Many of the rivers are navigable and are used for inland

transportation. There are over 1200 miles of railway, connecting the chief centers of trade within the country with those of Argentina, and in proportion to its size, Uruguay has more miles of good roads than most other South American countries. The imports consist of foodstuffs, cotton and woolen goods, clothing, machinery and other manufactured products. The exports include meats, hides, tallow, cattle, wool and a few other agricultural products.

The government is a republic. The president is elected for four years, and the legislative power is vested in a Senate, composed of one member from each of nineteen departments, elected for six years, and a Chamber of Deputies of 69 members, elected for three years. The Roman Catholic Church is the State Church, and most of the inhabitants are members of it, but other sects are tolerated. The University of Uruguay, at Montevideo, is the leading educational institution. It has about 400 students and 100 instructors, and it maintains an art school and an industrial school. Its library and museum are of considerable value. The public schools are poor. There is a compulsory education law, but it is not enforced, and the proportion of illiteracy is very large.

Uruguay was long in dispute between Spain and Portugal, and it finally became a Spanish possession, forming a part of the viceroyalty of Buenos Ayres. Later Brazil attempted to enforce the Portuguese claim and for a short time occupied the country, but in 1828 Uruguay became independent. Within recent years the country has suffered from internal dissensions and revolutions, which have nearly paralyzed her industries. The capital and chief city is Montevideo, which is described under its title. Population, in 1911, 1,177,560, consisting largely of a mixed race of indian and Spanish and Portuguese blood. Spanish is the prevailing language.

Uruguay River, a river of South America, which rises in the southeastern part of Brazil, flows westward, then southward, and enters the estuary of the Rio de la Plata. It forms a part of the boundary between Brazil and Argentina and forms the entire boundary between Argentina and Uruguay. Its length is about 950 miles, and in the lower part of its course it is from six to nine miles wide. It is navigable for large vessels as far as Paysandu, and for smaller vessels, for a considerably longer distance.

Us′beks or **Uzbeks,** members of a Turkish tribe, which at one time formed the ruling class throughout western Turkestan, but which are now completely under the influence of Russia. In many districts they still are the nobility.

Usury, *u'zhu ry,* iniquitous, excessive or illegal interest; formerly, interest of any kind on money lent. From earliest times there has been disagreement, not only as to the right of the State to limit the rate of interest, but as to the right of an individual to accept interest at all (See INTEREST). Within two centuries, sentiment has passed through all stages regarding this question, but in recent years most countries have passed laws fixing a maximum rate of interest. In most states of the Union, there are now so-called *usury laws.* The penalty for charging usury varies under these statutes from none at all to the forfeiture of principal and interest, the invalidation of the contract, the forfeiture of twice or three times the excess of interest over a certain percentage, and in a few instances, fine and imprisonment. The table below gives the legal rate of interest in each of the states, and also the rate permitted if both parties agree to it.

STATES	LEGAL RATE	CONTRACT RATE	STATES	LEGAL RATE	CONTRACT RATE
	Per cent	Per cent		Per cent	Per cent
Alabama	8	8	Nebraska	7	10
Arkansas	6	10	Nevada	7	*
Arizona	6	12	N. Hampshire	6	6
California	7	*	New Jersey	6	6
Colorado	8	*	New Mexico	6	12
Connecticut	6	6	New York	6	6
Delaware	6	6	North Carolina	6	6
D. of Columbia	6	10	North Dakota	7	12
Florida	8	10	Ohio	6	8
Georgia	7	8	Oklahoma	6	10
Idaho	7	12	Oregon	6	10
Illinois	5	7	Pennsylvania	6	6
Indiana	6	8	Rhode Island	6	*
Iowa	6	8	South Carolina	7	8
Kansas	6	10	South Dakota	7	12
Kentucky	6	6	Tennessee	6	6
Louisiana	5	8	Texas	6	10
Maine	6	*	Utah	8	12
Maryland	6	6	Vermont	6	6
Massachusetts	6	*	Virginia	6	6
Michigan	5	7	Washington	6	12
Minnesota	7	10	West Virginia	6	6
Mississippi	6	10	Wisconsin	6	10
Missouri	6	8	Wyoming	8	12
Montana	8	*			

*Any rate on which both parties may agree.

U'tah, the SALT LAKE STATE, one of the Rocky Mountain states, bounded on the n. by Idaho and Wyoming, on the e. by Colorado and Wyoming, on the s. by Arizona and on the w. by Nevada. It is nearly rectangular in shape, extending from north to south 350 mi. and from east to west 280 mi., with an area of 84,990 sq. mi. Population in 1910, 373,351.

SURFACE AND DRAINAGE. The surface is greatly diversified, containing high mountains, broad, arid valleys and desert plateaus. Near the middle of the northern boundary, the Wasatch Mountains enter the state and extend southward along the middle line, finally degenerating into plateaus. This is the principal mountain range of the state, and its position marks the highest land, from which, as a watershed, the streams flow eastward and westward, the former to the Colorado, the latter to sink in the Great Basin. Eastward from the Wasatch, along the northern boundary of Utah, stretches a broad, massive range, known as the Uintah. Great Salt Lake, with its extraordinary percentage of saline matter in solution, is but the remnant of a vast body of fresh water, which once covered western Utah. The principal stream of eastern Utah is the Colorado. This is formed by the junction of Green River, which rises in the Wind River Mountains of Wyoming, and the Grand, whose sources are in the snow fields on Long's Peak, in Colorado. The Green and the Colorado receive numerous branches from the Uintah and Wasatch ranges, among them the Uintah, the Price, the Fremont, the San Rafael and the Virgin.

CLIMATE. The mean annual temperature ranges from 48°, in the north, to 51°, in the south. The mean temperature at Frisco is 51°. The average rainfall is 16 inches. If the snow chances to fall early in the winter, it becomes compact, and the melting is retarded. A fall of snow late in the season lies loosely on the mountain sides, and the water reaches the valleys before the crops are ready to receive its full benefit.

MINERAL RESOURCES. Next to agriculture, mining is the chief industry of Utah. Silver is found in nearly all the mountains, and the annual output is over 11,000,000 ounces, placing Utah third among the silver states. The gold product is about $4,000,000. The copper output approximates $13,400,000. Other important metals are lead, iron and zinc. There are extensive coal fields in Emery, Carbon and Summit counties; the largest sulphur deposits in the world are in Millard and Washington counties, and a superior quality of onyx is found on the west shore of Utah Lake. Salt is mined in Juab County and is obtained from evaporation of brine along Great Salt Lake. Other mineral products are asphalt, building stone, mica, graphite and gypsum. The state also has a natural gas area.

AGRICULTURE. The agricultural districts of the state are chiefly in the valleys immediately west of the Wasatch Mountains, in the Great Basin. Elsewhere, except in a few favored spots, the altitude or the insufficient water supply east of the Wasatch range, prevents successful farming. This vast area is used only for grazing.

Irrigation in the Great Basin of Utah was the first important enterprise of the kind by Anglo-Saxons in the arid West. In 1847, the Mormon pioneers turned the waters of City Creek upon the parched soil of Salt Lake Valley, and now, out of 1,250,000 acres of improved land, about 1,000,000 acres are irrigated (See IRRIGATION). The wheat, oats, barley, hay and rye are of superior quality, and the yield is large. In most localities the nights are too cool for successful corn-growing. Potatoes, beets and other vegetables are profitably raised. Fruits are abundant. Among these are apples, peaches, plums, apricots, cherries and grapes; and in the south oranges, lemons and figs are grown. The cattle industry of Utah is extensive and is growing yearly. Many sheep are exported, and the annual output of wool exceeds 15,000,000 pounds.

MANUFACTURES. The leading manufacturing industry is the smelting and refining of ores. Other industries, in the order of their importance, are the manufacture of beet sugar, flour and grist milling, construction and repair of railroad cars and locomotives, the manufacture of butter and cheese and malt liquors, the canning of fruits and vegetables, the manufacture of boots and shoes and of salt. The drying of fruits is an important industry.

TRANSPORTATION. The state has railway communication with all the great cities, east and west. The principal roads are the Union Pacific, the Southern Pacific, the Denver & Rio Grande, the San Pedro, Los Angeles & Salt Lake and the Western Pacific. Short lines connect the mining towns with the principal cities. In all, the state has about 2000 miles of railway lines. Utah has a considerable local commerce. The state exports, however, a large proportion of the products of the mines and ranges.

GOVERNMENT. The legislature consists of a senate and a house of representatives. The number of senators can never exceed 30, and the number of representatives cannot exceed three times, nor fall below twice, the number of senators. Both senators and representatives are apportioned by districts, one-half of the senators being elected every two years, for a term of four years, and the representatives being elected for two years. The executive department consists of a governor, a secretary of state, an auditor, a treasurer, an attorney-general and a superintendent of public instruction, elected for four years. The state courts comprise a supreme court, consisting of three or five judges, elected for six years, and district courts in each of the seven judicial districts. In each district from one to three judges are elected for four years.

EDUCATION. The present educational system dates from 1890, when a uniform system of public schools was established, taking the place, to quite an extent, of schools that had been maintained by various church organizations. High schools are supported in all of the larger towns and cities, and there is a state university at Salt Lake City, with which the state normal school is connected. The state agricultural college is at Logan, with experiment stations in the Saint George region and at Nephi. The Mormon Church also has an educational system peculiarly its own, and well organized. At the head of this are the Latter Day Saints' University, in Salt Lake City, Brigham Young College, at Logan, and Brigham Young Academy, at Provo. Schools are also maintained by other denominations.

INSTITUTIONS. There is a hospital for the insane at Provo City, a penitentiary at Salt Lake City and a reform school at Ogden.

CITIES. The chief cities are Salt Lake City, the capital; Ogden, Provo City and Logan, each of which is described under its title.

HISTORY. The first white visitors to Utah were the members of Coronado's expedition in 1540, but the territory was not settled for nearly three hundred years. In 1824 Great Salt Lake was discovered by James Bridger, and soon afterwards trading posts were set up in its vicinity. The real history of Utah begins with the coming of the Mormons in 1847. In the following year the United States gained possession, under the Treaty of Guadalupe Hidalgo, and in 1849 a constitution for the "State of Deseret" was adopted. Though Congress refused admission to the new state, it organized the Territory of Utah, including a much greater area than the state now has. The attempt of the Mormons to keep other settlers out of the territory led to an expedition of Federal troops in June, 1858, which took possession of Salt Lake City. The practice of polygamy among the Mormons was viewed with disfavor by Congress, and a law making it a crime was passed in 1862, but was not seriously enforced for many years. Finally, twenty years later, the Edmunds bill, disfranchising polygamists and placing the territory under a commission of five men, was passed. This was made more stringent in 1887 and again in 1890, but in the latter year the Mormon Church declared that it no longer countenanced polygamy. Finally, in 1894, a constitution was adopted, and the state was admitted to the Union two years later.

Utah, UNIVERSITY OF, a state university established at Salt Lake City in 1850, as the University of the State of Deseret. Soon after its establishment, the school was closed until 1867, owing to lack of funds. The present charter was secured in 1894, when a grant of sixty acres of land and a state appropriation of $300,000 for buildings were made. The university maintains a school of arts and science, a state school of mines and a state normal school. The faculty has a membership of over seventy, and the average enrollment is about 1100, not including pupils of the normal training school. The university has productive funds to the amount of $400,000, and the annual income, chiefly from state appropriations, is about $250,000.

Utah Lake, a fresh-water lake, situated in the north central part of Utah. Its length is about 24 miles, and its width, about 8 miles. It is in a valley bordered by mountains and discharges into Great Salt Lake through the Jordan River. Next to Great Salt Lake, this is the largest body of water in Utah.

Ute, a tribe of indians of the Shoshonean family, living in New Mexico, Utah, Colorado and Nevada. They hunt and fish, but rarely engage in agriculture. They have now sold most of their lands to the United States government, retaining a large reservation, however, in the southwest corner of Colorado.

U'tica, an ancient city of Africa, located northeast of Carthage. According to some accounts it was founded about 1100 B. C. For a long time Utica resisted Carthage successfully, and it was never contented under the latter's rule. In the third Punic War Utica submitted to Rome, and it was made the capital of the Province of Africa, after the fall of Carthage. It was at Utica that Cato killed himself, after Caesar's victory at Thapsus. The Arabs destroyed the city in the seventh century.

Utica, N. Y., the county-seat of Oneida co., 96 mi. w. by n. of Albany and 53 mi. e. of Syracuse, on the Mohawk River, on the Erie Canal and on the New York Central, the West Shore, the Delaware, Lackawanna & Western and the New York, Ontario & Western railroads and several electric lines. The city has an elevation of about 500 feet above the sea and is laid out with wide streets, which are well paved and well kept. There is a large public library, besides that of the Oneida Historical Society, and law, medical, Y. M. C. A. and Hebrew libraries. Other educational institutions are the Utica Catholic Academy, Assumption Academy, the

New School and a number of other private schools. The many charitable institutions have caused the place to be called the "City of Charities." They include the Saint Luke's Homeopathic, the Faxton and the general hospitals; a state hospital for the insane; Saint Elizabeth's Hospital and Home; the state Masonic Home and various homes for orphans, aged and homeless. There are about fifty churches, some of which are fine buildings. The school buildings of the city are among the best in the state and the educational standing is very high. Prominent structures are the county courthouse, the state armory, the Federal building and the high school.

Utica has good transportation facilities and ships large quantities of cheese and other dairy products, roses, hops, fruit, livestock and manufactured goods. The principal manufactures are cotton and woolen cloth, men's clothing, hosiery and knit goods, furnaces, machine shop and lumber products, cutlery and iron pipe. During the French and Indian War a fort was erected here, to control the fording place on the Mohawk, and was named in honor of Philip Schuyler. A settlement grew up around it, and it was known as Old Fort Schuyler until its incorporation as the village of Utica in 1798. The city was chartered in 1832. Population in 1910, 74,419.

Util'ita'rianism, a term given to that system of ethics and philosophy whose fundamental principle is that the standard of right and wrong is the happiness of mankind; that is, that an act is good only to the extent that it proves itself serviceable in promoting the welfare or happiness of society. This theory is of modern origin, having been first definitely stated by John Stuart Mill and accepted by such later philosophers as Spencer and Sir Leslie Stephen. However, it is the natural outgrowth of the philosophy of such men as Hume, Locke, Bentham and Hobbes. See PHILOSOPHY.

Uto'pia (Greek, "no place"), the title of a political romance written by Sir Thomas More, and the name that he gave to an imaginary island, which he represented to have been discovered by a companion of Amerigo Vespucci, and in which existed a perfect society. In this happy island all the property belonged to the commonwealth, to which every one contributed by his labor and from which he received all his supplies. Its penal code was of wonderful mildness (in striking contrast to that which prevailed at that period in England), and the people had learned to tolerate diversity of opinion in religious matters. Promotion also was according to merit, and the citizens rose through all the gradations of their existence, from form to form, as in a great public school. *Utopia* was published in Latin in 1516, and it was translated into English by Bishop Burnet. It attained a wide popularity, its name furnishing the familiar epithet *Utopian*, which is commonly applied to projects of reform in religion, government or society, which are felt to be visionary and impossible.

Utrecht, *u'trekt*, a city of the Netherlands, capital of the province of the same name, situated on the Old Rhine, where the Vecht branches from it, 23 mi. s. e. of Amsterdam. The city is traversed by two canals and is the chief railway center of the Netherlands. It has a cathedral, begun in the middle of the thirteenth century; the Church of Saint Catharine's, begun in 1524, and Saint John's Kirke, which dates from the eleventh century, besides a number of modern churches. The University of Utrecht is the chief educational institution and dates from early in the seventeenth century. Its library contains over 250,000 volumes. The city also has a number of learned societies, a museum of paintings by the old masters and an archiepiscopal museum, which contains a collection of sacred relics. The principal industry is the manufacture of carpets, velvets, floor cloths, cottons, linens, cigars, chemicals, musical instruments and machinery. The trade is important. Utrecht is of importance because of its historical associations. It was here, in 1579, that the Union of Utrecht was formed. This union established the Dutch Republic upon a firm foundation, and in 1713 the Peace of Utrecht was concluded, which terminated the War of the Spanish Succession. Population in 1911, 121,317.

Utrecht, PEACE OF, a series of separate treaties, agreed upon at Utrecht by the powers which had been engaged in the War of the Spanish Succession (See SUCCESSION WARS, subhead *War of the Spanish Succession*). In April, 1713, the States-General, Prussia, Portugal and Savoy signed separate treaties with France. The emperor refused to accede to the peace, and his differences with France were subsequently adjusted by the treaties of Rastadt and Baden, in 1714. By the treaty with England, France, among other things, recognized the Hanoverian succession, engaged never to unite the crowns of France and Spain, and ceded to Britain, Nova Scotia, Newfoundland and Hudson Bay and Strait. Gibraltar and Minorca were also ceded to England. Holland retained the Spanish Netherlands until a barrier treaty was arranged with Austria. Louis XIV recognized the title of the king of Prussia and the right of the House of Hanover to the English throne. Savoy and Nice were restored to the duke of Savoy, who was recognized as presumptive heir to the Spanish monarchy, and who received the title of king. Philip V was not recognized till the conclusion of these treaties, but France treated for Spain, and formal treaties corresponding with those with France were afterward signed with that power.

Uz, in the Old Testament, the scene of the story of Job, a region probably lying east or southeast of Palestine.

Uzbeks, See USBEKS,

V, the twenty-second letter of the English alphabet, was used interchangeably with *u* in Latin, and in English until the seventeenth century. The sound of *v* is always the same, and the letter which is most closely allied to it is *f*, with which it is often interchanged in related languages. In English this close connection of the two letters is shown by the plural of such words as wi*f*e, wi*v*es; hal*f*, hal*v*es.

As a Roman numeral, V means five; with a line above it, it stands for 5000.

Vaccination, *vak'se na'shun,* inoculation with the cowpox—a disease akin to, but much less severe than, smallpox—in order to prevent a person from catching the latter, or to make the attack much less severe. The practice of vaccination was introduced by Jenner, and it soon came into common use, instead of the common inoculation of one person from the sores of another. The usual method in vaccination is to make, upon the upper part of the arm, a few scratches across one another, with a clean lancet point. The virus from cowpox eruptions is then rubbed on the skin where the scratches have been made. If the vaccination proves successful, a small inflamed sore appears about the third day and increases in size until the tenth day. On the eighth day the constitutional effects manifest themselves by a slight pain in the part, headache, shivering and loss of appetite. These subside spontaneously in one or two days. Afterward the fluid in the pustule dries up, and a scab forms, which disappears about the twentieth day, leaving a scar in the skin. Few things have been more definitely proved in medicine than that vaccination is a preventive of smallpox. To secure perfect immunity, repeated vaccinations at intervals of several years are necessary in most cases. There is no danger in vaccination if pure virus is used and if the wound is kept free from infection. The wise plan is to have the vaccination made by a good physician, who will treat the wound properly and prevent any injurious results.

Vac'uum, an empty space. The term is usually applied to a space from which air or other gases have been exhausted. An absolute vacuum is impossible, since, however completely the gases may be exhausted from an enclosed space, it will still be filled with ether (See ETHER). However, in the ordinary use of the term, a vacuum is said to be produced when the air is removed from a space as completely as possible by means of an air pump. Such vacuums are sufficiently perfect for common experiments. The most perfect vacuum formed in practice is that above the mercury in a barometer tube, which is produced by first filling the tube with mercury and then allowing this to settle, until the column sustained is equal to the weight of an equal column of atmosphere (See BAROMETER). Other practical applications of the vacuum are found in the vacuum brake and the vacuum pan. See AIR BRAKE; VACUUM PAN.

Vacuum Pan, a closed vessel, from which a portion of the air and steam can be removed from the surface of a boiling liquid. Heat is usually supplied to the vacuum pan by steam coils, which are placed in the lower part of the vessel. The upper part is connected with an air pump, which exhausts the air and then the steam as fast as it is formed. Vacuum pans are used for evaporating syrup in sugar refineries and in the manufacture of other substances, where evaporation at a low temperature is required. The principle upon which they work is that the boiling point of a liquid is lowered as the pressure upon its surface decreases. See BOILING POINT; VACUUM.

Vacuum Tubes. See GEISSLER'S TUBES.

Valdai, *val di',* **Hills,** a range of hills, situated in western Russia, and forming the chief watershed of that part of Europe. They are dome-shaped elevations, consisting of hills and plateaus, with an average altitude of from 8000 to 9000 feet, the highest summit reaching an elevation of 11,000 feet. They contain the sources of the Volga, the Dnieper and the Düna.

Valdivia, *val de've a,* a seaport of Chile, capital of the province of the same name, situated on the Valdivia River, 16 mi. from its mouth. The seaport of the town is known as Valdivia Port, or Coral. Population in 1910, 17,681.

Valdos'ta, GA., the county-seat of Lowndes co., 156 mi. s. w. of Savannah, on the Georgia Southern & Florida, the Atlantic Coast Line and other railroads. The city is in a farming region, producing cotton, sugar cane, rice, corn, fruit and sweet potatoes. There are manufactures of cloth and various lumber products. The municipality has six churches and three banks, and it owns and operates the waterworks. The town was settled in 1859. Population in 1910, 7656.

Valencia, *va len'she a*, a city of Spain, situated on the Guadalaviar, 200 mi. from its mouth and 190 mi. e. by s. of Madrid. The city is characterized by narrow streets, medieval buildings and churches with tinted domes. The most prominent structure is the cathedral, which occupies the central part of the old town. The Church of Saint Martin, dating from the fifteenth century, is also of interest, since it was constructed from a mosque that dates from the thirteenth century. The city maintains a botanical garden that is considered the best in Spain. Its leading educational institution is the University of Valencia. The principal industries are the manufacture of tobacco, silk goods, velvets, linen, fans, tiles and pottery. Population in 1910, 233,348.

Valencia, a city of Venezuela, situated 24 mi. s. e. of Puerto Cabello, with which it is connected by rail. Its chief buildings include a cathedral, a university and a national college. It is an important commercial center and has a large trade in agricultural products, cattle, hides and sugar. Population in 1910, about 40,000.

Va'lens (328–378), Roman emperor, declared emperor of the East by his brother, Valentinian I, who had already been elected emperor. The chief event of his reign was the war with the Goths, which lasted during the period. In 377, driven southward by the Huns, the Goths asked and received permission to settle on Roman territory, but, irritated by the treatment they received at the hands of the imperial officials, they soon took up arms, defeated Valens and destroyed the greater part of his army. Valens was never heard of afterward.

Val'entine, SAINT, a saint of the Roman calendar, said to have been martyred in 306 A. D. The custom of choosing valentines on his day (February 14) has been accidentally associated with his name. On the eve of Saint Valentine's day, young people of both sexes used to meet, and each of the men drew from a number of names of the opposite sex. Each gentleman thus

got a lady for his valentine, and he became the valentine of a lady, to whom he was bound to be faithful for a year. A similar custom prevailed in the Roman Lupercalia, to which the modern custom has, with probability, been traced. The day is now celebrated by sending anonymously, through the post, sentimental or ludicrous missives, specially prepared for the purpose.

Val'entin'ian I, a Roman Emperor. On the death of Jovian, in 364, he was chosen emperor by the army. He shared the Empire with his brother Valens, who ruled the East, Valentinian reserving the Western province for himself. Although chiefly occupied throughout his reign in repelling invasions of the barbarians, he proved himself a firm and just ruler. His sons, Gratianus and Valentinian II, succeeded him.

Valentinian III, Roman emperor from 425 to 455. He was made emperor by Theodosius II, but he never really exercised the imperial power, leaving it in the hands of his mother, Placidia, until her death in 450, and then in the hands of the eunuch Heraclius. Although the barbarians who were constantly harassing the Empire were repeatedly defeated by Aëtius, Spain, Africa, Gaul and other provinces were lost to Rome, and it became evident that the Empire was growing steadily weaker. Valentinian was finally assassinated.

Vale'rian, a plant, native of Europe, which grows abundantly by the sides of rivers and in ditches and moist woods from Vermont to Michigan. The root has a very strong smell, which is dependent on a volatile oil. It is used in medicine, especially for nervous diseases. Cats and rats are very fond of valerian.

Valet'ta, the capital of the island of Malta, situated on the northeast coast of the island, on an elevated neck of land, which commands a commodious harbor on each side of the town. The city contains a number of beautiful squares, and upon the wharves are some excellent buildings. The most important buildings are the governor's residence and the cathedral. The city also is the site of a university, with an astronomical observatory, and it has a botanical garden and a military hospital. It is the headquarters for the British forces in the Mediterranean. Population in 1911, 44,029.

Valhal'la, in Northern mythology, the palace of immortality, inhabited by the souls of heroes slain in battle, who here spent much of their time in drinking and feasting. The name is applied figuratively to any edifice which is the final resting place of many of the heroes or great men of a nation. It is specifically given to an edifice built by Ludwig I of Bavaria, a few miles from Ratisbon. See VALKYRIES.

Valkyries, *val kir' eez*, in Northern mythology, the attendants of Odin, who, at his command, hovered over battlefields and bore the souls of the bravest of the slain to Valhalla. Odin's great

A VALKYRIE

hall. Here the Valkyries waited upon the heroes, serving them mead in vessels made from skulls. They were sometimes regarded as the personification of the clouds, especially of storm clouds.

Valladolid, *vahl'ya do leed'*, MEXICO. See MORELIA, Mexico.

Valladolid, a city of Spain, situated on the Pisuerga River, 100 mi. n. w. of Madrid. It is an old town and contains a number of interesting structures, among them the house in which Columbus died and the house which Cervantes occupied. The city has a fine park and a university, which was founded about the middle of the fourteenth century. The industries include textile, glove, paper and pottery manufactures. Population in 1910, 71,066.

Vallejo, *val ya' ho*, CAL., a city of Solano co., situated on the northeastern shore of San Pablo Bay, 23 mi. n. e. of San Francisco and on the Southern Pacific railroad. It is noted for its large and deep harbor, which admits the largest ocean ships. The city is built on the slopes of a hill, and the surrounding country is devoted to fruit raising. The public institutions include an orphans' home, Saint Vincent's Academy and the sailors' clubhouse. There are a few manufactures and some tanneries. Vallejo is an important shipping port for grain and is near the United States navy yard on Mare Island. Population in 1910, 11,340.

Valley, a strip or tract of low land, bordered by hills, mountains or bluffs. The term is applied to low land between mountains and to an area drained by rivers, but the first meaning is the one ordinarily used in physiography.

The largest and most important valleys have been formed by the upheaval and folding of the earth's crust. Such are the valleys found among mountain systems. They are long and narrow, and their floor may have an elevation several hundred or several thousand feet above the sea level. The simplest valleys of this sort are found in the Jura Mountains, where the strata were not broken in folding and where the slopes are remarkably uniform and even. Many of the so-called basins in the Rocky Mountain plateau are also valleys formed by the folding of strata, but most of these are irregular and are crossed by transverse ranges, showing that the movements by which they were formed were very complex.

Valleys running parallel to the mountain ranges are known as *longitudinal* valleys; those running across the ranges are *transverse* valleys. Transverse valleys may be due to breaks in the folded strata, but most of them have been formed by erosion. They are usually narrow, with very steep sides, and the floor is only wide enough for the stream which flows in it. When of high altitude these valleys are known as *passes*. Among the most celebrated of these passes are the Kabul Pass in the Himalayas and the Simplon Pass. When of low altitude, transverse valleys are frequently known as *water gaps*, as the Delaware Water Gap.

Valleys in volcanic regions are usually due to volcanic action and are found in the side or on the summit of mountains, around the crater. They are small and of comparatively little importance. River valleys are formed by erosion, but their location was first determined by the formation of mountains and valleys by folding. Glacial valleys are those which have been formed or modified by the action of glaciers. They are found in mountainous regions, and most of them were undoubtedly river gorges, previous to the glacial period. The lochs and firths of Scotland and the fiords of Norway are good illustrations. See FIORD; GLACIERS; MOUNTAIN;

River. Consult Shaler's *Aspects of the Earth* and Davis's *Physical Geography*.

Valley City, N. D., the county-seat of Barnes co., 58 mi. w. of Fargo, is situated on the Sheyenne River and on the Northern Pacific and the Minneapolis, Saint Paul & Sault Sainte Marie railroads. The surrounding country produces large quantities of wheat, flax and vegetables. A state normal school is located here. Among the other noteworthy buildings are the county courthouse and the high school. The city has a large trade in merchandise and produce. Near by is a viaduct of the Northern Pacific Railroad, 164 feet high and 4000 feet long. Population in 1910, 4606.

Valley Forge, a village in Chester County, Pa., famous as the site of the quarters of the American colonial army under George Washington in the winter of 1777 and 1778. The army was 11,000 strong when it went into camp, December 17, but owing to mismanagement the sup-

WASHINGTON'S HEADQUARTERS AT VALLEY FORGE

piles were totally inadequate, and fully half the men were soon unfit for duty. The suffering of the soldiers during the winter and following spring was almost incredible and tried the patriotism of even the most loyal friends of the colonial cause. Washington remained with his men throughout this period, and with the aid of Baron Steuben brought the army to a high state of efficiency. Camp was broken June 18, 1778, and the army then occupied Philadelphia.

Valois, *val wah',* a dynasty which ruled France from 1328 to 1589. In 1285 Philip III gave the county of Valois to his younger son, Charles, and upon the extinction of the Capet dynasty, in 1328, the eldest son of this Charles of Valois ascended the French throne as Philip VI, and founded the Valois dynasty.

Valparaiso, *val pa ri' zo,* a seaport of Chile and the chief commercial center on the Pacific coast of South America, situated on a bay on the Pacific Ocean, 75 mi. n. w. of Santiago, with which it is connected by rail. Back of the city rise hills and mountains, on the lower slopes of which a considerable portion of the town is built. The city is well laid out, and the streets are regular and attractive. The lower town contains the principal business houses and the city park. The other buildings are mostly constructed of stone and are of a substantial character. The educational institutions include a naval school, a number of colleges and a school for marines. The city maintains a hydrographic bureau and a museum of natural history. The industrial establishments include foundries, machine shops, bottling works, distilleries, sugar refineries and railroad shops. The harbor is spacious, and the city has an extensive foreign trade, being connected by regular lines of steamers with the Pacific ports of America and the leading ports of Europe. On August 16 and 17, 1906, the city suffered severely from an earthquake and fire, which destroyed a large part of the city, killed more than a thousand persons and rendered at least 75,000 homeless. At the same time Santiago, the capital, was badly damaged, and Quillota, a neighboring town of 60,000 people, was almost totally demolished. Population in 1910, 179,815.

Valparaiso, Ind., the county-seat of Porter co., 44 mi. s. e. of Chicago, on the Grand Trunk, the Pennsylvania and other railroads. It is a residence place, in a rich farming section. The Northern Indiana Normal School, the Valparaiso College and Saint Paul's Academy are located here, and the city has a fine courthouse. There are manufactures of mica, paint, dairy products, educational specialties and other goods. It was settled in 1826 and was incorporated in 1856. Population in 1910, 6987.

Val'ue, one of the fundamental conceptions of political economy, has been variously defined, but is now generally considered to be the power, given by an article to its possessor, to command, in exchange for it, the labor or the product of labor of others. Obviously, a multitude of influences and qualities enter into the value of an article, and the number and relation of these factors have been the source of many controversies. Some have declared that *usefulness* is the one characteristic feature of valuable articles, but it has been justly replied that air is eminently useful, but has no economic value, since it cannot be exchanged, except under extraordinary conditions. Again, the labor cost of an article, it has been claimed, is really the source of its value, and the scientific socialists base their whole system upon this theory. Others have said that scarcity, or the difficulty of attainment, regulates value.

Most modern economists agree that the two fundamental factors in value are *utility*, that is, the quality by which an article satisfies a human desire, and *scarcity*, or difficulty of attainment, which makes it necessary for a person to sacrifice labor or the product of labor in order to obtain it. These two factors, considered together, constitute what is known as the "law of supply and demand." Value, then, depends upon the relation between demand and supply, if demand is understood to mean the quantity of a given article which would be taken at a given price, and supply to mean the quantity of that article which could be had at that price. Evidently there can be no absolute standard of value, as there can be no absolute measure of desire or of difficulty; but to avoid rapid and violent fluctuation, values are measured by reference to some one article, that is, an article is said to be more or less valuable than a given article, according as its possessor would be willing to give more or less of it in exchange for the given article. Usually this article, or medium of measurement of value, is a precious metal and is called *money*. The expression of the value of an article in money is generally called its price. See POLITICAL ECONOMY.

Valve, a kind of movable lid, or cover, adapted to the orifice of some tube or passage, and so formed as to open communication in one direction and to close it in the other. Valves are used to regulate the admission or escape of a fluid, such as water, gas or steam. Some valves are self-acting, that is, they are so contrived as to open in the required direction by the pressure of the fluid upon their surface, and immediately to shut and prevent the return of the fluid, when the direction of its pressure changes. Others are operated by some independent external force. Examples of the former kind are presented in the valves of pumps, and in the safety valves of steam boilers. Examples of the latter are the slide valves appended to the cylinder of a steam engine, for the purpose of regulating the admission and escape of the steam. The construction of valves admits of an almost endless variety. See PUMP; STEAM ENGINE.

Vam'pire, in the folklore of the Slavs, a corpse which leaves its grave during the night and sucks the blood of living human beings, particularly of young people and children. The victims gradually lose strength and finally die from no

apparent malady, while the vampire retains all the appearance of a living human being. Vampires are supposed to be either criminals or wizards or, perhaps, totally innocent persons who have been the victims of vampires. The only way to destroy a vampire is to dig up the body and burn it with a stake driven through the heart.

Vampire Bat, a name for certain bats which inhabit South America. The name was given from the blood-sucking habits attributed to these bats, but how many of them really attack animals and suck blood from them is not quite clear. These bats have large leathery ears, an erect, spear-like appendage on the tip of the nose, and wings which, when extended, measure twenty-eight inches. There is little doubt that they attack horses and cattle, and sometimes they even attack man in his sleep. These bats seem to be generally distributed throughout the warmer parts of South America, from Chile to Guiana.

Vana'dium, a metal, discovered in 1830, although what was at first considered the metal was really an oxide. It has a strong metallic luster, considerably resembling silver, but still more like molybdenum. When in mass it is not oxidized, either by air or water, but the fine-powdered metal quickly takes up oxygen from the air.

Van Bu'ren, MARTIN (1782–1862), an American statesman, eighth president of the United States, born at Kinderhook, N. Y. He became office boy to a village lawyer, studied law in New York City and was admitted to the bar in 1803 Long before this, however, he had developed an interest in politics, and at the age of eighteen he was already a member of a nominating convention. In 1812 he was elected to the state senate, and from 1815 to 1819 he was state attorney-general, being removed because of a disagreement with Governor De Witt Clinton. In 1821 he entered the United States Senate, of which he was a member until his election, in 1828, to the governorship of New York. In the same year he zealously supported Jackson for the presidency, and in 1829 he was rewarded with the portfolio of secretary of state, which he resigned in 1831 to accept appointment as minister to England, though the Senate refused to confirm his nomination after he sailed. Two years later he was elected vice-president, and in 1835 he was made president by an electoral majority of 97. During all his political career he was a conspicuous figure in the so-called Albany Regency, a group of men who, though often not office-holders, controlled the Democratic party and the policy of New York State.

Van Buren's four years of office were darkened by a financial panic; but what one man could do, he did to lighten it, by wringing from Congress its assent to a measure for a treasury independent of private banks. This, and his firm adherence to neutrality during the Canadian rebellion of 1837, showed him to be a far-seeing statesman; but both cost him popularity, and in 1840 he and his party were overwhelmingly defeated by the

MARTIN VAN BUREN

Whigs. He lost the nomination in 1844, and his nomination by the Free-Soil party in 1848 only secured the return of the Whig candidate, by dividing Democratic support. He supported Pierce in 1852 and Buchanan in 1856, though remaining an uncompromising opponent of slavery.

Van Buren was a master of the politician's arts, but he used his great skill for what he counted the highest ends. He was intensely partisan, yet his political enmities did not destroy his warm private friendship for great opponents, such as Henry Clay. Consult Shepard's *Van Buren*, in the American Statesmen Series.

Vance, ZEBULON BAIRD (1830–1894), an American soldier and politician, born in Buncombe County, N. C. He attended Washington College in Tennessee, studied law and was admitted to the bar in 1852. Two years later he was elected to the state legislature, and in 1858 he went to Congress as a Whig. Though opposing secession, he followed his state into the Con-

federacy and served at the head of North Carolina troops in the Peninsula Campaign. He was elected governor in 1862, served with energy and ability and was imprisoned at the end of the war, but was released on parole. Elected to the United States Senate in 1870, he was refused admission and resigned two years later. In 1876 he was elected governor, and three years later he became United States senator. He served until his death.

Vancouver, WASH., the county-seat of Clarke co., is situated on the Columbia River and on the Northern Pacific, Union Pacific and other railroads, 6 mi. n. of Portland, Oregon. It is the United States military headquarters for Washington, Oregon and Alaska. It is an important distributing point for the surrounding country. The leading industries include a barrel factory, shipyard, foundry and shoe factory. Population in 1910, 9300.

Vancouver, *van koo'vur*, a city of British Columbia, situated on Burrard Inlet. It is the western terminus of the Canadian Pacific railway. The city has a number of fine parks and important public buildings, as well as many beautiful residences. The leading industrial establishments include railroad shops; manufactories of wagons and machinery, furniture and glass; sugar refineries, canneries, breweries and distilleries. It is the seat of the University of British Columbia, formerly affiliated with McGill University. The harbor is extensive, and there is regular steamship connection with Pacific ports of the United States and with China and Japan. Population in 1911, 100,401.

Vancouver Island, an island in the Pacific Ocean, situated off the coast of British Columbia, from which it is separated by the Gulf of Georgia and Queen Charlotte Sound; it is separated from the United States by the Strait of Juan de Fuca. The length from northwest to southeast is 275 miles; its greatest breadth, 65 mi.; and its area, about 12,000 sq. mi. The island is generally mountainous, being formed by a continuation of the Coast Ranges. It has a temperate climate, and in the south and east its soil is fertile and well suited to agriculture and fruit growing. The mountains are generally covered with heavy forest. The interior is well adapted to grazing, and large numbers of horses, cattle, sheep and swine are raised. The fishing interests along the shores of the streams and lakes are also of considerable importance. The mineral resources include coal, gold and copper. The coal mines are extensively worked and supply a good portion of the coal used on the Pacific coast of North America. The chief town is Victoria, the capital of British Columbia. The island was visited by Vancouver, an officer of the British navy, in 1792, and it was named for him. When the Oregon boundary question was settled in 1846, it became a possession of Great Britain.

Van'dals, a German people, from the region between the Vistula and the Oder. Thence they moved southward and settled in Pannonia, where they became Christians of the Arian faith. But at the beginning of the fifth century they entered Gaul and crossed the Pyrenees into Spain. One section settled in Galicia and were almost entirely destroyed in the struggle with the Goths and Suevi; the other settled in a part of Baetica, which has received from them the name *Andalusia.* In 429 they crossed the Strait of Gibraltar, under their dreaded leader, Genseric, carrying devastation and ruin from the shores of the Atlantic to the frontiers of Cyrene. So destructive were they that the word *vandal* is still applied to a person who wilfully destroys a work of art.

Van'derbilt, CORNELIUS (1794–1877), an American capitalist and financier, born on Staten

CORNELIUS VANDERBILT

Island, N. Y. At the age of sixteen he bought a boat and ferried passengers and goods across to the city. Gradually extending his enterprise, by the age of forty he had become the owner of a fleet of sound and river steamers running to Boston and up the Hudson. In 1849 he founded a

steamship and transfer line by way of Lake Nicaragua to California, and during the Crimean War he established a line of ocean steamships to Havre. A little later he transferred his capital from steamships to railroads, and he gradually obtained a controlling interest in a large number of roads, extending his system to Chicago by securing the Lake Shore, the Canada Southern and Michigan Central roads. The Grand Central depot in New York City was erected by him. At his death he left a fortune of about $100,000,-000 to his son, William Henry Vanderbilt. He left $1,000,000 to found Vanderbilt University at Nashville, Tenn.

Vanderbilt, CORNELIUS (1843–1899), an American financier and capitalist, son of William Henry Vanderbilt and grandson of "Commodore" Cornelius Vanderbilt, born at New Dorp, Staten Island. He was first employed as a banking clerk, but soon entered the service of the New York & Maryland railroad, becoming its treasurer; later he was made first vice-president of the New York Central. He became connected as director, president or in other official capacities, with all the lines known as the "Vanderbilt system," and he largely increased their value. He was a liberal patron of Vanderbilt University, Yale University and other educational and philanthropic institutions.

Vanderbilt, WILLIAM HENRY (1821–1885), an American capitalist and financier, the son of "Commodore" Vanderbilt, born at Brunswick, N. J. He received a grammar school and private education and became a bank clerk at the age of eighteen. Years later, as receiver of the Staten Island railroad, he soon cleared it from debt and established it on a firm paying basis, being chosen its president. He then became a partner with his father in vast financial enterprises and was practically manager of most of the Vanderbilt railroads. At the death of "Commodore" Vanderbilt, in 1877, W. H. Vanderbilt became president of the New York Central & Hudson River lines and extended his interest over a large number of competing and connecting lines, until it included the Michigan Central, the Lake Shore & Michigan Southern, the Canada Southern, the Chicago & Northwestern, the Nickel Plate and the West Shore railroads. He made large gifts to Vanderbilt University and to Columbia University.

Vanderbilt, WILLIAM KISSAM (1849–   ), an American capitalist, born on Staten Island, son of William Henry Vanderbilt. He received an elementary education, then studied in Geneva

Switzerland, and, returning to America, became interested with his father in the New York Central and Hudson River railroads and other enterprises, being made chairman of the board of directors of several of the subsidiary Vanderbilt lines. At the death of his father, he became the active head of the Vanderbilt interests and was a conspicuous figure in the financial contests and expansion which characterized the following years.

Vanderbilt University, a coeducational institution, established at Nashville, Tenn., in 1872, under the auspices of the Methodist Episcopal Church, and named in honor of Cornelius Vanderbilt, who gave $1,000,000 for the purpose of establishing the school. The present organization includes the following departments: academic, legal, medical, biblical, pharmacy, dentistry and engineering. The university also maintains a summer school and carries on correspondence work in its biblical department. In 1912 the faculty numbered 120, and there were over 1100 students. The endowment is about $1,750,000, the annual income is about $200,000, and the library contains 50,000 volumes.

Van' der Stucken, *stoo'ken*, FRANK (1858–), an American musician and conductor, born in Texas. He received his education in Europe and early began to compose, but without remarkable success. He succeeded Leopold Damrosch as director of the Arion Club, New York City, and later he became director of the conservatory of music at Cincinnati and conductor of the Cincinnati Symphony Orchestra. Among his popular compositions are *The Festival March* and *The Inauguration March.*

Van Dyck or **Vandyke,** *van dike'*, ANTHONY, Sir (1599–1641), a famous portrait painter of the Flemish school, born at Antwerp, where his father was a merchant. He studied painting, first under Van Balen and then under Rubens, quitting the studio of the latter after a few years, to proceed to Italy, where he spent about five years, chiefly at Genoa, Venice and Rome, returning to Antwerp about 1627. Having acquired a great reputation as a portrait painter, he was invited to England by Charles I, who bestowed upon him the honor of knighthood and a considerable annuity. In 1636 he was united in marriage to Mary Ruthven, a grandaughter of the earl of Gowrie. Shortly afterward he died and was buried in Saint Paul's Cathedral, London. Van Dyck's great strength lay in portrait painting, but he also excelled in the knowledge of
175

chiaroscuro. His best-known works are *Portrait of Charles I*, bought by the duke of Marlborough for $85,000, *Children of Charles I, Elevation of the Cross* and *Crucifixion.*

Van Dyke, HENRY (1852–), an American poet, essayist and educator. He was born at Germantown, Pa., and graduated at Princeton and at Princeton Theological Seminary. In 1878 he became pastor of the United Congregational church of Newport, R. I., and five years later he was called to the Brick Presbyterian church of New York, where he remained until 1900, when he became professor of English literature

HENRY VAN DYKE

ature in Princeton University. He has written extensively, and always attractively, in various fields. *The Builders and Other Poems* and *Music and Other Poems* are among his volumes of poetry. *The Gospel for an Age of Doubt* and *Sermons to Young Men* are examples of his religious work; *The Blue Flower* and *The Ruling Passion* are some of his charming works of fiction, and *Fisherman's Luck* and *Little Rivers* include his best work in the field of essays. In 1913 Dr. Van Dyke was appointed minister to the Netherlands by President Wilson.

Vane, HENRY, Sir (1613–1662), an English statesman, educated at Oxford and at Geneva. While at the latter place, he became a Puritan and a Republican. He went to New England in 1635, and in the following year he was made governor of Massachusetts, but was not elected a second time, because his religious views differed from those of the leaders of the colony. On his return to England he was elected to Parliament, and during the war against Charles I he took an active part on the side of Parliament. He was not in favor of the death of the king, and from the first he was opposed to Cromwell's policy. After the dissolution of the Rump Parliament, in 1653, he retired from politics. At the Restoration, he was tried for treason and beheaded.

Van Hise', CHARLES RICHARD (1857–   ), an American geologist and educator, born at Fulton, Wisconsin, educated in the University of Wisconsin. Soon after graduation he became connected with the faculty of the same institution, where he served successively as instructor in chemistry, assistant professor of metallography and professor of geology. In 1903 he was chosen president of the university. Professor Van Hise was made a member of the United States Geological Survey in 1883. He won recognition as the highest authority on rocks of the Algonkian and Archaean Systems and especially on the ore-bearing rocks of the Lake Superior region. Some of his most important publications are *The Penokee Iron-Bearing Series of Michigan and Wisconsin, Principles of North American Pre-Cambrian Geology, The Marquette Iron-Bearing District of Michigan, The Crystal Falls Iron-Bearing District of Michigan, The Iron Ores of the Lake Superior Region, The Lead and Zinc Deposits of the Mississippi Valley* and *The Conservation of Natural Resources in the United States.*

Vanil'la, a genus of plants belonging to the orchid family, which furnish the well-known flavoring extract. They are climbing plants and are most common in Mexico, but they are also found in Central and South America and in the East Indies. The vine climbs by means of aërial roots and has large white, red or greenish, fragrant flowers. The fruit is a long, brown, shiny bean, which is filled with a dark, oily, odorous pulp. This is gathered before it is fully ripe, and the oil is extracted by a slow process, which brings out its peculiar odor and flavor. It is used in medicine as a stimulant, but its chief use is in the preparation of liquors and perfumery and in flavoring candy and other confections. The vanilla plant produces a crop every three years and continues bearing for thirty or forty years. Vanilla is produced artificially by several methods; and as the beans are very expensive, the artificial product is very common.

Van Rensselaer, *vahn ren'se lahr*, STEPHEN (1764–1839), an American politician, the eighth "patroon" of the vast estate near Albany, now forming three entire counties, which was first

acquired by Killian Van Rensselaer (1595–1644). He was born in New York and was educated at Harvard, and in 1783 he married a daughter of General Philip Schuyler. He was a leader of the Federalists in his state and served in the state senate and assembly, and in Congress from 1823 to 1829. He was a moving spirit in the construction of the Erie and Champlain canals, and he was president of their boards from 1811 till their completion, in 1825. In 1824 he founded at Troy the Rensselaer Polytechnic Institute.

Van Wert, *wurt'*, OHIO, the county-seat of Van Wert co., 78 mi. s. w. of Toledo, on the Pennsylvania and the Cincinnati Northern rail-

VANILLA

roads. The city is in a rich farming section and contains railroad shops, piano factories, lumber mills and other factories. It has two banks, several public parks and the Brumback Library. The waterworks are owned by the city. Population in 1910, 7157.

Va'por, in physics, the gas-like form which either solids or liquids take when heated to a sufficiently high temperature. In their structure and physical properties, there is practically no difference between vapors and gases (See GAS), but in ordinary usage the term *vapor* is applied to those gases that are formed by the action of heat on liquids and solids, as steam and the vapor of camphor, while the term *gas* is applied to those substances which remain in gaseous form under ordinary conditions of temperature and pressure, as air or oxygen. The water vapor formed on the surface of the land is always present in the atmosphere, and when it meets with a reduction of temperature it condenses into water, in the form of rain or dew. See RAIN.

Va'riable Quantity, in mathematics, a quantity regarded as being subject to continual increase or diminution, in opposition to those which are *constant*, remaining always the same; also, a quantity which, in a given problem, may have an infinite number of values. For instance, $\frac{1}{x}$, when the value of x constantly increases or diminishes, is a variable quantity, for as the value of x increases the value of $\frac{1}{x}$ constantly decreases, and *vice versa*.

Varicose, *var e kose'*, **Veins,** dilated veins, which are marked by knotty swellings at the valves. The disease commonly affects the lower limbs and sometimes becomes very painful and even dangerous, from the bursting of the veins, though it often is merely an inconvenience. Rest and support in an elevated position and the application of proper bandages are elements in the treatment.

Vari'ety, in scientific classifications, a subdivision of a species of animals or plants: an individual or group of individuals differing from the rest of the species to which it belongs in some accidental circumstances, which are not essential to the species. Varieties are considered as less permanent than species, and those naturalists who look upon species as strictly distinct in their origin consider varieties as modifications of them, arising from particular causes, of climate, nourishment, cultivation and the like. In naming plants and animals, the name of the variety is placed third, following the name of the species; as, *Ranunculus multifidus*, variety, *terrestris*. Here, *Ranunculus multifidus* is the common, yellow, water crowfoot, and the variety *terrestris* is a form growing on the ground.

Va'rioloid, a mild form of smallpox, induced by inoculation. See SMALLPOX.

Varna, *vahr'na*, a town of Bulgaria, situated on the west shore of the Black Sea. It is the principal seaport between Kustendje and the Bosporus. It has railway connections with the important cities of Europe, and its trade is extensive. Near it is the summer residence of the czar of Bulgaria. Population in 1910, 41,419.

Var'nish, a liquid made by dissolving a resin in alcohol, turpentine or other oil. It is used to form a thin, transparent coat over surfaces, to protect them from air and moisture or to make them more beautiful. The resinous substances most commonly employed for varnishes are mastic, lac, copal, amber and asphalt; and the solvents are fixed oil, volatile oil and alcohol. Varnishes are colored with arnotto, gamboge, saffron, dragon's blood and other substances.

The base of varnish is gum copal, or the fossil gum found in Zanzibar, Sierra Leone, New Zealand and the Philippine Islands. The best gum is found in Zanzibar. When the gum is received in the varnish factory, it is broken up into pieces about the size of small egg coal. As it is being broken up, it is selected, for in one chunk of the amber-like material there may be both transparent and almost opaque streaks; the white transparent gum goes into the making of the best grades of varnish, and the dark-colored gum goes into the poorer grades. After the gum copal is broken, it is run through a series of hand sieves, which divide it into block, nut, chip and dust, for convenience in handling. The gum is then ready for the kettle.

For first-class varnish, only Calcutta linseed oil is used. This oil is made from the flaxseed of India. The turpentine used for thinning the varnish is of the best and purest grade. The copper kettles in which the melting and mixing are done are on truck wheels, so that they can be rolled over a fire or taken off easily. The melting gum is constantly stirred; after it has melted, a tool somewhat like an egg-beater is introduced, and the melted gum is whipped, preparatory to letting in the boiled linseed oil. When the oil has been mixed with the liquid gum, the kettle is run back over the fire once more, and the gum and oil are boiled again. Then it is set away to cool, after which the kettle is taken to a room where a quantity of turpentine is mixed with the gum and oil and the varnish is made. The varnish is strained through cotton before it is pumped into the storage tanks, where it is left to age for at least six months and often for two years.

Shellac varnish is made in churns, or barrels, revolving on journals. The shellac as it comes from India looks like amber-colored mica, for it is in thin sheets and is almost transparent. This shellac is mixed with the proper amount of alcohol, to dissolve it and form the varnish.

Var'ro, MARCUS TERENTIUS (116–27 B. C.), one of the most learned men and prolific writers of ancient Rome. He served in the army and subsequently filled several public offices. Varro was the intimate friend of Cicero and was proscribed by Antony, but he escaped and returned to Rome under Augustus. Of his numerous writings, chiefly on language, history and philosophy, only one has come down to us entire— a treatise on agriculture. Fragments of a treatise on the Latin language are also extant.

Va'rus, PUBLIUS QUINTILIUS, a Roman general. In 7 B. C. he received from Augustus the command to introduce the Roman jurisdiction into the German territory just conquered by Drusus, and he was carrying out this mission when he was suddenly attacked by a force under Arminius. His whole army was destroyed, and Varus put an end to his own life. See ARMINIUS.

Vas'co da Gam'a. See GAMA, VASCO DA.

Vase, a name applied to certain vessels of an ornamental character. Vases were made in ancient times of all materials, but those which have come down to us in greatest numbers are the so-called Etruscan vases, made of terra cotta and adorned with painted figures (See ETRUSCAN VASES). Such vases have been found in most Greek cities, as well as in Etruria, and all are really the productions of Greek art. The Greek vases of the oldest style come chiefly from Corinth and the islands of Thera and Melos; and those of the late rich style have been almost exclusively discovered in Lower Italy, Apulia and Lucania. They were probably manufactured there, chiefly in the fourth and third centuries B. C. Chased metal vases were in use in ancient times, among both the Greeks and the Romans, and many of the more valuable and beautiful kinds of stone were used in making vases. Murrine vases were highly esteemed at Rome. Another favorite kind of vases at Rome was that called cameo vases, made of two layers of glass, the outer of which was opaque and cut down so as to leave figures standing out upon the lower layer as a ground. The celebrated Portland vase is an example of this kind. At a later period, glass vases, surrounded with a delicate filigree work, were introduced. Italy, France and Germany in the sixteenth and seventeenth centuries produced many vases which are the perfection of artistic form and execution, and since the fifteenth century many masterpieces of the glass art in the form of vases have issued from the Venetian manufactories. From India, China and Japan also have been obtained vases of various materials, especially of porcelain, vying in elegance of form and beauty of ornamentation with those produced in Europe. Of late, also, some highly artistic vases have been produced in the United States, which compare favorably with those made in foreign lands. Until recently, however, but little attention has been paid in this country to the development of the more artistic designs in connection with the making of vases.

Vaseline, *vas'e lin* or *vas'e leen,* a name given to a product obtained from petroleum after the hydrocarbons are driven off. It is composed of a mixture of parafines. It is used as a base for ointments, pomades and cold cream, and is employed for coating surgical instruments and steel surfaces, generally to protect them from rust. See PETROLEUM.

Vas'sar, MATTHEW (1792–1868), an American philanthropist, founder of Vassar College, born at Norfolk, England. He came to America when four years of age and settled at Poughkeepsie, N. Y. He succeeded his father in the brewing business and made a large fortune. In 1861 he donated $400,000 for the endowment of a school for the higher education of women, and in his will he provided for a further appropriation of $400,000, for the support of the institution, which is known as Vassar College. See VASSAR COLLEGE.

Vassar College, an institution for the higher education of women, established near Poughkeepsie, N. Y., in 1865. It is named from Matthew Vassar, who bequeathed 210 acres of land and $800,000 for founding the institution. The main building provides accommodation for 300 students. In addition to this, there are other residence halls, a museum, an observatory, a conservatory, laboratories and a library containing over 68,000 volumes. The regular course provides for the degree of Bachelor of Arts, and advanced courses prepare for the degrees of Master of Arts and Doctor of Philosophy. The faculty numbers over 100, and the yearly attendance is over 1000.

Vat'ican, the most extensive palace of modern Rome, and the residence of the pope. It is built upon the Vatican Hill, from which it has received its name, and it stands north of the Cathedral of Saint Peter's. It is a long rectangular edifice, lying north and south, with an irregular cluster of buildings at each end. The present building was begun by Pope Eugenius III (1145–1153) and has been enlarged and embellished by many subsequent popes, down to Pius IX.

It now possesses twenty courts, and, it is said, 1100 rooms. Immense treasures are stored away in it, including celebrated collections of pictures of many of the great masters, and museums in which all periods of the arts are represented by many of their most perfect productions. Among its noblest art treasures are the frescoes on the ceiling of the Sistine Chapel, painted by Michelangelo, representing scenes and figures connected with sacred history; the frescoes painted by Raphael on the ceilings and walls of certain apartments, known as Raphael's *stanze*, the subjects being biblical and allegorical. Since the return of the popes from Avignon, the Vatican has been their principal residence, and here the conclaves always meet for the election of new popes. The Vatican Library was first constituted by Pope Nicholas V (1447–1455) and was added to and enlarged by Leo X, Pius IV, Pius V and other popes. The most important part of the library is the manuscript collections, which are said to contain about 25,600 manuscripts. The number of printed volumes has been estimated at from 150,000 to 220,000, including 2,500 fifteenth century editions and a great number of bibliographical rarities.

Vatican Council, the Ecumenical Council of the Church of Rome, which met in the Vatican under Pope Pius IX, Dec. 8, 1869, and adjourned July 18, 1870. No council had ever been attended by so large a number of ecclesiastics. It declared the personal infallibility of the pope, when speaking *ex cathedra*, to be a doctrine of the Church.

Vaudeville, *vode'vil*, a kind of drama, in which dialogue is interspersed with dancing, comic acting and songs of the day. Originally the name was given to a popular humorous drinking song, and it is a corruption of *Vaux de Vire*, the name of two valleys in Normandy, where such songs first were composed. In the United States, to-day, vaudeville, is merely a series of singing, acting and dancing numbers, which pretend to no unity and to no relation with the drama.

Vaughan, *vawn*, HERBERT (1832–1903), an English churchman, born at Gloucester and educated at Stonyhurst and on the Continent. He succeeded Cardinal Manning as archbishop of Westminster and was soon afterwards made cardinal. Saint Joseph's College for foreign missions, at Mill Hill, Hendon, was founded by this eloquent preacher.

Vault, in architecture, a continued arch, or an arched roof, so constructed that the stones, bricks or other materials of which it is composed, sustain and keep one another in place. Vaults are of various kinds, cylindrical, elliptical, single, double, cross, diagonal or Gothic.

Vecellio, TIZIANO. See TITIAN.

Vedas, *va'das*, (from a Sanskrit word meaning *know*), the oldest sacred writings of India. Their date is unknown, but it is probably not long after 1500 B. C. They are four in number, called, respectively, the *Rig-Veda*, *Yajur-Veda*, *Sama-Veda* and *Atharva-Veda*. Of these the *Rig-Veda* is the oldest and most important. It consists of more than one thousand hymns, most of them celebrating the deeds and begging the blessing of the greater gods. The *Sama-Veda* contains also a number of hymns, but as most of them appear in the *Rig-Veda*, this second of the Vedas is of less importance than the others. The chief difference seems to be that in the *Sama-Veda* the stanzas are arranged in the order in which they are used in the liturgy. In the *Yajur-Veda* are given all the formulae which are employed during sacrifices, with the blessings intended for each sacrificial instrument and vessel, while the *Atharva-Veda* contains not only blessings, but curses and charms against witches. Some scholars question whether the last should be regarded as a Veda, as it is superstitious, rather than religious. All the Vedas are believed to be inspired and are held by the Brahmans in the highest respect. The religious system of the Vedas is at bottom monotheistic. It derives a polytheistic appearance from the mention of the deity by various names, according to the difference in his manifestations and attributes; but the unity of the supreme being is expressly asserted in more than one passage. Varying greatly in age, the Vedas represent many stages of thought and worship, the earliest being the simplest, the later following and reflecting the development of the Brahmanical system, with its superstitions and rites.

Ved'das, a wild race, about four hundred in number, residing in the interior of Ceylon, and said to be different from any other living race. Some live in trees and caves and subsist on game, which they kill with rude bows and arrows; others live in villages. The two classes do not intermarry, and each has its own chief, whom they elect and obey.

Ved'der, ELIHU (1836–   ), an American artist, born in New York. He studied in Paris and then went to Italy, where the greater part of his life has been passed. A wonderful imagination is evident in most of his work, which is often weird and almost always powerful. Among his best-known works are the *Cumean Sibyl*; the *Lair of the Sea Serpent*, which, with several others, is in the Boston Museum; *Samson*; *Good and Bad Government*, in the Library of Congress at Washington, and a famous series of illustrations for Fitzgerald's translation of, the *Rubaiyat* of Omar Khayyam.

Vega Carpio, *va'ga kahr'pe o*, FELIX LOPE DE (1562–1635), a Spanish poet and dramatist, best-known as Lope de Vega. In 1582 he joined the army, and in 1588 he accompanied the Invincible Armada. After being twice married and twice a widower, he became a priest, and subsequently he entered the order of Saint Francis. He had already published various poems, but his dramatic and poetical productions now multiplied with extraordinary rapidity. He enjoyed an immense popularity and received marks of distinction from the king of Spain and from Pope Urban VIII. About three hundred of his dramatic works have been printed. They reveal an inexhaustible, but ill-regulated, imagination, a strong mixture of the sublime and the ridiculous and extraordinary facility in versification. He wrote, altogether, upward of eighteen hundred comedies, but only four hundred fifty are extant in print or manuscript.

Vegetable, *vej'e ta b'l*, **I'vory.** See IVORY PALM.

Vegetables, in the most general sense, a synonym for plants. In a more limited and more common sense the term refers to plants used and cultivated for food, such as the cabbage, the potato, the turnip and the bean. In a loose way vegetables are distinguished from fruits by the fact that the former need cooking, while the latter can be eaten raw. The parts of the plant used for food are many and various. In some, as the turnip, the roots are the parts used; in others, as the onion, the bulbs. The tubers of the potato and artichoke; the stems of asparagus; the leaves of the lettuce and cabbage; the flower buds of the cauliflower; the green fruit of the cucumber; the ripe fruit of the tomato; the seeds of corn, peas and beans, are common vegetable foods.

The principal components of vegetables are water, protein, fat, nitrogen, starch and certain indigestible refuse, like fiber and ash. The proportions of these constituents vary among different vegetables, but in all, the principal element is water. The amount of water varies from 58.9 per cent, in green beans, to 95.4 per cent, in the cucumber. The per cent of protein varies from .4 per cent, in the watermelon, to 9.4 per cent, in green beans.

The amount of fat varies from .1 per cent, in the pumpkin, the radish, the potato, celery and the beet, to 1.1 per cent in green corn. The amount of nitrogen varies from 2.2, in lettuce, to 26.1, in the sweet potato.

Of fresh vegetables, green shelled beans have the highest fuel value, and the cucumber has the lowest, the value of the latter being about one-ninth that of the former. Others which contain a high fuel value are sweet potatoes, green peas, green corn, sugar peas and parsnips. In the cooking of vegetables, besides the loss of water content, there are chemical changes which often detract materially from the food value.

Vegetables are a valuable article of diet, and it has been claimed by many persons that a well-balanced vegetable diet is more healthful than the combination of vegetables and meat. Most authorities, however, do not accept this theory, claiming that the diet should be mixed; that meat gives greater strength and greater power of resisting disease, and that investigation proves that races living wholly on vegetables and those living wholly on meats are not the physical or mental equals of those who use both vegetable and animal foods. See VEGETARIANISM.

Vegetarianism, *vej'e ta'ri an iz'm*, the theory and practice of living solely on vegetables. The doctrines and practice of vegetarianism are as old as the time of Pythagoras, and they have for ages been strictly observed by many of the Hindus; Plato, Rousseau, Shelley and Swedenborg were also vegetarians. The practice of living wholly upon vegetable food came prominently before the public about the middle of the nineteenth century, its followers claiming that man lives longer, has a happier life and is stronger, both mentally and physically, if animal food is not eaten; that a vegetable diet is cheaper, less liable to communicate disease and to excite a fierce disposition. Those who believe in a mixed diet claim that man's stomach, intestines and teeth show that he was intended to eat animal and vegetable food, and that he can accomplish more work with less exhaustion on a mixed diet.

Veii, *ve'yi*, an ancient Etruscan town, about twelve miles from Rome. The Romans and the Veientines were constantly at war, and because the latter were uniformly unsuccessful in pitched battles, they adopted the plan of shutting themselves up in the city when the Romans approached and of going out to plunder when they were safe from attack. The family of Fabius, who had taken upon themselves the defense of

Roman territory against the Veientines, were decoyed into an ambush and put to death. Camillus took the city about 396 B. C. See CAMILLUS, MARCUS FURIUS.

Vein, *vane*, in geology, a formation of igneous rock, occupying a fissure in other rock, as represented by the nearly perpendicular layers in the figure. Veins were formed by rock in molten condition, and they often contain metals. They usually

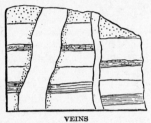

VEINS

have well-defined walls, and many of them extend into the earth for hundreds of feet. Miners call a metal-bearing vein a *lode*. Small veins are often seen in boulders and pebbles, where they can be easily studied. See DIKE; GEOLOGY.

Veins, a system of canals, or tubes, distributed throughout the bodies of animals, for the purpose of returning the impure blood to the heart and lungs, after it has been carried to the various parts by the arteries. Veins originate in the capillaries as tiny tubes, and as they unite they decrease in number and increase in size, till all those from the head, neck and upper extremities form the *superior vena cava* and those from the other parts of the body form the *inferior vena cava*. Both these large veins empty into the right auricle of the heart. The walls of the veins, like those of the arteries, are composed of three coats, but they are less elastic and have no pulsation. They collapse readily when empty. The distinguishing parts of a vein are the valves, which are made of folds in the internal coat and are arranged in pairs. They lie against the walls when the blood is flowing onward, but if from any cause the flow is obstructed, the valves are forced upward till they meet in the middle of the vein, and so they prevent the blood from going backward. The action of the valves may be shown by pressing on some vein near the surface, thus preventing the flow of the blood toward the heart, when the valves will make little elevations in the vein. Valves are not found in the very smallest veins, nor in those of the abdomen, lungs and brain.

The blood flowing from a wounded vein is dark in color and comes out in an even stream. To check the flow, press on the vein below the wound or between it and the extremity.

See ARTERIES; CIRCULATION; CAPILLARIES; WOUND.

Velazquez or **Velasquez,** *va lahs'kaith*, DON DIEGO RODRIGUEZ DE SILVAY (1599–1660), an eminent Spanish historical and portrait painter, born at Seville, of Portuguese parents. He studied first under Francisco Herrara the elder, and afterward under Francisco Pacheco. In 1622 he went to Madrid, and the result of this visit was an appointment as principal painter to Philip IV. Through the advice and intercession of Rubens, in 1629 Velazquez went to Italy, where he closely studied the works of Michelangelo, Raphael and Titian and the contemporary painters, especially Guido Reni, whose influence is evident to a marked degree in Velazquez's works. On his return to Spain, in 1631, he was received with great distinction, and in 1658 the king raised him to the dignity of a noble. His chief characteristic is naturalism. He was never imaginative, but painted just what he saw. His compositions exhibit strong expression, freedom of pencil and admirable coloring. Among his best works are the *Aguador*, or *Water Carrier*; a *Nativity*, or *Adoration of the Shepherds*; the *Brothers of Joseph*; *Moses Taken from the Nile*; portraits of Philip IV and of Elizabeth, his queen, Pope Innocent X and other dignitaries, and many pictures from history and from common life.

Velocipede, *ve los'e peed*, a light vehicle, or carriage, impelled by the feet of the rider himself. One of the older forms of this carriage consisted of two wheels, of nearly equal size, placed one before the other, connected by a beam, on which the driver's seat was fixed. The rider, sitting astride the machine, propelled it by the thrust of each foot on the ground. This form dates from the early part of the nineteenth century. About half a century later, treadles, operating cranks on the axle of the front wheel, came into use. See BICYCLE.

Velocity, *ve los'e ty*, the rate at which a body changes its position in space. Velocity is popularly expressed as so many miles per hour or as so many feet per second. The velocity of a body is *uniform*, when it passes through equal spaces in equal times; it is *variable*, when the spaces passed through in equal times are unequal; it is *accelerated*, when during each portion of time it passes through a greater space than during the preceding equal portion; it is *retarded*, when a less space is passed through in each successive portion of time.

Vel'vet, one of the most familiar of those cloths known as pile fabrics. It is produced by adding to the usual warp and weft threads of plain weaving, an additional row of warp yarns, which are woven into the ground of the cloth and passed over wires on the surface. In the case of a loop pile, the wires are simply drawn out, but for velvet or other cut pile, a knife is first passed along a groove on the top of each wire to cut the pile before the wire is withdrawn. Real velvet is made entirely of silk, but a kind is made with a silk face on a cotton basis. Cotton and woolen goods, woven in this manner, are called *velveteen* and *plush*, respectively. Some of the richest and most artistic of the many splendid textiles woven on Italian looms in the fifteenth and sixteenth centuries were made, in part at least, of velvet. Similar stuffs were also made in Spain and Flanders. Many of these were for ecclesiastical vestments and altar cloths, as well as for hangings. Plain velvets were likewise woven. The effect of a raised pattern in velvet, on a plain or figured silk ground, is very beautiful. Sometimes a design is formed of a long, upon a short, pile, called *velvet upon velvet*, and this, too, has a fine effect. Choice examples of these old velvet fabrics are preserved in some industrial art collections. Velvet is believed to have been first made in China.

Velvet Leaf. See INDIAN MALLOW.

Vendée, *vahN day'*, a department of France, in the western part, on the Bay of Biscay. Its area is almost 2585 square miles, and its population is 441,311. In 1793, during the French Revolution, an insurrection broke out in the Vendée, on the proclamation by the Republic that 300,000 men were to be drafted for military service. The most frightful excesses marked the rising, which the officers sent by the French government seemed utterly unable to put down. At length, late in the year, the Vendeans were defeated, and their punishment was severe. For three or four years, however, there was trouble in the Vendée.

Vendet'ta (Italian, from Latin *vindicta*, revenge), a blood feud; the practice of the nearest of kin executing vengeance on the murderer of a relative. In Corsica the vendetta is regarded as a duty incumbent on the relatives of the murdered man, to take vengeance on the murderer or his relatives. The practice exists, although to a more limited extent, in parts of Italy and among many less civilized peoples.

Veneer', a thin layer of choice hard wood, such as mahogany, rosewood or maple, glued to the surface of wood of a commoner sort, such as fir or pine, so as to give the whole the appearance of being made of the more valuable material. It is used for furniture and some interior finishings, and owing to recent improvements in sawing machinery, layers almost as thin as paper can be obtained.

Venetian, *ve ne'shan*, **School of Painting.** See PAINTING.

Venezuela, *ven'e zwe'la*, a country of South America, lying between 1° and 14° 20' north latitude and between 60° and 73° 20' east longitude. Its length from northeast to southwest is about 925 mi., and from north to south, 725 mi. Because of dispute over boundary lines, the area is not definitely settled, but is given by the latest authorities at 593,943 sq. mi., making the country a little larger than Alaska.

SURFACE AND DRAINAGE. Venezuela is naturally divided into three surface regions. These are the highland region in the northwest, the Guiana highlands in the southeast and the Orinoco valley between. The highland region, in the northwest, is formed by two ranges of the Andes Mountains, one of which extends directly north and south and forms the boundary between Venezuela and Colombia. This range contains some summits with an altitude of 10,000 feet. The other range enters the country near the headwaters of the Orinoco and extends northeasterly to the Gulf of Triest. This range contains the highest land in the country; some of the peaks have an altitude of over 15,000 feet and are capped with perpetual snow. Between these ranges of the Andes is the low depression occupied by Lake Maracaibo, which is directly connected with the sea. The boundary between Venezuela and Brazil is formed by the Parima and Pacarima mountains, which rise to altitudes varying from 6000 to 11,000 feet. From these ranges the land gradually descends to the basin of the Orinoco. This great interior is divided into the lowlands, along the lower part of the river's course, and the llanos, which lie chiefly north of the river and between it and the Andes. A portion of this region is yet unexplored, but it is supposed to consist of rolling plains and hills, heavily covered with forests.

Venezuela is supposed to have over 1000 rivers and is perhaps more completely watered than any other country of South America. Chief among these rivers is the Orinoco, flowing through the middle of the country, and its chief tributaries, the Apure, the Meta and the Negro, the last of which is connected with the Amazon by the Cassiquiare. The Orinoco and its chief tributaries, all of which are navigable, furnish an outlet not only for the interior of Venezuela, but for a portion of Colombia as well (See ORINOCO). There are a number of less important streams flowing into the Caribbean Sea. Of the lakes, Maracaibo, in the northwestern part, is the largest and most important.

CLIMATE. The climate of Venezuela depends upon altitude more than upon latitude. The varying elevations of the country divide it into three climatic regions. The first is the lowland region, which extends from sea level to an altitude of 2300 feet. This has a hot, tropical climate, with a mean annual temperature of about 77°. The second is the region of the interior, ranging in altitude from 2300 to 6500 feet. This region has a salubrious, temperate climate, with a mean temperature of about 65° and with a comparatively narrow range of temperature, the thermometer seldom rising above 80° or falling below 60°. In the highlands of the mountains is a cold region, which ranges in mean temperature from near freezing point to that of perpetual snow. There are two seasons, the rainy and the dry. During the rainy season the lowlands and most of the interior receive copious rain, in some sections sufficient to flood the country. Along the coast and the lower courses of the rivers the climate is somewhat unhealthful, but the temperate regions of the interior are pleasant and healthful, even to those who are accustomed to temperate latitudes.

MINERAL RESOURCES. The country contains large deposits of minerals. Gold is found in the Yuruari territory and is mined to a considerable extent, the annual output being about 60,000 ounces. Silver mines occur in the central, southern and southwestern parts of the country, while copper and iron are widely distributed. Some tin is also found. Other minerals of importance are sulphur, coal and kaolin. There are a number of salt mines in the country, and they are worked by the government. Petroleum is found in the southwestern part of the country, in the State of Los Andes. There are valuable deposits of asphalt on the island of Trinidad, in the vicinity of Maracaibo and in the State of Bermudez. Granite, marble and other building stones are widely distributed over the country. Lack of capital and transportation facilities has thus far prevented the exploitation of the mineral industries of the country.

AGRICULTURE. Agriculture is the chief occupation of the inhabitants. However, only about one-ninth of the surface is under cultivation. The chief crops are coffee, cacao, sugar cane, cereals, fruits, beans, potatoes and other vegetables. Tobacco is successfully cultivated in the lowlands, and the forests furnish valuable products for export, chief among which are copaiba, vanilla and rubber. In general, agriculture is in a backward state. Primitive implements and methods are used, and but poor returns are received for the capital and labor invested. The large areas of pasture land particularly adapt the country to cattle raising, and this is one of the most important branches of agricultural industry. The country also has large numbers of horses, goats and sheep.

MANUFACTURES. The manufactures are comparatively unimportant and are confined to the larger cities. The chief industries are the manufacture of cotton goods, shoes, hats, carriages, furniture and agricultural implements. The country also has a number of breweries and distilleries. The most important manufacturing industries are exploited by foreign capital and are under foreign management.

TRANSPORTATION. The interior is reached by the Orinoco and its numerous navigable tributaries. Roads are few and poor and, except in the vicinity of large cities, are merely mule paths. Caracas is joined with its seaport, La Guira, by railway. A few other interior towns are also connected with seaports in this way. In all, the country has about 530 miles of railway in operation. Through a French cable it has communication with the rest of the world. The leading seaports are connected by steamer with the ports of Europe and the United States. The commerce of the country is not as great as its resources and population would warrant. The chief article of export is coffee. Other important exports include cacao, hides, deer and goat skins, rubber, tobacco, fustic and some other forest products. Some cattle are shipped to Cuba. Most of the coffee and hides go to the United States. The imports consist of foodstuffs, manufactured goods and machinery.

INHABITANTS AND LANGUAGE. The inhabitants consist almost wholly of indians and people of mixed Spanish, indian and negro blood. Two-thirds of the indian population are civilized. The country is very unevenly populated, most of the people living within the agricultural and mountainous regions of the northwest. The interior is largely unexplored and uninhabited. Spanish is the language in general use.

EDUCATION. Education is free and compulsory, but the laws are poorly enforced, and outside of the large towns schools are few and poor.

It is estimated that not over one-fourth of the inhabitants can read and write. The public schools are maintained by the government and the different states. In addition to these there are nine barrack schools, four normal schools and schools of arts and trades. The country also maintains two universities, twenty-two federal colleges and eleven colleges for girls, one school of fine arts and schools of music. There are also a polytechnic school and a nautical school, besides several private colleges. The national library at Caracas contains 32,000 volumes.

GOVERNMENT AND RELIGION. The government is a republic. The present constitution, adopted in 1904, is the fifteenth under which the government has been administered since the country was formed. The head of the executive department is the president, who is elected for six years and is assisted by six ministers and a Federal Council of nineteen members. The members of the council are appointed by Congress every two years, and the president is chosen by this council from among its own members. Neither the president nor members of the Federal Council can be elected for a succeeding term. The legislative power is vested in a Congress of two houses, a Senate and a House of Representatives. The members of the Senate are apportioned two to each state and district and are elected for six years by the legislature of the state. The representatives are apportioned according to population, one to every 40,000, and are elected by universal suffrage. Each province or state has its own legislature and executive, while the unorganized territories and colonies are governed by an executive appointed by the national government.

Roman Catholicism is the State religion and is embraced by nearly all of the people. Other religions are tolerated, but public exercise of them is forbidden.

CITIES. The chief cities are Caracas, the capital; Valencia, Maracaibo, Barquisimeto, Barcelona and Ciudad Bolivar, each of which is described under its title.

HISTORY. The coast of Venezuela was first seen by Columbus in 1498. The following year it was more carefully examined by Vespucius, who gave the region the name it now bears, which means *Little Venice*; it was applied because of the discovery of an indian village built on palisades over the waters of Lake Maracaibo. The first Spanish settlement was made in 1527, and for more than two centuries the country was a Spanish colony, during which time it suffered from

change of rulers and internal dissensions. The early Spaniards treated the natives in a most cruel manner and enslaved many of them. The struggle for independence began early in the nineteenth century and was completed by the efforts of the patriots under Bolivar in 1821, when Venezuela and New Granada united under one government and formed the country of Colombia. In 1829 Venezuela seceded and became an independent republic. The country has always suffered from frequent revolutions and rebellions. It has also had several disputes with European powers concerning boundary lines. The last of these assumed such importance that in 1894 the United States recognized the seriousness of the contention between Venezuela and Great Britain and suggested to the latter country that the dispute be settled by arbitration. This was finally agreed to, and the question was submitted to a special tribunal, which in 1899 made final settlement of the boundary line between Venezuela and British Guiana. In 1897 a serious political disturbance began, which led, two years later, to a rebellion. This became so widespread that it threatened the existence of the established government, but in October, 1902, the revolutionists suffered a serious defeat, and their army was dispersed. The country later had a serious dispute with France, Germany and Great Britain over the payment of claims due subjects of these several nations, and in December Great Britain and Germany combined in a naval demonstration and blockaded some of the Venezuelan ports. Through the intercession of the United States, however, all parties agreed to submit the dispute to the court of arbitration at The Hague, and the points in dispute were satisfactorily adjusted. Population in 1909, 2,685,606. Consult Scruggs' *The Columbian and Venezuelan Republics* and Curtis's *Venezuela*.

Venice, *ven'is*, a city of northern Italy and capital of the province of the same name, situated on a number of islands in the northwest part of the Adriatic Sea, 164 mi. by rail e. of Milan. The city is built upon a cluster of 120 islands and is about 7 miles in circumference. It is reached by railway over a viaduct nearly $2\frac{1}{4}$ miles long. Venice is noted for its beauty, its many interesting buildings and its treasures of art. It is unique among the cities of the world, for its streets are canals and its conveyances are gondolas and steamers. Horses and carriages are unknown. The Grand Canal, which is the principal thoroughfare, passes through the city in the form of a letter *S* and divides it into two nearly

equal parts. This canal is crossed by four bridges, the chief of which is the Rialto. There are 146 smaller canals, by means of which all parts of the city can be reached by boat.

The Piazza, or Square of Saint Mark's, is the center of interest. This is the great center of business and amusement. It is 576 feet long, 269 feet wide on one side and 185 feet wide on the other. The east side is faced by the Cathedral of Saint Mark's, one of the most renowned structures of its kind in the world (See SAINT MARK, CATHEDRAL OF). On the north and south sides of the square are the palaces formerly occupied by the procurators of the cathedral, and they now form a part of the royal palace.

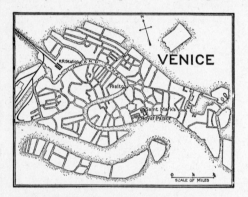

These buildings contain many rare paintings by some of the most celebrated artists of Venice, including Tintoretto and Paul Veronese. The famous Campanile, which fell in 1902, also faced this square. It is now being rebuilt. Another object of interest facing the square is the clock tower, built in 1496 and surmounted by two bronze figures, which strike the hours on a large bell. Another church of interest is the Church of Santa Maria della Salute, which contains excellent paintings by Titian. Among these are his masterpiece, *The Assumption of the Virgin*, and *The Presentation in the Temple*. The Church of San Sebastiano is celebrated for its altarpieces by Paul Veronese, and the Friari, a church built for the friars, is interesting for its size and because it is a good representation of the Italian Gothic style of architecture. It contains many monuments and pictures. The palaces are of no less interest than the churches. Of these the Palace of the Doges, originally built in 800, but several times destroyed and rebuilt, is the most important. During the time of Venice's greatest prosperity, this was the residence of her rulers. It now contains

many treasures of art. From the rear of this palace the celebrated "Bridge of Sighs" leads to the prison, which is still in use. Many of the palaces are now used for other purposes, serving as hotels, museums and office buildings. The Academy of Fine Arts is also of great interest, because it contains one of the most valuable collections of paintings found in Europe. The Rialto is the principal commercial street and typically represents the life of the city. The bridge of this name crosses the Grand Canal at the point where the first settlement was made.

Modern Venice is of considerable commercial importance, being second only to Genoa as a seaport of Italy. The manufactures include lace, tapestries, mosaics, bronzes, jewelry and woodcarvings among its finer wares, and cotton and woolen goods, chemicals, heavy machinery and clocks among its larger industries. There is also some shipbuilding, and glassware is manufactured on the island of Murano.

The islands occupied by the city were formerly a refuge from the hordes of barbarians which invaded Italy from the north. It is supposed that the first settlement was made about the middle of the fifth century, but there is no authentic record of the fact. In the sixth century Venice was independent, though it was tributary to the Eastern Empire. It was obliged to defend itself from pirates and from the Lombards of Italy, and because of this an organized government was formed and the leader or ruler, entitled *doge*, was selected. The Crusades gave the city a great impetus, because it became a commercial center for these military movements. During the Middle Ages Venice had increased in commercial importance and power until considerable surrounding territory of the mainland was under her control, and just previous to the discovery of America she was the leading commercial city of Europe. From that time her influence began to wane. The Turks captured Constantinople and cut off much of her trade from the East. A route to India around the Cape of Good Hope also brought much of that trade to Portugal, and the commerce which had entered Europe through her harbors now came through Genoa and other cities to the west. In 1797 the Venetian Republic was deprived of its independence by Napoleon, and most of the possessions were given to Austria. Within a few years the Austrians ceded Venice to Italy. Between this time and 1866, the city was alternately under the rule of Austria and Italy, until finally by vote of the inhabitants it was joined to Italy, with which it has since remained. Population in 1911, 160,-719.

Ventilation, *ven ti la' shun.* See HEATING AND VENTILATION.

Ventril'oquism, the art of speaking in such a way as to cause a hearer to believe that the sound comes, not from the person speaking, but from a different source. Practice alone is necessary to carry this act of illusion to a high degree of perfection. The sounds are formed by the ordinary vocal organs—the larynx, the palate, the tongue and the lips. The art of the ventriloquist consists merely in this: After drawing a long breath, he breathes it out slowly and gradually, dexterously modifying and diminishing the sound of the voice; besides this he moves his lips as little as possible, and by various contrivances he diverts the attention of his auditors. This art was known to the ancient Greeks.

Ve'nus, in Roman mythology, the goddess of love and beauty, called Aphrodite by the Greeks. By some accounts she was the daughter of Jupiter, but the most popular legend tells that she was born from the sea foam. She was brought up by the nymphs in their ocean caves, and when she had attained the fulness of her size and beauty, she was conducted to Olympus, where she excited the greatest admiration. All of the gods wished to marry her, but she scorned them all, and as a punishment she was compelled by Jupiter to marry Vulcan, the ugliest of the gods. He gained no great happiness from the union, for Venus always despised him and bestowed her love on Mars and on the mortals Adonis and Anchises. Cupid was her son by Mars, and Aeneas was her son by Anchises. Venus was the special protectress of all young people who were in love, but she does not seem to have continued her interest in their affairs after they were once married. She was consequently chiefly worshiped by young people.

Venus, the second planet from the sun, its orbit lying between Mercury and the Earth. It is the most brilliant planetary body, and on clear, moonless evenings it may be seen to cast a shadow. It is often called the *evening star* and the *morning star,* because of its brilliancy at those times. To the ancients, Venus was known by the corresponding terms, *Lucifer* and *Hesperus.* Its diameter is about 7700 miles, and in size, surface and density, Venus is not much different from the Earth. Like Mercury, it is situated so near the sun as to make observation difficult. Like the moon, it has various phases,

according to the various positions it occupies, appearing as a thin crescent, gradually increasing to a full circle and then decreasing till it disappears. At fixed intervals Venus is seen to pass across the sun's disk. This happened for the last time in December, 1882; the next will be June 8, 2004, and the second time June 6, 2012. So rare an occurrence as this becomes of great interest to the scientific world, and expeditions to study the transit of Venus have been fitted out on a large scale by most of the great nations. It is thought that the atmosphere surrounding Venus is far more dense than that of the earth—so dense, in fact, that astronomers cannot hope to see the surface of the planet.

Venus's Flower Basket, a beautiful sponge, whose skeleton looks like spun glass, woven into an exquisite pattern, so delicate and white that one can scarcely believe it to be a natural skeleton. It is found in the deep sea near the Philippine Islands.

Venus's Fly'trap or **Dionaea,** *di o ne'a,* an insectivorous plant, found along sandy coasts of

VENUS'S FLYTRAP

North Carolina. It belongs to the same order as the droseras, or sundews (See SUNDEW). The leaves are grouped in a rosette at the base. Each leaf is divided into two parts, the lower, flat and blade-like in appearance, and the upper, a roundish portion, consisting of two lobes, divided by a midrib. The upper portion is constructed like a trap, the two halves snapping together and the bristles around the edges closing up. There are a few sensitive, hair-like feelers on the surface of the leaf, and when the insect touches one of these, the trap shuts up and the insect is caught. When the soft parts of the insects' body are absorbed, the leaf opens up and is ready for a second capture, though it seems to have lost some of its power and rarely acts but two or three times.

Ver'a Cruz, *krooz,* the chief seaport of Mexico, situated on the Gulf of Mexico, 190 mi. e. by s. of the City of Mexico, with which it is connected by rail. The site is low and sandy, and the climate is somewhat unhealthful, but these conditions have recently been improved by the construction of a sea wall and by improved sanitation. The buildings and city wall are constructed almost entirely of coral, which gives the city a unique appearance. The buildings of interest are the government house, the customhouse and a large hospital. The harbor is protected by breakwaters and has accommodations for the largest ocean vessels. The foreign trade is considerable, and regular lines of steamers ply between Vera Cruz and the Atlantic ports of the United States, the West Indies and European ports. The city was founded by Cortez in 1520, on the spot where he first landed. It was captured by the Americans in 1847 and in 1914. Population in 1910, 45,021.

Verb, *vurb,* in grammar, that part of speech whose essential function is to predicate or assert something in regard to the subject or thing spoken of; as, the boy *runs,* the man *lifts* the stone, fishes *swim,* he *suffers* much. Verbs usually have the power of indicating time and mode, by means of tenses and moods, these varying in the different languages, as does also the conjugation, or system of verbal inflections and forms as a whole. Verbs are known as *active* or *neuter,* according as they predicate action or state, and active verbs are divided into *intransitive* and *transitive,* according as the action is confined to the actor or passes from him to an object. Intransitive verbs often take an objective of their own nature; as, he *runs* a race; he *sleeps* the sleep of death. When a verb may be used either transitively or intransitively, as, he *walks* the horse, he *walks* to church, the verb in the former use is said to be causative. Many causative verbs are distinguished from their corresponding intransitives by a change of form, as *sit, set; lie, lay; fall, fell.* Passive verbs affirm suffering or endurance of what another does. Hence, only verbs which take an object

after them can have a passive voice, because it can be said of objects, only, that they suffer or endure the action directed on or toward them by the subject of the active verb.

Verbena, *vur be'na,* a genus of plants, containing about eighty species, most of which are American. They usually grow in masses and have hairy stems and leaves and compact clusters of flowers. Several species are cultivated for the great beauty of their flowers, being fine border plants. Common vervain, a plant abounding in England, and widely distributed, was once held in great repute for its medicinal virtues and was used in various charms and love philters. The verbena of the perfumers is the lemon grass, from which the "oil of verbena" is extracted.

Verdi, *ver'de,* GIUSEPPE (1813–1901), the greatest modern Italian musical composer. His first production was the opera *Oberto, Conte di San Bonifazo,* and in 1842 he brought out with great success, at Milan, his *Nabaco,* followed by

GIUSEPPE VERDI

I Lombardi, Ernani, Rigoletto, Il Trovatore, La Traviata, Un Ballo in Maschera, Aida, Montezuma, Otello and *Falstaff.* The last is among the greatest of comic operas. Verdi had a fine dramatic gift, and his melodies are brilliant and attractive.

Verdigris, *vur'de grees,* a greenish substance that forms on copper when exposed to acetic acid. It is used principally in the composition of paints, in the manufacture of dyes and as an ointment, or liniment. Verdigris is poisonous.

Vergil, *vur'jil,* (70–19 B. C.), the common designation of Publius Vergilius Maro, a great Roman poet, author of the *Aeneid.* He was born near Mantua, in northern Italy, and was the son of a small land-owner. His education, which was careful and thorough, was received at Cremona, Milan, Naples and Rome, where he became thoroughly acquainted with the Epicurean philosophy. A naturally retiring disposition and a delicate constitution, together with the fact of his not being by birth a Roman citizen, would have checked any aspirations he might have had to the calling of the soldier, the orator or the statesman. He retired to his father's estate, with the intention of passing his life in the pursuit of poetry and agriculture, but was rudely disturbed by the allotment of his farm to the soldiers of Octavius, after the Battle of Philippi (42 B. C.). He recovered it through the aid of Asinius Pollio, the Roman governor; but further troubles arose, and he abandoned it, going at the instance of friends to Rome, where soon afterward he became acquainted with Maecenas and Octavius, to whom Pollio had recommended him. Through these powerful friends he received an estate in Campania and was enabled to devote his life to his favorite pursuits.

Vergil had become a great favorite of Octavius, and when, after the Battle of Actium (31 B. C.), the latter became Augustus, the poet was not forgotten. It was under the encouragement and patronage of the emperor that Vergil's greatest work, the *Aeneid,* was written; and indeed only the firm establishment of the Empire and the glorious achievements of Augustus in war and peace could have produced such an epic. During the years of its composition the poet recited selections before the imperial household. When the *Aeneid* was brought to a close, Vergil went to Athens, intending to spend a few years in revising the poem and completing certain unfinished parts. Soon afterward Augustus arrived in Athens from the East, and he induced Vergil to accompany him to Italy. Under the strain of seasickness and exposure to the strong sea air, his delicate constitution broke down, and he barely lived to reach Italy, dying at Brundusium, Sept. 21, 19 B. C. Rather than leave his life-work, the *Aeneid,* imperfect and incomplete, he ordered it burned, but finally yielded to the request of Augustus, that its revision might be entrusted to his friends Tucca and Varius, who edited it with the ut-

most care. The first of Vergil's poems of which the authorship is certain are the *Bucolics,* or *Eclogues.* While based on the model of the *Idyls* of Theocritus, these ten poems are by no means solely pastoral in character. Many contain allusions or are entirely devoted to current political events or to matters concerning the poet, the background and language alone being pastoral. The *Georgics* comprise four books of didactic poems on agricultural subjects. Book I deals with the tilling of the soil; Book II, with the cultivation of fruit trees; Book III tells of horses and cattle, and Book IV treats of bees. The *Georgics* are addressed to Maecenas and were said by some to have been written at his patron's request; the work is the most finished of all Vergil's poetry.

The *Aeneid,* the composition of which probably occupied most of the twelve years between the beginning of Augustus's reign and the poet's death, is Vergil's greatest work, although it is not as highly polished as some of his other poems. In general treatment of character and incident, it is inferior to its Greek models, the *Iliad* and the *Odyssey;* but certain parts are very successfully handled; and the whole poem is conceived in a spirit of delicacy, true culture and noble patriotism. In refinement of expression and elegant metrical construction, Vergil has not been surpassed. For an outline of the poem, see AENEID.

Verlaine, *vair layn',* PAUL (1844–1896), a French poet. His first volume of verse was published when he was but twenty-one, and from the outset he exercised a real influence on French poetry. He lived the life of a vagabond, spending much of his time in the hospital or in prison, and all of these experiences he made use of in his writing. Before his death he was recognized as the greatest of the French symbolists, or decadents, and as one of the foremost modern French poets.

Vermejo, *vair may'ho,* or **Rio Grande,** a river of Argentina, which rises on the frontier of Bolivia, flows southeast and joins the Paraguay about 50 mi. n. e. of Corrientes. Its length is about 750 miles, and it is navigable for flat-bottomed boats through most of its course.

Vermes, *vur'meez,* or **Worms,** one of the great branches into which the animal kingdom is divided. Most of the animals of this division have long, flat or cylindrical bodies, which are divided more or less distinctly into segments which have no limbs. Many of the Vermes are parasites, and some live in the intestines of human beings, where they give great discomfort. Occasionally some species cause death. See Tape-worm; Earth Worm; Leech; Trichina; Worms.

Vermicelli, *vur′me chel′le* or *vur′me sel′le.* See Macaroni.

Vermiform, *vur′me form,* **Appen′dix,** a long, slender, wormlike organ, which opens from the colon near its lower end. It is normally from three to six inches in length and is hollow to its tip. It is in the right side of the lower abdomen and projects upward and inward in most cases. Little is known of its function, which is probably unimportant. See Appendicitis.

Vermil′ion, a bright red pigment, named from a French word meaning *little worm,* because formerly crimson, or carmine, was obtained from a small red worm. The vermilion of commerce is obtained by mixing together in a revolving drum, mercury, sulphur and a solution of potash in water, and heating the mixture to about 115°, when it gradually assumes a red color. Vermilion is a permanent color and can be used with water or oil, but volatilizes at red heat and cannot be used for enamels. Cinnabar, a sulphide of mercury which occurs in large quantities in California, Brazil, Spain, China and other countries, is also a valuable source of vermilion.

Vermont′, the Green Mountain State, one of the New England states, bounded on the n. by the Province of Quebec, on the e. by New Hampshire, from which it is separated by the Connecticut River, on the s. by Massachusetts and on the w. by New York. For more than a hundred miles the western boundary follows the deepest channels of Lake Champlain, giving more than one-half of the lake to Vermont. Its length from north to south is 140 mi.; its width, from 40 to 90 mi.; its area, 9564 sq. mi. Population in 1910, 355,956.

Surface and Drainage. The entire state is mountainous, owing to the presence of the Green Mountain range, which extends from the Canadian border into Massachusetts, and to numerous parallel ranges, which extend in a nearly north and south direction. South and west of the main range is the Taconic range, and north and east are several short ranges. The highest peaks of the main range from north to south are Jay, Sterling, Mansfield, Camel's Hump, Lincoln, Pico, Killington, Shrewsbury, Stratton and Haystack, of which Mount Mansfield, with an altitude of 4364 feet, is the highest. All of the mountains of the parallel ranges are comparatively low, have rounded summits and are well timbered. These various ranges are separated by low,

broad valleys, through which one or more streams flow and which have fairly fertile soil. The lowest point in the state is the valley of Lake Champlain, which has an altitude of only 100 feet above sea level.

The eastern half of the state is drained by the Connecticut River and its tributaries, the most important of these being the Passumpsic, the Waitess White, the Ottauquechee, the Williams, the Saxtons and the West. The western part of the state is drained into Lake Champlain and thence into the Saint Lawrence River. The most important streams flowing into the lake are the Missisquoi, the Lamoille, the Winooski and the Otter Creek, the last being the largest river wholly within the state. The southwestern section is drained into the Hudson River, but the streams are small and unimportant.

Vermont contains a number of mountain lakes, all of which are noted for their beautiful scenery and clear waters. The most important of these is Lake Champlain, more than half of which belongs to Vermont. Other lakes in the Champlain valley are Bomoseen, Saint Catherine and Dunmore. In the northeastern part of the state is Lake Memphremagog, a portion of which is in Vermont and the remainder in Canada. Southeast of this is Willoughby Lake, renowned for its peculiar surroundings. The lake is about six miles long and lies between two mountains which seem to have been rent asunder in some past geological age. This region also contains numerous other smaller lakes, frequently known as ponds. All of these bodies of water have become favorite summer resorts.

Climate. The climate of Vermont is subject to extreme and sudden changes. In summer the temperature varies from 65° to 90°; in winter it ranges from 18° to 45°. At Burlington the mean annual temperature is 45°. The climate is milder in the Champlain Valley than east of the Green Mountains. During the winter there is often much snow, which in the colder parts of the state covers the ground for three months. The average annual rainfall is 33 inches. The air is clear and pure.

Mineral Resources. Ores of copper, silver, lead, gold, manganese and iron occur. A large amount of copper is obtained at the Ely mines, on the eastern side of the state. The chief mineral wealth of the state is in its quarries. No other state in the Union produces so great a variety or quantity of marble and granite, and Vermont has practically become the center of the marble and granite industries. Roofing and other slate is obtained in very large quantities and is of fine quality, and there are large beds of soapstone.

AGRICULTURE. The soil in the valleys along the streams and at the foot of the mountains and hills is usually fertile, though but very little of it compares favorably in this respect with the soil of the great prairie states in the Mississippi Basin. Agriculture is the leading industry of the state. The farms are comparatively small, averaging less than 200 acres, and most of them are tilled by their owners. Formerly Vermont was known for its production of wheat, oats, corn and potatoes, but since the development of the great agricultural states in the Mississippi valley, the New England states have been unable to compete in the markets which the western producers could reach; consequently, since 1875 methods and products have been radically changed. Now intensified farming is generally practiced, and the raising of wheat has given way to the raising of corn, which is very generally used as ensilage. Dairying is the chief agricultural industry. Excellent qualities of butter and cheese are made, and these find ready market in Boston and other eastern cities. Vermont has always been famed for the excellent breeds of horses produced there, and horses are still raised in large numbers. In some sections the raising of garden vegetables and apples for market is also a profitable industry, and Vermont is unsurpassed in the amount and quality of maple sugar produced.

MANUFACTURES. The chief manufacturing industries consist in dressing stone, particularly marble and granite; in the manufacture of scales in Saint Johnsbury and in Rutland, in the production of flour and other grist mill products, and in the manufacture of textiles, particularly woolen goods. Since the introduction of electrical power, many small factories have been established within the state, obtaining their power from mountain streams which were previously useless. This has increased the output of manufactures very materially since 1890.

TRANSPORTATION. The northwestern part of the state finds a ready outlet by water through Lake Champlain and the Richelieu River, but these are closed to navigation during the winter season. Lines of railway traverse the state from north to south, both on the eastern and western sides. There are also numerous cross-lines, so that every county has good railway facilities, and nearly every town is on a line of railway or within ready access of it. The railways of the

state are under the control of the Rutland, the Boston & Maine and the Grand Trunk systems.

GOVERNMENT. The legislature consists of a senate of 30 members and a house of representatives of 246 members, the latter containing one representative for each town and city within the state. Both senators and representatives are elected every two years. The legislature meets biennially. The executive department consists of the governor and the lieutenant governor. These officers, together with the secretary of state, the state treasurer, the auditor of accounts and the attorney-general, are elected by the people for two years. The courts consist of a state supreme court of seven judges, a chancery court and county courts. The judges of the supreme court, the superintendent of education and some other officers are elected by the legislature for a term of two years.

EDUCATION. The superintendent of education is at the head of the public school system. The township system is in vogue, in which the town constitutes the smallest unit for school purposes. County examiners are appointed by the governor and superintendent of education, and town superintendents are appointed by the town school boards. It is the duty of the examiners to examine and license teachers, and town superintendents inspect the schools of the towns. Graded schools are maintained in all of the larger towns and villages, most of which have high schools. The higher institutions of learning are the University of Vermont, at Burlington, with which is connected the state agricultural college; Middlebury College, at Middlebury, and Norwich University, at Northfield. Montpelier Seminary, at Montpelier; Goddard Seminary, at Barre; Saint Johnsbury Academy, at Saint Johnsbury; Vermont Academy, at Saxton's River, and Brigham Academy, at Bakersfield, are among the most prominent academies. There are normal schools at Randolph, Johnson and Castleton.

INSTITUTIONS. The deaf, dumb and blind are educated by the state in institutions of other states. The hospitals for the insane are at Waterbury and Brattleboro. The state prison is at Windsor, the house of correction is at Rutland and the state industrial school is at Vergennes.

CITIES. The chief cities and towns are Montpelier, the capital; Burlington, Rutland, Saint Albans, Brattleboro, Barre and Saint Johnsbury, each of which is described under its title.

HISTORY. The first white man to enter the territory of Vermont was probably Champlain (1609), but no settlements were made until

1665, when French trading posts were established on the western border. It was the scene of numerous expeditions by both French and English during the French and Indian Wars. After the middle of the eighteenth century, the territory was a cause of dispute between New Hampshire and New York, each claiming jurisdiction over it, by reason of charters and royal grants. On account of the grants of lands made there by New Hampshire, Vermont came to be known as the *Hampshire Grants.* It was finally decided by England that New York had jurisdiction, but the settlers of Vermont, by means of organized militia, known as "Green Mountain Boys," resisted the establishment of the authority of New York. This resulted in several skirmishes and considerable bloodshed. During the Revolution, Vermont organized its own forces and fought with great effect against the indians and British in the north. Meantime it set up a claim of independent statehood, and in 1791 was admitted to the Union. Its progress during the nineteenth century was consistent. Its government in most respects was rather more Democratic than that of other New England states. During the Civil War it furnished its full quota of troops, and it was the scene of the operations of the Fenians in 1866 and 1870. In 1852 an amendment prohibiting the sale of intoxicating liquors was adopted, but was repealed in 1902, high license and local option being substituted.

Consult Robinson's *Vermont,* in the American Commonwealths Series.

Vermont, UNIVERSITY OF, an institution of learning, founded in 1791 at Burlington, Vt. The university comprises departments of liberal arts; civil, mechanical and electrical engineering; chemistry and agriculture; commerce and economics, and medicine. The faculty numbers over 100, and there are about 600 students. The library contains over 85,000 volumes.

Verne, *vairn,* JULES (1828–1905), a popular French romancer. He studied law for some time, but afterward began writing short pieces for the stage. In 1862 he published *Five Weeks in a Balloon,* and the vein of the marvelous, tinged with a quasi-scientific truthfulness, was later used by him with great success. His most popular works are *Twenty Thousand Leagues under the Sea, From the Earth to the Moon, Around the World in Eighty Days, Michael Strogoff* and *The Mysterious Island.* Most of his books have been translated into the various European languages, and some even into Arabic

and Japanese. They will long remain popular for their ingenuity and their lively style.

JULES VERNE

Vernier, *vur'ne ur,* an index, fitted to slide along the edge of a scale, with divisions marked upon it, by means of which, readings may be taken to small fractions of the parts actually marked on the scale. For instance, the scale is divided into inches and tenths of an inch, and the index is $\frac{9}{10}$ of an inch and is divided into 10 divisions. Suppose, in one case of measurement, the end of the index is past the 8 figure on the scale; the reader writes down 8; if it is past 3 of the tenth spaces and part of another, he adds .3; then, looking up the index, if he finds that its sixth division most nearly coincides with a division on the scale, he adds .06. The position of the index is marked 8.36 inches.

Verona, *va ro'na,* a city of northern Italy, capital of the province of the same name, situated on the Adige River, 62 mi. w. of Venice. The city has a beautiful site and is noted for its medieval palaces and its many statues. The town occupies both sides of the river, which is crossed by a number of bridges. There are also interesting remains of a Roman amphitheater erected by the emperor Diocletian, and some of the churches contain valuable paintings by the old masters. The city is the reputed home of Romeo and Juliet, immortalized by

Shakespeare. It contains a number of academies of painting and sculpture and has a municipal library of 160,000 volumes. Next to Venice, Verona is the most important town in the State of Venetia. Population in 1911, 81,909.

Veronese, *va'ro nay'za,* PAUL (1528–1588), the popular name of Paolo Cagliari, an eminent Italian artist, born at Verona. He studied painting under his uncle, Antonio Badile, and worked successively in Venice, Rome and other cities of Italy; but Venice was his chief residence. Some idea of his talent may be gained from the fact that he was soon recognized as a rival of Titian and Tintoretto. He was an excellent colorist, as were most of the Venetian school, and he was distinguished by the richness and fertility of his imagination. His pictures are exceedingly numerous and varied in subject. Among his masterpieces are *The Marriage at Cana* (now in the Louvre), *The Calling of Saint Andrew to the Apostleship, The Rape of Europa, The Family of Darius at the Feet of Alexander, Adoration of the Magi, Consecration of Saint Nicholas and Saint Helena* and *The Vision of the Invention of the Cross.* The last five mentioned are in the National Gallery. Veronese died at Venice in the full maturity of his genius.

Veron'ica, SAINT, a female saint, who, according to legend, met Jesus Christ bending under the weight of the cross and offered him her veil to wipe the sweat from his brow. The divine features were found miraculously impressed on the cloth, and this veil was brought from Palestine to Rome, where it is still preserved by the canons of Saint Peter's. Milan and other places claim they have the genuine veil.

Verrazano, *ver a tsah'no,* GIOVANNI DA (1480?–1527), a Florentine navigator, about whose life little is known. About 1523 he made his first voyage of discovery, and in 1524 he voyaged to America, probably touching the coast of North Carolina. He wrote a letter to Francis I, describing this voyage, and this letter is almost the only source of information concerning his discoveries. Some accounts relate that Verrazano was hanged as a corsair; others state that he died while preparing for another expedition to America.

Versailles, *ver'sah'y',* a city of France, situated 10 mi. s. w. of Paris. The city is regularly laid out, with streets crossing at right angles. It is of note because of the magnificent palace erected here in 1661 by Louis XIV, and occupied by him and his successors as a royal residence until the time of Louis Philippe, when it was converted into a national museum. The palace now contains extensive collections of statues and paintings of unusual historical and artistic interest. The park surrounding it is also of remarkable beauty, because of its numerous vases, statues, terraces and fountains. From 1871 to 1879 Versailles was the seat of government of the Republic of France. Population in 1911, 60,458.

Versailles, PALACE OF, a famous palace, built for a residence, in 1661, by Louis XIV, at Versailles. The palace is particularly imposing because of its beautiful façade, which is a quarter of a mile long. The building is used principally as an historical museum and is filled with a great number of historical paintings and other valuable relics. The works of David, Delacroix and Vernet are represented here. The palace is interesting from an historical point of view; here the preliminary treaty that closed the American Revolution and gave the United States independence was signed; in the French Revolution, the mob fought its way up the marble stairs and sacked the palace; during the winter of 1870 the king of Prussia made it his headquarters, and in 1871 he was there proclaimed emperor of Germany, as William I.

Verse, *vurs,* a line of poetry, or, more commonly but less correctly, a stanza composed of several lines. The term is also used, in its broader sense, to mean the measured and cadenced form of speech or composition adopted in poetry. Verse, as simply cadenced lines, is of great antiquity, but the use of rhymed cadences is a comparatively modern invention. Blank verse is verse in which the lines do not end in rhymes. For the divisions of verse on the basis of meter, see METER.

Vertebrata, *vur'te bray'ta,* the highest and most important branch of the animal kingdom (See ZOOLOGY). The vertebrates have a skeleton which consists of a skull and a backbone, composed of vertebrae, ribs, and bones for supporting the jointed limbs. The chief function of the skull is to enclose the brain and the organs of sight, hearing, smell and taste. The bones of the head and face, and generally the vertebrae of the spinal column, are more numerous in the lower vertebrates than in the higher. The spine supports the body and forms a tube, through which runs the spinal cord, the great nerve trunk of the body. The ribs are attached to the vertebrae and form an expansible box, in which are stored the heart, lungs, stomach and other important organs. In the vertebrates the two sides of the body are alike, or nearly so. The digestive system is complicated, consisting of mouth, pharynx, oesophagus, stomach and intestines, all of which are modified in different families. Digestive fluids are secreted by various glands, and the oxygen necessary for the purification of the blood is obtained through gills, in the case of water-breathing animals, and through lungs, by those that breathe air directly. The body is covered by a skin of several thicknesses, from which grow scales, hair, feathers or other devices for the purpose of protection or ornament. For a further discussion of this great branch, see FISHES; BATRACHIANS; REPTILES; BIRDS; MAMMALIA, and the articles referred to in these.

Vertigo, *vur'te go,* an attack of giddiness, in which stationary objects appear to move in various directions, the person affected finding it difficult to maintain an erect position. It is a common symptom of excessive or defective supply of blood to the brain, as well as of nervous and general debility, though it also frequently arises from the disturbance of the digestive organs. Rapidly whirling the body will produce a severe form of vertigo.

Vertum'nus, a Roman deity, who presided over crops and orchards. He was generally represented as a young man, crowned with flowers, holding in his right hand fruit, and in his left a horn of plenty. He was the husband of Pomona.

Vespasian, *vez pa'zhe an,* (9–79), emperor of Rome. After serving with distinction in Germany and in Britain, as commander of a legion, he was made consul. He afterward became proconsul of Africa; and on the rebellion of the Jews, he was sent with an army into Judea. He reduced nearly all Galilee and was preparing to attack Jerusalem when he received news of Nero's death (68 A. D.). Then followed the emperors Galba, Otho and Vitellius, and in 69 A. D. Vespasian was himself elected emperor by the army. He left the siege of Jerusalem to his son Titus and returned to Rome. He immediately reformed the discipline of the army, purified the senatorial and equestrian orders and improved the administration of justice. He was the patron of learned men, particularly Quintilian, Pliny and Josephus. He rebuilt a part of the city, restored the capitol and erected the gigantic amphitheater, the ruins of which are still celebrated under the name of the *Colosseum.*

Vespucci, *ves poot'che,* AMERIGO. See AMERICUS VESPUCIUS.

Vest, GEORGE GRAHAM (1830–1904), an American statesman, born in Frankfort, Ky. He graduated from Center College and studied law at Transylvania University. Removing to Missouri, he became a member of the Missouri legislature in 1860 and served for three years in the Confederate congress. In 1879 he was elected United States senator for Missouri and served continuously until 1903, gaining prominence as an orator and debater. He was a leader of the Democratic representation in Congress.

Ves'ta, a Roman divinity, the goddess of the hearth. She was worshiped, along with the Penates, at every family meal, when the household assembled round the hearth, which was in the center of the room. Her public sanctuary was in the Forum, and the sacred fire was kept constantly burning in it by the vestal virgins, her priestesses. A special building, near the temple, was set aside as the dwelling of the vestals. Each community had a hearth, on which was kept constantly alight the sacred fire of Vesta, and colonists setting out from a city took with them some of the old fire to kindle a flame in their new home. Few legends are connected with Vesta.

Vesu'vius, an active volcano, situated in Italy, on the Bay of Naples, about 10 mi. s. e. of the city of Naples. The mountain varies in height from 3900 to 4350 feet, according to the amount of material thrown out or carried away by eruptions. Vesuvius, with its neighboring peak, Somma, on the north, stands alone. The main mountain rises by a gradual slope for about 2500 feet and is then surmounted by a cone nearly 1500 feet in altitude. The lower slopes of the mountain are quite generally covered with gardens and orchards, except in places where the fall of lava has produced a rough, rocky surface; but the cone is bare.

Vesuvius is the only active volcano on the continent of Europe, and for centuries it has been an object of interest to travelers. The mountain can be ascended by a bridle path, by carriage road, on foot or by means of a cable railway, which hauls one car up as another goes down. Accompanied by experienced guides, one can frequently descend into the crater to some distance, though it is not safe for those who are unacquainted with the mountain to attempt this alone. The mountain is supposed to be of comparatively recent origin. The first record of an eruption from this mountain is that of the eruption of 79 A. D., in which the cities of Pompeii and Herculaneum were buried. Many authorities believe that this eruption occurred from Somma, and that the cone now known as Vesuvius has risen since that date. The mountain was quiet from 1500 to 1631. Since that time there have been numerous eruptions, which, on account of their extent, attracted general attention. Between these periods of intense activity there have been numerous minor eruptions, and the crater always gives forth cinders and poisonous gases. When seen from a distance, these have the appearance of smoke. Of the more recent eruptions of importance, those of 1895, 1903 and 1905 are specially worthy of mention. An observatory is located on the western shoulder of the mountain, at an elevation of over 2200 feet. See HERCULANEUM; NAPLES; POMPEII; VOLCANO.

Vetch, a common name, rather loosely applied to several genera of climbing plants that are natives of the temperate zones. Many of them have been cultivated as forage plants for ages, and some yield edible seeds. Recently several species have been introduced into the United States for winter forage; the *hairy vetch* makes a good crop and, under favorable conditions, will grow from year to year.

Vet'erinary Medicine, the art which deals with the nature, causes and treatment of the disorders of domestic animals. The first veterinary school was instituted in 1762 at Lyons, France; in 1766 that at Alfort, near Paris, was opened. A similar institution was established at London in 1791, and in the year following, one in Berlin. In the United States veterinary chairs have been added to the University of Pennsylvania, Cornell University and to several other leading universities, as well as to many of the schools of agriculture. Besides these, there are many private schools that give thorough instruction. Recently the requirements of admission to veterinary courses have been materially advanced, and in the better schools four year courses of study are required.

The development of veterinary medicine has kept pace with that of the general practice of human medicine, and measures for preventing the spread of contagious diseases among animals are applied as rigorously as among men. The bureau of animal industry, in the United States department of agriculture, takes care of veterinary questions that come before the government, and the states and large cities have veterinarians who investigate diseases and attend to the enforcement of the veterinary laws of the districts in which they have power. Important documents are issued for public circulation by the bureau of animal industry and by the experiment

stations and boards of agriculture in the several states. *The American Veterinary Review* is a prominent journal. Among the many books relating to this subject may be mentioned Smith's *Physiology of Domestic Animals,* Hopkins's *Veterinary Elements* and Moore's *Pathology of the Infectious Diseases of Animals.*

Ve'to (Latin, "I forbid"), the power which one branch of the legislature of a state has to negative the resolutions of another branch; or the right of the executive branch of government to reject measures proposed by the legislature. The president of the United States may veto any measure passed by Congress, but the rejected bill may become law by being passed by two-thirds of each of the houses of Congress. The same rule usually obtains in state governments.

Vi'aduct, a bridge-like structure, for carrying a roadway across a valley, lowland or over a public street or highway. Viaducts are made of wood, stone, brick or iron, but the most recent ones are of iron and consist of several spans, supported on substantial piers of steel, well braced and riveted, resting on concrete or stone foundations. The longest viaduct in the world is at Des Moines, Iowa, and was built in 1901. It is 2685 feet long and is used by the Chicago & Northwestern railroad. Other great viaducts are those at Gokteik, Burma, and across the Pecos River in Texas, near the Rio Grande. See BRIDGE.

Vic'ar, in a general sense, a representative or deputy of another officer. The pope calls himself *vicar of Christ on earth.* In the Church of England a vicar is the priest of a parish, who receives only the smaller tithes, or a salary. A *vicar apostolic,* in the Roman Catholic Church, is a bishop who possesses no diocese, but who exercises jurisdiction over a certain district by direct authority of the pope; *vicar-general* is the official assistant of a bishop or archbishop.

Vicenza, *ve chen'tsa,* a city of Italy, situated on the Vacchiglione, 40 mi. w. of Venice. It is enclosed by a wall and contains a number of important buildings. Around the square, or Piazza de Signori, is the Basilica, with a number of grand colonnades that enclose the townhall. Another noted structure is the Municipio, and others are the Theatro Olympico and the Palazzo Chiericati, which contains the municipal museum. All of these structures are the work of the famous architect Palladio. Among the famous churches are the Church of Madonna del Monte, dating from the fifteenth century; the cathedral, and the Dominican Church of Santa Corona. These and other churches contain a number of valuable paintings by the ancient masters. The city maintains an academy of sciences and arts, a technological school, a municipal museum and a library of 175,000 volumes. The leading industries include the manufacture of silk, machinery, musical instruments and other articles. Population of the commune in 1911, 54,555.

Vice-President, the person second in authority to the president. The vice-president of the United States is chosen in the same way and for the same length of term as the president. A candidate for vice-president must be a natural-born citizen of the United States, must have reached the age of 35 years and must have been for 14 years a resident of the United States. He is inaugurated in the Senate chamber at Washington on the same day and immediately following the inauguration of the president. His chief duty is to preside over the sessions of the senate. He is not allowed to vote, except in case of a tie. He becomes president if the president dies or is permanently incapacitated from performing the duties of his office. Tyler, Fillmore, Johnson, Arthur and Roosevelt succeeded to the presidency in this manner. The salary of the vice-president is $12,000 a year.

Vicks'burg, Miss., the county-seat of Warren co., 43 mi. w. of Jackson, on the Mississippi River, a few miles below the mouth of the Yazoo, and on the Queen & Crescent and the Yazoo & Mississippi Valley railroads. The city is situated on a high bluff overlooking the river, and the streets are well kept and have many shade trees. Cotton is the principal product of the surrounding region, and the chief manufacturing establishments are cottonseed oil mills, lumber mills, railroad shops, foundries and other factories. The principal buildings are the courthouse, the Federal building and the charity hospital. The educational institutions include the Saint Aloysius College for boys, the Cherry Street College for colored students, an academy, and public and parish schools for both races. The large national cemetery is also of interest. The town was laid out on the plantations of John Lane and William Vick, and the city was incorporated in 1840. During the early part of the Civil War it was strongly fortified, and after a long siege it was surrendered to General Grant on July 4, 1863 (See VICKSBURG CAMPAIGN, THE). In 1876 high water caused some damage, but the government has since made considerable improvements in the river channel. Population in 1910, 20,-814.

Vicksburg Campaign, THE, a series of opera-tions in 1862 and 1863, whose object was the capture of Vicksburg by the Union troops, and ultimately the termination of the Confederate control of the Mississippi. The American forces, numbering about 48,000, were commanded by General Grant, supported by General Sherman. The campaign was begun December 20 by an expedition by Sherman down the Mississippi and a simultaneous advance by Grant toward Vicksburg from the land side. Sherman was repulsed at Chickasaw Bluffs, and the campaign was abandoned. In the following January, Grant planned another advance. Sherman was sent to take the right end of the Confederate position at Haines's Bluff; McClernand and McPherson were to move south along the west bank of the river, to effect a crossing, under the protection of a bombardment by gunboats under Commodore Porter, and to advance upon Vicksburg from the south. It was April 30 before the crossing was made, but on the following day the Federals won a decided victory at Port Gibson, causing the Confederates to contract their lines. Meantime General Joseph Johnston had marched toward Vicksburg to join Pemberton's force. Grant now attempted to prevent this union. He overtook Pemberton, who was retreating toward Clinton, to join Johnston, and administered two severe defeats, at Champion's Hill and Big Black River, finally compelling him to retire within his fortifications at Vicksburg.

Failing to take the city by direct assault, Grant established a siege, but maintained almost continuous bombardment. The condition of the soldiers and the citizens of Vicksburg soon became desperate. Famine and disease made great inroads upon their numbers, and at last Pemberton surrendered 29,500 men, 170 cannon and 50,000 small arms. His casualties during the campaign had been fully 10,000. The surrender occurred on July 4, the day after the final victory at Gettysburg. The two events were the turning points in the Civil War, and mark the beginning of the downfall of the Confederacy.

Vic'tor Emman'uel II (1820–1878), king of Sardinia, the son of Charles Albert. His aptitude for a military career became evident when he commanded the Savoy brigades against Austria (1848–1849), and he distinguished himself in the Battle of Goito by his reckless valor. After the battle of Novara his father abdicated, and Victor Emmanuel ascended the throne of Sardinia. He had then to negotiate with Austria under most unfavorable circumstances, but he steadily refused to give up the principle of representative government in the Sardinian constitution, and this gained for him the good will of the Italian people. Under the advice of his

VICTOR EMMANUEL III

celebrated minister, Cavour, he regulated the finances, reorganized the army and secularized the Church property, for which he was excommunicated by the pope. He took part in the Crimean War against Russia, and in 1859, assisted by France, he renewed the contest with Austria, winning the battles of Magenta and Solferino. By the Treaty of Villafranca and the Peace of Zurich, which followed these successes, Lombardy was added to his dominions, but he had to cede Savoy and Nice to France. Parma, Modena and Tuscany now became united to Sardinia, and Garibaldi's successes in Sicily and Naples brought the whole of southern Italy over to Victor Emmanuel. Early in 1861, he assumed the title of king of Italy. By the Peace of Vienna (1866) Austria ceded Venetia, and on the withdrawal of the French garrison from Rome in 1870 that city annexed itself to Italy. The king entered Rome on July 2, 1871, and took up his residence in the Quirinal. He was succeeded by his son Humbert.

Victor Emmanuel III (1869–   ), king of Italy, son of Humbert I. He entered the army in 1887 and was steadily advanced in rank. At the coronation of Nicholas II of Russia, in 1896, and at Queen Victoria's jubilee, in the following year, he was present as his father's representative. In 1896 he married Princess Helena of Montenegro. When his father was assassinated in 1900, he succeeded to the throne, and he proved a just and liberal ruler.

Victo′ria (1819–1901), queen of the United Kingdom of Great Britain and Ireland, and empress of India. She was the daughter of Edward, duke of Kent, fourth son of George III, and was born at Kensington palace. The duke died when Victoria was only eight months old, and she was brought up by her mother with exceptional prudence and care. Upon the death of William IV, June 20, 1837, she ascended the throne and was crowned at Westminster, June 28, 1838. The English people knew little of their young queen, who had been brought up in seclusion, but she soon proved herself possessed of the clear judgment and moderation which a sovereign needs, and of a thorough goodness which won the hearts of her subjects.

During the reign of Victoria there were eighteen changes of government, the following pre-

QUEEN VICTORIA

miers taking office at the dates given: 1835, Melbourne; 1841, Peel; 1846, Russell; 1852, Derby; 1852, Aberdeen; 1855, Palmerston; 1858, Derby; 1859, Palmerston; 1865, Russell; 1866, Derby;

1868, Disraeli; 1868, Gladstone; 1874, Disraeli; 1880, Gladstone; 1885, Salisbury; 1886, Gladstone; 1886, Salisbury; 1892, Gladstone; 1895, Salisbury.

The leading events of the reign were the confederation of Canada; the Opium War in China; the abolition of the corn laws, under the administration of Sir Robert Peel; the successive steps in parliamentary reform; the enfranchisement of the Jews; the Catholic Emancipation act; the assumption of the government of India by the Crown; the Crimean War; the wars with Afghanistan, Abyssinia, the Zulu tribes and Egypt; the long struggle on the Irish home-rule question; the beginning of the South African War, and the Australian federation.

In February, 1840, Victoria was married to her cousin, Prince Albert of Saxe-Coburg-Gotha, and the marriage proved an unusually happy one. On the death of her husband, in 1861, she withdrew from social life, and for many years her social duties were performed by her daughter-in-law, Alexandra. Victoria and Albert had four sons and five daughters: Victoria, Princess Royal, born in 1840, married in 1858 to Frederick William, afterward emperor of Germany, died in 1901; Albert Edward, Prince of Wales, born in 1841, married to Alexandra, daughter of the king of Denmark, succeeded to the throne on the death of his mother; Alice, born in 1843, married in 1862 to Prince Frederic William of Hesse, died in 1878; Alfred, born in 1844, married in 1874 to Marie, daughter of the czar of Russia, died in 1901; Helena, born in 1846, was married in 1866 to Prince Christian of Denmark; Louise, born in 1848, was married in 1871 to the Marquis of Lorne; Arthur, born in 1850, was married in 1879 to Princess Louise Marguerite of Prussia; Leopold, born in 1853, married in 1882 to Princess Helena of Waldeck, died in 1884; Princess Beatrice, born in 1857, was married in 1885 to Prince Henry of Battenberg.

During the reign of Queen Victoria, Great Britain enjoyed a long era of uninterrupted prosperity; peace and contentment prevailed at home, and, with very rare exceptions, relations of amity were maintained with foreign powers. In length her reign was unprecedented in the world's history. It is true that Louis XIV of France ruled over a longer period than she, but subtracting the years during which he was under a regent, his responsible tenure of the crown was shorter than hers. Although George III nominally ruled sixty years, owing to his insanity a portion of his reign was also under a regent.

In 1887 the people of Great Britain and the colonies celebrated the golden jubilee, or fiftieth year of Queen Victoria's reign. In 1897 they celebrated the diamond jubilee of her reign, by ceremonies more imposing than have ever attended any similar event. Representatives of all the colonies were present, and a grand procession, viewed by millions, moved through the streets of London. Victoria died January 22, 1901, and her death was mourned over the entire world. She was buried at Windsor.

Victoria, a genus of water lilies, of which the best known species is the *royal water lily,* called the *Victoria regia,* the largest of all known water lilies. It is a native of tropical regions of South America and grows usually in the still waters of the Amazon. Its leaves are like large circular trays, about twelve feet across, with edges turned up two or three inches. They are bright green above and deep violet on the lower surface. The flowers, which are sometimes more than a foot across, are of all shades, from white to pink, and are very fragrant. This plant, though sometimes seen in public gardens, is rare and difficult to cultivate.

Victoria, a state of the Australian Commonwealth, situated in the southeastern part of Australia. It is bounded on the n. by New South Wales, on the s. and s. e. by the Indian Ocean and on the w. by South Australia. Its area is 87,884 sq. mi., or a little less than Virginia and North Carolina combined. It has about 600 miles of sea coast, with a considerable number of bays and indentations, especially about the middle, where Port Phillip Bay, with an area of 875 square miles and an entrance barely 2 miles wide, affords shelter sufficient for the largest fleet. The interior, though diversified by mountains, is chiefly distinguished by vast, unwooded plains, mostly occupied as pasture. There is one principal mountain range, a portion of the Great Dividing Range of Eastern Australia, running from east to west through the colony, with various offshoots. The eastern portion of it, called the Australian Alps, with numerous northern and western ramifications, rises to 6500 feet in Mount Bogong and to 6100 feet in Mount Hotham, and has several other peaks exceeding 5000 feet in height. The most westerly portion, called the Grampians, runs north and south, and in Mount William reaches a height of 5600 feet. The Grampians and the Australian Alps are connected by such ranges as the Pyrenees and Hume Range, containing numerous cones and extinct craters. This is the region of the gold fields.

The rivers are numerous, but they are generally small and dry up in summer, leaving the country parched. The chief is the Murray, which rises in the Australian Alps and forms the northern boundary of the state for 980 miles. It is 1300 miles long and is navigable for several hundred miles. See MURRAY RIVER.

The climate of Victoria is temperate, but liable to sudden changes, and hot winds blow at intervals from November to February, causing great discomfort. The hottest period is in January and February, when the thermometer sometimes rises to 108° in the shade.

Victoria is the principal gold-producing colony of Australia, the output in 1904 being valued at $15,805,000. Tin, antimony, copper and coal are also among the minerals worked.

General farming is quite extensively followed. The chief crops are wheat, oats and barley, among the cereals. Hay is grown, and forage crops are also raised. Among fruits, grapes take the lead, and considerable attention is given to the manufacture of wine. Stock raising is important, and wool growing is the chief branch of agricultural industry. The state has nearly 11,000,000 sheep, and the annual output of wool averages over 53,000,000 pounds.

The manufacturing industries are quite generally distributed, and include the manufacture of textiles, machinery, food preparations, butter and cheese and malt and spirituous liquors.

Most of the commerce is with Great Britain, and in its foreign trade Victoria is the second state of the commonwealth. The chief exports are wool, gold, dairy products and wheat. Railway lines extend to all the most important trade centers and connect these directly or indirectly with Melbourne, the chief city and commercial port. In all, there are over 3200 miles of railway in the state.

The governor is appointed by the British sovereign. The legislature consists of a council of 48 members, who are chosen for six years, and an assembly of 95 members, elected for three years. Suffrage is restricted by property and professional qualifications. The state is second in population, and Melbourne, its capital, is the largest city of Australia. Population in 1911, 1,315,551. See AUSTRALIA.

Victoria, the capital of British Columbia, situated on the southeastern extremity of Vancouver Island, on the Strait of San Juan de Fuca, 75 mi. n. w. of Seattle, Wash. It is within 3 miles of Esquimault, which is one of the finest harbors on the Pacific coast. The town is well laid out and has good streets; excellent roads connect it with the surrounding country. The public buildings include the parliament house, the government offices and the provincial museum and library, the city hall, the courthouse, a marine hospital, the Anglican Cathedral and exposition buildings. The town is an important industrial center and has lumber mills, breweries, distilleries, potteries, powder works and other manufactories. It also has a large trade in salmon and is engaged in shipbuilding. Population in 1911, 31,660.

Victoria Bridge. See BRIDGE, subhead *Tubular Bridges*.

Victoria Cross, a British military decoration, instituted at the close of the Crimean War in 1856, in imitation of the French cross of the Legion of Honor. It is granted to soldiers and sailors of any rank, for a single act of valor in presence of the enemy. It is a Maltese cross of bronze, with a royal crown in the center, surmounted by a lion, and the words "For Valour" are indented on a scroll below the crown. The ribbon is red for the army and blue for the navy. A pension of £50 a year accompanies the decoration.

Victoria Falls, a celebrated cataract in the Zambezi River, 225 mi. n. w. of Bulawayo. After flowing for a long distance over a rough and broken plateau, covered with brush and stunted trees, the Zambezi plunges suddenly into a chasm nearly 400 feet deep. The falls are 3000 feet in width and 360 feet in height. At low water the fall is broken by projecting rocks and is described by an observer as resembling a film of delicate lace, but when the river is swollen during the rainy season, an unbroken sheet of water is hurled over the ledge, forming a cataract unequaled elsewhere in the world. The roar of the falls can be heard for several miles, and the cloud of spray thrown into the air is visible for twenty miles. Because of this cloud, the natives named the cataract *Mosi-oa-tuni*, which means *roaring smoke*. Below the cataract the Zambezi flows for a long distance through a narrow gorge, with nearly perpendicular walls of basalt. Just below the falls the Cape-to-Cairo railway crosses the river on a magnificent steel bridge, 600 feet long and 420 feet above the water; it is the highest structure of the kind in the world. From this bridge a magnificent view of the falls is obtained.

Victoria Nyan'za or **Ukerewe,** a large lake, situated in East Central Africa and forming the principal source of the Nile. It lies in German East Africa and British East Africa, between which territories it is about equally divided. The area is about 26,000 square miles, and that of the Catchment Basin is computed to include 70,-000 square miles in addition. Several streams flow into the lake, the most important being the Kagera from the west. As the Nile issues from the lake, it forms the Rippon Falls, which are about 1200 feet across. Next to the Great Lakes in North America, Victoria Nyanza is the largest body of fresh water on the globe. It was discovered by Captain Speke in 1858. Steamers now ply upon its waters, and its northeastern shore is reached by the Uganda railway, at Port Florence.

Vicuna, *ve koo'nya,* a small species of the guanaco, found in the mountains of South America. It is valuable, especially, because of its soft, silky wool, which is of a better quality even than that of the alpaca. It is a gregarious animal and lives in herds of twelve or fifteen, is very timid and has never been domesticated. See Alpaca; Llama.

Vienna, *ve en'na,* the capital and chief city of Austria-Hungary, and fourth city of Europe in

VIENNA

importance, situated on the south bank of the Danube, 330 mi. s. s. e. of Berlin and 630 mi. e. of Paris. The city is built upon a plain, bordered by mountains, whose bases are covered with magnificent forests. A branch of the Danube, known as the Danube Canal, traverses the city from northwest to southeast. This canal is spanned by many bridges. Vienna is built upon the plan of the old European cities, containing an inner, or central, city, surrounded by suburbs, which are now incorporated in the city and di-

vided into districts. The old town, or **Innere Stadt**, occupying the center of the city, was formerly enclosed by a wall and fortifications. In 1858 these were removed, and a magnificent boulevard, the Ringstrasse, was erected upon their site. This is one of the finest streets in Europe, and upon it are found most of the important public buildings of the city. In the newer parts the streets are broad, and there are a number of boulevards and parks. Chief among these is the Prator, in the southeastern quarter, having an area of over 4000 acres. The streets, parks and bridges are decorated with numerous statues and monuments. The buildings are noted for their beauty and elegant ornamentation, and Vienna is considered one of the finest cities of Europe.

In the center of the Innere Stadt is the Cathedral of Saint Stephen, which dates from the thirteenth century and is one of the finest Gothic structures in Europe. Other buildings of importance in and about the Ringstrasse are the imperial palace, in the southeastern quarter, noted for its age and size, rather than for its beauty; the townhall, a magnificent building adorned with many statues; the imperial museums of natural history and of art, with a monument to Maria Theresa between them; the houses of parliament; the palace of justice; the imperial opera house; a number of churches, noted for their statuary and paintings, and the University of Vienna, with its numerous structures (See Vienna, University of). Among the noted monuments not already mentioned are the monument to Mozart, the equestrian statues of Archduke Charles and Prince Eugene of Savoy and the monument to the Archduches Christines.

The educational institutions include the University of Vienna, a polytechnic institute, an agricultural college, a geological institute, the academy of sciences, the conservatory of music and the military geographical institute, besides a large number of trade schools, which prepare their students for such occupations as printing, bookbinding and other mechanic arts. The imperial library contains 900,000 volumes, besides a large number of manuscripts and engravings, and the library of the university has 650,000 volumes. These are supplemented by other libraries in the various institutions. The collections in the academy of art and the museums are among the best in the world, while the armory contains a large collection of weapons and other instruments of war. The charitable institutions include the general hospital, one of the largest and most famous institutions of its kind in the world; the asylum for the insane, and a number of smaller hospitals and homes for the blind and the deaf and dumb.

Vienna is situated at the crossing of the great commercial routes from London, Berlin and Paris to Constantinople and from Saint Petersburg to Rome. Its situation has made it an important industrial and commercial center. Among the leading industries are the manufacture of silks, woolens and other textiles, clothing, machinery, railway cars, locomotives and supplies, musical instruments, furniture, scientific and surgical instruments, pottery, jewelry, leather goods, malt liquors and numerous other products. It has an extensive trade with the surrounding country and with the leading commercial centers of Europe, though since the granting of the independent constitution to Hungary, this has fallen off to some extent.

Vienna occupies the site of an ancient Roman camp, known as Vindobona. It first became prominent as the capital of the duchy of Austria, and for about 150 years from the middle of the sixteenth century it was the capital of the German Empire. It was the seat of the celebrated Congress of Vienna that reorganized Europe after the fall of Napoleon, and it has always been one of the leading political and intellectual centers of Europe. Population in 1910, 2,031,498.

Vienna, CONGRESS OF, a congress which assembled late in 1814, to reorganize the political system of Europe after the first overthrow of Napoleon. The principal powers represented in it were Austria, Russia, Prussia, England and France; Spain, Portugal, Sweden and other minor powers were consulted on matters more nearly concerning them. The leading territorial adjustments effected by the congress were the following: Austria recovered Lombardy and Venice, while the king of Sardinia recovered Piedmont and Savoy. Murat retained Naples, but the Bourbons were soon reinstated. Holland and Belgium were erected into a kingdom for the prince of Orange, William I. Hanover was returned to the king of England, and Great Britain retained Malta, Helgoland and several conquered colonies. A federative constitution, with a diet at Frankfort, was established for Germany. Prussia received the duchy of Posen, Swedish Pomerania, the Rhine province and a part of Saxony. Russia received the greater part of the duchy of Warsaw, Cracow becoming a free state, protected by Russia, Austria and Prussia.

Sweden retained Norway, and Denmark was indemnified with Lauenburg. The congress was suddenly broken up by Napoleon's escape from Elba (February, 1815); but its acts were signed by the powers interested on June 9, 1815.

Vienna, UNIVERSITY OF, an educational institution established in Vienna by Duke Rudolph IV, in 1365. About twenty years later, the institution was strengthened by the addition of a department of theology. In 1623 it passed under the control of the Jesuits, who erected a number of buildings and enlarged the work in various other ways. While not always enjoying the greatest prosperity, the university continued to exist through the turbulent times of the Middle Ages and was reorganized by Joseph II as a State institution. In the middle of the nineteenth century, important reforms were introduced, and since that time it has increased in prestige and strength. The present organization includes faculties of law and political science, theology, medicine and philosophy. The medical department is one of the oldest in existence and is especially well fitted with laboratories, clinics and other appliances. It has attained a worldwide reputation and is considered second to no medical school in the world. The present attendance upon all departments of the university is about 7000. The library contains 600,000 volumes, besides a large number of pamphlets and manuscripts.

Vieuxtemps, *vyö tahN',* HENRI (1820–1881), a famous Belgian violinist and composer. He toured Germany in 1833 and made several later successful tours through Europe and America, appearing in the United States first in 1844 and for the last time in 1870. He was considered, both for his ability as a player and as a composer, among the world's greatest violinists. During the later part of his life he was professor in Brussels Conservatory.

Vigilance, *vij'i lans,* **Societies.** See LYNCH LAW; KU-KLUX KLAN; WHITECAPS.

Vigny, *ve nye',* ALFRED, Count de (1799–1863), a French poet and novelist. He entered the royal guard in 1816, but retired from military service in 1828, and devoted himself exclusively to literature. His *Poems* and his epic of *Eloa* placed him among the leaders of the new romantic school of poets. In 1826 he published *Poems, Ancient and Modern,* and an historical novel, *Cinq-Mars,* which attracted much attention. In 1835 his celebrated drama, *Chatterton,* appeared. He also wrote *Stello* and *Destinées,* a philosophical poem published after his death.

Vi'kings. See NORTHMEN.

Vi'las, WILLIAM FREEMAN (1840-1908), an American statesman and lawyer, born at Chelsea, Vt. He removed with his parents to Madison, Wis., in 1851, and graduated from the State University. He then went to Albany, N. Y., where he took up the study of law and was admitted to the bar in 1860. At the outbreak of the Civil War, he entered the Union service and rose to the rank of lieutenant colonel, but in 1863 he resigned, to begin the practice of law at Madison, Wis. From 1881 to 1885 he was professor of law in the University of Wisconsin. He was a member of the state legislature for one term, and in 1884 he was permanent chairman of the national Democratic convention. In the following year he was appointed postmaster-general by President Cleveland, and later he was made secretary of the interior. He was elected to the United States Senate in 1891. In 1896 he joined in the National (Gold) Democratic movement, but later he returned to the Democratic party.

Villeins, *vil'linz*, a class of feudal serfs, who were allowed to hold portions of land at the will of their lord, on condition of performing menial and non-military services. It frequently happened that lands held in villeinage descended in uninterrupted succession from father to son, until at length the occupiers or villeins became entitled, by prescription or custom, to hold their lands so long as they performed the required services. And although the villeins themselves acquired freedom, the villein services were still the condition of the tenure. These customs were preserved and evidenced by the rolls of the several courts in which they were entered, or by the immemorial usage of the several manors in which the lands lay. And as such tenants had nothing to show for their estates but the entries into those rolls, or copies of them, they at last came to be called *tenants by copy of court roll,* and their tenure was known as a *copy-hold.* See FEUDAL SYSTEM.

Vil'li, minute projections covering the mucous lining of the small intestine. Each villus contains an artery, a vein, a capillary, or a network of capillaries, and a lacteal. The office of the villi is to absorb the nutritious matter from the digested food in the intestines, after which the digested fats are carried to the thoracic duct, and the sugars, water, proteids and inorganic salts are carried by the portal vein to the liver.

Vilna, *veel'na,* a city of Russia, situated on the Viliya River, 225 mi. n. e. of Warsaw. The city is irregularly built and has narrow streets, but it contains some public buildings of interest. Among these are several palaces of the former Polish nobility; a Roman Catholic cathedral, dating from the fourteenth century; Saint John's Church, also dating from the fourteenth century, and a castle which is the residence of the governor-general. The city maintains a library of 200,000 volumes and a museum of antiquities. The industries are of comparatively little importance, but Vilna holds an important position from an historical point of view. It became prominent in the latter part of the Middle Ages, as the capital of Lithuania, and it was later an important city of Poland, but on the dismemberment of that country it became a Russian possession. Population in 1910, 190,210.

Vincennes, *vin senz',* IND., the county-seat of Knox co., 117 mi. s. w. of Indianapolis, on the Wabash River and on the Vandalia, the Baltimore & Ohio Southwestern, the Cleveland, Cincinnati, Chicago & Saint Louis and other railroads. It is in an agricultural, lumbering and coal-mining region, and it has manufactures of flour, lumber and clay products, novelties, paper, stoves, implements and various other articles. The city contains the Vincennes University, Saint Rose Female College, a cathedral library and a public library. Other interesting features are the house in which William Henry Harrison lived when he was governor of the territory, the old legislative house, the courthouse, the city hall, the Catholic cathedral, the Federal building, the Vincennes Sanatorium, the Harrison Park and several indian mounds near the city. Vincennes is the oldest city in the state and is located on the site of an ancient indian village, called Chip-kaw-kay. The French erected a fort here about 1702, and a regular settlement soon grew up. It was at first called The Post, but later it was given its present name, in honor of François Morgan de Vinsenne. The place was taken by the British in 1763, was captured by Virginian troops in 1779 and was turned over to the United States in 1783. It was the capital of Indiana Territory from 1801 to 1816 and was made a city in 1856. Population in 1910, 14,895.

Vincent, GEORGE EDGAR (1864–   ), an American educator and sociologist, son of Bishop John H. Vincent. He graduated from Yale University in 1885, and was made literary editor of the *Chautauqua Press.* He became vice-principal of the Chautauqua System two years later, and in 1907 became its president. From 1892 to 1911 he was a member of the faculty of the University of Chicago, in turn as fellow, assistant professor, professor, dean of the junior colleges and dean of the faculties. In 1911 he was elected president of the University of Minnesota.

GEORGE E. VINCENT

Vincent, *vin'sent,* JOHN HEYL (1832–   ), a Methodist Episcopal bishop, born in Tuscaloosa, Ala. He attended the academies of Lewisburg and Milton, Pa., and the Wesleyan Institute in Newark, N. J. In 1865 he established the *Sunday School Quarterly* and the following year he founded the *Sunday School Teacher.* He is the author of a large number of Sunday School publications. In 1874 he established the Chautauqua Assembly. He was elected bishop in 1888 at the General Conference, and he was appointed resident bishop in Europe, 1900. With four other bishops Vincent was retired by vote of the Quadrennial Conference in 1904. His works include *Studies in Young Life* and *The Earthly Footsteps of the Man of Galilee.*

Vinci, *vin'che,* LEONARDO DA (1452–1519), one of the greatest Italian painters, also distinguished as sculptor, architect, civil and military engineer and scientific inventor. His singular talents in the arts of design led his father to place him in the studio of Andrea Verocchio, a celebrated painter and sculptor. At the age of thirty da Vinci entered the service of Ludovico il Moro, duke of Milan, by whom he was employed in engineering, as well as in artistic work. The greatest work of all

that he had executed up to that time was the *Last Supper.* The original has been wholly defaced, but judging from copies and engravings, this work is universally regarded as one of the greatest ever produced.

After the occupation of Milan by Louis XII (1499), Leonardo retired to Florence, and soon afterward he became chief engineer of Caesar Borgia. While in Florence he painted his celebrated portrait of *Mona Lisa del Gioconda,* known as *La Gioconda,* which was bought after the death of the artist by Francis I for 4000 gold crowns, or $8600, an enormous sum in those days. Directly after this began the rivalry between Leonardo and the great Michelangelo, which lasted until the death of Leonardo. In 1502 he was appointed chief engineer and architect of the pope's army, and he visited many of the fortified posts in the papal dominions. It appears that Leonardo was not satisfied in Rome. He had been accustomed to hold the first rank as an artist wherever he lived, but here at Rome he found himself one of many, among whom were Michelangelo and Raphael; so at length he left Rome and went to Pavia, where the French king, Francis I, then held court. Here he was received with great honor and shown every favor. He died at Cloux, near Amboise, in his sixty-seventh year.

Vine. See GRAPE.

Vin'egar, a weak acetic acid, made from fermented juices of fruits and vegetables. Vinegar can be obtained from almost any liquid that will ferment, as sugar and water, or cold tea to which yeast has been added; but the vinegar of commerce is made from wine, cider and malt. Most of the so-called white wine vinegar is made from grain which is first malted, then treated as malt is treated in the manufacture of malt liquors (See BREWING), except that the fermentation is allowed to continue until the alcohol is all driven off and the liquid is turned to vinegar. Real wine vinegar is made from wine of a poor quality. Cider vinegar is made by allowing the cider to ferment until considerable alcohol is formed in it. It is then drawn from the barrels and placed in tanks or other casks, where the fermentation is completed. By far the largest part of the vinegar used in the United States is made from cider. Ohio, New York, Michigan and Missouri lead in the industry.

Cheap grades of vinegar are adulterated by having sulphuric acid mixed with them. Since this acid is intensely sour, a small quantity of it added to water and a little coloring matter makes an imitation of vinegar, but it is very unhealth-

MONA LISA

Executed by Da Vinci, and possibly now the most famous painting in the world. It was stolen by an Italian from the
Louvre, Paris, in 1912 and not found for two years. The picture is almost priceless;
probably an offer of $500,000 would not secure it

ful and should not be used. The presence of the acid can be detected by boiling a mixture of vinegar and potato starch. When this becomes cool, add a small quantity of iodine. If the vinegar is pure, the mixture will turn blue on the addition of the iodine; if the sulphuric acid is present, the color will not be changed. Vinegar is used for table sauces, in the manufacture of pickles and, to a very limited extent, in medicine.

Vin'land, the name given to that part of North America which is said to have been visited by the Norse about 1000. Its exact location is not known, different investigators placing it at points from Delaware to Labrador. It is believed, however, that the Norsemen did settle at some point in America and that they built homes, which they deserted because of the hostility of indians. The former popular belief that the old mill at Newport and the Dighton Rock are evidences of their visit has long since been discarded, the former having been erected by an early governor of Rhode Island and the latter being the work of Algonquin indians.

Vi'ol, a class of ancient musical instruments, which may be regarded as the precursors of the modern violins. They were fretted instruments, with three to six strings, and were played with a bow. There were three instruments in a set, differing in pitch; these were the treble, tenor and bass viols, and in concerts they were commonly played in pairs—two treble, two tenor and two bass. The bass viol, or *viol da gamba,* developed into the modern *violoncello.*

Vi'olet, the popular name given to a genus of plants, of which there are many species. They are favorite flowers in all northern and temperate climates, and many of them are among the first to make their appearance in the spring. The greatest favorites are the common sweet violet and the heart's-ease, the former being especially esteemed for its fragrance. The well-known pansies, so common as garden flowers, are but varieties of one species, produced by cultivation. In different localities, various species are called johnny-jump-ups. The so-called dog-tooth violet belongs to the lily family.

Violin', a musical instrument, consisting of four catgut strings, the lowest of which is covered with silvered copper wire, stretched, by means of a bridge, over a hollow wooden body, and played with a bow. It is considered the most perfect of musical instruments, on account of its capabilities of fine tone and expression and of producing all the tones in any scale in perfect tune. It forms, with the viola, the violoncello, or bass vio-

lin, and the double bass, the main element of all orchestras. The principal parts of the violin are the *scroll,* or *head,* in which are placed the pins for tuning the strings; the *neck,* which connects the scroll with the body, and to which is attached the *fingerboard,* upon which the strings are stopped by the fingers of the left hand, as it holds the neck in playing; the *belly,* over which the strings are stretched, and which has two *f*-shaped sound holes, one on each side; the *back,* or under side; the *sides,* or *ribs,* uniting the back and belly; the *tailpiece,* to which the strings are fastened, and the *bridge.* The back, neck and sides are generally of sycamore, the belly of deal, the fingerboard and tailpiece of ebony. Almost all the different pieces are fastened together with glue. The four strings of the violin are tuned at G, on the upper space of the base staff, D, A, E, reckoning upward. Every intermediate semitone in a compass of 3½ octaves may be produced by stopping the strings with the fingers, and the compass may be almost indefinitely extended upward by touching the strings lightly. The *viola,* or tenor violin, has four strings, tuned to C (in the second space of the base staff), D, A, G, reckoning upward; it is an octave higher than the violoncello and a fifth lower than the violin. The finest violins are by old makers and cannot be imitated, though the precise cause of their superiority has never been satisfactorily explained. The Cremona violins stand in the first rank, the celebrated makers being the Stradivari (Stradivarius), Amati and Guarneri (Guarnerius).

Violoncello, *vi'o lon chel'lo* or *vi'o lon sel'lo,* a powerful and expressive bow instrument, of the violin kind, held by the performer between the knees. It fills a place between the violin and the double bass. It has four strings, the two lowest covered with silver wire. It is tuned to C (on the second line below the bass staff), G, D, A, reckoning upward, and is an octave lower than the viola, or tenor violin. Its ordinary compass is from C, on the second line below, to A on the second space of the treble staff, but soloists frequently play an octave higher.

Vi'per, a name applied to various venomous serpents, characterized, like other members of the family, by having no teeth in the upper jaw, save the two hollow poison fangs. The *common viper,* or *adder,* the only venomous serpent which occurs in Great Britain, appears to be local in its distribution. It is generally of a brownish-yellow color, with zigzag markings and black triangular spots. Its bite is, as a rule, not fatal, but may induce pain, sickness and fever. The food consists of frogs, mice, birds and eggs. Among other vipers are the *black viper* of North America; the *death viper*, or *adder*, of Australia; the *horned viper*, or *asp*, and the *plumed viper* of North Africa. See ADDER; ASP.

Virchow, *veer' Ko*, RUDOLF (1821–1902), a German physician and pathologist, born in Pomerania. He studied medicine at Berlin and early became famous as a lecturer on pathological anatomy at Berlin University. His advanced liberal opinions during the movement of 1848 induced the government to deprive him, temporarily, of his appointment. In 1849 he accepted a chair at Wurzburg, where he remained seven years, at the end of which time he returned to Berlin as professor in the university and director of the pathological institute attached to it. In 1858 he published *Cellular Pathology*, in which he showed that pathological tissues are a collection of cells. Virchow rendered immense service to medical science by his discoveries in regard to inflammation, ulceration, tuberculosis and other diseases, and he has had great influence on the whole of modern medicine, including hospital reform and sanitary science. He was a voluminous writer, not only on scientific, but also on political subjects, and many of his works have been translated into the English and other European languages.

Vir'eo, a common name of a small family of birds, whose plumage is generally of a greenish shade. They are sometimes called greenlets, and about a dozen species are found in the United States. The *warbling vireo* is a plain little bird, with a charming song. The *yellow-throated* has a bright olive-green back and yellow throat and breast, fading off into pure white. One of the best-known species is the *red-eyed vireo*, which is larger than the others and has a white line over its red eye. All of them build deep, neatly constructed nests, which they ornament with lichens and other plants.

Virgil, *vur'jil*. See VERGIL.

Virgin Islands, a group of islands in the West Indian Archipelago and lying between Porto Rico and the Caribbees. Saint Croix, Saint John and Saint Thomas belong to Denmark. Vieques, or Crab Island, and Culebra belong to the United States. Tortola, Virgin, Gorda and Anegada belong to Great Britain. During McKinley's administration the United States tried to purchase the Danish islands, but failed. Culebra is one of the Porto Rican naval stations. Its government is administered as a department of Porto Rico. It has a population of a little over 700. These islands were discovered by Columbus on his second voyage. He gave the name *Saint Ursula* to the largest and called the others "the 11,000 Virgins" because they appeared innumerable. It is from this incident that the islands take their name.

Virginia, *vur jin' e a*, the OLD DOMINION, one of the South Atlantic states, bounded on the n. by West Virginia and Maryland, on the e. by Chesapeake Bay and the Atlantic Ocean, on the s. by North Carolina and Tennessee and on the w. by Kentucky. The state has a triangular shape, with the apex pointing northward. Its greatest length is the southern boundary line, 440 mi.; its greatest breadth from north to south is 192 mi.; its area is 42,627 sq. mi., of which 2365 sq. mi. are water. Population in 1910, 2,061,612.

SURFACE AND DRAINAGE. There are six natural divisions of Virginia, which differ greatly in scenery, soil and productions. Named in their order, from east to west, they are the tidewater country, middle Virginia, the Piedmont section, the Blue Ridge, the valley and Appalachia. The tidewater country consists of lowlands, extending about 100 miles westward from the ocean; it is divided by Chesapeake Bay and deeply cut by smaller bays, estuaries and rivers. Middle Virginia, extending from the tidewater to the eastern outlying spurs of the Appalachian system, is an undulating plain, increasing in elevation toward its western limits. The Piedmont section is a narrow belt, lying at the foot of the Blue Ridge. Its mountains and hills extend in every direction, enclosing picturesque valleys of every shape. The Blue Ridge, from 3 to 20 miles wide, broken by gorges and a series of beautiful peaks and expanding into an elevated plateau toward the south, is the principal range. The highest peak is Balsam Mountain, near the Tennessee line. The valley, between the Blue Ridge and the Alleghanies, is the garden spot of the state. The limestone formations in the central part of this valley contain several noted caverns, besides the famous Natural Bridge, considered one of the wonders of the world (See LURAY CAVERNS; NATURAL BRIDGE). Appalachia, the westernmost section, is a mountainous region, crossed by numerous narrow ranges, inclosing trough-like valleys.

The Potomac, which forms a portion of the boundary between Virginia and Maryland, drains the northern and eastern parts of the state. Its chief tributaries from Virginia are the South Branch and the Shenandoah. The important streams flowing into Chesapeake Bay, from the north southward, in their order, are the Rappahannock, the York and the James. The Roanoke flows into the state near the central point of the southern boundary and proceeds eastward for a number of miles and then returns to North Carolina. This, with its tributaries, drains the south central region. The southwestern part of the state is drained into the Tennessee, and the northwestern, into the Ohio. The chief streams flowing through this region are the Big Sandy, which forms a part of the boundary between Virginia and Kentucky, and the Great Kanawha. Many of the mountain streams are characterized by deep gorges and beautiful waterfalls.

CLIMATE. The climate is diversified according to the natural divisions of surface. In general, the state is free from intense heat and severe cold, although sudden changes are common in most localities. The mean annual temperature is 56°. The average annual rainfall is 43 inches. The climate is healthful the year round.

MINERAL RESOURCES. The Appalachian region contains valuable coal measures, and mines are worked in a number of places. While Virginia does not produce as much coal as some of her neighboring states, the output is nearly 5,000,000 tons a year. These mines yield bituminous coal of good quality, a large part of which is used in the manufacture of coke. There are also valuable deposits of brown hematite in this part of the state, and Virginia mines produce more of this iron ore than any others in the country. The Piedmont region contains slate quarries and other building stones. There are numerous mineral springs distributed over the state, many of which are valuable for their medicinal qualities.

AGRICULTURE. Over one-half the population of Virginia is engaged in agriculture. Corn, wheat, oats, hay and tobacco are the staple products. The Virginia Leaf, the finest tobacco raised in the United States, has a world-wide reputation for excellence. It thrives best in Middle Virginia and in the Piedmont section. In amount of tobacco produced, the state ranks third. The cotton crop amounts to about 10,000 bales a year. Other important productions are sweet potatoes, peanuts, apples, peaches, grapes and small fruits. Early vegetables and small fruits are sent in great quantities to the northern markets. Western Virginia is a famous grazing region.

MANUFACTURES. The iron mines, forests and tobacco and cotton fields of Virginia furnish abundant raw materials for manufactures. Its water power is extensive and has been developed largely at Richmond, Fredericksburg and Petersburg. Moreover, the best of steam coal is found in abundance in the Pocahontas field, while the navigable rivers and constantly increasing railway facilities encourage manufactures. The manufacture of tobacco is the leading industry. The manufactures of flouring and grist-mill products rank second. Other industries, in the order of their importance, are the manufactures of lumber and timber products, iron and steel products, cars and foundry and machine-shop products, the tanning of leather, and the manufacture of fertilizers and of textiles. Many people living along Chesapeake Bay are engaged in the oyster industry. Richmond is the leading manufacturing city.

TRANSPORTATION. There are over 4500 miles of railroad in operation. Some of the main lines are the Chesapeake & Ohio, the Southern, the Norfolk & Western, the Baltimore & Ohio and the Atlantic Coast Line. Coastwise steamers run regularly between Virginia ports and New York, Philadelphia, Baltimore and Boston, and a line of freighters plies between Newport News and Liverpool. Hampton Roads, at the mouth of the James River, is one of the finest harbors along the Atlantic coast. There is a large interstate traffic, both by rail and water. The exports consist of tobacco and its manufactured products, cotton, fruit, vegetables, coal and iron, and the imports are manufactured goods and food products.

GOVERNMENT. The legislature consists of a senate, which cannot exceed 40 members or have less than 33 members, and a house of delegates of not less than 90, or more than 100, members. The senators are elected for four years, and the delegates for two. The executive department consists of a governor, a lieutenant governor, a secretary of state, a treasurer and an auditor, each elected for four years; the auditor is chosen by the legislature, the others are elected by the people. Other state officers are appointed by the governor and confirmed by the senate, except division superintendents of schools, who are appointed by the board of education and confirmed by the senate. The state courts consist of a supreme court of appeals, of five judges, chosen by the legislature for twelve years, and circuit courts, which are held in 24 judicial districts, each of which has a judge, elected by the legislature for eight years. Lower courts are established for cities and towns.

EDUCATION. The school system is under the control of a superintendent of public instruction, elected by the people, and a state board of education of eight members, which consists of the governor, the superintendent of public instruction, the attorney-general, three representatives of higher institutions, chosen by the legislature, and two superintendents chosen by this group of six. The revenue for school purposes is provided almost wholly by local and state taxation. Separate schools are maintained for colored and white children, and the law requires that each district must have at least five months' school during the year. Notwithstanding the difficulties under which Virginia labored after the Civil War, the schools of the state have made continual advancement. The state maintains the University of Virginia, the Virginia Polytechnic Institute, the Virginia Military Institute, William and Mary College (the second oldest university in the United States), the Virginia Normal and Collegiate Institute, at Petersburg, and a state female normal school, at Farmville. Normal courses are given in William and Mary College and other institutions. Among the other higher institutions of learning are Washington and Lee University, Richmond College, Randolph-Macon College, Randolph-Macon College for Women, Sweet Briar Institute, Hollins Institute, Union Theological Seminary, the Episcopal Seminary at Alexandria, Virginia Union University and Hampton Normal and Agricultural Institute, the last devoted to the education of negro and indian youth.

INSTITUTIONS. The school for the deaf, dumb and blind is at Staunton, the hospitals for the insane whites are at Staunton, Williamsburg and Marion, and those for colored patients are at Petersburg. There is a soldiers' home at Richmond. The penal institutions include the state penitentiary, at Richmond, and the industrial reform school for boys, at Laurel.

CITIES. The chief cities are Richmond, the capital; Norfolk, Petersburg, Roanoke, Newport News, Lynchburg, Portsmouth and Danville, each of which is described under its title.

HISTORY. The shores of Virginia were probably first visited by Sebastian Cabot in 1498, but no attempt at settlement was made until late in the following century, when Sir Walter Raleigh sent out several expeditions without success. The London Company was formed in 1606, and in the following spring a colony was established at Jamestown. Its leading spirit was Captain John Smith, whose energy and ability saved the settlement from early destruction by famine and indian attacks. In 1610 Lord Delaware was sent to the colony as governor, and under his wise administration the settlement prospered. The year 1619 witnessed the introduction of negro slavery by Dutch traders, as well as the establishment of the first representative assembly in America. From this time forward many immigrants, driven from England by the persecution of the Puritans, arrived in Virginia; but at the outbreak of the Puritan revolution, in 1642, William Berkeley, a stanch royalist, became governor and promptly suppressed the rebellious spirit. At this time an influx of royalists also began, which led to serious opposition to the Cromwell régime in England and to the joyful recognition of the return of the Stuarts to the throne. However, within the next few years discontent with economic conditions and the policy of the administration led to a serious insurrection, known as Bacon's Rebellion (See BACON'S REBELLION), in 1676.

The eighteenth century in Virginia was marked by remarkable development, especially in the westward districts of the colony. During the French and Indian Wars, Virginia took an exceptionally prominent part, but she was also a leader in the resistance to Parliamentary taxation, her Assembly passing some of the earliest and most important measures of the period. Virginia also furnished some of the most conspicuous figures of the time, such as Washington, Jefferson, Patrick Henry, the Lees and Madison. The state took a prominent part in the Revolution, and the war ended on Virginia soil, in the surrender of Cornwallis. During the early years of the Republic, the state was stanchly Anti-Federalist (See KENTUCKY AND VIRGINIA RESOLUTIONS); but eight out of the first nine terms as president were filled by Virginians.

The state was at first favorable to the liberation of the slaves, but under the influence of states' rights theories and of agricultural conditions, she finally adhered to the policies of the lower South, and in the Civil War Virginia not only furnished the ablest generals in the Confederate armies, but became the battle ground of the great struggle. She at first opposed secession, but finally passed the resolution, April 17, and from that time forward the state was a continuous fighting ground between the two armies, many of the most important actions of the war, including Lee's surrender at Appomattox, taking place within its borders. A new constitution, framed in 1863, was adopted, but an amendment allowing negro suffrage was rejected in 1868, and the state was not readmitted until 1870. In 1902 a constitutional provision was adopted, limiting suffrage. Since the Civil War the state has been almost continuously Democratic in both state and national politics. Consult Cooke's *Virginia*, in the American Commonwealths Series.

Virginia, MINN., a city of Saint Louis co., on the Great Northern, the Duluth & Iron Range and other railroads, 54 mi. n. n. w. of Duluth. The surrounding district yields much iron, and the interests of Virginia are chiefly connected with iron industries. Population in 1910, 10,473.

Virginia, UNIVERSITY OF, an institution of higher learning, located near Charlottesville, Va., in 1819. It maintains the following departments: the college, engineering, law, medicine and agriculture. As at present organized, the university comprises twenty-eight independent schools, whose courses are elective under the group system. The university was opened for matriculation March 7, 1825. Its annual income is $270,000, $75,000 being from the state and the remainder from fees and endowment funds. It is under the government of a board of visitors, nine in number, appointed by the governor of the state and ratified by the state senate. The faculty and teaching staff include about 100 members, and there are over 800 students. The library contains about 75,000 volumes. This university was founded by the State of Virginia, through the influence of Thomas Jefferson, in 1819, and it owes much of its efficiency to his interest and care. In October, 1903, the visitors created the office of president, and in June, 1904, Edwin Anderson Alderman was elected the first president of the university.

Virginia City, NEV., the county-seat of Storey co., 52 mi. s. e. of Reno, on the Virginia & Truckee railroad. The city is on an elevation of about 7800 feet, noted for its extensive mineral deposits. The famous Comstock lode was discovered in 1859, and the city grew up around it. The principal buildings are the courthouse and the Miners' Union Library. The settlement was first known as Ophir and later was called Silver City. It received its present name from James Fenimore, an early settler, who was familiarly known as "Old Virginia." The city was incorporated in 1864. The population in 1880 was 10,917, and the decrease has been mostly due to the fall in the price of silver. Population in 1910, 2244.

177

Virginia Creep'er, an American vine, known as *American ivy*, or *woodbine*, often grown on the fronts of houses in Great Britain and continental Europe, as an ornamental creeper. The tendrils terminate in a peculiar kind of sucker, and the autumn foliage is rich in varied colors of light and dark green, brown, red and yellow. By its five leaflets, it may be distinguished from poison ivy, which has but three.

Virginia Resolutions. See KENTUCKY AND VIRGINIA RESOLUTIONS.

Virginius, *vur jin'e us,* **Mas'sacre,** THE. The *Virginius* was an American merchantman, commanded by an American, which was carrying arms, ammunition and men to the aid of the Cuban insurgents, in October, 1873. It was captured by a Spanish war ship and taken to Santiago. There four Cuban leaders, who were found on board, were immediately executed, and some days later Captain Frye, thirty-six members of the crew and sixteen passengers were executed. The affair created the greatest indignation in the United States, but war was averted by negotiation. The *Virginius* and the survivors of her passengers and crew were released and started for New York City. The boat was overtaken by a storm and was abandoned off Cape Fear.

Virgo, *vur'go,* (the virgin), the sixth sign of the zodiac, entered by the sun about August 20. In ancient astrology, the symbol (♍) was supposed to represent a wing.

Vi'rus, a term rather loosely used to indicate the product of a contagious disease, by which the disease is communicated from one person to another. Physicians usually restrict the term to such diseases as scarlet fever and measles, while popularly it is the name of the lymph used in vaccination. See ANTITOXIN; GERM THEORY OF DISEASE.

Vise, a tool for holding tight, material upon which work is being done, especially carpentry or smithing. A vise has two jaws, a handle, a center piece and a shank, or plate, by which it is fastened to the bench. The movable jaw is worked by a screw or a lever, which draws it against the fixed jaw with such force as to hold the object firmly in position. Vises are used by blacksmiths, carpenters, machinists and jewelers. (See illustration on next page.)

Vish'nu, the second of the three great Hindu gods, by his special worshipers considered to be the greatest. In the early Vedas he was not regarded as the most exalted deity, but this rank was accorded to him by the later writers. The myths relating to Vishnu are characterized by the idea that whenever a great physical or moral disorder affected the world, Vishnu descended to set it right. He is generally represented as having four hands, in which he holds a conchshell, blown in battle; a disk, the symbol of su-

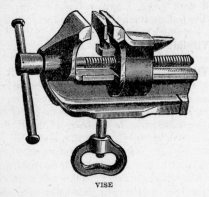

VISE

preme power; a mace, the emblem of punishment, and a lotus, the sign of the creative power. Often he is shown as riding on a being, half man and half bird. See BRAHMA; SIVA.

Visible Speech, a term applied by Prof. A. Melville Bell, its inventor, to a system of alphabetical characters, designed to represent every possible articulate utterance of the organs of speech. The system is based on an exhaustive classification of the possible actions of the speech organs, each organ and every mode of action having its appropriate symbol. It is said that this invention is of great utility in teaching the deaf and dumb to comprehend spoken words and in enabling learners of foreign languages to acquire their pronunciation from books.

Visigoths, *viz'e goths.* See GOTHS.

Vision, *vizh'un,* the act of seeing. As an optical instrument, the eye closely resembles a

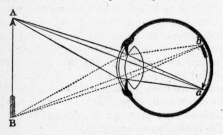

camera, the cornea and crystalline lens corresponding to the lens of a camera, and the retina corresponding to the screen (See EYE; CAMERA). The rods and cones of the retina are sensitive only to the light, and their great number and vari-

ety enable the perfect eye to respond to light waves producing all colors (See LIGHT; COLOR). Rays of light entering the eye through the pupil are refracted, and they cross just back of the lens, the rays from A coming to a focus on the retina at a, and those at B coming to a focus at b, thus forming an inverted image on the retina (See LENS, subhead *Double Convex Lens*). After carefully cutting away the sclerotic coat from around the optic nerve of an eye taken from one of the lower animals, exposing the retina over an area about the size of a dime, and then holding the eye towards a lighted lamp in a darkened room, an observer can plainly see an image of the lamp inverted on the retina.

PHYSIOLOGY OF VISION. The foregoing description deals with vision purely from the physical point of view, and it speaks of the eye purely as an optical instrument, but vision also includes physiological and mental action. While the image can fall on the retina of a dead eye, as well as on that of a living one, unless life stimulates the optic nerve to action, there is no vision. This action is physiological, and in order to understand it, a knowledge of the structure of the optic nerve is necessary.

The sensory fibers of the optic nerve originate in the optic centers of the brain. These fibers meet and cross at the base of the brain, forming the *optic commissure,* from which the optic nerves extend to each eye. In the commissure, half of the fibers cross, so that each optic nerve consists of half of the fibers from its own optic center and half of the fibers from the optic center on the opposite side of the brain. On reaching the eye, these fibers are so distributed that those from the right optic center form the right half of the retina in each eye, and those from the left center form the left half. When the rods and cones are stimulated, impulses are transmitted along the optic nerves and optic tracks to the centers of unconscious sight in the brain. From these centers, other nerves extend to the centers of vision, and when the stimuli are strong enough to cause impulses to be transmitted to these centers, the person becomes conscious of them and sees the object. This is completed vision, and the image is retained in memory for a greater or less length of time, depending upon the strength of the stimuli and the mental condition at the time the vision occurs (See MEMORY). Consciousness and memory are mental activities, so that vision depends upon mental, as well as physical action.

Vis'tula, a river of Europe, which rises in eastern Silesia, flows northeast, then north, northwest, and again northeast, emptying into the Frisches Haff and the Baltic Sea through several arms. For a part of its length, it forms the boundary between Galicia and Russian Poland. Among the cities on its banks are Cracow, Warsaw and Danzig. The river is about 630 miles in length, and it is navigable for a considerable part of this distance.

Vi'tascope. See KINETOSCOPE.

Viti, *ve'te,* **Islands.** See FIJI ISLANDS.

Vit'riol, OIL OF, the common name of strong sulphuric acid. See SULPHURIC ACID.

Viv'isec'tion, the practice of operating with the knife upon living animals, for the purpose of learning some fact in anatomy or something relating to health or disease, which cannot be otherwise investigated. It is also practiced in schools, in order to illustrate previously known facts, and to enable students to acquire skill in operating. Vivisection for the latter purpose is generally condemned in the United States, but it is carried on in the veterinary colleges in France. Though the term vivisection strictly is applicable to cutting operations only, it is generally employed for all scientific experiments performed on living animals, whether they consist of cutting operations, the compression of parts by ligatures, the administration of poisons, the inoculation of disease, the subjection to special conditions of food, temperature or respiration, or the action of drugs and medicines.

Vladivostok, *vlah'dye vohs tohk',* a Russian port on the Pacific, the capital of the Maritime Province of Siberia. It is a well-built town and has a safe, commodious harbor, which is blocked by ice but three months of the year. Its strong fortifications and the fact that it is a terminus of the Trans-Siberian railway make it of great importance. Population in 1910, 91,464.

Vocational Training, training for some special pursuit in life, not including, however, professional or higher technical training. The vast majority of children never pass beyond the elementary grades in school. The training they receive is along cultural lines, and they are in no way fitted for home making or for earning a livelihood in agriculture, commerce, or the industries. To remedy this, the attempt is being made to determine, during the latter years of school life, the field of activity for which the youth is fitted, and continue his education along practical lines in the chosen direction, so as to render him an efficient worker. To provide for this further training, special schools are being established, where vocational instruction can be imparted by teachers who have, in addition to a liberal education, experience and skill in the industry they attempt to teach. The value of this new system of education is self-evident. It is an intelligent response to the needs of our social and economic conditions. See CONTINUATION SCHOOLS.

Voice, the audible sound produced in the larynx of those animals which possess that organ. In man, it is produced by the true vocal cords, which consist of two elastic folds of mucous membrane, so attached to the cartilages of the larynx and to muscles, that they may be stretched or relaxed and otherwise altered, so as to modify the sounds produced by their vibration. The range of voice depends upon the amount of tension which the cords can undergo; the higher the note produced, the greater the tension of the cords. In ordinary speaking, the notes have nearly all the same pitch, and the variety of the sounds is due rather to articulation in the mouth than to definite movements of the glottis and vocal cords. A passage from high to low notes, without intervals, or from low to high notes, is exemplified in crying and howling, both in man and in lower animals. The true musical tones have vibrations corresponding in relative proportions to the notes of the musical scale. The male voice is classed as tenor and bass, and the female as soprano and contralto. The lowest female note is about an octave or so higher than the lowest note of the male voice, and the female's highest note is about an octave above that of the male. The compass of both voices taken together is about four octaves. The chief difference between male and female voices, besides that of pitch, is in the quality, or timbre. The difference of pitch is due to the length of the vocal cords, while the difference in timbre appears to result from differences in the nature and extent of the walls and cavity of the larynx, the throat and the mouth. A boy's voice is either alto or soprano, because the vocal cords are only about two-thirds as long as a man's, and the angle of the thyroid cartilage is no greater than that in the female. See LARYNX.

Vo'lapük, the name given to a universal language, invented about 1879 by Johann Martin Schleyer, of Constance, after twenty years' labor. The name, which means *world speech,* is based on the English *world* and *speak.* In structure the language is simple and extremely regular, and the orthography is entirely phonetic, the words being pronounced as they are written. The study of Volapük has made some progress; there are a number of periodicals written in it, and many associations are devoted to its dissemination.

Volca'no, a mountain that has an opening, through which heated matter is thrown from the interior. The parts of a volcano are the base, the cone, the crater and the vent, or chimney. The base comprises the walls of the mountain and often blends with the cone so completely that no line of separation can be discovered. The term *cone* is usually applied to the upper and more recently formed portion of the volcano. In its summit is the opening called the *crater*. Leading from the crater down into the interior of the mountain is the *vent*, or *chimney*.

The form of the volcano depends quite largely upon the material thrown out. If this is ashes or thick viscid lava, that does not flow rapidly, the slopes of the mountain are steep and may be quite regular, as in the case of Vesuvius, Aetna and many of the volcanoes of the Andes. If the material is of molten lava, that flows freely, a low, flat mountain, with gentle slopes, is formed. The volcanoes of Hawaii are the best illustrations of this type. In these volcanoes the flow of lava seldom takes place through an opening at the summit, but an outlet is forced through one or more crevices in the sides of the mountain. The crater is large and shallow and contains numerous vents, surrounded by small cones. Between these may also be found pools of molten lava.

In size, volcanoes vary from low mountains, comparatively small, like those in the vicinity of the Mediterranean, to great peaks, whose summits are from 17,000 to 20,000 feet above the sea, as is seen in the volcanoes of the Andes and the highest peaks of the Rocky Mountains, which are extinct volcanoes.

Volcanoes are classified as active, dormant and extinct. *Active* volcanoes are those either in continuous or frequent action. *Dormant* volcanoes are those which are active only at long intervals, and *extinct* volcanoes are those which have ceased action altogether. There is, however, no absolute division, as a volcano may pass from one class into another without warning, that is, a dormant or extinct volcano may become active, and an active volcano may become extinct.

The nature of the eruption is determined by the character of the material thrown out, and its violence is usually proportional to the length of time the mountain has been quiet. Volcanoes accustomed to throw out molten lava seldom eject ashes in large quantities. At the beginning, the lava flows rapidly, but as it cools it crusts over and flows more and more slowly until its motion

ceases. The flow destroys everything in the path of the fiery stream, and the eruption often causes great devastation, suffering and loss of life. Some eruptions are characterized only by solid matter and steam. The solid matter is in the form of masses of rock, gravel, sand and dust, or ashes. These rise to a great height and are often carried through the atmosphere for many miles.

The cause of volcanic action is not well understood; but it is generally believed to be the contact of water with highly heated portions of the earth's interior. The violence of the action is supposed to be due to the expansive force of steam that has suddenly been released from great pressure. The steam forces out the ashes. The flow of lava is probably caused by its being squeezed into the fissure by the movements of the earth's crust. An eruption is usually preceded by an increase in temperature of the land at the base and on the sides of the mountain, the drying up of springs and wells and frequently by local earthquakes. The most disastrous eruptions, as affecting loss of life, were the eruption of Vesuvius, 79 A. D.; Krakatoa, in 1883, and Mont Pelee, on the island of Martinique, in 1902. At this eruption over thirty thousand people lost their lives within a few hours. See ETNA; KRAKATOA; PELEE, MONT; VESUVIUS. Consult Shaler's *Aspects of the Earth*, Redway's *Physical Geography*, Geikie's *Text Book of Geology*, Bonney's *Volcanoes* and Russell's *Volcanoes of North America*.

Volcano Islands, three small islands in the Pacific Ocean, since 1891 a part of Japan. They are also known as the Magellan Archipelago and in Japanese are called Kwazan-retto (meaning a series of volcanic islands). The islands rise to a maximum altitude of 3021 feet in the extreme south. Arzobispo, an island to the north, is sometimes included in the group. The islands are uninhabited.

Vole, a genus of rodents belonging to the same family as the lemmings, the muskrats and several related genera, distributed over Europe and North America. The *water vole* is about the same size as the brown rat, and it is often called a rat. It has dark brown or black fur, a tail about half the length of the body, and very strong hind feet, with five rounded pads on the lower surfaces. It burrows by the banks of streams and feeds for the most part on vegetable food. The *field vole*, or *short-tailed field mouse*, is about the size of a common mouse, but the body is stouter and the tail shorter. It has brownish-gray fur; its hind feet have six pads. It lives in fields and woods, feeds on vegetable food, is very prolific and often does much dam-

FIELD VOLE

age. The *bank vole* is like the field vole, but has a rusty-colored back, larger ears and a longer tail.

Vol'ga, the largest river in Europe. It rises near the Valdai Hills, in the northwestern part of Russia, and flows in a circuitous course eastward and then southward, entering the Caspian Sea through a broad delta, a few miles below Astrakhan. The length of the river is about 2200 miles, and it is navigable for nearly its entire course. The chief tributaries from the north and east are the Oka, the Sura and the Sarpa, and from the west, the Tvertsa, the Mologa, the Sheksna, the Kostroma, the Vetluga, the Kama and the Samara. At ordinary stages, the width of the river varies from 420 feet to 700 feet and even 2400 feet, at Nijni Novgorod. During the spring it is liable to overflow, when its width varies from $1\frac{1}{4}$ to 3 miles. By means of canals the Volga is connected with the Black, the Baltic and the White seas, and with other important navigable rivers, so that it constitutes one of the most important inland waterways of Europe.

Volt, the unit employed in measuring electric pressure, such a pressure as will produce a flow of one ampere per second against a resistance of one ohm.

Volta, *vohl'ta,* ALESSANDRO (1745–1827), an Italian natural philosopher, born at Como. Two treatises, in which he gave a description of a new electrical machine, laid the foundation of his fame. He was successively professor of physics at the gymnasium in Como and in the University of Pavia, where he invented the electrophorus and the electroscope. He also devised several other electrical appliances, and in 1800 he invented the voltaic pile (See ELECTRIC BATTERY). In 1810 he was created a senator of Italy, with the title of count, and later he was made director of the philosophical faculty of Padua.

Volta'ic Cell or **Voltaic Battery.** See ELECTRIC BATTERY; ELECTRICITY, subhead *Voltaic Electricity.*

Voltaic Pile, Volta's arrangement for producing a current of electricity, consisting of a pile of alternate disks of two dissimilar metals. as copper and zinc, zinc and silver, zinc and platinum, separated by pieces of flannel or pasteboard, moistened with salt water or with water acidulated with sulphuric acid. See ELECTRIC BATTERY.

Voltaire, *vol tair',* the assumed name of Jean François Marie Arouet (1694–1778), a French writer and philosopher, born at Paris. His father was a notary, and he was destined for the legal profession, but abandoned the law for letters. In 1718 a tragedy named *Oedipus* was brought out by him and was most enthusiastically received. He now became a fashionable poet and resided mainly at Paris, leading a life of gaiety and pleasure in the most brilliant society. In 1726 he was imprisoned in the Bastille, for sending a challenge to the Chevalier Rohan, by whom he had been insulted, but he was liberated within a month and allowed to go to England. Here he resided till 1729, in friendship with some of the chief literary men of the day, and he acquired a good knowledge of English literature. His *Henriade,* an epic celebrating the exploits of Henry IV of France, was completed and published by subscription in England, but was not permitted in France.

After his return to France, he lived chiefly at Paris till 1734. During this period he raised himself from very moderate circumstances to a condition of affluence by successful monetary speculations. From 1734 to 1749 he resided with Madame du Châtelet at Cirey, in Lorraine, and he produced many plays during this period. After the death of Madame du Châtelet, Voltaire accepted the oft-repeated invitations of Frederick the Great to come and live at his court, at Potsdam. Here he was received with great honor, but a series of disagreements with the king ended in Voltaire's retirement from the Prussian court in 1753. After some unsettled years he fixed his residence with his niece, Madame Denis, at Ferney, near the boundary of the Republic of Geneva, and here he received a constant succession of distinguished visitors and maintained a correspondence which included in its range most of the crowned heads of Europe. In February, 1778, he went to Paris, where he was received with enthusiasm by all classes. But the excitement of the occasion hastened his death.

Voltaire's works embrace almost every branch of literature—poetry, the drama, romance, history, philosophy and even science. Hatred of fanaticism and superstition was his chief characteristic, and nearly all his works are strongly animated by a spirit of hostility to the priests and the religion they represented. He was one of the foremost of that band of writers whose revolt against conventions, openly and most forcefully expressed, was preparing the way for the French Revolution. It is the commonly accepted opinion that he was an atheist, but this has never been proved. Voltaire's literary fame chiefly rests on his philosophical novels, *Zadig, Candide, L'Ingénu*; his histories, *The Age of Louis XIV, The History of Charles XII*; his correspondence, and more than all, perhaps, on his poetical epistles, satires and occasional light poems, all of which exhibit wit, gaiety, vivacity and grace.

Volt′me′ter, an instrument for measuring the pressure of an electric current. It consists of a permanent steel horseshoe magnet, with a piece of soft iron attached to each pole. Between the poles, a soft iron cylinder is suspended, so that it can rotate vertically. Around this cylinder is a light rectangular frame of copper, wound with a coil of insulated wire. Spiral springs are attached at each end of this frame, and a needle, which moves over a graduated dial, is attached to the upper end of the axis. When an electric current passes through the coil or wire, it causes the copper frame to turn upon its axis. The springs furnish an amount of resistance that must be overcome by the current, and the position of the needle on the dial indicates the pressure. Voltmeters are used with dynamo electric machines. See VOLT.

Volunteers′, citizens who, of their own accord, offer the state their services in a military capacity. The oldest volunteer force in Great Britain is the Honorable Artillery Company of the city of London, which received its charter of incorporation from Henry VIII. In case of a war of magnitude, the United States has always relied on its volunteer soldiery. During the Civil War, including the re-enlistments, there were 2,656,533 union men in the field—the great body of whom were volunteers. They were paid by the United States, but the states appointed field and line officers. See ARMY.

Volunteers of America, formerly a branch of the Salvation Army in America. The society was chartered in 1883 under Ballington Booth, son of Gen. William Booth, and in 1896 it severed its connection with the Salvation Army and began an independent existence, with Ballington Booth and his wife, Maud Ballington Booth, as leaders. There are now about 675 corps, or societies, in the United States, and about 2,200 officers. Christian literature is distributed in state prisons, hospitals, soldiers' homes and many other public places. The Volunteers also conduct sewing classes and boys' fresh-air camps, and they furnish hospital nurses and Christmas dinners and perform many other worthy acts.

Vom′iting, the forcible expulsion of matter from the stomach, through the oesophagus, or gullet. It is not a disease in itself, but it is a symptom common to numerous diseases, or as an accompaniment of extreme nervous sensitiveness. The treatment of vomiting depends upon its cause and upon the disease, if any, which accompanies it. Lying down, the application of mustard to the pit of the stomach, small doses of soda, ice, whisky or coffee will sometimes relieve it. While sudden and violent vomiting in a healthy person is an indication of some poisonous substance in the stomach, yet very frequently vomiting is nature's method of relieving an overloaded stomach.

Von Holst, *hohlst′*, HERMANN EDUARD. See HOLST, HERMANN EDUARD VON.

Vor′hees, DANIEL WOLSEY (1827–1897), an American politician, born in Butler County, Ohio, educated at De Pauw University and admitted to the bar. He began his practice at Covington, Ind., in 1851, soon entered politics and became noted as a Democratic stump speaker. He was elected to Congress in 1861, served three terms and was again elected in 1869, serving until 1875. Two years later Vorhees succeeded Oliver P. Morton as United States senator and was re-elected and served continuously until 1897, being throughout his congressional career an acknowledged leader of the Democratic party.

Voronezh, *vo ro′nyezh*, a city of Russia, situated on the Voronezh River, near its confluence with the Don, 130 mi. e. of Kursk. It is an important railway center and has manufactures of woolen and linen goods, soap, vitriol and leather. Its trade is also large. The city is of interest historically, because it was here that Peter the Great began the construction of his fleet for the Black Sea. Population in 1910, 79,000.

Vorticella, *vor′te sel′la*, or **Bell Animalcule,** a genus of infusorians, which have a bell-shaped disk, or head, the opening of which is surrounded by cilia which are constantly in rapid motion, and which are used to draw in particles of food. The head is fixed by a stem, which is capable of being coiled in a spiral form. The species are very numerous in fresh water and are generally microscopic.

Vosges, *vohzh*, **Mountains,** a chain of mountains about 100 mi. long, extending in a north-northeast direction along the frontiers of France and Alsace, their course being nearly parallel with that of the Rhine. They are separated from the Jura Mountains by the valley of the Doubs on the south. The Vosges are composed chiefly of granite and are covered with forests of pine and beech to a height of about 3600 feet, beyond which their summits are covered with grass. Most of the summits are rounded in form. The highest peak is Ballon de Guebwiller, 4067 feet. These mountains contain considerable silver, copper, lead and coal and large quantities of rock salt.

Voss, *johs*, JOHANN HEINRICH (1751–1826), a German poet and translator. Between 1785 and 1802 he published several volumes of original poems, the best of which is the idyl *Luise*. As a translator Voss exhibited great skill in the handling of meters, and a wonderful command of language. Among his translations, that of Homer's works is undoubtedly the greatest, being the classical German version of these great epics. A translation of Shakespeare, which he undertook with his sons, was less successful.

Vote. See ELECTION; BALLOT.

Voting Machine, a machine for automatically registering and counting votes. Several different patterns of voting machines have been in more or less general use in large cities for ten years, the first trial being given in New York City in 1892. All, however, have the same advantages, namely, avoidance of repeating of votes, absolute secrecy, simplicity, rapidity of registration and counting, and cheapness. The principle upon which all work is much the same. The voter enters the booth, and not till all the curtains are closed will the machine register his vote. The names of the candidates are arranged in order, either by parties or alphabetically. The voter can either vote a straight ticket or can vote for individual candidates. In the former case, either by the use of a key or by means of a lever, he registers a vote and thus locks the mechanism, so that he cannot vote further, unless, by turning back the lever, he cancels his first vote. If he wishes to split the ticket, he turns a lever or key for one candidate for each office, and he is prevented thereby from voting for any other candidate for any office. As he leaves the booth, by opening the curtains or doors at the exit he resets the machine for the next voter. Each vote cast for each office or for a straight ticket is registered by a patent device on a slip of paper, so that as soon as the last vote is cast, the final returns are ready to be announced. Many states have authorized the use of voting machines at the option of the local authorities, but none has yet officially adopted the appliance.

Vow'el, a simple articulated sound, which is produced merely by the voice proceeding from the larynx, modified by a greater or less elevation or depression, expansion or contraction, of the tongue, and contraction or expansion of the lips. The vowel sounds of the English alphabet are imperfectly represented by five letters, *a, e, i, o, u* (and sometimes *w* and *y*). Vowels are distinguished from consonants, in that they result from an open position of the vocal organs, while consonants are the result of an opening or shutting action of the organs; thus the former may be pronounced by themselves, while consonants require to be sounded with the aid of a vowel.

Vul'can, called by the Greeks Hephaestus, in classical mythology, the god who presided over fire and the working of metals, and who patronized handicraftsmen of every kind. He was the son of Jupiter and Juno, but, unlike the other gods, he was seriously lame. By some writers he was said to have been born lame, and for that reason he was believed to have been thrown by his mother from Olympus; but by others his lameness is attributed to his having been thrown from Olympus by Jupiter, for interfering in Juno's behalf in a quarrel between her and Jupiter.

Vul'gate, the Latin translation of the Bible, which has, in the Roman Catholic Church, official authority, and which the Council of Trent, in its fourth session, on May 27, 1546, declared "shall be held as authentic in all public lectures, disputations, sermons and expositions; and that no one shall presume to reject it under any pretense whatsoever." Even in the early period of the Church, a Latin translation of the Old Testament existed, made not from the Hebrew, but from the Septuagint. Saint Jerome found that this translation was not always accurate, and between 385 and 405 A. D. he made a new Latin translation from the Hebrew, with the aid of the best Greek translations. This at first met with the greatest opposition, as the Septuagint was regarded as an inspired translation, and any deviation from it was considered sac-

rilegious. Before his death Jerome had justi-
fied himself and proved the purity of his inten-
tions, but it was not until the ninth century that
his version came to be used throughout the
Church and not until centuries later that it was
authorized. The version now in use is the edition published by Clement VIII in 1592.

Vul′ture, the common name for a class of
birds of prey, characterized by necks destitute
of feathers and by elongated beaks, with curved
upper mandibles. Their talons are not relatively
strong, and in tearing their prey they make more
use of their beaks than of their claws. Vultures
are usually of a cowardly disposition and live
chiefly on dead and decaying animal matter.
They have a marvelous power of vision, which
enables them, while flying high in the air, to
detect a dead animal quickly. Upon this they descend and gorge themselves till they can scarcely
fly, and if disturbed they usually vomit before
trying to escape. They are, however, valuable
scavengers in all warm and tropical countries.
The California vulture has a long, flat, orange-
colored head and dull black plumage, with a
grayish wing band. It builds a loose nest of
sticks, in a hollow in a tree or cliff, and lays one
round, greenish-white egg. The Egyptian species, called "Pharaoh's hen," is found in the
countries bordering the Mediterranean. See
CONDOR; TURKEY BUZZARD.

VULTURES
1, Griffin; 2, Pondicherry

W, the twenty-third letter of the English alphabet. It is formed, as its name indicates, by doubling the *u* or *v*, and before it appeared as a separate character in English its sound was sometimes represented by *uu* or *vv*. At the end of words or syllables it is either silent, as in *low*, or it modifies the preceding vowel, as in *new*, *how*, having then the power of a vowel.

Wabash, *waw'bash*, a river rising in the western part of Ohio, flowing northwestward, westward and then southward. It crosses Indiana, in the latter part of its course forms a part of the boundary between Indiana and Illinois, and enters the Ohio about 30 miles below Evansville, Ind. Its length is 550 miles, and it is navigable during high water as far as Lafayette, Ind., and in ordinary stages to Covington. Its chief tributary is the White River. Some of the principal towns on its banks are Wabash, Peru, Logansport, Lafayette, Covington, Terre Haute and Vincennes.

Wabash, IND., the county-seat of Wabash co., 90 mi. n. e. of Indianapolis, on the Wabash River and on the Cleveland, Cincinnati, Chicago & Saint Louis and the Wabash railroads. It is in an agricultural and stock-raising region and it also contains railroad shops, bridge and iron works, carriage factories, woolen and lumber mills and various other factories. The city has three parks, a public library and a school library. Wabash was settled and incorporated in 1837, and it was chartered as a city in 1866. Population, 1910, 8687.

Wacht Am Rhein, DIE (the watch on the Rhine), a German patriotic song. The words were written by Max Schneckenburger in 1840, when the left bank of the Rhine seemed in danger of falling into the hands of France. The music by Karl Wilhelm was composed in 1854.

Wa'co, TEX., the county-seat of McLennan co., 238 mi. n. w. of Galveston, on the Brazos River and on the Texas Central, the Missouri Kansas & Texas, the Saint Louis Southwestern and several other railroads. The city is reg-ularly laid out, with the residence section on the more elevated region above the river. Many artesian wells furnish water, which contains medicinal properties that have made the city a popular health resort. Baylor University is located here, and the city also has the Paul Quinn College, the Texas Christian University, Saint Basil's College, Douglas-Shuler School, the Academy of Sacred Heart and two business colleges. Other important features are the Waco Natatorium, the Federal building, the courthouse, the Masonic Temple and several large bridges across the river. The city has a number of important banks. The surrounding region is agricultural, producing grain, cotton and live stock, and the city contains saddlery and harness works, grain elevators, flour mills, bottling works, manufactures of cotton products and various other establishments. Waco was laid out in 1849 and was incorporated the next year. Population in 1910, 26,425.

Wadai, *wah di'*, a native state in the central part of Africa, and now a French protectorate. It borders upon Lake Tchad on the north and upon an extension of the French Kongo on the south, known as Upper Ubangui. The boundaries are indefinite. The surface is mostly of a desert character, but there are oases scattered through the region, and in some sections are fertile tracts covered with forests. The population, estimated at 2,000,000 is composed chiefly of negroes and Arabs, who are Mohammedans. The capital is Abeshr, and is connected with Bengeazi by caravan route.

Wade, BENJAMIN FRANKLIN (1800–1878), an American statesman, born near Springfield, Mass. In 1821 he removed to Ohio, was admitted to the bar and began the practice of law as a partner of Joshua R. Giddings. In 1837 he was elected state senator, and in 1847 he was appointed judge of the third judicial district of Ohio. In 1851 he was elected United States senator as a Whig and was reëlected by the Republicans in 1857 and again in 1863. In the Senate he constantly opposed slavery, voted to repeal the Fugitive Slave Law and worked against the Kansas-Nebraska Bill. During and after the Civil War, he was one of the most radical Republicans in his view of reconstruction; he was joint author of the Wade-Davis Bill, which President Lincoln vetoed, and he consistently opposed President Johnson's policy.

Wadsworth, *wahds'wurth,* JAMES SAMUEL (1807–1864), an American soldier, born at Geneseo, N. Y. He studied at Hamilton College and at Harvard and Yale, studied law under Daniel Webster and other noted lawyers and was admitted to the bar in 1833. However, he never practiced, devoting himself to the management of the large family estates. In 1861, as a member of the peace convention, he opposed a compromise granting important concessions to the South, and after the outbreak of the war he entered the Federal service, as major on the staff of General McDowell. He fought at Bull Run, Fredericksburg, Chancellorsville and Gettysburg, taking a conspicuous part in all of these battles and being promoted, meantime, to the rank of brigadier general. In December, 1862, he was made military governor of Washington, and in the same year he was the candidate of the Republicans for governor of New York, but was defeated by Horatio Seymour. He was mortally wounded in the Battle of the Wilderness. He was brevetted major general of volunteers in May, 1864.

Wager, *wa'jur,* a bet, or something staked on the result of a contest or on the decision of some unsettled question. The party whose opinion proves to be correct receives what has been staked by both. By statutes of England, Scotland and the United States, all contracts or agreements, whether oral or in writing, depending on wagers, are null and void, and money due thereon cannot be recovered in any court of law. A wager is therefore called a *debt of honor,* since it cannot be collected except through the good faith of the parties.

Wages, *way'jez,* in political economy, the return to labor from production, that is, the share of a product which goes to the labor employed in production. It is distinguished from *rent,* which is the share of the product returned to landowners by virtue of the use of land in production, and *interest,* the share of production returned to capital. The term *wages* is commonly used in a much more restricted sense, that is, to include only the amount paid to hired labor, or, in a still narrower sense, to refer to the remuneration of those engaged in manual labor, as distinguished from the professional classes. In economics,

however, no such distinctions are recognized. In the compilation of statistics and in general economic reasoning, a distinction is made between so-called *nominal wages* and *real wages,* the former being the wages expressed in money or as an absolute quantity, the latter, in terms of purchasing power.

The earliest theory in regard to the nature and origin of wages was that of the so-called physiocrats of France, who held that the return to labor from production always tended to the level at which laborers would consent to live, owing to the tendency of population always to press upon the means of subsistence. This theory, though now generally discarded, has been vigorously upheld by the modern socialists, who find in it one of their chief arguments for the overturning of the present social order. A more recent theory is that known as the *wages fund theory,* which had the support of such distinguished economists as John Stuart Mill, McCulloch and, by inference, Ricardo. These economists declared that wages are advanced from capital; that, therefore, total wages must be limited by the amount of capital existing, or rather by that part of capital which is devoted to the payment of labor. This so-called *wages fund* being limited, the average rate of wages depended upon the number of laborers competing. But this theory in turn has been largely superseded by another, whose first conspicuous advocate in this country was Francis A. Walker. It also received vigorous defense at the hands of Henry George. According to this theory the reward of labor, or wages, is drawn invariably from the product of labor, wages being therefore dependent upon the productivity of labor. The rate of wages is determined by the product of the laborer in the least advantageous situation, since if employers must pay one class of laborers a certain wage, other laborers, though in more advantageous positions, will not consent to labor for less. This rate of wages will evidently be dependent upon many causes, such as the following: An increase in the amount of land available for industry will open a new remunerative field for employment, thus increasing the product of the laborer in the least advantageous position and raising the general rate of wages; labor-saving inventions, by increasing the productivity of labor, will in the long run increase wages. These rules of course do not apply where special circumstances place the laborer on an unequal footing with his employer. See CAPITAL; RENT; INTEREST; POLITICAL ECONOMY.

Wagner, *vahg'nur,* WILHELM RICHARD (1813–1883), the most celebrated of modern composers, born at Leipzig. He received his education at Leipzig and Dresden, and after 1834 he filled various musical engagements at Magdeburg, Riga and Königsberg. In 1839 he went to Paris and London and there composed his operas *Rienzi* and *The Flying Dutchman.* The brilliant success of the operas secured him the conductorship at the Royal Opera of Dresden in 1843. He joined the insurrectionary movement of 1848 and was compelled to exile himself. Until his return to Germany, in 1864, he spent most of his time in Switzerland, Italy, Paris and London. His *Tannhauser* and *Lohengrin* appeared in 1845 and 1850, respectively. The king of Bavaria, Louis II, became an enthusiastic patron of Wagner, and the theater at Baireuth, especially built for Wagner by the contributions of Wagner societies throughout the world, was chiefly supported from the king's purse. Here the famous tetralogy *Der Ring des Nibelungen,* consisting of *Das Rheingold,*

WILHELM RICHARD WAGNER

Die Walküre, Siegfried and *Götterdämmerung,* was first performed in 1876. About a year before his death Wagner produced his last creation, *Parsifal,* which has since been produced with emphatic success. He gave to his works a

national character by selecting his subjects from old German legends. His theory, founded upon the ideas of Gluck and Weber, was that in a perfect musical drama, the three arts, poetry, music and dramatic representation, should be welded together into one well-balanced whole. His particular views on music are embodied in a well-known work, entitled *Oper und Drama.* See OPERA.

Wag'on, the name given a four-wheeled vehicle used for carrying merchandise. Wagons

ROAD WAGON

are constructed of a great variety of patterns, the body being adapted to the particular use for which the vehicle is intended. Farm wagons usually have long rectangular boxes, so made that they can be taken off or put on the gear at will. Most of these wagons can also have the running-gear extended or shortened, to suit the purpose for which the wagon is needed. Road wagons have a light running-gear, springs and upholstered seats. Some of them contain seats which can be placed upon the body. These seats are usually mounted upon steel springs. See CARRIAGE.

Wag'tail, the name of birds included in the family of warblers, so called from their habit of jerking their long tails when running or perching. The wagtails frequent muddy lands and pastures, running rapidly along the edge of water and catching the insects which they find there. Though there are several species common in Europe, they are rarely seen in the United States.

Wahabis, *wah hah'beez,* **Wahhabees** or **Wahabites,** a reforming Mohammedan sect, founded in Arabia about 1760 by Abd-el-Waháb, an Oriental scholar of high attainments. The latest statistics of Islamism estimate their number at four million.

Wah'peton, N. D., the county-seat of Richland co., 46 mi. s. of Fargo, on the Red River of the North and on the Great Northern, the Northern Pacific and the Chicago, Milwaukee &

Saint Paul railroads. The city has grain elevators, a flour mill, lumber yards and various mercantile establishments. There are seven churches, three banks, a college and waterworks, electric light and sewage systems. Population in 1910, 2467.

Waite, MORRISON REMICK (1816–1888), an eminent American jurist, born at Lyme, Conn. He graduated at Yale in 1837 and was admitted to the bar two years later. He practiced successfully in Maumee City and Toledo, Ohio, was elected to the legislature and in 1871 was sent to Geneva as United States counsel in the Alabama case. President Grant appointed him to succeed Salmon P. Chase as chief justice of the Supreme Court of the United States in 1874. He held the position until his death, winning universal esteem for his impartiality and learning. Among the important questions presented to the Supreme Court and decided during Chief Justice Waite's term were those affecting polygamy, election laws, the civil rights of negroes, the Bell telephone case, the power of removal by the president and the Chicago anarchist cases.

Wake, a term corresponding originally to vigil, and applied to a festival held on the anniversary of the day on which the parish church was consecrated and dedicated to a saint. A *lyke-wake* is the watching of a dead body by night, by the relatives and friends of the deceased. The practice, once general, is now confined to the lower Irish classes and is frequently accompanied by scenes much out of keeping with the occasion.

Wakefield, MASS., a town in Middlesex co., about 10 mi. n. of Boston, on the Boston & Maine railroad. It contains rattan works, foundries, a piano factory, a shoe factory, a flour mill, machine shops and other works. There are two banks, a public library and a town high school. It was settled about 1639, was incorporated as South Reading in 1812 and was given its present name in 1868. Population in 1910, 11,404.

Wake-Robin. See TRILLIUM.

Walburga, *vahl boor'ga.* See WALPURGA.

Walcheren, *vahl' Keren,* the most westerly island of the Netherlands, in the Province of Zealand, situated at the mouth of the Scheldt. It is low and level, and a portion of it, being below the high-water mark, is protected by dikes. The island is 13 miles long and 10 miles wide. The inhabitants are engaged in agriculture and cattle-raising. The chief town is Middelburg. Population, about 42,000.

Waldeck-Rousseau, *val dek'roo so',* PIERRE MARIE ERNEST (1846–1904), a French statesman. He served in the Chamber of Deputies and for several terms in the cabinet, and in 1894 he was elected to the Senate. In 1895 he was a candidate for the presidency of France. In 1899 he became premier, with the portfolio of the interior, and his administration was noteworthy for several measures, among them the proclamation of an amnesty law for all connected with the Dreyfus case, and the curtailment of the powers of religious associations by the Association Bill of 1901. Waldeck-Rousseau resigned his office in 1902.

Waldenses, *wol den'seez,* a Christian sect which owes its origin to Peter Waldus (Waldo), a rich citizen of Lyons. About 1170 Waldo sold his movable goods for the support of the poor and went about preaching by the wayside. His followers were known as the Poor Men of Lyons. They suffered many persecutions. Their chief strongholds were, and still are, in the mountain tract of the Cottian Alps, southwest of Turin, where, since 1848, they (about 10,000) enjoy the same religious and political rights as the Roman Catholics of Italy. The design of the founder was to reform the clergy and to preach the word of God freely to every one in his native language; but his followers went far beyond the original plan. They made the Bible alone the rule of their faith, renounced entirely the doctrines, usages and traditions of the Roman Church, and formed a separate religious society.

Waldersee, *vahl' dur zay,* ALFRED, Count (1832–1904), a German soldier. He served in the Seven Weeks' War and in the Franco-Prussian War and won honors for the ability and bravery he displayed. Several offices, both diplomatic and military, were conferred upon him, and in 1900 he was made field marshal. He had command of the German army, and also of the allied forces, during the Boxer trouble in China in 1900.

Waldstein, *vahlt' stine,* ALBRECHT EUSEBIUS WENZEL VON. See WALLENSTEIN, ALBRECHT EUSEBIUS WENZEL VON.

Wales, *waylz,* a principality in the southwest of the island of Great Britain, forming a peninsula between Bristol Channel, on the south, and the Irish Sea, on the north, and having an area of 7446 sq mi., or a little less than that of the State of New Jersey. The surface of the country is very mountainous, particularly in the north, where the ranges of England enter it. These run in nearly a north and south or northeast and southwest direction and are parallel to each other. They are low mountains, the highest peak having an altitude of only 3571 feet. The country is rich in minerals, particularly coal, iron, copper and slate, and to these Wales owes its chief wealth. The coal trade is the most important and extensive, and Cardiff is one of the largest coal ports in the world. The presence of coal and iron ore has given rise to large iron and steel plants, and there are also quite extensive copper works. The other manufactures include woolen goods, especially flannel, coarse cloth and hosiery.

Previous to the Roman occupation, Wales appears to have been chiefly inhabited by three British tribes, called the Silures, the Dimetae and the Ordovices. During the latter part of the Roman occupation one of the four provinces into which the island was divided included Wales and was called *Britannia Secunda*. After the invasion of the Saxons the country acquired a distinctly national character, because it became the refuge of the conquered Britons, who were gradually driven to the west and who for a long time maintained their independence. However, the country was finally conquered by Edward I, who established the title of prince of Wales for his son, whom he made ruler, and that title has ever since been conferred upon the heir to the British crown. The inhabitants are mostly of Celtic origin and are descendants of the early Britons. The language is Welsh, which is a branch of the Celtic, different from that used by the Irish and the Scotch Highlanders. See CELTS.

Wales, PRINCE OF, a British title, first conferred by Edward I on his son, at the time of his conquest of the principality of Wales. Edward III was never prince of Wales, but the title has been conferred on all the male heirs apparent to the English throne from the time of Edward the Black Prince, son of Edward III. The heir apparent is made prince of Wales and earl of Chester by special creation and investiture or by proclamation. As heir to the crown of Scotland, the prince of Wales bears the titles of *prince and high steward of Scotland, duke of Rothsay, earl of Carrick, baron of Renfrew and lord of the Isles*. The title of earl of Dublin was also borne by Albert Edward when he was prince of Wales.

Walhalla, *val hahl'la*, or **Temple of Fame,** a magnificent and sumptuously decorated Doric octostyle temple, on the Danube, near Ratisbon, built in 1830 by Ludwig I as a national pantheon. The pediments and frieze contain sculptures representing the history of the Teutonic people. The idea of the erection is derived from the Walhalla, or Valhalla, the ancient paradise of Odin and the Scandinavian deities.

Walker, *wauk'ur*, AMASA (1799–1875), an American political economist, born in Woodstock, Conn. He engaged in commercial pursuits from 1814 to 1842, and thereafter, for several years, he lectured on political economy in Oberlin College, later at Harvard and Amherst. He was elected to the Massachusetts legislature in 1848, became secretary of state of Massachusetts in 1851 and was elected to Congress in 1862. He was president of the Boston Temperance Society and was one of the founders of the Free-Soil party. In 1857 he published *Nature and Uses of Money*, and in 1866 *The Science of Wealth* appeared.

Walker, FRANCIS AMASA (1840–1897), an American economist and statistician, born at Boston, Mass., the son of Amasa Walker. He graduated at Amherst College and afterward studied law. He served in the Union army in the Civil War and was made brigadier general for gallantry at Chancellorsville, where he was wounded. From 1865 to 1867 he taught Latin and Greek at Williston Seminary, and in 1869 he was appointed chief of the bureau of statistics at Washington. Mr. Walker supervised the census of 1870, was appointed United States indian commissioner in 1872 and from 1873 to 1881 was professor of political economy in the Sheffield Scientific School of Yale College. In the latter year he became president of the Massachusetts Institute of Technology. He published many works, including volumes on the *Indian Question, Political Economy, The Wages Question, Money, International Bimetallism* and *The Making of the Nation*.

Walker, FREDERICK (1840–1875), an English painter, born at London. At an early age he began drawing, and after spending about eighteen months in an architect's office he became a student at the Royal Academy and commenced designing for wood engravers. The illustrations he supplied between 1860 and 1864 to the *Cornhill Magazine* and *Once a Week* are full of life and rank high as specimens of this kind of draughtsmanship. Some of these drawings he reproduced in water color, in which medium he produced a number of exquisite pictures. His best works in oil are *The Bathers, By the Plow, Philip in Church, The Wayfarers* and *Vagrants*. Originality, poetic feeling, graceful drawing and remarkable purity and range of color characterize his paintings.

Walker, WILLIAM (1824–1860), a famous American adventurer and filibuster, born at Nashville, Tenn. He graduated at the University of Nashville, was admitted to the bar and later studied medicine at Edinburgh and Heidelberg. Returning to America, he engaged in journalism, but in the summer of 1853 he organized an expedition to conquer the State of Sonora, Mex. After capturing several towns and proclaiming himself president, he was forced to flee from Mexico on account of a lack of provisions and ammunition and was arrested by United States authorities at San Diego. He was tried for violating neutrality, but was acquitted. He soon started upon an expedition to Nicaragua, then engaged in a civil war. There he was made secretary of war and commander in chief of the government forces, but quarreled with the president and condemned him to death for conspiracy. Walker then directed a brief and triumphant war with Costa Rica and proclaimed himself president. His arbitrary conduct, however, resulted in his expulsion from the country, and he again surrendered to United States authorities. As soon as possible, however, he returned to Nicaragua with a force of Americans and natives and was again driven from the country. After several attempts he later made an expedition to Honduras, but was compelled to surrender to the Honduran government, was condemned by court martial and executed in 1860.

Walking Stick, a long, slender, cylindrical insect which resembles a small twig covered with green or black bark. The long, delicate legs of the insect add to the illusion. There are several species in the United States, but more live in tropical countries. *Mule killer* and *devil's riding horse* are popular names. See LEAF INSECTS.

Wallace, *wawl'ase,* IDAHO, a city in Shoshone co., about 110 mi. east of Spokane, Wash., on Placer Creek and on the Northern Pacific railroad and the line of the Oregon Railroad and Navigation Company. It is in the famous Coeur d'Alene mining region, which produces gold, silver and lead. The city contains sampling works, lumber mills and yards, breweries, a foundry and other establishments. There are four churches, two banks, three newspapers, four hotels, two hospitals and a public high school. Population in 1900, 2265; estimated in 1905, 3000.

Wallace, ALFRED RUSSELL (1822-1913), an English naturalist, born at Usk, Monmouthshire, and educated at Hertford Grammar School. He spent many years in traveling, especially in South America and the Asiatic islands, and the valuable material collected in these scientific explorations he embodied in *Travels on the Amazon and Rio Negro, The Malay Archipelago, Tropical Nature* and *The Geographical Distribution of Animals.* His observation of animal life and his philosophical nature led him to investigate the causes and reasons of things, and as a result he formulated his theories of development and natural selection. Before Darwin gave his famous work to the world Wallace had published his *Specu-*

ALFRED RUSSELL WALLACE

lation on the Origin of Species. His share in establishing the theory has been acknowledged by Darwin. But while Darwin, in his later editions of the *Origin of Species,* somewhat modified his original conclusions, Wallace, in a late work, *Darwinism, an Exposition of the Theory of Natural Selection, with Some of its Applications,* strongly insists upon the complete controlling power of these primary laws and conditions. Wallace, however, differs from Darwin on the subject of the intellectual, moral and spiritual nature of man. He contends that the higher faculties have been developed, not under the law of natural selection, but under a higher law, which has come in imperceptibly; and that the Darwinian theory, instead of opposing, "lends a decided support to a belief in the spiritual nature of man." He claims to be at once a true Darwinian and an antimaterialist. In later years Wallace also paid some attention to social questions, wrote on the land question and against compulsory vaccination. He published his autobiography, entitled *My Life*. His last books, *Social Environment and Moral Progress* and *The Revolt of Democracy*, state his views on the progress, or lack of it, of civilization. See EVOLUTION.

Wallace, LEWIS (1827–1905), an American soldier and novelist, generally known as Lew Wallace. He was born in Brookville, Ind., received a common school education and began the study of law, which he practiced at intervals in Crawfordsville, Ind. He took part in the Mexican War, with rank of lieutenant, and was a member of the Indiana state legislature in 1848. At the outbreak of the Civil War he entered the service as colonel of an Indiana regiment, was appointed brigadier general in 1861 and was made major general for distinguished services at Fort Donelson in 1862. He was removed from command by Halleck, but was reinstated by Grant. He was sent to Mexico on secret diplomatic service in 1866, was elected governor of New Mexico in 1878 and was made minister to Turkey in 1881. His best-known works are *Ben Hur, The Fair God, The Prince of India* and *The Boyhood of Christ*.

Wallace, WILLIAM, Sir (about 1272–1305), a Scotch patriot, about whose early years little definite is known. He is described as a man of herculean proportions and strength, and it is certain that he possessed in a high degree the qualifications of a commander. He is represented as having been for some years engaged in a partisan war against the English, before what is represented by his biographer, Blind Harry, as the turning point in his career, the slaughter of Haselrig, in revenge for the murder of his wife. Henceforth he continued in open resistance to the English, and having collected a considerable force, he was besieging the castle of Dundee when he heard that Surrey and Cressingham were advancing upon Stirling with a large army. He met them in the vicinity of that town and gained a complete victory (1297). After this Wallace gained the title of guardian of the kingdom and conducted a series of organized raids into England. In 1298 Edward I entered Scotland, and Wallace retired before him, wasting the country, but he was at length overtaken at Falkirk and was compelled to fight; after a gallant resistance, he was defeated. He succeeded in escaping, and little is known of his movements thenceforth. He was excluded from the peace granted by Edward to the Scots in 1304, and when he fell into the hands of the

English he was conveyed to London, was found guilty of treason and rebellion and was executed.

Walla Walla, *wol′a wol′a*, WASH., the county-seat of Walla Walla co., about 150 mi. s. w. of Spokane, on the Walla Walla River, 28 mi. e. of the Columbia River, and on branch lines of the Northern Pacific and the Union Pacific railroads. The city is built at an altitude of 1060 feet, about fifteen miles west of the Blue Mountain range, and it is surrounded by a beautiful fertile valley. The agricultural region produces large quantities of wheat, oats, barley, fruits and vegetables. Walla Walla is the commercial center of the southeastern part of the state, and the industrial establishments include implement works, flour mills, gas and electric power plants and lumber mills. The city contains the state penitentiary and the Federal land office, weather bureau office and district court. It also has a state Odd Fellows' Home, the Stubblefield Home for widows and orphans, the Saint Mary's and the Walla Walla hospitals and a public library. The important educational institutions are the Whitman College, two seminaries for girls and an academy for boys, and Walla Walla College, which is two miles west of the city. The city has a good system of electric railway. A United States fort was established here in 1857, and a trading post grew up around it. The settlement was at first called Steptoeville, but was incorporated as the town of Walla Walla in 1859. Population in 1910, 19,364.

Wallenstein, *vahl′en stine*, or **Waldstein,** ALBRECHT EUSEBIUS WENZEL VON, duke of Friedland, Sagan and Mecklenburg (1583–1634), a famous leader in the Thirty Years' War, born at Hermanic, in Bohemia. Both his father and mother belonged to the Bohemian Evangelical Church, but shortly after their early death Wallenstein went over to the Roman Catholic faith. He finished his studies at the Universities of Bologna and Padua and traveled in Italy, Germany, France, Spain, England and the Netherlands. He took service in the Austrian army in the struggle against the Turks, and when the Thirty Years' War broke out in Bohemia (1618), he joined the imperial forces against his native country. With a large army, which he raised to assist the emperor against the Protestant League, he defeated Count Mansfield at Dessau (1626) and compelled Bethlen Gabor, of Transylvania, to conclude a truce. He also conquered Silesia and bought from the emperor, partly with military services, partly with plunder, the duchy of Sagan and other extensive estates.

In September, 1630, owing to the jealousy of the nobles and the license of his followers, he was deprived of his command and retired to his duchy of Friedland, until the emperor was compelled to seek his aid against Gustavus Adolphus. Wallenstein then obtained almost absolute power, and his behavior thenceforth leaves no doubt that the emperor's interests were second to his own, and that he would not have hesitated to join the emperor's enemies, to secure his own independence and the crown of Bohemia. After some partial successes he encountered the king of Sweden at Lützen in 1632, and in the battle which took place Wallenstein was defeated and Gustavus was killed. Wallenstein had unsuccessfully treated on his own account with the Swedish king, and he now secretly reopened negotiations with France and the German princes, occasionally taking the field to display his military power. The court at Vienna was well aware of his double dealing, but the emperor was not strong enough to remove him, and he therefore had him assassinated at Eger, whither he had retreated for safety.

Waller, *wol'lur*, EDMUND (1606–1687), an English poet. He was early left an orphan with a considerable estate, and was educated at Eton and King's College, Cambridge. It is stated that Waller wrote poetry at eighteen, but his first collection of poems did not appear until 1645. As an elegant amatory and panegyrical poet, a brilliant talker and wit, he was a great favorite at court, in Parliament and in society. Best remembered of his poems are the lines *On a Girdle* and the song beginning "Go, lovely rose."

Wallingford, *wol'ling furd*, CONN., a borough in New Haven co., 12 mi. n. e. of New Haven, on the Quinnipiac River and on the New York, New Haven & Hartford railroad. The streets are broad and regularly laid out, and they are shaded by large elm trees. The city contains the Phelps School for girls and a public library, and it owns the waterworks and electric light plant. There are manufactures of silver goods, silverplated ware, insulated wire and nickel, brass, rubber and other goods. The place was settled by planters from New Haven in 1670. In 1851 the Wallingford Community was established here, after the plan of the Oneida Community, but a Masonic home is now located on the grounds. Population in 1910, 8690.

Wall of China, THE GREAT. See GREAT WALL OF CHINA.

Walloons, *wal loonz'*, descendants of the ancient Belgians, who now occupy southern Belgium. They are superior in physique to their Flemish compatriots, and a large proportion of them have black hair and eyes. Their language, also called Walloon, is a French dialect, retaining numerous Gallic words, but it varies somewhat in the different provinces. There are about 2,750,000 Walloons now in Belgium.

Wall Paper, paper used for decorating the walls and ceilings of rooms. The use of paper hangings originated among the Chinese and was not introduced into Europe until the eighteenth century. The papers at first were imitations of the leather, tapestry and velvet hangings which had long been common as wall decorations, but gradually the designs became original and varied. Most of the processes are by machinery similar to that used in calico printing, but there is also much hand work done in the finer qualities. The paper is prepared in strips, which are made fast to the wall by paste. The skill of the workman consists in matching the strips and laying the paper so as to avoid wrinkles.

Walnut, *wol'nut*, a small family of trees that includes the American walnut, butternut and hickory. Of the walnut proper, about ten species are known, but only two are common in the United States, namely, the *black walnut*, which is a native of the Mississippi Valley, and the *Persian*, or *English*, *walnut*, which is cultivated in New England and California for its fruit. Black walnut produces one of the best timbers of the United States, of great value because of its durability and the fine polish which it takes. So great has been the demand for it, however, that the tree is becoming scarce. In 1900 the product in the United States was valued at $1,500,000. The fruit of this species is rich and oily, and by some it is esteemed as a food, but it is not comparable to the nut of the English species.

Walpole, *wawl'pole*, HORACE, fourth earl of Orford (1717–1797), an English man of letters, the son of Sir Robert Walpole. He received his education at Cambridge, and following his graduation he spent several years in travel. In 1741 he entered Parliament. His first publication was *A Catalogue of Royal and Noble Authors*, which was followed in 1764 by *The Castle of Otranto*, a romance abounding in mystery, which was at the time of its publication very popular. Walpole is, however, chiefly remembered for his *Letters*, which give entertaining pictures of the society of his day. While in general these pictures are true to life, they are of little value to accurate historians, on account of their untruthfulness. Many editions of these letters have been published.

Walpole, Robert, Sir, earl of Orford, (1676–1745), an English statesman. He was educated at Eton and at King's College, Cambridge, succeeded to his father's estate in 1700 and entered Parliament as member for Castle Rising. In 1702 he was elected for King's Lynn, became an active member of the Whig party and soon distinguished himself by his business capacity and by his ease in debate. He was successively secretary of war, paymaster of the forces and first lord of the treasury, chancellor of the exchequer and prime minister. This latter office he held for over twenty-one years, and during his long administration the Hanoverian succession became firmly established, a result to which his prudence and political sagacity largely contributed. He promoted by an enlightened

bishop of Eichstädt, Bavaria, she was induced to go to Germany to found convents, and about 750 she became abbess of Heidenheim, a convent within her brother's bishopric. She died at the latter place about 780, but was buried at Eichstädt. Her shrine was visited by many pilgrims and was the scene of many miracles. The eve of May 1, associated with some of the most popular witch superstitions of Germany, is called *Walpurgis night*; then the witches are supposed to ride on goats and broomsticks to places of judgment in the hills, where they offer sacrifice. The Brocken, the highest hill of the Harz, was made the scene, by Goethe, of his witches' sabbath in Faust. The feast of Walpurga falls properly on February 25.

Walrus, *wol'rus*, a marine flesh-eating mammal, related to the seal, and inhabiting the colder climates. It has two large, pointed tusks, from

WALRUS

policy the commercial prosperity of the nation and relieved the weight of taxation by many improvements in the tariff. Although he was constantly accused of corruption in office and was once even sent to the Tower on such a charge, the fact that he became no wealthier through his long term of office, shows that the reports of his contemporaries were certainly exaggerated.

Walpurga, *val poor'ga*, **Walburga** or **Walpurgis**, a female saint, born in England early in the eighth century. She was for many years a nun in the Dorsetshire convent. As a niece of Saint Boniface and sister of Saint Wilibald, first

fifteen inches to two feet in length, directed downward and slightly outward from the upper jaw. The tusks are used in digging up clams and other food from the bottom of the sea. The animals are valuable because of their hides and oil. They are either killed with rifles or taken with harpoons.

Walsingham, *wol'sing am*, Francis, Sir (about 1530–1590), an English statesman. Under Elizabeth, Burleigh secured his services for the Crown, and he became one of the principal secretaries of state. He feared constantly that Catholic plots might grow up in England, under the encouragement of Spain, and he had numerous spies at home and abroad, who kept him informed as to the movements of the Catholics. He discovered the Babington plot against Elizabeth and produced the letters supposed to have been written by Mary Queen of Scots, which implicated her in the plot. Mary accused Walsingham of having forged these letters.

Waltham, *wol'tham,* MASS., a city in Middlesex co., 10 mi. w. of Boston, on the Charles River and on the Boston & Maine railroad and several electric railways. It is well known for its extensive manufacture of watches. There are also large cotton mills, saddlery works, machine shops, foundries and other factories. The city has about fifteen churches, a large public library, a state school for feeble-minded, a training school for nurses, a normal school, a commercial college and several church schools. There is one large park, known as Prospect Hill, and several small squares. It was originally a part of Watertown, but was set off as a separate town in 1738 and was chartered as a city in 1884. Population in 1910, 27,834.

Walton, *wawl'ton,* IZAAK (1593–1683), the author of the famous *Compleat Angler*. For a number of years he was in business in London, whether as a linen draper or an ironmonger is not known, but he retired at the age of fifty and devoted his remaining forty years to a life of cultured ease and pleasure. His first edition of *The Compleat Angler* appeared in 1653. It is to his exquisite delineations of rural scenery, the ease and unaffected humor of his dialogue and the delightful simplicity of his style that *The Compleat Angler* owes its charm.

Waltz, *wawlts,* a dance of Bohemian origin, executed with a rapid whirling motion, the gentleman having his arm round his partner's waist. The music is written in triple time and consists of phrases of eight or sixteen bars. Several of these phrases are now usually united, to prevent monotony. Johann Strauss and his son of the same name are the most noted composers of waltzes. The *valse a deux temps* is a form of waltz in which two steps are made to each bar of three beats. *Classical waltzes* are musical compositions in waltz form, not intended for dance tunes. Of this style the composer Chopin is the greatest master.

Wampanoag, *wom'pa no'ag,* a tribe of indians who once occupied the lands east of Narragansett Bay, as far north as Massachusetts. See MASSASOIT; KING PHILIP.

Wampum, *wom'pum,* the name given by New England tribes to the white and purple shell beads which were used for ornament and which circulated as money among the tribes east of the Mississippi. Because of the fixed value which wampum strings held, they came to be accepted by the settlers in exchange for their own coins. It was the custom of the indians to weave wampum beads into belts, in such a manner that the figures formed permanent records. Few transactions of any sort were considered complete without the passing of the belts, and wampum records were used with binding force in great treaties.

Wanamaker, *wahn'a ma'kur,* JOHN (1838–), an American merchant, political leader and philanthropist, born in Philadelphia, Pa. He received a common school education and began his business career as errand boy in a book store; later he was salesman, and in 1861 he established a clothing house on his own account, which he enlarged into a general department store in 1876. A large branch was opened in New York in 1896. He helped to organize the Christian Commission, which assisted the soldiers during the Civil War; was chairman of Irish famine, yellow fever and other relief committees, and was prominent in the management of the Centennial Exposition. Mr. Wanamaker was appointed postmaster-general in 1889 and performed his duties with energy and administrative talent. He also took great interest in religious work, actively supported the Young Men's Christian Association and was the founder and for fifty years the superintendent of Bethany Presbyterian Sunday School in Philadelphia.

Wandering Jew. A legend, well known in almost all parts of the Christian world, says that while Christ was on his way to Calvary, bearing his cross, he was mocked by a Jew, who told him not to rest, but to hurry on with his burden. In reply, Christ said, "I go, but thou shalt tarry till I come." In consequence, the man has continued since to wander about the earth. He passes through his lifetime like any ordinary man, till he reaches one hundred years, and then he suffers a terrible sickness, after which he comes forth again young. This legend has been the subject of many literary works in prose, poetry and the drama. The most notable novel is *The Wandering Jew* by Eugene Sue.

Wap'iti, a large deer, native of North America, living now only in the northwestern United States and in Canada. It is related to the

European red deer, which it resembles in color, shape and form, though it is larger and has larger antlers. Its flesh and its hide are valuable.

WAPITI

In the United States it is usually called *elk.* See DEER.

War, *wawr,* a contest between nations or states (international war), or between parties in the same state (civil war), carried on by force of arms. It usually arises in the first case from disputes about territorial possessions and frontiers, unjust dealings with the subjects of one state by another, questions of race and sentiment, jealousy of military prestige or mere lust of conquest; rarely nowadays it springs from the whim of a despot. In the second case, it is owing to the claims of rival contenders for supreme power in the state, or to attempts to establish some important point connected with civil or religious liberty. In all cases the aim of each contending party is to overthrow or weaken the enemy, by the defeat or dispersion of his army or navy, by the occupation of important parts of his country, such as the capital or principal administrative and commercial centers, or by the ruin of his commerce, thus cutting off his sources of recuperation in men, money and material.

International, or public, war is always understood to be authorized by the sovereign powers of the nations; when it is carried into the territory of a hitherto friendly power, it is called an *aggressive,* or *offensive, war;* and when carried on to resist such aggression, it is called *defensive.* Previous to the outbreak of hostilities between states, the power taking the initiatory step

issues a *declaration of war,* which now usually takes the form of an explanatory manifesto, addressed to neutral governments.

During the progress of the struggle, certain laws, usages or rights of war have come to be generally recognized; such laws permit the destruction or capture of armed enemies, the destruction of property likely to be serviceable to them, the stoppage of all their channels of traffic and the appropriation of everything in an enemy's country necessary for the support and subsistence of the invading army. On the other hand, though an enemy may be starved into surrender, wounding, except in battle, mutilation and all cruel and wanton devastation are contrary to the usages of war, as are also bombarding an unprotected town, the use of poison in any way and the employment of torture to extort information from an enemy. Generally, the tendency in all laws and usages of war is becoming gradually more favorable to the cause of humanity at large.

When two nations are at war and it becomes necessary for them to communicate, it is customary to request the services of the embassies of some neutral powers, and the belligerents themselves do not meet until preliminary arrangements have been made by the neutrals; as, for instance, in the Russo-Japanese War, negotiations were carried on by the government of the United States. While terms of peace are being considered, or when for any reason the belligerents wish to meet, an *armistice,* or *truce,* is declared, during which there is a cessation of hostilities. Of course, if one nation completely conquers another, the war will cease; though even then many matters are settled by a *treaty* or by *grant,* and it is not customary now for the conquering nation to disturb the mode of life of the conquered people any more than is necessary. Property rights are respected in general, unless there is a good reason for a contrary course.

While in the progress of war it may be necessary to destroy public property of the enemy or even to raze whole towns, destroy provisions and private property everywhere, yet such things as works of art and the industries of peace and those things which aid the advance of civilization are usually regarded as exempt. Napoleon disregarded this rule; the British in 1814 burned the records at Washington, and Sherman destroyed property wantonly on his famous march to the sea, but these things meet now with universal disapproval. See ARMY;

CANNON, and articles therein referred to; also, NEUTRALITY; INTERNATIONAL LAW.

War, DEPARTMENT OF, that one of the executive departments of a government which has to do primarily with military affairs. The chief of the department in the United States is the secretary of war, who is a member of the president's cabinet and who carries out the orders of the president, commander in chief of the army. The war department consists of a number of different bureaus, over the chiefs of which the secretary has general control. The affairs of the war department, however, are not confined strictly to military matters, for it exercises control over pensions, sea coast forts, river and harbor improvements, the military academy and the government of island possessions which require military supervision. The principal bureau chiefs are the adjutant-general, the inspector-general, the judge-advocate-general, the quartermaster-general, the commissary-general, the sergeant-general, the paymaster-general and the chiefs of ordnance, signal office, engineers and pensions.

Warbeck, *wawr'bek*, PERKIN (1474–1499), the son of a Flemish Jew, set up by Margaret of York, dowager duchess of Burgundy, as a pretender to the crown of England against Henry VII. For this purpose she recognized him as her nephew, Richard Plantagenet, duke of York, the younger of the two princes who were murdered in the Tower by Richard III. He was accepted in France and in Scotland, married a kinswoman of the Scottish king, James IV, and made several fruitless invasions of England and Ireland. After an attempt on Cornwall, he was taken prisoner and confined to the Tower, where, as he continued his plotting, he was executed.

War'blers, the name of a large family of small, sprightly birds, closely related to the thrushes. They are perching birds and have long, sharp beaks. Many of them are remarkable for the clearness, sweetness and flexibility of their songs, and many are also notable for the brilliant coloring of patches of feathers upon different parts of the body. They are widely distributed, being found throughout both the Old and New World. Their migration northward is made with great regularity, and by the middle of May they are for a few days common everywhere in the Northern states; soon they move to their nesting places, which vary in latitude with the species. Among the handsomest of the American warblers are the cerulean warbler, the *redstart*, the *Blackburnian warbler*, the *yellow warbler* and the *black-throated blue warbler*. The American warblers are not as attractive songsters as those of Europe. Among the latter are the *blackcap*, the *goldcrest*, the *willow warbler* and the *green warbler*. The nests of the warblers are usually rather rude, though some construct finely formed, dainty little nests, like those of the humming bird. The Blackburnian warbler and the redstart are typical warblers. The summer yellow bird, or summer warbler, is found in all parts of America. It is lively, unsuspicious and almost familiar. While building the nest the female sings nearly as well as the male.

Ward, ARTEMUS. See BROWNE, CHARLES FARRAR.

Ward, ARTEMUS (1727–1800), an American soldier and jurist, born at Shrewsbury, Mass. He graduated at Harvard, served in the French and Indian Wars and at the outbreak of the Revolution commanded the Massachusetts forces. He conducted the siege at Boston until the arrival of Washington and was appointed second in command of the Continental army, but resigned at the close of 1776. He became chief justice of the court of common pleas, later was president of the Massachusetts executive council and for sixteen years was a member of the legislature. In 1791 he was elected to Congress, where he served two terms.

Ward, ELIZABETH STUART PHELPS (1844–1911), an American author and philanthropist, born at Andover, Mass. Besides lecturing and engaging in work for the advancement of women and for social reforms, she also wrote a number of stories, including *The Gates Ajar* (1868), which passed through twenty editions in the year of its publication, *Beyond the Gates*, *The Gates Between*, *Hedged In*, *The Silent Partner*, *The Story of Avis*, *A Singular Life* and, in conjunction with her husband, the Rev. Herbert D. Ward, *Come Forth* and *The Master of the Magicians*.

Ward, MRS. HUMPHREY (1851–   ), an English novelist, born in Tasmania, the niece of the poet and essayist, Matthew Arnold. In 1856 her family returned to England, and in 1872 she married Thomas Humphrey Ward. After writing much for periodicals and publishing two works of fiction, which were not especially noteworthy, she brought out in 1888 *Robert Elsmere*, a novel which became immensely popular and which won the favorable notice of critics. After that time she published *The*

History of David Grieve, Marcella, The Story of Bessie Costrell, Sir George Tressady, Helbeck of Bannisdale, Eleanor, Lady Rose's Daughter and *The Marriage of William Ashe*. The principal criticism which has been passed on Mrs.

MRS. HUMPHREY WARD

Ward's novels, especially on her earlier ones, is that the purpose is made too prominent. But her characters are clearly drawn, her literary execution is excellent and her topics are always vital.

Ward, JOHN QUINCY ADAMS (1830–1910), an American sculptor, born at Urbana, Ohio. He was a student in Washington and New York, and for the four years preceding the breaking out of the Civil War, he lived in Washington and made portrait busts of the leading public men. At this time he modeled his statuette of *The Freedman*, which became very popular, on account both of its subject and of the excellence of his design. Copies of it were widely sold. He made many studies among the indians, and *The Indian Hunter*, in Central Park, New York City, is the finest result of his work. A colossal figure of a uniformed soldier, a bronze statue of Shakespeare, a seated figure of Horace Greeley, statues of Senator Conkling, William Dodge and George Washington are to be seen in New York City. In Boston a group called *The Good Samaritan* commemorates the discovery of the use of ether as an anesthetic.

Ware, MASS., a town in Hampshire co., 25 mi. w. of Worcester, on the Ware River and on the Boston & Albany and the Boston & Maine railroads. It contains extensive cotton and woolen mills and boot, shoe and other factories. There are seven churches, two banks, a public library and municipal waterworks. The place was settled about 1673, and the town was incorporated in 1775. Population in 1910, 8774.

War Game or **Kriegsspiel,** a game of German origin, played with maps, on a large scale, and colored metal blocks, on the same scale as the map, representing bodies of troops of various strength (brigades of infantry, battalions of rifles, regiments of cavalry, besides artillery, engineers, pontoon troops, telegraph troops, etc.). The players are usually two on each side, and the game forms an exact miniature of tactical operations. It is played by alternate moves. Each move represents the lapse of two minutes, and rules are given to determine the distance that each branch of the service may move over in that time. When two bodies of men on opposite sides come into contact, the weaker in numbers and position is held to be defeated; but when they are equal in these respects, victory is determined to one side or the other by the use of a die. The game is a favorite one in the German army. Modified forms of the game prevail in the United States, where it is regarded as giving excellent practice in strategy.

Waring, *wair'ing,* GEORGE EDWIN, JR. (1833–1898), an American soldier and engineer, who is especially noted for his work as the head of the street-cleaning department in New York City. His early studies were in agriculture and agricultural chemistry, and at one time he managed the farm of Horace Greeley at Chappaqua, N. Y. Later he became drainage engineer of Central Park, New York City. During the Civil War he did good service, both on the field and in raising troops. In 1878 the city of Memphis, wishing to adopt a new drainage system, on account of a severe epidemic of yellow fever which had just passed, employed Waring, and the system which he introduced proved thoroughly satisfactory. As commissioner of street cleaning in New York, he made the city really clean, a thing which had been believed almost impossible. He died of yellow fever, contracted while on a visit to Havana as drainage commissioner. His publications include several books on the subject of drainage and sanitation.

Warm'ing. See HEATING AND VENTILATION.

War'ner, CHARLES DUDLEY (1829–1900), an American editor and critic, born at Plainfield, Mass. He received his degree at Hamilton College in 1852, was admitted to the bar and for a time practiced law in Chicago. Entering journalism, he became, in 1860, editor of the Hartford *Press* and later of the *Courant*. He made an extensive tour in Europe, as correspondent of American papers, and on his return, in 1884, became one of the editors of *Harper's Magazine*, to which he contributed until his death. The first book by which he attained prominence was *My Summer in a Garden*, a volume of sketches, which was followed by *Backlog Studies, Being a Boy* and *As We Were Saying*. Among his other works are *The Gilded Age*, a drama in which he collaborated with Samuel L. Clemens, and *A Little Journey in the World*, a novel with a moral purpose.

Warner, SETH (1743–1784), an American soldier, one of the commanders of the Green Mountain Boys. He was second in command at the Battle of Ticonderoga, and a few days later he took Crown Point with its garrison, for which he received a colonel's commission. He was at the Battle of Bennington and continued in the service until 1782, when he retired on account of ill health.

Warner, SUSAN (1819–1885), an American novelist, who wrote under the name of Elizabeth Wetherell. Her first book, *The Wide, Wide World*, appeared in 1850, and it attained almost immediately an extraordinary popularity in the United States and in England. Another book, *Queechy*, which appeared in 1852, was almost equally popular, but none of her other works won special favor with the public.

War of 1812, the name given to the struggle between the United States and Great Britain in the years 1812–1814. The general cause of the war was the attitude of Great Britain in relation to American shipping. Her claims to the right to board and search American vessels for the purpose of impressing British citizens, found in their crews, into the British service; her decrees and orders to the detriment of American commerce; her disregard of American protests, which had been a cause for grievance to the Americans for many years, at last compelled them to attempt to secure reparation by force. The same haughty actions regarding American commerce had been taken by France, and it was long a question as to which of the two powers the United States

would fight first; but the proximity of Canada, which seemed to offer an attractive field for conquest, and the old ill-feeling toward England, resulting from the Revolution, finally caused the declaration of war against Great Britain, on June 18, 1812. Five days later the British government withdrew the "Orders in Council," which had been probably the most objectionable features of their whole policy, since they established a paper blockade of European ports and practically excluded American commerce from the seas.

At the outset the land forces of the United States made little headway. Great Britain, with her vastly superior resources, was prepared for war, having been at war with France for many years, while the United States government had shown a shameful lack of appreciation of the dangers attending the new republic and had al-

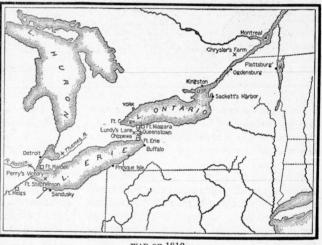

WAR OF 1812

lowed the navy and war departments to deteriorate almost out of existence. The first military movement was that of General Hull, who invaded Canada with two thousand men, but soon retreated before an inferior force under General Brock and surrendered at Detroit, August 16. In October of the same year, General Van Rensselaer made another invasion of Canada near Niagara Falls, and after the Battle of Queenstown, in which the British general, Brock, was mortally wounded, the Americans were again driven back with great loss. Meantime, on the sea the United States vessels had held their own. The *Constitution* had captured the British frigate *Guerriere* (August 19). The *Wasp*, after a sharp battle, took the *Frolic*. The *United States* captured the *Macedonian*, and in December the

Constitution compelled the surrender of the *Java*. American gunners had shown great superiority to their English opponents.

In the fall of this year, Madison was reëlected, with Elbridge Gerry as vice-president. In the following spring, General Dearborn, who had been placed at the head of affairs in the Northwest, invaded Canada for the third time, with an army of 1700 men, and captured York. He was relieved by Generals Wilkinson and Hampton, who made an attempt to take Montreal, but without success. In May an advance of the British into New York State was repulsed at Sackett's Harbor, and in September Commodore Perry fought the famous Battle of Lake Erie, by which he captured the most important British fleet upon the Great Lakes (See ERIE, LAKE, BATTLE OF). This victory enabled General Harrison to invade Canada. There he defeated General Proctor, in the Battle of the Thames.

In 1814 General Jacob Brown again invaded Canada, captured the British Fort Erie and defeated the force under General Riall at Chippewa. Then followed the Battle of Lundy's Lane and the withdrawal of the Americans to Fort Erie, where they were besieged. In the following September, General Prevost led 14,000 men in an invasion of New York, by way of Lake Champlain. The fleet which he had got together was disastrously defeated near Plattsburg by an American fleet under Commodore McDonough, while the land force was also repulsed. At about the same time, the British fleet ascended Chesapeake Bay, defeated the hastily summoned American militia at Bladensburg, entered Washington and sacked the government buildings, in retaliation for the sack of York at its capture. The British had maintained a rather effective blockade of all important American ports during the whole war.

Meanwhile, General Andrew Jackson had been fighting the Creek indians in the extreme South and had gathered together a considerable army of Kentucky and Tennessee frontiersmen. In January, 1815, this force was confronted by an army sent direct from England, under General Pakenham, and consisting of the veterans of Wellington's campaign against Napoleon. The result was the famous Battle of New Orleans, which was a brilliant victory for the Americans. The battle was fought two weeks after peace had been concluded.

On the sea the Americans continued to gain the upper hand, though the *Chesapeake* was captured by the *Shannon*, and other small American vessels were taken. Probably the most memorable event upon the sea during this period was the famous cruise of the American frigate *Essex*, which, after a long and brilliant career against British merchantmen, was compelled to surrender to the *Phoebe* and the *Cherub* in the Pacific Ocean, March 28, 1814. The very month in which the treaty of peace was signed, December, 1814, the Federalists of New England gathered in a convention at Hartford, Conn., to declare their opposition to the war and to the administration (See HARTFORD CONVENTION). The Treaty of Ghent did not provide for the withdrawal of the British claims regarding the right of search, the paper blockade and the laws of neutrality. However, it was approved by all parties in the United States. See UNITED STATES, subhead *History*.

War'rant, an instrument, or document, authorizing certain acts, which without it would be illegal. The most common forms of judicial warrants are the *warrant of arrest*, usually issued by a justice of the peace for the apprehension of those accused or suspected of crimes; and the *search warrant*, granting authority to police officers to search certain specified private premises, to find certain specified goods, which are held contrary to law or to the command of the court.

War'ranty, in law, a guarantee, or security; a promise, or covenant, made by a bargainer, for himself and his heirs, to warrant, or secure, the bargainee and his heirs against all men in the enjoyment of an estate or other thing granted. It is especially applied to a conveyance of land, a deed in which the title is guaranteed to be perfect being called a *warranty deed*. See DEED.

War'ren, OHIO, the county-seat of Trumbull co., 53 mi. s. e. of Cleveland, on the Mahoning River and on the Erie, the Pennsylvania and the Baltimore & Ohio railroads. The city is in a farming country, and it contains rolling mills and manufactories of electrical supplies, tubing, flour, automobiles and other articles. There are five banks, a high school and a public library. Warren was founded in 1799 and was incorporated in 1834. Population in 1910, 11,081.

Warren, PA., the county-seat of Warren co., 70 mi. s. e. of Erie, on the Allegheny River, at the mouth of the Conewango Creek, and on the Pennsylvania and the Dunkirk, Allegheny Valley & Pittsburg railroads. The borough is in a natural gas and oil region, and it contains oil refineries, furniture factories and various steel and iron works. A state hospital for the insane is located here. There are fifteen churches, five banks and a free library. Warren was settled in 1795 and was incorporated in 1832. Population in 1910, 11,080.

Warren, R. I., a town in Bristol co., 10 mi. s. e. of Providence, on the Warren River, on Narragansett Bay and on the New York, New Haven & Hartford railroad. Manufacturing is the principal industry, and the products include cotton goods, twine, braid and other articles. The town has the Hall Library and a public high school. Warren was settled by whites early in the seventeenth century, on the site of the indian village Sowamset. It was on ground that was for a time in dispute between Rhode Island and Massachusetts. The town was incorporated in 1746. During the Revolution it was pillaged by the British and partly burned. Population in 1910, 6585.

Warren, GOUVERNEUR KEMBLE (1830–1882), an American soldier, born at Cold Spring, N. Y., and educated at West Point. He joined the engineering force of the United States army and served in indian campaigns. Later he became professor of mathematics at West Point. At the outbreak of the Civil War, he was made lieutenant colonel of New York volunteers, fought in the Peninsula campaign and at Antietam, was made brigadier general of volunteers and subsequently became chief engineer of the Army of the Potomac. In May, 1863, he was made major general of volunteers. At the Battle of Gettysburg he took a conspicuous part, especially in choosing the Federal position, and was brevetted colonel in the regular army for his promptness and bravery. In command of a corps, he was with Grant in his famous Virginia campaign. After the war he was engaged on government surveys.

Warren, JOSEPH (1741–1775), an American patriot, born at Roxbury, Mass. He graduated at Harvard in 1759, taught school for a time and finally began the practice of medicine at Boston. He soon became a leader of the patriot forces in Massachusetts and delivered the addresses at the anniversary celebration of the Boston Massacre in 1772 and 1775. He drafted the Suffolk Resolves in 1774 and in the following year became president of the provincial congress, with practically dictatorial powers. It was he who dispatched Paul Revere upon his famous ride to Lexington, April 18, 1775. After the first battle he became major general of Massachusetts militia and fought as a vol-

unteer at Bunker Hill, declining supreme command of the American army. In the last charge during that battle, he was mortally wounded. The monument at Bunker Hill stands near the spot where he fell.

War'saw, a city of Russia, the capital of Russian Poland, is situated on the left bank of the Vistula, 625 mi. s. of Saint Petersburg and 320 mi. e. of Berlin. The city is built upon a hill, which slopes toward the river, and is connected with its suburb, Praga, by an iron bridge. The old part of the town is characterized by narrow, winding streets and quaint buildings, erected during the Middle Ages. It is enclosed by a wall, which is entered through a number of gates. Around this part of the town are the suburbs, which are of a more modern structure. In Castle Square stands the castle of the old Polish kings, now used as a residence for the governor-general. The Roman Catholic cathedral of Saint Johns, dating from the thirteenth century; the Church of the Holy Virgin, dating from the fifteenth century, and the Church of Saint Anne, of about the same date, are also of interest. The city contains a number of public monuments, among them an obelisk, which was erected to the memory of the Polish generals who fell in 1830. The educational institutions include a university, an observatory, a polytechnic institute, a conservatory of music and a museum of fine arts.

Warsaw is an important industrial center, and its leading manufactures include machinery, chemicals, food products, matches, spirits, tobacco and boots and shoes. Population in 1911, 872,478.

War'ship, a vessel designed especially for battle (See NAVY and articles therein referred to). From the earliest times ships were protected against the enemy; at first by leather, brass, lead or rope, or, best of all, by oaken bulwarks, which proved sufficient until the explosive shell came into use; then steel and iron armor became necessary (See ARMOR PLATE). This was developed until now about one-fourth of the weight of a battleship consists of armor. When the United States battleship *Connecticut* was launched, in 1904, it was the most formidable warship in the world. In 1906 the completion of the British battleship *Dreadnought* marked a new era in naval construction. Battleships are now classed as pre-dreadnoughts, or those built before 1906, and dreadnoughts, those built since. So great is the difference in the fighting power of these two classes of ships that in estimating the relative

strength of the world's navies only the dreadnoughts are now counted. The dreadnought
carries a main battery of large guns of uniform
calibre, whereas the earlier ships carry a mixed
armament. The dreadnoughts are much larger
and maintain a much higher rate of speed. The
warships built since 1910 show a further remarkable increase in size, and are naturally enough
called super-dreadnoughts.

The British *Dreadnought* was for a time the
most powerful battleship afloat. It is 490 feet
long, has a breadth of 82 feet, a displacement of
17,900 tons and a speed of 21.6 knot per hour.
Hardly was the *Dreadnought* off the ways when
construction was begun on ships which should
be even larger and more powerful. Great Britain,
Germany and the United States have taken the
lead in this policy. The *Queen Elizabeth*, completed in 1913, is the most powerful British
battleship. It carries a main battery of eight
15-inch guns, besides sixteen 6-inch guns and
twelve 3-inch guns for use against aeroplanes.
The British navy now has over 20 ships more
powerful then the original *Dreadnought*, and is
building three or four more each year. Germany
is building two, and occasionally three, a year.

The first American dreadnoughts were the
Michigan and *South Carolina*, laid down in 1906.
These are 450 feet long, 80 feet 3 in. in beam and
have a displacement of 17,620 tons. The main
battery is composed of eight 12-inch guns,
mounted in pairs, two pairs forward and two
pairs aft; there are also twenty-two small guns
for use against torpedoes. The sides of the ships
are protected by Krupp armor from 8 to 12
inches thick, tapering to 4 inches at the bow and
stern. The later dreadnoughts have a greater
displacement and a larger number of big guns.
The newest ship afloat is the *Texas*, laid down
in 1911 and completed in 1914. The *Texas*
has a displacement of 27,000 tons, is 573 feet
long and 95 feet on the beam. Her boilers are
a combination of coal and oil burners and her
speed is 21 knots an hour. The main battery
comprises ten 14-inch guns, mounted in pairs
in electrically controlled turrets. These big
guns have a range of 21,000 yards, about four
miles, and a broadside may be fired from either
side. The shells, which weigh 1400 pounds
each, can penetrate steel armor 16 inches thick
at a distance of two miles. The *Texas* also carries
twenty-five 5-inch guns against torpedo attack.
The sister-ship of the *Texas* is the *New York*.

The *armored cruiser*, occupying a position
between the battleship and the scouting boat,

partakes of the qualities of both. The tendency has been to increase the speed and size of
the cruisers, especially in Great Britain. The
British cruiser *Tiger*, launched in December,
1913, has a displacement of 28,000 tons and a
speed of 28 knots. Though officially a cruiser,
it resembles the *Queen Elizabeth*. It carries
eight thirteen 5-inch and twelve 6-inch guns.
Greater speed is desirable in a cruiser, whose
function is the pursuit of the enemy's ships.

The cruiser *Colorado*, completed in 1904, is
representative of the United States warships of
this class. It is 502 feet long and 70 feet broad,
and it has a maximum displacement of slightly
over 15,000 tons and a speed of nearly 23 knots.
It is protected along the entire water line by a
belt of armor over 7 feet high and from 3½ to
6 inches thick. The armor is arranged much
like that on a battleship, but is somewhat
lighter. The central citadel encloses ten 6-inch
rapid-fire guns, separated from one another by
steel walls 2½ inches thick. At each corner of
this citadel, another 6-inch gun is mounted, to
fire ahead or astern. The largest guns carried
by the *Colorado* are four 8-inch rifles, mounted
in barbette turrets, one in the fore, and one in
the after, part of the vessel. In the more recent
cruisers, the *Montana* and the *Washington*,
these turrets are occupied by 10-inch guns.
The *Colorado* also carries a number of 3-inch
rifles, 3-pounders, 1-pounders and automatic
guns.

The distinguishing features of the *protected
cruiser* are a curved deck of 1 to 4-inch steel,
under the guns, but above the magazines and
engines; and a main battery of 5-inch, 6-inch
or 8-inch guns, with a proportionate battery of
smaller calibers. The *unprotected cruiser* averages about 3000 tons in displacement, has no armor other than its steel hull and deck, of about
¾-inch steel, and mounts no larger rifles than 5-
inch. The sea-going gunboat is a cruiser of
about 1000 tons displacement, without armor
and with no guns above 4 or 6-inch calibers.

Wart Hog, a name common to certain members of the hog family living in Africa. The
head is very large and broad. Immense tusks
project from the mouth outward and upward,
and the cheeks are furnished with flesh-like protuberances, resembling warts. Wart hogs feed
on roots of plants, which they dig up with their
tusks. (See illustration on next page.)

War'wick, R. I., a town in Kent co., 5 mi. s.
of Providence, on Narragansett and Cowesett
bays, on the Pawtuxet and Providence rivers

and on the New York, New Haven & Hartford railroad. It is an important industrial center and contains cotton factories, foundries, machine shops and other establishments. The place was settled in 1642 and was called Shawomet until named in honor of the earl of Warwick, in 1648. Nathaniel Greene was born in the town. Population in 1910, 26,629.

Warwick, RICHARD NEVILLE, Earl of, called the *Kingmaker* (1428–1471), a great English nobleman. He was the son of the earl of Salisbury and became earl of Warwick by marrying the heiress of the Warwick title and estates. Taking the Yorkist side in the Wars of the Roses,

WART HOG

he was the main instrument in placing Edward IV on the throne in 1461, in place of Henry VI, and he became the most powerful nobleman in the kingdom. He quarreled with Edward, however, on account of the latter's marriage, went over to Henry's side and was able to place him again on the throne, but was defeated and slain at the Battle of Barnet.

Washburn, *wawsh'burn,* CADWALLADER COLDEN (1818–1882), an American soldier, politician and capitalist, born at Livermore, Maine. He removed to Iowa in 1839 and later to Illinois, where he studied law, and finally began practice at Mineral Point, Wis. He made a fortune in lumbering and was one of the first to engage in flour milling on a large scale. In 1854 he was elected to Congress as an anti-slavery man and was twice reëlected. At the outbreak of the Civil War he raised a regiment of cavalry in Wisconsin and entered the Federal service in February, 1862, serving first in Arkansas and then as major general of volunteers, at the head of a division of the Army of Tennessee. He served in the Vicksburg campaign and was then placed at the head of various western military districts, remaining in the service until May, 1865. He again entered Congress two years later, and in 1872 he was elected governor

of Wisconsin. Washburn was a liberal patron of education, was the founder of an orphan asylum at Minneapolis and gave an astronomical observatory to the University of Wisconsin.

Washburn, WILLIAM DREW (1831–   ), an American manufacturer and political leader, born in Livermore, Maine. He graduated at Bowdoin College and soon removed to Minnesota, where he practiced law. He became interested in flour and lumber mills and accumulated a large fortune by his connection with the Washburn-Crosby, and later the Pillsbury-Washburn, flouring mills, the largest in the world. He also was promoter and chief stockholder of the Minneapolis & Saint Louis and the Minneapolis, Saint Paul & Sault Saint Marie railroads. Mr. Washburn was a member of the state legislature for two terms, of Congress for three terms (1879–1885) and of the United States Senate for one term (1889–1895).

Washburne, ELIHU BENJAMIN (1816–1887), an American statesman, born at Livermore, Maine. He began life as a printer's apprentice and afterward taught a district school, later becoming editor of the Kennebec *Journal.* In 1836 he began the study of law at Kent's Hill Seminary, and later he attended the Harvard Law School. He was admitted to the bar in 1840 and began the practice of law in Galena, Ill. He became prominent in the Whig party in Illinois, was elected to Congress in 1852 and served continuously until 1869. During the Civil War he was a warm friend and supporter of General Grant, and was appointed secretary of state in Grant's first cabinet. Washburne soon resigned, however, to become minister plenipotentiary to France, which office he held during the Franco-German War, exhibiting, as the representative of German interests at Paris, remarkable diplomatic ability. His *Recollections of a Minister to France* was published in 1887.

Washington, *wawsh'ing ton,* the EVERGREEN STATE, the most northwestern state of the Union, bounded on the n. by British Columbia, on the e. by Idaho, on the s. by Oregon and on the w. by the Pacific Ocean. Its extent from east to west is about 350 miles and from north to south, about 240 miles. The area is 69,127 sq. mi. of which 2291 sq. mi. are water. Population in 1910, 1,141,990.

SURFACE AND DRAINAGE. The Cascade Mountains cross the state from north to south about 120 miles east of the coast, and divide it into two unequal parts, Eastern Washington and Western

Washington. These mountains form the chief physiographic feature of the state and have a mean elevation of about 8000 feet. Their eastern slope rises gradually from the interior plateau, but the western slope is steep and broken. The range contains a number of lofty peaks whose summits are covered with perpetual snow. The most noted among these are Mount Rainier, 14,-526 feet, now enclosed in a national park, Mount Adams, 12,307 feet, Mount Baker, 10,827 feet and Mount Saint Helens, 10,000 feet. Eastern Washington, which includes nearly two-thirds of the state, contains the Columbia River Basin, which is by far the largest natural division of surface within the state. Within this basin are the great irrigated and grain growing districts and a number of fertile valleys. In the southeastern part of the state the Blue Mountains rise to an altitude of about 6000 feet. Western Washington is naturally divided into three physiographic regions—the Puget Sound Basin, including the territory between the Olympic and Cascade Mountains, and surrounding the great inland sea, Puget Sound; the Olympic Peninsula, including that portion of the state containing the Olympic Mountains and the region extending from them to the Pacific; and the southwestern division, which occupies the region fronting on the Columbia River and Pacific Ocean and extending northward until it meets the Olympic Peninsula.

The eastern section of the state, or Eastern Washington, is drained entirely by the Columbia River and its tributaries. This river enters the state near the northeastern corner and flows south by west, then westward in an irregular course, then southward and southeastward until it reaches the southern boundary, when it makes a sharp turn to the west and pursues its course to the Pacific. These changes in direction form what is known as the Great Bend in the Columbia River, and this is for a part of the way the western boundary of the plateau. The chief tributaries of the Columbia are Clark Fork, from Idaho; the Snake, which flows through the southeastern corner of the state; the Spokane, the Okanogan, the Methow, the Wenatchee and the Yakima. Western Washington is drained into Puget Sound and the Pacific. In this part of the state all of the rivers are short and comparatively unimportant, the most important being the Cowlitz, flowing southward into the Columbia, the Chehalis, flowing directly into the Pacific, and the Skagit, which enters Puget Sound. The state contains a number of mountain lakes, the largest being Lake Chelan.

CLIMATE. The Cascade Mountains divide the state into two climatic regions. Eastern Washington is characterized by hot summers, cold though not severe winters and light rainfall, the annual average being about 16 inches. In many sections irrigation is necessary to successful agriculture. Except upon the high altitudes, there are many hot days during the summer. During the winter there are heavy falls of snow, which are welcomed by the farmers, because as the snow on the lowlands melts, it is absorbed by the soil, and that upon the mountains during the summer feeds the streams which supply water for irrigation. The climate of Western Washington is mild and moist. Here the annual rainfall varies from 20 to 132 inches. The winters are mild and the summers are free from extreme heat.

MINERAL RESOURCES. There are extensive deposits of coal in the Puget Sound Basin, notably in King, Pierce, Kittitas, Lewis, Whatcom and Thurston counties. These are now well developed, and over 3,000,000 tons of coal are mined annually. Both bituminous and lignite varieties are found. Veins of ore producing gold, silver, copper, lead, quicksilver and a number of rare metals occur throughout the mountainous regions. Gold and silver are mined in Whatcom, Skagit, Snohomish, King, Pierce, Lewis, Skamania, Cowlitz, Okanogan, Chelan, Kittitas, Yakima, Klickitat, Ferry and Stevens counties. Iron ore, and marble, granite, onyx, serpentine, limestone and sandstone occur in large quantities. There are also beds of fire clay, kaolin, talc and asbestos, which may be considered among the valuable resources of the state.

FISHERIES. The waters of Puget Sound, the Columbia River and the indentations along the Pacific coast abound in excellent food-fish, and in the lakes and streams are found large quantities of fresh water fish. The most important branch of the fisheries is catching and curing salmon (See SALMON). Second in point of value are the halibut fisheries. Large quantities of oysters, shrimp, clams and cod are also taken.

AGRICULTURE. Washington has a wide variety of soils. On the uplands of Eastern Washington wheat and other cereals are raised in large quantities. In the diked lands along Puget Sound oats are raised, and in the southeastern part of the state barley constitutes the important crop. Rye, buckwheat and flax are also grown, and in some counties hops are a staple product. Many large irrigated areas east of the mountains are devoted to alfalfa, and it is estimated that the state produces a million tons of hay annually. Potatoes, beets and other vegetables thrive and yield large returns.

Washington is also becoming one of the most important fruit growing states of the Union. In the valleys of Eastern Washington there are thousands of orchards, and they are increasing each year in number and extent. This region is especially valuable for the raising of apples, pears, peaches, plums and cherries. In the western part of the state small fruits are raised in large quantities, and grapes are grown upon both sides of the mountains.

The mild winters and excellent pasturage make the raising of live stock profitable, and large numbers of cattle, horses, sheep and hogs are found. For all of these there is a ready market. Dairying is also profitable and can be practiced under ideal conditions.

MANUFACTURES. Washington has abundant water power and a vast forest area. Because of these conditions, lumbering and its allied industries—the manufacture of doors, sash, shingles and furniture, constitute a leading manufacturing industry, in which over 100,000 men are employed. Lumber mills are quite generally distributed through the forest regions, but the most extensive establishments are found in the large forests of Western Washington.

In the Puget Sound Basin large quantities of lime are produced. Granite is quarried in Snohomish and Spokane counties. In other localities valuable sandstone occurs, and onyx of great variety and beauty is quarried in Stevens County. In King County are factories for the manufacture of brick, tile, terra cotta, stoneware and sewer pipe. Portland cement is produced in Skagit County, and iron and steel in Jefferson County.

TRANSPORTATION. Puget Sound and the Pacific Ocean have a coast line exceeding 2000 miles in extent. The largest ocean ships can sail on the Sound as far as Seattle and Tacoma, which are the chief harbors of the state. Three transcontinental lines of railway, the Great Northern, the Chicago, Milwaukee & Puget Sound and the Northern Pacific cross the state from east to west. Railway lines extend north and south from the great centers of trade on Puget Sound, and connect all important cities and towns in the state and with cities in British Columbia.

GOVERNMENT. The legislature consists of a house of representatives, that cannot exceed 99 members or be less than 63, and a senate, whose number cannot exceed one-half, or be less than

one-third, of the number of representatives. The representatives are elected for two years, and the senators are elected for four years. The legislature meets biennially, and the regular sessions are limited to sixty days. The executive department consists of a governor, a lieutenant-governor, a secretary of state, a treasurer, an auditor, an attorney-general, a superintendent of public instruction and a commissioner of public lands, elected for four years. The courts consist of a supreme court of nine judges, elected for six years, and a superior court in each county, presided over by a judge elected for four years.

EDUCATION. The public schools are under the direction of the superintendent of public instruction and a board of education. The schools are organized on the district plan, and each district must maintain a school for at least five months in the year. Cities and towns have good graded schools. The school fund is derived from state and local taxes and from income from the permanent fund derived from the sale and lease of school lands. The state university is at Seattle, and normal schools are maintained at Bellingham, Cheney and Ellensburg. The state college is at Pullman. A number of schools are maintained by religious denominations. Chief among these is Gonzaga College, at Spokane, and Whitman College, at Walla Walla.

INSTITUTIONS. The schools for the deaf and the blind are at Vancouver. The hospitals for the insane are at Fort Steilacoom and Medical Lake, and there is a soldiers' home at Orting and a veterans' home at Port Orchard. The penal institutions consist of the penitentiary at Walla Walla and the reformatory at Monroe. The state training school is located at Chehalis.

CITIES. The chief cities are Olympia, the capital; Seattle, Spokane, Tacoma, Bellingham, Walla Walla and Everett, each of which is described under its title.

HISTORY. For early history, see OREGON, subhead *History*. The territory of Washington was separated from Oregon in 1853, and soon afterward the discovery of gold led to an influx of population, which in turn induced the Indians to plan a massacre, known as the Washington-Oregon War, in 1855. Indian troubles continued to appear from time to time, but the constant influx of white population finally led to the abandonment of the territory by the Indians. After the Civil War, there were violent anti-Chinese agitations, which for a time retarded this territory's growth. Numerous attempts were made to secure statehood, and in 1889 the Omnibus Statehood Bill, admitting the two Dakotas, Montana and Washington, was signed by the president, and Washington became a state. The growth in the population and wealth of Washington since its admission has been phenomenal.

Washington, UNIVERSITY OF, a co-educational college founded at Seattle, Washington, in 1861, and supported by the state. It maintains a college of liberal arts, college of engineering, a school of forestry, a school of mines, colleges of pharmacy and law and a graduate department. The faculty numbers about 150, and there are over 2500 students. The library contains 55,000 volumes and the annual income exceeds $450,000.

Washington. The city of Washington, capital of the United States, lies on the left, or east, bank of the Potomac River, 156 mi. from Chesapeake Bay and 185 mi. from the Atlantic Ocean. It is situated in the District of Columbia, which covers an area of about 70 sq. mi. The Eastern Branch of the Potomac joins the larger stream and forms the southeastern boundary of the city. Rock Creek, a fine little stream, running between high, picturesque banks, is the northwestern boundary. Naturally the location was not beautiful, but the mingling of low, level lands with hills and streams gave an opportunity for building one of the most beautiful cities in the country.

The plan is unique, and though the growth has not been in accordance with expectations, yet the city has kept largely within the limits of the original scheme. The Capitol is the center of the great design. It stands on a hill in the center of a square park, the sides of which face the points of the compass. From the middle of the four sides of the square extend four great streets, which separate the city into quarters, known as North West, North East, South West and South East. These four streets are known as North and South Capitol and East and West Capitol streets. The streets running parallel to East and West Capitol Street are named, both north and south, for the letters of the alphabet. The streets parallel to North and South Capitol Street are numbered consecutively east and west. Broad avenues, named for the states, traverse the city from northwest to southeast and from northeast to southwest. All of this will be clearly understood if the reader will study the accompanying map. While at first glance the plan may seem confusing, yet it is really an excellent one, to afford ready

communication to all parts of the city, and it lends itself admirably to making Washington a great and beautiful residence city. In locating any place it is necessary, of course, to mention the quarter of the city. When this is done, the location is very definite; for instance, 1850 F Street N. W., would be known to lie between Eighteenth and Nineteenth Streets on F Street, in the northwestern part of the city. In the addressing of mail to the North West section, it is customary to omit the letters *N. W.*, but those for the other three sections should always be written.

The North West quarter of the city contains most of the business houses, the finest residence section and most of the government buildings. Pennsylvania Avenue, the principal business street, extends northwest from the Capitol for about a mile to the Treasury building; there it bends sharply to the north and again to the west, here passing in front of the Executive Mansion and the State, War and Navy building; beyond that it turns again to the northwest and extends into Georgetown. Seventh, Ninth and F, N. W., are among the important business streets. (See subhead *Parks and Boulevards.*)

Washington is connected with Baltimore (40 miles distant), New York (226 miles), Philadelphia (136 miles), Chicago (811 miles) and other large cities, east and west, by the Baltimore & Ohio, the Pennsylvania and other railroads. All trains will eventually be brought to the magnificent union station, north of Capitol Hill. Within the city, transportation is rendered easy by fine systems of electric railways, which run through all the principal streets and to the public buildings. Electric railways also connect Washington with Mount Vernon, Anacostia, Georgetown and Arlington.

PARKS AND BOULEVARDS. The park surrounding the Capitol occupies sixteen city blocks, crowning a hill 58 feet high, overlooking the west half of the city. It is laid out with drives and walks, bordered by magnificent trees and beautiful shrubbery, interspersed with beds, in which blossom the flowers of the season. The small ornamental buildings, fountains and statuary lend a peculiar charm to the whole park. From the west front of the Capitol a person looks down upon the broad Mall, which extends about a mile, to the imposing Washington Monument, and is four blocks wide throughout. In the immediate foreground, between the Mall and the Capitol, are the government conservatory and botanical gardens, in which may be seen foreign and native herbs, shrubbery and trees in profusion. Native and foreign trees, shrubs and plants beautify the walks and drives of the Mall, also, along whose west side are grouped several of the finest public buildings. Running north from the west end of the Mall are the Executive grounds, a magnificent tract, which, with the private gardens of the White House, cover about twenty city squares. In

logical Park, which in time will become one of the greatest in the world. North of this extends Rock Creek Park, a tract which is preserved in all its natural beauty. In the spring, when the foliage is fresh and the flowers in the parks in full bloom, no more beautiful city is to be found, for the streets are all broad and open and, in the better parts of the city, smoothly paved with asphalt.

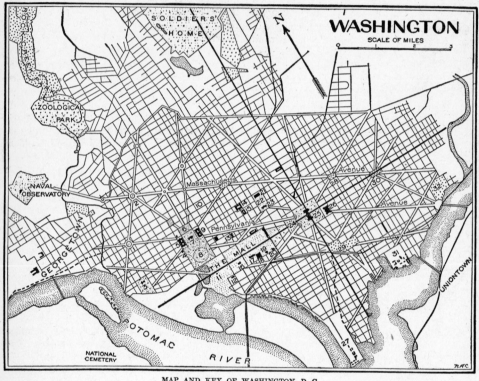

MAP AND KEY OF WASHINGTON, D. C.

1. Washington Circle.
2. Dupont Circle.
3. Old Naval Observatory.
4. New Corcoran Art Gallery.
5. State, War and Navy Building.
6. Lafayette Square.
7. White House.
8. Executive Grounds.
9. Treasury Department.
10. Franklin Square.
11. Washington Monument.
12. Bureau of Printing and Engraving.
13. General Postoffice.
14. Patent Offices.
15. Land Office.
16. Agricultural Department Building.
17. Smithsonian Institution.
18. National Museum.
19. Medical Museum.
20. Fish Commission.
21. Pension Office.
22. Judiciary Square.
23. City Hall.
24. Botanical Garden.
25. United States Capitol.
26. Library of Congress.
27. Arsenal.
28. Stanton Park.
29. Garfield Park.
30. Lincoln Park.
31. Navy Yard.
32. Congressional Cemetery.

front of the White House and across Pennsylvania Avenue is Lafayette Square, another exquisite park, adorned with fine statuary. The intersections of the avenues and streets throughout the city form squares and circles which are public gardens filled with statuary, flowers and shrubs. Other parks in different parts of the city afford resting places for visitors, and out beyond Rock Creek is the great National Zoö-

PUBLIC BUILDINGS AND INSTITUTIONS. Chief of all the public buildings is the Capitol, which because of its towering dome is conspicuous from any direction in which one approaches the city. The original plans for the Capitol were drawn by Doctor Thornton, a native of the West Indies, but they were redrawn by Stephen H. Hallet; they were followed in the construction of the first building, which little resembled the Capitol of to-day. The north wing, which contains the Supreme Court rooms, was finished in 1800, but the opposite wing was not ready until eleven years later. A wooden passageway then connected them. After the British burned the Capitol in 1814, the new central structure was planned, and the original building was completed in 1827, at a cost of not quite $2,500,000. In 1851 the building was remodeled, and in 1856 the erection of the present iron dome was begun. The Capitol as it now stands, together with its approaches, has cost about $15,000,000. The building is 751 feet long and 350 feet in its greatest width, and it covers nearly four acres of ground. Within the magnificent building are the two chambers occupied by the Senate and the House of Representatives, rooms for the Supreme Court and apartments for the various committees and officials who meet at the Capitol, and other rooms, made necessary by the great amount of business transacted there. The rotunda, the marble stairways and the dome are decorated with choice statuary and paintings by famous American artists. Most of the paintings depict great events in the nation's history. The famous doors, designed by Randolph Rogers, which guard the east entrance, are ornamented, in high relief, with historic scenes from the life of Columbus. The old Hall of Representatives is now called Statuary Hall, and around its walls are statues of men whose names have become household words in the nation. Most of these statues have been donated by the legislatures of the states to which the men belonged.

Along the Mall are the buildings of the fish commission, the Medical Museum, the great National Museum, the Smithsonian Institution, the agricultural department and the bureau of engraving and printing (See NATIONAL MUSEUM OF THE UNITED STATES; SMITHSONIAN INSTITUTION). East of the White House is the low, massive treasury department building, while west of it rises the magnificent building of the state, war and navy departments (See WHITE HOUSE). The government printing office, the pension office and the interior department are in different localities of the North West quarter. Near the Capitol, and east of it, is the Library of Congress, the grandest library building in existence (See LIBRARY OF CONGRESS). Within the library are housed more than 1,000,000 books and pamphlets and nearly 500,000 pieces of music, photographs and manuscripts. It is a rich collection in every department and is open to the public during library hours, but only members of Congress and a few government officials may take books away from the building.

To the north, and in a space adjoining the Capitol grounds, a magnificent granite building is in process of erection, in which is to be located offices for the senators, and to the south, another building of white marble, which will contain offices for the members of the House of Representatives. These great structures will constitute a notable addition to the splendid group of buildings which now crowns Capitol Hill.

The United States navy yard occupies a large tract of land on the east branch of the Potomac, and the arsenal is on the peninsula where the two rivers join. The old naval observatory was in a park on the Potomac, some distance west of the Executive buildings, but the present observatory is on a reservation north of Georgetown. The government has been generous with its public buildings and institutions, and no adequate idea can be given of them or their contents in any description. Most of the departmental buildings contain museums illustrating their particular activities, and these are open to inspection for the thousands of tourists who visit the city. The government sustains a hospital for the insane and various other hospitals, almshouses and public and charitable institutions. On a beautiful reservation, north of the city, is the Soldiers' Home, where disabled veterans of the army pass their last days in comfort. Near the State, War and Navy building is the new building of the Corcoran Art Gallery, a beautiful marble structure, which, with its priceless collection of paintings and statuary, was given to the public by W. W. Corcoran.

GOVERNMENT, COMMERCE AND INDUSTRIES. The government of the city, which is that of the District of Columbia, is directly in the hands of Congress, who act through a board of three commissioners appointed by the president (See DISTRICT OF COLUMBIA). In this respect Washington differs, with one exception, from any other city in the United States, or, in fact, in the world. It is peculiarly the capital of the United States, and its life and activities are all controlled by national influences. It is the official residence of the president, the members of the cabinet, members of both houses of Congress and the host of government employes who work in the various offices and departments. When Congress is in session, the whole city is permeated by its influence, and all its industries are affected. There are few manufactures of any importance, and little commerce is carried on with outside cities. The business is almost entirely a retail trade with the people who live in the city. Naturally, the shifting population creates a demand for hotels, and they are to be found in great numbers, ranging from the lavish new buildings of the region east of the Executive Mansion to simple, inexpensive hotels and boarding houses, scattered everywhere throughout the city.

EDUCATIONAL INSTITUTIONS. Washington is rapidly becoming a great educational center. It has an excellent public school system, which has the distinction of having been organized in 1800 under a board of trustees of which Thomas Jefferson was the first president.

The leading universities of the capital are Georgetown University, George Washington University, the Catholic University, with its affiliated colleges of the religious orders, and Howard University, an institute for colored youth.

On a commanding site near the city, the buildings of the new American University, established by the Methodist Church, are in course of erection.

Supplementing the universities are the great scientific bureaus and institutions for research maintained by the government, such as the Bureau of Fisheries, the Bureau of Standards, the Geological Survey, the Bureau of Labor, the scientific bureaus of the Department of Agriculture, the Bureau of Education, the Army Medical Museum, the National Museum, the Library of Congress and a large number of small libraries connected with various departments of the government.

The Smithsonian Institution, founded by James Smithson, an Englishman, who gave half a million dollars for its establishment, and the more recent Carnegie Institution, with an endowment of $10,000,000, are the leading private foundations for the advancement of knowledge.

The capital thus affords opportunities for advanced students, especially, in law, medicine, political economy or scientific research, such as are perhaps to be found in no other city.

HISTORY. Washington enjoys the distinction of having been designed and built for the capital of a great nation. Rome, London, Paris and Berlin grew out of the national conditions surrounding them and became the capitals of great empires, but the capital of the United States was located in a region sparsely populated and almost wholly wild; it was built from plans that were

created before any city was in existence there. The site was selected by the great president whose name was given the city, and he watched over its early days with a personal care and interest. In fact, it was he who employed Pierre Charles L'Enfant, a French civil engineer, to prepare the plans for the proposed city. It is said that L'Enfant rode over the ground with the president and commissioners and grew enthusiastic over the location, deeming it a fit site for the capital of a "mighty empire." Jefferson furnished L'Enfant with plans of the great cities of Europe, but the French engineer, faithful to the inspiration he had received from Versailles, filled his noble plans with broad avenues, vistas, streets and parkings, which eclipse anything in the world and make Washington truly the "City of Magnificent Distances." The Capitol was located on the hill, which was then a thick wood, and the lines of latitude and longitude which marked its center were carefully surveyed, and the streets and avenues were laid from this point with mathematical exactness. It was manifestly the intention that the chief front of the Capitol should be toward the east, and that the public buildings should be placed about that side; but many forces contributed to change this idea, and now the west front, with its great terraces topping the hill and with its magnificent stairways extending far down the side, dwarfs into comparative insignificance the east front and the flat court before it. Major L'Enfant was of an erratic temperament and was unable to agree with the commissioners, so that for a long time his plans were scorned by Congress, but more recently the value of his services has come to be appreciated. The city grew until 1814, when after a weak resistance by our troops at Bladensburg, it was captured by the British, who set fire to the public buildings and some private residences, with the expectation of destroying the entire city. A storm put out the conflagration, and the next day the British, in a panic of unnecessary fear, retreated, leaving Washington to be immediately rebuilt. At the breaking out of the Civil War, it contained about 61,000 inhabitants. The land through the northwestern part of the city fell into the hands of speculators of acute intelligence, and from time to time Congress was compelled to spend large sums of money in opening streets and beautifying that section of the city, so that now it surpasses the other parts as much as the west front of the Capitol does the east.

POPULATION. Naturally the actual popula-

GEORGE WASHINGTON—*Stuart*
The unfinished portrait in the Athenaeum, Boston

ion of Washington varies at different times of the year, the city being crowded during the winter, when Congress is in session, and thousands of visitors, friends of the members of Congress and government attaches throng the national capital. The census of 1910 gave the population at 331,-069, a gain of about 8000 in ten years.

Washington, IND., the county-seat of Daviess co., 85 mi. s. w. of Indianapolis, on the Baltimore & Ohio Southwestern and the Evansville & Indianapolis railroads. It is in a farming and stock-raising district, containing, also, extensive deposits of coal, kaolin and fire clay. The city has lumber and flour mills, brick and tile works, railroad shops, foundry and machine shops and other factories. The municipality has a high school, a public library and the Saint Simon's Academy, and it owns and operates the electric light plant. Population in 1910, 7854.

Washington, PA., the county-seat of Washington co., 25 mi. s. w. of Pittsburg, on the Pennsylvania, the Baltimore & Ohio and other railroads. It is the seat of Washington & Jefferson College, and it also contains the Washington Female Seminary, Trinity Hall and two commercial colleges. The borough contains the Citizens' Library, a county law library and that of the Y. M. C. A. There are oil wells in the vicinity, as well as extensive deposits of coal and limestone. The manufactures include tubing, steel products, glass, brick and other articles. The place was settled in 1768 and was originally called Bassetton. It received its present name in 1784 and was chartered as a borough in 1852. Population in 1900, 7670; in 1910 it was 18,-778.

Washington, BOOKER TALIAFERRO (about 1858–), an American negro educator. He was born a slave, and at the close of the Civil War he began work in a salt furnace in West Virginia. At this time he attended night school and obtained the rudiments of an education. He finally reached Hampton Normal and Agricultural Institute, where he remained for three years. After this he engaged in teaching at his former home, then he entered Wayland Seminary in Washington, D. C. On completing his course of study there, he was chosen one of the instructors at Hampton and given charge of the work of the indian pupils and of the night school. His success was phenomenal, and in 1881 he was selected by General Armstrong, principal of the institute, to start a normal school at Tuskegee, Ala. Mr. Washington began his work in an old building, with thirty pupils, but in the course of

the year he purchased the plantation where the Tuskegee Normal and Industrial Institute is now located. Under his management this school has developed into the largest and most influential industrial school for colored people in the world (See TUSKEGEE NORMAL AND INDUSTRIAL INSTITUTE). Mr. Washington is the leader in the movement for industrial education of the negro, and he firmly believes that it is only through intelligent application to the common occupations of life that the race will ever reach a high standard. He has traveled extensively and lectured throughout the United States and Europe. He is a forceful and eloquent speaker and is regarded as the foremost representative of his race. He is the author of *The Future of the American Negro, Up from Slavery* (his autobiography), *Character Building, The Story of My Life* and *Working with the Hands.* Consult *Up from Slavery* and *The Story of My Life.*

Washington, GEORGE (1732–1799), an American statesman, the hero of American independence. He was born in Westmoreland County, Va., February 22, 1732, the son of Augustine Washington, a well-to-do farmer, and the eldest of a second family of children. As a boy he possessed a fine physique, was athletically inclined and was especially graceful and expert as a rider. He was not by nature a scholar but was thoughtful and studious. His education was limited to the elementary subjects, but he acquired a fine knowledge of mathematics and surveying, chiefly by self-study. He desired to enter the British navy, but his widowed mother prevailed upon him to abandon the idea; he thereupon adopted surveying as a profession, became public surveyor in 1748, and by his sensible, business-like manner and conduct of the office he gained the esteem of his neighbors and of the government officials.

His military career began at the age of nineteen, when he was appointed adjutant general of one of the military districts of Virginia. He soon showed in operations against the French and indians that he united in an eminent degree the qualities of a successful commander. However, in 1754, when in command of a regiment upon the frontier, he was forced to surrender to a superior French force at Fort Necessity. In 1755 Washington accompanied General Braddock upon his ill-fated expedition to Fort Duquesne and was almost the only officer who returned safe from that expedition. Indeed, it appears that the unfortunate ending of the enterprise was due largely to Braddock's disregard of Washington's wise counsel, and but for the bravery and skill of Washington and his Virginia troops in the action, the British force would probably have been totally annihilated. In 1758 he again took an important part in an expedition that captured Fort Duquesne.

In the meantime, extensive estates at Mount Vernon had come into his possession, through the death of his half-brother Lawrence. To these possessions he added largely by marrying, in 1759, Mrs. Martha Custis, a wealthy young widow. He then devoted himself to the management of his lands, though he sat for some years in the Virginia assembly. He soon gained a preëminent position in the colony and became one of the wealthiest men in America. In the pre-Revolutionary struggle against England, he sympathized with the patriots, but counseled moderation and urged war as the last resort.

In 1774 Washington was elected to the Continental Congress, and shortly after the outbreak of war he was chosen commander in chief of the American forces. He accepted the commission reluctantly and refused all pay for his services, asking only that his necessary expenses be repaid, when possible, after the war. The details of his campaigns constitute the story of the Revolutionary War, which will be found in a separate article. It is sufficient to say that the struggle was carried on by him under extraordinary disadvantages, but with such rare skill and patience that the success which finally resulted seems now an inevitable consequence and certainly was no more than a just reward of his stupendous efforts.

When peace was signed, in 1783, Washington retired to Mount Vernon, where he devoted himself to the care and extension of his property. He was sent as a delegate to the constitutional convention in 1787 and was unanimously chosen its president. In that position he used his rare tact and judgment to bring all parties to agreement upon what he considered the prerequisites of a satisfactory instrument.

He was chosen first president of the United States under the Constitution and took the oath of office April 30, 1789, at New York. From the first he displayed in civil affairs the same qualities of leadership and invariable good judgment which he had shown during his military career. He set about informing himself concerning all that had happened during the period of the Confederation—the relations of the new government to foreign nations, and the questions of internal ad-

ministration and finance, which were soon to become pressing issues. He also chose a remarkably strong cabinet, including Thomas Jefferson and Alexander Hamilton, who, though directly opposite in their political opinions, were acknowledged leaders in the political life of the country. He was reëlected in 1793 in spite of his express wish. During his administrations some of the most important problems which have ever been presented to the American government arose, while the president had also to contend with the additional strain necessarily attendant upon the foundation of a new government and the establishment of official precedents.

In view of all the conditions, the advance of the prosperity of the Republic during Washington's terms and the almost uniform success which attended his efforts in improving the financial, industrial and political condition of the people, were phenomenal. Among the important events of his administrations were the admission of Vermont, Kentucky and Tennessee; the chartering of the first Bank of the United States; the indian wars in the northwest territory, in which General Saint Clair was disastrously defeated and General Wayne won an important victory; the assumption by the government of the debt contracted by the states during the Revolution; the establishment of the national mint; the Whisky Insurrection (See WHISKY INSURRECTION), and important diplomatic difficulties with both England and France (See GENET, EDMUND CHARLES; JAY TREATY).

Washington declined a third election, issued his famous farewell address and retired to Mount Vernon in 1797. Thereafter he devoted himself to agriculture, though in 1798, at the prospect of the war with France, he was chosen commander in chief of the United States army and accepted, though he was not called into the field. He died in December, 1799, from illness brought on by long exposure in the saddle. The news caused almost as widespread mourning in Europe as in America. The greatest statesmen and soldiers of every nation united in paying him tribute as a man, general, statesman and friend of humanity. The words of his old friend and companion, "Lighthorse Harry" Lee, "First in war, first in peace and first in the hearts of his countrymen," were without question literally true. He had avoided the snares of factional and partisan politics, had generously overlooked the harshest criticisms and had respected and used the abilities of his severest critics and opponents. Though a slave-holder at his death, he was in favor of the gradual abolition of slavery by legislation, and by his will he arranged that his one hundred twenty-five slaves should be emancipated at the death of his wife, so that the negroes of the two estates who had intermarried might not be separated.

Consult Lodge's *George Washington*, in the American Statesmen Series, and Fiske's *Washington and His Country*, a condensed and simplified edition of Washington Irving's *Life of Washington*.

Washington, MARTHA (1732–1802), the wife of George Washington, formerly Mrs. Martha Custis. She was born in New Kent County, Va., and married her first husband, Daniel Parke Custis, in 1749. She was married to George Washington in 1759. As mistress of the White House her amiable character won her a firm place in the hearts of the people. She died at Mount Vernon two years and a half after the death of President Washington.

Washington, TREATY OF, the treaty between the United States and Great Britain, signed in 1871, providing for the settlement of several subjects of dispute between the two countries, chief of which were the Alabama claims. A commission, which consisted of five representatives of Great Britain, headed by Earl de Gray and Sir John MacDonald, and five representatives of the United States, headed by Hamilton Fish and E. R. Hoar, began its meetings May 8 at Washington. It referred the Alabama Claims to a special court, which was to meet at Geneva (See ALABAMA, THE; GENEVA ARBITRATION). It provided for the establishment of a mixed commission, to discuss and decide upon the northwestern fisheries question, and it submitted the northwest boundary dispute to the arbitration of the emperor of Germany. It also laid down certain rules regarding neutrality in war, which were to govern the Geneva Tribunal in deciding the Alabama question and which have since been considered the true principles of international law upon the subject.

Washington and Lee University, a higher institution of learning, founded at Lexington, Va., in 1782, as an academy. It was afterwards christened Washington University, and later it received its present name, in honor of General Robert E. Lee, who after the Civil War became its president. He is buried in the college chapel, where a recumbent statue in marble marks his resting-place.

Washington Arch, a beautiful memorial building, erected to commemorate the first inauguration of George Washington as president of the United States. It stands at the foot of Fifth Avenue, New York, and was designed by Stanford White. It is of marble, 77 feet high and 62 feet broad, with a single archway 47 feet high and 30 feet broad. Its cost of $128,000 was met by popular subscription.

Washington Court House, OHIO, the county-seat of Fayette co., 40 mi. s. w. of Columbus, on the Paint Creek and on the Baltimore & Ohio Southwestern, the Detroit Southern, the Cincinnati, Hamilton & Dayton and other railroads. The city is in a farming region and ships considerable poultry. It contains manufactories of boots, shoes, woolen goods, flour and other articles. There are four banks, a high school, a public library and a private business college. Population in 1910, 7277.

Washington Elm, a famous elm, standing near the northwest corner of the Common, in Cambridge, Mass. It was under this tree that Washington assumed command of the American army in July, 1775. It is now carefully protected, but is rapidly decaying.

Washington Monument, an imposing marble obelisk in Washington, D. C., measuring 550 feet in height. It is famous as the tallest monument in the world, excepting the Eiffel Tower in Paris. It was begun in 1848, but was not dedicated until 1885, on Washington's birthday. The top, from which a magnificent view of the surrounding country is obtained, is reached by an elevator and also by an interior iron stairway. The monument covers an area of 16,000 square feet and cost $1,187,710.

Washington University, an institution of higher learning at Saint Louis, Mo., first chartered in 1853. It comprises a college of liberal arts and departments of law, engineering, architecture, fine arts, medicine, dentistry and manual training; it also maintains two preparatory schools. The faculty numbers about 150, and the attendance is over 1300. The library contains 130,000 volumes. The university is on the grounds occupied by the Louisiana Purchase Exposition, and the buildings were used for the anthropological exhibit and for administrative purposes.

Washita, *wosh'e ta,* **River** or **Ouachita River,** a river that rises in the western part of Arkansas, flows southeast and then south into Louisiana and discharges into the Red River, about 15 mi. above the confluence of that stream with the Mississippi. The Washita is connected with the Mississippi by a series of bayous. Its length is 550 miles, and it is navigable for steamboats for about 350 miles.

Wasp, *wahsp,* a common insect, which resembles the bee in many respects. The body is usually bluish in color, with yellow markings; sometimes it is black, marked with white or yellow. The common wasps live in societies, or colonies, composed of males, females and workers, or neuters. The females are armed with an extremely powerful and venomous sting. The wasps build nests, some of which are very ingenious, both as regards material and construction. Having selected a convenient and safe place in the ground or on walls or trees, oval nests are constructed of paper, which they manufacture. Within these nests the combs are enclosed completely, except for the small opening where the wasps enter. The cells of the comb, in which the larvae and pupae are reared, are six-sided and arranged in tiers, with the mouth downward or sidewise. Wasps are voracious insects, living upon sugar, meat, fruit, honey or the juices of other insects. Certain species of wasps live solitary lives, each mother making its own nest and caring for its own eggs and larvae.

Watau'ga Association, a name given in American history to an association of settlers in the eastern part of Tennessee, just west of the Alleghany Mountains. It provided a scheme of government for that region, with a legislature, consisting of thirteen councilors, of whom five constituted the judicial and executive branch of the government, one of their number being the supreme chairman. The government was given no jurisdiction over others than the signers of the compact, and the territory soon swarmed with outlaws and adventurers. In order to secure adequate protection, the signers asked representation in the North Carolina Assembly, as Washington District.

Watch, a pocket timepiece. The first watch was probably made at Nuremberg, about the end of the fifteenth century. In its adaptation to the keeping of time, the watch resembles a clock. It has about the same number of wheels, geared in the same manner. It differs from the clock in having a hairspring and a balance wheel, in place of a pendulum, and in having its parts much smaller and more nicely adjusted, so that it can be confined in a small circular case, easily carried in the pocket.

MECHANISM. A watch consists of two parts, the case and the works. The case is of metal, usually gold or silver, and it is made with one or two covers. The works consist of two plates,

perforated for the purpose of holding the wheels in position, and so arranged that they contain, between them, all of the wheels except the balance wheel. The lower plate, known as the pillar plate, rests next to the dial. The upper plate may be in one or in several pieces, but in the best-made watches it is usually in one piece. These plates are bored and chiseled so that each wheel fits perfectly into its place. The perforations, in which the minute axles of the wheels rest, are usually set in jewels, the ruby, sapphire and other hard stones being used for this purpose. They prevent wear. There are four wheels in the watch; these are (1) the barrel wheel, within which the mainspring is attached, (2) the first wheel, (3) the second wheel and (4) the third wheel, which is attached to the pinion of the escapement wheel. The motion is imparted by the uncoiling of the spring and is regulated by the escapement, which is kept in operation by the action of the mainspring and the hairspring combined, the two giving it an oscillating movement. The wheel which meshes into the pinion of the escapement wheel revolves once a minute and has sixty teeth upon its circumference. The pinion of this wheel meshes into the circumference of the wheel which gives the motion to the minute hands, and this meshes into the pinion of the center wheel, which gives the motion to the hour hands. The watch is regulated by a lever device, connected with the hairspring. By moving this to the right or left, the tension is lessened or strengthened.

WATCH MAKING. The works of a watch have for their foundation two plates of an alloy of brass and nickel. These plates are cut at the foundry, where the metal is cast, from dies furnished by the watch factory.

The rough plates are passed under trimming, or stripping, punches, which smooth off the roughness. Indentations absolutely exact are then made in the foundation plate, to allow room for the little wheels. The plate is placed under the lathe portion of a machine, and a steel copy of what it is to be is fastened to another part. The machine follows the outline of the steel model, gradually cutting out the foundation plate, so that the various parts of the mechanism of the watch will be thrown into proper position. The thickness of the plate and the depth of the indentations are measured so as to be perfect, according to a gauge, two degrees of which equal the thousandth part of an inch. The necessary screw holes and apertures for the settings are then drilled into the plate. The work on the upper plate is done in the same manner. The plates are then polished and smoothed down, on an Ayr stone, which is a cross between a soapstone and an emery stone, being harder than the former and softer than the latter, and capable of polishing without scratching.

The jewels used are garnets, rubies, sapphires and diamonds. Garnets are the ordinary jewels and are cut with diamond points into minute disks; they are then smoothed and pierced. These disks are set in larger disks of gold. The foundation plates are given an ordinary heavy plating of gold, by the battery process, and the jewels with their settings are fitted and fastened into the plate by exceedingly small screws. The wheels of a watch are stamped out of sheets of brass, with the exception of one or two pieces. The screws and springs are made from sheet steel, the screws being cold-drawn from wire. In tempering some of the screws, the workman uses a thermometer of a peculiar sort, in order to regulate accurately the temperature to which they are to be heated and cooled, respectively. Others are regulated by a careful observation of their color. The figures are printed on the dial by a process resembling lithography (See LITHOGRAPHY). The base of the dial is of copper and is stamped out of a thin sheet of the metal, in such a manner that a rim is left turned up for a short distance all around. Powdered enamel is spread on the disk, and it is then fired, like pottery or china. Steel plates are engraved with the design to be executed, and the lines are filled with a mineral paint of the desired color. The plate is then passed under a roller, covered with sheet rubber, and the dial receives the impression from the rubber on the roller. It is again fired, and when fancy colors are employed, each color requires a separate impression and firing. The balance wheel requires forty different steps in its manufacture. When all the parts are assembled, the watch is taken to a refrigerator and subjected to cold. This is followed by a stay in a hot air compartment, the two tests ranging from 40° to 103° F. Since the advent of the machine-made watch, the United States has reached the foremost position as a watch-manufacturing country. The largest watch factory in the world is at Waltham, Mass., and another, nearly as large, is at Elgin, Ill. See CLOCK.

Water, *waw'tur*, a universally diffused liquid. It was classed among the elements until the close of the last century, when Lavoisier, profiting by the experiments of Cavendish, proved it to be a compound of hydrogen and oxygen, in the proportion of two volumes of the former gas to one volume of the latter, or, by weight, 2 parts of hydrogen to 16 parts of oxygen; hence, its formula is H_2O. Pure water is a colorless, tasteless, inodorous liquid; it is a powerful refractor of light and is a bad conductor of heat and electricity; it is very slightly compressible, its absolute diminution for a pressure of one atmosphere being only about 51.3 millionths of its bulk. Although water is colorless in small quantities, it is blue, like the atmosphere, when viewed in mass. It takes a solid form, that of ice or snow, at 32° Fahrenheit (0° Centigrade) and all lower temperatures; and it takes the form of vapor or steam at 212° F. (100° C.) under a pressure of 29.9 inches of mercury, and it retains that form at all higher temperatures. Under ordinary conditions, water possesses the liquid form only at temperatures lying between 32° and 212°. It is, however, possible to cool water very considerably below 32° F. and yet maintain it in the liquid form. Water may also be heated, under pressure, many degrees above 212° F., without passing into the state of steam. The specific gravity of water is 1 at 39.2° F., (that is, one cubic centimeter of water weighs one gram), and it is the unit to which the specific gravities of all solids and liquids are referred, as a convenient standard; one cubic inch of water, at 62° F. and 29.9 inches barometrical pressure, weighs 252.458 grains. Distilled water is 815 times heavier than atmospheric air. Water is at its greatest density at 39.2° F. (4° C.), and in this respect it presents a singular exception to the general law of expansion by heat. If water at 39.2° F. be cooled, it expands as it cools, till reduced to 32°, when it solidifies; and if water at 39.2° F. be heated, it expands as the temperature increases, in accordance with the general law.

From a chemical point of view, water is a neutral fluid and shows in itself neither acid nor basic properties; but it combines with both acids and bases, forming *hydrates*, and with neutral salts. Water also enters, as a liquid, into physical combination with the greater number of all known substances. Of all liquids, water is the most powerful and general solvent, and on this important property its use depends. In consequence of the great solvent power of water, it is never found pure in nature. Even in rain water, which is the purest, there are always traces of carbonic acid, ammonia and sea salt. Where the rain water has filtered through rocks and soils and reappears as spring or river water, it is always more or less charged with salts derived from the earth, such as sea salts, gypsum and chalk. When the proportion of these is small, the water is called *soft*; when larger, it is called *hard water*. The former dissolves soap better and is therefore preferred for washing; the latter is often pleasanter to drink. Some springs contain a considerable quantity of foreign ingredients, which impart to the water particular properties (See MINERAL WATERS). The only way to obtain perfectly pure water is to distill it, but matter simply held in suspension may be taken out by suitable filtration. The great reservoirs of water on the globe are the seas and lakes, which cover more than three-fifths of its surface, and from which water is raised by evaporation. Uniting with the air in the state of vapor, it is wafted over the earth, ready to be precipitated in the form of rain, snow or hail. Water, like air, is absolutely necessary to life, and healthy human life requires that it should be free from contamination; hence, an ample and pure water supply is considered as one of the first laws of sanitation. See ICE; STEAM.

Waterbury, *waw'tur ber ry*, CONN., a city in New Haven co., 18 mi. n. by w. of New Haven, on the Naugatuck River and on three lines of the New York, New Haven & Hartford railroad. It is a very important manufacturing center. Brass ware of various kinds is the most valuable product, and the famous Waterbury watches are made here. There are also large button factories, foundries, machine shops, knitting mills, clock factories, bottling works, publishing houses and engraving establishments. The city is located in a beautiful valley and has three parks and a cemetery of considerable natural beauty. Among the educational institutions are Saint Margaret's School for girls, Convent of Notre Dame, Gerard School, two business colleges and a public high school. Other important features are the Bronson Public Library, Waterbury Hospital, St. Mary's Hospital, Southmayd Home for old ladies, the city hall and the Masonic Temple. The place was settled in 1677 and was known by the indian name of Mattatuck until its incorporation as a town, in 1686. It was chartered as a city in 1853. In 1691 it suffered from a flood; in 1712 an epidemic proved fatal to about one-tenth of the population, and in 1902 a large portion of the business section was destroyed by fire. The town and city of Waterbury were consolidated in 1900. Population in 1910, 73,141.

Water Clock, an early form of clock. See CLEPSYDRA; CLOCK.

Water Colors, pigments mixed and ground with water and mucilage, gum size or some other adhesive substance, instead of oil. The water colors used in painting pictures are generally prepared in the form of small, dry and hard cakes, while those used in coloring walls and the like are simply mixed up with glue or size. The quick drying of water colors is favorable to rapid execution, and a greater clearness is obtained than in an oil painting.

Water Dog. See MUD PUPPY.

Waterfall. See CATARACT.

Water Gas. See GAS, ILLUMINATING.

Water Glass, a substance which, when solid, resembles glass, but which is slowly soluble in boiling water, although it remains unaffected by ordinary atmospheric changes. It is the silicate of sodium, the silicate of potassium or a mixture of both. Among the many purposes to which water glass is applied are painting on glass; coating stone or wood and other materials, to render them waterproof and fireproof; glazing scenery and paintings, and fixing wall paintings. It is also used in the manufacture of an artificial stone and in the manufacture of earthenware.

Waterhouse, *waw'tur hows*, ALFRED (1830–), an English architect, born at Liverpool. He studied architecture in Manchester, and his first work of importance was the design for the Manchester Assize Courts, for the Owens College and for the townhall in that city. Among his chief works in London are the Natural History Museum at South Kensington, the New University Club, the National Liberal Club, the New Saint Paul's Schools and the City and Guilds' Institute. He also partly reconstructed Balliol College, Oxford, and Caius and Pembroke, Cambridge. He was elected a royal academician in 1885.

Waterloo', IOWA, the county-seat of Black Hawk co., on the Red Cedar River and on the Chicago, Rock Island & Pacific, the Illinois Central, the Great Western, the Dubuque & Sioux City and the Waterloo, Cedar Falls & Northern railroads. It is in an agricultural and stock raising district, and it contains foundries, malleable iron works, machine shops, gasoline engine works, farm implement factories, packing houses, canneries and cream separator factories. The principal structures are the government building, courthouse, municipal buildings, Presbyterian and Serphic Heights hospitals and about 30 churches. There are two high schools, Our Lady of Victory Academy and two colleges. The inhabitants are mostly American born, with some German, Irish and Scandinavians. The city was settled about 1845. Population in 1910, 26,693.

Waterloo, BATTLE OF, the famous battle, fought June 18, 1815, near Waterloo, a village in Belgium about eleven miles south of Brussels,

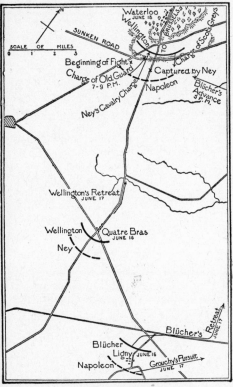

BATTLE OF WATERLOO

between Napoleon and the allied forces under Blücher and Wellington. It was Napoleon's last battle, and it put an end finally to his power (See HUNDRED DAYS). There had been two preliminary battles on the 16th, one at Quatre-Bras, by which Ney, although forced to retire, prevented Wellington from joining his Prussian allies, and one at Ligny, in which the Prussians under Blücher were defeated by Napoleon. On the morning of the eighteenth the main French army was drawn up near Waterloo, opposite the allied British, Dutch and German forces, under Wellington. Blücher, with the Prussian army, was absent at the opening of the fight. The French army numbered about 72,000, the allied army about 67,000, of which number many were untrained troops. Napoleon's plan was to defeat Wellington before Blücher could

come up with his troops, but the ground was in such a condition from the rain that had fallen all night that he was obliged to delay opening battle until almost noon. Wellington, on the contrary, simply aimed to hold out until the Prussians arrived, when a combined attack might be made on the French. In accordance with these plans, the struggle throughout the day consisted chiefly of charges, brilliant but unsuccessful, on the part of the French, and firm resistance on the part of the English. The French cavalry, charging during the afternoon, plunged into an unseen sunken road, and unable to check their rush, they filled the great ditch with troopers, over whom the remainder rode on. These repeated charges, although stubbornly resisted, had their effect, and the outcome of the battle remained doubtful until late in the day, when the arrival of the Prussians, at a time when both armies were about exhausted, completely turned the tide against the French. Napoleon's last effort was the charge of the Old Guard, the picked veterans from the Imperial Guard, late in the evening. Its rout was complete, and many of its squares, refusing to surrender or retreat, fell to the last man. Wellington now gave the order for a general advance, and the French, utterly overpowered, gave way at every point. The army broke up in confusion, and the disastrous retreat, with the Prussians in pursuit, lasted through the night. Napoleon himself escaped by flight. The French lost in this battle probably thirtyone thousand in killed, wounded and missing, while the allies lost over twenty-two thousand.

The importance of the Battle of Waterloo as the means of finally crushing Napoleon has been somewhat exaggerated. Even had he been successful on that day, he could never have regained his old power—it would not have been permitted by the allies. But the accomplishment of his overthrow that early in his campaign was fortunate for the allies and for the French, as it saved further bloodshed.

Watermelon, a creeping variety of gourd. The rind of the fruit is smooth and dark green when ripe; the inside of the melon is a coarse red or yellowish pulp, which contains over 90 per cent water. Its native home was Africa, but it has been widely cultivated from remote times. It is very popular in the United States, where it has become a most important crop for the fruitgrowers of the South Atlantic and Gulf states, in which sections thousands of acres are devoted to raising melons for the northern market. Watermelons in smaller quantities are raised as far north as southern Ontario. The ideal soil for melon culture is light, sandy loam, which is naturally dry or else thoroughly drained. An average melon weighs from 20 to 50 pounds.

Water Po'lo, a ball game, on the same general principles as hockey, but played by swimmers, with a round ball, which is filled with air, so that it will float. It is a good game for swimming tanks and is played generally throughout the country during the winter season. The object of the game, of course, is for one side to carry, push or throw the ball to the opponent's goal line, at the end of the tank.

Waterproofing, *waw' tur proof ing*, rendering cloth and other articles proof against water. Fabrics are treated with a solution of rubber, spread over the goods, after which the cloth is doubled, pressed and finished, the waterproof layer being in the center. This process is used in the preparation of mackintoshes and other wearing apparel. Such goods are impervious both to water and to air, and from a sanitary point of view they are not desirable for constant wear. A new process has been introduced, which renders the fabrics proof against water, but does not obstruct ventilation. The materials are saturated with soap and then dipped in an alum solution. Still another process, by which the same result is obtained, consists of treating the fibers of the cloth, instead of the manufactured, woven fabric, with the solution. The use of paraffin for this purpose is also extensive. Leather, wood and various kinds of articles are rendered waterproof by keeping them in hot, molten paraffin for a time. Paper is made waterproof by immersing it in a solution of shellac in borax, which causes it to resemble parchment paper.

Waterspout, a whirling column of water, extending from a cloud to the surface of a body of water, like the ocean or a lake. The presence of this column is marked by the cloud of vapor which it contains. This cloud is formed by the rapid condensation of the moisture in the atmosphere, due to expansion and rapid cooling, caused by the low pressure in the area occupied by the column. If the conditions continue a sufficient length of time, rain is produced and sometimes falls in such quantities as to constitute a small deluge. In waterspouts over the ocean, the lower part of the column may contain vapor from salt water, but usually the vapor is that of fresh water. Waterspouts are caused in the same way as whirlwinds. See WHIRLWIND.

Watertown, *waw'tur town*, MASS., a town in Middlesex co., 7 mi. w. of Boston, on the Charles River and on the Boston & Maine railroad. There are also a number of electric railways. It is a prominent residence place, but also has extensive manufactures of woolen goods, paper, stoves, furnaces, needles and various other articles. The large Mount Auburn Cemetery contains the graves of many noted men. The place was settled in 1630. The provincial congresses of Massachusetts met here in 1775 and 1776. Population in 1910, including several villages, 12,875.

Watertown, N. Y., the county-seat of Jefferson co., 70 mi. n. by e. of Syracuse, on the Black River and on two lines of the New York Central railroad. The city is in a fertile farming and dairying region, which contains, also, extensive deposits of iron and limestone. The river furnishes extensive water power, and there are large paper and pulp mills, foundries, machine shops, silk mills and other establishments. The principal buildings include the Y. M. C. A. building, the high school, the Flower Memorial Library, the postoffice, the courthouse, an armory and several large business blocks. The city has two hospitals, two orphanages and a home for the aged. Watertown was settled in 1800, was made the county-seat in 1805 and was chartered as a city in 1869. Population in 1910, 26,730.

Watertown, S. D., the county-seat of Codington co., about 100 mi. n. by w. of Sioux Falls, on the Big Sioux River and on the Chicago, Rock Island & Pacific, the Chicago & Northwestern, the Great Northern and other railroads. The city is surrounded by attractive scenery and is about three miles from Lake Kampeska, one of the most picturesque bodies of water in the state. It has a valuable trade with the adjacent wheat-growing and cattle-raising country, and it contains large grain elevators, warehouses, flour mills, stockyards, machine shops, leather works, implement factories and other manufacturing establishments. There are eight churches, three national banks and a public high school. Population in 1910, 7010.

Watertown, WIS., a city in Jefferson and Dodge cos., 44 mi. w. by n. of Milwaukee, on the Rock River and on the Chicago & Northwestern and the Chicago, Milwaukee & Saint Paul railroads. The river furnishes considerable water-power, and there are machine shops, a large shoe factory, a flour mill, a foundry, a brewery, creameries and other factories. The city contains the Northwestern University, Sacred Heart College, a high school and a public library. The place was settled by Timothy Johnson in 1836, and the city was chartered in 1853. Population in 1910, 8829.

Waterville, MAINE, a city in Kennebec co., 17 mi. n. by e. of Augusta, on the Kennebec River and on the Maine Central and other railroads. There are also several electric railways to neighboring places. Colby College is located here, and the city also contains the Coburn Classical Institute, the Ursuline Academy, a Carnegie library, a high school and nine churches. The principal industrial establishments are cotton mills, woolen mills, railroad shops and a shirt factory. A number of the inhabitants are French Canadians, but the majority are natives. The first settlement was made here about 1760, but remained a part of Winslow until 1802. The city was chartered in 1888. Population in 1910, 11,458.

Watervliet, *waw tur vleet'*, N. Y., a city in Albany co., on the Hudson River, opposite Troy, near the terminals of the Erie and Champlain canals, and on the Delaware & Hudson railroad. A United States arsenal was established here in 1807 on a reservation of 109 acres. It is now one of the largest plants for the construction of war materials. The city also contains manufactures of woolen goods and iron, lumber and other products. There are ten churches, Saint Patrick's Academy, an orphanage and public and high school libraries. The place was originally called West Troy. It was incorporated as a village in 1836 and as a city in 1897. Population in 1910, 15,074.

Water Wheels, motors for operating machinery by the pressure of water. The old style water wheels were large wooden structures, rotating upon a horizontal axis. They were constructed of two frames, from four to six feet apart, joined at their circumferences, with buckets or floats attached, as occasion required.

OVERSHOT WHEEL

They were known as *overshot* or *undershot* wheels, according to the method of operating, the overshot wheel receiving water at the top, and the undershot at the bottom. Each of these is described under its respective title.

The *breast* wheel has the water admitted to the floats at a point horizontally opposite the axle.

A recent modification of the undershot wheel consists of a small iron wheel, with cups or buckets upon its circumference, the whole enclosed in an iron box. This is often known as the *impact wheel*, or *water motor*. The water issues from a small nozzle under very high pressure, and as it strikes the box it causes the wheel

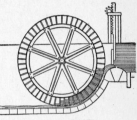

BREAST WHEEL

to revolve with great rapidity. These wheels are convenient, because of their small size and the ease with which they can be placed in almost any desirable position, but they are of use only in cities where the waterworks enable a high pressure to be obtained. Another form of wheel in common use is the turbine. See TURBINE WHEEL.

Waterworks, the appliances arranged for supplying a community with water for domestic use, manufacturing purposes, fire protection and street and lawn sprinkling. Large cities are usually supplied with water from lakes or rivers. Smaller towns often obtain their supply from springs or wells. The selection of a source of supply should be made with great care, because the water must be free from decaying animal and vegetable matter and other organic impurities. It must also be free from sewage contamination. In general, rivers are considered a better source of supply than lakes, since, when not contaminated by sewage, running water is usually free from impurities. Cool water is better than warm, because it will not propagate life so readily. Large cities consume very large quantities of water. The average daily consumption per capita is over 120 gallons. In New York it is 116 gallons; in Chicago, 190 gallons, and in Philadelphia, 229 gallons.

Where the source of supply is a long distance from the city, a large reservoir is usually constructed, and this is connected with the city by an aqueduct which empties into one or more reservoirs, as is shown in the New York plant. From these reservoirs the water is distributed through mains to different portions of the city, and from the mains to the consumers. When situated near a suitable source of supply, the water is pumped directly from this source through the mains, as is the case in Chicago. Small cities often use standpipes for reservoirs. These are constructed of iron or steel and mounted on a strong foundation of masonry. They sometimes rise to the height of 125 or 150 feet. They are not, however, considered safe, since the least accident to the lower part of the standpipe would cause the portion of the city in which it is located to be flooded.

Watson, *wat'son,* JOHN (1850-1907), well-known under the pen name of Ian Maclaren, an English author and clergyman, born at Manningtree, in Essex, of Scotch parents. He graduated in 1870 at the University of Edinburgh, and studied theology at New College, Edinburgh, and at Tübingen. His first charge was at Logiealmond, in Perthshire. In 1877 he became associate pastor of Saint Matthew's Church, Glasgow, and he took charge of the Sefton Park Presbyterian Church, Liverpool, in 1880. A number of sketches of humble Scottish life, which were published in the *British Weekly,* were in 1894 collected into a little volume called *Beside the Bonnie Brier Bush,* and it is by this work that he is best known. Among his other writings are *The Days of Auld Lang Syne, Kate Carnegie, The Mind of the Master* and *A Doctor of the Old School.*

Watson, THOMAS E. (1856–   ), an American lawyer, politician and journalist, born in Columbia County, Ga. He studied at Mercer College, taught school for a time and was admitted to the bar in 1875, beginning practice in Thompson, Ga. He was elected to the state legislature and to Congress in 1891 as a Populist. He was defeated in the two following elections. During his term he fought for and secured the first appropriation for rural free delivery. In 1896 he was the Populist candidate for vice-president of the United States, and in 1904 he was made the candidate of the party for president. Though making an active campaign, he received no electoral votes. In 1905 he began the publication of *Tom Watson's Magazine* in New York, as an organ of radical democracy, but in November, 1906, he resigned from the editorship. He has written several important works, including a *Life of Napoleon,* a *Life of Thomas Jefferson* and a *History of France.*

Watt, *wot,* JAMES (1736-1819), the celebrated improver of the steam engine, born at Greenock, Scotland. Having determined to adopt the trade of making mathematical instruments, Watt went to London, at the age of eighteen, to learn the art; but ill health compelled him to return after only a year's apprenticeship. Shortly after his return he was appointed maker of mathematical instruments for the university. Resigning this position, he acted as a civil engineer; he made several surveys for canals and harbors, and some of his plans were afterward carried into execution. Between 1764 and 1774 Watt conceived and gave shape to his improvements on the steam engine, which have rendered his name famous. To give his inventions practical form, he associated himself with Mathew Boulton, who fur-

JAMES WATT

nished the capital, the firm of Boulton & Watt having their works at Soho, Birmingham. Watt was a fellow of the Royal Societies of London and Edinburgh, and he was a member of the National Institute of France. Besides improving the steam engine, he invented or improved a variety of mechanical appliances, including a letter-copying press. See STEAM ENGINE.

Watteau, *vah to',* JEAN ANTOINE (1684-1721), a French painter, born at Valenciennes, of poor parents. In 1702 he went to Paris and earned his living by working for decorative painters. For many years he struggled in obscurity, but his talent once recognized, he rapidly became popular and prosperous and was a great favorite of Frederick the Great of Prussia. In 1717 he was received at the Academy and was enrolled as a painter of *fêtes galantes,* that is, pleasure parties, balls, masquerades, and the like, subjects in which he excelled. Lightness, elegance and brilliancy form the chief attractions of his style. Some of his works are *Embarkation for the Island of Cytherea, The Village Bride* and *The Village Fête.*

Watterson, *waw'tur son*, HENRY (1840–) an American journalist, born in Washington, D. C. He was educated by private tutors and began his career as a journalist in his native city. He removed to Nashville in 1861, where he edited the *Republican Banner,* and during the Civil War he served in the Confederate army. The *Republican Banner* was revived after the close of the war; and in 1867 Watterson went to Louisville, where he founded the *Journal,* later consolidated with the *Courier,* and then known as the *Courier-Journal.* He steadily refused office, but in 1876 he accepted a seat in Congress, serving with distinction and declining reëlection. He delivered the dedicatory oration at the opening of the World's Columbian Exposition in 1893.

Watts, *wots,* GEORGE FREDERICK (1817–1904), an English artist. In 1842 he secured prizes for the decoration of the Houses of Parliament. After this he visited Italy, and in his study he was influenced by the Venetian school, from which he learned the skill of coloring. Among his more important pictures are *Love and Death,* now in Washington; *Life's Illusion, The Window Seat* and *Sir Galahad.* He is one of the most subtle and powerful of portrait painters, among his successful work in this line being portraits of Tennyson, Millais, Sir Frederick Leighton, Cardinal Manning and Browning. More than almost any other artist, he devoted himself to the artistic interests of the nation, gratuitously decorating the dining hall of Lincoln's Inn and giving the best of his work to form the nucleus of the National Gallery of British Art. The principles of his art are best summed up in his own words, "The end of art must be the expression of some weighty principle of spiritual significance, the illustration of great truth."

Watts, ISAAC (1674–1748), an English clergyman and writer, noted for his hymns. He was born at Southampton. He injured his health by study, while in an academy in London, was afterward tutor for six years and in 1702 became minister of the Independent Church in Mark Lane. After a severe illness, Watts spent the remainder of his life with Sir Thomas Abney, at Theobalds. Among his works are *Divine and Moral Songs for Children, Hymns and Spiritual Songs, Psalms of David Imitated and Horae Lyricae,* the last three containing nearly five hundred hymns and versions. "When I survey the wondrous cross" is said to be Watts's finest hymn, and with Ken's *Morning Hymn,* Charles Wesley's "Hark, the Herald Angels" and Toplady's "Rock of Ages," it stands at the head of all hymns in the English language.

Wauke'gan, ILL., the county-seat of Lake co., 35 mi. n. of Chicago, on Lake Michigan and on the Chicago & Northwestern railroad and several electric railways. The streets are well paved and well shaded, and the city has a pleasant situation, on a bluff about 100 feet above the lake. It has a good harbor and a considerable trade in farm and dairy products. There are large wire-works, sugar refineries, brass and iron works, a tannery, wood-working establishments, scale works and various other factories. Some of the prominent buildings are the courthouse, the Jane McAllister Hospital and a Carnegie library. The place was settled by Thomas Jenkins in 1835, and the city was chartered in 1859. Population in 1910, 16,069.

Wau'kesha, WIS., the county-seat of Waukesha co., 17 mi. w. of Milwaukee, on the Fox River and on the Chicago, Milwaukee & Saint Paul, the Chicago & Northwestern, the Wisconsin Central and several electric railways. The city has numerous mineral springs, possessing medicinal properties, and it has become a prominent health resort. Carrol College and the state industrial school for boys are located here. Other features of interest are the Waukesha Springs, Rest Haven, the courthouse, a public library and three parks. The city has iron works, steel bridge works, a cannery and other factories. The place was settled in 1836. Population in 1910, 8740.

Wau'sau, WIS., the county-seat of Marathon co., about 175 mi. n. w. of Milwaukee, on the Wisconsin River and on the Chicago & Northwestern and the Chicago, Milwaukee & Saint Paul railroads. It is in a lumbering, agricultural and dairying section, which also has extensive granite quarries. The river furnishes good water power, and the city contains large sawmills, sash and blind factories, machine shops, box factories, canneries, flour mills and other establishments. There are about a score of churches, three banks, electric lights, well-paved streets and a fine natural park. The county maintains a training school for teachers, a school of agriculture and domestic science and an asylum for the insane. The city also has a public library, a fine courthouse and a city hall. The place was settled in 1842, and at first it was known as Big Bull Falls. It was chartered as a city in 1872. Population in 1910, 16,560.

Waves, *wayvz,* disturbances in matter, which result in carrying force from point to point, often to a great distance. Waves are of two classes, visible and invisible. *Visible* waves are those produced by disturbing the surface of liquid, as water, or striking a cord stretched between two supports. *Invisible* waves are those minute vibrations produced in a body, either by striking it or by some other means of agitation. These waves are manifest through their results, as in sound, heat and light. When waves are produced by the disturbance of a small quantity of liquid, as by throwing a pebble into a pool, they appear to advance from the point where the pebble strikes, in widening, concentric circles, the height of the wave decreasing gradually as the circle enlarges. There is, however, no progressive motion of the liquid itself, as may be seen by watching a body floating on its surface. Only the motion rolls onward, while the body rises and falls as the waves pass, but does not move on with them. This is true of large, as well as small, waves, and the waves of the ocean, which sometimes reach a height of over forty feet, do not cause the water to move forward. Breakers are caused by the friction of the water on the bottom of the sea, which retards the motion at the base of the wave and causes the crest to break over it. Breakers never occur in deep water.

Wax, a solid, secreted by bees and a few other insects and by certain plants. Beeswax is the most common form in which we see wax, and it is obtained by heating honeycomb in water (See BEESWAX). Wax is also obtained from various plants and in large quantities from a species of palm known as the wax palm. Japan wax is obtained from the wax tree in Japan, and *lacquer* is a wax of fine quality also obtained from a Japanese tree. Wax is solid at ordinary temperatures, and in its natural condition it is usually of a yellowish or brownish color, but it can be bleached by exposure to the sun and air. It melts at about 155° F., is insoluble in water and dissolves only sparingly in alcohol or ether. It is used in making candles, in polishing furniture and floors and in the manufacture of certain cements used by chemists. It also is employed as a vehicle for colors.

Wax Myrtle or **Wax Tree.** See CANDLE-BERRY.

Wax Palm, a species of palm, yielding a resinous wax. It is a native of the Andes Mountains, where it is a magnificent tree, sometimes reaching a height of 160 feet.

Wax'wing, a handsome singing bird, of a reddish-brown color, deriving its name from the little red appendages attached to the quill feathers of the wings, which have the appearance of red sealing wax. The under parts of the birds are yellowish, the chin is black, and a handsome crest decorates the head. The bird is also known as the

WAXWING

cedar bird, because of its fondness for the fruit of cedar trees. It is common in the United States, and in winter it gathers in flocks, often remaining until cold weather sets in. The *Bohemian waxwing* is a European representative, which lives in high northern latitudes of both hemispheres, and sometimes it comes south into the United States.

Way'cross, GA., the county-seat of Ware co., 96 mi. s. w. of Savannah, on the Atlanta & Birmingham railroad and several branches of the Atlantic Coast Line. The town is in a cotton and sugar cane region, and it also contains extensive railroad shops and manufactories of naval stores, lumber, implements and other articles. The city contains two banks and two high schools, and it owns and operates the waterworks. Population in 1910, 14,485.

Way'land, FRANCIS (1796–1865), an American educator, born in New York City and educated at Union College and Andover Theological Seminary. After preaching for several years, he was chosen professor of mathematics and natural history at Union College. From this position he was elected president of Brown University, and he held this office for twenty-eight years. During his administration the scope of the university was greatly enlarged, and the requirements for admission were changed to meet the growing demands of science and of industrial life. Doctor Wayland is the author of *Elements of Moral Science, Elements of Polit-*

ical Economy, The Elements of Intellectual Philosophy and a number of other works.

Wayne, Anthony (1745–1796), an American revolutionary general, born at Easton, Pa. He was prominent in the patriotic movements before the Revolution, served in the Pennsylvania legislature and in 1775 was a member of the Committee of Safety. When the war broke out he joined the army, was colonel of a volunteer regiment and early in 1776 accompanied the expedition to Canada. For some time he was in command of a fort at Ticonderoga, and he afterward took part in the battles of Brandywine, Germantown and Monmouth. His most brilliant achievement was the victory at Stony Point, where he took the fortress by storm, without firing a shot. It was through such daring exploits as this that he won the name of "Mad Anthony" Wayne. After the surrender of Cornwallis at Yorktown, at which he was present, he served for a time in Georgia and South Carolina. After the close of the war he held a number of civil offices in Pennsylvania and then removed to Georgia. In 1791 and 1792 he represented Georgia in Congress. In 1792 he was made general in chief of the United States army and was given command of an expedition against the indians in the West. He defeated them at Fallen Timbers in August, 1794, and he concluded with them the Treaty of Greenville, by which the United States gained a large tract of land.

Waynesboro, *waynz'bur ro*, Pa., a borough in Franklin co., 48 mi. s. w. of Harrisburg, on the Cumberland Valley and the Western Maryland railroads. It contains manufactories of engines, boilers, implements, creamery products and various kinds of machinery. The Confederate army passed through here on the way to the Battle of Gettysburg, and the battlefields of South Mountain and Antietam Creek are near the borough. Population in 1910, 7199.

Weasel, *we'zel*, a small, carnivorous animal, a native of almost all the temperate and cold parts of the northern hemisphere. The body is extremely slender, the head small and flattened, the neck long and the legs short. It preys upon mice, birds and other small animals and is very destructive to poultry. The weasel is usually nocturnal in its habits. It is a fine hunter, having a very keen scent and sharp sight, and, being unwearying in pursuit of its victim, it often wears to exhaustion animals larger than itself. Several species are common in the United States, and others are found in most parts of the temperate zones. The *long-tailed,* or *New York, weasel* is one of the most familiar species in North America. It is dark brown above and white beneath, and in winter in cold climates it turns pure white, except for the tip of the tail, which is black. See Polecat; Ferret; Ermine; Sable.

Weather Bureau, *weth'ur bu'ro*, a government organization, for the purpose of making systematic meteorological observations, forecasting the weather and giving information of the approach of storms, floods and the like. Weather bureaus are now maintained by the governments of all civilized countries, the most efficient being those of the United States, Great Britain, Germany, France and Japan.

Previous to the Civil War several attempts to maintain a systematic weather service were made, but on the breaking out of that conflict all these were abandoned. The United States weather bureau was organized in 1870 as a division of the signal service in the war department. The organization was under the supervision of General Albert J. Myer, chief signal officer of the army, and it was adopted by Congress as a national service. Under General Myer's management, *signal stations,* as they were then called, were established throughout the country and were under the direction of a corps of trained weather observers. In 1891 the weather department of the signal service was made a bureau of the department of agriculture.

The weather bureau contains a number of divisions, each of which carries on its special line of work. The most important of these divisions are:

(1) *The Forecast Division,* which receives twice a day reports from all stations in the United States, the West Indies and the southern portions of the British provinces, and makes charts showing the conditions embodied in these reports. These charts are the regular weather maps of the bureau and include forecasts for the entire country and for the Atlantic coast as far as the Grand Banks. Their predictions are for twenty-four or forty-eight hours.

(2) *The Division of River and Flood Service,* which obtains information concerning the amount of rainfall, ice and snow in the basins of the principal rivers, whether navigable or not. The information which this division gives is for facilitating commerce and especially for protecting river valleys from floods, of which it aims to give ample warning.

(3) *The Division of Climate and Crops.* This division maintains a staff of about 3000 voluntary observers, who give reports of the temperature, rainfall and other important data pertaining to the welfare and growth of crops in different parts of the country. This information is published in weekly and monthly crop bulletins, which are regarded as the highest authority on crop conditions of the country and are of the greatest benefit to agricultural interests.

(4) *Other Divisions.* These include divisions which have charge of examining and testing all instruments used, a division of rec-

the central station of the district and to the office at Washington, from each of which maps are issued and reports transmitted to the country. These stations and numerous other sub-

FIG. 1

stations indicate the local weather conditions by the display of signals. A white flag (1 in Fig. 1) indicates fair weather. A flag with the

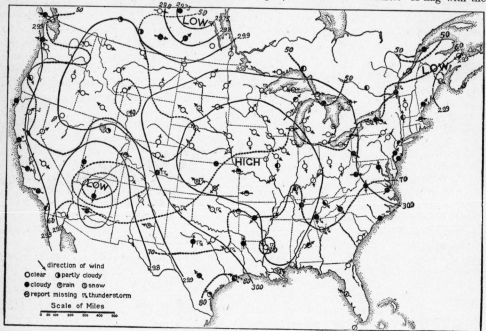

UNITED STATES WEATHER MAP

ords and divisions of telegraphy, publications and supplies.

The official organ of the bureau is the *Monthly Weather Review*, each issue of which contains statements of the weather conditions, their influence on crops in different parts of the country and various other articles pertaining to the work of the bureau and of general interest to the public.

There are over 200 regular meteorological stations in the United States. Each of these is in charge of trained observers and is equipped with a full set of instruments. These observations are taken at 8 A. M. and 8 P. M. Washington time, and the results are telegraphed to

upper half white and the lower half blue (2 in Fig. 1) indicates local rain or snow. A full blue flag (3 in Fig. 1) indicates general rain or snow. A triangular blue flag (4 in Fig. 1) indicates change of temperature. When placed below another flag it indicates colder, and when placed above, warmer. A white flag with a black square in the center (5 in Fig. 1) indicates a cold wave, which means a drop in temperature of from 15° to 20°.

The direction of winds is indicated by triangular flags, which are generally used in connection with storm warnings. The warning flag is red, with a black square in the center. When this is displayed with a triangular white flag above it, it indicates a storm with wind from the northwest. With the white flag below, it indicates a wind from the southwest (See Fig. 2). The warning flag with a dark triangle above indicates storm with wind from the northeast, and with the dark triangle below, storm with a wind from the southeast (See Fig. 3). The hur-

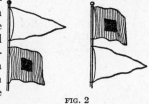

FIG. 2

ricane warning consists of two red flags with black centers, one above the other (See Fig. 4). Forecasts are also displayed in post offices and other public places, and in some sections of

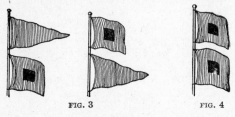

FIG. 3   FIG. 4

the country they are given by a series of signals by the whistles of locomotives.

Through telegraphic reports received from all parts of the country twice each day the United States Weather Bureau constructs, twice daily weather charts showing areas of high and low barometric pressure, the former generally indicating centers of storm disturbance; the general temperature of the different sections of the country, those of equal temperatures being connected by lines called isotherms; the direction of winds and the condition of the atmosphere, the latter being denoted as cloudy, partly cloudy or clear, and including presence of rain, snow or thunderstorms. By comparing the map under construction with previous maps and with the latest reports from the various stations, the forecaster is able to tell in what directions the areas of low pressure are moving, and at what speed, and can thus predict, with reasonable certainty, changes of weather in all parts of the country. As to changes in temperature and the velocity and the direction of winds, information furnished by the bureau is almost never far wrong, but so many influences affect the condition of the atmosphere that it is more difficult to predict changes in this respect. The weather map shown here is an exact copy of one furnished by the government.

See CLIMATE; STORMS; METEOROLOGY. Consult Davis's *Elementary Meteorology* and the publications of the weather bureau.

Weatherford, *weth'ur furd,* TEXAS, the county-seat of Parker co., situated 31 mi. w. of Fort Worth, on the Texas & Pacific and other railroads. The leading educational institutions are Texas Female Seminary and Rutherford College. The industries include cotton gins and presses, cotton mills and flouring mills. The mining of coal is also of considerable importance. Population in 1910, 5074.

Weaver, *we'vur,* JAMES BAIRD (1833-), an American political leader, born at Dayton, Ohio. He graduated from the law school of Ohio University in 1854, served in the Civil War and was brevetted brigadier general at its close. He removed to Iowa, entered journalism, as editor of the Iowa *Tribune,* at Des Moines, and became a member of Congress in 1879 and again in 1885. In 1880 he was made the Greenback candidate for president of the United States, and in 1892 he was the candidate of the People's or Populist party, receiving 22 electoral votes.

WEAVER BIRD

Weaver Bird, a name given to various members of the finch family, because of their

SOCIABLE WEAVER BIRD'S NEST

remarkable nests, which are woven of various vegetable fibers. Some species, including the *yellow weaver*, or *baya*, of India, build long, bottle-like nests and hang them separately and singly from slender branches of trees and shrubs, often over the water, where it is impossible for anything but a bird to enter them. Other species, known as the *sociable weaver bird*, build a large dome-shaped structure, or roof, suspended from the branches of a tree, and underneath this a great many families build their single nests, each having a separate entrance.

BAYA'S NEST

While all members of the community work on the roof, each pair works alone on its own nest. See BAYA.

Weaving, *we'ving*, the art of making cloth by means of a loom, from threads or yarn. It is not known when weaving was first practiced,

JACQUARD LOOM

but it is certain that it is one of the earliest of the arts, and it seems probable that looms were invented independently by several of the ancient nations. The Greeks and Romans brought the art to a high degree of perfection, and among modern countries Italy was the first to acquire fame for the manufacture of woolen and cotton cloths. Since the fiber of wool is much more easily worked than are those of cotton or flax, woolen cloth has always been made among the more primitive peoples of the temperate regions, before they attempted the manufacture of cotton or linen fabrics.

In weaving, two sets of threads are necessary, one running lengthwise of the cloth, and called the *warp*, the other running crosswise, and called the *weft*, or *woof*. The threads of the warp are arranged on the loom by being wound on a yarn beam, at the back, and stretched evenly to the front, where they are fastened to another beam, upon which the cloth is to be wound. In passing from one beam to the other, the warp threads are laid through the *heckles* and also through a comb on the batten. In laying the warp, every other thread passes through one heckle, and the alternate thread passes through the other. The weft is wound upon bobbins, which are placed in the shuttle, by means of which the weft is laid in position. Weaving by hand loom includes the following steps: (1) Pressing a treadle, which is connected with the heckles by a cord that passes over a pulley on the top of the loom. This spreads the threads of the weft, raising one-half and lowering the others, so that they form an angle called the *shed*. (2) Throwing the shuttle across the warp and thus laying the thread of the weft in position. (3) Striking this thread with the batten, so as to drive it close up against the one previously laid. (4) Springing down the opposite treadle and thus preparing the web for the second thread of the weft.

Simple as the hand loom is, it contains the elements of all looms operated by power and designed for weaving the most complex patterns. The complexity of the pattern may be increased by placing more than two frames in the heckle and dividing the weft into more parts, also by inventions which raise certain threads in the warp at one time and certain others at another. An invention known as the *Jacquard* loom is a very ingenious device which operates upon this plan. A series of hooks is attached to the warp in such a way as to raise the threads necessary to produce any desired pattern. Any number of cords can be used, so that a pattern of any degree of complexity is possible. When one cord has been used, it drops and gives place to the one following. Since all cords are tied together in the form of an endless chain, the pattern can be repeated indefinitely. It is on looms of this sort that portraits, landscapes, flowers and other interesting devices are woven. England, Germany, France and the United States are the leading countries in the weaving industry, and in them, with rare exceptions, all weaving is now done on power looms.

Webb, ALEXANDER STEWART (1835–1911), an American soldier, born and educated in New York City. He graduated at West Point in 1855 and was appointed assistant professor of mathematics there two years later. In 1861 he was made major of the First Rhode Island Artillery. He was in the first Battle of Bull Run and later participated in the Peninsula Campaign of the Army of the Potomac and in the Maryland and Rappahannock campaigns. He was commissioned brigadier general of volunteers, was wounded at the Battle of Gettysburg and received from General Meade a bronze medal for personal gallantry. He was brevetted lieutenant colonel in 1863, and major general of the United States Army in 1865. He was discharged from the service in 1870 at his own request. He contributed articles on the war to the *Century Magazine* and published *The Peninsula: McClellan's Campaign of 1862.*

Webb City, Mo., a city in Jasper co., 160 mi. s. of Kansas City, on the Frisco and the Missouri Pacific railroads. It is in the lead and zinc district of the southwestern part of the state, and there are more than 200 mining plants in the vicinity. Farming and fruit raising are also important industries. The city contains iron works, a large foundry, a flour mill and other factories. There are ten churches, two banks, municipal waterworks, electric lights and electric street railways. Population in 1910, 11,817.

Web'er, KARL MARIA FRIEDRICH ERNST VON (1786–1826), a German musical composer, born at Eutin in Holstein. His father was a musician and gave him a good musical education. In 1800 he wrote an opera, and in 1803 he visited Vienna, where he became acquainted with Haydn and the Abbé Vogler, from whom he received great help in his studies. The latter procured him a musical directorship in Breslau, on which he entered in 1804, leaving it only to accept, successively, several more important positions. In 1820, at Berlin, he produced *Der Freischütz,* the most celebrated of his compositions. It was performed in London and Paris two years later. In 1822 *Euryanthe* was brought out, and in 1826 Weber visited London to superintend the production of *Oberon,* which he had composed for Covent Garden Theater. It was enthusiastically received. The composer, however, was seriously ill, and he died in London.

180

Besides the operas mentioned, Weber wrote a large number of works for the piano, notably the *Invitation a la Valse* and the E♭ *major Polonaise.* He was the forerunner, in style, of Wagner, whom he influenced decisively.

Web'ster, MASS., a town in Worcester co., 16 mi. s. by w. of Worcester, on the French River and on the Boston & Albany and the New York, New Haven & Hartford railroads. It contains extensive cotton and woolen mills and other factories. There are eleven churches, two banks, a public library and a large, attractive lake. It was incorporated in 1832 from parts of the towns of Oxford and Dudley. Population in 1910, 11,509.

Webster, DANIEL (1782–1852), an American orator and statesman, born in the township of Salisbury, N. H. His father was a backwoods farmer, who had previously been a hunter and soldier, and Daniel owed his first education to his mother. Later, in the intervals of farm work, he attended village school, and when he had reached the age of fifteen, his father made some generous sacrifices to send him to Dartmouth College, where he remained four years. After studying privately and in a Boston law office, he entered the law in 1804, settled at Portsmouth, N. H., and rose rapidly in his profession.

Webster at first took little interest in politics, but in 1812, having already established a commanding reputation, he was elected to Congress by the anti-war party. He was placed on the committee of foreign affairs, and his maiden speech, delivered on June 10, 1813, upon the Berlin and Milan decrees, took the House and country by surprise by its display of rhetorical power and wealth of historical knowledge. His subsequent speeches on the increase of the navy, which he warmly recommended, and the repeal of the embargo, placed him in the first rank of debaters.

He removed to Boston in 1816 and retired for a time from political life, to devote himself to his profession. For nearly seven years afterward, with a single exception, he filled no public office, but as an advocate and counselor he achieved a preëminent position at the American bar. His strongest powers were displayed in arguing points of constitutional law, and his achievements in this direction drew upon him the attention of the whole country. In 1820, on the celebration of the bicentenary of the landing of the Pilgrim Fathers, he delivered an oration which added greatly to his fame as a powerful speaker, and he continued to gain in public esteem through other great addresses, notably those at the laying of the cornerstone of Bunker Hill Monument in 1825 and at the memorial service for Adams and Jefferson in 1826.

In 1822 he was elected to Congress, and he was reëlected in 1824 and 1826. At the end of his last term he was chosen senator for Massachusetts. In January, 1830, he delivered a remarkable speech in favor of the nationalist view of the Constitution, in reply to a speech by Robert Y. Hayne of South Carolina. The address created a great sensation throughout the Union and probably was more widely circulated throughout the country than any other in American history. Webster was strongly opposed to the nullification movement of Calhoun and the South Carolina school, and his eloquence in support of Jackson's energetic measures did

DANIEL WEBSTER

much to prevent secession. In 1836 he was the unsuccessful candidate for the presidency, but from 1841 to 1843 he was secretary of state under Harrison and 'Tyler. The chief event of this period was the negotiation of the famous Webster-Ashburton treaty with England, which was equally advantageous and honorable to both parties. Webster generously supported Clay's candidacy for the presidency in 1844; and he was himself an unsuccessful aspirant for the Whig nomination in 1848. In 1845 he was reëlected to the Senate, and in the struggle over the admission of Texas and California he strongly favored the Northern, or anti-slavery, side. Afterward, however, when public excitement had reached a dangerous height, he supported a policy

of compromise, and March 7, 1850, he made a speech in favor of obedience to the Fugitive Slave Law. The same year he was appointed a second time secretary of state, and he held the office until his death.

Webster's guiding principle in politics was the preservation of the Union, for which he was ready to make all sacrifices, opposing the nullifiers, on the one hand, and the abolitionists, on the other. He possessed a fine physique and was always fond of out-of-door sports and of practical agriculture. His biography has been written by George Ticknor Curtis.

Webster, Noah (1758–1843), an American lexicographer, author of the original *Webster's Dictionary* and of *Webster's Spelling Book*. He was educated at Yale and prepared for the law, but gave it up for teaching. His experience in schools led to the composition of his *Spelling Book*, which was published in 1784, and of which it is said that 62,000,000 copies have been sold. About 1807 he began work upon his *American Dictionary of the English Language*. In preparing this work he visited England and worked for some months at Cambridge. The first edition of the dictionary was finished in 1828, and a second edition was published by Webster in 1840. This work was the basis of the standard *Webster's International Dictionary*.

Webster-Ashburton Treaty, a treaty concluded at Washington in 1842 by Daniel Webster, then secretary of state, and Lord Ashburton, the minister of Great Britain to the United States. It defined the northeastern boundary between the United States and Canada, which for years had been the source of acrimonious controversies.

Wedgwood, *wej'wood*, Josiah (1730–1795), a celebrated English potter. He received little education and went to work in his brother's factory at the age of eleven. An incurable lameness, the result of smallpox, which subsequently compelled him to have his right leg amputated, forced him to give up the potter's wheel. He removed for a time to Stoke, where he entered into a partnership, and where his talent for ornamental pottery was first displayed. Returning in 1759 to Burslem, he set up a small manufactory of his own, in which he made a variety of fancy articles. His business improving, he turned his attention to white stoneware and to the cream-colored ware for which he became famous, and he succeeded in producing a ware so hard and durable as to render it almost indestructible.

Wedgwood Ware, a superior kind of glazed pottery, capable of taking on the most brilliant and delicate colors, which are produced by fused metallic oxides and ochers. The ware was named after the inventor, Josiah Wedgewood. It is much used for ornamental ware, and, owing to its hardness and property of resisting the action of all corrosive substances, it is commonly used for mortars in laboratories. See POTTERY.

Wednesday, *wenz'day,* (Woden's day), the fourth day of the week.

Weed, THURLOW (1797–1882), an American journalist, born at Cairo, N. Y. At the age of twelve he began to learn the printer's trade in Catskill, N. Y., and at the age of twenty-two he edited the *Agriculturist,* at Norwich. Two years later he founded the Onondaga County *Republican,* and in 1824 he became editor and owner of the Rochester *Telegraph.* In 1826 he was elected to the legislature, and at the close of his second term he established the Albany *Evening Journal,* which he edited for thirty-three years as a Whig. During the Civil War, at the instance of President Lincoln, he was sent to Europe on a semi-official mission, and he did much to remove the misapprehensions as to the war, and to induce foreign governments to refrain from interference. In 1867 he became editor of the New York *Commercial Advertiser,* which position he resigned on account of failing health. He was the author of *Letters from Europe and the West Indies* and an *Autobiography.*

Weeds, a term applied to plants growing wild in uncultivated grounds and in most cases very troublesome. Many plants when grown and cultivated in gardens, as the goldenrod and the dandelion, are classed as flowers, while the same plants, running wild in uncultivated ground, are considered as weeds. The chief ways in which weeds are injurious are: (1) They increase the labor necessary to cultivate the soil; (2) they take up food from the soil, which should go to useful plants; (3) their foliage smothers the young plants; (4) they sometimes are poisonous to cattle. Care should be taken to eradicate them as soon as they begin to grow. There are various ways to prevent the growth, different weeds requiring different methods. Planting of pure seed, diligent tillage of the soil, rotation of crops, cultivation of all open land with crops, are some of the means used. Some weeds while young can be destroyed without injury to the crop, by spraying the field with certain chemicals, called *herbicides.* Weeds are often of service to a farmer, in aiding him to know the needs of his land, since many kinds grow only where the conditions are peculiarly adapted to them. See HERBICIDES.

Week, a period of seven days, one of the common divisions of time, the origin of which is doubtful. Among the nations who adopted the week as a division of time, the Chinese, the Hindus, the Egyptians, the Chaldeans, the Jews, the Persians and the Peruvians have been mentioned, but in some cases the antiquity of the practice is doubtful, and in others the name has been applied to other cycles than that of seven days. The nations with whom the weekly cycle has been traced with certainty to the greatest antiquity are the Egyptians and the Hebrews. The use of the week was introduced into the Roman Empire from Egypt, about the first or second century of the Christian era, and it had been recognized independently of Christianity before the emperor Constantine confirmed it by enjoining the observance of the Christian Sabbath. With the Mohammedans, the week has also a religious character, Friday being observed by them as a Sabbath.

Wee'ver or **Stingfish,** a name of several fishes, included by many authorities among the perches. Two species are found in the Atlantic along European coasts and are considered good food-fish. They inflict severe wounds with the spines of their first dorsal fin, but the sting is not poisonous.

Wee'vil, a little beetle, easily recognized by its elongated snout. The *wheat weevil,* which is about one-eighth of an inch long, bores a hole into a grain of wheat and lays therein an egg that hatches into a destructive little grub. No other insect does so much damage to stored grain, largely because of the fact that several generations are produced in a single year.

Weighing, *way'ing,* **Scale,** a device for weighing. The simplest forms of weighing machines are the balance and the steelyard, both of which are described under their respective titles. The *even weight* scale, used by grocers and druggists, is only a modified form of the balance. In this pattern the scale pans are above the beam. A weight is placed in one pan, and a sufficient quantity of the article purchased to balance it is placed in the other. The weighing scale in common use consists of a weighing beam, attached to a frame, convenient for use on a counter. The article to be weighed is usually placed in a peculiarly shaped pan, which accompanies the scale. A set of weights, each of which balances a certain number of pounds in the pan, is also furnished. A sliding weight, moving on the long arm of the lever, marks the fractions of a pound. The platform scale is an arrangement of several levers, placed side by side, so that the short arm of one rests upon the

WEIGHING SCALES

long arm of another, by means of pivots which extend on each side of the lever. The last lever of the series has its long arm connected with the short arm of the weighing beam, which is furnished with weights and is balanced by a sliding weight. This scale is the invention of Mr Thaddeus Fairbanks of Vermont, and it was patented in 1831. From this patent, numerous patterns have been devised, but all depend upon the principle of the compound lever.

Weight, *wayt,* the measure of the force by which any body or a given portion of any substance gravitates or is attracted to the earth; in a more popular sense, the quantity of matter in a body, as estimated by the balance, or expressed numerically with reference to some standard unit. In determining weight in cases where very great precision is desired, due account must be taken of temperature, elevation and latitude. Hence, in fixing exact standards of weight, a particular temperature and pressure of air must be specified; thus the standard brass pound of Great Britain is directed to be used when the Fahrenheit thermometer stands at 62° and the barometer at 30 inches. See also GRAVITATION; WEIGHTS AND MEASURES; METRIC SYSTEM.

Weights and Measures, the standards used in measuring quantities. Most of the common standard units have been chosen arbitrarily, though efforts have always been made to have the units conform to some natural rule. Evidences of this fact remain in the names of both ancient and modern units, such as the *cubit* of the Egyptians and Hebrews, which was the length of the forearm, and the *foot* of the Greeks, which was the length of a man's foot. The

so-called *English* system of weights and measures dates from a law passed in 1266 in England, which provided that an English penny should equal in weight 32 wheat corns, taken from the middle of the ear; that 20 pence should make an ounce, 12 ounces a pound, 8 pounds a gallon of wine and 8 gallons of wine a London bushel. Before this time, two pound units had grown up; one, the *Troy* pound, introduced into England by William the Conqueror, weighed considerably less than that before used in England, and its introduction created such dissatisfaction that an average pound of sixteen ounces, now known as the *avoirdupois* pound, was made the standard unit for articles in common trade, while the Troy pound, of twelve ounces, was retained as the unit of weight for gold, silver, gems and apothecaries' supplies. The units of length, capacity, weight and volume have often varied and are not yet entirely uniform, but the common standards of the English system are as follows: Of length, the *yard*, consisting of 3 *feet*, each foot containing 12 *inches*; 5½ yards equal 1 *rod*; 320 rods equal 1 *mile*. In England, the rod is called a *pole* or a *perch*. The units of square and cubical measure are respectively the square and cubes of the linear units, as *square yard*, *cubic inch*, etc. The *acre*, used in the measurement of land, contains 160 square rods. A square mile equals 640 acres. Of capacity, dry, 1 *quart* is divided into 2 *pints*, each pint into 4 *gills*; 8 quarts equal 1 *peck*; 4 pecks equal 1 *bushel*. Capacity, liquid, is measured by the same units as capacity, dry, except that 4 quarts equal 1 *gallon*. There are numerous terms in use in special occupations, such as the *hand*, a unit used in measuring the height of an animal, and equivalent to about 4 inches; the *fathom* (2 yards), used in measuring the depth of water; the *knot*, or *geographical mile* (6088.27 feet), used to designate distance at sea; the *chain* (4 rods), used in surveying; the *furlong* (10 chains); a *link* (.01 of a chain); the *ell* (3¾ feet); the *barrel* (31½ gallons); the *hogshead* (2 barrels). In England the barrel equals 36 gallons, and the hogshead is the same.

The *metric system* of weights and measures, which originated in France, is based upon the meter, the standard unit of length. It was originally equal to one ten-millionth part of a quarter of the meridian of the earth, but it has now been changed to an arbitrary standard of about 39.37 inches (See METRIC SYSTEM).

Standards of weights and measures are maintained by the governments of all countries, the standard units being carefully preserved at the capitals (See UNIT). For definitions of the various units and of the systems of which they are the bases, see articles upon those units, such as POUND; QUART; MILE.

Weimar, *vi'mahr,* a city of Germany, the capital of the Grand Duchy of Saxe-Weimar, situated on the Ilm, about 50 mi. w. s. w. of Leipzig. The town is famous for its association with the classical epoch of German literature. Goethe, Schiller, Wieland and Herder lived here, and Goethe and Schiller are buried in the cemetery in the southern part of the town. Goethe's house is now the Goethe National Museum, and Schiller's house is also the property of the city and is open to the public. The Goethe-Schiller monument in bronze is in front of the famous court theater. The most striking building in the city is the grand ducal palace, which was partially constructed under the supervision of Goethe. Weimar has an excellent school system, including an art school, an industrial school, a music school and other special schools. Stoves, straw hats, leather and cloth are manufactured, and the book trade is considerable. Population in 1910, 34,582.

Weir, ROBERT WALTER (1803–1889), an American painter, born in New Rochelle, N. Y. He studied painting in New York and went to Italy in 1824, remaining several years. He was elected a member of the National Academy of Design in 1829, and three years later he was appointed professor of drawing in the West Point military academy, holding the position for forty-two years. Among his best-known paintings, most of which are historical subjects, are *Landing of Henry Hudson, Embarkation of the Pilgrims* and the *Belle of the Carnival.* He also designed the stained glass windows of Trinity Chapel and Calvary Church in New York City.

Weismann, *vise'mahn,* AUGUST (1834–   ), a German biologist, born at Frankfort-on-the-Main. He attended the gymnasium until his eighteenth year, afterward studying medicine at Göttingen, Vienna and Paris. In 1864 he published *Development of the Diptera,* a work on the embryology of flies and the metamorphosis of insects. He studied zoölogy at the University of Giessen under Leukart, and he later became professor at Freiburg, in Breisgau. He devoted himself to studies in regard to the theory of descent and natural selection, and became an ardent follower of Darwin's theory. His works have been translated into English and include *Studies in the Theory of Descent, The Germ*

Plasm and *Germinal Selection.* See EMBRYOLOGY; EVOLUTION.

Weld'ing, the process of uniting two pieces of a substance when softened by heat. In the arts the term is restricted to splicing such metals as iron and platinum, though glass and several other substances can be welded as readily as these metals. The simplest method of welding iron is that employed in the ordinary blacksmith shop. The smith hammers the ends of the bars to be welded into a wedge-like form, heats them white hot, and just as they begin to soften, he covers them with borax or some other flux, to prevent the formation of oxide. The hot ends are then laid together and hammered, the soft surfaces unite, and the joint formed is usually as strong as any other portion of the bar. In large manufactories, electricity is now very generally used for welding, a current of sufficient power to heat and soften the metals being employed. By means of this current, copper can be welded, as well as iron and steel.

Wel'land Canal, a canal on the Canadian side of the Niagara River, connecting lakes Erie and Ontario. It was completed in 1833 and was enlarged in 1871. It constitutes an import-

A LOCK ON THE WELLAND CANAL

ant link in the chain of canals extending from Lake Superior to Montreal. Its total cost was about $27,300,000, and its annual revenues are about $220,000. The annual tonnage is about 3,000,000. Until 1912 the canal had an average width of 160 feet and a depth of 15 feet throughout its length of 26¾ miles. In that year great improvements were begun. The new canal will be 25 feet deep and 200 feet wide, and will have only seven locks instead of 25 as

WELLAND CANAL
1, new canal; 2, old canal; 3, feeders

formerly. The estimated cost of these improvements is $30,000,000. This expenditure will enable the Welland Canal to compete effectively with the Erie Canal, and will provide a Canadian outlet for shipments from the west.

Well' Boring, a method of sinking wells of small diameter, for the purpose of obtaining water, petroleum or natural gas, or for discovering veins of ore. Well boring is done by machinery, which is operated by steam power. The outfit consists of a derrick, shaped like a square pyramid, about 20 feet across at the base, 4 feet across at the top and from 70 to 75 feet high; an engine for operating the machinery; a windlass for raising and lowering the drill; a walking beam, and the boring machinery, which consists of bits and drills of different sizes and styles. The drill is attached to a large rope, which runs over a pulley at the top of the derrick and down to a drum on the windlass. A few feet above the surface, this rope is grasped by a clamp, which is attached to a screw, called the *temper* screw. This screw is about five feet in length and is used to regulate the motion of the drill. The drill is attached to one end of the walking beam, which is operated by the engine and works the drill up and down. The rotary motion is given the drill by the operator's turning the handle a little at every stroke. When the drill has descended the length of the temper screw, it is drawn out by the windlass. If the well is dry, water is then run into it, and a bucket, called the *sandpipe*, is lowered, to draw out the mud and crushed rock. This bucket is a hollow cylinder, about sixteen feet long, with a bottom that opens upward. As it descends, the bottom opens and allows the

cylinder to be filled. When the cylinder is drawn out, the weight of the mud closes the valve, and in this way the well is emptied. As fast as the hole is drilled, it is cased with a steel tube. Bored wells in the oil regions vary in size from five feet to eight feet in diameter. Artesian wells are usually smaller.

Wells may be bored as deep as 3000 or 4000 feet. Difficulty in well boring increases with the depth, and deep wells are very expensive. See ARTESIAN WELL; PETROLEUM.

Welles, *welz,* GIDEON (1802–1878), an American statesman, born at Glastonbury, Conn. He early entered politics and became a power in the Democratic party, as editor of the *Hartford Times.* He was an admirer and supporter of Andrew Jackson. From 1827 to 1835 he sat in the state legislature, where he advocated such liberal principles as the abolition of imprisonment for debt. He was made comptroller of the state in 1835 and later served in minor administrative capacities in the national government. He joined the Republican party soon after its organization, and in 1861 he was made secretary of the navy by President Lincoln. There he displayed remarkable executive ability, managed the navy with consummate skill and efficiency during the war and advised the president on numerous questions of general policy. He also served throughout Johnson's term. In 1872 he supported the Liberal Republican movement, and in 1876 he used his influence for Samuel J. Tilden.

Wellesley, *welz'ly,* RICHARD COLLEY WELLESLEY, Marquis (1760–1842), a British general and statesman, brother of the Duke of Wellington. He served for three years in the Irish House of Peers, before being elected to the English House of Commons. In 1797 he was made governor-general of India, and for his suppression of the insurrection of Tippu Sahib of Mysore, and for the capture of Seringapatam, he was made Marquis Wellesley in the Irish peerage. He was also successful in the struggle with the Mahrattas in 1803–1805. His administration in India, which ended in 1805, was one of the most important in the history of British rule in India, owing to his financial reforms and his military victories. In 1808, Wellesley was made minister to Spain, and in the following year he became secretary of state for foreign affairs. He was chosen prime minister in 1812, but was unsuccessful in his attempt to form a cabinet. From 1821 to 1828 and from 1830 to 1834 he was lord lieutenant of Ireland.

Wellesley College, an institution for the higher education of women, founded in 1875 at Wellesley, Mass. The courses are largely elective and lead to the degrees of Bachelor of Arts and Master of Arts. The college is a contributor to the American Schools of Classical Study at Rome and Athens, to the zoölogical station at Naples and to the marine biological laboratory at Wood's Hole, Mass. The faculty includes about 125 instructors; the attendance is over 1400, and the library contains 75,000 volumes.

Wel'lington, the capital of New Zealand, situated on Port Nicholson, on North Island. The important buildings include the government building, the museum, the buildings of Victoria University College, the Wellington branch of the New Zealand Institute and an observatory. The town has tramways and botanic gardens and some manufactures. Population in 1911, 64,372.

Wellington, ARTHUR WELLESLEY, Duke of (1769–1852), a British general and statesman,

DUKE OF WELLINGTON

son of the earl of Mornington, educated at Eton, at Brighton and finally at the Military College of Angers, in France. In 1787 he received a commission as ensign in the army, and after a rapid series of changes and promotions, he attained, by 1796, the rank of colonel. During 1794 and 1795 he served with his regiment under the duke of York in Flanders, and in 1797 his

regiment was dispatched to Bengal. War had just been declared against Tippu Sahib, and Colonel Wellesley's regiment had an important part in the Battle of Malavelly and the storming of Seringapatam. After this he was appointed to the administration of Mysore, and in 1803 he was given the command of a force engaged in a war against the Mahrattas. His successes compelled the submission of the Mahrattas, and peace was restored on conditions drawn up by the successful general.

In 1805 Wellesley returned to England, was shortly afterward elected to Parliament for Rye and in 1807 was appointed secretary of state for Ireland. In August, 1807, he received the command of a division in the expedition to Copenhagen, and he directed the only land operation of importance. In 1808 he attained the rank of lieutenant general and received the command of a force destined to operate in the north of Spain and Portugal. He was subsequently superseded; but before giving up the command he gained the Battle of Vimeiro over Junot, the campaign being brought to a close with the Convention of Cintra, by which the French agreed to evacuate Portugal. In 1809 Wellesley was appointed to take the chief command in the peninsula, which had been overrun by the French. The passage of the Douro, and the defeat of Soult, which followed, fittingly opened this masterly campaign. For the victory at Talavera (July 28), the first of many which he won in the peninsula, the government raised Wellesley to the peerage, as Viscount Wellington. Toward the end of 1810 he fought the Battle of Busaco, which was followed by the famous fortification and defense of the lines of Torres Vedras. Before these fortifications the French encamped for months, but they were finally compelled, by lack of supplies, to evacuate Portugal. A little later (in 1811) occurred the victory of Fuentes de Onoro. Early in 1812 Wellington took Ciudad Rodrigo and Badajoz by storm, fought the Battle of Salamanca, accounted one of his most famous victories, and in August entered Madrid. For his brilliant conduct of the campaign, he received the thanks of Parliament and was raised to the dignity of marquis. Next followed the Battle of Vittoria (1813), battles in the Pyrenees, the capture of San Sebastian and the forced retreat of Soult.

In 1814 a victory over Soult was gained, and in the same year the Battle of Toulouse, in which Soult's best troops were routed, opened the way for the British troops to the heart of France.

Napoleon abdicated on April 12, and a few days later the war was brought to a close by the signing of conventions with Soult and Berthier. The triumphant general was created marquis of Douro and duke of Wellington and was given the thanks of both houses of Parliament. In July he went as ambassador to France and succeeded Lord Castlereagh as British representative in the Congress of Vienna, and when Napoleon returned, Wellington took command of the army assembled in the Netherlands to oppose him, winning the great victory of Waterloo. On his return to England, after the restoration of peace, he accepted the post of master-general of the ordnance, with a seat in the cabinet of Lord Liverpool. In 1822 he represented Great Britain in the Congress of Verona, and six years later he accepted the premiership, resigning the command of the forces to Lord Hill. The growing discontent throughout the country on the subject of Parliamentary reform, which Wellington steadily opposed, caused the resignation of the government in 1830. He held office under Sir Robert Peel as secretary of state, and in 1846 he helped to carry the repeal of the corn laws, which till then he had opposed. He died Sept. 14, 1852, and was buried in Saint Paul's Cathedral.

Wellington, KAN., the county-seat of Sumner co., is on Slate Creek, 30 mi. s. w. of Wichita, and on the Santa Fé and the Chicago, Rock Island & Pacific railroads. It is an important shipping point for the surrounding country. The city has flour mills, grain elevators, a plow factory and other industries. Population in 1910, 7034.

Wells, *welz,* DAVID AMES (1828-1898), an American political economist. He was born at Springfield, Mass., graduated at Williams College and from the Lawrence Scientific School of Harvard. The first work which won him recognition as an economist was *Our Burden and Our Strength,* published in 1864, and this was followed by *Our Merchant Marine, Practical Economics* and *Recent Economic Changes.*

Wells'ton, OHIO, a city in Jackson co., about 80 mi. s. e. of Columbus, on the Cincinnati, Hamilton & Dayton, the Detroit Southern, the Baltimore & Ohio Southwestern and other railroads. It is in a coal-mining region and contains foundries, blast furnaces, machine shops, cement works, brick plants and other factories. There are two banks, a high school and a public library. Wellston was settled in 1871 and was incorporated in 1876. Population in 1910, 6875.

Wells'ville, OHIO, a city in Columbiana co., 39 mi. n. of Wheeling, W. Va., on the Ohio River and on the Pennsylvania railroad. Coal is mined and valuable fire clay is found in the vicinity. The city contains railroad shops, pottery works, brickyards, foundries, machine shops and other establishments. There are three banks, nine churches, a high school, a public library and municipal waterworks. Population in 1910, 7769.

Welwitschia, *wel wich' e a,* a remarkable plant, growing in the dry regions of southern Africa. It consists of a stem, which forms a woody mass, rising not more than a foot above the ground and having a diameter of from four inches to as many feet. From this mass grow two enormous leaves, which become dry and are often split up into shreds, but which do not fall off. Every year several short flower stalks grow up from the base of these leaves, but no other leaves are ever produced.

Wentworth, *went' wurth,* THOMAS, Earl of Strafford. See STRAFFORD, THOMAS WENTWORTH, Earl of.

Werwolf, *wur' woolf,* or **Werewolf,** *weer'-woolf,* according to an old superstition, a man who, either temporarily or permanently, became a wolf. The change might be voluntary, or it might be the result of enchantment, but in any case it gave to a man all the appetites and powers of a wolf. These werwolves were exceedingly dangerous, as their appetite for human flesh was particularly strong. The superstitions about werwolves were most widespread in Germany, but they existed in many other countries.

Weser, *va'zur,* a river of Germany, formed by the junction of the Fulda and the Werra at Münden It flows generally in a northwest direction, and after a winding course it enters the North Sea through a broad estuary. Its length is about 300 miles, and it is navigable for light boats throughout its course, while vessels drawing 16 feet of water can ascend as far as Bremen. Its principal tributaries are the Aller from the east and the Hunte from the west.

Wes'ley, CHARLES (1708-1788), the younger brother of John Wesley, born at Epworth and educated at Westminster School and Christ Church, Oxford. He accompanied his brother to Georgia as an ordained clergyman, but after his return to England he became, in 1738, a preacher in the Methodist connection and materially assisted the success of the movement by his numerous hymns, large collections of which have been frequently published. Two of his sons, Charles and Samuel, were celebrated for musical genius.

Wesley, John (1703–1791), the founder of Wesleyan Methodism, born at Epworth, Lincolnshire (his father being rector of the parish), and educated at the Charterhouse and at Christ Church, Oxford. He took his degree of B. A. in 1724, was ordained deacon in 1725, became a fellow of Lincoln College and lecturer and moderator in classics in 1726 and took priest's orders in 1728. He now gathered together a number of pupils and companions, among whom were Hervey, Whitefield and Law, the author of the *Serious Call to the Unconverted,* who met regularly for religious purposes, and by so doing they acquired the name of Methodists. In 1725 Wesley accepted an invitation from General Oglethorpe to go to America to preach to the colonists of Georgia. He returned to England (February, 1738), and in the following May an important event took place in his inner religious life—his conversion. In June he paid a visit to Herrnhut, the Moravian settlement, returning to England in September. Early in the following year (1739) he began open-air preaching, in which he was closely associated with Whitefield, from whom, however, he soon separated, though their friendship was not broken.

Having now the sole control of the religious body which adhered to him, he devoted his entire life without intermission to the work of its organization, in which he showed much practical skill and admirable method. His labors as an itinerant preacher were incessant. He would ride from forty to sixty miles and preach four or five times in a day, reading and writing during the journeys. It is said 30,000 persons would wait hours for him to come to them on horseback. He married, in 1750, Mrs. Vizelle, a widow with four children, but the union was unfortunate, and they finally separated. He held strongly to the principle of episcopacy, and he never formally separated from the Church of England. His collected works were published after his death in thirty-two octavo volumes. He contributed to a collection of hymns, the greater part of which were written by his brother Charles. He founded an orphans' home at Newcastle, a dispensary at Bristol and charity schools in London.

Wes'leyan University, a university established at Middletown, Conn., in 1831, under the auspices of the Methodist Episcopal Church. This is the oldest college of the denomination in the country. It provides classical, Latin-scientific and scientific courses. The university is coeducational, but the number of women admitted to the college in any year is limited to twenty per cent of the total enrollment of the previous year. The faculty numbers thirty-six, and there are about 350 students. The library contains 85,000 volumes, the endowment is $1,444,000 and the annual income is $114,000.

West, Benjamin (1738–1820), an American painter, born at Springfield, Pa. He showed great precocity in his aptitude for painting, and at the age of eighteen he established himself as a portrait painter at Philadelphia. In 1760 he visited Italy, and settling in Rome he painted *Cimon and Iphigenia* and *Angelica and Medora.* He visited England in 1763 and was so well patronized that he determined to make it his future residence. He painted *Hector and Andromache, The Return of the Prodigal Son* and an historical painting of *Agrippa Landing with the Ashes of Germanicus,* the last for the archbishop of York, who introduced him to George III, who became his steadfast patron and gave him commissions to the extent of about $5000 a year for upward of thirty years. He painted a series of historical works for Windsor, and for the oratory there he produced a series on the progress of revealed religion. On the death of Sir Joshua Reynolds, in 1792, he was elected president of the Royal Academy. He afterward painted a number of religious and historical pictures of large size, among them being *Christ Healing the Sick, The Crucifixion, The Ascension* and *Death on the Pale Horse. The Death of General Wolfe at Quebec* and *The Battle of La Hogue* are accounted the best of his historical pieces.

West Allis, Wis., a village of Milwaukee co., a few miles west of Milwaukee, on the Chicago, Milwaukee & Saint Paul Railroad. There are manufactories of engines, steam pumps and machinery and other industries. Population in 1910, 6645.

West Bay City, Mich., formerly a city in Bay co., about 4 miles from Saginaw Bay, on the Saginaw River, opposite Bay City, and on the Grand Trunk and the Michigan Central railroads. Since 1905 it has been a part of Bay City. Population in 1905, 13,000. See Bay City.

Westboro, *west'bur ro,* Mass., a town in Worcester co., 12 mi. e. of Worcester, on the Boston & Albany railroad. It contains manufactures of straw and rubber goods, shoes, automobiles and other articles. There are five churches, a public library, a hospital for the insane and the Lyman Reform School. The place was settled about 1659 and was known as Chauncy, but was incorporated under the present name in 1717. Population in 1910, 5446.

West′brook, MAINE, a city in Cumberland co., 6 mi. n. e. of Portland, on the Presumpscott River and on the Boston & Maine and the Maine Central railroads. There are also several electric railways. The river furnishes some water power, and the principal manufactures are silk and cotton goods, paper, flour and other articles. There are eight churches, the Walker Memorial Library and a convent. Westbrook was a part of Falmouth until separately incorporated in 1814. It was chartered as a city in 1889. Population in 1910, 8281.

West Ches′ter, PA., the county-seat of Chester co., 25 mi. w. of Philadelphia, on the Pennsylvania railroad, with trolleys to Philadelphia and other points. A state normal school is located here, also Darlington Seminary, two Friends' schools, a hospital and a public library. Other features of interest are the Marshall Square, with its rare trees, the old Turk's Head Hotel, the fine classic building of the National Bank of Chester County and the county buildings. It is in a fine agricultural region, has the largest cream separator works in the country, large wheel works and extensive nurseries. West Chester was settled in 1784 and was made a borough in 1799. The Battle of Brandywine was fought four miles south of the city. Population in 1910, 11,767.

Wes′terly, R. I., a town in Washington co., 44 mi. s. w. of Providence, on the Pawcatuck River and on the New York, New Haven & Hartford railroad. It has granite quarries and contains manufactures of cotton and woolen goods and other articles. The waterworks are owned by the municipality, and there are six banks, three savings institutions and a large public library. The place was at first called by the indian name of Misquamicut, but it was incorporated in 1669 as the town of Westerly. Population in 1910, including five villages, 8696.

Western Austra′lia, a state of the Australian Commonwealth, occupying all of that portion of the continent west of the 129th meridian east longitude. Its greatest extent from north to south is 1480 mi., and from east to west, 1000 mi. The area is estimated at 975,-920 sq. mi., making it the largest of the Australian states. The interior is a low plateau, varying in altitude from 700 to 1000 feet and occasionally rising to greater height. It is mostly sterile, with little or no vegetation. Most of the eastern part of this division belongs to the great Victorian desert.

The western coast line is bordered by highlands or mountains, which are from 50 to 100 miles from the coast. These mountains also extend into the northern or Kimberley division. They are low, and their highest summits do not exceed 3580 feet. The productive regions of the colony are in the west and southwest. Here there is sufficient rainfall to sustain vegetation, and extensive forests of eucalyptus, sandalwood and other Australian trees occur. The lands are also well suited to grazing and agriculture, and wheat, barley, corn, oats, potatoes and hay are raised in paying quantities. Apples, peaches, oranges, lemons, grapes and other fruits are also cultivated. Considerable live stock is raised and wool growing is an important branch of agricultural industry. Other resources of the state are timber, and mineral wealth, consisting largely of gold.

The government is similar to that of other Australian states. The governor is appointed by the British sovereign and the legislature consists of a legislative council of 30 members and an assembly of 50 members. The members of the council are chosen for six years, and of the assembly, for three years. Perth is the capital. Population in 1911, 282,114. See AUSTRALIA, COMMONWEALTH OF.

Western Reserve, the name given to a part of northern Ohio, reserved by Connecticut in 1786, when that state yielded its claims to the other western lands to the United States. The Reserve was 120 miles long and had an area of more than 8000 square miles. These claims were based on the Connecticut charter of 1662, which gave to the colony a strip from sea to sea. The fund derived from the sale of the Western Reserve in 1796 was devoted to the maintenance of Connecticut's public schools.

Western Reserve University, an institution of higher learning at Cleveland, Ohio, founded in 1826. It comprises Adelbert College, a graduate school, a medical college and law, dental and library departments. The faculty numbers over 225, the enrollment is about 1000, and the library contains over 90,000 volumes.

West′field, MASS., a town in Hampden co., 9 mi. w. of Springfield, on the Westfield River and on the Boston & Albany and the New York, New Haven & Hartford railroads. It is in the beautiful Westfield River valley, has a park, an excellent water supply and a good sewage system. The manufactures include paper, thread, bicycles, whips, cigars and other articles. A state normal school is located here, and the town has public and parish schools and kindergartens, a hospital and a public library. There are four banks and two savings banks, and the municipality owns the water works, electric light and gas plants. It was settled in 1642 and was known by the indian name of Woronoco until its incorporation in 1669. Population in 1910, 16,044.

West Ha'ven, CONN., a borough in New Haven co., on New Haven Bay at the mouth of the West River, opposite the city of New Haven, and on the New York, New Haven & Hartford railroad. It is a residence place, has a public square of seven acres, and contains good municipal buildings. There are manufactures of pianos, buckles, safes, fertilizers and other articles. Savin Rock, on Long Island Sound, is a well-known summer resort. West Haven was separated from New Haven in 1822. Population in 1910, 8543.

West Ho'boken, N. J., a town in Hudson co., adjoining Hoboken, near Jersey City. It is located on high lands above the river and has silk mills and other factories. The cultivation of flowers is also extensively carried on. The principal buildings are the Saint Michael's Monastery and the Dominican Convent. There are public and parish schools, a high school and a Catholic theological seminary. West Hoboken was a part of Bergen until its incorporation in 1861. Population in 1910, 35,403.

West Indies, in'diz, or **Antilles,** an til'leez, an archipelago lying between North America and South America, and forming the northern and eastern boundary of the Caribbean Sea. Its area is about 92,000 sq. mi. It contains a number of groups of islands, including the Bahamas, the Greater Antilles and the Lesser Antilles (See ANTILLES). The islands have a tropical climate, and most of them are high. Geologically, they are supposed to be elevations caused by the projection of the eastern mountain system of North America. Politically, Cuba and Haiti, the latter divided between Haiti and Santo Domingo, are free. The others are colonial possessions, distributed among the different countries as follows:

GREAT BRITAIN: Bahamas, Jamaica, Cay-

mans, Virgin Gorda, Tortola, Anegada, Sombrero, Anguilla, Barbuda, Saint Christopher (Saint Kitts), Antigua, Nevis and Redonda, Montserrat, Dominica, Saint Lucia, Saint Vincent, Barbados, Grenada and the Grenadines, Tobago, Trinidad.

UNITED STATES: Porto Rico.

FRANCE: Martinique, Guadeloupe, Désirade, Saint Martin (in part), Marie Galance, Saint Bartholomew, Les Saintes.

DENMARK: Saint Thomas, Saint John, Santa Cruz (Saint Croix).

NETHERLANDS: Saint Martin (in part), Saint Eustatius, Saba, Curaçao, Aruba, Buen Ayre.

VENEZUELA: Margarita, Tortuga, Hermanos.

INDEPENDENT: Cuba and Isle of Pines, Haiti. The large islands and different groups are described under their respective titles. See BAHAMA ISLANDS; CUBA; HAITI; JAMAICA; PORTO RICO; WINDWARD ISLANDS.

West Indies, DANISH, a group of three islands in the West Indies, a colonial possession of Denmark. It comprises the islands, Saint Thomas, Saint Croix and Saint John. The cultivation of sugar is the chief industry, and an extensive trade is also carried on in rum. The capital is Christiansted, on Saint Croix, and the chief town is Charlotte Amalie, on Saint Thomas. Population in 1911, 27,086.

West'inghouse, GEORGE (1846-1914), an American inventor and engineer, the inventor of the air brake. He was born in Schoharie co., N. Y., and was educated in the public schools of Schenectady. He spent much time in his father's machine shop and invented, when but fifteen years of age, a rotary engine. During 1863 and 1864 he served in the Union army, and later he studied in Union College. His inventions include a device for replacing railroad cars on the track; the air brake, which he invented in 1868 and subsequently improved, and a number of signaling devices. Alternating current machinery was introduced in America largely through his efforts. He built the great generators at Niagara Falls and those for the elevated railway and the rapid transit system in New York, and he established in Europe and in the United States large works for the manufacture of air brakes and other machines. See AIR BRAKE.

West'minster, England. See LONDON.

Westminster Abbey, a famous church in London, called "Abbey" because up to the time of Henry VIII it was a Benedictine monastery, presided over by an abbot. It is situated near the Thames, adjoining the Houses of Parliament. In 1065 a church was built here, in the Norman style, by Edward the Confessor, but the main building, as it now stands, was begun in 1220 by Henry III and was practically completed by Edward I. Various additions, however, were made down to the time of Henry VII, who built the chapel which bears his name, while the upper parts of the two towers were designed by Sir Christopher Wren. The extreme length of the church is 423 feet, the roof is 102 feet high, and the towers are 225 feet high. The coronation of English kings takes place in the choir of Westminster Abbey, where the coronation stone brought by Edward I from Scotland, is placed beside the coronation chairs of the English sovereigns. Westminster Abbey is distinguished as the burial place of numerous English kings, from Edward the Confessor to George II. The north transept is occupied chiefly by monuments to warriors and statesmen, while in the south transept is the *Poets' Corner*, where are monuments to most of England's great poets, from Chaucer to Robert Browning. Longfellow is the only American poet whose memorial has been placed in Westminster Abbey.

Westminster Hall, the hall of the old palace of Westminster, erected by Richard II on the foundations of a structure built byWilliam Rufus. It is 290 feet long, 68 feet wide and 90 feet high, and it has a fine porch, and a roof of carved timber which is considered the most notable of its kind. This building is closely associated with many stirring events in English history; but it is chiefly remarkable as the place where were held such great state trials as those of the Chancellor More, Lady Jane Grey, the earl of Strafford, King Charles I and Warren Hastings, and as the center of the highest English courts of law, till these were removed to the new buildings recently erected for their accommodation. The hall, which is the only part of the Houses of Parliament which remained standing after the fire of 1834, serves as a vestibule to the present Houses of Parliament.

West New York, N. J., a town of Hudson co., adjoining West Hoboken. Like numerous other towns in its vicinity, it is interested chiefly in the manufacture of silk. Population in 1910, 13,560.

West Orange, *or'anj*, N. J., a town in Essex co., 5 mi. n. w. of Newark and 12 mi. w. of New York City, on the Erie railroad. It has a pleasant location along the base of Orange Mountain, and it contains well-paved streets and two public parks. There are manufactures of phonographs, electrical supplies and other goods. Population in 1910, 10,980.

Westphalia, *west fa'le a*, PEACE OF, the treaty which closed the Thirty Years' War. Many states had been involved in this contest and two separate conventions were held to decide upon terms of peace. The representatives of the Empire, France and Spain and the Catholic electors and princes of the Empire met at Münster, and the representatives of Sweden, the Empire and the German Protestants at Osnabrück. Each of these conventions signed a treaty in 1648, and in October of that year the general treaty was signed at Westphalia, by the representatives of all the powers. One of the important provisions of the treaty was the extension to the Calvinists of the religious liberty which had by the Peace of Augsburg been allowed only to the Lutherans. It was provided, also, that all territory which, in the Palatinate, Württemberg and Baden in 1618 and in the other states in 1624, had been held by Catholics, was to remain Catholic, and that all which at that time had been held by the Protestants was to remain Protestant. A prince might decide as to the religion of the state, but the people might emigrate if dissatisfied. The Upper Palatinate was added to the duchy of Bavaria; the Lower Palatinate was given to the son of the elector Palatine, and Western Pomerania was ceded to Sweden. Brandenburg received certain cessions of territory to make up for the loss of Pomerania; France was given Alsace, with Metz, Toul and Verdun; Spain recognized the independence of the United Provinces of the Netherlands, and Austria recognized the independence of Switzerland. This treaty, chiefly by weakening Austria, made France the first power in Europe.

West Pitt'ston, PA., a borough in Luzerne co., on the Susquehanna River opposite Pittston, with which it is connected by two bridges. It is primarily a residence place and has wide streets and many attractive homes. There are also some manufacturing establishments. Population in 1910, 6848.

West Point', N. Y., a village in Orange co., on the west bank of the Hudson, 55 mi. n. of New York City, and at the opening of the Highlands. The village is beautifully situated on an elevated plateau and is noted as the seat of the United States Military Academy, which occupies a site covering 2300 acres. The buildings are grouped upon a plateau of about 200 acres, adjoining which is a large parade ground. Among the important buildings are the library, the hospital, the riding hall, the superintendent's hall and Cullom Memorial Hall, completed in 1897 and containing a museum of war trophies and portraits and busts of distinguished Americans and a new memorial to General Grant. The grounds are also adorned with numerous statues of American generals and with a beautiful monument, surmounted by a figure of "Victory" and erected to the memory of the officers and men in the regular army who perished during the Civil War. Under a recent act of Congress, ample provision was made for rebuilding and enlarging the various buildings of the academy. See MILITARY ACADEMY, UNITED STATES.

In the early history of the country West Point was of considerable strategic importance, and during the Revolution it was fortified under the direction of the Polish engineer Kosciusko. It was given into the command of Benedict Arnold (See ARNOLD, BENEDICT), who treacherously attempted to surrender it to the British; but the discovery of the plot prevented its being successfully carried out. It was selected as the site of the military academy by Congress in 1802.

West Spring'field, MASS., a town in Hampden co., on the Connecticut River opposite Springfield, and on the Boston & Albany railroad. It is chiefly a residence place, but there are also flour and paper mills, machine shops and railroad shops. Market gardening is extensively carried on. The municipality has a public library and owns and operates the waterworks. Population in 1910, including several villages, 9224.

West Virginia, the PAN-HANDLE STATE, one of the South Atlantic states, bounded on the n. by Ohio, Pennsylvania and Maryland, on the e. by Pennsylvania, Maryland and Virginia, on the s. by Virginia and Kentucky and on the w. by Kentucky and Ohio. The outline is very irregular, but the general shape of the state is that of an oval. The greatest extent from northeast to southwest is 210 mi., and from east to west, 125 mi. The area is 24,170 sq. mi. The population in 1910 was 1,221,119.

SURFACE AND DRAINAGE. The surface as a whole is very uneven and in the eastern portion it is mountainous. The mountain region occupies more than one-third of the state, and the ranges extend in a northeast-southwest direction. Between the mountain ranges on the eastern and western sides are broad valleys, narrowing into ravines as they approach the hill region. The ridges in the eastern part of the state are cut by numerous transverse valleys, and in the southern part these valleys are so numerous as to cut the mountain ranges into broad domes with spurs running in various directions, leaving but few definite ridges. The average elevation of the state is 1500 feet. This is the highest average of any state east of the Mississippi River. The highest point is Spruce Knob in Pendleton County, which has an elevation of 4860 feet, and the lowest point is Harpers Ferry, with an elevation of 260 feet. Some of the other prominent peak are Bald Knob, 4800 feet, and High Knob, 4170 teet. West of the mountains there is a belt of broad, flat hills, ranging from 1000 to 2000 in elevation. These hills are followed by a more gently rolling country, sloping toward the Ohio River.

The Ohio River furnishes steam navigation along the whole western boundary and receives all the principal streams of the state, except the Potomac and its affluents. The largest rivers flowing into the Ohio are the Guyandotte, the Great Kanawha, the Little Kanawha, the Big Sandy and the Monongahela. The chief streams flowing into the Potomac are the North and South branches.

CLIMATE. The climate is remarkably equable, with no extremes of heat or cold. The mean annual temperature at Morgantown is 54°. The average rainfall in the highest elevation is 35 inches, and in the lowest, 55 inches.

MINERAL RESOURCES. West Virginia is one of the leading mining states. It contains extensive measures of bituminous coal and large fields of petroleum and natural gas. The productive area of its coal fields is 12,930 square miles. The mining of coal is the chief mineral industry, and the output for twelve months, ending June 30, 1910, was 59,274,553 tons. Mines are worked in twenty-one counties. Much of this coal is used in the manufacture of coke. The oil fields are a continuation of the oil fields of Pennsylvania, and the output is about 12,000,-000 barrels a year. The yield of natural gas is also quite large, its value being over $16,000,000 annually. Building stone and clays are widely distributed over the state and are quarried for local purposes.

AGRICULTURE. The western part of the state contains a fertile soil, well suited to tillage, but the hills in the eastern part are better suited to grazing. Diversified farming is practiced, and no one crop can be said to lead. Buckwheat, oats and rye are the cereals raised in largest quantities. Hay is produced to a considerable extent, and tobacco and sorghum are cultivated on a small scale. Potatoes and other vegetables are raised with profit, as are orchard fruits. The state has a large forested area, producing $20,000,000 worth of lumber yearly.

MANUFACTURES. The manufacturing industries are concentrated mainly at Wheeling, the largest city, on the Ohio, in the northern part of the state; the products consist mainly of iron and steel, coke, flour and grist mill products, lumber and leather.

TRANSPORTATION. The state finds water communication through the Monongahela and the Great Kanawha, both of which are navigable, and most of the commerce finds an outlet through the Ohio valley. Several trunk lines of railway traverse the state from east to west, one in the northern, another in the central and two in the southern section. Lines also extend north and south, connecting these in several places, and there are numerous cross-lines and spurs, so that the northern and central parts of the state are well supplied with railway facilities. There are over 3600 miles of railroad in the state. There are a few counties in the west central and southern parts that are without railway communication.

GOVERNMENT. The legislature consists of a senate and a house of delegates, the former having 30 members, and the latter, 86. One-half of the senators are elected every two years for a four-year term, and the delegates are elected for two years. The legislature meets biennially, and the session is limited to forty-five days. The executive department consists of a governor, a secretary of state, a superintendent of free schools, a treasurer and an attorney-general, each elected for four years. The courts consist of 1 supreme court of appeals, 18 circuit courts and 38 courts of limited jurisdiction, together with courts of county commissioners, justices of the peace and city courts.

EDUCATION. Separate schools are maintained for white and colored pupils. The system of public instruction is in charge of the superintendent of free schools. The higher institutions of learning are the University of West Virginia, at Morgantown; the normal schools at Athens, Fairmont, Glenville, Huntington, Shepherdstown and West Liberty; Bethany College; West Virginia Wesleyan College; Morris Harvey College; the West Virginia Colored Institute and Bluefield Colored Institute.

INSTITUTIONS. The school for the deaf and blind is at Romney; the hospitals for the insane are at Weston, Spencer and Huntington. There is a hospital for incurables at Huntington, and miners' hospitals are maintained at Fairmont, McKendree and Welch. The penal institutions consist of a penitentiary at Moundsville, a reform school for boys at Pruntytown, and a girls' industrial school at Salem.

CITIES. The chief cities are Charleston, the capital; Wheeling, Huntington, Parkersburg, Martinsburg, Fairmont, Grafton, Morgantown and Moundsville, each of which is described under its title. There are 14 towns ranging between 2000 and 5000 in population.

HISTORY. The State of West Virginia was, until 1863, a part of the State of Virginia (For early history, see VIRGINIA, subhead *History*). At the outbreak of the Civil War, many of the counties in the western part of that state had Union sympathies, while the remainder wished to secede and join the Confederacy. Therefore, in June, 1861, representatives of forty counties declared independence of the State of Virginia, established a provisional government, under Francis H. Pierpont, as governor, and a legislature, elected representatives to Congress and adopted a constitution in April, 1862. Meantime, a "reorganized" provisional government of Virginia had given its consent to the formation of the state, and West Virginia was formally admitted June 20, 1863. It was the scene of some of the earliest fighting in the Civil War and furnished far more than its quota to the Federal armies. After the war there was rapid development of the resources of the state and a great increase in population. It was uniformly Democratic in politics from 1872 to 1892, but it has been generally Republican since that time.

West Virginia, UNIVERSITY OF, a state university, established at Morgantown, W. Va., in 1868, by the consolidation of the West Virginia Agricultural College, Woodburn Seminary and Monongahela Academy. It includes colleges of arts and sciences, engineering and mechanic arts, agriculture and law, schools of music, military science and tactics and commerce, and preparatory schools at Keyser, Montgomery and Morgantown. There are seventy instructors and about 1100 students. The income derived from state and government appropriations amounts to $250,000. The institution is coeducational, and all departments are open to women on equal terms with men.

Weyler, *va e lair'*, Nicolau Valeriano, Marquis of Teneriffe (1838–　), a Spanish general. During the Civil War he was in the United States as an attaché of the Spanish legation, and he was with Sheridan on some of his cavalry raids. He gained a reputation for excessive barbarity at the time of the Carlist War in Spain and during the African War against the Moors. He was captain-general of Catalonia, in Spain, and was in 1896 appointed to the charge of Cuban affairs, to succeed Martinez Campos. The United States protested against his methods, and he was recalled in 1897. After the Spanish-American War he was for a time captain-general of Madrid, and he held office as minister of war in Sagasta's cabinet.

Weyman, *wi'man* or *way'man*, Stanley John (1855–　), an English novelist. He was educated at Shrewsbury and Christ Church, Oxford, and was for a time classical instructor in King's School, Chester. After studying law he was admitted to the bar in 1881. His literary work began with contributions to the *Cornhill Magazine*, and he published his first romance, *The House of the Wolf*, in 1889. Later he published *The New Rector, A Gentleman of France*, which has been translated into several languages, *The Man in Black, My Lady Rotha, Under the Red Robe* and *The Red Cockade*.

Weymouth, *way'muth*, Mass., a town in Norfolk co., 12 mi. s. e. of Boston, on Boston harbor, and on the New York, New Haven & Hartford and several electric railroads. It contains extensive shoe factories, wool-scouring plants, railroad shops and other factories. There are two libraries, a town high school and municipal waterworks. The first permanent settlement was made about 1623, and the present name was adopted in 1635, when the town was incorporated. Population in 1910, including several villages, 12,895.

Whale, the common name given to the larger mammals of the order Cetacea (See Cetacea). Their abode is in the sea or the great rivers, and they resemble the fishes so closely in external appearance that some of the earlier zoölogists regarded them as belonging to that class. The whales are usually divided into two families, the whalebone whales and the whales having teeth. In the whalebone whales the place of teeth is taken by *baleen*, or whalebone. The typical representative of this family is the *common*, or *Greenland, whale*, valuable on account of the oil and whalebone which it furnishes. It is principally found in the Arctic seas, but it is also found in considerable numbers in many other parts of the world. Its length is usually about 60 feet, and its greatest circumference is from 30 to 40 feet. Allied to the Greenland whale is the *rorqual*, which often measures about 100 feet in length and from 30 to 35 feet in circum-

GREENLAND WHALE

ference. Of the toothed whales the best-known species is the *sperm whale*, or *cachalot*, which averages from 50 to 70 feet in length.

Whale fisheries have been important for many years and have been prosecuted with such vigor that the Greenland whale is now nearly exterminated. Previous to the discovery of petroleum, whale oil was extensively used in lamps, but the substitution of kerosene and illuminating gas lessened the demand for this product, and whales are now sought more for their whalebone than for their oil. Since the middle of the eighteenth century, whale fishing has rapidly declined, and it is now prosecuted by only a few vessels of any nation.

Whalebone, *hwale'bone*, or **Baleen'**, a term applied to the horny plates attached to the palate of the whalebone whale. They are arranged in a double row on the upper jaw and hang down in parallel plates into the cavity of the mouth. The length of the plates varies from a few inches to twelve feet, and in number there are about 200 on each side of the mouth. The color varies according to the species, some kinds being black, some yellowish-white and others gray, striped with black or black and white. The whole apparatus acts as a kind of sieve, or strainer, for the small animals on which the whale feeds. From its strength, lightness and flexibility, whalebone has become an important article of commerce, being used for many purposes, as in the manufacture of corsets, ribs for umbrellas, whips and surgical instruments.

Wharf, *hwawrf*, a platform of either wood or stone, alongside of which ships are moored, for loading and unloading. Wharves may be parallel with the shore, in which case they are called *quays*; or they may be built out into the water at right angles to the shore line, when they are known as *piers*. Many wharves are built of piles, driven into the bottom of the harbor and covered with a plank flooring. The construction of wharves is under the control of the government. In the United States this means the state government, and in other countries the national government. According to common law, the land of tide waters, between high and low water marks, belongs to the state, and individuals or corporations wishing to establish wharves must obtain permission from the state, otherwise the wharf would be declared a public nuisance. Most of the states lease the harbors to the cities in which they are located, and the cities lease the wharves to corporations and private individuals, who charge a rental to ships that use them.

Wharton, *hwawr'ton,* EDITH (1862–   ), one of the more important of the contemporary American novelists. Among her most noteworthy writings are *The Touchstone, The Valley of Decision, Italian Villas and their Gardens* and *The House of Mirth.* Her novels are marked by a true insight into character and a power for psychological analysis.

Wharton, FRANCIS (1820–1899), an American jurist, born in Philadelphia. He graduated from Yale, studied law and was admitted to the bar in 1843. In 1845 he became assistant district attorney in Philadelphia, and eleven years later he was made professor of logic and rhetoric at Kenyon College, Ohio. On his return from a visit to Europe, he was ordained in the Episcopal Church and became rector of a church in Brookline, Mass., holding at the same time the chairs of ecclesiastical and international law at the Cambridge Divinity School and Boston University. In 1885 he was made counsel to the United States department of state, and in 1888 he was made editor of the Revolutionary diplomatic correspondence of the United States. His publications include *A Treatise on the Criminal Law of the United States,* his best-known work; *A Treatise on the Law of Homicide in the United States; A Treatise on the Conflict of Laws, or Private International Law; A Treatise on Theism and Modern Skeptical Theories,* and *The Silence of Scripture.*

Whately, *hwate'ly,* RICHARD (1787–1863), archbishop of Dublin, born in London. He was educated at Bristol and Oriel College, Oxford; was elected a fellow in Oriel College in 1811; became a college tutor in 1815 and was made archbishop of Dublin in 1831. He vigorously opposed the Tractarian Movement, was a

Liberal in politics and religion and worked for a system of religious instruction that would be unsectarian. While he was unpopular with some, because of his freedom of speech and sarcastic wit, his charity, honesty, justice and strong sense of duty won respect and warm friends.

Wheat, one of the most valuable and widely distributed grains. It grows readily in almost every climate and constitutes an important crop in Russia, Germany, France, India, Australia, Argentina, Canada and the United States. While wheat has a wide range of climate, it thrives best in a temperate climate, where there is a medium rainfall. It requires a rich, clay soil or heavy loam. Wheat is supposed to be a native of western Asia, but it has been cultivated so many centuries that the place of its origin is not fully known. There are many varieties. In accordance with their method of growth these are divided into *bearded* wheat and *bald* wheat. The first has glumes attached to the seeds, while the second has none. In regard to the color of the kernel, the varieties are divided into *light-colored* and *dark-colored,* or *white* and *red* wheats. Classified according to the time of planting, all wheats are grouped under *winter* wheat and *spring* wheat. In each of these classes we find hard and soft wheats. The winter wheat is planted in the fall and is harvested early the following summer. It is well suited to warm temperate climates that have mild winters. The spring wheat is planted early in spring and matures the same season. It is adapted to the short season of the cool temperate regions. It is usually a hard wheat and of better quality than any varieties of winter wheat.

The United States is the leading wheat-producing country of the world, and the raising of this grain is carried on in Minnesota, North Dakota, South Dakota, Kansas, Oklahoma and some other states on an extensive scale. The wheat farms or ranches are large, some of them embracing more than 25,000 acres. These are divided into sections, each of which has its stables for teams, sheds for storing machinery, and other buildings, and each is under the direction of a foreman. In the spring-wheat region the land is plowed in the fall, and the wheat is planted as early in the spring as the condition of the ground will admit. In the winter-wheat section the ground is plowed as soon as possible after the crop has been harvested. The time of planting depends upon the location. In the warmest regions it is later than in the cool por-

WHEAT

1, Harvesting.	3, Steel Elevator.	5, Wheat Plants.
2, Threshing.	4, Interior of Flour Mill.	6, Products.

tions of the winter wheat belt. All of the work is done by machinery. The land is plowed by gang plows and is pulverized by wheel harrows, and the seed is planted by seeders or drills (See Sowing Machine). The grain is harvested by the self-binding harvesters (See Reaping Machine) and is thrashed by machines operated by steam engines of such capacity as to thrash from 1200 to 1500 bushels in a day (See Thrashing Machine). The wheat is hauled directly from the thrasher to the local elevators or to cars for shipment. From the local elevators it is transported to the great wheat centers, such as Minneapolis, Duluth, Chicago and Buffalo, where it is stored in large elevators, some of which have a capacity of nearly 2,000,000 bushels; there it is kept until needed for use. The average production in the United States is about 700,000,000 bushels a year, though in 1913 the crop was 753,233,000 bushels.

Other important wheat-producing countries are Russia, Austria-Hungary, France, India, Argentina and Canada. See Flour; also Chinch Bug.

Wheat Midge, a small, yellowish insect, with a dark back, related to the Hessian fly, but differing in habits. The wheat midge, which is now common in the Mississippi Valley, probably came from Europe and has occasioned a great deal of damage to wheat, especially in warm and moist seasons. The damage is done by the little orange-yellow larvae, which destroy the embryos of the grain and prevent the heads from filling. As the larvae can live for several months without either moisture or food, they are carried about in the wheat heads, and so the species is distributed.

Wheat'on, Henry (1785–1848), an American lawyer and diplomat, born at Providence, R. I. He graduated at Brown University, was admitted to the bar and spent several years of study in Europe. He began the practice of law at Providence and later removed to New York City, where he also entered journalism. In 1816 he became reporter of the United States Supreme Court and served until 1827, his twelve volumes of reports being of special value. At the close of this service he was sent as *chargé d'affaires* to Denmark. He was later made minister resident to the court of Prussia, and from 1837 to 1846 he acted as minister plenipotentiary. He is perhaps best known for his *Elements of International Law*, one of the greatest extant authorities on the subject. It has been translated into French, Chinese and Japanese. He also wrote numerous other works of importance.

181

Wheat'stone, Charles, Sir (1802–1875), an English scientist and inventor. His early occupation led him to give attention to the laws of sound, and later he published a work on the subject, which secured him an appointment as professor of experimental philosophy at King's College, London. Among his inventions are the stereoscope and an electric telegraph, the latter in conjunction with Cook, but this invention was not put into practical use until after the telegraph had been invented by Morse. Wheatstone was also the inventor of several other electric appliances, one of which enabled a system of clocks to be regulated from a central clock, by means of electro-magnets.

Wheel, an instrument of torture, formerly employed in France and Germany. The criminal was placed on the wheel with his face upward, and his legs and arms extended along the spokes. On the wheel being moved round, the executioner broke the wretch's limbs by successive blows with a hammer or iron bar; and after a more or less protracted interval he put an end to the sufferings of his victim by two or three severe blows, called *coups de grace* (mercy strokes), on the chest or stomach, or by strangling him. In Germany the wheel was occasionally used till the beginning of the nineteenth century.

Wheel and Ax'le, a sort of continuous lever of the first class (See Lever), consisting of a wheel and axle, fastened to the same axis. The radius of the wheel is the power arm, and the radius of the axle, the weight arm, of the lever. The law of equilibrium is that the power multiplied by the radius of the wheel is equal to the weight multiplied by the radius of the axle. In the figure, A represents the circumference of the wheel, C is the circumference of the axle, R the radius of the wheel, and r the radius of the axle. If  the wheel has a diameter of three feet, and the axle has a radius of one foot, a power of one pound will balance a weight of three pounds. In making the computations, the same results are obtained, whether the radius of the wheel is compared with the radius of the axle, or the diameter of the wheel with the diameter of the axle. The most common use of the wheel and axle is in the windlass, for raising water. Here the crank often takes the place of a wheel, but the device operates on the same principle. Combinations of the wheel and axle often occur in machinery where great power is required. In these combinations the axle of the wheel to which the power is applied is fitted with teeth, which mesh into those on the rim of the next wheel, and so on until the entire combination has been used. Derricks and shears used for cutting iron bars and plates afford good illustrations of these combinations.

Wheel'er, BENJAMIN IDE (1854–   ), an American educator. He was educated at Colby Academy and Brown University and spent four years of study in the universities of Leipzig, Heidelberg, Jena and Berlin. He taught in the Providence High School, Brown University and Harvard and in 1886 became a professor in Cornell University, holding, successively, the chairs of comparative philology and Greek. In 1899 Wheeler became president of the University of California. His written works include *Analogy and the Scove of its Application in Language,*

BENJAMIN IDE WHEELER

Introduction to the Study of the History of Language and *Principles of Language Growth.*

Wheeler, JOSEPH (1836–1906), an American soldier, born at Augusta, Ga. He was educated at the West Point military academy, was appointed lieutenant of cavalry and served in New Mexico. When the Civil War broke out he joined the Confederate army. His efficient serv-

JOSEPH WHEELER

ices caused him to be rapidly promoted until he reached the rank of lieutenant general. He was in the Battle of Shiloh, rendered distinguished service at Chickamauga and was noted for the annoyance he caused Sherman on his march through Georgia and South Carolina. After the war he settled in Alabama, and in 1880 he was sent to Congress. He represented his district until 1898, when he reëntered the army as major general of volunteers, with command of the cavalry in the Army of Santiago. He rendered valiant service in the battles of Las Guasimas and San Juan Hill, and he was senior member of the commission which arranged for the surrender of Santiago. Later he served in the Philippines, until he was retired under the age limit.

Wheeler, WILLIAM ALMON (1819–1887), an American statesman, born at Malone, Franklin County, N. Y. He studied for a time at the University of Vermont, studied law in his native town and was admitted to the bar. Later he engaged in banking. He was a member of the state legislature for two terms, and in 1860 he was sent to Congress, where he served continuously until 1877. He was nominated for the vice-presidency by the Republican party in 1876 and was elected with President Hayes. He returned to Malone at the expiration of his term in 1881. Mr. Wheeler rendered invaluable service to his country during reconstruction days by his conciliatory attitude as chairman of the committee on Southern affairs.

Wheel′ing, W. Va., the county-seat of Ohio co., 63 mi. s. w. of Pittsburg, Pa., on the Ohio River and on the Pennsylvania, the Baltimore & Ohio, the Wheeling & Lake Erie and several electric railroads. One ward of the city is built on Zane's Island in the river, the island being connected with the main part of the city by a large steel bridge and a suspension bridge more than 1000 feet long. The city has a large public library, and other features of interest are the site of old Fort Henry, the Krugar Monument, the customhouse, the postoffice, the city hall and the courthouse. The principal educational institutions are Linsley Institute, Mount de Chantal Academy, Saint Joseph's Academy, Wheeling Female Academy and the Wheeling Business College. There are about forty-five churches, two public hospitals, several private hospitals and a home for the aged.

The city is the largest in the state, has excellent transportation facilities and conducts a large trade. Extensive coal fields are found in the vicinity, and there are large iron and steel works, glass factories, potteries, tobacco works, lumber mills and various other factories. The place was settled by Ebenezer Zane in 1770 and was the first on the Ohio River. It was incorporated as a town in 1806 and was chartered as a city in 1836. Fort Henry was built here in 1774. The people of Virginia who were opposed to secession met here in 1861 at the Wheeling Convention and established "the restored government of Virginia." The Constitutional Convention of West Virginia also met in Wheeling, and the city was the state capital from 1863 to 1870 and from 1875 to 1885. It has had a steady growth. Population in 1910, 41,641.

Whig, in English history, the name which formerly was applied to the political party that advocates changes in the constitution in the direction of democracy. The term is of Scottish origin, but was early brought to England, where it was used as the name of the political party opposed to the *Tories,* or government party. The term *Liberals* is now generally applied to the representatives of the party formerly known as Whigs.

The Whig party in the United States opposed the Democratic party from about 1835 to 1856, when the Northern wing of the Whigs was merged in the new Republican party. See Political Parties in the United States.

Whip′ple, Henry Benjamin (1822–1901), a Protestant Episcopal bishop of Minnesota, born at Adams, N. Y. He became rector of the Church of the Holy Comforter, in Chicago, in 1857, and was consecrated the first bishop of Minnesota in 1859. Bishop Whipple became

HENRY BENJAMIN WHIPPLE

famous as the friend and apostle of the indians; he was influential in settling the Sioux outbreak in 1862, and many times he pleaded the cause of the red man before the government officials at Washington.

Whip′-poor-will, an American bird, so named because of its night call, which resembles the

WHIP-POOR-WILL

words *whip-poor-will*, repeated rapidly at intervals many times over. The prevailing color of the bird is a brownish-gray, with sharp black streaks on the head and back. The wings are barred with reddish-brown. The whip-poor-will is a night bird, capturing insects on the wing, which it is enabled to do with ease on account of the wide gape of its bill and the long hairs which line it. During the day the birds retire into the woods, where they sit lengthwise on a limb, as their short legs are of little value and their toes are not clasping.

Whirlpool, *whurl'pool*, a current of water, moving in a circular direction, and usually having a funnel-like shape. Small whirlpools occur in rivers and are caused either by the forcing of the current into a circular core in the channel or by an opening in the bank of the stream which draws the water down to a lower level. Sometimes the position of rocks and the direction of currents in the sea cause large and dangerous whirlpools. The most noted of these is the Maelstrom, off the coast of Norway, and the Charybdis, near Sicily. The most celebrated river whirlpool is that of the Niagara River, below the falls.

Whirl'wind, a small local wind, with a circular direction, usually noticeable for a column of dust and other light objects which it raises from the ground. Whirlwinds are caused by the meeting of currents of air which are moving in different directions. The chief source is usually a small area, which is more highly heated than the land around it. The air over this becomes heated and rises, and the currents, rushing in from all sides to fill this area of low pressure, cause a whirling motion. Whirlwinds never occur when the wind is blowing and are seldom seen on rough or uneven ground. Very large whirlwinds are known as tornadoes and cyclones. See CYCLONE; TORNADO.

Whis'ky, the name applied to an ardent spirit, distilled generally from barley, but sometimes from corn, wheat, rye, sugar or molasses. There are two chief varieties of whisky, namely, malt whisky and grain whisky. The former variety is of finer quality and is made chiefly from malted barley or bere, and sometimes, though rarely, from rye. The latter variety is made from various substances, as sugar, molasses, potatoes, but principally from unmalted grain, as indian corn, barley and oats, dried and ground. The grain most largely used is indian corn. Grain whisky requires the same process of fermentation and distillation as malt whisky, but it is cheaper, from its greater yield, and because it saves the expensive process of malting. Though coarser, it is stronger, but if kept long enough, it is equally good. See DISTILLATION.

Whisky In'surrec'tion, the name given to a revolt against the Federal government in western Pennsylvania in 1794. It was the result of the excise law passed by Congress in 1791, imposing a tax on whisky. This tax was a peculiarly heavy burden to the people of western Pennsylvania, most of whom were dependent for support largely upon the manufacture of whisky. They successfully resisted the attempts of the government to collect the tax and haughtily rejected the offer of amnesty in return for a promise of submission. Finally, in October, 1794, Washington sent 15,000 militia to the scene of the disturbance, and the insurrectionists promptly subsided. Two of the leaders were found guilty of treason, but they were pardoned by President Washington.

Whisky Ring, a term given in American history to a combination of distillers and Federal revenue collectors, who conspired to defraud the government of the excise tax on whisky. This "ring" began operations in Saint Louis, where the revenue officers, having knowledge of technical violations of the law, blackmailed the distillers, under threats of prosecution. The decline in the revenue receipts was immediately noticeable, but all efforts at finding the conspirators failed, on account of the presence of their friends in the treasury department at Washington. It was only after the most thorough investigation by Benjamin H. Bristow, the secretary of the treasury, that evidence sufficient to convict was found. The disclosures implicated the chief clerk of the treasury department and O. E. Babcock, President Grant's private secretary, but neither was convicted. About two hundred forty distillers and revenue officers pleaded guilty or were convicted in court, but most of the leading ones were pardoned. The total frauds amounted to fully $1,650,000.

Whist, a well-known game at cards, first clearly described by Edmond Hoyle, in his *Short Treatise on the Game of Whist* (1743). The game is played with the full pack of fifty-two cards, by four persons, two being partners against the other two, each player receiving thirteen cards, dealt out one by one in rotation. The last card dealt is turned face up and is called the trump card; it gives a special power to the suit to which it belongs. The cards rank ace (highest), king, queen, knave, and the others rank according to their number of spots. Play is commenced by the person on the left hand of the dealer, who lays down a card face up on the table; the other players follow in succession, with cards of the same suit, if they have them. When all have played, the player who has laid the highest card takes the four cards laid down, which constitute a trick. The winner of the trick then leads, as the first of a new trick, the winner of which becomes the leader, and so on. When a player cannot play a card of the same suit, he may play one of the trump suit and take the trick, or he may lay one of a different suit, which gives him no chance of winning the trick. When the hand is played out, the score is taken as follows: The partners who conjointly gain the majority of tricks score 1 point for every trick taken above six. The ace, king, queen and knave of the trump suit are called honors, in some systems of play, and count 1 each for the side who holds them; if one side hold three honors, they count 2 by honors, as the opposite side can have but one honor; if one side hold all the honors, 4 by honors is counted; should the honors be equally divided, neither side counts. In *long whist*, ten of these points make a game. In *short whist*, the number has been reduced to five, and in this form it is common to count by tricks alone. A rubber consists of a series of three games and is won by the side that secures two of them. In *duplicate whist* the game is played with as many sets of cards as desired. Each hand, as it is played, is laid aside, and at the close of the series of games the hands are exchanged, so that each game is played a second time, partners playing the hands of their opponents. The side that makes the greater number of points in the series wins.

BRIDGE WHIST, or, more commonly, BRIDGE, is played in the same manner as whist except that the dealer or his partner declares what shall be trumps, and that the dealer's partner takes no further part in the playing of that particular hand. If the dealer feels that his own hand does not permit a satisfactory declaration of trumps, he may "bridge it" to his partner, whose duty it then is to make the trump. A hand may be played without trumps if the dealer or his partner prefer. The dealer's partner lays his hand face up on the table after his opponent has led his first card.

Scoring: If "no trumps" is the declaration, each trick over six (a "book") counts twelve points; if hearts, eight points; if diamonds, six points; if clubs, four points; if spades, two points. The side first scoring 30 points wins a game.

The "honor" score is more complicated than in whist. The honor cards are the ace, king, queen, knave or jack and ten of the trump suit. If the declaration is "no trumps," the four aces are counted honors. The honor score is kept separately from the game score, and is only added in at the end of the rubber to determine the winner of the rubber. *Chicane* occurs when a player holds no trumps; his side adds to its honor score twice the value of a trick. When one side takes all 13 tricks, it makes a *grand slam*, which adds 40 points to the honor score; if 12 tricks are taken, it is a *little slam*, and adds 20 points to the honor score.

In "no trumps" each honor counts ten, provided one side holds at least three aces, but four aces held in one hand count 100. The following table shows the value of the remaining various combinations of honors:

	Spades	Clubs	Diamonds	Hearts
Three honors, called "simple"	4	8	12	16
Four honors (in 2 hands)	8	16	24	32
Four honors (in 1 hand)	16	32	48	64
Five honors (in 2 hands)	18	36	54	72
Five honors (in 1 hand)	20	40	60	80

Doubling. A player may "double" the value of a trick. A "double" means that he believes he can take more tricks than the dealer and his partner. The dealer or his partner may "redouble," in which case each trick counts four times the original value. It is customary to limit the value of a trick to 100.

Royal Spades. This is a common variety of declaring trumps. If spades are trumps under the ordinary rules, a strong spade hand is practically worthless. The dealer only may declare "royal spades" trumps; in this case each trick counts ten.

Auction Bridge. This is a variety of bridge which has almost displaced ordinary bridge. The methods of play are exactly the same, except that each of the players bids in turn, for the privilege of declaring what shall be trump. The method of scoring is slightly different. The rules for the play of cards in all forms of bridge are so complex that considerable study is required to make one a proficient bridge player. The game requires a good memory; expert players can recall at any stage of the game just which cards have already been played.

Authoritative books on bridge have been written by Elwell, Foster and Dalton.

Whistler, *whis'lur,* JAMES ABBOTT MCNEILL (1834–1903), an American artist, born at Lowell, Mass., and educated at West Point. He studied art in England and France, and became associated with Du Maurier, who, in his *Trilby,* represented Whistler as one of the young artists. In 1902 Whistler moved to England, where he died the next year. His etchings are universally praised, and his paintings show talent and originality, but they are to many persons incomprehensible. He called his paintings "nocturnes" and "symphonies," loving, especially, pearly gray and soft pink tones, the results of which were subtle and dreamy effects. Among the best are *The White Girl*, now owned in America; *Old Battersea Bridge, Sea and Rain, Portrait of Carlyle, Little Wild Rose* and a portrait of Whistler's mother.

White, ANDREW DICKSON (1832–), an American educator, author and diplomat, born in Homer, N. Y. He was educated at Yale, the College of France and the University of Berlin. For a time he was professor of history and literature in the University of Michigan, and on the establishing of Cornell University he was chosen its president. He retained this position for eighteen years, and when he resigned he bequeathed the institution his historical library of 30,000 volumes. In recognition of this and other bequests, the departments of history and economics at Cornell were reorganized as the White School of History and Political Science. While president of Cornell, Doctor White served on several important government appointments. He obtained leave of absence and was United States minister to Germany from 1879 to 1881. After he severed his connection with the university, he served the government in several important diplomatic posts, being minister to Russia, one of the commissioners to investigate the Venezuela boundary and for five years ambassador to Germany. He was also president of the United States delegation to the Hague Peace Conference. He is the author of numerous works on political and diplomatic subjects and of a large number of magazine articles. Among his most important works are *The Warfare of Science against Theology, Studies in General History, The New Germany, The European Schools of History, Chapters from My Diplomatic Life* and *Seven Great Statesmen*.

White, EDWARD DOUGLASS (1845–), an American jurist, born at Lafourche, La. He was educated at Mount Saint Mary's in Maryland, at the Jesuit college in New Orleans and at Georgetown (D. C.) College. He served during the Civil War in the Confederate army, was admitted to the bar in December, 1868, and was appointed associate justice of the state supreme court ten years later. In 1891 he was chosen to the United States Senate as a Democrat. In 1894 he was appointed an associate justice of the

Supreme Court of the United States, and in 1911 he became chief justice.

White, RICHARD GRANT (1821–1885), an American scholar and critic. He was educated for the law, but his literary tendencies drew him from a legal career, and his writings on Shakespeare soon made him recognized as one of the most prominent of Shakespearean scholars. Among his works are *Words and Their Uses, Everyday English, England Without and Within, Studies in Shakespeare* and the *Riverside Edition of Shakespeare*.

White, STEWART EDWARD (1873–), an American novelist, born in Grand Rapids, Mich., and educated at the University of Michigan. He spent his boyhood among the rivermen of Michigan and early acquired a liking for the forest, which he has so vividly described in his books. He has written many short stories, as well as several novels. Among his books are *The Blazed Trail, Conjuror's House, The Mountains, The Silent Places* and *The Rules of the Game*.

White, WILLIAM ALLEN (1868–), an American editor and writer, born in Emporia, Kans., and educated at the University of Kansas. He entered upon newspaper work when twenty-two years old, becoming owner and editor of the Emporia *Gazette* in 1894. An editorial of his, entitled *What's the Matter with Kansas?* was widely copied and first brought him into prominence. He has published *The Real Issue, and Other Stories* and *Stratagems and Spoils*, both collections of intense stories of political life.

White Ant. See TERMITES.

Whitebait, *white'bayt*, a name given to the young fish of the herring tribe, of whatever species they may be. These very small fish are caught by the thousands, cooked entire and considered a great delicacy, especially in England.

White Caps, the name given to bodies of men in various parts of the United States, who take into their hands the punishment of offenses, either real or imaginary, against the community. They have adopted all methods, from warning and intimidation to actual violence. The chief reason for the rise of such organizations is the slowness with which the law is often administered and the injustice arising therefrom. The name is derived from the disguise which these men commonly assume.

Whitefield, *whit'feeld*, GEORGE (1714-1770), founder of the Calvinistic Methodists, born at Gloucester. At the age of eighteen he entered, as servitor, Pembroke College, Oxford, where he became acquainted with the Wesleys, and he joined the "Holy Club," which became known as Methodists. In 1738 he came to America and settled in Georgia, where his ministrations gave great satisfaction to the colonists. In the following year he returned to England to procure subscriptions for building an orphan house in the settlement. The clergy opposed him and would not allow him to preach in the parish pulpits. Whitefield then began preaching in the open air and met with great success by his earnest manner and eloquence. In 1739, having collected £1000 for his orphanage, he again went to America and made a tour through several of the provinces, preaching with great effect to immense crowds. He made seven visits to America and tours through England, Scotland and Wales. In Lanarkshire one of the greatest revivals of modern times was the result of his efforts. He died at Newburyport, Mass.

Whitefish, a very important food fish of the salmon family. Many species are to be found in northern waters of both hemispheres. They are greenish-blue above and white below. The common whitefish is found in the Great Lakes and is the most important fresh-water fish in the United States. The yield of this fish for a single year has been more than 30,000,000 pounds, valued at $1,500,000.

White House, called also the EXECUTIVE MANSION, the residence of the president of the United States, at Washington. It is on Pennsylvania Avenue, near the treasury and the State, War and Navy building, and it is surrounded by a fine park. The first house was occupied by President Adams in 1800. In 1814 the British army burned it, and the present building was completed in 1829. Extensive modifications have recently been made, and the building has been finished, practically according to the plans of the architect, James Hoban, who designed it in 1792. It fronts upon the Potomac, though the entrance on Pennsylvania Avenue is the one in general use. The mansion is in the colonial style, with long wings and an Ionic portico. It has large reception rooms, a dining room, a conservatory, offices and apartments for the president and his family and for guests. The East Room, the Blue Room and the Green Room are elegantly furnished, contain some things of historical interest and are generally open to the public. While not to be compared with the great royal palaces of Europe, yet it is a fine, commodious building, suitable for the president of a great nation.

White Lead, a compound of lead and carbon dioxide, used in the manufacture of white paint and as the basis of many colored paints. White lead is made of coils of sheet lead, placed in earthen pots containing acetic acid, and buried in tan bark that has been used or in horse manure. In about two months the metal is changed to white lead, which is in the form of a white powder. In the manufacture of white paint, this powder is ground with oil. White lead is used as the body of most paints that are not mineral paints. It also makes a durable white paint, but turns dark when exposed to gases containing sulphur. In general, lead paints are much more durable than mineral, for either outside or inside surfaces. See PAINT.

White Mountains, a group of mountains belonging to the Appalachian system, and situated in the northern part of New Hampshire, where they form parts of Grafton, Coös and Carroll counties. The mountains rest upon a plateau about 45 miles long, 30 miles wide and 1600 feet above sea level. Upon this elevation some twenty peaks rise to varying heights. Some of these are separated from one another by narrow valleys, called notches. The mountains are clustered in two groups, of which the eastern is generally known as the White Mountains, and the western, as the Franconia Mountains. These groups are separated by a tableland, varying in width from 10 to 20 miles. The principal peaks in the White Mountains are in the Presidential range, so named from the names of the peaks. Of these, Mount Washington, 6286 feet, is the highest and is also the fourth highest in the Appalachian system. The other important peaks are Adams, Jefferson, Clay, Monroe and Madison, all of which exceed 5000 feet, while Franklin, Pleasant, Clinton and Webster have an altitude of 4000 feet or more. In the Franconia group the most prominent peaks are Lafayette, 5269 feet, and Moosilaukee, Liberty and Profile, all exceeding 4000 feet. Intermingled with these prominent peaks in each group are numerous other lower mountains.

The White Mountains are traversed by the famous Crawford Notch, a narrow defile, lined with walls 2000 feet high, through which the Saco River wends its way toward the sea. The other objects of special interest in this group of mountains are Tuckerman's Ravine, a deep gorge on the south side of Mount Washington, which is always partially filled with snow, and the summit of Mount Washington, which is reached both by carriage road and by railway. This railway was completed in 1869 and was the first structure of its kind ever built. It consists of three rails, the middle rail being constructed in the form of a ladder, with iron rounds, about four inches apart. A cog wheel on the locomotive meshes into these rounds and thus enables the engine to push the car up the mountain. On the summit is a hotel and a station of the United States weather bureau.

The principal object of interest in the Franconia Mountains is the Profile, or Old Man of the Mountains. This is a representation of the human face, formed by the projection of three rocks from the face of a nearly perpendicular cliff on the east of Cannon Mountain. One rock forms the forehead; the second, the nose and mouth, and the third, the chin. The Profile is about 1200 feet above the road from which it is seen, and it is 90 feet in length. It was an object of worship to the Indians for centuries before it was known to white men, and it is supposed to have given Hawthorne the inspiration which enabled him to write his beautiful allegory, *The Great Stone Face*. Near by is Echo Lake, a beautiful sheet of water, so enclosed by hills that an ordinary tone of the voice is repeated five times.

The summits of the White Mountains are bare and are composed of a variety of rock known as mica schist. The reflection of the sunlight upon this rock, when seen at a distance, gives the mountains the appearance of being covered with snow; hence the name, White Mountains or White Hills.

White Plains, N. Y., the county-seat of Westchester co., 22 mi. n. e. of the center of New York City, on the Harlem division of the New York Central railroad. The village has many fine residences, a public library, a county law library and the Bloomingdale Asylum for the Insane. Here the Battle of White Plains was fought. Population in 1910, 15,949.

White Plains, BATTLE OF, an important battle in the Revolutionary War, fought October 28, 1776, at White Plains, near New York City, after the American evacuation of Long Island. The battle was a defeat for the Americans.

White River, a river of Arkansas, which rises in the northwestern part of the state, where it is formed by several small streams, and flows northeastward into Missouri, returning into Arkansas and, after a general southeast and southerly course, entering the Mississippi 14 miles above the mouth of the Arkansas. Its length is about 800 miles, and it is navigable for river steamers for about 350 miles.

White River, a river of Indiana, a tributary of the Wabash. It is formed, at the border of

Pike co., by the junction of two streams, and it is about 50 miles in length. Its length, including the West Fork, is 350 miles.

White Sea, a large gulf of the Arctic Ocean, penetrating into northern Russia to the distance of between 300 and 400 miles. It has an area of about 47,000 square miles, with a coast-line of 1000 miles. It is navigable only from the middle of May to the end of September, being frozen over the rest of the year. About thirty rivers, among which the principal are the Northern Dwina, the Onega and the Mezene, empty themselves into the sea. Two canals, uniting the Dwina with the Volga and the Dnieper, connect the White Sea with the Caspian and Black seas.

Whiting, IND., a city of Lake co., is situated on the Lake Shore & Michigan Southern and other railroads, 17 mi. s. e. of Chicago. It was established by the Standard Oil Company. It has an oil refinery, paint works, lumber mills and other manufacturing establishments. Population in 1910, 6587.

Whit'man, MASS., a town in Plymouth co., 20 mi. s. by e. of Boston, on the New York, New Haven & Hartford Railroad. It has manufactories of boots, shoes, tacks, nails, boxes and other articles. There are seven churches, two banks and a public library. It was a part of Abington until its incorporation as South Abington in 1875. The present name was adopted in 1886. Population in 1910, 7292.

Whitman, MARCUS (1802–1847), an American physician and missionary, born at Rushville, N. Y. In 1835 he was sent by the American Board on an exploring trip to Oregon, and he became one of the leaders in founding Christian missions in Oregon. Whitman attained notoriety by a remarkable journey which he made from Oregon to Washington, D. C., in the dead of winter. It was supposed that this journey was taken to induce the government to hold Oregon against British claims, but more recent investigations have proved that the journey was for missionary purposes.

Whitman, WALT (1819–1892), an American poet, born at West Hills, Long Island, N. Y. He had little education and early began to learn the carpenter's trade. Later he worked as printer, as a school teacher and as general writer for the press. In these early years, as later, he was very fond of the society of workingmen, and spent much time studying their methods of life. During the war he gave splendid service in the hospitals of Virginia and Washington and permanently injured his health. From the close of the war to 1874 he was a clerk in the interior and treasury departments, but a stroke of paralysis compelled him to resign.

In 1855 the first edition of his *Leaves of Grass* had been issued, and much of his later life was given up to the enlargement of this originally small volume. Whitman's avowed purpose is to be the prophet of the democratic spirit of independence and of the common brotherhood of man. In his desire to free himself from all poetic trammels, his poetry often becomes almost ridiculous, and as it lacks both rhyme and meter it has never been popularly accepted as poetry. At times it does attain, however, to great heights, and Whitman is fast becoming recognized as one of the most representative poets of the United States.

Whit'ney, ADELINE DUTTON TRAIN (1824–1906), a writer of stories and poems for young people, born in Boston, Mass. In 1843 she married Seth D. Whitney of Milton, Mass. Her works, which comprise more than twenty volumes, are wholesome, pleasant reading for young people. It is believed that one of Mrs. Whitney's earlier novels, in which the heroine went to live among the poor and accomplished much good among them, had a great deal to do with the beginning of social settlement work in America. Some of her stories are *We Girls, Faith Gartney's Girlhood* and *Real Folks*.

Whitney, ELI (1765–1825), an American inventor, born at Westborough, Mass., and educated at Yale College. After graduation he went to Georgia as a teacher; later, he took up the study of law. Meantime, he became interested in the problem of cleaning cotton. The cotton culture at this period, especially that of the best kind, the "green seed," was limited by the slow and difficult work of separating the cotton from the seed by hand. Whitney set to work to remedy this under great disadvantages, for he had to make his own tools; but the reports of his success prompted some lawless people to break into his workshop and steal his machine and to get others made before he could secure a patent. He, however, formed a partnership with one Miller in 1793 and went to Connecticut to manufacture cotton gins; but the lawsuits in defense of his rights carried off all his profits, besides $50,000 voted him by the State of South Carolina. Finally, in 1798, he got a government contract for the manufacture of firearms. He made a fortune by this manufacture, carried out with ingenious machinery, while he made little

or no profit from the cotton gin, one of the most important of the whole series of inventions con-

ELI WHITNEY

nected with cotton manufacture. See COTTON GIN.

Whitney, WILLIAM COLLINS (1841–1904), an American politician and capitalist, born at Conway, Mass., and educated at Yale and Harvard. He settled in New York City, was admitted to the bar and took an active part in Democratic politics, being conspicuous in the opposition to the "Tweed Ring." Elected corporation counsel in New York City in 1875, he completely reorganized the office and saved vast sums during his administration. In 1885 he was appointed secretary of the navy by President Cleveland and was instrumental in beginning and furthering the construction of a larger navy. Upon retiring from the cabinet, he engaged in large financial affairs and managed the successful Democratic campaign in 1892.

Whitney, WILLIAM DWIGHT (1827–1895), a distinguished American philologist, born at Northampton, Mass., and educated at Williams College and Yale College, where he gave special attention to the study of Sanskrit. He continued his study in Germany, and on returning to America he was appointed professor of Sanskrit at Yale in 1854, a position he held the remainder of his life. Among his works may be mentioned *Language and the Study of Language, Oriental* *and Linguistic Studies, Life and Growth of Language, Sanskrit Grammar,* a very important work, and a *German Grammar.* He was editor of the *Century Dictionary* of the English language.

Whit′tier, JOHN GREENLEAF (1807–1892),· one of the foremost American poets. He was born near the town of Haverhill, Mass., Dec. 17, 1807. His parents were Quakers, who were always anxious to advance the interests of their children. The old farm house was not far from the Merrimac River and near it was the little brook whose "liquid lip" was companionship to them. In *The Barefoot Boy* Whittier tells of some of the advantages he had as a child:

> "I was rich in flowers and trees,
> Humming-birds and honey-bees;
> For my sport the squirrel played,
> Plied the snouted mole his spade;
> For my taste the blackberry cone
> Purpled over hedge and stone;
> Laughed the brook for my delight
> Through the day and through the night."

The young Whittier worked on his father's farm and learned the shoemaker's trade. He had little early education, except a few terms in the district school, and the wider training he received from his father and mother. Of books he had few and those not the best adapted to a child. The Bible, however, was thoroughly studied and its literary treasures fully appreciated. A volume of Burns fell into his hand and gave him the poetic inspiration. At the age of eighteen Whittier began writing for the press. One of his poems which appeared in the Newburyport *Free Press* attracted the attention of William Lloyd Garrison, its editor. Garrison visited the young poet at his home and induced him to give his pen and his life to the cause of freedom. This was the beginning of a life-long friendship. Garrison urged Whittier to obtain a better education, and assisted him in securing it. Although Whittier had had comparatively little schooling, he had read widely and was well fitted to become, as he did, the chief poet of the abolition movement. In 1835 and 1836 he was a member of the legislature of Massachusetts, but ill health compelled him to resign and to give up also the editorship of a paper which he was managing. In 1836 he moved to Amesbury, and some years later he went to Philadelphia, where he edited the *Pennsylvania Freeman,* an anti-slavery paper, the office of which was burned by a mob after he had been at work on it but four days. This did not compel Whittier, however, to give up the work, which he continued for two years. After his

return to Amesbury, his poems on freedom continued to appear, and in 1843 a volume of ballads was published. Among his notable poems of these years, which appeared in *The National Era,* the *New England Magazine* and the *Atlantic Monthly,* were *Songs of Labor, Maud Muller* and *Barbara Frietchie. Snowbound,* publish d in 1865, brought great increase to Whittier's popularity and also an improvement in his worldly circumstances. He had no family, however, and most of his money was spent in charity. He died while on a visit to Hampton Falls, N. H.

Whittier's poems on slavery were too thoroughly inspired by the occasion for which they were written, too much given over to argument on this subject, to be permanently great poetry, but their energy and sincerity made them most effective aids toward the ends to which they were directed. Among his other poems, *The Barefoot Boy, Telling the Bees, Snowbound* and *Among the Hills* are most notable. They have a homely truth to life, a fineness of sentiment, a freshness and a quiet power which will make them live.

Whooping Cough, *hoop′ing kof,* a contagious disease that frequently becomes epidemic and usually affects children only, though adults may have it. It begins with the symptoms of a severe cold, which after a week or ten days develops into a peculiar cough, that ends with a whoop, caused by a forcible indrawing of the breath. These coughing paroxysms occur at rather short intervals, but in the intervals the person feels reasonably well, and after three or four weeks the attacks occur less frequently, and within two months they disappear entirely. The cause of the disease is not thoroughly understood, and it is not usually attended with fatality except where other complications, such as pneumonia and bronchitis, set in. In severe epidemics, however, the mortality has been great.

Whortleberry, *hwurt′l′ber′ry.* See HUCKLEBERRY.

Wichita, KAN., the county-seat of Sedgwick co., 157 mi. s. w. of Topeka, on the Arkansas River and on the Atchison, Topeka & Santa Fé, the Chicago, Rock Island & Pacific, the Frisco, the Missouri Pacific and other railroads. It is located on rolling prairie land, contains broad, well-shaded streets and has excellent waterworks and sewage systems. It has many attractive residences and good public buildings, including a commodious courthouse, a city hall and a Federal building. The city has Fairmount College, Friends' University, All Hallow's Academy, Lewis Academy, two commercial colleges, a pub-

JOHN GREENLEAF WHITTIER

lic library, a high school and fourteen ward school buildings. There are more than thirty churches, two hospitals, eight banks and several children's homes. The city is in a fertile agricultural region, producing wheat, corn, hogs and cattle. It has a large wholesale and jobbing trade and contains extensive packing houses, stockyards, flour mills, foundries, machine shops, wood-working plants, stove works, grain elevators, implement factories, a creamery and other establishments. Wichita was settled by indian traders in 1869 and was chartered as a city in 1872. Population in 1910, 52,450.

Wichita Falls, TEX, the county-seat of Wichita co., is on the Wichita River and on the Fort Worth & Denver City and other railroads. It has important grain and lumber interests and manufactories. Population in 1910, 8200.

Wic'lif, JOHN. See WYCLIFFE, JOHN.

Wic'opy or **Moosewood.** See LEATHERWOOD.

Widgeon, *wij'un,* a genus of birds related to the ducks. There are but few species, though there are representatives in both Europe and

WIDGEONS

America. The American widgeon, which is most abundant in the south, is often called the *bald pate,* from the white on the top of its head.

Wieland, *ve'lahnt,* CHRISTOPH MARTIN (1733-1813), a German romance writer and poet. He was educated at the University of Tübingen and was appointed professor of philosophy in 1769 at Erfurt. Three years afterward he went to Weimar, as teacher to the sons of Duchess Anna Amalie. Here, or in the immediate neighborhood, he resided till his death, being a member of the circle to which Goethe, Schiller and Herder belonged. The early period of his literary life was devoted to pietistic, or at least serious, poetry, such as the *Experiences of a Christian;* in the second period he produced the romances *Agathon* and *Don Sylvio de Rosalva,* the poem *Musarion* and a prose translation of Shakespeare, the first in German; in the third and ripest period were written the romantic epic of *Oberon, The Republic of Fools, Peregrinus Proteus* and *Aris-*

tippus. He also published translations of Horace, Lucian and the *Letters* of Cicero.

Wiesbaden, *vees'bah den,* a city of Prussia, situated in the valley of the Salzbach, about 2 mi. from the Rhine and 5 mi. n. n. w. of Mainz. The town has a beautiful location and is one of the most celebrated watering places in Germany. It contains a number of churches of historic interest, and the educational institutions include a museum, a picture gallery, a public library of 145,000 volumes, agricultural and industrial schools and an institution for the blind. The industries are unimportant. Population in 1910, 109,002.

Wig'gin, KATE DOUGLAS. See RIGGS, KATE DOUGLAS WIGGIN.

Wight, *wite,* ISLE OF, an island in the English Channel, directly off Southampton and separated from the mainland by the Solent and the Spithead. Its length from east to west is 23½ mi., and its greatest breadth is 13 mi. The area is 147 sq. mi. Off the western end of the island are the chalk cliffs, small islands known as The Needles. The island is noted for its beautiful scenery and mild temperate climate, and it is visited by large numbers of tourists. Population in 1911, 90,000.

Wigwam, *wig'wom,* a North American indian cabin or hut, generally of a conical shape, formed of bark or mats, laid over saplings planted in the ground and converging at the top, where there is an opening for the escape of the smoke.

Wilberforce, *wil'bur fors,* SAMUEL (1805-1873), an English clergyman, born at Clapham, son of the anti-slavery philanthropist, who wrote many letters to his son, six hundred of which are extant. Wilberforce entered Oriel College, graduating in 1826 with first-class honors in mathematics and second-class honors in classics. He was successively curate of Checkendon church; rector of Brightstone, Isle of Wight; archdeacon of Surrey; rector of Alverstoke and canon of Winchester; chaplain to the prince, a position gained through an anti-slavery speech; dean of Westminster; bishop of Oxford, where he remained twenty-four years. Wilberforce, because of his cleverness, self-reliance, fascinating manner, persuasive power, facility and expediency, was sometimes called "Soapy Sam." He acknowledged the title as just, saying, "I am always in hot water, and always come out of it with clean hands." Among his writings are *Letters and Journals of Henry Martyn, Agathos, Rocky Island* and *History of American Church;* with his brother he wrote the life of his **father.**

Wilberforce, WILLIAM (1759–1833), an English statesman and philanthropist, born at Hull, in Yorkshire. After completing his education at Saint John's College, Cambridge, he was in 1780 elected member of Parliament. In 1789 he brought forward in Parliament resolutions condemning the slave trade. In 1792 he succeeded in getting a bill for the gradual abolition of slavery through the House of Commons, but it was rejected by the House of Lords. Year after year he pressed this measure, but it was always defeated until 1807, when it was passed, during the short administration of Fox. He then devoted his energies to bringing about the total abolition of slavery, and three days before his death he was informed that the House of Commons had passed a bill which abolished slavery in the British colonies.

Wil'cox, ELLA WHEELER (1855–   ), an American poet and essayist. She was born in Wisconsin, was educated at the University of Wisconsin and was married in 1884 to Robert M. Wilcox. From her girlhood she contributed freely to newspapers and magazines, and some of her writings have acquired considerable popularity. Her volumes of verse include *Poems of Pleasure, Poems of Passion, Poems of Power* and *Maurine;* while among her prose works are *An Ambitious Man; Men, Women and Emotions* and *A Woman of the World.*

Wild Barley or **Squirrel-Tail Grass,** a grass of the United States, common in the neighborhood of the upper Great Lakes, in the south and in the west. The flowers are greenish in color, and each bears a bristle, about two inches long. This weed is especially injurious to sheep, since the clinging seeds imbed themselves in the

WILD CAT

hide. In this way, also, the seeds are distributed. Another common injury arises when the leaves and flowers stick in the throat of grazing animals, causing choking. Cultivation, sowing of clean seed and prevention of the plants' seeding are the usual methods of eradication. See WEEDS.

Wild Cat or **Catamount,** a name given in the United States to the lynx, in India to the jungle cat, and in other regions to various animals of the cat family. In Europe the wild cat proper, from which may have sprung our domestic cat, is a large animal, with longer body and limbs, but a shorter tail than the domestic cat.

Wil'derness, BATTLE OF THE, the first important battle of Grant's famous Virginia campaign in 1864, between a force of 120,000 men under General Meade, supported by Warren, Sedgwick and Hancock, and with General Grant in supreme command, and the Army of Northern Virginia, under Lee, comprising about 62,000 men under Ewell, Hill and Longstreet. The Federals were encamped on the northern bank of the Rapidan River, near Culpeper Court House, while the Confederates were south of the river, on the edge of the Wilderness, where Lee had completely baffled Hooker's army after the Battle of Chancellorsville. Grant began crossing the river on May 3, without a contest, Lee being confident that he could defeat the Federals when they had once become entangled in the Wilderness. In the morning of May 5 General Warren, who was in the van of the Federal force, was met by General Ewell, and an all-day's battle resulted, with little advantage to either contestant. Grant at first believed that he was confronting only a part of Lee's army, but soon ordered Hancock to come up from Chancellorsville. Upon his arrival, he confronted General Hill, and another severe battle ensued, which paused at nightfall, only to recommence at dawn. It ended in a drawn battle; Grant had failed to make progress toward Richmond; Lee had failed to crush the opposing army. The losses of the Union forces were about 18,000; of the Confederates, from 10,000 to 12,000. See CIVIL WAR IN AMERICA.

Wilhelmina, *vil' hel me' na,* (1880–   ), queen of the Netherlands, born at The Hague. On the death of her father, William III, she succeeded to the throne (1890), her mother serving as regent until 1898. She was married to Duke Henry Frederick of Mecklenburg-Schwerin, in February, 1901. (See illustration on next page.)

Wilkes, *wilks,* CHARLES (1798–1877), an American naval officer and explorer, born in New York City. He was educated in the common schools, entered the United States navy in 1818 and became a lieutenant in 1826. In 1838, in charge of an expedition authorized by Congress to explore the Southern Ocean, he visited most of the important southern countries, including New South Wales, New Zealand, Fiji and other Australasian regions. The scientific data which he collected were of the greatest importance and value. He was made commander in 1843 and became a captain in 1855. Upon the outbreak of the Civil War he was given command of the frigate *San Jacinto.* On November 8, 1861, he overtook the English mail steamer *Trent* and arrested Mason and Slidell,

QUEEN WILHELMINA

the Confederate commissioners (see TRENT AFFAIR.) He was retired in 1864, and became rear admiral in 1866.

Wilkes, JOHN (1727–1797), an English politician and agitator. He was returned to Parliament as member for Aylesbury in 1757, and several years later he attained considerable notoriety by the publication of a paper entitled the *North Briton,* in Number 45 of which he commented severely on the king's speech to Parliament. The home secretary in consequence issued a general warrant ordering the arrest of the printers, publishers and authors of the article, and Wilkes, with others, was taken and committed to the Tower, but was released by Chief Justice Pratt, who declared the prosecution illegal. On the next meeting of Parliament, however, a special law was passed to sanction his prosecution, and in 1764 he was expelled from the House of Commons. As he had by this time withdrawn to France and did not appear to receive

sentence, he was outlawed. He returned to England at the election of 1768, however, was sent to Parliament as representative of Middlesex, but was expelled from the House and committed to prison. Three times after this he was reëlected within a few months by the same constituency, but the House of Commons persisted in keeping him out, giving rise to a formidable agitation in favor of "Wilkes and liberty." He was released from prison in 1770, having been elected alderman of London, and he was next appointed sheriff of Middlesex, lord mayor of London and again (1774) member of Parliament for Middlesex. This time he was allowed to take his seat. His struggle with Parliament is important, because it established the right of constituencies to return to Parliament whom they will.

Wilkesbarre, *wilks′bar ray,* PA., the countyseat of Luzerne co., 145 mi. n. by w. of Philadelphia and 175 mi. w. by n. of New York City, on the north branch of the Susquehanna River. Nine railroads enter the city, four being trunk lines. It is an important electric railroad center. The Laurel line, a third-rail road to Scranton, is said to be the finest electric road in the United States. The city is beautifully located, well laid out and paved and has many fine public and private buildings.

The educational institutions include the Harry Hillman Academy for boys, the Wilkesbarre Institute for girls and several Catholic schools; the well-known Wyoming Seminary is at Kingston, just across the river. The public schools are excellent, including a first-class high school. The Boys' Industrial Association is a unique institution, of an educational and social nature. The Osterhaut Free Library has more than 30,-000 volumes, and the Wyoming Historical and Geological Society has a reference library and a notable collection of indian relics and geological specimens and fossils. There are homes for children and aged women and two well-equipped hospitals, while a United Charities Association cares for the deserving poor in a systematic manner. Many of the churches of the city are notable structures. Other important buildings are the new $1,000,000 courthouse, the city hall, the armory, the postoffice, Grand Army hall, the Y. M. C. A. building, two theaters, several hotels and a number of business blocks.

Anthracite coal was first discovered in Luzerne county and was first used for domestic fuel in Wilkesbarre in 1808. Mining is now the principal industry, but the cheap fuel has made the city a very important manufacturing center. There are large axle, wire rope and lace curtain factories, besides manufactories of locomotives, cutlery, silk, automobiles, flour, malt liquors and other goods. In 1900 $10,000,000 of capital was invested in manufactures, and their products were valued at $10,000,000.

The first settlement was made in 1769 by men from Connecticut. It was named in honor of John Wilkes and Issac Barré, members of the British Parliament who advocated the cause of the colonists before and during the Revolution. In 1784, during the controversy between Pennsylvania and Connecticut over the sovereignty of the Wyoming Valley, the settlement was burned. The Wyoming Monument marks the site of the conflict of the Americans with the loyalists and indians, July 3, 1778. Wilkesbarre was made the county seat in 1786 and was incorporated as a borough in 1806. After the Civil War it grew rapidly and was chartered as a city in 1871. Population in 1900, 51,721; in 1910, 67,105. There are many contiguous and near-by boroughs that are estimated to make a total business and social community of nearly 200,000 people.

Wil'kie, DAVID, Sir (1785–1841), one of the most famous painters of the British school. He received his early art training at the Trustee's Academy, Edinburgh, and entered the schools of the Royal Academy, London, in 1805. He first exhibited there, in the next year, *The Village Politicians,* which at once established his reputation. His first works were genre paintings, in which, by close study of the Dutch masters, he learned how to produce proper color effects. In his later work, after his visits to Italy and Spain, he showed the influence of Titian and Velasquez and changed his theme to historical and portrait subjects. In 1811 he was made a member of the Royal Academy. Among his pictures are the *Blind Fiddler, Rent Day, The Village Festival, Penny Wedding, Cotter's Saturday Night, Duncan Gray, Blind Man's Buff, John Knox Preaching before the Lords of the Congregation* and *Wellington Writing a Dispatch.*

Wil'kins, MARY ELEANOR. See FREEMAN, MARY E. WILKINS.

Wil'kinsburg, PA., a borough in Allegheny co., 5 mi. e. of Pittsburg, on the Pennsylvania railroad. It is a residence suburb of Pittsburg. The place was previously called McNairville and then Rippeyville, but was given its present name in honor of William Wilkins, who was secretary of war under President Tyler. Population in 1910, 18,924.

Wil'kinson, JAMES (1757–1825), an American soldier, born in Maryland. He served in the Continental army during the Revolution, being promoted from private to brevet brigadier general, but was implicated in the Conway Cabal. In 1784 he moved to Kentucky, where he had an influential part in politics and was probably connected with Spanish intrigues to gain possession of Louisiana. Nevertheless he was appointed to a commission in the army in 1791 and did valuable service in the indian wars, becoming commander in chief in 1796. Upon the acquisition of Louisiana, Jefferson appointed Wilkinson governor of Upper Louisiana, and in the following years he was an accomplice of Burr's in his scheme to found an empire in the southwest. He avoided punishment by turning state's evidence, but his conduct was later investigated by several Congressional committees, and though acquitted, he never regained the confidence of the people (See BURR, AARON). Early in the War of 1812 he displayed inability as a general, as well as moral laxity; at its close he was tried, but was acquitted and honorably discharged. He spent his last years in Mexico, in promotion of adventurous schemes.

Will, in law, the legal declaration of a person's wishes as to the distribution of property after his death. Technically, a *will* can dispose only of real property, the document relating to the disposal of personal property being called a *testament.* In most states of the Union, no will or testament is valid unless it is in writing and signed at the end by the maker, or *testator,* or by some person in his presence and by his direction. This signature must be made and the document acknowledged by the testator, in the presence of two or more witnesses, not beneficiaries by the will, present at the same time, and such witnesses must attest and sign the will in the presence of the testator. The will usually names one or more persons, known as executors, to direct the execution of its provisions. If none such is named, or if no will is made, the court appoints an administrator to the estate. In the latter case the property goes to lineal descendants (For the rules for the disposal of the estate in the latter case, see DESCENT). Any alteration in the will must be duly signed by the testator and the witnesses. An addition to the will is known as a *codicil.* A will may be revoked by canceling, obliteration, tearing or burning, by a new will expressly revoking the former, or by one containing provisions inconsistent with it. The destruction of a later will revives a former will. At the death of the testator the will is recorded in the probate court. See PROBATE.

Will, in psychology, the mental power on which all purposive action depends; the power of choice. Feeling is the foundation of will, and the two are so closely related that there is no well-defined line of separation between them. See FEELING.

DEVELOPMENT OF WILL. In the infant, will exists only as a possibility. The first actions of a young child are impulsive and instinctive, and are impelled without thought or purpose; yet it is from such actions that will is developed (See INSTINCT). Every idea contains a motor element. This is readily seen in the motor effect of such ideas as that of a worm or of a mountain. The idea "worm," when entertained, causes one to cast the eye downward; the idea "mountain" causes one to look upward. One seldom thinks of this element in ideas, but self-examination soon reveals it. It is from this motor element that impulse arises. The child, from watching others, soon learns to imitate their actions. At first these imitations are impulsive, but when the impulse has been repeated a number of times it leads to a wish on the part of the child to perform the act. This wish is a *desire*, which has been developed from the impulse and is now directed to a definite end. The accomplishment of this desire calls for voluntary action, hence the will is brought into play.

But the mind often entertains two or more desires at the same time, and these may be so related as to oppose each other. This is readily illustrated in the case of a child who is at play with a toy in which he is interested. On the table in the room is an apple which he desires. He cannot obtain this without climbing upon a chair. While he desires the apple, he also desires to continue playing with the toy. He may have been told that he must not climb upon chairs, and, possibly, that he must not touch the apple. He desires to obey his mother's command, but he also desires the apple. This he cannot obtain, without disobeying his mother and leaving his toy. His desires are in conflict, and this leads to another step in the development of will—deliberation. He weighs the desires—shall he continue playing with his toy, or shall he get the apple? During the deliberation he hesitates. He finally decides to get the apple, and with the acceptance of this desire, the others are dropped. In making this decision comes the

fourth step in an act of will—choice. The desire which was chosen now becomes a motive, which leads to the final step—action. Without this, however strong his desire may be, the child would never obtain the apple.

These successive steps—impulse, desire, deliberation, choice and action—are all included in an act of will, but in the mature mind, the most common voluntary acts have become habitual to such an extent that the deliberative phase is scarcely noticed. In choosing between desires, one holds in mind past experiences and the desires under consideration, and one also imagines the conditions that will arise from the choice of each one of the desires in conflict. This process frequently makes choice a difficult step, and one occasionally calls upon others to decide for him. Choosing a certain course of action is based upon a desire of a peculiarly personal nature, and no one except the person involved is likely to make a satisfactory choice. For this reason each one should make his own choices. The ability to choose varies widely with different people. Some make right choices quickly, while others after long deliberation make unwise choices. Still others choose without deliberation and are liable to spend considerable time in attempting to extricate themselves from undesirable conditions.

The will is impelled to action through ideas received through the senses and through ideas developed by the mental processes; that is, there are two sources leading to will activity—the world without and the self. The ideas derived from the second source are those which usually lead to sudden action for the accomplishment of the different purposes in life, and indirectly these often lead to action upon ideas obtained through the senses. If a man has determined to become a carpenter, he will guide his actions to this end, and his relation to such material as wood, iron and other substances used in building will be different from the relations of one who has determined to become an artist.

INHIBITION. One of the highest functions of the will is to prevent action. This function is known as *inhibition*. Its action depends upon conflicting perceptions. If one stoops to pick an apple from the ground, and, as he is about to grasp it, discovers a hornet upon it, his action is instantly arrested, because the injury which he would probably receive from the hornet conflicts with the satisfaction he would obtain from possessing the apple. Action is also arrested by the memory of past experiences. One who has been burned by coming in contact with a flame or a hot stove will not voluntarily come in contact with such an object again. Finally, the power of inhibition is called forth by the conflict of ideas, which necessitates deliberation and choice. This principle has already been illustrated, in describing the conflict of desires. Inhibition is characteristic of a well-trained will. It develops late, and in children and uncivilized people it seldom reaches full development. Such persons act upon impulse, while the man with a disciplined mind delays action until after careful deliberation. One in vigorous health and full of energy is more liable to act without deliberation than one whose physical conditions are the opposite. One who is hopeful is more liable to act than one who is doubtful. Because of their lack of experience, children and young people often attempt to perform the impossible, and it is only by repeated failures that they learn the value of deliberation.

RELATION OF THE WILL TO OTHER MENTAL POWERS. The will is the highest power of the mind, and when properly trained, it holds all the other powers under its sway. It first asserts itself by securing control of the muscles, then by getting control of mental processes. In other words, it is developed towards muscular movements and mental action. All voluntary acts are conscious and are preceded by ideas, one of which is the cause of the act. The act is more or less clearly defined in the mind of the one who executes it, and the means by which it is to be performed are usually decided upon before beginning. Without the action of the will, the other mental powers would fail of development beyond the most elementary stages which characterize infants.

CULTURE OF THE WILL. The will is one of the most important of the mental powers, and upon its right development depends one's success or failure in life. Because of this, those having care of young children should give the training of the will careful attention. The following principles are helpful in securing desired results in will training:

(1) The power to act lies within the nervous system. During childhood and youth this system is plastic and is easily guided in any line of action.

(2) The greatest function of the will is in the formation of habits. Habits formed during childhood are the seeds of character. The parent and teacher cannot give too careful attention to habits formed in the home and the school. See HABIT.

(3) The child is a bundle of impulses and is filled to overflowing with nervous energy. He must act, and it is the duty of poth parent and teacher to furnish definite ends toward which his activity may he directed.

(4) Ability to make right choices is important in the formation of character. This ability is acquired and strengthened by practice, and children should be led to make right choices as early in life as possible and to continue the practice until it becomes habitual.

(5) Environment has much to do with the choices made by both children and adults. No one likes to go against the sentiment of his community; hence the proper home atmosphere and school atmosphere are important factors in training the will.

(6) Attention is a fundamental act of will. The child's power of attention should be cultivated and strengthened day by day. See ATTENTION.

(7) All right choices should be acted upon. When a choice is made, it should be carried out. Failure to act has a disastrous effect upon the character, and those who let their desires evaporate without action become the do-nothings of society.

(8) Will is strengthened by effort; therefore, within the limits of their ability, children should frequently be assigned difficult tasks, both at home and at school. Without this training they will never form the habit of persistent effort, which is necessary to success.

(9) Stubbornness is not evidence of a cultured will or of a strong will. One with a cultured will decides after due deliberation and in accordance with the best judgment a person can exercise. The stubborn person decides in accordance with his feelings and without deliberation.

See PSYCHOLOGY. Consult Compayre's *Lectures on Pedagogy*, Halleck's *Psychology and Psychic Culture* and Baldwin's *Mental Development*.

Willamette, *wil lah'met*, a river of Oregon, formed by the junction of the McKenzie and the Middle Fork. It flows northward and empties into the Columbia River. Its total course is about 250 miles, and while it is directly navigable only to Portland, canals have been built around the obstructing falls to Eugene.

Wil'lard, EMMA HART (1787–1870), an American educator, born at Portland, Conn. She became principal of a girls' academy at Middlebury, Vt., and later married Dr. John

FRANCES E. WILLARD

WILLIAM II, EMPEROR OF GERMANY

vision of the king. It was at Versailles, during
the siege of Paris, in 1871, that William was pro
claimed German emperor.

William II (1859-   ), king of Prussia and
emperor of Germany, the eldest son of Frederick
III and Victoria, princess royal of England. He
was thoroughly trained in military affairs and
studied law and political science at the University of Bonn. Later he served in the army
of Emperor William I, where he reached the
rank of major general. In 1881 he married
Augusta Victoria of Schleswig-Holstein-Augus-
tenburg, and in 1888, on the death of his father,
he succeeded to the throne. Two years after his
accession his determined opposition to the policy
of Bismarck led to the retirement of the chancellor. Emperor William has taken considerable interest in social questions and was at his
accession inclined to conciliate the socialists.

William I, PRINCE OF ORANGE, COUNT OF
NASSAU, called THE SILENT (1533-1584), founder
of the Dutch Republic. He was brought up in
the Catholic religion, although both of his parents
were Protestants. In 1544 he inherited from his
cousin the principality of Orange, along with
large estates in the Netherlands. Under Charles
V he served as commander of the army of the
Netherlands and governor of Holland, Zealand
and Utrecht, and Philip II employed him in various offices, without, however, really trusting him.
One of William's achievements was the negotiation of the Treaty of Câteau-Cambrésis with
France. On his return from Spain to the Netherlands, he took part in the movement for the removal of Granvella from the Netherlands, and
as stadtholder of Holland, Utrecht and Zealand,
he refused to allow the Inquisition to be introduced there.

When the duke of Alva entered the Netherlands, William withdrew to Germany, and he
refused to appear when summoned before the
council by Alva. His first open resistance to
Spain was an invasion of Brabant in 1568. This
was unsuccessful, and a second attempt in 1572
met with no better fate. William had been before this time chosen stadtholder by Holland,
Utrecht, Zealand, Gelderland and Overyssel,
and in 1576 he succeeded in bringing about the
"pacification of Ghent," whereby the southern
provinces united with the northern, to expel the
Spaniards and secure religious liberty. The
southern provinces shortly broke away from their
allegiance to William, but in 1579, by the Union
of Utrecht, the seven northern provinces, Holland, Zealand, Gelderland, Friesland, Utrecht,

Groningen and Overyssel, were formed into a
league, which two years later formally deposed
Philip and declared itself a republic, with William
as hereditary stadtholder. A price had been set
by the king of Spain on William's head, and several unsuccessful attempts were made to assassinate him; but in 1584 he was shot at Delft.

William and Mary College, next to Harvard, the oldest institution of higher learning in
the United States, having been established in
1693, at Williamsburg, Virginia. It suffered
heavily, during both the Revolution and the Civil
War, and for a period between 1881 and 1888 it
was so crippled financially that it had to close its
doors. But in 1888 a state appropriation enabled it to reopen, and an indemnity of $64,000,
granted it by Congress in 1893, for its losses in
the Civil War, put it again on a firm foundation.
The college offers two courses, a collegiate and a
normal course. It has about 200 students.

Williams, JOHN SHARP (1854-   ), an
American politician, born at Memphis, Tenn.
His father was killed at the Battle of Shiloh,
while in the service of the Confederates, and the
family moved to Yazoo County, Miss., where
young Williams received a fair education at private schools. He later studied at the Kentucky
Military Institute at Frankfort, at the University of the South in Sewanee, Tenn., at the University of Virginia and at the University of Heidelberg, in Germany. He also studied law and
was admitted to practice in 1877 in Tennessee.
In the following year, he removed to Yazoo City,
Miss., where he practiced law and also became a
planter. Taking an active part in Democratic
politics, he was elected to Congress in 1893 and
served continuously for eighteen years, becoming
the leader of the Democratic party in the House.
In 1911 he became United States senator from
Mississippi.

Williams, ROGER (1604 or 1605-1683), a
Puritan divine, founder of the colony of Rhode
Island, born of Welsh or Cornish parents. He
was sent as a scholar to the Charter House,
afterward studied either at Oxford or Cambridge
and is said to have taken orders in the English
Church; but because of his Puritan beliefs he
emigrated in 1631 to New England. Here he
became pastor of a church at Salem, but his extreme views regarding the jurisdiction of the
civil magistrate caused him to be banished from
the colony of Massachusetts, and he went with a
few companions to Rhode Island and founded a
settlement, which he called Providence. Here
he formed the first Baptist church in America.

He was twice in England, in connection with a charter for the colony, and there he made the acquaintance of Milton and other prominent Puritans. He published *A Key into the Language of the Indians of America, The Bloudy Tenent of Persecution for the Cause of Conscience, The Bloudy Tenent yet more Bloudy* and *George Foxe Digged out of His Burrowes.*

Wil'liamsburg, VA., the county-seat of James City co., 48 mi. e. by s. of Richmond, on the Chesapeake and Ohio railroad. William and Mary College is located here. The town has interesting historical associations. It was settled in 1632, became the capital of Virginia in 1698 and in 1722 received its charter, being the first city in the state to do so. During the Civil War the first important engagement of the Peninsular campaign took place at Williamsburg. This was a battle on May 5, 1862, between the Confederates under Longstreet and the Federals under Sumner. The battle was indecisive, and the Confederates continued their retreat toward Richmond.

Williams College, an institution of higher learning, developed from a free school by Colonel Ephraim Williams, at Williamstown, Mass., and chartered in 1793. The college has a faculty of over 50 members, an average attendance of about 600 and a valuable library, containing over 67,000 bound volumes and 17,000 pamphlets. The prosperity and high rank of the institution are largely due to the work and influence of Mark Hopkins, who was its president from 1836 to 1872. See HOPKINS, MARK.

Wil'liamsport, PA., the county-seat of Lycoming co., 95 mi. n. of Harrisburg, on the West Branch of the Susquehanna River, and on the Pennsylvania, the Philadelphia & Reading, the New York Central and other railroads. The city is on the Alleghany plateau, in an agricultural, mining and lumbering section. It contains numerous lumber mills, clothing factories, steel works, furniture factories and manufactories of rubber goods, machinery, wire rope, shoes, silks, sewing machines and other articles. There is also an extensive trade in lumber products and coal. The city has four parks, and some of the prominent buildings are the city hall, the opera house, the Federal building, a hospital, a home for the friendless and the Masonic Temple. There are more than fifty churches, good public schools, two large parish schools, two commercial colleges, seven banks and the Dickinson Seminary. The place was settled in 1779, was incorporated as a borough in 1806, and was chartered as a city in 1866. Population in 1910, 31,860.

Wil'liamstown, MASS., a town in Berkshire co., 5 mi. w. of North Adams, on the Hoosac and Green rivers and on the Boston & Maine railroad. Williams College is located here, and the town has a public library and Mission Park. It is chiefly a residence place, but also has a bleaching establishment and a cotton mill. Market gardening is an important industry. The place was settled in 1753 and was called West Hoosic until its incorporation in 1765, when it was named in honor of Ephraim Williams. Population in 1910, including several villages, 3708.

Wil'liman'tic, CONN., a city in Windham co., 16 mi. n. w. of Norwich, at the confluence of the Willimantic and the Natchaug rivers and on the New York, New Haven & Hartford and the Central Vermont railroads. A state normal school is located here, and the city has the public and the Dunham Hall libraries. There is good water power, and the manufacture of cotton thread is the principal industry. Cotton goods, silk goods, machinery and other articles are also produced. It was settled about 1822, was incorporated as a borough in 1833 and was chartered as a city in 1893. Population in 1910, 11,230.

Wil'lis, NATHANIEL PARKER (1806–1867), an American author, born at Portland, Maine, educated at Andover and at Yale. During his college days he attracted some attention by his verse, and after his graduation he was employed by S. G. Goodrich to edit *The Legendary* and *The Token.* The *American Monthly Magazine,* from its establishment to its consolidation with the New York *Mirror,* was under his control. Willis traveled for some years as correspondent of the *Mirror* in France, Italy, Greece, Turkey, Asia Minor and England, and of the famous men whom he met he wrote in *Pencilings by the Way.* Many of these articles caused offense by their personal tone. After his return to America, he conducted several journals, none of which was very successful. His works include *Loiterings of Travel, Famous Persons and Places, Outdoors at Idlewild* and *The Convalescent.*

Will'-o'-the-Wisp. See IGNIS FATUUS.

Wil'low, the common name of a family of shrubs and trees, of which many species are found throughout the greater part of the northern hemisphere. They usually grow in moist soil and are common along the banks of streams. The leaves are slender, and the flowers are usually borne in catkins, appearing before or with the leaves. Those catkins which are clothed with long, glossy hairs are popularly known as pussy-willows. On account of the flexible nature of the shoots of many species and the toughness of their wood and fibers, they have always been used as materials for weaving baskets, hoops and crates. Baseball bats, hoe handles and many similar articles are made from the wood of the white willow, and wooden shoes, pegs and other small objects are constructed from other species. The *weeping willow*, which is a native of China, is a fine ornamental tree that is often planted in cemeteries, as symbolical of sorrow.

Wil'mington, DEL., the county-seat of New Castle co., 27 mi. s. w. of Philadelphia, Pa., and 70 mi. n. e. of Baltimore, Md., on the Delaware River, at the junction of the Christiana and the Brandywine rivers, and on the Baltimore & Ohio, the Philadelphia & Reading and the Philadelphia, Baltimore & Washington railroads. Four steam lines make connection here for passengers and freight. The city is picturesquely situated on hilly ground and extends about four miles back from the Delaware River. The city contains the Friends' School, a military academy, the Hebbs School, Goldey College, the Ursuline Academy and two business colleges. The libraries include the public, the law and that of the historical society. There are more than 80 churches of various denominations, among which the Methodist Episcopal predominates. Holy Trinity Church, built by the Swedes in 1698, is said to be the oldest one in continuous occupation in the United States. Some of the charitable institutions are the industrial school for girls; the Ferris Industrial School for boys; the Delaware and the Homeopathic hospitals; a home for friendless children; Saint Peter's Orphanage; Saint Joseph's Home; two homes for aged men and women, and the state hospital for the insane and the county almshouse, which are two miles south of the city. Other prominent buildings are the courthouse, the postoffice, the customhouse, the Auditorium and the Equitable Guarantee and Trust Company's building.

The falls of the Brandywine afford considerable water power for manufacturing. The city contains numerous iron and steel works, foundries, machine shops, rolling mills, shipbuilding yards, railroad shops, brick yards, breweries and manufactures of brick-making machinery, furniture and other goods. About a score of leather plants have made it the center of the morocco industry in the United States, and about four miles from the city is one of the largest powder mills in the world.

The first settlement here was made by Swedes, on Christiana Creek, where they built a fort in 1638 and established the village of Christianaham. It was taken by the Dutch in 1655 and was renamed Fort Altena. They were in turn succeeded by the English in 1664, and soon the place was brought under the control of William Penn's proprietorship. A town was laid out about 1731 by Thomas Willing and was called Willingstown, but it was later changed to Wilmington, in honor of the English peer of that name. It was incorporated as a borough in 1739 and was chartered as a city in 1832. The Battle of the Brandywine was fought at Chadd's Ford, just 12 miles from the city. Population in 1910, 87,411.

Wilmington, N. C., the county-seat of New Hanover co., 148 mi. s. by e. of Raleigh, on the Cape Fear River, 30 mi. from its mouth, and on the Seaboard Air Line and several divisions of the Atlantic Coast Line railroad. It is primarily a commercial city, is a port of entry and conducts a large foreign and coastwise trade. The principal exports are cotton, rice, turpentine, vegetables, lumber and naval supplies. There are extensive manufactures of lumber and cotton products, fertilizers, ice, foundry goods and various other articles. Some of the prominent structures are the Federal building, the courthouse and the Masonic Temple. Other important institutions are the Cape Fear Academy, the county hospital, the United States Marine Hospital, a house of correction, a home for aged women and a public library. The place was settled in 1830 and was called New Liverpool and later Newtown. It was incorporated in 1739 as the town of Wilmington, and it was the capital of the province after 1743. Before the Revolution it was one of the first to resist British authority, and during the Civil War the port was one of the most important in the Southern states. Fort Fisher, protecting the harbor, was captured by Federal forces on January 15, 1865, and the town itself was entered by General Terry on February 22. Wilmington was chartered as a city in 1866. Population in 1910, 25,748. Consult Lyman P. Powell's *Historic Towns of the Southern States*.

Wil'mot, DAVID (1814–1868), an American politician and jurist, born at Bethany, Pa. He was admitted to the bar in 1834 and began his practice at Towanda. He became a prominent Democrat and served in the House of Representatives from 1845 to 1851. There he opposed the extension of slavery into the territory acquired from Mexico and was the sponsor for the famous Wilmot Proviso (See WILMOT PROVISO). He later joined the Republican party, was an unsuccessful candidate for governor of Pennsylvania in 1857, served in the Senate for two years (1861–1863), and thereafter until his death was judge of the United States court of claims.

Wilmot Provi'so, a name commonly given to an amendment presented in Congress in 1846 to a bill providing for the purchase of territory from Mexico. It was offered by David Wilmot, a Democrat from Pennsylvania, and provided that "neither slavery nor involuntary servitude shall ever exist in any part of such territory, except for crime whereof the party shall first be duly convicted." The amendment was adopted in the House, but did not come to a vote in the Senate, and in the next Congress the bill was finally passed without the amendment. The debate in Congress over the question resulted in a breach between Northern and Southern Democrats, which led to the adoption by that party of the doctrine of popular sovereignty. This in turn resulted in the withdrawal of many Northerners, who joined the Free-Soilers and later became prominent in the Republican party.

Wil'son, ALEXANDER (1766–1813), an American ornithologist, born at Paisley in Scotland. He emigrated to America in 1794, assisted in editing the American edition of Rees's *Cyclopaedia* and determined to write and illustrate a work on American birds. The result of his labor was the American *Ornithology,* a work which was completed by Ord, with a continuation by Lucien Bonaparte.

Wilson, HENRY (1812–1875), an American statesman, born in Farmington, N. H. His original name was Jeremiah Jones Colbraith, but he abandoned the name upon reaching manhood. He was first employed on a farm, later learned the shoemaking trade, earned money to pay for an academic education and finally engaged in the manufacture of shoes at Natick, Mass. In 1840, as the "Natick cobbler," he addressed political meetings, winning wide fame, and in that year he was elected to the Massachusetts legislature. In 1848 he began to edit the Boston *Recorder,* as a Free-Soil organ. In 1855 he was chosen United States senator, as a Free-Soiler or Know-Nothing, to succeed Edward Everett. His speeches against slavery are among the most important of the period. He served for a short time on the staff of General McClellan

in the Civil War. In 1872 he was elected vice-president, on the ticket with President Grant, but died before completing his term.

Wilson, JAMES (1742–1798), an American jurist, signer of the Declaration of Independence. He was born in Scotland, was educated at Saint Andrews, Glasgow and Edinburgh and came to America in 1763, removing to Philadelphia three years later. There he taught Latin at the University of Pennsylvania and at the same time studied law under John Dickinson, being admitted to the bar in 1767. He was elected twice to the Continental Congress, and in 1785 he was a member of the Congress of the Confederation. He became advocate-general of the French government in America in 1779 and also participated in important private trials in all parts of the country. In the constitutional convention of 1787 he was a conspicuous member of the strong government party, and later he did much to secure the ratification of the Constitution by Pennsylvania. He has been called one of the foremost political thinkers of his age. From 1789 until his death Wilson was associate justice of the United States Supreme Court.

Wilson, JAMES (1835–   ), an American politician and administrator, born in Ayrshire, Scotland. He emigrated to the United States in 1852, settling in Connecticut. Three years later he moved to Iowa, where he engaged in farming, was elected to the state legislature and became speaker of the assembly. In 1872 he was chosen to Congress, served for three non-consecutive terms and for a time was on the state railway commission. He was secretary of agriculture from 1897 to 1913, a longer term than any other cabinet member has ever served.

Wilson, JAMES HARRISON (1837–   ), an American soldier, born at Shawneetown, Ill. He graduated at West Point in 1860 and entered the engineering service of the army. He served in the Civil War, being brevetted major general in the regular army "for gallant and meritorious services." He was especially distinguished for exceptional achievements as officer of engineers, notably in the Vicksburg and Chattanooga campaigns. He fought at Antietam, Vicksburg, Chattanooga and the Wilderness, was with Sherman in his marches to Atlanta and to the sea and was present at the capture of Jefferson Davis. He was honorably discharged in December, 1870, and engaged in railroad and engineering enterprises, but at the outbreak of the Spanish-American War, in May, 1898, he was made major general of United States volunteers and served

PRESIDENT WOODROW WILSON

in the Cuban and Porto Rican campaigns. In 1900 he was sent to China with the American relief expedition and commanded the American forces at Peking. He was the special representative of the United States army at the coronation of King Edward VII and retired in 1901, with the rank of brigadier general in the regular army.

Wilson, JOHN (1785–1854), a Scottish writer, better known as Christopher North. He was born at Paisley, educated at Glasgow University and at Oxford and on leaving college settled on an estate on Lake Windermere, where he gave himself up to literary work. Wordsworth, Southey and Coleridge were among his acquaintances. His first independent publication was a poem called *The Isle of Palms*, and this was followed by *The City of the Plague*, a second book of poems. When *Blackwood's Magazine* was established, in 1817, Wilson became one of its contributors, and for many years he wrote some of the most notable articles in that periodical. In 1820 he was appointed to the chair of moral philosophy in Edinburgh University, a position which he held for thirty-one years. Most famous, perhaps, of the writings of Wilson are the *Noctes Ambrosianae*, which abound in graceful humor and sentiment. Among his other works are three novels, *The Lights and Shadows of Scottish Life, The Trials of Margaret Lyndsay* and *The Foresters*.

Wilson, JOHN (1804–1875), an English missionary and Oriental scholar, born at Lauder, Berwickshire. He was educated at the University of Edinburgh, went to Bombay in the service of the Scottish Missionary Society and later transferred his labors to the mission work of the Free Church of Scotland. He established numerous schools, became vice chancellor of the University of Bombay, contributed largely to the abolition of the practice of suttee, traveled all over India, establishing missionary centers, and was universally honored and beloved by the natives. His linguistic ability was remarkable, and his contributions to literature included *The Parsi Religion, India Three Thousand Years Ago, Memoirs on the Cave Temples of India, The Lands of the Bible Visited and Described* and *Indian Caste*.

Wilson, JOHN M. (1837–), an American soldier, born in the District of Columbia and educated at West Point. He entered the Union service in the Civil War as an engineer and attained the rank of brevet major in the regular army, for bravery at Gaines's Mill and Malvern Hill. At the close of the war, he was brevetted colonel in both the volunteer and regular service, for his conduct at Mobile. After the war he constructed important engineering works for the government, had charge of the completion of the Washington Monument and of other memorials and in August, 1889, became superintendent of the United States Military Academy. He retired in April, 1901, with the rank of brigadier general.

Wilson, WILLIAM LYNE (1843–1900), an American politician and educator, born in Jefferson County, Va. He graduated at Columbian College, Washington, studied at the University of Virginia and served in the Confederate army. Later he became professor of Latin at Columbian College and practiced law from 1871 to 1882, when he was chosen president of the University of West Virginia. In 1883 he entered Congress as a Democrat and served twelve years. As chairman of the ways and means committee, he led in the repeal of the Sherman silver purchase law and was the author of the famous Wilson Tariff Bill (See TARIFF). In 1895 he was made postmaster-general by President Cleveland, and at the close of his term he became president of Washington and Lee University.

Wilson, WOODROW (1856–), an American educator and statesman, twenty-eighth president of the United States, born at Staunton, Virginia, on December 28, 1856. After his graduation from Princeton in 1879, he studied law at the University of Virginia, and then practiced for two years in Atlanta, Ga. From 1883 to 1885 he took a post-graduate course at Johns Hopkins University, where he received the degree of Ph. D. For three years he was professor of history and political economy at Bryn Mawr College, and for the next two years he held a similar position at Wesleyan University. In 1890 he was appointed professor of jurisprudence and politics at Princeton, a position in which he acquired a reputation not only as a scholar and teacher but as an understanding friend of the students and their problems. In 1902, Mr. Wilson was unanimously elected president of Princeton University, being the first layman ever elected to that office. In 1910 he resigned the presidency of Princeton and received the Democratic nomination for governor of New Jersey. After an aggressive campaign Mr. Wilson was elected by a large plurality. As governor he made a brilliant record in securing the passage of progressive legislation on such subjects as direct primaries, public utilities, public health, and the reform of laboring conditions.

Mr. Wilson's prominence as a Democratic governor of a Republican state and his success in securing the passage of progressive legislation quickly made him a national figure in politics. By the end of 1911 he was acknowledged the strongest candidate for the Democratic nomination for President of the United States. He received the nomination at the Convention at Baltimore in June, and in November was elected president by the greatest electoral majority ever received by a presidential candidate. Of a total electoral vote of 531 votes he received 446, and his popular vote was over 6,000,000, a heavy plurality over each of his leading opponents, Roosevelt and Taft, but about a million short of a majority of all the votes cast.

Mr. Wilson is the author of a number of important books on history and government, besides many contributions to periodicals. Besides *Congressional Government*, his works include *The State: Elements of Historical and Practical Politics; An Old Master and Other Political Essays; Division and Reunion*, in the epochs of American History series. His most important work is a *History of the American People*, in five volumes, in many respects the best work of its kind.

Win'chell, ALEXANDER (1824–1891), an American geologist, born in Dutchess County, New York. He graduated from the Wesleyan University at Middletown, Conn., and taught the natural sciences in several schools before becoming, in 1853, professor of physics and civil engineering at the University of Michigan. From 1859 to 1862 and from 1869 to 1871 he was state geologist of Michigan. In 1873 he became chancellor of Syracuse University, but he held this position only one year, becoming professor of geology, zoölogy and botany in Vanderbilt University. The University of Michigan made him professor of zoölogy and paleontology in 1881, and this position he held until his death. He published, among other books, *The Doctrine of Evolution, Pre-Adamites, Sketches of Creation*, and *Sparks from a Geologist's Hammer*.

Win'chendon, MASS., a town in Worcester co., 35 mi. n. w. of Worcester, on Miller's River and on the Boston & Maine and the Boston & Albany railroads. It contains manufactures of wooden ware, cotton goods and machinery. The place was settled in 1752 and was incorpor-

ated as a town in 1764. Population in 1910, including several villages, 5678.

Win'chester, KY., the county-seat of Clark co., 18 mi. s. e. of Lexington, on the Chesapeake & Ohio, the Louisville & Nashville and other railroads. The Kentucky Wesleyan College is located here. The city is in the blue-grass region and contains flour and planing mills and other factories. It has a good system of waterworks, two electric light plants, three banks, two building and loan associations and about seventeen churches. Population in 1910, 7156.

Winchester, MASS., a town in Middlesex co., 8 mi. n. w. of Boston, on the Boston & Maine railroad. It is a residence suburb of Boston and contains manufactures of watch hands, leather and felt goods, flour and other articles. The town has two banks, a public library, a home for aged people and a state aviary. The large state park, known as Middlesex Fells, is near by. The place was settled in the early part of the seventeenth century and was known under various names until the adoption of the present one in 1850. Population in 1910, 9309.

Winchester, VA., the county-seat of Frederick co., 80 mi. w. by n. of Washington, on the Baltimore & Ohio and the Cumberland Valley railroads. The city is in an agricultural and stock-raising section and contains lumber, flour, paper and woolen mills, tanneries, glove works and other factories. It has the Valley Female College, the Shenandoah Valley Academy, Fairfax Hall, two public high schools and a public library. The National and Confederate cemeteries are also of interest. Fort Loudoun, built by Washington during the French and Indian War, may still be seen. The city was an important strategic point in the Civil War, and several engagements were fought in the vicinity. General Philip H. Sheridan made his famous ride from here to Cedar Creek. Population in 1910, 5864.

Wind, air in motion, with any degree of velocity. Winds are caused by the unequal heating of the atmosphere at different places on the earth's surface. The unequal heating produces inequality in pressure, and this gives rise to motion. The temperature is highest and the atmospheric pressure is lightest at the equator, and at the poles the temperature is lowest and the air is most dense. The heating of the air at the equator produces an upward current, which continues until the rising air reaches layers of atmosphere of the same density, when the vertical motion is changed to a horizontal one, and currents set in toward the poles. As the warm air over the equator rises, the cool air on either side moves in to take its place, so that there are in the equatorial regions two sets of currents, blowing in opposite directions—a surface current blowing towards the equator, and an upper current blowing towards the poles. When the upper current reaches the latitude of the tropics of Cancer and Capricorn, it becomes of the same density as the air near the surface and descends, forming a surface current. See CALMS, REGIONS OF.

Were it not for the rotation of the earth, these currents would blow directly north and south. As it is, each is deflected from its course. The wind blowing toward the equator is blowing into regions having a greater velocity of rotation than

ate latitudes and become nearer equal in temperature and pressure, they are subject to many local influences and become very irregular; hence, no theory of wind which accounts for the general circulation of the atmosphere is sufficient to explain the prevailing winds in many localities, and the accounting for these is one of the most difficult problems with which the meteorologist has to contend.

A wind is named from the direction from which it blows; an easterly wind blows from the east, a westerly blows from the west. The force of the wind depends upon its velocity, which is determined by the anemometer. See STORMS; WEATHER BUREAU. Consult Archibald's *Story of the Atmosphere* and Tarr's *Physical Geography*.

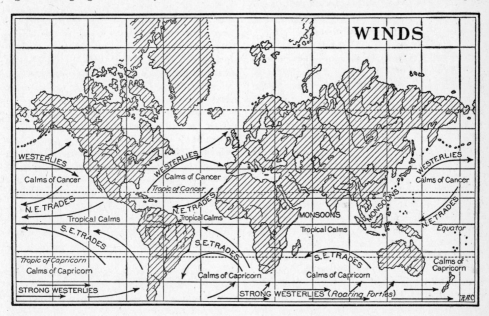

those from which it came. It is unable at once to acquire this velocity and, as it were, lags behind, producing a wind blowing toward the west, or what is known as an easterly wind; that is, a wind blowing in a direction contrary to that of the earth's rotation (See TRADE WINDS). Winds blowing toward the poles are constantly entering regions having a lower velocity of rotation, and their eastward motion is greater than that of the land; hence they become westerly winds. In the northern hemisphere they blow from the southwest, and in the southern hemisphere, from the northwest. See PREVAILING WESTERLIES.

In and near the tropics, these currents are quite regular, but as they approach the temper-

Winder, *wine′dur,* WILLIAM HENRY (1775–1824), an American soldier, born in Somerset County, Md., educated at the University of Pennsylvania and admitted to the bar. He served in the War of 1812 and was commissioned brigadier general in March, 1813. He was captured at Stony Creek and was not released until 1814. In the following fall he opposed the advance of the British against the city of Washington, but, having a totally inadequate force, was defeated at Bladensburg, allowing the British to enter the capital. He was afterwards court-martialed, but was acquitted.

Windermere, *win′dur meer,* the largest lake of England, situated in Westmoreland and Lancashire counties, in the northwestern part of the country. It is 10½ miles long and from ¾ to 1 mile in width. It has a group of islands in its center and is noted for the beauty of its surroundings.

Windhover, *wind'huv ur.* See KESTREL.

Wind'lass, a machine for raising weights, by winding a chain or rope around a cylinder. The windlass is a modification of the wheel and axle, and in its simplest form it contains a mounted roller, several inches in diameter, with square holes at each end, into which bars, called handspikes, can be inserted for turning it. As the roller is turned, it winds a rope or chain, which raises the weight. The windlass used for raising buckets of water from a well has a winch at one or both ends of the roller. The power can be greatly increased by fastening a cog wheel to one end of the roller, into which a smaller wheel fits, to which a winch is attached. See DERRICK.

Wind'mill, a mill which receives its motion from the impact of wind upon sails, and which is used for grinding corn, pumping water, and for other purposes requiring light power. In structure, the windmill is a conical or pyramidal tower, and from the position of the sails in relation to the wind shaft, it is described as either *vertical* or *horizontal.* In the former the wind is made to act upon sails or vanes, attached, by means of rectangular frames, to the axle, or *wind shaft,* of the mill. This axle is placed nearly horizontal, so that the sails by the pressure of the wind revolve in a nearly vertical plane, thus giving a rotary motion to the driving wheel, fixed to the wind shaft. The movement thus produced is transferred by means of bevel wheels to the main shaft, which is connected with the machinery of the mill. As the sails, to be effective, must always face the wind, this is accomplished in modern mills by a self-adjusting cap, moved by a fan, or flyer, attached to the projecting framework at the back of the cap. By means of a pinion on its axis, motion is given to the inclined shaft and to the wheel on the vertical spindle of the pinion; this latter pinion engages the cogs on the outside of the fixed rim of the cap, and by these means the sails are kept constantly to the wind, when the wind causes the fan to revolve.

The American windmill, which has come into use since the middle of the nineteenth century, has now completely replaced the old style Dutch mill, in both the United States and all the other countries of the world. It has a small wheel, in which wood or iron slats take the place of the canvas sails of the Dutch mill. These slats are so arranged that the wind strikes them slantingly, as it blows between them. This forces the slats along and causes the wheel to revolve. A vane, attached to the opposite side of the frame, causes the wheel to face the wind at all times. Most of these mills revolve at a high rate of speed in the ordinary windmill, and they are constructed so as to develop as high as four horsepower. Most mills in use for pumping water and running feed cutters and churns on farms have about one-fourth of one horse-power.

Win'dom, WILLIAM (1827-1891), an American statesman, born at Waterford, Ohio. He was educated at Mount Vernon Academy, studied law and was admitted to the bar in 1850. In 1855 he removed to Winona, Minn., and four years later he was elected to Congress as a Republican, serving in the lower house for ten years He was appointed United States senator in 1870. was elected in 1871 and again in 1877. He served in Garfield's cabinet as secretary of the treasury until the president's death, when he returned to the Senate. Resuming private practice in 1883, he was made secretary of the treasury by President Harrison in 1889 and filled the office until his death.

Win'dow, an opening in the wall of a building, to admit light and air into the interior. In dwelling houses in ancient times the windows were narrow slits, and it was not until about the end of the twelfth century that glass was generally used in private houses in England. In Egypt windows were in common use in domestic and military architecture, but rare in the religious edifices. In Greece they were in use from ancient times, most of them being simple rectangular openings. Amongst the Romans, windows were very common, both in their private dwellings and in their temples. There was a great variety of form and decoration, and glass and transparent stones were used. The window reached its highest development in the Gothic architecture, where it constitutes a distinguishing and characteristic feature. In this style, large pointed and circular windows were used, decorated with tracery and filled with beautiful stained glass, representing various designs, so as to rival wall paintings. This art of stained glass prevailed in France most extensively and also in England and Germany in the Middle Ages, but declined after the fifteenth century. It has been revived in the United States by the use of methods which enable the artist to excel even the finest effects of the Middle Ages. In modern houses, windows are generally closed with clear glass, set in a frame, or *sash*, usually of wood or metal. They are often decorative, stained glass being used, and are made in nearly all styles. See STAINED GLASS.

Wind'pipe. See TRACHEA.

Windsor, *win'zur*, ONTARIO, a city, situated on the Detroit River, directly opposite Detroit, Mich., with which it is connected by railroad ferries. It is on the Grand Trunk, the Canadian Pacific, the Michigan Central and other railroads. The industries include the manufacture of salt, chemicals, silverware, bicycles, baskets and malt liquors. Population in 1911, 17,829.

Windsor Castle, one of the most magnificent royal palaces in the world, situated at Windsor on the Thames, about twenty miles from London. Windsor was the residence of the Saxon kings before the Conquest. William the Conqueror first built a royal residence there, and succeeding rulers have added to, torn down and rebuilt, until the present structure was completed in the reign of George IV, at a cost of $4,500,000. The castle consists of buildings surrounding two great courts, between which is the round tower, or keep, the oldest part of the structure, built by Edward III. Saint George's chapel, an imposing part of the castle, is a fine example of Gothic flamboyant architecture. It has a vault, in which are buried many members of the royal family, among whom are Henry VI, Edward IV, Henry VIII, Jane Seymour, Charles I and George IV. Adjoining this is the Albert Chapel, one of the most beautiful memorial buildings in the world. Henry VII built this, as a mausoleum for himself. Under James II it was used as a Roman Catholic chapel, and after this it was neglected until George III rebuilt it as a royal tomb. It was Queen Victoria who finished it in the most sumptuous manner, as a memorial to her husband, Prince Albert. Besides the private rooms of the royal family, there are in the castle richly furnished state apartments, in which are many treasures of art.

Wind ward Islands, a term frequently applied to the most southerly islands of the Lesser Antilles (See ANTILLES), including Martinique, Saint Lucia, Saint Vincent, the Grenadines and Grenada. The islands are so called because they are exposed on their eastern sides to the trade winds. The name is also applied to a British colony including the same islands. See LEEWARD ISLANDS.

Wine, the term particularly applied to the fermented juice of the grape. However, in its broadest sense it may be applied to the fermented juice of any fruit. Wine is made by crushing the ripe grapes, then allowing the juice and pulp to ferment. When the grapes come to the winery, they are crushed by running them through a machine containing two corrugated cylinders, which crush the grapes, but do not crush the seeds. This forms the *must*, which is forced by pumps through hose to the vats, or tanks, in which fermentation takes place. These are made of oak in the old countries, but in California, of redwood, and have capacities varying from 25 to 100 or more barrels each. The fermentation must be watched with the greatest care, since upon it depends the quality of the wine. It is hastened by raising the temperature or by placing in the must a small quantity of fermented pulp from another vat. When the fermentation is completed, the juice is strained from the pulp and placed in large reservoirs, called *tuns*, where it remains until the wine is ripe, when it is drawn into casks or bottles and is ready for market.

Wines are known as *dry* when complete fermentation takes place and all the sugar is changed to alcohol. They are known as *sweet*, or *fruity*, when fermentation is arrested before it is complete and some of the sugar remains. A sparkling wine is one which effervesces when the bottles are uncorked. Champagne is a good illustration. In such wines fermentation has been arrested before all of the carbonic acid has escaped. In color, wines are known as *red* or *white*. The red color is obtained from the skins of the grapes, which have been allowed to remain in the vat during fermentation. White wines are made by removing the skins before fermentation begins. They are usually made from white grapes. The amount of alcohol in wine varies from 16 to 25 parts in 100. In light wines it may be from 7 to 12 parts in 100.

Wines are manufactured in almost endless variety, and many of them are named from the locality in which they are made, such as Port, Burgundy, Bordellais and Rhenish wines. The leading countries in the world in the manufacture of wine are France, Spain, Italy and the United States, in which the wine-producing region is confined to California. See CHAMPAGNE; PORT WINE; GRAPE.

Win'field, KAN., the county-seat of Cowley co., 40 mi. s. e. of Wichita, on the Walnut River and on the Atchison, Topeka & Santa Fé, the Frisco and the Missouri Pacific railroads. There are natural gas wells in the vicinity, and the city contains flour mills, grain elevators, ice works, machine shops and other establishments. It has a large trade with the surrounding agricultural and stock-raising region, and the quarrying of limestone is also an important industry. The Southwest Kansas College, the Saint John's Lutheran College and the state imbecile asylum are located here. The city also has a business college, public and school libraries, an opera house and eleven churches. A large Chautauqua assembly is held annually. Winfield was settled in 1870 and was incorporated the next year. Population in 1910, 6700.

Winged Lion, a winged lion in bronze, on one of the columns in the Piazzetta at Venice. The lion with wings is the emblem of Saint Mark, who is the patron saint of Venice, which city accordingly put the winged lion on her coat of arms. The bronze statue of the winged lion was taken by Napoleon in 1797, but was restored in 1815.

Winkelried, *vin'kel reet*, ARNOLD, a Swiss patriot, much celebrated in legend. According to the popular story, during the Battle of Sempach, when the Swiss were contending for liberty against their Austrian oppressors, Winkelried threw himself into the Austrian ranks, gathered as many spears as he could in his arms and pressed them into his breast. The breach thus made enabled the Swiss to make a successful attack. It has been asserted by some authorities that Winkelried is a mythical character, but it is by no means certain.

Win'neba'go, an important Siouan tribe, now numbering about 2000, who live in Wisconsin and northeastern Nebraska. When the Jesuits met the Winnebagos, they held a broad tract in central Wisconsin, near Green Bay and Lake Winnebago. They were a tractable people, but many of them died from the ravages of smallpox, and their numbers have grown very small.

Winnebago, a lake in eastern Wisconsin, about 28 miles in length and from 3 to 11 miles wide. It empties through the Fox River into Green Bay. It is navigable by steamers and is of importance commercially. The chief towns on its banks are Oshkosh and Fond du Lac.

Win'nipeg, CANADA, the capital of Manitoba, is situated at the junction of the Assiniboine and Red rivers, 1425 mi. w. of Montreal and 1481 mi. e. of Vancouver. Winnipeg is the most important city and chief railway center in Western Canada. It has 22 main and branch lines of railway radiating from it in every direction.

There are 156 factories, the annual value of whose output exceeds $25,000,000. Winnipeg is also an important wholesale and jobbing center, being the chief distributing point for Manitoba, Saskatchewan and Alberta. It has 60 banks, with 41 branches, 122 churches and missions, 32 public schools, 6 parachial schools, a number of colleges, including the University of Manitoba, a Presbyterian, an Anglican and a Roman Catholic college and a medical school. The city is well built, with wide, regular streets and many beautiful buildings, among which are the city hall, the parliament buildings, the courthouse, Carnegie Library, two large and modern railway stations and exposition buildings. Its water works, sewage and lighting systems are of the best. Population in 1911, 136.035.

Winnipeg, LAKE, a lake situated in the north central part of Manitoba and the southern part of Keewatin. The southern half is in the form of a narrow arm, which extends southward to within about 30 miles of the city of Winnipeg. Its entire length is 260 miles, and its greatest width, about 60 miles. The shores are low, and in general the lake is shallow, seldom exceeding 70 feet in depth. It receives the Winnipeg, the Red River of the North and the Assiniboine on the south, and the Saskatchewan on the west. Its outlet is by the Nelson River, which, after flowing through several small lakes, reaches Hudson Bay.

Win'o'na, MINN., the county-seat of Winona co., 103 mi. s. e. of Saint Paul, on the Mississippi River and on the Chicago, Burlington & Quincy, the Chicago & Northwestern, the Chicago Great Western and other railroads. The city has excellent transportation facilities and conducts a large trade in grain, lumber and live stock. It contains extensive sawmills, railroad shops, breweries, flour mills, wagon works and shoe and other factories. A state normal school is located here, and the city has a seminary for young women, a business college and a public library. There are many fine residences, and the streets are lined with large shade trees. The prominent public structures include the Federal building, the courthouse, the city hospital, the opera house and the Margaret Simpson Home. The place was settled in 1851, and the city was chartered in 1857. Population in 1910, 18,583.

Wins'low, JOHN ANCRUM (1811–1873), an American naval officer, born at Wilmington, N. C., a descendant of Governor Edward Winslow of Plymouth Colony. He entered the navy in 1827 and became commander in 1855. At the outbreak of the Civil War he served under Commodore Foote and later was made captain of the *Kearsarge*. Proceeding to Europe in search of Confederate privateers, he overtook the *Alabama*, under Semmes, at the port of Cherbourg, France. He accepted the challenge of the Confederate vessel to a combat, managed the *Kearsarge* with exceptional skill and compelled the surrender of the *Alabama*. He was promoted to the rank of commodore and received a vote of thanks from Congress. After the war, Winslow commanded the Gulf squadron and was raised to the rank of rear admiral in March, 1870.

Winsor, *win'zur,* JUSTIN (1831–1897), an American librarian and historian, born in Boston and educated at Harvard, at Paris and at Heidelberg. From 1868 to 1877 he was superintendent of the public library at Boston, and in the latter year he became librarian of Harvard, a position which he held until his death. He published a *Narrative and Critical History of America, The Reader's Handbook of the American Revolution* and *Christopher Columbus*.

Win'sted, CONN., one of the county-seats of Litchfield co., 28 mi. n. w. of Hartford, on the Mad and the Still rivers and on the Central New England and the New York, New Haven & Hartford railroads. The borough contains the Gilbert Home for poor children, the Litchfield County Hospital and the Memorial and Gilbert School libraries. There is good water power, and the manufactures include clocks, pins, hosiery, brass goods, tools, cutlery and other articles. The place was settled about 1756, and the borough was incorporated in 1858. Population in 1910, 7754.

Win'ston Sa'lem, N. C., twin cities and the county-seat of Forsyth co., 30 mi. w. of Greensboro, on the Norfolk & Western and two lines of the Southern railroad. They have separate municipal governments, but only one postoffice, and they practically form one city. They are in a tobacco-growing region and contain large tobacco factories, cotton and flour mills and other manufactories. Electric power is now transmitted from the Yadkin River. The educational institutions include the Salem Female Academy and the Slater Industrial Academy and Normal School. Salem was founded in 1766 by the Moravians and was governed for a time as a Church community. Population in 1910, 17,167.

Win'ter, the season of the year between autumn and spring, beginning with the winter

solstice, about December 22, and ending with the vernal equinox, about March 21. In the United States, winter is said to cover the months December, January and February.

Winter, WILLIAM (1836–   ), an American poet and dramatic critic, born at Gloucester, Mass. After graduating from the Harvard Law School, he was admitted to the bar, but the success of his articles, contributed to various papers, led him to take up journalistic work, and he became finally dramatic critic on the New York *Tribune*. In this capacity he served after 1865. He has written a number of books on dramatic subjects, including *Shadows of the Stage, The Life and Art of Joseph Jefferson* and *The Stage Life of Mary Anderson*; and he has also published *Gray Days and Gold* and *Wanderers*, a collection of verse.

Win'tergreen, a name of several plants, including a genus of perennial plants, with short stems, broad evergreen leaves and usually white or pink flowers. This is the common wintergreen which grows in the pine woods of the northern United States and Canada. It has pretty, white, bell-shaped flowers and bears a red berry. An oil is obtained from the leaves, which is used in flavoring candy and for medicinal purposes.

Win'throp, MASS., a town in Suffolk co., about 5 mi. n. e. of Boston, on Massachusetts Bay and on the Boston, Revere Beach & Lynn railroad. It is a residence suburb of Boston and a popular summer resort. It was originally a part of the city, and was separately incorporated in 1852. The town has the Frost Library. The West Shore Reservation, Ingall's Park, forts Heath and Banks and the old Dean Winthrop house are of interest. Population in 1910, including several villages, 10,132.

Winthrop, JOHN (1588–1649), first governor of Massachusetts Bay Colony, after the removal of the seat of government from England to America. He was a native of Suffolk County, England, and early became a man of influence in the community, but he joined the Congregational movement against the Church of England and finally decided to go to Massachusetts, to escape political and religious persecution. Winthrop was governor of the colony from 1630 until his death, with the exception of short intervals when the party of radical opposition to England was in power. He took a prominent part in the formation of the New England Confederation and became its first president. He was one of the most admirable characters in early American history.

Winthrop, ROBERT CHARLES (1809–1894), an American politician, born at Boston and educated at Harvard University. He studied law in the office of Daniel Webster, being admitted to the bar in 1831. Three years later he entered the state legislature and from 1840 to 1850 was a member of the national House of Representatives, being speaker for one term. He was appointed United States senator upon the death of Daniel Webster, but was defeated for election by Charles Sumner. During his career in Congress he consistently opposed slavery and denounced the Mexican War, but favored the compromise measures of 1850 and refused to join the Republican party, supporting Fillmore in 1856, Bell in 1860 and McClellan in 1864. After the Civil War he devoted himself to administering the Peabody Educational Fund, and was for thirty years president of the Massachusetts Historical Society.

Wire, a bar of metal drawn to an even thread or slender rod of uniform diameter, by being passed between grooved rollers or drawn through holes in a plate of steel. Wire is usually cylindrical, but it is also made of various other forms. The metals most commonly drawn into wire are gold, silver, copper and iron; but the finest wire is made from platinum. The metal to be drawn is first hammered into a bar, and then passed through a series of holes in a hardened steel plate, successively diminishing in diameter. Some fine gold wires and platinum wires for the spider lines of telescope micrometers have a diameter of only $\frac{1}{18000}$ of an inch.

WIRE MAKING. The steel or iron from which the wire is made is delivered to the wire mills in billets, four inches square and about three feet long. These billets are heated in a furnace to a white heat and are then put through several trains of rolls, in exactly the same way as that in which a bar of iron is made. When the metal comes from the last train of rolls, it is about a quarter of an inch in diameter. A billet of steel weighing 150 pounds makes a rod about 850 feet long. The steel rod is coiled upon an iron reel as it comes from the rolls and while the metal is still hot. When the coils have become thoroughly cold, they are taken to the cleaning room, where they are lowered into circular wooden vats, sunk into the floor and filled with heated sulphuric acid. Here they are allowed to boil for fifteen or twenty minutes, for the purpose of cleaning away all foreign substances. The steel absorbs some of the acid, which renders it brittle, and in order to remove all trace of the acid, the rods are piled in stacks on the grating floor, and clear water is turned on them, until all the acid on the outside is washed off. The rods are then lowered into a vat filled with lime and water, kept hot by steam coils, and are allowed to remain until a coating of lime adheres to them. They are then piled on trucks and run into brick ovens, where they are allowed to bake for two hours at a low temperature. They are taken from the oven to the scales, where they are weighed and turned over to the wire drawer.

Before each workman on a bench or table is a cast-iron reel. By means of cog wheels, connected with a shaft, this reel is made to revolve with considerable force. To one side of this reel is the wire plate, through which the wire is drawn. Through the middle of the plate are two rows of holes, six in a row, through which the wire is passed. The workman takes a coil of rods and puts the end in a pointing machine, for a distance of 3 or 4 inches. This machine, which is really a small steam hammer, pounds the end down to a small size. The wire drawer then pushes this end through one of the holes in the wire plate, and with a pair of pincers, attached to a lever, he pulls the wire through the plate far enough so that it can be fastened to the cast-iron reel. The reel is then put in motion and the wire is pulled through the plate with irresistible force. In order that the wire may be annealed, or softened, the coils are piled on a spindle, and the spindle with the wire is lowered into what is called the annealing pot. This pot is fitted with an iron cover and is sealed with fire clay, to make it air-tight. It is then put into a brick oven, the fire is started under the pot and allowed to heat until the wire is cherry red, the workmen being able to tell from the appearance of the cast-iron pot the condition of the wire. The wire is kept at this heat for several hours and is then slowly cooled. The wire used in making small springs is not annealed, nor is that used in making wire nails, for in that case the nail would double up under the stroke of the hammer.

Wire is used for so many purposes that only a few of the most important uses can be noticed. The most important are for telegraph and telephone lines, for trolley wires and electric cables, for fencing and for the manufacture of wire nails (See NAILS). Wire designed for outdoor use, such as telegraph and telephone lines and fencing, is galvanized, to prevent rusting (See GALVANIZED IRON). Much of the wire intended for fencing is made into barb wire, the manufacture of which has become an important industry. Over 500,000 tons of wire are made into nails in the United States each year.

Wire Glass, a glass used in buildings and consisting of wire and glass. The glass has wire netting embedded in the center during the process of manufacture. The wire is embedded in the molten glass at a temperature sufficiently high to insure adhesion of the glass to it, so that the two materials are strongly bound together and if the glass is broken it will remain practically in shape. The surface of the pane can be finished in such style as to adapt the glass for different uses. It may be ribbed, polished or "rough rolled." Wire glass is strong, and is used for window panes where ordinary glass is liable to be broken. It is also one of the most efficient safeguards against fire, since, if broken by heat, it retains its shape and position instead of falling out of the sash and leaving an opening through which air can enter. Two inventors claim the honor of being the first to make wire glass, Frank Schuman of Philadelphia and Leon Appert of France.

Wireless Tel'egraph. See TELEGRAPH, WIRELESS.

Wireworms, *wire'wurmz,* a name given by farmers to the larvae, or grubs, of several species of click beetles. The worms are said to live for years, during all which time they are destructive to vegetation. See CLICK BEETLE.

Wirt, *wurt,* WILLIAM (1772–1834), an American lawyer, statesman and writer, born at Plattsburg, Md. He received a grammar school education, studied law and began the practice of his profession in Virginia. He soon attained some note as a writer of essays in a light and satirical vein. He settled in Richmond in 1806, prosecuted with great skill the case against Aaron Burr and as a warm supporter of Jefferson was elected to the state legislature. In 1817 he was appointed, by James Monroe, attorney-general of the United States and held the office through the administration of John Quincy Adams. In 1832, having removed meanwhile to Baltimore, he became the candidate of the anti-Masonic party for the presidency.

Wiscon'sin, the BADGER STATE, one of the North Central states, bounded on the n. by Minnesota and Michigan, on the e. by Michigan, on the s. by Illinois and on the w. by Iowa and Minnesota. Nearly all of the western boundary is formed by the Saint Croix and Mississippi rivers; a part of the northern boundary line lies in Lake Superior, and the eastern boundary line is in

Lake Michigan. The greatest length of the state from north to south is 315 mi., the greatest width, 294 mi., and the area, 56,066 sq. mi., of which 810 sq. mi. are water. Population in 1910, 2,333,860.

SURFACE AND DRAINAGE. The surface of Wisconsin is generally a great rolling plain. A low height of land extends through the state north and south, a little east of the middle line, and at a point about 30 miles south of Lake Superior it meets another elevation extending east and west. The highest altitudes of this ridge are about 1800 feet. These ridges form watersheds, from which the land slopes in all directions. There are no high mountains, but the rivers flow through well-worn valleys in some localities, and along the Mississippi and other streams there are bluffs. There is also a considerable bluff along Green Bay. The lowest part of the state borders on Lake Michigan, which is a little less than 600 feet above sea level.

Wisconsin is divided into three drainage areas. The northwestern part of the state is drained into Lake Superior by a few short rivers, chief of which are the American and the Bois Brulé. The portion east of the watershed extending north and south is drained into Lake Michigan, and with the exception of the Fox, all of the rivers in this drainage area are short. Some of the most important are the Menominee, forming a good part of the boundary between Wisconsin and the northern peninsula of Michigan, the Peshtigo and the Oconto. Nearly three-fourths of the state is drained into the Mississippi River. The chief tributaries are the Saint Croix, forming a part of the western boundary, the Chippewa, the Black and the Wisconsin, which flows through the central part of the state and is the largest river wholly within its boundaries. Each of these rivers has numerous tributaries, but none of them is navigable for large boats. Through a part of its course the Wisconsin has cut its way through sandstone bluffs, forming the Dalles, noted for their beautiful scenery. In the southeastern, north central and northern parts of the state are numerous lakes, which are favorite resorts for summer residence and also for hunters and fishermen. The largest of these is Lake Winnebago, almost directly south of Green Bay.

CLIMATE. The winters are long and severe, but of uniform temperature, with many dry, clear days; the summers are short and hot. But the cold of winter and the heat of summer are in the eastern section tempered by the waters of Lake Michigan. In northern Wisconsin, snow usually falls early in the winter and covers the ground until late in the spring; in the south there is often little snow. The average rainfall is 30 inches; the mean temperature at La Crosse is 44°.

MINERAL RESOURCES. Wisconsin is one of the leading states in the production of iron ore, the mines being located in the valley of the Menominee River and along the Gogebic range in the northern part of the state. This ore is similar to that found in Michigan and Minnesota and is shipped by lake steamers. In the southwestern part of the state are important deposits of lead and zinc, and the zinc mines near Plattville are among the most important in the country. Building stone and clay suitable for making brick and tiling are widely distributed, and the manufacture of cream-colored brick is one of the important industries of the state. Granite is found in Marquette County, in the central part of the state, and valuable quarries of a reddish-brown sandstone are found in Bayfield County.

AGRICULTURE. Originally a large part of the state was covered with forests. In the north these were of pine, and the intervening regions consist of marsh or land covered with boulders; hence this part of the state is not well suited to general agriculture, but it is well adapted to dairying, and that industry is being rapidly developed. The middle and southern portions consist of fertile prairie lands. They are supplied with an abundance of moisture, and the temperature is suitable to growing all crops produced in a medium or cool temperate climate; hence all of the central and southern part of Wisconsin is under tillage and produces abundant crops. Hay and forage are extensively grown, and among the cereals the leading crops are oats, corn, wheat, barley and rye. Other crops of importance are buckwheat, potatoes, peas, beans and tobacco. The region around Green Bay and Manitowoc is specially adapted to the growing of peas, and a large canning industry has been developed. Dairying and the raising of live stock are important branches of agricultural industry. Large numbers of cattle, horses and swine are raised every year, and as a dairy state Wisconsin is one of the foremost in the Union, the yearly output of dairy products being valued at over $70,000,000, practically all of this amount being received for the sale of milk.

MANUFACTURES. In recent years the manufacturing industries of Wisconsin have developed with remarkable rapidity. The most important of these is the manufacture of lumber and of lumber and timber products, in which Wisconsin is one of the leading states, the annual output of this industry exceeding $60,000,000. Next in importance is the manufacture of flour and grist mill products, followed by foundry and machine shop products, malt liquors, wood pulp and paper, and dairy products, including butter, cheese and condensed milk. Tanning and currying leather, slaughtering and meat packing are also important industries. Others of importance are the manufacture of agricultural implements, boots and shoes, furniture, iron and steel, and the construction and repair of railway cars.

TRANSPORTATION AND COMMERCE. The western part of the state has an outlet through the Saint Croix and the Mississippi, and the northwestern section, through Lake Superior, while the eastern portion, bordering its entire length upon Lake Michigan, has communication with the Great Lakes through Racine, Milwaukee, Sheboygan, Manitowoc, Sturgeon Bay and a number of other points. The state is well supplied with railways, there being about 7500 miles of lines within its borders. The leading lines are the Chicago, Milwaukee & Saint Paul, the Chicago & Northwestern, the Wisconsin Central, the Minnesota, Saint Paul & Sault Sainte Marie, the Green Bay & Western, the Chicago, Burlington & Quincy and the Northern Pacific. A canal connects the Fox and Wisconsin rivers at Portage, and a canal at Sturgeon Bay connects Green Bay with Lake Michigan.

The commerce of the state is extensive. Iron, dairy products, live stock, lumber and its manufactured products, flour and grist mill products, potatoes and other vegetables are exported in large quantities. The imports consist of manufactured goods and machinery. Milwaukee is the chief center of trade on Lake Michigan and for the state at large, while Superior is the chief commercial center for the northwestern part of the state.

GOVERNMENT. The legislature consists of a senate and a house of representatives, the senate having 33 members, and the house, 100. The members of the assembly are elected for two years; of the senate, for four years. The sessions are biennial and are unlimited as to time. The executive department consists of a governor, a lieutenant governor, a secretary of state, a treasurer, an attorney-general and an insurance commissioner, each elected for two years, and the state superintendent, elected at a spring election for four years. The courts consist of a supreme court of seven judges, elected for ten years, and circuit courts in the judicial circuits established by the legislature, each circuit having one judge elected by the people. Local administration is by counties.

EDUCATION. The school system is under the administration of the superintendent of public instruction. Wisconsin expends over $13,000,000 annually on its public schools and maintains one of the best systems in the Union. The University of Wisconsin at Madison is at the head of the system and is directly affiliated with the high schools throughout the state. There are also normal schools at Milwaukee, Oshkosh, Plattville, River Falls, Stevens Point, Superior, Whitewater and La Crosse. The higher institutions of learning not under state administration are Beloit College at Beloit, Lawrence University at Appleton, Ripon College at Ripon, Milton College at Milton and Milwaukee-Downer College at Milwaukee. Wisconsin was the first state in the Union to establish a system of county training schools for the preparation of teachers for the country schools; there are now 24 of these schools. It was also the first state to establish county schools of agriculture and domestic economy for rural communities; there are now five of these in operation. Additional schools of both types are being established from year to year. In connection with its educational department, Wisconsin maintains an excellent system of school libraries, which are so managed as to bring a large list of the best books within reach of every inhabitant of the state, at practically no expense. The traveling libraries have no connection with the educational department, being promoted by the state library commission. The library of the historical society at Madison is also one of great value.

INSTITUTIONS. The school for the blind is at Janesville; that for the deaf and dumb is at Delavan; the school for the feeble-minded is at Chippewa Falls, and the state public school for dependent children is at Sparta. Hospitals for the insane are at Mendota and Winnebago, and the incurable insane are cared for in county institutions which receive state aid. A state tuberculosis sanitarium was established at Wales in 1905. There is a state soldiers' home at Waupaca and a national soldiers' home at Milwaukee. The penal and reformatory institutions consist of a state prison at Waupun, a state reformatory near Green Bay, an industrial school for boys at Waukesha, and a

183

house of correction and industrial school for girls at Milwaukee.

CITIES. The chief cities are Madison, the capital; Milwaukee, Superior, Oshkosh, Racine, La Crosse, Sheboygan, Green Bay, Eau Claire, Marinette, Appleton and Fond du Lac, each of which is described under its title.

HISTORY. Probably the first white man to enter the territory of Wisconsin was Jean Nicolet, who was dispatched in 1634 by Champlain and traversed the southern part of the state. Other traders and missionaries followed, including Radisson and Groseilliers, Father Allouez and Marquette and Joliet. Meantime, several missions had been established, one at La Pointe on Lake Superior in 1665 and one at the site of De Pere in 1669. By the Treaty of Paris, in 1763, the territory, with all the northwest, was transferred to Great Britain and, after the Revolution, to the United States, where it formed a part of the Northwest Territory (See NORTHWEST TERRITORY; ORDINANCE OF 1787). However, the French and indians in the region still remained hostile to the United States and fought against it during the War of 1812. The discovery of lead mines led eventually to rapid influx into the territory, and after the defeat of Black Hawk (See BLACK HAWK WAR) there was a large agricultural immigration. Wisconsin was successively joined to Indiana, Michigan, Illinois and again to Michigan Territory, and it was erected into a separate territory in 1836. In 1847, the population of the state having been vastly increased, a constitution was adopted, and Wisconsin was admitted to the Union in the following year. For a time the chief incident in the political history of the state was the scandal arising from the promiscuous granting and sale of public lands to railroads. One of the first movements leading to the Republican party was a convention at Ripon, Wis., in 1854. The state was consistently opposed to slavery, and its supreme court declared that the Fugitive Slave Law was unconstitutional in the state. During the Civil War, Wisconsin furnished more than its quota. Since that time large areas have twice been devastated by forest fires, but the state has otherwise enjoyed phenomenal prosperity. It has been almost consistently Republican in politics. Consult Thwaites's *The Story of Wisconsin.*

Wisconsin, UNIVERSITY OF, a state institution of higher learning, located at Madison, Wis., in 1838. The university stands at the head of the educational system of the state and gives free tuition to students who are residents of Wisconsin, in all departments, except in the summer. The university comprises the colleges of letters and science, agriculture and engineering, the law, medical and graduate schools, and the extension division. The faculty numbers over 500, and the resident enrollment exceeds 5500. The buildings and grounds are valued at over $2,500,000. The library building is one of the finest in the United States and contains the University library of 175,000 volumes; the library of the Wisconsin State Historical Society, 250,000 volumes, and the library of the Academy of Sciences, Arts and Letters, 5,000 volumes, besides thousands of valuable documents and pamphlets.

Wisconsin River, a river which rises on the boundary between Michigan and Wisconsin, in Lake Desert, and flows southward to Portage City, thence in a southwest direction, entering the Mississippi River 4 mi. s. of Prairie du Chien. Its length is about 600 miles, and it is navigable for steamboats to Portage City, about 200 miles. At this point it is united with the Fox River by a short canal. Its passage through some deep gorges forms the celebrated Dalles of the Wisconsin, near Kilbourn City.

Wiseman, *wize'man,* NICHOLAS PATRICK STEPHENS (1802-1865), a British churchman, born of Irish parents at Seville. He was educated at Waterford and at the Roman Catholic College, Ushaw, near Durham, and he joined the English College, then newly formed at Rome. He became professor of Oriental languages and rector of the English College, returned to England and was appointed, successively, rector of Ushaw, vicar apostolic of the central district of England and Roman Catholic archbishop of Westminster. He was the author of *Lectures on the Connection between Science and Revealed Religion, Letters on Catholic Unity, Papal Supremacy, Fabiola* and the *Four Last Popes,* and he was joint editor of the Dublin *Review* for many years.

Wista'ria, a genus of plants belonging to the same family as the pea. The species are twining and climbing shrubs, natives of China and North America. Several have been introduced into England, and, when in flower, they form some of the most beautiful of garden plants. The Chinese and American species in the United States are much used for garden ornament.

Wis'ter, OWEN (1860–), an American novelist and story-writer, born in Philadelphia, educated at Harvard and admitted to the bar in Philadelphia. After two years, however, he gave up law work for literature and has won wide notice by his stories of western life. Of these *The Virginian* was most popular. He has written biographies of *Ulysses S. Grant,* of *Oliver Wendell Holmes* and of *Benjamin Franklin,* and he has contributed to magazines both short stories and verse. Among his latest books are *Lady Baltimore, The Simple Spelling Bee* and *The Seven Ages of Washington.*

Witch'craft, a supernatural power or influence, supposed to be acquired by certain persons over others, by reason of their holding some connection or entering into some league with the Devil or other powers of darkness. The belief in witchcraft was universal in the civilized world up to the sixteenth century, and even in the succeeding century, one of the judges of the Court of Queen's Bench in England declared that witchcraft was one of the crimes recognized by the common law of that realm. So great a man as Roger Bacon believed in witches, and the best men in all ages have participated in the delusion. Various tests were applied in olden times to ascertain whether or not the person was a witch, such as pricking the body of the victim all over, until the particular spot that was bewitched was found; throwing supposed witches into deep water, under the presumption that they would float if possessed.

In 1648 the witchcraft frenzy, which had been extensively prevalent in England and Scotland during a full century, broke out among the Puritans of New England. In Salem, Mass., Cotton Mather, a clergyman of wide influence and great power as a pulpit orator, wrote a work entitled *Memorable Providences Relating to Witchcraft and Possessions* and another entitled *Wonders of the Invisible World.* By the distribution of his writings and his utterances in the pulpit, he succeeded in arousing the superstitious element to its utmost tension. Many of the teaching men of the province were influenced by his writings and sermons, and, as clergymen in those days constituted a part of the magisterial authority, he succeeded in procuring the execution of nineteen persons. The good sense of the Puritans at last revolted against these atrocities, and a reaction set in. Samuel Parris, a clergyman, who was one of the chief persecutors, made a confession; others also relented, and nothing of importance has since been heard of witchcraft in the United States.

Witenagemot, *wit'e nah ge mote',* in English history, the name given to the old Anglo-Saxon assembly, which consisted of the king, the ealdormen, the higher ecclesiastics and the thanes. This body had power to elect the king, when a succession was in dispute, or to depose a king if it saw fit, to make treaties, to collect revenue and to enact laws. Under a weak king it was able to exercise all of these functions, but a strong king might easily make most of them merely nominal. The Norman Conquest put an end to this assembly, and the Parliament which grew up later in England was a separate institution, though it had its roots in this early body.

With'erspoon, JOHN (1722–1794), an American clergyman and publicist, signer of the Declaration of Independence. He was born in Gifford, Scotland. In 1768 he became president of Princeton College, identified himself with the cause of the colonists and was elected to the Continental Congress, where his patriotic work was arduous and of supreme importance.

Wit'ness, in law, (1) one who signs his name as evidence of the genuineness of another signature; (2) a person who gives testimony or evidence under oath or affirmation in a judicial proceeding. In the latter case, any person can be compelled to appear before a court to give evidence, failing which, he is liable to punishment for contempt (See CONTEMPT). The summons by which he is ordered to appear is called a *subpoena*; if he is ordered to bring a document or other thing in his possession, he is summoned by a *subpoena duces tecum* (bring with you under penalty).

Witte, *vit'te,* SERGEI YULIEVITCH (1840–   ). a Russian statesman and diplomat, born at Tiflis. After his graduation from the New Russian University at Odessa, he first took up journalism and later was engaged by the government in railway service. In the Russo-Turkish War Witte was given charge of the transportation of troops on the Odessa railway and so distinguished himself that he was given a position on the Southwestern railway, of which he became general manager in 1886. Two years later he was made chief of the Imperial Railway department and president of the tariff commission. His next promotion was to the office of minister of finance, a position which he held until 1903. His policy in this office led to the rapid development of manufacturing industries in Russia. He introduced the gold standard, made the sale of alcohol a government monopoly, concluded several important commercial treaties especially with Germany, and made large foreign loans, whereby the Trans-Siberian railway could be built. In 1903 Witte was made president of the

Committee of Ministers and a member of the Council of the Empire. At the Treaty of Portsmouth, N. H., at the close of the Russo-Japanese War, Witte was especially prominent, having won the only victory gained by Russia, when his stand resulted in the withdrawal by the Japanese

SERGEI WITTE

of all disputed points and the conclusion of peace. When he returned to Russia, the Czar conferred upon him the title of count. In 1905 he was appointed prime minister of Russia, but in 1906 he resigned this position, being succeeded by Goremykin.

Wittenberg, *vit'ten berK,* a town of Prussia, situated on the Elbe, 59 mi. s. w. of Berlin. The place is of special historical interest, because of its association with Luther and Melanchthon. It was to the door of the Schlosskirche that Luther nailed his celebrated theses, and within this church both Luther and Melanchthon are buried. For a time Luther was professor in the University of Wittenberg (See LUTHER, MARTIN; REFORMATION). The town contains a number of educational institutions, but its industries are unimportant. Population in 1910, 20,332.

Woad, *wode,* a plant of the mustard family, formerly cultivated on account of the blue dye extracted from its leaves. The leaves are dried and marketed in this form, or they are made into a paste, which is dried before marketing. This dye is now, however, displaced by indigo, which gives a stronger and finer blue. The ancient Britons are said to have colored their bodies with the dye procured from the woad plant. See DYER'S WEED.

Woburn, woo'burn, MASS., a city in Middlesex co., 10 mi. n. w. of Boston, on the Boston & Maine railroad. It is well laid out, has many fine homes and is an attractive residence place. There are twelve churches, three banks, a good high school and a public library, with a valuable art collection. The manufacturing of leather is the principal industry, while shoes, chemicals and machinery are also produced. The first settlement was made in 1640, and was known as Charleston Village. It was incorporated as a town in 1642 and was chartered as a city in 1888. Population in 1910, 15,308.

Woden, vo'den. See ODIN.

Wolf, a carnivorous animal, very closely related to the dog. The common European

WOLF

wolf, found almost everywhere in North America, also, is yellowish-gray, with a blackish band, or streak, on the fore legs. The hair is harsh and strong, the ears are erect and pointed, the tail is straight, or nearly so. The height at the shoulder is about two and a half feet. The wolf is swift of foot and crafty, a destructive enemy to sheep and poultry. It associates in packs, to hunt the larger quadrupeds, such as the deer and the elk. When hard pressed with hunger, these packs have been known to attack isolated travelers and even to enter villages and carry off children. In general, however, wolves are cowardly and stealthy. They are still plentiful in some parts of Europe and the United States. They probably ceased to exist in England about the end of the fifteenth century. The small *prairie wolf* or *coyote*, living on the western plains of the United States, is a burrowing animal. The Tasmanian wolf is a marsupial.

Wolfe, JAMES (1727–1759), a British general, the hero of Quebec. He entered the army early, and his rise was rapid, owing to the ability which he showed during the war in Germany and in Flanders and in the defeat of Charles Edward Stuart. When it was decided, in 1758, to send an expedition to Cape Breton, Wolfe was appointed by Pitt brigadier general. He advised an attack on Quebec and was selected to lead the enterprise, in which capacity he showed wonderful courage and genius. Driven back from the fortress, he led his men, by a steep, narrow path, to the Heights of Abraham, above the city, and here he met the French under Montcalm. While leading a charge, he had one of his wrists shattered by a shot, but he did not stop. Another shot struck him, and he still advanced, but a third lodged in his breast and proved fatal. His last words, when he was told that the French were giving way, were, "Now God be praised; I die in peace." By the surrender of Quebec, Canada was lost to the French.

Wolf Fish, a savage fish, that has a mouth armed with sharp, strong teeth of large size. When captured, the fish is said to bite the nets and even to attack the fishermen. Around the coasts of Great Britain it attains a length of six or seven feet, but in more southern seas it grows to a still larger size. The flesh is palatable and is generally eaten in Iceland. The skin is durable and is manufactured into a kind of shagreen, used for making pouches and like articles.

Wolseley, woolz'ly, GARNET JOSEPH, Sir, Viscount (1833–1913), a British general, born in Ireland. He entered the army as ensign in 1852, took part in the second Burmese War (1852–1853), where he was severely wounded, and served with distinction in the Crimea. He engaged in the siege and capture of Lucknow during the Indian mutiny of 1857–1858 and was employed in 1860 in the Chinese War. In the following year he was dispatched to Canada, and in 1870 he carried the Red River expedition to a successful issue. Three years afterward he was appointed to the command of an expedition to punish the king of Ashantee, and after a brief campaign he entered Kumassi and received the submission of the king. After the defeat of a British force by the Zulus in South Africa, in 1879, he was dispatched as high commissioner, but before his arrival the Zulus had been defeated and little remained for him to do. His next command was in Egypt, in 1882, where his forces successfully stormed the lines of Tel-el-Kebir and captured Arabi Pasha. For this he received the thanks of Parliament, was created a baron and was promoted to the rank of general. When the Mahdi subdued the Sudan and held General Gordon prisoner in Khartum, Wolseley was dispatched with a relief expedition, but before the arrival of his advance force, the place had fallen. On his return to England he was created a viscount. In 1890 he was made commander of the troops in Ireland, and in 1895 he was raised to the supreme command of the British army.

Wolsey, *wool'zy,* THOMAS, Cardinal (1475?-1530), said to have been the son of a butcher, was born at Ipswich. He was educated at Magdalen College, Oxford, where he took his degree as a scholar of distinction. When Henry VIII became king, the advancement of Wolsey was rapid. Successively he was appointed canon of Windsor, dean of York, bishop of Lincoln, archbishop of York, lord chancellor of the kingdom, cardinal and pope's legate. He was twice a candidate for the papacy, and his power in England and his revenues were only equaled by those of the crown. Part of his immense revenues he expended in display, and part for the advancement of learning, as he endowed the College of Christ Church at Oxford, which he intended to call Cardinal College. He founded several lectures and built the palace at Hampton Court, which he presented to the king. This rapid preferment by the king was largely the result of a remarkable series of diplomatic victories, in which Wolsey had been the means of enabling Henry to hold the balance between Francis I and Emperor Charles V. His success in the region of politics terminated in the splendors of the Field of the Cloth of Gold (1520). In his ambitious career the cardinal had made many enemies, who were held in check so long as he retained the favor of his royal master. This favor Wolsey lost when he failed to obtain from Pope Clement a decision granting the king's divorce from Catharine of Aragon. The enemies of the fallen prelate now succeeded in banishing him from court and stripping him of his dignities. Being found guilty of a praemunire, he was sentenced to imprisonment. Finally, after a brief respite, during which he was restored to some of his offices and had returned to his see of York, he was arrested at Cawood Castle on a charge of high treason, and on his way to London, as a prisoner, he died at Leicester Abbey.

Wolverene or **Wolverine,** *wool vur een'.* See GLUTTON.

Woman's Christian Temperance Union, THE NATIONAL, a woman's organization. founded in Cleveland, Ohio, in 1874. It was the outgrowth of the famous 'woman's crusade' for that purpose Its purpose was to unify the work of women in temperance and social reform The organization now has state, district, county and local societies in every state and territory, and it contains a membership of over 300,000. It is the largest organization exclusively of women that has ever been effected and has over forty distinct lines of work, each under the management of national state, district, county and local superintendents. The society has been instrumental in securing in nearly every state the enactment of laws requiring the public schools to give instruction in the effects of stimulants and narcotics on the human system; through their influence many laws for the better protection of girls and women have also been passed, and industrial homes for girls and houses of refuge for fallen women have been established. The official organ is the *Union Signal,* published at Chicago, with a circulation of over 80,000. Headquarters of the society are at Evanston, Ill.

The World's Christian Temperance Union was formed in 1883, through the influence of Frances E. Willard, It now has local organizations in most Christian countries. The badge of all Woman's Christian Temperance Union members is the white ribbon.

Woman's Relief Corps, a patriotic society, organized in July, 1883, as an auxiliary to the Grand Army of the Republic. Mothers, wives, daughters and sisters of Union soldiers, and those who assisted in the field during the Civil War, compose largely its membership, though all loyal women are eligible. The society is divided into 35 *departments* and 2978 *corps,* with a total membership of over 152,000. Its purpose is to help perpetuate the memory of Union soldiers, to extend aid to widows and orphans and to inculcate lessons of patriotism in the rising generation. The society has expended about $2,000,-000 in charities.

Woman Suffrage, the right of women to vote on an equality with men. The agitation to give women a political status equal to that of men is merely one phase of the great movement to make woman in every way possible—legally, socially, intellectually, morally, politically—the equal of man. In the field of business this agitation for a fair and equal opportunity for women has made more progress than in any other field. In nearly all departments of skilled labor, in clerical positions, in the professions, women are efficient and successful workers. The first woman suffrage convention in the United States was held in 1848, Lucretia Mott and Elizabeth Cady Stanton being present. From that source has come the present situation. Since 1869, when Wyoming granted full suffrage to women, Colorado, Utah, Idaho, Washington, California, Arizona, Kansas and Oregon have followed this example. In Illinois women may vote for all officers not mentioned in the state constitution. Women are allowed to vote on school matters in nineteen other states, and on municipal questions in several others. In Alaska women have full suffrage.

Wom'bat, a clumsy marsupial animal, with short, stout legs and a short, stumpy tail. It feeds on roots during the night and lives in burrows during the day. Several species are found in Australia.

WOMBAT

Women's Clubs. With the increase in facilities for the education of women and with woman's growing share in public life, came the feeling of the necessity for coöperation along lines in which women were interested. The first societies of women were religious and charitable societies. These were followed by patriotic societies and by organizations of other sorts. At present there exist in the United States a great number of clubs for women, which may be considered as falling under three general heads, *educational, social* and *practical.* The first two divisions are explained by the names. The clubs which may be classified as *practical* include charitable organizations, societies for civic improvement or for the furthering of schools and libraries, and such organizations as have for their object

the securing, by legislation, of improved conditions for working women and children.

In 1889 an invitation was issued by a prominent club in New York to different clubs throughout the United States to a general meeting. In the following year the General Federation of Women's Clubs was formed, the membership consisting originally of sixty-three clubs. At present the General Federation holds meetings every two years in some large city. There were in the United States, at the last enumeration, considerably over 200,000 women belonging to clubs.

The idea of women's clubs has been popular in England, in which country there are a number of important clubs. On the continent the idea has never been very favorably received.

A special branch of this same movement is represented by the working girls' clubs in the large cities. These are usually founded and guided by influential women, although occasionally the clubs are started by the working girls themselves. Some of these societies simply provide rest rooms and lunch rooms, where excellent meals can be procured at a very low rate. Others have permanent club rooms.

Wood, LEONARD (1860–   ), an American soldier, born at Winchester, N. H. He graduated from Harvard Medical School in 1884, entered the army two years later as assistant surgeon, served in the campaign against Geronimo in 1886 and at the outbreak of the Spanish-American War in 1898 assisted Roosevelt in recruiting the first regiment of United States volunteer cavalry, known as the Rough Riders. He was raised to the rank of brigadier general of volunteers for gallantry at San Juan, later became major general of volunteers and in December, 1899, was appointed military governor of Cuba. This position he held for three years, and he exhibited the greatest energy and ability in administration, especially in improving the sanitary conditions of Santiago and Havana. In 1903 he was made a major general in the regular army and was assigned to command in the Philippines. From 1910 to 1914 he was chief of staff.

Wood Al'cohol or **Methyl Alcohol,** a colorless liquid, with a peculiar odor. It is obtained by heating water in retorts, where it cannot come in contact with the air, and by chemical refining of the products afterwards. Wood alcohol, mixed with ordinary alcohol in the proportion of about one to nine, forms methylated spirit, a cheaper compound than ordinary alcohol, but having most of its properties. Wood alcohol is also used in large quantities in the manufacture of varnishes.

Wood'berry, GEORGE EDWARD (1855–   ), an American poet and critic, born at Beverly, Mass. He graduated from Harvard and became professor of English in the University of Nebraska. Later he devoted himself to literary work, contributing to magazines and serving on the editorial staff of the *Nation* and other journals. In 1891 he was appointed professor of comparative literature in Columbia University, and he held this position until he resigned in 1904. He is the author of *America in Literature, Heart of Man, Makers of Literature,* lives of *Edgar Allan Poe* and *Nathaniel Hawthorne,* and *Collected Poems.*

Wood'bury, LEVI (1789–1851), an American jurist, born at Francestown, N. H. He graduated at Dartmouth College, was admitted to the bar and in 1816 became judge of the state superior court. In 1823 he was elected governor of New Hampshire and two years later was chosen to the United States Senate, where he became a close friend and supporter of President Andrew Jackson. He entered Jackson's cabinet in 1831 as secretary of the navy, and from 1834 to 1841 he was secretary of the treasury. Upon retiring from that office he was elected to the United States Senate, but resigned in 1845, to accept an appointment to the United States Supreme Court, to succeed Joseph Story.

Wood Carving, the art of producing sculpture in wood. Wood carving was probably the earliest form of sculpture. As far as known, the Egyptians were the first nation to practice the art. Specimens of their work, made more than 4000 B. C., are still in existence, and it is quite probable that the Greeks obtained their first ideas of sculpture from the wood carving of these people. The Romans also carved many of their early statues from wood. In the first century of the Christian era wood carving was used in the decoration of churches, and many pieces still in existence show the remarkable skill of the artists and workmen of that time. From the early centuries of the Christian era wood carving fell into disuse, until about the eleventh century, when it was again revived, and used, as before, in the decoration of churches.

Wood carving as practiced to-day is confined to the ornamentation of altars, pulpits and choir stalls for churches; to a few articles of the most expensive furniture; to the decoration of expensive interiors of dwellings and public halls, and to ornaments. Among European nations the art is practiced with the greatest skill in Tyrol, Switzerland, and some of the provinces of Italy and Germany. Among the Eastern nations the Hindus are remarkably skilful in carving wood. Nearly all their designs represent some form of leaf or vine. The work is finely executed, but shows a tendency to overcrowding, which mars the general effect. The Chinese and Japanese also produce wood carvings of decided merit.

All the finest work is done by hand, with small chisels, shaped for the purpose. Oak, mahogany, ebony and many of the softer woods are used. Before carving, the wood should be thoroughly seasoned. The completed work is usually finished by rubbing down in oil or shellac or some other varnish. In the United States, but little hand carving is done, though in some manual training schools it is now a part of the course of instruction. Most of the ornamental woodwork used for interiors is made by machine tools. Inlaid work constitutes wood mosaic and should not be classed with wood carvings.

Wood'chuck, the popular name of an animal of the squirrel family, common in the United States and Canada. The woodchuck is the American marmot and is often called the *ground hog.* It is of a heavy form, from fifteen to eighteen inches long, blackish or grizzled above and chestnut red below. It forms burrows, in which it sleeps through the winter. It feeds on vegetables and is very destructive to crops of red clover and alfalfa.

Wood'cock, a bird belonging to the same family as the snipe. In its several species it is widely

WOODCOCK

distributed over North America, Europe and northern Asia, extending as far east as Japan. The woodcocks are brown birds, marked with black and gray. A very peculiar appearance is given to their heads by their eyes, which are large and set very far back. The American woodcock is smaller than the European species, but quite similar in its habits. It is seen frequenting low grounds and leaf-strewn woods and feeding mostly by night, when with its long slender bill it searches skilfully for worms, which it readily extracts from the ground. The young are often carried about between the thighs of the parents.

Wood Engraving. See ENGRAVING, subhead WOOD ENGRAVING.

Wooden Horse. The Greeks in their attempts to conquer Troy had been ten years before the city without gaining an entrance, and at the end of that time they saw that an entrance could be effected only by strategy. They accordingly built a huge wooden horse, in the hollow body of which were concealed a number of Greek soldiers. This horse was left near the Trojan gates, and the Greeks withdrew to await developments. When the Trojans came from the gates of the city, to look at the wooden horse, they were persuaded by a Greek, who had remained behind for the purpose, to take it into the city and offer it as a sacrifice to Neptune. Once within the city, the Greeks inside of the horse crept during the night from their hiding-place and threw open the gates of Troy to the Grecian army.

Wood'pecker, the name of a large group of climbing birds, of which there are a number of

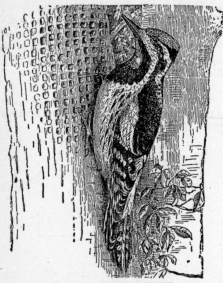

YELLOW-BELLIED SAP SUCKER

different species. They have long, straight, angular beaks, adapted to perforating the bark of trees. Their tongues are long, slender and armed with a barbed, horny tip. They can thrust their tongues far out of their mouths and so spear insects in the depths of their burrows. Their tongues are also covered with a sticky,

slimy substance, that helps to hold their prey. When feeding, they usually ascend the tree spirally, aided by the spiny points which terminate their tail-feathers. They tap here and there on the tree-trunk, searching for the holes in which insects are hidden, and often tear away large parts of rotten trees, for the larvae concealed in them. The *sap sucker* is a species that is fond of the sap of trees and bores round holes, which it arranges with geometrical exactness in broad bands around the trunk of a tree. It especially favors the pines, and in feeding it moves about over the checkerboard of holes, taking the sap from them regularly, as it accumulates. The *ivory-billed woodpecker* of the southern United States is a large bird, about twenty-one inches long, bright black and white in color, the male having a large bright scarlet crest. Like most of the other woodpeckers, this one excavates its nest in suitable dead trees. The *red-headed woodpecker*, the *black and white woodpecker*, the *hairy woodpecker* and the *downy woodpecker* are well known in the Northern states. The red-headed woodpecker often lights on the shingles of houses or on a hollow branch and strikes his bill in a noisy clatter, stopping now and then to call out his hoarse, rough note. The woodpeckers are found in almost every part of the globe, excepting Australia and Egypt. See FLICKER.

Wood Pe'wee, a familiar little bird, resembling the phoebe bird, but distinguished by a greenish-yellow belly and a grayish band across the wings. It has a rapid flight and catches insects with the skill of its genus. Its slow, plaintive little note, *pee-a-way,* may be heard in the woods, all through the long summer, at early dawn and during the twilight hours. See PHOEBE.

Wood Sor'rel. See OXALIS.

Wood Spirit. See METHYLATED SPIRIT.

Wood'stock, a city of Ontario and the county-seat of Oxford co., situated on the Thames River, at its junction with Cedar Creek, 30 mi. e. n. e. of London and on the Canadian Pacific and the Grand Trunk railways. Its leading industries include the manufacture of wagons, furniture, leather, pianos and organs and automobiles. It is also an important summer resort. Population in 1911, 9,320.

Wool, the soft hair which grows on sheep, the alpaca and some species of goats. In fineness, wool sometimes approaches to fur. Wool is divided into two classes—*short,* or *carding, wool,* seldom reaching a length of more than 3 or 4 inches, and *long,* or *combing, wool,* varying in

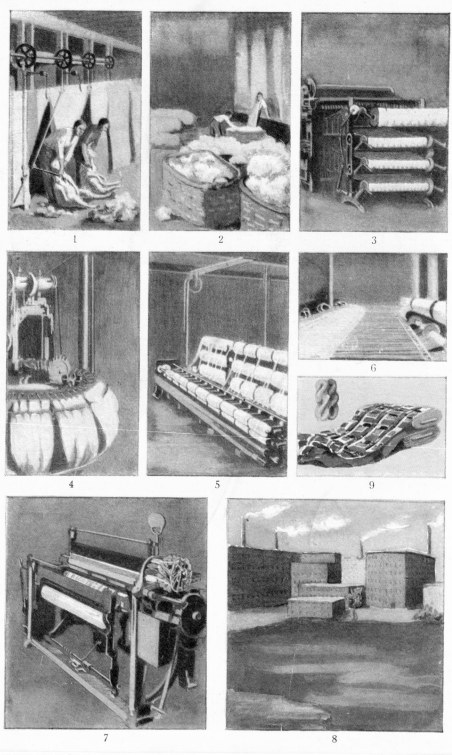

WOOL

1, Shearing of sheep.	4, Combing.	7, Weaving.
2, Sorting and grading.	5, Drawing.	8, Woolen factory.
3, Carding.	6, Spinning.	9, Products.

length from 4 to 8 inches, each class being subdivided into a variety of sorts, according to the fineness and soundness of the staple. Wools which unite a high degree of fineness and softness with considerable length of staple, bear a high price. The finest carding wools were formerly extensively obtained from Spain, the native country of the merino sheep, and at a later period extensively from Germany, where that breed had been successfully introduced and cultivated. The leading countries in the production of wool are Australia, the United States, Argentina and British South Africa. The United States produces about one-fourth of the world's supply. See Sheep.

Wool, John Ellis (1788–1869), an American soldier, born at Newburg, N. Y. He studied law, but entered the United States army and served during the War of 1812, becoming major of regulars, on account of gallantry at Queenstown. He also won distinction at Plattsburg and was raised to the rank of lieutenant colonel. In 1841 he was made brigadier general, and in the Mexican War he fought under General Taylor with remarkable skill and bravery, being brevetted major general. At the outbreak of the Civil War he performed notable service in saving Fortress Monroe to the Union, but retired in August, 1863, with the rank of major general of regulars.

Woolen Manufacture. The use of wool as an article of clothing dates from the earliest times, and woolen fabrics were well known to the ancient Jews, the Greeks and the Romans. It was undoubtedly the last-named people who introduced the manufacture of woolen cloth into England, though the industry did not reach importance for several centuries after its introduction.

In the making of woolen cloth, the following are the chief processes: When the wool is brought to the factory, it is carefully sorted, and that having the same grade of fiber is placed together. It is then thoroughly cleaned by being dusted, scoured with soap or lye and hot water, and then rinsed. After this, if colored cloth is to be made, the wool is dyed. It is then dried and is ready for the second important step in the process, that of preparing it for the loom.

The dried wool is first run through a machine, which removes any burs that may have adhered to the fiber. It is then run through the *picker*, which pulls all of the little tufts of wool apart and also enables the manufacturer to mix wools of different colors in any proportion desired. By mixing white and brown or blue and black or blue and gray, many very pleasing effects are obtained. After picking, the wool passes through the carding machines, of which there are usually three. Each of these draws out the fiber and straightens it and places the wool in the form of a loose band, or roll. Each successive machine straightens the fiber and reduces the size of this band, making it each time proportionately stronger. When the wool leaves the third card, it is in the form of an untwisted yarn a little larger than the heavy crocheting yarn. As it comes from this machine it is wound upon large spools or bobbins and is ready for spinning.

The spinning is done on the mule jenny or the ring frame, and thus a large number of threads are spun at a time. The size of the thread and the hardness of the twist depend upon the way in which the machine is gauged. For a fine thread that is hard twisted, a machine which revolves very rapidly and also draws the thread out rapidly, is necessary. The spun yarn is wound upon spools ready for being placed in the loom. The arrangement for this consists of frames, upon which these spools are placed in such a position that the thread unwinds from them directly, to make the warp of a width and number of threads desired (See Weaving). The woven cloth is finished in the style desired, possibly re-dyed, pressed and wound into bundles containing about fifty yards each, in which form it is placed upon the market. The woolen industry of the United States is one of great importance; the value of its yearly output is about $430,000,000. See Cloth; Spinning; Worsted.

Wool'sey, Theodore Dwight (1801–1889), an American educator, born in New York. He was educated at Yale College and at Princeton Theological Seminary. He began his career as a tutor in Yale College, then studied in Europe, and on his return he was made professor of Greek at Yale. In 1846 he was elected president, and he held that position for twenty-five years. He was chairman of the American committee of revisers for the New Testament and was the author of a number of editions of Greek plays. His best-known works are *Introduction to the Study of International Law, Essays on Divorce and Divorce Legislation, Political Science, Religion of the Past and of the Future* and *Communism and Socialism.*

Woon'socket, R. I., a city in Providence co., 15 mi. n. w. of Providence, on the Blackstone River and on several lines of the New York, New Haven & Hartford railroad and a number of electric railways. It is an important manufacturing place, containing cotton and woolen mills, foundries, machine shops, rubber works, worsted and hosiery mills, wagon works and other factories. There are public and parish schools, the Sacred Heart College for men, an academy for girls and the Harris Institute Library. A magnificent bridge crosses the river here, and there are fair grounds and three parks. The present city was incorporated in 1888. It was formed by the consolidation of several factory villages, although the original village of Woonsocket was not included. Population in 1910, 38,125.

Woos'ter, OHIO, the county-seat of Wayne co., 50 mi. s. by w. of Cleveland, on Killbuck Creek and on the Baltimore & Ohio and the Pennsylvania railroads. It is the seat of the University of Wooster and also contains a state agricultural experiment station, a high school, two libraries and three banks. The city is in an agricultural and stock-raising region and has manufactures of lumber products, flour, engines and other articles. Wooster was laid out in 1808 and was chartered as a city in 1868. Population in 1910. 6136.

Worcester, *woos'ter*, MASS., one of the county seats of Worcester co., the second city in size in the state, is on the Blackstone River, 44 mi. w. by s. of Boston and on the Boston & Albany branch of the New York Central, the Boston & Maine and the New York, New Haven & Hartford railroads. It is also connected by electric lines with Boston, Springfield, Fitchburg and other towns. The city is situated in a valley surrounded by low hills. It is well laid out, has good streets and ten public parks, the largest of which is Lake Park, with an area of 110 acres, and Elm Park, with 86 acres. The city is noted for its large number of excellent buildings. Chief among these are the city hall, the courthouse, the public library, which contains over 137,000 volumes, the postoffice, the art museum, the state armory, a state asylum for the insane and the buildings of the women's club, the American Antiquarian Society, the Worcester Society of Antiquity and the Young Men's and Young Women's Christian associations, besides a number of prominent business blocks. The educational institutions include Clark University, Clark College, College of the Holy Cross (Roman Catholic), the Worcester Polytechnic Institute, the Worcester Academy, the Highland Military Academy and a state normal school.

The city is one of the most important manu-

facturing centers in New England and has the largest wire factory in the world, employing more than four thousand men. Other important industries include manufactures of envelopes, emery wheels, elevators, tools, carpets, firearms, railway cars, boots and shoes, cotton and woolen goods, clothing and prepared foods. There are also a large number of minor industries. There are a number of pleasant summer resorts in the vicinity, including Lake Quinsigamond and Mount Wachusett, which are connected with Worcester by electric railway.

The first settlement was made in 1673, but was abandoned on the outbreak of King Philip's War two years later. A second attempt in 1684 was also given up because of indian depredations, and the first permanent settlement was not made until 1713. In 1722 Worcester was incorporated as a town, and in 1848 it was chartered as a city. Worcester is the birthplace of the historian George Bancroft. It was also the home of Isaiah Thomas, and at one time it was one of the most important publishing centers in the United States. Population in 1910, 145,986.

Wor'den, JOHN LORIMER (1818–1897), an American naval officer, born in Westchester County, N. Y. He entered the navy in 1835 and became a lieutenant eleven years later. In March, 1862, he was in command of the *Monitor* during the famous battle with the *Merrimac*, or *Virginia*, in Hampton Roads. During this engagement his eyesight was seriously impaired by the explosion of a shell, but he was given other commands and served with gallantry until the close of the war. In 1870 he became head of the Annapolis Naval Academy and was made rear admiral in 1872. He retired in 1886.

Wordsworth, *wurdz'wurth*, WILLIAM (1770–1850), an English poet, born at Cockermouth, Cumberland. While at a grammar school at Hawkshead, he spent much time in solitary rambles, and the deep love of nature begun at this time grew throughout his life and was his most prominent characteristic. He graduated from Cambridge in 1791, without having distinguished himself in any way, and later in the same year he crossed to France. He exhibited the most ardent sympathy with he Revolution and remained in France for over a year. But the excesses into which the Revolution afterward ran shocked him greatly, and as time went on he settled down to a staid conservatism. Many of his contemporaries, ardent republicans like Byron and Shelley, condemned him severely for the change. Shortly after his return from France,

Wordsworth published his first poems, *An Evening Walk* and *Descriptive Sketches taken during a Pedestrian Tour among the Alps*, which, although they were written somewhat after the manner of Pope, yet contained signs of the new poet's peculiar genius. In 1795, Wordsworth, with his sister Dorothy, settled at Racedown in Dorset, where among other experiments he began his tragedy of *The Borderers*. In this retreat

WILLIAM WORDSWORTH

they were visited (1797) by Coleridge, who induced them to remove to Alfoxden, in the immediate neighborhood of his own residence at Nether Stowey. Here the two poets held daily intercourse, and after a twelvemonth they published *Lyrical Ballads*, in literary copartnership. This volume contained as Coleridge's contribution *The Ancient Mariner*, and as Wordsworth's, among others, *We are Seven* and *Lines on Tintern Abbey*. Although the poems were received with almost complete public indifference, yet Wordsworth felt that he had found his mission, and after a winter spent in Germany, he and his sister settled at Grasmere, one of the most beautiful places in England, where he gave himself up to literary work. Thenceforth his life was marked by few incidents. Those worth noting are his marriage, in 1802, with Mary Hutchison; his appointment, in 1813, to an inspectorship of stamps, and his removal to Rydal Mount; several

journeys into Scotland and to the continent; his acceptance of a D. C. L. degree, conferred upon him in 1839 by the University of Oxford, and his accession, in 1843, to the laureateship, on the death of Southey.

The public and the critics were slow to recognize Wordsworth's ability, refusing utterly to accept his idea that poetry may deal with simple and natural subjects, presented in simple and natural language. Coleridge, Lamb, De Quincey, Southey, Keats and others were always his strong admirers, however, and his faith in his own mission was too strong to be shaken. His great philosophic poem, which, in his own phrase, was to be the Gothic cathedral of his labor, received only a fragmentary accomplishment in *The Prelude, The Excursion* and *The Recluse*. Yet enough was achieved in his smaller poems to justify his own conception of himself as a "dedicated spirit," and to set him apart among the greatest of England's poets. His intense sympathy with nature and his firm belief in the brotherhood of man find expression in all of his poems; and his language, although always simple, sometimes rises far above what he insisted it should be, the unadorned language of prose. Among the most beautiful of Wordsworth's poems are the *Ode on the Intimations of Immortality, Ode to Duty, The Solitary Reaper, To a Highland Girl, I wandered lonely as a cloud* and *Yarrow Revisited*. His sonnets are among the finest ever produced by an English poet.

Work'house, a house in which paupers are maintained at public expense, those who are able-bodied being compelled to work. In these establishments the pauper inmates are employed according to their capacity and ability. Religious and secular instruction is supplied, while habits of industry, cleanliness and order are enforced. In the United States the name is often applied to a place where short prison sentences are served, the offenders being compelled to do manual labor during their confinement. These houses are more properly known as *houses of correction*.

World's Columbian Exposition, an international exposition of arts and industries, in commemoration of the four hundredth anniversary of the discovery of America by Columbus. It was built in Jackson Park, Chicago, on the shore of Lake Michigan, and was open from May 1 till November 1, 1893. The construction of the exposition occupied two years, besides the time consumed in preparatory work, such as study, investigation and advertising. The exposition was formally opened May 1, 1893, Grover Cleveland, then president of the United States, setting the intricate machinery in motion by pressing a button connected with electrical appliances. His opening address was listened to by an assemblage estimated at fully 400,000 people. The exhibition comprised over 400 buildings, covering fully 200 acres of ground. Fifteen of these buildings were occupied by special classes of exhibits, of individuals, firms, states and nations, every important nation on the globe being represented in some one or more departments. The largest building was the Manufactures and Liberal Arts Building, 787 by 1687 feet in size, covering nearly forty acres, including the surrounding colonnade, and costing $1,500,000. Its enormous roof was supported by the largest steel arches ever used in building construction. Besides the buildings used for the exposition proper, nearly every state in the Union and many foreign nations erected buildings for social and exhibition purposes.

The architectural beauty of the whole exposition was one of its greatest triumphs, and, indeed, it has rarely, if ever, been excelled. The center of the main group of buildings was the Court of Honor, consisting of a wide plaza, with a lagoon in its center, having at one end a beautiful electric fountain, sculptured by McMonnies, and terminated at the other by a graceful peristyle.

The whole cost of the exposition to its managers before the opening was more than $18,000,-000, the cost of operation exceeded $7,000,000, while the expenditures by states and foreign nations were not less than $8,000,000. Adding to this enormous sum the expenses incurred by private exhibitors, the total cost of the exposition was probably $40,000,000. The attendance from the opening to the closing day was 27,539,-041, or slightly less than the attendance at the Paris Exposition of 1889. The largest attendance upon any one day was on Chicago Day, October 9, when 716,881 people passed through its gates. One of the most novel and interesting features of the exposition was the Midway Plaisance, a boulevard 600 feet wide, connecting Jackson and Washington Parks. Along the sides of this avenue was arranged a motley collection of amusement enterprises, the most interesting consisting of representative scenes from the life of various peoples of Europe, Africa and the Orient.

An interesting and important feature of this fair was the World's Congress Auxiliary, consisting of special congresses on all the main topics of human interest, social, physical, industrial, educational, philosophical, commercial and religious. The congresses of religion presented features of peculiar interest, being attended by representatives of the Hindu, Buddhist, Shintoo, Mohammedan, Zoroastrian and various other religions of Asia and Africa, as well as by the most illustrious divines of Europe and America.

Worms, *wurmz,* a term loosely applied to many small, rather long, creeping animals, lacking feet entirely, or having very short ones, including such various forms as the earthworm, the grubs of certain insects and intestinal parasites. The zoölogist, however, confines the term to animals belonging to the branch known as Vermes, and accordingly he excludes the larvae of all insects. See Vermes.

Worms, *vorms,* a city of Germany, situated on the Rhine, 26 mi. s. e. of Mainz and 20 mi. n. w. of Heidelberg. It is an old city and contains many objects which are of interest because of their antiquity. Among these is the cathedral, which dates from the twelfth century, the Paulus Kirche, of about the same date, and a synagogue, which is still older. On Luther Platz is a monument to Luther, and it was in this city that he appeared before the diet in 1521 and refused to retract his theses (See Luther, Martin). The industries include the manufacture of textiles, leather, machinery, chemicals and chicory. Population in 1910, 46,819.

Wormwood, *wurm'wood,* the common name of several plants, members of the Compositae family. Common wormwood, a well-known plant, is celebrated for its intensely bitter tonic and stimulating qualities, which have led to its use as an ingredient in various medicinal preparations and even in the preparation of liquors. It is also useful in destroying worms in children. The French make absinthe from wormwood.

Worsted, *woos'ted* or *wur'sted,* a variety of woolen yarn or thread, spun from long staple wool, which has been combed, and which in the spinning is twisted harder than ordinary. Formerly the use of worsted was confined to stockings, carpets and other coarse fabrics, but it is now extensively used in the manufacture of cloth for men's and women's clothing. See Woolen Manufacture.

Worth, *wurth,* William Jenkins (1794–1849), an American soldier, born in Hudson, N. Y. He served in the War of 1812, winning special distinction at Chippewa and Lundy's Lane, where he was severely wounded. Later he served in campaigns against the Seminole, and during the Mexican War he fought under General Taylor, being brevetted major general for gallantry at Monterey. He then served under General Scott, distinguished himself at Cerro Gordo, Churubusco, Molino del Rey and Chapultepec, and conducted the preliminary negotiations for the surrender of the City of Mexico. After the close of the war, he commanded the Department of Texas until his death.

Wounds, *woondz* or *wowndz,* injuries to any of the soft parts of the body, occasioned by external violence and attended by a greater or less amount of bleeding. Wounds have been classified as follows: (a) *Cuts, incisions,* or *incised wounds,* which are produced by sharp-edged instruments; (b) *stabs,* or *punctured wounds,* made by the thrusts of pointed weapons; (c) *contused wounds,* produced by hard, blunt, obtuse bodies; (d) *lacerated wounds,* in which there is tearing or laceration, as by some rough instrument; (e) all those common injuries called *gunshot wounds;* (f) *poisoned wounds,* those complicated with the introduction of some poison or venom into the part. If wounds are of such a nature that the edges can be brought together closely, and if then bacteria can be kept out, healing "by first intention" takes place rapidly and with little inflammation. When wounds are deep and open, they are slower in healing (See GRANULATION). Wounds poisoned by chemicals or by bacteria are liable to be serious, and sometimes an apparently trifling injury of this sort results in death.

The first step to be taken in the treatment of any of the wounds mentioned above is to stop the bleeding by binding tight the artery or vein which has been opened. Then thoroughly cleanse the wound with warm water, removing all foreign matter, and wash with some good antiseptic, such as boric acid in saturated solution. Finally, bandage the wound with perfectly clean gauze or light cloth. These bandages should be removed frequently, and the wound should again be cleaned, disinfected and redressed.

Wrang'ler, in Cambridge University, the name given to those who have attained the first class in the public examination, for honors in mathematics, commonly called the *mathematical tripos.* The student taking the first place is called the *senior wrangler.* See CAMBRIDGE, UNIVERSITY OF.

Wren, a very active little bird, of the creeper family. A number of different species are common in America, Europe and Asia. The wrens are distinguished by their small size, slender beaks, short, rounded wings, mottled plumage and erect tails. The common *house wren* of the United States builds its nest in boxes prepared for it, or in crevices, wherever it can find them, seeming to have no fear of human beings and never hesitating to attack cats, dogs, swallows

WREN

and other birds, whenever they near its habitation. The eggs are from three to nine in number and are white or spotted. The song of the wren is melodious and flute-like, and its amusing ways make it a great favorite everywhere. It destroys large numbers of noxious insects; it is therefore a friend of the farmer and amply repays any care that may be taken of it.

Wren, CHRISTOPHER, Sir (1632–1723), one of the greatest of English architects, born in Knowle, Wiltshire. He was educated at Waldham College, Oxford, became a fellow of All Souls in 1653, was appointed professor of astronomy at Gresham College later, and afterward was elected Savilian professor of astronomy at Oxford. He had been appointed by Charles II to restore old Saint Paul's, but after the great fire in 1666, it became necessary to rebuild the cathedral. In preparing his plans he was considerably hampered by the ecclesiastical authority, but with the king's permission he modified and improved the design as the building proceeded. Among the other notable buildings which Wren designed are the modern part of the palace at Hampton Court; the library of Trinity College, Cambridge; the hospitals of Chelsea and Greenwich; the Church of Saint Stephen's, Walbrook; those of Saint Mary-le-bow and Saint Michael, Cornhill; that of Saint Bride, Fleet Street, and the campanile of Christ Church, Oxford. In 1680 he was chosen president of the royal works, and from 1685 to 1700 he represented various boroughs in Parliament. Over the north doorway of Saint Paul's is a memorial tablet, on which are the well-known words, *Si* *monumentum requiris, circumspice* (If thou seek his monument, look about thee).

Wrench, a tool, consisting of a bar of metal with jaws adapted to catch upon the head of a bolt or a nut. in order to turn it. Some wrenches

WRENCH

have a variety of jaws, to suit different sizes and shapes oi nuts and bolts, and others, as the monkey-wrench, have an adjustable inner jaw.

Wrestling, *res'ling*, a sport of great antiquity, in which one person tries to throw another to the ground. In all the Greek athletic contests, wrestling bore a prominent part, the contestants going into the combats with their bodies oiled and made as slippery as possible. Among the Romans the sport was equally popular, and all through the Middle Ages wrestling bouts were common; but they grew to be very rough and so dangerous that frequently men were maimed or even killed. In England the sport died out during the Reformation, but was revived again, and of recent years it has come to be extremely popular. A number of different methods are well recognized. *Collar and elbow wrestling* is a system in which the opponents stand facing each other, before beginning the contest, and seize each other by the clothing at the collar and elbow. To count a *fall*, either two hips and one shoulder, or two shoulders and one hip, must be on the carpet at the same time. If either man loses his hold with one or both hands, in order to save himself from a fall, he is counted as losing the fall. A bout usually consists of three or five falls, with intervals of rest of from ten to twenty minutes between. In *Graeco-Roman wrestling* the contestants do not wear the heavy jacket and trousers of the collar and elbow class, but are usually clothed only with the trunks of the athlete. Any hold whatever above the waist is permissible, and a fall is counted whenever two shoulders strike the ground simultaneously. The men are not allowed to strike or scratch or to clasp their own hands together, nor to interlace their fingers, but they may grasp their own wrists. *Catch-as-catch-can wrestling* is a further modification, in which any hold is permissible. In the Graeco-Roman and catch-as-catch-can styles, no clothing for the feet is allowed excepting socks or thin slippers. The men are not allowed to do anything to injure an opponent,

but even under the rules, the catch-as-catch-can is a rough, strenuous affair, suitable only for the strong. A fall is won when the opponent has two shoulders on the mat at the same time. There are a number of recognized "holds," which give a wrestler great advantage over his opponents; such, for instance, as the *grape-vine lock*, the *chancery*, the *half-Nelson* and the *hammer-lock*. What these terms mean can be learned from the manuals on the subject.

One of the best methods of wrestling for boys and youths is that which belongs particularly to Cumberland, England, and is known as the *back-hold catch*. The opponents stand close together, each with his chin on the shoulder of the other, and each grasping the other about the body, the right arm of each under the left arm of his opponent. At a signal the wrestling begins, and every means is allowed except kicking or any unnecessary roughness or brutality. If one of the contestants unclasps his hands, or if he is thrown so that both shoulders touch the floor, he loses. In this kind of wrestling the first step to certain success is to get the right shoulder beneath the armpit of the opponent.

Wright, *rite*, CARROLL DAVIDSON (1840–1909), an American economist, statistician and legislator, born at Dunbarton, N. H. He received an academic education, was admitted to the bar and served in the Civil War, becoming colonel of volunteers. He was elected to the Massachusetts senate in 1872 and in the following year became chief of the state bureau of labor statistics. From 1885 to 1902 he was United States commissioner of labor, being responsible for the publication of many exceedingly valuable bulletins and studies of phases of the labor problem. In 1895 he was appointed honorary professor of social economics at the Catholic University of America; in 1900 he was professor of statistics and social economics in Columbian University, also lecturer at Harvard; and in 1902 he became president of the college department of Clark University, Worcester, Mass. He was the author of many works on labor questions, and in 1902 he was appointed by President Roosevelt a member and recorder of the United States Anthracite Strike Commission. He was also made one of the trustees of the Carnegie Institution at Washington, at its foundation.

Wright, HORATIO GOUVERNEUR (1820–1899). an American soldier, born at Clinton, Conn., and educated at West Point. He entered the engineering department of the army, and after the opening of the Civil War he performed important service at Bull Run. He was made brigadier general of volunteers in September, 1861, having command in Florida. He also commanded a division during Lee's second invasion of Pennsylvania in 1863 and was with Grant during his Virginia campaign in the following spring. He was wounded at Spottsylvania and was brevetted colonel for gallantry in that battle. In July, 1864, General Wright commanded the corps which opposed Early's advance upon Washington. He later took part in the Shenandoah campaign, under General Sheridan, and was wounded at Cedar Creek, but later returned to Grant's army and led the final assault against the Confederate works, April 2, 1865.

Wright, ORVILLE (1871–   ), WILBUR (1867–1912), two brothers who have won distinction in the United States and Europe by their inventions and exploits in aviation. Orville was born in Dayton, Ohio, and Wilbur in Millville, Indiana. Both were educated in the public schools. They began to study aeronautics in 1896. At this time they had a small shop in Dayton, Ohio, where they made and repaired bicycles. In 1900 they began experiments in aviation with machines of their own invention and manufacture, and three years later they had produced a machine which would remain in the air over a minute. The perfection of this machine resulted in the celebrated Wright biplane, now in successful use in navigating the air. In 1909 the Wright aeroplane was accepted by the United States government for use in the army, and it has been brought to such a degree of perfection that flights of several hundred miles are becoming known. See FLYING MACHINES.

Writ, in law, a written command, issued by the authority and in the name of the sovereign or the state, for the purpose of compelling a person to do something therein mentioned. It is issued by a court or other competent authority, and action under it must be accounted for to the same. It must be under seal and attested by the proper officer, and it is directed to the sheriff or some other officer legally authorized to execute it. Among the most common writs are the following: The writ of *habeas corpus* (See HABEAS CORPUS); of *summons*, commanding an authorized officer to notify a person to appear in court to answer to a complaint; of *replevin*, an order permitting the recovery of goods illegally seized; of *mandamus*,

commanding a person, corporation or inferior court to do something pertaining to their office or duty; of *injunction* (See INJUNCTION); of *capias* (See CAPIAS); of *quo warranto*, a command to show by what right an act is done or an office held; of *error*, issued to remove an action to a higher court, by reason of error in the proceedings of the inferior court; of *certiorari*, issued by a court of review, requiring the record of a case to be sent up from an inferior court for examination; of *subpoena* (See WITNESS); of *attachment* (See ATTACHMENT).

Writing, the art of recording thoughts, by means of visible signs on some material substance. It is usually divided into *ideographic* writing, in which signs represent ideas, and *phonetic* writing, in which signs represent sounds. Ideographic writing, in its earliest form, is supposed to have been an attempt to convey ideas by copying objects direct from nature, and this form of it has thus acquired the name of picture writing. After this came symbolical writing, in which abbreviated pictures were used as arbitrary symbols, first of things and still later of sounds and words. This indicates the transition into phonetic writing, in which the signs may either represent a whole syllable or only a single sound, in which case they are called alphabetic symbols. Of the systems of writing in which sounds represent syllables, the best-known is the Chinese. In a system of this kind, of course, a single sound may have various meanings, and it is often necessary to add to a syllable some sign to indicate what meaning is intended. Various systems of writing differ, also, in the way in which the symbols are arranged. Thus the Chinese signs are read in columns from top to bottom, the Mexican picture writing is read from bottom to top, the Hebrew writing is from right to left, and Latin, Greek and all modern European languages, as well as Sanskrit, from left to right.

Writing was introduced to the Western nations by the Phoenicians, and the Phoenician system was based on the Egyptian (See HIEROGLYPHICS). The cuneiform writing, another ancient system, invented by the Akkadian inhabitants of Chaldea, was also adapted to several languages, as the Assyrian and the Persian, in a variety of ways, ideographic, syllabic and alphabetic. From the hieratic writing, the second of the three distinct kinds of Egyptian writing, the Phoenician and other Semitic systems of writing were derived. The leading Semitic forms are the Samaritan, or ancient Hebrew; the Chaldee, or East Aramaic; the Syriac, or West Aramaic; the Kufic, or early Arabic, and the Neshki, or modern Arabic. At what time writing was introduced into Greece is not known with certainty, but the ancient belief was that Cadmus had brought with him to Boeotia the Phoenician system of writing, about the seventeenth century B. C.; and the resemblance of certain Greek letters to the corresponding Phoenician letters shows that there was undoubtedly a connection. Like the Semites, the Greeks originally wrote from right to left. The Greek forms spread to Sicily and to Italy and were modified in various ways as they spread.

Before the spread of Greek and Roman influence in Europe systems of writing existed in various countries. Thus the Gauls are known to have practiced writing, and the ancient inhabitants of Britain are said by Caesar to have employed it. No remains of it exist, however. In medieval manuscripts a variety of styles were adopted in different epochs and countries. Capitals were not then used, as now, to distinguish prominent words, but whole manuscripts were written in large or small capitals. Uncial letters, which prevailed from the seventh to the tenth century, were rounded capitals, with few hair strokes. Gothic characters, which were merely fanciful deviations from the Roman types, became common in inscriptions from the thirteenth to the fifteenth century, and were employed in church books from the time of Saint Louis. In England, a variety of styles called Saxon prevailed in the early Middle Ages. A mixed style was formed of a combination of Roman, Lombardic and Saxon characters; the Norman style came in with William the Conqueror, and the English court hand, an adaptation of Saxon, prevailed from the sixteenth century to the reign of George II.

There have been various attempts made to introduce systems of phonetic writing, in which each sound should be reproduced by one invariable sign. Systems of shorthand writing are generally phonetic.

Writ of Assis'tance, in American history, a writ issued by a court, instructing a competent official to search premises for goods smuggled into the colonies. These writs differed from search warrants in not naming the particular premises which the officers were authorized to search, in not being limited as to time and in not requiring a report from the officer. The first writ of this kind was issued in 1761 and aroused the greatest opposition. James Otis, advocate-general of the colony of Massachusetts, resigned his office and became leading attorney in a case in opposition to the issuance of the writs. In his appeal to the court he uttered radical sentiments in opposition to the king and Parliament. The writ was declared legal, but it was rarely, if ever, used. See WARRANT.

Wry'neck, a small bird of the woodpecker family, characterized by a rounded tail of soft

WRYNECK

feathers. The common wryneck is the European bird, about seven inches long, which feeds on insects, especially upon ants. It takes its name from its peculiar habit of moving its neck in an undulating, snake-like manner.

Württemberg, *vürt'em berK*, a kingdom of Germany, situated in the southern part of the Empire, and bounded on the e. and s. by Bavaria and on the s. w. and n. by Baden. It has an area of 7528 sq. mi., and in 1910 its population was 2,437,574. The government is a constitutional monarchy, the executive power being vested in a sovereign and the legislative power devolving jointly upon the sovereign and the parliament, which is composed of an upper and a lower chamber. The lower house is composed of 93 members, elected every six years. The kingdom is represented by 4 members in the Bundesrat and by 17 members in the Reichstag. In the Middle Ages, Württemberg was a county. It was erected into a duchy in 1495 and became a kingdom in 1806. At the formation of the German Empire, in 1871, it became a member of that government. For surface, climate and products, see GERMANY.

Würzburg, *vürts'boorK*, a city of Bavaria, situated on the Main, 140 mi. n. w. of Munich and 60 mi. s. e. of Frankfort. The city contains a number of churches that are of interest because of their antiquity, one dating from the eleventh century and another from the fourteenth. The educational institutions include the university, an art museum and a picture gallery. The town also maintains a botanical garden and a school of music. The industries include the manufacture of machinery, tobacco, wines, liquors, vinegar and chocolate. Population in 1910, 84,496.

Wu Ting-Fang, *woo'ting'jahng'*, (1842–   ), a Chinese statesman. In 1874 he went to England to study law and became a barrister. As secretary of the peace commission which made the treaty at the close of the war with Japan, he won such distinction that he was appointed minister to the United States in 1896. During the siege of Peking, in 1900, Minister Wu succeeded in sending a dispatch in cipher to Minister Conger, of the United States legation, and received a reply. This assured the powers that the legations were alive and averted a war of devastation. In 1902 Minister Wu was placed at the head of foreign affairs in the Chinese government. In 1908 he was returned to the United States, remaining for two years.

Wyandotte, *wi'an dot.* See HURON.

Wyandotte, MICH., a city in Wayne co., 12 mi. s. by w. of Detroit, on the Detroit River and on the Lake Shore & Michigan Southern, the Michigan Central and other railroads. It contains extensive chemical works, a steel shipbuilding plant, salt works, a fur coat factory, breweries and various other factories The city has a public library and owns and operates the waterworks and electric light plant. The place was settled in 1850, and the city was incorporated in 1867. Population in 1910, 8287.

Wyandotte Cave, a natural cavern, situated in Crawford co., Ind., 5 mi. n. w. of Leavenworth. It is next to Mammoth Cave in size and has been explored for about 23 miles. It is noted for its large chambers, some of which are 200 feet high and 300 feet broad. The stalactite formations in this cave are of unusual magnitude and beauty. Those in the room known as the Pillared Palace are of unusual interest, while Monument Mountain is a collection of stalagmites 175 feet high.

Wy'ant, ALEXANDER H. (1836–1892), an American landscape painter, born at Port Washington, Ohio. He studied at Düsseldorf, Germany, under Hans Gude, and made attractive studies in Ireland of the lakes of Killarney. His studies of autumn effects in American forests and views of nature in the Adirondacks and along

184

the Ohio River brought him more than American fame. Among his oil paintings are *View on Lake George, An October Day* and *Landscape.*

Wycliffe or **Wiclif,** *wik'lif*, JOHN, (about 1320–1384), an English reformer, born at Hipswell, in Yorkshire, England. Of his early life we know nothing. At sixteen he entered Oxford and soon became a fellow of Merton College, which was distinguished for the great learning of its faculty. Under Thomas Bradwardine he studied Aristotelian philosophy, scholastic theology and law, and he became master of Balliol College and warden of Canterbury Hall. He zealously applied himself to the study of the Scriptures, which he subjected to the most critical analysis, and he early manifested a skepticism in regard to ecclesiastical doctrine and discipline. Disputes were going on at this period between Edward III and the Papal court, concerning tribute exacted from King John, and the English Parliament had resolved to support the sovereign in his refusal to submit to the vassalage. Wycliffe took a prominent part in this affair, urging King Edward to refuse the tribute to the Holy See. Pope Gregory XI, on learning of Wycliffe's defiant attitude toward the Church in regard to this matter, wrote letters to the king, to the archbishop of Canterbury and to the University of Oxford, to have him tried for heresy. In subsequent sermons, Wycliffe attacked the higher clergy, accusing them of having assumed undue power and unbecoming arrogance. In February, 1378, he appeared before Archbishop Courtenay in Canterbury Cathedral, attended by John of Gaunt and other friends. The people who were present became so angered against Wycliffe that he and his friends had to flee for their lives. He retained the favor of the king and soon afterward was awarded a pro essorship of divinity in the University of Oxford. In 1380 he opposed the doctrine of transubstantiation at Oxford, and two years later he was summoned to appear before a commission of bishops and doctors at London. He refused to attend, taking advantage of the privileges of the university. The trial went on without his presence. Ten out of twenty-four articles culled from his writings were condemned as heretical, and fourteen were declared to be erroneous. By an order from the crown, he was deprived of his professorship and expelled from the university. He returned to Lutterworth, in Leicestershire, where Edward had given him a rectory. Here he labored zealously and unweariedly, as a preacher and pastor. Part of his time was spent in translating the Bible from the Vulgate, with the assistance of some of his friends. He continued to write unceasingly and boldly against the papal claims, upholding the Scripture itself as the highest explanation of the divine law and urging the importance of teaching it to every Christian and hence the duty of giving it to the world in the common tongue of the people. He sent out young men with the Bible, to preach the plain, straightforward word of God. These men were known as *poor priests*, and the people heard them gladly.

On Dec. 28, 1384, while hearing mass, he was seized with paralysis and died a few days later.

Wycliffe's followers were active in spreading his teachings, which for about a generation after his death acted as a powerful religious and political factor among the English people. Before Wycliffe's time there had been no systematic attempt to translate the whole Bible into English, and hence the vast importance of the version known as Wycliffe's Bible. Aside from its value from a theological point of view, Wycliffe's Bible was one of the most important contributions to the growing standard of English prose.

Wyo'ming, the EQUALITY STATE, one of the Plateau states, bounded on the n. by Montana, on the e. by South Dakota and Nebraska, on the s. by Colorado and Utah and on the w. by Utah, Idaho and Montana. From east to west the length is 355 mi.; the width from north to south is 276 mi. and the total area is 97,914 sq. mi. Population in 1910, 145,965.

SURFACE AND DRAINAGE. The surface of the state, for the most part, is composed of mountains and plateaus. The great plains of the Mississippi valley slope away from the foothills in the east. The elevation varies from 3500 to 14,000 feet. The main axis of the Rocky Mountains, which forms the Continental Divide, extends from north to south across the state. The northern group of these mountains finds here its greatest development and is noted for its wild and rugged character and for its picturesque scenery. Yellowstone National Park, 3600 square miles in area, occupies the northwestern corner of the state (See YELLOWSTONE NATIONAL PARK). In the west central part are the Wind River Mountains; in the north central part, the Big Horn Mountains, and in the extreme northeast, the Black Hills, extending into South Dakota; in the southeast is the Laramie range; in the south, the Medicine Bow Mountains, and in the west the Teton, Gros Ventre and Shoshone

ranges. The southwestern portion of the state slopes towards the Pacific Ocean and forms a part of the Grand River valley. From the eastern and western slopes of the Rocky Mountains, several rivers take their rise, among them the North Platte, the Green, the Snake, the Laramie and the Shoshone.

CLIMATE. Wyoming has the typical climate of the mountainous region of the northwest. The air is pure and dry, clear weather prevails and the high altitude is for many healthful. The average annual temperature is 45.5°; the mean annual rainfall, 12.98 inches.

MINERAL RESOURCES. In every mountain range of Wyoming, gold, silver, lead and copper ores are to be found, but as yet the resources have not been largely developed. Coal mining is most important, the annual output being over 6,000,000 tons, and there are over 20,000 square miles of coal lands, from which a steadily increasing amount is being mined. Valuable iron deposits are found in various localities in the state, but the mines are as yet undeveloped. Petroleum has been found in Fremont and Natrona counties, and several wells have been bored, but the development of the oil industry awaits better transportation facilities. Extensive phosphate beds are found in Uinta County. The state also possesses extensive deposits of soda and an abundance of valuable building stone.

AGRICULTURE. Below the timber line, the mountains are covered with forests of coniferous trees. Between the mountain ranges are broad plateaus, with arable soils, which by means of proper irrigation yield prolific crops. On account of the slight rainfall it has been supposed that only a small part of the state was capable of cultivation. However, modern methods of moisture conservation have brought vast areas under cultivation. Irrigation ditches also have been carried long distances from the source of water supply. The result has been an immense increase in the tillable area. The raising of livestock is the most important agricultural industry. The nutritive grasses which so abundantly cover the great ranges of pasturage support many thousands of cattle and sheep.

Irrigation is being largely extended. The Shoshone project, the greatest in the state, includes a remarkable dam, 328 feet high, across a narrow canyon. The dam is only 85 feet long at the bottom and 200 feet at the top. A smaller dam diverts the waters of the Shoshone River, through a tunnel 3¼ miles long, into a canal which for 40 miles passes only the upper edge of a broad and fertile valley containing 150,000 acres. Near Douglas, in Converse county, and in Johnson and Sheridan counties there are large irrigated areas.

MANUFACTURES. As Wyoming is an agricultural and mineral state and still in the first steps of material development, it has no distinctive manufacturing interests. The most important manufacturing industry is car construction and railway repair, and next in importance is the manufacture of lumber and timber products.

TRANSPORTATION. The principal railroads are the Union Pacific, the Chicago, Burlington & Quincy and the Chicago & Northwestern. The total operative mileage is about 1600. A system of local railway, which will make possible the development of the various resources of the state, is much needed. From railway terminals to interior towns, transportation is by means of cattle, mule or horse equipment.

GOVERNMENT. The legislature is composed of a senate of 28 members and a lower house of 56 members, elected for two years. The sessions are biennial, and are limited to forty days. The executive department consists of a governor, a secretary of state, an auditor, a treasurer and a superintendent of public instruction, each elected for four years. The courts consist of a supreme court, consisting of a chief justice and two associates, and such inferior courts as the legislature may establish.

EDUCATION. The University of Wyoming, chartered in 1886, is situated at Laramie and is the leading educational institution. The expenses of the public school system are provided for in part by the rental of government lands which are set aside for school purposes. The total extent of lands which may be so used is 3,600,000 acres. The course of instruction throughout the state has been made uniform, and free text-books are supplied by the state. There are several valuable libraries. The State Law Library numbers 20,000 volumes and that of the state university, 30,000 volumes. Provision is made by the state for a library in each county, and most of the school districts have small libraries.

INSTITUTIONS. There is a soldiers' home at Buffalo, a hospital for the insane at Evanston and a state hospital at Rock Springs. The penitentiary is at Rawlins.

CITIES. The chief cities are Cheyenne, the capital; Laramie, Rock Springs, Sheridan, Rawlins, Casper and Douglas.

HISTORY. The territory of Wyoming was a part of the Louisiana Purchase, but at that time it contained no permanent settlements, the first being established in 1834. The discovery of gold after the Civil War led to an increase of population, and Wyoming was organized into a territory in 1869. After that time several indian outbreaks occurred. Yellowstone National Park was created in 1872, and Wyoming was admitted as a state in 1890. In 1892 occurred the "Johnson County raid," when a band of fifty armed cattlemen invaded the central part of the state with the announced intention of shooting all the men considered to be cattle thieves. After killing two settlers supposed thieves, the cattlemen were besieged in some ranch buildings by a superior number of settlers. The siege was finally raised by a troop of United States cavalry, who took the cattlemen as prisoners to Cheyenne. They were held for murder, but were later released without trial. This was but an incident in the long conflict between the cattlemen and the settlers who broke up the free range and sometimes stole calves and unbranded cattle. In 1912 Wyoming had the greatest crops in its history.

Wyoming, UNIVERSITY OF, a state university open to both sexes and founded at Laramie in 1886. It maintains preparatory and collegiate departments. In 1910 its faculty numbered 40 and there were 300 students. The library contains 30,000 volumes and the annual income is $180,000.

Wyoming Valley Mas'sacre, a fearful massacre in the Wyoming Valley, Pa., on July 3 and 4, 1778, perpetrated by an English and indian force against the Yankee inhabitants of the valley. A vast majority of the inhabitants, including women and children, were slain during the two days, and the rest fled eastward to the nearest settlements. The valley was not settled again for several years.

X, the twenty-fourth letter of the alphabet and the representative of what might as well be denoted by *ks* or *gs*. The letter *x* was until a late date the last in the Roman alphabet, but *y* and *z* were finally added from the Greek. As an initial letter, it is pronounced like *z*, as in *Xenophon*.

In algebra, *x* is the usual symbol for the unknown quantity. In Roman numerals X signifies ten, perhaps from the fact that it represents a V standing upon a second V inverted.

Xalapa, *ha lah'pa*. See JALAPA.

Xanthippe, *zan thip'pe*, the scolding wife of the philosopher Socrates, whose forbearance with her quarrelsome temper was a salient trait in his character. The name has become proverbial as that of a scolding shrew.

Xanthus, *zan'thus*, the capital of ancient Lycia, situated on the river Xanthus, in the s. w. corner of Asia Minor, near the present village of Gunik. The city was twice destroyed by the Persians, the last time in 546 B. C. It was sacked by the Romans under Brutus in 43 B. C. At the time of its greatest prosperity, it was a place of remarkable magnificence. Excavations have disclosed sculptures and architectural ornaments which show something of its former grandeur. One of these sculptures, known as the Harpy Tomb, is now in the British Museum. The friezes of other buildings represent battles, sports and banquets, while other excavations have revealed works of Roman origin. The date of these works is unknown, but it is supposed that many of them are of a period nearly five hundred years before the beginning of the Christian era.

Xavier, *zav'e ur*, FRANCISCO (1506–1552), now spelled *Javier*, a missionary and saint of the Roman Catholic Church, usually styled the "Apostle of the Indies." He was a native of northern Spain, the son of a nobleman whose family seat was Xavier. He was sent to Paris to be educated, and with Loyola he founded the Society of Jesus. In the early part of 1540, he

was chosen for the mission to India. From Goa, where he arrived in May, 1542, he extended his labors southward to Ceylon, Malacca and Celebes. He spent two years in Japan and returned to Goa to organize a mission to China, but before he could overcome the difficulties in his way, he died. Xavier was canonized in 1619, and in 1747 Benedict XIV declared him the Protector of India.

Xenia, *ze'ne a*, OHIO, the county-seat of Green co., 16 mi. e. by s. of Dayton, on the Cincinnati, Hamilton & Dayton, the Pennsylvania and several electric railroads. The city is pleasantly located on rolling ground, surrounded by a productive farming region. There are extensive cordage works, shoe factories, powder mills, machine shops and automobile and other works. It is the seat of the Xenia Theological Seminary and of the Ohio Soldiers' and Sailors' Orphans' Home. It contains a good courthouse, a Carnegie library, sixteen churches and two banks. Three miles northeast of the town is Wilberforce University, an institution for colored students, containing college and industrial departments. Xenia was settled in 1803 and was incorporated five years later. Population in 1910, 8706.

Xenophon, *zen'o fon*, (about 434–about 355 B. C.), an Athenian historian and general, one of the pupils of Socrates. When about forty, he joined the expedition of Cyrus against Artaxerxes, and after the Battle of Cunaxa he led the ten thousand Greek mercenaries, who had belonged to the army of Cyrus, back to the coast of the Black Sea. After his return he was banished from Athens, either because of his part in the expedition of Cyrus, or because he aided the Spartans, and he passed the latter years of his life in exile. Xenophon wrote numerous works, and all of these, it would seem, have come down to us. The chief are the *Anabasis*, which describes the expedition of Cyrus already referred to, especially the retreat of the Ten Thousand; the *Memorabilia*, a record of the life and teachings of Socrates; the *Hellenica*, which gives a somewhat dull account of forty-eight years of Grecian history and is a continuation of the history of Thucydides, and the *Cyropaedia*, a fictitious biography of Cyrus the Elder of Persia. Of Xenophon it may be said, that of all the classic writers he is the most commonplace. He was a man of strong, though not of great, mind. He is sensible, lively and natural; moreover, he is one of the best sources of information regarding some of the most important events that have ever happened and the greatest people the world has ever seen.

Xerxes, *zurk'seez,* (about 519–465 B. C.), a celebrated Persian king, probably the Ahasuerus of the Bible. He was the son of Darius. On his father's death, in 485, he came to the throne and immediately prepared to carry out the invasion of Greece, the preparations for which had been begun by his father. These preparations were on the most enormous scale. Provisions were stored up on the intended route for three years, a transport fleet was collected, the engineering skill of the day was exerted to remove land obstacles and the resources of the vast Persian Empire were taxed to the utmost to produce an armament sufficient to crush Greece. According to ancient computation, the invading army numbered over two million, and although this, possibly, is an exaggeration, it must have been numerically the greatest army on record. At the head of his enormous host, Xerxes advanced unopposed till he came to Thermopylae, but here his fleet was seriously damaged by a storm, while the narrow pass was effectually held by Leonidas, at the head of a determined, though small, band of Spartans. At last the passage was effected through treachery, and Xerxes marched on through Phocis and Boeotia to Athens, which he entered without opposition. In the meantime the Persian fleet had met with several mishaps. In two engagements with the Greek ships at Artemisium, it had suffered considerable damage, and a storm which occurred between the two conflicts was the cause of still greater loss. Finally, at Salamis (480 B. C.) a naval battle was fought, one of the most decisive in the history of the world, in which the Persians were defeated with terrible loss. Xerxes, who from a lofty eminence had watched the destruction of his fleet, gave up the command of the invading army to Mardonius and fled panic-stricken to Sardis. He spent the rest of his life in obscurity and was finally murdered by Artabanus, the commander of his bodyguard, who was plotting to make himself king of Persia.

Ximenes, *ze mee'neez,* Francisco or **Ximenes de Cisneros** (1436–1517), called Cardinal Ximenes, a Spanish churchman, born at Torredelaguna in New Castile. Queen Isabella chose him as her confessor, because of his piety and learning; he was appointed archbishop of Toledo in 1495, but was too modest to accept until he was commanded to by the pope. He founded the University of Alcala de Henares and directed the preparation of a Polyglot Bible, called the *Complutensian.* On the death of Philip, in 1506, he was appointed regent and guardian of Queen Joanna, who was insane. He made the citizens of towns form militia regiments, and this, while it reduced the power of the nobles, promoted that of the Crown. In 1507 he was made cardinal, and in 1516 he became, by the will of Ferdinand, regent of all Castile, during the absence of King Charles.

Xingu, *sheen goo',* **River,** a large river of Brazil, which rises in the south central part of the country, where it is formed by the union of four smaller streams, and flows in a northerly direction, joining the Amazon 230 miles southwest of Para. Its length is about 1200 miles. Its course is frequently interrupted by falls and rapids, so that the river is of but little use to navigation.

X-Ray. See Roentgen Rays.

Xylophone, *zi'lo fone,* a musical instrument, composed of graduated bars of wood, played

XYLOPHONE

by being struck with small hammers or rubbed with resined gloves.

X Y Z Cor'respon'dence, the name given to the dispatches sent in 1797–1798 to the United States government by its commissioners, Charles Pinckney, John Marshall and Elbridge Gerry, in Paris. These men were sent to France to settle certain difficulties with that government. On their arrival they were not received officially, but were compelled to communicate with the government through three agents, who informed them that the first step toward negotiation would be the payment of a large sum of money to the Directory, which was then in control of French affairs. The American commissioners, with the exception of Gerry. promptly withdrew and transmitted the correspondence to President Adams. who, in turn, laid it before Congress. substituting for the names of the French commissioners the letters X Y Z. The correspondence aroused the bitterest feeling in the United States, and a naval war with France was actually begun. but the French government receded from its position and thus averted a struggle.

Y, the twenty-fifth letter of the English alphabet, resembling in its form the Greek upsilon. It is, like *w*, both a consonant and a vowel, but it differs from *w* in that it is often used by itself as a vowel, as in *by*, *deny*, *pony*. In this use it is superfluous, as it might be replaced by *i*.

In algebra, *y* stands for the second of the unknown quantities.

Y, THE, an arm of the Zuider Zee, on its west side, in the Province of North Holland. It is 21 miles in length, with an average breadth of little over a mile. The city of Amsterdam is situated on its south shore.

Yablonoi, *yah blo noi'*, **Mountains,** a system of mountains, situated in eastern Siberia and extending in a north-northeast direction. Their length is about 1000 miles. They appear to merge into the Stanovoi. The highest points are in the southwest and are over 8000 feet in altitude.

Yacht, *yot*, a sailing boat kept for pleasure, as for traveling or for racing. There are three principal rigs for yachts—cutter, schooner and yawl. A cutter has one mast and a running bowsprit and usually carries four sails, namely, mainsail, gaff-topsail, foresail and jib (See SAIL). A square sail is also frequently set by the larger vessels of this class. A schooner has two masts, mainmast and foremast, a standing bowsprit and jibboom, or not infrequently, instead of these, a running bowsprit, like that of a cutter. A yawl is rigged exactly like a cutter, with the addition of a small mizzenmast. It is a very convenient cruising rig and is becoming common for yachts of over 50 tons. Steam yachts are common, and in many localities they are put to practical uses by their owners. The speed attained by some is remarkable. See YACHTING.

Yachting, the sport of racing in yachts and boats with sails, for money or for prizes; also, the pastime of cruising for pleasure in sailing or steam vessels. The history of yachting is the history of yacht-racing, inasmuch as competition improved yachts, just as horse racing improved horses. In America, yachting has become a national sport, about one hundred leading clubs being in existence at the present time. Steam launches and yachts and naphtha launches are also extensively in use. The largest American steam yacht is the *Alva*, owned by W. K. Vanderbilt, which is 285 feet long and has a 32-foot beam. Yacht racing is an old-time amusement. The first of yacht clubs was established in 1720, though a race is recorded between Charles II, king of England, and his brother, duke of York, in 1661. In 1843 Queen Victoria began giving cups for racing prizes, and since that time the sport has been well established in England. International races began in 1851, at which time the *America* defeated fifteen English yachts in their own waters. The prize, which was a silver cup valued at $500, was given to the New York Yacht Club, to be kept thereafter as a trophy. From time to time the New York Yacht Club has been challenged for this cup, and races of world-wide interest have been sailed. In 1870 the *Cambria* was defeated. In 1885 the *Genesta* was defeated by the *Puritan*, and a year later the *Galatea* by the *Mayflower*. The *Volunteer*, the *Defender*, the *Reliance* are yachts that have more recently been successful in keeping the cup still in American hands. The principal competitors have been vessels constructed for the purpose by Sir Thomas Lipton, called the *Shamrock*, I, II and III. The races are usually sailed off Sandy Hook. See YACHT.

Yafa, *yah'fah*. See JAFFA.

Yak, an animal of the ox tribe, found only in Tibet, Asia. It is found wild and is the ordinary domestic animal of the inhabitants of that region, supplying milk, food and raiment, as well as serving as a beast of burden. The size is that of a small ox. The horns are long, nearly cylindrical, smooth and pointed at the ends, and they have a peculiar and characteristic curve. Some of the domestic yaks are hornless. Their most remarkable external characteristic is the excessive growth and peculiar distribution of the hair.

The upper parts of the body and sides are clothed with a thick, soft, woolly hair, more fully developed along the middle of the back, especially on the shoulders, where it forms a great bunch. From the upper parts of the limbs and the whole of the lower surface of the body hangs a thick growth of long, straight hair, in old animals sweeping the ground and almost concealing the somewhat short legs. The tail is profusely covered with a thick mass of such hairs. The wild animals are nearly uniformly black; the domestic yaks are often quite white. The silky and tough hair and the skins are often used in the manufacture of caps, coats, blankets and ropes.

Yakima, *yah'ke ma*, a name now given to those indians who live in Oregon, Washington and northern Idaho, south of the Columbia River. The Yakima proper live on the Yakima reservation in the foothills of the Cascade Mountains.

Yale, ELIHU (1648–1721), an English merchant and philanthropist, born near Boston. His father was one of the original settlers of New Haven, Connecticut. The son was educated in England and began his career as a merchant, engaging in trade in India. From 1687 to 1692, he was governor of the East India Company's fort at Madras. He then returned to England. Mr. Yale became interested in the school founded at Saybrook and afterwards located at New Haven, Connecticut. During his life he made several bequests to this institution, and in 1718 he announced a large gift. The trustees then honored him by naming the school Yale College. This has since become Yale University.

Yale University, formerly Yale College, a school established in 1701 by ten ministers of the colony of Connecticut, and located at Saybrook. In 1716 it was removed to New Haven, where it was permanently located, and two years later it was given the name Yale College in honor of Elihu Yale, who bestowed upon it a large sum of money. The beginning of the present organization dates from the administration of Timothy Dwight, who was president from 1795 to 1817. During this time, permanent professorships were established, the college grounds were extended and professional schools were planned, but only the medical school was established. President Dwight's successors continued his plan and the other professional schools were organized as rapidly as funds could be provided for their maintenance. The present organization includes departments of philosophy and arts, theology, medicine and law. Each department is under the direct supervision of its faculty.

The department of philosophy and arts is organized in two divisions, known as the academic department and the Sheffield Scientific School. It also includes the school of fine arts, the departments of music, the forest school and the graduate school. In addition to its regular work, the university maintains a large number of lecture courses, either under the immediate supervision of the university or under the supervision of various departments. The faculty numbers over 450, and the enrollment in all departments exceeds 3000. The general library contains 350,-000 volumes, while the libraries of the various departments bring the grand total up to 900,000 volumes, besides a large number of pamphlets.

Yalu River, a river of Asia, which rises on the eastern borders of China and flows southwestward and southward, forming during its entire course a part of the boundary between China and Korea. Its length is about 300 miles, and it is navigable for about 30 miles. At the mouth of this river a famous naval battle was fought in 1894, during which the Japanese destroyed the Chinese fleet. The forcing of the passage of this river at its mouth by the Japanese in 1904 was the first movement in the land operations of the Russo-Japanese War. See RUSSO-JAPANESE WAR.

Yam, a tropical plant, with twining stem and large, edible roots. These resemble the sweet potato, but because of their coarseness and lack of flavor, they are not generally marketed in the North, but in all southern countries and in the southern portion of the United States they are cultivated extensively. Some wild varieties of yam are poisonous. (See illustration on next page.)

Yancey, *yan'sy*, WILLIAM LOWNDES (1814–1863), an American publicist and orator, born in Georgia. He studied law, was admitted to the bar in 1834 and practiced law, at the same time editing a Unionist paper. He removed to Alabama in 1836, became prominent as a lawyer and Whig orator and entered the legislature. Elected to Congress in 1844, he espoused the Southern cause, and after his retirement two years later he became the recognized leader and orator of the radical element in the South. In the convention, which met at Montgomery, Ala., January 7, 1861, he reported the ordinance of secession. He left New York City in March, as a Confederate commissioner, to seek for recognition in Europe, but was unsuccessful, and, returning in February, 1862, he served in the Confederate Senate until his death.

Yang-tse-Kiang, *yahng'tse kyahng'*, one of the largest rivers of Asia. It rises in the south central part of the continent, in the plateau of Tibet, flows northeastward, then southeastward, then northeastward; after an irregular course, it enters the Yellow Sea through an estuary about 30 miles wide. Its length is about 3000 miles. The upper part of the course is between mountains, and the channel is narrow and the stream rapid, often interrupted by rapids and falls. The tide ascends the river for 450 miles, and it is navigable for 600 miles. The chief tributaries

YAM

are the Han, from the north, and the Wu, the Heng and the Kan, from the south. Some of these are navigable for considerable distances. The Yang-tse-Kiang brings down large quantities of sediment, and it is estimated that the amount deposited each year is equal to about five-sixths of the amount deposited by the Mississippi. It is connected with the Hoang-ho by the Grand Canal, and it is one of the most important waterways in the Chinese Empire.

Yank'ee, in America, the popular name for a New Englander, in Great Britain often applied indiscriminately to the whole population of the United States. In its origin it was a corruption of the word *English* as pronounced by the indians. It seems to have been first applied about 1775 by the British soldiers, as a term of reproach to

the New Englanders, who themselves afterward adopted it. Since the Civil War the southern population have applied it to the northern people generally.

Yank'ee Doo'dle, a national song of the United States, of uncertain origin. The words were probably written by Doctor Schuckbrugh, a surgeon in the French and Indian War, and the music is probably an English tune, which has been considerably modified.

Yank'ton, S. D., the county-seat of Yankton co., 62 mi. s. w. of Sioux Falls, on the Missouri River and on the Great Northern, the Chicago & Northwestern and the Chicago, Milwaukee & Saint Paul railroads. The city is the commercial center of a large agricultural and stock-raising district, and it has cement works, flour mills, grain elevators, brickyards, breweries, packing houses, woolen mills, stockyards and other establishments. It contains Yankton College, Saint Joseph Academy and public and parish schools. The South Dakota Hospital for the Insane is located here, and the Sisters of Saint Benedict have a hospital. There are eight churches and four banks, and the waterworks are owned and operated by the city. The place was settled in 1862, and the city was chartered in 1883. Until 1883 it was the capital of the territory of Dakota. Population in 1910, about 5000.

Yapura, *yah poo rah'*. See JAPURA.

Yarkand, *yahr kahnd'*, a city situated in the chief oasis of Chinese Turkestan, 100 mi. s. e. of Kashgar. It is at an elevation of over 3800 feet, is enclosed by a wall and surrounded by a moat. The buildings are constructed of stone and clay, and most of them are of one story. The city has numerous bazaars, mosques and caravansaries. It is also the seat of some Mohammedan colleges. Formerly Yarkand was an important commercial center, but the construction of railway lines has diverted much of its trade. The industries include the manufacture of carpets, silks, linens, cottons, woolens and dye stuffs. Population, estimated at from 75,000 to 100,000.

Yarmouth, *yahr'muth*, Nova Scotia, the county seat of Yarmouth co., situated on a small bay, 205 mi. s. w. of Halifax, and on the Dominion & Atlantic and the Halifax & Yarmouth railroads. It has manufactures of boots and shoes, cotton goods and also foundries and shipbuilding industries. It is an important fishing port and has quite an extensive trade. It has also become a prominent summer resort. Population in 1911, 6600.

Yarmouth or **Great Yarmouth,** a seaport and watering place of England, situated on the east coast, 19 mi. e. of Norwich. The town occupies a narrow peninsula between the Yare River and the North Sea and is connected by bridges with Suffolk and other places on the right bank of the Yare. The river is lined with extensive piers and Yarmouth is an important commercial port. It is also the chief center of the herring fishery of England. The industries include shipbuilding and the manufacture of ropes, nets and sails. Population in 1911, 55,905.

Yarn. See SPINNING.

Yaroslav, *yahr′os lahf′*, a town in Russia, capital of the government of the same name, on the Volga, 162 mi. n. e. of Moscow. Among the chief manufactures are cotton, tobacco and white lead. The Demidoff Juridical Lyceum is its chief educational institution. Population, 70,610.

Yar′row, a small river in the southern part of Scotland, rising in Selkirkshire and joining the Ettrick. It is famous for its beautiful scenery, which has many times been praised in the poems of Scott, Wordsworth and others.

Yates, EDMUND HODGSON (1831–1894), a British journalist. He wrote several novels of merit and was the theatrical critic of the *Daily News* for six years; he edited the *Temple Bar Magazine,* was the first editor of *Tinsley's Magazine* and was a constant contributor to *All the Year Round.* In 1873 he was appointed London representative of the New York *Herald,* which post he resigned in July, 1874, when he established *The World.* He published two volumes of *Recollections and Experiences,* besides several novels.

Yates, RICHARD (1818–1873), an American political leader, born in Warsaw, Ky., but taken in childhood to Springfield, Ill. He graduated at Illinois College in Jacksonville and began the practice of law at Springfield, where he became a prominent Whig. He was elected to the state legislature, serving from 1842 to 1849, and he was a member of Congress from 1851 to 1855. He became a Republican at the organization of the party and was elected governor of Illinois in 1860. During five years' service, he gained fame as one of the greatest of the war governors and was a close friend and adviser of President Lincoln. In 1865 he was elected to the United States Senate, where he served one term. His son, Richard Yates (1860–   ), was governor of Illinois from 1901 to 1905.

Yaws, the name in use in the British West Indies, on the West Coast of Africa and in tropical countries, wherever negroes have been taken, for a peculiar, contagious disease of the skin, marked by yellow spots and by a reddish, fungous growth beneath them. Mercury is the active ingredient of all West Indian remedies for this disease.

Yaz′oo, a river of Mississippi, formed by the Tallahatchie and the Yalabusha. It has a winding course to the south and southwest and enters the Mississippi about five miles above Vicksburg. Its length is 300 miles, and it is navigable for steamboats throughout its course.

Year, the period of time during which the earth makes one complete revolution in its orbit, or the period which elapses between the sun's leaving either equinoctial point, or either tropic, and its return to the same. This is the *tropical,* or *solar,* year, which is the year in the strict and proper sense of the word. This period comprehends what are called the twelve calendar months, and it is usually considered to commence on January 1, and to end on December 31. It is not quite uniform, but its mean length is about 365 days, 5 hours, 48 minutes and 51.6 seconds. In popular usage, however, the year consists of 365 days, and every fourth year of 366. The *civil year* is the ordinary year of 365 days. The *ecclesiastical year* is from Advent to Advent. The *lunar year* is a period consisting of 12 lunar months. The *lunar astronomical year* consists of 12 lunar synodical months, or 354 days, 8 hours, 48 minutes, 36 seconds. The *common lunar year* consists of 12 lunar civil months, or 354 days.

Yeast, *yeest,* a minute fungus in the form of a single, somewhat egg-shaped cell, which consists of a speck of protoplasm, surrounded by walls. These cells are so small that 3000 of them, laid end to end, would scarcely measure an inch. Under favorable conditions, the plants multiply very rapidly. Yeast thrives in a warm temperature, and as the plants grow they break up the sugar in the substance upon which they feed, setting free carbonic acid gas and forming alcohol. This is one of the processes of fermentation, and yeast is known as a *ferment.* Yeast is used in the manufacture of malt liquors and in making bread. See BREAD; BREWING; FERMENTATION.

Yeats, WILLIAM BUTLER (1865–   ), an Irish poet and dramatist, born in Dublin. He was educated in private schools. At first he studied art, but after three years he turned his attention to literature. He became the leading spirit in the new Irish literary movement. His poems are the embodiment of Irish thought and feeling, and his dramatic works are vivid sketches of Irish life. He has visited the United States several times. His best known works are *Wanderings of Oisin, The Shadowy Waters, Cathleen ni Hoolihan, Hour Glass* and *Deirdre.*

Yed′do, Japan. See TOKYO.

Yellow, one of the three primary colors. Lemon and canary yellow may be taken as pure yellows. Chrome yellow has a slight orange tint. A peculiarity of yellow is that an increase of light seems to strengthen the color, while an increase of light on blue makes it paler, and on all other colors gives them a yellowish tint. Yellow is the national color of the Chinese Empire.

Yel′lowbird. See AMERICAN GOLDFINCH.

Yellow Fever (locally, Yellow Jack), a peculiar, infectious disease, that has its origin in tropical Africa and America. Yellow fever is a very dangerous disease, the mortality varying in different localities and in different epidemics, from ten to seventy per cent. Persons who survive an attack, however, are generally immune from the disease for the remainder of their lives and do not appear to be the worse for their sufferings. Sometimes the disease is very quickly fatal, while in other cases it lasts for several days, but rarely for more than a week. It has been certainly proved that the disease is introduced into the human system through the bite of a mosquito, and it is claimed that that is the only way in which the disease is communicated. Everything seems to indicate that yellow fever is a bacterial disease, but as yet the specific germ has not been recognized, although the most skilled physicians have sought it.

The history of yellow fever in Cuba shows what may be accomplished by proper sanitary measures. When the United States occupied Cuba in 1898, the disease was prevalent in the island, and in fact for many years the island had not been free from it. The government took immediate measures to cleanse and purify the cities by drainage and proper sewerage and by insisting upon the destruction of garbage and the improvement of methods of living in crowded localities. Every case of yellow fever was promptly isolated, and the patient was protected by screens and in other ways from being bitten by mosquitoes. At the termination of every case, the houses were thoroughly disinfected, all the mosquitoes that could be found were killed, and so, gradually, the disease was

conquered, and Cuba was free from the scourge. Several serious epidemics have visited the southern part of the United States, entering usually by way of New Orleans or other Gulf ports, but physicians feel certain now of their ability to cope with these epidemics, and that the time will come when this disease will entirely disappear. See MOSQUITO.

Yel′low-ham′mer, the common name in the United States for the *flicker,* but in Europe the name for the *yellow bunting.* See FLICKER.

Yellow Jacket, the common name for any wasp whose body is marked with yellow. See WASP.

Yellow Jasmine, *jas′min.* See GELSEMIUM.

Yel′lowlegs, the common name of two species of snipe, both of which are prized by huntsmen. These species resemble each other so very closely that they are often confused, unless the two are together, when the difference in size becomes at once apparent. They are sometimes known as *tattlers,* because of the unusual way in which they alarm other birds at the approach of hunters.

Yellow Race. See MONGOLIAN RACE.

Yellow Sea, a branch of the Pacific Ocean, situated between China, on the west, Manchuria, on the north, and Korea, on the east. The northern projections constitute the gulfs of Korea, Liao-tung and Pe-chi-li. Its greatest width is 400 miles, and its narrowest span is about 115 miles. The chief rivers flowing into it are the Hoang-ho, the Liao and the Yalu. In general the sea is shallow, and it is named for the large quantity of yellow mud deposited in it by the inflowing streams.

Yel′lowstone National Park, a government reservation, situated in the northwestern part of Wyoming, and celebrated for its volcanic phenomena. Yellowstone National Park, as created by the act of Congress in 1872, has a length from north to south of 62 mi., and a breadth from east to west of 54 mi., and it contains an area of 3300 sq. mi. On the north and west it includes narrow strips of land from Montana and Idaho, respectively. In 1891 a forest reserve, lying to the south and east of the park, was created by presidential proclamation and placed under the control of the park authorities. The total area of the two reservations is about 5500 sq. mi.

SURFACE. The central portion of the park consists of a broad plateau, ranging in altitude from 7000 to 8500 feet. This plateau is bordered by a number of mountain ranges, in which peaks rise to a height of 11,000 to 12,000 feet. Of these the most important ranges are Absarokas, on the east; the Snowy Mountains, on the northeast; the Gallatin Range, on the north and west, and the Tetons, on the south. The loftiest mountain in the park is Electric Peak, which has an altitude of 11,155 feet. The highest land in the vicinity is Mount Hayden, more commonly known as the Grand Teton, the highest peak of the Teton Range, having an altitude of 13,671 feet. This stands on the south of the park, just a few miles beyond the boundary. The mountains are separated from one another by broad plateaus or valleys, and the intermingling of these features gives a diversity to the scenery of the region which is remarkably pleasing. The great valleys are Junction Valley, on the east, which, with its branches, includes the Yellowstone and the Lamar rivers; Hayden Valley, occupying an important tract along the Yellowstone, between Yellowstone Lake and the Great Fall; the Madison Valley and its extensions, through which flow the Firehole and Gibbon rivers, and in which are located the geyser regions; Swan Lake Flats, Willow Park, the Shoshone and the Paul's River basins.

RIVERS. The Yellowstone National Park is drained into three river systems, the Yellowstone, the Missouri and the Snake. The first two find an outlet on the Atlantic slope, while the third reaches the Pacific. The rivers flowing into the Missouri are the Madison, formed by the Gibbon and the Firehole, and the Gallatin. These drain the northwest and west central portions of the park. The southwestern and most of the south central portions are drained into the Snake River, and thence to the Columbia. The eastern and southeastern portions are drained into the Yellowstone, and thence to the Missouri. Between these river systems the Continental Divide passes, in an irregular line, entering the park near the southeastern corner and extending in a northwesterly direction to a point just west of the center, then extending westward, then southward, southwestward and again northwestward, leaving the western boundary near its middle point. This divide is a plateau, varying in altitude from 7000 to 8500 feet. In the southeastern part of the park is the Two Ocean Plateau, so named because rivers having their source in it flow respectively to the Atlantic and to the Pacific, and in one locality these come so near each other that during high water, streams flowing

in both directions may be fed from the same source.

The rivers are characterized by their clear water, swift current, deep canyons and beautiful cascades. Among the minor canyons worthy of mention are the Golden Gate, the Canyon of the Gibbon and the Canyon of the Gardiner. But surpassing all of these in beauty and grandeur is the Grand Canyon of the Yellowstone, a gorge nearly 20 miles in length and in places over 1400 feet deep. The upper part of this canyon, for about 5 miles, consists of bare rocks, noted for the variation and brightness of their coloring. Prominent among the colors are red, terra cotta, yellow and gray. At the head of this gorge is the Great Fall of the Yellowstone, where the stream makes a perpendicular descent of 310 feet. While other canyons are larger, it is generally conceded by travelers that nowhere else in the world is there a natural gorge which, for beauty and grandeur combined, equals this.

FALLS. There are over 30 waterfalls in the park. Some of these are small cascades, scarcely worthy of notice, while others are cataracts seldom surpassed for their beauty and grandeur. Among the falls worthy of mention are Gibbon Falls, 80 feet in height; Firehole Falls, upon Firehole River, 60 feet; Kepler Cascade, 80 feet; the Osprey Falls, 150 feet; Tower Falls, 132 feet, and the Falls of the Yellowstone, the upper fall of 112 feet and the lower of 310 feet. The last are the largest and by far the grandest falls of the park.

LAKES. Foremost among the bodies of water in the park is Yellowstone Lake. This sheet of water has an altitude of 7741 feet and is the largest body of fresh water in the country at so great an altitude. Its area is 139 square miles, and its maximum depth, 300 feet. It has a shore line of about 100 miles. Its waters are cold and swarm with fish. On the shore of the western projection, known as The Thumb, is seen the peculiar proximity of hot and cold water for which this region is noted. Here are several hot springs, whose cones have been built up within the lake, so that they are surrounded by cold water, and one can easily catch fish from the lake and, without moving from his tracks, immerse them in a spring hot enough to cook them. Other lakes of importance are Shoshone, to the south and west of Yellowstone; Louis Lake, south of Shoshone, and Jackson Lake, just across the southern boundary.

HOT SPRINGS AND GEYSERS. Within the boundaries of the park are found no fewer than

GREAT FALLS AND POINT LOOKOUT, YELLOWSTONE NATIONAL PARK

The unobstructed fall of water is 310 feet

4000 hot springs and 100 geysers (See THERMAL SPRINGS; GEYSER). The temperature of these springs varies from 60° to 175°. Many of them boil and, to a casual observer, would appear to have the temperature of ordinary boiling water; however, much of the ebullition is due to the escape of gas. The most prominent of the hot springs are the Mammoth Hot Springs, situated about 5 miles from the entrance of the Park at Gardiner, and near Fort Yellowstone, which is the administrative headquarters. These springs are noted for the beautiful terraces which they have formed. In all, these cover an area of nearly 200 acres and vary in altitude from a few feet to nearly 350 feet. These terraces have been formed by the overflow of the water from the springs. The water is charged with limestone, which, while still hot, is held in solution; as the water overflows and runs down the side of the crater, it evaporates and deposits minute particles of the solidified lime. Thus, as the years go by, the spring builds up its crater, raising the level of the water higher and higher and increasing the height and extent of the walls which enclose it. These terraces are objects of rare beauty, because of their great variety of coloring. Some are bright yellow; others of a terra cotta hue, while others are nearly white; many have a variety of colors. The water in the springs is remarkably clear, and because of the reflection from the crater it has a peculiar blue color, seen nowhere else. Aside from the Mammoth Hot Springs, the smaller springs are quite generally distributed through-

out the park, though they are the most numerous in three localities, where they intermingle with the geysers. These localities are the Norris Geyser Basin, the Lower Geyser Basin and the Upper Geyser Basin. Most of the hot springs are merely quiescent pools and are of interest because of the beauty of their coloring. The contrast in coloring is remarkable and is due entirely to the reflection of light from the crater of the spring, since in all cases the water

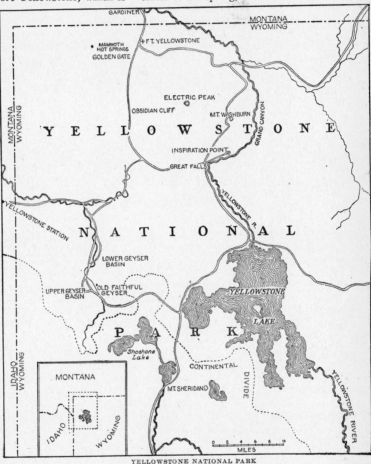

YELLOWSTONE NATIONAL PARK

taken from them is transparent. Among these springs of special note are the Turquois Spring, in the Middle Geyser Basin; Prismatic Lake, a pool of hot water over 150 feet across, under ordinary conditions reflecting all the tints of the rainbow; the Morning Glory Spring, Emerald Pool; Sapphire Pool, and the Punch Bowl, so named because of the form of its crater.

The geysers are divisible into two classes, the geysers proper and those known as the *fountains*.

The fountains are distinguished by an eruption, in which all of the water in the crater is thrown out in the form of a great fountain, leaving the crater empty. The eruption of such a geyser lasts but a few moments and will not be repeated until the crater is refilled. The most remarkable geysers of this type are the Fountain and the Great Fountain, both in the Lower Geyser Basin. Of the true geysers, Old Faithful, which has an eruption every 70 minutes and throws a jet of water varying from 75 to 125 feet high; the Beehive; the Giant; the Giantess; the Castle, and the Riverside are the most noted. The Giant, when in eruption, expels a column of water 5 feet in diameter to a height of nearly 250 feet and continues in operation for an hour and a half. The Giantess is even larger, but the eruptions are much less frequent. In general, the larger the geyser the longer the interval between periods of eruption. Most of the interesting geysers are found in the Upper Geyser Basin, where, within an area less than a mile square, nearly all of the large geysers are located. Interspersed among the large geysers are numerous small ones, some of which erupt every few minutes.

OTHER OBJECTS OF INTEREST. The greater part of the park is covered with beautiful forests of pine, through which the tourist passes on his way from one point of interest to another. The Park is a game preserve. Hunting is strictly prohibited, and the forests now abound in large game, including bears, elk and antelopes. There are also a few wild buffalo, and their number is increasing every year. The care taken of these animals has, in a measure, removed the timidity which generally characterizes them, and they are frequently seen by tourists, while the bears in many instances become very tame. In addition to the more striking features described above, there are many minor objects of interest, such as Obsidian Cliff, a mountain of volcanic glass from 250 to 300 feet in height; the Paint Pots, which are really hot springs, expelling colored clay from their craters, and mud geysers and volcanoes, differing from the other geysers in ejecting turbid water. Roaring Mountain is a hill several hundred feet high, from the openings in whose sides issue jets of steam with such force that they can be heard at quite a distance. In each of the hot spring regions are also found vents, known as *fumeroles*, through which steam escapes with a terrific force.

The roads through the park have been constructed by the United States government and are the best in the country. Transportation companies have erected a number of large hotels at convenient stages and at the most interesting points, so that tourists can make the trip of the park as comfortably as they can travel the same number of miles in any other part of the country. The park is entered from three gateways, Gardiner, on the north; Monida, on the west, and Cody, on the east, but Gardiner is the most desirable gateway. The regular trip includes a carriage drive of 150 miles and requires six days. Consult Chittenden's *The Yellowstone National Park;* Langford's *Discovery of Yellowstone Park.*

Yellowstone River, a river of the United States, the largest tributary of the Missouri. It rises in Wyoming, in the Continental Divide, flows northeast through Montana and empties into the Missouri a short distance beyond the boundary of North Dakota. Its length is about 1100 miles. Throughout most of its course the river is followed by the Northern Pacific railroad.

Yen, the monentary unit of Japan, equivalent to about 50 cents of United States money. The yen was formerly coined in both gold and silver, but in 1897 Japan adopted a gold standard and since that time few silver yens or single gold yen have been coined. The most common Japanese coins are the 20-yen piece in gold, equivalent to $9.97 in United States money; the sen in bronze, equal to one-hundreth yen; 5-sen, in nickel; 10-sen, 20-sen and 50-sen, in silver, and the 5-rin, in bronze, equal to one-half sen.

Yenisei, *yen' e say'e,* a river of Asia, which rises in the north central part of Mongolia, flows westward, then northward, across Siberia, and enters the Arctic Ocean. Its length is about 3000 miles, and it is navigable for river steamers for 1750 miles. In the lower course the river is from 4 to 5 miles broad and is deep, and during the spring high water is usually about 30 feet above the average level of the river. The area of the Yenisei basin is about 1,000,000 square miles.

Yew, an evergreen tree of the pine family, with dense, spreading branches, thickly covered with very dark green linear leaves. The common yew of Europe is very long-lived, and in England it is planted in cemeteries and is considered an emblem of immortality. The leaves and seeds are poisonous, but the red berries are not. The tough, elastic wood was used for making bows in the days before firearms were invented. The American yew is commonly known as *ground hemlock,* and is a low shrub, with straggling branches, common in dense forests.

Yezo. See JAPAN.

Yggdrasil, *ig'dra sil,* in Norse mythology, the enormous ash-tree which binds together heaven, earth and the under world. It was the tree of life, fate, time and space.

Yokohama, *yo'ko hah'ma,* a treaty port of Japan and the chief commercial center of the Empire, situated on the east coast of Hondo, on the Bay of Tokyo, 17 mi. s. w. of the latter city. It is on a large harbor, which is protected by breakwaters. The city is well planned and has a number of excellent public buildings. Most important of these are the customhouse, the post-office, the courthouse and the railway station. The city has a number of modern churches and in most respects resembles a European town. The harbor is lined with massive docks, and the surrounding heights are occupied by fine residences. The city is the center of a large silk industry, as well as of foreign trade. It is in direct communication with all of the leading ports of the world. Population in 1908, 394,303.

Yokosuka, *yo kose'ka,* an important naval station of Japan, situated on the island of Hondo, 13 mi s. w. of Yokohama, with which it is connected by rail. The town has large dockyards, arsenals and shipbuilding works. Population in 1910, 70,964.

Yonge, *yung,* CHARLOTTE MARY (1823–1901), an English author, whose writings, consisting of fiction and historical and educational works, comprise about one hundred twenty-five volumes. She is said, with the proceeds of two of her novels, to have fitted out a missionary ship and to have founded a missionary college in New Zealand. Her best-known books are *The Heir of Redcliffe, The Daisy Chain, The Dove in the Eagle's Nest* and a life of Hannah More.

Yon'kers, N. Y., a city in Westchester co., on the east bank of the Hudson River, adjoining New York, and on the New York Central railroad, 15 miles from the New York City terminal. There are also several electric railways. The city has a pleasant location, opposite the Palisades, on an elevation which affords excellent views across and up and down the Hudson. The streets are broad, well paved and well shaded, and there are many fine residences. There are thirty churches, three hospitals, an orphanage, a home for the aged and good municipal and Federal buildings. Other prominent institutions include a large public library, the Hollywood Inn for working men, with its library, the Woman's Institute Library, and a training school for nurses. The city hall, which was for-merly the Philipse Manor House, built in 1682, and Greystone, once the residence of Samuel J. Tilden, are of historic interest. Yonkers is also an important industrial and commercial center. It contains many foundries and machine shops, a large sugar refinery and manufactories of hats, carpets, rugs, patent medicines, furniture, roofing and other articles. There are shipbuilding yards, lumber mills, grain elevators and large coal-yards. The place was settled by the Dutch about 1650. After 1672 it was part of Philipse Manor, until the township of Yonkers was organized in 1788. The settlement itself was called Philipsburg until its incorporation into the village of Yonkers in 1855. In 1872 the northern part of the township was chartered as the city of Yonkers, and the southern part was later annexed to New York City. Population in 1910, 79,803.

York, a city of England, situated on the Ouse, at its confluence with the Foss, 175 mi. n. n. w. of London. The town has narrow streets and old houses, some of which were erected during the Middle Ages. It is surrounded by walls, which are entered by numerous gates. The object of greatest interest is the Minster or York Cathedral, which is considered one of the finest specimens of Gothic architecture in the world. It was built during the thirteenth and fourteenth centuries and is noted for its central tower, the western façade, the chapter house and its windows of stained glass. The manufactures include glass, iron-ware and linen. Population in 1911, 82,282.

York, NEB., the county-seat of York co., 50 mi. w. of Lincoln, on the Chicago & North-western and two lines of the Chicago, Burlington & Quincy railroad. The city is in an agricultural and stock-raising district and contains a flour mill, a machine shop, a foundry, stock-yards, grain elevators and other establishments. York College is located here, and the city has an academy, a public high school and public and school libraries. There are two national banks, a fine courthouse and a public park. The place was settled in 1871, and the city was incorporated in 1880. Population in 1910, 6235.

York, PA., the county-seat of York co., 100 mi. w. of Philadelphia, on Codorus Creek and on the Western Maryland, the Northern Central and the Maryland & Pennsylvania railroads. The city is regularly laid out on rolling ground, has excellent drainage and contains broad, well-paved streets and three parks. Some of the prominent institutions are the York Collegiate

Institute, the county academy, an orphans' home, a hospital, a public library, a law library, about sixty churches and ten banks. Other important buildings are the postoffice, the courthouse, the municipal building, the high school, the opera house, the jail, the Masonic Temple and four market buildings. The city is in a productive farming region and is an important industrial center. It contains foundries, machine shops, tobacco factories, silk mills, implement works, planing mills, breweries, brickyards, paper mills and manufactories of wagons, furniture and various other articles. York was settled by Germans in 1734, and the town was laid out in 1741. The Continental Congress met here from September, 1777, to June, 1778, when it was driven from Philadelphia by the approach of Howe's army. The borough was incorporated in 1787, and the city was chartered in 1887. Population in 1910, 44,750.

York, HOUSE OF, a royal family of England, which attempted in the Wars of the Roses to wrest the crown from the Lancastrian House, as represented by the king, Henry VI (See ROSES, WARS OF THE). The Yorkists had, indeed, the superior claim, as Richard, duke of York, was descended from a third son of Edward III, while Henry VI was descended from a fourth son. Richard died in 1460, and his son continued the struggle; after a short time he was crowned king as Edward IV. With the exception of a short interval, Edward was king until 1483, and after his death his son was crowned king as Edward V. Richard, duke of Gloucester, the brother of Edward IV, killed his royal nephew and was made king, but was overthrown by the earl of Richmond, the head of the Lancastrian House, who united the claims of the two families by marrying the daughter of Edward IV.

York River, a river which rises in the eastern part of Virginia, being formed by the Pamunkey and the Mattapony. It flows in a southeasterly direction and enters Chesapeake Bay opposite Cape Charles. Its length is 40 miles, and its greatest width is about 2½ miles. It was the scene of numerous military operations in the Civil War.

York'town, SIEGES OF, two notable sieges about Yorktown, Va. The more important was that of 1781, which ended in the surrender of Cornwallis and his English army, and which practically terminated the Revolutionary War. After a long campaign in the Carolinas, Corn-

wallis had been driven into Virginia and to Yorktown by General Greene. Lafayette had taken up a position overlooking the British quarters, and Admiral De Grasse and his French fleet had arrived in the vicinity, to shut off the British retreat by sea. Washington, by

SIEGE OF YORKTOWN, 1781

a brilliant march from the vicinity of New York to Chesapeake Bay, a distance of 400 miles, completed the investment of the town, bringing the American force to 16,000 men. The British fleet attempted to rescue the garrison, but was defeated by the French after a hard struggle, on October 19. After a number of brave but futile sorties, the British surrendered more than seven thousand troops and a large number of guns. A handsome monument has been erected to commemorate this event.

The second siege of Yorktown was during the Civil War, when the Confederates, under General Magruder, with about 15,000 men, had occupied and strongly fortified the town. They were reënforced by General Johnston, who assumed command and brought the total Confederate force to about 55,000 men. The siege was begun by General McClellan on April 5, 1862, with about 50,000 troops, but this number was augmented until it reached 95,000. In spite of the overwhelming Union force, Johnston evacuated Yorktown on the night of May 3 and retreated toward Richmond, pursued by Federal troops. He was forced to give battle at Williamsburg on May 5.

Yorktown is the county-seat of York co., Va., and is on the south bank of the York River, 10 mi. from Chesapeake Bay and about 60 mi. from Richmond. The oldest customhouse in America still stands in the town. Population in 1910, 136.

Yosemite, *yo sem'e te,* **Valley,** a valley of the Merced River, in Mariposa County, Cal. It is nearly in the center of the state and is about 150 miles in a direct line east by south of San Francisco, though in order to reach it from that city, one has to travel a much greater distance. Yosemite Valley is noted for its peculiar formation and high walls. It is about 8 miles long and in width varies from $\frac{1}{4}$ to $1\frac{1}{4}$ miles. The floor of the valley is about 3800 feet above the sea, and the cliffs rise upon each side of this to altitudes of from 3000 to 5000 feet. The sides are nearly perpendicular. The floor of the valley is carpeted with grass and flowers, and numerous trees spring forth along the foot of the cliffs. The scenery is characterized by grandeur, solemnity and marked contrasts, making the valley unique. So far as known, there is no other place in the world like it. Among the most important features are El Capitan, a peak near the eastern entrance, which rises to the height of over 3000 feet and presents a remarkably bold appearance, because it is separated from the surrounding mountains; Cathedral Rocks, which have an altitude of over 4000 feet above the valley, so called because when seen from a distance their summits present the appearance of two spires. Another object of interest is Sentinel Rock, 3043 feet high. The Three Brothers, Washington Column and the South Dome are other peaks of great interest and of imposing grandeur, but perhaps the most interesting feature of the valley consists in the falls. Of these, Yosemite Fall is the most prominent. This is formed by Yosemite Creek and has a total height of 2600 feet, which is divided into three falls. The first is a vertical fall of 1500 feet; the second, a series of cascades of 626 feet, and the third, a vertical fall of 400 feet. The Bridal Veil Fall is a delicate cascade 900 feet high, and receives its name from the fact that before the water reaches the base of the cliff, it is dissipated in spray, which closely resembles a long white lace veil. Vernal Fall has a height of 400 feet, and the Nevada Fall has a descent of about 600 feet, though it is not vertical. Another object of interest is Mirror Lake, near the west entrance of the valley, named from

185

its beautiful reflections of the surrounding scenery.

Yosemite Valley was discovered in 1851 by a party in pursuit of a band of indians, who made it their hiding place, supposing it to be inaccessible to white men. In 1864, by act of Congress, it was granted to California for a state park, upon condition that it should be kept for the use of the public and that its scenery should never be injured. The Mariposa grove of big trees, adjoining the valley, was also granted the state at the same time. Since 1890 it has been known as the Yosemite National Park. The most desirable months in which to visit the valley are June, July and the early part of August. Later in the season a number of the streams become dry, and their falls disappear.

Yoshi-hito (1879-   ), mikado or emperor of Japan, succeeded to the throne on the death of his father, Mutsuhito, July 29, 1912. The name Yoshi-hito means "good man." Yoshi-hito was named heir to the throne on his eighth birthday, his mother being one of the royal princesses of the emperor's household. He was educated at the school for children of the royal family at Tokyo, and speaks three foreign languages, English, French and German. He was married in 1900 to his cousin, Princess Sada.

Young, *yung,* BRIGHAM (1801-1877), the founder of the Mormon settlement in Utah, for many years the able leader of the Mormons. His father was a Vermont farmer, and he himself learned the trades of painter and glazier. Early in life he joined the Baptists, but was converted to Mormonism and joined the sect at Kirtland, Ohio, in 1832. In 1835 he was ordained an elder and sent forth among the twelve apostles. On the death of Joseph Smith, in 1844, he was unanimously chosen president and prophet. When the sect were expelled from Nauvoo, he led them through toils and dangers, over the plains and tablelands to the splendid valley where, between the Wasatches and the Great Salt Lake, he founded (July, 1847) the present Salt Lake City. In 1849 an attempt was made to organize a state, to be called the State of Deseret, that being the name given by the Mormons to the district. The government refused to sanction the new state, but Utah was organized as a territory, and Young was appointed governor for four years. In 1854 he was superseded by a "Gentile" and this move led to considerable trouble with the United States government, since the

Mormons were unwilling to submit to the authority of one not of their own sect. By some, Young is considered to be the founder of polygamy, but others declare the doctrine to have been promulgated by Joseph Smith. Young continued ruler of his sect until his death in 1877. He was a man of strong character, remarkable foresight and unusual executive ability.

Young, CHARLES AUGUSTUS (1834–1907), an American astronomer, who graduated at Dartmouth in 1853 and after teaching at Phillips Academy, Andover, in 1856 became professor of natural philosophy and mathematics in the Western Reserve College, Ohio. In 1877 he was appointed professor of astronomy and natural philosophy at Princeton, after serving in the same capacity at Dartmouth. Young made the first observation of the spectrum of the solar corona in August, 1869, and made many other important observations and discoveries. In 1870 he was one of the Winlock party that observed the total eclipse at Jerez, Spain. *The Sun* and *General Astronomy* are among his publications, which include also textbooks and papers on miscellaneous scientific subjects.

Young, EDWARD (1683–1765), an English poet, famous as the author of *Night Thoughts*. He had published many poems and several tragedies, one of which, *Revenge*, was very popular, before the *Night Thoughts on Life, Death and Immortality* made him famous. This series of poems, in the main too melancholy to be entirely pleasing, contains many fine passages and many expressions which have become proverbial in the language, such as "Procrastination is the thief of time."

Young, ELLA FLAGG (1845–   ), a prominent American educator. Mrs. Young was educated in the public schools of Chicago, graduating from a Chicago high school and from the Chicago Normal School. In 1900 she received the degree of Ph.D. from the University of Chicago. She began teaching in 1862, making rapid advancement in her profession. From 1887 until 1899 she was district superintendent of schools in Chicago, and from 1899 until 1905, she held a professorship in the University of Chicago in the department of education. In 1905 she was chosen principal of the Chicago Normal School, and was one of the most efficient principals that institution ever had. In 1909 she was unanimously elected superintendent of schools in Chicago, one of the most important educational positions in the United States. Her work as super-

intendent of schools has been such as to command the highest admiration. In 1910 Mrs. Young had the honor of being elected to the presidency of the National Education Association, being the first woman to hold that position. In the same year she was also elected president of the Illinois State Teachers' Association.

Young, JOHN RUSSELL (1841–1899), an American journalist. He was educated in the public schools of Philadelphia and the New Orleans high school, began his newspaper career as a copy boy on the Philadelphia *Press*, and when the Civil War began was sent as correspondent to Virginia. After the war he returned to Philadelphia and was given editorial charge of the *Press*. He made two unsuccessful attempts to start a paper, and in 1871 he went to Europe as correspondent of the New York *Herald*. For the latter paper he went with President Grant around the world, and when he returned to New York he took a position on the editorial staff. In 1882 he was appointed minister to China and filled the post until Cleveland's election. He was appointed librarian of Congress in 1897.

Young, SAMUEL BALDWIN MARKS (1840–   ), an American soldier, born in Pittsburg, Pa. He entered the army as a private in 1861, became colonel in 1864 and was brevetted brigadier general in 1865. He was later brevetted major, lieutenant colonel and colonel in the regular army. In 1898 he became brigadier general of volunteers in the Spanish-American war, and he served with ability at Santiago under Shafter. In 1899 he was sent to the Philippines, and after his return he commanded the Department of California. In 1903 he became chief of staff of the United States army, retiring in 1904.

Young Italy, a society founded by Mazzini in 1831 for the purpose of freeing Italy from Austrian rule and uniting the different states as a republic. The first open movement, the invasion of Savoy in 1834, failed, and this fact lessened the influence of the society. Its work was not entirely vain, however, as it contributed greatly to the growth of the patriotism which resulted later in the unification of Italy.

Young Men's Christian Association, THE, an organization of men, established for the purpose of promoting evangelical work and preaching the gospel to all, in the home and fields throughout the United States and in many portions of Europe and the East. Active membership is held only by members of evangelical churches; associate and honorary members are, however, admitted, but they are prohibited from holding office and from voting upon constitutional questions. The first of these associations was formed during 1845, when George Williams of London, England, a clerk sixteen years of age, persuaded his fellow clerks to meet for prayer and Bible study. But similar movements had existed in England from 1632. The first American Association was formed in Boston in December, 1851. Since that date, associations have been organized in nearly every city, town and village of the United States and Canada, many of them occupying buildings of the most substantial character and owning real estate and personal property representing hundreds of thousands of dollars in value. The objects of the association, in addition to those stated, are to improve young men, by the conversion of their souls and the consecration of their lives to the love and service of Jesus Christ; to unite Christians of the various churches in this and other work that will be promoted by united action; to carry the gospel among the railroad and other employes of the country; to unite college students for active Christian work; to coöperate with foreign Christian young men for the salvation of their fellows; to bring together in sympathy and companionship for Christian work the young men of every section of the country and Canada; to secure the services of, and financial aid from, Christian laymen in spreading the gospel, and generally to promote the common cause and extend religion among all orders and conditions of men. In pursuit of the accomplishment of these objects, the association has founded missions, secured positions for young men, strangers and penniless in cities and in the country; acted in capacities of nurses and humanitarians; secured legislation against the publication and circulation of obscene literature; officiated as almoners for the distribution of funds, food and clothing among the deserving poor; established schools, libraries and lectures, and exerted a powerful influence for the general good. Many of the associations have become incorporated under the laws of the several states wherein they are domiciled and are clothed with powers and privileges of corporate bodies. In 1883 the international committee, composed of twenty-seven members, was incorporated under the laws of the State of New York, and in 1888 delegates from the United States were in attendance upon the international convention held at Stockholm, Sweden. The headquarters of the central international committee are at Geneva, Switzerland, and the committee is composed of representatives from America, Aus-

tralia, Austria-Hungary, Belgium, Denmark, England, France, Germany, Italy, Netherlands, Norway, Russia, Spain, Sweden and Switzerland. The total membership of American associations is 381,982; they occupy 517 buildings of their own, valued at $50,919,000, and have 728 libraries, containing 550,592 volumes. They employ 2103 general secretaries, and they expended in 1910 for expenses—local, state and international—$8,297,689. There are 2017 associations in America and 8098 in the world. The movement has made some headway in Asia, but not much progress in Africa.

Youngs'town, OHIO, the county-seat of Mahoning co., 67 mi. e. by s. of Cleveland, on the Mahoning River and on the Erie, the Pennsylvania, the Baltimore & Ohio and other railroads. The city is an important industrial center, containing rolling mills, blast furnaces, steel mills, bridge works and furniture, engine, automobile, wagon and other factories. It has several parks, one of which contains about 450 acres. Some of the important institutions are the Macmillan Library, a children's home, several free kindergartens, two hospitals and many churches. Other prominent structures are the Y. M. C. A. building, the Park Theater and the halls of the Elks and Odd Fellows. The first settlement was made by John Young in 1797. It became the county-seat in 1876. Population in 1910, 79,066.

Young Women's Christian Association, THE WORLD'S, an association of women, organized in 1894. Eleven national associations are now affiliated with it, with headquarters in London. The American committee was formed in 1886. The office of the international committee of the women's association is at Chicago, Ill. The work of the associations among women is fourfold—physical, including systematic training in the gymnasium, health talks, holiday excursions and outing clubs; social, including receptions and socials in homelike rooms, musical and literary entertainments, helpful companionships, noon rest, lunch rooms, boarding clubs and employment bureaus; intellectual, furnishing libraries and reading rooms, educational classes, lecture courses, concerts and musical and art clubs; spiritual, through Bible training classes, evangelistic meetings, personal work and Gospel meetings. Seven annual conferences are held, to train volunteer workers in Bible study and association work. They meet at Lake George, N.Y.; Lake Geneva, Wis.; Asheville, N. C.; Capitola, Cal.; Waterloo, Iowa; Lakeside, Iowa, and

Seaside, Ore. *The Evangel* is the official organ, published in Chicago. Connected with the American committee is a membership of 100,252.

Ypsilanti, *ip'se lan'te,* MICH., a city in Washtenaw co., 30 mi. s. w. of Detroit, on the Huron River and on the Michigan Central and the Lake Shore railroads. It is the business center for a considerable agricultural region and is connected by several electric railways with other cities. The principal manufactures are flour, paper, dairy products and agricultural implements. The Michigan State Normal College is located here, and the city has nine churches, two banks, a business college and public and school libraries. The town was laid out in 1824 on the site of an indian trading post. It was chartered as a city in 1858. Population in 1910, 6230.

Yttrium, *it're um,* the name of a rare metal, found only in a few scarce minerals. It was first obtained by Gadolin in 1794 from the ytterbite, or gadolinite, of Sweden. It occurs in a gray powder, that has the metallic luster of iron.

Yuan Shi Kai, Chinese statesman, first president of the Chinese Republic. As a young man his fondness for military life led him to active service in Korea, where his work attracted the notice of Li Hung Chang, and brought him the office of resident-commissioner of trade. His rise was now rapid, and during the Boxer rebellion he gained an international reputation for his efforts to protect foreigners. Though a supporter of the monarchy, Yuan Shi Kai was a reformer. His innovations finally led to his dismissal from power in 1908, but in 1911 he was recalled to the office of premier. He tried to bring about a compromise between the Manchus, the constitutional reformers and the revolutionists. After the abdication of the emperor early in 1912, Yuan Shi Kai, recognized as "the strong man of China," was elected first president of the Chinese Republic. See CHINA, subhead *History.*

Yucatan, *yoo'ka tahn',* a peninsula comprising the Mexican states of Yucatan and Campeche, occupying the extreme southeastern part of Mexico and extending between the Gulf of Mexico on the north and the Caribbean Sea on the east. Its northern extremity is washed by the Yucatan channel. The area is 55,400 square miles. Within the peninsula interesting remains of the former Aztec and Toltec civilizations are found. For climate and products, see MEXICO; see, also, INDIANS, AMERICAN.

Yuc'ca, a genus of plants belonging to the lily family, some of which are remarkable for their stately appearance. They occur in greatest frequency in Mexico and the southwestern states of America, extending also into Central America and occurring in such numbers in some places as to form straggling forests. A coarse fiber is obtained by the Mexicans from the stem and foliage, which they use for cordage and matting. The juicy fruits, which resemble small bananas, are cooked as an article of diet, and the roots contain matter used as a substitute for soap. The names given to different species are dagger weed, Spanish bayonet, soap weed and banana plant.

Yu'kon, a district of Canada, situated in the extreme northwestern part of the Dominion. It is bounded on the north by the Arctic Ocean, on the east by the District of Mackenzie, on the south by British Columbia and on the west by Alaska. The Rocky Mountains form most of the eastern boundary, and the district is nearly triangular in outline. The area is 196,976 square miles. The population in 1901 was 27,-219. The country is more or less mountainous and is of interest, chiefly, because of the rich gold deposits found in the Klondike region (See KLONDIKE). The chief town and the seat of government is Dawson.

Yukon River, one of the largest rivers of North America. It rises in the west central part of the District of Yukon, Canada, flows northward and northwestward into Alaska, then westward and southwestward, entering Bering Sea 60 miles southwest of Michael. Its total length is about 2200 miles, and it is one of the largest rivers of the continent. It is fed by numerous streams, which are the outlets of marshes and lakes. In some places the current is swift and the river is obstructed by rapids. Small steamers have descended all these rapids, but those at White Horse form an impassable barrier to up-river steamers, so that the river is divided into two navigable sections, which are now connected by railway. The discovery of gold in the Klondike region and along the banks of the Yukon has brought this stream into special prominence since 1896. During the open season steamers make regular trips as far as White Horse, and smaller boats go to Dawson.

Yu'ma, a small tribe of indians, now living on a reservation in the southeastern corner of California. They are a fine-looking family and, like most of the agricultural tribes, are friendly and peaceful when not imposed upon. They were originally a large tribe living along the Colorado River. They tattooed their bodies and wore feather headdresses and shell ornaments.

Z, the twenty-sixth and last letter of the English alphabet, occupying the same position as in Latin. It is derived, through the Greek and Latin, from the Phoenician alphabet, in which, however, it was the seventh character. In English, *z* was little used before the fifteenth century. It is properly a double consonant, compounded of *d* and *s,* but it has acquired the pronunciation of the hard terminal *s. S* or *ss* is, indeed, frequently used in the place of *z,* as in *choose, dissolve.*

Zac′ate′cas, a city of Mexico and capital of the state of the same name, situated in the south central part of the country, 350 mi. n. w. of the City of Mexico. The chief buildings are a municipal palace, a cathedral and the buildings of a number of educational institutions. The city also has a mint and a number of hospitals. It is built in the vicinity of silver mines and has manufactures of pottery of some importance. Population in 1910, 25,905.

Zacyn′thus. See ZANTE.

Zalin′ski, EDMUND LOUIS GRAY (1849–1909), an American soldier and inventor, born in Poland. He was brought to the United States in 1853, and when fifteen years of age he entered the Union army, serving first as volunteer aid-de-camp on the staff of General Miles. Later he was commissioned second lieutenant in the Second New York Artillery, for bravery at the Battle of Hatcher's Run, Va. He remained on General Miles's staff until the surrender of Lee, and after the close of the war he was commissioned second lieutenant in the Fifth United States Artillery. Captain Zalinski's name is widely known in connection with the development of the dynamite gun and the invention of an electrical fuse.

Zambe′zi, a river of southern Africa, which rises in the eastern part of Angola, where it is formed by the union of several smaller streams, generally known as the Seven Springs. It flows southward, eastward, northeastward and then southeastward, finally entering the Mozambique Channel through a number of delta arms. For a portion of its course it forms the boundary between Rhodesia and German Southwest Africa. Its upper course is through an expanse of country clothed with grass and forest, and just after entering Rhodesia it plunges over a precipice nearly 400 feet high, forming the celebrated Victoria Falls (See VICTORIA FALLS). Below the falls the river has a winding course of about 80 miles through a deep canyon, with almost perpendicular banks, whence it reaches open country. Its entire length is about 1650 miles. It is navigable for large steamers to the first series of rapids, 400 miles from the sea. Above this point another section is navigable to Zumbo, on the western border of Portuguese East Africa. Several lines of steamers ply regularly upon the river, and the Cape-to-Cairo railway crosses it on a magnificent steel bridge erected just below Victoria Falls. The Zambezi is the fourth river of Africa in size and, together with its tributaries, exceeds 4000 miles in length. It was discovered by Livingstone in 1854.

Zanesville, *zaynz′vil,* OHIO, the county-seat of Muskingum co., 59 mi. e. of Columbus, on the Muskingum River, at the mouth of the Licking, and on the Baltimore & Ohio, the Wheeling & Lake Erie, the Ohio River & Western and other railroads. The city has an attractive location, in the river valleys between lofty hills. Six parks, several bridges, the courthouse, the jail, Memorial Hall, the Masonic Temple, two opera houses, the high school, the Clarendon Hotel and several business blocks are prominent features. The surrounding country is a farming region and also has deposits of limestone, clay and coal. The rivers furnish good water power, and there are potteries, terra cotta works, railroad shops, implement works, flour mills and other factories. The town was founded by Jonathan Zane and John McIntire in 1799. Population in 1910, 28,026.

Zang′will, ISRAEL (1864–   ), a British author, of Jewish parentage. He showed a decided turn for literature at an early age. Among his works are *The Children of the Ghetto, Ghetto Tragedies, Dreamers of the Ghetto, They That Walk in Darkness* and *The Mantle of Elijah,* works of fiction, and *Without Prejudice,* a collection of essays. His fame rests on the faithfulness of his portrayal of Hebrew life and character.

Zan'te or **Zacyn'thus,** one of the Ionian Islands, situated in the Mediterranean Sea, west of the northern part of the southern peninsula of Greece. It has an area of 167 square miles. It produces currants, olives, oranges, lemons and other semi-tropical fruits. The inhabitants manufacture considerable wine. Formerly the island is supposed to have belonged to Ulysses, ancient king of Ithaca. Population, 1907, 42,502.

Zan'zibar, or *zahn ze bahr',* or **Zanguebar,** an island off the eastern coast of Africa, in the Indian Ocean, forming a part of the British protectorate of Zanzibar. Its area is 640 square miles, and it is mostly low, the highest point being only 1000 feet above the sea. The island is fertile and well cultivated. Cloves, cocoanuts and other tropical products are grown. The population in 1911 numbered 115,000, and includes numerous races, among which are Arabs, Persians and representatives of most of the native tribes of eastern Africa. There are only a few Europeans.

Zanzibar, the capital and chief town of the island, contains the palaces of the sultan, the barracks, the fort, hospitals and a number of mission stations. It is an important port in the Eastern trade and has some manufactories. The population is about 60,000.

Zealand, *ze'land.* See SEELAND.

Ze'bra, a wild animal of South Africa, closely

ZEBRA

related to the wild ass and the horse. Its body is gray, but there are conspicuous dark stripes

across the head, body and legs. The true zebra is now almost extinct. The most abundant species now is the *quagga,* known also as Burchell's zebra. Its color is usually dull yellow, and the stripes rarely continue below the main body. It roams in large herds over the plains to the north of the Orange River, but in yearly diminishing numbers. Other species exist in smaller numbers. See QUAGGA.

Ze'bu, a species of ox, a native of India, whence it has spread into Persia, Arabia and eastern Africa. It is remarkable for a convex forehead, short horns, large, drooping ears and a fatty hump on the back. It is very gentle and

ZEBU

docile and is used as a beast of burden. Zebus vary greatly in size, the smallest being no larger than a large dog, while others are the size of a large ox. The sacred bulls of the Hindus are zebus.

Zebu, *za boo'.* See CEBU.

Zeb'ulun, one of the twelve tribes of Israel, derived, according to *Gen.* xxx, 20, from the sixth son of Jacob and Leah. The tribe was distinguished for its warlike spirit, scientific skill and commercial enterprise. The country of Zebulun lay in the fertile hilly country north of the plain of Jezreel.

Zechariah, *zek'a ri'a,* son of Berechiah, son of Iddo, appeared as a prophet in Jerusalem, along with Haggai, in the second year of Darius Hystaspes (520 B. C.), to warn and encourage the Jews to commence the restoration of the Temple.

Zed'eki'ah, last king of Judah, the son of Josiah. He succeeded Jehoiachim, was captured at the siege of Jerusalem by the Chaldeans, 588 B. C., was blinded, and died in captivity in Babylon.

Zemst'vo, the governing body of a province or district in Russia. It is composed of representatives chosen by the peasants, the householders of the towns and the landed proprietors. This body is presided over by the president of the nobility of the district or province, and it is charged with the administration of economic affairs. The executive power of the zemstvo is entrusted to an *upraba*, who is elected by the assembly. See RUSSIA, subhead *Government*; DUMA.

Zenana, *ze nah'na*, the part of the house set apart for women, among Hindus. The typical zenana is found in Bengal, where it is in a separate building, at the rear of that occupied by the men. The Indian Zenana Mission has done noble and extended work among the inhabitants of zenanas.

Zend-Aves'ta, the original document of the religion of Zoroaster, still used by the Parsees as their bible and prayer book. It is usually translated "authorized text," and the term Zend is applied to the language in which it is written. It was first translated in 1771 by Anquetil Duperron, a French scientist.

Ze'nith, a term used in astronomy to indicate the point in the heavens directly over our heads. It is the opposite of Nadir.

Ze'no (about 340–260 B. C.), the founder of the Stoic school of philosophy, born of a merchant family of Citium, in Cyprus. After studying twenty years under various masters, he established himself at Athens as a teacher. His school derived its name from the *stoa*, or porch, where its doctrines were expounded. During his long life Zeno won much renown and was highly regarded by the public and by his many disciples. After his death his followers systematized the Stoic doctrines. See STOICISM.

Zeno'bia, queen of Palmyra, who succeeded to the throne as regent for her son, on the murder of her husband, Odenathus, in 267 A. D. She aimed at a dominion which should include Egypt, Syria and Asia Minor, and should make good her title of "Queen of the East." The accession of Aurelian, in 270, once more placed a soldier at the head of the Roman Empire, and in 272 the armies of Zenobia were defeated. Palmyra was taken, and its queen was made prisoner. She resembled Cleopatra in her talents and personal fascination, but she far surpassed her in purity and elevation of character.

Zephaniah, *zef'a ni'a*, a Hebrew prophet, who flourished in the reign of Josiah, 600 B. C. He is the ninth, in order, of the twelve "minor prophets." His little book of three chapters predicts the desolation of Judea, as a punishment for idolatry and worldliness.

Zeppelin, FERDINAND, Count (1838–   ), a celebrated aeronaut, born in Constance, Germany. He was educated at the Polytechnical School in Stuttgart and the military school at Ludwigsburg. At twenty he became an officer in the army, and rendered valuable service in the Seven Weeks' War and the Franco-Prussian War. He began the study of airships with the idea of using them in war, and as a result developed the dirigible balloon. His success led the German government to purchase two of his airships at a price of $537,500, and to present him with $100,000. See FLYING MACHINES.

Zeram'. See CERAM.

Ze'ro, in mathematics, a symbol (0) denoting the absence of quantity or value; also, the symbol of an infinitesimal quantity (See INFINITY AND INFINITESIMAL). The same term is used to represent the point from which measurement is recorded on a scale, as in thermometers or barometers. In a scale of numbers in algebra, the positive numbers proceed from 0 to infinity in one direction, and the negative numbers proceed from 0 to infinity in the opposite direction.

Zeus, *zuse.* See JUPITER.

Zeuxis, *zuke'sis*, a famous Greek painter, probably born at Heraclea, on the Euxine, about 450 B. C. Among his masterpieces are his *Hercules Strangling the Serpent, Jupiter among the Gods, Marsyas Bound, Pan* and *Helen.*

Zhitomir, *zhit o'mur*, a town of Russia, capital of the Government of Volhynia, on the left bank of the Teterev, 80 mi. w. of Kiev. It is a commercial center and carries on an active trade. The chief manufactures are tobacco, spirits and gloves. Population in 1910, 87,200

Zinc or **Spelter,** the name of an important, useful metal, and of the element of which the metal consists. Zinc, as a component of brass, had currency in metallurgy long before it became known as an individual metal. In 1597 Libavius described a "peculiar kind of tin," which was prepared in India and of which a friend had given him a quantity. It is not known to whom the discovery of isolated zinc is due; but we do know that the art of zinc smelting was practiced in England from about 1730. The various zinc ores are known as *red zinc ore, franklinite, calamine, electric calamine, willemite* and *zinc blende.* Large deposits of zinc ore occur in New Jersey, Pennsylvania, Wisconsin, Tennessee, Arkansas, Missouri and Kansas. The Missouri and Kansas mines are the most important.

The uses of zinc are varied and important. It

is very extensively consumed in the form of amalgamated plates, in the construction of voltaic batteries. It is also largely used in preparing galvanized iron, which consists of sheet or wire iron, coated with zinc, by dipping or passing the iron, previously rendered chemically clean, through a bath of molten zinc, the surface of which is protected by a covering of sal ammoniac. In some cases a thin film of tin is first deposited on the iron surface by electric action before galvanizing, and sometimes a little tin is added to the zinc bath. The metal also forms a series of valuable alloys, the most important of which are brass and German silver. Pure zinc, a bluish-white metal, on cooling, deposits crystals, and at last it freezes into a compact crystalline solid, which may be brittle or ductile, according to circumstances. According to some authorities, pure zinc always yields ductile ingots. Commercial *spelter* always breaks under the hammer; but it is susceptible of being rolled out into a very thin sheet. Such a sheet, if once produced, remains flexible when cold. Oxide of zinc is prepared chiefly in two ways—(1) by burning the metal, a method now being carried out industrially, the zinc vapor being sometimes produced from a mixture of roasted ore and carbon, and (2) by heating the basic carbonate. Oxide of zinc is used in the arts as a white pigment. It is used also in medicine, chiefly externally. Sulphate of zinc, or white vitriol, is prepared by the dissolution of the ordinary metal in dilute sulphuric acid. Sulphate of zinc is used in medicine, chiefly externally. In the arts it is employed in the preparation of varnishes and as a mordant for the production of colors on calico. Chloride of zinc is produced by heating the metal in dry chlorine gas. It is used as a caustic and disinfectant.

Zinc Etch'ing, a process for making a printing plate from a drawing or lettering. The drawing is first made in black on white paper or cardboard that possesses a rough surface; a printed page of type may take the place of the drawing. A photograph is taken of this drawing or print, and this is reversed on a sensitized plate (See PHOTOGRAPHY), which is in turn placed on a plate of highly polished zinc, that has been treated with a solution of albumen, water and bichromate of ammonia. The negative is then clamped to this plate and is subjected for a few minutes to an electric light or to sunlight. The negative is then removed, and the image on the zinc plate is developed in a manner somewhat similar to that used in developing the negative

in photography. After this the plate is prepared by etching, in a manner similar to that used in preparing halftone plates (See HALFTONE). It is then nailed to a block, to make it the same height as type, and is ready for printing. Zinc etchings are used for the reproduction of designs and for small black and white drawings; but they cannot reproduce fine shading, such as is seen in engravings and photographs. They are cheap, convenient and quickly made, and for these reasons are quite generally used for the illustrations in daily papers.

Zinc White, a compound of zinc, used for white paint. Zinc white is a compound of zinc and oxygen, known as an oxide. It was formerly made by the burning of pure zinc, the vapor being collected, but it is now made by roasting zinc ore and burning the vapor in the same furnace. The ore is mingled with anthracite coal and is spread on a hearth that has openings through it. After the coal is ignited, a blast of air is forced through the fire, which causes the zinc to rise from the ore in the form of vapor, which burns the vapor in the upper chamber of the furnace. The zinc white, which forms as a powder, is collected as it passes through the openings lined with coarse cloth. It is mixed with linseed oil and placed upon the market as a pure white paint, which is extensively used for interiors. Zinc white makes a clearer color than white lead, but it is not suitable for exteriors, as it does not withstand the action of the weather.

Zinzendorf, *tsin'tsen dorf,* NICOLAUS LUDWIG (1700–1760), count of Zinzendorf and Pottendorf, a German religious reformer. He established an order of worship in 1727, and soon afterward he founded an organization, which has been described in the article *Moravian Brethren.* He traveled widely in its interests, visiting America in 1741–1742 and spending some time in London in 1750.

Zi'on. See JERUSALEM.

Zi'onist Movement, a movement which had its beginning in a pamphlet, in which Doctor Herzl of Vienna advocated the purchase of Palestine from the Sultan, for use as an independent Jewish state. The first Zionist Congress, composed of delegates from Austria, Germany, Russia, France and England, met at Basel, Switzerland, in August, 1897. A program of the Congress stated that "Zionism aims at establishing for the Jewish people a publicly and legally assured home in Palestine"; and it seeks the practical encouraging of the colonization of the country by Jewish farmers, artisans and tradesmen.

All Hebrews were asked to contribute to the general fund. The Lovers of Zion, a society formed after the Russian riots of 1881, do not intend to go back to the Holy Land in a body. Through the influence of the Rothschilds and Baron de Hirsch, 25 Jewish colonies have been founded in Palestine. They do not pay yet, but the work is progressing steadily. The sixth Zion Congress met in Basel, in August, 1903. About 600 delegates were present, coming from nearly every place in the world where Jews reside. The British government at this time offered a grant of land, lying along the Uganda railway in British East Africa, for the Jewish state. A committee of experts was appointed to survey and study the territory and report on it. A letter was also received from Von Plehve of Russia, in which he said he would not oppose a Jewish state in Palestine, but would oppose any effort to form one on Russian territory. In 1903 there were nearly 400,000 Zionists, with 900 societies in Russia and 250 in America. Max Nordau and Israel Zangwill greatly favor the movement. Theodore Herzl, the leader, died in 1904.

Zirco'nium, a rare element, closely allied to titanium. In 1789 Klaproth analyzed zircon and found it to contain a new earth, which he called "zirconia." This has been utilized for the construction of a new kind of gas lamp, in which a colorless flame, produced by the combustion of a mixture of gas and air, serves to heat a hollow cylinder of zirconia, suspended over it by means of platinum gauze.

Zith'er, a common, stringed musical instrument, especially popular in Austria and the Tyrol. It is a flat instrument, with a wooden frame and a flat sounding board, over which are stretched about thirty gut and wire-bound silk strings. It is placed on a table or on the knees; the strings are played with the right hand, the thumb being armed with a metallic plectrum, to bring out the melody more prominently.

ZITHER

Zo'diac, the name given to a zone of the visible heavens, extending in breadth to certain equal distances on both sides of a great circle of the celestial sphere, in the plane of the ecliptic or of the earth's orbit produced. The zodiac is the region containing the paths of the sun, moon and planets. It was marked out by early astronomers into twelve parts, each with its constellations, and these twelve constellations came to be denoted, for brevity's sake, by certain signs. When the sun appears to cross the equator going north, it is said to enter the first sign of the zodiac, or Aries. The twelve signs of the zodiac are Aries (♈), the Ram; Taurus (♉), the Bull; Gemini (♊), the Twins; Cancer (♋), the Crab; Leo (♌), the Lion; Virgo (♍), the Virgin; Libra (♎), the Balance; Scorpio (♏), the Scorpion; Sagittarius (♐), the Archer; Capricornus (♑), the Goat; Aquarius (♒), the Waterman; Pisces (♓), the Fishes.

Zodi'acal Light, usually described as a cone-shaped glow of nebulous light, seen after sunset or before sunrise, extending upward from the position of the sun, nearly in the direction of the sun's equator. The causes of this light are not determined.

Zola, *zo lah'*, EMILE (1840–1902), a noted French author. He had published several novels and won considerable notice before beginning, in 1869, his great series on the "Rougon-Macquart" family. This series was, as he stated, to give the "physiological and social history of a family under the Second Empire," and as finally completed it comprised twenty volumes, which dealt with the appearance, in every member of the Rougon family, of an irresistible tendency to crime and vice. The early volumes of the series created little stir; but with the publication of *L'Assommoir,* in 1878, Zola became famous. The strongest remaining members of the series are *Germinal,* the *Human Beast, The Earth* and *The Downfall.* Of his later works the most important were the two series, *Lourdes, Rome, Paris,* and *Fruitfulness, Labor, Truth* and *Justice,* this last unfinished at his death.

Zola championed the cause of Captain Dreyfus, accused of fraud the court which had convicted Dreyfus and dared the authorities to prosecute him. He was brought to trial and sentenced to a fine and imprisonment, but the decision was set aside on an error, and a new trial was begun. Again he was convicted, but the sentence was not carried out, and he went into voluntary exile, returning in 1899.

Zol'licof'fer, FELIX KIRK (1812–1862), an American soldier, born in Tennessee. He served during the Seminole War, held various political offices after its close and on the outbreak of the Civil War entered the Confederate service, with the rank of brigadier general. He was killed at the Battle of Mill Springs, Ky.

Zollverein, *tsole' je rine,* (German, "customs-union"), a union formed for certain fiscal purposes among the smaller German states, under the leadership of Prussia, in 1818. Its purpose was to enable all the contracting states to act for certain purposes as one. All import duties were collected on a common frontier, and the funds thus received were divided among the states in proportion to their several populations. Since October 15, 1888, all the German states, except the port of Bremen and part of Hamburg, have joined together under the Zollverein.

Zone, in geography, one of the five great divisions of the earth, bounded by imaginary circles, which are parallel to the equator. The zones are named according to the prevailing temperature in each. The torrid zone extends 23° 30' north and 23° 30' south of the equator, thus being 47° wide. It is bounded on the north by the Tropic of Cancer and on the south by the Tropic of Capricorn. The north temperate zone extends from the Tropic of Cancer to the Arctic Circle and is 43° wide. The south temperate zone extends from the Tropic of Capricorn to the Antarctic Circle and is of the same width as the north temperate zone. The north frigid zone extends from the Arctic Circle to the North Pole, and the south frigid zone from the Antarctic Circle to the South Pole. While the parallels named mark the arbitrary boundaries of these zones, the climate of each merges so gradually into that of the zones adjoining upon either side, that no distinct climatic boundary exists between them. See CLIMATE; ANTARCTIC CIRCLE; ARCTIC CIRCLE; EQUATOR; TROPICS.

Zoölogical, *zo'o loj'i cal,* **Garden,** a park or other large enclosure where live animals are kept for exhibition. The Jardin des Plantes, in Paris, founded in 1804, was the first of such establishments, and the number has increased steadily, until at present many of the large cities in Europe and the United States maintain zoölogical collections of some sort. Germany has taken the lead in the development of such institutions, and the one at Berlin is the most important zoölogical garden in the world. The gardens at London, Antwerp, Vienna and Amsterdam are also among the best in the world. Most of the European collections are maintained by societies or corporations, the city merely furnishing the land. In the United States many cities have municipal "zoos," the largest being those at Lincoln Park, in Chicago, and at Highland Park, in Pittsburg. Philadelphia, Cincinnati, New York and Washington have well-equipped zoölogical gardens, the one in New York occupying a tract of 261 acres in Bronx Park. The National Zoölogical Park at Washington is under the control of the Smithsonian Institution and is supported by the government.

Zoölogy, *zo ol'o jy,* the science that deals with animals, their structure, classification and habits. It is a part of natural history, and with botany it forms the science of biology. The more complex living things are either animals or plants, but the simpler ones, mostly microscopic in size, possess in common so many of the properties of both groups that they justify the belief that plants and animals have had a common ancestry.

Zoölogy includes several sub-sciences, the most important of which are (1) systematic zoölogy, the description and classification of animal species; (2) distributional zoölogy, the study of the distribution of animals over the globe at present or in the past; (3) animal morphology, the study of the structure and form of animals; (4) animal physiology, dealing with the uses of the parts of animals; (5) ecologic zoölogy, the study of the relations of animals to one another and to their surroundings, and (6) evolutionary zoölogy, the body of doctrines which attempt to explain how animals have come to their present state (See ANIMAL).

The earliest important zoölogical writings are from the Greek philosopher Aristotle. Among the Romans, Pliny was the most noted natural historian. After the dark ages and with the revival of letters, zoölogy was again cultivated. The rude descriptions of animals by such naturalists as Gesner (1516–1565) were improved and systematized by Linnaeus, who published the first complete descriptive classification of all the species of animals known at his time. He also devised the binomial system of naming animals, a system which is now universally adopted and by which the name of each species consists of two Latin words, a generic name and a specific name (See GENUS; SPECIES; VARIETY). Linnaeus described over 4000 species of animals; at present about 500,000 species are known. The revival of dissection by Vesalius was the germ from which the morphology of to-day has sprung. Swammerdam described the anatomy of many of the lower animals, but the modern school of comparative anatomy was founded by Cuvier, who showed that the different parts of a given animal were often fundamentally related, an idea that was very fruitful in the study of fossil remains. Comparative anatomy was subsequently much advanced by the researches of Owen, Agassiz, Huxley and Gegenbaur. The study of developing animals, often called embryology, was founded by Von Baer and vigorously promoted by Agassiz and Balfour. Animal physiology, as a distinct sub-science, had its beginning in the discovery of the circulation of the blood by Harvey; it was systematized by Haller and was much advanced in the last century by the researches of Johann Müller. Evolutionary zoölogy received its initial impulse from Lamarck, but its most noted advocate was Darwin, whose theories were expounded and popularized by Huxley in England, Haeckel in Germany and the botanist Gray in America. Much interesting information as to the researches and discoveries in zoölogy can be found in the biographies of celebrated zoölogists, such as those of Owen, Agassiz, Darwin and Huxley.

Zoölogists generally agree in dividing the animal kingdom into the following fifteen subkingdoms, or phyla: (1) *Protozoa*, animals composed of one cell or several similar cells, usually microscopic in size and devoid of special organs (See AMOEBA; FORAMINIFERA; VORTICELLA); (2) *coelenterata*, animals whose bodies are bell-shaped or sac-shaped, composed of two layers of cells and with organs usually arranged in 4 or 6 rays (See JELLYFISH; HYDRA; POLYP; CORAL); (3) *porifera*, attached, sac-like animals, often in colonies, with many small lateral pores into which water is drawn, and one large opening through which the water is driven out; (4) *ctenophora*, more or less globular animals, of the consistency of jelly, with a branched digestive cavity and eight rows of swimming plates; (5) *platyhelminthes*, animals with a flattened, worm-like body, and a branched digestive system, or none (See TAPEWORM); (6) *nemathelminthes*, animals with a round, unsegmented, worm-like body (See TRICHINA); (7) *rotatoria*, small externally segmented animals, in which the mouth is provided with ciliated lobes, which in action look like wheels; (8) *annelida*, animals with long, segmented bodies, and with the usual systems of organs, but without jointed limbs (See EARTHWORM); (9) *arthropoda*, animals with segmented bodies, in which the segments differ; each segment may carry a pair of jointed limbs; this subkingdom includes more than half of all the known species of animals (See CRUSTACEA; ARACHNIDA; MYRIAPODA; INSECTA); (10) *bryozoa*, small animals living in colonies, and known as moss animals; with U-shaped digestive tubes, and mouths provided with ciliated tentacles; (11)

brachiopoda, animals possessing a dorsal and a ventral shell, and known as lamp- and tongue-shells; (12) *echinodermata*, rough-skinned animals, whose organs are arranged on a system of five rays (See SEA URCHIN; STARFISH; CRINOIDEA); (13) *mollusca*, animals with a soft, unsegmented body, usually protected by a shell (See MOLLUSCA; CLAM; OYSTER; SNAIL; NAUTILUS); (14) *tunicata*, small sac- or barrel-shaped animals known as sea squirts, whose young have in their bodies a supporting rod, such as is found in the more primitive vertebrates; (15) *vertebrata*, animals that usually possess an internal skeleton, composed of a backbone and skull, and bones for the limbs, of which there are never more than two pairs. The vertebrates include the largest and the most highly specialized animals known (See VERTEBRATES; FISHES; BATRACHIANS; REPTILES; BIRDS; MAMMALIA).

Besides such larger works as *The Standard Natural History, The Cambridge Natural History* and *Lankester's Treatise on Zoölogy*, the following texts will be found of service for reference and general reading: Hertwig's *Manual of Zoölogy*, Linville and Kelly's *Text-book in General Zoölogy* and Jordan and Kellogg's *Animal Life*. Of a more popular character are the following works: J. Burroughs's *Wake-Robin*, W. H. Gibson's *Highways and Byways* and *Sharp Eyes*, B. Torrey's *The Rambler's Lease* and *Every-day Birds*, M. O. Wright's *Fourfooted Americans*, H. K. Job's *Wild Wings*, F. M. Chapman's *Bird Life*, F. H. Herrick's *The Home Life of Wild Birds*, F. M. Bailey's *Birds of Village and Field*, M. C. Dickerson's *The Frog Book*, A. F. Arnold's *The Sea Beach at Ebb Tide*, E. T. Seton's *The Trail of the Sandhill Stag* and W. T. Hornaday's *The American Natural History*. For younger readers the following will be found appropriate: A. M. Dalton's *Wings and Stings*, A. W. Gould's *Mother Nature's Children*, A. B. Kelley's *Short Stories of Our Shy Neighbors* and Kipling's *Jungle Books*. A good collection of verses will be found in E. V. Lucas's *The Open Road*. White's *Natural History of Selbourne* and Walton's *Compleat Angler* are among the quaintest of English classics on these subjects.

Zo'roas'ter, whom the Persians called *Zerdusht*, and the Greeks *Zoroastres*, the founder of the Magian, or Parsee, religion, was one of the greatest of religious teachers. He lived about 660–583 B. C., under a king called Gushtasp, who has been incorrectly identified with Darius Hystaspes by many Parsee scholars. Spitama was his family name; Zarathustra is a more correct and conventional title, apparently equal to "high priest." Zoroaster, according to legend, spent fifteen years in preparing for his work, during which time he was tempted by the evil spirit Ahriman, but came off conqueror. The Parsis and Guebers are his followers to-day.

Zouaves, *zwahvz* or *zoo ahvz'*, originally a body of troops in the French army. It derived its name from a tribe of Kabyles inhabiting the mountain of Jurjura, in the Algerian province of Constantine. General Clausel, of the French army in Algiers, created, in 1830, two battalions of Zouaves, in which each company consisted of French and Kabyles in certain proportions, officers, subalterns and soldiers being selected from either race. The zouaves, though retaining their Moorish dress, were armed and disciplined after the European fashion, and the battalions were recruited by voluntary enlistment. The native Algerian contingent are known as Zurcos. In the United States the zouave uniform was popular during the Civil War, and the name is memorable for the bravery of the Ellsworth Zouaves and the New York Fire Zouaves, two Union regiments.

Zuccaro or **Zucchero,** *tsook'ka ro*, the name of two Italian painters: (1) TADDEO ZUCCARO (1529–1566), one of the most popular painters of the so-called Roman mannerist school. His best frescoes were an historical series painted on the walls of a new palace at Caprarola, built for Cardinal Alessandro Farnese. (2) FEDERIGO ZUCCARO (1543–1609), the younger brother and pupil of Taddeo. His first important commission was to complete the *Last Judgment*, begun by Vasari, and later he was called upon to carry out Michelangelo's designs for decorating the Pauline Chapel. In 1574 Federigo went to England, where his fame was already known, so that he at once received a large number of commissions to paint the portraits of various distinguished persons, among them Queen Elizabeth, Mary Queen of Scots, Sir Nicholas Bacon, Sir Francis Walsingham, Lord Howard and others. From 1585 to 1588, he was employed by Philip II of Spain, in decorating the Escurial.

Zuider Zee, *zoi' dur zay*, or **Zuyder Zee,** a gulf of the North Sea, projecting into the coast of the Netherlands. It has an area of 1365 square miles and is nearly enclosed by land. Near the middle it is divided by narrows into an inner and outer basin. Its depth varies from 12 to 40 feet, and some portions of it have been reclaimed for cultivation.

Zululand, *zoo'loo land*, a region of southeastern Africa, which forms a province of the British colony of Natal. Its area is about 10,460 square miles, and its population is about 130,000, the most of whom are natives. See NATAL; ZULUS.

Zulus, *zoo'looz*, a brave and intelligent branch of the Bantu division of the human family. The men are given to field sports and to foraging expeditions and bloody warfare among themselves. The chiefs are elected and hold office at the will of the people. As a race, the Zulus are conspicuous for their morality. The pursuits of the people are pastoral. Trading is little known, and the arts are limited to simple ironwork, pottery and ornaments of copper, ivory, horn or wood. Tshaka, the chief ruler, during the first quarter of the nineteenth century dominated South Africa, from the Zambezi to the Cape Colony. Cetewayo reigned from 1874 until 1878, and by his depredations he embroiled his people in war with England. For a time the fierce Zulus successfully resisted the British, but they were ultimately subdued and are gradually becoming civilized.

Zuni, *zoo'nye*, the largest and most important of the Pueblo indian tribes, living near the Arizona line, in western New Mexico. When the Spaniards explored this country in 1539, seven villages were discovered, in most of which, at a later period, missions were established. The indians did not take kindly to the intrusion of the whites, and there were at intervals serious outbreaks, at each of which the indians took refuge in their citadels on Thunder Mountain, where they could not easily be overcome. When peaceful relations were again established, they would come down from the mountain and reoccupy their villages. There are now about 1600 of the Zuni living in three farm villages. See PUEBLO.

Zurich, *zoo'riK*, a town of Switzerland, capital of the Canton of Zurich and the largest city of the Republic. It is on the Limmat, at the northern end of Lake Zurich, 60 mi. n. e. of Bern. The city is divided by the Limmat into two parts, known respectively as the Little City and the Great City. The old historical quarter of Zurich is picturesque, with its steep, narrow streets and quaint, dark houses, but the newer part of the city has handsome buildings and wide, attractive streets. Among the more noteworthy buildings are the old Wasserkirche, which now holds the municipal library; the old church known as the Grossmünster, of which Zwingli was pastor; the townhall, and the university buildings. The Swiss national museum is the largest museum in Switzerland and contains a fine collection of stained glass. The educational institutions of the town include the university, with about 800 students, and the Federal Polytechnic, which has about 1100 regular students, besides special students who attend lectures. Commercially and industrially, Zurich is of considerable importance. The silk industry is large, and cotton, paper and machinery are also manufactured. During the Middle Ages the town of Zurich was prosperous and important. It was the scene of the beginning of Zwingli's reformation. Population in 1910, 189,088.

Zurich, Lake, a lake of Switzerland, lying mostly within the Canton of Zurich, but extending for a short distance into Schwyz and Saint Gall. It is about 25 miles in length and from $\frac{1}{2}$ to $2\frac{1}{2}$ miles in width and is somewhat in the shape of a crescent. Its scenery is picturesque and charming, although not as grand as that of some of the other lakes of Switzerland.

Zuyder Zee, *zoi' dur zee.* See Zuider Zee.

Zwingli, *tsving' lee,* Ulric or Huldreich (1484–1531), an illustrious Swiss reformer. In 1506 he was ordained by the bishop of Constance, becoming in the same year pastor of the large parish of Glarus. His studies in the ment gradually led him to question m doctrines in which he had been trained degrees he became known as an ardent re as well as a prominent patriot. He had no communication with Luther, but by 1516 he had begun a work in Switzerland very similar to that which had been started by the great German reformer. In 1522 he demanded of the bishop of Constance and all the governments of the confederation the abolition of the law imposing celibacy upon the priests, and his suggestions for one reform after another widened his breach with the Church. In 1529 he went to Marburg, to confer with Luther and the other German reformers, upon the possibility of uniting the reform movements, that a stronger resistance might be made to their opponents. Zwingli was willing to make concessions, but Luther objected to the fact that the religious movement in Switzerland was allied with a movement for civil reform, and this, together with their differing views on the Lord's Supper, prevented coöperation. In 1531, when open war broke out between the Catholic and the Protestant cantons of Switzerland, Zwingli accompanied the Zurich regiment as chaplain and was killed at the Battle of Kappel.